Master the NCERT

Line by Line MCQs from Latest NCERT Books

for NEET/JEE

CHEMISTRY XI

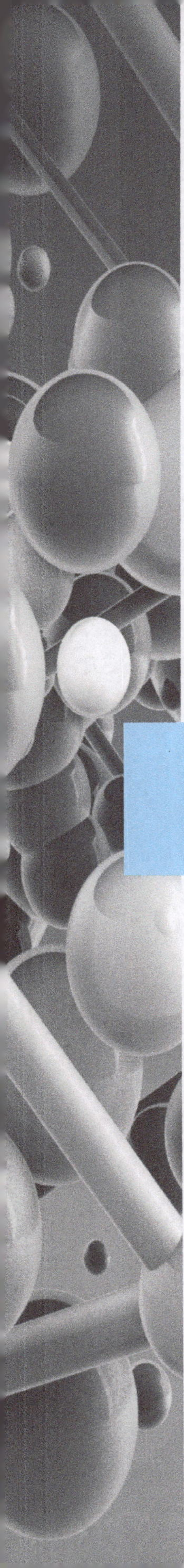

Master the

NCERT

Line by Line MCQs from Latest NCERT Books

for NEET/JEE

CHEMISTRY XI

DR. NARENDRA JHA

Co-Authored by

SWATI CHAUHAN

HARSH KUMAR

arihant

SUCCESS AND NOTHING LESS

arihant
SUCCESS AND NOTHING LESS

Arihant Prakashan (Series), Meerut

Administrative & Production Offices

Regd. Office
'Ramchhaya' 4577/15, Agarwal Road, Darya Ganj, New Delhi -110002
Tele: 011- 47630600, 43518550

Head Office
Kalindi, TP Nagar, Meerut (UP) - 250002
Tel: 0121-7156203, 7156204

Sales & Support Offices

Agra, Ahmedabad, Bengaluru, Bareilly, Chennai, Delhi, Guwahati, Hyderabad, Jaipur, Jhansi, Kolkata, Lucknow, Nagpur & Pune.

PRICE ₹350.00

PO No : TXT-XX-XXXXXXX-X-XX

Published by Arihant Publications (India) Ltd.

For further information about the books published by Arihant, log on to www.arihantbooks.com or e-mail at info@arihantbooks.com

Follow us on

Preface...

For any aspirant of competitions, a proper grip over NCERT books is the necessity now. After rationalisation of syllabus in competitions like NEET, JEE Main and their syncing with different State Boards, it is very much expected that their test papers will contain most of the questions from NCERT. To cater this situation the need of dual synchronous preparation, i.e. study of NCERT for school and competitive exams simultaneously is increasing day by day.

Arihant's Master the NCERT Series is framed, developed and now revised with the same philosophy of such synchronous preparation. These books serve as the complete resource for gripping NCERT with learning, practice and assessment tools. The specialised features of this revised edition are-

- **3 level Chapter Analysis** is incorporated in the beginning of each Chapter.
- **Key Notes** are more elaborative and enriched with NEET/JEE exclusive features like **NEET PYQ markings, Marks Maximiser, Mnemonics, Caution Points & PYQ Notes.**
- **Concept Master** is present at places as concept explanatory videos of key notes.
- Major key points of the chapter are further mapped as multicoloured **Chapter at a Glance** for better visualisation and quick revision.
- Exercise portion is scientifically designed for step-by-step mastering through **Concept Builders,** followed by **Topical MCQs, Assertion – Reason, Statement Based, Matching, Numericals, NCERT Exemplar's, Past Exams'** and **Skill Boosters.**
- Questions of Exercises are tagged with NCERT page numbers.
- For Assessment of self-preparation levels **MCQs Based Online Chapter Tests** and **3 Online Mock Tests** (2 NEET & 1 JEE Main pattern) are incorporated with this revised edition.

The variety in types of questions framed will also be helpful in analysis of self – performances and exposure to face tough problems of competitive exams.

Huge efforts have been made from our side to keep this book error free, but inspite of that if any error or whatsoever is skipped, then that will be purely incidental. Please write to us your feedbacks for further improvement of the book.

Authors

Key Features

3 Level Chapter Analysis

On the first page of each chapter NEET Analysis of 5 years is given on following 3 basis -

(i) Topics

(ii) Special format Questions

(iii) Chapter weightage

Topicwise No. of Ques asked in 5 Years (NEET)

Topics	No. of Questions				
	2024	2023	2022	2021	2020
Why do we Need to Classify Elements, Genesis of Periodic Classification	–	–	–	–	–
Modern Periodic Law and Present Form of Periodic Table	–	1	–	–	–
Nomenclature of Elements with Atomic Number > 100	–	–	1	–	1
Electronic Configurations of Elements and the Periodic Table	–	–	–	–	1
Electronic Configurations and Types of Elements: s-, p-, d-, f-Block	–	–	–	–	–
Periodic Trends in Properties of Elements	2	1	1	1	2

Special Type of Ques asked in 5 Years

Types	Years				
	2024	2023	2022	2021	2020
A-R	–	–	–	–	–
Statement Based	–	–	–	–	–
Matching	–	–	–	–	3

Last 5 Years Weightage (NEET)

Marks Maximizer

- **Nature of oxides** Along period, the nature of the oxides varies from basic to acidic.

Oxide	Na_2O	MgO	Al_2O_3	SiO_2	P_4O_{10}	Cl_2O_7
Appearance and nature	White, alkaline	White, basic	White, Amphoteric	Transparent Crystal, Acidic	White, acidic	Colourless, acidic

- The acidic character of the oxides of a non-metal increases with increase in oxygen content in it. e.g.

$$N_2O_3 < N_2O_5;\ SO_2 < SO_3,\ Cl_2O < Cl_2O_3 < Cl_2O_7$$

Marks Maximiser

Specialised box matter with NEET/JEE exclusive important Information which may or may not be present in NCERT.

Mnemonics

Specialised learning tricks as easy to memorise sentences for retaining concepts and avoiding confusions.

Mnemonics Recall General Trends of different Properties in the Periodic Table

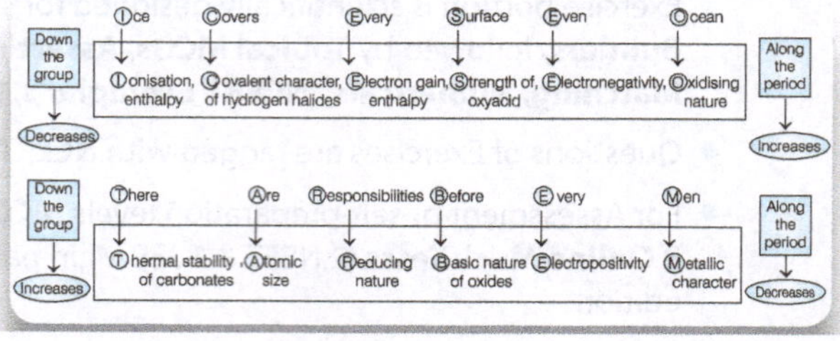

Ionisation Enthalpy

For Concept Master *Video*

- It represents the energy required to remove an electron from an isolated gaseous atom in its ground state. It is expressed in kJ mol^{-1}. NEET 2019
- The first ionisation enthalpy for an element Y.

$$Y(g) \longrightarrow Y^+(g) + e^- \quad \text{NEET 2024}$$

- The second ionisation enthalpy for most loosely bound electron.

$$Y^+(g) \longrightarrow Y^{2+}(g) + e^-$$

- Energy is always required to remove electrons from an atom and hence, ionisation energy is always positive.

Chemistry Through Concept Master

Unique video support to explain difficult Topics/Concept of NCERT in simple and easy to understand language.

Key Features

PYQ Notes

1. Moseley's observation on characteristic X-ray spectra of elements relates frequency (ν) of X-ray emitted to the atomic number by the relation. $\sqrt{\nu} = a(Z - b)$. The plot of $\sqrt{\nu}$ *vs* Z is linear straight lines. **JEE Main 2023, 8 April Shift-II**

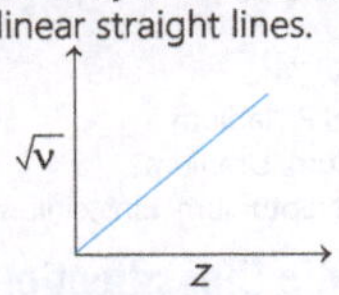

2. van der Waals' radius > Metallic radius > Covalent radius (For an atom). **NEET 2014**

PYQ Notes

NEET/JEE specific important points, which were asked in past years but not incorporated in present Rationalised NCERT .

Chapter at a Glance

Fully Coloured Glorified Infographics to map all the key points of a chapter for quick review. These are present at the end of chapters.

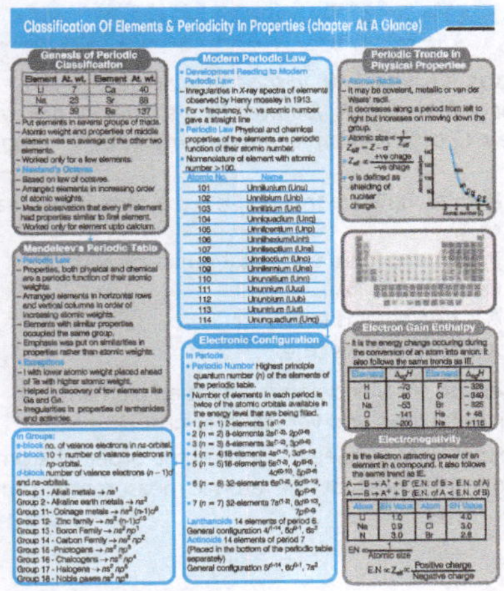

Step by Step

Mastering NCERT

- Concept Builders
- Topical Questions
- Assertion-Reason
- Statement Type
- Matching Type
- Numerical Value
- NCERT Exemplar's
- Past Exams'
- Skill Boosters

Concept Builders

1. The periodic classification follows as a logical consequence of the .... of atoms.
2. In Dobereiner triads, the average weight of the 1st and the 3 3rd element is equal to that of the second one. [T/F]
3. According to Newlands' law of octaves, the properties of Li were similar to .... (Na/Mg).
4. Give the formula of oxide of gallium predicted by Mendeleev along with their formulas.
5. Henry Moseley developed a relationship between $\sqrt{\nu}$ (ν = frequency of X-rays emitted) and atomic weight (Z). [T/F]
6. The horizontal rows in Mendeleev's periodic table is called .... while in modern periodic table, these are called ....
7. Write the IUPAC nomenclature of seaborgium.
8. The elements of *s*-block are reactive metals with high ionisation enthalpies. [T/F]

18. The energy required to remove an electron from the outermost orbit of an isolated gaseous atom (X) in its ground state is called .... and it is expressed in the units of ....
19. The effective nuclear charge experienced by the valence electrons in an atom will be more than the actual charge on the nucleus. [T/F]
20. An element 'P' has atomic number 56. What will be the formula of its halide?
21. In period II elements, it is easier to remove the fourth 2*p*-electrons from .... than to remove one of the three 2*p*-electrons from ....
22. Na > Mg > Be > Si is the correct trend regarding metallic character. [T/F]

Step by Step Mastering NCERT

The scientifically designed practice exercise with all possible type of questions to be asked in competition like NEET/JEE.

Concept Builders

1. The periodic classification follows as a logical consequence of the .... of atoms.
2. In Dobereiner triads, the average weight of the 1st and the 3 3rd element is equal to that of the second one. [T/F]
3. According to Newlands' law of octaves, the properties of Li were similar to .... (Na/Mg).
4. Give the formula of oxide of gallium predicted by Mendeleev along with their formulas.
5. Henry Moseley developed a relationship between $\sqrt{\nu}$ (ν = frequency of X-rays emitted) and atomic weight (Z). [T/F]
6. The horizontal rows in Mendeleev's periodic table is called .... while in modern periodic table, these are called ....

Concept Builders

These are present as simple teasers like T/F, Fill ups and one word question. Thus, structured to build foundation stone of NCERT concepts.

Key Features

Topical Question

NEET/JEE like MCQs form line by line text of NCERT with complete tagging of pages. All these MCQs are arranged as per the Topic headings of NCERT.

Topical Questions

Why do we Need to Classify Elements?

1 Which of the following is a set containing man-made elements?
(a) Gold, Mercury, Zinc
(b) Gold, Radium, Palladium
(c) Curium, Osmium, Uranium
(d) Technetium, Neptunium, Einsteinium

Genesis of Periodic Classification

2 Which of the following statements is correct? NCERT Pg 75
(a) Dobereiner arranged elements by the help of triads methods.
(b) Law of triads seemed to work for large number of elements.

A-R Questions

Most Important special format MCQs category. All of these are also tagged with NCERT page numbers as well .

Assertion-Reason Questions

Directions (Q. Nos. 1-10) *In the following questions a statement of Assertion* (A) *followed by a statement of Reason* (R) *is given. Choose the correct answer out of the following choices.*

(a) Both A and R are true and R is the correct explanation of A.
(b) Both A and R are true but R is not the correct explanation of A.
(c) A is true but R is false.
(d) A is false but R is true.

1 **Assertion** (A) Mendeleev's arranged elements in horizontal rows and vertical columns.
Reason (R) Mendeleev's ignored the order of atomic weight thinking that the atomic measurements might be incorrect. NCERT Pg 76

Statement type Question

In NEET Chemistry paper 3 types of statement based questions are asked
(i) Statement I & II
(ii) 4 statements with codes
(iii) 5 statements with codes
All these 3 categories are overed in step by step practice with NCERT page tagging.

Statement Type Questions

Directions (Q. Nos. 1-5) *In the following questions, two statements (I & II) are given. In the light of the given statements, choose the correct option given below.*

(a) Both Statement I and Statement II are false.
(b) Statement I is true but Statement II is false.
(c) Statement I is false but Statement II is true.
(d) Both Statement I and Statement II are true.

1 **Statement I** Zn is not a transition element whereas Cu is a transition element.
Statement II Zn belongs to group 12(IB) and Cu belong to group 11 (IB) in the periodic table. NCERT Pg 79, 84

Matching Type Questions

Step by step practice includes both the matching type MCQs (with and without codes. These are placed just after statement based MCQs and all are tagged with NCERT page numbers.

Matching Type Questions

1 Match the Column I with Column II and choose the correct option using the codes given below. NCERT Pg 79

Column I	Column II
A. 3*d*-transition series	1. Cerium ($Z = 58$)
B. 4*d*-transition series	2. Actinium ($Z = 89$)
C. 4*f*-inner transition series	3. Zinc ($Z = 30$)
D. 5*f*-inner transition series	4. Yttrium ($Z = 39$)

Key Features

NCERT Exemplar Questions

1 Which important property did Mendeleev use to classify the elements in his periodic table?
(a) Atomic weight (b) Atomic number
(c) Melting point (d) Boiling point

2 In terms of period and group, where would you locate the element with, $Z = 114$?
(a) Period-5, Group- 6
(b) Period-7, Group-14
(c) Period-5, Group-10
(d) Period-3, Group-13

NCERT Exemplar's Questions

NCERT Exemplar books are considered as one of the best problem books for competitive exams. Each chapter has selected exemplar problems to provide consolidation for preparations.

Past Exams' Questions

NEET Archive

1 Arrange the following elements in increasing order of electronegativity **NCERT Pg 91, NEET 2024**

N, O, F, C, Si

Choose the correct answer from the options given below:
(a) Si < C < N < O < F (b) Si < C < O < N < F
(c) O < F < N < C < Si (d) F < O < N < C < Si

2 Arrange the following elements in increasing order of first ionisation enthalpy : **NCERT Pg 88, NEET 2024**

Li, Be, B, C, N

Choose the correct answer from the options given below:
(a) Li < Be < B < C < N (b) Li < B < Be < C < N
(c) Li < Be < C < B < N (d) Li < Be < N < B < C

Past Exams' Question

Selected PYQs with NCERT page tagging are present as the final check of preparation.

Skill Boosters

1 The first ($\Delta_i H_1$) and the second ($\Delta_i H_2$) ionisation enthalpies in kJ mol^{-1} of a few elements are given as

Elements	$\Delta_i H_1$	$\Delta_i H_2$	$\Delta_{eg} H$
A	520	7300	−60
B	419	3051	−48
C	1681	3374	−328
D	1008	1846	−295
E	2372	5251	+48
F	738	1451	−53

Which of the given elements is most reactive and least reactive metal respectively?
(a) *A*, *C* (b) *F*, *D* (c) *B*, *E* (d) *F*, *E*

Skill Boosters

Brain Teasers present at the end of step by step practice to provide extra edge for preparation.

Step by Step

Decoding the Questions

Concept Builders

1 electronic configuration
2 True 3 Na
4 Ga_2O_3 5 False
6 series, periods 7 Unnilhexium
8 False 9 Hydrogen
10 high reactivity 11 Sn
12 Cd, transition 13 True
14 $120 \rightarrow [Uuo]_{118} 8s^2$ 15 False
16 increases, decreases
17 114 pm
18 ionisation energy, kJ mol^{-1}
19 False 20 PX_2
21 oxygen, nitrogen

- This law is true for both physical and chemical properties.

4 (*b*) 5 (*b*)
6 (*b*) All the properties of Mendeleev's periodic table are correct except (b). Its correct form is as follows
He could not assign the proper positions for isotopes.
7 (*b*)
8 (*b*) Statement (b) is correct, while the other statements are incorrect. Their correct form are as follows
- According to modern periodic law, the seventh period is incomplete.
- Subsequent periods consist of 2, 8, 8, 18, 18 and 32 elements.

15 (*b*) Scandium ($Z = 21$) which has electronic configuration $= [Ar]3d^1 4s^2$ and zinc ($Z = 30$) has electronic configuration $= [Ar]3d^{10} 4s^2$.
16 (*d*) All the given statements are correct except (d) the correct form is as Hydrogen shows similarity more with Ist group than VIIth group.
17 (*a*) The elements in a vertical column of the periodic table constitute a group or family and exhibit similar chemical behaviour. This similarity arises because these elements have the same number and same distribution of electrons in their outermost orbitals.

Decoding the Questions

Answers and explanatory solutions of selected questions for better gripping of NCERT concepts.

Contents

01

Scan for Chemistry Through Concept Master Videos

Some Basic Concepts of Chemistry

Topicwise No. of Ques asked in 5 Years (NEET)

Topics	No. of Questions				
	2024	2023	2022	2021	2020
Development, Importance of Chemistry and Nature of Matter	–	–	–	–	–
Laws of Chemical Combinations	–	–	–	–	–
Dalton's Atomic Theory, Atomic and Molecular Masses	–	–	1	1	1
Mole Concept, Molar Mass and Percentage Composition	2	1	–	–	2
Stoichiometry and Stoichiometric Calculation	1	1	–	–	–

Special Type of Ques Asked In 5 Years (NEET)

Types	Years				
	2024	2023	2022	2021	2020
A-R	–	–	–	–	–
Statement Based	–	–	–	–	–
Matching	–	–	–	–	–

Last 5 Years Weightage (NEET)

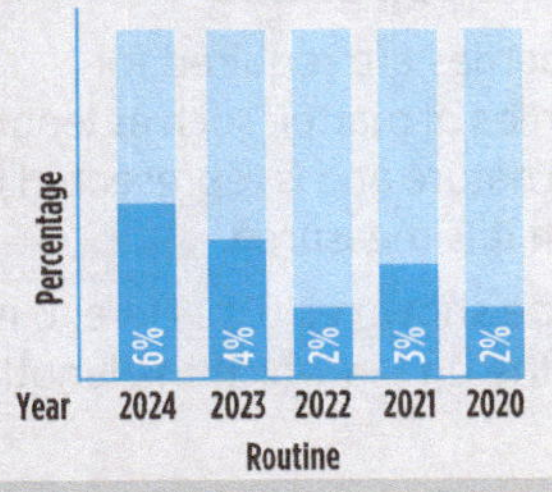

Development of Chemistry

- Chemistry, as we understand it today, is not a very old discipline.
- Chemistry was not studied for its own sake, rather it came up as a result of search for two interesting things :
  - (i) **Philosopher's stone** (Paras) which would convert all baser metals e.g. iron and copper into gold.
  - (ii) **'Elexir of life'** which would grant immortality.
- Chemistry developed mainly in the form of alchemy and iatrochemistry (medicine chemistry) during 1300-1600 CE.
- In ancient India, chemistry was called Rasayan Shastra, Rastantra, Ras Kriya or Rasvidya.

Importance of Chemistry

- **Chemistry** is the science of molecules and their transformation. It deals with the studies of preparations, properties, structure (compositions) and reactions of material substances. It plays a key role in science and is often closely connected to the remaining branches of science.
- Principles of chemistry are applicable in diverse areas such as weather patterns, functioning of brain and operation of a computer, production in chemical industries, manufacturing fertilizers, alkalis, acids, salts, dyes, polymers, drugs, soaps, detergents, metals, alloys etc., including new materials.
- Chemistry provides methods for isolation of life saving drugs from natural sources and makes possible synthesis of such drugs. Some of these drugs are ***cis*-platin** and **taxol** which are effective in cancer therapy. The drug **AZT** (Azidothymidine) is used for helping **AIDS** patients.

- Safer alternatives of environmentally hazardous refrigerants like CFC's (Chlorofluorocarbons) responsible for ozone depletion in the stratosphere, have been successfully synthesised.

Nature of Matter

Anything that occupies space and has mass is called matter. Everything around us for example, boot, pen, all living beings etc., are composed of matter.

States of Matter

Matter exists in three physical states, i.e. **solid, liquid** and **gas.**

(i) In **solids**, the particles are held very close to each other in an orderly arrangement and there is not much freedom of movement.

Due to such arrangement, solids have definite volume and definite shape.

(ii) In **liquids**, the particles are close to each other but they can move around. Liquids possess definite volume but do not possess definite shape.

(iii) In **gases**, the particles are far apart as compared to those present in solid or liquid states and their movement is easy and fast. They have neither definite volume nor definite shape.

These **three states of matter are interconvertible**, by changing the condition of temperature and pressure.

$$\text{Solid} \underset{\text{Cool}}{\overset{\text{Heat}}{\rightleftharpoons}} \text{Liquid} \underset{\text{Cool}}{\overset{\text{Heat}}{\rightleftharpoons}} \text{Gas}$$

Classification of Matter

On the basis of chemical composition, matter is classified as **mixture** or **pure substances.** They can further be divided as shown below.

I. **Pure substances** contain all constituent particles of a substance are same in chemical nature. Constituent particles of pure substances have fixed composition.

- These can further be classified into **elements** and **compounds**.
- Particles of an **element** consist of only one type of atoms. These particles may exist as **atoms** or **molecules**.
- Some elements such as sodium, copper etc., contain atoms and all atoms are of same type, whereas in **some others** such as hydrogen, nitrogen and oxygen gases, the constituent particles are molecules which are formed by two or more atoms.
- When two or more atoms of different elements combine together in a definite ratio, the molecule of a **compound** is obtained, e.g. water, ammonia, sugar etc. The constituents of a compound cannot be separated into simpler substances by physical methods. However, these can be separated by chemical methods.
- The atoms of different elements are present in a compound in a fixed and definite ratio. The properties of a compound are different from those of its constituent elements. e.g. H_2 and O_2 are gases, whereas the compound formed by their combination, i.e. water is a liquid.

II. **Mixture** contains particles of two or more pure substances which may be present in it in any ratio. Their composition is variable. It may be **homogeneous** or **heterogeneous**.

- In a **homogeneous mixture**, the components completely mix with each other. This means, particles of components of the mixtures are uniformly distributed throughout the bulk of the mixture which cannot be seen separately and its composition is uniform throughout, e.g. salt dissolved in water.
- In a **heterogeneous mixture**, the composition is not uniform throughout and sometimes different components are visible, e.g. salt and sand in water.

*Properties of Matter and their Measurement

Each substance is associated with some unique set of characteristics, which are collectively called the properties of matter. They are categorised into two types as given below.

Physical Properties

Those properties which can be measured or observed without changing the identity or the composition of the substance are called physical properties, e.g. colour, odour, melting point, boiling point, density etc.

Chemical Properties

Those properties which require a chemical change to occur for their measurement or observation are known as chemical properties. e.g. Characteristic reactions of different substances ; these include acidity, basicity, combustibility etc.

Measurements of Physical Properties

Quantitative measurements of properties are required for scientific investigation. Many properties of matter, such as length, area, volume etc., are quantitative in nature and is represented by a number followed by units in which it is measured.

For example, length of a room can be shown as 6 m. Here, 6 is the number and m denotes metre, the unit in which the length is measured.

The International System of Units (SI)

Many systems of measurements exist, among them the English and the **metric systems** are widely used. The scientific community has agreed to have a uniform and common system throughout the world which is abbreviated as SI units. The SI system has seven base units. These are as follows

Base Physical Quantities and their Units

Base physical quantity	Symbol for quantity	Name of SI unit	Symbol for SI unit
Length	l	metre	m
Mass	m	kilogram	kg
Time	t	second	s
Electric current	I	ampere	A
Thermodynamic temperature	T	Kelvin	K
Amount of substance	n	mole	mol
Luminous intensity	I_v	candela	cd

Some physical quantities are either too small or too large. To change the order of magnitude, the S.I. system allows the use of prefixes to indicate the multiples or submultiples of a unit. Some prefixes are listed as follows

Prefixes Used in SI System

Multiple	Prefix	Symbol	Multiple	Prefix	Symbol
10^{-1}	deci	d	10^{1}	deca	da
10^{-2}	centi	c	10^{2}	hecto	h
10^{-3}	milli	m	10^{3}	kilo	k
10^{-6}	micro	μ	10^{6}	mega	M
10^{-9}	nano	n	10^{9}	giga	G
10^{-12}	pico	p	10^{12}	tera	T
10^{-15}	femto	f	10^{15}	peta	P
10^{-18}	atto	a	10^{18}	exa	E
10^{-21}	zepto	z	10^{21}	zeta	Z
10^{-24}	yocto	y	10^{24}	yotta	Y

Mass and Weight

- The amount of matter present in a substance is called **mass**, while the force exerted by gravity on an object is called **weight**.
- The mass of a substance is constant, whereas its weight may vary from one place to another due to change in gravity.
- The SI unit of mass is kilogram (kg). The mass of a substance can be determined accurately by using analytical balance.

Volume

- It is the amount of space occupied by a substance. In SI system, its unit is m^3.
- A common unit, litre (L) is used for measurement of volume of liquids. $1L = 1000$ mL, $1000 \text{ cm}^3 = 1 \text{ dm}^3$
- In laboratory, the volumes of liquids or solutions can be measured by graduated cylinders, burette, pipette etc.
- A volumetric flask is used to prepare a known volume of a solution.

Density

- It is the amount of mass per unit volume.

$$\text{Density} = \frac{\text{Mass}}{\text{Volume}}$$

- Its SI unit is kg m^{-3}.
- Density of a substance tells us about how closely its particles are packed. If it is more, it means particles are more closely packed.

Temperature

- It is the measure of hotness or coldness of a body.
- There are three common scales to measure temperature °C (degree Celsius), °F (degree Fahrenheit) and K (Kelvin).
- The temperature on Fahrenheit scale and Celsius scale are related to each other by following relationship.

$$°F = \frac{9}{5}(°C) + 32$$

- The Kelvin scale is related to Celsius scale as follows

$$K = °C + 273.15$$

- Temperature below 0°C are possible in Celsius scale but in Kelvin scale, negative temperature is not possible.

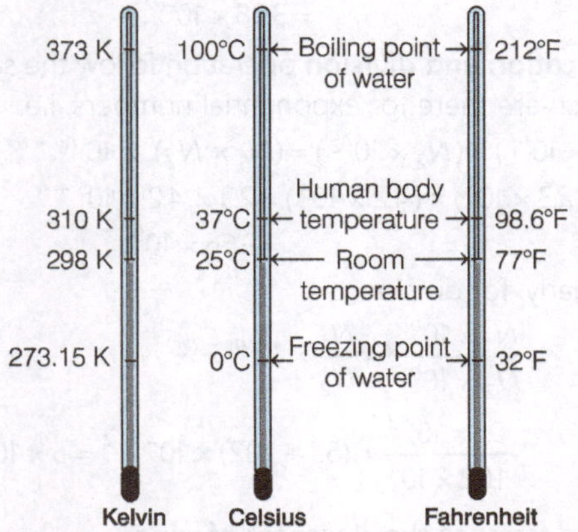

Thermometers using different temperatures scales

Uncertainty in Measurement

- A convenient system of expressing the numbers in **scientific notation** is used, i.e. exponential notation in, which any number can be represented in the form $N \times 10^n$, where n is an exponent having positive or negative values and N is a number (called digit term) which varies between 1.000 and 9.999.

  e.g. We can write 829.402 as 8.29402×10^2 in scientific notation. The decimal had to be moved to the left by two places, then same is the exponent (2) of 10 in scientific notation.
- Similarly, 0.00042 can be written as 4.2×10^{-4}. Here, the decimal has to be moved to four places to the right. (– 4) is the exponent in scientific notation.
- While performing mathematical operations on numbers expressed in scientific notation, following points should be kept in mind.
- In **addition and subtraction**, first the number are written in such a way that they have the same exponents. After that, the coefficients (digit terms) are added or subtracted as the case may be
  (i) Let the two numbers be $N_1 \times 10^n$ and $N_2 \times 10^n$, then

  Addition $(N_1 \times 10^n) + (N_2 \times 10^n) = (N_1 + N_2) \times 10^n$

  Subtraction $(N_1 \times 10^n) - (N_2 \times 10^n) = (N_1 - N_2) \times 10^n$

  (ii) Thus, for adding 7.32×10^4 and 3.92×10^3, exponent is made same for both the numbers. So, these numbers can be added as

  $$(7.32 + 0.392) \times 10^4 = 7.712 \times 10^4$$

  (iii) Similarly the subtraction of two numbers can be done as

  $$(3.5 \times 10^{-2}) - (4.2 \times 10^{-3}) = (3.5 \times 10^{-2}) - (0.42 \times 10^{-2})$$
  $$= (3.5 - 0.42) \times 10^{-2}$$
  $$= 3.08 \times 10^{-2}$$
- **Multiplication and division** operation follow the same rule which are there for exponential numbers, i.e.

  (i) $(N_1 \times 10^{n_1}) \times (N_2 \times 10^{n_2}) = (N_1 \times N_2) \times 10^{(n_1 + n_2)}$

  e.g. $(2.3 \times 10^5) \times (4.2 \times 10^4) = 2.3 \times 4.2 \times 10^{5+4}$
  $= 9.66 \times 10^9$

  (ii) Similarly, for division

  $$\frac{N_1 \times 10^{n_1}}{N_2 \times 10^{n_2}} = \frac{N_1}{N_2} \times 10^{(n_1 - n_2)}$$

  e.g. $$\frac{5.1 \times 10^{-3}}{1.02 \times 10^4} = (5.1 \div 1.02) \times 10^{-3-4} = 5 \times 10^{-7}$$
- **Precision** refers to the closeness of various measurements for the same quantity.
- **Accuracy** is the agreement of a particular value to the true value of the result.

Significant Figures

These are the meaningful digits which are known with certainty plus one which is estimated or uncertain.

Rules for counting significant figures are as follows

(i) All non-zero digits and zero present between two non-zero digits are significant.
(ii) Zeros preceding to first non-zero digit are not significant.
(iii) Zeros at the end or right of a number are significant, provided they are on the right side of the decimal point.
(iv) Terminal zeros are not significant if there is no decimal point.
(v) Exact numbers have an infinite number of significant figures.
(vi) While addition and subtraction of significant figures, the result cannot have more digits to the right of the decimal point than either of the original numbers.

The **rules for rounding off** the result to the required number of significant figures are as follows

- In **addition** and **subtraction**, the answer is rounded off to match the same number of decimal places as the quantity with the least number of decimal places.
- In **multiplication** and **division** of significant figures, the result must be reported with no more significant figures as in the measurement with the few significant figures.
- While **limiting the results** to the required number of significant figures. The following points should be kept in mind : If the rightmost digit to be removed is
  (i) more than 5, then the preceding number is increased by 1. e.g. 1.487 is rounded off as 1.49.
  (ii) less than 5, then the preceding number is not changed. e.g. 5.443 is rounded off as 5.44.
  (iii) equal to 5, then the preceding number is not changed, if it is even. However it is increased by one if it is an odd number. e.g. 6.315 is rounded off as 6.32 and 6.345 is rounded off as 6.34.

Dimensional Analysis

- The method used to convert units from one system to the other is called **factor label method** or **unit factor method** or dimensional analysis.

  For example, to convert inches into cm or *vice-versa*. We can write, 1 inch = 2.54 cm

  So, $\frac{1 \text{ inch}}{2.54 \text{ cm}} = 1 = \frac{2.54 \text{ cm}}{1 \text{ inch}}$
- The quantities such as 2.54 cm per inch or one inch per 2.54 cm are called **'unit conversion factors'**.

  Quantity required = Quantity given × C.F. (Conversion Factor)

* *This topic is not include in latest NEET syllabus, but it is given in latest rationalised NCERT.*

Marks Maximizer

Conversion factor is a factor 1 that converts a quantity in one unit to the same quantity in another unit. Some conversion factors are given below.

- 1 Å (Angstrom) $= 10^{-8}$ cm $= 10^{-10}$ m $= 10^{-1}$ nm $= 10^{2}$ pm
- 1 amu (atomic mass unit) $= 1.6605 \times 10^{-24}$ g $= 931.48$ MeV
- 1 atm (atmosphere) 760 torr = 760 mm Hg = 76 cm Hg $= 1.01325 \times 10^{5}$ Pa
- 1 cal (calorie) = 4.18 J $= 2.613 \times 10^{19}$ eV
- 1 Joule $= 10^{7}$ erg = 0.2390 cal
- 1 Faraday $= 9.6487 \times 10^{4}$ coulomb
- 1 dyne $= 10^{-5}$ N
- 1 electron volt $= 1.6021 \times 10^{-19}$ J $= 3.827 \times 10^{-20}$ cal
- 1 esu (electrostatic unit) $= 3.33564 \times 10^{-10}$ C

Laws of Chemical Combinations

Elements combine to form compounds in accordance to the following five basic laws of chemical combinations.

(i) **Law of conservation of mass** (Antoine Lavoisier)
Matter can neither be created nor be destroyed during a chemical reaction.

(ii) **Law of definite proportions** (Joseph Proust)
It is also called as **law of definite composition.**
A given compound always contains exactly the same proportion of elements by weight.

(iii) **Law of multiple proportions** (John Dalton)
If two elements can combine to form more than one compound, the masses of one element that combine with a fixed mass of the other element, are in the ratio of small whole numbers.

(iv) **Gay Lussac's law of gaseous volumes** (Joseph Louis Gay Lussac)
When gases combine or are produced in a chemical reaction, they do so in a simple ratio by volume, provided all gases are at the same temperature and pressure.

(v) **Avogadro's law** (Avogadro)
Equal volumes of all gases at the same temperature and pressure should contain equal number of molecules.

Marks Maximizer

Law of reciprocal proportions states that, when two different elements combine separately with a fixed mass of third element, then the ratio between their masses in which they combine will be either same or simple multiple of the ratio in which they combine with each other.

Dalton's Atomic Theory

The main postulates of this theory are as follows

- Matter consists of indivisible atoms.
- All atoms of a given element have identical properties including identical mass. Atoms of different elements differ in mass.
- Compounds are formed when atoms of different elements combine in a fixed ratio.
- Chemical reactions involve reorganisation of atoms. These are neither created nor destroyed in a chemical reaction.

Demerit It could not explain the laws of gaseous volumes. It could not provide the reason for combining of atoms, which was later answered by other scientists.

Atomic and Molecular Masses

- The present system of **atomic masses** is based on carbon-12 (^{12}C) as the standard which is one of the isotopes of carbon.
- In this system, ^{12}C is assigned a mass of exactly 12 **atomic mass unit** and masses of all other atoms are given relative to this standard.
- One atomic mass unit is defined as a mass exactly equal to one-twelfth of the mass of one carbon-12 atom. At present, 'amu' has been replaced by 'u' which is known as **unified mass**.

$$1 \text{ amu} = 1.66056 \times 10^{-24} \text{ g}$$

- Many naturally occurring elements exist as more than one isotope. When we take into account the existence of these isotopes and their relative abundance, the **average atomic mass** of the element can be computed.

Average atomic mass =

$$\frac{(\text{Relative abundance} \times \text{Atomic mass})_1 + (\text{Relative abundance} \times \text{Atomic mass})_2}{(\text{Relative Abundance})_1 + (\text{Relative abundance})_2}$$

Isotope	Relative abundance (%)	Atomic mass (amu)
^{13}C	98.892	12
^{13}C	1.108	13.00335
^{14}C	2×10^{-10}	14.00317

- **Molecular mass** is the sum of atomic masses of the elements present in a molecule. It is obtained by multiplying the atomic mass of each element by the number of its atom and adding them together. NEET 2022

$$\text{Molecular mass} = \frac{\text{Average mass of one molecule}}{\frac{1}{12} \times \text{Mass of an atom of C - 12}}$$

- Some substances, such as sodium chloride do not contain discrete molecules as their constituent units. The formula such as NaCl is used to calculate **the formula mass** instead of molecular mass as in the solid state sodium chloride does not exist as a single entity.

Mole Concept and Molar Masses

- **One mole** is the amount of a substance that contains as many particles or entities as there are atoms in exactly 12g of the ^{12}C isotope, i.e. 6.022×10^{23} atoms/mol. NEET 2020, 2024
- 6.022×10^{23} is called **Avogadro's number** or **Avogadro's constant**. It is denoted by N_A.
- The mass of one mole of a substance in grams is called its **molar mass** which is numerically equal to atomic/molecular/formula mass expressed in **u**.

Marks Maximizer

- 1 molar mass = 22.4 L of gas at STP
  $= 6.022 \times 10^{23}$ particles/1 mole
- Gram molecular mass = 1 gram molecule
  $= N_A$ molecules $= 6.022 \times 10^{23}$ molecules
- Gram atomic mass = 1 gram atom $= N_A$ atoms
  $= 6.022 \times 10^{23}$ atoms

Percentage Composition

For determining the percentage composition of each element in a compound.

Mass % of an element

$$= \frac{\text{Mass of that element in the compound}}{\text{Molar mass of the compound}} \times 100$$

Empirical Formula and Molecular Formula

- An **empirical formula** represents the simplest whole number ratio of various atoms present in a compound. NEET 2021, 2024
- The **molecular formula** shows the exact number of different types of atoms present in a molecule of a compound.

Steps to Find Empirical and Molecular Formula

***Step* I** Conversion of mass percent to grams.

***Step* II** Convert into number of moles of each element.

***Step* III** Divide each of the mole values obtained above by the smallest number amongst them.

***Step* IV** Write down the empirical formula by mentioning the numbers after writing the symbols of respective elements.

***Step* V** Multiply empirical formula by n to obtain molecular formula.

where, $n = \dfrac{\text{Molar mass}}{\text{Empirical formula mass}}$

Stoichiometry and Stoichiometric Calculations

- **Stoichiometry** deals with the calculation of masses (sometimes volumes also) of the reactants and the products involved in a chemical reaction. It can be determined with the knowledge of balanced chemical equation. NEET 2019, 2023
- A balanced chemical equation has the same number of atoms of each element on both sides of the equation.
- In the balanced equation,

$$CH_4(g) + 2O_2(g) \longrightarrow CO_2(g) + 2H_2O(g),$$

  the coefficients 2 for O_2 and H_2O are called **stoichiometric coefficients**. Similarly, for CH_4 and CO_2, stoichiometric coefficient is 1.
- Stoichiometric coefficient represent the number of molecules (and moles as well) taking part in a reaction (like above reaction) as follows
  - (i) One **mole** of $CH_4(g)$ reacts with two **moles** of $O_2(g)$ to give one **mole** of $CO_2(g)$ and two **moles** of $H_2O(g)$.
  - (ii) One **molecule** of $CH_4(g)$ reacts with 2 **molecules** of $O_2(g)$ to give one **molecule** of $CO_2(g)$ and 2 **molecules** of $H_2O(g)$.
  - (iii) 22.7 L of $CH_4(g)$ reacts with 45.4 L of $O_2(g)$ to give 22.7 L of $CO_2(g)$ and 45.4 L of $H_2O(g)$.
  - (iv) 16 g of $CH_4(g)$ reacts with 2×32 g of $O_2(g)$ to give 44g of CO_2 and 2×18 g of $H_2O(g)$.

  From the above data we can say that,

  mass $\rightleftharpoons$ moles $\rightleftharpoons$ number of molecules

- The reactant which gets consumed first and limits the amount of product formed in a chemical reaction is called the **limiting reagent**. NEET 2024

For Concept Master *Video*

Reactions in Solutions

The concentration of a solution or the amount of substance present in its given volumes can be expressed in any of the following ways shown in below table:

Comparison between Concentration Terms

	Mass per cent or weight per cent (*w/w* %)	Mole fraction (χ)	Molality (m)	Molarity (M)
Definition	It is the mass of the element or solute divided by the mass of the compound or solution.	The ratio of number of moles of a particular component to the total number of moles of the solution.	The number of moles of solute present in 1 kg of solvent. NEET 2019	The number of moles of the solute in 1 litre of the solution. For Concept Master Video
Formula	$\frac{w_{solute}}{W_{solution}} \times 100$ where, w_{solute} = Mass of solute $W_{solution}$ = Mass of solution	$\chi_{solute} = \frac{n_{solute}}{n_{solute} + n_{solvent}}$ $\chi_{solvent} = \frac{n_{solvent}}{n_{solute} + n_{solvent}}$ $\chi_{solute} + \chi_{solvent} = 1$ where, χ_{solute} = Mole fraction of solute n_{solute} = Number of moles of solute $\chi_{solvent}$ = Mole fraction of solvent $n_{solvent}$ = Number of moles of solvent	$m = \frac{n_{solute}}{W_{solvent}(\text{in g})} \times 1000$ $= \frac{w_{solute}(\text{in g}) \times 1000}{Mw_{solute} \times w_{solvent}(\text{in g})}$ n_{solute} = Number of moles of solute w_{solute} = Mass of solute $W_{solvent}$ = Mass of solvent Mw_{solute} = Molecular weight of solute	$M = \frac{n_{solute}}{V_{solution}(\text{in L})}$ $M = \frac{w_{solute}(\text{in g})}{Mw_{solute} \times V_{solution}(\text{in L})}$ where, n, w, W nd M_w are same as is molality. $V_{solution}$ = Volume of solution Molarity of solution after dilution = $M_1V_1 = M_2V_2$
Units	Unitless	Unitless	mol/kg	mol/L

Note (Effect of temperature on concentration) Molality and mole fraction are preferred over molarity. It is because molality and mole fraction do not change with temperature. As they involve masses of the solute and the solvent which do not change with temperature, whereas, molarity changes with temperature as it involves volume of the solution which changes with temperature.

Marks Maximizer

- Normality (N) = $\frac{\text{Gram-equivalents of the solute}}{\text{Volume of the solution in litre (L)}}$
  $= \frac{w \times 1000}{\text{GEM} \times V_{(mL)}}$
  where, GEM is gram equivalent mass.
- Equivalents = $\frac{\text{Mass of compound}}{\text{Gram equivalent weight}}$
- Gram equivalent weight $= \frac{\text{Molar mass}}{n\text{-factor}}$
- Molarity (M) × GMM (solute) = Normality (N) × GEM (solute), where, GMM is gram molecular mass.
- Normality and molarity equations = $N_1V_1 = N_2V_2$; $M_1V_1 = M_2V_2$ (for dilution)

PYQ Notes

1. % purity of substance $= \frac{\text{Weight of pure substance}}{\text{Weight of impure sample}} \times 100$ **NEET 2022, 2015**
2. Number of atoms (n) $= \frac{\text{Mass (in g)} \times \text{Atomicity of the molecule}}{\text{Gram molar mass } (M)} \times N_A$
   where, N_A = Avogadro's number **NEET 2020**
3. Number of moles $= \frac{\text{Mass of substance (g)}}{\text{Molar mass (g mol}^{-1})}$ **NEET 2018, 2015**
4. Number of moles $= \frac{\text{Volume of gas (L)}}{22.4}$ **NEET 2018**
5. One mole = 22.4 L of gas at STP **NEET 2014**
6. Atomic mass = Equivalent mass × Valency **NEET 2019**
7. Molecular mass = 2 × Vapour density **NEET 2017**

Step by Step

Mastering NCERT

- Concept Builders
- Topical Questions
- Assertion-Reason
- Statement Type
- Matching Type
- Numerical Value
- NCERT Exemplar's
- Past Exams'
- Skill Boosters

Concept Builders

1 Gypsum cement contains lime, sand and traces of ....

2 Chemistry is also called the science of atoms and molecules. [T/F]

3 The drug *cis*-platin is effective in cancer therapy. [T/F]

4 The drug .... is used for helping AIDS patients.

5 Write the name of the hazardous chemical responsible for ozone depletion in the stratosphere.

6 The physical states of matter can be change by changing the conditions of temperature and pressure. [T/F]

7 Mixture of salts is an example of .... mixture.

8 Carbon, hydrogen and oxygen are the constituents of glucose which can be separated by simple physical methods. [T/F]

9 Atoms of different elements are present in a compound .... and definite ratio.

10 Write the name of the SI unit of luminous intensity.

11 Boiling point of water is 312°F. [T/F]

12 The division of 2.7×10^{-3} and 5.5×10^{4} is .... in scientific notation.

13 The number of significant figures in Avogadro's number is ....

14 The term which refers to the closeness of various measurements for the same quantity.

15 A jug contains 2 L of milk. So, the volume of the milk is 2×10^{-3} cm^3. [T/F]

16 A nuclear reaction is an example of law of conservation of mass. [T/F]

17 Joseph Proust, a French chemist introduces the law of ....

18 Name the law which is an application of law of definite composition for volume.

19 Dalton's atomic theory completely satisfies the law's of chemical combinations. [T/F]

20 The mass exactly equal to one-twelfth of the mass at one carbon-12 atom is ....

21 The molecular mass of glucose ($C_6H_{12}O_6$) is ....

22 The mole was introduced as fifth base quantity for the amount of a substance. [T/F]

23 Write the % of carbon in ethanol.

24 The empirical formula represents the simplest whole number ratio of various atoms present in a compound. [T/F]

25 The stoichiometric coefficient of oxygen in the combustion at methane is ....

26 The limiting reagent for the reaction is ....

$$CH_4(g) + 2O_2(g) \longrightarrow CO_2(g) + 2H_2O(g)$$

27 A solution is prepared by adding 2 g of a substance *A* to 18 g of water. The mass percent of the solute *A* is ....

28 In molarity equation ($M_1V_1 = M_2V_2$), the number of moles remains the same. [T/F]

29 Write the mole fraction of solute with moles '*n*' in a solution with moles of solvent N.

30 Molality of solution changes with change in temperature. [T/F]

Topical Questions

Development, Importance of Chemistry and Nature of Matter

1 Chemistry was not studied for its own sake, rather it came up as a result of search for Elexir of life and .... NCERT Pg 1

(a) Philosopher's stone (b) Charaka Samhita
(c) Rasopanishada (d) R Sarnavam

2 Which of the following is not described in Charaka Samhita? NCERT Pg 2, 3

(a) Preparation of nitric acid and oxides of Cu, Sn and Zn.
(b) Use of various parts of plant for the preparation of Asavas.
(c) Preparation of perfumes and cosmetics.
(d) Use of Bhasma of metals for treatment of ailments

3 The two effective drugs which act as life saving drugs for cancer therapy and AIDS victims respectively are NCERT Pg 4

(a) AZT (azidothymidine) and taxol
(b) Taxol and *cis*-platin
(c) Taxol and AZT (azidothymidine)
(d) AZT (azidothymidine) and *cis*-platin

4 Which of the following substances have neither definite volume nor definite shape? NCERT Pg 4

(a) Water (b) Oxygen
(c) Salt (d) Oil

Properties of Matter and Their Measurement

5 Consider the following units of volume,
$A:1\text{L} \quad B:1\text{ mL} \quad C:1\text{cm}^3 \quad D:1\text{dm}^3$
The correct relation is NCERT Pg 9

(a) $A=B=C=D$ (b) $A=D>B=C$
(c) $A>B>C=D$ (d) $A=D<B=C$

6 Few quantities with their units are given below. Mark the unit which is not correctly converted. NCERT Pg 9

(a) $1\text{ km}=10^6\text{mm}$ (b) $1\text{ mg}=10^{-6}\text{ kg}$
(c) $1\text{ mg}=10^{10}\text{ng}$ (d) $1\text{ mL}=10^{-3}\text{dm}^3$

7 The correct conversion of the following into basic units. NCERT Pg 9

(i) 28.7 pm (ii) 15.15 μs (iii) 25365 mg

(a) (i) $\rightarrow 28.7\times10^{-11}$m, (ii) $\rightarrow 1.515\times10^{-6}$s, (iii) $\rightarrow 2.5365\times10^{-3}$kg
(b) (i) $\rightarrow 2.87\times10^{-11}$m, (ii) $\rightarrow 1.515\times10^{-5}$s, (iii) $\rightarrow 2.5365\times10^{-2}$kg
(c) (i) $\rightarrow 2.87\times10^{-10}$m, (ii) $\rightarrow 1.515\times10^{-5}$s, (iii) $\rightarrow 2.5365\times10^{-3}$kg
(d) (i) $\rightarrow 2.87\times10^{-10}$m, (ii) $\rightarrow 1.515\times10^{-6}$s, (iii) $\rightarrow 2.5365\times10^{-2}$kg

8 Few prefixes with their multiples are listed below. Mark the units which are not correctly matched. NCERT Pg 9

(i) Pico : 10^9
(ii) Femto : 10^{-15}
(iii) milli : 10^{-3}
(iv) giga : 10^{-12}
(v) hecto : 10^2

(a) (i) and (iv) (b) (i), (ii) and (iv)
(c) (ii) and (v) (d) (iii) and (v)

Uncertainty in Measurement

9 The scientific notation of some figures are given below. Which of the following options is not correct? NCERT Pg 11

(a) $8008=8.008\times10^3$ (b) $208=2.08\times10^2$
(c) $5000=5.0\times10^3$ (d) $0.0034=3.4\times10^3$

10 In scientific notation, 0.00016 can be written as NCERT Pg 11

(a) 1.6×10^{-4} (b) 1.6×10^{-3}
(c) 1.6×10^{-2} (d) 1.6×10^{-1}

11 The addition of numbers 6.65×10^4 and 8.95×10^3 and subtraction of numbers 2.5×10^{-2} and 4.8×10^{-3}, respectively in terms of scientific and notation will be NCERT Pg 12

(a) $7.545\times10^4, 2.02\times10^{-2}$
(b) $75.43\times10^3, 2.02\times10^{-3}$
(c) $745.5\times10^2, 2.02\times10^{-1}$
(d) $75.45\times10^0, 2.02\times10^0$

12 Which set of figures will be obtained after rounding up the following upto three significant figures? NCERT Pg 13

36.217, 0.04597, 10.4107

(a) 36.3, 0.0461, 10.4 (b) 36.2, 0.046, 10.4
(c) 36.20, 0.460, 10.40 (d) 36.21, 4.597, 1.04

13 Mark the rule, which is not correctly stated about the determination of significant figures. NCERT Pg 13

(a) Zeros preceding to first non-zero digit are not significant.
(b) Zeros between two non-zero digits are not significant.
(c) Zeros at the end or right of the number are significant, if they are on the right side of decimal point
(d) The terminal zeros are not significant, if there is no decimal point.

14 Which of the following statement is incorrect regarding significant figures? NCERT Pg 12

(a) All non-zero digits are significant.
(b) Significant figures are meaningful digits which are known with certainty.
(c) Zeros between two non-zero digits are significant.
(d) Zeros at the end or right of a number are not significant.

15 Which of the following rules regarding the significant figures and their calculations is incorrect? **NCERT Pg 12**

(a) The result of an addition or substraction is reported to the same number of decimal places as present in number with least decimal places.

(b) Result of multiplication or division should have same number of significant figures as present in most precise figure.

(c) The result of multiplication or division should be rounded off to same number of significant figures as present in least precise figure.

(d) The non-significant figures in the measurements are rounded-off.

16 *A* refers to the closeness of various measurements for the same quantity. *B* is the agreement of a particular value to the true value of the result. *A* and *B* respectively are **NCERT Pg 13**

(a) $A \rightarrow$ significant figures, $B \rightarrow$ accuracy

(b) $A \rightarrow$ accuracy, $B \rightarrow$ precision

(c) $A \rightarrow$ precision, $B \rightarrow$ accuracy

(d) $A \rightarrow$ significant figures, $B \rightarrow$ precision

17 Given that, the true value for a result is 2.00 g. Three students *A*, *B* and *C* take two measurements and report the result, data to illustrate precision and accuracy as given below. **NCERT Pg 13**

Student	Measurement (in g)		
	1	2	Average (in g)
Student *A*	1.95	1.93	1.940
Student *B*	1.94	2.05	1.995
Student *C*	2.01	1.99	2.000

Which of the following students got the values which are both precise and accurate?

(a) Student *A* (b) Student *B*

(c) Student *C* (d) None of these

18 Look at the addition of significant figures given below. **NCERT Pg 13**

$$\begin{array}{r} 12.11 \\ 18.0 \\ 1.012 \\ \hline 31.122 \end{array}$$

The result reported in this addition should be

(a) 31.12 (b) 31.1 (c) 31.122 (d) 31.10

19 The result reported in the following multiplication of significant figures, $2.5 \times 1.25 = 3.125$ should be **NCERT Pg 13**

(a) 3.125 (b) 3.1 (c) 3.12 (d) 3.10

20 The result of which of the following has/have least significant figure(s)? **NCERT Pg 13**

(a) $\dfrac{0.02856 \times 298.15 \times 0.112}{0.5785}$

(b) 5×5.364

(c) $0.0125 + 0.7864 + 0.0215$

(d) All have same number of significant figures.

21 A worker had done has work for 2.5 days. How many seconds he inverted in his complete work? **NCERT Pg 14**

(a) 21600 seconds (b) 216000 seconds

(c) 2116000 seconds (d) 211600 seconds

Laws of Chemical Combinations

22 4.88 g of $KClO_3$ when heated, produces 1.92 g of O_2 and 2.96 g of KCl. Which law is illustrated by the above experiment? **NCERT Pg 14**

(a) The result illustrates the law of conservation of mass.

(b) The result illustrates the law of multiple proportion.

(c) The result illustrates the law of constant proportion.

(d) The result illustrates the law of definite proportions.

23 If 6.3 g of $NaHCO_3$ are added to 15.0 g CH_3COOH solution, the residue is found to weigh 18.0 g. What will be the mass of CO_2 released in the reaction? **NCERT Pg 14**

(a) 4.5 g (b) 3.3 g (c) 2.6 g (d) 2.8 g

24 Proust worked with the two samples of cupric carbonate, one of which was of natural origin and the other was synthetic one. He found that, the composition of elements present in it was same for both the samples as shown below. **NCERT Pg 15**

Sample	% of Cu	% of C	% of O
Natural sample	51.35	9.74	38.91
Synthetic sample	51.35	9.74	38.91

Which law is in favour of the above data?

(a) Law of multiple proportions

(b) Gay Lussac's law of gaseous volumes

(c) Avogadro's law

(d) Law of definite proportions

25 Zinc sulphate contains 22.65% zinc and 43.9% water of crystallisation. If the law of constant proportions is true then the weight of zinc required to produce 20 g of the zinc sulphate crystals will be **NCERT Pg 15**

(a) 45.3 g (b) 4.53 g

(c) 0.453 g (d) 453 g

26 Among the following how many pairs which illustrate the law of multiple proportions is. **NCERT Pg 15**

A. PH_3, HCl B. $CuCl_2$, $CuSO_4$ C. PbO, PbO_2

D. H_2S, SO_2 E. NO, N_2O

Choose the correct option.

(a) 1 (b) 2 (c) 3 (d) 4

27 Which of the following statements illustrate the law of multiple proportions? **NCERT Pg 15**

(a) 3.47 g of $BaCl_2$ reacts with 2.36 g of Na_2SO_4 to give 3.88 g of $BaSO_4$ and 1.95 g of NaCl.

(b) Hydrogen sulphide contains 5.89% hydrogen, water contains 11.1% hydrogen and sulphur dioxide contains 50% oxygen.

(c) An element forms two oxides, XO and XO_2 containing 50% and 60% oxygen respectively. The ratio of masses of oxygen which combines with 1 g of element is 2 : 3.

(d) 20 mL ammonia gives 10 volumes N_2 and 30 volumes H_2 at constant temperature and pressure.

28 According to Avogadro's law, two volumes of hydrogen combine with one volume of oxygen to give two volumes of water without leaving any **NCERT Pg 15**

(a) mass of oxygen. (b) residual mass of oxygen.
(c) reacted oxygen. (d) unreacted oxygen.

29 Consider the given figure, **NCERT Pg 16**

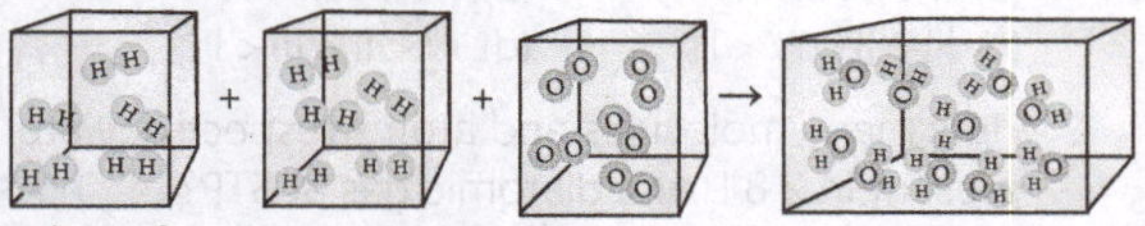

Two volumes of hydrogen react with one volume of oxygen to give two volumes of water vapour.

Hydrogen + Oxygen $\longrightarrow$ Water
100 mL A 100 mL

The volumes of hydrogen and oxygen which combine together bear a simple ratio of ...B... .
The missing terms A and B respectively are

(a) $A \rightarrow 25$ mL, $B \rightarrow 1:2$ (b) $A \rightarrow 50$ mL, $B \rightarrow 1:2$
(c) $A \rightarrow 50$ mL, $B \rightarrow 2:1$ (d) $A \rightarrow 25$ mL, $B \rightarrow 2:1$

Dalton's Atomic Theory, Atomic and Molecular Masses

30 Which of the following postulates of Dalton's atomic theory explains the law of multiple proportion? **NCERT Pg 16**

(a) Atoms of two elements may combine with one another to form more than one compound.
(b) Atoms combine in the ratio of small whole numbers to form compounds.
(c) The relative numbers and kinds of atoms are constant.
(d) All atoms of a given element have identical properties, including identical mass. Atoms of different elements differ in mass.

31 According to John Dalton's atomic theory, atoms are **NCERT Pg 16**

(a) indivisible and indestructible particles.
(b) made up of protons, neutrons and electrons.
(c) composed of positively charged protons and negatively charged electrons.
(d) always in motion around the nucleus.

32 Which of the following statement is correct? **NCERT Pg 16**

(a) Atoms of a given element are non-identical in mass and chemical properties.
(b) Atoms combine in the ratio of small natural number to form compounds.
(c) The relative number and types of atoms are constant in a given element.
(d) Matter consists of very tiny particles named as atom.

33 An element have three isotope and their atomic masses are 11, 12, 13 unit respectively and their percentage of occurrence in nature is 85, 10, 5 respectively, then average atomic mass is **NCERT Pg 17**

(a) 22.4 (b) 11.2 (c) 10 (d) 12

34 Oxygen occurs in nature as a mixture of isotopes ^{16}O, ^{17}O and ^{18}O having atomic masses of 15.995 u, 16.999 u and 17.999 u and relative abundance of 99.763%, 0.037% and 0.200% respectively. What is the average atomic mass of oxygen? **NCERT Pg 17**

(a) 15.999 u (b) 16.999 u
(c) 17.999 u (d) 18.999 u

35 Carbon has the following three isotopes with relative abundances and masses (amu) shown in the table. **NCERT Pg 17**

Isotopes	Relative abundance (%)	Atomic mass (amu)
^{12}C	98.892	12
^{13}C	1.108	13.00335
^{14}C	2×10^{-10}	14.00317

On the basis of above data, the average atomic mass of carbon will be

(a) 12.000 u (b) 12.011 u (c) 12.015 u (d) 13.000 u

36 Use the data given in the following table to calculate the molar mass of naturally occurring argon. **NCERT Pg 17**

Isotope	Isotopic molar mass	Abundance
^{36}Ar	35.96755 g mol^{-1}	0.337%
^{38}Ar	37.96272 g mol^{-1}	0.063%
^{40}Ar	39.9624 g mol^{-1}	99.600%

The molar mass of argon is

(a) 39.948 (b) 39.504 (c) 39.0 (d) 37.482

37 Packing of K^+ and Cl^- ions in potassium chloride is depicted by the given figure. Which of the following statement is correct regarding formula mass of potassium chloride. **NCERT Pg 17**

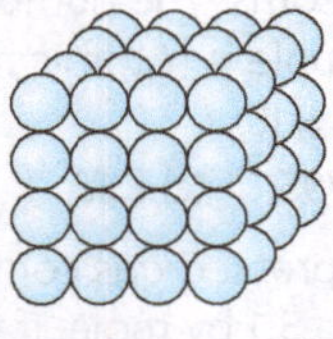

(a) In the solid state, potassium chloride as a single entity.
(b) Potassium chloride contains discrete molecule.
(c) Formula mass of KCl is 74.6 u.
(d) Formula mass of KCl is the multiplication of atomic masses of K and Cl.

38 Given that, the abundances of isotopes ^{54}Fe, ^{56}Fe and ^{57}Fe are 5%, 90% and 5% respectively, the average atomic mass of Fe is **NCERT Pg 17**

(a) 55.85 (b) 55.95
(c) 55.75 (d) 56.05

Mole Concept, Molar Mass and Percentage Composition

39 Which of the following statements about the molecular formula is not correct? **NCERT Pg 18**

(a) Molecular formula shows the exact number of different types of atoms present in a molecule.
(b) Molecular formula can be obtained from empirical formula if molar mass is known.
(c) Percentage composition of a compound can be calculated from its molecular formula.
(d) Molecular formula represents the simplest whole number ratio of various atoms present in a compound.

40 In order to determine the mole precisely, the mass of a carbon *A* was determined by a *B* and found to be equal to *C* g. *A*, *B* and *C* respectively are **NCERT Pg 18**

(a) $A \rightarrow$ 12 atom, $B \rightarrow$ mass spectrometer, $C \rightarrow 1.992648 \times 10^{-23}$
(b) $A \rightarrow$ 14 atom, $B \rightarrow$ atomic spectrometer, $C \rightarrow 1.992648 \times 10^{-21}$
(c) $A \rightarrow$ 1 mole, $B \rightarrow$ Infrared spectrometer, $C \rightarrow 1.992648 \times 10^{-20}$
(d) $A \rightarrow$ 12 atom, $B \rightarrow$ mass spectrometer, $C \rightarrow 1.992 \times 10^{-19}$

41 What will be the weight of CO having the same number of O-atoms as present in 22 g of CO_2? **NCERT Pg 18**

(a) 28 g (b) 22 g
(c) 44 g (d) 72 g

42 How many aluminium ions are present in 0.051 g of aluminium oxide? **NCERT Pg 18**

(a) 6.023×10^{23} (b) 6.023×10^{31}
(c) 6.023×10^{20} (d) 6.023×10^{24}

43 A sample of ammonia phosphate, $(NH_4)_3PO_4$ contains 6.36 moles of H-atoms. The number of moles of O-atom in the sample is (Atomic mass of N = 14.04, H = 1, P = 31 and O = 16) **NCERT Pg 18**

(a) 0.265 (b) 0.795 (c) 2.12 (d) 4.14

44 A cylinder of compressed gas contains nitrogen and oxygen in the ratio 3:1 by mole. If the cylinder is known to contain 2.5×10^4 g of oxygen, what is the total mass of the gas mixture? **NCERT Pg 18**

(a) 781.25 (b) 6.5625×10^4
(c) 9.0625×10^4 (d) 6.023×10^5

45 Number of oxygen atoms in 0.2 g molecules of Na_2SO_3 is **NCERT Pg 18**

(a) 0.2 (b) 0.4
(c) 0.4 N_A (d) 0.6 N_A

46 Arrange the following in the order of increasing mass (Atomic mass of O = 16, Cu = 63 and N = 14). **NCERT Pg 18**

I. One atom of oxygen
II. One atom of nitrogen
III. 1×10^{-10} mole of oxygen
IV. 1×10^{-10} mole of copper

(a) II < I < III < IV (b) I < II < III < IV
(c) III < II < IV < I (d) IV < II < III < I

47 How many molecules and atoms respectively are present in 2.8 L of a diatomic gas at STP? **NCERT Pg 18**

(a) 6.023×10^{23}, 7.5×10^{23}
(b) 6.023×10^{23}, 15×10^{22}
(c) 7.5×10^{22}, 15×10^{22}
(d) 15×10^{22}, 7.5×10^{23}

48 Number of carbon atoms in 0.2 mol of $C_6H_{12}O_6$ is **NCERT Pg 18**

(a) 0.2 N_A (b) 1.2 N_A
(c) 2.4 N_A (d) 3.2 N_A

49 Maximum number of atoms are present in **NCERT Pg 18**

(a) 8 g CH_4 (b) 18 g $C_6H_{12}O_6$
(c) 25 g $CaCO_3$ (d) 28 g CO

50 Fill in the blanks by choosing the correct option. **NCERT Pg 18**

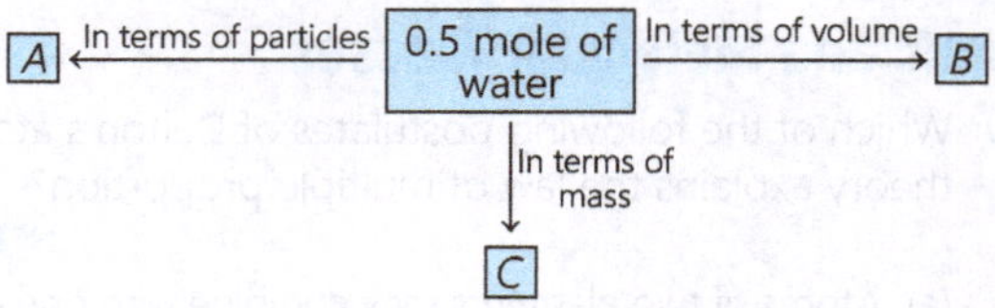

	A	*B*	*C*
(a)	3.011×10^{23} atoms/molecules	11.2L at STP	9g
(b)	6.023×10^{23} atoms/molecules	22.4L at STP	18g
(c)	3.011×10^{23} atoms/molecules	22.4L at STP	24g
(d)	6.011×10^{23} atoms/molecules	11.2L at STP	18g

51 If 1 mL of water contains 20 drops then number of molecules in a drop of water is **NCERT Pg 18**

(a) 6.023×10^{23} molecules
(b) 1.376×10^{26} molecules
(c) 1.67×10^{21} molecules
(d) 4.346×10^{20} molecules

52 An oxide of iodine (atomic mass = 127) contains 25.4 g of iodine and 8 g of oxygen. Its formula would be **NCERT Pg 19**

(a) I_2O_3 (b) I_2O
(c) I_2O_5 (d) I_2O_7

53 An organic compound on analysis was found to contain 10.06% carbon, 0.84% hydrogen and 89.10% chlorine. What will be the empirical formula of the substance? NCERT Pg 19
(a) CH_2Cl_2 (b) $CHCl_3$
(c) CCl_4 (d) CH_3Cl

54 The empirical formula of the compound if $M = 68\%$ (atomic mass = 34) and remaining 32 % oxygen will be NCERT Pg 19
(a) MO (b) M_2O (c) MO_2 (d) M_2O_3

55 A compound contains 69.5% oxygen, 30.5% nitrogen and its molecular weight is 92. The formula of compound is NCERT Pg 19
(a) N_2O (b) NO_2 (c) N_2O_4 (d) N_2O_5

56 A spherical ball of radius 7 cm contains 56 w% iron. Find out the number of moles of iron present approximately in the ball ($d = 1.4$ g cm^{-3}; atomic mass = 56 g mol^{-1}) NCERT Pg 19
(a) 15.1 (b) 20.1
(c) 25.1 (d) 35.1

57 280 mL of sulphur vapours at NTP weights 3.2 g. The molecular formula of the sulphur vapour is NCERT Pg 19
(a) S (b) S_2 (c) S_4 (d) S_8

58 An organic compound has an empirical formula (CH_2O). Its vapour density is 45. The molecular formula of the compound is NCERT Pg 19
(a) CH_2O (b) C_2H_5O (c) C_2H_2O (d) $C_3H_6O_3$

59 An organic compound containing C, H and O has 49.3% carbon, 6.84% hydrogen and its vapour density is 73. Molecular formula of the compound is NCERT Pg 19
(a) $C_3H_5O_2$ (b) $C_4H_{10}O_2$
(c) $C_6H_{10}O_4$ (d) $C_3H_{10}O_2$

60 0.0833 mole of carbohydrate of empirical formula CH_2O contain 1 g of hydrogen. The molecular formula of the carbohydrate is NCERT Pg 19
(a) $C_5H_{10}O_5$ (b) $C_3H_4O_3$
(c) $C_{12}H_{22}O_{11}$ (d) $C_6H_{12}O_6$

61 In a compound, C, H and N are present in the ratio of 9 : 1 : 3.5 by weight. If molecular weight of the compound is 108, then the molecular formula of the compound is NCERT Pg 19
(a) $C_2H_6N_2$ (b) $C_3H_4N_2$
(c) $C_6H_8N_2$ (d) $C_9H_{12}N_3$

62 A compound contains 54.55% carbon, 9.09% hydrogen and 36.36% oxygen .The empirical formula of this compound is NCERT Pg 19
(a) C_3H_5O (b) $C_4H_8O_2$
(c) $C_2H_4O_2$ (d) C_2H_4O

63 If 300 g of C_2H_6 is burnt in excess of oxygen, then the mass of CO_2 produced is NCERT Pg 20
(a) 110 g (b) 220 g (c) 440 g (d) 880 g

64 The volume occupied by 14 g of N_2 gas at STP will be NCERT Pg 20
(a) 22.4 L (b) 11.2 L
(c) 33.6 L (d) 5.6 L

65 For the following reaction, the mass of water produced from 445 g of $C_{57}H_{110}O_6$ is

$$2C_{57}H_{110}O_6(s) + 163O_2(g) \longrightarrow 114CO_2(g) + 110H_2O(g)$$

NCERT Pg 20
(a) 490 g (b) 495 g
(c) 445 g (d) 890 g

66 A gas has vapour density equal to 11.2. The volume occupied by 1 g of the gas at STP will be NCERT Pg 20
(a) 11.2 L (b) 22.4 L (c) 1 L (d) 10 L

67 The mass of 80% pure $CaCO_3$ required to produce 11.2 L of CO_2 at STP.

$$CaCO_3(s) \xrightarrow{\Delta} CaO(s) + CO_2(g)$$

NCERT Pg 20
(a) 50 g (b) 40 g
(c) 60 g (d) 62.5 g

68 In transforming 0.01 mole of PbS to $PbSO_4$,

$$PbS + 4H_2O_2 \longrightarrow PbSO_4 + 4H_2O$$

the volume of 10 volume H_2O_2 required is NCERT Pg 20
(a) 11.2 mL (b) 22.4 mL
(c) 44.8 mL (d) 33.6 mL

69 1 g of a metal carbonate (M_2CO_3) on treatment with excess HCl produces 0.01186 mole of CO_2. The molar mass of M_2CO_3 in g mol^{-1} is NCERT Pg 20
(a) 1186 (b) 84.3 (c) 118.6 (d) 11.86

70 A mixture of $CaCl_2$ and NaCl weighing 4.44 g is treated with sodium carbonate solution to precipitate all the Ca^{2+} ions as calcium carbonate. The calcium carbonate so obtained is heated strongly to get 0.56 g of CaO. The percentage of NaCl in the mixture is (Atomic mass of Ca = 40) NCERT Pg 20
(a) 75 (b) 30.6 (c) 25 (d) 69.4

Stoichiometry and Stoichiometric Calculation

71 Stoichiometric ratio of sodium dihydrogen orthophosphate and sodium hydrogen orthophosphate required for the synthesis of $Na_5P_3O_{10}$ is NCERT Pg 20
(a) 1.5 : 3 (b) 3 : 1.5 (c) 1 : 1 (d) 2 : 3

72 2.76 g of silver carbonate on being strongly heated yield a residue of weighing NCERT Pg 20
(a) 2.16 g (b) 2.48 g
(c) 2.64 g (d) 2.32 g

73 The decomposition of a certain mass of $KHCO_3$ gave 11.2 dm^3 of CO_2 gas at STP. The mass of KOH required to completely neutralise the gas is NCERT Pg 20
(a) 56 g (b) 28 g
(c) 42 g (d) 20 g

74 x g of Ag was dissolved in HNO_3 and the solution was treated with excess of NaCl, when 2.87g of AgCl was precipitated. The value of x is **NCERT Pg 20**

(a) 1.08 g (b) 2.16 g (c) 2.70 g (d) 1.62 g

75 $CH_4(g) + 2O_2(g) \longrightarrow CO_2(g) + 2H_2O(g)$ **NCERT Pg 20**

According to the above chemical reaction, following information have been given.

(i) One mole of $CH_4(g)$ reacts with two moles of $O_2(g)$ to give one mole of $CO_2(g)$ and two moles of $H_2O(g)$.

(ii) One molecule of $CH_4(g)$ reacts with 2 molecules of $O_2(g)$ to give one molecule of $CO_2(g)$ and 2 molecules of $H_2O(g)$.

(iii) 22.7 L of $CH_4(g)$ reacts with 45.4 L of O_2 to give 22.7 L of $CO_2(g)$ and 45.4 L of $H_2O(g)$.

(iv) 16 g of $CH_4(g)$ reacts with 2×32 g of $O_2(g)$ to give 44 g of $CO_2(g)$ and 2×18 g of $H_2O(g)$.

From these information the correct interconversion should be

(a) mass $\longrightarrow$ moles $\longrightarrow$ number of molecules
(b) mass $\rightleftharpoons$ moles $\rightleftharpoons$ number of molecules
(c) mass $\longrightarrow$ moles $\rightleftharpoons$ number of molecules
(d) mass = moles = number of molecules.

76 When zinc reacts with dilute nitric acid, nitrous oxide is produced. What mass of the gas is evolved by treating 325 g zinc with excess of nitric acid? **NCERT Pg 20**

(a) 44 g (b) 66 g (c) 55 g (d) 33 g

77 'X' litre of carbon monoxide is present at STP. It is completely oxidised to CO_2. The volume of CO_2 formed is 11.2 litres at STP. What is the value of 'X' in litres? **NCERT Pg 20**

(a) 22.4 (b) 11.2
(c) 5.6 (d) 44.8

78 In the reaction,

$2Al(s) + 6HCl(aq) \longrightarrow 2Al^{3+}(aq) + 6Cl^-(aq) + 3H_2(g)$ **NCERT Pg 20**

(a) 6 L HCl (aq) is consumed for every 3L $H_2(g)$ produced.
(b) 33.6 L $H_2(g)$ is produced regardless of temperature and pressure for every mole Al that reacts.
(c) 67.2 L $H_2(g)$ at STP is produced for every mole Al that reacts.
(d) 11.2 L $H_2(g)$ at STP is produced for every mole HCl(aq) consumed.

79 $KMnO_4$ reacts with oxalic acid according to the equation, **NCERT Pg 20**

$2MnO_4^- + 5C_2O_4^{2-} + 16H^+ \longrightarrow 2Mn^{2+} + 10CO_2 + 8H_2O$

Here, 20 mL of 0.1 M $KMnO_4$ is equivalent to

(a) 20 mL of 0.5 M $H_2C_2O_4$
(b) 50 mL of 0.1 M $H_2C_2O_4$
(c) 50 mL of 0.01 M $H_2C_2O_4$
(d) 20 mL of 0.1 M $H_2C_2O_4$

80 What mass of $Mg(OH)_2$ is required to neutralize 125 mL of 0.136 M HCl solution? **NCERT Pg 20**

(a) 0.248 g (b) 0.992 g
(c) 1.98 g (d) 0.496 g

81 When 22.4 litres of $H_2(g)$ is mixed with 11.2 litres of $Cl_2(g)$, each at S.T.P, the moles of HCl(g) formed is equal to **NCERT Pg 20**

(a) 1 mol of HCl (g) (b) 0.5 mol of HCl (g)
(c) 2 mol of HCl (g) (d) 1.5 mol of HCl (g)

82 The weight of iron which will be converted into its oxide (Fe_3O_4) by the action of 18 g of steam on it will be (Atomic weight of Fe = 56) **NCERT Pg 20**

(a) 168 g (b) 84 g
(c) 42 g (d) 21 g

83 1.0 g of Mg is burnt with 0.56 g O_2 in a closed vessel. Which reactant is left in excess and how much? **NCERT Pg 20, 21**

(a) Mg; 0.44 g (b) O_2; 0.28 g
(c) Mg; 0.16 g (d) O; 16 g

84 For a reaction,

$N_2(g) + 3H_2(g) \longrightarrow 2NH_3(g)$, identify dihydrogen ($H_2$) as a limiting reagent in the following reaction mixtures.

(a) 56 g of N_2 + 10 g of H_2 **NCERT Pg 20, 21**
(b) 35 g of N_2 + 8 g of H_2
(c) 14 g of N_2 + 4 g of H_2
(d) 28 g of N_2 + 6 g of H_2

85 If 0.5 mole of $BaCl_2$ is mixed with 0.20 mole of Na_3PO_4, the maximum number of $Ba_3(PO_4)_2$ that can be formed is **NCERT Pg 20, 21**

(a) 0.70 (b) 0.50 (c) 0.20 (d) 0.10

86 3 g of Mg is burnt in a closed vessel containing 0.5 g of O_2. Which reactant is limiting reagent and how much of the excess reactant will be left? **NCERT Pg 22**

(a) Mg is a limiting reagent and O_2 is in excess by 0.5 g.
(b) O_2 is a limiting reagent and Mg is in excess by 0.5 g.
(c) O_2 is a limiting reagent and Mg is in excess by 0.25 g.
(d) Mg is a limiting reagent and O_2 is in excess by 1 g.

87 If mole fraction of methanol in acetone is 0.2, then molality of methanol in the solution will be **NCERT Pg 23**

(a) 4.3 m (b) 5.8 m
(c) 2.0 m (d) 9.2 m

88 6.02×10^{20} molecules of urea are present in 100 mL of its solution. The concentration of solution is **NCERT Pg 23**

(a) 0.02 mol L^{-1} (b) 0.01 mol L^{-1}
(c) 0.001 mol L^{-1} (d) 0.1 mol L^{-1}

89 Mole fraction of the solute in a 1.00 molar aqueous solution is **NCERT Pg 23**

(a) 0.0177 (b) 0.0344
(c) 1.7700 (d) 0.1770

90 Molality of urea in an aqueous solution is 5 molal. Mass percentage of urea in the solution **NCERT Pg 23**
(a) 12.2% (b) 23% (c) 32.2% (d) 18%

91 A sample of nitric acid is 69% by mass and it has a concentration of 15.44 moles per litre. Its density is **NCERT Pg 23**
(a) 1.86 g/cc (b) 1.41 g/cc
(c) 2.60 g/cc (d) 1.02 g/cc

92 What volume of water is to be added to 100 cm^3 of 0.5 M NaOH solution to make it 0.1 M solution? **NCERT Pg 23**
(a) 200 cm^3 (b) 400 cm^3
(c) 500 cm^3 (d) 100 cm^3

93 Dissolving 120 g of urea (mol. wt. 60) in 1000 g of water gave a solution of density 1.15 g/mL. The molarity of the solution is **NCERT Pg 23**
(a) 1.78 M (b) 2.00 M (c) 2.05 M (d) 2.22 M

94 8 g of NaOH is dissolved in 18 g of H_2O. Mole fraction of NaOH in solution and molality (in mol kg^{-1}) of the solution respectively are **NCERT Pg 23**
(a) 0.2, 11.11 (b) 0.167, 22.20
(c) 0.2, 22.20 (d) 0.167, 11.11

95 100 g of lime stone on heating produced 22 g of CO_2. The percentage of $CaCO_3$ in lime stone is **NCERT Pg 23**
(a) 80% (b) 60% (c) 50% (d) 87.66%

96 How many grams of concentrated nitric acid solution should be used to prepare 250 mL of 2.0 M HNO_3? The concentrated acid is 70% HNO_3. **NCERT Pg 23**
(a) 45.0 g conc. HNO_3
(b) 90.0 g conc. HNO_3
(c) 70.0 g conc. HNO_3
(d) 54.0 g conc. HNO_3

97 Air contains 20% O_2 by volume. How much volume of air will be required for combustion of 100 cc of acetylene? **NCERT Pg 22**
(a) 500 cc (b) 1064 cc
(c) 212.8 cc (d) 1250 cc

98 If 20 g NaOH is present in 500 mL aqueous solution then molarity of Na^+ ions will be **NCERT Pg 23**
(a) 1 M (b) 0.2 M
(c) 0.5 M (d) 2 M

99 Molality of urea in an aqueous solution is 2 m. Mole fraction of urea in the solution is **NCERT Pg 24**
(a) 0.035 (b) 0.632
(c) 0.124 (d) 0.966

100 The molality of the solution obtained by dissolving 5.85 g NaCl in 100 g water is **NCERT Pg 24**
(a) 0.0001 m (b) 0.001 m
(c) 0.1 m (d) 1 m

Assertion-Reason Questions

Directions (Q. Nos. 1-10) *In the following question Assertion (A) followed by Reason (R) is given below. Choose the correct option out of the choices given below.*

(a) Both A and R are true and R is the correct explanation of A.
(b) Both A and R are true but R is not the correct explanation of A.
(c) A is true but R is false.
(d) A is false but R is true.

1 **Assertion** (A) Hydrogen burns with a pop sound and oxygen is a supporter of combustion but water is used as a fire extinguisher.
Reason (R) The properties of a compound are different from those of its constituent elements. **NCERT Pg 6**

2 **Assertion** (A) The ratio by volume of $NH_3 : HCl : NH_4Cl$ is 1:1 in the reaction.

$$NH_3(g) + HCl(g) \longrightarrow NH_4Cl(s)$$

Reason (R) Gay-Lussac's law deals with gaseous reactants and products only. **NCERT Pg 15**

3 **Assertion** (A) Matter consists of divisible molecules.
Reason (R) Atoms of different elements differ in mass. **NCERT Pg 16**

4 **Assertion** (A) Equal moles of different substances contain same number of constituent particles.
Reason (R) Equal weights of different substances contain the same number of constituent particles. **NCERT Pg 18**

5 **Assertion** (A) An organic compound containing 24 mg of carbon, 6 mg of hydrogen and 32 mg of oxygen has the empirical formula CH_3O.
Reason (R) Empirical formula gives the simplest ratio of masses at the various elements present in one molecule of the compound. **NCERT Pg 19**

6 **Assertion** (A) Equivalent weight of ozone in the change $O_3 \longrightarrow O_2$ is 8.
Reason (R) 1 mole of O_3 on decomposition gives 3/2 moles of O_2. **NCERT Pg 21**

7 **Assertion** (A) The empirical mass of ethene is half of its molecular mass.

Reason (R) The empirical formula represents the simplest whole number ratio of various atoms present in a compound. NCERT Pg 19

8 **Assertion** (A) One atomic mass unit is defined as one twelfth of the mass of one carbon-12 atom.

Reason (R) Carbon-12 isotope is the most abundant isotope of carbon and has been chosen as standard. NCERT Pg 15

9 **Assertion** (A) Significant figures for 0.200 is 3 whereas for 200 it is 1.

Reason (R) Zero at the end or right of a number are significant provided they are not on the right side of the decimal point. NCERT Pg 16

10 **Assertion** (A) Combustion of 16 g of methane gives 18 g of water.

Reason (R) In the combustion of methane, water is one of the products. NCERT Pg 16

Statement Type Questions

Direction (Q. Nos. 1-5) *In the following questions, two statements (I & II) are given. In the light of the given statements, choose the correct option given below.*

(a) Both Statement I and Statement II are false.
(b) Statement I is true but Statement II is false.
(c) Statement I is false but Statement II is true.
(d) Both Statement I and Statement II are true.

1 **Statement I** Average atomic mass of an element depends mainly on the heavier isotope.

Statement II Average atomic mass is obtained by multiplying the atomic mass on the heavier isotope with its fractional abundance. NCERT Pg 28

2 **Statement I** One mole is the amount of a substance that contains as many particles or entities as there are atoms in exactly 12 g of the C-12 isotope.

Statement II One mole of different substances contain different number of particles. NCERT Pg 18

3 **Statement I** Both 44 g CO_2 and 16 g CH_4 have the same number of carbon atoms.

Statement II 12 g of carbon contains $6.023 \times 10^{23} \times 12$ carbon atoms. NCERT Pg 18

4 **Statement I** A reagent that is entirely consumed when a reaction goes to completion is known as limiting reagent.

Statement II The amount of limiting reagent present in a reaction limits the amount of product formed. NCERT Pg 2

5 **Statement I** Molality, mole fraction and mass fraction changes with temperature.

Statement II Molarity does not change with temperature. NCERT Pg 23, 24

6 Consider the following statements regarding compound. NCERT Pg 5, 6

I. Glucose has a fixed composition, so it is a pure substance.
II. A compound retains the physical properties of its constituent elements.
III. The constituents of a compound cannot be separated by physical methods of separation.
IV. A molecule of a compound has atom of different elements.
V. Observation of chemical properties of a matter can be observed by a chemical change.

Choose the correct answer from the options given below.

(a) I and III only (b) I, III and IV
(c) I, II and V (d) I, III, IV and V

7 Which of the following statement is incorrect? NCERT Pg 8, 9, 10

I. The weight of a substance can be determined very accurately by using an analytical balance.
II. Volume is denoted in dm^3 units.
III. Density of a substance is its amount of mass per unit volume.
IV. Candela is the luminous intensity, that emits monochromatic radiation of frequency, 540×10^{12} Hz.
V. The smallest unit of time is yocto second.

Choose the correct answer from the options given below.

(a) I, II and III (b) Only I
(c) III, IV and V (d) Only III

8 Select the correct statement from the following. NCERT Pg 15, 16

I. Matter consist of very small indivisible particles named as atom.
II. Gay Lussac's law is an application of law of definite proportions by weight.

III. Fractions of atoms do not take part in a chemical reaction.
IV. Atoms in a chemical reactions are neither created nor destroyed but they get reorganised.
V. Formation of water or hydrogen peroxide by hydrogen and oxygen follows definite proportions.

Choose the correct answer from the option given below.
(a) I, II and V (b) I, II and III
(c) I, II, III, IV and V (d) I, III and IV

9 Select the incorrect statement from the following. **NCERT Pg 16, 17**

I. 'amu' has been replaced by unified mass 'u'.
II. Mass of H-atom in terms of amu is 1.0080 amu.
III. Mass of an atom is very big in magnitude.
IV. One atomic mass unit is a mass exactly equal to one-twelfth the mass of one carbon-12 atom.
V. The formula such as NaCl is used to calculate the molecular mass.

Choose the correct answer from the options given below.
(a) I, II and IV (b) III and V
(c) II, IV and V (d) I, II and V

10 Choose the incorrect statement from the following statements. **NCERT Pg 16, 17, 18**

I. The atoms of different elements are present in a compound in a fixed and definite ratio.
II. In compounds like NaCl, the positive and negative entities are arranged in two dimensional structure.
III. In NaCl, one Na^+ ion is surrounded by 12 Cl^- ions and *vice-versa*.
IV. In SI system, mole was introduced as seventh base quantity for the amount of a substance.
V. Carbon has 3 isotopes which helps to determine it's average atomic mass.

Choose the correct answer from the options given below.
(a) I, II and IV (b) II and III (c) IV and V (d) I, II and III

Matching Type Questions

1 If we write a result as 11.2 mL then match the items of Column I with Column II and choose the correct option from the codes given below. **NCERT Pg 12**

Column I (Indication of uncertainty)		Column II (Number associated with uncertainty)
A. Certain digit is	1.	2
B. The uncertain digit is	2.	± 1
C. The uncertainty in the last digit would be	3.	11

Codes

	A	B	C
(a)	3	1	2
(b)	1	2	3
(c)	3	2	1
(d)	2	1	3

2 Match the Column I with Column II and choose the correct option from the codes given below. **NCERT Pg 18**

Column I	Column II
A. Mass of H_2 produced when 0.5 mole of zinc reacts with excess of HCl.	1. 3.01×10^{23} molecules
B. Mass of all atoms of a compound with formula $C_{70}H_{22}$.	2. 6.023×10^{23} molecules
C. Number of molecules in 35.5 g of Cl_2.	3. 1.43×10^{-21} g
D. Number of molecules in 64 g of SO_2.	4. 1g

Codes

	A	B	C	D
(a)	2	1	4	3
(b)	1	2	3	4
(c)	4	3	1	2
(d)	4	3	2	1

3 Match the following Column I with Column II and choose the correct codes from the option given below. **NCERT Pg 18**

Column I	Column II
A. 46 g of Na	1. 0.01 mol
B. 6.022×10^{23} molecules of H_2O	2. 2 mol
C. 0.224 L of O_2 at STP	3. 1 mol
D. 84 g of N_2	4. 3 mol

Codes

	A	B	C	D
(a)	2	3	1	4
(b)	1	2	3	4
(c)	4	2	1	3
(d)	2	4	3	1

4 Match the Column I with Column II and choose the correct option from the codes given below. **NCERT Pg 20**

Column I	Column II
A. $10\text{ g } CaCO_3 \xrightarrow[\text{Decomposition}]{\Delta}$	1. 0.224 L CO_2
B. $1.06\text{ g } Na_2CO_3 \xrightarrow{\text{Excess HCl}}$	2. 4.48 L CO_2
C. $2.4\text{ g C} \xrightarrow[\text{combustion}]{\text{Excess } O_2}$	3. 0.448 L CO_2
D. $0.56\text{ g CO} \xrightarrow[\text{combustion}]{\text{Excess } O_2}$	4. 2.24 L CO_2

Codes

	A	B	C	D
(a)	4	1	2	3
(b)	4	2	1	3
(c)	4	1	3	2
(d)	1	4	2	3

5 Match the items of Column I with Column II and choose the correct codes from the options given below. NCERT Pg 23, 24

Column I		Column II	
A.	Mole fraction	1.	$M_2 \times V_2$
B.	Molarity	2.	The solution of higher concentration.
C.	Molality	3.	It is defined as the number of moles of solute present in 1 kg of solvent.
D.	$M_1 \times V_1$	4.	It is the ratio of number of moles of a particular component to the total number of moles of the solution.
E.	Stock solution	5.	It is defined as the number of moles of the solute in 1 L of the solution.

Codes

	A	B	C	D	E
(a)	1	2	3	4	5
(b)	4	5	3	1	2
(c)	1	2	5	4	3
(d)	3	2	1	4	5

Numerical Value Questions

1 A solution of sugar is obtained by mixing 200 g of its 25% solution and 500 g of its 40% solution (both by mass). The mass percentage of the resulting sugar solution is .... (Nearest integer) NCERT Pg 18

2 Among the following species, the number of species having same number of molecules as in 16 g of oxygen is NCERT Pg 18

(i) 16 g of CO (ii) 28 g of N_2
(iii) 14 g of N_2 (iv) 1.0 g of H_2
(v) 22 g of CO_2

3 The volume of hydrogen liberated at STP by treating 2.4 g of magnesium with excess of hydrochloric acid is .... $\times 10^{-2}$ L. NCERT Pg 20

[Given : Molar volume of gas is 22.4L at STP. Molar mass of magnesium is 24 g mol^{-1}.]

4 Consider the following reaction :

$$MnO_2 + 4HCl \longrightarrow MnCl_2 + 2H_2O + Cl_2$$

2 moles of MnO_2 react with 4 moles of HCl to form 11.2L Cl_2 at STP. Thus, percent yield of Cl_2 is .... NCERT Pg 23

5 5 g of NaOH was dissolved in deionised water to prepare a 450 mL stock solution. What volume (in mL) of this solution would be required to prepare 500 mL of 0.1 M solution .... NCERT Pg 23

[Given, molar mass of Na, O and H is 23, 16 and 1 g mol^{-1} respectively.]

NCERT Exemplar's Questions

1 Which of the following statements about a compound is/are incorrect?

I. A molecule of a compound has atoms of different elements.
II. A compound cannot be separated into its constituent elements by physical methods of separation.
III. A compound retains the physical properties of its constituent elements.
IV. The ratio of atoms of different elements in a compound is fixed.

(a) Only III (b) Only II
(c) I and IV (d) III and IV

2 A measured temperature on Fahrenheit scale is 200°F. What will this reading be on Celsius scale?

(a) 40 °C (b) 94 °C
(c) 93.3 °C (d) 30 °C

3 If the density of a solution is 3.12 g mL^{-1}, the mass of 1.5 mL solution in significant figures is ....

(a) 4.7 g (b) 4680×10^{-3} g
(c) 4.680 g (d) 46.80 g

4 Which of the following reactions is not correct according to the law of conservation of mass?

(a) $2Mg(s) + O_2(g) \longrightarrow 2MgO(s)$
(b) $C_3H_8(s) + O_2(g) \longrightarrow CO_2(g) + H_2O(g)$
(c) $P_4(s) + 5O_2(g) \longrightarrow P_4O_{10}(s)$
(d) $CH_4(g) + 2O_2(g) \longrightarrow CO_2(g) + 2H_2O(g)$

5 Match the following.

List-I		List-II	
A.	88 g of CO_2	1.	0.25 mol
B.	6.022×10^{23} molecules of H_2O	2.	2 mol
C.	5.6 L of O_2 at STP	3.	1 mol
D.	96 g of O_2	4.	6.022×10^{23} molecules
E.	1 mole of any gas	5.	3 mol

6 One mole of any substance contains 6.022×10^{23} atoms/molecules. What will be number of molecules of H_2SO_4 present in 100 mL of 0.02 M H_2SO_4 solution?

(a) 12.044×10^{20} molecules (b) 6.022×10^{23} molecules
(c) 1×10^{23} molecules (d) 12.044×10^{23} molecules

7 The number of atoms present in one mole of an element is equal to Avogadro's number. Which of the following element contains the greatest number of atoms?
(a) 4 g He (b) 46 g Na
(c) 0.40 g Ca (d) 12 g He

8 What is the mass per cent of carbon in carbon dioxide?
(a) 0.034% (b) 27.27% (c) 3.4% (d) 28.7%

9 The empirical formula and molecular mass of a compound are CH_2O and 180 g respectively. What will the molecular formula of the compound?
(a) $C_9H_{18}O_9$ (b) CH_2O
(c) $C_6H_{12}O_6$ (d) $C_2H_4O_2$

10 What will be the molarity of a solution, which contains 5.85 g of NaCl (*s*) per 500 mL?
(a) 4 mol L^{-1} (b) 20 mol L^{-1}
(c) 0.2 mol L^{-1} (d) 2 mol L^{-1}

11 If the concentration of glucose ($C_6H_{12}O_6$) in blood is 0.9 g L^{-1}, what will be the molarity of glucose in blood?
(a) 5 M (b) 50 M
(c) 0.005 M (d) 0.5 M

12 What will be the molality of the solution containing 18.25 g of HCl gas in 500 g of water?
(a) 0.1 m (b) 10 m (c) 0.5 m (d) 1 m

13 If 500 mL of a 5 M solution is diluted to 1500 mL, what will be the molarity of the solution obtained?
(a) 1.5 M (b) 1.66 M (c) 0.017 M (d) 1.59 M

14 Which of the following statements is correct about the reaction given below?

$$4Fe(s) + 3O_2(g) \longrightarrow 2Fe_2O_3(g)$$

(a) Total mass of iron and oxygen in reactants = total mass of iron and oxygen in product, therefore, it follows law of conservation of mass.
(b) Total mass of reactants = total mass of product, therefore, law of multiple proportions is followed.
(c) Amount of Fe_2O_3 can be increased by taking any one of the reactants (iron or oxygen) in excess.
(d) Amount of Fe_2O_3 produced will decrease if the amount of any one of the reactants (iron or oxygen) is taken in excess.

15 Which of the following statement indicates that, law of multiple proportion is being followed?
(a) Sample of carbon dioxide taken from any source will always have carbon and oxygen in the ratio 1 : 2.
(b) Carbon forms two oxides namely CO_2 and CO, where masses of oxygen which combine with fixed mass of carbon are in the simple ratio 2 : 1.
(c) When magnesium burns in oxygen, the amount of magnesium taken for the reaction is equal to the amount of magnesium in magnesium oxide formed.
(d) At constant temperature and pressure, 200 mL of hydrogen will combine with 100 mL oxygen to produce 200 mL of water vapour.

16 Match the following physical quantities with units.

	Physical quantity		Unit
A.	Molarity	1.	g mL^{-1}
B.	Mole fraction	2.	mol
C.	Mole	3.	Pascal
D.	Molality	4.	Unitless
E.	Pressure	5.	mol L^{-1}
F.	Luminous intensity	6.	Candela
G.	Density	7.	mol kg^{-1}
H.	Mass	8.	Nm^{-1}
		9.	kg

17 Two students performed the same experiment separately and each one of them recorded two readings of mass which are given below. Correct reading of mass is 3.0 g.

Student	Readings	
	I	II
A	3.01	2.99
B	3.05	2.95

On the basis of given data, mark the correct option out of the following statement.
(a) Results of both the students are neither accurate nor precise.
(b) Result of student *A* are both precise and accurate.
(c) Results of student *B* are precise but not accurate.
(d) Results of student *B* are both precise and accurate.

Past Exams' Questions

NEET Archive

1. The highest number of helium atoms is in NCERT Pg 18, NEET 2024
(a) 4 moles of helium
(b) 4 u of helium
(c) 4 g of helium
(d) 2.271098 L of helium at STP

2. 1 g of sodium hydroxide was treated with 25 mL of 0.75 M HCl solution, the mass of sodium hydroxide left unreacted is equal to NCERT Pg 20. NEET 2024
(a) 750 mg (b) 250 mg (c) zero mg (d) 200 mg

3. A compound *X* contains 32% of *A*, 20% of *B* and remaining percentage of *C*. Then, the empirical formula of *X* is (Given, atomic masses of $A = 64; B = 40; C = 32$ u) NCERT Pg 19, NEET 2024
(a) A_2BC_2 (b) ABC_3
(c) AB_2C_2 (d) ABC_4

4 The right option for the mass of CO_2 produced by heating 20 g of 20% pure limestone is (Atomic mass of Ca = 40) NCERT Pg 20, NEET 2023

$$CaCO_3 \xrightarrow{1200\text{ K}} CaO + CO_2$$

(a) 1.76 g (b) 2.64 g (c) 1.32 g (d) 1.12 g

5 Weight (g) of two moles of the organic compound, which is obtained by heating sodium ethanoate with sodium hydroxide in presence of calcium oxide is NCERT Pg 20, NEET 2023
(a) 32 (b) 30
(c) 18 (d) 16

6 An organic compound contains 78% (by wt.) carbon and remaining percentage of hydrogen. The right option for the empirical formula of this compound is [At. wt. of C is 12, H is 1] NCERT Pg 19, NEET 2021
(a) CH (b) CH_2 (c) CH_3 (d) CH_4

7 Which one of the following has maximum number of atoms? NCERT Pg 18, NEET 2020
(a) 1 g of Mg(*s*) [Atomic mass of Mg = 24]
(b) 1 g of $O_2(g)$ [Atomic mass of O = 16]
(c) 1 g of Li(*s*) [Atomic mass of Li = 7]
(d) 1 g of Ag(*s*) [Atomic mass of Ag = 108]

8 The number of moles of hydrogen molecules required to produce 20 moles of ammonia through Haber's process is NCERT Pg 20, NEET 2019
(a) 20 (b) 30 (c) 40 (d) 10

9 The density of 2 M aqueous solution of NaOH is 1.28 g/cm^3. The molality of the solution is [Given that molecular mass of NaOH = 40 g mol^{-1}]
(a) 1.20 m (b) 1.56 m NCERT Pg 24, NEET 2019
(c) 1.67 m (d) 1.32 m

10 A mixture of 2.3 g formic acid and 4.5 g oxalic acid is treated with conc. H_2SO_4. The evolved gaseous mixture is passed through KOH pellets. Weight (in g) of the remaining product at STP will be NCERT Pg 20, NEET 2018
(a) 2.8 (b) 3.0 (c) 1.4 (d) 4.4

11 In which case is the number of molecules of water maximum? NCERT Pg 18, NEET 2018
(a) 0.00224 L of water vapours at 1 atm and 273 K
(b) 0.18 g of water
(c) 18 mL of water
(d) 10^{-3} mol of water

12 Suppose the elements *X* and *Y* combine to form two compounds XY_2 and X_3Y_2. When 0.1 mole of XY_2 weighs 10 g and 0.05 mole of X_3Y_2 weighs 9 g, the atomic weights of *X* and *Y* are NCERT Pg 16, NEET 2016
(a) 40, 30 (b) 60, 40 (c) 20, 30 (d) 30, 20

13 When 22.4 L of $H_2(g)$ is mixed with 11.2 L of $Cl_2(g)$, each at STP, the moles of HCl(*g*) formed is equal to NCERT Pg 18, NEET 2014
(a) 1 mole of HCl(*g*) (b) 2 moles of HCl(*g*)
(c) 0.5 mole of HCl(*g*) (d) 1.5 mole of HCl(*g*)

JEE Main Archive

14 A sample of $CaCO_3$ and $MgCO_3$ weighed 2.21 g is ignited to constant weight of 1.152 g. The composition of mixture is (Given, molar mass in g mol^{-1} $CaCO_3$: 100, $MgCO_3$: 84) NCERT Pg 18, JEE Main 2024
(a) 1.187 g $CaCO_3$ + 1.187 g $MgCO_3$
(b) 1.023 g $CaCO_3$ + 1.187 g $MgCO_3$
(c) 1.187 g $CaCO_3$ + 1.023 g $MgCO_3$
(d) 1.023 g $CaCO_3$ + 1.023 g $MgCO_3$

15 Number of moles of methane required to produce 22 g $CO_2(g)$ after combustion is $x \times 10^{-2}$ moles. The value of *x* is .... NCERT Pg 18, JEE Main 2024

16 Mass of methane required to produce 22 g of CO_2 after complete combustion is .... g. (Given, molar mass in g mol^{-1} C = 12.0, H = 1.0, O = 16.0) NCERT Pg 20, JEE Main 2024

17 The quantity which changes with temperature is NCERT Pg 24, JEE Main 2024
(a) molality (b) mole fraction
(c) mass percentage (d) molarity

18 The number of molecules and moles in 2.8375 litres of O_2 at STP are respectively NCERT Pg 18, JEE Main 2023
(a) 7.525×10^{23} and 0.125 mol (b) 1.505×10^{23} and 0.250 mol
(c) 7.525×10^{22} and 0.250 mol (d) 7.525×10^{22} and 0.125 mol

19 A metal chloride contains 55.0% of chlorine by weight. 100 mL vapours of the metal chloride at STP weight 0.57 g. The molecular formula of the metal chloride is (Given, atomic mass of chlorine is 35.5 u) **NCERT Pg 18, JEE Main 2023**

(a) MCl_4 (b) MCl_2 (c) MCl (d) MCl_3

20 Given below are two statements, one is labelled as Assertion (A) and the other is labelled as Reason (R). **NCERT Pg 23, JEE Main 2023**

Assertion (A) 3.1500 g of hydrated oxalic acid dissolved in water to make 250.0 mL solution will result in 0.1 M oxalic acid solution.

Reason (R) Molar mass of hydrated oxalic acid is 126 g mol^{-1}.

In the light of the above statements, choose the correct answer from the options given below.

(a) A is true but R is false.
(b) Both A and R are true and R is the correct explanation of A.
(c) A is false but R is true.
(d) Both A and R are true but R is not the correct explanation of A.

21 Match List-I with List-II. **NCERT Pg 18, 19, JEE Main 2023**

List-I	List-II
A. 16 g of $CH_4(g)$	I. Weighs 28 g
B. 1 g of $H_2(g)$	II. 60.2×10^{23} electrons
C. 1 mole of $N_2(g)$	III. Weighs 32 g
D. 0.5 mol of $SO_2(g)$	IV. Occupies 11.4 L volume at STP

Choose the correct answer from the options given below.

(a) A-I, B-III, C-II, D-IV (b) A-II, B-IV, C-I, D-III
(c) A-II. B-III, C-IV, D-I (d) A-II, B-IV, C-III, D-I

22 $\underset{(20\ g)}{N_2(g)} + \underset{(5\ g)}{3H_2(g)} \longrightarrow 2NH_3(g)$ **NCERT Pg 20, JEE Main 2022**

Consider the above reaction, the limiting reagent of the reaction and number of moles of NH_3 formed respectively are

(a) H_2, 1.42 mol (b) H_2, 0.71 mol
(c) N_2, 1.42 mol (d) N_2, 0.71 mol

23 Consider the reaction, **NCERT Pg 20, JEE Main 2022**

$$4HNO_3(l) + 3KCl(s) \longrightarrow Cl_2(g) + NOCl(g) + 2H_2O(g) + 3KNO_3(s)$$

The amount of HNO_3 required to produce 110.0 g of KNO_3 is (Given, atomic masses of H, O, N and K are 1, 16, 14 and 39 respectively.)

(a) 32.2 g (b) 69.4 g
(c) 91.5 g (d) 162.5 g

24 250 g solution of D-glucose in water contains 10.8% of carbon by weight. The molality of the solution is nearest to (Given: Atomic weights are, H, 1u; C, 12u; O, 16u) **NCERT Pg 24, JEE Main 2022**

(a) 1.03 (b) 2.06 (c) 3.09 (d) 5.40

25 Haemoglobin contains 0.34% of iron by mass. The number of Fe-atoms in 3.3 g of haemoglobin is (Given, atomic mass of Fe is 56 u, $N_A = 6.022 \times 10^{23}\ mol^{-1}$) **NCERT Pg 18, JEE Main 2022**

(a) 1.21×10^5 (b) 12.0×10^{16}
(c) 1.21×10^{20} (d) 3.4×10^{22}

Skill Boosters

1. Two gases, A and B having equal mass are kept in two separate vessels under identical conditions of temperature and pressure. If the ratio of their molecular masses be 2 : 3. The ratio of the volumes of the vessels is

(a) 1 : 2 (b) 2 : 3 (c) 3 : 2 (d) 1 : 1

2. A 100 mL solution of 0.1 N HCl was titrated with 0.2 N NaOH solution. The titration was discontinued after adding 30 mL of NaOH solution. The remaining titration was completed by adding 0.25 N KOH solution. The volume of KOH required for completing the titration is

(a) 70 mL (b) 32 mL (c) 35 mL (d) 16 mL

3. A person has as many notes as number of oxygen atom in 24.8 g $Na_2S_2O_3 \cdot 5H_2O$ (mol. wt. = 248). A note counting machine counts 48 million notes per day. How many days it would take to count these notes?

(a) 10^{12} (b) 10^{14} (c) 10^{16} (d) 10^{18}

4. In Haber process, 30 litres of dinitrogen were taken for reaction which yielded only 50% of the expected product. What will be the composition of the gaseous mixture under the aforesaid condition in the end?

(a) 20 litres NH_3, 25 litres N_2, 20 litres H_2
(b) 10 litres NH_3, 25 litres N_2, 15 litres H_2
(c) 20 litres NH_3, 10 litres N_2, 30 litres H_2
(d) 20 litres NH_3, 25 litres N_2, 15 litres H_2

5. 2.30 g of an optically active L-amino acid (A) is reacted with $NaNO_2$/HCl at 0°C. 500 cm^3 of nitrogen gas at STP is evolved. A sample of protein has 0.30% of this amino acid by mass. The molar mass of the protein is

(a) 36500 g/mol
(b) 32500 g/mol
(c) 38680 g/mol
(d) 34346.66 g/mol

6. A welding fuel gas contains carbon and hydrogen only. On burning a small sample of it, with oxygen gives 3.38 g of CO_2, 0.690 g of H_2O and no other products. A volume of 10.0 litre (measured at STP) of this welding gas is found to weigh 11.6 g. The molar mass and molecular formula of the gas is
(a) 30 g/mol, C_2H_6 (b) 26 g/mol, C_2H_2
(c) 28 g/mol, C_2H_4 (d) 44 g/mol, C_3H_8

7. In human digestion process, stomach digest food by producing gastric juice which is a unique combination of HCl, lipase and pepsin. It is observed, gastric juice contains 3.0 g of HCl per litre. If a person produces 2.5 litre of gastric juice per day. How many antacid tablets each containing 400 mg of $Al(OH)_3$ are needed to neutralise all the HCl produced in one day?
(a) 18 (b) 14
(c) 20 (d) 17

8. Calcium carbonate reacts with aqueous HCl to give $CaCl_2$ and CO_2 according to the reaction given below.
$CaCO_3(s) + 2HCl(aq) \longrightarrow CaCl_2(aq) + CO_2(g) + H_2O(l)$
What mass of $CaCl_2$ will be formed when 250 mL of 0.76 MHCl reacts with 1000 g of $CaCO_3$? Name the limiting reagent and calculate the number of moles of $CaCl_2$ formed in the reaction.
(a) $CaCO_3$, 0.01 mol (b) HCl, 0.08 mol
(c) HCl, 0.095 mol (d) $CaCO_3$, 0.080 mol

Correct Codes

Topical Questions

1. (a)	2. (c)	3. (c)	4. (b)	5. (b)	6. (c)	7. (b)	8. (a)	9. (d)	10. (a)
11. (a)	12. (b)	13. (b)	14. (d)	15. (b)	16. (c)	17. (c)	18. (b)	19. (b)	20. (a)
21. (b)	22. (a)	23. (b)	24. (d)	25. (b)	26. (b)	27. (c)	28. (d)	29. (c)	30. (a)
31. (a)	32. (d)	33. (b)	34. (a)	35. (b)	36. (a)	37. (c)	38. (b)	39. (d)	40. (a)
41. (a)	42. (c)	43. (c)	44. (c)	45. (d)	46. (a)	47. (c)	48. (b)	49. (a)	50. (a)
51. (c)	52. (c)	53. (b)	54. (a)	55. (c)	56. (b)	57. (d)	58. (d)	59. (c)	60. (d)
61. (c)	62. (d)	63. (d)	64. (b)	65. (b)	66. (c)	67. (d)	68. (c)	69. (b)	70. (a)
71. (a)	72. (a)	73. (a)	74. (b)	75. (b)	76. (c)	77. (b)	78. (d)	79. (b)	80. (d)
81. (a)	82. (c)	83. (c)	84. (a)	85. (d)	86. (c)	87. (a)	88. (b)	89. (a)	90. (b)
91. (b)	92. (b)	93. (c)	94. (d)	95. (c)	96. (a)	97. (d)	98. (a)	99. (a)	100. (d)

Assertion-Reason

1. (a)	2. (d)	3. (d)	4. (c)	5. (c)	6. (a)	7. (a)	8. (b)	9. (c)	10. (d)

Statements Type

1. (a)	2. (b)	3. (b)	4. (d)	5. (a)	6. (d)	7. (b)	8. (d)	9. (b)	10. (b)

Matching Type

1. (a)	2. (c)	3. (a)	4. (a)	5. (b)

Numerical Value

1. (36)	2. (3)	3. (224)	4. (50)	5. (180)

NCERT Exemplar's

1. (a) 2. (c) 3. (a) 4. (b) 5. A-2, B-3, C-1, D-5, E-4 6. (a) 7. (d) 8. (b)
9. (c) 10. (c) 11. (c) 12. (d) 13. (b) 14. (a) 15. (b) 16. A-5, B-4, C-2, D-7, E-3,8, F-6, G-1, H-9
17. (b)

Past Exams'

1. (a)	2. (b)	3. (b)	4. (a)	5. (a)	6. (c)	7. (c)	8. (b)	9. (c)	10. (a)
11. (c)	12. (a)	13. (a)	14. (c)	15. (50)	16. (8)	17. (d)	18. (d)	19. (b)	20. (b)
21. (b)	22. (c)	23. (c)	24. (b)	25. (c)					

Skill Boosters

1. (c)	2. (d)	3. (c)	4. (b)	5. (d)	6. (b)	7. (b)	8. (c)

Step by Step

Decoding the Questions

Concept Builders

1 $CaCO_3$
2 True
3 True
4 azidothymidine
5 Chlorofluorocarbons
6 True
7 heterogeneous
8 False
9 fixed
10 Candela
11 False
12 4.909×10^{-8}
13 4
14 Precision
15 False
16 False
17 definite proportions
18 Gay Lussac's law
19 False
20 atomic mass unit
21 180.162 u
22 False
23 52.17
24 True
25 2
26 methane
27 10%
28 True
29 $\frac{n}{(n+N)}$
30 False

Topical Solutions

1 (*a*) Chemistry was not studied for its own sake, rather it came up as a result of search for two interesting things :

(i) 'Philosopher's stone' which would convert all baser metals, e.g. iron and copper into gold.

(ii) 'Elexir of life' which would grant immortality.

2 (*c*) The preparation of perfumes and cosmetics were described in Brihat Samhita.

3 (*c*) Taxol and AZT (azidothymidine) are two effective drugs which act as life saving drugs for cancer therapy and AIDS victims, respectively.

4 (*b*) Oxygen is a gas, which has neither definite volume nor definite shape.

5 (*b*) Relation between units of volume is given as,

$$1 L = 1000 mL$$

$$1000 cm^3 = 1 dm^3 ; 1 mL = 1 cm^3$$

Hence, the correct order is

$$A = D > B = C.$$

6 (*c*) The incorrect option is (c). It's correct form is as follows

$$1 mg = 10^6 ng$$

$$(1 mg = 10^{-6} kg = 10^6 ng)$$

7 (*b*) (i) $28.7 pm \times \frac{10^{-12} m}{1 pm} = 2.87 \times 10^{-11} m$

(ii) $15.15 \mu s \times \frac{10^{-6} s}{1 \mu s} = 1.515 \times 10^{-5} s$

(iii) $25365 mg \times \frac{1 g}{1000 mg} \times \frac{1 kg}{1000 g} = 2.5365 \times 10^{-2} kg$

8 (*a*) The incorrect match is (i) and (iv). It is correct form is

$$\text{Pico} = 10^{-12}; \quad \text{Giga} = 10^9$$

9 (*d*) The correct scientific notation of 0.0034 is 3.4×10^{-3}.

10 (*a*) 0.00016 can be written as 1.6×10^{-4} in scientific notation.

11 (*a*) The addition of numbers

$$6.65 \times 10^4 + 8.95 \times 10^3$$
$$= (6.65 + 0.895) \times 10^4 = 7.545 \times 10^4$$

Also, substraction of numbers

$$2.5 \times 10^{-2} - 4.8 \times 10^{-3}$$
$$= 2.5 \times 10^{-2} - (0.48 \times 10^{-2}) = 2.02 \times 10^{-2}$$

The scientific notation will be 7.545×10^4 and 2.02×10^{-2} respectively.

12 (*b*) To round up a given number, ignore the last digit as such if the digit next to it is less than 5, then increase it by 1, if the next digit is greater than 5.

(i) $36.217 \rightarrow 36.2$

(ii) $0.04597 \rightarrow 0.046$

(iii) $10.4107 \rightarrow 10.4$

13 (*b*) Zeros between two non-zero digits are significant.

14 (*d*) Statement given in option (d) is incorrect. Its correct form is zeros at the end or right of a number are significant.

15 (*b*) Statement (b) is incorrect. It's correct form is as follows

Result of multiplication or division is rounded off to the same number of significant figures as possessed by the least precise term in the calculation.

16 (*c*) *A* and *B* are precision and accuracy, respectively.

17 (*c*) Given that, the true value for a result is 2.00 g and student '*A*' takes two measurements and report the result as 1.95 g and 1.93 g.

The values are precise as they are close to each other but are not accurate.

Another student (*B*) repeats the experiment and obtains 1.94 g and 2.05 g as the results for two measurements. These observations are neither precise nor accurate.

The third student (*C*) repeats these measurements and reports 2.01 g and 1.99 g as the result, these values are both precise and accurate.

18 (*b*) In addition or subtraction, for the following digits

$$\begin{array}{r} 12.11 \\ 18.0 \\ 1.012 \\ \hline 31.122 \end{array}$$

Here, 18.0 has only one digit after the decimal point and, therefore the result should be reported only upto one digit after the decimal point which is 31.1.

19 (*b*) In the given multiplication

$$2.5 \times 1.25 = 3.125$$

Since, 2.5 has two significant figures, the result should not have more than two significant figures, thus it is 3.1.

20 (*a*) The result of $\frac{0.02856 \times 298.15 \times 0.112}{0.5785}$ has least significant figures.

21 (*b*) 2.5 days $\times \frac{24 \text{ hrs}}{1 \text{ day}} \times \frac{60 \text{min}}{1 \text{hr}} \times \frac{60 \text{ second}}{1 \text{min}}$

$W = 2.5 \times 24 \times 60 \times 60 = 216000$ seconds

22 (*a*) $\underset{4.88 \text{ g}}{2KClO_3} \longrightarrow \underset{2.96 \text{ g}}{2KCl} + \underset{1.92 \text{ g}}{3O_2}$

Since, mass of the products (2.96 +1.92) is equal to the mass of the reactant, thus result illustrates the law of conservation of mass.

23 (*b*) According to law of conservation of mass,

mass of reactants = mass of products

$\therefore \quad 6.3 + 15.0 = 18.0 + x$

or $\quad x = 21.3 - 18.0 = 3.3$ g

24 (*d*) Law of definite proportions was given by a French chemist, Joseph Proust.

He stated that, a given compound always contains exactly the same proportion of elements by weight.

25 (*b*) To prepare 20 g zinc sulphate crystals,

zinc required $= \frac{22.65}{100} \times 20 = 4.53$ g

26 (*b*) In (PbO, PbO_2), oxygen (16g, 32g) combines with a fixed mass of lead (Pb), bearing a simple ratio, 16 : 32 or 1 : 2.

In (NO, N_2O), N and O combine to form two compounds NO and N_2O

27 (*c*) The statement (c) illustrate the law of multiple proportions.

28 (*d*) According to Avogadro's law, two volumes of hydrogen combine with one volume of oxygen to give two volumes of water without leaving any unreacted oxygen.

29 (*c*) 100 mL of hydrogen combines with 50 mL of oxygen to give 100 mL of water vapour.

30 (*a*) The postulate (a) explains the law of multiple proportions.

31 (*a*) According to Dalton's atomic theory, atoms are indivisible particles and cannot be created in a chemical reaction.

32 (*d*)

33 (*b*) Average atomic mass

$= F_1M_1 + F_2M_2 + \ldots + F_nM_n$

where, $F_1, F_2, \ldots F_n$ is the fraction representing the natural abundance of the isotope and M is the weight of the isotope.

So, the average atomic mass

$= (0.85 \times 11) + (0.10 \times 12) + (0.05 \times 13)$

$= 9.35 + 1.2 + 0.65 = 11.2$

Hence, the average atomic mass = 11.2

34 (*a*) Atomic mass of oxygen

$= \frac{(99.763 \times 15.995) + (0.037 \times 16.999) + (0.200 \times 17.999)}{100}$

= 15.999 u

35 (*b*) From the given data in question, the average atomic mass of carbon will come out to be (0.98892) (12 u) + (0.01108) (13.00335 u) + (2×10^{-12}) (14.00317 u) = 12.011 u.

36 (*a*) Average molar mass of (Ar)

$= \sum fi \times A_i$

$= (0.00337 \times 35.96755) + (0.00063 \times 37.96272) + (0.99600 \times 39.9624)$

$= 0.121 + 0.024 + 39.802$

$= 39.947 \text{ g mol}^{-1}$

37 (*c*) The correct statement is (c) while other statements are incorrect.

The correct form is as follows

(a) In the solid state, potassium chloride does not exist as a single entity.

(b) Potassium chloride do not contain discrete molecules.

(d) Formula mass of KCl is the addition of atomic masses of K and Cl.

38 (*b*) Average atomic mass

$= \frac{54 \times 5 + 56 \times 90 + 57 \times 5}{100}$

$= 55.95$

39 (*d*) The incorrect statement is (d). Its correct form is, empirical formula represents the simplest whole number ratio of various atoms present in a compound.

40 (*a*) The mass of a carbon -12 atom was determined by a mass spectrometer and found to be equal to 1.992648×10^{-23} g.

41 (*a*) Molar mass of $CO_2 = 44$ g

44 g of CO_2 = 1 mol of CO_2

22 g of CO_2 = 0.5 mol of CO_2

1 mole of CO_2 contains

$= 2 \times 6.023 \times 10^{23}$ O-atoms

$\therefore$ 0.5 mole of CO_2

$= 6.023 \times 10^{23}$ O-atoms

Number of O-atoms in CO

$= 6.023 \times 10^{23}$

$\therefore$ Molar mass of CO = 12 + 16 = 28 g

$\therefore$ 28 g of CO contains 6.022×10^{23} atoms of oxygen.

The weight of CO is 28 g having the same number of oxygen atoms as are present in 22 g of CO_2.

42 (*c*) Mass of $Al_2O_3 = 2 \times 27 + 3 \times 16$

= 102 g

Moles in 0.051 g of $Al_2O_3 = \frac{0.051}{102}$

= 0.0005 mol

1 mole of Al_2O_3 contains

$= 2 \times 6.023 \times 10^{23}$ Al^{3+} ions,

0.0005 mole of Al_2O_3 contains

$= 2 \times 0.0005 \times 6.023 \times 10^{23}$ Al^{3+} ions

$= 6.023 \times 10^{20}$ Al^{3+} ions

43 (*c*) 12 moles of H-atoms = 1 mole of $(NH_4)_3PO_4$

$\therefore$ 1 mole of H-atom

$= \frac{1}{12}$ moles of $(NH_4)_3PO_4$

$\therefore$ 6.36 moles of H-atom $= \frac{1}{12} \times 6.36$

$= \frac{6.36}{12}$ moles of $(NH_4)_3PO_4$

1 mole of $(NH_4)_3PO_4$ contains 4 moles of oxygen

So, $\frac{6.36}{12}$ moles of $(NH_4)_3PO_4$

$= \frac{4 \times 6.36}{12}$ moles of oxygen

$= 2.12$ moles of oxygen

44 (c) Number of moles of oxygen in the cylinder

$= \frac{\text{Mass (in g)}}{\text{Molecular mass (in g mol}^{-1})}$

$= \frac{2.5 \times 10^4}{32} = 781.25$ mol

$\therefore$ Number of moles of N_2

$= 3 \times 781.25 = 2343.75$

Mass of nitrogen in the cylinder

$= 2343.75 \times 28$

$= 65625 \text{ g} = 6.5625 \times 10^4 \text{g}$

Total mass of the gas in the cylinder

$= 2.5 \times 10^4 + 6.5625 \times 10^4$

$= 9.0625 \times 10^4$ g

45 (d) In Na_2SO_3, 1 mol of $Na_2SO_3 \longrightarrow$ 3 mol 'O' atoms

So, number of oxygen atoms

$=$ Atomicity $\times$ No. of moles $\times N_A$

(where, N_A = Avogadro number)

$= 3 \times 0.2 \times N_A = 0.6\, N_A$

46 (a) I. Mass of one atom of oxygen

$= \frac{16}{6.022 \times 10^{23}} = 2.66 \times 10^{-23}$ g

II. Mass of one atom of nitrogen

$= \frac{14}{6.022 \times 10^{23}} = 2.32 \times 10^{-23}$ g

III. Mass of 1×10^{-10} mole of oxygen $= 16 \times 10^{-10}$ g

IV. Mass of 1×10^{-10} mole of copper $= 63 \times 10^{-10}$ g

Hence, the order of increasing mass

II < I < III < IV.

47 (c) Number of molecules of gas at STP

$= \frac{6.023 \times 10^{23} \times 2.8}{22.4}$

$= 7.5 \times 10^{22}$ molecules

Number of atoms in diatomic molecule $= 2 \times 7.5 \times 10^{22}$

$= 15 \times 10^{22}$ atoms

48 (b) Number of C atoms is

$= 0.2 \times 6 \times N_A = 1.2\, N_A$

49 (a) Maximum number of atoms are present in 8 g CH_4.

As, for 8 g of CH_4

Moles $= \frac{8}{16} = \frac{1}{2}$

Number of molecules $= \frac{N_A}{2}$

Number of atoms in $CH_4 = \frac{5}{2} N_A$

Similarily, for 18 g of

$C_6H_{12}O_6 = \frac{24}{10} N_A$

For 25 g of

$CaCO_3 = \frac{25 \times 5}{100} N_A = \frac{5}{4} N_A$

For 28 g of $CO = 2N_A$

50 (a) 1 mole of water contains 6.022×10^{23} atoms of oxygen

$\therefore$ 0.5 mole of water contains

$\frac{6.022 \times 10^{23}}{2}$ atoms of oxygen

$= 3.011 \times 10^{23}$ atoms of oxygen:

1 mole of water at STP occupies a volume of 22.4L

0.5 mole of water at STP

$= \frac{1}{2} \times 22.4 = 11.2$ L

Mass (g) = Molar mass $\times$ Mole

$= 0.5 \times 18 = 9$ g

51 (c) Given, 1 mL of water contains 20 drops.

(But, 1 mL = 1 g)

1 g water contains 20 drops of water.

1 drops of water contains $\frac{1}{20}$ g of water.

18 g of water contains 6.023×10^{23} molecules.

So, $\frac{1}{20}$ g of water contains

$= \frac{6.023 \times 10^{23}}{18 \times 20}$ molecules

Hence, 1 drop of water contains

$= \frac{6.023 \times 10^{23}}{360} = 0.0167 \times 10^{23}$

or 1.67×10^{21} molecules

52 (c)

Element	Mass	Mole ratio	Simple ratio
Iodine	25.4	$\frac{25.4}{127} = 0.2$	2
Oxygen	8	$\frac{8}{16} = 0.5$	5

The formula of oxide is I_2O_5.

53 (b)

Element	%	Atomic mass	Molar ratio	Simpler molar ratio
C	10.06%	12	$\frac{10.06}{12} = 0.84$	$\frac{0.84}{0.84} = 1$
H	0.84%	1	$\frac{0.84}{1} = 0.84$	$\frac{0.84}{0.84} = 1$
Cl	89.10%	35.5	$\frac{89.10}{35.5} = 2.5$	$\frac{2.5}{0.84} = 3$

Thus, the empirical formula of the substance is $CHCl_3$.

54 (a) Given, % of element $(M) = 68\%$

and of oxygen (O) $= 32\%$

Atomic mass of $M = 34$

Atomic mass of O = 16

Thus, empirical formula of M_xO_y is

element $\longrightarrow$ % of mass $\longrightarrow$ moles (n)

$M \longrightarrow 68 \longrightarrow 68/34 = 2$

$O \longrightarrow 32 \longrightarrow 32/16 = 2$

Hence, empirical formula of given compound is M_2O_2 or MO.

55 (c)

Element	%	% at. wt.	Molar ratio	Ratio
N	30.5	$\frac{30.5}{14} = 2.18$	$\frac{2.18}{2.18} = 1$	1
O	69.5	$\frac{69.5}{16} = 4.34$	$\frac{4.34}{2.18} = 1.99$	2

Empirical formula $= NO_2$

Empirical formula weight = 46

$\therefore \quad n = \frac{92}{46} = 2$

Molecular formula

$= (NO_2)_2 = N_2O_4$

56 (*b*) Volume of spherical ball $=\frac{4}{3}\pi r^3$

$$=\frac{4}{3}\times\frac{22}{7}\times(7)^3$$

$\because$ Mass $= V \times d$

$$=\frac{4}{3}\times\frac{22}{7}\times 7\times 7\times 7\times 1.4$$

As, the ball contains 56% Fe. Then,

$$\text{Mass}=\frac{4}{3}\times\frac{22}{7}\times(7)^3\times 1.4\times\frac{56}{100}\text{ g}$$

$$=1126.86\text{ g}$$

$$\text{No. of moles of Fe}=\frac{\text{given mass}}{\text{molecular mass}}$$

$$=\frac{1126.86\text{ g}}{56\text{ g/mol}}=20.1\text{ mol}$$

57 (*d*) Let, the molecular formula of

$$S = S_x$$

$$\text{mole of } S_x \text{ in 280 mL at NTP}=\frac{280}{22400}$$

$$\therefore \text{Weight of } S_x=\frac{28}{2240}\times 32x=3.2$$

(Given, weight of sulphur = 3.2 g)

$$x=\frac{224}{28}=8$$

$\therefore$ Molecular formula of sulphur $= S_8$

58 (*d*) Molecular weight = 2 × vapour density = 2 × 45 = 90

Empirical formula weight

$$=12+2+16=30$$

$$\because\ n=\frac{\text{Mol. wt.}}{\text{Empirical formula wt.}}$$

$$=\frac{90}{30}=3$$

$\therefore$ Molecular formula of the compound $=(CH_2O)_3 = C_3H_6O_3$

59 (*c*)

Element	%	Relative number of atom	Simplest ratio
C	49.3	$\frac{49.3}{12}=4.1$	$\frac{4.1}{2.74}=1.5\times 2=3$
H	6.84	$\frac{6.84}{1}=6.84$	$\frac{6.84}{2.74}=2.5\times 2=5$
O	43.86	$\frac{43.86}{16}=2.74$	$\frac{2.74}{2.74}=1\times 2=2$

Thus, the empirical formula is $C_3H_5O_2$.

Empirical formula weight

$$=3\times 12+5\times 1+2\times 16$$

$$=36+5+32=73$$

Molecular weight of the compound

$$=2\times \text{VD}=2\times 73=146$$

$$n=\frac{\text{mol. wt.}}{\text{empirical formula wt.}}$$

$$=\frac{146}{73}=2$$

Molecular formula = Empirical formula × 2

$$=(C_3H_5O_2)\times 2=C_6H_{10}O_4$$

60 (*d*) 0.0833 moles of carbohydrate has hydrogen = 1g

$\therefore$ 1 mole of carbohydrate has

$$\text{hydrogen}=\frac{1}{0.0833}=12\text{ g}$$

Given, empirical formula of carbohydrate (CH_2O) has 2 g of hydrogen, $n=12/2=6$

$\therefore$ Molecular formula of carbohydrate is $(CH_2O)_n$

$$=(CH_2O)\times 6=C_6H_{12}O_6.$$

61 (*c*)

	C	H	N
Ratio	9	1	3.5
Molar ratio	$\frac{9}{12}=0.75$	$\frac{1}{1}=1$	$\frac{3.5}{14}=0.25$
Simpler molar ratio	$\frac{0.75}{0.25}=3$	$\frac{1}{0.25}=4$	$\frac{0.25}{0.25}=1$

So, empirical formula $=C_3H_4N$

Empirical formula weight

$$=(3\times 12+4\times 1+14)=54$$

$$n=\frac{108}{54}=2$$

$$\text{Molecular formula}=(C_3H_4N)_2=C_6H_8N_2$$

62 (*d*)

Element	%	At. weight	% Atomic weight	Simplest molar ratio
C	54.55	12	$\frac{54.55}{12}=4.54$	$\frac{4.54}{2.27}=2$
H	9.09	1	$\frac{9.09}{1}=9.09$	$\frac{9.09}{2.27}=4$
O	36.36	16	$\frac{36.36}{16}=2.27$	$\frac{2.27}{2.27}=1$

$\therefore$ Empirical formula is C_2H_4O.

63 (*d*) The equation is

$$C_2H_6+\frac{7}{2}O_2\longrightarrow 2CO_2+3H_2O$$

Here, C_2H_6 is burnt in excess of oxygen. The mass of CO_2 produced will only depends upon C_2H_6.

As we know,

Number of moles

$$=\frac{\text{Given mass in grams}}{\text{Molar mass in g/mol}}$$

$\because$ Molar mass of C_2H_6 = 30 g/mol

$$\text{So, } n_{C_2H_6}=\frac{300\text{g}}{30\text{ g/mol}}=10\text{ mol}$$

1 mole of C_2H_6 gives 2 moles of CO_2.

$\therefore$ 10 moles of C_2H_6 gives 20 moles of CO_2.

Mass of CO_2 produced = Number of moles × Molar mass of CO_2

$$=20\text{ mol}\times 44\text{ g/mol}=880\text{ g}$$

64 (*b*) Volume occupied by N_2 at S.T.P.

= No. of moles × molar volume

Hence, volume occupied by N_2 at S.T.P = 0.5 × 22.4 = 11.2 litres

65 (*b*) Molecular mass of 2 molecules of $C_{57}H_{110}O_6$

$$=2\times(12\times 57+1\times 110+16\times 6)\text{ g}$$

$$=1780\text{ g}$$

Molecular mass of 110 molecules of $H_2O=110(2+16)=1980$ g

1780 g of $C_{57}H_{110}O_6$ produced = 1980 g of H_2O

445 g of $C_{57}H_{110}O_6$ produced

$$=\frac{1980}{1780}\times 445\text{ g of } H_2O$$

$$=495\text{ g of } H_2O$$

66 (*c*) $\because$ Molecular mass

= 2 × vapour density

= 2 × 11.2 = 22.4 g

Molecular mass = 22.4 L at S.T.P

$\therefore$ 22.4 g = 22.4 L at S.T.P

$$\therefore\quad 1\text{ g}=\frac{22.4}{22.4}\times 1=1\text{ L}$$

67 (*d*) 1 mole of calcium carbonate degrades to form 1 mole of calcium oxide along with carbon dioxide gas.

100 g of $CaCO_3$ = 22.4 L of CO_2

x g of $CaCO_3$ = 11.2 L of CO_2

Number of moles of $CaCO_3$

$$= \frac{80}{100} \times \frac{x}{100}$$

$$\text{So, } x \times \left(\frac{80}{100}\right) \times 22.4 = 11.2 \times 100$$

$$x = 62.5 \text{ g}$$

Hence, 62.5 g of calcium carbonate is required here.

68 (*c*) 0.04 mol of H_2O_2 is required to react with 0.01 mol PbS.

Molarity of H_2O_2 may be calculated as,

Volume strength = Molarity × 11.2

$$10 = M \times 11.2$$

$$M = 0.892$$

$$\text{Number of moles} = \frac{MV}{1000}$$

$$= 0.04 = \frac{0.892 \times V}{1000}$$

$$V = 44.8 \text{ mL}$$

69 (*b*) $\underset{1\text{ g}}{M_2CO_3} + 2HCl \longrightarrow 2MCl + H_2O + \underset{0.01186 \text{ mole}}{CO_2}$

Number of moles of M_2CO_3 reacted = Number of moles of CO_2 evolved

$$1/M = 0.01186$$

[M = molar mass of M_2CO_3]

$$M = \frac{1}{0.01186} = 84.3 \text{ g mol}^{-1}$$

70 (*a*) Weight of CaO = 0.56 g

0.56 g of CaO contains 0.40 g of calcium.

Molar mass of $CaCl_2$ = 40 + 71 = 111

Therefore, 0.4 g of calcium present

$$\text{in } \frac{(0.40 \times 111)}{40} = 1.11 \text{ g of } CaCl_2.$$

Amount of NaCl present in mixture = 4.44 − 1.11 = 3.33 g

Therefore, percentage of

$$NaCl = \frac{3.33}{4.44} \times 100 = 75\%$$

71 (*a*) $NaH_2PO_4 + 2Na_2HPO_4 \longrightarrow Na_5P_3O_{10} + 2H_2O$

Hence, the stoichiometric ratio of sodium dihydrogen orthophosphate and sodium hydrogen orthophosphate is 1 : 2 or 1.5 : 3.

72 (*a*) $\underset{2 \times 276\text{ g}}{2Ag_2CO_3} \xrightarrow{\Delta} \underset{4 \times 108 \text{ g}}{4Ag} + 2CO_2\uparrow + \frac{1}{2}O_2\uparrow$

∵ 2×276 g of Ag_2CO_3 gives = 4×108 g Ag

$$\therefore 1 \text{ g of } Ag_2CO_3 \text{ gives} = \frac{4 \times 108}{2 \times 276} \text{ g Ag}$$

∴ 2.76 g of Ag_2CO_3 gives

$$= \frac{4 \times 108 \times 2.76}{2 \times 276} = 2.16 \text{ g Ag}$$

73 (*a*) $CaCO_3 \longrightarrow CaO + \underset{(22.4 \text{ L})}{CO_2}$

$$2KOH + CO_2 \longrightarrow K_2CO_3 + H_2O$$

Here, 2 moles of KOH required to neutralise 1 mol or 22.4 L of CO_2.

So, 11.2 L of CO_3 required 1 mole at KOH.

Mass of 1 mole KOH is = 39 + 16 + 1 = 56 g

74 (*b*)

∵ 143.5 g AgCl contains Ag = 108 g

∴ 2.87 g AgCl contains Ag

$$= \frac{108 \times 2.87}{143.5} = 2.16 \text{ g}$$

75 (*b*) From the given relationships, the data can be interconverted as,

mass ⇌ moles ⇌ number of molecules

76 (*c*) $\underset{\substack{4 \times 65 \text{ g} \\ = 260 \text{ g}}}{4Zn} + 10HNO_3(\text{dil.}) \longrightarrow 4Zn(NO_3)_2 + \underset{44 \text{ g}}{N_2O} + 5H_2O$

∴ The gas evolved by treating 260 g Zn with excess of nitric acid = 44 g

∴ The gas evolved by treating 325 g of Zn with excess of nitric acid = (44/260) × 325 = 55 g

77 (*b*) The reaction is as

$$CO + \frac{1}{2}O_2 \longrightarrow CO_2$$

The complete oxidation of 1 mole (22.4 L) of CO gives 1 mole (22.4 L) of CO_2.

Thus, 11.2 L of CO_2 will be produced by complete combustion of

$$11.2 \times \frac{22.4}{22.4} = 11.2 \text{ L of CO.}$$

78 (*d*) 3 × 22.4 L $H_2(g)$ at STP is produced by 6 moles of HCl (*aq*).

Hence, 11.2 L $H_2(g)$ at STP is produced by 1 mole of HCl (*aq*) consumed.

79 (*b*) $2MnO_4^- + 5C_2O_4^{2-} + 16H^+ \longrightarrow 2Mn^{2+} + 10CO_2 + 8H_2O$

20 mL of 0.1 M $KMnO_4$ = 20 × 0.1 = 2 mmol

∵ 2 mmol of $KMnO_4$ = 5 mmol of $C_2O_4^{2-}$

50 mL of 0.1 M $H_2C_2O_4$ or 50 × 0.1 = 5 mmol

Hence, 20 mL of 0.1 M $KMnO_4$ = 50 mL of 0.1 M $H_2C_2O_4$

80 (*d*) The balanced chemical reaction is

$$Mg(OH)_2 + 2HCl \longrightarrow MgCl_2 + 2H_2O$$

From the equation, it is clear that we need 2 moles of HCl to neutralise 1 mole of $Mg(OH)_2$.

Now, there is 0.136 M of HCl for every 100 mL.

So, the sample will have

$$125 \text{ mL} \times \frac{0.136 \text{ moles HCl}}{1000 \text{ mL}}$$

$$= 0.017 \text{ moles of HCl}$$

So, for complete neutralisation,

$$= 0.017 \text{ moles of HCl} \times \frac{\text{Molar mass of } Mg(OH)_2}{2 \text{ moles HCl}}$$

$$= 0.0085 \times 58.33 = 0.496$$

So, 0.496 g of $Mg(OH)_2$ is required to neutralise 125 mL of 0.136 M HCl solution.

81 (*a*) At S.T.P 1 mole of any gas occupies a volume of 22.4 L.

The balanced chemical reaction is

$$\underset{(22.4 \text{ L})}{H_2} + \underset{(11.2 \text{ L})}{Cl_2} \longrightarrow 2HCl$$

Here, limiting reagent is Cl_2.

1 mole of Cl forms 2 moles of HCl.

Hence, 0.5 moles of chlorine will form 1 mole of HCl.

82 (*c*) $\underset{\substack{3 \times 56 \text{ g} \\ = 168 \text{ g}}}{3Fe} + \underset{\substack{4 \times 18 \text{ g} \\ = 72 \text{ g}}}{4H_2O} \longrightarrow Fe_3O_4 + 4H_2$

∵ 72 g steam required Fe = 168 g

$\therefore$ 18 g steam required Fe

$$= \frac{168 \times 18}{72} = 42 \text{ g}$$

83 (c) The balanced chemical equation is

$$\underset{24\text{ g}}{Mg} + \underset{16\text{ g}}{\frac{1}{2}O_2} \longrightarrow \underset{40\text{ g}}{MgO}$$

From the above equation, we note that 24 g Mg reacts with 16 g O_2.

Therefore, 1.0 Mg reacts with

$$\frac{16}{24} \text{ g } O_2 = 0.67 \text{ g } O_2$$

However, only 0.56 g of O_2 is available. Thus, O_2, is the limiting reagent.

16 g O_2 then reacts with 24 g Mg.

$\therefore$ 0.56 g O_2 will react with Mg

$$= \frac{24}{16} \times 0.56 = 0.84 \text{ g}$$

The amount of Mg left unreacted

$$= 1.0 - 0.84 \text{ g}$$
$$= 0.16 \text{ g Mg}$$

Hence, Mg is present in excess and 0.16 g Mg is left behind unreacted.

84 (a) $\underset{\substack{56\text{ g}\\(2\text{ mol})}}{N_2(g)} + \underset{\substack{10\text{ g}\\(5\text{ mol})}}{3H_2(g)} \longrightarrow 2NH_3(g)$

Actually, 6 moles of H_2 is required but only 5 moles present, so, it is limiting reagent.

85 (d)

$$\underset{0.5}{3BaCl_2} + \underset{0.2}{2Na_3PO_4} \longrightarrow Ba_3(PO_4)_2 + 6NaCl$$

As, 3 moles of $BaCl_2$ required

$$= 2 \text{ moles of } Na_3PO_4$$

$\therefore$0.5 moles of $BaCl_2$ required

$$= \frac{2}{3} \times 0.5$$

$$= 0.33 \text{ moles of } Na_3PO_4$$

$\therefore$ Na_3PO_4 is the limiting reagent.

$\because$ 2 moles of Na_3PO_4 gives

$Ba_3(PO_4)_2 = 1$ mol

$\therefore$ 0.2 mole of $Na_3(PO_4)$ gives

$$Ba_3(PO_4)_2 = \frac{1}{2} \times 0.2 = 0.10 \text{ mol}$$

86 (c) $\underset{2\times 24}{2Mg} + \underset{2\times 16}{O_2} \longrightarrow \underset{2(24+16)}{2MgO}$

48 g of Mg requires 32 g of O_2

$$1 \text{ g of Mg requires} = \frac{32}{48}$$
$$= 0.66 \text{ g of } O_2$$

Oxygen available = 0.5 g

Hence, O_2 is limiting reagent.

32 g of O_2 reacts with 48 g of Mg

$$0.5 \text{ g of } O_2 \text{ reacts with } \frac{48}{32} \times 0.5$$
$$= 0.75 \text{ g of Mg}$$

Excess of Mg = (1.0 − 0.75) = 0.25 g

87 (a) Given, $x_B = 0.2$, $x_A = 0.8$

$$\text{Now, molality } (m) = \frac{x_B \times 1000}{x_A \times M_A} \quad \text{...(i)}$$

(M_A = molar mass of solvent)

$\therefore$ Molar mass of solvent (acetone)

= 58.08 g/mol

Now, by putting the value of x_A, x_B and M_A in Eq. (i)

$$\text{Then, the molarity } (m) = \frac{0.2 \times 1000}{0.8 \times 58.08}$$
$$= \frac{200}{46.464}$$
$$= 4.30 \text{ m}$$

88 (b) $\therefore$ $\text{Number of moles} = \frac{6.02 \times 10^{20}}{N_A}$

$$= \frac{6.02 \times 10^{20}}{6.023 \times 10^{23}} = 1 \times 10^{-3} \text{ mol}$$

Volume of the solution = 100 mL = 0.1 L

Concentration of urea solution (in mol L^{-1})

$$= \frac{1 \times 10^{-3}}{0.1} \text{ mol } L^{-1}$$
$$= 1 \times 10^{-2} \text{ mol } L^{-1}$$
$$= 0.01 \text{ mol } L^{-1}$$

89 (a) 1.00 molar aqueous solution

= 1.0 mole in 1000 g water

$$n_{solute} = 1; w_{solvent} = 1000 \text{ g}$$

$$n_{solvent} = \frac{1000}{18} = 55.56$$

$$\Rightarrow \quad \chi_{solute} = \frac{n_{solute}}{n_{solute} + n_{solvent}}$$

$$\chi_{solute} = \frac{1}{1 + 55.56} = 0.0177$$

90 (b) Given, Molality = 5 molal

As we know, Mass% of urea

$$= \left(\frac{\text{Mass of solute}}{\text{Mass of solution}}\right) \times 100 \text{ ...(i)}$$

Mass of solvent = 1 kg = 1000 g

Mass of urea (solute)

= mole × molar mass

= 5 × 60 = 300

$$\text{Mass of solution} = M_{solute} + M_{solvent}$$
$$= 300 + 1000 = 1300$$

Now, by putting the values in equation (i) we get,

$$\text{Mass \% of urea} = \frac{300}{1300} \times 100$$
$$= 23.07\% \approx 23\%$$

91 (b) Volume of 100 g sample

$$= \frac{\text{Mass}}{\text{Density } (d)} = 100/d$$

$$\text{Molarity} = \frac{\text{Mass of solute}}{\text{Molar mass of solute}} \times \frac{1000}{\text{Volume of solution (in mL)}}$$

$$\text{Molarity} = \frac{69}{63} \times \frac{1}{100/d} \times 1000$$

$$15.44 = \frac{69}{63} \times \frac{1}{100/d} \times 1000$$

$$d = \frac{63 \times 15.44}{69 \times 10}$$

$$= 1.409 \text{ g/cc} \approx 1.41 \text{ g/cc}$$

92 (b) $M_1V_1 = M_2V_2$

$$0.5 \times 100 = 0.1 \times V_2$$

$$\Rightarrow \quad V_2 = 500 \text{ cm}^3$$

Volume of water to be added to 100 cm^3 of solution = 500 − 100

= 400 cm^3

93 (c) Molarity (M)

$$= \frac{\text{Moles of solute}}{\text{Volume of solution (in L)}}$$

Moles of urea = 120/60 = 2

Weight of solution = Weight of solvent + Weight of solute

= 1000 + 120 = 1120 g

$$\Rightarrow \text{Volume} = \frac{1120 \text{ g}}{1.15 \text{ g / mL}} \times \frac{1}{1000 \text{ mL}}$$

= 0.973 L

$\therefore$ Molarity = 2/0.973 = 2.05 M

94 (d) Moles of NaOH $= \frac{8}{40} = 0.2$ mol

Moles of $H_2O = \frac{18}{18} = 1$ mol

Mole fraction $(\chi_{NaOH}) = \frac{0.2}{0.2+1}$

$= 0.167$

Molality (NaOH) $= \frac{0.2 \times 1000}{18}$

$= 11.11 \text{ mol kg}^{-1}$

95 (c) The balanced chemical reaction is

$$CaCO_3 \xrightarrow{\Delta} CaO + CO_2$$

0.5 mol of $CaCO_3$ produce 0.5 more of CO_2

Mass of $CaCO_3$ used is $= 0.5 \times 100$

$= 50$ g

The percentage of $CaCO_3$ in lime stone is $= \frac{50}{100} \times 100 = 50\%$

96 (a) Molarity

$= \frac{\text{Weight of } HNO_3}{\text{Molecular mass of } HNO_3 \times \text{Volume of solution (in L)}}$

$\therefore$ Weight of HNO_3

$=$ Molarity $\times$ Molecular mass $\times$ Volume (in L)

$= 2 \times 63 \times \frac{250}{1000} = 31.5$ g

It is the weight of 100% HNO_3.

But the given acid is 70% HNO_3 is

$= \frac{31.5}{70} \times 100 \text{ g} = 45.0$ g conc. HNO_3

97 (d) $C_2H_2 + \frac{5}{2}O_2 \longrightarrow 2CO_2 + H_2O$

1 mole of C_2H_2 reacts with $\left(\frac{5}{2}\right)$ mole of oxygen

$\therefore$ 1 oxygen vol. of C_2H_2 will react with $\left(\frac{5}{2}\right)$ vol. of 100 cc of C_2H_2 will react with $= \frac{5}{2} \times 100 = 250$ cc of O_2

$\therefore$ Volume of required air

$= \frac{250 \times 100}{20} = 1250$ cc

98 (a) Number of moles of NaOH

$= \frac{20}{40} = 0.5$ mol

Hence, molarity $= \frac{0.5}{500} \times 1000 = 1$ M

99 (a) 2m urea solution means 2 moles of urea are present in 1 kg or 1000 g solvent.

$n_{urea} = 2$ mol

$n_{H_2O} = \frac{\text{given mass}}{\text{molar mass}} = \frac{1000}{18}$

$= 55.55$ mole

Mole fraction of urea,

$x = \frac{n_{urea}}{n_{urea} + n_{H_2O}}$

$= \frac{2}{2 + 55.55} = 0.035$

100 (d) Molality $(m) = \frac{5.85 \times 1000}{58.44 \times 100}$

$= 1.001 \approx 1$ m

Assertion-Reason

1 (a) Both A and R are true and R is the correct explanation of A.

2 (d) A is false but R is true.

The correct explanation of A is :

Gay-Lussac's law deals only with gaseous reactants and products at same temperature and pressure.

As, $NH_3(g) + HCl(g) \longrightarrow NH_4Cl(s)$

So, the ratio is 1 : 1 : 0. Because the products is a solid.

3 (d) A is false but R is true. Matter consists of indivisible atoms.

4 (c) A is true but R is false.

The correct form of R is :

Equal weights of different substances do not contain the same number of constituent particles.

5 (c) A is true but R is false.

The correct form of R is :

Empirical formula gives the simplest ratio of the atoms of the various elements present in one molecule of the substance.

6 (a) Both A and R are true and R is the correct explanation of A.

$2O_3 \longrightarrow 3O_2$ (Balanced equation)

2 moles of $O_3 \equiv 3$ moles of O_2

$= 3 \times 2$ eq. O_2

$E_{O_3} = M/6 = 48/6 = 8.$

7 (a) Both A and R are true and R is the correct explanation of A.

The molecular formula of ethene is C_2H_4 and its empirical formula is CH_2. Thus, molecular formula = empirical formula × 2.

8 (b) Both A and R are true but R is not the correct explanation of A.

Atomic masses of the elements obtained by scientists by comparing with the mass of carbon comes out to be close to whole number value.

9 (c) A is true but R is false.

0.200 contains 3 while 200 contains only one significant figure because zero at the end or right of a number are significant provided they are on the right side of the decimal point.

10 (d) A is false but R is true.

Combustion of 16 g of methane gives 36 g of water.

$$\underset{\substack{1\text{mol}\\=16\text{g}}}{CH_4} + 2O_2 \longrightarrow CO_2 + \underset{\substack{2\text{ mol}\\=36\text{g}}}{2H_2O}$$

Statement Type

1 (a) Both Statements I and II are false.

Their correct form is :

I. Average atomic mass depends upon the atomic masses at different isotopes and their fractional abundances.

II. Average atomic mass is obtained by multiplying atomic masses of the isotopes with their corresponding fractional advances and then adding them.

2. (b) Statement I is true but Statement II is false.

The correct form at Statement II is:

One mole at a substance always contains the same number of entities, no matter what the substances may be.

3. (*b*) Statement I is true but Statement II is false.

The correct form of Statement II is :

44 g of CO_2 = 1 mole = 12 g of C

16 g of CH_4 = 1 mole = 12 g of C

12 g of C contains 6.023×10^{23} carbon atoms.

4. (*d*) Both Statements I and II are true.
5. (*a*) Both Statements I and II are false.
6. (*d*) Among the given options I, III, IV and V are correct statements while II is incorrect.

The correct form of Statement II is :
The properties of a compound are quite different from the properties of constituent elements.

7. (*b*) Statement I is incorrect while II, III, IV and V are correct.

The correct form of Statement I is :
The mass of a substance can be determined very accurately by using an analytical balance.

8. (*d*) Statements I, III and IV are correct while Statements II and V are incorrect.

Their correct form is :

II. Gay Lussac's law is an application of law of definite proportions by volume.

V. Formation of water of hydrogen peroxide by combination of hydrogen and oxygen is an example at law of multiple proportions.

9. (*b*) Statements I, II and IV are correct, while statements III and V are incorrect.

Their correct form is :

III. Mass of an atom is very small in magnitude because atoms are extremely small.

V. The formula such as NaCl is used to calculate the formula mass instead of molecular mass as in solid state NaCl does not exist as a single entity.

10 (*b*) Statements II and III are incorrect while I, IV and V are correct.

Their correct form is :

II. In compounds like NaCl positive (Na^+ ion) and negative (Cl^- ion) entities are arranged in a three-dimensional structure.

III. In NaCl, one Na^+ ion surrounded by 6 Cl^- ions and *vice-versa*.

Matching Type

1 (*a*) The correct match is A-3, B-1, C-2.

2 (*c*) The correct match is

A-4, B-3, C-1, D-2.

A. $Zn + 2HCl \longrightarrow ZnCl_2 + H_2$.

1 mole of Zn produces 2 g of H_2

0.5 mole of Zn will produce 1 g of H_2.

B. $C_{70}H_{22} = 70 \times 12 + 22 \times 1 = 862$

Molar mass = 862

$$\text{Mass of atoms} = \frac{862}{6.023 \times 10^{23}} = 1.43 \times 10^{-21} \text{ g}$$

C. 71 g of $Cl_2 = 6.023 \times 10^{23}$ molecules

35.5 g of $Cl_2 = 3.01 \times 10^{23}$ molecules

D. Molar mass of SO_2 = 64 g = 1 mole

64 g of $SO_2 = 6.023 \times 10^{23}$ molecules

3 (*a*) The correct match is

A-2, B-3, C-1, D-4.

4 (*a*) The correct match is

A-4, B-1, C-2, D-3.

5 (*b*) The correct match is

A-4, B-5, C-3, D-1, E-2.

Numerical Value

1 (*36*) Total mass of sugar in the given mixture is = $0.25 \times 200 + 0.40 \times 500$ = 250 g

Now, total mass of solution = 200 + 500 = 700 g

$$\text{So, mass \% of sugar} = \frac{250}{700} \times 100 = 35.7\% \approx 36\%.$$

2 (*3*) Number of molecules

$$= \frac{\text{Mass}}{\text{Molar mass}} \times N_A$$

$$16 \text{ g of } O_2 = \frac{16}{32} \times N_A = \frac{N_A}{2}$$

(i) $16 \text{ g of } CO = \frac{16}{28} \times N_A = \frac{4}{7} N_A$

(ii) $28 \text{ g of } NO_2 = \frac{28}{28} \times N_A = N_A$

(iii) $14 \text{ g of } N_2 = \frac{14}{28} \times N_A = \frac{N_A}{2}$

(iv) $1 \text{ g of } H_2 = \frac{1}{2} \times N_A = \frac{N_A}{2}$

(v) $22 \text{ g of } CO_2 = \frac{22}{44} \times N_A = \frac{N_A}{2}$

3 (*224*) $\underset{1\text{ mol}}{Mg} + \underset{2\text{ mol}}{2HCl} \longrightarrow \underset{1\text{ mol}}{MgCl_2} + \underset{1\text{ mol}}{H_2\uparrow}$

$$\text{No. of moles} = \frac{\text{Mass of Mg}}{\text{Molar mass of Mg}} = \frac{2.4}{24} = 0.1 \text{ mol}$$

So, 1 mole of Mg will give 1 mole of H_2

1 mole of gas at STP = 22.4 L

$\therefore$ 0.1 mole of gas = $0.1 \times 22.4 = 2.24$ L or 224×10^{-2} L.

Thus, volume of hydrogen liberated is 224×10^{-2} L.

4 (*50*) The given reaction is

$\underset{2\text{ mol}}{MnO_2} + \underset{4\text{ mol}}{4HCl} \longrightarrow MnCl_2 + 2H_2O + \underset{\substack{1\text{ mol}\\(22.4\text{ mL})}}{Cl_2}$

Actual yield is 11.2.L

$$\therefore \text{Percentage yield} = \frac{11.2}{22.4} \times 100 = 50\%$$

5 (*180*) $\text{Molarity} = \frac{5 \times 1000}{40 \times 450}$

Let x mL is required from $\frac{5 \times 1000}{40 \times 450}$ M NaOH solution to prepare 500 mL 0.1 M solution.

$$\therefore \left(\frac{5 \times 1000}{40 \times 450}\right) x = 0.1 \text{ M} \times 500 \text{ mL}$$

$$(\because M_1V_1 = M_2V_2)$$

$$x = \frac{0.1 \times 500 \text{ mL} \times 40 \times 450}{5 \times 1000} = 180 \text{ mL}$$

NCERT Exemplar's

1 (*a*) Statement III is incorrect. It's correct form is as follows

A compound do not retains the physical and chemical properties of its constituent elements.

2 (c) We know that, $°F = \frac{9}{5} t°C + 32$

Putting the values in above equation,

$$200 - 32 = \frac{9}{5} t°C$$

$$\Rightarrow \quad \frac{9}{5} t°C = 168$$

$$\Rightarrow \quad t°C = \frac{168 \times 5}{9} = 93.3°C$$

3 (a) For a solution,

Mass = Volume × Density

$= 1.5 \text{ mL} \times 3.12 \text{ g mL}^{-1} = 4.68 \text{ g}$

The digit 1.5 has only two significant figures, so the answer must also be limited to two significant figures. So, it is rounded off to reduce the number of significant figures.

Hence, the answer is reported as 4.7 g.

4 (b) $C_3H_8(g) + O_2(g) \longrightarrow CO_2(g) + H_2O(g)$

This reaction is not correct according to the law of conservation of mass, because it is not a balanced chemical equation.

5 A-(2), B-(3), C-(1), D-(5), E-(4)

A. Number of moles of CO_2 molecule

$$= \frac{\text{Weight in gram of } CO_2}{\text{Molecular weight of } CO_2}$$

$$= \frac{88}{44} = 2 \text{ mol}$$

B. 1 mole of a substance $= N_A$ molecules $= 6.022 \times 10^{23}$ molecules

= Avogadro number

$= 6.022 \times 10^{23}$ molecules of $H_2O = 1$ mol

C. 22.4L of O_2 at STP = 1 mol

5.6 L of O_2 at STP

$$= \frac{5.6}{22.4} \text{ mol} = 0.25 \text{ mol}$$

D. Number of moles of 96 g of O_2

$$= \frac{96}{32} \text{ mol} = 3 \text{ mol}$$

E. 1 mole of any gas = Avogadro number $= 6.022 \times 10^{23}$ molecules.

6 (a) One mole of any substance contains 6.022×10^{23} atoms/ molecules.

Hence, number of moles of H_2SO_4

= Molarity × Volume (in L)

$= 0.02 \times 100 \times 10^{-3} = 2 \times 10^{-3}$ mol

Number of molecules

= number of moles × N_A

$= 2 \times 10^{-3} \times 6.022 \times 10^{23}$

$= 12.044 \times 10^{20}$ molecules

7 (d) 12 g of He (3 moles of He) contains the greatest number of atoms.

12 g of He contains

$$= \frac{6.023 \times 10^{23}}{4} \times 12$$

$= 18.069 \times 10^{23}$ atoms of He.

8 (b) % of C in $CO_2 = \frac{12}{44} \times 100$

$= 27.27\%$

9 (c) Empirical formula mass = CH_2O

$= 12 + 2 \times 1 + 16 = 30$

Molecular mass = 180

$$n = \frac{\text{Molecular mass}}{\text{Empirical formula mass}}$$

$= 180/30 = 6$

∴ Molecular formula

= n × empirical formula

$= 6 \times CH_2O = C_6H_{12}O_6$

10 (c) 1 mole of NaCl contains = 58.5 g

Molarity of a solution

$$= \frac{0.1 \times 1}{2} = 0.2 \text{ mol/L}$$

11 (c) Mol. mass of $C_6H_{12}O_6 = 180$ g

Molarity of glucose

$$= \frac{0.9}{180} \text{ mol/L} = 0.005 \text{ M}$$

12 (d) Molality (m)

$$= \frac{\text{Moles of solute}}{\text{Mass of solvent (in kg)}} \quad \text{...(i)}$$

$$\text{Moles of HCl} = \frac{18.25}{36.5} = 0.5$$

$$\text{Molality} = \frac{0.5}{0.5} = 1 \text{ mol/kg}$$

[from Eq. (i)]

13 (b) $M_1V_1 = M_2V_2$

$5 \times 500 = M_2 \times 1500$

$$\frac{5 \times 500}{1500} = M_2 \Rightarrow M_2 = 1.66 \text{ M}$$

14 (a) According to the law of conservation of mass,

Total mass of reactants = Total mass of products

15 (b) The masses of oxygen combine with a fixed mass of carbon (12 parts) in CO_2 and CO are 32 and 16 respectively.

These masses of oxygen bear a simple ratio of 32 : 16 or 2 : 1 to each other.

This is an example of law of multiple proportion.

16 A-(5), B-(4), C-(2), D-(7), E-(3,8), F-(6), G-(1), H-(9)

17 (b) Average readings of student,

$$A = \frac{3.01 + 2.99}{2} = 3.00$$

Average readings of student,

$$B = \frac{3.05 + 2.95}{2} = 3.00$$

Correct reading = 3.00

For both the students, average value is close to the correct value.

Hence, readings of both are accurate.

Readings of student *A* are close to each other (differ only by 0.02) and also close to the correct reading, hence readings of *A* are precise also.

But readings of *B* are not close to each other (differ by 0.1) and, hence are not precise.

Past Exams'

1 (a) In 4 moles of He, number of He atom $= 4 \times N_A$

In 4u of He, number of He atom = 1

In 4g of He, number of He atom $= N_A$

In 2.271098 L of He, number of He atom $= \frac{2.27}{22.7} \times N_A = 0.1 N_A$

Hence, option (a) is correct.

2. (b) $NaOH + HCl \longrightarrow NaCl + H_2O$

Given, mass of NaOH = 1g

$$\text{Mole of NaOH} = \frac{1}{40} \text{ mol} = 0.025 \text{ mol}$$

Mole of HCl $= \dfrac{0.75 \times 25}{1000} = 0.01875$ mol

Now finding the limiting reagent (LR)

value $= \dfrac{\text{Given amount}}{\text{Stoichiometry coefficient}}$

NaOH : HCl

$\dfrac{0.025}{1} > \dfrac{0.01875}{1}$

So, limiting reagent (LR) will be HCl

Unreacted moles of NaOH

$= 0.025 - 0.01875 = 0.00625$ mol

Unreacted mass $= 0.00625 \times 40$ g

$= 0.25$ g $= 250$ mg

3. (*b*)

Element	%	Mole	Simple ratio
A	32	$\frac{32}{64} = \frac{1}{2}$	1
B	20	$\frac{20}{40} = \frac{1}{2}$	1
C	46	$\frac{48}{32} = \frac{3}{2}$	3

Empirical formula $= ABC_3$

4 (*a*) Molar mass ($CaCO_3$) = 100 g/mol

20 g of 20% pure limestone on heating gives $\dfrac{20 \times 20}{100} = 4$ g

Moles of $CO_2 = \dfrac{4}{100} = 0.04$

Mass of CO_2 produces = Moles × Molecular mass of CO_2

$= 0.04 \times 44 = 1.76$ g

5 (*a*) $CH_3 - \underset{\underset{O}{\|}}{C} - \overset{-}{O}\overset{+}{Na} + NaOH$

Sodium ethanoate

$\xrightarrow[\text{Decarboxylation}]{\text{CaO, }\Delta} CH_4 + Na_2CO_3$

The product formed in above reaction is CH_4.

Thus, weight of two moles of CH_4 is 2×16, i.e. 32.

6 (*c*)

Element	%	Atomic mass	Relative number of moles	Simple ratio of moles	Simplest whole number ratio
C	78	12	$\frac{78}{12} = 6.5$	$\frac{6.5}{6.5} = 1$	1
H	22	1	$\frac{22}{1} = 22$	$\frac{22}{6.5} = 3.3$	3

The empirical formula of the organic compound is CH_3.

7 (*c*) Number of atoms (*n*)

$= \dfrac{\text{Mass in g (1 g)} \times \text{Atomicity of the molecule}}{\text{Gram molar mass } (M)} \times N_A$

(a) $n_{Mg} = \dfrac{1}{24} \times N_A$

(b) $n_{O_2} = \dfrac{2N_A}{32} = \dfrac{1}{16} N_A$

(c) $n_{Li} = \dfrac{1}{7} N_A$

(d) $n_{Ag} = \dfrac{1}{108} N_A$

Thus, 1 g of Li has maximum number of atoms.

8 (*b*) According to Haber's process,

$N_2(g) + 3H_2(g) \rightleftharpoons 2NH_3(g)$

∵ 2 moles of ammonia (NH_3) require $= 3$ moles of H_2

∴ 1 mole of NH_3 require $= 3/2$ moles of H_2

or, 20 moles of NH_3 require

$= \dfrac{3}{2} \times 20$ moles of H_2

$= 30$ moles of H_2.

9 (*c*) Mass of solution

$= d \times V = 1.28 \times 1000 = 1280$ g

Mass of solute $= n \times$ Molar mass

$= 2 \times 40 = 80$ g

Mass of solvent

$= (1280 - 80) = 1200$ g

Number of moles of solute $= \dfrac{80}{40} = 2$

∴ Molality $= \dfrac{2 \times 1000}{1200} = 1.67$ m

10 (*a*) $\underset{2.3\text{g}\left(\frac{1}{20}\text{mol}\right)}{HCOOH} \xrightarrow{\text{Conc. } H_2SO_4} \underset{\frac{1}{20}\text{mol}}{CO(g)} + H_2O(l)$

$\underset{4.5\text{ g or}\left(\frac{1}{20}\text{mol}\right)}{\begin{matrix}COOH\\|\\COOH\end{matrix}} \xrightarrow{\text{Conc. } H_2SO_4} \underset{\frac{1}{20}\text{mol}}{CO(g)} + \underset{\frac{1}{20}\text{mol}}{CO_2(g)} + \underset{\frac{1}{20}\text{mol}}{H_2O(l)}$

Gaseous mixture formed is CO and CO_2. When it is passed through KOH, only CO_2 is absorbed. So, the remaining gas is CO, product CO is $\dfrac{2}{20} \times 28 = 2.8$ g

11 (*c*) The correct option is (c). As,

(1) Moles of water $= \dfrac{0.00224}{22.4} = 10^{-4}$

Molecules of water = moles $\times N_A = 10^{-4} N_A$

(2) Mass of water = 0.18 g

Molecules of water = mole $\times N_A = \dfrac{0.18}{18} N_A = 10^{-2} N_A$

(3) Mass of water $= 18 \times 1 = 18$ g

Molecules of water = moles $\times N_A$

$= \dfrac{18}{18} N_A = N_A$

(4) Molecules of water = moles $\times N_A$ $= 10^{-3} N_A$

12 (*a*) Let atomic masses of *X* and *Y* be A_X and A_Y, respectively

For XY_2, $n_{XY_2} = 0.1 = \dfrac{10}{A_X + 2A_Y}$

or $A_X + 2A_Y = 100$ ...(i)

For X_3Y_2, $n_{X_3Y_2} = 0.05 = \dfrac{9}{3A_X + 2A_Y}$

or $3A_X + 2A_Y = 180$ ...(ii)

On solving Eqs. (i) and (ii), we get,

$A_X = 40$ g mol^{-1}

⇒ $A_Y = 30$ g mol^{-1}

13 (*a*) Moles of $H_2 = \dfrac{22.4}{22.4} = 1$ mol

Moles of $Cl_2 = \dfrac{11.2}{22.4} = 0.5$ mol

Reaction is as,

	$H_2(g)$ +	$Cl_2(g)$ ⟶	$2HCl(g)$
Initial	1 mol	0.5 mol	0
Final	$(1-0.5)$ = 0.5 mol	$(0.5-0.5)$ = 0 mol	2×0.5 1 mol

Here, Cl_2 is limiting reagent. So, 1 mole of HCl (*g*) is formed.

14. (c) The reaction involved are

$CaCO_3(s) \xrightarrow{\Delta} CaO(s) + CO_2(g)$

$MgCO_3(s) \xrightarrow{\Delta} MgO(s) + CO_2(g)$

Let the weight of $CaCO_3$ be *x* g.

∴ Weight of $MgCO_3 = (2.21 - x)$ g

Moles of $CaCO_3$ decomposed

= Moles of CaO formed

$$\frac{x}{100} = \text{Moles of CaO formed}$$

$\therefore$ Weight of CaO formed $= \frac{x}{100} \times 56$

Moles of $MgCO_3$ decomposed

$= $ Moles of MgO formed

$$\frac{2.21 - x}{84} = \text{Mole of MgO formed}$$

$\therefore$ Weight of MgO formed

$$= \frac{2.21 - x}{84} \times 40$$

$$\frac{2.21 - x}{84} \times 40 + \frac{x}{100} \times 56 = 1.152$$

$\therefore \quad x = 1.1886\,g \approx 1.187\,g$

$= $ Weight of $CaCO_3$

Weight of $MgCO_3 = 1.0214$ g

≈ 1.023 g

Hence, option (c) is correct.

15. (50) $CH_4(g) + 2O_2(g) \longrightarrow CO_2(g) + 2H_2O(l)$

$$n = \frac{22}{44} = \frac{1}{2} \text{ mol of } CO_2$$

as 1 mol CH_4 form 1 mol CO_2

So, $n_{CH_4} = \frac{1}{2}$ mol $= 0.5$ mol

$n_{CH_4} = 50 \times 10^{-2}$ mol

So, the value of x is 50.

16. (8) The combustion reaction of methane is,

$CH_4 + 2O_2 \longrightarrow CO_2 + 2H_2O$

Moles of $CO_2 = \frac{22}{44} = 0.5$ mol

1 mole of CO_2 is produced from 1 mole of CH_4.

So, 0.5 mole of CO_2 will be produced from 0.5 mole of CH_4.

Mass of CH_4 formed

$= $ Moles $\times$ Molar mass

$= 0.5 \times 16 = 8$ g

17 (*d*) Concentration terms such as mass percentage mole fraction and molality and independent of temperature.

However, molarity is a function of temperature. Since, it depend on the total volume of the solution.

$$\text{Molarity} = \frac{\text{Mole of solute}}{\text{Volume of solution}}$$

18 (*d*) No. of moles of O_2

$$= \frac{2.8375}{22.7} = 0.125 \text{ moles}$$

Now, number of molecules = Moles $\times$ Avogadro's number

$= 0.125 N_A = (0.125) \times (6.02 \times 10^{23})$

$= 7.525 \times 10^{22} \approx 7.525 \times 10^{22}$

19 (*b*) Molecular weight of metal chloride is given by

$$= \frac{0.57}{100} \times 22700 = 129.39$$

Weight or mass of

Cl $= 129.39 \times 0.55 = 71.1645$ u

Now, number of moles of

$$\text{Cl} = \frac{71.1645}{35.5} \approx 2$$

Thus, the molecular formula is MCl_2.

20 (*b*) Both A and R are true and R is the correct explanation of A.

21 (*b*) The correct match is A-II, B-IV, C-I, D-III.

A. 16 g of $CH_4 = 1$ mole CH_4 contains $10 \times 6.02 \times 10^{23}$ electrons $= 60.2 \times 10^{23}$

B. 1 g $H_2(g) = 0.5$ mole H_2 gas occupy 11.2 litre volume at STP.

C. 1 mole of $N_2(g) = 28$ g

D. 0.5 mole of $SO_2(g) = 32$ g

22 (*c*) Moles of $N_2 = \frac{20}{28}$ mol

Moles of $H_2 = \frac{5}{2}$ mol

Limiting reagent

$$= \frac{\text{Number of moles}}{\text{Stoichiometric coefficient}}$$

For $N_2 = \frac{20}{28}$

For $H_2 = \frac{5}{2 \times 3} = \frac{5}{6}$

Clearly, $\frac{20}{28} < \frac{5}{6}$ so, N_2 is a limiting reagent.

1 mole of N_2 forms 2 mole of NH_3.

So, $\frac{20}{28}$ mole of N_2 forms

$$= 2 \times \frac{20}{28} = \frac{20}{14} = \frac{10}{7} = 1.42 \text{ mol.}$$

23 (*c*) The given reaction is

$$4HNO_3(l) + 3KCl(s) \longrightarrow Cl_2(g) + NOCl(g) + 2H_2O(g) + 3KNO_3(s)$$

Amount 'x'g 110 g moles $x/63$ ... $\frac{110}{101}$

So, the amount of HNO_3 required to produce $\frac{110}{101}$ moles of KNO_3 is $\frac{4}{3} \times \frac{110}{101}$ moles.

$$\therefore \quad \frac{x}{63} = \frac{4}{3} \times \frac{110}{101}$$

$$\Rightarrow \quad x = \frac{4 \times 110 \times 63}{3 \times 101} = 91.5 \text{ g}$$

24 (*b*) $C_6H_{12}O_6 \longrightarrow$ Glucose

$$\frac{\text{Mass of C}}{\text{Mass of glucose}} = \frac{72}{180}$$

Given % of C = 10.8

$$= \frac{\text{Mass of C}}{\text{Mass of solution}} \times 100$$

$$= \frac{10.8 \times 250}{100} = \text{Mass of C}$$

Mass of C = 27g

$\therefore$ Mass of glucose = 67.5 g

Mass of solvent = 250 − 67.5 g

= 182.5 g

$$\therefore \text{ Molality} = \frac{0.375}{0.1825} = 2.055 \approx 2.06$$

25 (*c*) Since, 100 g of haemoglobin has

$= 0.34$ *g* of Fe

Therefore, 3.3 g haemoglobin

$= \frac{0.34}{100} \times 3.3$ *g* of Fe

$= 0.01122$ g of Fe

Since, 56 g (1 mole) of Fe has $= 6.022 \times 10^{23}$ atoms of Fe

Therefore, 0.01122 g of Fe has

$= \frac{6.022 \times 10^{23}}{56} \times 0.01122$ atoms of Fe

$= 1.21 \times 10^{20}$ atoms of Fe

Skill Boosters

1 (*c*) Let M_A and M_B be the molar masses at *A* and *B* respectively.

As, per given data, $M_A : M_B = 2 : 3$

$\therefore M_A = \frac{2}{3} \times M_B$

Here, mass of *A* = mass of *B* = *W*

$\therefore$ In mass of weight of each gases A and B, the ratio of number of moles.

$$n_A : n_B = \frac{W}{M_A} : \frac{W_{M_B}}{M_B} = \frac{M_B}{M_A}$$

$$= \frac{M_B}{\frac{2}{3} \times M_B} = \frac{3}{2} = 3:2$$

Since, under the identical conditions at temperature and pressure, the volumes at gases are directly proportional to their number of moles, (because according to Avogadro's law, $V \propto n$ at the same temperature and pressure).

The ratio of volumes of two vessels is

$$V_A : V_B = n_A : n_B = 3:2$$

2 (d) $N_1V_1 = N_2V_2 + N_3V_3$

i.e. $0.1 \times 100 = 0.2 \times 30 + 0.25V_3$

$$0.25V_3 = 4$$

or $V_3 = 16$ mL

3 (c) 24.8 g of $Na_2S_2O_3 \cdot 5H_2O$

$$= \frac{24.8}{248} \text{ mol} = 0.1 \text{ mol}$$

1 mol of $Na_2S_2O_3 \cdot 5H_2O$ contains O-atoms = 8 mol

$\therefore$ 0.1 mol of $Na_2S_2O_3 \cdot 5H_2O$ will contain O-atoms 0.8 mol

$= 0.8 \times 6.02 \times 10^{23}$ atoms

$= 4.816 \times 10^{23}$ atoms

Thus, number at notes $= 4.816 \times 10^{23}$

$$\text{Days taken} = \frac{4.816 \times 10^{23}}{48 \times 10^6} = 10^{16}$$

4 (b) $N_2(g) + 3H_2(g) \rightleftharpoons 2NH_3(g)$

1 L of N_2 reacts with 3 L of H_2 to form 2 L of NH_3.

Thus, N_2 is the limiting reactant.

10 L N_2 will react with 30 L H_2 to form 20 L NH_3, as actual yield is 50% of the expected value, NH_3 formed = 10 L, N_2 reacted = 5 L.

H_2 reacted = 15 L

$\therefore$ Mixture will contain 10 L NH_3, 25 L N_2, 15 L H_2.

5 (d) L-amino acid (A) $\xrightarrow[0°C]{NaNO_2 + HCl} N_2\uparrow$

1 mole of L-amino acid $\longrightarrow$ 1 mol at N_2

$\therefore$ 22400 cm^3 at N_2 at STP

500 cm^3 of N_2 = 2.30 g of L-amino acid

22400 cm^3 of $N_2 \equiv x$ g of L-amino acid

$$x = \frac{2.30 \times 22400}{500}$$

$= 103.04$ g of L-amino acid

Sample of protein has 0.3% amino acid.

Amino acid	**Protein**
0.30	100
103.04	y

$$y = \frac{103.04 \times 100}{0.30}$$

$y = 34346.66$ g/mol

6 (b) Given, 3.38 g of carbon dioxide is obtained, the mass at C present in the sample of welding fuel gas is

$$\frac{12 \times 3.38}{44} = 0.92 \text{ g}$$

Since, 0.690 g of water is obtained, the mass of hydrogen present in the welding fuel gas sample is

$$\frac{2 \times 0.690}{18} = 0.077 \text{ g}$$

$$\text{The \% of C is} = \frac{0.92 \times 100}{0.077 + 0.92} = 92.30$$

$$\text{The \% at H is} = \frac{0.077}{0.077 + 0.92} \times 100$$

$= 7.72\%$

The no. of moles of carbon

$$= \frac{92.30}{12} = 7.7$$

The no. of moles of hydrogen

$$= \frac{7.70}{1} = 7.7$$

The mole ratio C : H = 7.7 : 7.7 = 1 : 1

Hence, the empirical formula of the gas is CH.

The weight of 10.0 L of gas at N.T.P. is 11.6 g.

22.4 L of gas at N.T.P. will weight

$$= \frac{11.6}{10.0} \times 22.4 = 26 \text{ g/mol}$$

The empirical mass of the welding fuel gas = 13 g /mol

$\therefore$ Molecular mass = (empirical formula mass) $\times n$

$$\therefore \quad n = \frac{26}{13} \approx 2$$

$$\left(\text{Molecular mass is } = \frac{22.4 \times 11.6}{10} = 25.98 \approx 26\right)$$

$\therefore$ Molecular formula is $= (CH)_n = C_2H_2$.

7 (b) Gram equivalent of HCl

$$= \frac{3}{36.5} \times 2.5 = 0.20548$$

= Gram eq. of $Al(OH)_3$

$$\text{Weight of } Al(OH)_3 = \frac{0.20548 \times 78}{3}$$

$= 5.342$ g $= 5342$ mg

Number of tablets

$$= \frac{5342}{400} = 13.35 \simeq 14 \text{ tablets}$$

8 (c) Number as moles of HCl

$$= 250 \text{ mL} \times \frac{0.76}{1000} = 0.19 \text{ mole}$$

Mass of $CaCO_3$ = 1000 g

$$\text{Number of moles of } CaCO_3 = \frac{1000 \text{ g}}{100 \text{ g}}$$

$= 10$ mole

According to the equation, 1 mole of $CaCO_3$ requires 2 moles of HCl.

Hence, for the reaction at 10 mole of $CaCO_3$ number of moles of HCl requird would be

$$10 \text{ mol } CaCO_3 \times \frac{2 \text{ mol HCl}}{1 \text{ mol } CaCO_3}$$

$= 20$ moles HCl

There is only 0.19 moles of HCl available, hence HCl is a limiting reagent.

Therefore, the amount of $CaCl_2$ formed will depend on the amount of HCl would give

$$0.19 \text{ mol of HCl} \times \frac{1 \text{ mol } CaCl_2}{2 \text{ mol HCl}}$$

$= 0.095$ mole $CaCl_2$

02

Scan for **Chemistry Through Concept Master** *Videos*

Structure of Atom

- The atomic theory of matter was first proposed by John Dalton in 1808, called Dalton's atomic theory, which regarded the atom as the ultimate indivisible particle of matter.
- This theory was able to explain the law of conservation of mass, law of constant composition and law of multiple proportion.
- However, it failed to explain the results of many experiments. For example, it was known that substances like glass or ebonite, when rubbed with silk or fur get electrically charged.

Topicwise No. of Ques asked in 5 Years (NEET)

Topics	No. of Questions				
	2024	2023	2022	2021	2020
Discovery of Sub-atomic Particles	–	1	–	–	–
Atomic Models	–	–	–	–	1
Developments Leading to the Bohr's Model of Atom	–	–	–	–	–
Bohr's Model for Hydrogen Atom	–	–	1	–	–
Towards Quantum Mechanical Model of Atom	1	–	–	1	–
Quantum Mechanical Model of Atom	1	1	1	–	1

Special Type of Ques asked in 5 Years

Types	Years				
	2024	2023	2022	2021	2020
A-R	–	–	–	–	–
Statement Based	–	1	1	–	–
Matching	–	–	–	–	–

Last 5 Years Weightage (NEET)

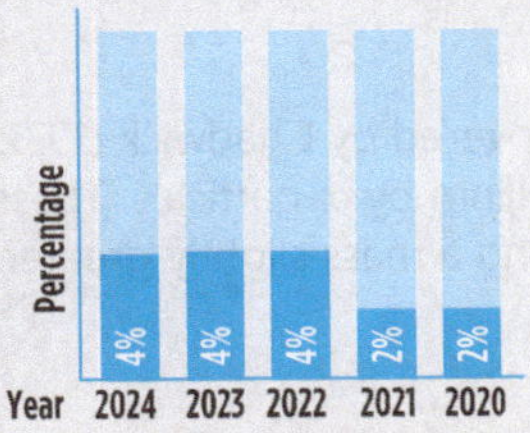

*Discovery of Sub-atomic Particles

In the end of 19th century and beginning of 20th century, it was discovered that atoms consist of sub-atomic particles, i.e. electrons, protons and neutrons, are also known as **fundamental particles**.

Discovery of Electron

Electrons were discovered by J.J. Thomson, by utilising Faraday's study of electrical discharge in partially evacuated tubes known as **cathode ray discharge tubes**.

- **Cathode ray discharge tube experiment** A cathode ray tube is made of glass containing two electrodes sealed in it.
- At very low pressure and high voltage current start flowing from negative electrode (cathode) to positive electrode (anode). These current rays were called **cathode rays** or **cathode ray particles**.
- Further, the flow of current was checked by making a hole in the anode and coating the tube behind anode with phosphorescent material ZnS, when the cathode ray strike the other end of the glass tube it develop a bright spot on the coating.

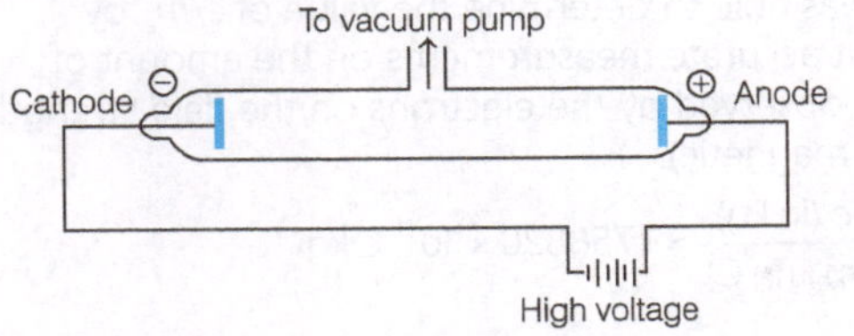

A cathode ray discharge tube

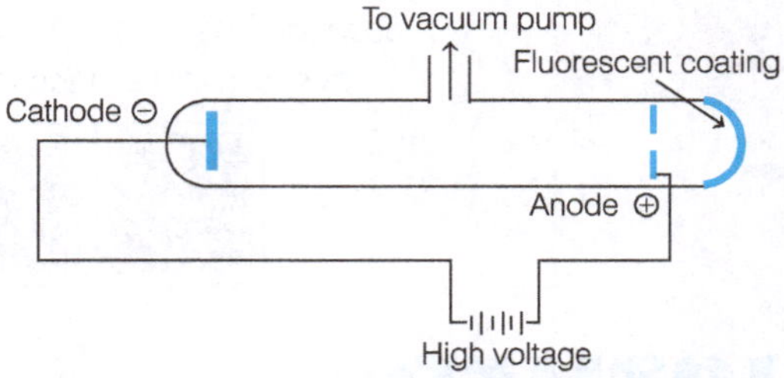

A cathode ray discharge tube with perforated anode

The results of the experiment are summarised below.

- The cathode rays starts from cathode and move towards the anode.
- Cathode rays themselves are not visible but their behaviour can be observed with the help of certain type of materials (fluorescent or phosphorescent).
- Cathode rays travel in straight lines in the absence of electrical or magnetic field.
- In the presence of electrical or magnetic field, the behaviour of cathode rays are similar to that expected from negatively charged particles, suggesting that these rays consist of negatively charged particles called **electrons**.
- The characteristics of cathode rays (electrons) do not depend upon the material of electrodes and the nature of the gas present in the cathode ray tube. Thus, it can be conclude that electrons are basic constituent of all the atoms.

Charge to Mass Ratio of Electron

In 1897, British Physicist J.J. Thomson determined the ratio of electrical charge (e) to the mass of electron (m_e) by using cathode ray tube under the influence of electrical and magnetic field. These field are perpendicular to each other as well as to the path followed by electrons.

Thomson, demonstrate that the amount of deviation of the particles from their path in presence of electrical or magnetic field depends upon following factors.

- Greater the **magnitude of the charge on the particle**, greater is the interaction with the electric or magnetic field thus, greater is the deflection.
- The **mass of the particle**-lighter the particle, greater is the deflection.
- **Strength of the field** The deflection of electrons from its original path increases with the increase in the voltage across the electrode or magnetic field strength.
- Thomson was able to determine the value of e/m_e by carrying out accurate measurements on the amount of deflections observed by the electrons on the field strength (electric or magnetic).

$$\frac{e\text{ (in kg)}}{m_e\text{ (in C)}} = 1.758820 \times 10^{11}\ \text{C kg}^{-1}$$

where, m_e is the mass of electron and e is the magnitude of the charge on the electron.

Charge on the Electron

- R.A Millikan devised a method known as **oil drop experiment**, used to determine the charge on the electron.
- The charge on an electron was found to be -1.6×10^{-19} C.
- The present accepted value of electrical charge is $-1.602176 \times 10^{-19}$ C.

The mass of electron $(m_e) = \dfrac{e}{\dfrac{e}{m_e}} = \dfrac{1.602176 \times 10^{-19}\text{C}}{1.758820 \times 10^{11}\text{C kg}^{-1}}$

$= 9.1094 \times 10^{-31}$ kg

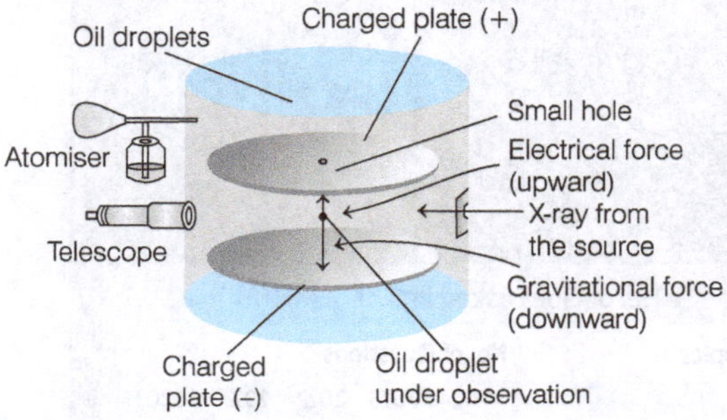

Millikan oil drop apparatus

Discovery of Protons (Canal Rays)

Modified cathode ray tube experiment was carried out which led to the discovery of **canal rays** carrying positively charged particles called **protons**. This was discovered by Goldstein. Their characteristics are as follows

- Unlike cathode rays, the mass of positively charged particles depends upon the nature of gas taken in the cathode ray tube. These are simply positively charged gaseous ions.
- Charge to mass ratio of particles depends on the gas from which these originate.
- Some of the positively charged particles carry a multiple of the fundamental unit of electrical charge.
- Behaviour of positively charged particles in electrical or magnetic field is opposite to that observed for cathode rays.

Discovery of Neutrons

These are neutral particles and discovered by Chadwick (1932) by bombarding a thin sheet of beryllium by α-particles. These are electrically neutral particles having a mass slightly greater than that of protons.

Properties of Fundamental Particles

Name	Symbol	Absolute charge/C	Relative charge	Mass/kg	Mass/u	Approx. mass/u
Electron	e	$-1.602176 \times 10^{-19}$	–1	9.109382×10^{-31}	0.00054	0
Proton	p	$+1.602176 \times 10^{-19}$	+1	$1.6726216 \times 10^{-27}$	1.00727	1
Neutron	n	0	0	1.674927×10^{-27}	1.00867	1

Atomic Models

Different atomic models were proposed to explain the distribution of charged particles. These are as follows

Thomson Model of Atom

- In 1898, J.J. Thomson explained that an atom has a structure like sphere (pudding) in which the positive charge is uniformly distributed with a number of electrons (negative charge like raisin) scattered throughout the sphere in such a manner which is sufficient to neutralise the positive charge and give the most stable electrostatic arrangement. This model has some other names as **plum pudding, raisin pudding** or **watermelon model.**
- An important feature of this model is that the mass of atom is assumed to be uniformly distributed over the atom.
- **Demerit** Although this model was able to explain the overall neutrality of the atom, but was not consistent with the results of later experiments.

Marks Maximizer

- Henri Becqueral observed that there are certain elements which emit radiation (α, β and γ) on their own. These elements were named as radioactive elements and the phenomenon is called **radioactivity**.
- **Penetrating Power of Rays** γ-rays > X-rays > β-rays > α-rays

  As regards penetrating power, α-particles are the least, followed by β-rays (100 times that of α-particles) and γ-rays (1000 times that of α-particles).

Rutherford's Nuclear Model of Atom

Thomson's model of atom was proved wrong by Rutherford's α-particles scattering experiment which was carried out in 1909. In this, a thin gold foil was bombarded with fast moving α-particles.

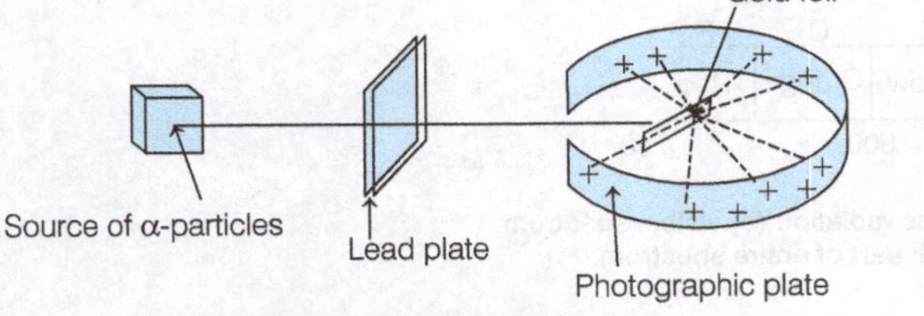

Rutherford's scattering experiment

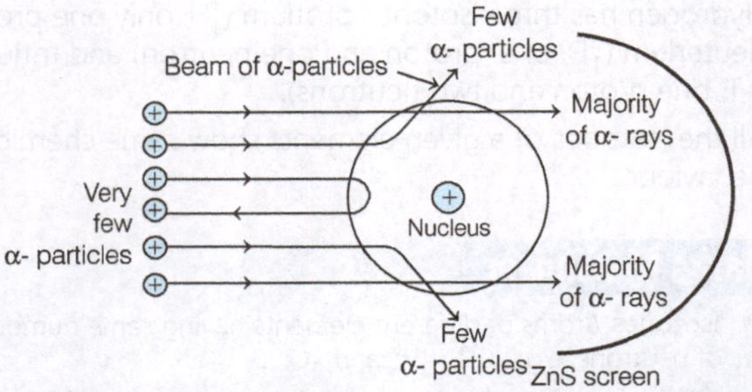

Schemetic atomic view of the α-particles scattering experiment

The main observation and conclusion of this model are as follows

- Most of the α-particles passed through the foil undeflected, which indicated that most of the space in atom is empty.
- Some of them were deflected, but only at small angles. This shows that there is something positively charged at the centre.
- Few particles were deflected at small angles. It means that in the atom, mass and positive charge is centrally located in extremely small region, this very small portion of the atom was called **nucleus** by Rutherford.
- Nucleus has a radius of 10^{-15} in order, while atom has radius of the order of 10^{-10} m.
- The nucleus is surrounded by electrons that move around the nucleus with a very high speed in circular paths called **orbits**. Thus, Rutherford's model of atom resembles the solar system in which the nucleus plays the role of sun and the electrons that of revolving planets.
- Electrons and the nucleus are held together by electrostatic force of attraction.

Atomic and Mass Number

- The number of protons present in the nucleus of an atom is **equal to atomic number** (Z). NEET 2020

  Atomic number (Z) = number of protons in the nucleus of an atom = number of electrons in a neutral atom.
- The protons and neutrons present in the nucleus are collectively known as **nucleons**. The total number of nucleons is termed as **mass number** of the atom.

  Mass number (A) = number of protons (Z) + number of neutrons (n).

Isobars and Isotopes

- **Isobars** are the atoms with same mass number, but different atomic number, e.g. $^{14}_{6}C$ and $^{14}_{7}N$.
- The species with same atomic number but different mass number are called **isotopes**, e.g. $_6C^{12}$ and $_6C^{14}$.
- Hydrogen has three isotopes protium (^1_1H, only one proton), deuterium (^2_1D, one proton and one neutron) and tritium (^3_1T, one proton and two neutrons).
- All the isotopes of a given elements show same chemical behaviour.

Marks Maximizer

- **Isotones** Atoms of different elements having same number of neutrons, e.g. $_6C^{14}$, $_7C^{15}$ and $_8O^{16}$.
- **Isodiaphers** The elements which have same value of $(n-p)$ are called isodiaphers, e.g. $^{235}_{92}U$, $^{231}_{90}Th$.
- **Isosteres** Molecules having same number of atoms and electrons. e.g. CO_2, N_2O.
- **Isomorphous** The two different types of compounds which contain same crystalline structure are called isomorphous and this property is called **isomorphism**.

Drawbacks of Rutherford Model

- According to the electromagnetic theory of Maxwell, charged particles when accelerated should emit electromagnetic radiation. (This feature does not exist for planets since they are uncharged). Therefore, an electron in an orbit will emit radiation, the energy carried by radiation comes from electronic motion. The orbit will thus continue to shrink.
- Calculations show that it should take an electron only 10^{-8} s to spiral into the nucleus. But this does not happen. Thus, Rutherford's model was failed to account for the stability of the atom.
- The model does not give any information about how electrons are distributed around nucleus and what are the energies of these electrons.

* *This topic not include in latest NEET syllabus, but it is given in latest rationalised NCERT.*

Developments Leading to the Bohr's Model of Atom

Bohr utilised some results observed from the studies proposed by Rutherford. Two developments play an important role in the formulation of Bohr's model of atom. There were, dual nature of electromagnetic radiation of both (particle as well as wave like properties) experimental results regarding atomic spectra.

Wave Nature of Electromagnetic Radiation

- James Maxwell suggested that when electrically charged particle under acceleration alternate. These fields are transmitted in the form of waves are called **electromagnetic waves** or **electromagnetic radiations.**
- The electric and magnetic field components of an electromagnetic wave have the same wavelength, frequency, speed and amplitude, but they vibrate in two mutually perpendicular planes.
- There are many types of electromagnetic radiations which differ from one another in wavelength or frequency. These constitute **electromagnetic spectrum.**
- The small portion in the electromagnetic spectrum around 10^{15} Hz and wavelength (750 to 400 nm) is called **visible light.**
- All these radiations travel with the **speed of light** and do not require any medium for their propagation or transmission.

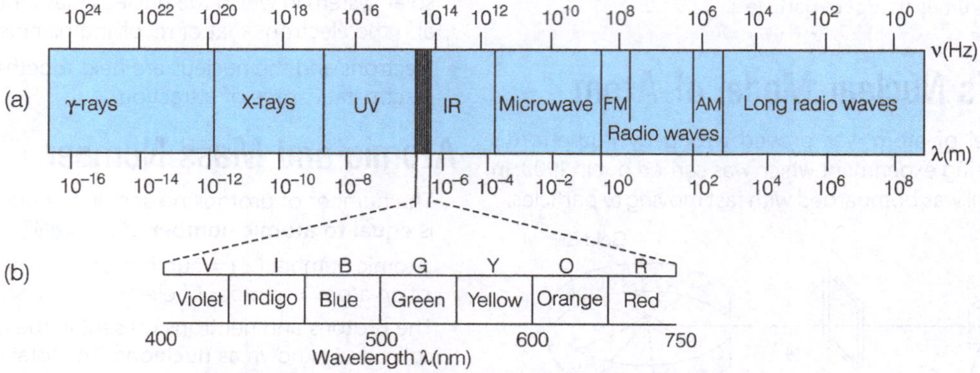

(a) The spectrum of electromagnetic radiation (b) visible spectrum. The visible region is only a small part of entire spectrum.

Properties of Electromagnetic Waves

- **Frequency** Number of waves that pass a given point in one second and its SI unit is Hertz (Hz). ($1 \text{ Hz} = 1 \text{ s}^{-1}$)
- **Wavelength** Distance between successive crests or troughs of a wave. The SI unit of wavelength is metre. It is measured in terms of Å(10^{-10} m), pm(10^{-12} m), nm(10^{-9} m) or cm(10^{-2} m). In vacuum, all types of electromagnetic waves travel with same speed, i.e. $3 \times 10^8 \text{ ms}^{-1}$ (speed of light).
- The **frequency (ν), wavelength (λ) and velocity of light (c) are related** by the equation, $c = \nu\lambda$.
- **Wave number** is defined as the number of wavelengths per unit length. Its commonly used unit is cm^{-1}.
- Relation between wave number and wavelength, $\bar{\nu} = \frac{1}{\lambda}$

Particle Nature of Electromagnetic Radiation : Planck's Quantum Theory

- The ideal body, which emits and absorbs radiations of all frequencies is called a **black body** and the radiation emitted by such a body is called **black body radiation**.
- According to **Planck's quantum theory**, the energy which is emitted or absorbed in the atom in small discrete packets of energy known as **quantum** and in case of light, the quantum of energy is called photons.
- The energy of each quantum is directly proportional to frequency of the radiation, i.e.

$$E = h\nu \text{ or } E = h\frac{c}{\lambda}$$

where, h = Planck's constant = 6.626×10^{-34} Js

E = Energy of photon or quantum

- The energy can take any one of the values from the following set, but cannot take on any values between them.

$$E = 0,\ h\nu,\ 2h\nu \text{ .... } nh\nu$$

Photoelectric Effect

In 1887, H. Hertz performed an experiment in which electrons were ejected from a metal surface, when light of certain frequency strikes on it. This phenomenon is called photoelectric effect. Some results of this effect are as follows

- For each metal, there is a characteristic minimum frequency, known as **threshold frequency** (ν_0) below which photoelectric effect is not observed.
- When a photon of sufficient energy strikes an electron in the atom of the metal, it transfers its energy instantaneously to the electron during the collision and the electron is ejected.
- The number of electrons ejected is proportional to the intensity or brightness of light.
- On the basis of the conservation of energy principle, the **kinetic energy of ejected electron** is given by the equation,

$$h\nu = h\nu_0 + \frac{1}{2} m_e v^2 \qquad (h\nu_0 = \text{Work function})$$

Dual Behaviour of Electromagnetic Radiation

Light possesses both particle and wave like properties. Whenever radiation interacts with matter, it displays particles, like properties and when it propagates, it displays wave like properties.

Evidence for the Quantised Electronic Energy Level : Atomic Spectra

Spectrum

A ray of white light consists of wave with all the wavelengths in the visible range is spread out into a series of coloured bands through prism is called as spectrum.

A spectrum can be of following types

Atomic Spectra

When the radiation (or energy) absorbed/emitted by an atom, it shows atomic spectra.

Molecular Spectra

When the radiation absorbed/emitted by a molecule due to more involvement in electronic transitions compared to atoms and are more complex than atomic spectra.

Continuous Spectra

A white light shows this type of spectra because it contains all the wavelength in a particular region of spectrum.

e.g. VIBGYOR it is continuous due to each and every light (colour) merge simultaneously as step by step. It ranges from 7.5×10^{14} Hz to 4×10^{14} Hz.

Discontinuous Spectra

In this type of spectra some wavelength are missing and it contains some certain wavelengths. e.g. VBYR is discontinuous spectra in which IGO wavelength are missing.

Emission Spectra

Spectrum of radiation emitted by a substance that has absorbed energy is called an emission spectrum. It indicates the wavelengths emitted by an excited species (atoms, molecules or ions). Each spectral line of this spectra is attribute to one electronic transition from higher energy level to lower energy level.

Absorption Spectra

It represents the wavelength (or frequencies) absorbed by an atom or molecule. It is like a photographic negative of an emission spectrum. A continuous radiation is passed through a sample which absorbs radiation of certain wavelengths.

Line Emission Spectra

This spectra is obtained in those species in which number of electronic transitions is less and each line corresponds to one electronic transition. It contains only some specific lines and appear as the bright lines in the spectra.

Line Spectrum of Hydrogen

- When an electric discharge is passed through gaseous hydrogen, the H_2 molecules dissociate and the energetically excited hydrogen atoms produced emit electromagnetic radiation of discrete frequencies.
- The **line spectra of hydrogen** lies in three regions of electromagnetic spectrum, i.e. infrared, visible and UV-region.
- The set of lines in the visible region is known as **Balmer series.**
- The Swedish spectroscopist, Johannes Rydberg noted that all series of lines in the hydrogen spectrum could be described by the following formula,

$$\bar{\nu} = 109677\left[\frac{1}{n_1^2} - \frac{1}{n_2^2}\right]\text{cm}^{-1}$$

where, $n_1 = 1, 2 \ldots$ and $n_2 = n_1 + 1, n_1 + 2 \ldots$

- The value 109677 cm^{-1} is called the **Rydberg constant**.
- The first five series of lines that correspond to $n_1 = 1, 2, 3, 4, 5$ are known Lyman, Balmer, Paschen, Bracket and Pfund series respectively.

Spectral Lines for Atomic Hydrogen NEET 2019

Series	n_1	n_2	Spectral regions	Number of possible transition
Lyman	1	2, 3, 4...	Ultraviolet	$n_2 - 1$
Balmer	2	3, 4, 5...	Visible	$n_2 - 2$
Paschen	3	4, 5, 6...	Infrared	$n_2 - 3$
Brackett	4	5, 6, 7...	Infrared	$n_2 - 4$
Pfund	5	6, 7...	Infrared	$n_2 - 5$

Bohr's Model for Hydrogen Atom

Neils Bohr (in 1913) was the first to explain quantitatively general features of the structure of hydrogen atom and its spectrum. The main postulates for Bohr's model are

- The electron in the hydrogen atom can move around the nucleus in a circular path of fixed radius and energy. These paths are called **orbits**, stationary states or allowed energy states.
- The energy is **absorbed** when an electron move from lower stationary state to a higher stationary state or energy is **emitted** when an electron jumps from higher energy level to lower energy level.
- Energy of electron in a orbit does not change with time.
- The frequency of radiation absorbed or emitted when transition occurs between two stationary states that differ in energy by ΔE is given by

$$\nu = \frac{\Delta E}{h} = \frac{E_2 - E_1}{h}$$

where, E_1 and E_2 are the energies of the lower and higher allowed energy states respectively. This expression is commonly known as **Bohr's frequency rule.**

- The **angular momentum of an electron** is quantised. In a given stationary state, it can be expressed as,

$$m_e vr = n \cdot \frac{h}{2\pi}, \quad n = 1, 2, 3 \ldots$$

Angular momentum $= m_e vr$

Significance of Bohr's Model

This model is useful to explain the following facts

- The stationary states for electron are numbered, $n = 1, 2, 3 \ldots$. These integral numbers are known as **principal quantum numbers.**
- The radii of the stationary states are expressed as $r_n = n^2 a_0$ where, $a_0 = 52.9$ pm. Thus, the radius of the first stationary state of the **Bohr's orbit** is 52.9 pm. NEET 2022
- **Energy of stationary state for n^{th} state** is given as,

$$E_n = -R_H\left(\frac{1}{n^2}\right), \; n = 1, 2, 3 \ldots$$

where, R_H is called **Rydberg constant** and its value is equal to 2.18×10^{-18} J.

- Bohr's theory can also be applied to the ions containing only one electron, e.g. He^+, Li^{2+}, Be^{3+} and so on.
- The energy of the stationary states associated with these hydrogen like species is given by,

$$E_n = -2.18 \times 10^{-18}\left(\frac{Z^2}{n^2}\right)\text{J}$$ NEET 2024

and radii by the expression, $r_n = 52.9\,\frac{n^2}{Z}$ pm

Marks Maximizer

Electron orbits and their energy

- Radius of permitted n^{th} orbits,

$$r_n = \frac{n^2h^2}{4\pi^2 mKZe^2} \Rightarrow r_n \propto n^2$$

- Velocity of electron in n^{th} orbit,

$$v_n = \frac{2\pi KZe^2}{nh} \Rightarrow v_n \propto \frac{1}{n}$$

- Energy of electron in n^{th} orbit,

$$E_n = \frac{-2\pi^2 mK^2Ze^4}{n^2h^2} \Rightarrow E_n \propto \frac{1}{n^2}$$

Explanation of Line Spectrum of Hydrogen

- The energy gap between the two orbits higher to lower is given by equation,

$$\Delta E = 2.18\times 10^{-18}\,\text{J}\left(\frac{1}{n_i^2}-\frac{1}{n_f^2}\right), \text{ where, } \Delta E = E_f - E_i$$

- The frequency associated with the absorption and emission of the photon can be evaluated by using equation,

$$\nu = \frac{\Delta E}{h} = \frac{R_H}{h}\left(\frac{1}{n_i^2}-\frac{1}{n_f^2}\right)$$

and in terms of wave numbers ($\bar{\nu}$)

$$\bar{\nu} = \frac{R_H}{hc}\left(\frac{1}{n_i^2}-\frac{1}{n_f^2}\right)$$

- In case of absorption spectrum, $n_f > n_i$, ΔE is +ve (energy absorbed) and in case of emission spectrum, $n_i > n_f$, ΔE is (energy released) –ve.

Limitations of Bohr's Model

- Bohr's model did not explain the fine structure of atom, spectrum of multi-electron system, Zeeman effect and Stark effect (splitting of spectral lines under the influence of magnetic and electric field respectively) and ability of atoms to form molecules by chemical bonds.
- It does not satisfactorily explain the distribution of electrons in an atom.
- Dual nature of particle and the uncertainty principle was ignored in the Bohr's model.

Towards Quantum Mechanical Model of Atom

In view of shortcoming of the Bohr's model, two important developments, i.e. **dual behaviour of matter** and **Heisenberg uncertainty principle came into existence.**

Dual Behaviour of Matter

- de-Broglie explains the dual nature of electron (i.e. wave nature as well as particle nature)

$$\lambda = \frac{h}{mv} = \frac{h}{p}$$ NEET 2021, 2019

where, λ = wavelength, v = velocity of particle, m = mass of particle, p = momentum

- Every object in motion has a wave character.
- The wavelength associated with ordinary objects are so short (because of their large masses) that their wave properties cannot be detected.
- The wavelength associated with electrons and other subatomic particles (with very small mass) can however be detected experimentally.

Heisenberg's Uncertainty Principle (1927)

- This states that "it is impossible to determine at any given instant, both the momentum and the position of subatomic particles like electron simultaneously".

For Concept Master Video

Mathematically, it can be given as

$$\Delta x \cdot \Delta p_x \geq \frac{h}{4\pi} \quad \text{or} \quad \Delta x \cdot \Delta v_x \geq \frac{h}{4\pi m}$$

Δx = Uncertainty in position
Δp_x = Uncertainty in momentum
Δv_x = Uncertainty in velocity

- **Significance of uncertainty principle** Heisenberg uncertainty principle rules out the existence of definite paths or trajectories of electrons and other similar particles.
- The effect of Heisenberg uncertainty principle is significant only for motion of microscopic objects and is negligible for that of macroscopic objects. This is because in dealing with milligram sized or heavier objects, the associated uncertainties are hardly of real consequence.
- In case of microscopic object like an electron, $\Delta v \cdot \Delta x$ obtained is much larger and such uncertainties are of real consequence.
- The precise statement of the position and momentum of electrons have to be replaced by the statements of probability that the electron has at a given position and momentum.
- **Reason for failure of Bohr model** In Bohr's model, an electron is regarded as a charged particle moving in well defined circular orbits around the nucleus.

  Thus, Bohr's model not only ignores the dual behaviour of matter but also contradicts Heisenberg uncertainty principle.

Quantum Mechanical Model of Atom

- The branch of science that takes into account the dual behaviour of matter is called **quantum mechanics.**
- Schrodinger derived an equation for an electron which describes the wave motion of an electron associated with particles. For a system (such as an atom or molecule whose energy does not change with time), the **Schrodinger equation** is written as $\hat{H}\psi = E\psi$,
  where, $\hat{H}$ is a mathematical operator called **Hamiltonian.**
- ψ has no physical significance but ψ^2 describes the probability of finding an electron within an atom.
- An **atomic orbital** is the space around the nucleus, where the probability of finding an electron is maximum.

Marks Maximizer

Schrodinger wave equation is written in its simplest form as

$$\frac{\partial^2\psi}{\partial x^2}+\frac{\partial^2\psi}{\partial y^2}+\frac{\partial^2\psi}{\partial z^2}+\frac{8\pi^2 m}{h^2}(E-V)\,\psi = 0$$

Important Features of the Quantum Mechanical Model of Atom

- The energy of electrons in atoms is quantised (i.e. can only have certain specific values).
- The existence of quantised electronic energy levels is a direct result of the wave like properties of electrons and are allowed solutions of Schrodinger wave equation.
- Both the exact position and exact velocity of an electron in an atom cannot be determined simultaneously.
- An atomic orbital is the wave function ψ for an electron in an atom.
- The probability of finding an electron at a point within an atom is proportional to the square of the orbital wave function $|\psi|^2$ at that point, which is known as probability density and is always positive.
- From the value of $|\psi|^2$ at different points within an atom, it is possible to predict the region around the nucleus, where electron will most probably be found.

For Concept Master Video

Orbitals and Quantum Numbers

A large number of orbitals are possible in an atom. These atomic orbitals are precisely distinguished by **quantum number.** NEET 2024

	Quantum number	Symbol	Allowed values	Represents/Defines
1.	Principal quantum number	n	Positive integer (1, 2, 3, 4 etc.) ↓ ↓ ↓ ↓ Shell K L M N	• It represents the number of shell. • Size and energy of orbital. Larger the value of n, greater is the distance from the nucleus and energy of electron. • Number of orbitals in n^{th} shell $= n^2$.
2.	Azimuthal/ Subsidiary/ Orbitals Angular momentum Quantum number	l	For a particular value of n, $l = 0$ to $(n-1)$ For, $l = 0$, s-subshell $l = 1$, p-subshell $l = 2$, d-subshell $l = 3$, f-subshell	• It represents the number of subshells/sub-levels present in the shell. • 3D shape of orbitals. • $(2l + 1)$ no. of orbitals of each type in a subshell. • Energy of the subshell in a multielectron atom.
3.	Magnetic quantum number	m_l	For a particular value of l, $m = -l$ to $+l$	• Spatial orientation of the orbital with respect to standard set of co-ordinate axis. • Number of orbitals present in any subshell. • For any subshells, $(2l + 1)$ value of m_l are possible. NEET 2023
4.	Electron spin quantum number	m_s	$+\frac{1}{2}(\uparrow), -\frac{1}{2}(\downarrow)$ [Two spin states of electrons]	• Orientation of the spin of the electron.

Shapes of Atomic Orbitals

- Shape of an orbital is given by total probability density ψ^2 including both radial part as well as angular part.
- According to the German physicist, Max Born, the square of the wave function at a point gives the probability density of the electron at that point.
- For 1s-orbital the probability density is maximum at the nucleus and it decreases sharply as we move away from it. On the other hand, for 2s-orbital the probability density first decreases sharply to zero and again starts increasing. After reaching a small maxima it decreases again and approaches zero as the value of r increases further. The region where this probability density function reducesy to zero is called **nodal surfaces** or **simply nodes.**

For an atom of principal quantum number, n

Radial or Spherical nodes $= n - l - 1$

Angular or Planar nodes $= l$ NEET 2020, 2019

Total no. of nodes $= n - 1$

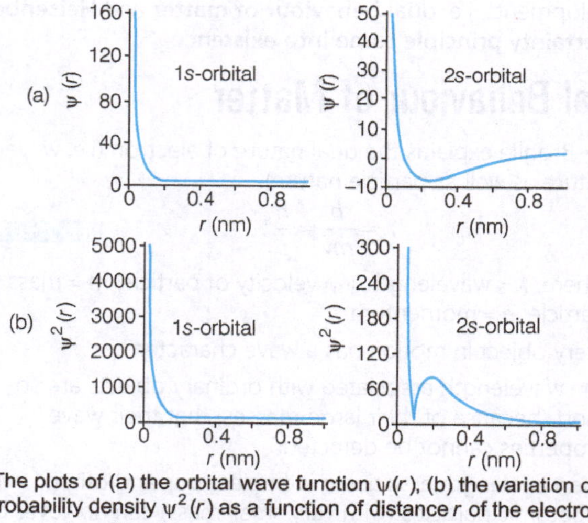

The plots of (a) the orbital wave function $\psi(r)$, (b) the variation of probability density $\psi^2(r)$ as a function of distance r of the electron from the nucleus for 1s and 2s-orbitals

Shape of *s*-orbital

- Boundary surface diagram of a *s*-orbital is actually a sphere centred on the nucleus, i.e. the probability of finding the electron is the same in all directions, i.e. 90%.
- The size and energy of *s*-orbital with increasing *n* will be $1s < 2s < 3s < 4s$.

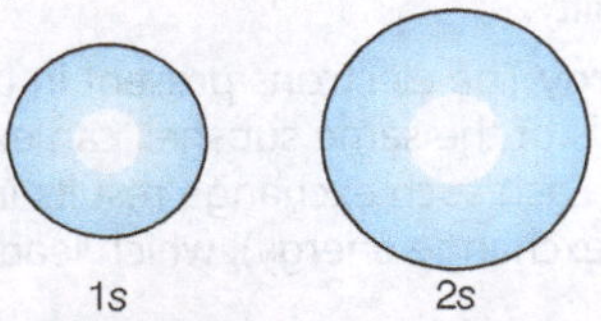

Boundary surface diagram for 1*s* and 2*s*- orbitals

Shape of *p*-orbital

- For *p*-orbital ($l = 1$), which means that there are three *p*-orbitals which are represented by p_x, p_y, p_z.
- Each *p*-orbital have two sections which are called its **lobes.** These lobes lie on either side of the plane that passes through the nucleus.
- These three *p*-orbitals are identical in size, shape and energy but differ in orientation of lobes.

  The order of the energy of various *p*-orbitals is $4p > 3p > 2p$.

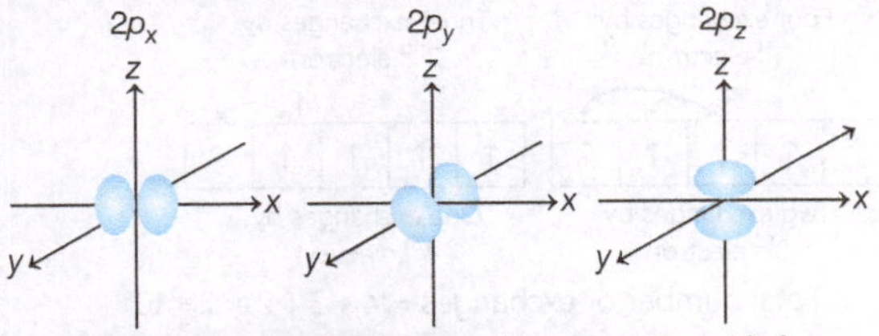

Boundary surface diagrams of the three 2*p*-orbitals

Shape of *d*-orbital

- For *d*-orbital, $l = 2$ which means m_l have five values (–2, –1, 0, +1 and +2) thus there are five *d*-orbitals. The boundary surface diagram of these five *d*-orbitals are given below.

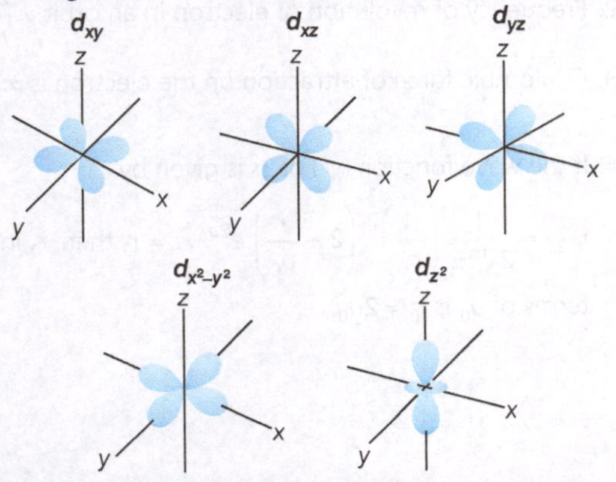

Boundary surface diagrams of the five 3*d*-orbitals

- The five *d*-orbitals are designated as $d_{xy}, d_{yz}, d_{xz}, d_{x^2-y^2}$ and d_{z^2} and are of equal energy, i.e. degenerate. The first four *d*-orbitals have similar shape but the shape of fifth one, i.e. d_{z^2}, is different from that of the other. NEET 2022

Energies of Orbitals

- For hydrogen and hydrogen like species, all the orbitals within a same shell have same energy. Thus, the energy of the orbitals in hydrogen atom increases as follows

  $$1s < 2s = 2p < 3s = 3p = 3d < 4s = 4p = 4d = 4f < \ldots$$

- The orbitals having same energy are called **degenerate orbitals.**
- For hydrogen atom, the 1*s* orbital corresponds to the most stable condition and is called the **ground state** and an electron residing in this orbital is most strongly held by the nucleus. An electron in the 2*s*, 2*p* or higher orbitals in a hydrogen atom is said to be in **excited state.**
- In a multi-electron atom, energies of orbitals depends said to be upon the values of principal quantum number (shell) and azimuthal quantum number (subshell). The lower the value of $(n + l)$ for an orbital, the lower its energy.
- If two orbitals have the same $(n + l)$ value, the orbital with lower value of *n* has the lower energy.
- The shielding of the outer shell electrons from the nucleus by the inner shell electrons and as a result the net positive charge experienced by the outer electrons is known as effective nuclear charge (Z_{eff}).
- Energies of the orbitals in the same subshell decreases with increase in the atomic number *Z*.

  e.g. $E_{2s}(H) > E_{2s}(Li) > E_{2s}(Na) > E_{2s}(K)$.

Filling of Orbitals in Atom

Filling of electrons into the orbitals of different atoms takes place according to the following discussed rules.

- **Aufbau principle** In the ground state of the atoms, the orbitals are filled in order of their increasing energies. 1*s*, 2*s*, 2*p*, 3*s*, 3*p*, 4*s*, 3*d*, 4*p*, 5*s*, 4*d*, 5*p*, 6*s*, 4*f*, 5*d*, 6*p*, 7*s*. NEET 2019
- **Pauli's exclusion principle** No two electrons in an atom can have the same set of four quantum numbers. It can also be stated as, "only two electrons may exist in the same orbital and these electrons must have opposite spins".
- The maximum number of electrons in the shell with principal quantum number *n* is equal to $2n^2$.
- **Hund's rule of maximum multiplicity** It states that "pairing of electrons in the orbitals belonging to the same subshell (*p*, *d* or *f*) does not take place until each orbital belonging to that subshell has got one electron each, i.e. it is singly occupied."

Electronic Configuration of Atoms

Distribution of electrons in different orbitals in accordance to rule which governs the filling of orbitals is known as **electronic configuration**. There are following two ways to assign the electronic configuration of different atoms. These ways are as

(i) $s^a p^b d^c$ ...notation (ii) Orbital diagram

Stability of Completely Filled and Half-filled Subshells

Some elements show exceptional electronic configuration because of the stability associated with half-filled and fully-filled orbitals. e.g.

$^{24}Cr: 1s^2 2s^2 2p^6 3s^2 3p^6 4s^2 3d^4$: Expected configuration

$1s^2 2s^2 2p^6 3s^2 3p^6 4s^1 3d^5$: Actual configuration

$^{29}Cu: 1s^2 2s^2 2p^6 3s^2 3p^6 4s^2 3d^9$: Expected configuration

$1s^2 2s^2 2p^6 3s^2 3p^6 4s^1 3d^{10}$: Actual configuration

This is due to the following reasons

- **Symmetry** The half-filled and completely filled configurations are more symmetrical because of symmetrical distribution of electrons and symmetry leads to greater stability.
- **Exchange energy** The electrons present in the different orbitals of the same subshell can exchange their positions. Each such exchange results in release of energy (called exchange energy), which leads to a greater stability.

  As the number of exchange that can be take place is maximum in the exactly half-filled and completely filled arrangements (i.e. more in d^5 than in d^4), therefore exchange energy is maximum in these two cases and hence the stability is maximum.

Possible Exchange for d^4 and d^5 Configuration

d^4 configuration

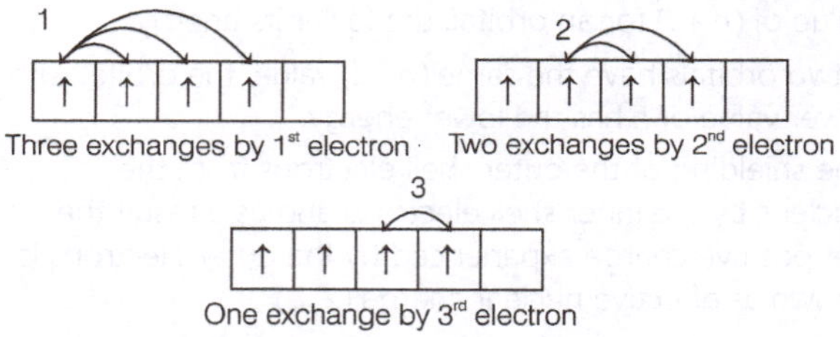

Total number of exchanges = 3 + 2 + 1 = 6

d^5 configuration

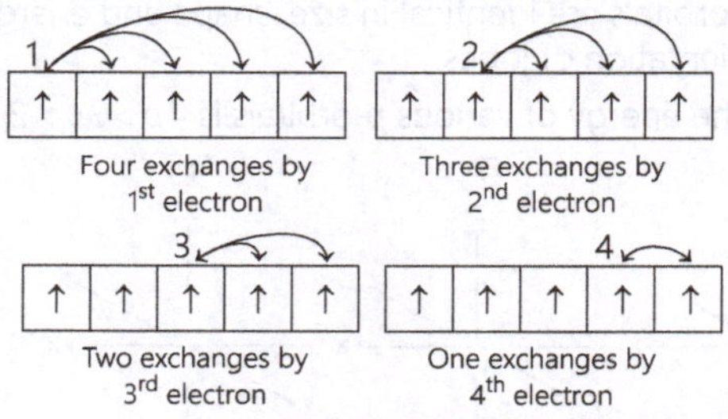

Total number of exchanges = 4 + 3 + 2 + 1 = 10

Caution Points

- For shortest wavelength or maximum energy or maximum frequency, n has to be maximum and for longest wavelength or minimum energy or minimum frequency, n has to be minimum.
- Heisenberg's uncertainty principle is applicable only when the location and momentum are along the same axis, i.e. if Δx is uncertainty in position along the z-axis than ΔP must also be uncertainty in momentum along the z-axis.
- ψ is not to be confused with probability factor, ψ^2 which describes the probability of finding an electron within a small space.
- If the orbitals are only singly occupied, all electrons must have same spin quantum number, i.e. spinning in the same direction.

PYQ Notes

1. Orbital angular momentum of an electron can be calculated as $\mu_l = \sqrt{l(l+1)}\dfrac{h}{2\pi}$. **NEET 2015**
2. Frequency of revolution of electron in an orbit $\propto \dfrac{Z^2}{n^3}$.
3. Coulombic force of attraction on the electron is $\propto \dfrac{Z^3}{n^4}$. **JEE 2021**
4. If the wave function (ψ) of $2s$ is given by

   $$\psi_{2s} = \frac{1}{2\sqrt{2\pi}}\left(\frac{1}{a_0}\right)^{\frac{1}{2}}\left(2 - \frac{r}{a_0}\right)e^{\frac{-r}{2a_0}},\ r = r_0 \text{ then, } r_0 \text{ in}$$

   terms of a_0 is $r_0 = 2a_0$. **JEE 2023**

Step by Step

Mastering NCERT

- Concept Builders
- Topical Questions
- Assertion-Reason
- Statement Type
- Matching Type
- Numerical Value
- NCERT Exemplar's
- Past Exams'
- Skill Boosters

Concept Builders

1 What is the optimum conditions required to study the conduction of electricity through gases?

2 Which experiment is responsible for an insight of the structure of atom?

3 In cathode ray experiment, the tube behind anode was coated with phosphorescent material, i.e. zinc sulphide. [T/F]

4 The characteristics of cathode rays do not depend upon the size, material of electrodes and ....

5 Greater the magnitude of the charge on the particles .... (greater/lower) is the interaction with the electrical or magnetic field.

6 Lighter the particles, greater will be its deflection in electric/magnetic field. [T/F]

7 R.A. Millikan devised a method known as oil drop experiment to determine ......

8 According to Millikan's experiment, the magnitude of electrical charge on droplets is always an even number multiple of electrical charge. [T/F]

9 The behaviour of positively charged particles in electrical or magnetic field is ...... (same as/opposite to) electron or cathode rays.

10 Which type of forces in an atom are responsible for arrangement and stability of electrons according to J.J. Thomson?

11 Write the name of the phenomenon of the spontaneous emission of radiations from an element.

12 The correct order of penetrating power of the rays is

$\gamma_{rays} > X_{rays} > \beta_{rays} > \alpha_{rays}$. [T/F]

13 The radius of an atom is about 10^{-10} m while radius of nucleus is 10^{-20} m. [T/F]

14 Who introduced the terms 'nucleus' and 'orbits'?

15 The least abundant isotope of hydrogen is ....

16 The number of neutrons have large effect on the chemical properties of an elements. [T/F]

17 Thermal radiations consist of electromagnetic waves of various frequencies. [T/F]

18 Who give the explanations about the event as, 'light waves are associated with oscillating electric and magnetic character?

19 Electromagnetic waves do not require medium and can move in vacuum. [T/F]

20 The wavelength (λ) of visible spectrum ranges from .... nm to .... nm.

21 Which parameter is responsible for the dependency of the intensities of radiations of different wavelengths emitted by hot body?

22 An ideal body which emits and absorbs radiations of all frequencies uniformly is called a black body. [T/F]

23 The number of electrons ejected in photoelectric effect is directly proportional to the .... (velocity/intensity) of light.

24 Kinetic energy of the electrons increases with increase in frequency of light used. [T/F]

25 Name the spectrum of radiation emitted by a substance that has absorbed energy.

26 Write the name of the spectra which is used for the study of electronic structure.

27 An electron can move only in those orbits for which its angular momentum is integral multiple of $h/2\pi$. [T/F]

28 What is the values of radius and the energy associated with the first orbit of He^{+}?

29 According to the dual behaviour of matter concept, just like photon, electrons should also have .... as well as ....

30 Spin angular momentum of the electron is a scalar quantity. [T/F]

Topical Questions

Discovery of Subatomic Particles

1 Michael Faraday showed that, if electricity is passed through a solution of an electrolyte, chemical reactions occurred at the electrodes which resulted in NCERT Pg 30
(a) liberation of rays at the electrodes
(b) liberation and deposition of matter at the electrodes
(c) emission of energy at the electrodes
(d) release of O_2 at electrode

2 The electrical discharge through the gases could be observed only at NCERT Pg 30
(a) very low pressure and very low voltage
(b) very high pressure and very high voltage
(c) very high pressure and very low voltage
(d) very low pressure and very high voltage

3 Which of the following substance, shows the properties of phosphorescent? NCERT Pg 30
(a) Zinc sulphide
(b) Zinc sulphate
(c) Zinc nitrate
(d) Zinc chloride

4 Which of the following statements are correct about cathode rays. NCERT Pg 30
I. These moves from cathode to anode.
II. These are visible rays.
III. Television picture tubes are cathode rays tubes.
IV. In the absence of electrical or magnetic field, these rays travel in a straight line.

Choose the most appropriate answer from the options given below.
(a) I, II and III (b) II, III and IV
(c) I, III and IV (d) I, II, III and IV

5 According to Thomson, the amount of deviation of the particles from their path in the presence of electrical or magnetic field does not depend upon NCERT Pg 31
(a) the magnitude of the negative charge on the particle
(b) the mass of the particle
(c) the strength of the electrical or magnetic field
(d) temperature

6 Cathode rays have same charge to mass (e/m_e) ratio as β-rays, which is equal to NCERT Pg 31
(a) 1.758820×10^{10} C kg^{-1}
(b) 17.58820×10^{12} C kg^{-1}
(c) 17.58820×10^{11} C kg^{-1}
(d) 1.758820×10^{11} C kg^{-1}

7 Consider the following image. NCERT Pg 31

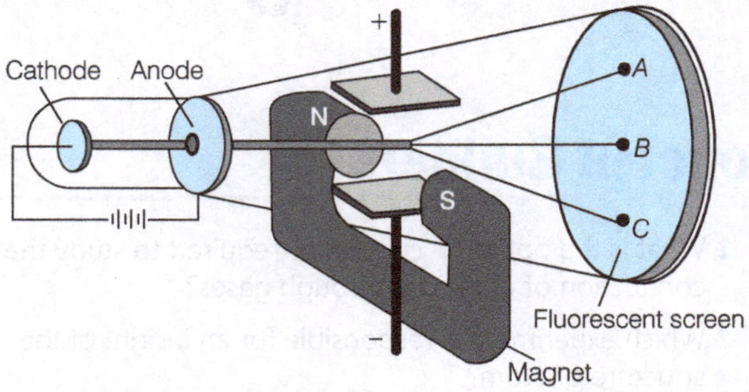

Which of the following statements regarding above image is incorrect?
(a) Electric and magnetic field are perpendicular to each other.
(b) When magnetic field is applied, the electrons deviate from their path and hit the cathode ray tube at *A*.
(c) When electric field is applied, electron strikes the cathode ray tube at point *A*.
(d) In equilibrium state, of magnetic and electrical field strength, electron hit the screen at *B*.

8 Increasing order for the values of e/m_e for electron (e), proton (p), neutron (n) and α-particles is NCERT Pg 31
(a) $e < p < n < \alpha$ (b) $n < \alpha < p < e$
(c) $n < p < e < \alpha$ (d) $n < p < \alpha < e$

9 Which role did the electric field play in Millikan's oil drop experiment? NCERT Pg 32
(a) To suspend the droplets.
(b) To accelerate the droplets.
(c) To change the direction of the droplets.
(d) To break the droplets into smaller particles.

10 Which of the following statement regarding the characteristics of positively charged particle canal rays is incorrect? NCERT Pg 32
(a) Unlike cathode rays, mass of positively charged particles depends upon the nature of gas present in the cathode ray tube.
(b) The charge to mass ratio of these particles depends on the gas from which these originate.
(c) The behaviour of these particles in electric or magnetic field is same as that observed for electron or cathode rays.
(d) Some of the positively charged particles carry a multiple of the fundamental unit of fundamental charge.

11 Which of the following statement is incorrect regarding the oil droplets experiment? NCERT Pg 32

(a) Oil droplets in the form of mist, produced by the atomiser were allowed to enter through tiny hole in the upper plate of electrical condenser.

(b) The air inside the chamber was ionised by passing a beam of X-ray through it.

(c) The fall of these charged oil droplets can be retarted, accelerated or made stationary.

(d) Magnitude of electric charge, 'q' on the droplets is always fractional multiple of the electrical charge (e).

Atomic Models

12 Which of the following statements about thomson model of atom is incorrect? NCERT Pg 33

(a) An atom possesses an spherical shape in which the positive charge is uniformly distributed.

(b) The electrons are embedded into it in such a manner as to give the most stable electrostatic arrangement.

(c) Mass of the atom is assumed to be uniformly distributed over the atom.

(d) This model was unable to explain the overall neutrality of the atom.

13 Consider the following statements regarding the Thomson's model of atom. NCERT Pg 33

I. The electrons are embedded in the nucleus, so as to give the most stable electrostatic arrangement.

II. The model was able to explain the overall neutrality of the atom.

III. The other name of this model are plum pudding model, raisin pudding model or watermelon model.

Choose the most appropriate answer from the options given below.

(a) I and II (b) II and III (c) I, II and III (d) I and III

14 Wilhelm Roentgen showed that when electrons strike a material in the cathode ray tubes, some rays are produced.

Consider the following statements regarding these rays.

I. These can cause fluorescence in the fluoroscent materials placed outside the cathode ray tubes.

II. These rays are named as X-rays.

III. These rays are deflected by both, electric and magnetic fields.

IV. These are used to study interior of the objects.

Choose the incorrect statement(s) appropriate answer from the options given below.

(a) I and III (b) Only III NCERT Pg 33

(c) Only IV (d) I, II and IV

15 According to Rutherford's scattering experiment, it can be concluded that NCERT Pg 34

(a) most of the α-particles passed through the gold foil deflected

(b) a small fraction of the α-particles was deflected by small angles

(c) a very large number of α-particles were bounced back

(d) every (~1 in 20000) at α-particles were deflected

16 On bombarding a beam of α-particles on the atom of the gold sheet, few particles get deflected, whereas most of them go straight and remains undeflected. This is due to NCERT Pg 34

(a) the nucleus occupy much smaller volume as compared to the volume of atom

(b) the force of repulsion on fast moving α-particles is very small

(c) the neutrons in the nucleus do not have any effect on α-particles

(d) the force of attraction on α-particles by the oppositely charged electron is not sufficient

17 An element E loses one α and two β-particles in three successive stages. The resulting element will be

(a) an isobar of E (b) an isotope of E NCERT Pg 35

(c) an isotone of E (d) E itself

18 Which of the following pairs will have same chemical properties? NCERT Pg 35

(a) ${}^{14}_{6}C$ and ${}^{15}_{7}N$ (b) O^{2-} and F^{-}

(c) ${}^{40}_{18}Ar$ and ${}^{40}_{19}K$ (d) ${}^{35}_{17}Cl$ and ${}^{37}_{17}Cl$

19 Which of the following atoms contains the least number of neutrons? NCERT Pg 35

(a) ${}^{235}_{92}U$ (b) ${}^{238}_{92}U$

(c) ${}^{239}_{93}Np$ (d) ${}^{240}_{93}Np$

20 The number of protons, neutrons and electrons in ${}^{80}_{35}Br$.

(a) Protons = 80, electrons = 80, neutrons = 35 NCERT Pg 35

(b) Protons = 35, electrons = 55, neutrons = 80

(c) Protons = 35, electrons = 35, neutrons = 80

(d) Protons = 35, electrons = 35, neutrons = 45

21 An element with a mass number of 150 contains 42% more neutrons compared to protons. Determine the symbol of the atom is NCERT Pg 35

(a) ${}^{150}_{60}Nd$ (b) ${}^{150}_{62}Sm$ (c) ${}^{150}_{64}Gd$ (d) ${}^{150}_{61}Pm$

22 Which of the following statements are not correct? NCERT Pg 35

I. The presence of positive charge on the nucleus is due to the presence of protons and neutrons in the nucleus.

II. The number of protons present in the nucleus is equal to the atomic number.

III. In order to keep the electrical neutrality, the number of electrons in an atom is equal to the number of proton in an atom.

IV. Protons, neutrons and electrons present in the atom are collectively called nucleons.

Choose the most appropriate answer from the options given below.

(a) II and III (b) I, II and III (c) I and IV (d) III and IV

23 Rutherford's nuclear model of an atom is like a small scale solar system. Further, coulombic force between electron and the nucleus is mathematically similar to the **NCERT Pg 36**

(a) gravity $\left(\frac{Gr^2}{m_1 m_2}\right)$

(b) gravity $\left(\frac{G m_1 \cdot m_2}{r}\right)$

(c) gravitational force $\left(\frac{Gm_1 \cdot m_2}{r^2}\right)$

(d) gravitational force $\frac{Gm_1 m_2}{r}$

24 Rutherford model could explain **NCERT Pg 36**

(a) electronic structure of an atom

(b) stability of an atom

(c) that most of the space in atom is empty

(d) spectrum of hydrogen atom

25 According to the electromagnetic theory of Maxwell, which one is correct? **NCERT Pg 36**

(a) Charged particles when accelerated should emit electromagnetic radiation.

(b) Charged particles when accelerated should absorb electromagnetic radiation.

(c) Charged particles when retarded should emit EMR.

(d) Charged particles when retarded should absorb EMR.

Development Leading to the Bohr's Model of Atom

26 Which of the following statement is incorrect about the graph given below? **NCERT Pg 38**

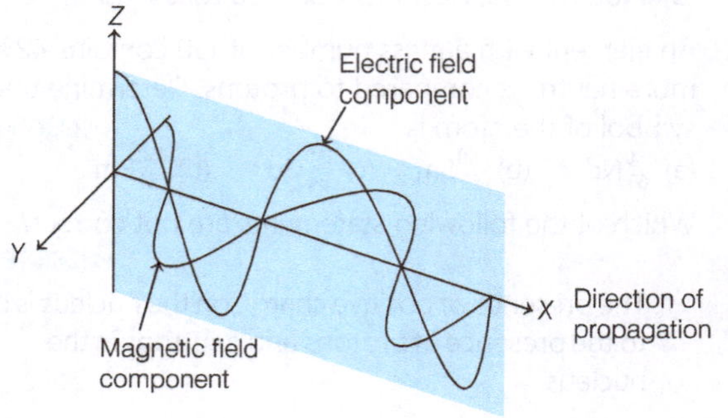

(a) Electric and magnetic field are perpendicular to the direction of propagation of the EM wave.

(b) Electromagnetic waves do require medium to travel.

(c) The constitute of different wavelength or frequency electromagnetic radiations is called electromagnetic spectrum.

(d) Different units are used to represent electromagnetic radiation.

27 Major developments responsible for the formulation of Bohr's model of atom was **NCERT Pg 37**

(a) dual character of the electromagnetic radiation

(b) experimental results regarding atomic spectra

(c) electronic structure of atom

(d) particle nature of electromagnetic radiation

28 Many types of electromagnetic radiations, differ from one another in wavelength (or frequency) constitute a spectrum known as **NCERT Pg 38**

(a) electromagnetic spectrum

(b) line spectrum

(c) continuous continous spectrum

(d) atomic spectrum

29 The wave number which corresponds to electromagnetic radiations of 600 nm is equal to **NCERT Pg 39**

(a) 1.66×10^4 cm^{-1} (b) 0.16×10^4 cm^{-1}

(c) 16×10^4 cm^{-1} (d) 160×10^4 cm^{-1}

30 Consider the following graph. **NCERT Pg 40**

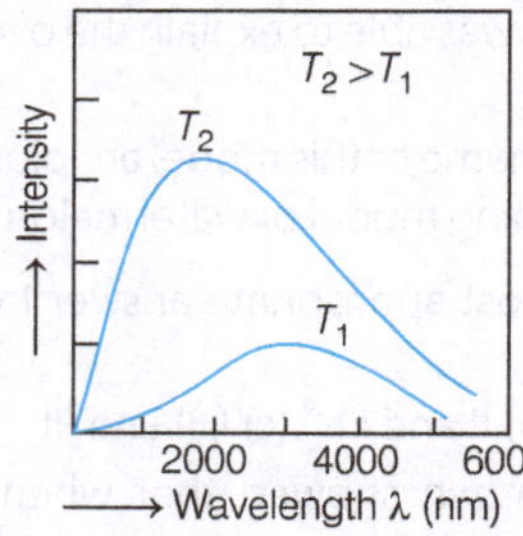

Select the incorrect statement from the following.

(a) As the temperature increases, maxima of the curve shift to short wavelength.

(b) The amount of light emitted (i.e. intensity of radiation from a black body and its spectral distribution depends only on its temperature.

(c) For the given graph T_1 is greater than T_2.

(d) At a given temperature, intensity of radiation emitted increases with the increase of wavelength, reaches a maximum value at a given wavelength and then starts decreasing with further increase of wavelength.

31 Which of the following figure represents a black body? **NCERT Pg 40**

(a) 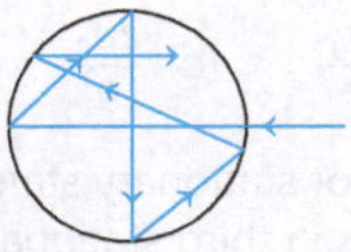 (b) 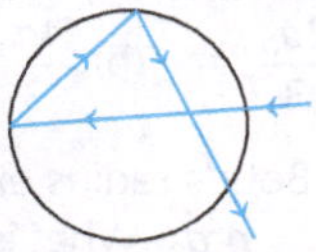

(c) 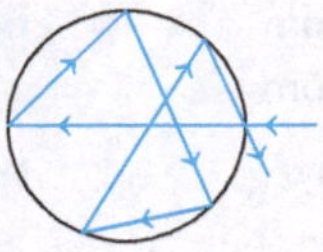 (d) 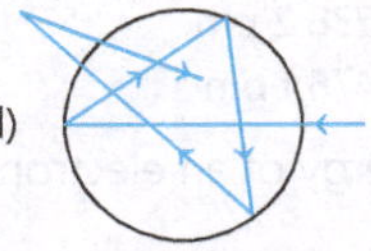

32 The energies E_1 and E_2 of two radiations are 25 eV, and 50 eV, respectively. The relation between their wavelengths, i.e. λ_1 and λ_2 will be **NCERT Pg 41**

(a) $\lambda_1 = \frac{1}{2}\lambda_2$ (b) $\lambda_1 = \lambda_2$

(c) $\lambda_1 = 2\lambda_2$ (d) $\lambda_1 = 4\lambda_2$

33 Which of the following statement is incorrect? **NCERT Pg 41**

(a) The energy of a quantum of radiation is proportional to its frequency (ν) is expressed by equation, $E = h\nu$.

(b) With the help of quantum theory, Planck explained the distribution of intensity in the radiation from black body as a function of frequency or wavelength at different temperatures.

(c) In photoelectric effect, there is no time lag between the striking of light beam and the ejection of electrons from metal surface.

(d) The energy of a quantum of radiation is proportional to its frequency and is expressed by equation $E = 3h\nu$.

34 The value of Planck's constant is 6.63×10^{-34} Js. The speed of light is 3×10^{17} nm s^{-1}. Which value is closest to the wavelength (in nm) of a quantum of light with frequency of $6 \times 10^{15} s^{-1}$? **NCERT Pg 41**

(a) 10 (b) 25 (c) 50 (d) 75

35 Number of photons emitted by a 100 W (Js^{-1}) yellow lamp in 1.0 s is (λ of yellow light is 560 nm) **NCERT Pg 41**

(a) 1.6×10^{18} (b) 1.4×10^{18}

(c) 2.8×10^{20} (d) 2.1×10^{20}

36 The energy required to break one mole of Cl—Cl bonds in Cl_2 is 242 kJ mol^{-1}. The largest wavelength of light capable of breaking a single Cl—Cl bond is **NCERT Pg 41**

(a) 700 nm (b) 494 nm

(c) 596 nm (d) 640 nm

37 The work function of a metal is 4.2 eV. If radiation of 2000Å fall on the metal then the kinetic energy of the fastest photoelectron is **NCERT Pg 42**

(a) 1.6×10^{-19} J (b) 16×10^{-10} J

(c) 3.2×10^{-19} J (d) 6.4×10^{-10} J

38 Kinetic energy of the ejected electron is **NCERT Pg 42**

(a) equal to the frequency of the electromagnetic radiation

(b) proportional to the frequency of the electromagnetic radiation

(c) more than the frequency of the electromagnetic radiation

(d) inversely proportional to the frequency of the electromagnetic radiation

39 What is the work function of the metal, if a light of wavelength 4000 Å generates photoelectrons of velocity 6×10^5 ms^{-1} from it? **NCERT Pg 42**

(a) 4.0 eV (b) 2.1 eV

(c) 0.9 eV (d) 3.1 eV

40 In a photoelectric effect experiment the Threshold wavelength of light is 380 nm. If the wavelength of incident light is 260 nm, the maximum kinetic energy of emitted electrons will be [Given : $E \text{ (in eV)} = \frac{1237}{\lambda \text{(in nm)}}$]

NCERT Pg 43

(a) 15.1 eV (b) 4.5 eV

(c) 1.5 eV (d) 3.0 eV

41 The emission spectra of atoms in the gaseous phase do not show a continuous spread of wavelength from red to violet, rather they emit light only at specific wavelengths with dark spaces between them. Such spectra is called **NCERT Pg 44**

(a) line spectra (b) continuous spectra

(c) absorption spectra (d) emission spectra

42 The type of spectrum which is illustrated by the following figure is **NCERT Pg 45**

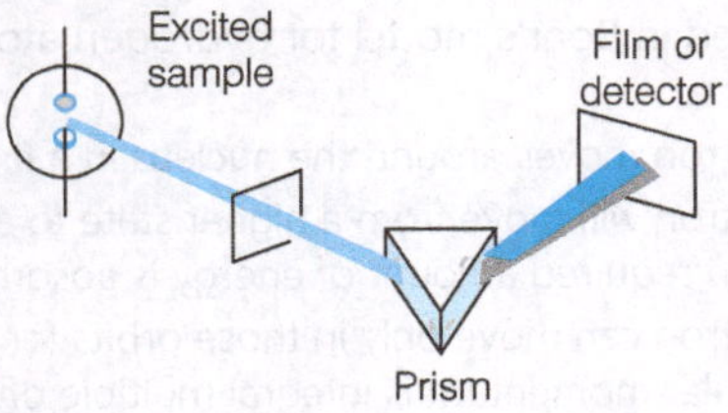

(a) Atomic emission spectra

(b) Continuous spectra

(c) Atomic absorption spectra

(d) Discontinuous spectra

43 The ratio of the shortest wavelength of two spectral series of hydrogen spectrum is found to be about 9. The spectral series are **NCERT Pg 45**

(a) Lyman and Paschen

(b) Brackett and Pfund

(c) Paschen and Pfund

(d) Balmer and Brackett

44 Which of the following relation correctly described all the lines in the hydrogen spectrum? **NCERT Pg 45**

(a) $\bar{\nu} = \frac{1}{109677}\left[\frac{1}{n_1^2} - \frac{1}{n_2^2}\right] \text{cm}^{-1}$

(b) $\bar{\nu} = 109677\left[\frac{1}{n_2^2} - \frac{1}{n_1^2}\right] \text{cm}^{-1}$

(c) $\bar{\nu} = 109677\,[n_1^2 - n_2^2]\ \text{cm}^{-1}$

(d) $\bar{\nu} = 109677\,[n_2^2 - n_1^2]\ \text{cm}^{-1}$

45 The electronic transition from $n=2$ to $n=1$ will produce the shortest wavelength in (where, n = principal quantum number) **NCERT Pg 45**

(a) He^+ (b) H (c) H^+ (d) Li^{2+}

46 Consider the given figure. **NCERT Pg 46**

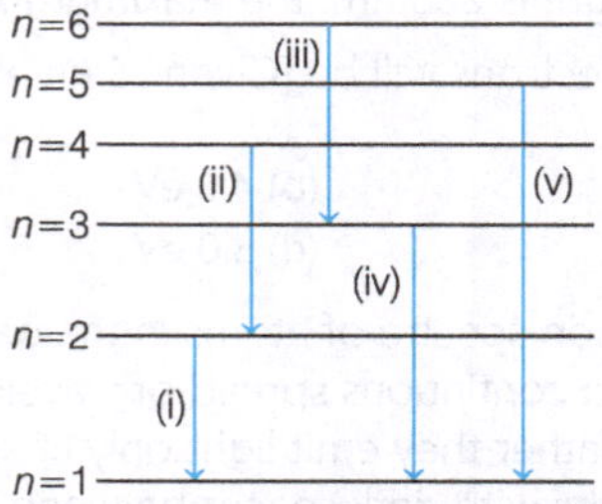

How many spectral lines will have frequency of same order?

(a) 4 (b) 5 (c) 3 (d) 2

Bohr's Model for Hydrogen Atom

47 Which of the following statement is not correctly described in Bohr's model for hydrogen atom? **NCERT Pg 46**

(a) Electron moves around the nucleus in a fixed orbit.

(b) Electron will move from a higher state to a lower state when required amount of energy is absorbed.

(c) Electron can move only in those orbits for which its angular momentum is integral multiple of $h/2\pi$.

(d) The frequency of radiation absorbed or emitted when transition of e^- occurs between two stationary states is $\nu = \frac{\Delta E}{h}$

48 The expression for Bohr's frequency rule is **NCERT Pg 46**

(a) $\nu = \frac{E_2 - E_1}{h}$ (b) $v = E_2 - E_1 \cdot h$

(c) $\frac{v}{h} = (E_2 - E_1) + h$ (d) $\frac{v}{h} = E_1 - E_2$

49 An electron can move only in those orbits for which its angular momentum is integral multiple of **NCERT Pg 46**

(a) $\frac{h}{4\pi}$ (b) $\frac{h}{2\pi}$ (c) $\frac{h}{\sqrt{2\pi}}$ (d) $h \cdot 2\pi$

50 The radius of the second Bohr orbit in terms of the Bohr radius, a_0, in Li^{2+} is **NCERT Pg 47**

(a) $\frac{2a_0}{3}$ (b) $\frac{4a_0}{3}$ (c) $\frac{4a_0}{9}$ (d) $\frac{2a_0}{9}$

51 The Bohr's radius expression for stationary states given by $r_n = n^2 a_0$. What is the radius in third stationary state? **NCERT Pg 47**

(a) 238.2 pm (b) 388 pm

(c) 476.1 pm (d) 506 pm

52 Energy of an electron is given by **NCERT Pg 48**

$$E = -2.178 \times 10^{-18}\left(\frac{Z^2}{n^2}\right) \text{J}$$

Wavelength of light required to excite an electron in an hydrogen atom from level $n=1$ to $n=2$ will be ($h = 6.62 \times 10^{-34}$ Js and $c = 3.0 \times 10^8\ \text{ms}^{-1}$)

(a) 1.216×10^{-7} m (b) 2.816×10^{-7} m

(c) 6.500×10^{-7} m (d) 8.500×10^{-7} m

53 The ionisation enthalpy of hydrogen atom is $1.312 \times 10^6\ \text{J mol}^{-1}$. The energy required to excite the electron in the atoms from $n_1 = 1$ to $n_2 = 2$ is **NCERT Pg 48**

(a) $6.56 \times 10^5\ \text{J mol}^{-1}$ (b) $9.84 \times 10^5\ \text{J mol}^{-1}$

(c) $7.56 \times 10^5\ \text{J mol}^{-1}$ (d) $8.51 \times 10^5\ \text{J mol}^{-1}$

54 The kinetic energy of an electron in the second Bohr orbit of a hydrogen atom is [a_0 is Bohr radius] **NCERT Pg 48**

(a) $\frac{h^2}{4\pi^2 m a_0^2}$ (b) $\frac{h^2}{16\pi^2 m a_0^2}$

(c) $\frac{h^2}{32\pi^2 m a_0^2}$ (d) $\frac{h^2}{64\pi^2 m a_0^2}$

55 The energy of the electron in a hydrogen atom has a negative sign because **NCERT Pg 48**

(a) the energy of the electron in the atom is lower than the energy of a free electron at rest

(b) a free electron at rest is an electron that is infinitely far away from the nucleus

(c) the energy value assigned to free electron at rest is zero

(d) the electron will be tightly bound to the nucleus

56 The radius of the second Bohr orbit for hydrogen atom is (Planck's constant (h) = 6.6262×10^{-34} Js; mass of electron = 9.1091×10^{-31} kg; charge of electron (e) = 1.60210×10^{-19} C; permitivity of vacuum (ϵ_0) = $8.854185 \times 10^{-12}\ \text{kg}^{-1}\text{m}^{-3}\text{A}^2$) **NCERT Pg 48**

(a) 1.65 Å (b) 4.76 Å (c) 0.529 Å (d) 2.12 Å

57 The energy of an electron in first Bohr orbit of H-atom is −13.6 eV. Which of the following energy value(s) of excited state(s) for electrons in Bohr orbits of hydrogen is correct? **NCERT Pg 48**

(a) − 3.4 eV (b) − 4.2 eV (c) − 6.8 eV (d) + 6.8 eV

58 The frequency (ν) associated with the absorption and emission of the photon can be evaluated by equation **NCERT Pg 48**

(a) $\nu = \frac{\Delta E}{h} = \frac{R_H}{h}(n_i^2 - n_f^2)$

(b) $\nu = \frac{\Delta E}{h} = R_H \cdot h\left(\frac{1}{n_i^2} - \frac{1}{n_f^2}\right)$

(c) $\nu = \frac{\Delta E}{h} = \frac{R_H}{h} \cdot \left(\frac{1}{n_i^2} - \frac{1}{n_f^2}\right)$

(d) $\nu = \frac{\Delta E}{h} = R_H \cdot h(n_i^2 - n_f^2)$

59 The first line in the Balmer series in the H-atom will have the frequency **NCERT Pg 48**

(a) $3.29 \times 10^{15}\ s^{-1}$ (b) $4.57 \times 10^{14}\ s^{-1}$
(c) $8.22 \times 10^{15}\ s^{-1}$ (d) $8.02 \times 10^{14}\ s^{-1}$

60 For emission line of atomic hydrogen from $n_i = 8$ to $n_f = n$, the plot of wave number (ν) against $\left(\frac{1}{n^2}\right)$ will be (The Rydberg constant, R_H is in wave number unit) **NCERT Pg 48**

(a) non-linear (b) non-linear with slope
(c) linear with slope R_H (d) linear with intercept $-R_H$

61 Which of the following is not correctly matched?

(a) Energy associated with Bohr's orbit, **NCERT Pg 48**

$$E = \frac{-3.18 \times 10^{-18}\ J \times Z^2}{n^2}$$

(b) Energy gap between two orbits,

$$\Delta E = R_H\left[\frac{1}{n_1^2} - \frac{1}{n_2^2}\right]$$

(c) Kinetic energy of the ejected electron,

$$h\nu = h\nu_0 + \frac{1}{2}mv^2$$

(d) Energy of one mole of photons, $E = N_A \frac{hc}{\lambda}$

62 The emission spectrum of hydrogen is found to satisfy the expression for the change in energy is $\Delta E = 2.18 \times 10^{-18}\left(\frac{1}{n_1^2} - \frac{1}{n_2^2}\right)$ J. The spectral lines corresponds to bracket series if. **NCERT Pg 48**

(a) $n_1 = 4$ and $n_2 = 5, 6, 7 \ldots$
(b) $n_1 = 3$ and $n_2 = 4, 5, 6 \ldots$
(c) $n_1 = 1$ and $n_2 = 2, 3, 4 \ldots$
(d) $n_1 = 2$ and $n_2 = 3, 4, 5 \ldots$

63 The colour corresponding to the wavelength of the light emitted when the electron in a hydrogen atom undergoes transition from $n = 5$ to $n = 2$ is **NCERT Pg 49**

(a) red (b) green
(c) blue (d) yellow

64 The phenomenon of splitting of spectral lines under the influence of the electric field is called **NCERT Pg 49**

(a) Stark effect (b) photoelectric effect
(c) Zeeman effect (d) electromagnetic effect

65 Zeeman effect is due to **NCERT Pg 49**

(a) splitting up the lines in an emission spectrum in the presence of an external electrostatic field
(b) random scattering of light by colloidal particles
(c) splitting up of the spectral lines in an emission spectrum in the presence of magnetic field
(d) emission of electrons from metals when light falls upon them

66 Which of the following is not the limitation of Bohr model? **NCERT Pg 49**

(a) It fails to account for the finer details of the hydrogen atom spectrum observed by using sophisticated spectroscopic techniques.
(b) It is unable to explain the spectrum of atoms other than hydrogen.
(c) It is unable to explain the ability of atoms to form molecules by chemical bonds.
(d) It is unable to explain continuous atomic spectra.

Towards Quantum Mechanical Model of the Atom

67 If a 300 g cricket ball is thrown with a speed of 2×10^4 cm s^{-1} then its de-Broglie's wavelength is **NCERT Pg 50**
($h = 6.6 \times 10^{-27}$ g $cm^2\ s^{-1}$)

(a) 1.1×10^{-24} cm (b) 1.1×10^{-33} cm
(c) 0.55×10^{-36} cm (d) 11.0×10^{-35} cm

68 A body of mass x kg is moving with velocity of 100 m s^{-1}. Its de-Broglie wavelength is 6.62×10^{-35} m. Hence, x is

(a) 0.25 (b) 0.15 (c) 0.2 (d) 0.1 **NCERT Pg 50**

69 Which of the following statement is incorrect regarding Bohr's model of hydrogen atom? **NCERT Pg 48**

(a) Energy of the electrons in the orbit is quantised.
(b) The electron in the orbit nearest to the nucleus has the lowest energy.
(c) Electrons revolve in different orbits around the nucleus.
(d) The position and velocity of the electrons in the orbit cannot be determined simultaneously.

70 The mass of a photon with wavelength 3.6 Å is **NCERT Pg 51**

(a) 6.135×10^{-27} kg (b) 6.135×10^{-28} kg
(c) 6.135×10^{-33} kg (d) 6.135×10^{-30} kg

71 The effect of Heisenberg uncertainty principle is significant **NCERT Pg 51**

(a) only for motion of microscopic objects
(b) only for motion of macroscopic objects
(c) for motion of both microscopic and macroscopic objects
(d) only when the objects are stationary

72 In atom, an electron is moving with a speed of 600 m/s with an accuracy of 0.005%. Certainty with which the position of the electron can be located is ($h = 6.6 \times 10^{-34}$ kg m^2 s^{-1}, mass of electron, $e_m = 6.6 \times 10^{-31}$ kg) NCERT Pg 51

(a) 1.52×10^{-4} m (b) 5.10×10^{-3} m
(c) 1.92×10^{-3} m (d) 3.84×10^{-3} m

73 The uncertainties in the velocities of two particles *A* and *B* are 0.05 and 0.02 ms^{-1} respectively. The mass of *B* is five times to that of mass *A*. What is the ratio of uncertainties $(\Delta x_A / \Delta x_B)$ in their positions? NCERT Pg 51

(a) 2 (b) 0.25 (c) 4 (d) 1

74 Uncertainty in the position of an electron (mass = 9.1×10^{-31} kg) moving with a velocity 300 ms^{-1}, accurate upon 0.001% will be ($h = 6.63 \times 10^{-34}$ J-s) NCERT Pg 51

(a) 19.2×10^{-2} m (b) 5.76×10^{-2} m
(c) 1.93×10^{-2} m (d) 3.84×10^{-2} m

75 If E_A, E_B and E_C represent kinetic energies of an electron, alpha particle and proton respectively and each moving with same de-Broglie wavelength, then choose the correct increasing representation. NCERT Pg 51

(a) $E_A = E_B = E_C$ (b) $E_A > E_B > E_C$
(c) $E_B > E_C > E_A$ (d) $E_A < E_C < E_B$

Quantum Mechanical Model of Atom

76 The effect of Heisenberg uncertainty principle is not significant for macroscopic objects because NCERT Pg 52

(a) $\Delta v \Delta x$ is extremely small (b) Δv is extremely large
(c) Δx is infinite (d) $\Delta v \Delta x$ is extremely large

77 A car with a mass of 1000 kg is moving at a speed of 30 m/s. Given that the speed can be measured with an accuracy of 5%, then the uncertainty in speed and position respectively are NCERT Pg 52

(a) 1.5 m/s and 3×10^{-20} m
(b) 1.5 m/s and 3.51×10^{-38} m
(c) 15 m/s and 5×10^{-38} m
(d) 150 m/s and 1×10^{-38} m

78 What was the primary reason that the Bohr's model couldn't account for the atomic structure? NCERT Pg 52

(a) Lack of experimental evidence
(b) Inconsistency with dual behaviour of matter
(c) Theoritical limitations of orbits
(d) Absence of nuclear force

79 In the Schrodinger equation, $\hat{H}$ is NCERT Pg 53

(a) a mathematical operator called Schrodinger Laplacian operator
(b) introduced by Schrodinger from the expression for the total energy of the system
(c) introduced by Schrodinger from the expression for the kinetic energy of the system
(d) introduced by Schrodinger from the expression for the momentum of the system

80 Consider the following statements about wave function. NCERT Pg 53, 54, 55, 56

I. When an electron is in energy state, the wave function corresponds to that energy state, which contains all information about the electron.
II. It is a mathematical function whose value depends upon the coordinates of the electron in the atom and does not carry any physical meaning.
III. Wave functions of hydrogen or hydrogen like species with one electron are called atomic orbitals.
IV. Wave functions pertaining to one-electron species are called one-electron systems.
V. It is denoted by $|\psi|^2$.

The correct statements are

(a) I, II and III (b) III and IV
(c) I and II (d) I, II, III and IV

81. Which of the statement about quantum numbers is wrong? NCERT Pg 55

(a) If the value of $l = 0$, the electron distribution is spherical.
(b) The shape of the orbital is given by subsidiary quantum number.
(c) The Zeeman's effect is explained by magnetic quantum number.
(d) The spin quantum number gives the orientation of electron cloud.

82 The number of *d*-electrons in Fe^{2+} ($Z = 26$) is not equal to the number of electrons in which one of the following? NCERT Pg 55

(a) *s*-electrons in Mg ($Z = 12$)
(b) *p*-electrons in Cl ($Z = 17$)
(c) *d*-electrons in Fe ($Z = 26$)
(d) *p*-electrons in Ne ($Z = 10$)

83 Which of the following sets of quantum numbers represents the highest energy of an atom? NCERT Pg 55

(a) $n = 3, l = 0, m = 0, s = +\frac{1}{2}$
(b) $n = 3, l = 1, m = 1, s = +\frac{1}{2}$
(c) $n = 3, l = 2, m = 1, s = +\frac{1}{2}$
(d) $n = 4, l = 0, m = 0, s = +\frac{1}{2}$

84 Consider the following statements concerning the quantum numbers, **NCERT Pg 55, 56**

I. Angular quantum number determines the three dimensional shape of the orbital.

II. The principal quantum number determines the orientation and energy of the orbital.

III. Magnetic quantum number determines the size of the orbital.

IV. Spin quantum number of an electron determines the orientation of the spin of electron.

The correct set of statements are

(a) I and II (b) I and IV

(c) III and IV (d) II, III and IV

85 Which of the following statements are correct? **NCERT Pg 55, 56**

I. The shape of the orbitals is given by magnetic quantum number.

II. In an atom, all electrons travel with the same velocity.

III. If the value of $l = 0$, the electron distribution is spherical.

IV. Angular momentum of 1*s*, 2*s*, 3*s* electrons are equal.

Choose the most appropriate answer from the options given below.

(a) II and IV (b) I and III

(c) I and II (d) III and IV

86 The correct set of four quantum numbers for the valence electrons of rubidium atom ($Z = 37$) is **NCERT Pg 56**

(a) $5, 0, 0, +\frac{1}{2}$ (b) $5, 1, 0, +\frac{1}{2}$

(c) $5, 1, 1, +\frac{1}{2}$ (d) $5, 0, 1, +\frac{1}{2}$

87 The graph between $|\psi|^2$ and r (radial distance) is shown below. **NCERT Pg 57**

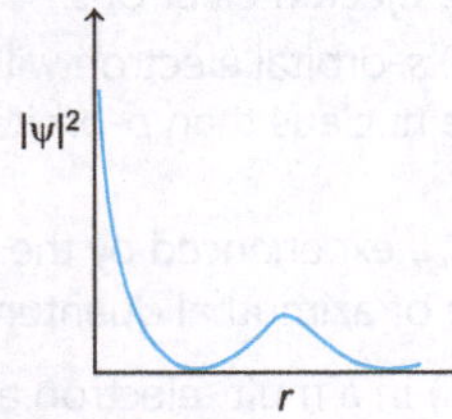

This represents

(a) 1*s*-orbital (b) 2*p*-orbital

(c) 3*s*-orbital (d) 2*s*-orbital

88 The number of orbitals associated with quantum numbers $n = 5$, $m_s = +\frac{1}{2}$ is **NCERT Pg 58**

(a) 25 (b) 50

(c) 15 (d) 11

89 Given below are some boundary surface diagram of the 3*d* orbitals. **NCERT Pg 59**

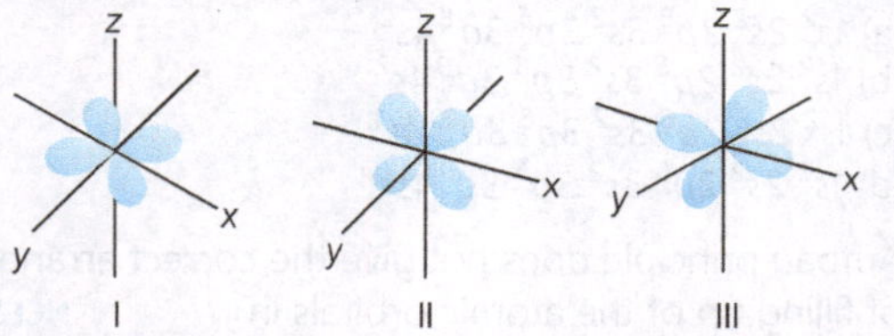

Boundary surface diagrams of the three 3*d*-orbitals

Choose the correct answer from the option given below

(a) I-$d_{x^2-y^2}$, II-d_{yz}, III-d_{xz} (b) I-d_{xy}, II-d_{xz}, III-d_{yz}

(c) I-d_{xz}, II-d_{xy}, III-d_{yz} (d) I-d_{yz}, II-d_{xz}, III-d_{xy}

90 Out of the following pairs of electrons, identify the pairs of electrons present in degenerate orbitals. **NCERT Pg 57, 60**

(a) (i) $n = 3, l = 1, m_l = -1, m_s = -\frac{1}{2}$

(ii) $n = 3, l = 2, m_l = -1, m_s = -\frac{1}{2}$

(b) (i) $n = 3, l = 1, m_l = 1, m_s = +\frac{1}{2}$

(ii) $n = 3, l = 2, m_l = 1, m_s = +\frac{1}{2}$

(c) (i) $n = 4, l = 1, m_l = 1, m_s = +\frac{1}{2}$

(ii) $n = 3, l = 2, m_l = 1, m_s = +\frac{1}{2}$

(d) (i) $n = 3, l = 2, m_l = +2, m_s = -\frac{1}{2}$

(ii) $n = 3, l = 2, m_l = +2, m_s = +\frac{1}{2}$

91 Identify the correct order of increase in the energy of the orbitals for hydrogen atom. **NCERT Pg 60**

(a) $1s < 2s = 2p < 3s = 3p = 3d < 4s = 4p = 4d = 4f$

(b) $1s > 2s = 2p > 3s = 3p = 3d > 4s = 4p = 4d = 4f$

(c) $1s = 2s = 3s = 4s > 2p = 3p = 4p > 3d = 4d > 4f$

(d) $1s = 2s = 3s = 4s < 2p = 3p = 4p < 3d = 4d < 4f$

92 Consider the following statements. **NCERT Pg 60, 61**

I. The attractive interactions of an electron increases with increase of positive charge (Z_e) on the nucleus.

II. Due to the presence of electrons in the inner shells, the electrons in the outer shell will not experience the full positive charge of the nucleus (Z_e).

III. The effect will be lowered due to the partial screening of positive charge on the nucleus by the inner shell electrons.

IV. The net negative charge experienced by the other electrons is known as effective nuclear charge (Z_{eff}).

The correct statements are

(a) I, II and III (b) II, III and IV

(c) I, III and IV (d) I and IV

93 Which of the following does not represent ground state electronic configuration of Cu atom? NCERT Pg 64

(a) $1s^2\ 2s^2\ 2p^6\ 3s^2\ 3p^6\ 3d^8 4s^2$
(b) $1s^2\ 2s^2\ 2p^6\ 3s^2\ 3p^6\ 3d^9 4s^2$
(c) $1s^2\ 2s^2\ 2p^6\ 3s^2\ 3p^6\ 3d^{10} 4s^1$
(d) $1s^2\ 2s^2\ 2p^6\ 3s^2\ 3p^6\ 3d^5 4s^1$

94 Aufbau principle does not give the correct arrangement of filling up of the atomic orbitals in NCERT Pg 64

(a) Cu and Zn (b) Co and Zn (c) Mn and Cr (d) Cu and Cr

95 The electronic configuration with maximum exchange energy will be NCERT Pg 65

(a) $3d^1_{xy}\ 3d^1_{yz}\ 3d^1_{zx}\ 4s^1$
(b) $3d^1_{xy}\ 3d^1_{yz}\ 3d^1_{zx}\ 3d^1_{x^2-y^2}\ 3d^2_{z^2}\ 4s^2$
(c) $3d^2_{xy}\ 3d^2_{yz}\ 3d^2_{zx}\ 3d^2_{x^2-y^2}\ 3d^1_{z^2}\ 4s^1$
(d) $3d^2_{xy}\ 3d^2_{yz}\ 3d^2_{zx}\ 3d^2_{x^2-y^2}\ 3d^2_{z^2}\ 4s^1$

96 With the saturation of 3*d*-orbitals, the filling of the 4*p*-orbitals start at *A* and is completed at *B*. Here, *A* and *B* refer to NCERT Pg 66

(a) $A \rightarrow$ Ga; $B \rightarrow$ Kr
(b) $A \rightarrow$ Ga; $B \rightarrow$ Xe
(c) $A \rightarrow$ Zn; $B \rightarrow$ Br
(d) $A \rightarrow$ Zn; $B \rightarrow$ Kr

97 The atomic numbers of elements *X*, *Y* and *Z* are 19, 21 and 25 respectively. The number of electrons present in the *M*-shell of these elements follow the order NCERT Pg 66

(a) $Z > X > Y$ (b) $X > Y > Z$
(c) $Z > Y > X$ (d) $Y > Z > X$

98 What is the atomic number of an element which has $3d^5$ as its outermost configuration? NCERT Pg 66

(a) 25 (b) 23 (c) 11 (d) 36

Assertion-Reason Questions

Directions (Q. Nos. 1-10) *In the following question Assertion (A) followed by Reason (R) is given below. Choose the correct option out of the choices given below.*

(a) Both A and R are true and R is the correct explanation of A.
(b) Both A and R are true but R is not the correct explanation of A.
(c) A is true but R is false.
(d) A is false but R is true.

1 **Assertion** (A) X-rays are used to study the interior of the objects. NCERT Pg 33

Reason (R) X-rays are not deflected by the electric and magnetic fields and have very high penetrating power through the matter.

2 **Assertion** (A) In the Rutherford experiment most of the space in the atoms is empty. NCERT Pg 34

Reason (R) Most of the α-particles passed through the foil remain undeflected.

3 **Assertion** (A) Electromagnetic waves can move in vacuum. NCERT Pg 38

Reason (R) They do not require medium to propagate.

4 **Assertion** (A) Iron rod, heated in a furnace, first turns to dull red, intense red, white and then become blue as the temperature becomes high. NCERT Pg 40

Reason (R) The frequency of emitted radiation goes from a higher frequency to a lower frequency as the temperature increases.

5 **Assertion** (A) Greater the energy possessed by the photon, lesser will be transfer of energy to the electron and the kinetic energy of the ejected electron. NCERT Pg 41

Reason (R) The kinetic energy of the ejected electron is proportional to the frequency of the electromagnetic radiation.

6 **Assertion** (A) Classical mechanics fails to explain the behaviour of microscopic particles. NCERT Pg 42

Reason (R) It ignores the concept of dual behaviour of matter.

7 **Assertion** (A) Red light of any brightness may shine on a piece of potassium-metal for hours but no photoelectrons are ejected. But as soon as even a very weak yellow light shines on the potassium-metal, the photoelectric effect is observed. NCERT Pg 42

Reason (R) The number of electrons ejected depends upon the brightness of light and not on the kinetic energy of the ejected electrons.

8 **Assertion** (A) *s*-orbital electron will be more tightly bound to the nucleus than *p*-orbital electron. NCERT Pg 59, 60

Reason (R) Z_{eff} experienced by the electron decreases with increase of azimuthal quantum number (*l*).

9 **Assertion** (A) In a multi-electron atom, the electrons in different subshell have different energies. NCERT Pg 61

Reason (R) Energy of an orbital depends upon $(n + l)$ value.

10 **Assertion** (A) Energy of the orbital increases with increase of principal quantum number. NCERT Pg 60

Reason (R) Energy is required in shifting away the negatively charged electron from the positively charged nucleus.

Statement Type Questions

Direction (Q. Nos. 1-6) *In the following questions, two statements (I & II) are given. In the light of the given statements, choose the correct option given below.*

(a) Both Statement I and Statement II are false.
(b) Statement I is true but Statement II is false.
(c) Statement I is false but Statement II is true.
(d) Both Statement I and Statement II are true.

1 **Statement I** Emitted radiation will fall in visible range when an electron jump from $n = 4$ to $n = 2$ in H-atom. **NCERT Pg 45**

Statement II Balmer series radiations belong to the visible range for hydrogen atoms only.

2 **Statement I** Energies of the orbitals in hydrogen or hydrogen like species depend only on the quantum number '*n*'. **NCERT Pg 46**

Statement II Energies of the orbitals in multielectron atoms depend on quantum numbers '*n*' and '*l*'.

3 **Statement I** ψ is constant over the boundary surface.

Statement II The boundary surface for $|\psi|^2$ and $|\psi|$ are different. **NCERT Pg 58**

4 **Statement I** Orbital having *xz* plane as node may be $3d_{xy}$.

Statement II $3d_{xy}$ has two radial nodes. **NCERT Pg 59**

5 **Statement I** The effective nuclear charge experienced by an electron within a multi-electron atom increases as the principle quantum number (n) decreases. **NCERT Pg 61**

Statement II Electrons with the same principle quantum number (n) but different azimuthal quantum numbers (l) experience the same effective nuclear charge within an atom.

6 **Statement I** Fe^{2+} ion has 24 electrons and its electronic configuration represents that of Cr. **NCERT Pg 63**

Statement II All the five unpaired electrons, in the 3rd subshell give stability to the ion.

7 Which of the following statements is/are correct? **NCERT Pg 37, 38, 39**

I. The speed of light does not depend upon the nature of the medium through which it passes.
II. The beam of light is deviated or refracted from its original path as it passes from one medium to another.
III. When a ray of white light is passed through a prism, the wave with shorter wavelength bends more than the one with a longer wavelength.
IV. Qualitatively, the magnitude of velocity of electron increases with increase of positive charge on the nucleus.
V. Magnitude of velocity of electron decreases with increase of principal quantum number.

Choose the correct answer from the options given below.

(a) I, II, III and V (b) II, III, IV and V
(c) I and III (d) II and V

8 Which of the following statements are correct? **NCERT Pg 38, 46, 51, 55, 57**

I. Angular quantum number signifies the size of the orbital.
II. Total number of nodes for 3*s*-orbital is three.
III. The radius of the first orbit of He^+ is half that of the first orbit of hydrogen atom.
IV. X-rays have larger wave number than microwaves.
V. The exact position and exact momentum of an electron cannot be determined simultaneously.

Choose the correct answer from the options given below.

(a) I and II (b) II, III and IV
(c) III, IV and V (d) I and V

9 Which of the following statements is/are incorrect? **NCERT Pg 35, 40, 61, 62**

I. Photon have easiest access to the surface of a caesium metal.
II. All isotopes of a given element show same type of chemical behaviour.
III. Black body is an ideal body that emits and absorbs radiations of all frequencies.
IV. The two electrons in an orbital create opposite magnetic fields.
V. Energy of $4s < 3d$ is decided by Aufbau principle.

Choose the correct answer from the options given below.

(a) I only (b) II and III
(c) II, III, IV and V (d) IV and V

10 Which of the following statements is/are incorrect? **NCERT Pg 48, 49, 50, 51**

I. Bohr's theory can also be applied to species He^+, Li^{2+}, Be^{3+} and energy of stationary states associated with these kind of ions is given as, $E_n = 2.18 \times 10^{-18} (Z^2/n^2)$ J
II. In case of absorption spectrum, $n_i > n_f$ and in case of emission spectrum $n_f > n_i$.
III. de-Broglie suggested that matter like radiation should also exhibit dual behaviour.
IV. Heisenberg uncertainty principle rules out existence of definite path or trajectories of electrons.

Choose the correct answer from the options given below.

(a) I and II (b) II and III (c) Only IV (d) Only II

Matching Type Questions

1 Match the Column I with Column II and choose the correct options from the codes given below. **NCERT Pg 33**

Column I (Type of rays)	Column II (Characteristics)
A. α-ray	1. Negatively charged particles similar to electrons.
B. β-ray	2. X-ray, neutral in nature.
C. γ-ray	3. Two units of positive charge and four units of atomic mass.

Codes

	A	B	C		A	B	C
(a)	3	2	1	(b)	1	2	3
(c)	2	1	3	(d)	3	1	2

2 Match the Column I with Column II and choose the correct options from the codes given below. **NCERT Pg 38**

Column I	Column II
A. 10^6 Hz	1. Satellite, radar
B. 10^{10} Hz	2. Broadcasting
C. 10^{13} Hz	3. Solar radiation
D. 10^{16} Hz	4. Heat, remote

Codes

	A	B	C	D
(a)	1	2	3	4
(b)	3	1	2	4
(c)	2	1	4	3
(d)	4	3	1	2

3 Match the Column I with Column II and choose the correct options from the codes given below. **NCERT Pg 56**

Column I (n, l)	Column II (Subshell notation)
A. $n = 1, l = 0$	1. $4f$
B. $n = 2, l = 0$	2. $4s$
C. $n = 3, l = 1$	3. $3p$
D. $n = 3, l = 2$	4. $3d$
E. $n = 4, l = 3$	5. $1s$
F. $n = 4, l = 0$	6. $2s$

Codes

	A	B	C	D	E	F
(a)	5	6	3	4	1	2
(b)	6	5	4	3	2	1
(c)	1	2	3	4	5	6
(d)	3	6	4	2	1	5

4. Match the Column I with Column II and choose the correct options from the codes given below. **NCERT Pg 56, 57**

Column I	Column II
A. Number of sub-shells in a shell.	1. $2(2l + 1)$
B. Maximum number of electrons in a sub-shell.	2. $n - l - 1$
C. Number of spherical nodes.	3. n
D. Number of spectral lines in Lyman series for a gas (for n to 1 transition).	4. $(n - 1)$

Codes

	A	B	C	D		A	B	C	D
(a)	3	1	4	2	(b)	3	1	2	4
(c)	1	2	3	4	(d)	1	4	2	3

5 Match the Column I with Column II and choose the correct options from the codes given below. **NCERT Pg 59**

Column I (Boundary surface diagram) — **Column II** (d-orbital)

A.
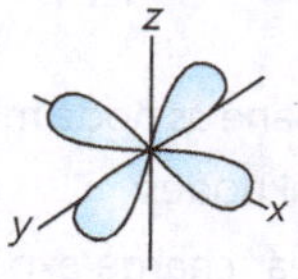

1. d_{z^2}

B.
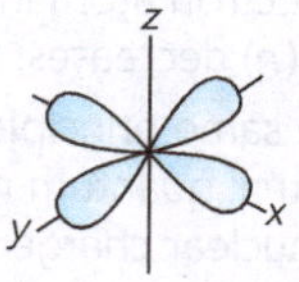

2. d_{xy}

C.
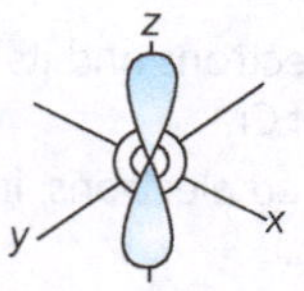

3. $d_{x^2-y^2}$

D.
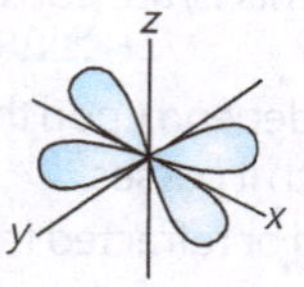

4. d_{yz}

Codes

	A	B	C	D		A	B	C	D
(a)	1	2	3	4	(b)	3	4	1	2
(c)	2	4	1	3	(d)	4	3	1	2

Numerical Value Questions

1 The ground state energy of hydrogen atom is – 13.6 eV. The energy of second excited state of He^+ ion in eV is – x eV. The value of x is .... (Nearest integer) NCERT Pg 48

2 In a hydrogen atom the wavelength of the radiation emitted, when electron falls from infinity to stationary state 1, would be (Rydberg constant $= 1.097 \times 10^7\ m^{-1}$) .... nm. NCERT Pg 48

3 The total number of orbitals associated with the principal quantum number 5 is .... NCERT Pg 55

4 The number of atomic orbitals from the following having 5 radial nodes is ....

6*p*, 7*s*, 7*p*, 8*p*, 8*d* NCERT Pg 59

5 The number of radial nodes in 5*d*-orbital is .... NCERT Pg 59

NCERT Exemplar's Questions

1 Which of the following statements about the electron is incorrect?
(a) It is a negatively charged particle.
(b) The mass of electron is equal to the mass of neutron.
(c) It is a basic constituent of all atoms.
(d) It is a constituent of cathode rays.

2 Which of the following statement is incorrect about the characteristics of cathode rays?
(a) They start from the cathode and move towards the anode.
(b) They travel in a straight line in the absence of an external electrical or magnetic field.
(c) Characteristics of cathode rays do not depend upon the material of electrodes in cathode ray tube.
(d) Characteristics of cathode rays depend upon the nature of gas present in the cathode ray tube.

3 Which of the following conclusions could not be derived from Rutherford's α-particle scattering experiment?
(a) Most of the space in the atom is empty.
(b) The radius of the atom is about 10^{-10} m while that of nucleus is 10^{-15} m.
(c) Electrons move in a circular path of fixed energy called orbits.
(d) Electrons and the nucleus are held together by electrostatic forces of attraction.

4 Which of the following properties of an atom could be explained correctly by Thomson's model of atom?
(a) Overall neutrality of atom
(b) Spectra of hydrogen atom
(c) Position of electrons, protons and neutrons in atom
(d) Stability of atom

5 Two atoms are said to be isobars, if
(a) they have same atomic number but different mass number
(b) they have same number of electrons but different number of neutrons
(c) they have same number of neutrons but different number of electrons
(d) sum of the number of protons and neutrons is same but the number of protons is different

6 Which of the following is responsible to rule out the existence of definite paths or trajectories of electrons?
(a) Pauli's exclusion principle
(b) Heisenberg's uncertainty principle
(c) Hund's rule of maximum multiplicity
(d) Aufbau principle

7 If travelling at same speeds, which of the following matter waves have the shortest wavelength?
(a) Electron (b) Alpha particle (He^{2+})
(c) Neutron (d) Proton

8 Which of the following options does not represent ground state electronic configuration of an atom?
(a) $1s^2\ 2s^2\ 2p^6\ 3s^2\ 3p^6\ 3d^8\ 4s^2$
(b) $1s^2\ 2s^2\ 2p^6\ 3s^2\ 3p^6\ 3d^9\ 4s^2$
(c) $1s^2\ 2s^2\ 2p^6\ 3s^2\ 3p^6\ 3d^{10}\ 4s^1$
(d) $1s^2\ 2s^2\ 2p^6\ 3s^2\ 3p^6\ 3d^5\ 4s^1$

9 The pair of ions having same electronic configuration is
(a) Cr^{3+}, Fe^{3+} (b) Fe^{3+}, Mn^{2+}
(c) Fe^{3+}, Co^{3+} (d) Sc^{3+}, Cr^{3+}

10 Total number of orbitals associated with third shell will be ......
(a) 2 (b) 4 (c) 9 (d) 3

11 Orbital angular momentum depends on......... .
(a) l (b) n and l
(c) n and m (d) m and s

12 The number of radial nodes for 3*p*-orbital is.......... .
(a) 3 (b) 4 (c) 2 (d) 1

13 Number of angular nodes for 4*d* orbital is ....
(a) 4 (b) 3 (c) 2 (d) 1

Past Exams' Questions

NEET Archive

1 Match List I with List II. **NCERT Pg 54, NEET 2024**

List I (Quantum number)		List II (Information provided)	
A.	m_l	I.	Shape of orbital
B.	m_s	II.	Size of orbital
C.	l	III.	Orientation of orbital
D.	n	IV.	Orientation of spin of electron

Choose the correct answer from the options given below.

(a) A-I, B-III, C-II, D-IV (b) A-III, B-IV, C-I, D-II
(c) A-III, B-IV, C-II, D-I (d) A-II, B-I, C-IV, D-III

2. The energy of an electron in the ground state ($n = 1$) for He^+ ion is $-x$ J, then that for an electron in $n = 2$ state for Be^{3+} ion in J is **NCERT Pg 48, NEET 2024**

(a) $-x$ (b) $-\frac{x}{9}$ (c) $-4x$ (d) $-\frac{4}{9}x$

3 Select the correct statements from the following.

I. Atoms of all elements are composed of two fundamental particles.
II. The mass of the electrons is 9.10939×10^{-31} kg.
III. All the isotopes of a given element show same chemical properties.
IV. Protons and electrons are collectively known as nucleons.
V. Dalton's atomic theory, regarded the atom as an ultimate particle of matter.

Choose the correct answer from the options given below. **NCERT Pg 29, 31, 35, NEET 2023**

(a) III, IV and V (b) I and V (c) II, III and V (d) I, II and III

4 The relation between n_m, (n_m = the number of permissible values of magnetic quantum number (m)) for a given value of azimuthal quantum number (l), is **NCERT Pg 55, NEET 2023**

(a) $l = 2n_m + 1$ (b) $n_m = 2l^2 + l$ (c) $n_m = l + 2$ (d) $l = \frac{n_m - 1}{2}$

5 If radius of second Bohr orbit of the He^+ ion is 105.8 pm, what is the radius of third Bohr orbit of Li^{2+} ion? **NCERT Pg 48, NEET 2022**

(a) 15.87 pm (b) 1.587 pm (c) 158.7 Å (d) 158.7 pm

6 Identify the incorrect statement from the following. **NCERT Pg 59, NEET 2022**

(a) All the five 5d-orbitals are different in size when compared to the respective 4d-orbitals.
(b) All the five 4d-orbitals have shapes similar to the respective 3d-orbitals.
(c) In an atom, all the five 3d-orbitals are equal in energy in free state.
(d) The shapes of d_{xy}, d_{yz} and d_{zx}-orbitals similar to each other; and $d_{x^2-y^2}$ and d_{z^2} are similar to each other.

7 A particular station of All India Radio, New Delhi, broadcasts on a frequency of 1,368 kHz (kilohertz). The wavelength of the electromagnetic radiation emitted by the transmitter is
[Speed of light, $c = 3.0 \times 10^8$ ms^{-1}] **NCERT Pg 39, NEET 2021**

(a) 219.3 m (b) 219.2 m (c) 2192 m (d) 21.92 cm

8 From the following pairs of ions which one is not an isoelectronic pair? **NCERT Pg 35, NEET 2021**

(a) Fe^{2+}, Mn^{2+} (b) O^{2-}, F^- (c) Na^+, Mg^{2+} (d) Mn^{2+}, Fe^{3+}

9 The number of protons, neutrons and electrons in $^{175}_{71}Lu$, respectively are **NCERT Pg 35, NEET 2020**

(a) 71, 104 and 71 (b) 104, 71 and 71
(c) 71, 71 and 104 (d) 175, 104 and 71

10 The number of angular nodes and radial nodes in 3s-orbital are **NCERT Pg 59, NEET (Oct.) 2020**

(a) 0 and 2 respectively (b) 1 and 0 respectively
(c) 3 and 0 respectively (d) 0 and 1 respectively

11 Which of the following series of transitions in the spectrum of hydrogen atom falls in visible region? **NCERT Pg 46, AIPMT 2019**

(a) Brackett series (b) Lyman series
(c) Balmer series (d) Paschen series

12 4d, 5p, 5f and 6p-orbitals are arranged in the order of decreasing energy. The correct option is **NCERT Pg 60, NEET (National) 2019**

(a) $6p > 5f > 5p > 4d$ (b) $5p > 5f > 4d > 5p$
(c) $5f > 6p > 4d > 5p$ (d) $5f > 6p > 5p > 4d$

13 Which one is a wrong statement? **NCERT Pg 63, NEET 2018**

(a) The electronic configuration of N-atom is

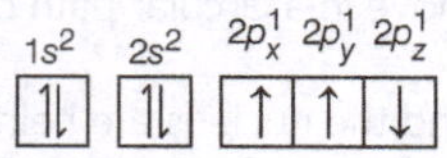

(b) An orbital is designated by three quantum numbers while an electron in an atom is designated by four quantum numbers.
(c) Total orbital angular momentum of electron in 's' orbital is equal to zero.
(d) The value of m for d_{z^2} is zero.

14 Which one is the wrong statement? **NCERT Pg 60, NEET 2017**

(a) The uncertainty principle is $\Delta E \times \Delta t \geq \frac{h}{4\pi}$
(b) Half-filled and fully-filled orbitals have greater stability due to greater exchange energy, greater symmetry and more balanced arrangement.

(c) The energy of 2s-orbital is less than the energy of 2p-orbital in case of hydrogen like atoms.

(d) de-Broglie's wavelength is given by $\lambda = \frac{h}{mv}$, where, m = mass of the particle, v = group velocity of the particle.

15 Two electrons occupying the same orbital are distinguished by **NCERT Pg 56, NEET (Phase I) 2016**

(a) magnetic quantum number
(b) azimuthal quantum number
(c) spin quantum number
(d) principal quantum number

JEE Main Archive

16 The number of electrons present in all the completely filled subshells having $n = 4$, and $s = +\frac{1}{2}$ is ....
(where, n = principal quantum number and s = spin quantum number) **NCERT Pg 56, JEE Main 2024**

17 The four quantum numbers for the electron in the outermost orbital of potassium (atomic no. 19) are **NCERT Pg 56, JEE Main 2024**

(a) $n = 4, l = 2, m = -1, s = +\frac{1}{2}$ (b) $n = 2, l = 0, m = 0, s = +\frac{1}{2}$
(c) $n = 4, l = 0, m = 0, s = +\frac{1}{2}$ (d) $n = 3, l = 0, m = 1, s = +\frac{1}{2}$

18 The number of radial nodes for 3p-orbital is **NCERT Pg 59, JEE Main 2024**

(a) 1 (b) 2 (c) 4 (d) 3

19 Match List-I with List-II. **NCERT Pg 46, JEE Main 2024**

List I (Spectral series for hydrogen)		List II (Spectral region \ higher energy state)	
A.	Lyman	I.	Infrared region
B.	Balmer	II.	UV region
C.	Paschen	III.	Infrared region
D.	Pfund	IV.	Visible region

Choose the correct answer from the options given below.

(a) A-I, B-III, C-II, D-IV (b) A-II, B-IV, C-III, D-I
(c) A-I, B-II, C-III, D-IV (d) A-II, B-III, C-I, D-IV

20 Given below are two statements.

Statement I According to Bohr's model of hydrogen atom, the angular momentum of an electron in a given stationary state is quantised.

Statement II The concept of electron in Bohr's orbit, violates the Heisenberg uncertainty principle.

In the light of the above statements, choose the most appropriate answer from the options given below. **NCERT Pg 46, JEE Main 2023**

(a) Statement I is incorrect but Statement II is correct.
(b) Statement I is correct but Statement II is incorrect.
(c) Both Statement I and Statement II are incorrect.
(d) Both Statement I and Statement II are correct.

21 The energy of an electron in the first Bohr orbit of hydrogen atom is -2.18×10^{-18} J. Its energy in the third Bohr orbit is .... **NCERT Pg 48, JEE Main 2023**

(a) three times of this value (b) $\frac{1}{9}$th of this value
(c) one third of this value (d) $\frac{1}{27}$ of this value

22 If the radius of the first orbit of hydrogen atom is a_0, then de-Broglie's wavelength of electron in 3rd orbit is **NCERT Pg 47, JEE Main 2023**

(a) $3\pi a_0$ (b) $\frac{\pi a_0}{3}$ (c) $6\pi a_0$ (d) $\frac{\pi a_0}{6}$

23 Given below are two statements, one is labelled as Assertion (A) and the other is labelled as Reason (R).

Assertion (A) In the photoelectric effect, the electrons are ejected from the metal surface as soon as the beam of light of frequency greater than threshold frequency strikes the surface. **NCERT Pg 41, JEE Main 2023**

Reason (R) When the photon of any energy strikes an electron in the atom, transfer of energy from the photon to the electron takes place.

In the light of the above statements, choose the most appropriate answer from the options given below.

(a) A is true but R is false.
(b) Both A and R are true and R is the correct explanation of A.
(c) A is false but R is true.
(d) Both A and R are true but R is not the correct explanation of A.

24 Arrange the following orbitals in decreasing order of energy. **NCERT Pg 61, JEE Main 2023**

A. $n = 3, l = 0, m = 0$ B. $n = 4, l = 0, m = 0$
C. $n = 3, l = 1, m = 0$ D. $n = 3, l = 2, m = 1$

The correct option for the order is

(a) D > B > A > C
(b) A > C > B > D
(c) B > D > C > A
(d) D > B > C > A

25 The minimum energy that must be possessed by photons in order to produce the photoelectric effect with platinum metal is [Given, the threshold frequency of platinum is $1.3 \times 10^{15}\ s^{-1}$ and $h = 6.6 \times 10^{-34}$ Js] **NCERT Pg 41, JEE Main 2022**

(a) 3.21×10^{-14} J (b) 6.24×10^{-16} J
(c) 8.58×10^{-19} J (d) 9.76×10^{-20} J

26 Given below are two statements. One is labelled as Assertion (A) and the other is labelled as Reason (R).

Assertion (A) Energy of 2*s*-orbital of hydrogen atom is greater than that of 2*s*-orbital of lithium.

Reason (R) Energies of the orbitals in the same subshell decrease with increase in the atomic number.

In the light of the above statements, choose the correct answer from the options given below:

NCERT Pg 61, JEE Main 2022

(a) Both A and R are true and R is the correct explanation of A.
(b) Both A and R are true but R is not the correct explanation of A.
(c) A is true but R is false.
(d) A is false but R is true.

27 If the radius of the 3rd Bohr's orbit of hydrogen atom is r_3 and the radius of 4th Bohr's orbit is r_4. Then

NCERT Pg 48, JEE Main 2022

(a) $r_4 = \frac{9}{16} r_3$ (b) $r_4 = \frac{16}{9} r_3$ (c) $r_4 = \frac{3}{4} r_3$ (d) $r_4 = \frac{4}{3} r_3$

28 Consider the following statements.

I. The principal quantum number '*n*' is a positive integer with values of '*n*' = 1, 2, 3, ...
II. The azimuthal quantum number '*l*' for a given '*n*' (principal quantum number) can have values as '*l*' = 0, 1, 2,... *n*.
III. Magnetic orbital quantum number 'm_l' for a particular '*l*' (azimuthal quantum number) has $(2l + 1)$ values.
IV. $\pm 1/2$ are the two possible orientations of electron spin.
V. For $l = 5$, there will be a total of 9 orbital.

Which of the above statements are correct?

NCERT Pg 55, 56, JEE Main 2022

(a) I, II and III (b) I, III, IV and V
(c) I, III and IV (d) I, II, III and IV

29 Which of the following is the correct plot for the probability density $\psi^2(r)$ as a function of distance '*r*' of the electron from the nucleus for 2*s*-orbital?

NCERT Pg 57, JEE Main 2022

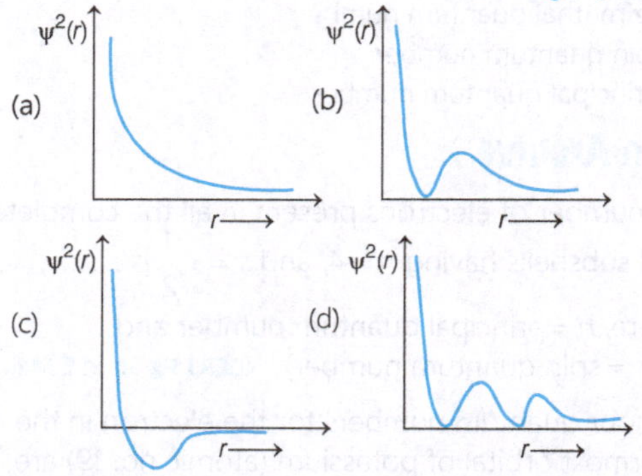

30 Given below are two statements.

Statement I Rutherford's gold foil experiment cannot explain the line spectrum of hydrogen atom.

Statement II Bohr's model of hydrogen atom contradicts Heisenberg's uncertainty principle.

In the light of the above statements, choose the most appropriate answer from the options given below :

(a) Both statements I and II are false. NCERT Pg 49, JEE Main 2021
(b) Statement I is false but statement II is true.
(c) Both Statements I and II are true.
(d) Statement I is true but statement II is false.

Skill Boosters

1 Raman had just finished studying the chapter named 'structure of atom'. Right after that he saw a car moving in a straight road. The possible reason behind the car not travelling in a wave fashion on the road is

(a) wavelength is very large (b) velocity is very high
(c) mass is very large (d) angle with road is very large

2 A student had learnt a concept based on Bohr's model of hydrogen atom. He thought about the findings of the time taken for an electron to complete one revolution in Bohr orbit of hydrogen atom and the velocity of electron present in first Bohr orbit of hydrogen atom, respectively are

(a) $\frac{2\pi mr}{n^2h^2}$, 2.18×10^{-4} m/s (b) $\frac{h}{2\pi mr}$, 2.18×10^{-5} m/s

(c) $\frac{4\pi^2 mr^2}{nh}$, 2.18×10^{6} m/s (d) $\frac{nh}{4\pi^2 mr}$, 2.18×10^{-8} m/s

3 Samar was playing the tennis ball game and he thought about the concept of the structure of atom so, he consider the tennis ball as a moving particle. He asked himself as what will be de-Broglie wavelength of a tennis ball of mass 60 g moving with a velocity of 10 meters per second (approximately)?

(a) 10^{-16} meters (b) 10^{-25} meters
(c) 10^{-33} meters (d) 10^{-31} meters

4 Three bodies of different characteristics are as follows

Body A It is not a perfect radiator of radiant energy.

Body B The energy absorbed from its surrounding is the same amount of energy radiates per unit area.

Body C At a fixed temperature, intensity of radiation emitted decreases with increase of wavelength.

Choose the 'Black body' among the given bodies.
(a) Body A (b) Body B (c) Body C (d) A, B and C

5 A student had studied the Thomson atomic model and found it incomplete or wrong after the learning of Rutherford's gold foil experiment. Suppose that if the Thomson model was correct, then the result of Rutherford's model would have been
(a) all of the α-particle pass through the gold foil without decrease in speed.
(b) all α-particles get bounced back by 180°.
(c) α-particles are deflected over a wide range of angles.
(d) α-particles pass through the gold foil deflected by small angles and with reduced speed.

6 A hydrogen atom is having ground state energy is –13.6 eV. Consider an electronic state ψ of He^+ whose energy and azimuthal quantum number are – 3.4 eV and 2 respectively. From which of the following state is this belong?
(a) $3d$-state (b) $4d$-state
(c) $5d$-state (d) $6d$-state

7 A hydrogen-like species Li^{2+} is in a spherically symmetric state S_1 with one radial node. Upon absorbing light the ion undergoes transition to a state S_2. The S_1 and S_2 state respectively are
(a) 1s and 0 (b) 2s and 1
(c) 2p and 2 (d) 3s and 3

Correct Codes

Topical Questions

1 (b)	2 (d)	3 (a)	4 (c)	5 (d)	6 (d)	7 (b)	8 (b)	9 (a)	10 (c)
11 (d)	12 (d)	13 (c)	14 (b)	15 (b)	16 (a)	17 (b)	18 (d)	19 (a)	20 (d)
21 (b)	22 (c)	23 (c)	24 (c)	25 (a)	26 (b)	27 (a)	28 (a)	29 (a)	30 (c)
31 (a)	32 (c)	33 (d)	34 (c)	35 (c)	36 (b)	37 (c)	38 (b)	39 (b)	40 (c)
41 (a)	42 (a)	43 (a)	44 (a)	45 (d)	46 (c)	47 (b)	48 (a)	49 (b)	50 (b)
51 (c)	52 (a)	53 (b)	54 (c)	55 (a)	56 (d)	57 (a)	58 (c)	59 (b)	60 (c)
61 (a)	62 (a)	63 (c)	64 (a)	65 (c)	66 (d)	67 (b)	68 (d)	69 (d)	70 (c)
71 (a)	72 (c)	73 (a)	74 (c)	75 (d)	76 (a)	77 (b)	78 (b)	79 (c)	80 (d)
81 (d)	82 (b)	83 (c)	84 (b)	85 (d)	86 (a)	87 (d)	88 (a)	89 (b)	90 (d)
91 (a)	92 (a)	93 (b)	94 (d)	95 (d)	96 (a)	97 (c)	98 (a)		

Assertion-Reason

1. (a)	2. (a)	3. (a)	4. (c)	5. (d)	6. (a)	7. (a)	8. (a)	9. (a)	10. (a)

Statement Type

1. (d)	2. (d)	3. (b)	4. (b)	5. (b)	6. (c)	7. (b)	8. (c)	9. (a)	10. (d)

Matching Type

1. (d)	2. (c)	3. (a)	4. (b)	5. (d)

Numerical Value

1. (6)	2. (91)	3. (25)	4. (2)	5. (2)

NCERT Exemplar's

1. (b)	2. (d)	3. (c)	4. (a)	5. (d)	6. (b)	7. (b)	8. (b)	9. (b)	10. (c)
11. (a)	12. (d)	13. (c)							

Past Exams'

1. (b)	2. (a)	3. (c)	4. (d)	5. (d)	6. (d)	7. (a)	8. (a)	9. (a)	10. (a)
11. (c)	12. (d)	13. (a)	14. (c)	15. (c)	16. (16)	17. (c)	18. (a)	19. (b)	20. (d)
21. (b)	22. (c)	23. (a)	24. (d)	25. (c)	26. (a)	27. (b)	28. (c)	29. (b)	30. (c)

Skill Boosters

1. (c)	2. (c)	3. (c)	4. (b)	5. (d)	6. (b)	7. (b)

Step by Step

Decoding the Questions

Concept Builders

1 Low pressure and high voltage

2 Experiment on electrical discharge through gases

3 True

4 nature of the gas

5 greater

6 True

7 charge on the electrons

8 False

9 opposite to

10 Electrostatic forces

11 Radioactivity

12 True

13 False

14 Rutherford

15 tritium ($_1H^3$) or ($_1T^3$)

16 False

17 True

18 James Maxwell

19 True

20 400 nm to 750 nm

21 Temperature

22 True

23 Intensity of light

24 True

25 Emission spectrum

26 Line emission spectra

27 True

28 0.02645 nm and -8.72×10^{-18} J

29 momentum, wavelength

30 False

Topical Solutions

1 (*b*) Electricity is passed through a solution of an electrolyte, chemical reactions occurred at the electrodes which resulted in the liberation and deposition of matter at the electrodes.

2 (*d*)

3 (*a*)

4 (*c*) Statements I, III and IV are correct, while statement II is incorrect. It's correct form is as follows :

These rays themselves are not visible but their behaviour can be observed with the help of certain kind of materials (fluorescent or phosphorescent) which glow when hit by them.

5 (*d*)

6 (*d*) Thomson was able to determine the charge to the mass ratio of cathode rays, which is same as β-rays (electron) by carrying out accurate measurements on the amount of deflections observed by the electrons on the electric field strength or magnetic field strength as,

$$e/m_e = 1.758820 \times 10^{11} \text{C kg}^{-1}$$

7 (*b*) Among the given statements, option (b) is incorrect. The correct form of (b) is :

When only magnetic field is applied, electron strikes the cathode ray tube at point *C*.

8 (*b*) Electrons (*e*) and protons (*p*) have the same charge (1.602×10^{-19} C) but protons are 1840 times heavier than electrons. e/m_e of any particle decreases, if the mass is increased. So, the e/m_e of electron is higher than the proton.

Alpha particle (α) is a helium nucleus which consists of two protons and two electrons. It has +2 charge and the mass of 4 protons. So, the α-particle has the least e/m_e because of its large mass. Neutron (*n*) has no charge thus its e/m_e is zero.

Thus, the increasing order of e/m_e values is $n < \alpha < p < e$.

9 (*a*) In Millikan's oil drop experiment, the electric field is applied to suspend the oil droplets.

By applying an electric field between two plates, one could counteract the force of gravity acting on the droplets, effectively suspending them in mid-air.

10 (*c*) Statement (c) is incorrect.

It's correct form is as follows

The behaviour of these particles in the magnetic or electric field is opposite to that observed for electron or cathode rays.

Rest other statements are correct.

11 (*d*) Statement (d) is incorrect.

It's correct form is as follows

Millikan concluded that the magnitude of electrical charge *q*, on the droplets is always an integral multiple of the electrical charge, *e*, that is, $q = ne$, where, $n = 1,2,3$.

Rest other statements are correct.

12 (*d*) Among the given options, option (d) is incorrect. The correct form of (d) is :

According to Thomson model of an atom, the explanation of overall neutrality of the atom is possible.

13 (*c*) All the given statements are correct about Thomson's model of atom.

14 (*b*) Statement III is incorrect.

It's correct form is as follows

X-rays are not deflected by electric and magnetic fields and have a very high penetrating power through the matter.

Rest other statements are correct.

15 (*b*) Among the given conclusions, option (b) is correct whereas, option (a), (c) and (d) are incorrect. The correct form of (a), (c) and (d) are

(a) Most of the α-particles passed through the gold foil undeflected.

(c) A very few α-particles were bounced back.

(d) Every (~1 in 20000) at α-particles were bounced back.

16 (*a*) Rutherford observed that most of α-particles pass through the gold foil undeflected. It signifies that nucleus occupy much smaller volume as compared to the volume of atom.

17 (*b*) $${}^{A}_{Z}E \xrightarrow{-\alpha} {}^{A-4}_{Z-2}X \xrightarrow{-\beta} {}^{A-4}_{Z-1}Y \xrightarrow{-\beta} {}^{A-4}_{Z}W$$

Both elements *E* and *W* have same atomic number but different mass numbers. Hence, both are isotopes. So, the resulting element will be an isotope of E.

18 (*d*) $^{35}_{17}Cl$ and $^{37}_{17}Cl$ are isotopes, so they will have same chemical properties.

19 (*a*) The number of neutrons in different species is

Mass number (A) = no. of protons (Z) + no. of neutrons (n)

$^{235}_{92}U = 235 = 92 + n \Rightarrow n = 143$

$^{238}_{92}U = 238 = 92 + n \Rightarrow n = 146$

$^{239}_{93}U = 239 = 93 + n \Rightarrow n = 146$

$^{240}_{93}U = 240 = 93 + n \Rightarrow n = 147$

So, $^{235}_{92}U$ has the least no. of neutrons.

20 (*d*) In $^{80}_{35}Br$

Number of protons = Number of electrons = 35 = Atomic number

Number of neutrons = Mass number (A) − Number of proton $= (80 - 35) = 45$

21 (*b*) Mass number of the element = 150

Neutrons = 42% more than protons

Mass (A) is sum of protons and neutrons (N) : $A = P + N$

$$A = P + P + \frac{42P}{100}$$

$$150 = \frac{242P}{100}$$

$$\Rightarrow \quad P = 61.98 \approx 62$$

So, the symbol of atom is $^{150}_{62}Sm$.

22. (*c*) Among the given Statements I and IV are incorrect.

Their correct form are as follows

I. The presence of positive charge on the nucleus is due to the presence of protons in the nucleus.

IV. Protons and neutrons present in the nucleus is collectively known as nucleons.

23 (*c*)

24 (*c*) Rutherford model can explain that the most of the alpha particles passed the foil undeflected, which indicated that most of the space in atom is empty.

25 (*a*)

26 (*b*) Among the given options, option (b) is incorrect. The correct form of (b) is EM waves do not require medium to travel.

27 (*a*) Major developments responsible for the formulation of Bohr's model of atom were dual character of the electromagnetic radiation which means that radiations possess both wave like and particle like properties.

28 (*a*)

29 (*a*) Calculation of wave number $(\bar{\nu})$

$\lambda = 600 \text{ nm} = 6000 \text{ Å} = 6000 \times 10^{-10}$ m

$$\bar{\nu} = \frac{1}{\lambda} = \frac{1}{6000 \times 10^{-10}}$$

$$\bar{\nu} = 1.66 \times 10^{6} \text{ m}^{-1}$$

or $\quad \bar{\nu} = 1.66 \times 10^{4} \text{ cm}^{-1}$

30 (*c*) For the given graph, $T_2 > T_1$.

31 (*a*) A cavity with a tiny hole, that has no other opening, can be considered as a black body. Any ray of light entering the hole would be reflected by the walls of the cavity and ultimately absorbed by it.

32 (*c*) $\frac{E_1}{E_2} = \frac{\lambda_2}{\lambda_1}$

$$\frac{25 \text{ eV}}{50 \text{ eV}} = \frac{\lambda_2}{\lambda_1} \Rightarrow \lambda_1 = 2\lambda_2$$

33 (*d*) The energy of a quantum of radiation is proportional to its frequency is expressd by $E = nh\nu$

34 (*c*) We know that, $\nu = \frac{c}{\lambda}, \lambda = \frac{c}{\nu}$

$$= \frac{3 \times 10^{17}}{6 \times 10^{15}} = 0.5 \times 10^{2} \text{ nm} = 50 \text{ nm}$$

35 (*c*) As we know that,

$$E = nh\nu = n\frac{hc}{\lambda} \Rightarrow n = \frac{E\lambda}{hc} \quad ...(i)$$

$$E = 100 \text{ W (Js}^{-1}) \times 1 \text{ s} = 100 \text{ J}$$

Putting the value in Eq. (i) we get

$$n = \frac{100 \text{ J} \times 560 \times 10^{-9} \text{ m}}{6.626 \times 10^{-34} \text{ Js} \times 3 \times 10^{8} \text{ ms}^{-1}}$$

$$= 2.82 \times 10^{20} \approx 2.8 \times 10^{20}$$

36 (*b*) Energy required for one

$$Cl_2 \text{ molecule} = \frac{242 \times 10^{3}}{N_A} \text{ J}$$

$$\lambda = \frac{hc}{E}$$

$$= \frac{6.626 \times 10^{-34} \times 3 \times 10^{8} \times 6.02 \times 10^{23}}{242 \times 10^{3}}$$

$$= 494 \times 10^{-9} \text{ m} = 494 \text{ nm}$$

37 (*c*) Given, $E_0 = 4.2$ eV

$$= 4.2 \times 1.60 \times 10^{-19} \text{ J}$$

$$= 6.72 \times 10^{-19} \text{ J}$$

We know that, $c = 3 \times 10^{8}$ m/s $\quad [1 \text{ Å} = 10^{-10} \text{ m}]$

$$\because \quad E = h\nu = \frac{hc}{\lambda}$$

$$\therefore \quad E = \frac{6.63 \times 10^{-34} \text{ Js} \times 3 \times 10^{8} \text{ ms}^{-1}}{2000 \times 10^{-10} \text{ m}}$$

$$= 9.94 \times 10^{-19} \text{ J}$$

∴ Kinetic energy of electron emitted

$$= (9.94 - 6.72) \times 10^{-19} \text{ J}$$

$$= 3.22 \times 10^{-19} \text{ J}$$

38 (*b*)

39 (*b*) Work function of metal $(\phi) = h\nu_0$

where, ν_0 = threshold frequency

Also, $\frac{1}{2} m_e v^2 = h\nu - h\nu_0$

or $\quad \frac{1}{2} m_e v^2 = h\nu - \phi = \frac{hc}{\lambda} - \phi \quad ...(i)$

Thus, on substituting all the given values in Eq. (i), we get

$$\frac{1}{2} \times 9 \times 10^{-31} \text{ kg} \times (6 \times 10^{5} \text{ ms}^{-1})^2$$

$$= \frac{6.626 \times 10^{-34} \text{ J s} \times 3 \times 10^{8} \text{ms}^{-1}}{4000 \times 10^{-10} \text{ m}} - \phi$$

$$\therefore \phi = 4.96 \times 10^{-19} \text{ J} - 162 \times 10^{-21} \text{ kgm}^2\text{s}^{-2}$$

$$= 3.34 \times 10^{-19} \text{ J} \quad [1 \text{ kg m}^2\text{s}^{-2} = 1\text{J}]$$

$$= 2.1 \text{ eV}$$

40 (*c*) $\lambda_0 = 380$ nm

$$K_{max} = h(\nu_i - \nu_0)$$

$$= h\left[\frac{c}{\lambda_i} - \frac{c}{\lambda_o}\right] = hc\left[\frac{\lambda_0 - \lambda_i}{(\lambda_0 \lambda_i)}\right]$$

$$= 1237\left[\frac{(380 - 260)}{380 \times 260}\right] = 1.5 \text{ eV}$$

41 (*a*)

42 (*a*) The light emitted by a sample (excited hydrogen atom or any other element), which is passed through a prism and then separated into certain discrete wavelength is called atomic emission spectra.

43 (*a*) According to Rydberg's equation,

$$\frac{1}{\lambda}=\frac{R_H}{hc}\left(\frac{1}{n_1^2}-\frac{1}{n_2^2}\right) \text{ or } \frac{1}{\lambda}\propto\left(\frac{1}{n_1^2}-\frac{1}{n_2^2}\right)$$

For shortest wavelength, i.e. highest energy spectral line, n_2 will be (∞).

The lowest energy state of Lyman series, $n=1$.

The lowest energy state of Paschen series, $n=3$.

For the given spectral series, ratio of the shortest wavelength of two spectral series can be calculated as follows

$$\frac{\lambda_L}{\lambda_P}=\frac{\frac{1}{3^2}-\frac{1}{\infty^2}}{\frac{1}{1^2}-\frac{1}{\infty^2}}=\frac{\frac{1}{9}-0}{1-0}=\frac{1}{9}$$

Thus, Lyman series and Paschen series forms the ratio of about 9.

44 (*a*)

45 (*d*) The electronic transition from $n=2$ to $n=1$ will produce the shortest wavelength in Li^{2+}.

The exact value can be calculated *via* Rydberg formula $\left(\because Z\propto\frac{1}{\lambda}\right)$

More the atomic number, the shortest will be the wavelength. The atomic number of lithium is 3 and is the highest of all. So, it will have the shortest wavelength.

46 (*c*) The spectral line (ii), (iv) and (v) in spectrum is of same order of frequency, i.e. of 10^{16} Hz.

47 (*b*) Among the given statements, statement (b) is incorrectly described. The correct form is electron will move from a lower stationary state to a higher stationary state when required amount of energy is absorbed.

48 (*a*) 49 (*b*)

50 (*b*) According to Bohr model, radius of orbit $r_n=\frac{a_0\times n^2}{Z}$

For, Li^{2+}, $Z=3$ and $n=2$

$$\therefore \quad r=\frac{2^2\times a_0}{3}=\frac{4a_0}{3}$$

51 (*c*) The radius of the stationary states are expressed as, $r_n=n^2a_0$

$$n=3,\ a_0=52.9 \text{ pm}$$
$$r_3=(3)^2\times 52.9 \ [r_3=476.1 \text{ pm}]$$

$\because$ Hence, the radius of the 3rd stationary state is 476.1 pm.

52 (*a*) Given, $E=-2.178\times 10^{18}\left[\frac{Z^2}{n^2}\right]$ J

For hydrogen, $Z=1$

So, $E_1=-2.178\times 10^{-18}\text{ J}\left[\frac{1}{1^2}\right]$

$$E_2=-2.178\times 10^{-18}\text{ J}\left[\frac{1}{2^2}\right]$$

Now, E_2-E_1
$$=\Delta E=2.178\times 10^{-18}\left(\frac{1}{1^2}-\frac{1}{2^2}\right)=\frac{hc}{\lambda}$$

i.e. $2.178\times 10^{-18}\left(\frac{1}{1^2}-\frac{1}{2^2}\right)$
$$=\frac{6.62\times 10^{-34}\times 3.0\times 10^8}{\lambda}$$
$$\therefore \quad \lambda\approx 1216\times 10^{-7}\text{ m}$$

53 (*b*) Ionisation enthalpy of hydrogen atom is 1.312×10^6 J mol^{-1}. It suggests that the energy of electron in the ground state (first orbit) is -1.312×10^6 J mol^{-1}.

$$\Delta E=E_2-E_1$$
$$=\left(\frac{-1.312\times 10^6}{2^2}\right)-\left(\frac{-1.312\times 10^6}{1}\right)$$
$$=9.84\times 10^5 \text{ J mol}^{-1}$$

54 (*c*) According to Bohr's model,

$$\Rightarrow \quad \text{KE}=\frac{1}{2}mv^2=\frac{n^2h^2}{8\pi^2r^2m} \quad \text{...(i)}$$

Also, Bohr's radius for H-atom is,
$$r=n^2a_0$$

On substituting '*r*' in Eq. (i), we get

$$\text{KE}=\frac{h^2}{8\pi^2n^2a_0^2m}$$

when, $n=2$, $\text{KE}=\frac{h^2}{32\pi^2a_0^2m}$

55 (*a*)

56 (*d*) Bohr radius $(r_n)=n^2\frac{a_0}{Z}$

Radius of *n*th Bohr orbit for H-atom $=0.53\,n^2$ Å [$Z=1$ for H-atom]

$\therefore$ Radius of 2nd Bohr orbit for H-atom $=0.53\times(2)^2=2.12$ Å

57 (*a*) Energy of electron in H-atom is determined by the expression :

$$E_n=-\frac{13.6}{n^2}\text{eV}$$

In excited states, $E_2=-\frac{13.6}{4}=-3.4$ eV

58 (*c*)

59 (*b*) Frequency of first line in Balmer series can be calculated as

$$\nu=3.29\times 10^{15}\left[\frac{1}{n_1^2}-\frac{1}{n_2^2}\right]\text{s}^{-1}$$
$$=3.29\times 10^{15}\left[\frac{1}{(2)^2}-\frac{1}{(3)^2}\right]\text{s}^{-1}$$
$$=4.57\times 10^{14}\text{s}^{-1}$$

60 (*c*) According to Rydberg's formula,

wave number $(\bar{\nu})=R_HZ^2\left[\frac{1}{n_i^2}-\frac{1}{n_f^2}\right]$

Given, $n_i=n$, $n_f=8$

[$\because$ it is the case of emission]

$$\bar{\nu}=R_H\times(1)^2\left[\frac{1}{n^2}-\frac{1}{8^2}\right]=\frac{R_H}{n^2}-\frac{R_H}{64}$$

On comparing with equation of straight line, $y=mx+C$

We get, slope $=R_H$

intercept $=\frac{-R_H}{64}$

Thus, plot of wave number $(\bar{\nu})$ against $\frac{1}{n^2}$ will be linear with slope $(+R_H)$.

61 (*a*) The energy associated with Bohr's orbit is, $E=\frac{-2.18\times 10^{-18}\text{ J}\times Z^2}{n^2}$

62 (*a*) In the emission spectra of hydrogen atom, Bracket series is the one where the transition from higher energy states to fourth energy state takes place. i.e. $n_1=4$ and $n_2\geq 5$.

63 (c) From the Rydberg formula

$$\frac{1}{\lambda} = R_H\left(\frac{1}{n_1^2} - \frac{1}{n_2^2}\right)$$

$$\frac{1}{\lambda} = R\left(\frac{1}{2^2} - \frac{1}{5^2}\right) = R\left(\frac{25-4}{100}\right)$$

$$\Rightarrow \quad \lambda = 434 \times 10^{-9} = 434 \text{ nm}$$

So, the 434 nm wavelength is in the blue region of the visible spectrum.

64 (a) **65** (c) **66** (d)

67 (b) According to de-Broglie equation,

$$\lambda = \frac{h}{mv} = \frac{6.6 \times 10^{-27}}{300 \times 2 \times 10^4} = 1.1 \times 10^{-33} \text{ cm}$$

68 (d) The de-Broglie wavelength (λ) of a particle is given by the equation

$$\lambda = \frac{h}{mv} \Rightarrow m = \frac{h}{\lambda v}$$

On, substituting the values

$$x = \frac{6.626 \times 10^{-34}}{6.62 \times 10^{-35} \times 100} = 0.1 \text{ kg}$$

69. (d)

70 (c) Velocity of photon = Velocity of light

$$m = \frac{h}{\lambda v} = \frac{6.626 \times 10^{-34} \text{ Js}}{(3.6 \times 10^{-10} \text{ m})(3 \times 10^8 \text{ ms}^{-1})}$$

$$= 6.135 \times 10^{-33} \text{ kg}$$

71 (a)

72 (c) By Heisenberg's uncertainty principle,

$$\Delta x \cdot m\Delta v = \frac{h}{4\pi}$$

$$\Delta v = 0.005\% \text{ of } 600 \text{ m/s}$$

$$= \frac{600 \times 0.005}{100} = 0.03 \text{ m/s}$$

$$\Delta x \times 9.1 \times 10^{-31} \times 0.03 = \frac{6.6 \times 10^{-34}}{4 \times 3.14}$$

$$\text{Hence, } \Delta x = \frac{6.6 \times 10^{-34}}{4 \times 3.14 \times 0.03 \times 9.1 \times 10^{-31}}$$

$$= 1.92 \times 10^{-3} \text{ m}$$

73 (a) According to question,

$$\Delta x_A \times m \times 0.05 = \frac{h}{4\pi} \quad \text{...(i)}$$

$$\Delta x_B \times 5m \times 0.02 = \frac{h}{4\pi} \quad \text{...(ii)}$$

Divide Eq. (i) by Eq. (ii), then

$$\frac{\Delta x_A \times m \times 0.05}{\Delta x_B \times 5m \times 0.02} = 1$$

$$\Rightarrow \quad \frac{\Delta x_A}{\Delta x_B} = \frac{5m \times 0.02}{m \times 0.05} = 2$$

74 (c) $\Delta x \cdot \Delta v \geq \frac{h}{4\pi m}$

$$\Delta x = \frac{6.63 \times 10^{-34}}{4 \times 3.14 \times 9.1 \times 10^{-31} \times 300 \times 0.001 \times 10^{-2}}$$

$$= 0.01933 = 1.93 \times 10^{-2} \text{ m}$$

75 (d) As we know that,

$$\lambda = \frac{h}{mv} = \frac{h}{\sqrt{2m\text{KE}}}$$

$$\because \quad \lambda \propto \frac{1}{\sqrt{m}}$$

Mass of e, α and p are $m_e < m_p < m_\alpha$.

The correct order is $E_A < E_C < E_B$.

76 (a)

77 (b) Uncertainty in speed = Accuracy in measuring speed × Given speed

$\Delta v = 0.05 \times 30$ m/s $= 1.5$ m/s

By using Heisenberg's equation

$$= \Delta x \cdot \Delta p \geq \frac{h}{4\pi}$$

$$\Rightarrow \Delta x \cdot m\Delta v \geq \frac{h}{4\pi}$$

$$= \Delta x \cdot 1000 \times 1.5 \geq \frac{h}{4\pi}$$

$$\Rightarrow \quad \Delta x \geq \frac{6.626 \times 10^{-34}}{3.14 \times 4 \times 1500}$$

$$\Delta x \geq 3.51 \times 10^{-38}$$

$$\Delta x = 3.51 \times 10^{-38} \text{ m}$$

So, uncertainty in speed = 1.5 m/s

Uncertainty in position = 3.51×10^{-38} m

78 (b) **79** (c)

80 (d) All the given statements are correct except V.

The correct statement of V is Wave function is denoted by ψ.

81 (d) Spin quantum number describes the spin of electron in particular orbital.

Orientations of electron cloud is specified of a magnetic quantum number.

82 (b) Electronic configuration of Fe^{2+} is [Ar] $3d^6 4s^0$

∴ Number of d-electrons = 6

$Cl = 1s^2 2s^2 2p^6 3s^2 3p^5$ (11 p-electrons)

It does not match with the 6 d-electrons of Fe^{2+}.

Hence, Cl has 11p-electrons which does not matches in number with 6d-electrons of Fe^{2+}.

83 (c)

84 (b) Statements I and IV are correct, while the other statements are incorrect.

Corrected forms are as follow

II. The principal quantum number determines the size and to large extent the energy of the orbital.

III. The magnetic quantum number gives information about the spatial orientation of the orbital with respect to standard set of coordinate axis.

85. (d) Statements III and IV are correct, while the other statements are incorrect.

Their corrected forms are as follow

I. The shape of the orbitals are given by azimuthal quantum number.

II. In an atom, all electrons travel with the different velocity.

86 (a) Given, atomic number of Rb, $Z = 37$.

Thus, its electronic configuration is [Kr] $5s^1$. Since, the last electron or valence electron enter in 5s-subshell.

So, the quantum numbers are $n = 5$, $l = 0$, (for s-orbital) $m = 0 (\because m = +l \text{ to } -l)$, $s = +1/2$ or $-1/2$.

87 (d) The graphs between $|\psi|^2$ and r are radial density plots having $(n - l - 1)$ number of radial nodes.

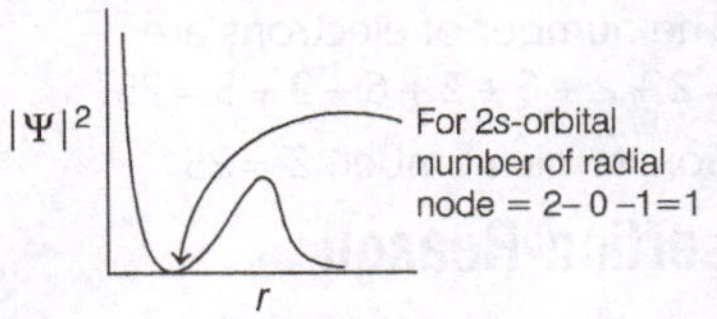

Thus, the given graph between $|\psi|^2$ and r represents 2s-orbital.

88 (*a*) Number of orbitals associated with $n = 5$ is $n^2 = 25$.

89 (*b*) Among the given option, (b) represents the correct *d*-orbitals. i.e. I-d_{xy}, II-d_{xz}, III-d_{yz}

90 (*d*) Degenerate orbitals mean the orbitals of the same subshell of the same shell, i.e. their *n* and *l* values should be same for both the given sets.

Thus, (d) represents pair of degenerate orbitals.

91 (*a*) The energy of the orbitals in hydrogen atom increases as follows

$$1s < 2s = 2p < 3s = 3p = 3d < 4s = 4p = 4d = 4f$$

92. (*a*) Statements I, II and III are correct but IV is incorrect. It's correct form is the net positive charge experienced by the other electrons is known as effective nuclear charge (Z_{eff}).

93 (*b*) The correct representation should be $1s^2 2s^2 2p^6 3s^2 3p^6 3d^{10} 4s^1$ for the copper which has atomic number 29. Due to extra stability of fully-filled orbital of *d*-subshell, the last electron enters into *d*-orbital instead of *s*-orbital.

94 (*d*) **95** (*d*)

96 (*a*) With the saturation of 3*d*-orbitals, the filling up of the 4*p*-orbitals starts at Ga and is completed at Kr.

97 (*c*)

Symbols	=	*K*	*L*	*M*	*N*
$_{19}X$	=	2	8	8	1
$_{21}Y$	=	2	8	9	2
$_{25}Z$	=	2	8	13	2

Hence, the order of number of electrons in *M*-shell is $Z > Y > X$.

98 (*a*) The complete electronic configuration will become $1s^2, 2s^2, 2p^6, 3s^2, 3d^6, 4s^2 3d^5$.

The number of electrons are $= 2 + 2 + 6 + 2 + 6 + 2 + 5 = 25$

So, atomic number, $Z = 25$.

Assertion-Reason

1 (*a*) Both A and R are true and R is the correct explanation of A.

2 (*a*) Both A and R are true and R is the correct explanation of A.

3 (*a*) Both A and R are true and R is the correct explanation of A.

4 (*c*) A is true but R is false.

The correct form of R is :

Frequency of emitted radiation goes from lower frequency to higher frequency as the temperature increases.
The red colour lies in the lower frequency while blue colour belongs to the higher frequency region of electromagnetic spectrum.

5 (*d*) A is false but R is true.

The correct form of A is :

Kinetic energy of the ejected electron is proportional to the frequency of the electromagnetic radiation.

∴ Greater the energy possessed by the photon, greater will be transfer of energy to the electron and greater the kinetic energy of the ejected electron.

6 (*a*) Both A and R are true and R is the correct explanation of A.

7 (*a*) Both A and R are true and R is the correct explanation of A.

8 (*a*) Both A and R are true and R is the correct explanation of A.

9 (*a*) Both A and R are true and R is the correct explanation of A.

10 (*a*) Both A and R are true and R is the correct explanation of A.

Statement Type

1 (*d*) Both the Statements I and II are true.

2 (*d*) Both Statement I and Statement II is true.
Energies of the orbitals in hydrogen or hydrogen like species depend only on the quantum number '*n*'. Energies of the orbitals in multielectron atoms depend on quantum numbers '*n*' and '*l*', i.e. more than 1 quantum number.

3 (*b*) Statement I is true but Statement II is false. If probability density $|\psi|^2$ is constant on a given surface, ψ is constant over the surface. The boundary surface for ψ^2 and ψ are identical.

4 (*b*) Statement I is true but Statement II is false.
No. of radial nodes $= (n - l - 1)]$
No. of angular nodes $(l) = 2$
Total no. of node, $n - 1$.
So, $3d_{xy}$ has $3 - 2 - 1 = 0$ radial node.

5 (*b*) Statement I is true but Statement II is false.

The correct form of Statement II is :
Electrons with the same principle quantum number (*n*) but different azimuthal quantum numbers (*l*) experience different effective nuclear charges within an atom.

6 (*c*) Statement I is false but Statement II is true.

The correct form of Statement I is :

The two configurations are different

$$Fe^{2+} = [Ar]\,3d^6$$
$$Cr = [Ar]\,4s^1 3d^5$$

7 (*b*) Among the given statements II, III, IV and V are correct, while the statement I is incorrect. It's correct form is as follows

The speed of light depends upon the nature of the medium through which it passes.

8 (*c*) Statements, III, IV and V are correct while Statements I and II are incorrect.

Their correct form are as follows

I. Angular quantum number signifies the shape of the orbital.

II. Total number of nodes for 3*s*-orbital is two.

9 (*a*) I is incorrect. Their correct form are as follows

I. In caesium, the electrons are most loosely held on the surface of the atom due to very small ionisation energy.

10 (*d*) Statement II is incorrect.
It's correct form is as follows
In case of absorption spectrum, $n_f > n_i$ and in case of emission spectrum $n_i > n_f$.
Rest other statements are correct.

Matching Type

1 (*d*) The correct match is
A-3, B-1, C-2.

2 (*c*) The correct match is
A-2, B-1, C-4, D-3.

3 (*a*) The correct match is
A-5, B-6, C-3, D-4, E-1, F-2.

4 (*b*) The correct match is
A-3, B-1, C-2, D-4.

5 (*d*) The correct match is
A-4, B-3, C-1, D-2.

Numerical Value

1 (6) Energy of electron in n^{th} orbital
$$= -13.6 \times \frac{Z^2}{n^2} \text{ eV}$$
For 2nd excited state of He^+, $n = 3$
$$\therefore E_3(He^+) = -13.6 \times \frac{2^2}{3^2} \text{ eV}$$
$$= -6.04 \text{ V} \approx -6$$

2 (91) $\frac{1}{\lambda} = R_H \left[\frac{1}{n_1^2} - \frac{1}{n_2^2}\right]$
$$= 1.097 \times 10^7 \left[\frac{1}{1^2} - \frac{1}{\infty^2}\right]$$
$$\lambda = 0.91 \times 10^{-7} = 91 \text{ nm}$$

3 (25) Number of orbitals can be calculated by using the formula $= n^2 = (5)^2 = 25$

4 (2) Number of radial nodes in an orbital is given as $n - l - 1$.
$6p : n = 6, l = 1 \Rightarrow 6 - 1 - 1 = 4$
$7s : n = 7, l = 0 \Rightarrow 7 - 0 - 1 = 6$
$7p : n = 7, l = 1 \Rightarrow 7 - 1 - 1 = 5$
$8p : n = 8, l = 1 \Rightarrow 8 - 1 - 1 = 6$
$8d : n = 8, l = 2 \Rightarrow 8 - 2 - 1 = 5$

5 (2) For 5*d*-orbital the value of $n = 5$ and $l = 2$
So, angular nodes $= l = 2$
radial nodes $= n - l - 1$
$$= 5 - 2 - 1 = 2$$

NCERT Exemplar's

1 (*b*) Statement (b) is incorrect. It's correct form is as follows
The mass of electron is not equal to the mass of neutron. It is much less than that of neutron.
Rest other statements are correct.

2 (*d*) Statement (d) is incorrect. It's correct form is as follows
Cathode rays do not depend upon the nature of gas present in the cathode rays tube.
Rest other statements are correct.

3 (*c*) Rutherford's model does not provide any idea about the movement of electrons in a circular path of fixed energy called orbits.

4 (*a*)

5 (*d*) Isobars have the same mass number (i.e. sum of protons and neutrons) but different atomic number (i.e. number of protons). e.g. $_{18}Ar^{40}$ and $_{19}K^{40}$ are isobars.

$_{18}Ar^{40}$	$_{19}K^{40}$
Atomic number = 18	Atomic number = 19
Mass number = 40	Mass number = 40

6 (*b*) 7 (*b*)

8 (*b*) Correct configuration should be $1s^2\ 2s^2\ 2p^6\ 3s^2\ 3p^6\ 3d^{10}\ 4s^1$ for the copper which has atomic number 29 ($_{29}Cu$).
Due to extra stability of full filled orbital of *d*-subshell, the last electron enter into *d*-orbital instead of *s*-orbital.

9 (*b*) $_{24}Cr$ = [Ar]$3d^5, 4s^1$; $_{24}Cr^{3+}$ = [Ar]$3d^3$
$_{26}Fe$ = [Ar]$3d^6, 4s^2$; $_{26}Fe^{3+}$ = [Ar]$3d^5$
$_{25}Mn$ = [Ar]$3d^5, 4s^2$; $_{25}Mn^{2+}$ = [Ar]$3d^5$
$_{27}Co$ = [Ar]$3d^7, 4s^2$; $_{27}Co^{3+}$ = [Ar]$3d^6$
$_{21}Sc$ = [Ar]$3d^1, 4s^2$; $_{21}Sc^{3+}$ = [Ar]
Thus, Fe^{3+} and Mn^{2+} have the same electronic configuration.

10 (*c*) Total number of orbitals associated with n^{th} shell $= n^2$
$\therefore$ Total number of orbitals associated with third shell $= (3)^2 = 9$

11 (*a*) Orbital angular momentum,
$$mvr = \frac{h}{2\pi}\sqrt{l(l+1)}.$$
Hence, it depends only on 'l'. l can have values ranging from 0 to $(n-1)$.

12 (*d*) For an atom there are $n - l - 1$ radial nodes and $(n-1)$ total nodes.
Number of radial nodes for 3*p*-orbital
$$= n - l - 1 = 3 - 1 - 1 = 1$$

13 (*c*) Number of angular nodes $= l$
For 4th orbital $n = 4$ and $l = 2$ for *d*-orbital.
$\therefore$ Number of angular nodes $= 2$

Past Exams'

1 (*b*) The correct match is
A-III, B-IV, C-I, D-II.

2 (*a*) $E \propto \frac{Z^2}{n^2} \Rightarrow \frac{E_1}{E_2} = \frac{Z_1^2}{n_1^2} \times \frac{n_2^2}{Z_2^2}$
$He^+ \longrightarrow n_1 = 1$ and $Z_1 = 2$
$Be^{3+} \longrightarrow n_2 = 2$ and $Z_2 = 4$
$$\frac{E_1}{E_2} = \frac{2^2}{1^2} \times \frac{2^2}{4^2} = 1 \Rightarrow E_1 = E_2$$
Hence, it will be same as $-x$J for Be^{3+} ion.

3 (*c*) Among the given statements II, III and V are correct while remaining are incorrect. The correct form of I and IV are as follows
I. Atoms of all elements are composed of three fundamental particles, i.e. electrons, protons and neutrons.
IV. Protons and neutrons are collectively known as nucleons.

4 (*d*) We know that, $n_m = 2l + 1$.
$$\therefore \quad 2l = n_m - 1 \text{ and } l = \frac{n_m - 1}{2}$$

5 (*d*) According to Bohr's atomic model
$$r \propto \frac{n^2}{Z}$$
For 2nd orbit of He^+, $n_2 = 2$
$$Z_2 = 2$$

For 3rd orbit of Li^{2+}, $n_1 = 3$

$Z_1 = 3$

From the above equation,

$$\frac{(r_3)_{Li^{2+}}}{(r_2)_{He^+}} = \frac{n_1^2 \times Z_2}{n_2^2 \times Z_1}$$

$$\frac{(r_3)_{Li^{2+}}}{105.8 \text{ pm}} = \frac{3 \times 3 \times 2}{2 \times 2 \times 3}$$

$$= 158.7 \text{ pm}$$

Hence, the radius of third Bohr orbit of Li^{2+} ion is 158.7 pm.

6 (*d*) The shapes of d_{xy}, d_{xz}, d_{yz} and $d_{x^2-y^2}$ are similar to each-other, while that of d_{z^2} is different from others. All five 3*d*-orbitals are equivalent in energy. The *d*-orbitals for which *n* is greater than 3 (4*d*, 5*d*, ...) also have shapes similar to 3*d*-orbital but differ in energy and size.

7 (*a*) Frequency of electromagnetic radiation

$$\nu = 1368 \text{ kHz} = 1368 \times 10^3 \text{ s}^{-1}$$

Speed of light, $c = 3 \times 10^8 \text{ ms}^{-1}$

Wavelength of electromagnetic radiation, $\lambda = \frac{c}{\nu} = \frac{3 \times 10^8 \text{ ms}^{-1}}{1368 \times 10^3 \text{ s}^{-1}}$

$$= 219.3 \text{ m}$$

8 (*a*) The species having same number of electrons are among the given pairs of ions, Fe^{2+} and Mn^{2+} are not isoelectronic as Fe^{2+} contains 24 electrons and Mn^{2+} contains 23.

9 (*a*) In $^{175}_{71}Lu$, number of electrons = Number of protons = Atomic number = 71

and No. of neutrons = Mass number − Atomic number = 175 − 71 = 104

10 (*a*) For 3 *s*-orbital, $n = 3, l = 0$

Number of radial nodes $= (n - l - 1) = 3 - 0 - 1 = 2$

Number of angular nodes $= l = 0$.

11 (*c*)

Series		**Region**
Lyman series	:	UV region
Balmer series	:	Visible region
Paschen series	:	IR region
Brackett series	:	IR region

12 (*d*) The order of energy of orbitals can be calculated from $(n + l)$ rule. The lower the value of $(n + l)$ for an orbital, lower is its energy. If two orbitals have same $(n + l)$ value, the orbital with lower value of *n* has the lower energy.

(i) $6p = n + l = 6 + 1 = 7$

(ii) $5f = 5 + 3 = 8$

(iii) $4d = 4 + 2 = 6$

(iv) $5p = 5 + 1 = 6$

∴ The order of decreasing energy will be $5f > 6p > 5p > 4d$.

13 (*a*) According to Hund's rule "the pairing of electrons in the orbitals of a particular subshell does not takes place until all the orbitals of a subshell are singly occupied. Moreover, the singly orbitals must have the electrons with parallel spin.

i.e. $1s^2$ [↑↓] $2s^2$ [↑↓] $2p_x^1 2p_y^1 2p_z^1$ [↑|↑|↑]

or

$1s^2$ [↑↓] $2s^2$ [↑↓] $2p_x^1 2p_y^1 2p_z^1$ [↓|↓|↓]

Hence, option (a) is the incorrect option.

14 (*c*) In case of hydrogen like atoms, energy depends on the principal quantum number, i.e. '*n*' only. Hence, 2*s*-orbital will have energy equal to 2*p*-orbital.

15 (*c*) Two electrons occupying the same orbital has equal spin but the directions of their spin are opposite.

Hence, spin quantum number, *s*, (represented +1/2 and −1/2) distinguishes them.

16 (16) Given, $n = 4, s = +\frac{1}{2}$

For $n = 4$ we have 4*s*, 4*p*, 4*d*, 4*f* subshell.

The total electrons are

$4s = 2$ electrons → (Total e^- with $+\frac{1}{2}$ spin = 1)

$4p = 6$ electrons → (Total e^- with $+\frac{1}{2}$ spin = 3)

$4d = 10$ electrons → (Total e^- with $+\frac{1}{2}$ spin = 5)

$4f = 14$ electrons → (Total e^- with $+\frac{1}{2}$ spin = 7)

Therefore, total number of electrons with $+\frac{1}{2}$ spin $= 1 + 3 + 5 + 7 = 16$

17 (*c*) Electronic configuration of potassium is

$$_{19}K = 1s^2 2s^2 2p^6 3s^2 3p^6 4s^1$$

Outermost orbital of K is 4*s* orbital.

For 4*s*, *n* = Principal quantum number orbital = 4

l = Azimuthal quantum number = 0

m_l = Magnetic quantum number = 0

s = Spin quantum number $= \pm\frac{1}{2}$

Hence, option (c) is correct.

18 (*a*) Number of radial nodes is given by $n - l - 1$

For 3*p*-orbital, the value of $n = 3, l = 1$

So, number of radial nodes $= 3 - 1 - 1 = 1$

19 (*b*) The correct match is A-II, B-IV, C-III, D-I.

A. Lyman series lies in UV region.

B. Balmer series lies in visible region.

C. Paschen and Pfund series lies infrared region.

20 (*d*) Both Statement I and Statement II are correct.

21 (*b*) Energy of hydrogen atom can be given as

$$E_1 = -2.18 \times 10^{-18} \text{ J / atom} \quad ...(i)$$

For 3rd orbit, $(n = 3)$ $(Z = 1)$

$$E_3 = -2.18 \times 10^{-18} \left[\frac{(1)^2}{(3)^2}\right]$$

$$= -2.18 \times 10^{-18} \left[\frac{1}{9}\right] \quad ...(ii)$$

Hence, the energy in the 3rd Bohr orbit is (1/9th) of the energy of electron in the first Bohr orbit.

22 (c) As we know,

$$\lambda = \frac{h}{mv} = \frac{2\pi r}{n}$$

de-Broglie wavelength of electron in 3rd orbit,

$$\lambda_3 = \frac{2\pi r_3}{n} \quad \text{...(i)}$$

Also radius of 3rd orbit, r_3 = radius of 1st orbit $\times n^2$

$$r_3 = a_0 \times n^2$$

$$\frac{r_3}{n} = a_0 \times n \quad \text{...(ii)}$$

From Eqs. (i) and (ii) $\lambda_3 = 2\pi a_0 \times n$

for 3rd orbit, $n = 3$

$$\therefore \quad \lambda_3 = 6\pi a_0$$

23 (a) A is true but R is false. Correct form is R is :

Emission of electron from metal surface take place only, when the photon with energy greater than threshold frequency strikes the metal surface. The ejected electrons leave with a specific amount of kinetic energy at a frequency $\nu > \nu_0$.

24 (d) The orbital with greater value of $n + l$ value will have higher energy.

$$\begin{matrix} n=3 & & n=4 & & n=3 & & n=3 \\ l=2 & > & l=0 & > & l=1 & > & l=0 \end{matrix}$$

$$\begin{matrix} n+l \to 5 & & 4 & & 4 & & 3 \\ D & > & B & > & C & > & A \end{matrix}$$

25 (c) For minimum kinetic energy

$$E = E_0 = h\nu_0$$
$$= 6.6 \times 10^{-34} \times 1.3 \times 10^{15}$$
$$= 8.58 \times 10^{-19} \text{ J}$$

26 (a) Both A and R are true and R is the correct explanation A.

27 (b) Radius of nth Bohr's orbit of hydrogen atom is given as

$$r = 0.529 \times \frac{n^2}{Z} \text{ Å} \quad (Z = 1 \text{ for hydrogen})$$

So, for 3rd Bohr's orbit

$$r_3 = 0.529 \times \frac{(3)^2}{1} = 0.529 \times 9 \quad \text{...(i)}$$

For 4th Bohr's orbit ($n = 4$)

$$r_4 = 0.529 \times \frac{(4)^2}{1}$$

$$r_4 = 0.529 \times 16 \quad \text{...(ii)}$$

From Eqs. (i) and (ii),

$$\frac{r_4}{r_3} = \frac{0.529 \times 16}{0.529 \times 9} = \frac{16}{9} \Rightarrow r_4 = \frac{16}{9} r_3$$

28 (c) Statements I, III and IV are correct while Statements II and V are incorrect.

II. Azimuthal quantum number 'l' can have values from 0 to $(n-1)$ for a given 'n'. It describes the subshell and orbital angular momentum.

V. For any value of 'l', total number of orbitals are given by $(2l+1)$ formula. So, for $l = 5$.

Total number of orbitals

$$= 2l + 1 = 2 \times 5 + 1 = 11$$

29 (b) The point at which the probability of finding an electron is zero is known as node or nodal surface. Number of nodes in any orbital $= n - l - 1$

In case of $2s$-orbital, number of nodes $= 2 - 0 - 1 = 1$

The correct plot for $\psi^2(r)$ as function of distance 'r'.

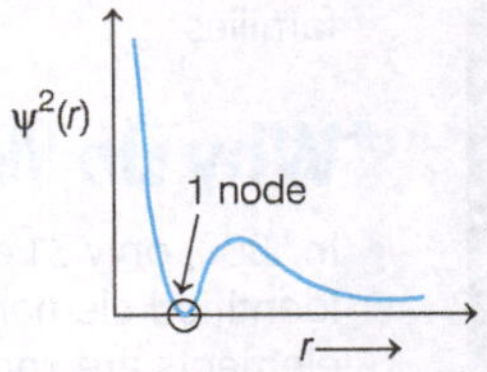

30 (c) Both Statement I and Statement II are true.

Skill Boosters

1 (c) According to de-Broglie's equation, $\lambda = \frac{h}{mv}$, i.e. $\lambda \propto \frac{1}{m}$ the mass of the car is very large and its wavelength (λ) or wave nature is negligible. Therefore, we do not see a car moving like a wave.

2 (c) Angular momentum

$$= mvr = \frac{nh}{2\pi}; \; v = \frac{nh}{2\pi mr}$$

$$T = \frac{2\pi r}{v} = \frac{2\pi r}{\frac{nh}{2\pi mr}} = \frac{4\pi^2 mr^2}{nh}$$

From Bohr's theory,

$$v = 2.18 \times 10^6 \times \frac{Z}{n} \text{ m/s}$$

$$\Rightarrow \quad = 2.18 \times 10^6 \text{ m/s}$$

3 (c) According to de-Broglie relation of wavelength with mass and velocity.

$$\lambda = \frac{h}{mv} = \frac{6.6 \times 10^{-34}}{60 \times 10^{-3} \times 10}$$

$$= 1.1 \times 10^{-33} \approx 10^{-33} \text{m}$$

4 (b) An ideal body, which emits and absorbs radiations of all frequencies uniformly is called a black body and the radiation emitted by such a body is called black body radiation.

In body B, the energy absorbed from its surroundings is the same amount of energy it radiates per unit area, which is a characteristics of a black body.

Hence, body B is a black body.

5 (d) α-particles pass through the gold foil deflected by small angles with reduced speed because it carries positive charge which due to repulsion from protons deflected by smaller angle.

6 (b) Energy of hydrogen atom

$$= -13.6 \text{ eV}$$

Energy of $He^+ = -3.4$ eV, $Z = 2$

$$-3.4 = \frac{-13.6 \times Z^2}{n^2} \text{ eV}$$

$$\Rightarrow \quad n = \sqrt{\frac{13.6 \times 4}{3.4}} = 4$$

Azimuthal quantum number $(l) = 2$ so, the subshell is d.

So, it belong to 4d state.

7 (b) It is given that S_1 is spherically symmetrical state, so it related to s-orbital.

Because it also has 1 radial node so,

$n - l - 1$ = Radial nodes

$$\Rightarrow n - 0 - 1 = 1 \Rightarrow n = 2$$

i.e. $S_1 = 2s$

If a state has 1 radial node and energy equal to hydrogen ground state energy. This condition is possible only when orbital is $3p$.

03

Scan for Chemistry Through Concept Master Videos

Classification of Elements and Periodicity in Properties

Topicwise No. of Ques asked in 5 Years (NEET)

Topics	No. of Questions				
	2024	2023	2022	2021	2020
Why do we Need to Classify Elements, Genesis of Periodic Classification	–	–	–	–	–
Modern Periodic Law and Present Form of Periodic Table	–	1	–	–	–
Nomenclature of Elements with Atomic Number > 100	–	–	1	–	1
Electronic Configurations of Elements and the Periodic Table	–	–	–	–	1
Electronic Configurations and Types of Elements: *s*-, *p*-, *d*-, *f*-Block	–	–	–	–	–
Periodic Trends in Properties of Elements	2	1	1	1	2

Special Type of Ques asked in 5 Years

Types	Years				
	2024	2023	2022	2021	2020
A-R	–	–	–	–	–
Statement Based	–	–	–	–	–
Matching	–	–	–	–	3

Last 5 Years Weightage (NEET)

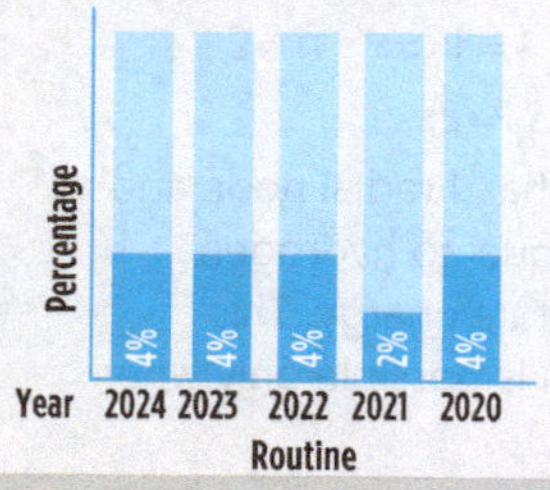

- Periodic table is most important concept in chemistry, both in principle and in practice.
- The foundation of classification or periodic table is a great achievement for the chemists to explore deeper into the subject.
- Periodic table is a remarkable demonstration of the fact that the chemical elements are well organised and lie together in families.

*Why Do We Need to Classify Elements?

- In 1800, only 31 elements were known. By 1865, the number of identified elements had more than doubled to 63. At present, 118 elements are known and some of them are man-made.
- With such a large number of elements it is difficult to study individually the chemistry of all these elements and their innumerable compounds individually. To ease out this problem, scientists searched for a systematic way to organise their knowledge by classifying the elements in the tabular form.
- This classification gives rise to a table, which is known as periodic table in which the elements with similar properties are grouped together.

Genesis of Periodic Classification

- **Dobereiner's triads** (1829) The German chemist Johann Dobereiner mentioned a similarity among the physical and chemical properties of several groups of three elements and called them as **triads**.
- In each triads of the elements, the atomic weight of the middle one is about half (or arithmetic mean) of the atomic weights of the other two.

Dobereiner's Triads

S.No.	Elements	Atomic wt.	Average atomic wt. of I and III elements
1.	I. Lithium (Li)	7	$\frac{7+39}{2}=23$
	II. Sodium (Na)	23	
	III. Potassium (K)	39	
2.	I. Calcium (Ca)	40	$\frac{40+137}{2}=88.5$
	II. Strontium (Sr)	88	
	III. Barium (Ba)	137	
3.	I. Chlorine (Cl)	35.5	$\frac{35.5+127}{2}=81.25$
	II. Bromine (Br)	80	
	III. Iodine (I)	127	

Newlands' law of octaves (1865) The English chemist John Alexander Newlands' arranged the elements in increasing order of their atomic weights and notice that every eighth element have properties similar to the first element, like the eighth note of musical scale.

A few octaves based on the Newlands' generalisation are tabulated below.

Musical note	Sa	Re	Ga	Ma	Pa	Dha	Ne
First row	Li	Be	B	C	N	O	F
At. wt.	7	9	11	12	14	16	19
Second row	Na	Mg	Al	Si	P	S	Cl
At. wt.	23	24	27	29	31	32	35.5
Third row	K	Ca					
At. wt.	39	40					

Note This law is true only for elements upto Ca.

Lothar Meyer's atomic volume curve (1869) He plotted a graph between the physical properties (i.e. atomic volume, melting point and boiling point) against atomic weight. He obtained that elements with similar properties occupied the similar positions on the graph.

Marks Maximizer

- In the curve, top position were occupied by most electropositive alkali metals or elements of group IA, i.e. Li, Na, K, Rb, Cs etc.
- The ascending portions of the curve were occupied by most electronegative elements, i.e. F, Cl, Br, I.
- The transition elements occupy minima of the curve.

- **Mendeleev's periodic law** (1869) It states that, "the physical and chemical properties of the elements are the periodic function of their atomic weights".
- In Mendeleev periodic table, there were eight vertical columns (excluding zero group of noble gases) named as groups.
- He arranged the elements on the basis of increasing atomic weights. So, that the elements with similar properties occupied the same **vertical column** or **group**.
- In this table, there were seven horizontal rows, named as periods.
- He kept elements having similar nature in the same vertical column or group with respect to atomic weight.
- He left the gap for the elements which were unknown at that time. He left the gap under aluminium and under silicon called these elements **Eka-Aluminium and Eka-Silicon** respectively.
- **Demerits of Mendeleev's periodic table** He did not give any separate place to isotopes.
- Position of hydrogen was anomalous, it shows resemblance with the elements of both I^{st} as well as VIIth group.
- Position of rare earth metals and actinoids could not be justified.
- Certain pairs of elements having higher atomic weights ($Co^{58.9}$) have been given position before the elements having lower atomic weights ($Ni^{58.6}$).

* *This topic not include in latest NEET syllabus, but it is given in latest rationalised NCERT.*

Modern Periodic Law and the Present Form of Periodic Table

- In 1913, the English physicist, **Henry Moseley** observed that a plot of frequency of X-rays emitted ($\sqrt{\nu}$) against atomic number (Z), gave a straight line and not the plot of ($\sqrt{\nu}$) *versus* atomic weight.
- He proposed a modified version of Mendeleev's law, which is known as **modern periodic law**. This law can be stated as, "The physical and chemical properties of the elements are periodic functions of their atomic numbers."
- The modern periodic law is essentially the consequence of the periodic variation in electronic configurations which determine the physical and chemical properties of elements and their compounds. A modern version is also called "long form" of the periodic table of the elements.
- **Long form of the periodic table** It consists of seven horizontal rows called **periods** and eighteen vertical columns called **groups** or **families**.
- Elements having similar electronic configuration in their atoms are arranged in groups. The period number corresponds to the highest principal quantum number (n) of the elements.
- The first period contains 2 elements. The subsequent periods consists of 8, 8, 18, 18 and 32 elements respectively.
- The seventh period is incomplete and like the sixth period would have theoretical maximum of 32 elements.

Representation of Periodwise Elements

Period/Elements	Quantum number (n)	Filling of orbitals	Elements present in the period	Comments
First [H(1) ⟶ He(2)]	1	1s	2	Very short period
Second [Li(3) ⟶ Ne(10)]	2	$2s\ 2p$	2 + 6 = 8	Short period
Third [Na(11) ⟶ Ar(18)]	3	$3s\ 3p$	2 + 6 = 8	Short period
Fourth [K(19) ⟶ Kr(36)]	4	$4s\ 3d\ 4p$	2 + 10 + 6 = 18	Long period
Fifth [Rb(37) ⟶ Xe(54)]	5	$5s\ 4d\ 5p$	2 + 10 + 6 = 18	Long period
Sixth [Cs(55) ⟶ Rn(86)]	6	$6s\ 4f\ 5d\ 6p$	2 + 14 + 10 + 6 = 32	Very long period
Seventh [Fr(87) ⟶ Og(118)]	7	$7s\ 5f\ 6d\ 7p$	2 + 14 + 10 + 6 = 32	Very long period

- In this form of periodic table, 14 elements of both sixth and seventh periods (lanthanoids and actinoids, respectively) are placed in separate panels at the bottom.

Representative elements (*s*-block elements) — GROUP NUMBER 1, 2; Group 1 → Alkali metals; Group 2 → Alkaline earth metals

Transition elements (*d*-block elements) — GROUP NUMBER 3–12

Representative elements (*p*-block elements) — GROUP NUMBER 13–17; Group 16 → Chalcogens; Group 17 → Halogens; Group 18 → Noble gases

Period number	1 IA	2 IIA	3 IIIB	4 IVB	5 VB	6 VIB	7 VIIB	8 VIII	9 VIII	10 VIII	11 IB	12 IIB	13 IIIA	14 IVA	15 VA	16 VIA	17 VIIA	18 0
1	1 H $1s^1$																	2 He $1s^2$
2	3 Li $2s^1$	4 Be $2s^2$											5 B $2s^22p^1$	6 C $2s^22p^2$	7 N $2s^22p^3$	8 O $2s^22p^4$	9 F $2s^22p^5$	10 Ne $2s^22p^6$
3	11 Na $3s^1$	12 Mg $3s^2$											13 Al $3s^23p^1$	14 Si $3s^23p^2$	15 P $3s^23p^3$	16 S $3s^23p^4$	17 Cl $3s^23p^5$	18 Ar $3s^23p^6$
4	19 K $4s^1$	20 Ca $4s^2$	21 Sc $3d^14s^2$	22 Ti $3d^24s^2$	23 V $3d^34s^2$	24 Cr $3d^54s^1$	25 Mn $3d^54s^2$	26 Fe $3d^64s^2$	27 Co $3d^74s^2$	28 Ni $3d^84s^2$	29 Cu $3d^{10}4s^1$	30 Zn $3d^{10}4s^2$	31 Ga $4s^24p^1$	32 Ge $4s^24p^2$	33 As $4s^24p^3$	34 Se $4s^24p^4$	35 Br $4s^24p^5$	36 Kr $4s^24p^6$
5	37 Rb $5s^1$	38 Sr $5s^2$	39 Y $4d^15s^2$	40 Zr $4d^25s^2$	41 Nb $4d^45s^1$	42 Mo $4d^55s^1$	43 Tc $4d^55s^2$	44 Ru $4d^75s^1$	45 Rh $4d^85s^1$	46 Pd $4d^{10}$	47 Ag $4d^{10}5s^1$	48 Cd $4d^{10}5s^2$	49 In $5s^25p^1$	50 Sn $5s^25p^2$	51 Sb $5s^25p^3$	52 Te $5s^25p^4$	53 I $5s^25p^5$	54 Xe $5s^25p^6$
6	55 Cs $6s^1$	56 Ba $6s^2$	57 La* $5d^16s^2$	72 Hf $4f^{14}5d^26s^2$	73 Ta $5d^36s^2$	74 W $5d^46s^2$	75 Re $5d^56s^2$	76 Os $5d^66s^2$	77 Ir $5d^76s^2$	78 Pt $5d^96s^1$	79 Au $5d^{10}6s^1$	80 Hg $5d^{10}6s^2$	81 Tl $6s^26p^1$	82 Pb $6s^26p^2$	83 Bi $6s^26p^3$	84 Po $6s^26p^4$	85 At $6s^26p^5$	86 Rn $6s^26p^6$
7	87 Fr $7s^1$	88 Ra $7s^2$	89 Ac** $6d^17s^2$	104 Rf $5f^{14}6d^27s^2$	105 Db $6d^37s^2$	106 Sg $6d^47s^2$	107 Bh $6d^57s^2$	108 Hs $6d^67s^2$	109 Mt $6d^77s^2$	110 Ds $6d^97s^1$	111 Rg $6d^{10}7s^1$	112 Cn $6d^{10}7s^2$	113 Nh $7s^27p^1$	114 Fl $7s^27p^2$	115 Mc $7s^27p^3$	116 Lv $7s^27p^4$	117 Ts $7s^27p^5$	118 Og $7s^27p^6$

Inner-transition elements (*f*-block elements)

Lanthanoids	58 Ce $4f^25d^06s^2$	59 Pr $4f^35d^06s^2$	60 Nd $4f^45d^06s^2$	61 Pm $4f^55d^06s^2$	62 Sm $4f^65d^06s^2$	63 Eu $4f^75d^06s^2$	64 Gd $4f^75d^16s^2$	65 Tb $4f^95d^06s^2$	66 Dy $4f^{10}5d^06s^2$	67 Ho $4f^{11}5d^06s^2$	68 Er $4f^{12}5d^06s^2$	69 Tm $4f^{13}5d^06s^2$	70 Yb $4f^{14}5d^06s^2$	71 Lu $4f^{14}5d^16s^2$
Actinoids	90 Th $5f^06d^27s^2$	91 Pa $5f^26d^17s^2$	92 U $5f^36d^17s^2$	93 Np $5f^46d^17s^2$	94 Pu $5f^66d^07s^2$	95 Am $5f^76d^07s^2$	96 Cm $5f^76d^17s^2$	97 Bk $5f^96d^07s^2$	98 Cf $5f^{10}6d^07s^2$	99 Es $5f^{11}6d^07s^2$	100 Fm $5f^{12}6d^07s^2$	101 Md $5f^{13}6d^07s^2$	102 No $5f^{14}6d^07s^2$	103 Lr $5f^{14}6d^17s^2$

Long form of the periodic table *of the elements with their atomic numbers and ground state outer electronic configurations. The groups are numbered 1-18 in accordance with the 1984 IUPAC recommendations. This notation replaces the old numbering scheme of IA-VIIA, VIII, IB-VIIB and 0 for the elements.*

Marks Maximizer

Groups 13, 14 and 15 are known as icosagens, crystallogens and pnictogens respectively.

Nomenclature of Elements with Atomic Numbers > 100

- The IUPAC has recommended a systematic nomenclature for the elements with $Z > 100$.
- The name of elements with $Z > 100$ are derived by using roots for the three digits in the atomic number of the elements followed by adding '–ium' at the end.
- Symbol is obtained from first letter of word used for each numerical digit.

Notation of IUPAC Nomenclature of Elements

S.No.	Digit	Name	Abbreviation
1.	0	nil	n
2.	1	un	u
3.	2	bi	b
4.	3	tri	t
5.	4	quad	q
6.	5	pent	p
7.	6	hex	h
8.	7	hept/sept	s
9.	8	oct	o
10.	9	enn	e

e.g. The element with atomic number 109 will be named as un-nil-ennium and symbolised as une (u for 1, n for 0 and e for 9).

Electronic Configurations of Elements and the Periodic Table

- An electron in an atom is characterised by a set of four quantum numbers and the principal quantum number (n) defines the main energy level known as **shell**.
- The distribution of electrons into orbitals of an atom is called its **electronic configuration**.
- An element's location in the periodic table reflects the quantum numbers of the last orbital filled.

Electronic Configurations in Periods

- The period indicates the value of n for the outermost or valence shell.
- Number of elements in each period is twice the number of atomic **orbitals** available in the energy level that is being filled.

  e.g. The first period ($n = 1$) starts with the filling of the lowest level (1s) and therefore has two elements hydrogen ($1s^1$) and helium ($1s^2$) when the first shell (K) is completed.

Period No.	Electronic configuration	Elements is period with atomic numbers
First ($n = 1$)	$1s^{1-2}$	H(1) and He(2)
Second ($n = 2$)	$2s^{1-2}\,2p^{0-6}$	Li(3) to Ne(10)
Third ($n = 3$)	$3s^{1-2}\,3p^{0-6}$	Na(11) to Ar(18)
Fourth ($n = 4$)	$4s^{1-2}\,3d^{0-10}\,4p^{0-6}$	K(19) to Kr(36)
Fifth ($n = 5$)	$5s^{1-2}\,4d^{0-10}\,5p^{0-6}$	Rb(37) to Xe(54)
Sixth ($n = 6$)	$6s^{1-2}\,4f^{0-14}\,5d^{0-10}\,6p^{0-6}$	Cs(55) to Rn(86)
Seventh ($n = 7$)	$7s^{1-2}\,5f^{0-14}\,6d^{0-10}\,7p^{0-6}$	Fr(87) to Og(118)

- f-block elements are divided in two separate periods called as $4f$ and $5f$ inner transition series. It can be explained as

	Electronic configuration	Elements in period with atomic numbers
Lanthanoids ($4f$)	$5d^{0-1}6s^2\,4f^n$	Ce(58) to Lu(71)
Actinoids ($5f$)	$6d^{0-2}7s^2 5f^n$	Th(90) to Lr(103)

Groupwise Electronic Configurations

The elements in the same vertical column or group of a periodic table exhibit similar properties, similar valence shell electronic configuration and the same number of electrons in the outer orbitals. e.g. The group 1 element (alkali metals) all have ns^1 valence shell electronic configuration as shown below.

At. no.	Symbol	Electronic configuration
3	Li	$1s^2 2s^1$ or [He] $2s^1$
11	Na	$1s^2 2s^2 2p^6 3s^1$ or [Ne] $3s^1$
19	K	$1s^2 2s^2 2p^6 3s^2 3p^6 4s^1$ or [Ar] $4s^1$
37	Rb	$1s^2 2s^2 2p^6 3s^2 3p^6 3d^{10} 4s^2 4p^6 5s^1$ or [Kr] $5s^1$
55	Cs	$1s^2 2s^2 2p^6 3s^2 3p^6 3d^{10} 4s^2 4d^{10} 5s^2 5p^6 6s^1$ or [Xe] $6s^1$
87	Fr	[Rn] $7s^1$

Electronic Configurations and Types of Elements: *s*, *p*, *d*, *f*-Blocks

- Elements are classified into four blocks *viz.* s, p, d and f-block depending on the type of atomic orbitals that are being filled with electrons.
- The Aufbau (build up) principle and the electronic configuration of atoms provide a theoretical foundation for the periodic classification.

- Helium belongs to the *s*-block but its positioning in the *p*-block along with other group 18 elements is justified because it has a completely filled valence shell ($1s^2$) and as a result, exhibits properties characteristic of other noble gases.
- Hydrogen has only one *s*-electron and hence can be placed in group 1 (alkali metals). It can also gain an electron to achieve a noble gas arrangement and hence it can behave similar to a group 17 elements.
- It is a special case, we shall place hydrogen separately at the top of the periodic table.

The *s*-Block Elements

Group 1 **(alkali metals)** and Group 2 **(alkaline earth metals)** elements belong to this block, their last electron enters in *s*-orbital. NEET 2023

Properties

- General electronic configuration of alkali metals is ns^1 and of alkaline earth metals is ns^2.
- These are all reactive metals with low ionisation enthalpies.
- They lose the outermost electron(s) and form +1 (in alkali metals) or +2 (in alkali earth metals) ions.
- The metallic character and the reactivity of *s*-block elements increase as we go down the group.
- They are highly reactive thus never found pure in nature.
- The compounds of *s*-block elements with the exception of those of lithium and beryllium are predominantly ionic.
- These are all soft metals and have low melting and boiling points.
- These are highly electropositive and act as strong reducing agents.
- They are strong reducing agents and good conductor of heat and electricity.

The *p*-Block Elements

Groups 13th to 18th excluding He, belong to this block. Their last electron enters in *p*-orbital. *s* and *p*-block elements together are known as representative elements or main group elements.

Properties

- General electronic configuration of *p*-block elements is ns^2np^{1-6}.
- **Halogens** (group 17) and **chalcogens** (group 16) elements have highly negative electron gain enthalpies and readily add one or two electrons respectively to attain the stable noble gas configuration.
- *p*-block includes non-metals, poor metals and metalloids. However, non-metals are predominant.
- The non-metallic character increases as we move from left to right across a period and metallic character increases as we go down the group.
- The noble gas elements exhibit very low chemical reactivity because of completely filled (ns^2np^6) electronic configuration. It is very difficult to alter this arrangement by the addition or removal of electrons. These elements are also called **inert gas** or noble gas. NEET 2023

The *d*-Block Elements (Transition Elements)

Elements of group 3rd to 12th in periodic table belong to *d*-block as their last electron enters in *d*-orbitals.

Properties

- General outer electronic configuration of *d*-block elements is $(n-1)d^{1-10}\ ns^{0-2}$ except Pd ($4d^{10}5s^0$).
- They are all metals. They mostly form coloured ions, exhibit variable valence (oxidation states) and also used as catalyst. e.g. Hg^+ and Hg^{2+}, Cu^+ and Cu^{2+}, Ti^{2+}, Ti^{3+} and Ti^{4+} etc.
- Zn, Cd and Hg have the electronic configuration $(n-1)d^{10}ns^2$, do not show most of the properties of transition elements.
- Transition metals form a bridge as they placed in between the chemically active metals of *s*-block elements and the less active elements of group 13 and 14 and thus these are called **"transition elements"**.
- Their ions and compounds are generally paramagnetic. These have one or more unpaired electrons in their atoms or ions and form both ionic and covalent compounds.
- These elements are metals so having high melting and boiling points.
- Most of the transition metals form alloys.

The *f*-Block Elements (Inner-Transition Elements)

- Elements in which the last electron enters in *f*-orbital of anti-penultimate shell.
- Two series 4*f* (lanthanoids) and 5*f* (actinoids) are included in '*f*' block elements.

Properties

- General configuration $(n-2)f^{1-14}(n-1)d^{0-1}ns^2$. NEET 2020
- **Lanthanoids**, Ce($Z=58$) to Lu($Z=71$) and **actinoids**, Th($Z=90$) to Lr($Z=103$), are the two rows of elements present at the bottom of the periodic table. Hence, also known as **inner-transition elements**.
- They are all heavy metals. Within each series, the properties of the elements are quite similar.

- The chemistry of early actinoids is more complicated than the corresponding lanthanoids due to the large number of oxidation states possible for these actinoid elements.
- The most common oxidation state is (+3) in *f*-block elements.
- Actinoid elements are radioactive in nature.
- The elements after uranium are called **transuranium elements**.

Metals, Non-metals and Metalloids

The elements can be broadly divided into metals, non-metals and metalloids on the basis of their physical and chemical properties.

Metals

- They comprise more than 78% of all known elements and appear on the left side of the periodic table.
- Metals are usually solids at room temperature [mercury is an exception].
- Metals usually have high melting and boiling points except gallium and caesium (303 K and 302 K respectively).
- They are good conductors of heat and electricity.
- They are malleable and ductile.

Non-metals

- They are located at the top right hand side of the periodic table.
- Non-metals are usually solids or gases at room temperature.
- They have low melting and boiling points [boron and carbon are exceptions].
- They are poor conductors of heat and electricity.
- Most non-metallic solids are brittle and are neither malleable nor ductile.
- The elements become more metallic as we go down a group. The non-metallic character increases as one goes from left to right across the periodic table.

Metalloids

The elements which show the properties of both metals and non-metals are termed as semi-metals or metalloids. NEET 2020

e.g. Silicon, germanium, arsenic, antimony and tellurium.

Periodic Trends in Properties of Elements

- There are so many remarkable patterns in the physical and chemical properties of elements as we go down the group or moving in a period of the periodic table.
- This trend can be understood by an example, like within a group of representative metals (alkali metals), reactivity increases down the group, while within a group of non-metals (halogens), reactivity decreases down the group.
- Further in a period, chemical reactivity tends to be high in group 1 metals, lower in elements towards the middle of the table and increases to a maximum in the group 17 non-metals.
- The recurrence of similar properties of the elements after certain definite intervals when the elements are arranged in order of increasing atomic numbers in the periodic table is called **periodicity**.

Trends in Physical Properties

Atomic Radius

- Atomic radii can be measured by X-ray or other spectroscopic methods.
- It is defined as the distance from the centre of the nucleus to the outermost shell of electrons. However, due to uncertainty in the position of the electron in atom, this definition is hypothetical in practical. It is referred to both **covalent** or **metallic radius** depending upon, whether the element is a non-metal or a metal respectively.
- Atomic radius generally decreases from left to right along a period and increases on moving down the group.
- **Covalent radius** is defined as the half of the internuclear distance between two identical or almost atoms of a non-metallic element bounded by a single covalent bond.
- **Metallic radius** is defined as half of the internuclear distance between two non-bounded adjacent atoms in closed packed crystal lattice. It is also known as crystal radius.

Marks Maximizer

- **van der Waals' radius** is defined as half of the internuclear distance between the nuclei of two non-bonded adjacent atoms belonging to different molecules having identical atoms.
- This radius is taken into consideration for those cases where intermolecular attractive forces are weak.
- In case of noble gases, van der Waals' radius and atomic radius are same, since they do not form molecules.

Ionic Radius

- This can be defined as the distance between the nucleus and the outermost shell of an ion.
- The trend of ionic radii in the periodic table is just same like, as atomic radii.
- The removal of an electron from an atom results in the formation of a cation and gain of an electron leads to an anion.

- The ionic radii can be estimated by measuring the distances between cations and anions in ionic crystal.
- The size of cation is smaller than its parent atom, because it has fewer electrons, while its nuclear charge remains same. e.g. $Ca > Ca^{+} > Ca^{2+}$.
- The size of an anion is greater than its parent atom, because it has more electron, the net repulsion of the electrons will outweigh the nuclear charge.
  e.g. $S^{2-} > S^{-} > S$.
- This theory of size can be explained on the basis of Z/e ratio, e.g. $\left(\frac{\text{nuclear charge}}{\text{no. of electrons}}\right)$, with the increase in Z/e ratio, the size decreases and when Z/e ratio decreases, the size increases.
- There are some species of atoms or ions having same number of electrons, but different nuclear charge are known as **isoelectronic species.** NEET 2021
  e.g. N^{3-}, F^{-}, Al^{3+}, Na^{+} all have 10 electrons.
- In isoelectronic species, the cation with greater positive charge will have a smaller radius and anion with the greater negative charge will have the larger radius.

Ionisation Enthalpy

For Concept Master Video

- It represents the energy required to remove an electron from an isolated gaseous atom in its ground state. It is expressed in kJ mol^{-1}. NEET 2019
- The first ionisation enthalpy for an element Y.

$$Y(g) \longrightarrow Y^{+}(g) + e^{-}$$ NEET 2024

- The second ionisation enthalpy for most loosely bound electron.

$$Y^{+}(g) \longrightarrow Y^{2+}(g) + e^{-}$$

- Energy is always required to remove electrons from an atom and hence, ionisation energy is always positive.
- The second ionisation enthalpy is always greater than the first and in similar way, the third ionisation enthalpy is greater than the second ionisation enthalpy and so, on because it is more complicated to pull out an electron from a positively charged ion than from a neutral atom.
  Successive ionisation energy is defined as the energy that is required to remove the electron one after the other.

$$IE_3 > IE_2 > IE_1$$

- On moving across a period from left to right, the ionisation enthalpy increases and decreases on going down the group.
- The ionisation enthalpy of elements of second group (Be) is higher than the corresponding element of thirteen group (B).
- Also, the ionisation enthalpy of elements of group 15 (N) is higher than that of corresponding elements of group 16 (O).
- **The screening effect or shielding effect** In a multielectron atom, valence shell electrons experience less attractive force due to repulsion between inner shell electrons and valence electrons.
- It is much difficult to remove the electrons from **completely filled or half-filled orbitals** because they are more stable.
- Ionisation enthalpy follows the trend for s, p, d, f-orbitals as

$$s > p > d > f$$

- **Factors affecting ionisation enthalpy**

  Size of atom : $IE \propto \frac{1}{\text{Size of atom}}$

  Nuclear charge : $IE \propto \text{Nuclear charge}$

  Screening effect : $IE \propto \frac{1}{\text{Screening effect}}$

Electron Gain Enthalpy

- It is the enthalpy change accompanied when an electron is added to a gaseous atom in its ground state to convert it into a negative ion. It is a measure of the ease with which an atom adds an electron to form anion. NEET 2023

$$Y(g) + e^{-} \longrightarrow Y^{-}(g)$$

- On moving down a group, the electron gain enthalpy become less negative, while on moving from left to right across a period, electron gain enthalpy becomes more negative.
- Depending on the element, the process of adding an electron to the atom can be either endothermic or exothermic.
- It is due to increasing the atomic number there is increase in effective nuclear charge.
- Group 17 elements (F, Cl, Br) have high negative electron gain enthalpy, whereas noble gases (He, Ne, Ar etc.) have high positive values.

Factors affecting electron gain enthalpy

- Magnitude of $\Delta_{eg}H \propto Z_{eff}$
- Magnitude of $\Delta_{eg}H \propto \frac{1}{\text{atomic size}}$
- Magnitude of $\Delta_{eg}H \propto$ penetrating power

Electronegativity

- A qualitative measure of the ability of an atom in a chemical compound to attract the shared pair of electrons towards itself is called electronegativity. It is not a measurable quantity.
- There are some numerical scales used to calculate the electronegativity of an element like Mulliken-Jaffe scale, Pauling scale, Allred-Rochow scale. Pauling scale is most widely used scale.

- Although the electronegativity of an element is not constant, it varies on the basis of bounded atom/element but it does provide a information about the nature of force that holds a pair of atoms together.
- Electronegativity generally increases across a period from left to right and decreases with increase in atomic radii on going down a group in the periodic table. NEET 2024
- Non-metallic elements have strong tendency to gain electrons. Therefore, electronegativity is directly related to non-metallic properties of the elements and is inversely related to the metallic properties of the elements.
- Across a period, non-metallic character increases with increase in electronegativity and down the group non-metallic character decreases with decrease in electronegativity.

Electronegativity Values (on Pauling Scale)

Atom (Period (II)	Li	Be	B	C	N	O	F
Electronegativity	1.0	1.5	2.0	2.5	3.0	3.5	4.0
Atom (Period III)	Na	Mg	Al	Si	P	S	Cl
Electronegativity	0.9	1.2	1.5	1.8	2.1	2.5	3.0

Marks Maximizer

- **Scales of Electronegativity**

1. Pauling scale (1931)
$$x_A - x_B = 0.1017\sqrt{\Delta}\ \text{kJ/mol}$$
$$\Delta = E_{A—B} - \sqrt{E_{A—A} \times E_{B—B}}$$
2. Mulliken scale (1934)
$$x = \frac{\text{I.E} + \text{EA}}{2}$$
$$x = \frac{\text{I.E} + \text{EA}}{2 \times 2.8}\ \text{eV}$$
$$x = \frac{\text{I.E} + \text{EA}}{2 \times 2.8 \times 96.5}\ \text{(in kJ/mol)}$$
3. Allred and Rochow scale
$$x_A = 0.744 + \frac{0.359\, Z_{\text{eff}}}{r^2}$$

- **Slater's rule for determination of Z_{eff}**
$$Z_{\text{eff}} = Z - \sigma^*$$
where, Z_{eff} = effective nuclear charge, Z = total nuclear charge and σ^* = Slater's screening constant.
σ^* = [0.35 × No. of other electrons in n^{th} shell + 0.85 × No. of electrons in $(n-1)^{\text{th}}$ shell + 1.00 × Total no. of electrons in the inner shells]

Periodic Trends in Chemical Properties

The periodicity of the valence state shown by elements and the anomalous properties of the second period elements (from Li to F) are covered in this section.

Periodicity of Valence or Oxidation States

- The valence is the most characteristics property of the elements that can be understood in terms of their electronic configurations.
- The valence of representative elements is usually equal to the number of electrons in the outermost orbitals or equal to eight minus the number of outermost electrons.
- The term oxidation state is frequently used for valence.
- The oxidation state of an element in a particular compound can be defined as the charge acquired by its atoms on the basis of electronegative consideration from other atoms in a molecule.
- Valency of the elements increases from 1 to 4 and then decreases from 4 to 0 in a period.
- When we move down the group, the number of valence electrons remains the same therefore, all the elements in a group exhibit the same valency.
- The transition elements and actinoids have the property to showing variable valency.

Anomalous Properties of Second Period Elements

For Concept Master Video

- The behaviour of lithium and beryllium is more similar with the second element of the following group, i.e. magnesium and aluminium. This sort of similarity is commonly referred to as **diagonal relationship** in the periodic properties.
- This anomalous behaviour in '*s*' and *p*-block is attributed to their small size, large charge/radius ratio and high electronegativity of elements.
- The maximum covalency of first member of each group in second period is 4 because they have only four valence orbitals (2*s* and 2*p*) available for bonding whereas the second member of the groups have nine valence orbitals. (3*s*, 3*p*, 3*d*) and, hence they can expand their valence shell to accommodate more than four pairs of electrons.

  e.g. Boron can only form $[BF_4]^-$, while aluminium can expand it's valence shell and form $[AlF_6]^{3-}$.
- Also, the first member of *p*-block elements displays greater tendency to form $p\pi$-$p\pi$ multiple bonds to itself and to other second period elements compared to subsequent members of the same group.

  e.g. C═C, C≡C, N═N, N≡N and C═O, C═N, C≡N, N═O etc.

Periodic Trends and Chemical Reactivity

- The periodicity of all chemical and physical properties are related to the electronic configuration reactivity of elements.
- There are some relationship between chemical reactivity of elements with their fundamental property.

- The atomic and ionic radii decrease in a period, ionisation enthalpy of the extreme left element in a period is the least and electron gain enthalpy of the element on the extreme right is the highest negative (except noble gases).
- The maximum chemical reactivity of the alkali metals (s^1) at the extreme left with their tendency to lose an electron, while at the extreme right halogens by the gain of an electron have maximum chemical reactivity.
- The centre part of the periodic table has the lowest chemical reactivity.
- The normal oxide formed by an element on the extreme left is most basic (Na_2O). Whereas, that formed by the element on extreme right is the most acidic (Cl_2O_7).
- Oxides of elements in the centre are amphoteric, (Al_2O_3), i.e. behave as acidic as well as basic oxides. NEET 2020
- Neutral oxides (CO, NO, N_2O etc.) have no acidic or basic properties. NEET 2019
- The reducing nature or metallic character of elements increases down the group, whereas oxidising nature or non-metallic character decreases.

Marks Maximizer

- **Nature of oxides** Along period, the nature of the oxides varies from basic to acidic.

Oxide	Na_2O	MgO	Al_2O_3	SiO_2	P_4O_{10}	Cl_2O_7
Appearance and nature	White, alkaline	White, basic	White, Amphoteric	Transparent Crystal, Acidic	White, acidic	Colourless, acidic

- The acidic character of the oxides of a non-metal increases with increase in oxygen content in it. e.g.
$$N_2O_3 < N_2O_5;\ SO_2 < SO_3,\ Cl_2O < Cl_2O_3 < Cl_2O_7$$
- The basic character of hydroxides decreases in the order:
$$CsOH > RbOH > KOH > NaOH > LiOH$$
- Non-metal oxides when dissolved in water form oxyacids, thus, they are called anhydrides of the acid, e.g. CO_2, N_2O_5, P_2O_3, P_2O_5.

Mnemonics

Recall General Trends of different Properties in the Periodic Table

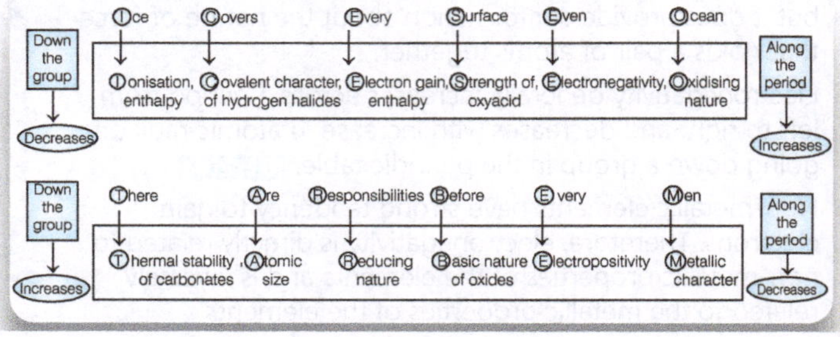

Caution Points

- The element with most negative electron gain enthalpy is chlorine, the one with most positive electron gain enthalpy is neon.
- Relation between electron affinity (A_e) and electron gain enthalpy ($\Delta_{eg}H$) at absolute 0 K is
$$\Delta_{eg}H = -A_e - \frac{5}{2}RT$$
- The $\Delta_{eg}H$ values (negative) of the elements of third period are higher than the $\Delta_{eg}H$ values of the elements of second period.
- First ionisation energy of group 2 (II A) elements is greater than the corresponding elements of group 13(III A).
- Electronegativity is a tendency and tendencies cannot be measured accurately.

PYQ Notes

1. Moseley's observation on characteristic X-ray spectra of elements relates frequency (v) of X-ray emitted to the atomic number by the relation. $\sqrt{v} = a(Z - b)$. The plot of $\sqrt{v}$ vs Z is linear straight lines. JEE Main 2023

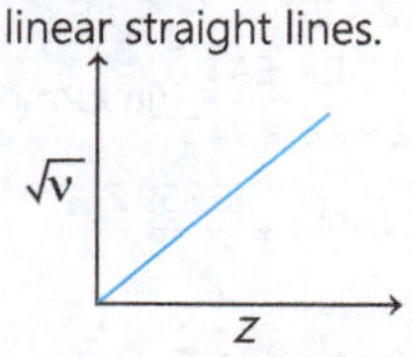

2. van der Waals' radius > Metallic radius > Covalent radius (For an atom). NEET 2014

Step by Step

Mastering NCERT

- Concept Builders
- Topical Questions
- Assertion-Reason
- Statement Type
- Matching Type
- Numerical Value
- NCERT Exemplar's
- Past Exams'
- Skill Boosters

Concept Builders

1. The periodic classification follows as a logical consequence of the .... of atoms.
2. In Dobereiner triads, the average weight of the 1st and the 3rd element is equal to that of the second one. [T/F]
3. According to Newlands' law of octaves, the properties of Li were similar to .... (Na/Mg).
4. Give the formula of oxide of gallium predicted by Mendeleev along with their formulas.
5. Henry Moseley developed a relationship between $\sqrt{v}$ (v = frequency of X-rays emitted) and atomic weight (Z). [T/F]
6. The horizontal rows in Mendeleev's periodic table is called .... while in modern periodic table, these are called ....
7. Write the IUPAC nomenclature of seaborgium.
8. The elements of s-block are reactive metals with high ionisation enthalpies. [T/F]
9. Name the element which can achieve noble gas configuration by gaining an electron but it is not a halogen.
10. s-block elements are never found pure in nature because of ....
11. Select the element which does not belong to pnictogens (N, P, As, Sn).
12. Zn, ... and Hg have $(n-1)d^{10}ns^2$ electronic configuration but do not show most of the properties of .... elements.
13. Actinoid elements are radioactive and made only in nanogram quantities. [T/F]
14. Write the electronic configuration of the element having atomic number 120.
15. Metals comprise more than 87% of all known elements and appear on the left side of the periodic table. [T/F]
16. The reactivity of metals .... on moving down the group, whereas the reactivity of non-metals .... down the group.
17. If the bond distance in bromine molecule (Br_2) is 228 pm, then what will be the atomic radius of bromine.
18. The energy required to remove an electron from the outermost orbit of an isolated gaseous atom (X) in its ground state is called .... and it is expressed in the units of ....
19. The effective nuclear charge experienced by the valence electrons in an atom will be more than the actual charge on the nucleus. [T/F]
20. An element 'P' has atomic number 56. What will be the formula of its halide?
21. In period II elements, it is easier to remove the fourth $2p$-electrons from .... than to remove one of the three $2p$-electrons from ....
22. Na > Mg > Be > Si is the correct trend regarding metallic character. [T/F]
23. Write the formulae of the binary compounds, formed by the combination of magnesium and nitrogen.
24. The first member of s- and p-block has only five valence orbitals available for bonding, whereas the second member has eight valence orbitals. [T/F]
25. Which member of every group of p-block elements has the ability to form $p\pi$-$p\pi$ multiple bond?
26. In compound $[AlCl(H_2O)_5]^{2+}$ the oxidation state of Al is .... and the covalency of Al is ....
27. The electronegativity of any given element is not constant, it varies depending on the element to which it is bound. [T/F]
28. The normal oxide formed by the element on extreme left is most acidic in nature. [T/F]
29. .... oxides behave as acidic with bases and as basic with acids.
30. The metallic character and oxidising property increases down the group. [T/F]

Topical Questions

Why do we Need to Classify Elements?

1 Which of the following is a set containing man-made elements?
(a) Gold, Mercury, Zinc
(b) Gold, Radium, Palladium
(c) Curium, Osmium, Uranium
(d) Technetium, Neptunium, Einsteinium

Genesis of Periodic Classification

2 Which of the following statements is correct? NCERT Pg 75
(a) Dobereiner arranged elements by the help of triads methods.
(b) Law of triads seemed to work for large number of elements.
(c) The properties of Br were in between those of Cl and F.
(d) Group 17 elements are known as alkali metals.

3 Which of the following statements is correct regarding Newlands' law of octaves? NCERT Pg 75
(a) It is an arrangement of the elements in increasing order of their atomic number.
(b) Every eighth element had properties similar to the first element.
(c) This law is true only for elements upto argon.
(d) It is true only for the physical properties.

4 Which of the following relationship proposed graphically by Lothar Meyer? NCERT Pg 75
(a) Chemical properties *vs* atomic weight
(b) Physical properties *vs* atomic weight
(c) Physical properties *vs* atomic number
(d) Chemical properties *vs* atomic number

5 Which of the following statements is incorrect regarding Mendeleev's periodic table? NCERT Pg 76
(a) He arranged elements in horizontal rows and vertical columns.
(b) He arranged elements in order of their increasing atomic number.
(c) Its system of classifying elements was more elaborate than that of Lothar Meyer.
(d) He arranged elements in order of their increasing atomic weight.

6 Which of the following is not a characteristic of Mendeleev's periodic table? NCERT Pg 76
(a) He dropped some gaps for some undiscovered elements yet predicted their properties previously.
(b) He put isotopes separately in his periodic table.
(c) This table helped in rectifying the atomic weights of some of the elements.
(d) He designed the periodic table consisting vertical and horizontal columns to shape it properly.

7 In Mendeleev's periodic table, iodine with lower atomic weight than that of tellurium was placed alongwith NCERT Pg 77
(a) iron, cobalt and nickel
(b) fluorine, chlorine and bromine
(c) oxygen, sulphur and selenium
(d) carbon, silicon and germanium

Modern Periodic Law and the Present form of the Periodic Table

8 Which of the following statements is correct regarding periodic table? NCERT Pg 78
(a) According to modern periodic law, the sixth period is incomplete.
(b) Total number of groups are 18.
(c) The subsequent periods consist of 2, 8, 8, 16, 32 elements.
(d) Second period consists of 2 elements.

9 Henry Moseley observed regularities in the characteristics X-ray spectra of the elements and plot a graph between frequency ($\sqrt{\nu}$) and atomic number (Z) as NCERT Pg 78

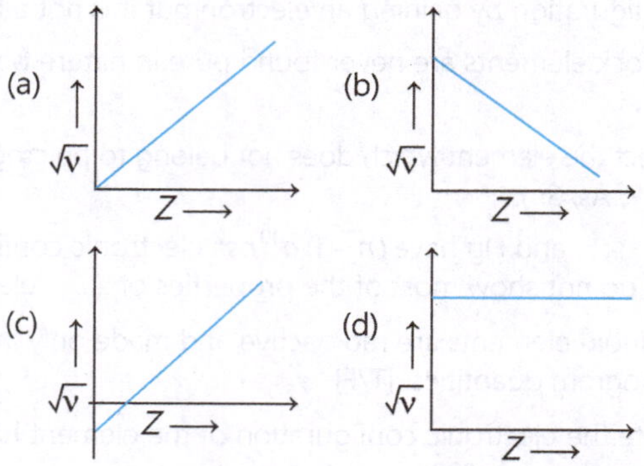

10 Which of the following in the periodic table corresponds to the highest principal quantum number (n) of the elements? NCERT Pg 78
(a) Group number
(b) Period number
(c) Atomic number
(d) Mass number

Nomenclature of Elements with Atomic Numbers > 100

11 The symbol and name according to the IUPAC system for the element with atomic number = 120, respectively are **NCERT Pg 80**

(a) Ubn and unbinilium
(b) Ubn and unbiunium
(c) Ubn and unnilbium
(d) Ubn and unnilium

12 Predict the symbol and name of the element with atomic number 115? **NCERT Pg 80**

(a) Dubnium, (Db) (b) Moscovium, (Mc)
(c) Rontgenium, (Rg) (d) Livernorium, (Lv)

13 Tennessine is the IUPAC official name of an element with atomic number. **NCERT Pg 80**

(a) 43 (b) 52 (c) 117 (d) 73

Electronic Configuration of Elements and the Periodic Table

14 Which factor among all does not effect the valence shell? **NCERT Pg 81**

(a) Nuclear charge (Z)
(b) Nuclear mass
(c) Number of valence electrons
(d) Principal quantum number (n)

15 $3d$-transition series of elements starts with Sc and ends at Zn. The electronic configuration of Sc and Zn are respectively. **NCERT Pg 81**

(a) [Ar] $3d^1 4s^1$ and [Ar] $3d^{10} 4s^1$
(b) [Ar] $3d^1 4s^2$ and [Ar] $3d^{10} 4s^2$
(c) [Ar] $3d^2 4s^1$ and [Ar] $3d^9 4s^2$
(d) [Ar] $3d^3 4s^2$ and [Ar] $3d^8 4s^2$

16 Which of following statements regarding the configuration of elements in a periodic table is/are incorrect? **NCERT Pg 81**

(a) The period indicates the value of n for the valence shell.
(b) The number of elements present in each period is twice the number of atomic orbitals available in the energy level that is being filled.
(c) First period starts with filling of the lowest level.
(d) Hydrogen has similarity with VIIth group more than Ist group.

17 The elements in a vertical column exhibit similar chemical behaviour. This is because **NCERT Pg 82**

(a) these elements have the same number of electrons in their outermost orbitals
(b) having the same principal quantum number
(c) these elements have no electrons in their outermost orbitals
(d) these elements have almost same atomic radius

18 An element having atomic number 79 will belong to **NCERT Pg 82**

(a) Group 8 (b) Group 9
(c) Group 11 (d) Group 13

Electronic Configuration and Types of Elements : *s*-, *p*-, *d*-, *f*-Blocks

19 Which of the following statements is incorrect? **NCERT Pg 84**

(a) The 4th period in the periodic table ends at krypton with the filling up of the $3p$-orbitals.
(b) The 5th period in the periodic table contains the $4d$-transition series.
(c) Starting element of $4d$-transition series is yttrium.
(d) Filling up of the $4f$-orbitals begins with cerium.

20 ns^1 and ns^2 are outermost electronic configuration of s-block elements. They are all reactive metals with **NCERT Pg 84**

(a) high electron gain enthalpy
(b) low ionisation enthalpy
(c) larger principal quantum number
(d) lower electropositive nature

21 The noble gases exhibit very low chemical reactivity due to **NCERT Pg 84**

(a) unavailability of valence electrons
(b) stable configuration
(c) availability of large number of valence electrons
(d) half-filled configuration

22 Which of the following groups of elements have highly negative electron gain enthalpy? **NCERT Pg 84**

(a) Group 13 (b) Group 17
(c) Group 14 (d) Group 18

23 Which of the following properties of p-block elements increases as we move from left to right across a period? **NCERT Pg 84**

(a) Metallic character (b) Non-metallic character
(c) Atomic size (d) Electropositivity

24 General outer electronic configuration of d-block elements is **NCERT Pg 84**

(a) $(n-1)\, d^{1-10} ns^2$ (b) $(n+1)\, d^{1-10} ns^{0-2}$
(c) $(n-1)\, d^{1-10} ns^{0-2}$ (d) $(n-1)\, d^0 ns^{0-2}$

25 Outer electronic configuration of f-block elements is **NCERT Pg 84**

(a) $(n-1)f^{1-14}(n-1)\, d^{0-1} ns^2$
(b) $(n-2)f^{1-14}(n+1)\, d^{0-1} ns^2$
(c) $(n-2)f^{1-14}(n-1)\, d^{0-1} ns^2$
(d) $(n-1)f^{1-14} nd^{0-1} ns^2$

26 An element A belongs to third period and fifteenth group of the periodic table. Which one of the following is correct regarding the outer electronic configuration of A? **NCERT Pg 84**

(a) It has completely filled s-orbital and p-orbital.

(b) It has partially filled d-orbitals and completely filled s-orbital.

(c) It has half-filled d-orbitals and completely filled s-orbitals.

(d) It has completely filled s-orbital and half-filled p-orbitals.

27 Consider the following statements. **NCERT Pg 84**

I. Transition metals form a bridge between chemically active metals of s-block elements and less active elements of groups 13 and 14.

II. The chemistry of the early actinoids is less complicated than the corresponding lanthanoids.

III. Actinoid elements are radioactive.

IV. The elements after uranium are called transuranium elements.

Choose the option with incorrect statement.

(a) I and III (b) Only II

(c) III and IV (d) II and III

28 Find the incorrectly matched pair out of the following? **NCERT Pg 84**

(a) $1s^2 2s^2 2p^6 3s^2 3p^6 3d^8 4s^2$ – A d-block element

(b) $1s^2 2s^2 2p^6 3s^2 3p^6$ – An element from 18th group

(c) $1s^2 2s^2 2p^6 3s^2 3p^3$ – An element belonging to 4th period and 6th group

(d) $1s^2 2s^2 2p^6 3s^2 3p^6 3d^5 4s^2$ – An element belonging to $3d$ series

29 In f-block, elements are arranged in two rows of 14 elements each in the periodic table. The reason behind this is that **NCERT Pg 84**

(a) there is space to conform 14 electrons only in these rows

(b) the discovery of only 28 inner transition elements till then have been done

(c) the values for magnetic quantum number of f-orbital is seven, thus 14 electrons can reside

(d) the maximum number of elements that any block can adopt is 28 only

30 Find the correctly matched pair out of the following. **NCERT Pg 85**

(a) Gold Crystalline non-metal $-4s^2 4p^6$

(b) Mercury Liquid metal-amalgam

(c) Iodine Liquid non-metal-blue colour

(d) Chlorine Crystalline non-metal-violet colour

31 Arrange the following elements in the decreasing order of metallic characters. Si, Be, Mg, Na and P. Select the correct answer. **NCERT Pg 85**

(a) Na > Be > Mg > P > Si (b) Na > Mg > Be > P > Si

(c) Na > Be > P > Mg > Si (d) Na > Mg > Be > Si > P

Periodic Trends in Properties of Elements

32 Half the internuclear distance separating the metal ions in the metallic crystal is termed as **NCERT Pg 86**

(a) metallic radius (b) atomic radius

(c) covalent radius (d) ionic radius

33 Which of the following is incorrect explanation regarding atomic radius? **NCERT Pg 86**

(a) Atomic radius changes, when the atom is present in different bonded states.

(b) The atomic radii can be measured by X-ray.

(c) Atomic radius can be determined precisely as atom has a defined boundary.

(d) The atomic radii can be measured by some spectroscopic methods.

34 In the given table, few values are mentioned in the direction from left to right and top to bottom.

Increases ↓	152	111	88	77	74	66
	186	Decreases →				
	231					
	244					
	262					

Which of the following property can be depicted in the table? **NCERT Pg 86**

(a) Atomic number (b) Atomic radius

(c) Ionisation enthalpy (d) Electron gain enthalpy

35 Consider the following graph.

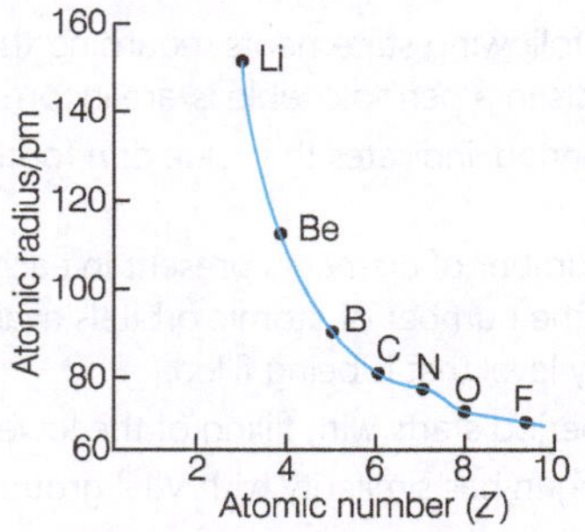

The plot has a steep slope from Li to Be but has much less steeper slope from O to F. This is due to the fact that **NCERT Pg 87**

(a) atomic number increases from Li to F

(b) nuclear charge increases from Li to F

(c) metallic character decreases from Li to F

(d) inter-electronic repulsion in atom increases from Li to F

36 Identify the incorrect statement in the following. **NCERT Pg 87, 86**

(a) Amongst isoelectronic species, smaller the positive charge on the cation, smaller is the ionic radius.
(b) Amongst isoelectronic species, greater the negative charge on the anion, larger is the ionic radius.
(c) Atomic radius of the elements increases as one moves down the group in the periodic table.
(d) Atomic radius of the elements decreases as one moves across from left to right in the 2nd period of the periodic table.

37 What effect is observed, on the size of an atom when an electron is removed and in another case when an electron is added to the same atom? **NCERT Pg 87**

(a) Remains constant
(b) Size decreases and increases respectively
(c) Size increases in both cases
(d) Size decreases in both cases

38 Consider the following compounds/species: **NCERT Pg 87**

I. NO_3^- II. SO_2 III. CO_3^{2-}
IV. SO_4^{2-} V. NO_2^-

The number of compounds/species which are isoelectronic is

(a) 2 (b) 4 (c) 3 (d) 5

39 The increasing order of the atomic radii of the following elements is **NCERT Pg 87**

(A) C (B) O (C) F (D) Cl (E) Br

(a) (A) < (B) < (C) < (D) < (E)
(b) (C) < (B) < (A) < (D) < (E)
(c) (D) < (C) < (B) < (A) < (E)
(d) (B) < (C) < (D) < (A) < (E)

40 Which of the following ions has larger size although they have the same number of electrons? **NCERT Pg 87**

(a) F^- (b) Na^+ (c) Mg^{2+} (d) O^{2-}

41 The ions with the greater positive charge or negative charge will have the radius, respectively with neutral atom **NCERT Pg 87**

(a) smaller or larger (b) larger
(c) remains same (d) smaller

42 Correct order of ionic radii is **NCERT Pg 87**

(a) $Mg^{2+} > Na^+ > O^{2-} > N^{3-}$
(b) $O^{2-} > N^{3-} > Mg^{2+} > O^{2-}$
(c) $N^{3-} > Na^+ > Mg^{2+} > O^{2-}$
(d) $N^{3-} > O^{2-} > Na^+ > Mg^{2+}$

43 Which of the following represents the correct order of increasing first ionisation enthalpy for Ca, Ba, S, Se and Ar? **NCERT Pg 88**

(a) Ca < S < Ba < Se < Ar (b) S < Se < Ca < Ba < Ar
(c) Ba < Ca < Se < S < Ar (d) Ca < Ba < S < Se < Ar

44 What is the order of successive ionisation enthalpies? **NCERT Pg 88**

(a) $IE_{III} > IE_{II} > IE_I$ (b) $IE_I > IE_{II} > IE_{III}$
(c) $IE_{II} > IE_I > IE_{III}$ (d) $IE_{III} > IE_I > IE_{II}$

45 Consider the following graph.

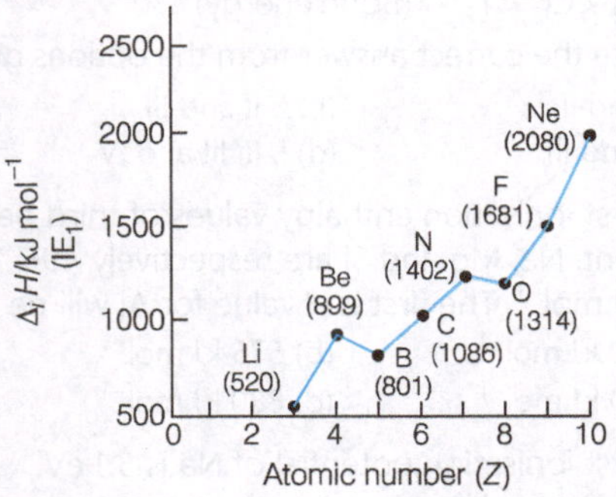

What could be the possible reason for a dip at boron (B) in the above plot? **NCERT Pg 88**

(a) Size of boron is smaller than Be.
(b) 2*p* electrons are more shielded as compared to 2*s* electrons.
(c) The penetration of a 2*s*-electron is less than that of a 2*p*-electron.
(d) Size of boron is equal to Be.

46 The element having greatest difference between its first and second ionisation energy is, **NCERT Pg 88**

(a) Ca (b) Sc (c) Ba (d) K

47 Which of the following statements are not correct? **NCERT Pg 88**

I. Ionisation energy is the energy required to remove an electron from an isolated gaseous atom from its ground state.
II. Ionisation energy can be either positive or negative.
III. The second ionisation enthalpy of Ca will be less than third but greater than first ionisation enthalpy.

Choose the most appropriate answer from the options given below.

(a) I and II (b) II and III (c) Only II (d) I, II and III

48 Ionisation enthalpy increases across the second period as we move from Li to F. This is because **NCERT Pg 88**

(a) shielding of the nuclear charge by the inner core of electrons increases very much from Li to F.
(b) increasing nuclear charge outweighs the shielding.
(c) increase in shielding outweighs the increasing nuclear charge.
(d) increase in electronegativity

49 Which of the following elements will have highest second ionisation enthalpy? **NCERT Pg 88**

(a) $1s^2 2s^2 2p^6 3s^2 3p^3$ (b) $1s^2 2s^2 2p^6$
(c) $1s^2 2s^2 2p^6 3s^1$ (d) $1s^2 2s^2 2p^6 3s^2$

50 Correct orders among the following are NCERT Pg 88, 89

I. $H^+ < H < H^-$ (Atomic/ ionic radii)

II. $O < N < F$ (First ionisation energy)

III. $Br_2 < Cl_2 < F_2$ (Oxidising power)

IV. $Br_2 < Cl_2 < F_2$ (Bond energy)

Choose the correct answer from the options given below.

(a) I and II (b) I, II and III
(c) II and III (d) I, II, III and IV

51 The first ionisation enthalpy values of third period element, Na, Mg and Si are respectively 496, 737 and 786 kJ mol^{-1}. The first $\Delta_i H$ value for Al will be close to NCERT Pg 89

(a) 760 kJ mol^{-1} (b) 575 kJ mol^{-1}
(c) 950 kJ mol^{-1} (d) 880 kJ mol^{-1}

52 The first ionisation potential of Na is 5.1 eV. The value of electron gain enthalpy of Na^+ will be NCERT Pg 89

(a) −2.55 eV (b) −5.1 eV
(c) −10.2 eV (d) +2.55 eV

53 Which of the following statement is incorrect? NCERT Pg 89

(a) Noble gases have large positive electron gain enthalpy.
(b) Electron gain enthalpy becomes more negative with increase in the atomic number across a period.
(c) The effective nuclear charge increases from left to right across a period.
(d) The process of adding electrons to the atom always be endothermic.

54 Which of the following statements is incorrect? NCERT Pg 89

(a) The removal of the outermost electron requires less energy down a group.
(b) The penetration capacity of a 2s-electron towords the nucleus is more than that of a 2p-electrons in boron.
(c) An electron is added to neutral gaseous atom to convert it into positive ion.
(d) Boron has a smaller first ionisation enthalpy than beryllium.

55 Which of the following statements is incorrect? NCERT Pg 90

(a) Electron gain enthalpy becomes more negative with increase in atomic number across a period.
(b) Effective nuclear charge increases from left to right across period.
(c) Electron gain enthalpy becomes less negative as we go up in a group.
(d) Electron gain enthalpy of selenium is less than sulphur excluding negative sign.

56 When the first electron gain enthalpy ($\Delta_{eg}H$) of oxygen is −141 kJ/mol, its second electron gain enthalpy is NCERT Pg 90

(a) a positive value
(b) a more negative value than the first
(c) almost the same as that of the first
(d) negative, but less negative than the first

57 The electron gain enthalpy (in kJ/mol) of fluorine, chlorine, bromine and iodine, respectively, are NCERT Pg 90

(a) −333, −325, −349 and −295
(b) −296, −325, −333 and −349
(c) −328, −349, −325 and −295
(d) −349, −333, −325 and −296

58 Which of the following pairs contain the least negative and most negative electron gain enthalpy respectively ? NCERT Pg 90

(a) P and Cl (b) S and Cl
(c) Cl and F (d) F and P

59 Which of the following statements is/are not correct? NCERT Pg 90

I. Group 17 elements have very high negative electron gain enthalpies.

II. Noble gases have large positive electron gain enthalpies.

III. Electron gain enthalpies have less negative values towards the upper left of the periodic table.

IV. Electron gain enthalpy is not a measurable quantity.

Choose the most appropriate answer from the options given below.

(a) I and III (b) II and IV (c) Only IV (d) Only III

60 Which of the following statements is/are correct? NCERT Pg 90

I. Electron gain enthalpy of noble gases are high positive value.

II. Electron affinity value of halogens are highly negative.

III. I^{st} electron gain enthalpy of most of the elements are negative and successive electron gain enthalpies are also negative.

IV. Electron affinity of Be and N are maximum positive.

Choose the most appropriate answer from the options given below.

(a) Only IV (b) I and II (c) I and III (d) I, II and III

61 In which of the following options the order arrangement does not agree with the variation of property indicated against it? NCERT Pg 90

(a) Li < Na < K < Rb (increasing metallic radius)
(b) $Al^{3+} < Mg^{2+} < Na^+ < F^-$ (increasing ionic size)
(c) B < C < N < O (increasing first ionisation enthalpy)
(d) I < Br < Cl < F (increasing electron gain enthalpy)

62 Which of the following statements is correct about the elements E_1, E_2 and E_3 with atomic number 11, 19 and 37 respectively? NCERT Pg 89

(a) E_2 would have an ionisation potential in between E_1 and E_3.
(b) E_3 would have the highest ionisation potential.
(c) E_2 would have the highest ionisation potential.
(d) Their ionisation potential would increase with increasing atomic number.

63 The correct order of electronegativity of N, O and F is NCERT Pg 91
(a) N > O > F (b) O > F > N
(c) O > N > F (d) F > O > N

64 The correct order of decreasing electronegativity values among the elements A-beryllium, B-oxygen, C-nitrogen and D-magnesium is NCERT Pg 91
(a) B > C > A > D (b) C > D > B > A
(c) A > B > C > D (d) A > B > D > C

65 In general, the properties that decrease and increase down a group in the periodic table, respectively are
(a) electronegativity and atomic radius NCERT Pg 91
(b) electronegativity and electron gain enthalpy
(c) electron gain enthalpy and electronegativity
(d) atomic radius and electronegativity

66 Which of the following statements is/are not correct? NCERT Pg 91, 92

I. Electronegativity generally increases across a period from left to right.
II. The attraction between the outer electrons and the nucleus increases as the atomic radius decreases in a period.
III. The increase in electronegativities across a period is accompanied by an increase in non-metallic properties.
IV. The valency of representative elements is always equal to the number of electrons in the outermost orbitals.

Choose the most appropriate answer from the options given below.
(a) Only IV (b) I, II and IV
(c) Only II (d) II and III

67 Oxidation state of oxygen in compounds OF_2 and Na_2O respectively are NCERT Pg 92
(a) +2, −2 (b) −2, +2
(c) −2, −1 (d) +1, −1

68 Predict the correct formula of compounds, by the following pair of elements like aluminium and sulphur with the help of oxidation states. NCERT Pg 92
(a) Al_2S_2 (b) Al_2S_3 (c) Al_3S_2 (d) Al_4S_2

69 Which of the following statements is/are correct? NCERT Pg 92

I. Metals comprise more than 78% of all known elements and appear on the left side of the periodic table.
II. Most non-metallic solids are brittle and are neither malleable nor ductile.
III. The elements become more metallic as we go down a group.
IV. The non-metallic character decreases as one goes from left to right across the periodic table.

Choose the most appropriate answer from the options given below.
(a) I, II and III (b) II, III and IV
(c) I and II (d) III and IV

70 Which of the following statements is/are not correct? NCERT Pg 92
(a) Non-metals are located at the top right hand side of the periodic table.
(b) In a horizontal row, the property of elements change from non-metallic character on the left to metallic character on the right.
(c) Chemical reactivity tends to be maximum at the both extremes (left as well as right) but lowest at the centre of the periodic table.
(d) Being monoatomic, the atomic radii of noble gases are very large.

71 Which of the following statement is incorrect? NCERT Pg 92
(a) Non-metals have strong tendency to gain electron.
(b) Electronegativity is directly related to non-metallic properties of elements.
(c) Electronegativity is inversely proportional to the metallic properties of elements.
(d) Increase in electronegativity down a group is accompanied by a decrease in non-metallic properties.

72 What is the molecular formula of the compound formed by an element '*E*' having atomic number 116.
(a) EF_3 (b) EF_2 (c) EF (d) EF_4 NCERT Pg 92

73 Which of the following types of elements show variable valency? NCERT Pg 93
(a) Transition elements (b) Alkali metals
(c) Alkaline earth metals (d) Halogens

74 In which of the following sets of compounds, hydrogen has same oxidation state? NCERT Pg 93
(a) CaH_2, LiH (b) LiH, H_2O
(c) NaH, HCl (d) NaH, H_2O

75 Boron behaves anomalously with respect to its other group members, because boron does not have comparatively NCERT Pg 93
(a) small size
(b) large charge to radius ratio
(c) high electronegativity
(d) vacant *d*-orbital

76 $[AlF_6]^{3-}$ exists, while $[BF_6]^{3-}$ does not. Choose the most appropriate reason. NCERT Pg 93
(a) Boron is smaller in size.
(b) Boron cannot expand its valence shell.
(c) Aluminium shows variable valency.
(d) Aluminium is more electropositive.

77 The first member of p-block elements displays greater ability to form NCERT Pg 93
(a) $p\pi$ - $d\pi$ multiple bonds (b) $p\pi$ - $p\pi$ multiple bonds
(c) single covalent bonds only (d) $d\pi$ - $d\pi$ multiple bonds

78 Which among the following sets of groups consist elements with high chemical reactivity? NCERT Pg 94
(a) Groups-1 and 11 (b) Groups-11 and 17
(c) Groups-1 and 17 (d) Groups-11 and 18

79 Within a group of alkali metals in the periodic table reactivity increases on moving NCERT Pg 94
(a) top to bottom (b) bottom to top
(c) left to right (d) right to left

80 The acidic, basic and amphoteric oxides, respectively are NCERT Pg 94
(a) Cl_2O, CaO, P_4O_{10} (b) N_2O_3, Li_2O, Al_2O_3
(c) Na_2O, SO_3, Al_2O_3 (d) MgO, Cl_2O, Al_2O_3,

81 Which of the following compounds is/are amphoteric in nature? NCERT Pg 94
(a) Cl_2O_7 (b) Al_2O_3
(c) N_2O_3 (d) Li_2O

82 During a chemical reaction with water, alkali metal oxide and halogen oxide behave respectively as NCERT Pg 94
(a) acidic oxide and basic oxide
(b) basic oxide and acidic oxide
(c) Both are neutral oxides
(d) Both are acidic oxides

83 Which of the following is the correct order of acidic character of oxides in fourth period of periodic table? NCERT Pg 94
(a) $BrO_2 < As_2O_3 < SeO_2 < GeO_2$
(b) $As_2O_3 < SeO_2 < BrO_2 < GeO_2$
(c) $GeO_2 < As_2O_3 < SeO_2 < BrO_2$
(d) $GeO_2 < SeO_2 < As_2O_3 < BrO_2$

Assertion-Reason Questions

Directions (Q. Nos. 1-10)Directions (Q. Nos. 1-10) *In the following question Assertion (A) followed by Reason (R) is given below. Choose the correct option out of the choices given below.*
(a) Both A and R are true and R is the correct explanation of A.
(b) Both A and R are true but R is not the correct explanation of A.
(c) A is true but R is false.
(d) A is false but R is true.

1 **Assertion** (A) Mendeleev's arranged elements in horizontal rows and vertical columns.
Reason (R) Mendeleev's ignored the order of atomic weight thinking that the atomic measurements might be incorrect. NCERT Pg 76

2 **Assertion** (A) The third period in the periodic table contains 18 elements and not 8 like 2nd in periodic table.
Reason (R) In third period, filling of electron starts from $3s^1$ and complete at $3p^6$. NCERT Pg 78

3 **Assertion** (A) Sixth and seventh periods in the periodic table contains 14 elements.
Reason (R) In the periodic table 14 elements each of sixth [from $Z = 58$ to $Z = 71$] and seventh periods [from $Z = 90$ to $Z = 103$] respectively are known as lanthanoids and actinoids. NCERT Pg 78

4 **Assertion** (A) The elements having $1s^2 2s^2 2p^6 3s^2$ and $1s^2 2s^2$ configuration belong to same period.
Reason (R) Both have same outermost electronic configuration. NCERT Pg 81

5 **Assertion** (A) Noble gases are highly reactive.
Reason (R) Noble gases have stable outer electronic configuration. NCERT Pg 84

6 **Assertion** (A) Na^+ and Al^{3+} are isoelectronic but the ionic radii of Al^{3+} is smaller than Na^+.
Reason (R) The nuclear attraction on the outermost shell electrons of Al^{3+} is greater than that of Na^+. NCERT Pg 87

7 **Assertion** (A) Helium has the highest first ionisation enthalpy in the periodic table.
Reason (R) Ionisation enthalpy decreases from top to bottom in a group. NCERT Pg 88

8 **Assertion** (A) Boron has a smaller first ionisation enthalpy than beryllium.
Reason (R) $2p$-electron of boron is more shielded from the nucleus by the inner core of electrons. NCERT Pg 89

9 **Assertion** (A) Electron gain enthalpy becomes less negative as we go down a group.
Reason (R) Size of the atom increases on going down the group and the added electron would be farther away from the nucleus. NCERT Pg 89

10 **Assertion** (A) In a group while going from top to bottom, oxidising nature of element decreases.
Reason (R) The tendency to accept electrons decreases, on moving down the group. NCERT Pg 95

Statement Type Questions

Directions (Q. Nos. 1-5) *In the following questions, two statements (I & II) are given. In the light of the given statements, choose the correct option given below.*

(a) Both Statement I and Statement II are false.
(b) Statement I is true but Statement II is false.
(c) Statement I is false but Statement II is true.
(d) Both Statement I and Statement II are true.

1 Statement I Zn is not a transition element whereas Cu is a transition element.

Statement II Zn belongs to group 12(IB) and Cu belong to group 11 (IB) in the periodic table. NCERT Pg 79, 84

2 Statement I In Cl_2 molecule the covalent radius is double of the atomic radius of chlorine.

Statement II Ionic radius of anionic species is always greater than their atomic radius. NCERT Pg 86

3 Statement I In a period, 2nd ionisation energy of alkali metal is minimum.

Statement II After losing one electron, alkali metals attains inert gas electronic configuration. NCERT Pg 88

4 Statement I Electronegativity is not a measurable quantity.

Statement II The electronegativity of any given element is not constant and it varies depending on the element to which it bounds. NCERT Pg 90, 91

5 Statement I Electronegativity is inversely related to the metallic properties of elements.

Statement II Decrease in electronegativity across a period is accompanied by an increase in non-metallic properties. NCERT Pg 92

6 Which of the following statements are correct?

I. Elements Be, B and S form a Dobereiner's triads.
II. Lothar Meyer plotted the physical properties against atomic volume.
III. Mendeleev predicted not only the existence of gallium and germanium, but also described some of their general physical properties.
IV. Henry Moseley showed that the atomic number is a more fundamental property of an element than its atomic mass.
V. The IUPAC name for the element with atomic number 120 is unbinilium.

Choose the most appropriate answer from the options given below. NCERT Pg 75, 76, 81

(a) I and V (b) I, II and IV
(c) II, III and V (d) III, IV and V

7 Which of the following statements are incorrect?

I. The Aufbau (build up) principle and the electronic configuration of atoms provide a theoretical foundation for the periodic classification.
II. The fifth period begins with caesium and has 18 elements in this period.
III. An elements location in the periodic table reflects the quantum number of the last orbital filled.
IV. The element with atomic number 120 will be placed in Group 2 (alkaline earth metals).
V. The compounds of the *s*-block elements, with the exception of only lithium are predominantly ionic in nature.

Choose the most appropriate answer from the options given below. NCERT Pg 84, 82, 81

(a) II and V (b) I and III
(c) II and III (d) III and IV

8 Select the correct statements from the following.

I. All metals are usually solids at room temperature and have high melting and boiling points.
II. Silicon, arsenic and antimony show the properties that are characteristic of both metals and non-metals.
III. There is no practical way by which the size of an individual atom can be measured.
IV. Atomic radii of noble gases should be compared with the van der Waals' radii of other elements.
V. Among isoelectronic species, the one with the larger positive nuclear charge will have a larger radius.

Choose the correct answer from the options given below. NCERT Pg 85, 86, 87

(a) III, IV and V (b) I, IV and V
(c) II, III and IV (d) I, II and IV

9 Select the incorrect statements from the following. NCERT Pg 79

I. A qualitative measure of the tendency of an element to lose electron is given by its ionisation enthalpy.
II. It is more difficult to remove an electron from a positively charged ion than from a neutral atom.
III. The effective nuclear charge experienced by a valence electron in an atom will be more than the actual charge on the nucleus.
IV. The penetration of a 2*s*-electron to the nucleus is less than that of a 2*p*-electron.
V. The variation in electron gain enthalpies of elements is less systematic than for ionization enthalpies.

Choose the correct answer from the options given below. NCERT Pg 89, 88, 87

(a) II and III (b) I and V (c) III, IV and V (d) I, III and IV

10 Which of the following statements are correct?

I. The elements on the extreme right of a period combine with oxygen to form basic oxide.

II. Arsenic oxide is an amphoteric oxide in nature.

III. The first ionisation enthalpy of Be is greater than that of Li.

IV. Every period of periodic table starts with a member of alkali group.

V. The valency is the most characteristic property of the elements and can be understood in terms of their electronic configurations.

Choose the most appropriate answer from the options given below. NCERT Pg 94, 92, 81

(a) II, IV and V (b) II, III and V
(c) I and III (d) I, IV and III

Matching Type Questions

1 Match the Column I with Column II and choose the correct option using the codes given below. NCERT Pg 79

Column I	Column II
A. 3d-transition series	1. Cerium ($Z = 58$)
B. 4d-transition series	2. Actinium ($Z = 89$)
C. 4f-inner transition series	3. Zinc ($Z = 30$)
D. 5f-inner transition series	4. Yttrium ($Z = 39$)

Codes

	A	B	C	D		A	B	C	D
(a)	1	2	3	4	(b)	1	2	4	3
(c)	3	4	2	1	(d)	3	4	1	2

2 Match the Column I with Column II and choose the Correct option using the codes given below. NCERT Pg 84

Column I (Element types)	Column II (General electronic configuration)
A. Inert gas elements	1. $(n-1)d^{1-10}\ ns^{0-2}$
B. Transition elements	2. ns^2np^6
C. Inner-transition elements	3. $(n-2)f^{1-14}(n-1)d^{0-1}\ ns^2$

Codes

	A	B	C		A	B	C
(a)	1	2	3	(b)	2	1	3
(c)	3	2	1	(d)	2	3	1

3 Match the Column I with Column II and choose the correct option using the codes given below. NCERT Pg 90, 88, 86

Column I	Column II
A. Ionisation potential	1. N > O > F
B. Electronegativity	2. N < O < F
C. Z_{eff}	3. O < N < F
D. Atomic size	4. O < N < C

Codes

	A	B	C	D		A	B	C	D
(a)	3	2	1	4	(b)	2	3	2	4
(c)	2	3	4	1	(d)	1	3	2	4

4 Match the Column I with Column II and choose the correct option using the codes given below. NCERT Pg 87, 90

Column I (Order)	Column II (Properties)
A. $Li^+ < Al^{3+} < Mg^{2+} < K^+$	1. EA (Electron affinity)
B. $Li^+ > Al^{3+} > Mg^{2+} > K^+$	2. Ionic radii
C. Cl > F > Br > I	3. EN (Electronegativity)
D. F > Cl > Br > I	4. ENC (Effective nuclear charge)

Codes

	A	B	C	D
(a)	2	4	3	1
(b)	2	4	1	3
(c)	4	2	3	1
(d)	4	2	1	3

5 Match the Column I with Column II and choose the correct option using the codes given below. NCERT Pg 90

Column I (Electronic configuration)	Column II (Electron gain enthalpy/kJ mol^{-1})
A. $1s^2\ 2s^2\ 2p^6$	1. − 53
B. $1s^2\ 2s^2\ 2p^6\ 3s^1$	2. − 328
C. $1s^2\ 2s^2\ 2p^5$	3. − 141
D. $1s^2\ 2s^2\ 2p^4$	4. + 116

Codes

	A	B	C	D
(a)	4	1	2	3
(b)	1	2	3	4
(c)	3	2	1	4
(d)	2	4	1	3

Numerical Value Questions

1 The sum of group number and number of valence electrons with atomic number 15 is .... **NCERT Pg 82**

2 How many ions are isoelectronic with argon? **NCERT Pg 87**
$Ba^{2+}, Sr^{2+}, K^{+}, S^{2-}, O^{2-}, F^{-}, Cl^{-}, Sc^{3+}, Mg^{2+}, Ca^{2+}$

3 The total number of isoelectronic species from the given set is .... **NCERT Pg 87**
O^{2-}, F^{-}, Al, Mg^{2+}, Na^{+}, O^{+}, Mg, Al^{3+}

4 How many pairs are in which first species has lower ionisation energy than second species? **NCERT Pg 87, 88**
(i) N and O (ii) Br and K (iii) Be and B
(iv) I and I^- (v) Li and Li^+ (vi) Ba and Se

5 IE and EA values of an element are 15.0 eV and 4.8 eV respectively. Its electronegativity on Pauling scale is .... (Nearest integer) **NCERT Pg 91**

NCERT Exemplar's Questions

1 Which important property did Mendeleev use to classify the elements in his periodic table?
(a) Atomic weight (b) Atomic number
(c) Melting point (d) Boiling point

2 In terms of period and group, where would you locate the element with, $Z = 114$?
(a) Period-5, Group- 6
(b) Period-7, Group-14
(c) Period-5, Group-10
(d) Period-3, Group-13

3 Mark the atomic number of the element present in the third period and seventeenth group of the periodic table.
(a) 17 (b) 18
(c) 19 (d) 20

4 The statement that is incorrect for periodic classification of elements is
(a) the properties of elements are periodic function of their atomic numbers
(b) non-metallic elements are less in number than metallic elements
(c) for transition elements, the 3*d*-orbitals are filled with electrons after 3*p*-orbitals and before 4*s*-orbitals
(d) the first ionisation enthalpies of elements generally increase with increase in atomic number as we go along a period

5 Match the correct atomic radius with the element.

	Element		Atomic radius (pm)
A.	Be	1.	74
B.	C	2.	88
C.	O	3.	111
D.	B	4.	77
E.	N	5.	66

6 The period number in the long form of the periodic table is equal to
(a) magnetic quantum number of any element of the period
(b) atomic number of any element of the period
(c) maximum principal quantum number of any element of the period
(d) maximum azimuthal quantum number of any element of the period

7 The elements in which electrons are progressively filled in 4*f*-orbital are called
(a) actinoids
(b) transition elements
(c) lanthanoids
(d) halogens

8 Which of the following is not an actinoid?
(a) Curium ($Z = 96$)
(b) Californium ($Z = 98$)
(c) Uranium ($Z = 92$)
(d) Terbium ($Z = 65$)

9 The electronic configuration of gadolinium (atomic number = 64) is
(a) [Xe] $4f^3 5d^5 6s^2$ (b) [Xe] $4f^7 5d^2 6s^1$
(c) [Xe] $4f^7 5d^1 6s^2$ (d) [Xe] $4f^8 5d^6 6s^2$

10 The order of screening effect of electrons of *s, p, d* and *f*-orbitals of a given shell of an atom on its outer shell electrons is
(a) $s > p > d > f$ (b) $f > d > p > s$
(c) $p < d < s > f$ (d) $f > p > s > d$

11 Which of the following is the correct order of size of the given species?
(a) $I > I^- > I^+$ (b) $I^+ > I^- > I$
(c) $I > I^+ > I^-$ (d) $I^- > I > I^+$

12 Consider the isoelectronic species, Na^+, Mg^{2+}, F^- and O^{2-}. The correct order of increasing length of their radii is

(a) $F^- < O^{2-} < Mg^{2+} < Na^+$
(b) $Mg^{2+} < Na^+ < F^- < O^{2-}$
(c) $O^{2-} < F^- < Na^+ < Mg^{2+}$
(d) $O^{2-} < F^- < Mg^{2+} < Na^+$

13 The first ionisation enthalpies of Na, Mg, Al and Si are in the order

(a) Na < Mg > Al < Si (b) Na > Mg > Al > Si
(c) Na < Mg < Al < Si (d) Na > Mg > Al < Si

14 Match the correct ionisation enthalpies and electron gain enthalpies of the following elements.

	Elements		ΔH_1	ΔH_2	$\Delta_{eg}H$
A.	Most reactive non-metal	1.	419	3051	− 48
B.	Most reactive metal	2.	1681	3374	− 328
C.	Least reactive element	3.	738	1451	− 40
D.	Metal forming binary halide	4.	2372	5251	+ 48

15 Among halogens, the correct order of amount of energy released in electron gain enthalpy is

(a) F > Cl > Br > I (b) F < Cl < Br < I
(c) F < Cl > Br > I (d) F > Br > Cl > I

16 Electronic configuration of four elements *A*, *B*, *C* and *D* are given below.

A. $1s^2\ 2s^2\ 2p^6$ *B*. $1s^2\ 2s^2\ 2p^4$
C. $1s^2\ 2s^2\ 2p^6\ 3s^1$ *D*. $1s^2\ 2s^2\ 2p^5$

Which of the following is the correct order of increasing tendency to gain electron?

(a) *A* < *C* < *B* < *D* (b) *A* < *B* < *C* < *D*
(c) *D* < *B* < *C* < *A* (d) *D* < *A* < *B* < *C*

17 The formation of oxide ion $O^{2-}(g)$, from oxygen atom requires first an exothermic and then an endothermic step as shown below.

$$O(g) + e^- \longrightarrow O^-(g); \Delta H^\ominus = -141 \text{ kJ mol}^{-1}$$
$$O^-(g) + e^- \longrightarrow O^{2-}(g); \Delta H^\ominus = +780 \text{ kJ mol}^{-1}$$

Thus, process of formation of O^{2-} in gas phase is unfavourable even though O^{2-} is isoelectronic with neon. It is due to the fact that

(a) oxygen is more electronegative
(b) addition of electron in oxygen results in larger size of the ion
(c) electron repulsion outweighs the stability gained by achieving noble gas configuration
(d) O^- ion has comparatively smaller size than O-atom

Past Exams' Questions

NEET Archive

1 Arrange the following elements in increasing order of electronegativity **NCERT Pg 91, NEET 2024**

N, O, F, C, Si

Choose the correct answer from the options given below:

(a) Si < C < N < O < F (b) Si < C < O < N < F
(c) O < F < N < C < Si (d) F < O < N < C < Si

2 Arrange the following elements in increasing order of first ionisation enthalpy : **NCERT Pg 88, NEET 2024**

Li, Be, B, C, N

Choose the correct answer from the options given below:

(a) Li < Be < B < C < N (b) Li < B < Be < C < N
(c) Li < Be < C < B < N (d) Li < Be < N < B < C

3 The element expected to form largest ion to achieve the nearest noble gas configuration is **NCERT Pg 87, NEET 2023**

(a) F (b) N (c) Na (d) O

4 Which one of the following arrangements represents the correct order of least negative to most negative electron gain enthalpy for C, Ca, Al, F and O? **NCERT Pg 89, 90, NEET 2023**

(a) Al < Ca < O < C < F
(b) Al < O < C < Ca < F
(c) C < F < O < Al < Ca
(d) Ca < Al < C < O < F

5 The IUPAC name of an element with atomic number 119 is **NCERT Pg 80, NEET 2022**

(a) unnilennium
(b) unununnium
(c) ununoctium
(d) ununennium

6 From the following pairs of ion which one is not an isoelectronic pair? **NCERT Pg 87, NEET 2021**

(a) O^{2-}, F^- (b) Na^+, Mg^{2+}
(c) Mn^{2+}, Fe^{3+} (d) Fe^{2+}, Mn^{2+}

7 Identify the incorrect match.

Name	IUPAC official name
(A) Unnilunium	(i) Mendelevium
(B) Unniltrium	(ii) Lawrencium
(C) Unnilhexium	(iii) Seaborgium
(D) Unununnium	(iv) Darmstadtium

NCERT Pg 80, NEET (Sep.) 2020

(a) (B) – (ii) (b) (C) – (iii) (c) (D) – (iv) (d) (A) – (i)

8 Match the element in Column I with that in Column II.

Column I	Column II
A. Copper	1. Non-metal
B. Fluorine	2. Transition metal
C. Silicon	3. Lanthanoid
D. Cerium	4. Metalloid

Codes NCERT Pg 84, 85, NEET 2020

	A	B	C	D		A	B	C	D
(a)	1	2	3	4	(b)	2	4	1	3
(c)	2	1	4	3	(d)	4	3	1	2

9 Match the following. NCERT Pg 94, NEET 2020

Oxide	Nature
A. CO	1. Basic
B. BaO	2. Neutral
C. Al_2O_3	3. Acidic
D. Cl_2O_7	4. Amphoteric

Which of the following is correct option?

	A	B	C	D		A	B	C	D
(a)	2	1	4	3	(b)	3	4	1	2
(c)	4	3	2	1	(d)	1	2	3	4

10 The element ($Z = 114$) has been discovered recently. It will belong to which of the following family/group and electronic configuration? NCERT Pg 79, 84, NEET 2017

(a) Halogen family, $[Rn]\,5f^{14}\,6d^{10}\,7s^2\,7p^5$
(b) Carbon family, $[Rn]\,5f^{14}\,6d^{10}\,7s^2\,7p^2$
(c) Oxygen family, $[Rn]\,5f^{14}\,6d^{10}\,7s^2\,7p^4$
(d) Nitrogen family, $[Rn]\,5f^{14}\,6d^{10}\,7s^2\,7p^6$

11 The species Ar, K^+ and Ca^{2+} contain the same number of electrons. In which order do their radii increase? NCERT Pg 87, CBSE-AIPMT 2015

(a) $Ar < K^+ < Ca^{2+}$ (b) $Ca^{2+} < Ar < K^+$
(c) $Ca^{2+} < K^+ < Ar$ (d) $K^+ < Ar < Ca^{2+}$

12 Which of the following orders of ionic radii is correctly represented? NCERT Pg 87, CBSE-AIPMT 2014

(a) $H^- > H > H^+$ (b) $Na^+ > F^- > O^{2-}$
(c) $F^- > O^{2-} > Na^+$ (d) $Al^{3+} > Mg^{2+} > N^{3-}$

JEE Main Archive

13 Match List I with List II. NCERT Pg 91, JEE Main 2024

List I (Elements)	List II (Properties in their respective groups)
A. Cl, S	I. Elements with highest electronegativity
B. Ge, As	II. Elements with largest atomic size
C. Fr, Ra	III. Elements which show properties of both metals and non-metal
D. F, O	IV. Elements with highest negative electron gain enthalpy

Choose the correct answer from the options given below : NCERT Pg 91, JEE Main 2024

(a) A-III, B-II, C-I, D-IV (b) A-II, B-III, C-IV, D-I
(c) A-IV, B-III, C-II, D-I (d) A-II, B-I, C-IV, D-III

14 If IUPAC name of an element is "unununnium" then the element belongs to nth group of periodic table. The value of n is .... NCERT Pg 80, JEE Main 2024

15 Given below are two statements:

Statement I The $4f$ and $5f$-series of elements are placed separately in the periodic table to preserve the principle of classification.

Statement II s-block elements can be found in pure form in nature. NCERT Pg 84, JEE Main 2024

In the light of the above statements, choose the most appropriate answer from the options given below.

(a) Statement I is true but Statement II is false.
(b) Both Statement I and Statement II are false.
(c) Both Statement I and Statement II are true.
(d) Statement I is false but Statement II is true.

16 The correct order of metallic character is NCERT Pg 95, JEE Main 2023

(a) K > Be > Ca (b) K > Ca > Be
(c) Be > Ca > K (d) Ca > K > Be

17 For elements B, C, N, Li, Be, O and F, the correct order of first ionisation enthalpy is NCERT Pg 88, JEE Main 2023

(a) B > Li > Be > C > N > O > F
(b) Li < B < Be < C < O < N < F
(c) Li < Be < B < C < O < N < F
(d) Li < Be < B < C < N < O < F

18 For electron gain enthalpies of the elements denoted as $\Delta_{eg}H$, the incorrect option is NCERT Pg 88, 87, JEE Main 2023

(a) $\Delta_{eg}H(Cl) < \Delta_{eg}H(F)$ (b) $\Delta_{eg}H(Te) < \Delta_{eg}H(Po)$
(c) $\Delta_{eg}H(Se) < \Delta_{eg}H(S)$ (d) $\Delta_{eg}H(I) < \Delta_{eg}H(At)$

19 The metal that has very low melting point and its periodic position is closer to a metalloid is
NCERT Pg 85, JEE Main 2022

(a) Al (b) Ga
(c) Se (d) In

20 Metals generally melt at very high temperature. Amongst the following, the metal with the highest melting point will be NCERT Pg 85, JEE Main 2022

(a) Hg (b) Ag
(c) Ga (d) Cs

21 Given below are two statements, one is labelled as Assertion (A) and the other is labelled as Reason (R).

Assertion (A) The first ionisation enthalpy for oxygen is lower than that of nitrogen.

Reason (R) The four electrons in $2p$ orbitals of oxygen experience more electron-electron repulsion.

In the light of the above statements, choose the correct answer from the options given below.
NCERT Pg 88, JEE Main 2022

(a) Both A and R are true and R is the correct explanation of A.
(b) Both A and R are true but R is not the correct explanation of A.
(c) A is true but R is false.
(d) A is false but R is true.

22 Given below are two statements. One is labelled as Assertion (A) and the other is labelled as Reason (R) .

Assertion (A) The ionic radii of O^{2-} and Mg^{2+} are same.

Reason (R) Both O^{2-} and Mg^{2+} are isoelectronic species.

In the light of the above statements, choose the correct answer from the options given below.
NCERT Pg 87, JEE Main 2022

(a) Both A and R are true and R is the correct explanation of A.
(b) Both A and R are true but R is not the correct explanation of A.
(c) A is true but R is false.
(d) A is false but R is true.

23 Given below are two statements one is labelled as Assertion (A) and the other is labelled as Reason (R).

Assertion (A) Metallic character decreases and non-metallic character increases on moving from left to right in a period.

Reason (R) It is due to increase in ionisation enthalpy and decrease in electron gain enthalpy, when one moves from left to right in a period.

In the light of the above statements, choose the most appropriate answer from the options given below.
NCERT Pg 91, 92, JEE Main 2021

(a) Both A and R are true and R is the correct explanation of A.
(b) Both A and R are true but R is not the correct explanation of A.
(c) A is true but R is false.
(d) A is false but R is true.

24 The set of elements that differ in mutual relationship from those of the other sets is NCERT Pg 93, JEE Main 2021

(a) Li-Mg (b) B-Si
(c) Be-Al (d) Li-Na

Skill Boosters

1 The first ($\Delta_i H_1$) and the second ($\Delta_i H_2$) ionisation enthalpies in kJ mol^{-1} of a few elements are given as

Elements	$\Delta_i H_1$	$\Delta_i H_2$	$\Delta_{eg} H$
A	520	7300	–60
B	419	3051	–48
C	1681	3374	–328
D	1008	1846	–295
E	2372	5251	+48
F	738	1451	–53

Which of the given elements is most reactive and least reactive metal respectively?

(a) *A*, *C* (b) *F*, *D* (c) *B*, *E* (d) *F*, *E*

2 In the given graph, a periodic property (R) is plotted against atomic numbers (Z) of the elements. Which property is shown in the graph and how it is correlated with reactivity of the elements?

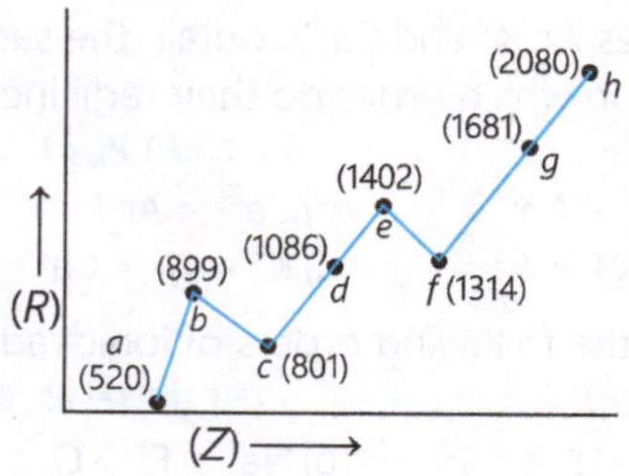

(a) Ionisation enthalpy in a group, reactivity decrease from $a \to h$.
(b) Ionisation enthalpy in a period, reactivity increase from $a \to h$.
(c) Metallic character in a group, reactivity increase from $a \to h$.
(d) Ionisation enthalpy in a group, reactivity increase from $a \to h$.

3 If one electron is present in the outermost orbit, there will be no screening in that orbital. Each electron contribute, 0.35 (total electrons minus one electron) present in the outermost shell. A contribution of 0.85 for each electron is taken in the $(n-1)^{th}$ shell. Find out the screening constant (σ) for a 4s electron of Mn ($Z = 25$).
(a) 22.6 (b) 30.35 (c) 20.25 (d) 22.95

4 The first (IE_1) and second (IE_2) ionisation enthalpies of element, *A* are given below.

	A
IE_1	995
IE_2	1600

In an experiment $\frac{1}{13}$ mole of A atom in vapour phase absorb 100 kJ of energy. So, that it forms a mixture of A^+ and A^{2+} ions. Energy utilised to form A^{2+} from A^+ in experiment is
(a) 995 kJ (b) 1600 kJ (c) 62.5 kJ (d) 23.46 kJ

5 Consider the following sequence of reaction.

$$A^- \xrightarrow{\Delta H_4} A \xrightarrow{\Delta H_1} A^+ \xrightarrow{\Delta H_2} A^{2+} \xrightarrow{\Delta H_3} A^{3+}$$
$$A \xrightarrow{\Delta H_5} A^- \qquad A^+ \xrightarrow{\Delta H_6} A$$

If the electronic configuration of element *A* is [Ne] $3s^1$, then which of the following order is incorrect regarding given enthalpies?
(a) $|\Delta H_1| = |\Delta H_6|$ (b) $|\Delta H_3| > |\Delta H_2|$
(c) $|\Delta H_2| > |\Delta H_3|$ (d) $|\Delta H_4| = |\Delta H_5|$

6 Along a period on moving left to right atomic/ionic radii and metallic character decreases while IE, EN, non-metallic character and oxidising power increases. However, $\Delta_{eg}H^\ominus$ becomes less negative down a group but more negative along a period. If the ionic radii of M^+ and X^- are about 135 pm, then expected values of metallic radii of *M* and *X* should be respectively.
(a) 65 and 230 pm
(b) 230 and 60 pm
(c) 230 and 135 pm
(d) 135 and 135 pm

7 Identify the elements which are correctly matched with their sequential ionisation energies.

Elements	ΔH_1 (kJ/mol)	ΔH_2 (kJ/mol)
E_1	900	1758
E_2	2372	5251
E_3	520	7297

	E_1	E_2	E_3
(a)	Noble gas	Alkali metal	Alkaline earth metal
(b)	Alkaline earth metal	Noble gas	Alkali metal
(c)	Alkali metal	Alkaline earth metal	Noble gas
(d)	Alkali metal	Noble gas	Alkaline earth metal

8 Periodic properties are directly or indirectly related to their electronic configuration and show a regular gradation on moving from left to right in a period or from top to bottom in a group. Generally, the first ionisation energy increases across a period. But there are some exceptions. The one which is not an exception is
(a) Na and Mg (b) Be and B
(c) N and O (d) Mg and Al

Correct Codes

Topical Questions

1. (d)	2. (a)	3. (b)	4. (b)	5. (b)	6. (b)	7. (b)	8. (b)	9. (a)	10. (b)
11. (a)	12. (b)	13. (c)	14. (b)	15. (b)	16. (d)	17. (a)	18. (c)	19. (a)	20. (b)
21. (b)	22. (b)	23. (b)	24. (c)	25. (c)	26. (d)	27. (b)	28. (c)	29. (c)	30. (b)
31. (d)	32. (a)	33. (c)	34. (b)	35. (d)	36. (a)	37. (b)	38. (c)	39. (b)	40. (d)
41. (a)	42. (d)	43. (c)	44. (a)	45. (b)	46. (d)	47. (c)	48. (b)	49. (c)	50. (b)
51. (b)	52. (b)	53. (d)	54. (c)	55. (c)	56. (a)	57. (c)	58. (a)	59. (c)	60. (d)
61. (d)	62. (a)	63. (d)	64. (a)	65. (a)	66. (a)	67. (a)	68. (b)	69. (a)	70. (a)
71. (d)	72. (b)	73. (a)	74. (a)	75. (d)	76. (b)	77. (b)	78. (c)	79. (a)	80. (b)
81. (b)	82. (b)	83. (c)							

Assertion-Reason

1. (b)	2. (d)	3. (d)	4. (d)	5. (d)	6. (a)	7. (b)	8. (a)	9. (a)	10. (a)

Statement Based

1. (b)	2. (c)	3. (c)	4. (d)	5. (b)	6. (d)	7. (a)	8. (c)	9. (d)	10. (b)

Matching Type

1. (d)	2. (b)	3. (a)	4. (b)	5. (a)

Numerical Value

1. (20)	2. (5)	3. (5)	4. (2)	5. (4)

NCERT Exemplar

1. (a)	2. (b)	3. (a)	4. (c)	5. A-3, B-4, C-5, D-2, E-1	6. (c)	7. (c)	8. (d)
9. (c)	10. (a)	11. (d)	12. (b)	13. (a)	14. A-2, B-1, C-4, D-3	15. (c)	16. (a)	17. (c)

Past Exams

1. (a)	2. (b)	3. (b)	4. (d)	5. (d)	6. (d)	7. (c)	8. (c)	9. (a)	10. (b)
11. (c)	12. (a)	13. (c)	14. (11)	15. (a)	16. (b)	17. (b)	18. (a)	19. (b)	20. (b)
21. (b)	22. (d)	23. (c)	24. (d)						

Skill Boosters

1. (c)	2. (b)	3. (a)	4. (d)	5. (c)	6. (b)	7. (b)	8. (a)

Step by Step

Decoding the Questions

Concept Builders

1 electronic configuration

2 True

3 Na

4 Ga_2O_3

5 False

6 series, periods

7 Unnilhexium

8 False

9 Hydrogen

10 high reactivity

11 Sn

12 Cd, transition

13 True

14 $120 \rightarrow [Uuo]_{118} 8s^2$

15 False

16 increases, decreases

17 114 pm

18 ionisation energy, kJ mol^{-1}

19 False

20 PX_2

21 oxygen, nitrogen

22 True

23 Mg_3N_2

24 False

25 First

26 +3, 6

27 True

28 False

29 Amphoteric

30 False

Topical Solutions

1 (*d*) Technetium, neptunium, einstenium are man-made elements. Technetium is the first man-made element.

2 (*a*) Among the given statements, only (a) is correct while other are incorrect. Their correct forms are as follow

- Law of triads, seemed to work only for few elements.
- The properties of Br were in between those of Cl and I.
- Group 17 elements are known as halogens.

3 (*b*) Statement (b) is correct, while the other statements are incorrect. Their correct forms are as follows

- He arranged the elements in the increasing order of their atomic weights.
- This law is true only for elements upto calcium.
- This law is true for both physical and chemical properties.

4 (*b*) 5 (*b*)

6 (*b*) All the properties of Mendeleev's periodic table are correct except (b). Its correct form is as follows

He could not assign the proper positions for isotopes.

7 (*b*)

8 (*b*) Statement (b) is correct, while the other statements are incorrect. Their correct form are as follows

- According to modern periodic law, the seventh period is incomplete.
- Subsequent periods consist of 2, 8, 8, 18, 18 and 32 elements.
- The second period consists of 8 elements.

9 (*a*) Moseley's observation on characteristic X-ray spectra of elements relates frequency (ν) of X-rays emitted to the atomic number by the relation $\sqrt{\nu} = a(Z-b)$. The plot of $\sqrt{\nu}$ *vs* Z is linear straight line.

10 (*b*) Period number is the highest principal quantum number in the periodic table.

11 (*a*)

12 (*b*) The element with atomic number 115 is having the electronic configuration $(Z) = [Rn] 5f^{14} 6d^{10} 7s^2 7p^3$ so the last electron goes to the *p*-block orbital and having 5 valence electron so, it belong to 15 group of nitrogen family and it is moscovium (Mc).

13 (*c*)

14 (*b*) Only nuclear mass is the one among all factors which does not affect the valence shell because nucleus consist of protons and neutrons. Protons, i.e. nuclear charge affect the valence shell but neutrons do not.

15 (*b*) Scandium ($Z = 21$) which has electronic configuration $= [Ar] 3d^1 4s^2$ and zinc ($Z = 30$) has electronic configuration $= [Ar] 3d^{10} 4s^2$.

16 (*d*) All the given statements are correct except (d) the correct form is as Hydrogen shows similarity more with I[st] group than VIIth group.

17 (*a*) The elements in a vertical column of the periodic table constitute a group or family and exhibit similar chemical behaviour. This similarity arises because these elements have the same number and same distribution of electrons in their outermost orbitals.

18 (*c*)

19 (*a*) Statement (a) is incorrect. It's correct form is as follows :

The 4th period in the periodic table ends at krypton with the filling up of the 4*p*-orbitals.

Rest other statements are correct.

20 (*b*)

21 (*b*) The shells in noble gases are completely filled by electrons and it is very difficult to alter this stable electronic configuration, hence, they show low chemical reactivity.

22 (*b*) The halogens (group 17) and the chalcogens (group 16) are two groups of elements having highly negative electron gain enthalpies.

23 (*b*) 24 (*c*) 25 (*c*)

26 (*d*) The element *A* can be phosphorus (P) and its electronic configuration is

$A(P) = 1s^2 2s^2 2p^6 3s^2 3p^3$

So, element '*A*' has completely filled *s*-orbital and half-filled *p*-orbitals.

27 (*b*) Statement II is incorrect. It's correct form is as follows

The chemistry of the early actinoids is more complicated than corresponding lanthanoids due to the large number of oxidation states possible for actinoid elements.

Rest other statements are correct.

28 (*c*) All the options are correctly matched except (c). The correct form of (c) is as follows

The element with electronic configuration $1s^2, 2s^2, 2p^6, 3s^2, 3p^3$ is the element which should belong to 3rd period and 15th group.

29 (*c*)

30 (*b*) Only (b) is correct while the other are incorrect. Their correct form are as follow

- Gold (Au) is a noble metal present with in transition metal.
- Iodine is a non-metallic, nearly black solid at room temperature and has a glittering crystalline appearance.
- Chlorine is a non-metal with electronic configuration $3s^2 3p^5$ and has highest electron gain enthalpy.

31 (*d*) Down the group metallic character increases, while in period from left to right metallic character decreases, but non-metallic character increases.

So, the correct order is

$$Na > Mg > Be > Si > P.$$

32 (*a*)

33 (*c*) Statement (c) is incorrect.

It's correct form is as follows

Atomic radii can't be measured precisely as atom has no sharp boundary.

Rest other statements are correct.

34 (*b*) Atomic radius is depicted in the table, as it decreases along the period and increases down the group.

35 (*d*) As we move left to right in a period, the number of electron in outer shell increases with increase in atomic number. This results in increase in inter-electronic repulsions in the outermost shell from Li to F.

Therefore, decrease in radius from O to F is not as much as in case of from Li to Be.

36 (*a*) Statement (a) is incorrect.

It's correct form is as follows

Amongst isoelectronic species, smaller the positive charge on the cation, larger is the ionic radius.

Rest other statements are correct.

37 (*b*) Size of an atom decreases when an electron is removed from it due to increased nucleus charge.

While, size of an atom increases with addition of an extra electron (formation of anion) due to increased repulsion among electrons.

38 (*c*) Among the given compounds, only three compounds (NO_3^-, CO_3^{2-} and SO_2) are isoelectronic.

- $NO_3^- \rightarrow 32$ electrons
- $SO_2 \rightarrow 32$ electrons
- $CO_3^{2-} \rightarrow 32$ electrons
- $SO_4^{2-} \rightarrow 50$ electrons
- $NO_2^- \rightarrow 24$ electrons

39 (*b*) Atomic radius generally decreases as we compare elements in a period from left to right,

$$\therefore \quad C > O > F$$

but elements present in next period are larger in size,

$$\therefore \quad Br > Cl > C > O > F.$$

So, the correct increasing order of the atomic radii

$$C < B < A < D < E.$$

40 (*d*) All the ions have 10 electrons and, thus are isoelectronic species. Size of O^{2-} is largest among $F^-, Na^+, Mg^{2+}, O^{2-}$ ions. This is due to the fact that, addition of one or more electrons would result in increased repulsion among the electrons and a decrease in effective nuclear charge.

41 (*a*) The ion with the greater positive charge will have a smaller radius because of the greater attraction in the electrons due to the nucleus and ions with the greater negative charge will have large radius due to net repulsion of electrons.

42 (*d*)

43 (*c*) I.E. of noble gases are maximum, whereas that of alkali metal is least. I.E. of alkaline earth metal is higher than alkali metal but lower than subsequent elements, thus the correct order is

$$Ba < Ca < Se < S < Ar.$$

44 (*a*)

45 (*b*) In boron (B), the electron is removed from p-orbital. The 2*p*-electrons of boron is more shielded from the nucleus by inner core of electrons than the 2*s*-electrons. Also, removal of one 2*p*-electron from boron leads to a comparatively stable configuration of $2s^2$, where the two electrons are paired.

Hence, the first ionisation energy of boron (B) is lower than both Be and C.

46 (*d*)

47 (*c*) Statement II is incorrect.

It's correct form is as follows

Ionisation enthalpies are always positive.

Rest other statements are correct.

48 (*b*)

49 (*c*) After losing one electron, the atom will get a stable configuration and its second ionisation energy will be very high.

50 (*b*) The correct order is represented in I, II and III while IV is incorrect. The correct order of bond energy is $F_2 < Br_2 < Cl_2$.

51 (*b*) First $\Delta_i H$ value for Al will be more close to 575 kJ mol^{-1}. The value for Al should be lower than that of Mg because of effective shielding of 3*p*-electrons from the nucleus by 3*s*-electrons.

52 (*b*) $Na \longrightarrow Na^+ + e^-$ [First IE]

$Na^+ + e^- \longrightarrow Na$ [Electron gain enthalpy]

Electron gain enthalpy of Na^+ is reverse of ionisation enthalpy because reaction is reverse, so

$$\Delta_{eg}H = -5.1 \text{ eV}$$

53 (*d*) Statement (d) is incorrect.
It's correct form is as follows
The process of adding electrons to the atom can be either endothermic or exothermic.
Rest other statements are correct.

54 (*c*) Statement (c) is incorrect.
It's correct form is as follows
An electron is added to neutral gaseous atom to convert it into negative ion.
Rest other statements are correct.

55 (*c*) Statement (c) is incorrect.
It's correct form is as follows
Generally, electron gain enthalpy becomes more negative as we go up in a group.
Rest other statements are correct.

56 (*a*) The expression of second electron gain enthalpy of oxygen will be,
$O^-(g) + e^- \longrightarrow O^{2-}(g), \Delta_{eg}H_2 = +\text{ ve}$
$\Delta_{eg}H_2$ of oxygen is positive, i.e. endothermic, because a strong electrostatic repulsion will be observed between highly negative O^- and the incoming electron (e^-). A very high amount of energy will be consumed (endothermic) by the system to overcome the electrostatic repulsion.

57 (*c*)

58 (*a*) Chlorine (Cl) has most negative electron gain enthalpy, while phosphorus (P) has least negative electron gain enthalpy.

59 (*c*) Statement IV is incorrect.
It's correct form is as follows
Electron gain enthalpy is a measurable quantity.
Rest other statements are correct.

60 (*d*) Among the given statements I, II and III are correct while statement IV is incorrect.
Its correct form is:
Be($1s^2\,2s^2$) has a filled valence shell, so it does not have the tendency to gain electrons. Thus its electron affinity is almost zero.

61 (*d*) All except (d) are correct. The correct order is I < Br < F < Cl.

62 (*a*) Elements E_1, E_2 and E_3 with atomic number 11, 19 and 37 lie in group 1 (alkali metals).
Within a group, ionisation energy decreases from top to bottom. Therefore, ionisation energy of E_2 could be in between of E_1 and E_3.

63 (*d*)

64 (*a*) Electronegativity values of given elements are as follows
Be-1.5(A), Mg-1.2(D), O-3.5(B), N-3.0(C)
Hence, the correct order
B > C > A > D.

65 (*a*) Electronegativity decreases and atomic radius increases down a group in the periodic table.

66 (*a*) Statement IV is incorrect.
It's correct form is as follows
The valency of representative elements is usually equal to the number of electrons in the outermost orbitals and/or equal to eight minus the number of outermost electrons.
Rest other statements are correct.

67 (*a*)

68 (*b*) Oxidation state of aluminium (Al) = + 3.
Oxidation state of sulphur = − 2 with respect to aluminium, hence correct formula is = Al_2S_3.

69 (*a*) Statements I, II and III are correct, while the statement IV is incorrect.
It's correct form is as follows
The non-metallic character increases as one goes from left to right across the periodic table.

70 (*a*) Statement II is incorrect.
It's correct form is as follows
In a horizontal row, the property of elements change from metallic character on the left to non-metallic character on the right.
Rest other statements are correct.

71 (*d*) Statement (d) is incorrect.
It's correct form is as follows
Decrease in electronegativity down a group is accompanied by a decrease in non-metallic properties of elements.
Rest other statements are correct.

72 (*b*) Element *E* with atomic number 116 will share two electrons to achieve stable noble gas electronic configuration. It resides in the oxygen family.
Fluorine (F) shares one electron to gain a stable noble gas electronic configuration. So, 1 atom of *E* combines with 2 atoms of F to form EF_2.
Hence, option (b) is correct.

73 (*a*) Transition elements show variable valency due to involvement of incomplete *d*-orbitals in addition to electrons of *ns*-orbital. So, the electrons from both the energy levels can be used for bonding.

74 (*a*) In CaH_2, LiH and NaH, the oxidation state of H is −1, while in H_2O and HCl, the oxidation state of H is +1.
Thus, same oxidation state of H is (−1) in CaH_2 and LiH.

75 (*d*) Boron behaves anomalously with respect to its other group members, because boron has comparatively small size, high electronegativity and large charge to radius ratio but does not have vacant *d*-orbital.

76 (*b*) The most appropriate reason is that, boron cannot expand its valence shell and its maximum valency is limited to 4, while Al can expand its valence shell and hence can form $[AlF_6]^{3-}$.

77 (*b*) The first member of *p*-block elements displays greater ability to form $p\pi$-$p\pi$ multiple bonds to itself (e.g. C=C, C≡C, N=N, N≡N) and to other second period elements (e.g. C=O, C=N, C≡N, N=O) compared to subsequent members of the same group.

78 (*c*)

79 (*a*)

80 (*b*) The acidic, basic and amphoteric oxides, respectively are N_2O_3, Li_2O and Al_2O_3.

81 (*b*) Among the given compounds, only Al_2O_3 is amphoteric in nature while Cl_2O_7 and N_2O_3 are acidic and Li_2O is basic in nature.

82 (*b*) During a chemical reaction with water, alkali metal oxide and halogen oxide behave respectively as basic oxide and acidic oxides.

83 (*c*) Ge, As, Se and Br are elements of period 4. As we move from Ge to Br the non-metallic character increases, thus acidic character of oxide is also increases.

Assertion-Reason

1 (*b*) Both A and R are true but R is not the correct explanation of A.
The correct form of A is:
Mendeleev arranged elements in horizontal rows and vertical columns in order of their increasing atomic weights in such a way that, the elements with similar properties occupied the same vertical column or group.

2 (*d*) A is false but R is true
The correct form of A is:
The third period in the periodic table contain 8 elements.

3 (*d*) A is false but R is true.
The correct form of A is:
Sixth period contains 32 elements and seventh period is incomplete and like sixth, the period would have 32 elements.

4 (*d*) A is false but R is true
The correct form of A is:
The elements having $1s^2 2s^2 2p^6 3s^2$ and $1s^2 2s^2$ electronic configuration belongs to same group not period.

5 (*d*) A is false but R is true
The correct form of A is:
Noble gases are very less reactive due to stable outer electronic configuration like ns^2np^6 or ns^2.

6 (*a*) Both A and R are true and R is the correct explanation of A.

7 (*b*) Both A and R are true but R is not the correct explanation of A. The correct form of A is:
Helium has the highest first ionisation enthalpy in the periodic table because greater force of attraction acts between nuclei and electrons of 1*s*-orbital.

8 (*a*) Both A and R are true and R is the correct explanation of A.

9 (*a*) Both A and R are true and R is the correct explanation of A.

10 (*a*) Both A and R are true and R is the correct explanation of A.

Statement Type

1 (*b*) Statement I is true but statement II is false. The correct form of Statement II is:
Zn belongs to group 12 (II B) and Cu belongs to group 11 (I B) in the periodic table.

2 (*c*) Statement I is false but Statement II is true. The correct form of Statement I is:
Covalent radius is half of the atomic radius of chlorine.

3 (*c*) Statement I is false but Statement II is true. The correct form of Statement I is : In a period, 2nd ionisation energy of alkali metal is maximum.

4 (*d*) Both Statements I and II are true.

5 (*b*) Statement I is true and Statement II is false. The correct form of Statement II is as follows
Increase in electronegativity across a period is accompanied by an increase in non-metallic properties.

6 (*d*) Among the given statements only III, IV and V are correct while the statements I and II are incorrect. Their correct form are as follow
- Elements Be, B and S do not form a Dobereiner triads because the atomic weight of the middle element (B) is not the arithmetic mean of the other two elements.
- Lothar Meyer plotted the physical properties against atomic weight.

7 (*a*) Among the given statements, only II and V are incorrect while the I, III and IV statements are correct. The correct form of II and V are
- The fifth period begins with rubidium and has 18 elements in this period.
- The compounds of the *s*-block elements, with the exception of lithium and beryllium are predominantly ionic in nature.

8 (*c*) Among the given statements, only II, III and IV are correct while the statements I and V are incorrect. Their correct form are as follow
- Metals are usually solids at room temperature except mercury and metals usually have high melting and boiling point except gallium and caesium.
- Among isoelectronic species, the one with the larger positive nuclear charge will have a smaller radius.

9 (*d*) Among the given statements, only I, III and IV are incorrect while II and V are correct. the correct form of I, III and IV are as follows
- A quantitative measure of the tendency of an element to lose electron is given by its ionisation enthalpy.
- The effective nuclear charge experienced by a valence electron in an atom will be less than actual charge on the nucleus.
- The penetration of a 2*s*-electron to the nucleus is more than that of a 2*p*-electron.

10 (*b*) Among the given statements, only II, III and V are correct while I and IV are incorrect. Their correct form are as follows
- The elements on the extreme right of a period combine with oxygen to form acidic oxide.
- Every period of the periodic table (except first period) starts with a member of alkali metals.

Matching Type

1 (*d*) The correct match is
A-3, B-4, C-1, D-2.

2 (*b*) The correct match is
A-2, B-1, C-3.

3 (*a*) The correct match is
A-3, B-2, C-1, D-4.

4 (*b*) The correct match is
A-2, B-4, C-1, D-3.

5 (*a*) The correct match is
A-4, B-1, C-2, D-3.

Numerical Value

1 (20) Number of valence electrons present in an atom decides the group number.
Electronic configuration of an element having atomic number = 15
$= 1s^2 2s^2 2p^6 3s^2 3p^3$
As five electrons are present in valence shell, its group number is 15.
∴Sum of group number and number of valence electrons = 15 + 5 = 20.

2 (5) Argon has 18 electrons. Among the given species only K^+, S^{2-}, Cl^-, Sc^{3+} and Ca^{2+} have 18 electrons. Hence, they are isoelectronic with argon.

3 (5) Among the given species, O^{2-}, F^-, Al^{3+}, Mg^{2+} and Na^+ are isoelectronic species having 10 electrons.

4 (2) Among the given pairs, only two pairs (v) and (vi) in which first species has lower ionisation energy than second species.

5 (4) As, $\chi_{Pauling} = \dfrac{\chi_{Mulliken}}{2.8}$
$$= \frac{I.E + EA}{2 \times 2.8}$$
$$= \frac{15.0 + 4.8}{2 \times 2.8} = \frac{19.8}{5.6}$$
$$= 3.53 \approx 4$$

NCERT Exemplar's

1 (*a*)

2 (*b*) The given element $_{114}Z$ has electronic configuration $_{86}[Rn]\, 7s^2, 5f^{14}, 6d^{10}, 7p^2$.
In the periodic table, the element with $Z = 114$ is located in *p*-block (as last electron enters in *p*-subshell).
Period – 7th (as $n = 7$ for valence shell)
Group – 14th (for *p*-block elements, group number = 10 + number of electrons in the valence shell).

3 (*a*)

4 (*c*) Statement (c) is incorrect.
It's correct form is as follows
In case of transition elements (or any elements), the order of filling of electrons in various orbital is
$$3p < 4s < 3d.$$
Thus, 3*d*-orbital is filled when 4*s*-orbital gets completely filled.
Rest other statements are correct.

5 The correct match is
A-3, B-4, C-5, D-2, E-1.

6 (*c*) 7 (*c*)

8 (*d*) Elements with atomic number, $Z = 90$ to 103 are called actinoids. Thus, terbium ($Z = 65$) is not an actinoid. Terbium belong to lanthanoids.

9 (*c*) 10 (*a*)

11 (*d*) Cation has smaller size but anion has bigger size than its neutral atom.
Thus, correct order of size is :
$$I^- > I > I^+.$$

12 (*b*) The ionic radii increases as the positive charge decreases or the negative charge increases.
Thus, the correct order of given isoelectronic species is
$$Mg^{2+} < Na^+ < F^- < O^{2-}.$$

13 (*a*)

14 The correct match is
A-2, B-1, C-4, D-3.

15 (*c*) 16 (*a*)

17 (*c*) Although, O^{2-} has noble gas configuration and isoelectronic with neon but its formation is unfavourable due to the strong electronic repulsion between the negatively charged O^- ion and the second electron being added.
Hence, the electronic repulsion outweighs the stability gained by achieving noble gas configuration.

Past Exams'

1 (*a*) Electronegativity increases in period from left to right. The electronegativity values of given elements are,
Si = 1.8, C = 2.5, N = 3.0, O = 3.5, F = 4
Hence, the correct sequence is
Si < C < N < O < F.

2 (*b*) First ionisation enthalpy is the energy required to remove the first most loosely bound electron from an isolated atom in its ground state.
The electronic configuration is,
$Li \rightarrow 2s^1$, $Be \rightarrow 2s^2$, $B \rightarrow 2s^2 2p^1$
$C \rightarrow 2s^2 2p^2$, $N \rightarrow 2s^2 2p^3$
The correct increasing order is,
Li < B < Be < C < N

3 (*b*) Among the given elements, nitrogen (N) expected to form largest ion, i.e. N^{3-} to achieve the nearest noble gas configuration.

4 (*d*) Electron gain enthalpy becomes less negative from top to bottom in a group while it becomes more negative from left to right with in a period. Hence, the order is
Ca < Al < C < O < F.

5 (*d*)

6 (*d*) Among the given pairs, only (d), i.e. (Fe^{2+} and Mn^{2+}) is not an isoelectronic pair.

7 (*c*) D-(iv) is the incorrect match. The correct match is:
Unununnium → 111 → Roentgenium (Rg).

8 (*c*) The correct match is
A-2, B-1, C-4, D-3.

9 (*a*) The correct match is
A-2, B-1, C-4, D-3.

10 (*b*)

11 (*c*) Ar, K^+ and Ca^{2+} are isoelectronic i.e. with same number of electrons, 18.
For isoelectronic species ionic radii decreases with increase in effective

(relative) positive charge. Hence the correct order is

$Ca^{2+} < K^{+} < Ar$

12 (a) Among the given options, only option (a) is correct while other are incorrect. Their correct order is

(b) $O^{2-} > F^{-} > Na^{+}$

(c) $O^{2-} > F^{-} > Na^{+}$

(d) $N^{3-} > Mg^{2+} > Al^{3+}$

13 (c) The correct match is A-IV, B-III, C-II, D-I

Cl, S ⇒ Element with highest negative electron gain enthalpy.

Ge, As ⇒ Elements which show property of both metal and non-metal.

Fr, Ra ⇒ Elements with largest atomic size.

F, O ⇒ Element with highest electronegativity.

14 (11) Unununium is the IUPAC name of Roentgenium.

Atomic number → 111

Group belong → 11th group.

Hence, it belongs to group 11.

15 (a) Statement I is true but Statement II is false.

The correct form of Statement II is as follows, *s*-block element never occurs in pure form in nature. As, they are highly reactive. Thus, they are found as ore or minerals.

16 (b) On moving from top to bottom in periodic table metallic character increases while on moving from left to right metallic character decreases.

Hence, the correct order of metallic character is K > Ca > Be.

17 (b) The correct order of first ionisation energy is

Li < B < Be < C < O < N < F.

On moving from left to right in a period, atomic size decreases, Z_{eff} increases, so ionisation enthalpy increases. But presence of half-filled and fully-filled configuration will make an ion more stable thus more will be the ionisation enthalpy.

18 (a) The incorrect option among the given options is (c).

Its correct form is $\underset{(-328)}{\Delta_{eg}H(F)} < \underset{(-349)}{\Delta_{eg}H(Cl)}$

19 (b)

20 (b) Mercury is a liquid at room temperature, so it has lowest melting point and Ga and Cs are liquid at slightly above room temperature and hence have melting points around 30°C. So, being solid, Ag has highest melting point.

21 (b) Both A and R are true but R is not the correct explanation of A. The correct explanation of A is

First ionisation enthalpy of oxygen is lower than nitrogen as N has half-filled electronic configuration.

22 (d) A is false but R is true. The correct form of A is:

The ionic radii of Mg^{2+} is smaller than O^{2-}.

23 (c) A is true but R is false. The correct form of R is:

On moving from left to right in periodic table, metallic character decreases while non-metallic character increases. This is due to decrease in ionisation enthalpy and increase in electron gain enthalpy.

24 (d) Li-Na pair is different from remaining three options as it do not shows diagonal relationship. Both Li-Na belongs to same group and are not placed diagonally.

Li-Mg, B-Si and Be-Al show diagonal relationship.

Skill Boosters

1 (c) Among the given elements, the element *B* would be the most reactive metal as it has the lowest I.E and low negative electron gain enthalpy. The element *E* would be the least reactive metal as it has very high I.E and positive electron gain enthalpy.

2 (b) In the given graph, ionisation enthalpy is plotted against atomic numbers (*Z*) of the elements.

As, ionisation enthalpy in a period increases and the reactivity is also increases.

3 (a) Electronic configuration of Mn ($Z = 25$) is

$$\underbrace{1s^2 2s^2 2p^6 3s^2 3p^6}_{\text{(Inner shell)}} \ \underbrace{3d^5}_{(n-1)\text{ shell}} \ \underbrace{4s^2}_{n^{th}\text{ shell}}$$

As we know,

σ = [0.35 × No. of electrons in the *n*th shell + (0.85 × No. of electrons in (*n* − 1)th shell) + (1.00 × Total no. of electrons in the inner shell)]

So, $\sigma_{4s} = (0.35 \times 1) + (0.85 \times 5) + (1.00 \times 18) = 22.6$

4 (d) Energy required to convert *A* to A^{+} is $= \frac{1}{13} \times 995 = 76.53$ kJ

Remaining energy to convert A^{+} to $A^{2+} = 100 - 76.53 = 23.46$ kJ

5 (c) Among the given options, option (c) is incorrect regarding given enthalpies for element Na, i.e. [Ne] $3s^1$.

As we know,

$\Delta H_3 > \Delta H_2 > \Delta H_1$ (Successive I.E. is generally higher than previous I.E.)

6 (b) Since, size of $M > M^{\oplus}$ (135 pm) and that of $X < X^{-}$ (135 pm) hence the expected values of metallic radii for *M* and *X* from the given options will be 230 and 60 pm respectively.

7 (b) Element 1 has a second lowest value of first ionisation energy among the given elements.

Hence, it is alkaline earth metals.

Element 2 has the highest value of first ionisation energy among the given elements.

Hence, it is a noble gas.

Element 3 has a very low value of first ionisation energy and a high value of second ionisation energy.

Hence, it is reactive alkali metal with lowest first ionisation energy.

8 (a)Among the given options, only Na and Mg is not an exception because there is no half-filled or completely filled orbital in them.

Topicwise No. of Ques asked in 5 Years

Topics	No. of Questions				
	2024	2023	2022	2021	2020
Kossel-Lewis Approach to Chemical Bonding	–	2	–	–	–
Bond Parameters	1	3	–	2	1
The Valence Shell Electron Pair Repulsion (VSEPR) Theory	1	–	1	–	–
Valence Bond Theory and Hybridisation	–	–	–	2	3
Molecular Orbital Theory	–	1	1	–	1
Hydrogen Bonding	–	–	–	–	–

Special Type of Ques asked in 5 Years

Types	Years				
	2024	2023	2022	2021	2020
A-R	–	–	–	–	–
Statement Based	–	–	1	–	–
Matching	1	–	–	1	1

Last 5 Years Weightage (NEET)

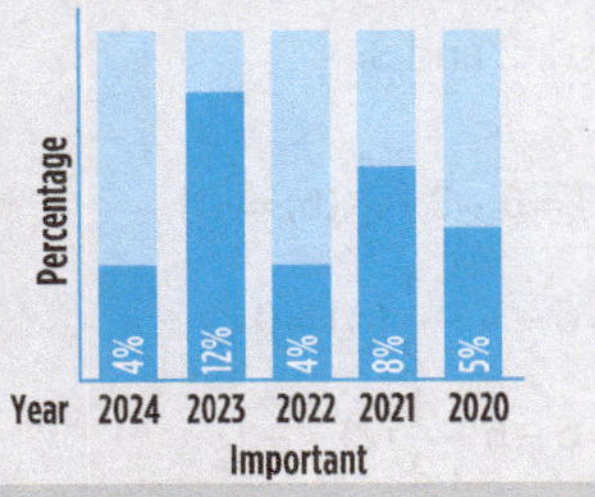

04

Scan for **Chemistry Through Concept Master** *Videos*

Chemical Bonding and Molecular Structure

The attractive force which holds various constituents (atoms, ions, etc.) together in different chemical species is called a **chemical bond**.

The factors due to which atoms interact with each other are

- Tendency to acquire minimum energy to attain stability.
- Tendency to achieve nearest noble gas configuration.

Kossel-Lewis Approach to Chemical Bonding

- Lewis pictured the atom in terms of a positively charged **Kernel** (the nucleus plus the inner electrons) and the outer shell that could accommodate a maximum of eight electrons which is called the **valence shell**. The electrons present in valence shell are called the **valence electrons** which can be represented by **Lewis symbol** (•).
- Lewis postulated that atoms achieve the stable octet (or duplet in case of H, He) when they are joined through chemical bonds.

Octet Rule

- Atoms can combine either by transfer of valence electrons from one atom to another (gaining or losing) or by mutual sharing of valence electrons in order to have an octet in their valence shells. This is known as **octet rule**.

  There are two ways by which the atoms can acquire the stable inert gas configuration.

(i) When transfer of electrons takes place from one atom to another and the bond formed in this process is known as **ionic bond**.

(ii) When sharing of electrons takes place. In this process two types of bond can be formed **covalent** and **coordinate bond**.

Covalent Bond

The bond which is formed between two combining atoms by the mutual sharing of electron pair(s) is called covalent bond.

Important Points Regarding Covalent Bonds

- Each bond is formed as a result of sharing of an electron pair between the atoms.
- Each combining atom contribute atleast one electron to the shared pair.
- The combining atom attains the outer shell noble gas configuration as a result of the sharing of electrons.
- Depending upon the number of electron pair 1, 2 or 3 shared between two atoms, a covalent bond is called **single, double** or **triple bond** respectively.

Lewis Representation of Simple Molecules (The Lewis Structure)

The structures in which valence electrons are represented by 'dots' around the atom are called Lewis dot structure.

e.g. Formation of chlorine molecule.

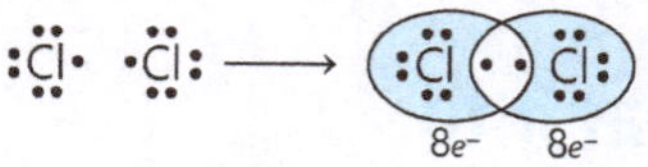

or Cl—Cl
Single bond

The Lewis dot structures provide a picture of bonding in molecules and ions in terms of the shared pair of electrons and the octet rule.

Lewis dot structures can be written by adopting the following steps :

- The total number of electrons required for writing the structures are obtained by adding the valence electrons of the combining atoms.
- For anions, each negative charge would mean addition of one electron. Similarly, for cations, each positive charge would result in subtraction of one electron from total number of valence electrons.
- In general, the least electronegative atom occupies the central position in the molecule/ion.
- The basic requirement is that each bonded atom gets an octet of electrons.

Lewis Representations of Few Molecules/Ions

Molecule/Ion	Lewis representation	
H_2	H:H*	H—H
O_2	:Ö::Ö:	:Ö=Ö:
O_3		
NF_3		
CO_3^{2-}	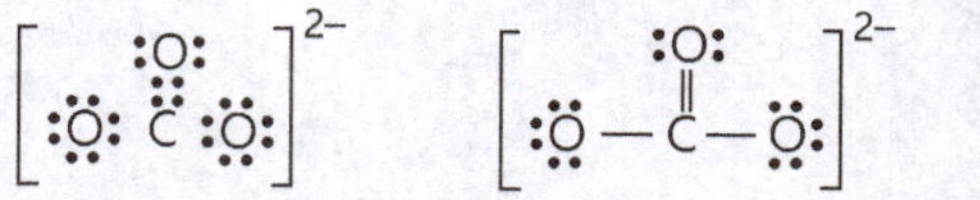	
HNO_3		
N_2	:N⋮⋮N:	:N≡N:

* Each H-atom attains the configuration of helium (a duplet of electrons).

Formal Charge

- It can be defined as the difference between the number of valence electrons of that atom in an isolated or free state and the number of electron assigned to that atom in the Lewis structure.
- Formal charge on an atom in a molecule/ion

$$F.C. = V - N - \frac{B}{2}$$

F.C = formal charge

V = total number of valence electrons in the free state

N = number of non-bonding (lone pair) valence electrons

B = total number of bonding (shared) electrons

- The Lewis structure of O_3 may be drawn as

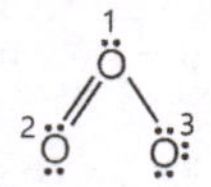

The atoms have been numbered as 1, 2 and 3.

The formal charge on

(i) The central O-atom marked $1 = 6 - 2 - \frac{1}{2}(6) = +1$

(ii) The end O-atom marked $2 = 6 - 4 - \frac{1}{2}(4) = 0$

(iii) The end O-atom marked $3 = 6 - 6 - \frac{1}{2}(2) = -1$

Hence, we represent O_3 along with the formal charges as follows

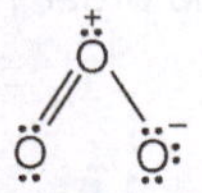

- Formal charges help in the selection of the lowest energy structure from a number of possible Lewis structures for a given species.
- Generally, the lowest energy structure is the one with the smallest formal charges on the atom.

Limitations of the Octet Rule

The different types of exceptions to the octet rule are discussed below

- **Incomplete octet of the central atom** In some compounds, the central atom is surrounded by less than eight electrons.
  Especially, in case with elements having less than four valence electrons. e.g. LiCl, BeH_2, BCl_3, $AlCl_3$, BF_3 etc. NEET 2023
- **Odd-electron molecules** Molecules like NO, NO_2 etc., have odd number of electrons.
- **Expanded octet molecules** Elements of the third and higher periods, can accommodate more than $8e^-$ shows expansion of octet. e.g. PF_5, SF_6, H_2SO_4, IF_7 the central atom, P, S, S, I contains $(10e^-)$, $(12e^-)$, $(12e^-)$, $(14e^-)$ respectively.
- It does not explain the shape, relative stability and the energy of the molecules.
- It is based upon the chemical inertness of noble gases, however noble gases like Xe and Kr also combine with O_2 and F_2 to form a number of compound like XeF_2, KrF_2 etc.

Marks Maximizer

Sugden's concept of singlet linkage Sugden put forward the view that octet rule is never violated. He suggested that in case of molecules like PCl_5, SF_6 etc., some atoms are linked to the central atom by covalent bonds while other are linked by singlet bonds. A singlet bond is formed by one sided sharing of only one electron between the two atoms and is therefore, represented by the half arrow (⇀) pointing from donor to acceptor.

e.g.

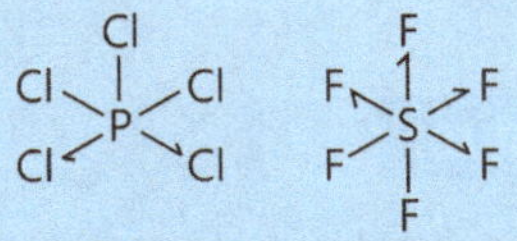

Ionic or Electrovalent Bond

It is formed as a result of electrostatic force of attraction between an electropositive atom and an electronegative atom due to complete transfer of electrons to fulfill the octet.

Exception The ammonium ion, NH_4^+ is made up of two non-metallic elements.

- Ionic bonds will be formed more easily between elements with comparatively low ionisation enthalpies and elements with comparatively high negative value of electron gain enthalpy.
- A qualitative measure of the stability of an ionic compound is provided by its enthalpy of lattice formation and not simply by achieving octet of electron around the ionic species in gaseous state.

Lattice Enthalpy

The lattice enthalpy of an ionic solid is defined as the energy required to completely separate one mole of a solid ionic compound into gaseous constituent ions.

Factors affecting lattice enthalpy

(a) Charge on the ions (b) Size of the ions.

$$\text{Lattice enthalpy} \propto \text{Charge on the ions} \propto \frac{1}{\text{Size of the ions}}$$

Bond Parameters

The various characteristics shown by a bond are called bond parameters. These are as follows

Bond Length

- It is defined as the equilibrium distance between the nuclei of two bonded atoms in a molecule.
  Generally, it is expressed in picometer (1 pm $=10^{-12}$ m).
- **Covalent radius** is measured as the radius of an atom's core which is in contact with the core of an adjacent atom in a bonded situation.

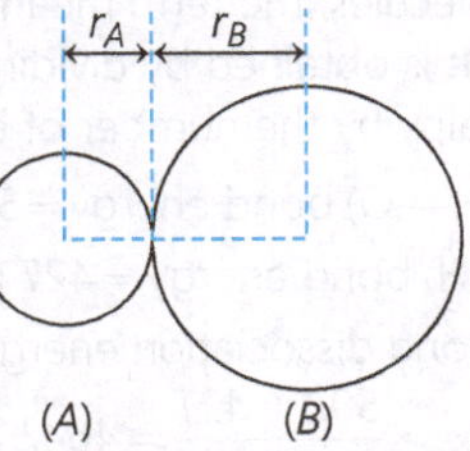

The bond length in a covalent molecule *AB*.
$R = r_A + r_B$ (*R* is the bond length r_A and r_B are the covalent radii of atoms *A* and *B* respectively)

- The **van der Waals' radius** represents the overall size of the atom which includes its valence shell in a non-bonded situation.

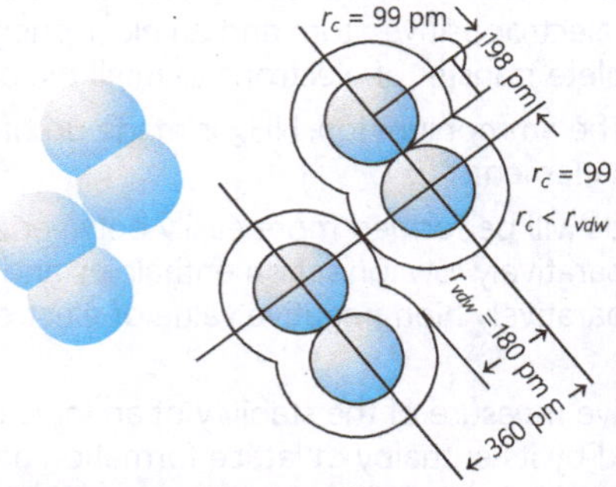

Covalent and van der Waals' radii in a chlorine molecule. The inner circles correspond to the size of the chlorine atom (r_{vdw} and r_c are van der Waals' and covalent radii respectively).

Bond Angle

- It is defined as the angle between the orbitals containing bonding electron pairs around the central atom in a molecule/complex ion.
- It gives some idea regarding the distribution of orbitals around the central atom in a molecule/ complex ion and hence it helps us in determining its shape. e.g. H—O—H bond angle in water is 104.5°.

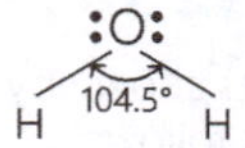

Bond Enthalpy

- It is defined as the amount of energy required to break one mole of bonds of a particular type between two atoms in a gaseous state. It is also called as **bond dissociation enthalpy**.

  Its unit is kJ mol^{-1}.

  Bond enthalpy $\propto$ bond multiplicity NEET 2021
- In polyatomic molecules, the term mean or average bond enthalpy is used. It is obtained by dividing total bond dissociation enthalpy by the number of bonds broken.

  e.g. In H_2O, first (H—O) bond energy = 502 kJ mol^{-1} and second (O—H) bond energy = 427 kJ mol^{-1}.

  Hence, average bond dissociation energy

  $$= \frac{502 + 427}{2} = 464.5 \text{ kJ mol}^{-1}$$

Bond Order

It is given by the number of bonds between the two atoms in a molecule.

$$\text{Bond order} \propto \frac{1}{\text{bond length}} \propto \text{bond enthalpy}$$

Isoelectronic molecules and ions have identical bond order.

e.g. F_2 and O_2^{2-} have bond order 1 and N_2, CO and NO^+ have bond order 3.

Resonance Structures

According to this concept, whenever a single Lewis structure cannot describe all the properties of a molecule, a number of canonical structures with similar energy, positions of nuclei, bonding and non-bonding pairs of electrons are taken to describe the molecule accurately. The intermediate of these canonical structure is known as resonance hybrid and the different individual structures are termed as **resonating structures** or **canonical forms**. This phenomenon is called **resonance**.

Resonance Structures of carbonate ion, CO_3^{2-}

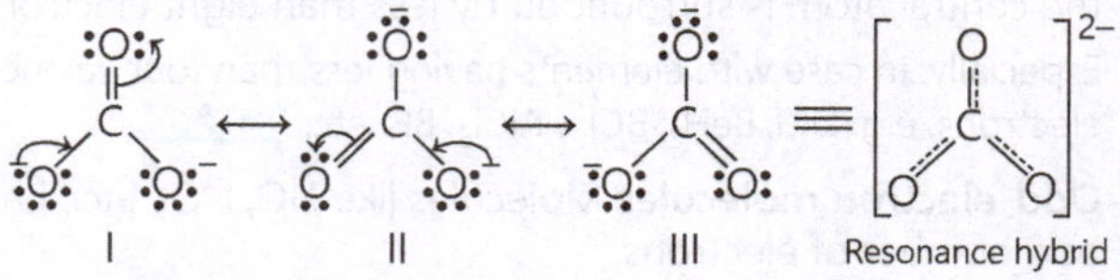

Salient Characteristics of Resonance

- Resonance stabilises the molecule as the energy of the resonance hybrid is less than the energy of any single canonical structure.
- Resonance averages the bond characteristics as a whole.
- Hybrid structure is more stable than any of the resonating structures.

Misconceptions Related to Resonance

- The canonical forms have no real existance.
- The molecule does not exist for a certain fraction of time in one canonical form and for other fractions of time in other canonical forms.
- The molecule as such has a single structure which is the resonance hybrid of the canonical forms and which cannot as such be depicted by a single Lewis structure.
- There is no such equilibrium between the canonical forms as we have between tautomeric forms (keto and enol) in tautomerism.

Marks Maximizer

The molecules or ions having resonance, their bond order can be calculated as follow

$$\text{Bond order} = \frac{\text{Total number of bonds between two atoms in all the structures}}{\text{Total number of resonating structure}}$$

Polarity of Bonds

- If a covalent bond is formed between two similar atoms having same electronegativity, the shared pair of electrons is equally attracted by the two atoms. And as a result electron pair is situated exactly between the two identical nuclei. This type of bond is called **non-polar covalent bond**. e.g. H_2, O_2, Cl_2, N_2 and F_2 etc.
- In case of a heteronuclear molecule like HF, the shared electron pair between the two atoms gets displaced more towards fluorine since the electronegativity of fluorine is far greater than that of hydrogen. The resultant covalent bond is a **polar covalent bond**.
- The polarity of covalent bonds results in the formation of electric dipole possessing a **dipole moment** (μ).

NEET 2019, 2020, 2021

- Dipole moment is a vector quantity thus, indicated by the symbol ($+\!\!\!\longrightarrow$) pointing towards the negative end.

e.g. $\overset{\delta+}{H} +\!\!\!\longrightarrow \overset{\delta-}{Cl}$

Dipole moment (μ) = charge (q) × distance of separation (d)

Unit of dipole moment is Debye (D).

$$1\text{D} = 3.33564 \times 10^{-30} \text{ Cm (Coulomb metre)}.$$

- Molecules with regular geometry have zero dipole moment, while molecules with irregular geometry (having bond pair and lone pair) possess a definite dipole moment.
- **Dipole moment of NH_3 and NF_3** Although F is more electronegative than H, the resultant dipole moment of NH_3 is much more than that of NF_3. As the lone pair of nitrogen opposes the dipole moment of NF_3 whereas, it add to the dipole moment of NH_3. It can be concluded from the following diagrams. NEET 2024

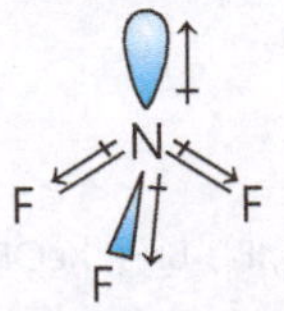

NF_3 (Dipole moment $= 0.80 \times 10^{-30}$ C m)

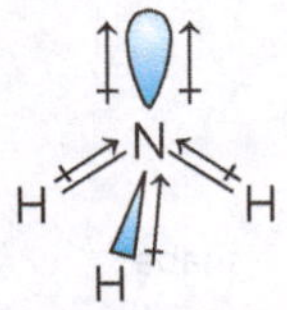

NH_3 (Dipole moment $= 4.90 \times 10^{-30}$ C m)

- Just as all the covalent bonds have some partial ionic character, the ionic bonds also have some partial covalent character. The partial covalent character of ionic bonds was discussed by Fajan in terms of rules called Fajans rule.

Marks Maximizer

- Net dipole moment of the molecule,
$$\mu = \sqrt{\mu_1^2 + \mu_2^2 + 2\mu_1\mu_2\cos\theta}$$
where, μ_1 and μ_2 are the bond dipole moments of various bonds present in the molecule, θ is the bond angle between two bonds in a given molecule.
- Dipole moment can be used to determine
$$\%\text{ ionic character} = \frac{\mu_{\text{observed}}}{\mu_{\text{theoretical}}} \times 100$$
- The dipole moment of CO molecule is greater than expected. This is because of the presence of a dative (coordinate) bond.

Fajans' rule According to this rule, the magnitude of covalent character in an ionic bond depends upon the extent of polarisation caused by cation.

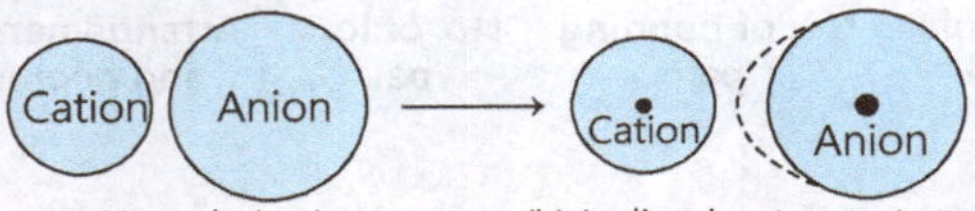

(a) No polarisation

(b) Inclined outermost e^- cloud of anion. Polarised anion by cation.

- The smaller the size of the cation and the larger the size of the anion, shows greater covalent character of an ionic bond.
- The greater the charge on the cation, the greater the covalent character of the ionic bond.
- Among two cations of similar size, the polarising power of cation with noble gas configuration $ns^2np^6nd^{10}$ is larger than cation with noble gas configuration ns^2np^6.
- The polarising power of the cation, the polarisability of the anion and the extent of distortion (polarisation) of anion are the factors, which determine the percent covalent character of the ionic bond.

The Valence Shell Electron Pair Repulsion (VSEPR) Theory

This theory was developed and redefined by Nyholm and Gillespie in 1957. The main postulates of this theory are

- The number of valence shell electron pairs (bonded or non-bonded) present around the central atom decides the shape of the molecule.
- Electron pairs in valence shell repel one another to make their electron clouds negatively charged.

For Concept Master Video

- The repulsion between the different electron pairs follow the order

  Lone pair – Lone pair > Lone pair – Bond pair
  > Bond pair – Bond pair

- These electron pairs arrange themselves in such a way that there is minimum repulsion and maximum distance in between them.
- The valence shell is considered as a sphere in which the electron pairs are localised on the spherical surface at maximum distance from one another.
- A multiple bond is treated as if it is a single electron pair and the two or three electron pairs of a multiple bond are treated as a single super pair.
- If a molecule has several resonating structures, the VSEPR model is applicable to any such structure.

Geometrical shape of different molecules according to VSEPR theory and geometry of molecules in which central atom has no lone pair of electrons are as follows

- Linear (e.g. $BeCl_2$) = 2 electron pairs.
- Trigonal planar (e.g. BF_3) = 3 electron pairs.
- Tetrahedral (e.g. CH_4, NH_4^+) = 4 electron pairs.
- Trigonal bipyramidal (e.g. PCl_5) = 5 electron pairs.
- Octahedral (e.g. SF_6) = 6 electron pairs.
- Pentagonal bipyramidal (e.g. IF_7) = 7 electron pairs.

NEET 2021, 2022, 2024

Shape of some molecules or ions with central ions having one or more lone pairs of e^- on the basis of VSEPR theory.

Molecule type	No. of bonding pair	No. of lone pair	Arrangement of electron pairs and geometry of molecule	Shape	Examples
AB_2E	2	1	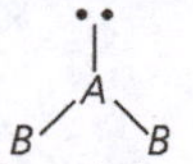 Trigonal planar	Bent (V-shape)	SO_2, O_3, $SnCl_2$, $PbCl_2$, NO_2^+
AB_3E	3	1	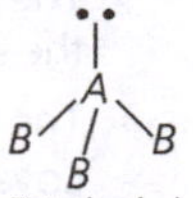 Tetrahedral	Trigonal pyramidal	PH_3, $BiCl_3$, NH_3, PCl_3, $AsCl_3$, XeO_3, ClO_3^-, SO_3^{2-}, $P(CH_3)_3$
AB_2E_2	2	2	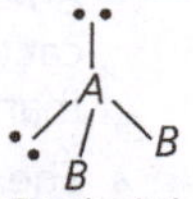 Tetrahedral	Bent (V-shape)	H_2S, NH_2, H_2O, OF_2, Cl_2O, $Cl_2\dot{O}$, ClO_2^-, $Cl\dot{O}F$, SCl_2
AB_4E	4	1	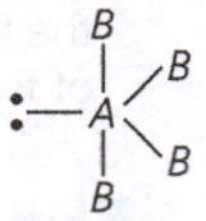 Trigonal bipyramidal	*See-saw*	SF_4, SCl_4, $TeCl_4$, XeO_2F_2
AB_3E_2	3	2	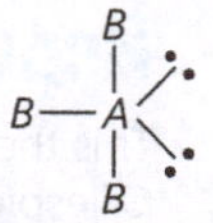 Trigonal bipyramidal	T-shape	ClF_3, IF_3, BrF_3, $XeOF_2$
AB_5E	5	1	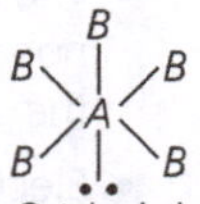 Octahedral	Square pyramidal	IF_5, BrF_5, SbF_5^{2-}
AB_4E_2	4	2	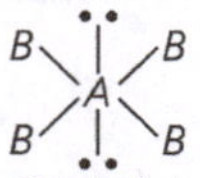 Octahedral	Square planar	XeF_4, ICl_4^-

Note *E* is the number of lone pair around central metal atom *A*.

Valence Bond Theory

- This theory (VBT) was introduced by **Heitler** and **London** in 1927 and further improved by **Pauling** and others.
  It is based on the knowledge of atomic orbitals, electronic configurations of elements, the criteria of overlapping of atomic orbitals and the hybridisation of atomic orbitals and the principles of variation and superposition.
- Attractive forces tend to bring the combining atoms close to each other whereas, repulsive forces tend to push them apart.
- Bond formation is accompanied by release of energy and this accounts for the stability of the bond.
- The molecule has minimum energy at the equilibrium distance known as the intermolecular distance. Larger the decreases in energy, stronger will be the bond formed.

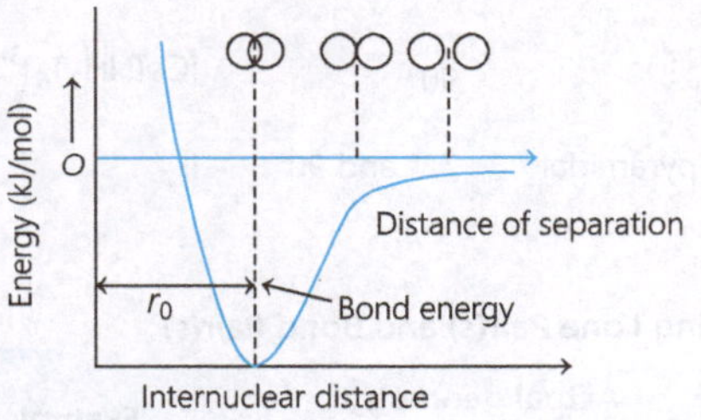

NEET 2020

- The extent of overlap decides the strength of a covalent bond. In general, greater the overlap the stronger is the bond formed between two atoms.

Orbital Overlap Concept

- According to **orbital overlap concept**, the formation of a covalent bond between two atoms results by pairing of electrons present in the valence shell having opposite spins.
- The VBT explains the formation and **directional properties of bonds** in polyatomic molecules in terms of overlap and hybridisation of atomic orbitals like CH_4, NH_3 and H_2O etc.

Overlapping of Atomic Orbitals

When orbitals of two atoms overlap to form bond, their overlap may be positive, negative or zero. It depends upon the sign and direction of orientation of amplitude of orbital wave function in space.

- Orbitals forming bond should have same sign (phase) and orientation in space.

Types of Overlapping and Nature of Covalent Bonds

The overlapping of orbitals may be classified into two types

- **Sigma (σ) bond** is formed by the end to end (head on) overlap of bonding orbitals along the internuclear axis. This is called as head on overlap or axis overlap, e.g. *s-s*, *s-p*, *p-p* overlapping.
- **Pi (π) bond** is formed when the atomic orbitals overlap in such a way that their axis remain parallel to each other and perpendicular to the internuclear axis, e.g. p_y-p_y and p_z-p_z orbitals.

Strength of Sigma and Pi-Bonds

σ-bonds are always stronger than π-bonds because extent of overlapping occurs to a smaller extent in π-bond.

In the formation of multiple bonds between two atoms of a molecule, π-bond(s) is formed in addition to a σ-bond.

Hybridisation

The concept of hybridisation was put forward by **Linus Pauling** (1931). He proposed that the atomic orbitals mix together to generate a new set of equivalent orbitals, called the **hybrid orbitals** or **hybridised orbitals**. These orbitals are used in bond formation and the phenomenon is called hybridisation.

The main features of hybridisation are as follows

- The number of hybrid orbitals generated is equal to the number of atomic orbitals that get hybridised.
- The hybridised orbitals are always equivalent in energy and shape.
- The hybrid orbitals are more effective in forming stable bonds than the pure atomic orbitals.
- These hybrid orbitals arrange themselves in space in such a way so that there is minimum repulsion between electron pairs and to attain a stable arrangement.

Important conditions for hybridisation are as follows

- The orbitals present in the valence shell of the atom are hybridised.
- The orbitals undergoing hybridisation should have nearly same energies.
- Promotion of electron is not essential condition prior to hybridisation.
- It is not necessary that only half-filled orbitals participate in hybridisation.

Types of Hybridisation

There are many types of hybridisation involving *s*, *p* and *d*-orbitals. Hybridisation of some important molecules are summarised below.

Hybridisation and Structures of Molecules having Bond Pairs Only NEET 2020

No. of atomic orbitals involved in hybridisation	Type of hybridisation	No. of hybrid orbitals formed	Shape of molecules	Bond angles	Examples
2	*sp* (one *s* and one *p*)	2	Linear	180°	$BeCl_2$, BeF_2
3	sp^2 (one *s* and two *p*)	3	Planar triangular	120°	BF_3, BCl_3 NEET 2021
4	sp^3 (one *s* and three *p*)	4	Tetrahedral	109° 28′	CH_4, CCl_4
4	dsp^2 one $(n-1)$ '*d*' usually $(d_{x^2-y^2})$, one '*s*' and two '*p*'	4	Square planar	90°	$[Ni(CN)_4]^{2-}$, $[PtCl_4]^{2-}$
5	sp^3d one '*s*', three '*p*' and one '*d*' usually d_{z^2}	5	Trigonal bipyramidal	120° and 90°	PCl_5
6	sp^3d^2 one '*s*', three '*p*' and two '*d*' usually $d_{x^2-y^2}+d_{z^2}$	6	Octahedral	90°	SF_6
	d^2sp^3 (same as sp^3d^2 in reverse order)	6	Octahedral	90°	$[Co(NH_3)_6]^{3+}$
7	sp^3d^3 one '*s*', three '*p*' and three '*d*' $d_{x^2-y^2}$, d_{z^2} and any one d_{xy}, d_{yz}, d_{zx}	7	Pentagonal bipyramidal	72° and 90°	IF_7

Hybridisation and Structures of Molecules having Lone Pair(s) and Bond Pair(s) NEET 2019, 2020

Type of molecules	No. of bond pair(s)	No. of lone pair(s)	Hybridisation	Bond angle	Expected geometry	Actual geometry (Shape)	Examples
AB_2L	2	1	sp^2	< 120°	Trigonal planar	V-shape or Bent	SO_2, $SnCl_2$, $PbCl_2$
AB_2L_2	2	2	sp^3	< 109°28′	Tetrahedral	V-shape or Bent	H_2O, H_2S, NH_2^-, SCl_2, OF_2, Cl_2O, ClO_2^-, $ClOF$
AB_2L_3	2	3	sp^3d	180°	Trigonal bipyramidal	Linear	XeF_2, I_3^-, ICl_2^-
AB_3L_2	3	2	sp^3d	90°	Trigonal bipyramidal	T-shape	ClF_3, IF_3, BrF_3, $XeOF_2$
AB_3L	3	1	sp^3	< 109°28′	Tetrahedral	Pyramidal	NH_3, PH_3, PCl_3, $BiCl_3$, $AsCl_3$, XeO_3, ClO_3^-, SO_3^{2-}, XeO_4
AB_4L	4	1	sp^3d	120°, 90°	Trigonal bipyramidal	*See-saw* or Distorted tetrahedron	SF_4, SCl_4, $TeCl_4$, XeO_2F_2
AB_4L_2	4	2	sp^3d^2	—	Octahedral	Square planar	XeF_4, ICl_4^-
AB_5L	5	1	sp^3d^2	< 90°	Octahedral	Square pyramidal	IF_5, BrF_5, SbF_5^{2-}
AB_6L	6	1	sp^3d^3	—	Pentagonal bipyramidal	Distorted octahedral	XeF_6

Note $d_{x^2-y^2}$ orbital is involved in d_{sp^2}, d_{z^2} in sp^3d, $d_{x^2-y^2}$ and d_{z^2} in sp^3d^2 or d^2sp^3 and $d_{x^2-y^2}$, $d_{z^2}d_{xy}$, d_{yz} or d_{xz} in sp^3d^3 hybridisation.

Molecular Orbital Theory

This theory was developed by **F. Hund** and **R.S. Mulliken** in **1932**. The main features of Molecular Orbital Theory (MOT) are as follows

- The electrons in a molecule occupy various molecular orbitals as the electrons of atoms are present in various atomic orbitals.
- Molecular orbitals are obtained when atomic orbitals of comparable energies and proper symmetry combine together.
- An atomic orbital is **monocentric**, while a molecular orbital is **polycentric**.
- The number of molecular orbital formed is equal to the number of combining atomic orbitals.

For Concept Master Video

- When two atomic orbitals combine, two types of molecular orbitals are obtained one is **bonding molecular orbital** and other is **anti-bonding molecular orbital**.
- The bonding molecular orbital have greater stability than the corresponding antibonding molecular orbital.
- A molecular orbital shows the electron probability distribution around a group of nuclei in a molecule.
- The molecular orbitals are filled in accordance with the Aufbau principle obeying the Pauli's exclusion principle and the Hund's rule.

Marks Maximizer

- If the molecular orbital is symmetrical, then it is called gerade '*g*' orbital while if it is unsymmetrical it is called ungerade and is represented by the symbol 'μ'. All σ-bonding molecular orbitals are gerade while all (σ*) antibonding molecular orbitals are ungerade.
- All (π*) anti-bonding MO are gerade whereas all π-bonding MO are ungerade.

Formation of Molecular Orbitals Linear Combination of Atomic Orbitals (LCAO)

The most convenient way of working out the wave functions for molecular orbitals is to adopt the method of LCAO.

- Molecular orbitals are formed by the addition or subtraction of wave functions of the atomic orbitals.

$$\psi_{MO} = \psi_A \pm \psi_B; \sigma = \psi_A + \psi_B; \sigma^* = \psi_A - \psi_B$$

- The molecular orbital with lower energy formed by the addition of atomic orbitals is called **bonding molecular orbitals** and are represented by σ and π.
- The molecular orbital with higher energy formed by the subtraction of atomic orbitals is called **anti-bonding molecular orbitals** are represented by σ^* and π^*.

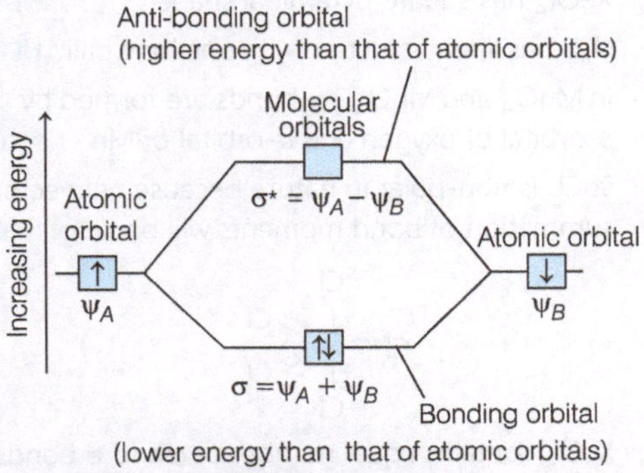

Formation of bonding (σ) and anti-bonding (σ*) molecular orbitals by the linear combination of atomic orbitals ψ_A and ψ_B centered on two atoms *A* and *B* respectively.

Conditions for the Combination of Atomic Orbitals

The Linear Combination of Atomic Orbitals (LCAO) to form molecular orbitals is possible only when the following conditions are satisfied :

- The combining atomic orbitals must have the same or nearly the same energy.
- The combining atomic orbitals must have the same symmetry about the molecular axis.
- The combining atomic orbitals must overlap to the maximum extent.

Types of Molecular Orbitals

In case of diatomic molecules, molecular orbitals are designated as σ (sigma), π (pi), δ (delta) etc.

- If the molecular orbital is symmetrical about the internuclear axis (or bond axis) it is called **σ-molecular orbital** and if it is not symmetrical about the internuclear axis, it is called a **π-molecular orbital**.
- If internuclear axis is taken to be in the *z*-direction, it can be seen that a linear combination of $2p_z$-orbital of two atoms also produces two sigma molecular orbitals designated as $\sigma 2p_z$ and $\sigma^* 2p_z$ while $2p_x$ and $2p_y$ form π and π^*.

Energy Level Diagram for Molecular Orbitals

- The energy order of molecular orbitals for O_2 and F_2 is as follows

$$\sigma 1s < \sigma^* 1s < \sigma 2s < \sigma^* 2s < \sigma 2p_z < (\pi 2p_x = \pi 2p_y) < (\pi^* 2p_x = \pi^* 2p_y) < \sigma^* 2p_z.$$

- For B_2, C_2, N_2 (i.e. upto total = 14 electrons), the energy of $\sigma 2p_z$ molecular orbital is higher than that of $\pi 2p_x$ and $\pi 2p_y$ molecular orbitals. NEET 2023

$$\sigma 1s < \sigma^* 1s < \sigma 2s < \sigma^* 2s < (\pi 2p_x = \pi 2p_y) < \sigma 2p_z < (\pi^* 2p_x = \pi^* 2p_y) < \sigma^* 2p_z.$$

Electronic Configuration and Molecular Behaviour

The distribution of electrons among various molecular orbitals is called the **electronic configuration of the molecule**. Electronic configuration gives the important information about the molecule as discussed below.

- **Stability of molecules** If the number of electrons occupying bonding orbitals are represented by N_b and the number of electrons occupying the antibonding orbitals by N_a then,
  - the molecule is stable, if $N_b > N_a$ and
  - the molecule is unstable, if $N_b < N_a$.
- **Bond Order** (B.O) $= \dfrac{N_b - N_a}{2}$
  - If $N_b > N_a$; B.O is positive ⇒ molecule is stable.
  - If $N_b < N_a$; B.O is negative and molecule is unstable.
  - If $N_b = N_a$; B.O = 0, molecule is unstable.

∴ B.O should be positive, otherwise molecule does not exist.

- **Nature of the bond** If bond order is 1, 2 or 3 it shows the presence of single, double or triple bonds respectively.
- **Bond length** decreases as the bond order increases.
- **Magnetic nature** Molecules/ions (like H_2) having no unpaired electrons gives rise to **diamagnetic** character. Molecules/ions (like O_2) having unpaired electrons gives rise to **paramagnetic** character.

Bonding in Some Homonuclear Diatomic Molecules

In this section we shall discuss bonding and molecular orbital configurations of some molecules/ions.

- $H_2 : \sigma 1s^2$
  Bond order $= \frac{1}{2}(2-0) = 1$ (diamagnetic)
- $H_2^+ : \sigma 1s^1$
  Bond order $= \frac{1}{2}(1-0) = 0.5$ (paramagnetic)
- $He_2 : \sigma 1s^2\ \sigma^* 1s^2$
  Bond order $= \frac{1}{2}(2-2) = 0$ (does not exist)
- Similarly, Be_2 does not exist.
- $Li_2 : \sigma 1s^2\ \sigma^* 1s^2\ \sigma 2s^2$
  Bond order $= \frac{1}{2}(4-2) = 1$ (diamagnetic) NEET 2020
- $C_2 : \sigma 1s^2 \sigma^* 1s^2 \sigma 2s^2 \sigma^* 2s^2 \pi 2p_x^2 = \pi 2p_y^2$
  Bond order $= \frac{1}{2}(8-4) = 2$ (diamagnetic) NEET 2019
- $O_2 : \sigma 1s^2 \sigma^* 1s^2 \sigma 2s^2 \sigma^* 2s^2 \sigma 2p_z^2\ \pi 2p_x^2 = \pi 2p_y^2\ \pi^* 2p_x^1 = \pi^* 2p_y^1$
  Bond order $= \frac{1}{2}(10-6) = 2$ (paramagnetic)
- $O_2^+ : \sigma 1s^2\ \sigma^* 1s^2 \sigma 2s^2 \sigma^* 2s^2 \sigma 2p_z^2 \pi 2p_x^2 = \pi 2p_y^2 \pi^* 2p_x^1$
  Bond order $= \frac{1}{2}(10-5) = 2.5$ (paramagnetic)
- $O_2^- : \sigma 1s^2\ \sigma^* 1s^2 \sigma 2s^2 \sigma^* 2s^2 \sigma 2p_z^2 \pi 2p_x^2 = \pi 2p_y^2 \pi^* 2p_x^2 = \pi^* 2p_y^1$
  Bond order $= \frac{1}{2}(10-7) = 1.5$ (paramagnetic)

Hydrogen Bonding

- The attractive force which binds hydrogen atom of one molecule with the highly electronegative atom (F, O or N) of the same or another molecule is called hydrogen bonding.
- The magnitude of H-bonding depends on the physical state of the compound.
- **Intermolecular hydrogen bond** is formed between two different molecules of the same or different compounds.
  e.g. In HF, *R*OH or H_2O etc.
  $\overset{\delta+}{H}—\overset{\delta-}{F} \ldots\ldots \overset{\delta+}{H}—\overset{\delta-}{F} \ldots\ldots \overset{\delta+}{H}—\overset{\delta-}{F} \ldots\ldots \overset{\delta+}{H}—\overset{\delta-}{F} \ldots\ldots$
- **Intramolecular hydrogen bond** is formed when hydrogen atom is in between the two highly electronegative (F, O, N) atoms present within the same molecule.
  e.g. In *o*-nitrophenol the hydrogen is in between the two oxygen atoms.

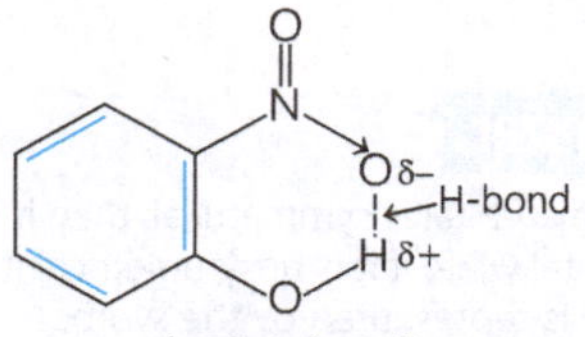

(*o*-nitrophenol)

Caution Points

- M.O electronic configuration of diatomic species upto 14 electrons, $\sigma 2p_z$ orbitals (considering *z*-as the internuclear axis) is greater than $\pi 2p_y$ and $\pi 2p_x$ orbitals.
  For species more than 14 electrons, $\sigma 2p_z$ orbital is lower in energy than $\pi 2p_x$ and $\pi 2p_y$ orbitals.
- To forms an ionic bond, the electronegativity difference between two atoms should be ≥ 1.9.
- Lone pair does affect the shape of a molecule.
- Species having same number of electrons have same bond order.

PYQ Notes

1. Hybridisation $= \frac{1}{2}$ [number of valence electrons + number of side atoms – positive charge + negative charge] NEET 2021
2. SO_4^{2-} and CrO_4^{2-}, $SiCl_4$ and $TiCl_4$ are isostructural pairs. JEE 2021
3. $XeOF_4$ has square pyramidal shape. NEET 2020
4. N_2O has linear structure with one lone pair. NEET 2020
5. In MnO_4^- and MnO_4^{2-} π-bonds are formed by *p*-orbital of oxygen and *d*-orbital of Mn. NEET 2019
6. $SbCl_5$ is non-polar in nature because net vector summation of bond moments will be zero. NEET 2021

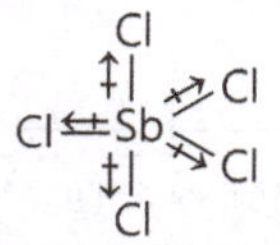

7. XeO_4 contains equal number of σ and π-bonds. NEET 2015

Step by Step

Mastering NCERT

- Concept Builders
- Topical Questions
- Assertion-Reason
- Statement Type
- Matching Type
- Numerical Value
- NCERT Exemplar's
- Past Exams'
- Skill Boosters

Concept Builders

1 According to Lewis, nucleus together with inner electrons is termed as 'Kernel' of the atom. [T/F]

2 The negative and positive ions are stabilised by .... attraction.

3 Write the name of bond present in CaF_2.

4 Write the Lewis representation of CO_3^{2-} ion.

5 The formal charges on oxygen atoms in O_3 are –1, 0, +1. [T/F]

6 A compound of sulphur of type AB_6 which has expanded octet is ....

7 The octet theory does not explain the relative stability of the molecule. [T/F]

8 The ionic bonds will be formed more easily between element with comparatively .... ionisation energy and element with comparatively .... negative electron gain enthalpy.

9 Bond enthalpy of N_2 is less than NO. [T/F]

10 Resonance stabilises the molecule as the energy of the resonance hybrid is less than the energy of any single canonical structure. [T/F]

11 Dipole moments is usually expressed in .... unit and symbolise as ....

12 According to Fajans's rule, cation of transition element is more polarising than that of alkali earth metal cations. [T/F]

13 The sum of the bond angles both (equatorial and axial) in PCl_5 molecule is ....

14 The number of bond pairs and lone pairs are present in a compound AX_5 of shape square pyramid.

15 The compound is said to be stable if lone pairs are present at axial and bond pairs are present at equatorial positions. [T/F]

16 When the net force of attraction balances the forces of repulsion, then the system acquires .... (maximum/minimum) energy.

17 The result of overlap when two orbitals with different phases overlap with each other is ....

18 It is necessary that only half-filled orbitals participate in hybridisation because they are involved in bonding. [T/F]

19 The % of *p*-character in hybrid orbitals of PF_5 molecule is ....

20 The total number of sp^3 hybridised carbon present in $CH_3—C(CH_3)_2—C(CH_3)_2—CH_3$ is ....

21 The bonding molecular orbital has lower energy and greater stability than the corresponding antibonding molecular orbital. [T/F]

22 To overcome the difficulty of solving wave function for multi-electron orbitals we adopted a method called ....

23 π^*-antibonding molecular orbital lacks electron density because of presence of node between the nuclei. [T/F]

24 Write the number of molecular orbitals which are formed by 2*s* and 2*p* atomic orbitals.

25 If $N_b > N_a$, the molecule is .... and bond order is ....

26 Name the molecule which has both π-electrons in the formation of π-bond in it.

27 C_2 is paramagnetic while O_2 is diamagnetic. [T/F]

28 The bond order of Be_2 is .... and the number of unpaired electron is ....

29 Hydrogen bond is weaker than covalent bond. [T/F]

30 The number of hydrogen bonds can formed by a water molecule is ....

Topical Questions

Kossel-Lewis Approach to Chemical Bonding

1 Consider the following atoms with their electronic configuration : NCERT Pg 101

$L(1s^2\,2s^2\,2p^1)$; $M(1s^2\,2s^2\,2p^5)$; $Q(1s^2\,2s^2\,2p^6\,3s^1)$;

$R(1s^2\,2s^2\,2p^2)$

The element that would readily form a diatomic molecule is

(a) Q (b) M

(c) R (d) L

2 Which theory can be best understood by considering the formation of the chlorine molecule, Cl_2? NCERT Pg 102

(a) Lewis theory

(b) Langmuir theory

(c) Lewis-Langmuir theory

(d) Kossel theory

3 Consider two elements P and Q. If P has 2 and Q has 6 electrons in their outermost shell, then formula of compound is NCERT Pg 102

(a) PQ (b) P_2Q

(c) P_2Q_3 (d) PQ_2

4 The number and types of bonds present in NH_4^+ are NCERT Pg 102

(a) four covalent bonds.

(b) two covalent bonds and two ionic bonds.

(c) three covalent bonds and one ionic bond.

(d) three covalent bonds and one coordinate bond.

5 Select the molecule which does not follow octet rule NCERT Pg 102

(a) NH_3 (b) H_2O

(c) CCl_4 (d) PCl_5

6 Choose the incorrect statement for Lewis dot structure of covalent compounds. NCERT Pg 102

(a) Each bond is formed as a result of sharing of an electron pair between the atoms.

(b) Each combining atom contributes atleast one electron to the shared pair.

(c) The combining atoms attain the outer shell noble gas configurations as a result of the sharing of electrons.

(d) Lewis dot structure cannot be drawn for molecules with more than two atoms.

7 Which of the following statements is incorrect for writing the Lewis dot structure? NCERT Pg 103

(a) The total number of electrons required for writing the structure are obtained by adding the valence electrons of the combining atoms.

(b) It is easy to distribute the number of electrons in a compound as bonding shared pairs between the atoms in proportions to the total bonds.

(c) In general, the least electropositive atom occupies the central position in the molecule/ion.

(d) After accounting for the shared pairs of electrons for single bonds, the remaining electron pairs are either utilised for multiple bonding or remain as the lone pairs.

8 How many number of electrons are involved in the formation of oxygen molecule? NCERT Pg 103

(a) 2 (b) 4 (c) 8 (d) 6

9 What is the formal charge on N atom in SCN^- ion ? NCERT Pg 104

(a) + 1 (b) – 1 (c) 0 (d) – 2

10 Lewis dot structure of CO, NO_2^- ion and CO_3^{2-} ion are I, II and III respectively. NCERT Pg 104

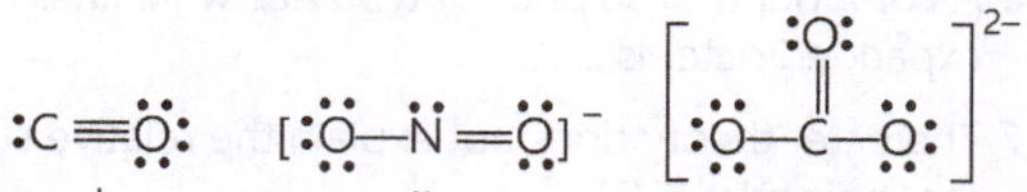

I II III

Which of the above structure(s) is/are wrong?

(a) Only I (b) II and III

(c) Only III (d) I and II

11 Consider the following molecules : NCERT Pg 104

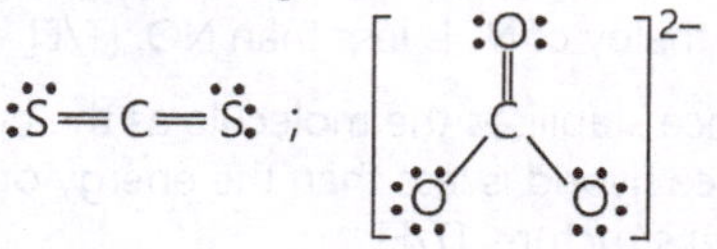

The formal charge on C in CS_2 and CO_3^{2-} respectively are

(a) 0, –2 (b) 0, 0 (c) +2, –2 (d) +1, – 1

12 Which of the following has octet around central atom? NCERT Pg 105

(a) PF_5 (b) SF_6 (c) CCl_4 (d) BF_3

13 Ionic bonds will be formed more easily between elements with comparatively NCERT Pg 106

(a) low ionisation enthalpy and high negative value of electron gain enthalpy

(b) high ionisation enthalpy and high negative value of electron gain enthalpy

(c) low ionisation enthalpy and low positive value of electron gain enthalpy

(d) high ionisation enthalpy and low positive value of electron gain enthalpy

14 Ionic compounds in the crystalline state consist of orderly three-dimensional arrangements of cations and anions held together by NCERT Pg 106
(a) coulombic interaction energies
(b) van der Waals' force
(c) dipole-dipole interactions
(d) electron lattice energies

15 The species in which bond is non-directional is NCERT Pg 106
(a) NCl_3 (b) RbCl
(c) $BeCl_2$ (d) BCl_3

16 Which of the following statement is incorrect? NCERT Pg. 103, 105, 106
(a) Lewis dot structures provide a picture of bonding in molecules and ions in terms of shared pair of electrons and octet rule
(b) Lowest energy structure is the one with highest formal charges on the atoms.
(c) Octet rule is not applied in odd-electron molecules, molecules with expanded octet and incomplete octet of the central atom.
(d) Energy required to completely separate one mole of a solid ionic compound into gaseous constituent ions is called lattice enthalpy.

17 Which of the following statements is incorrect? NCERT Pg 106
(a) The positive and negative ions from the neutral atoms are formed by losing or gaining of electrons respectively.
(b) The formation of positive and negative ions involve ionisation enthalpy and electron gain enthalpy respectively.
(c) Ionisation enthalpy is always positive.
(d) The formation of positive and negative ions involve electron gain enthalpy.

18 Which of the following statement is/are incorrect? NCERT Pg 107
I. In the case of a covalent bond, the contribution from each atom is called the covalent radius of that atom.
II. The covalent radius is equal to the distance between two similar atoms joined by a covalent bond in the same molecule.
III. The covalent radius is measured approximately as the radius of an atom core which is in contact with the core of an adjacent atom in a bonded situation.

Choose the correct answer from the options given below.
(a) Only I (b) Only II
(c) Only III (d) I, II and III

Bond Parameters

19 The correct order of increasing bond length of C—H, C—O, C—C and C=C is NCERT Pg 107
(a) $C-H < C-O < C-C < C=C$
(b) $C-H < C=C < C-O < C-C$
(c) $C-C < C=C < C-O < C-H$
(d) $C-O < C-H < C-C < C=C$

20 Which of the following molecule has the highest bond energy? NCERT Pg 108
(a) H_2 (b) O_2 (c) Cl_2 (d) N_2

21 In case of H_2O molecule, the enthalpy needed to break the two O—H bonds is not the same, i.e. NCERT Pg 109
$H_2O(g) \longrightarrow H(g) + OH(g);\ \Delta_a H_1^{\ominus} = 502\ \text{kJ mol}^{-1}$
$OH(g) \longrightarrow H(g) + O(g);\ \Delta_a H_2^{\ominus} = 427\ \text{kJ mol}^{-1}$
What should be the mean bond enthalpy of O—H bonds in case of H_2O molecule?
(a) 75 kJ mol^{-1} (b) –75 kJ mol^{-1}
(c) 464.5 kJ mol^{-1} (d) 929 kJ mol^{-1}

22 Amongst the following, the total number of molecules which have same bond order is NCERT Pg 109
$\underset{I}{H_2}, \underset{II}{Cl_2}, \underset{III}{CO}, \underset{IV}{Br_2}, \underset{V}{N_2}, \underset{VI}{CH_4}, \underset{VII}{NO}$
Choose the correct option.
(a) 1 (b) 4 (c) 3 (d) 5

23 Which of the following is correct? NCERT Pg 109
(a) Bond order $\propto \dfrac{1}{\text{bond length}} \propto \dfrac{1}{\text{bond enthalpy}} \propto$ stability
(b) Stability $\propto \dfrac{1}{\text{bond order}} \propto \dfrac{1}{\text{bond length}} \propto \dfrac{1}{\text{bond enthalpy}}$
(c) Stability $\propto$ bond order $\propto$ bond length $\propto$ bond enthalpy
(d) Stability $\propto$ bond order $\propto$ bond enthalpy $\propto \dfrac{1}{\text{bond length}}$

24 Which of the following molecules does not show resonance? NCERT Pg 109
(a) NH_3 (b) CO_3^{2-} (c) O_3 (d) SO_3

25 The isoelectronic set of ions is NCERT Pg 109
(a) F^-, Li^+, Na^+ and Mg^{2+}
(b) N^{3-}, Li^+, Mg^{2+} and O^{2-}
(c) Li^+, Na^+, O^{2-} and F^-
(d) N^{3-}, O^{2-}, F^- and Na^+

26 Which of the following pairs of ions is isoelectronic and isostructural? NCERT Pg 109
(a) CO_3^{2-}, NO_3^- (b) ClO_3^-, CO_3^{2-}
(c) SO_3^{2-}, NO_3^- (d) ClO_3^-, NO_3^-

27 The polarity of the covalent bond among the following is maximum in NCERT Pg 110
(a) F—F (b) O—F (c) N—F (d) C—F

28 Resonance stabilises the molecule as the energy of the resonance hybrid is NCERT Pg 110
(a) more than the energy of the single canonical structure
(b) less than the energy of the single canonical structure
(c) less than the energy of the single Lewis structure
(d) more than the energy of a single Lewis structure

29 Which of the following structures of CN_2^{2-} is not correct? NCERT Pg 110
(a) $[:\underset{..}{\ddot{N}}—C\equiv N:]^{2-}$ (b) $[:\underset{..}{N}=C=\underset{..}{N}:]^{2-}$
(c) $[:N\equiv C—\underset{..}{\ddot{N}}:]^{2-}$ (d) $[:\underset{..}{\ddot{N}}=C=\underset{..}{\ddot{N}}:]^{2-}$

30 Consider the following statements. NCERT Pg. 110
I. The canonical forms have no real existence.
II. The molecule does not exist for a certain fraction of time in one canonical form and for other fractions of time in other canonical forms.
III. There is a equilibrium between the canonical forms as we have between tautomeric forms (keto and enol) in tautomerism.
IV. The molecule as such has a single structure which is the resonance hybrid of the canonical forms and which cannot such as be depicted by a single Lewis structure.

Which of the above statement is incorrect?
(a) I and II (b) II and IV (c) Only III (d) Only IV

31 In case of polyatomic molecules, dipole moment is NCERT Pg 111
(a) only depends upon the individual dipole moments of bonds
(b) vector sum of the dipole moments of various bonds
(c) subtraction of dipole moments of various bonds
(d) multiplication of the dipole moment of various bonds

32 Arrange the following molecules from most to least polar. NCERT Pg 111
I. CH_4 II. CH_3Cl III. CH_2Cl_2
IV. CCl_4 V. $CHCl_3$
(a) II > III > V > IV = I (b) II > V > III > IV > I
(c) III > II > V > IV > I (d) V > III > II > IV = I

33 Which of the following molecules has the maximum dipole moment? NCERT Pg 111
(a) CO_2 (b) CH_4 (c) NH_3 (d) NF_3

34 Compound which has both polar and non-polar bonds is NCERT Pg 111
(a) XeF_4 (b) H_2O_2 (c) PCl_5 (d) CO_2

35 In a diatomic molecule, the inter-atomic spacing is 1 Å. Its dipole moment is 1.8 D. The charge on each atom (in C) is NCERT Pg 111
(a) 6×10^{-20} (b) 0.25
(c) 1.8×10^{-10} (d) 6×10^{-18}

36 The decreasing order of dipole moments of the molecules HF, H_2O, BeF_2, NF_3 is NCERT Pg 112
(a) HF > H_2O > BeF_2 > NF_3 (b) H_2O > HF > NF_3 > BeF_2
(c) BeF_2 > NF_3 > HF > H_2O (d) NF_3 > BeF_2 > H_2O > HF

37 Consider the following compound, NCERT Pg 112
NaCl, $MgCl_2$, $AlCl_3$
The correct increasing order of covalent character is
(a) NaCl < $MgCl_2$ < $AlCl_3$ (b) $MgCl_2$ < NaCl < $AlCl_3$
(c) $AlCl_3$ < $MgCl_2$ < NaCl (d) NaCl < $AlCl_3$ < $MgCl_2$

38 Among CaH_2, BeH_2, BaH_2, the order of ionic character is NCERT Pg 112
(a) BeH_2 < BaH_2 < CaH_2 (b) CaH_2 < BeH_2 < BaH_2
(c) BeH_2 < CaH_2 < BaH_2 (d) BaH_2 < BeH_2 < CaH_2

39 Which of the following set of molecules will have zero dipole moment? NCERT Pg 112
(a) Boron trifluoride, hydrogen fluoride, carbon dioxide, 1, 3-dichlorobenzene.
(b) Nitrogen trifluoride, beryllium difluoride, water, 1, 3-dichlorobenzene
(c) Boron trifluoride, beryllium difluoride, carbon dioxide, 1, 4-dichlorobenzene.
(d) Ammonia, beryllium difluoride, water, 1, 4-dichlorobenzene.

40 Which of the following statements is incorrect regarding Fajans' rule? NCERT Pg 112
(a) It discussed the partial covalent character of ionic bonds.
(b) Smaller the size of cation and larger the size of anion, the greater is the covalent character of an ionic bond.
(c) Greater the charge on the cation, the greater the covalent character of the ionic bond.
(d) For cations of same size and charge, the one with electronic configuration of noble gas is more polarising than the one with transition metals configuration.

The Valence Shell Electron Pair Repulsion (VSEPR) Theory

41 The bond angle in H_2O molecule is less than that of NH_3 molecule because NCERT Pg 112
(a) the hybridisation of O in H_2O and N in NH_3 is different
(b) the atomic radii of N and O are different
(c) there is one lone pair on O and two lone pairs on N.
(d) there are two lone pairs on O and one lone pair on N.

42 Which of the following postulate of VSEPR theory is incorrect? **NCERT Pg 113**
(a) The shape of a molecule depends upon the number of valence shell electron pairs around the central atom.
(b) Pairs of electrons in the valence shell repel one another since their electron clouds are negatively charged.
(c) These pairs of electrons tend to occupy such positions in space that minimise repulsion and thus maximise distance between them.
(d) The valence shell is taken as a sphere with the electron pairs localising on the spherical surface at minimum distance from one another.

43 VSEPR theory suggests that bond length and bond angle depend upon the presence or absence of pairs. If the bond angle of H—O—H in H_2O is 105° (approx), then the bond angle of F—O—F in F_2O will be **NCERT Pg 113**
(a) greater than 105°
(b) lesser than 105°
(c) equal to 105°
(d) equal to 180°

44 The ideal shape of H_2O and NH_3 molecules differ due to **NCERT Pg 113**
(a) same hybridisation
(b) different hybridisation
(c) repulsive effect
(d) inductive effect

45 Which of the following molecules has trigonal bipyramidal geometry with bond angles 120° and 90°? **NCERT Pg 114**
(a) SF_6 (b) PCl_5 (c) CH_4 (d) BF_3

46 Which one of the following species contains three bond pairs and one lone pair around the central atom? **NCERT Pg 114**
(a) H_2O (b) BF_3
(c) NH_2^- (d) PCl_3

47 Which of the following is correctly matched? **NCERT Pg 115**
(a) $SO_3^{2-} \Rightarrow$ Tetrahedral
(b) $NO_2^- \Rightarrow$ Trigonal planar
(c) $ClO_4^- \Rightarrow$ Tetrahedral
(d) $NH_3 \Rightarrow$ Trigonal planar

48 The shapes of I_3^+, $XeF_5^{\ominus}$ and $SnCl_2$ are **NCERT Pg 115**
(a) octahedral, trigonal bipyramidal and bent
(b) linear, pentagonal planar and linear
(c) bent, pentagonal planar and angular
(d) *see-saw*, T-shaped and linear

49 Which of the following shows correct molecule and shape? **NCERT Pg 116, 117**
(a) AB_2E, T-shape
(b) AB_2E_2, T-shape
(c) AB_3E_2, Bent-shape
(d) AB_3E_2, T-shape

50 Which of the following structure is most stable?

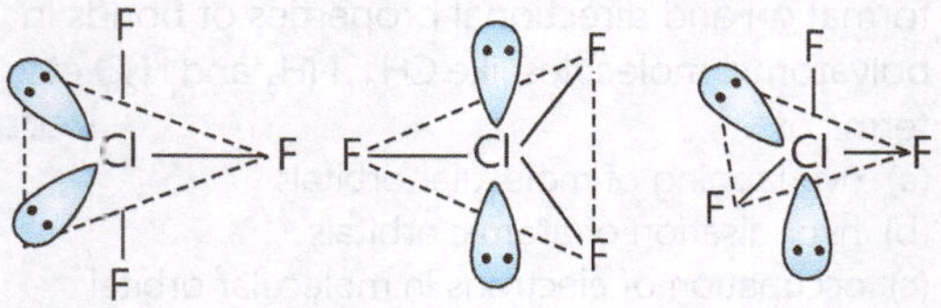

I II III

Choose the correct option. **NCERT Pg 117**
(a) Only I (b) Only II (c) Only III (d) I and II

51 Consider the following statements. **NCERT Pg 116, 117**
I. H_2O molecule has V-shape with two lone pairs of electrons.
II. SF_4 molecule has *see-saw* shape with one lone pair of electrons.
III. ClF_3 is bent-shaped molecule with three lone pairs of electrons.

Which of the above statements are incorrect?
(a) I and II (b) Only III (c) II and III (d) Only II

Valence Bond Theory and Hybridisation

52 Valence bond theory (VBT) is not based on the **NCERT Pg 117**
(a) knowledge of atomic orbitals and electronic configuration of elements
(b) overlapping criteria and the hybridisation of atomic orbitals
(c) the principles of variation and superposition
(d) energy of the molecule

53 Consider the following graph : **NCERT Pg 118**

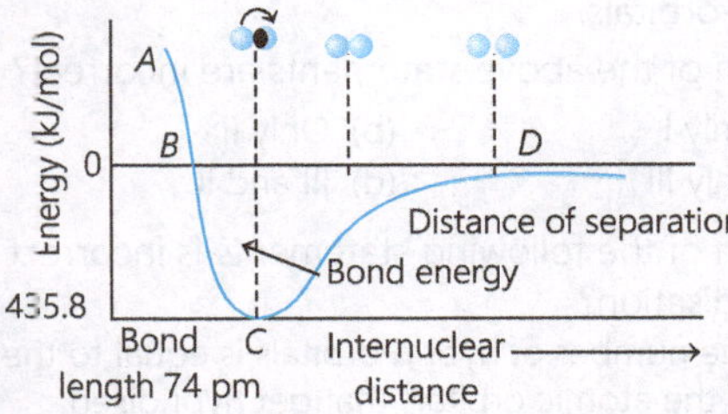

The above potential energy curve is given for the formation of H_2 molecule as a function of internuclear distance of H-atoms. At what point in the curve H_2 is found in the most stable state?
(a) *A* (b) *B* (c) *C* (d) *D*

54 The formation of hydrogen molecule takes place when **NCERT Pg 118**
(a) the energy state is maximum
(b) two hydrogen atomic orbitals undergo large extent of overlapping
(c) two 2*s*-orbital undergo overlapping
(d) the energy state is neutral

55 The valence bond theory explains the shape, the formation and directional properties of bonds in polyatomic molecules like CH_4, NH_3 and H_2O etc., in terms of **NCERT Pg 119**
(a) overlapping of molecular orbitals
(b) hybridisation of atomic orbitals
(c) occupation of electrons in molecular orbital
(d) energy of the molecule

56 Which of the following does not represent positive overlap? **NCERT Pg 119**

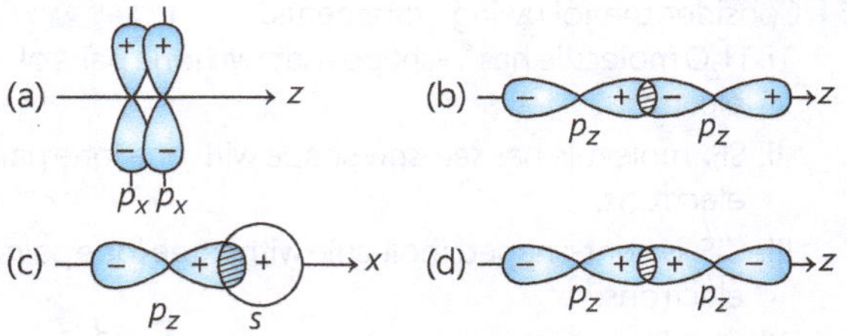

57 Which of the following molecules having all the atoms in same plane? **NCERT Pg 119**
(a) NH_3 (b) CH_4
(c) BF_3 (d) PF_3

58 Consider the following statements. **NCERT Pg 120**
I. In F_2 molecule, F—F σ-bond is formed by axial overlapping of two *p*-orbitals.
II. In O_2 molecule, one σ-bond is formed by axial overlap of *p*-orbitals and one π-bond is formed by lateral overlap of *p*-orbitals.
III. In N_2 molecule, one σ and two π-bonds, i.e. all the three bonds are formed by lateral overlap of *p*-orbitals.

Which of the above statements are incorrect?
(a) Only I (b) Only II
(c) Only III (d) III and II

59 Which of the following statements is incorrect regarding hybridisation? **NCERT Pg 120**
(a) The number of hybrid orbitals is equal to the number of the atomic orbitals that get hybridised.
(b) The hybridised orbitals are always equivalent in energy and shape.
(c) The hybrid orbitals are less effective in forming stable bonds than the pure atomic orbitals.
(d) Hybridisation occurs only between orbitals of similar energy.

60 The fluorine molecule is formed by **NCERT Pg 120**
(a) *p-p* overlapping
(b) *sp-sp* overlapping
(c) *s-s* overlapping
(d) sp^3-sp^3 overlapping

61 The two *sp*- hybrid points in the opposite direction along the *z*-axis with projecting lobes are of size (taking positive sign as overlapping end) **NCERT Pg 121**
(a) more negative and less positive
(b) same positive and negative
(c) more positive and less negative
(d) only positive

62 Which of the following pair have same hybridisation? **NCERT Pg 121**
(a) NO_2^- and NH_2^- (b) NO_2^- and NO_3^-
(c) NH_4^+ and NO_3^- (d) SCN^- and NH_2^-

63 The hybridisation which is also known as diagonal hybridisation is **NCERT Pg 121**
(a) sp^3- hybridisation
(b) sp^2- hybridisation
(c) *sp*- hybridisation
(d) sp^2d- hybridisation

64 Which of the following is not an important condition for hybridisation? **NCERT Pg 121**
(a) The orbitals present in the valence shell of the atom are hybridised.
(b) The orbitals undergoing hybridisation should have almost equal energy.
(c) For hybridisation to take place, it is not necessary that the electrons should be excited and promoted to higher energy.
(d) It is not necessary that only half-filled orbitals participate in hybridisation.

65 Consider the following compounds. **NCERT Pg 121, 122**
I. H_2O II. NH_4^+ III. BF_3 IV. PCl_6^-
V. SO_4^{2-} VI. ClO_4^- VII. BrF_5
The number of compounds which have sp^3-hybridisation.
(a) 2 (b) 3 (c) 4 (d) 5

66 Which one of the following conversions involve change in both hybridisation and shape? **NCERT Pg 122**
(a) $CH_4 \longrightarrow C_2H_6$
(b) $NH_3 \longrightarrow NH_4^+$
(c) $BF_3 \longrightarrow BF_4^-$
(d) $H_2O \longrightarrow H_3O^+$

67 The hybridisation of N-atom and shape of $(SiH_3)NCO$ around N is **NCERT Pg 124**
(a) sp^2, planar (b) sp^3, planar
(c) sp^3, pyramidal (d) *sp*, linear

68 Considering the state of hybridisation of C-atoms, find out the molecule among the following which is linear? **NCERT Pg 123, 124**
(a) $CH_3—CH_2—CH_2—CH_3$
(b) $CH_3—CH=CH—CH_3$
(c) $CH_3—C\equiv C—CH_3$
(d) $CH_2=CH—CH_2—C\equiv CH$

69 The acetylene molecule contains **NCERT Pg 124**
(a) 2 sigma and 2 pi-bond
(b) 2 sigma and 1 pi-bond
(c) 1 sigma and 2 pi-bonds
(d) 3 pi-bonds

70 Which of the following shows sp^3d hybridisation and a trigonal bipyramidal shape ? **NCERT Pg 124**
(a) PF_5 (b) BrF_5
(c) SF_6 (d) $[PtCl_4]^{2-}$

71 Which of the following statements is incorrect regarding PCl_5? **NCERT Pg 125**
(a) Axial bonds suffers more repulsion from the equatorial bond.
(b) The bond angle is 90° only for a bond in an axial plane.
(c) Axial bonds are slightly weaker than equatorial bonds.
(d) All five P—Cl bonds are of same bond length.

Molecular Orbital Theory

72 Which of the following statements is incorrect regarding the conditions for the combination of atomic orbitals? **NCERT Pg 126**
(a) The combining atomic orbitals must have the same or nearly the same energy.
(b) The combining atomic orbitals must have the same symmetry about the molecular axis.
(c) The combining atomic orbitals must overlap to the minimum extent.
(d) Atomic orbitals having same or nearly the same energy will not combine if they do not have the same symmetry.

73 Consider the following statements. **NCERT Pg 126, 127**
I. The electrons in a molecule are present in various molecular orbitals as electrons of atoms are present in various atomic orbitals.
II. Atomic orbital is monocentric while molecular orbital is polycentric.
III. If internuclear axis is taken to be in z-direction, linear combination of $2p_z$-orbitals of two atoms produces $\sigma 2p_z$ and $\sigma^* 2p_z$.
IV. In case of diatomic molecules, molecular orbitals are designated as s, p, d etc.

Choose the incorrect statement.
(a) I and II (b) Only II (c) III and IV (d) Only IV

74 Which of the following statement is not correct from the view point of molecular orbital theory?
(a) Be_2 is not a stable molecule.
(b) He_2 is not stable but He_2^+ is expected to exist.
(c) Bond strength of N_2 is maximum amongst the homonuclear diatomic molecules belonging to the second period.
(d) The order of energies of molecular orbitals in N_2 molecule is $\sigma 2s < \overset{*}{\sigma} 2s < \sigma 2p_z < (\pi 2p_x \simeq \pi 2p_y) < (\pi^* 2p_x \simeq \pi^* 2p_y) > \sigma^* 2p_z$.

75 $2s$ and $2p$ atomic orbitals combine to give how many molecular orbitals? **NCERT Pg 127**
(a) 2 (b) 4 (c) 8 (d) 6

76 Considering x-axis as the intermolecular axis, which of the following will not form sigma bond? **NCERT Pg 127**
(a) $2s$ and $2s$ (b) $2p_x$ and $2s$
(c) $2p_x$ and $3p_x$ (d) $2p_y$ and $2p_y$

77 In case of bonding molecular orbital, the electron density is located **NCERT Pg 127**
(a) away from the space between nuclei of the bonded atom
(b) in between the nuclei of the bonded atoms
(c) in the outer shell
(d) in the inner orbital

78 The electrons placed in antibonding molecular orbital destabilise the molecule. This is because **NCERT Pg 127**
(a) mutual repulsion of electrons > attraction between electrons and nuclei
(b) the repulsion between the nuclei is high
(c) the repulsion between the nuclei is low
(d) mutual repulsion of electrons < attraction between electrons and nuclei

79 $2p_z$-orbital of an atom can not overlap with the $2p_x$ or $2p_y$-orbitals of other atom. Because **NCERT Pg 127**
(a) they possesses same energy
(b) the symmetry of p_x, p_y and p_z is same
(c) the energy of p_x, p_y and p_z is different
(d) symmetry of p_x, p_y and p_z is different

80 If internuclear axis is taken to be in z-direction then, which of the following orbital does form σ-bond? **NCERT Pg 127**
(a) p_x-orbitals (b) p_y-orbitals
(c) p_z-orbitals (d) s and p_x-orbitals

81 Which one of the following combination is not allowed in LCAO method for the formation of a molecular orbital? (Consider z-axis as the molecular axis). **NCERT Pg 127**
(a) $s + p_z$ (b) $p_x + p_x$
(c) $p_z + p_z$ (d) $s + p_x$

82 According to molecular orbital theory, which of the following will not be a viable molecule? **NCERT Pg 129**
(a) He_2^{2+} (b) He_2^+ (c) H_2^- (d) H_2^{2-}

83 Which of the following order is correct in terms of increasing bond order? NCERT Pg 129

(a) $N_2^- < N_2^{2-} < N_2$ (b) $N_2^- < N_2 < N_2^{2-}$

(c) $N_2^{2-} < N_2^- < N_2$ (d) $N_2 < N_2^{2-} < N_2^-$

84 The number of anti-bonding electrons present in O_2^+ ion is NCERT Pg 129

(a) 5 (b) 6 (c) 7 (d) 4

85 According to molecular orbital theory, which of the following is true with respect to Li_2^+ and Li_2^-? NCERT Pg 129

(a) Both are unstable.

(b) Li_2^+ is unstable and Li_2^- is stable.

(c) Both are stable.

(d) Li_2^+ is stable and Li_2^- is unstable.

86 Which of the following species has only π-bonds according to MOT? NCERT Pg 130

(a) C_2 (b) N_2 (c) O_2 (d) F_2

87 Which of the following has minimum bond length? NCERT Pg 129, 130

(a) O_2 (b) O_2^+

(c) O_2^- (d) O_2^{2-}

88 In which of the following processes, the bond order has increased and paramagnetic character has changed to diamagnetic? NCERT Pg 129, 130

(a) $O_2 \rightarrow O_2^+$ (b) $N_2 \rightarrow N_2^+$

(c) $O_2 \rightarrow O_2^{2-}$ (d) $NO \rightarrow NO^+$

89 When O_2 is converted into O_2^{2+}, what will happen? NCERT Pg 130

(a) Both paramagnetic character and bond order increase.

(b) Bond order decreases.

(c) Paramagnetic character increases.

(d) Paramagnetic character decreases and bond order increases.

90 Four diatomic species are listed below. Arrange them in the increasing order of bond order. NCERT Pg 130

(a) $NO < O_2^- < C_2^{2-} < He_2^+$

(b) $O_2^- < NO < C_2^{2-} < He_2^+$

(c) $C_2^{2-} < He_2^+ < O_2^- < NO$

(d) $He_2^+ < O_2^- < NO < C_2^{2-}$

91 The bond order and the magnetic characteristics of CN^- are respectively. NCERT Pg 130

(a) 3, diamagnetic (b) $2\frac{1}{2}$, diamagnetic

(c) 3, paramagnetic (d) $2\frac{1}{2}$, paramagnetic

92 O_2^+ has same bond order as of NCERT Pg 130

(a) N_2 (b) N_2^+ (c) CO (d) O_2^-

93 Identify a molecule which does not exist NCERT Pg 130

(a) N_2 (b) Li_2

(c) Be_2 (d) B_2

Hydrogen Bonding

94 Which of the following molecule does not show hydrogen bonding? NCERT Pg 131

(a) HF (b) H_2O

(c) NH_3 (d) H_2S

95 Which of the following statement is incorrect? NCERT Pg 132

(a) Magnitude of H-bonding is maximum in solid state and minimum in gaseous state.

(b) Intermolecular hydrogen bond is formed between two different molecules of same or different compounds.

(c) Intramolecular hydrogen bond is formed when hydrogen atom is in between the two highly electronegative atoms present with in the same molecule.

(d) Magnitude of H-bonding does not depends on the physical state of the compound.

96 Which of the following observations can be explained on the basis of hydrogen bonding? NCERT Pg 132

I. H—F has higher boiling point than other halogen acids.

II. H_2O has highest boiling point among hydrides of group 16 elements.

III. NH_3 has lower boiling point than PH_3.

(a) I, II and III (b) I and III

(c) II and III (d) I and II

97 Which of the following hydrogen bond is strongest in vapour phase? NCERT Pg 132

(a) HF .... HF

(b) HF .... HCl

(c) HCl ... HCl

(d) HI .... HF

98 Which of the following molecules exhibit intermolecular hydrogen bonding? NCERT Pg 132

(a) *ortho*-nitrophenol

(b) *ortho*-hydroxybenzaldehyde

(c) orthoboric acid

(d) *ortho*-nitrobenzoic acid

Assertion-Reason Questions

Directions (Q. Nos. 1-10) *In the following question Assertion (A) followed by Reason (R) is given below. Choose the correct option out of the choices given below.*

(a) Both A and R are true and R is the correct explanation of A.

(b) Both A and R are true and R is not the correct explanation of A.

(c) A is true but R is false.

(d) A is false but R is true.

1 **Assertion** (A) Sodium chloride formed by the action of chlorine gas on sodium metal is a stable compound.

Reason (R) Sodium and chloride ions acquire octet in sodium chloride formation. NCERT Pg 102

2 **Assertion** (A) The correct Lewis structure of O_3 may be drawn as

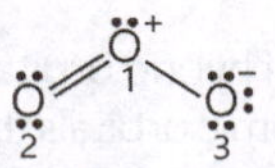

Reason (R) In O_3, the formal charges on atom 1, 2 and 3 are +1, 0 and –1, respectively. NCERT Pg 103, 105

3 **Assertion** (A) NH_4^+ ion is not a cation for ionic compounds.

Reason (R) Cations of ionic compounds are formed from metallic elements. NCERT Pg 106

4 **Assertion** (A) F—F bond has low bond dissociation energy.

Reason (R) The fluorine has least reactivity. NCERT Pg 108

5 **Assertion** (A) Among the two O—H bonds in H_2O molecule, the energy required to break the first O—H bond and the other O—H bond is the same.

Reason (R) This is because the electronic environment around oxygen is not the same even after breakage of one O—H bond. NCERT Pg 109

6 **Assertion** (A) NaCl is more ionic than LiCl.

Reason (R) Greater the size of cation, greater is the polarising power. NCERT Pg 112

7 **Assertion** (A) CH_2Cl_2 is a non-polar molecule while CCl_4 is a polar molecule.

Reason (R) Molecules with zero dipole moment are non-polar in nature. NCERT Pg 112

8 **Assertion** (A) The structure of H_2O is similar to SO_2.

Reason (R) In both molecules (H_2O and SO_2), the central atom has one lone pair of electrons. NCERT Pg 115, 116

9 **Assertion** (A) BrF_5 and SF_6 both have same hybridisation but different shape.

Reason (R) In SF_6, all the six valence electrons are used for bonding. NCERT Pg 126

10 **Assertion** (A) In N_2 molecule, last electron enters into $\pi 2p_y$ molecule.

Reason (R) There is $2s$-$2p$ mixing in orbitals of N_2 molecule. NCERT Pg 131

Statement Type Questions

Direction (Q. Nos. 1-6) *In the following questions, two statements (I & II) are given. In the light of the given statements, choose the correct option given below.*

(a) Both Statement I and Statement II are false.

(b) Statement I is true but Statement II is false.

(c) Statement I is false but Statement II is true.

(d) Both Statement I and Statement II are true.

1 **Statement I** The octet rule holds true for H_2SO_4.

Statement II In H_2SO_4, central atom has 8 valence electrons around it. NCERT Pg 102

2 **Statement I** Orbitals forming bond should have same phase and orientation in space.

Statement II A covalent bond forms between orbitals having electrons with opposite spins. NCERT Pg 118, 119

3 **Statement I** If equatorial place in PCl_5 molecule is the X—Y plane, the orbital hybridising to produce axial bonds are p_y and p_z.

Statement II In PO_4^{3-} ion, number of bond pairs and lone pairs of electrons on phosphorus atom are 4, 1 respectively. NCERT Pg 125

4 **Statement I** Molecules N_2, CO and NO^+ do not have equal bond order.

Statement II The lowest unoccupied molecular orbitals for N_2, is $\sigma^* 2p_z$. NCERT Pg 129, 130

5 **Statement I** H-bonding is maximum in gaseous state and minimum in solid state.

Statement II *o*-hydroxybenzaldehyde shows intramolecular H-bonding. NCERT Pg 131

6 **Statement I** Dipole-dipole interactions are the only non-covalent interactions, resulting in hydrogen bond formation.

Statement II Hydrogen bond in HF are symmetrical
NCERT Pg 131

7 Select the correct statements from the following.
NCERT Pg 103, 106, 109, 127, 131

I. In the CH_4 molecule there are eight valence electrons available for bonding.
II. Sigma molecular orbitals are symmetrical around the bond axis.
III. The formation of positive and negative ions involve electron gain enthalpy.
IV. Hydrogen bonding is the characteristic features of all polar molecules.
V. Resonance hybrid has lower energy than other canonical structures.

Choose the correct answer from the options given below.

(a) I, II and V (b) Only I
(b) II and IV (d) I, II and IV

8 Select the incorrect statement from the following.
NCERT Pg 102, 113, 129, 131

I. The angle between the hybridised orbitals gradually increases when the hybridisation state of carbon atom shifts from sp^3 to sp to sp^2.
II. Hydrogen bond is weaker than the covalent bond.
III. Cl and N have comparable electronegativities yet there is no H-bonding in HCl because size of Cl is large.
IV. The order of stability is $H_2 < Li_2 < O_2 < N_2$.
V. $AlCl_3$, SF_6 and CO_2 show deviation from octet rule.

Choose the correct answer from the options given below.

(a) III and V (b) II, IV and V
(c) I and V (d) I, II and IV

9 Select the correct statements from the following.

I. The molecular geometry of ClF_3 is trigonal bipyramidal according to VSEPR theory.
II. The repulsive interaction of electron pairs decrease in the other *lp-lp* > *lp-bp* > *bp-bp*.
III. PCl_5 molecule has trigonal bipyramidal geometry with no lone pairs of electrons on phosphorus atom.
IV. The molecular geometry of BF_3 is linear.
V. The VSEPR theory model is not applicable for the molecules which have two or more resonance structures.
NCERT Pg 113, 114, 115

Choose the correct answer from the options given below.

(a) I, III and IV (b) I, II and III
(c) I, II and V (d) II, III and IV

10 Which of the following statements are incorrect?

I. Lewis structure of H_2SO_4 shows the limitation of octet rule.
II. According to VSEPR theory, the pairs of electrons tends to occupy such positions that minimise repulsions.
III. Ionic bond is possible between similar and dissimilar atoms.
IV. The number of hybrid orbitals is more than the number of atomic orbitals that are hybridised.
V. Molecular orbitals like atomic orbitals obey Aufbau principle for filling of electrons.
NCERT Pg 105, 106, 113, 120, 126

Choose the correct answer from the options given below.

(a) I, II and V (b) II and III
(c) III and IV (d) I, II and IV

11 Which of the following statements are correct?

I. N_2 has lower bond dissociation enthalpy than O_2.
II. SO_3^{2-} and SF_4 molecules has same number of lone pairs at central atom.
III. d^2sp^3-hybrid orbitals are directed towards the corners of a regular octahedron.
IV. The atomic orbitals of comparable energies and proper symmetry combine to form molecular orbitals.
V. Bond length of HBr is more than HI.
NCERT Pg 108, 114, 125, 126, 129

Choose the correct answer from the options given below.

(a) I and II (b) I, II and III
(c) III and V (d) II, III and IV

Matching Type Questions

1 Match Column I with Column II. NCERT Pg 129

	Column I (Molecule)		Column II (Bond order)
A.	N_2^{2-}	1.	1/2
B.	CO	2.	2
C.	Be_2^+	3.	3
D.	NO	4.	5/2

Codes

	A	B	C	D		A	B	C	D
(a)	3	2	1	4	(b)	2	3	1	4
(c)	2	4	1	3	(d)	3	4	1	2

2 Match the following columns and choose the correct option from the codes given below : NCERT Pg 114

	Column I		Column II
A.	Triagonal planar	1.	PCl_5
B.	Tetrahedral	2.	NH_4^+
C.	Trigonal bipyramidal	3.	SF_6
D.	Octahedral	4.	BF_3

Codes

	A	B	C	D		A	B	C	D
(a)	1	2	3	4	(b)	4	3	2	1
(c)	4	2	1	3	(d)	3	1	2	4

3 Match the following columns and choose the correct option from the codes given below. NCERT Pg 115

	Column I (Molecule type)		Column II (Shape)
A.	AB_4E	1.	Square planar
B.	AB_2E_2	2.	Bent
C.	AB_5E	3.	Square pyramidal
D.	AB_4E_2	4.	*See-saw*

Codes

	A	B	C	D
(a)	1	3	2	4
(b)	4	2	3	1
(c)	3	2	4	1
(d)	2	1	3	4

4 Match the species in Column I with the type of hybrid orbitals in Column II and choose the correct option from the codes given below. NCERT Pg 121, 122, 123, 124

	Column I		Column II
A.	SF_4	1.	sp^3d^2
B.	IF_5	2.	sp
C.	NO_2^+	3.	sp^3d
D.	NH_4^+	4.	sp^3

Codes

	A	B	C	D		A	B	C	D
(a)	1	4	2	3	(b)	3	1	2	4
(c)	2	4	3	1	(d)	4	2	3	1

5 Match the following columns and choose the correct option from the codes given below. NCERT Pg 129, 130

	Column I		Column II
A.	He_2	1.	Paramagnetic
B.	O_2	2.	Diamagnetic
C.	Li_2	3.	Does not exist

Codes

	A	B	C		A	B	C
(a)	1	2	3	(b)	1	3	2
(c)	3	1	2	(d)	3	2	1

Numerical Value Questions

1 The total number of lone pairs of electrons on oxygen atoms of ozone is .... NCERT Pg 105

2 Amongst BeF_2, BF_3, H_2O, NH_3, CCl_4 and HCl, the number of molecules with non-zero net dipole moment is .... NCERT Pg 111

3 The maximum number of lone pairs of electrons on the central atom in the following species is ....

ClO_3^-, XeF_4, SF_4 and I_3^- NCERT Pg 112, 113

4 The number of species having a square planar shape from the following is ....

XeF_4, SF_4, SiF_4, BF_4^-, BrF_4^-, $[Cu(NH_3)_4]^{2+}$, $[FeCl_4]^{2-}$, $[PtCl_4]^{2-}$ NCERT Pg 124

5 The number of species from the following which have square pyramidal structure is ....

PF_5, BrF_4^-, BrF_5, $XeOF_4$, ICl_4^-, IF_5 NCERT Pg 124

6 Among the following species:

N_2, N_2^+, N_2^-, N_2^{2-}, O_2, O_2^+, O_2^-, O_2^{2-}

The number of species showing diamagnetism is .... NCERT Pg 129

NCERT Exemplar's Questions

Direction (Q. Nos. 1-4) *The electronic configurations of the elements A, B and C are given below. Answer the questions from 1 to 4 on the basis of these configurations.*

A	$1s^2$	$2s^2$	$2p^6$		
B	$1s^2$	$2s^2$	$2p^6$	$3s^2$	$3p^3$
C	$1s^2$	$2s^2$	$2p^6$	$3s^2$	$3p^5$

1 Stable form of *A* may be represented by the formula
(a) *A* (b) A_2 (c) A_3 (d) A_4

2 Stable form of *C* may be represented by the formula
(a) *C* (b) C_2 (c) C_3 (d) C_4

3 The molecular formula of the compound formed from *B* and *C* will be
(a) *BC* (b) B_2C (c) BC_2 (d) BC_3

4 The bond between *B* and *C* will be
(a) ionic (b) covalent
(c) hydrogen (d) coordinate

5 The electronic configuration of the outermost shell of the most electronegative elements is
(a) $2s^2 2p^5$ (b) $3s^2 3p^5$
(c) $4s^2 4p^5$ (d) $5s^2 5p^5$

6 If the electronic configuration of an element is $1s^2 2s^2 2p^6 3s^2 3p^6 3d^2 4s^2$, the four electrons involved in chemical bond formation will be
(a) $3p^6$ (b) $3p^6, 4s^2$
(c) $3p^6, 3d^2$ (d) $3d^2, 4s^2$

7 In PO_4^{3-} ion the average formal charge on the oxygen atom is
(a) + 1 (b) – 1 (c) – 0.75 (d) + 0.75

8 Polarity in a molecule and the dipole moment depends primarily on electronegativity of the constituent atoms and shape of a molecule. Which of the following has the highest dipole moment?
(a) CO_2 (b) HI (c) H_2O (d) SO_2

9 Match the species in Column I with the geometry/shape in Column II.

Column I		Column II	
A.	H_3O^+	1.	Linear
B.	$HC{\equiv}CH$	2.	Angular
C.	ClO_2^-	3.	Tetrahedral
D.	NH_4^+	4.	Trigonal bipyramidal
		5.	Pyramidal

10 In NO_3^- ion, the number of bond pairs and lone pairs of electrons on nitrogen atom are
(a) 2, 2 (b) 3, 1
(c) 1, 3 (d) 4, 0

11 Which of the following species has tetrahedral geometry?
(a) BH_4^- (b) NH_2^-
(c) CO_3^{2-} (d) H_3O^+

12 In which of the following molecule/ion all the bonds are not equal?
(a) XeF_4 (b) BF_4^-
(c) C_2H_4 (d) SiF_4

13 Number of π- bonds and σ- bonds in the following structure is

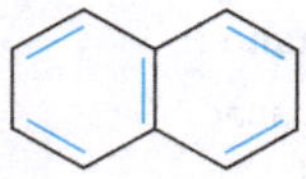

(a) 6, 19 (b) 4, 20
(c) 5, 19 (d) 5, 20

14 Match the species in Column I with the bond order in Column II.

Column I		Column II	
A.	NO	1.	1.5
B.	CO	2.	2.0
C.	O_2^-	3.	2.5
D.	O_2	4.	3.0

15 Which of the following order of energies of molecular orbitals of N_2 is correct?
(a) $(\pi 2p_y) < (\sigma 2p_z) < (\pi^* 2p_x) \approx (\pi^* 2p_y)$
(b) $(\pi 2p_y) > (\sigma 2p_z) > (\pi^* 2p_x) \approx (\pi^* 2p_y)$
(c) $(\pi 2p_y) < (\sigma 2p_z) > (\pi^* 2p_x) \approx (\pi^* 2p_y)$
(d) $(\pi 2p_y) > (\sigma 2p_z) < (\pi^* 2p_x) \approx (\pi^* 2p_y)$

16 Which molecule/ion out of the following does not contain unpaired electrons?
(a) N_2^+ (b) O_2
(c) O_2^{2-} (d) B_2

17 Which of the following options represents the correct bond order?
(a) $O_2^- > O_2 > O_2^+$
(b) $O_2^- < O_2 < O_2^+$
(c) $O_2^- > O_2 < O_2^+$
(d) $O_2^- < O_2 > O_2^+$

18 The types of hybrid orbitals of nitrogen in NO_2^+, NO_3^- and NH_4^+ respectively are expected to be
(a) sp, sp^3 and sp^2 (b) sp, sp^2 and sp^3
(c) sp^2, sp and sp^3 (d) sp^2, sp^3 and sp

19 Isostructural species are those which have the same shape and hybridisation. Among the given species identify the isostructural pairs.
(a) [NF_3 and BF_3] (b) [BF_4^- and NH_4^+]
(c) [BCl_3 and $BrCl_3$] (d) [NH_3 and NO_3^-]

20 Hydrogen bonds are formed in many compounds, e.g. H_2O, HF, NH_3. The boiling point of such compounds depends to a extent on the strength of hydrogen bond and the number of hydrogen bonds. The correct decreasing order of the boiling points above compounds is
(a) $HF > H_2O > NH_3$
(b) $H_2O > HF > NH_3$
(c) $NH_3 > HF > H_2O$
(d) $NH_3 > H_2O > HF$

Past Exams' Questions

NEET Archive

1 Match List I with List II. **NCERT Pg 114, NEET 2024**

	List I (Compound)		List II (Shape/Geometry)
A.	NH_3	I.	Trigonal pyramidal
B.	BrF_5	II.	Square planar
C.	XeF_4	III.	Octahedral
D.	SF_6	IV.	Square pyramidal

Choose the correct answer from the options given below:
(a) A-I, B-IV, C-II, D-III (b) A-II, B-IV, C-III, D-I
(c) A-III, B-IV, C-I, D-II (d) A-II, B-III, C-IV, D-I

2 The correct order of energies of molecular orbitals of N_2 molecule, is **NCERT Pg 129, NEET 2023**
(a) $\sigma 1s < \sigma^* 1s < \sigma 2s < \sigma^* 2s < \sigma 2p_z < (\pi 2p_x = \pi 2p_y) < (\pi^* 2p_x = \pi^* 2p_y) < \sigma^* 2p_z$
(b) $\sigma 1s < \sigma^* 1s < \sigma 2s < \sigma^* 2s < \sigma 2p_z < \sigma^* 2p_z < (\pi 2p_x = \pi 2p_y) < (\pi^* 2p_x = \pi^* 2p_y)$
(c) $\sigma 1s < \sigma^* 1s < \sigma 2s < \sigma^* 2s < (\pi 2p_x = \pi 2p_y) < (\pi^* 2p_x = \pi^* 2p_y) < \sigma 2p_z < \sigma^* 2p_z$
(d) $\sigma 1s < \sigma^* 1s < \sigma 2s < \sigma^* 2s < (\pi 2p_x = \pi 2p_y) < \sigma 2p_z < (\pi^* 2p_x = \pi^* 2p_y) < \sigma^* 2p_z$

3 Amongst the following which one will have maximum 'lone pair - lone pair' electron repulsions? **NCERT Pg 112, NEET 2022**
(a) IF_5 (b) SF_4 (c) XeF_2 (d) ClF_3

4 Which amongst the following is incorrect statement? **NCERT Pg 130, NEET 2022**
(a) C_2 molecule has four electrons in its two degenerate π-molecular orbitals.
(b) H_2^+ ion has one electron.
(c) O_2^+ ion is diamagnetic.
(d) The bond orders of O_2^+, O_2, O_2^- and O_2^{2-} are 2.5, 2, 1.5 and 1 respectively.

5 BF_3 is planar and electron deficient compound. Hybridisation and number of electrons around the central atom, respectively are **NCERT Pg 121, NEET 2021**
(a) sp^3 and 4 (b) sp^3 and 6
(c) sp^2 and 6 (d) sp^2 and 8

6 Match List-I with List-II. **NCERT Pg 115, 114, NEET 2021**

	List-I		List-II
A.	PCl_5	I.	Square pyramidal
B.	SF_6	II.	Trigonal planar
C.	BrF_5	III.	Octahedral
D.	BF_3	IV.	Trigonal bipyramidal

Choose the correct answer from the options given below.

	A	B	C	D
(a)	IV	III	I	II
(b)	II	III	IV	I
(c)	III	I	IV	II
(d)	IV	III	II	I

7 From the following pairs of ion which one is not an isoelectronic pair? **NCERT Pg 109, NEET 2021**
(a) O^{2-}, F^- (b) Na^+, Mg^{2+}
(c) Mn^{2+}, Fe^{3+} (d) Fe^{2+}, Mn^{2+}

8 Among the compounds shown below which one revealed a linear structure? **NCERT Pg 114, NEET 2020**
(a) NO_2 (b) HOCl (c) O_3 (d) N_2O

9 Identify the wrongly matched pair. **NCERT Pg 114, 115, NEET 2020**

	Molecule	Shape of geometry of molecule
(a)	PCl_5	Trigonal planar
(b)	SF_6	Octahedral
(c)	$BeCl_2$	Linear
(d)	NH_3	Trigonal pyramidal

10 Identify a molecule which does not exist. **NCERT Pg 130, NEET 2020**
(a) Li_2 (b) C_2
(c) O_2 (d) He_2

11 Which of the following diatomic molecular species has only π-bonds according to molecular orbital theory? NCERT Pg 130, NEET (National) 2019

(a) N_2 (b) C_2 (c) Be_2 (d) O_2

12 Which of the following is paramagnetic? NEET (Odisha) 2019

(a) N_2 (b) H_2 (c) Li_2 (d) O_2

13 In the structure of ClF_3, the number of lone pairs of electrons on central atom 'Cl' is NCERT Pg 117, NEET 2018

(a) four (b) two
(c) one (d) three

14 Consider the following species :

CN^+, CN^-, NO and CN NCERT Pg 129, NEET 2018

Which one of these will have the highest bond order?

(a) CN^+ (b) CN^- (c) NO (d) CN

15 Which of the following pairs of compounds is isoelectronic and isostructural? NCERT Pg 109, NEET 2017

(a) $BeCl_2$, XeF_2 (b) TeI_2, XeF_2
(c) IBr_2^-, XeF_2 (d) IF_3, XeF_2

16 Consider the molecules CH_4, NH_3 and H_2O. Which of the given statements is false? NCERT Pg 122, NEET 2016

(a) The H—O—H bond angle in H_2O is larger than the H—C—H bond angle in CH_4.
(b) The H—O—H bond angle in H_2O is smaller than the H—N—H bond angle in NH_3.
(c) The H—C—H bond angle in CH_4 is larger than the H—N—H bond angle in NH_3.
(d) The H—C—H bond angle in CH_4, the H—N—H bond angle in NH_3 and the H—O—H bond angle in H_2O are all greater than 90°.

JEE Main Archive

17 Number of molecules ions from the following in which the central atom is involved in sp^3 hybridisation is ......

NO_3^-, BCl_3, ClO_2^-, ClO_3 NCERT Pg 122, JEE Main 2024

(a) 3 (b) 2 (c) 1 (d) 4

18 Sum of bond order of CO and NO^+ is ...... NCERT Pg 109, JEE Main 2024

19 The number of species from the following in which the central atom uses sp^3hybrid orbitals in its bonding is ....

NH_3, SO_2, SiO_2, $BeCl_2$, CO_2, H_2O, CH_4, BF_3 NCERT Pg 122, JEE Main 2024

20 Identify from the following species in which d^2sp^3 hybridisation is shown by central atom. NCERT Pg 124, JEE Main 2024

(a) $[Pt(Cl)_4]^{2-}$ (b) $[Co(NH_3)_6]^{3+}$
(c) BrF_5 (d) SF_6

21 What is the number of unpaired electrons in the highest occupied molecular orbital of the following species N_2; N_2^+; O_2; O_2^+? NCERT Pg 129, JEE Main 2023

(a) 2, 1, 2, 1 (b) 0, 1, 0, 1
(c) 2, 1, 0, 1 (d) 0, 1, 2, 1

22 Resonance in carbonate ion (CO_3^{2-}) is

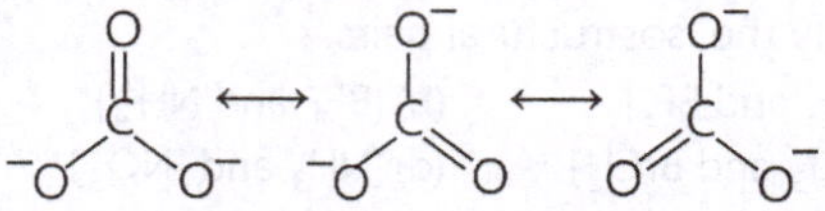

Which of the following is true? NCERT Pg 110, JEE Main 2023

(a) Each structure exists for equal amount of time.
(b) It is possible to identify each structure individually by some physical or chemical method.
(c) All these structures are in dynamic equilibrium with each other.
(d) CO_3^{2-} has a single structure, i.e. resonance hybrid of the above three structures.

23 Order of covalent bond;

A. KF > KI; LiF > KF
B. KF < KI; LiF > KF
C. $SnCl_4$ > $SnCl_2$; CuCl > NaCl
D. LiF > KF; CuCl < NaCl
E. KF < KI; CuCl > NaCl

Choose the correct answer from the options given below. NCERT Pg 112, JEE Main 2023

(a) Only B, C (b) Only A, B
(c) Only C, E (d) Only B, C, E

24 Which of the following pair of molecules contain odd electron molecule and an expanded octet molecule? NCERT Pg 105, JEE Main 2022

(a) BCl_3 and SF_6
(b) NO and H_2SO_4
(c) SF_6 and H_2SO_4
(d) BCl_3 and NO

25 Consider the species CH_4, NH_4^+ and BH_4^-. Choose the correct option with respect to these species. NCERT Pg 109, JEE Main 2022

(a) They are isoelectronic and only two have tetrahedral structures.
(b) They are isoelectronic and all have tetrahedral structures.
(c) Only two are isoelectronic and all have tetrahedral structures.
(d) Only two are isoelectronic and only two have tetrahedral structures.

26 Bonding in which of the following diatomic molecule(s) become(s) stronger, on the basis of MO theory, by removal of an electron?

A. NO B. N_2 C. O_2 D. C_2 E. B_2

Choose the most appropriate answer from the options given below. NCERT Pg 129, JEE Main 2022

(a) A, B and C (b) B, C and E
(c) A and C (d) Only D

27 The compound(s) which will show significant intermolecular H-bonding is/are

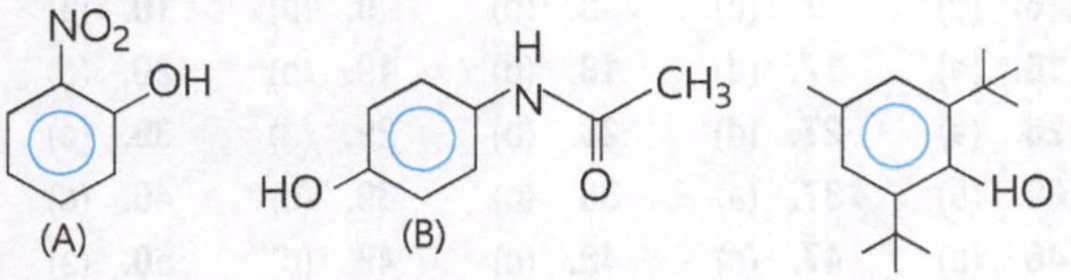

(A) (B) (C)

NCERT Pg 132, JEE Main 2021

(a) Only *B* (b) Only *C*
(c) *A* and *B* (d) *A*, *B* and *C*

28 Which of the following are isostructural pairs ? NCERT Pg 109, JEE Main 2021, 24

A. SO_4^{2-} and CrO_4^{2-}
B. $SiCl_4$ and $TiCl_4$
C. NH_3 and NO_3^-
D. BCl_3 and $BrCl_3$

Choose the most appropriate answer from the options given below.

(a) A and B (b) A and C
(c) B and C (d) C and D

29 The hybridisations of the atomic orbitals of nitrogen in NO_2^-, NO_2^+ and NH_4^+ respectively are NCERT Pg 121, JEE Main 2021

(a) sp^3, sp^2 and sp (b) sp, sp^2 and sp^3
(c) sp^3, sp and sp^2 (d) sp^2, sp and sp^3

Skill Boosters

1 Rajat has taken an organic compound for experiment the compound contains 92.3% C and 7.7% H, then number of sp^3, sp^2 and sp hybridised carbon atoms in all possible structures of this compound respectively are (molecular mass = 52 g/ mol)

(a) 1, 2, 5 (b) 0, 4, 4 (c) 0, 8, 4 (d) 1, 0, 2

2 The radius and charge of each of six ions are shown in the table:

Ion	J^+	L^+	M^{2+}	X^-	Y^-	Z^{2-}
Radius/nm	0.14	0.18	0.15	0.14	0.18	0.15

The ionic solids *JX*, *LY* and *MZ* are of the same lattice type. What is the correct order of their lattice energies placing the one with the highest numerical value first?

(a) *JX* > *LY* > *MZ* (b) *JX* > *MZ* > *LY*
(c) *LY* > *MZ* > *JX* (d) *MZ* > *JX* > *LY*

3 In a School laboratory, a teacher gives four anions O_2^{2-}, CO_3^{2-}, CN^- and NCS^- to his students. Along with it he given four neutral molecule to them. He told his students to find out the molecule which has the same geometry and the same arrangement of the bonding electrons as in CO_3^{2-}. The molecule is ....

(a) Cl_2 (b) BF_3 (c) CO (d) H_2O

4 A salt of copper is formed by copper sulphate and water. The salt obtained is used as a pesticide in soil. The colour of the salt and the number of co-ordinate bonds present in the salt will be

(a) blue, 4 (b) colourless, 3
(c) red brown, 5 (d) dark brown, 6

5 A AB_2L_2 type molecule is observed in which a highly electronegative atom *A* of electronegativity 3.44 is placed as central atom. The molecule is a polar molecule. In the observation value of dipole moment of the molecule is found to be 1.840. What is the bond angle of *B*—*A*—*B* in AB_2L_2, given that dipole moment at *A*—*B* bond is 1.5 D ?

(a) 104°.33′ (b) 106°.26′
(c) 107°.01′ (d) 110°.36′

6 In certain polar solvents PCl_5 undergoes an ionisation reaction in which Cl^- ion leaves one PCl_5 molecule and attaches itself to another.

$$2PCl_5 \rightleftharpoons PCl_4^+ + PCl_6^-$$

By observing this reaction; what are the changes in the geometrical shape that occurs in this ionisation and the formal charges on P-atom of both the ions.

(a) sp^3d to sp^2 and d^2sp^3, 0 to – 1 and + 1
(b) sp^3d to sp^3 and sp^3d^2, 0 to + 1 and – 1
(c) sp^2 to sp^3d and sp^3d^3, 1 to 0 and – 1
(d) sp^3d to dsp^3 and d^2sp^3, 2 to – 2 and 0

7 A student is trying to perform an activity in the lab for which he took two ice cubes, which are pressed over each other until they write to form one block. To force dominates for holding them together is

(a) covalent attraction force
(b) dipole-dipole interaction force
(c) hydrogen bond formation
(d) van der Waals' forces

Correct Codes

Topical Questions

1. (b)	2. (c)	3. (a)	4. (d)	5. (d)	6. (d)	7. (c)	8. (b)	9. (b)	10. (a)
11. (b)	12. (c)	13. (a)	14. (a)	15. (b)	16. (b)	17. (d)	18. (b)	19. (b)	20. (d)
21. (c)	22. (c)	23. (d)	24. (a)	25. (d)	26. (a)	27. (d)	28. (b)	29. (d)	30. (c)
31. (b)	32. (a)	33. (c)	34. (b)	35. (a)	36. (b)	37. (a)	38. (c)	39. (c)	40. (d)
41. (d)	42. (d)	43. (b)	44. (c)	45. (b)	46. (d)	47. (c)	48. (c)	49. (d)	50. (a)
51. (b)	52. (d)	53. (c)	54. (b)	55. (b)	56. (b)	57. (c)	58. (c)	59. (c)	60. (a)
61. (c)	62. (b)	63. (c)	64. (c)	65. (c)	66. (c)	67. (d)	68. (c)	69. (c)	70. (a)
71. (d)	72. (c)	73. (d)	74. (d)	75. (c)	76. (d)	77. (b)	78. (a)	79. (d)	80. (c)
81. (d)	82. (d)	83. (c)	84. (a)	85. (d)	86. (a)	87. (b)	88. (d)	89. (d)	90. (d)
91. (a)	92. (b)	93. (c)	94. (d)	95. (d)	96. (d)	97. (a)	98. (c)		

Assertion-Reason

1. (a)	2. (a)	3. (d)	4. (c)	5. (d)	6. (c)	7. (d)	8. (c)	9. (a)	10. (d)

Statement Type

1. (a)	2. (d)	3. (a)	4. (a)	5. (c)	6. (c)	7. (a)	8. (c)	9. (b)	10. (c)
11. (d)									

Matching Type

1. (b)	2. (c)	3. (b)	4. (b)	5. (c)

Numerical Value

1. (6)	2. (3)	3. (3)	4. (4)	5. (3)	6. (2)

NCERT Exemplar's

1. (a)	2. (b)	3. (d)	4. (b)	5. (a)	6. (d)	7. (c)	8. (c)	9. A-5, B-1, C-2, D-3
10. (d)	11. (a)	12. (c)	13. (c)	14. A-3, B-4, C-1, D-2	15. (a)	16. (c)	17. (b)	18. (b)
19. (d)	20. (b)							

Past Exams'

1. (a)	2. (d)	3. (c)	4. (c)	5. (c)	6. (a)	7. (d)	8. (d)	9. (a)	10. (d)
11. (b)	12. (d)	13. (b)	14. (b)	15. (c)	16. (a)	17. (b)	18. (6)	19. (4)	20. (b)
21. (b)	22. (d)	23. (d)	24. (b)	25. (b)	26. (c)	27. (a)	28. (a)	29. (d)	

Skill Boosters

1. (c)	2. (d)	3. (b)	4. (a)	5. (a)	6. (b)	7. (c)

Step by Step

Decoding the Questions

Concept Builders

1 True 2 electrostatic

3 Electrovalent or ionic bond

4 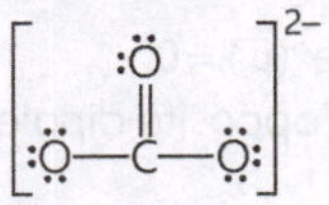

5 True 6 SF_6

7 True 8 low, high

9 False 10 True

11 Debye, μ 12 True

13 210° 14 5 *bp*, 1 *lp*

15 False 16 minimum

17 negative overlap

18 False 19 60%

20 8 21 True

22 linear combination of atomic orbitals

23 True 24 8

25 stable, positive

26 C_2 27 False

28 0, 0 29 True 30 4

Topical Solutions

1 (*b*) The element that would readily form a diatomic molecule is *M*. By sharing of 1 electron each, both the atoms of *M* will get a completed octet.

2 (*c*) The formation of chlorine molecule, (Cl_2), can be understood by Lewis-Langmuir theory.

3 (*a*) Valence electrons in $P = 2$

Valence electrons in $Q = 6$

$$P \longrightarrow P^{2+} + 2e^-$$

$$Q + 2e^- \longrightarrow Q^{2-}$$

So, $P^{2+} + Q^{2-} \longrightarrow PQ$

Since, both show a valency of 2. So, the formula for the compound will be *PQ*.

4 (*d*) In NH_4^+ molecule, there are 2 type of bonds, three covalent bonds and one coordinate bond (N—H).

5 (*d*) Among the given molecules, PCl_5 does not follow octet rule because central P-atom is surrounded by 10 electrons.

6 (*d*) Among the given statements, only statement (d) is incorrect. The correct form is :

Lewis dot structure can be drawn for the molecules which contains more than two atoms like methane.

7 (*c*) Statement (c) is incorrect. It's correct form is as follows

In general, the least electronegative atom occupies the central position in the molecule/ion.

Rest other statements are correct.

8 (*b*) Oxygen molecule is diatomic and contains double bond between two O-atoms O=O. So, that total four electrons are involved in the formation of O_2 molecule.

9 (*b*) $F.C = V - N - \frac{B}{2}$

$$\text{As, } F.C = \left(5 - 4 - \frac{1}{2} \times 4\right) = -1$$

So, formal charge on N-atom in SCN^-.

10 (*a*) The correct Lewis dot structure of CO is

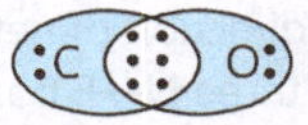 or :C≡O: (Correct)

11 (*b*) Formal charge on C-atom of CS_2

$$F.C = V - N - \frac{B}{2}$$

$$= 4 - 0 - \frac{1}{2} \times 8 = 0$$

Similarly, formal charge on C-atom of CO_3^{2-} is 0.

12 (*c*) Carbon tetrachloride (CCl_4) has octet around central atom. The number of bonded electrons in other given compounds are as follows

$PF_5(10e^-)$, $SF_6(12e^-)$, $BF_3(6e^-)$

13 (*a*) 14 (*a*)

15 (*b*) RbCl molecule bonds are non-directional because it is an electrovalent compound. Whereas others are covalent compounds.

16 (*b*) Statement (b) is incorrect. While other statements are correct. The correct form of (b) is :

The lowest energy structure is the one with the smallest formal charges on the atoms.

17 (*d*) Statement (d) is incorrect whereas other statements are correct. The correct form of (d) is :

The formation of negative ion involve electron gain enthalpy.

$$X(g) + e^- \longrightarrow X^-(g)$$

[addition of electron]

18 (*b*) Statements I and III are correct while Statement II is incorrect. It's correct form is :

The covalent radius is half of the distance between two similar atoms joined by a covalent bond in the same molecule.

19 (*b*) The C—H bond is the shortest due to small size of both atoms and large electronegativity difference. The double bonds are shorter than single bonds.

Hence, C=C bond is shorter than C—O and C—C. Due to electronegativity difference between C and O, the C—O bond length is shorter than C—C bond. Hence, the correct order is (b).

20 (*d*) $B.E \propto \frac{1}{B.L}$

$\therefore N_2$ has the highest bond energy among the given molecules. Because, N_2 has triple bond and the bond length of N_2 is the least.

21 (*c*) Average/mean bond enthalpy is

$$= \frac{502 + 427}{2} = 464.5 \text{ kJ mol}^{-1}$$

22 (*c*) In CO three shared electron pairs are present in between C and O thus, the bond order is 3. For N_2, bond order is 3. H_2, Cl_2 and Br_2 have bond order 1. NO has 2.5 bond order and CH_4 has 4 bond order.

23 (*d*)

24 (*a*) Ammonia (NH_3) do not show resonance because ammonia lacks a double bond. So, no resonance can be observed.

25 (*d*) The species with same number of electrons are isoelectronic species.

Hence, $N^{3-}(10e^-)$, $O^{2-}(10e^-)$, $F^-(10e^-)$ and $Na^+(10e^-)$.

26 (*a*)

Species	Total number of electrons	Structure	Shape
CO_3^{2-}	32	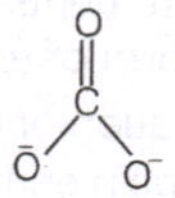	Trigonal planar
NO_3^-	32	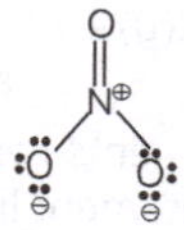	Trigonal planar

27 (*d*) In a Pauling scale the electronegativities of F = 4, C = 2.5, O = 3.5, N = 3.

Since, the electronegativity difference between C and F is maximum.

So, the C—F bond would have maximum polarity.

28 (*b*)

29 (*d*) The incorrect structure is (d). As,

$$[\ddot{N}=C=\ddot{N}]^{2-} \longleftrightarrow [:N\equiv C-\ddot{N}:]^{2-} \longleftrightarrow [:\ddot{N}-C\equiv N]^{2-}$$

30 (*c*) Statements I, II and IV are correct while Statement III is incorrect. It's correct form is :

There is no equilibrium exists between the canonical forms because they have no real existence, and equilibrium cannot exist between hypothetical structures.

31 (*b*)

32 (*a*) The correct decreasing order of dipole moment is

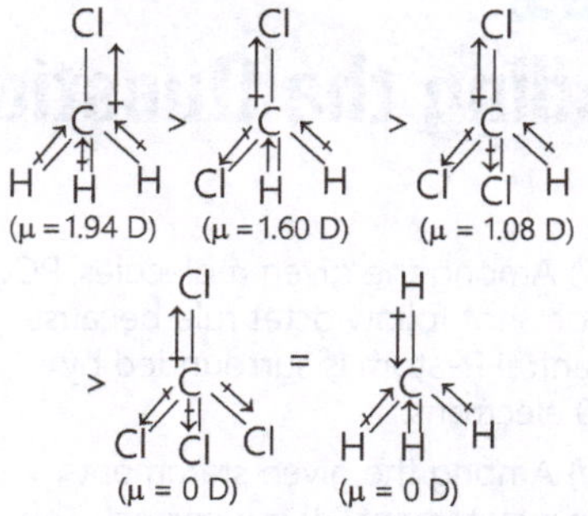

33 (*c*) In NH_3, the dipole moment is maximum because the dipole due to the lone pair being in the same direction as the resultant dipole moment of the N—H bonds.

34 (*b*) Among the given compounds, H_2O_2 contains both polar and non-polar covalent bonds.

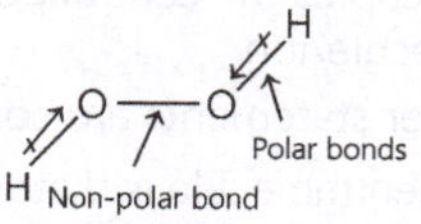

35 (*a*) Dipole moment (μ) = Charge $(Q) \times$ Distance (r)

$$\text{Charge } (Q) = \frac{\text{Dipole moment } (\mu)}{\text{Distance } (r)}$$

$$= \frac{1.8\text{ D}}{1\text{ Å}} = \frac{1.8 \times 3.335 \times 10^{-30}\text{ Cm}}{10^{-10}\text{ m}}$$

$$\simeq 6 \times 10^{-20}\text{ C.}$$

36 (*b*) BeF_2 has zero dipole moment as it is symmetrical in nature. H_2O has maximum dipole moment as it possess two lone pair of electrons.

In case of NF_3, the direction of net dipole moment of three N—F bonds is opposite to that of the dipole moment of the lone pair. The dipole moment of HF is larger than NF_3 but smaller than H_2O. Thus, the correct decreasing order is (b).

37 (*a*) The decreasing order of cation size is $Na^+ > Mg^{2+} > Al^{3+}$. Al^{3+} has maximum polarisation effect and Na^+ has least polarisation effect. So, the correct increasing order of covalent character is (a).

38 (*c*) According to Fajans' rule, since, the size of cation decreases in the following order :

$$Ba^{2+} > Ca^{2+} > Be^{2+}$$

Therefore, the correct order of ionic character is (c).

39 (*c*) The set of molecules which have zero dipole moment is

Boron trifluoride $(\mu) = 0$

Beryllium difluoride $(\mu) = 0$

Carbon dioxide $(\mu) = 0$

1, 4-dichlorobenzene $(\mu) = 0$

Due to cancelling of opposite dipole moments.

40 (*d*) Statement (d) is incorrect while other statements are correct. The correct form of (d) is as follows

For cations of the same size and charge, the one with electronic configuration $(n-1)d^n ns^0$, typical of transition metals is more polarising than the one with a noble gas configuration, ns^2np^6.

41 (*d*) NH_3 has only one lone pair and H_2O has two lone pairs. Hence, due to *lp-lp* repulsions, bond angle in H_2O is lower than that in NH_3.

42 (*d*) The incorrect postulate is (d). It's correct form is :

Valence shell is taken as a sphere with the electron pairs localising on the spherical surface at maximum distance from one another.

43 (*b*) In F_2O, F is more electronegative which attracts the bond pair electrons away from central oxygen atom which decreases the repulsion between bond pair of electrons, hence, bond angle decreases and lesser than 105°.

44 (*c*) **45** (*b*)

46 (*d*) $PCl_3 \Rightarrow$

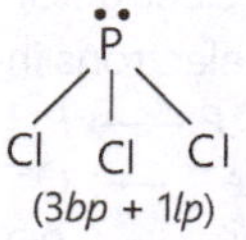

47 (*c*) Option (c) is correct.

ClO_4^- is tetrahedral.

Other options are incorrect. Corrected form are as follows

The structure with hybridisation of given compounds are as follows

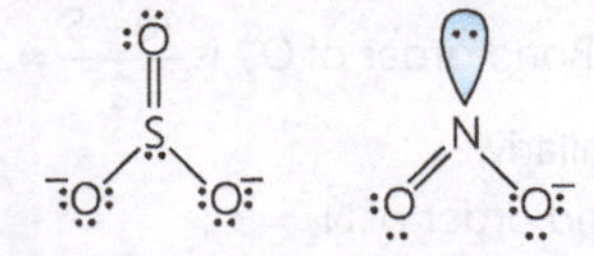

Sulphite ion (SO_3^{2-}) sp^2-trigonal planar   Nitrite ion (NO_2^-) sp^2-bent

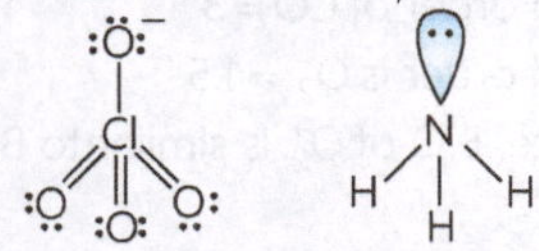

Perchlorate ion (ClO_4^-) sp^3-tetrahedral   Ammonia (NH_3) sp^3-pyramidal

48 (c) The shapes of I_3^+, XeF_5^- and $SnCl_2$ are

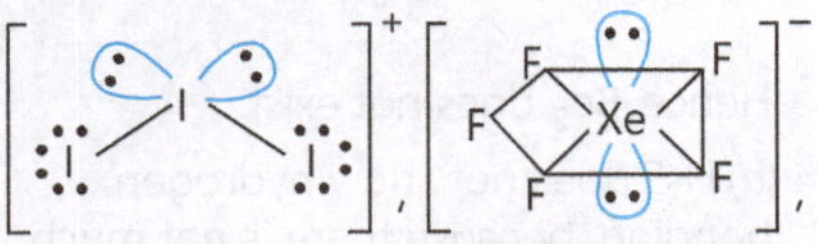

(Bent)   (Pentagonal planar)

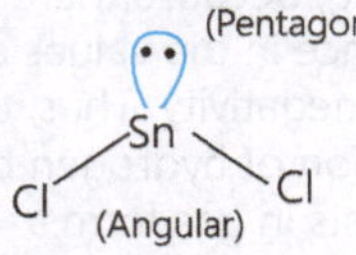

(Angular)

49 (d) Structures of AB_3E_2 type molecules are as follows

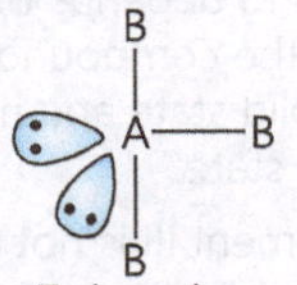

T-shaped (AB_3E_2)

AB_2E_2 and AB_2E has bent structure while AB_3E_2 has T-shaped.

50 (a) Structure I is the most stable because both the lone pairs are present at equatorial position. Due to which repulsion is minimum in molecule.

51 (b) Statements I and II are correct while Statement III is incorrect.

It's correct form is :

ClF_3 is T-shaped molecule with two lone pairs of electrons.

52 (d) The valence bond theory (VBT) is not perfect. It has its own sets of limitations. It fails to answer the energies of the molecules.

53 (c) At C point in the curve, H_2 is found in the most stable state due to minimum energy as the energy get released when bond is formed between two hydrogen atoms.

54 (b) During the formation of the H_2 molecule, the 1s orbitals of two hydrogen atoms containing one unpaired electron with opposite spin overlap with each other along the internuclear axis.

55 (b)

56 (b) Option (b) does not represent positive overlap.

It is an out of phase overlap. Thus, it shows negative overlap.

57 (c) The correct option is (c) BF_3. In this boron is sp^2-hybridised so all its atoms are co-planar.

58 (c) Statement I and II are correct but Statement III is incorrect.

It's correct form is as follows

In N_2 molecule, one σ-bond is formed by axial overlapping of p-orbitals and 2π-bonds are formed by lateral overlapping of p-orbitals.

59 (c) Statement (a), (b) and (d) are correct while (c) is incorrect. It's correct form is as follows

The hybrid orbitals are more effective in forming stable bonds than the pure atomic orbitals.

60 (a) The fluorine molecule is formed by 2p-2p overlapping.

61 (c) It projecting more positive lobes and less negative lobes, which provides more effective overlapping resulting in the formation of stronger bonds.

62 (b) NO_2^- and NO_3^- both have same hybridisation, i.e. sp^2-hybridisation.

63 (c) The sp-hybridisation is also called diagonal hybridisation because it possess linear geometry.

64 (c) Statement (c) is incorrect.

It's correct form is :

Promotion of electron is not essential condition prior to hybridisation.

65 (c) Among the given species, (H_2O, NH_4^+, ClO_4^- and SO_4^{2-}) has sp^3-hybridisation while other species BF_3, BrF_5, PCl_6^- have sp^2, sp^3d^2 and sp^3d^2 hybridisation respectively.

66 (c) The change in both hybridisation and shape is in

	$BF_3 \longrightarrow$	BF_4^-
	3 bp	4 bp
Hybridisation	sp^2	sp^3
Structure	Trigonal planar	Tetrahedral

67 (d) $H_3Si{=}N{=}C{=}O$

180° (linear structure)

Hence, in (SiH_3) NCO hybridisation of N-atom is sp and shape of the compound is linear.

68 (c) $H_3C-\underset{\uparrow\atop sp}{C}\equiv\underset{\uparrow\atop sp}{C}-CH_3$

is linear due to sp-hybridisation of the two symmetric carbon.

69 (c)

70 (a) Among the given options, PF_5 has sp^3d-hybridisation and trigonal bipyramidal shape.

71 (d) Statement (d) is incorrect. It's correct form is :

The two axial (P—Cl) bonds are slightly longer than the equatorial bonds.

72 (c) Statement (c) is incorrect, while other statements are correct.

The correct form of (c) is :

The combining atomic orbitals must overlap to the maximum extent.

73 (d) Statements I, II and III are correct, while the Statement IV is incorrect. It's correct form is :

In case of diatomic molecules, molecular orbitals are designated as σ(sigma), π(pi), δ(delta) etc.

74 (d) Option (d) is incorrect regarding molecular orbital theory.

The correct order of energies of molecular orbitals in N_2 molecule is

$$\sigma 2s < \sigma^* 2s < (\pi 2p_x \simeq \pi 2p_y) < \sigma 2p_z < (\pi^* 2p_x \approx \pi^* 2p_y) < \sigma^* 2p_z$$

75 (c) 2s and 2p atomic orbitals combine to give eight molecular orbitals. From 2s orbitals, σ2s and σ^*2s can be formed. From 2p orbital, $\sigma 2p_z$, $\sigma^* 2p_z$, $\pi 2p_x$, $\pi^* 2p_x$, $\pi 2p_y$ and $\pi^* 2p_y$ molecular orbitals can be formed.

76 (d) $2p_y$ and $2p_y$-orbitals will not form a sigma bond.

Taking, x-axis as the internuclear axis, $2p_y$ and $2p_y$-orbitals will undergo lateral overlapping. So, forming a pi(π)-bond.

77 (*b*) In bonding molecular orbital, the electron density is located between the nuclei of the bonded atoms.

78 (*a*) This is because the mutual repulsion of the electrons in this orbital is more than the attraction between the electrons and the nuclei, which causes a net increase in energy.

79 (*d*) $2p_z$ orbital of one atom can not overlap with the $2p_x$ or $2p_y$ orbitals because symmetry of p_x, p_y and p_z is different.

80 (*c*) If intermolecular axis is taken to be in z-direction then, p_z orbital form σ-bond whereas p_x and p_y form π-bond.

81 (*d*) s and p_x-orbitals do not have proper orientation to overlap and hence molecular orbital is not formed.

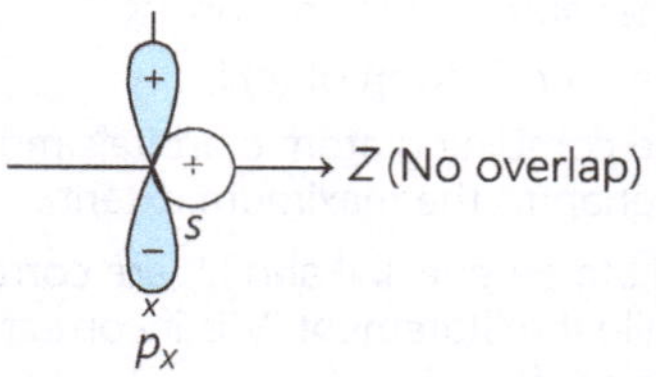

82 (*d*) According to MOT, if bond order of a molecule is zero the molecule will not exist.

Hence, among the given molecules, only H_2^{2-} has zero bond order.

$\because$ Bond order $= \dfrac{N_b - N_a}{2}$, B.O. of

$= \dfrac{2-2}{2} = 0$ hence, it does not exist.

83 (*c*)

	N_2	N_2^-	N_2^{2-}
Number of electron	14	15	16
Bond order	3	2.5	2

$\therefore$ The correct increasing bond order is $N_2^{2-} < N_2^- < N_2$.

84 (*a*) M.O. configuration of O_2^+ will be $\sigma 1s^2, \sigma^* 1s^2, \sigma 2s^2, \sigma^* 2s^2, \sigma 2p_z^2,$

$\pi 2p_x^2 = \pi 2p_y^2, \pi^* 2p_x^1$

Hence, number of anti-bonding electrons are 5.

85 (*d*) The electronic configuration of $Li_2^+ (Z=5) = \sigma 1s^2, \sigma^* 1s^2, \sigma 2s^1$

Bond order (BO)

$$= \frac{N_b - N_a}{2} = \frac{3-2}{2} = \frac{1}{2}$$

The electronic configuration of $Li_2^- (Z=7) = \sigma 1s^2, \sigma^* 1s^2, \sigma 2s^2, \sigma^* 2s^1$

Bond order (BO)

$$= \frac{N_b - N_a}{2} = \frac{4-3}{2} = \frac{1}{2}$$

For the species having the same value of BO, the species having lesser number of antibonding electrons [N_a] will be more stable.

So, Li_2^+ is stable and Li_2^- is unstable.

86 (*a*) C_2 has only π-bonds because of the presence of four electrons in two Pi molecular orbitals. Whereas others have sigma and π-bonds both.

87 (*b*) Bond order $\propto \dfrac{1}{\text{Bond length}}$

Thus, O_2^+ has minimum bond length as its bond order is maximum, i.e. 2.5.

88 (*d*) $NO \longrightarrow NO^+$

NO is paramagnetic (1 unpaired e^-) with B.O $=2.5$, NO^+ is diamagnetic with B.O $=3$.

89 (*d*) When O_2 is converted into O_2^{2+}, the paramagnetic character decreases and the bond order increases.

90 (*d*) Bond order $= \dfrac{N_b - N_a}{2}$

As, bond order (NO) $= \dfrac{5}{2} = 2.5$

Bond order (O_2^-) $= \dfrac{3}{2} = 1.5$

Bond order (He_2^+) $= \dfrac{1}{2} = 0.5$

Bond order (C_2^{2-}) $= \dfrac{6}{2} = 3$

Thus, the correct increasing order of bond order is (d).

91 (*a*) $CN^- = 14 e^-$

$CN^- : \sigma 1s^2\ \sigma^* 1s^2\ \sigma 2s^2\ \sigma^* 2s^2\ \pi 2p_x^2$

$= \pi 2p_y^2\ \sigma 2p_z^2$

$\therefore$ Bond order $= \dfrac{10-4}{2} = 3$

As there is no unpaired electron in CN^-, thus it is diamagnetic.

92 (*b*) Bond order of O_2^+ is $\dfrac{10-5}{2} = 2.5$

Similarly,

Bond order of $N_2 = 3$

Bond order of $N_2^+ = 2.5$

Bond order of $CO = 3$

Bond order is $O_2^- = 1.5$

Hence, B.O of O_2^+ is similar to B.O of N_2^+.

93 (*c*) If bond order of a molecule is zero, the molecule will not exist.

$Be_2(8e^-) = \sigma 1s^2 \sigma^* 1s^2 \sigma 2s^2 \sigma^* 2s^2$

$$\text{B.O.} = \frac{4-4}{2} = 0$$

Hence, Be_2 does not exist.

94 (*d*) H_2S does not show hydrogen bonding, because there is not much difference in the values of electronegativity. Thus, there is no formation of hydrogen bonding and H_2S exists in gas form.

95 (*d*) Statement (d) is incorrect. It's correct form is magnitude of H-bonding depends on the physical state of the compound. It is maximum in the solid state and minimum in the gaseous state.

96 (*d*) Statement III is not true since NH_3 has higher boiling point than PH_3 due to hydrogen bonding.

97 (*a*) A compound having maximum electronegative element will form strong hydrogen bond. F is the most electronegative element among halogens hence, form strongest hydrogen bond.

98 (*c*) Among the given option, orthoboric acid shows intermolecular hydrogen bonding

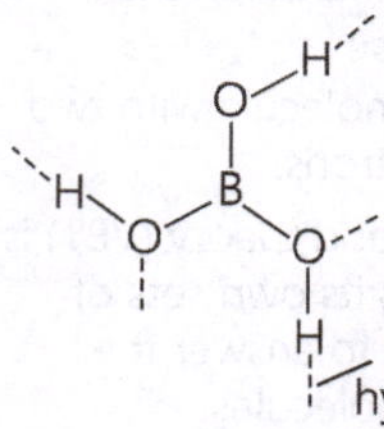

Intermolecular hydrogen bonding

while others show intramolecular hydrogen bonding.

Assertion-Reason

1 (*a*) Both A and R are true and R is the correct explanation of A.

2 (*a*) Both A and R are true and R is the correct explanation of A.

3 (*d*) A is false but R is true.

The correct form of A is :

Though NH_4^+ is a cation formed from non-metallic elements, it is a cation for a number of ionic compounds.

4 (*c*) A is true but R is false. The correct form of R is :

Fluorine is highly reactive because F—F bond has low bond dissociation energy.

5 (*d*) A is false but R is true.

The correct form of A is :

The bond enthalpies of two O—H bonds in H—O—H are not equal.

6 (*c*) A is true but R is false. The correct form of R is :

Smaller is the size of cation (Li) and larger is the size of anion (Cl) greater is the polarising power.

7 (*d*) A is false but R is true.

The correct form of R is :

The molecule CH_2Cl_2 is polar in nature and CCl_4 is non-polar in nature.

8 (*c*) A is true but R is false. The correct form of R is :

O has two lone pairs of electrons in H_2O while S has one lone pair of electron in SO_2.

9 (*a*) Both A and R are true and R is the correct explanation of A.

10 (*d*) A is false but R is true.

The correct form of A is :

In N_2 molecule, last electron enters into $\sigma 2p_z$ molecular orbital.

Statement Type

1 (*a*) Both Statements I and II are false.

Their correct form are

The octet rule does not hold true for H_2SO_4.

In H_2SO_4, central atom has 12 valence electrons around it.

2 (*d*) Both Statements I and II are true.

3 (*a*) Both Statements I and II are false.

Their correct form are as follows

If equatorial place in PCl_5 molecule is the *X*—*Y* plane, the orbital hybridising to produce axial bonds are p_z and d_{z^2}.

In PO_4^{3-} ion, number of bond pairs and lone pairs of electrons on phosphorus atom are 5 and 0 respectively.

4 (*a*) Both Statements I and II are false.

Their correct form are as follows

Molecules N_2, CO and NO^+ have equal bond order because they are isoelectronic.

The LUMO for N_2 is $\pi^* 2p_x$ and $\pi^* 2p_y$.

5 (*c*) Statement I is false but Statement II is true.

Correct form of Statement I is :

H-bonding is maximum in the solid state and minimum in gaseous state.

6 (*c*) Statement I is false but Statement II is true.

The corrected form of I is :

Dipole-dipole interactions are purely covalent interactions of dipolar covalent bonds.

7 (*a*) Statements I, II and V are correct whereas Statements III and IV are incorrect. Their correct form are as follows

III. The formation of positive ions involve ionisation enthalpy and negative ions involve electron gain enthalpy.

IV. Hydrogen bonding is the characteristic feature of those polar molecules which contain a covalent bond between H and any electronegative atoms among F, O, N.

8 (*c*) Statements I and V are incorrect while other are correct. The correct form of I and V are as follows

I. The angle between the hybridised orbital increases when hybridisation state of carbon atom shifts from sp^3 to sp^2 to sp.

V. $AlCl_3$, SF_6 deviate from octet rule but CO_2 follows octet rule.

9 (*b*) Among the given statements, I, II and III are correct, while the other statements IV and V are incorrect.

Their correct form are :

IV. The molecular geometry of BF_3 molecule is trigonal planar according to VSEPR theory.

V. The VSEPR model is applicable to such molecules which have two or more resonance structures.

10 (*c*) Among the given statements, statements III and IV are incorrect while the other statements are correct. Their correct form is

III. Ionic bond is not possible, between similar atoms.

IV. The number of hybrid orbitals is equal to the number at atomic orbitals that are hybridised.

11 (*d*) Among the given statements, Statements II, III and IV are correct while Statements I and V are incorrect.

Their correct form is

I. N_2 has higher bond dissociation enthalpy than O_2.

V. Bond length of HI is more than HBr.

Matching Type

1 (*b*) The correct match is A-2, B-3, C-1, D-4.

2 (*c*) The correct match is A-4, B-2, C-1, D-3.

3 (*b*) The correct match is A-4, B-2, C-3, D-1.

4 (*b*) The correct match is A-3, B-1, C-2, D-4.

5 (*c*) The correct match is A-3, B-1, C-2.

Numerical Value

1 (6) Oxygen has 6 lone pair of electrons in ozone molecule.

2 (3) Out of given molecules; H_2O, NH_3 and HCl are polar molecules and BeF_2, BF_3 and CCl_4 are non-polar molecules.

3 (3)

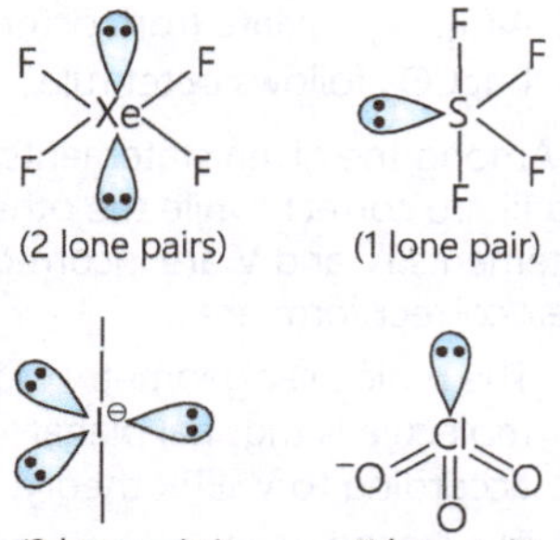

(2 lone pairs) (1 lone pair)

(3 lone pairs) (1 lone pair)

Among the given species I_3^- contains maximum number of lone pair electrons, i.e. 3.

4 (4)

Species	Hybridisation	Geometry
XeF_4	sp^3d^2	Square planar
BrF_4^-	sp^3d^2	Square planar
$[Cu(NH_3)_4]^{2+}$	dsp^2	Square planar
$[PtCl_4]^{2-}$	dsp^2	Square planar

So, total 4 species have square planar shape.

5 (3)

PF_5	sp^3d	Triangular pyramidal
BrF_4^-	sp^3d^2	Square planar
IF_5	sp^3d^2	Square pyramidal
BrF_5	sp^3d^2	Square pyramidal
$XeOF_4$	sp^3d^2	Square pyramidal
ICl_4^-	sp^3d^2	Square planar

Among the given species 3 species, (IF_5, BrF_5, $XeOF_4$) have square pyramidal structure.

6 (2) $N_2 : (\sigma 1s)^2(\sigma^* 1s)^2(\sigma 2s)^2(\sigma^* 2s)^2$ $(\pi 2p_x^2 = \pi 2p_y^2)(\sigma 2p_z)^2$; Diamagnetic
$O_2^{2-}: (\sigma 1s)^2(\sigma^* 1s)^2(\sigma 2s)^2(\sigma^* 2s)^2(\sigma 2p_z)^2$ $(\pi 2p_x^2 = \pi 2p_y^2)(\pi^* 2p_x^2 = \pi^* 2p_y^2)$; Diamagnetic

NCERT Exemplar's

1 (a) The given electronic configuration shows that *A* represents noble gas because the octet is complete. *A* is neon which has 10 atomic number.

2 (b) The electronic configuration of *C* represent chlorine. Its stable form is dichlorine (Cl_2), i.e. C_2.

3 (d) The electronic configuration show that *B* represents phosphorus and *C* represents chlorine. The stable compound formed is PCl_3, i.e. BC_3.

4 (b) The bond between *B* and *C* will be covalent. Both *B* and *C* are non-metal atoms. *B* represents phosphorus and *C* represent chlorine.

5 (a) The electronic configuration of the most electronegative element is $2s^2 2p^5$ (fluorine).

6 (d) The given electronic configuration shows that the element is titanium (Z = 22). In transition elements, i.e. *d*-block elements, electrons of *ns* and $(n-1)$ *d*-subshell take part in bond formation.

7 (c) In PO_4^{3-} ion, formal charge on each O-atom of P—O bond, i.e. average formal charge

$$= \frac{\text{total charge}}{\text{number of O -atoms}} = -\frac{3}{4} = -0.75$$

8 (c) Among all dipole moment is highest for H_2O as in it the central atom contains 2 lone pairs and also due to maximum electronegativity difference between H and O-atoms.

9 The correct match is A-5, B-1, C-2, D-3.

10 (d)

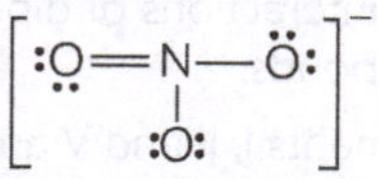

In NO_3^- ion, the no. of bond pair and lone pair are 4 and 0.

11 (a) $BH_4^{\ominus}$ has tetrahedral geometry.

12 (c) In C_2H_4 (ethene), all bonds are not equal. The molecule consist of one double bond and two single bonds. Double bond is shorter than single bond.

13 (c) The given compound will have the correct structure as

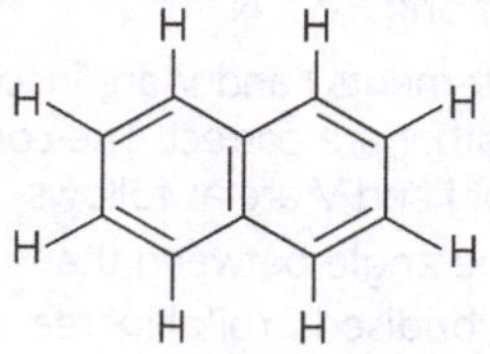

(Naphthalene)

There are 5 π-bonds and 8 C— H + 11C— C σ-bonds, i.e. 19 σ-bond are present in the above molecule.

14 The correct match is A-3, B-4, C-1, D-2.

15 (a) The correct increasing order of energies of molecular orbitals of N_2 is given below.

$$\sigma 1s < \overset{*}{\sigma} 1s < \sigma 2s < \overset{*}{\sigma} 2s < (\pi 2p_x \approx \pi 2p_y) < \sigma 2p_z < (\overset{*}{\pi} 2p_x \approx \overset{*}{\pi} 2p_y) < \overset{*}{\pi} 2p_z$$

16 (c) O_2^{2-} does not contain unpaired electrons.

17 (b) Electronic configuration of O_2 (16 electrons)

$$= \sigma 1s^2, \overset{*}{\sigma} 1s^2, \sigma 2s^2, \overset{*}{\sigma} 2s^2, \sigma 2p_z^2, \pi 2p_x^2 \approx \pi 2p_y^2, \overset{*}{\pi} 2p_x^1 \approx \overset{*}{\pi} 2p_y^1$$

$$\text{Bond order} = \frac{1}{2}(N_b - N_a) = \frac{1}{2}(10-6) = 2$$

Thus, the order of bond order is $O_2^- < O_2 < O_2^+$.

18 (b) The type of hybrid orbitals of nitrogen in NO_2^+, NO_3^- and NH_4^+ respectively are *sp*, sp^2 and sp^3 respectively.

19 (b) BF_4^- and NH_4^+ both are isostructural pairs. Both are tetrahedral and sp^3-hybridised.

20 (b) Strength of H-bond is in the order

$$\overset{\delta^+}{H} \ldots \overset{\delta^-}{F} > \overset{\delta^+}{H} \ldots \overset{\delta^-}{O} > \overset{\delta^+}{H} \ldots \overset{\delta^-}{N}$$

But each H_2O molecule is linked to four other H_2O molecules through H-bonds, whereas each HF molecule is linked only to two other HF molecules.

Hence, correct decreasing order of boiling points is (b).

Past Exams'

1 (a) The correct match is A-I, B-IV, C-II, D-III.

A. $NH_3 \longrightarrow sp^3$ hybridised with 1 lone pair $\longrightarrow$ trigonal pyramidal.

B. $BrF_5 \longrightarrow sp^3d^2$ hybridised with 1 lone pair $\longrightarrow$ square pyramidal

C. $XeF_4 \longrightarrow sp^3d^2$ hybridised with 2 lone pairs $\longrightarrow$ square planar

D. $SF_6 \longrightarrow sp^3d^2$ hybridised with zero lone pair $\longrightarrow$ octahedral

2 (*d*) The correct order of energies of molecular orbitals of N_2 molecule is (d).

3 (*c*) XeF_2

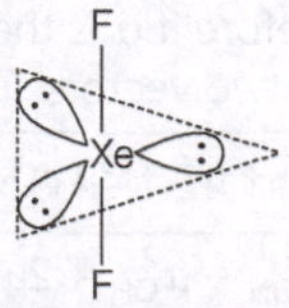

Among all the options XeF_2 has maximum number of lone pairs, i.e. 3. Hence, it will show maximum 'lone pair- lone pair' repulsion.

4 (*c*) Among the given options, the incorrect statement is option (c).

$O_2^+ = \sigma 1s^2 \sigma^* 1s^2 \sigma 2s^2 \sigma^* 2s^2 \sigma 2p_z^2$
$\pi 2p_x^2 = \pi 2p_y^2 \pi^* 2p_x^1$

O_2^+ ions have 15 electrons, so, it contains one unpaired electron. Hence, it is paramagnetic in nature.

5 (*c*) Electronic configuration of $B = 1s^2, 2s^2, 2p^1$

Number of valence electrons in B = 3 electrons in last shell

Number of side atoms in BF_3 = 3F-atoms.

So, hybridisation$= \frac{1}{2}(3+3) = \frac{1}{2} \times 6 = 3$.

Hybridisation of B in BF_3 is sp^2.

Number of electrons around central atom, B in BF_3 is equal to the number of electrons in three sigma bonds (B—F). i.e.

= 3 B—F bonds × 2 electrons in one σ-bond.

= 6 electrons

6 (*a*) The correct match is A-(IV); B-(III); C-(I); D-(II).

7 (*d*) Fe^{2+} $(24e^-)$ and Mn^{2+} $(23e^-)$ are not iso-electronic pair.

8 (*d*) $N_2O \Rightarrow :N \equiv \overset{sp}{N} \rightarrow O \rightarrow$ Linear structure

Hence, option (d) is correct.

9 (*a*)

(A) $PCl_5 \Rightarrow$ 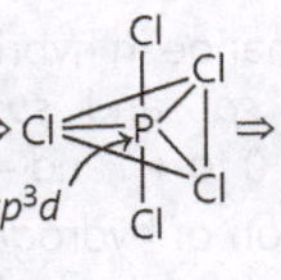 $\Rightarrow$ Geometry = shape = trigonal bipyramidal

sp^3d

10 (*d*) If bond order of a molecules becomes zero, the molecule will not exist.

Bond order $= \frac{N_b - N_a}{2}$

$He_2(4e^-) = \sigma 1s^2\ \sigma^* 1s^2$; $BO = \frac{2-2}{2} = 0$

So, He_2 does not exist.

11 (*b*) The molecular orbital configuration of C_2 is

$C_2(Z=12) = \sigma 1s^2, \sigma^* 1s^2, \sigma 2s^2, \sigma^* 2s^2, \pi 2p_x^2 = \pi 2p_y^2$.

Double bond in C_2 consists of both π-bonds because of the presence of last (valence) four electrons in two π-molecular orbitals.

12 (*d*) $O_2 (Z = 16)$

It is a paramagnetic molecule due to presence of unpaired electrons in each orbital of degenerate levels.

13 (*b*)The central atom Cl has seven electrons in the valence shell. Three of these will form electron pair bonds with three fluorine atoms leaving behind four electrons. Thus, there are three bond pairs and two lone pairs of electrons.

14 (*b*) CN^- : Central atom is C
[Total number of electrons= 14]

$\sigma 1s^2, \sigma^* 1s^2, \sigma 2s^2, \sigma^* 2s^2, (\pi 2p_x^2 \approx \pi 2p_y^2)\ \sigma 2p_z^2$

$B.O. = \frac{10-4}{2} = 3$

CN^- has highest B.O. While the species NO have (2.5), CN (2.5) and CN^+ (2) B.O respectively.

15 (*c*) Both IBr_2^- and XeF_2 are linear and number of valence electrons present in both the species is same, i.e. they are also isoelectronic.

16 (*a*) As the number of lone pair of electrons on central element increases, repulsion between those lone pair of electrons increases and therefore, bond angle decreases. So, H_2O has smaller bond angle as it has 2 lone pair.

17 (*b*) The hybridisation of central atom in the given molecules/ions are as follows

$NO_3^- \rightarrow sp^2$ 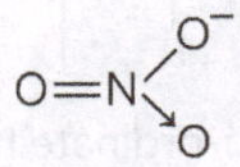

$BCl_3 \rightarrow sp^2$ 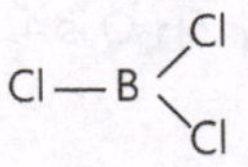

$ClO_2^- \rightarrow sp^3$ 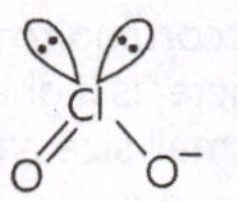

$ClO_3 \rightarrow sp^3$ 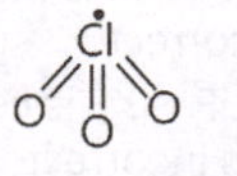

Thus, two molecules/ions, i.e. ClO_2^- and ClO_3 has sp^3-hybridisation.

18 (6) NO^+ and CO both are isoelectronic species and each of them is having bond order 3.

∴Sum of bond order of NO^+ and CO = Bond order (NO^+) + Bond order (CO) = 3 + 3 = 6

19 (4) The number of species that uses sp^3 hybrid orbitals in bonding are 4 i.e., H_2O, NH_3, SiO_2, CH_4.

While other species uses sp^2 and sp-hybrid orbitals which are as follows.

sp^2 — SO_2, BCl_3

sp — $BeCl_2$, CO_2

20 (*b*) Among the given options, only $[Co(NH_3)_6]^{3+}$ shows d^2sp^3 hybridisation.

Hybridisation of rest of the members are as follows

$BrF_5 = sp^3d^2$

$SF_6 = sp^3d^2$

$[PtCl_4]^{2-} = dsp^2$

21 (*d*) $N_2 = \sigma 1s^2 \sigma^* 1s^2\ \sigma 2s^2\ \sigma^* 2s^2 \pi 2p_x^2 = \pi 2p_y^2, \sigma 2p_z^2$

Number of unpaired electron present in HOMO = 0

$N_2^+ = \sigma 1s^2, \sigma^* 1s^2, \sigma 2s^2, \sigma^* 2s^2, \pi 2p_x^2 = \pi 2p_y^2, \sigma 2p_z^1$

Number of unpaired electron present in HOMO = 1

$O_2 = \sigma 1s^2, \sigma^* 1s^2, \sigma 2s^2, \sigma^* 2s^2, \sigma 2p_z^2, \pi 2p_x^2 = \pi 2p_y^2, \pi^* 2p_x^1 \approx \pi^* 2p_y^1$

Number of unpaired electron present in HOMO = 2

$O_2^+ = \sigma 1s^2, \sigma^* 1s^2, \sigma 2s^2, \sigma^* 2s^2, \sigma 2p_z^2, \pi 2p_x^2 = \pi 2p_y^2, \pi^* 2p_x^1 = \pi^* 2p_y^0$

Number of unpaired electron present in HOMO = 1

Thus, the number of unpaired electrons are 0, 1, 2, 1.

23 (*d*) According to Fajans' rule, covalent character is higher for large size anion and small size cation. Thus,

(A) KF > KI is incorrect, LiF > KF is correct.

(D) LiF > KF is correct, CuCl < NaCl is incorrect.

24 (*b*) NO contains 15 electrons.
Expanded octet molecule contains more than eight electrons in their valence shell. SF_6, PCl_5 and H_2SO_4 are examples of expanded octet molecules. BCl_3 and SF_6 are even electron molecules.

25 (*b*) Number of electron in given species

$CH_4 = 6 + 4 = 10$

$NH_4^+ = 7 + 3 = 10$

$BH_4^- = 5 + 4 + 1 = 10$

They all have same number of electron, i.e. are isoelectronic (species with same number of electron) and also have same structure, i.e. tetrahedral.

26 (*c*) Bond strength ∝ bond order
Removal of electron from antibonding MO increases B.O
∴ NO and O_2 has valence e^- in π^* orbital. So, these two form strong bond after removal of electron.

27 (*a*) Extensive H-bonding is observed in compound (b) as two H-atoms bonded to strongly electronegative atoms (nitrogen, oxygen) are present.

28 (*a*) If number of sigma bond (σ), co-ordinate bond and lone pair are same for given pairs, they are isostructural. Hence, SO_4^{2-}, CrO_4^{2-}, $SiCl_4$ and $TiCl_4$ have tetrahedral shape and are isostructural.

29 (*d*) Hybridisation of N in NO_2^-, NO_2^+, NH_4^+ are sp^2, sp, sp^3 respectively.

Skill Boosters

1 (*c*) Let amount of compound = 100 g

$$\text{No. of moles of C} = \frac{92.3}{12} = 7.69 = 7.77$$

$$\text{No. of moles of H} = \frac{7.7}{1} = 7.7$$

Empirical formula = CH

Empirical formula mass
$= 12 + 1 = 13$ g/mol

Molecular mass = 52 g/mol

$$n = \frac{52}{13} = 4$$

∴Molecular formula = Empirical formula × 4 = C_4H_4

Possible structures

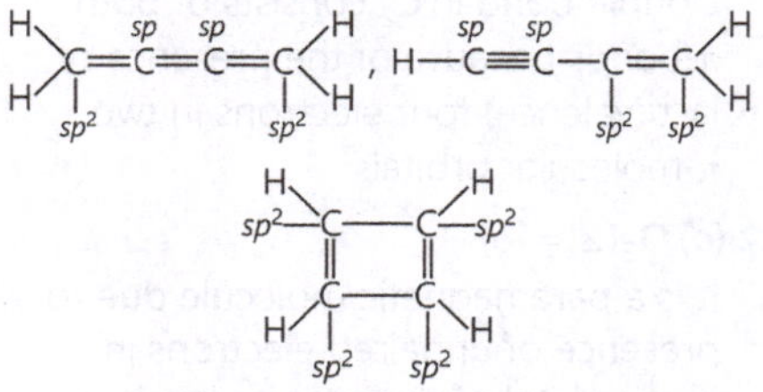

No. of sp^3 C = 0 ; No. of sp^2 C = 8
No. of sp C = 4

2 (*d*) The highest lattice energy is given by one with the highest ionic charges and smallest ionic sizes.

3 (*b*) CO_3^{2-} :

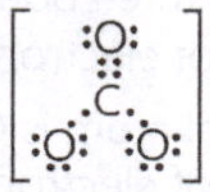

→ Geometry is trigonal planar and F •• B •• F (BF_3) also has trigonal planar. While Cl_2, CO have linear and H_2O has tetrahedral geometry.

4 (*a*) $\underset{\text{Copper sulphate}}{CuSO_4(s)} + \underset{\text{Water}}{5H_2O(l)} \longrightarrow \underset{\substack{\text{Copper sulphate}\\\text{pentahydrate}\\\text{(Blue vitriol)}}}{CuSO_4 \cdot 5H_2O(s)}$

The colour of copper sulphate pentahydrate is blue.
∴$CuSO_4 \cdot 5H_2O$ has ionic, covalent, co-ordinate and hydrogen bonds as shown below.

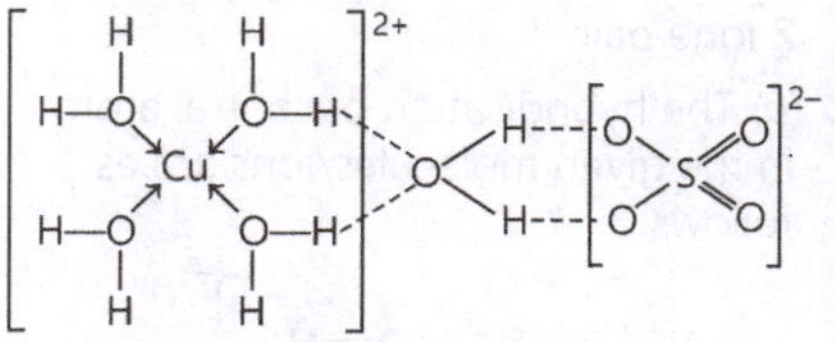

The co-ordinate bond present in $CuSO_4 \cdot 5H_2O$ is 4.

5 (*a*) The molecule AB_2L_2 is H_2O.
As, dipole moment of H_2O is the resultant of the two vectors (O—H bonds), therefore if α is the angle between the two vectors. Then,

$$\mu = \sqrt{\mu_1^2 + \mu_2^2 + 2\mu_1\mu_2 \cos\alpha}$$

$$\mu_{H_2O} = \sqrt{\mu_{OH}^1 + \mu_{OH}^2 + 2\mu_{OH}^2 \cos\alpha}$$

$$1.84 = \sqrt{(1.5)^2 + (1.5)^2 + 2(1.5)^2 \cos\alpha}$$

$3.3856 = 2.25 + 2.25 + 4.50 \cos\alpha$

$\cos\alpha = -0.2476$

∴ $\alpha = 104°3'$

6 (*b*) The hybridisation can be determined by $X = \frac{1}{2}[\text{V.E} + \text{M.A} - C + a]$

(V.C = Valence e^-
M.A = Monovalent atom
C = charge on cation
a = charge on anion)

PCl_5

$$X = \frac{1}{2}[5 + 5 - 0 + 0] = \frac{10}{2} = 5$$

∴ X is 5, therefore, sp^3d hybridisation.

PCl_4^+

$$X = \frac{1}{2}[5 + 4 - 1 + 0] = \frac{8}{2} = 4$$

∴ X is 4, therefore, sp^3 hybridisation.

PCl_6^-

$$X = \frac{1}{2}[5 + 6 + 0 + 1] = \frac{12}{2} = 6$$

The value of X is 6, therefore, the hybridisation is sp^3d^2.
Formal charge can be determined as

$$\text{F.C.} = \text{V} - \text{N} - \frac{B}{2}$$

PCl_5

$$\text{F.C} = 5 - 0 - \left(\frac{10}{2}\right) = 0$$

PCl_4^+

$$\text{F.C} = 5 - 0 - \frac{8}{2} = +1$$

PCl_6^- $\text{F.C} = 5 - 0 - \frac{12}{2} = -1$

∴Therefore, the change in hybridisation is from sp^3d to sp^3 and sp^3d^2 and informal charge is 0 to +1 and −1.

7 (*c*) Due to formation of hydrogen bond between two atoms (positively charged hydrogen atom and negatively charged oxygen atom) two cubes holds together.

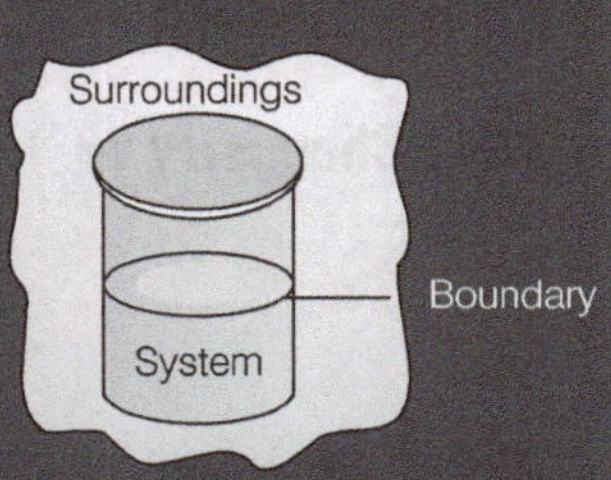

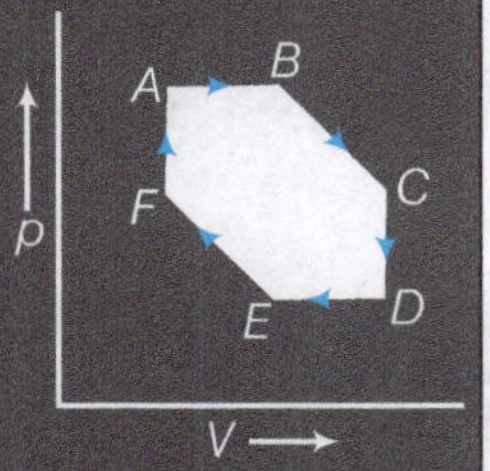

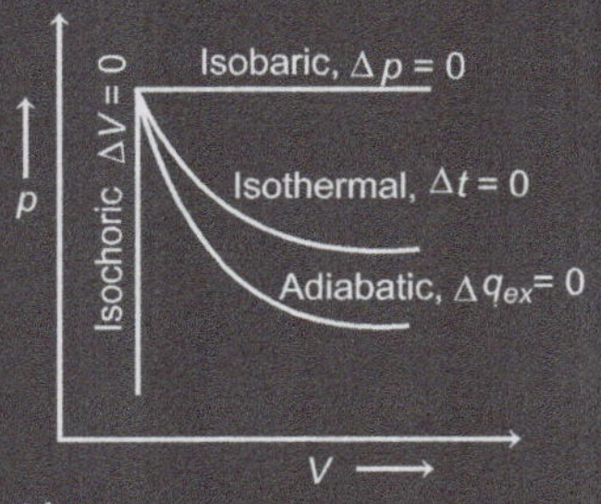

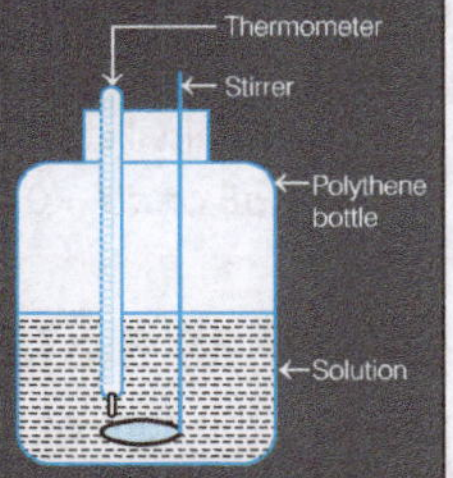

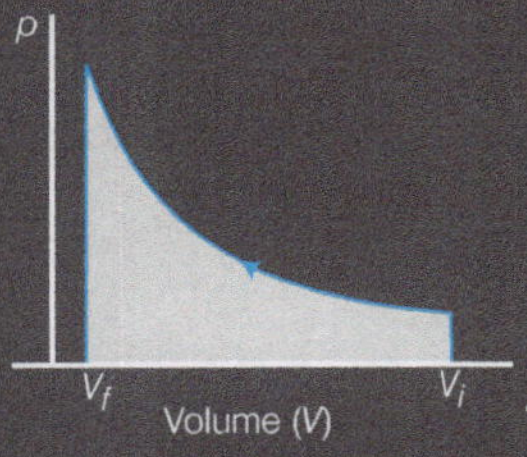

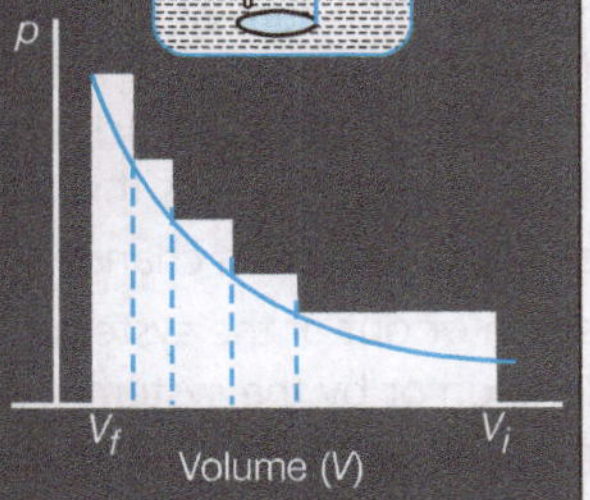

05

Scan for **Chemistry Through Concept Master** *Videos*

Thermodynamics

Thermodynamics deals with the study of different forms of energy and their transformation from one form to another.

The laws of thermodynamics deals with energy changes of macroscopic systems involving a large number of molecules rather than microscopic systems containing a few molecules.

- Thermodynamics is based on initial and final states of a system undergoing the change and not on the rate of energy transformation.
- Laws of thermodynamics apply only when a system is in equilibrium or moves from one equilibrium state to another equilibrium state.

Thermodynamic Terms

Some thermodynamic terms needs to understand the chemical reactions and the energy changes accompanying them. These are as follows

The System and the Surroundings

- A **system** in thermodynamics refers to that part of universe in which observations are made and remaining universe constitutes the **surroundings**.
- System and the surroundings together constitute the universe.
- The wall (real or imaginary) that separates the system from the surroundings is called boundary.

Types of the System

Depending upon the movement of matter and energy in or out of the system, the system can be classified as

- **Open system** In this system the energy and matter both can be exchanged between system and surroundings, e.g. presence of reactants in an open beaker.
- **Closed system** A system in which only energy can be exchanged not matter between system and surroundings, e.g. hot water kept in closed container.

Topicwise No. of Ques asked in 5 Years

Topics	No. of Questions				
	2024	2023	2022	2021	2020
Thermodynamics Terms	1	–	–	1	–
Applications	1	1	1	1	1
Measurement of ΔU and ΔH: Calorimetry	–	–	–	–	–
Enthalpy Change ΔH of a Reaction- Reaction Enthalpy	1	–	–	–	1
Enthalpies for Different Types of Reactions	–	–	–	–	–
Spontaneity	–	–	–	1	1
Gibbs Energy Change and Equilibrium	–	–	–	–	2

Special Type of Ques Asked In 5 Years (NEET)

Types	Years				
	2024	2023	2022	2021	2020
A-R	–	–	–	–	–
Statement Based	–	–	–	–	–
Matching	1	–	–	–	–

Last 5 Years Weightage (NEET)

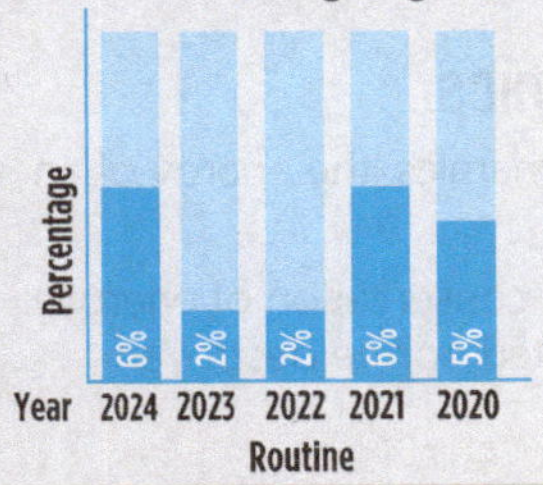

- **Isolated system** In this system neither matter nor energy can be exchanged between the system and surroundings, e.g. thermos flask.

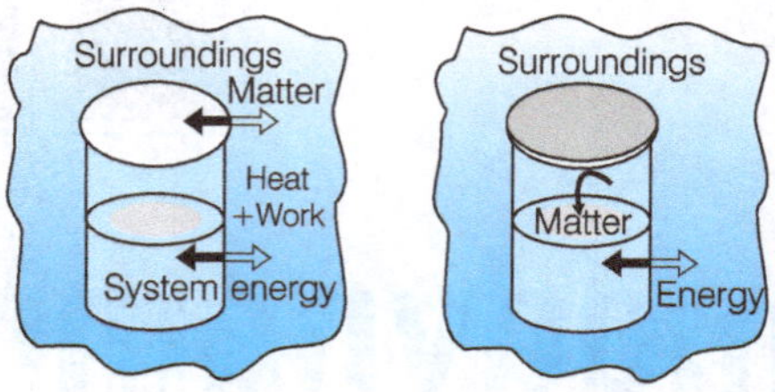

(a) Open system (b) Closed system

(c) Isolated system

The State of the System

- The state of a system is described by its measurable or macroscopic (bulk) properties that must be specified to make any useful calculations.
- The state of a gas can be described by quoting its pressure (p), volume (V), temperature (T), amount (n) etc. Variable like p, V, T are called **state variables** or **state functions** because their values depends only upon the state of the system and not on how it is reached.

Thermodynamic Process

The state of a system can be changed *via* thermodynamic process. These processes are of the following types NEET 2024

- **Adiabatic process** The process in which system does not exchange heat with its surroundings is called adiabatic process. For adiabatic process, $dq = 0$.
- **Isothermal process** This process is carried out at constant temperature, i.e. $dT = 0$ and thus, $dE = 0$.
- **Reversible process** It is a slow process in which direction can be reversed by infinite small changes in some properties of the surroundings. Such as pressure or temperature, e.g. states of matter.
- **Irreversible process** A process in which the system and the surroundings do not return to their original condition by an infinitiesimally small change in the conditions of the system unlike reversible processes.

Marks Maximizer

- **Isobaric process** In this process, change of state is brought about at constant pressure, i.e. $dp = 0$.
- **Isochoric process** In this process, volume of the system remains constant, i.e. $dV = 0$.
- **Cyclic process** It is a sequence of processes that bring the system back to its initial state.

$$dE \text{ or } dU = 0 \text{ and } dH = 0$$

Internal Energy as a State Function

In thermodynamics, the sum of all types (chemical, electrical or any type) of energies of the system arising from the microscopic motions and intractions of its particles (atoms, molecules or ions) is called internal energy (E or U). It is a state function.

Internal energy of the system change when

- heat passes in or out of the system,
- work is done on or by the system,
- matter enters or leaves the system.

Work

In an adiabatic system, the work (W_{ad}) required to bring about a change of state is equal to the difference between the value of internal energy (U) in one state and that in the other state, ΔU, i.e. $\Delta U = U_2 - U_1 = W_{ad}$.

- By conventions of IUPAC in chemical thermodynamics, W_{ad} **is positive when work is done on the system** and the internal energy of system increases.
- If **the work is done by the system,** W_{ad} **will be negative** because internal energy of the system decreases.

Heat

NEET 2024

- **Heat** (q) is defined as the quantity of energy which flows between system and surroundings on account of temperature difference.

  $\Delta U = q$, when no work is done at constant volume.
- When heat is transferred from the surroundings to the system and the internal energy of the system increases then, q is **positive**.
- When heat is transferred from system to the surroundings results in decrease of the internal energy of the system, then q is **negative**.

First Law of Thermodynamics

- According to first law of thermodynamics, the energy of an isolated system is constant.
- It is commonly states as the law of conservation of energy, i.e. the energy can neither be created nor be destroyed.

- The mathematical expression of first law of thermodynamics is given as,

$$\Delta U = q + W$$ NEET 2019

where, ΔU = change in internal energy, q = heat involved
W = work involved
- ΔU is path independent, q and W are not state functions.
- If there is no transfer of energy as heat or as work and no mass exchange (i.e. in a isolated system), ΔU will be zero.

Marks Maximizer

IUPAC Sign Convention
- q is +ve = heat is supplied to the system.
- q is – ve = heat is lost by the system.
- W is +ve = work done on the system.
- W is – ve = work done by the system
- ΔU is – ve = energy transfer from system to surrounding.
- ΔU is +ve = energy transfer from surrounding to system.

Applications

Work done on an ideal gas in a cylinder when it is compressed by a constant external pressure, p_{ext} is given by

$$W = -p_{ext}\,\Delta V$$

or

$$W = -p_{ext}(V_f - V_i)$$

$(V_f - V_i = -\text{ve due to compression})$ NEET 2019

The negative sign of this expression is required to obtain conventional sign for W, which will be positive.
- If the pressure is not constant, work done is given by two points
  - When the pressure changes in number of finite steps, then work done on the gas will be given as
  $$W = -\Sigma p\Delta V$$
  - When the pressure is not constant and changes in infinite steps (reversible conditions) during compression from initial volume, V_i to final volume V_f, work done on the gas is given by
  $$W_{rev} = -\int_{V_i}^{V_f} p_{ex} dV$$

  The work done during an isothermal reversible expansion is
  $$W_{rev} = -2.303\, nRT \log \frac{V_f}{V_i}$$ NEET 2020

  The work done during an isothermal reversible compression can be given as $\because p_iV_i = p_fV_f$
  $$W_{rev} = 2.303\, nRT \log \frac{p_i}{p_f}$$ NEET 2024
- **Free expansion** Expansion of a gas in vacuum ($p_{ext} = 0$) is called free expansion. No work is done during free expansion of an ideal gas whether the process is reversible or irreversible, i.e. $\Delta U = q - p_{ext}\,\Delta V$.
  At constant volume ($\Delta V = 0$), $\Delta U = q_V$
- **Isothermal and free expansion of an ideal gas**
  - For isothermal expansion of an ideal gas into vacuum; $W = 0$ Since, $p_{ext} = 0$
  - For isothermal irreversible change, $q = -W = p_{ext}(V_f - V_i)$
  - For isothermal reversible change; $q = -W$
  $$= 2.303\, nRT \log \frac{V_f}{V_i}$$
  - For adiabatic change; $q = 0$, $\Delta U = W_{ad}$

Enthalpy, *H* (A Useful New State Function)

- The total heat content of a system at constant pressure is called **enthalpy** (H) of **the system**.
- It is an extensive property.
- It is absolute value cannot be determined.
- It is a **state function** and is given by the expression
$$H = U + pV.$$
If H_2 is enthalpy in final state and H_1 in initial state then
$$\Delta H = (H_2 - H_1) = \Delta U + p\Delta V$$

Note $\Delta H = q_p$, heat absorbed by the system at constant pressure.

- At constant volume; $\Delta H = \Delta U = q_V$, i.e. heat supplied at constant volume.
- $\Delta H = -$ ve, exothermic reaction (heat evolved) and $\Delta H = +$ ve, endothermic reaction (heat absorbed).
- For solids and liquids, ΔH and ΔU is insignificant but for gases, if pressure and temperature remains constant, then
$$p\Delta V = \Delta n_g RT$$
Here, $\Delta n_g = n_P - n_R$
where, n_P = number of moles of product (gaseous)
n_R = number of moles of reactant (gaseous)
Moreover, $\Delta H = \Delta U + \Delta n_g RT$
or $q_p = q_V + \Delta n_g RT$ NEET 2023
- (i) If $\Delta n_g > 0$, then $\Delta H > \Delta U$
(ii) If $\Delta n_g < 0$, then $\Delta H < \Delta U$
(iii) If $\Delta n_g = 0$, then $\Delta H = \Delta U$
- For a reaction occurs only for the solids and liquids or carried out in a closed vessel ($\Delta V = 0$), $\Delta H = \Delta U$.

Extensive and Intensive Properties

- **Extensive properties** are those properties which depend upon the quantity or size of matter, e.g. mass, volume, internal energy, enthalpy, heat capacity etc.
- **Intensive properties** are those which do not depend upon the quantity or size of matter, e.g. pressure, temperature, density, concentration, viscosity, etc.

Note Ratio of two extensive properties become intensive in nature. e.g. The ratio of an object's mass and volume, which are two extensive properties, is density, which is an intensive property.

Molar property (x_m) is the value of an extensive property x of the system for 1 mole of the substance. If n is the amount of matter. $x_m = \frac{x}{n}$ is independent of the amount of matter.

e.g. Molar volume (V_m), Molar heat capacity (C_m).

Mnemonics (Recall the examples of extensive and intensive properties)

You can recall the examples of extensive and intensive properties just be remembering as sentence form

Extensive Property

Massive → Mass
Mole → Mole
Freely → Free energy
Enter → Entropy
In → Internal energy
Energetic → Enthalpy
Venue → Volume

Intensive Property

BP → Boiling point
OF → Freezing point
M → Melting point and molar heat capacity
R → Refractive index
V → Viscosity and vapour pressure
C → Concentration

Decreases → Density
When She → Surface tension, specific heat capacity
Travels → Temperature

Heat Capacity

- **Heat capacity** (C) of a system is defined as the amount of heat required to raise the temperature of the system by 1°C,
$$C = \frac{q}{\Delta T} \text{ or } q = C\Delta T$$
- **Molar heat capacity** (C_m) of the system is defined as the quantity of heat required to raise the temperature of one mole of the substance by one degree Celsius (or one Kelvin).
i.e. $$C_m = \frac{C}{n}$$
where, n = amount of substance (or number of moles)
- **Specific heat capacity** (C) is the quantity of heat needed to raise the temperature of one unit mass of a substance by 1°C or one K.
It is given as, $q = m \times c \times \Delta T = C\Delta T$
where, m = mass of the substance
c = specific heat of the substance
ΔT = temperature difference

Note Specific heat capacity of water = 1 cal g^{-1} K^{-1} or 4.18 J g^{-1} K^{-1}.

Relationship between C_p and C_V for an Ideal Gas

At constant volume, the heat capacity, C is denoted by C_V and at constant pressure, C denoted by C_p,

$$C_p - C_V = R$$ NEET 2021

where, $C_p = \frac{\Delta H}{\Delta T} = \frac{q_p}{\Delta T}$ and $C_V = \frac{\Delta U}{\Delta T} = \frac{q_V}{\Delta T}$

Marks Maximizer

- If q_p and q_V (ΔH or ΔV) are in calories,
$R = 1.987 \approx 2$ cal/degree/mol
In kcals, $R = 0.002$ kcal/degree/mol
In joules, $R = 8.314$ J K^{-1}mol^{-1}
In kJ, $R = 0.008314$ kJ K^{-1}mol^{-1}
- Poisson ratio, $\frac{C_p}{C_V} = \gamma$; For **monoatomic** gas, $\gamma = 1.66$
For **diatomic** gas, $\gamma = 1.40$; For **triatomic** gas, $\gamma = 1.33$.

Measurement of ΔH and ΔU: Calorimetry

- Energy changes associated with chemical or physical processes can be measured by an experimental technique called **calorimetry**.
- **Measurement of** (ΔU) Heat change occurs at constant volume, is measured by the bomb calorimeter.
- **Measurement of** (ΔH) Heat change occurs at constant pressure, is measured by the insulated calorimeter.
- The temperature inside the calorimeter depend on the reaction occured is exothermic or endothermic.

Enthalpy Change, $\Delta_r H$ of a Reaction–Reaction Enthalpy

- **Reaction enthalpy** is the enthalpy change that accommpanies a chemical reaction
$$\Delta_r H = \sum_i x_i H_{\text{products}} - \sum_i y_i H_{\text{reactants}}$$
where, x_i and y_i = stoichiometric coefficients of products and reactants respectively in a balanced chemical equation.
e.g. For the reaction,
$$CH_4(g) + 2O_2(g) \longrightarrow CO_2(g) + 2H_2O(l)$$
$$\Delta_r H = \Sigma x_i H_{\text{products}} - \Sigma y_i H_{\text{reactants}}$$
$$= [H_m(CO_2, g) + 2H_m(H_2O, l)] - [H_m(CH_4, g) + 2H_m(O_2, g)]$$
where, H_m is the molar enthalpy.

Note Enthalpy change of reaction can also be calculated by bond enthalpy as
$$\Delta_r H^\circ = \Sigma_{\text{bond enthalpies of reactants}} - \Sigma_{\text{bond enthalpies of products}}$$
or $\Delta_r H^\circ = \Sigma\, \Delta_f H^\circ_{\text{bonds enthalpy of products}} - \Sigma \Delta_f H^\circ_{\text{bonds enthalpy of reactants}}$

- **Standard enthalpy of reaction** is the enthalpy change for a reaction when all the participating substances are in their **standard states.**
- The standard state of a substance (compound) is the most stable physical state of it at 298 K and 1 atmospheric pressure (or 1 bar).
  - Ethanol is pure liquid at 298 K and 1 bar.
  - Iron is pure solid at 500 K and 1 bar.

Enthalpy Changes for Different Types of Processes (Based on IUPAC Recommendations)

Enthalpy	Definition	Examples
Standard enthalpy of fusion ($\Delta_{fus}H°$ or ΔH°_{fus})	One mole of liquid is formed from a solid in its standard state. All enthalpies of fusion are positive. In case of freezing, $\Delta_{freezing}H°$ is negative.	$H_2O(s) \longrightarrow H_2O(l)$, $\Delta_{fus}H° = 6.00$ kJ mol^{-1}
Standard Enthalpy of vaporisation $\Delta_{vap}H°$ or ΔH°_{vap}	One mole of the vapour formed from a liquid at its boiling temperature and under standard pressure.	$H_2O(l) \longrightarrow H_2O(g)$, $\Delta_{vap}H° = +40.79$ kJ mol^{-1}
Standard Enthalpy of sublimation ($\Delta_{sub}H°$ or ΔH°_{sub})	One mole of solid is converted into vapours without melting at a temperature below its melting point (and at 1 bar pressure).	$H_2O(s) \longrightarrow H_2O(g)$, $\Delta_{sub}H° = 73.0$ kJ mol^{-1}
Standard enthalpy of formation ($\Delta_f H°$ or $\Delta H°$)	One mole of the compound formed from its constituent elements, when they are in their most stable states of aggregation or reference states.	$H_2(g) + \frac{1}{2}O_2(g) \longrightarrow H_2O(l)$, $\Delta_f H° = -285.8$ kJ mol^{-1}
Standard enthalpy of combustion ($\Delta_c H°$)	One mole of the compound (fuel) is burnt completely in oxygen (oxidation) and all the reactants and products are in their standard states. $\Delta_c H°$ is always negative.	$C_4H_{10}(g) + \frac{13}{2}O_2(g) \longrightarrow 4CO_2(g) + 5H_2O(l)$; $\Delta_c H° = -2658.0$ kJ mol^{-1}
Enthalpy of atomisation $\Delta_a H°$ or ΔH°_a	One mole of the substance broken into isolated atoms in the gas phase.	$H_2(g) \longrightarrow 2H(g)$, $\Delta_a H° = 435.0$ kJ mol^{-1} (In this case enthalpy of atomisation is same as the bond dissociation enthalpy) $Na(s) \longrightarrow Na(g)$, $\Delta_a H° = 108.4$ kJ mol^{-1} (Here, enthalpy of atomisation is same as that of sublimation enthalpy.)
Bond dissociation enthalpy (bond A—B) (ΔH°_{A-B} or $\Delta_{bond}H°$) Mean bond enthalpy	One mole of covalent bonds of a gaseous covalent compound is broken to form products in the gas phase. In case of polyatomic molecules, instead of bond dissociation enthalpy, mean dissociation enthalpy of all the bonds present in the compound is taken.	**Diatomic** $H_2(g) \longrightarrow 2H(g)$; $\Delta_{H-H}H° = 435.0$ kJ mol^{-1} **Polyatomic** $CH_4(g) \longrightarrow (aq) + 4H(g)$; $\Delta_{C-H}H° = \frac{1}{4}(\Delta_a H°) = \frac{1665}{4} = 416$ kJ mol^{-1}
Lattice enthalpy ($\Delta_{lattice}H°$ or $\Delta H°_{lattice}$)	One mole of an ionic compound dissociates completely into its constituent ions in the gaseous phase.	$NaCl(s) \longrightarrow Na^+(g) + Cl^-(g)$; $\Delta_{lattice}H° = +788$ kJ mol^{-1}
Standard enthalpy of solution ($\Delta_{sol}H°$ or $\Delta H°_{sol}$ $\Delta_{sol}H° = \Delta_{lattice}H° + \Delta_{hyd}H°$)	One mole of the solute dissolved completely in specified amount of solvent. If a large excess of solvent is taken then the interaction between the ions (or solute molecules) are negligible and the enthalpy change is called enthalpy of solution at infinite dilution.	$NaCl(s) \longrightarrow Na^{\oplus}(aq) + Cl^{\ominus}(aq)$,
Standard enthlapy of dilution ($\Delta_{dil}H°$ or $\Delta H°_{dil}$)	Solution containing one mole of a substance is diluted from one concentration to another.	HCl (25 aq) + 15(aq) $\longrightarrow$ HCl (40 aq); $\Delta H° = -0.76$ kJ/mol

Note The most stable state of aggregation of an element at 25°C and 1 bar pressure is called its reference state, e.g. H_2 gas is the reference state for dihydrogen and O_2 gas is the reference state for dioxygen etc.

Marks Maximizer

- **Enthalpy of neutralisation** It is the amount of heat change when one gram equivalent of an acid is completely neutralised by one gram equivalent of a base in a dilute solution.

$$HCl(aq) + NaOH(aq) \longrightarrow NaCl(aq) + H_2O(l);\ [\Delta H = -ve]$$

- **Enthalpy of transition** It is the amount of energy released or absorbed in the transition of one phase to another

e.g. interconversion of allotropic forms of elements C (as graphite and diamond) or S (as monoclinic and rhombic)

- **Enthalpy of hydration** It is the amount of heat change when one mole of anhydrous substance combines with the required number of water to convert into hydrated compound.

$$CuSO_4(s) + 5H_2O \longrightarrow CuSO_4 \cdot 5H_2O(s);\ \Delta_{hyd}H = -78.2 \text{ kJ mol}^{-1}$$

During hydration, the physical state of the solid does not change.

Thermochemical Equation

A thermochemical equation is a balanced chemical equation in which the value of $\Delta_r H^\circ$ is also mentioned.

e.g. $C_2H_5OH(l) + 3O_2(g) \longrightarrow 2CO_2(g) + 3H_2O(l);$

$$\Delta_r H^\circ = -1367 \text{ kJ/mol}$$

Note Negative (–ve) sign indicates, it is an exothermic reaction.

Some conventions related to thermochemical equations are as follows

- The coefficients of different substances in a balanced thermochemical equation show only their number of moles (never molecules) of reactants or products involved in that reaction.
- On reversing a reaction, the sign of ΔH is also reversed but its magnitude remains the same.
- Enthalpy is an extensive property, thus if a thermochemical equation is multiplied or divided by an integer n, the value of $\Delta_r H^\ominus$ is also multiplied or divided by the integer n, respectively.

Hess's Law of Constant Heat Summation

According to this law, if a reaction takes place in several steps then its standard reaction enthalpy is the sum of the standard enthalpies of the intermediate reactions into which the overall reaction may be divided at the same temperature.

$$\Delta_r H = \Delta_r H_1 + \Delta_r H_2 + \Delta_r H_3 + \dots$$

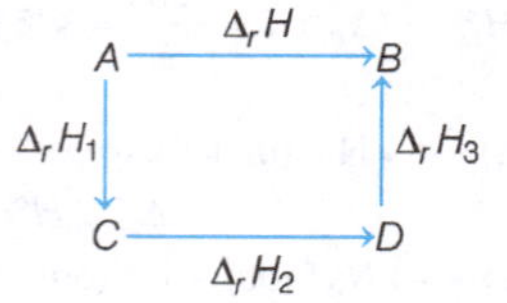

Born-Haber Cycle

Lattice enthalpy can be indirectly calculated by Born-Haber cycle as shown below.

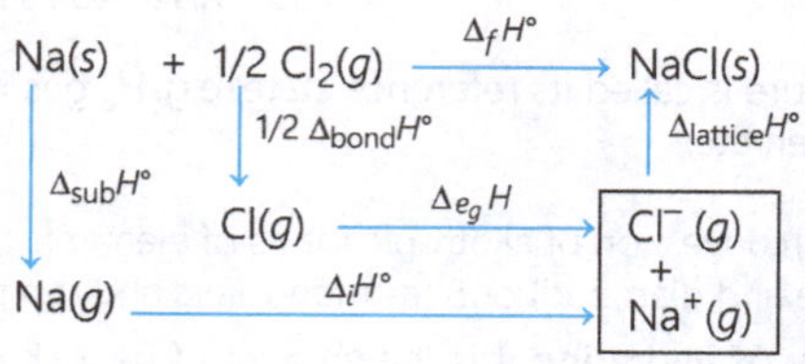

It is an approach to calculate energy involved during a process and is based on the Hess's law of constant heat summation.

Marks Maximizer

Expression for Ionisation Enthalpy (IE) and Electron Affinity (EA) Using Heat Capacities

Ionisation enthalpy and electron affinity are defined at absolute zero. At any other temperature, heat capacities are considered.

$$\Delta_r H^\circ(T) = \Delta_r H^\circ(0) + \int_0^T \Delta_r C_p^\circ dT \text{ and } \Delta_r C_p^\circ = +\frac{5}{2}R \quad \text{(for ionisation)}$$

$$\Delta_r C_p^\circ = -(5/2)R \text{ (for electron gain enthalpy)}$$

$$\therefore \Delta_r H^\circ \text{(ionisation enthalpy)} = E^\circ \text{(ionisation energy)} + (5/2)RT$$

$$\Delta_r H^\circ \text{(electron gain enthalpy)} = -A \text{ (electron affinity)} - \frac{5}{2}RT$$

Spontaneity

- Spontaneity means, having the potential to proceed without the assistance of external agency.
- A spontaneous process is an irreversible process and may only be reversed by some external agency, e.g. burning of carbon in dioxygen giving CO_2, heat flow, rolling ball, gas flow etc.
- Spontaneity does not tell about the rate of the reaction or process.
- A tendency to attain the minimum energy, i.e. **decrease in enthalpy** is responsible for the spontaneity or feasibility of a reaction but it is not true for all the cases.
- Different criteria of spontaneity in terms of changes a ΔS, ΔU, ΔH and ΔG. A process is spontaneous when $(dS)_{U,V} > 0$ or $(dU)_{S,V} < 0$ or $(dH)_{S,P} < 0$ or $(dG)_{P,T} < 0$ or $(dA)_{V,T} < 0$.

Entropy and Spontaneity

For Concept Master Video

- It is a measure of degree of randomness or disorderness in an isolated system and is represented by the symbol (S).
- The greater the degree of randomness, higher is the entropy. It is also a **state function**.
- In a chemical reaction, this entropy change can be attributed to rearrangement of atoms or ions from one pattern in the reactants to another (in the products). NEET 2020, 2019
- If the structure of the products is very much disordered than that of the reactants, there will be a resultant increase in entropy.
- For a given substance, the crystalline solid state is the most ordered state and, therefore has the lowest entropy, while gaseous state is the most disordered and has a state of highest entropy.
- For a reversible process, ΔS is related with q and T as

$$\Delta S_{\text{system}} = \frac{q_{\text{rev}}}{T}$$

- The total entropy change for the system and surroundings of a spontaneous process is given by

$$\Delta S_{total} = \Delta S_{sys} + \Delta S_{surr} > 0$$ NEET 2024

- The change in entropy at equilibrium, i.e. $\Delta S = 0$.
- For both reversible and irreversible expansion for an ideal gas, under isothermal conditions, $\Delta U = 0$ but ΔS_{total}, i.e. $\Delta S_{sys} + \Delta S_{surr}$ is not zero for irreversible process. NEET 2021
- Entropy changes during phase transformations are

$$\Delta_{fus} S = \frac{\Delta_{fus} H}{T_m}, \Delta_{vap} S = \frac{\Delta_{vap} H}{T_b} = \Delta_{sub} S = \frac{\Delta_{sub} H}{T}$$

where, T_m = melting point, T_b = boiling point

T = sublimation temperature.

$$\Delta_r S^\circ = \Sigma S^\circ_{products} - \Sigma S^\circ_{reactants}$$

Marks Maximizer

Some contradictions of entropy increase
- when a rubber band is stretched, entropy decreases because the macromolecules get uncoiled and hence arranged in a more order manner, i.e. randomness decreases.
- when an egg is boiled, the entropy decreases because denaturation occurs resulting into a change of proteins from helical form into random coiled form.
- for molecules which have same heat capacity and molecular mass, more symmetrical molecule has lower entropy than less symmetrical.

Gibbs Energy (*G*) and Spontaneity

- Gibbs function or Gibbs energy (*G*) is a quantity that is used to measure the maximum amount of work done in a thermodynamic system when the temperature and pressure are kept constant.

For Concept Master Video

$$G = H - TS$$

- Gibbs free energy is a state function. Hence, it doesn't depend on the path. So, change in Gibbs free energy is expressed as

$$\Delta G = \Delta H - T\Delta S$$ NEET 2020

It is an extensive property.

Standard free energy

$$\Delta_r G^\circ = \begin{bmatrix}\text{Sum of the standard free energy} \\ \text{of formation of products}\end{bmatrix} - \begin{bmatrix}\text{Sum of the standard free energy of} \\ \text{formation of reactants}\end{bmatrix}$$

$$= \Sigma \Delta_f G^\circ_{(products)} - \Sigma \Delta_f G^\circ_{(reactants)}$$

- The criteria of spontaneity through Gibbs free energies is as follows

At constant temperature and pressure.

(i) If ΔG is negative (< 0), the process is spontaneous.

(ii) If ΔG is positive (> 0), the process is non-spontaneous.

(iii) If ΔG is zero, the process is in equilibrium state.

- The various conditions in which a reaction occur spontaneously are tabulated below.

Effect of Temperature on Spontaneity of Reactions

$\Delta_r H^\ominus$	$\Delta_r S^\ominus$	$\Delta_r G^\ominus$	Description
–	+	– (at all T)	Reaction is spontaneous at all temperature.
–	–	– (at low T)	Reaction is spontaneous at low temperature.
–	–	+ (at high T)	Reaction is non-spontaneous at high temperature.
+	+	+ (at low T)	Reaction is non-spontaneous at low temperature.
+	+	– (at high T)	Reaction is spontaneous at high temperature.
+	–	+ (at all T)	Reaction is non-spontaneous at all temperature.

Entropy and Second Law of Thermodynamics

According to second law of thermodynamics, the entropy (*S*) of any natural and spontaneous process either increases or remains constant. $\Delta S = 0$ for reversible process, $\Delta S > 0$ for irreversible process.

*Absolute Entropy and Third Law of Thermodynamics

According to third law of thermodynamics, "The entropy of a pure crystalline substance approaches zero as the absolute zero of temperature is approached". It forms the basis from which entropies at other temperatures can be measured.

$$\lim_{T \to 0} S = 0$$

Note In case of CO and NO molecules in solid state, there is randomness occur even at 0 K due to their dipole moment hence, entropy in such cases is not zero even at 0 K.

* *This topic not include in latest NEET syllabus, but it is given in latest rationalised NCERT.*

Gibbs Energy Change and Equilibrium

The ΔG° is related to equilibrium constant of the reaction by the following equation, $\Delta G = \Delta G^\circ + RT \ln K$

$\because \quad \Delta G = 0$ [at equilibrium]

$\therefore \quad \Delta G^\circ = -RT \ln K = -2.303 RT \log K$ NEET 2020

Also, $\Delta G^\circ = \Delta H^\circ - T\Delta S^\circ = -RT \ln K$

Marks Maximizer

- Gibbs Helmholtz equation,

$$\Delta G = \Delta H + T\left[\frac{d(\Delta G)}{dt}\right]_p$$

or $\frac{\Delta G - \Delta H}{T} = \left[\frac{d(\Delta G)}{dt}\right]_p$ or $-\Delta S = \left[\frac{d(\Delta G)}{dt}\right]_p$

- Entropy change of an ideal gas (1 mol)

$$\Delta S = C_V \ln\frac{T_2}{T_1} + R\ln\frac{V_2}{V_1} = C_p \ln\frac{T_2}{T_1} + R\ln\frac{p_1}{p_2}$$

– At constant temperature $\Rightarrow \Delta S_T = R\ln\frac{V_2}{V_1} = R\ln\frac{p_1}{p_2}$

– At constant volume $\Rightarrow \Delta S_V = C_V \ln\frac{T_2}{T_1} = C_V \ln\frac{p_2}{p_1}$

– At constant pressure $\Rightarrow \Delta S_p = C_p \ln\frac{T_2}{T_1} = C_p \ln\frac{V_2}{V_1}$

$\Delta G°$	$\log K$	K	Explanation
$\Delta G° = 0$	$\log K = 0$	$K = 1$	When a mixture contains approx equal amount of reactants and products (at 1 atm and 1 M).
$\Delta G° < 0$ $\Delta G° = (-\text{ve})$	$\log K > 0$	$K >>> 1$	It is a case of exothermic reaction, $\Delta H°$ is large and (–ve).
$\Delta G° > 0$ $\Delta G° = (+\text{ve})$	$\log K < 0$	$K <<< 1$	It is a case of endothermic reaction, $\Delta H° = +\text{ve}$ but reaction does not takes place.

Caution Points

- Extensive properties are additive but intensive properties are not.
- For elementary substances in the standard state, the standard enthalpy of formation ($\Delta_f H°$) is taken as zero.
- Only those compounds are more stable than their elements whose $\Delta_f H°$ values are negative.

PYQ Notes

1. Entropy change is given as,

$$\Delta S = nC_p \ln\frac{T_f}{T_i} + nR\ln\frac{P_i}{P_f}$$

For isothermal process, $T_i = T_f$

$$\therefore \quad nC_p \ln\frac{T_f}{T_i} = nC_p \ln\frac{T_i}{T_i} = 0$$

NEET 2016

2. Enthalpy of bond dissociation of hydrogen and deuterium at 298.2 K.

$H_2 = 435.88\text{s kJ/mol}$

$D_2 = 443.35 \text{ kJ/mol}$

JEE Main 2021

3. Heat of neutralisation of strong acid (HCl) and weak base (MgO) is lower than – 57.33 kJ.

NEET 2015

Step by Step

Mastering NCERT

- Concept Builders
- Topical Questions
- Assertion-Reason
- Statement Type
- Matching Type
- Numerical Value
- NCERT Exemplar's
- Past Exams'
- Skill Boosters

Concept Builders

1 In an endothermic reaction, the value of ΔH is ....

2 Heat capacity is an .... property whereas pressure is .... property in the thermodynamics.

3 The absolute value of internal energy can be determined. [T/F]

4 Name the thermodynamic process during which no heat flows between the system and the surroundings.

5 Variables like p, V, T are called ....

6 Write mathematical statement of first law of thermodynamics.

7 For increase in volume, work done is more if the gas is allowed to expand reversibly at higher temperatures. [T/F]

8 Internal energy change of a system is the heat absorbed or evolved at constant .... whereas enthalpy change is that at constant ....

9 $\Delta U = q - W$, is represent to an adiabatic system. [T/F]

10 For the isothermal reversible expansion of an ideal gas from volume V_1 to volume V_2, the work done is given by W_{rev} = ... whereas for the irreversible expansion, it is given by W_{irrev} =

11 What is the relationship between q_p and q_V?

12 For a process which is carried out in a closed vessel, $\Delta H = \Delta U$. [T/F]

13 Molar heat capacity of aluminium will be .... times to its specific heat $JK^{-1}g^{-1}$.

14 Name the property which can be determined by a bomb calorimeter.

15 For exothermic reactions, the enthalpy of products is .... than enthalpy of reactant.

16 The standard heat of formation of diamond is not zero. [T/F]

17 The enthalpy of formation of gaseous iodine is 62.5 kJ mol^{-1} at 25°C. The enthalpy of sublimation of iodine at 25°C will be ....

18 Enthalpy of solution of anhydrous $CuSO_4(s)$ and hydrated salt, $CuSO_4 \cdot 5H_2O(s)$ are –66.5 kJ mol^{-1} and +11.7 kJ mol^{-1} respectively. The enthalpy of hydration of $CuSO_4(s)$ is ....

19 The bond energies of four C—H bonds present in CH_4 are equal. [T/F]

20 First law of thermodynamics cannot predict the .... of process (spontaneity/change in internal energy).

21 Write a general expression for the entropy change during a phase transformation.

22 For the given reaction,

$CaC_2O_4(s) \longrightarrow CaCO_3(s) + CO(g)$, ΔS will be ....

23 Water can be flowed into the water tank at the top of the house with the help of a pump, this process is non-spontaneous. [T/F]

24 Thermodynamic quantity which continuously increasing or decreasing for the universe is ....

25 The standard free energy change of a reaction is found to be zero. Its equilibrium constant will be ....

26 Free energy change (ΔG) is related to the change in enthalpy and the change in entropy as ....

27 ΔG and $\Delta G°$ for the reaction :

$A + B \rightleftharpoons C + D$ at 27°C will be (in kJ) (equilibrium constant (K) for this reaction $= 10^2$).

28 The reaction was non-spontaneous at high temperature but became spontaneous at low temperature. The reaction is ....

29 Absolute .... can be determined. (Internal energy, enthalpy, entropy)

30 Entropy of solutions and super cooled liquids is zero at 0 K. [T/F]

Topical Questions

Thermodynamics Terms

1 On which of the following factor(s) the internal energy of the system does not depend? **NCERT Pg 138**
(a) Matter enters or leaves the system
(b) Work is done on or by the system
(c) Heat passes into or out of the system
(d) Path taken by the system to reach final state

2 Among the following the set of parameters that represents path functions, is **NCERT Pg 138**
(A) $q + W$ (B) q
(C) W (D) $H - TS$
(a) (A) and (D) (b) (A), (B) and (C)
(c) (B), (C) and (D) (d) (B) and (C)

3 When the system does not exchange heat with the surroundings, the process is **NCERT Pg 138**
(a) isothermal (b) adiabatic
(c) thermal (d) isochoric

4 The enthalpy change of a reaction does not depend upon **NCERT Pg 143**
(a) state of reactants and products
(b) nature of reactants and products
(c) different intermediate reaction
(d) initial and final enthalpy change of a reaction

5 If we take water at temperature T_A in a container having thermally conducting walls and enclosed in a huge heat reservoir at temperature T_B. What is the correct expression of change in internal energy if no work is done at constant volume? **NCERT Pg 139**
(a) $\Delta U = U_B - U_A$ (b) $\Delta U = q$
(c) $\Delta U = W_{ad}$ (d) $\Delta U = -W_{ad}$

6 Which of the following statements/expressions is incorrect? **NCERT Pg 139**
(a) Internal energy change is equal to the adiabatic work done.
(b) $W_{ad} = +$ ve, when work is done on the system.
(c) $W_{ad} = -$ ve, when work is done by the system.
(d) ΔU is +ve, when energy is transferred from system to surrounding.

7 Select the correct statement. **NCERT Pg 139**
(a) $q = +$ve means heat is transferred from the system to the surroundings.
(b) $q = -$ve means heat is transferred from the surroundings to the system.
(c) $q = +$ve means heat is transferred from the surroundings to the system.
(d) $q = -$ve means heat is absorbed from the surroundings to the system.

8 Choose the correct expression for a closed system. **NCERT Pg 140**
(a) $\Delta U = W_{ad}$, (b) $\Delta U = -q$,
(c) $\Delta U = q - W$, (d) $\Delta U = -W$,

9 The change in the energy of system if 500 cal of heat energy are added to a system and system does 350 cal of work on the surroundings will be **NCERT Pg 140**
(a) − 150 cal (b) +150 cal (c) + 850 cal (d) − 850 cal

Applications

10 What will be the work done on an ideal gas enclosed in a cylinder, when it is compressed by a constant external pressure, p_{ext} in a single step as shown in figure? **NCERT Pg 140**

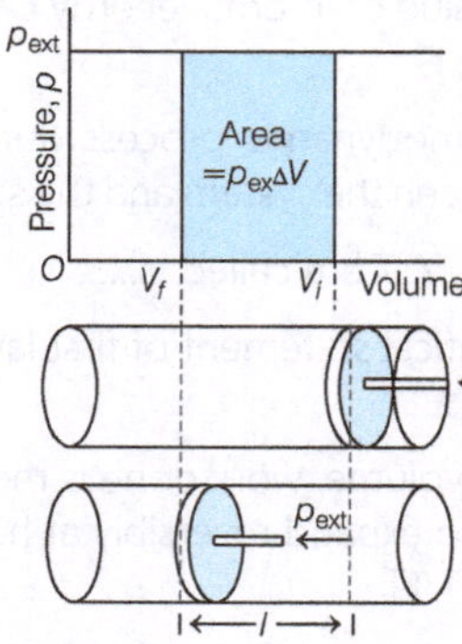

(a) Work done $= -p_{ext}(V_f - V_i)$
(b) Work done $= -p_{ext}(V_i - V_f)$
(c) Work done $= +p_{ext}(V_f - V_i)$
(d) Work done $= -p(V_f - V_i)$

11 Which of the following statement is correct? **NCERT Pg 140**
(a) The energy can be created.
(b) According to first law of thermodynamics, the energy of an isolated system is not constant.
(c) In an isolated system, $W = 0, q = 0, \Delta U \neq 0$.
(d) $\Delta U = q + W$, will depend only on initial and final state.

12 Select the incorrect statement about the graph.

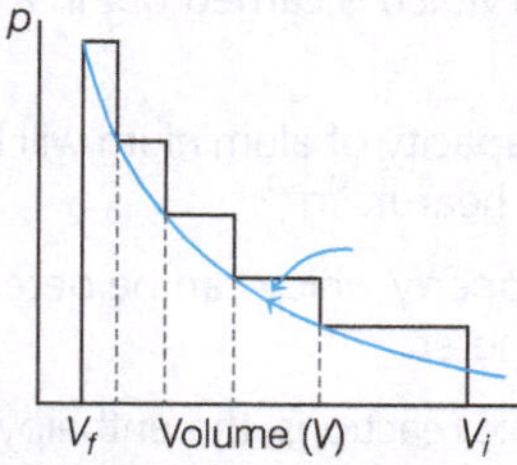

NCERT Pg 141
(a) It is an irreversible compression.
(b) Pressure is not constant and changes finite steps during compression from initial volume, V_i to final volume, V_f.
(c) Work done on gas will be equal to $-\sum p\Delta V$.
(d) It is a reversible expansion.

13 Consider the reversible isothermal expansion of an ideal gas in a closed system at two different temperatures T_1 and T_2 ($T_1 < T_2$). The correct graphical depiction of the dependence of work done (W) on the final volume (V) is **NCERT Pg 142**

(a)
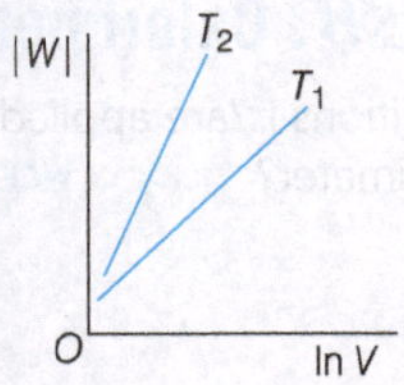

(b)
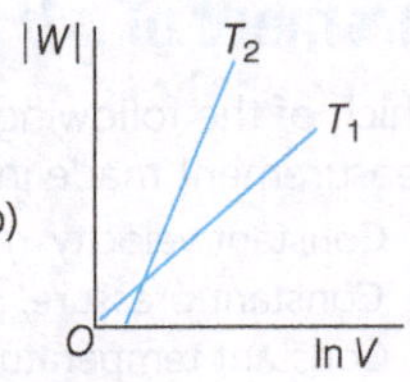

(c)
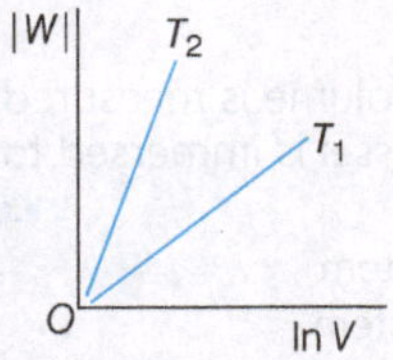

(d)
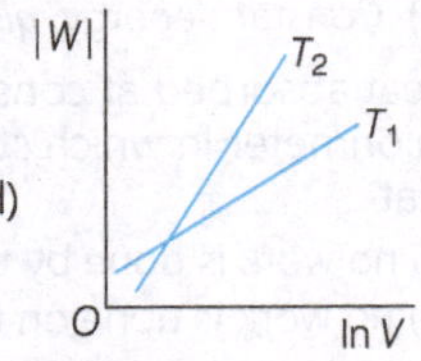

14 In an adiabatic expansion of ideal gas

(a) $W = -\Delta U$ (b) $W = \Delta U$
(c) $\Delta U = 0$ (d) $W = 0$

15 In an isolated system, an ideal gas is allowed to expand both reversibly and irreversibly. If the initial temperature is T_i and the final temperature is T_f, then which of the following statement is correct? **NCERT Pg 142**

(a) $T_f > T_i$ (reversible) but $T_f = T_i$ (irreversible)
(b) $(T_f)_{irrev} > (T_f)_{rev}$
(c) $(T_f)_{rev} = (T_f)_{irrev}$
(d) $T_f = T_i$ for both reversible and irreversible process.

16 No work is done on the system, but q amount of heat is taken out from the system and given to the surrounding. The change in internal energy of a system is **NCERT Pg 142**

(a) $\Delta U = -q$ (b) $\Delta U = +q$
(c) $\Delta U = W_{ad}$ (d) $\Delta U = q - W$

17 The work done in isothermal expansion of 2 litre of an ideal gas at 20 atm and 25°C into vacuum until its volume becomes 10 litre is **NCERT Pg 142**

(a) 0 (b) 160 L atm
(c) 80 L atm (d) 20 L tam

18 A piston filled with 0.04 mole of an ideal gas expands reversibly from 50.0 mL to 375 mL at a constant temperature of 37.0°C. As it does so, it absorbs 208 J of heat. The values of q and W for the process will be ($R = 8.314 J / mol K, \ln 7.5 = 2.01$) **NCERT Pg 142**

(a) $q = +208$ J, $W = -208$ J
(b) $q = -208$ J, $W = -208$ J
(c) $q = -208$ J, $W = +208$ J
(d) $q = +208$ J, $W = +208$ J

19 Find the value of maximum work done, if one mole of an ideal gas expands isothermally at 47°C from 25 L to 35 L. **NCERT Pg 142**

(a) 86.43 J (b) 42.92 J (c) 894.55 J (d) 322.26 J

20 When heat is absorbed by the system at constant pressure then **NCERT Pg 143**

(a) $\Delta H = q_v$ (b) $\Delta U = q_p$ (c) $\Delta H = q_p$ (d) $\Delta U = q_v$

21 When the expansion of a gas occurs in vaccum and at constant volume, then **NCERT Pg 143**

(a) $\Delta U = q_V$ (b) $\Delta U = q_p$
(c) $\Delta H = q_V$ (d) $\Delta H = q_p$

22 The combustion of benzene (l) gives $CO_2(g)$ and $H_2O(l)$. Given that heat of combustion of benzene at constant volume is -3263.9 kJ mol^{-1} at 25° C; heat of combustion (in kJ mol^{-1}) of benzene at constant pressure will be ($R = 8.314$ JK^{-1} mol^{-1}) **NCERT Pg 143**

(a) 4152.6 (b) −452.46
(c) 3260 (d) −3267.6

23 When 1 mole of ice melts at 0°C and at a constant pressure of 1 atm, 1440 cal of heat is absorbed by the system. If the molar volume of ice and water are 0.0196L and 0.0180L, then the value of ΔH and ΔU will be **NCERT Pg 143**

(a) 1440 cal, 1440.039 cal (b) 1440 cal, 1438 cal
(c) 1440.039 cal, 1440 cal (d) 1438 cal, 1440 cal

24 Argon (10 g) is compressed isothermally and reversibly at a temperature of 27°C from 10 L to 5 L. Choose the correct option for ΔH, ΔE, q and W **NCERT Pg 143**

	ΔH	ΔE	q	W
(a)	0	0	0	0
(b)	+103.980	0	−103.980 cal	0
(c)	0	−103.980	+103.980 cal	0
(d)	0	0	−103.980 cal	+103.980 cal

25 ΔH and ΔE for the reaction,

$$Fe_2O_3(s) + 3H_2(g) \longrightarrow 2Fe(s) + H_2O(l)$$

at constant temperature are related as **NCERT Pg 143**

(a) $\Delta H = \Delta E$ (b) $\Delta H = \Delta E + RT$
(c) $\Delta H = \Delta E + 3RT$ (d) $\Delta H = \Delta E - 3RT$

26 $\Delta U°$ of combustion of ethane is $-x$ kJ mol^{-1}. The value of $\Delta H°$ is **NCERT Pg 143**

(a) = 0 (b) = $\Delta U°$
(c) > $\Delta U°$ (d) < $\Delta U°$

27 At 25°C, 1 mole of butane is heated then CO_2 and H_2O liquid is formed. The work done for the given process is **NCERT Pg 143**

(a) 75.6 L atm (b) 85.6 L atm
(c) 50.3 L atm (d) 62.1 L atm

28 Consider the following equation, NCERT Pg 144

$$q = \text{coeff.} \times \Delta T$$

The magnitude of the coefficient does not depend
(a) size of system
(b) composition of system
(c) nature of the system
(d) concentration of system

29 The quantity of heat needed to raise the temperature of one mole of the substance by one degree celsius and heat required to raise the temperature of one unit mass of a substance by one degree celsius, respectively are NCERT Pg 144
(a) specific heat capacity and molar entropy
(b) molar heat capacity and specific heat capacity
(c) specific heat and molar enthalpy
(d) molar heat and molar entropy

30 Choose the incorrect equation. NCERT Pg 144
(a) $C_m = \dfrac{C}{n}$ (b) $q = c \times m \times \Delta T$
(c) $\Delta H = \Delta U + R\Delta T$ (d) $C_p + C_V = nR$

31 The correct inference that can be observed from the given figure II is NCERT Pg 144

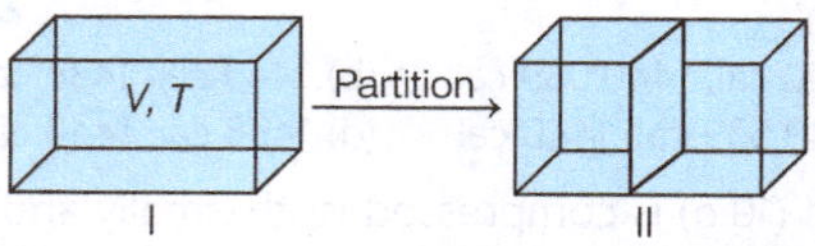

(a) Each part has double the temperature of the gas.
(b) Each part has the same temperature of the gas.
(c) Each part only have half the temperature of the gas.
(d) Each part has one-fourth the temperature of the gas.

32 Which of the following statement is incorrect? NCERT Pg 144
(a) The heat transferred to the system is directly related to increase in temperature.
(b) $q = C\,\Delta T$, the coefficient C is called the heat capacity.
(c) C_m is the quantity of heat needed to raise the temperature of one mole by one K.
(d) A small amount of energy is needed to raise the temperature of water.

33 Among the following, how many properties are extensive in nature? NCERT Pg 144
(i) Density (ii) Temperature (iii) Mass
(iv) Heat capacity (v) Internal energy
(a) 1 (b) 2 (c) 3 (d) 4

34 The molar heat capacity of water at constant pressure is 84 JK^{-1} mol^{-1}. When 1.0 kJ of heat is supplied to 100 g of water which is free to expand; the increase in temperature of water is NCERT Pg 145
(a) 3.8 K (b) 2.1 K (c) 4.8 K (d) 1.5 K

35 Calculate the difference between C_p and C_V for 10 moles of an ideal gas. NCERT Pg 145
(a) 83.14 J/K (b) 8.314 J/K
(c) 831.4 J/K (d) 0.831 J/K

Measurement of ΔU and ΔH: Calorimetry

36 Which of the following conditions is/are applied for the measurement made in calorimeter? NCERT Pg 145
(a) Constant velocity, q_v
(b) Constant pressure, q_p
(c) Constant temperature, q_T
(d) Constant energy, qE

37 Heat absorbed at constant volume is measured in a calorimeter in which steel vessel is immersed to ensure that NCERT Pg 145
(a) no work is done by the system
(b) no work is done on the system
(c) no heat is lost to the surrounding
(d) no heat is lost by the surrounding

38 Enthalpy of sublimation of iodine is 24 cal g^{-1} at 200°C. If specific heat of $I_2(s)$ and I_2(vap.) are 0.055 and 0.031 cal g^{-1} K^{-1} respectively, then enthalpy of sublimation of iodine at 250°C (in cal g^{-1}) is NCERT Pg 145
(a) 2.85 (b) 5.7
(c) 22.8 (d) 11.4

39 In a constant volume calorimeter, 3.5 g of gas with molecular weight = 28 was burnt in excess of oxygen at 298.0 K. The temperature of the calorimeter was found to increase from 298.0 K to 298.45 K due to the combustion process.
Given, that the heat capacity of the calorimeter is 2.5 kJ K^{-1}, the numerical value for the enthalpy of combustion of the gas in kJ mol^{-1} is NCERT Pg 145
(a) 7 (b) 9 (c) 0 (d) 8

40 A refrigerant CCl_2F_2 cooled 1.25 g sample at constant atmospheric pressure of 1 atm from 320 K to 293 K. During cooling the sample volume decreased from 274 to 248 mL. Calculate ΔH for the CCl_2F_2 for this process. (C_p = 80.7 J mol^{-1} K^{-1}). NCERT Pg 146
(a) 22.51 J (b) −19.83 J (c) 19.88 J (d) −22.51 J

Enthalpy Change, $\Delta_r H$ of a Reaction — Reaction Enthalpy

41 Which of the following statements is correct? NCERT Pg 146
(a) Unit of $\Delta_r H°$ is kJ mol^{-1}.
(b) Enthalpy is an intensive quantity.
(c) When a chemical equation is reversed the value of $\Delta_r H°$ remain same in sign.
(d) $\Delta_r H$ will be negative in an endothermic reaction.

42 Which of the following statements correctly represents the uses of the enthalpy change? **NCERT Pg 146**

(a) The enthalpy change is required to maintain an industrial chemical reaction at higher temperature.

(b) It is also required to calculate temperature dependence of equilibrium constant.

(c) The enthalpy change is required to maintain an industrial chemial reaction at lower temperature.

(d) It is required to calculate temperature independence of equilibrium constant.

43 For the combustion of methane (CH_4).
The correct expression for $\Delta_r H$ is **NCERT Pg 147**

(a) $[H_m(CO_2, g) + 2H_m(O_2, g)] - [2H_m(H_2O, l) + H_m(CH_4, g)]$
(b) $[2H_m(O_2, g) + H_m(CH_4, g)] - [H_m(CO_2, g) + 2H_m(H_2O, l)]$
(c) $[H_m(CO_2, g) + 2H_m(H_2O, l)] - [H_m(CH_4, g) + 2H_m(O_2, g)]$
(d) $[H_m(CO_2, g) + H_m(H_2O, l)] - [H_m(CH_4, g) + H_m(O_2, g)]$

44 The melting of ice **NCERT Pg 147**

(a) is a state transformation
(b) takes place at constant pressure and temperature
(c) takes place at 373 K
(d) increases with decrease in temperature

45 Standard enthalpy of vaporisation $\Delta_{vap}H°$ for water at 100°C is 40.66 kJ mol^{-1}. The internal energy of vaporisation of water at 100°C (in kJ mol^{-1}) is (Assume water vapour to behave like an ideal gas). **NCERT Pg 148**

(a) +37.56 (b) −43.76
(c) +43.76 (d) + 40.66

46 If the sublimation energy and enthalpy of fusion of I_2 are 57.3 kJ mol^{-1} and 15.5 kJ mol^{-1}, respectively then, the enthalpy of vaporisation of I_2 will be **NCERT Pg 148**

(a) −72.8 kJ mol^{-1}
(b) 72.8 kJ mol^{-1}
(c) − 41.8 kJ mol^{-1}
(d) +41.8 kJ mol^{-1}

47 Which of the following statement is incorrect? **NCERT Pg 147, 148**

(a) The standard enthalpy of reaction is the enthalpy change for a reaction when all the participating substances are in their standard states.
(b) The standard state of a substance at a specified temperature is its pure form at 1 bar.
(c) The standard state of solid iron at 298 K is equal to pure iron at 1 bar.
(d) Solid CO_2 or 'dry ice' sublimes at 195 K.s

48 Which one of the following is a correct equation? **NCERT Pg 148**

(a) $H_2 - H_1 + E_1 - E_1 = n_2RT - n_1RT$
(b) $E_2 - E_1 - H_2 + H_1 = n_2RT - n_1RT$
(c) $E_2 - E_1 - H_2 - H_1 = n_2RT - n_1RT$
(d) $H_2 - H_1 - E_2 + E_1 = n_2RT - n_1RT$

49 Which of the following statement is incorrect? **NCERT Pg 147, 149**

(a) The subscript in $\Delta_f H^\circ$ indicates that one mole of the compound is formed in its standard state.
(b) The standard state of an element is its most stable state of aggregation at 273K.
(c) The standard state for dihydrogen is H_2 in gaseous state and for sulphur is S in rhombic state.
(d) The standard state of solid iron at 500 K is pure iron at 1 bar.

50 The standard enthalpy of formation of $NH_3(g)$ is −81.9 kJ mol^{-1}. The amount of heat required to decompose 26 g of NH_3 (g) into its elements, is **NCERT Pg 149**

(a) 125.31 (b) 143.8
(c) 164.7 (d) 105.6

51 How much of heat is required by the chemical reaction in order to decompose $CaCO_3$ to lime and CO_2? (Standard molar enthalpies of formation is given in the table). **NCERT Pg 150**

Substance	$\Delta_f H°/(\text{kJ mol}^{-1})$
$CaCO_3(s)$	−1206.92
CaO (s)	− 635.09
$CO_2(g)$	−393.51

(a) 187 kJ mol^{-1} (b) 170.0 kJ mol^{-1}
(c) 178.3 kJ mol^{-1} (d) 173.8 kJ mol^{-1}

52 The standard enthalpies of combustion of $C_6H_6(l)$, $C_{(graphite)}$ and $H_2(g)$ are respectively −3270 kJ mol^{-1}, −394 kJ mol^{-1} and −286 kJ mol^{-1}. What is the standard enthalpy of formation of $C_6H_6(l)$ in kJ mol^{-1}? **NCERT Pg 150**

(a) − 48 (b) + 48
(c) − 480 (d) + 480

53 Consider the following conventions related to thermochemical equations. **NCERT Pg 150**

I. The coefficients of different substances in a balanced thermochemical equation show only number of moles involved in the reaction.

II. Enthalpy is an extensive property thus if a thermochemical equation is multiplied or divided by an integer n, the value of $\Delta_r H^\circ$ is also multiplied or divided by the integer, n.

III. On reversed a reaction, the sign of ΔH is also reversed and its magnitude also changes.

Select the correct statement and choose the correct option.

(a) Only I (b) Only III
(c) I and II (d) II and III

54 Which of the following statements is incorrect about the equation? **NCERT Pg 150**

$$C_2H_5OH(l) + 3O_2(g) \longrightarrow 2CO_2(g) + 3H_2O(l);$$
$$\Delta_r H° = -1367 \text{ kJ mol}^{-1}$$

(a) The reaction is an endothermic.
(b) The numerical value of $\Delta_r H°$ refers to the number of moles of substances specified by an equation.
(c) The coefficients in a balanced thermochemical equations refer to the number of moles (never molecules) of reactants and product involved in the reaction.
(d) The equation describes the combustion of liquid ethanol at constant temperature and pressure.

55 The reaction $A \longrightarrow C$ proceeds through two paths I and II as shown below : **NCERT Pg 152**

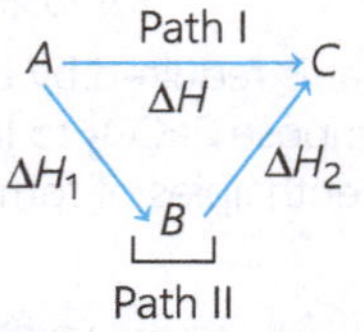

The correct relationship between ΔH, ΔH_1 and ΔH_2 will be

(a) $\Delta H = \Delta H_2 - \Delta H_1$
(b) $\Delta H = \Delta H_1 / \Delta H_2$
(c) $\Delta H = \Delta H_1 + \Delta H_2$
(d) $\Delta H = \Delta H_1 \times \Delta H_2$

56 A reaction takes place in a several sequential steps *A*, *B*, *C* and *D*. The value of enthalpy change for sequential steps are *p*, *q*, *r* and *s*, respectively. If *B* and *C* have equal values of enthalpy change with total enthalpy change *t*, then choose the incorrect symbolic equation among the following. **NCERT Pg 152**

(a) $q = r$
(b) $q + r = t - (s + p)$
(c) $2q = t - (s + p)$
(d) $q + r = p + s$

57 Based on following thermochemical reaction, **NCERT Pg 152**

$$H_2O(g) + C(s) \longrightarrow CO(g) + H_2(g); \Delta H = 131 \text{ kJ}$$
$$CO(g) + \frac{1}{2}O_2(g) \longrightarrow CO_2(g); \quad \Delta H = -282 \text{ kJ}$$
$$H_2(g) + \frac{1}{2}O_2(g) \longrightarrow H_2O(g); \quad \Delta H = -242 \text{ kJ}$$
$$C(s) + O_2(g) \longrightarrow CO_2(g); \quad \Delta H = x \text{ kJ}$$

The value of *x* will be

(a) – 393 kJ (b) – 655 kJ (c) + 393 kJ (d) + 655 kJ

Enthalpies For Different Types of Reactions

58 The heat of formations of $CO(g)$ and $CO_2(g)$ are – 26.4 kcal and – 94.0 kcal respectively. The heat of combustion of carbon monoxide will be **NCERT Pg 152**

(a) – 46.5 kcal
(b) 36.5 kcal
(c) – 36.5 kcal
(d) – 67.6 kcal

59 Given, **NCERT Pg 152**

$$C_{\text{diamond}} + O_2 \longrightarrow CO_2; \ \Delta H = -395.3 \text{ kJ/mol}$$
$$C_{\text{graphite}} + O_2 \longrightarrow CO_2; \ \Delta H = -393.4 \text{ kJ/mol}$$

The enthalpy change (ΔH) for the reaction,

$$C_{\text{graphite}} \longrightarrow C_{\text{diamond}} \text{ in kJ/mol is}$$

(a) + 1.9 (b) – 1.9 (c) + 3.8 (d) – 3.8

60 Which of the following statements is correct? **NCERT Pg 152**

(a) Combustion reactions are endothermic in nature.
(b) During complete combustion of 1 mole of butane, 2658 kJ of heat is released.
(c) Our body generates energy from food by the process of atomisation.
(d) Rate of combustion decreases if supply of O_2 is increases.

61 Which of the following statements is incorrect? **NCERT Pg 153**

(a) Mean C—H bond enthalpies differ slightly from compound to compound.
(b) The reaction enthalpies accompaning the breaking of old bonds and formation of the new bonds.
(c) $\Delta_r H° = \Sigma_{\text{bond enthalpies of reactants}} + \Sigma_{\text{bond enthalpies of products}}$
(d) Using Hess's law, bond enthalpies can be calcualted.

62 Find out the incorrect expression. **NCERT Pg 153**

(a) $\Delta_r H°(T) = \Delta_r H°(0) + \int_0^T \Delta_r C_p^° dT$
(b) $\Delta_r C_p^° = -\frac{5}{2} R$ (for ionisation)
(c) $\Delta_r H°$ (electron gain enthalpy) $= - A$ (electron affinity) $- \frac{5}{2} RT$
(d) $\Delta_r H°$ (ionisation enthalpy) $= E_0$ (ionisation energy) $+ \frac{5}{2} RT$

63 The bond dissociation energies of H_2, Cl_2 and HCl are 104, 58 and 103 kcal mol^{-1} respectively. The enthalpy of formation of HCl would be **NCERT Pg 154**

(a) – 22 kcal mol^{-1}
(b) – 44 kcal mol^{-1}
(c) +44 kcal mol^{-1}
(d) +22 kcal mol^{-1}

64 Find the multiple bond energy (kJ mol^{-1}) of a $C \equiv C$ bond in C_2H_2 molecule from the following data. (Take the bond energy of a C—H bond as 350 kJ mol^{-1}) **NCERT Pg 154**

$$2C(s) + H_2(g) \longrightarrow C_2H_2(g); \Delta H = 225 \text{ kJ mol}^{-1}$$
$$2C(s) \longrightarrow 2C(g); \Delta H = 1410 \text{ kJ mol}^{-1}$$
$$H_2(g) \longrightarrow 2H(g); \Delta H = 330 \text{ kJ mol}^{-1}$$

(a) 1165 (b) 837 (c) 865 (d) 815

65 Calculate the bond enthalpy of Xe—F bond as given in the equation. **NCERT Pg 155**

$$XeF_4(g) \longrightarrow Xe^{+}(g) + F^{-}(g) + F_2(g) + F(g)$$

[Given, $\Delta_r H = 292$ kcal mol^{-1}

Ionisation energy of Xe = 279 kcal/mol

Bond energy (F—F) = 38 kcal/mol

Electron affinity of F = 85 kcal/mol]

(a) 8.5 kcal/mol (b) 34 kcal/mol

(c) 24 kcal/mol (d) 2.5 kcal/mol

66 Enthalpy change for the reaction,

$$4H(g) \longrightarrow 2H_2(g) \text{ is } -869.6 \text{ kJ}$$

The dissociation energy of H—H bond is **NCERT Pg 155**

(a) –869.6 kJ (b) + 434.8 kJ

(c) + 217.4 kJ (d) – 434.8 kJ

67 Given that, for the reaction,

$$\frac{1}{2}H_2 + \frac{1}{2}Cl_2 \longrightarrow HCl$$

$\Delta H_f(HCl) = -93$ kJ/mol

$\Delta BE\ (H_2) = 434$ kJ/mol

$\Delta BE\ (Cl_2) = 242$ kJ/mol

The bond dissociation energy of HCl is **NCERT Pg 155**

(a) 232 kJ/mol (b) 331 kJ/mol

(c) 431 kJ/mol (d) 530 kJ/mol

68 Consider the reactions given below.

(i) $C_2H_4(g) + H_2(g) \longrightarrow C_2H_6(g)$

(ii) $C(g) + O_2(g) \longrightarrow CO_2(g)$

(iii) $H_2(g) + I_2(g) \longrightarrow 2HI(g)$

(iv) $N_2(g) + O_2(g) \longrightarrow 2NO(g)$

(v) $2SO_2(g) + O_2(g) \longrightarrow 2SO_3(g)$

In how many reactions ΔH is not equal to ΔU?

(a) 3 (b) 4

(c) 5 (d) 6

69

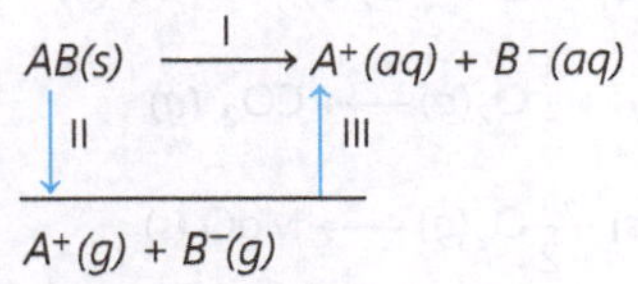

Identify I, II, III in the above diagram. **NCERT Pg 156**

	I	II	III
(a)	$\Delta_{lattice}H°$	$\Delta_{hyd}H°$	$\Delta_{sol}H°$
(b)	$\Delta_{lattice}H°$	$\Delta_{sol}H°$	$\Delta_{hyd}H°$
(c)	$\Delta_{sol}H°$	$\Delta_{lattice}H°$	$\Delta_{hyd}H°$
(d)	$\Delta_{sol}H°$	$\Delta_{hyd}H°$	$\Delta_{lattice}H°$

70 Consider the chemical equation, **NCERT Pg 156**

$$Na^{+}(g) + Cl^{-}(g) \longrightarrow Na^{+}Cl^{-}(s)$$

For 1 mole of NaCl(s),

Lattice enthalpy = +788 kJ mol^{-1}, $\Delta_{hyd}H° = -784$ kJ mol^{-1}

The enthalpy of solution is calculated as

(a) –4 kJ mol^{-1} (b) –8 kJ mol^{-1}

(c) +4 kJ mol^{-1} (d) –6 kJ mol^{-1}

71 The enthalpy of solution of $CuSO_4 \cdot 5H_2O(s)$ and $CuSO_4(s)$ are respectively – 11.7 and – 65.5 kJ/mol. The hydration enthalpy of anhydrous $CuSO_4$ will be **NCERT Pg 156**

(a) 53.8 kJ mol^{-1} (b) – 9.8 kJ mol^{-1}

(c) – 77.2 kJ mol^{-1} (d) – 53.8 kJ mol^{-1}

Spontaneity

72 Which of the following statements correctly represents the enthalpy of dilution? **NCERT Pg 156**

(a) The heat withdrawn from the system when additional solvent is added to solution.

(b) The heat withdrawn from the surroundings when additional solvent is added to solution.

(c) The heat withdrawn from the system when additional solute is added to solution.

(d) The heat withdrawn from the surroundings when additional solute is added to solution.

73 $C(\text{graphite}, s) + 2S(l) \longrightarrow CS_2(l);\ \Delta_r H° = +128.5$ kJ mol^{-1}

The above reaction is **NCERT Pg 158**

(a) exothermic and spontaneous

(b) exothermic and non-spontaneous

(c) endothermic and spontaneous

(d) endothermic and non-spontaneous

74 Which of the following pair(s) of conditions are certain to result in a spontaneous reaction? **NCERT Pg 158**

(a) Endothermic and decreasing order

(b) Exothermic and increasing disorder

(c) Endothermic and increasing disorder

(d) Exothermic and decreasing disorder

75 Which of the following statement is incorrect? **NCERT Pg 158**

(a) In case of chemical reactions, entropy change shows the rearrangement of atoms or ions from one pattern in the reactants to another.

(b) The greater the degree of randomness, higher is the entropy.

(c) The crystalline solid state is most ordered, while gaseous state is most disordered.

(d) Increase of regularity in structure would mean increase in entropy.

76 Which of the following statement is incorrect? NCERT Pg 158

(a) Heat (q) has randomising influence on the system.
(b) Entropy change varies directly with temperature.
(c) Entropy change is a state function.
(d) Temperature is the measure of average chaotic motion of the particle in the system.

77 Which of the following statement is incorrect regarding spontaneity of a reaction? NCERT Pg 158

(a) The flow of heat is undirectional from higher temperature to lower temperature.
(b) All naturally occurring processes tend to proceed spontaneously in any direction.
(c) The gas in a container will not spontaneously contract into one corner.
(d) Spontaneous reactions occurs immediately when contact is made between the reactants.

78 Which of the following statement is incorrect regarding entropy? NCERT Pg 158

(a) The greater the disorder in an isolated system, the lower is the entropy.
(b) The entropy change can be attributed to rearrangement of atoms or ions from one pattern in the reactants to another in the product.
(c) The gaseous state is the state of highest entropy.
(d) The change in entropy is independent of path.

79 Which of the following substance having highest value of entropy? NCERT Pg 158

(a) Water (H_2O)
(b) Hydrogen (H_2)
(c) Graphite (C)
(d) Mercury (Hg)

80 Which of the following reactions will have the value of ΔS with a negative sign? NCERT Pg 159

(a) $H_2O(l) \longrightarrow H_2O(g)$
(b) $2SO_2(g) + O_2(g) \longrightarrow 2SO_3(g)$
(c) $Cl_2(g) \longrightarrow 2Cl(g)$
(d) $CaCO_3(s) \longrightarrow CaO(s) + CO_2(g)$

81 Which set is correct for both reversible and irreversible expansion for an ideal gas, under isothermal condition, NCERT Pg 159

(a) $\Delta U = 0, \Delta S_{total} \neq 0$
(b) $\Delta U \neq 0, \Delta S_{total} = 0$
(c) $\Delta U \neq 0, \Delta S_{total} = 0$
(d) $\Delta U \neq 0, \Delta S_{total} \neq 0$

82 For an ideal gas, consider only ($p-V$) work on going from initial state A to final state C. The final state C can be reached by either of two paths as shown below. NCERT Pg 159

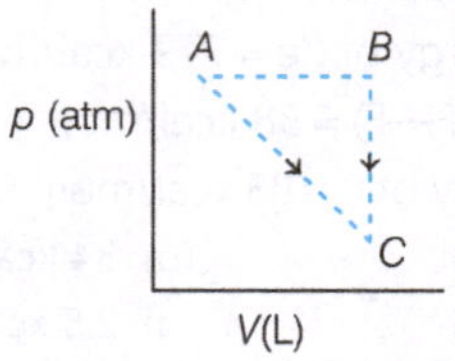

Which of the following option is correct? (Take ΔS as change in entropy and was work done.)

(a) $\Delta S_{A\to C} = \Delta S_{A\to B} + \Delta S_{B\to C}$
(b) $W_{A\to B\to C} = W_{A\to B} - W_{B\to C}$
(c) $W_{A\to B\to C} = W_{A\to B} + W_{B\to C}$
(d) $\Delta S_{A\to C} = \Delta S_{A\to B} - \Delta S_{A\to C}$

83 In the given equation,

$$4Fe(s) + 3O_2(g) \longrightarrow 2Fe_2O_3(s)$$

The entropy change is -549.4 JK^{-1} mol^{-1} at 298 K. ($\Delta_r H° = -1648 \times 10^3$ J mol^{-1}). The above reaction is NCERT Pg 159

(a) spontaneous (b) non-spontaneous
(c) reversible (d) irreversible

84 The process which occur spontaneously are

I. flow of heat from colder to warmer body.
II. gas expanding to fill the available volume.
III. gas in a container contracting into one corner.

Select the correct statements and choose the correct option. NCERT Pg 159

(a) Only I (b) Only II (c) Only III (d) I, II and III

85 In which of the following reactions, standard entropy changes ($\Delta S°$) is positive and standard Gibbs energy change ($\Delta G°$) become more negative with increasing temperature? NCERT Pg 160

(a) $C\text{ (graphite)} + \frac{1}{2}O_2(g) \longrightarrow CO\ (g)$

(b) $CO(g) + \frac{1}{2}O_2(g) \longrightarrow CO_2\ (g)$

(c) $Mg\ (s) + \frac{1}{2}O_2(g) \longrightarrow MgO\ (s)$

(d) $\frac{1}{2}C\text{(graphite)} + \frac{1}{2}O_2(g) \longrightarrow \frac{1}{2}CO_2\ (g)$

86 If the enthalpy change for the transition of liquid water to steam is 30 kJ mol^{-1} at 27°C, the entropy change for the process would be NCERT Pg 160

(a) 1.0 J mol^{-1} K^{-1} (b) 0.1 J mol^{-1} K^{-1}
(c) 100 J mol^{-1} K^{-1} (d) 10 J mol^{-1} K^{-1}

87 The entropy change for **NCERT Pg 160**

$$CH_4(g) + H_2O\,(g) \longrightarrow 3H_2(g) + CO\,(g)$$

using the following data is

Substance	$CH_4(g)$	$H_2O(g)$	$H_2(g)$	$CO(g)$
$S°/JK^{-1}mol^{-1}$	186.2	188.7	130.6	197.6

(a) $-46\ JK^{-1}\ mol^{-1}$ (b) $+46\ JK^{-1}\ mol^{-1}$
(c) $-214.5\ JK^{-1}\ mol^{-1}$ (d) $214.5\ JK^{-1}\ mol^{-1}$

88 The enthalpy of fusion of water is 1.435 kcal/mol. The molar entropy change for the melting of ice at 0° C is **NCERT Pg 161**

(a) 10.52 cal/mol K (b) 21.04 cal/mol K
(c) 5.260 cal/mol (d) 0.526 cal/mol K

89 A process will be spontaneous at all temperature if **NCERT Pg 161**

(a) $\Delta H > 0$ and $\Delta S < 0$ (b) $\Delta H < 0$ and $\Delta S > 0$
(c) $\Delta H < 0$ and $\Delta S < 0$ (d) $\Delta H > 0$ and $\Delta S > 0$

90 Select the incorrect expression from the following. **NCERT Pg 161**

(a) $\Delta S_{total} = \Delta S_{system} + \Delta S_{surr}$
(b) $\Delta S_{surr} = \dfrac{\Delta H_{surr}}{T}$
(c) $\Delta S_{total} < 0$ (spontaneous process)
(d) $\Delta G = \Delta H - T\Delta S$

91 For a reaction $P + Q \longrightarrow R + S$. The value of ΔH is -30 kJ mol^{-1} and ΔS is -100 J K^{-1}mol^{-1}. At what temperature the reaction will be at equilibrium? **NCERT Pg 161**

(a) 27°C (b) 52°C
(c) 30°C (d) 45°C

92 Dissolution of NH_4Cl in water is an endothermic reaction, yet it is a spontaneous process. This is due to the fact that **NCERT Pg 162**

(a) ΔH is +ve, ΔS is −ve
(b) ΔH is −ve, ΔS is +ve
(c) ΔH is +ve and $\Delta H > T\Delta S$
(d) ΔH is +ve, ΔS is +ve and $\Delta H < T\Delta S$

Gibbs Energy Change and Equilibrium

93 For the reaction,

$$CO(g) + \frac{1}{2}O_2(g) \longrightarrow CO_2(g)$$

If the standard entropy change at 298 K is -0.082 kJ mol^{-1} K^{-1} and standard Gibb's energy for formation of CO_2 and CO are -298.4 and -114.6 kJ/mol respectively, then the enthalpy change for the given reaction will be **NCERT Pg 162**

(a) -314.5 kJ/mol (b) -159.8 kJ/mol
(c) -208.24 kJ/mol (d) -418.3 kJ/mol

94 The equilibrium constant (K) of a reaction may be written as, **NCERT Pg 162**

(a) $K = e^{-\Delta H°/RT}$ (b) $K = e^{-\Delta G/RT}$
(c) $K = e^{-\Delta H/RT}$ (d) $K = e^{-\Delta G°/RT}$

95 The value of $\Delta_r G°$ is equal to **NCERT Pg 162**

(a) $-2.303\ RT \log K$ (b) $+2.303\ RT \log K$
(c) $\Delta_r H° - T\Delta_r S°$ (d) $\Delta_r H° - \Delta_r U°$

96 A process has $\Delta H = 200$ J mol^{-1} and $\Delta S = 40$ JK^{-1} mol^{-1}. Out of the values given below, choose the minimum temperature above which the process will be spontaneous **NCERT Pg 162**

(a) 20 K (b) 4 K (c) 5 K (d) 12 K

97 ΔH and ΔS for the reaction, $Br_2(l) + Cl_2(g) \longrightarrow 2BrCl(g)$ are 29.37 kJ and 104 JK^{-1}, respectively. The temperature at which the reaction will be in equilibrium. **NCERT Pg 162**

(a) Above 150 K (b) Above 282.4 K
(c) Above 153.5 K (d) Above 263.4 K

98 As $O_2(l)$ is cooled at 1 atm pressure, it freezes to form solid I at 54.5 K. At a lower temperature, solid I rearrange to solid II, which has a different crystal structure. Thermal measurements show that for the phase transition solid I to solid II, $\Delta H = -743.1$ J mol^{-1} and $\Delta S = -17$ JK^{-1} mol^{-1}. At what temperature are solids I and II in equilibrium. **NCERT Pg 162**

(a) 2.06 K (b) 31.6 K
(c) 43.7 K (d) 53.4 K

99 The value of logarithm of equilibrium constant K_p if the standard free energy change of a reaction is $\Delta G° = -115$ kJ at 298 K will be **NCERT Pg 162**

(a) 2.303 (b) 13.83 (c) 2.015 (d) 20.15

100 Which of the following graph represents an exothermic reaction? **NCERT Pg 162**

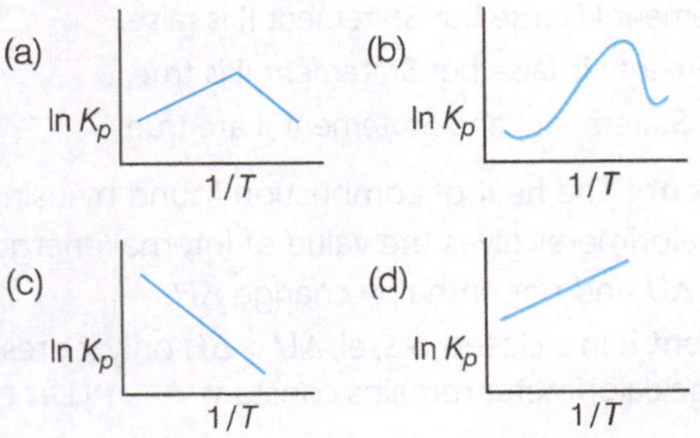

Assertion-Reason Questions

Directions (Q.Nos. 1-9) *In the following question Assertion (A) followed by Reason (R) is given below. Choose the correct option out of the choices given below.*

(a) Both A and R are true and R is the correct explanation of A.

(b) Both A and R are true but R is not the correct explanation of A.

(c) A is true but R is false.

(d) A is false but R is true.

1 **Assertion** (A) Volume of water in a pond is not a state function. NCERT Pg 138

Reason (R) Volume of water is independent of the route by which water is filled in the pond either by rain or by tubewell or by both.

2 **Assertion** (A) First law of thermodynamics is applicable to an electric fan or a heater. NCERT Pg 140

Reason (R) In an electric fan, the electrical energy is converted into mechanical work that moves the blades. In a heater, electrical energy is converted into heat energy.

3 **Assertion** (A) The difference between ΔH and ΔU is not significant for systems consisting of only solids or liquids. NCERT Pg 143

Reason (R) Solids and liquids do not suffer any significant volume changes upon heating.

4 **Assertion** (A) 1 mole of acetone requires more heat to vaporise than the 1 mole of water to vaporise. NCERT Pg 148

Reason (R) There is strong hydrogen bonds between water molecules but weaker intermolecular dipole-dipole interactions in acetone.

5 **Assertion** (A) The solubility of most salts in water increases with rise in temperature. NCERT Pg 156

Reason (R) For most of the ionic compounds, $\Delta_{sol} H°$ is positive and the dissociation process is endothermic.

6 **Assertion** (A) The phenomenon like flow of water down hill or fall of a stone on to the ground is an example of a spontaneous process. NCERT Pg 157

Reason (R) There is a net increase in potential energy in the direction of change.

7 **Assertion** (A) The dissolution of NH_4Cl in water is endothermic but it dissolves in water. NCERT Pg 156

Reason (R) On dissolution of NH_4Cl, entropy increases.

8 **Assertion** (A) The entropy decreases when the temperature of a crystalline solid is raised from 0 K to 115 K.

Reason (R) On raising temperature from 0 K to 115 K, the constituent particles begin to move. NCERT Pg 159

9 **Assertion** (A) Third law of thermodynamics is restricted to pure crystalline solids.

Reason (R) Practical and theoretical evidences have shown that entropy of solutions and supercooled liquids is not zero at 0 K. NCERT Pg 159

Statement Type Questions

Directions (Q. Nos. 1-5) *In the following questions, two statements (I & II) are given. In the light of the given statements, choose the correct option given below.*

(a) Both Statement I and Statement II are false.

(b) Statement I is true but Statement II is false.

(c) Statement I is false but Statement II is true.

(d) Both Statement I and Statement II are true.

1 **Statement I** The heat of combustion found by using bomb calorimeter gives the value of internal energy change ΔU and not enthalpy change ΔH.

Statement II In a closed vessel, $\Delta U > \Delta H$ only if pressure inside the calorimeter remains constant. NCERT Pg 145

2 **Statement I** During isothermal expansion of an ideal gas, there is no change in the internal energy.

Statement II During isothermal expansion of an ideal gas, as temperature remains constant, no heat enters or leaves the system. NCERT Pg 142

3 **Statement I** For every chemical reaction at equilibrium standard Gibbs energy of reaction is zero.

Statement II At constant temperature and pressure, chemical reactions are spontaneous in the direction of decreasing Gibbs energy. NCERT Pg 160

4 **Statement I** The enthalpy of formation of gaseous oxygen molecules at 298 K and under a pressure of one atm is zero. NCERT Pg 161

Statement II The entropy of formation of gaseous oxygen molecules under the same condition is zero.

5 **Statement I** Bond energy is the average value of the dissociation energies of similar bonds in a molecule, e.g. in CH_4.

Statement II All the C—H bonds in CH_4 do not have the same bond dissociation enthalpy. **NCERT Pg 153, 154**

6 Select the incorrect statements from the following.

I. The greater the disorder in an isolated system, the lower is the entropy.

II. The entropy change can be attributed to rearrangement of atoms or ions from one pattern in the reactants to another (in the product).

III. Decrease of regularity in structure would mean increase in entropy.

IV. The gaseous state is the state of highest entropy.

V. In a bomb calorimeter, heat absorbed at constant pressure can be measured. **NCERT Pg 145, 159**

Choose the correct answer from the options given below.

(a) II, III and V (b) I and V
(c) I, II and III (d) II, III and IV

7 Which of the followings statements are correct?

I. First law of thermodynamics does not tell anything about the spontaneity of a process.

II. A spontaneous process is a process which doesn't takes place by itself.

III. First law of thermodynamics deals only with different forms of energy.

IV. A spontaneous process may not be instantaneous.

V. For a reaction to be spontaneous at constant temperature and pressure the following condition should be satisfied $\Delta H > 0$ and $\Delta S < 0$. **NCERT Pg 140, 157**

Choose the correct answer from the options given below.

(a) I, II and III (b) I, III and IV
(c) II and V (d) III and IV

8 Select the correct statements from the following.

I. In polyatomic molecules, bond dissociation enthalpy is different for different bonds within the same molecules.

II. For most of the ionic compounds, $\Delta S_{sol} H°$ is positive and dissociation process is endothermic.

III. The enthalpy of formation of $H_2O(g)$ is greater than that of $H_2O(l)$.

IV. Combustion of N_2 to give NO is an endothermic reaction.

V. ΔH_f° of F_2 is taken as zero. **NCERT Pg 153, 156**

Choose the correct answer from the options given below.

(a) I and IV (b) I, II, IV and V
(c) III and IV (d) II, III and IV

9 Select the incorrect statements from the following.

I. The standard value of absolute entropy of elementary substances is takes as zero.

II. Work done in isothermal expansion is greater than that in the adiabatic expansion for same increase in volume.

III. During adiabatic expansion of a real gas there is no change in the enthalpy of the system.

IV. Expansion against vacuum is very large and hence, work done is also very large.

V. The difference between ΔH and ΔU is not usually significant for systems consisting of only solids.

Choose the correct answer from the options given below. **NCERT Pg 142, 143**

(a) I, IV and III (b) II, III and V
(c) I and V (d) III and IV

10 Which of the following statements are correct?

I. Absolute value of thermodynamic property can't be measured.

II. No work is done during free expansion of an ideal gas whether the process is reversible or irreversible.

III. Molar property (X_m) is an intensive property.

IV. The reference state of sulphur is $S_{rhombic}$.

V. A spontaneous process is an reversible process.

Choose the correct answer from the options given below. **NCERT Pg 140, 142, 144, 149, 157**

(a) I, II and V (b) II and III
(c) I, II and IV (d) II, III and IV

Matching Type Questions

1 Match the following Column I with Column II and choose the correct codes given below.

Column I	Column II
A. $p_{ext} = 0$	1. Free expansion of an ideal gas
B. $q = p_{ext}(V_f - V_i)$	2. Adiabatic change
C. $q = 2303\, nRT \log (V_f/V_i)$	3. Isothermal reversible change
D. $\Delta U = W_{ad}$	4. Isothermal irreversible change

Codes NCERT Pg 142

	A	B	C	D		A	B	C	D
(a)	1	4	3	2	(b)	1	2	3	4
(c)	1	3	4	2	(d)	1	3	2	4

2 The following cyclic process is represented by the graph given below. NCERT Pg 142

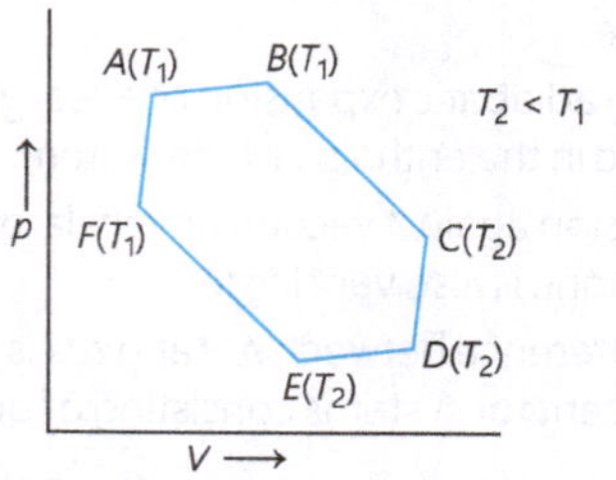

Match the following process given in Column I with changes take place given in Column II and choose the correct codes given below.

Column I (Process)	Column II (Type)
A. $A \to B$	1. Adiabatic contraction, temperature increases to T_1.
B. $C \to D$	2. Isothermal and isobaric expansion at T_1.
C. $E \to F$	3. Isochoric and isothermal (pressure falls).
D. $F \to A$	4. Isochoric and isothermal (pressure increases).

Codes

	A	B	C	D		A	B	C	D
(a)	1	2	3	4	(b)	2	3	1	4
(c)	2	4	1	3	(d)	4	2	3	1

3 Match the Column I with Column II and mark the option given in the codes below. NCERT Pg 152, 153, 155, 156

Column I	Column II
A. $CH_4(g) + 2O_2(g) \longrightarrow CO_2(g) + 2H_2O$	1. $\Delta_{sol}H°$
B. $H_2(g) \longrightarrow 2H(g)$	2. $\Delta_{lattice}H°$
C. $NaCl(s) \longrightarrow Na^+(g) + Cl^-(g)$	3. $\Delta_c H°$
D. $NaCl(s) \longrightarrow Na^+(aq) + Cl^-(aq)$	4. $\Delta_{bond}H°$

Codes

	A	B	C	D		A	B	C	D
(a)	4	3	1	2	(b)	2	1	4	3
(c)	1	2	3	4	(d)	3	4	2	1

4 Match of the following Column I with Column II and mark the correct option given below. NCERT Pg 143, 146, 157

Column I	Column II
A. Equilibrium	1. $\Delta H = (-ve)$
B. Cyclic	2. $\Delta G = (-ve)$
C. Exothermic	3. $\Delta H = 0, \Delta U = 0$
D. Spontaneous	4. $\Delta G = 0$

Codes

	A	B	C	D
(a)	1	2	3	4
(b)	4	3	1	2
(c)	4	2	1	3
(d)	2	3	4	1

5 Match of the following Column I with Column II and mark the correct option given below. NCERT Pg 144, 145

Column I	Column II
A. ΔH is equal to q	1. Entropy
B. ΔU is equal to q	2. Specific heat
C. Intensive property	3. At constant pressure
D. State function	4. At constant volume

Codes

	A	B	C	D		A	B	C	D
(a)	1	2	3	4	(b)	2	3	4	1
(c)	3	4	2	1	(d)	4	1	3	2

6 Match of the following Column I with Column II and mark the correct option given below. NCERT Pg 145, 146

Column I	Column II
A. $H_2(g) + Br_2(g) \longrightarrow 2HBr(g)$	1. $\Delta H = \Delta U + 3RT$
B. $N_2(g) + 3H_2(g) \longrightarrow 2NH_3(g)$	2. $\Delta H = \Delta U - 2RT$
C. $PCl_5(g) \longrightarrow PCl_3(g) + Cl_2(g)$	3. $\Delta H = \Delta U + RT$
D. $2N_2O_5(g) \longrightarrow 4NO_2(g) + O_2(g)$	4. $\Delta H = \Delta U$

Codes

	A	B	C	D
(a)	4	2	3	1
(b)	1	2	3	4
(c)	3	1	4	2
(d)	2	3	1	4

Numerical Value Questions

1 3000 J of heat is given to a gas at constant pressure of $2 \times 10^5 N/m^2$. If its volume increases by 10 litres during the process, the change in the internal energy of the gas is ..... J. **NCERT Pg 140**

2 30.4 kJ of heat is required to melt 1 mole of sodium chloride and the entropy change at the melting point is $28.4 JK^{-1} mol^{-1}$ at 1 atm. the melting point of sodium chloride is .... K. **NCERT Pg 161**

3 $A_2 + B_2 \longrightarrow 2AB; \Delta H_f^\circ = -200 \text{ kJ mol}^{-1}$.
AB, A_2 and B_2 are diatomic molecules. If the bond enthalpies of A_2, B_2 and AB are in the ratio 1 : 0.5 : 1, then the bond enthalpy of A_2 is ...... kJ/mol. **NCERT Pg 150**

4 The total number of intensive properties from the following are ....
Volume, Molar heat capacity, Molarity, E°_{cell}, Gibbs free energy change, Molar mass, Mole. **NCERT Pg 144**

5 The number of endothermic processes from the following is/are....... **NCERT Pg 152**

A. $I_2(g) \longrightarrow 2I(g)$,
B. $HCl(g) \longrightarrow H(g) + Cl(g)$
C. $H_2O(l) \longrightarrow H_2O(g)$
D. $C(s) + O_2(g) \longrightarrow CO_2(g)$
E. Dissolution of ammonium chloride in water.

NCERT Examplers' Questions

1 Thermodynamics is not concerned about
(a) energy changes involved in a chemical reaction.
(b) the extent to which a chemical reaction proceeds.
(c) the rate at which a reaction proceeds.
(d) the feasibility of a chemical reaction.

2 Which of the following statements is correct?
(a) The presence of reacting species in a covered beaker is an example of open system.
(b) There is an exchange of energy as well as matter between the system and the surroundings in a closed system.
(c) The presence of reactants in a closed vessel made up of copper is an example of a closed system.
(d) The presence of reactants in a thermos flask or any other closed insulated vessel is an example of a closed system.

3 The state of a gas can be described by quoting the relationship between
(a) pressure, volume, temperature
(b) temperature, amount, pressure
(c) amount, volume, temperature
(d) pressure, volume, temperature, amount

4 The volume of gas is reduced to half from its original volume. The specific heat will be
(a) reduce to half (b) be doubled
(c) remain constant (d) increase four times

5 During complete combustion of one mole of butane, 2658 kJ of heat is released. The thermochemical reaction for above change is

(a) $2C_4H_{10}(g) + 13O_2(g) \longrightarrow 8CO_2(g) + 10H_2O(l)$;
$\Delta_c H = -2658.0 \text{ kJ mol}^{-1}$

(b) $C_4H_{10}(g) + \frac{13}{2}O_2(g) \longrightarrow 4CO_2(g) + 5H_2O(l)$;
$\Delta_c H = -1329.0 \text{ kJ mol}^{-1}$

(c) $C_4H_{10}(g) + \frac{13}{2}O_2(g) \longrightarrow 4CO_2(g) + 5H_2O(l)$;
$\Delta_c H = -2658.0 \text{ kJ mol}^{-1}$

(d) $C_4H_{10}(g) + \frac{13}{2}O_2(g) \longrightarrow 4CO_2(g) + 5H_2O(l)$;
$\Delta_c H = +2658.0 \text{ kJ mol}^{-1}$

6 Match the following processes with entropy change and choose the correct codes given below.

Reaction	Entropy change
A. A liquid vaporises	1. $\Delta S = 0$
B. Reaction is non-spontaneous at all temperatures with positive ΔH	2. ΔS = positive
C. Reversible expansion of an ideal gas	3. ΔS = negative

7 In an adiabatic process, no transfer of heat takes place between system and surroundings. Choose the correct option for free expansion of an ideal gas under adiabatic condition from the following.
(a) $q = 0, \Delta T \neq 0, W = 0$ (b) $q \neq 0, \Delta T = 0, W = 0$
(c) $q = 0, \Delta T = 0, W = 0$ (d) $q = 0, \Delta T < 0, W \neq 0$

8 $\Delta_f U^\circ$ of formation of $CH_4(g)$ at certain temperature is -393 kJ mol^{-1}. The value of $\Delta_f H^\circ$ is
(a) zero (b) $< \Delta_f U^\circ$ (c) $> \Delta_f U^\circ$ (d) equal to $\Delta_f U^\circ$

9 The pressure-volume work for an ideal gas can be calculated by using the expression, $W = -\int_{V_i}^{V_f} p_{ext} dV$.

The work done can also be calculated from the pV-plot by using the area under the curve within the specified limits. When an ideal gas is compressed (a) reversibly or (b) irreversibly from volume V_i to V_f. Choose the correct option.

(a) W (= reversible) = W (= irreversible)
(b) W (= reversible) < W (= irreversible)
(c) W (= reversible) = W (= irreversible)
(d) W (= reversible) = W (= irreversible) + $p_{ext} . \Delta V$

10 The entropy change can be calculated by using the expression, $\Delta S = \frac{q_{rev}}{T}$. When water freezes in a glass beaker, choose the correct statement amongst the following.

(a) ΔS (system) decreases but ΔS (surroundings) remains the same.
(b) ΔS (system) increases but ΔS (surroundings) decreases.
(c) ΔS (system) decreases but ΔS (surroundings) increases.
(d) ΔS (system) decreases but ΔS (surroundings) also decreases.

11 The enthalpies of elements in their standard states are taken as zero. The enthalpy of formation of a compound

(a) is always negative (b) is always positive
(c) may be positive or negative (d) is never negative

12 On the basis of thermochemical equations (1), (2) and (3), find out which of the algebraic relationships given in options (a) to (d) is correct.

1. $C(\text{graphite}) + O_2(g) \longrightarrow CO_2(g); \Delta_r H = x \text{ kJmol}^{-1}$
2. $C(\text{graphite}) + \frac{1}{2}O_2(g) \longrightarrow CO(g); \Delta_r H = y \text{ kJmol}^{-1}$
3. $CO(g) + \frac{1}{2}O_2(g) \longrightarrow CO_2(g); \Delta_r H = z \text{ kJmol}^{-1}$

(a) $z = x + y$ (b) $x = y - z$ (c) $x = y + z$ (d) $y = 2z - x$

13 Match the following parameters with description for spontaneity and choose the correct codes given below.

	(Parameters $\Delta_r H^\circ$	$\Delta_r S^\circ$	$\Delta_r G^\circ$)	Description
A.	+	−	+	1. Non-spontaneous at high temperature
B.	−	−	+at high T	2. Spontaneous at all temperatures
C.	−	+	−	3. Non-spontaneous at all temperatures

14 Which of the following is not correct?

(a) ΔG is zero for a reversible reaction.
(b) ΔG is positive for a spontaneous reaction.
(c) ΔG is negative for a spontaneous reaction.
(d) ΔG is positive for a non-spontaneous reaction.

15 Consider the reactions given below. On the basis of these reactions find out which of the algebraic relationship given in options (a) to (d) is correct?

1. $C(g) + 4H(g) \longrightarrow CH_4(g); \Delta_r H = x \text{ kJmol}^{-1}$
2. $C(\text{graphite}, s) + 2H_2(g) \longrightarrow CH_4(g); \Delta_r H = y \text{ kJmol}^{-1}$

(a) $x = y$ (b) $x = 2y$ (c) $x > y$ (d) $x < y$

16 Enthalpy of sublimation of a substance is equal to

(a) enthalpy of fusion + enthalpy of vaporisation
(b) enthalpy of fusion
(c) enthalpy of vaporisation
(d) twice the enthalpy of vaporisation

17 Match the following:

(i) Entropy of vaporisation	(a) decreases
(ii) K for spontaneous process	(b) is always positive
(iii) Crystalline solid state	(c) lowest entropy
(iv) ΔU in adiabatic expansion of ideal gas	(d) $\frac{\Delta H_{vap}}{T_b}$

Past Exams' Questions

NEET Archive

1 Match List I with List II. NCERT Pg 142, NEET 2024

	List-I (Process)		List-II (Conditions)
A.	Isothermal process	I.	No heat exchange
B.	Isochoric process	II.	Carried out at constant temperature
C.	Isobaric process	III.	Carried out at constant volume
D.	Adiabatic process	IV.	Carried out at constant pressure

Choose the correct answer from the options given below:

(a) A-IV, B-III, C-II, D-I (b) A-IV, B-II, C-III, D-I
(c) A-I, B-II, C-III, D-IV (d) A-II, B-III, C-IV, D-I

2 The work done during reversible isothermal expansion of one mole of hydrogen gas at 25°C from pressure of 20 atmosphere to 10 atmosphere is (Given, $R = 2.0 \text{ cal K}^{-1}\text{mol}^{-1}$) NCERT Pg 142, NEET 2024

(a) 0 calorie (b) −413.14 calories
(c) 413.14 calories (d) 100 calories

3 In which of the following processes entropy increases?

A. A liquid evaporates to vapour. **NCERT Pg 158, NEET 2024**

B. Temperature of a crystalline solid lowered from 130 K to 0 K.

C. $2NaHCO_3(s) \longrightarrow Na_2CO_3(g) + CO_2(g) + H_2O(g)$

D. $Cl_2(g) \longrightarrow 2Cl(g)$

Choose the correct answer from the options given below:

(a) A and C (b) A, B and D
(c) A, C and D (d) C and D

4 Which of the following p-V curve represents maximum work done? **NCERT Pg 141, NEET 2022**

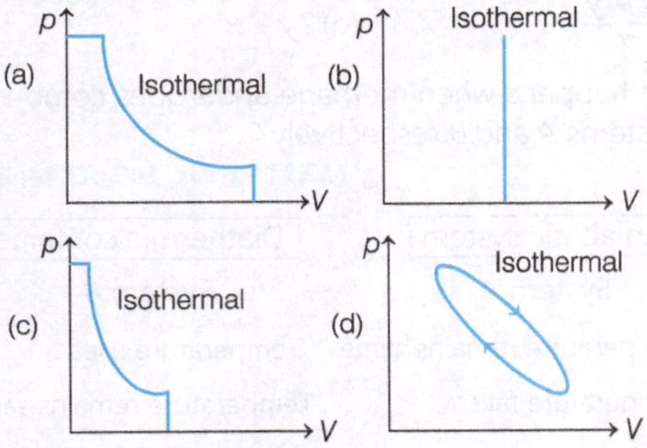

5 Which one among the following is the correct option for right relationship between C_p and C_V for one mole of ideal gas? **NCERT Pg 145, NEET 2021**

(a) $C_p + C_V = R$ (b) $C_p - C_V = R$
(c) $C_p = RC_V$ (d) $C_V = RC_p$

6 For irreversible expansion of an ideal gas under isothermal condition the correct option is **NCERT Pg 145, NEET 2021**

(a) $\Delta U = 0, \Delta S_{total} = 0$ (b) $\Delta U \neq 0, \Delta S_{total} \neq 0$
(c) $\Delta U = 0, \Delta S_{total} \neq 0$ (d) $\Delta U \neq 0, \Delta S_{total} = 0$

7 If for a certain reaction $\Delta_r H$ is 30 kJ mol^{-1} at 450 K, the value of $\Delta_r S$ (in JK^{-1} mol^{-1}) for which the same reaction will be spontaneous at the same temperature is **NCERT Pg 160, NEET 2020**

(a) 70 (b) −33
(c) 33 (d) −70

8 At standard conditions, if the change in the enthalpy for the following reaction is −109 kJ mol^{-1}.

$$H_2(g) + Br_2(g) \longrightarrow 2HBr(g)$$

Given that, bond energy of H_2 and Br_2 is 435 kJ mol^{-1} and 192 kJ mol^{-1} respectively, what is the bond energy (in kJ mol^{-1}) of HBr? **NCERT Pg 145, NEET 2020**

(a) 368 (b) 736
(c) 518 (d) 259

9 For the reaction, $2Cl(g) \longrightarrow Cl_2(g)$, the correct option is **NCERT Pg 154, NEET 2020**

(a) $\Delta_r H > 0$ and $\Delta_r S < 0$ (b) $\Delta_r H < 0$ and $\Delta_r S > 0$
(c) $\Delta_r H < 0$ and $\Delta_r S < 0$ (d) $\Delta_r H > 0$ and $\Delta_r S > 0$

10 In which case change in entropy is negative? **NCERT Pg 159, NEET 2019**

(a) Expansion of a gas at constant temperature
(b) Sublimation of solid to gas
(c) $2H(g) \longrightarrow H_2(g)$
(d) Evaporation of water

11 Under isothermal condition, a gas at 300 K expands from 0.1 L to 0.25 L against a constant external pressure of 2 bar. The work done by the gas is
(Given that 1 L bar = 100 J) **NCERT Pg 142, NEET 2019**

(a) 5 kJ (b) 25 J (c) 30 J (d) −30 J

12 An ideal gas expands isothermally from 10^{-3} m^3 to 10^{-2} m^3 at 300 K against a constant pressure of 10^5 Nm^{-2}. The work done on the gas is **NCERT Pg 142, NEET 2019**

(a) + 270 kJ (b) − 900 J
(c) + 900 kJ (d) − 900 kJ

13 Reversible expansion of an ideal gas under isothermal and adiabatic conditions are as shown in the figure.

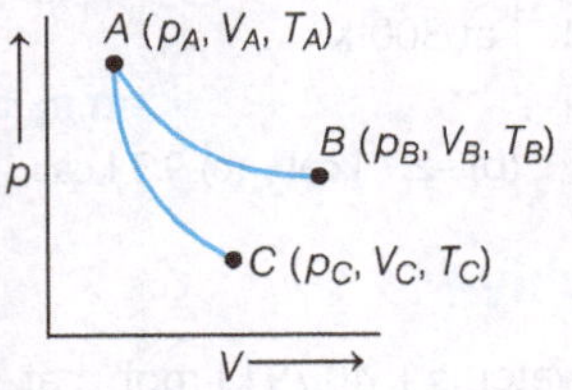

$AB \rightarrow$ Isothermal expansion $AC \rightarrow$ Adiabatic expansion

Which of the following option is not correct? **NCERT Pg 140, 145, NEET 2019**

(a) $\Delta S_{isothermal} > \Delta S_{adiabatic}$
(b) $T_A = T_B$
(c) $W_{isothermal} > W_{adiabatic}$
(d) $T_c > T_A$

14 The bond dissociation energies of X_2, Y_2 and XY are in the ratio of 1 : 0.5 : 1. ΔH for the formation of XY is −200 kJ mol^{-1}. The bond dissociation energy of X_2 will be **NCERT Pg 154, NEET 2018**

(a) 800 kJ mol^{-1} (b) 100 kJ mol^{-1}
(c) 200 kJ mol^{-1} (d) 400 kJ mol^{-1}

15 For a given reaction, $\Delta H = 35.5$ kJ mol^{-1} and $\Delta S = 83.6 JK^{-1}$ mol^{-1}. The reaction is spontaneous at (Assume that ΔH and ΔS do not vary with temperature) **NCERT Pg 160, NEET 2017**

(a) $T < 425$ K (b) $T > 425$ K
(c) All temperatures (d) $T > 298$ K

16 The correct thermodynamic conditions for the spontaneous reaction at all temperatures is NCERT Pg 162, NEET 2016

(a) $\Delta H > 0$ and $\Delta S < 0$ (b) $\Delta H < 0$ and $\Delta S > 0$
(c) $\Delta H < 0$ and $\Delta S < 0$ (d) $\Delta H < 0$ and $\Delta S = 0$

17 Which of the following statements is correct for a reversible process in a state of equilibrium? NCERT Pg 162, CBSE-AIPMT 2015

(a) $\Delta G = -2.303RT \log K$ (b) $\Delta G = 2.303RT \log K$
(c) $\Delta G° = -2.303RT \log K$ (d) $\Delta G° = 2.303RT \log K$

18 The heat of combustion of carbon to CO_2 is–393.5kJ/mol. The heat released upon the formation of 35.2 g of CO_2 from carbon and oxygen gas is NCERT Pg 149, CBSE-AIPMT 2015

(a) –315 kJ (b) +315 kJ (c) –630 kJ (d) –3.15 kJ

19 Which of the following statements is correct for the spontaneous adsorption of a gas? NCERT Pg 160, CBSE-AIPMT 2014

(a) ΔS is negative and therefore, ΔH should be highly positive.
(b) ΔS is negative and therefore, ΔH should be highly negative.
(c) ΔS is positive and therefore, ΔH should be negative.
(d) ΔS is positive and therefore, ΔH should also be highly positive.

20 For the reaction, $X_2O_4(l) \longrightarrow 2XO_2(g)$; $\Delta U = 2.1$ kcal, $\Delta S = 20$ cal K^{-1} at 300 K.

Hence, ΔG is NCERT Pg 160, CBSE-AIPMT 2014

(a) 2.7 kcal (b) –2.7 kcal (c) 9.3 kcal (d) –9.3 kcal

JEE Main Archive

21 $\Delta_{vap}H^{\ominus}$ for water is + 40.79 kJ mol^{-1} at 1 bar and 100 °C. Change in internal energy for this vaporisation under same condition is .... kJ mol^{-1}. (Integer answer) (Given $R = 8.3$ JK^{-1} mol^{-1}) NCERT Pg 143 JEE Main 2024

22 The enthalpy of formation of ethane (C_2H_6) from ethylene by addition of hydrogen where the bond-energies of C—H, C—C, C=C, H—H are 414 kJ, 347 kJ, 615 kJ and 435 kJ respectively is...... kJ. NCERT Pg 149 JEE Main 2024

23 If three moles of an ideal gas at 300 K expand isothermally from 30 dm^3 to 45 dm^3 against a constant opposing pressure of 80 kPa, then the amount of heat transferred is .... J. NCERT Pg 142 JEE Main 2024

24 The heat of combustion of solid benzoic acid at constant volume is – 321.30 kJ at 27°C. The heat of combustion at constant pressure is (–321.30 – xR) kJ, the value of x is ......

25 Which of the following relations are correct?

A. $\Delta U = q + p\Delta V$ B. $\Delta G = \Delta H - T\Delta S$
C. $\Delta S = \frac{q_{rev}}{T}$ D. $\Delta H = \Delta U - \Delta nRT$

Choose the most appropriate answer from the options given below. NCERT Pg 159, 60, JEE Main 2023

(a) A and B (b) C and D
(c) B and C (d) B and D

26 Given,

(A) $2CO(g) + O_2(g) \longrightarrow 2CO_2(g) \Delta H_1^\circ = -x$ kJ mol^{-1}
(B) $C(\text{graphite}) + O_2(g) \longrightarrow CO_2(g) \Delta H_2^\circ = -y$ kJ mol^{-1}

The $\Delta H°$ for the reaction,

$C(\text{graphite}) + \frac{1}{2}O_2(g) \longrightarrow CO(g)$ is NCERT Pg 151, 152, JEE Main 2023

(a) $\frac{x+2y}{2}$ (b) $\frac{x-2y}{2}$
(c) $\frac{2x-y}{2}$ (d) $2y - x$

27 What happens when methane undergoes combustion in systems A and B respectively? NCERT Pg 139, 140, JEE Main 2023

	Adiabatic system System A	Diathermic container System B
(a)	Temperature remains same	Temperature rises
(b)	Temperature falls	Temperature remains same
(c)	Temperature falls	Temperature rises
(d)	Temperature rises	Temperature remains same

28 Which of the following relation is not correct? NCERT Pg 140, 143, 159, 160, JEE Main 2022

(a) $\Delta H = \Delta U - p\Delta V$ (b) $\Delta U = q + W$
(c) $\Delta S_{sys} + \Delta S_{surr} \geq 0$ (d) $\Delta G = \Delta H - T\Delta S$

29 At 25°C and 1 atm pressure, the enthalpies of combustion are as given below.

Substance	H_2	C(graphite)	$C_2H_6(g)$
$\frac{\Delta_c H^{\ominus}}{kJ\ mol^{-1}}$	–286.0	–394.0	–1560.0

The enthalpy of formation of ethane is NCERT Pg 149, 150, JEE Main 2022

(a) +54.0 kJ mol^{-1} (b) –68.0 kJ mol^{-1}
(c) –86.0 kJ mol^{-1} (d) +97.0 kJ mol^{-1}

30 At 25°C and 1 atm pressure, the enthalpy of combustion of benzene (l) and acetylene (g) are –3268 kJ mol^{-1} and –1300 kJ mol^{-1}, respectively.

The change in enthalpy for the reaction

$3C_2H_2(g) \longrightarrow C_6H_6(l)$, is NCERT Pg 154, JEE Main 2022

(a) +324 kJ mol^{-1} (b) +632 kJ mol^{-1}
(c) –632 kJ mol^{-1} (d) –732 kJ mol^{-1}

31 Match List-I with List-II.

List-I	List-II
A. Spontaneous process	1. $\Delta H < 0$
B. Process with $\Delta p = 0$, $\Delta T = 0$	2. $\Delta G_{T,p} < 0$
C. $\Delta H_{reaction}$	3. Isothermal and isobaric process
D. Exothermic process	4. [Bond energies of molecules in reactants] – [Bond energies of product molecules]

Choose the correct answer from the options given below. **NCERT Pg 160, 142, 162, JEE Main 2022**

	A	B	C	D		A	B	C	D
(a)	3	2	4	1	(b)	2	3	4	1
(c)	2	3	1	4	(d)	2	1	3	4

32 The incorrect expression among the following is **NCERT Pg 142, 160, 162, JEE Main 2021**

(a) $\left(\frac{\partial G}{\partial T}\right)_P = -S$ (b) $\ln k = \frac{\Delta H° - T\Delta S°}{RT}$ (c) $k = e^{-\frac{\Delta G°}{RT}}$

(d) For isothermal process, $W_{reversible} = -nRT \ln \frac{V_f}{V_i}$

Skill Boosters

1 If 150 kJ of energy is needed for muscular work to walk a distance of one km, then how much of glucose, one has to consume to walk a distance of five km, provided only 30% energy is available for muscular work. [Given the enthalpy of combustion of glucose is 3000 kJ/mol^{-1}]

(a) 75 g (b) 30 g (c) 180 g (d) 150 g

2 Bond dissociation enthalpies of $H_2(g)$ and $N_2(g)$ are 436.0 kJ mol^{-1} and 941.8 kJ mol^{-1}, respectively and enthalpy of formation of $NH_3(g)$ is –46 kJ mol^{-1}. The enthalpy of atomisation of $NH_3(g)$ and the average bond enthalpy of N—H bond respectively (in kJ mol^{-1}) are

(a) 1170.9, 390.3 (b) 117, 300
(c) 300, 200 (d) 2000, 1975

3 A gaseous system is initially characterised by 500 mL volume and 1 atm pressure at 298 K. This system is allowed to do work as follows

(i) In isobaric conditions, it expands to 800 mL resulting a decrease in pressure and temperature to 0.6 atm and 273 K respectively.

(ii) In adiabatic conditions, it is allowed to expand upto 800 mL and results a decrease in pressure and temperature to 0.6 atm and 273 K respectively.

If Gibbs energy change in (i) is ΔG_a and in (ii) is ΔG_b, then what will be the ratio of $\frac{\Delta G_a}{\Delta G_b}$?

(a) 0 (b) 1 (c) Between 0-1 (d) > 1

4 A heating coil is immersed in a 100 g sample of $H_2O(l)$ at 1 atm and 100°C in a closed vessel. In this heating process, 60% of the liquid is converted into gaseous form at constant pressure of 1 atm. Densities of liquid and gaseous water under these conditions are 1000 kg/m^3 and 0.60 kg/m^3 respectively. Magnitude of the work done for the process is :

(a) 4997 J (b) 4970 J (c) 9994 J (d) 2830 J

5 A swimmer coming out from a pool is covered with a film of water weighing about 18 g. Assuming the water vapour to be a perfect gas.

(i) Calculate the internal energy change when 1 mole of water at 100°C and 1 bar pressure is converted to ice at 0°C.

(ii) How much heat must be supplied to evaporate this water by the swimmer at 298 K?

(Given, $\Delta_{vap}H°$ of water at 298 K = 44.01 kJ/mol^{-1} and $\Delta_{fus}H°$ of ice is 6.00 kJ mol^{-1}

Heat capacity of water = 4.2 J/g°C)

(a) –13.56 kJ mol^{-1}, 34.01 kJ (b) –20.61 kJ mol^{-1}, 18 kJ
(c) –13.56 kJ mol^{-1}, 44.01 kJ (d) –19.63 kJ mol^{-1}, 44.01 kJ

6 In a fuel cell (device used for producing electricity directly from a chemical reaction) methanol is used as a fuel and oxygen gas is used as an oxidiser. The standard enthalpy of combustion of methanol is –726 kJ mol^{-1}. The standard free energies of formation of $CH_3OH(l)$, $CO_2(g)$ and $H_2O(l)$ are –166.3, –394.4 and –237.1 kJ mol^{-1} respectively. Calculate the standard free energy, standard internal energy and standard entropy change accompanying the cell reaction.

(a) –702.3 kJ mol^{-1}, –723.42 kJ mol^{-1}, –19.1 JK^{-1} mol^{-1}
(b) –728.48 kJ mol^{-1}, –465.2 kJ mol^{-1}, –24.1 JK^{-1} mol^{-1}
(c) –702.3 kJ mol^{-1}, –724.76 kJ mol^{-1}, –19.1 JK^{-1} mol^{-1}
(d) –597.8 kJ mol^{-1}, –728.48 kJ mol^{-1}, +24.1 kJ mol^{-1}

7 Jatin an athlete, decides to go for a run on a winter day. He starts his run with an initial internal energy of 500 kJ and burns 100 kJ of energy during his exercise. However, due to low temperature, he loses 50 kJ of heat to his surroundings during his run.

Calculate the final internal energy of Jatin after his run, taking into account the exercise induced energy expenditure and the heat loss to the surroundings. Assume that the system is closed, an no other energy interactions occur during his run.
(a) 200 kJ
(b) 350 kJ
(c) 400 kJ
(d) 500 kJ

8 A student is conducting an experiment to determine the heat of combustion of new organic compound. They place 1.00 g of the compound in a bomb calorimeter containing 1000 g of water. The initial temperature of the water is 25°C. After igniting the compound, the final temperature of water is found to be 45°C.
The heat capacity of the bomb calorimeter is 8.0 kJ/°C. The heat of combustion of the compound in kJ/g will be (C = 4.18 J/g°C of water).
(a) 303.1 kJ/g (b) 404.32 kJ/g (c) 243.6 kJ/g (d) 289.66 kJ/g

Correct Codes

Topical Questions

1. (d)	2. (d)	3. (b)	4. (c)	5. (b)	6. (d)	7. (c)	8. (c)	9. (b)	10. (a)
11. (d)	12. (d)	13. (b)	14. (b)	15. (b)	16. (a)	17. (a)	18. (a)	19. (c)	20. (c)
21. (a)	22. (d)	23. (a)	24. (d)	25. (d)	26. (d)	27. (b)	28. (d)	29. (b)	30. (d)
31. (b)	32. (d)	33. (c)	34. (b)	35. (a)	36. (b)	37. (c)	38. (c)	39. (b)	40. (a)
41. (a)	42. (b)	43. (c)	44. (b)	45. (a)	46. (d)	47. (c)	48. (d)	49. (b)	50. (a)
51. (c)	52. (b)	53. (c)	54. (a)	55. (c)	56. (d)	57. (a)	58. (d)	59. (a)	60. (b)
61. (c)	62. (b)	63. (a)	64. (d)	65. (b)	66. (b)	67. (c)	68. (a)	69. (c)	70. (c)
71. (d)	72. (b)	73. (c)	74. (b)	75. (d)	76. (b)	77. (b)	78. (a)	79. (b)	80. (b)
81. (a)	82. (a)	83. (a)	84. (b)	85. (a)	86. (c)	87. (d)	88. (c)	89. (b)	90. (c)
91. (a)	92. (d)	93. (c)	94. (d)	95. (a)	96. (c)	97. (b)	98. (c)	99. (d)	100. (d)

Assertion-Reason

1. (d)	2. (a)	3. (a)	4. (d)	5. (a)	6. (c)	7. (b)	8. (d)	9. (a)

Statement Type

1. (b)	2. (d)	3. (c)	4. (b)	5. (d)	6. (b)	7. (b)	8. (b)	9. (a)	10. (c)

Matching Type

1. (a)	2. (b)	3. (d)	4. (b)	5. (c)	6. (a)

Numerical Value

1. (1000)	2. (1070)	3. (400)	4. (4)	5. (4)

NECERT Exemplar's

1. (c)	2. (c)	3. (d)	4. (c)	5. (c)	6. A-(2), B-(3), C-(1)	7. (c)	8. (b)	9. (b)
10. (c)	11. (c)	12. (c)	13. A-(3), B-(1), C-(2)	14. (b)	15. (c)	16. (a)		
17. (i)-(b,d), (ii)-(b), (iii)-(c), (iv)-(a)								

Past Exams'

1. (d)	2. (b)	3. (c)	4. (a)	5. (b)	6. (c)	7. (a)	8. (a)	9. (c)	10. (c)
11. (d)	12. (b)	13. (d)	14. (a)	15. (b)	16. (b)	17. (c)	18. (a)	19. (b)	20. (b)
21. (38)	22. (125)	23. (1200)	24. (150)	25. (c)	26. (b)	27. (d)	28. (a)	29. (c)	30. (c)
31. (b)	32. (b)								

Skill Boosters

1. (d)	2. (a)	3. (b)	4. (c)	5. (c)	6. (c)	7. (b)	8. (c)

Step by Step

Decoding the Questions

Concept Builders

1 positive

2 extensive, intensive

3 False

4 Adiabatic

5 state variables

6 $\Delta U = q + W$

7 True

8 volume, pressure

9 False

10 $W_{rev} = -2.303\, nRT \log \frac{V_2}{V_1}$,

$W_{irrev} = -p(V_2 - V_1) = -p\Delta V$

11 $q_p = q_V + \Delta n_g RT$

12 True

13 27

14 ΔU

15 less

16 True

17 62.5 kJ mol^{-1}

18 −78.2 kJ/mol

19 False

20 spontaneity

21 $\Delta S = \frac{q_{rev}}{T}$

22 +ve

23 True

24 entropy

25 1

26 $\Delta G = \Delta H - T\Delta S$

27 0, −11.488

28 exothermic

29 entropy

30 False

Topical Solutions

1 (*d*) Internal energy is a state function and does not depend on path.

2 (*d*) *q* (heat) and *W* (work) represents path functions.

3 (*b*) In adiabatic process, system does not exchange heat with surroundings.

4 (*c*) Enthalpy change is a state function.

So, it does not depend on the path taken by the reaction.

5 (*b*) In the given case, change in internal energy, $\Delta U = q$, as no work is done at constant volume.

6 (*d*) ΔU is −ve, when energy transferred from system to surrounding.

7 (*c*)

8 (*c*) $\Delta U = q - W$ (closed system)

9 (*b*) According to the first law of thermodynamics,

$$\Delta E = q + W = 500 + (-350) = +150\text{cal}$$

10 (*a*) Since, *W* is the work done on the system by movement of the piston, therefore

$$W = \text{force} \times \text{distance}$$
$$= p_{ext} \cdot A \cdot l$$
$$= p_{ext}(-\Delta V)$$
$$= -p_{ext}(V_f - V_i)$$

11 (*d*) Statement (d) is correct, while the other statements are incorrect. Their correct form are as follows

- Energy can neither be created nor destroyed but can be converted into one form to another.
- First law of thermodynamics which states that the energy of an isolated system is constant.
- In an isolated system, $W = 0$, $q = 0$ and, therefore $\Delta U = 0$.

12 (*d*) The option (d) is incorrect as the given graph represents an irreversible compression.

13 (*b*) For isothermal expansion

$$W = -nRT \ln \frac{V_f}{V_i}$$

$$|W| = nRT \ln \frac{V_f}{V_i}$$

As, $|W| = nRT \ln V_f - nRT \ln V_i$

By compairng with $y = mx - C$.

So, the slope of curve 2 is more than the slope of curve 1 and the intercept of curve 2 is more negative than the intercept of curve 1.

14 (*b*) Since the system is insulated, heat is not allowed to enter or leave the system.

Thus, $q = 0$, $\Delta U = q + W \Rightarrow \Delta U = W$.

15 (*b*)

16 (*a*) Internal energy of a system, $\Delta U = -q$ [work done = 0]

17 (*a*) $W = -\int p_{ext} dV = 0$

$\because p_{ext} = 0$ (vacuum)

18 (*a*) As, the process is carrying out at constant temperature, therefore this type of expansion is called isothermal reversible expansion. for which $\Delta U = 0$,

Hence $q = -W$

Thus, $q = +208$ J, $W = -208$ J

19 (*c*) $W_{rev} = -2.303\, nRT \log \frac{V_2}{V_1}$

$$= -2.303 \times 1 \times 8.314 \times (273 + 47) \times \log \frac{35}{25}$$

$$= -6127.08 \times 0.146 \times \log(1.4)$$

$$W_{rev} = -894.55 \text{ J}$$

[(−ve) sign shows work of expansion]

20 (*c*) $\Delta H = q_p$ (constant pressure)

21 (*a*) As we know that,

$$\Delta U = q - p_{ext}\Delta V$$

Now, if a process of expansion of a gas occurs in vacuum and at constant volume, then

$$\Delta U = q_V \quad (\because \Delta V = 0,\, p_{ext} = 0)$$

22 (*d*) From the equation,

$$C_6H_6(l) + \frac{15}{2}O_2(g) \longrightarrow 6CO_2(g) + 3H_2O(l)$$

Change in the number of gaseous moles i.e.

$$\Delta n_g = 6 - \frac{15}{2} = -\frac{3}{2} \text{ or } -1.5$$

$$\Delta H_p = \Delta U + n_g RT$$

So, $\Delta H_p = (-3263.9) + (-1.5) \times 8.314 \times 10^{-3} \times 298$

$= -3267.6 \text{ kJ mol}^{-1}$

23 (*a*) $\therefore \quad \Delta H = 1440$ cal

Given : $H_2O(s) \rightleftharpoons H_2O(l)$

$$\Delta V = (0.0180 - 0.0196)$$
$$= -0.0016 \text{ L}$$

$\therefore \quad p\Delta V = -1 \text{ atm} \times 0.0016 \text{ L}$

$= -0.0016$ L atm

$\simeq -0.039$ cal

($\because$ 1 L atm = 24.20 cal)

Using, $\Delta H = \Delta U + p\Delta V$

$\Delta U = \Delta H - P\Delta V$

$= 1440 - (-0.039)$

$= 1440.039$ cal

24 (*d*) $\because \; q = 2.303\, nRT \log (V_2/V_1)$

$R = 2$ cal/K-mol

$$\therefore q = 2.303 \times \frac{10}{40} \times 2 \times 300 \times \log\left(\frac{5}{10}\right)$$
$$= -103.980 \text{ cal}$$

For isothermal expansion, $\Delta U = 0$

$W = \Delta U - q$

$= 0 - (-103.980)$

$= +\ 103.980$ cal

When the temperature is constant,

$$p_1V_1 = p_2V_2$$
$$\Delta H = \Delta U + \Delta(pV)$$
$$= 0 + 0 = 0$$

25 (*d*) $\Delta H = \Delta E + \Delta n_g RT$

$\Delta n_g = 0 - 3 = -3$

$\therefore \; \Delta H = \Delta E + (-3)RT$

$\Delta H = \Delta E - 3RT$

26 (*d*) $C_2H_6(g) + \frac{7}{2}O_2(g) \longrightarrow 2CO_2(g) + 3H_2O(l)$

$$\Delta H^\circ = \Delta U^\circ + \Delta n_g RT$$
$$= \Delta U^\circ + \left[2 - \frac{9}{2}\right]RT$$
$$= \Delta U^\circ - \frac{5}{2}RT = x - \frac{5}{2}RT$$

$\therefore \quad \Delta H^\circ < \Delta U^\circ$

27 (*b*) Using gas equation,

$$p\Delta V = \Delta n_g RT$$

Temperature, $T = 25 + 273 = 298$ K

For the reaction,

$$C_4H_{10}(g) + \frac{13}{2}O_2(g) \longrightarrow 4CO_2(g) + 5H_2O(l)$$

$$\Delta n_g = 4 - \left(1 + \frac{13}{2}\right) = -\frac{7}{2}$$

Thus, $W = -\left[-\frac{7}{2} \times 0.0821 \times 298\right]$

$= 85.6$ L atm

28 (*d*) $q =$ coefficient $\times \Delta T$

The magnitude of the coefficient does not depend on concentration of system.

29 (*b*) Molar heat capacity and specific heat capacity.

30 (*d*) Option (d) is incorrect option. The correct from is $C_p - C_V = R$

31 (*b*) Temperature (T) will still remain the same, because volume is an extensive property and temperature is an intensive property.

32 (*d*) The option (d) is incorrect.

The correct form is as follows:

Water has a large heat capacity i.e. a lot of energy is needed to raise its temperature.

33 (*c*) Among the given properties, only 3 (mass, internal energy and heat capacity) properties are extensive in nature.

34 (*b*) Molar heat capacity of water per gram $= 84/18 = 4.7$J

Molar heat capacity (q)

$= m \times c \times \Delta T$

$\therefore \quad q = 100 \times 4.7 \times \Delta T$

$\therefore \quad 1000 = 100 \times 4.7 \times \Delta T$

$\Rightarrow \quad \Delta T = \frac{1000}{100 \times 4.7} = 2.1$ K

35 (*a*) $C_p - C_V = nR$

$C_p - C_V = 10 \times 8.314 = 83.14$ J/K

36 (*b*) The conditions applied for the measurement made in calorimeter are q_p.

37 (*c*) No heat is lost to the surrounding.

38 (*c*) $I_2(s) \longrightarrow I_2(g)$;

$\Delta H_1 = 24 \text{ cal g}^{-1}$ at 200°C

$\Delta H_2 = \Delta H_1 + \Delta C_p(T_2 - T_1)$

$= 24 + (0.031 - 0.055) \times 50$

$= 24 - 1.2$

$\Delta H_2 = 22.8 \text{ cal g}^{-1}$

39 (*b*) Energy release at constant volume due to combustion of 3.5 g of a gas.

$= C \times \Delta T = 2.5 \times 0.45$ kJ

Hence, energy released due to the combustion of 28g of a gas

$= 2.5 \times 0.45 \times \frac{28}{3.5} = 9 \text{ kJ mol}^{-1}$

40 (*a*) $\Delta H = q_p$ and C_p is the heat evolved or absorbed per mole for 1° fall or rise in temperature.

Here, fall in temperature is given,

$= 320 - 293 = 27$ K

Molar mass of $CCl_2F_2 = 121\text{g mol}^{-1}$

Thus, heat evolved from 1.25 g of the sample on being cooled from 320 K to 293 K at constant pressure will be

$= \frac{80.7}{121} \times 1.25 \times 27 = 22.51$ J

41 (*a*) Statement (a) is correct, while the other statements are incorrect. Their correct form are as follows

- Enthalpy is an extensive property.

- When a chemical equation is reversed, the value of $\Delta_r H°$ is also reversed in sign.
- $\Delta_r H$ will be positive in an endothermic reaction.

42 (*b*)

43 (*c*) For the reaction,

$$CH_4(g) + 2O_2(g) \longrightarrow CO_2(g) + 2H_2O(l)$$

$$\Delta_r H = \sum_i a_i H_{(\text{products})} - \sum_i b_i H_{(\text{reactants})}$$
$$= [H_m(CO_2, g) + 2H_m(H_2O, l)] - [H_m(CH_4, g) + 2H_m(O_2, g)]$$

where, H_m is the molar enthalpy.

44 (*b*) Phase transformations involve the energy changes e.g. ice, requires heat for melting. Normally, this melting takes place at constant pressure and during phase change, temperature remains constant (at 273 K).

45 (*a*) Given, $H_2O(l) \xrightarrow{100°C} H_2O(g)$

As we know that,

$$\Delta_{vap}H° = \Delta_{vap}U° + \Delta n_g RT$$

$\Delta_{vap}H°$ = enthalpy of vaporisation

$$= 40.66 \text{ kJ mol}^{-1}$$

For the above reaction,

$$\Delta n_g = n_p - n_r = 1 - 0 = 1$$

$$\therefore \; 40.66 \text{ kJ mol}^{-1} = \Delta_{vap}U° + 1 \times 8.314 \times 10^{-3} \text{ kJ} \times 373 \text{ K}$$

$$\Delta_{vap}U° = 40.66 - 3.1 = +37.56 \text{ kJ mol}^{-1}$$

46 (*d*)

(i) $I_2(s) \longrightarrow I_2(g)$; $\quad \Delta H_1 = +57.3 \text{ kJ mol}^{-1}$

(ii) $I_2(s) \longrightarrow I_2(l)$; $\quad \Delta H_2 = +15.5 \text{ kJ mol}^{-1}$

(iii) $I_2(l) \longrightarrow I_2(g)$; $\Delta H = ?$

Eq. (iii) will be obtained, if we substract Eq. (ii) from (i), i.e (iii) = (i) − (ii)

Now, $\Delta H = 57.3 - 15.5 = +41.8 \text{ kJ mol}^{-1}$

47 (*c*) Statement (c) is incorrect.

It's correct form is as follows

Standard state of solid iron at 500 K is equal to pure iron at 1 bar.

Rest other statements are correct.

48 (*d*) As we know that,

$$\Delta H = \Delta E + \Delta n_g RT$$
$$H_2 - H_1 = E_2 - E_1 + (n_2RT - n_1RT)$$
$$\text{or } H_2 - H_1 - E_2 + E_1 = n_2RT - n_1RT$$

49 (*b*) Only statement (b) is incorrect, while other are correct. The correct form is as follows

The standard state of an element is its most stable state of aggregation at 298 K.

50 (*a*) Moles of $NH_3 = \frac{26}{17} = 1.53$

Heat required to decompose 1 mol of $NH_3 = 81.9$ kJ/mol^{-1}

Now, heat of decomposition for 1.53 moles of NH_3.

= Number of moles × Standard enthalpy

$$= 1.53 \times 81.9 \approx 125.31 \text{ kJ}$$

51 (*c*) $CaCO_3(s) \longrightarrow CaO(s) + CO_2(g)$

$$\Delta_r H° = \sum_i a_i \Delta_f H°_{(\text{products})} - \sum_i b_i \Delta_f H°_{(\text{reactants})}$$

$$\Delta_r H° = \Delta_f H°[CaO(s)] + \Delta_f H°[CO_2(g)] - \Delta_f H°[CaCO_3(s)]$$

$$= 1(-635.1 \text{ kJ mol}^{-1}) + (1)(-393.5 \text{ kJ mol}^{-1}) - 1(-1206.9 \text{ kJ mol}^{-1}) = 178.3 \text{ kJ mol}^{-1}$$

52 (*b*)

(i) $C_6H_6 + \frac{15}{2}O_2 \longrightarrow 6CO_2 + 3H_2O$; $\quad \Delta H = -3270 \text{ kJ mol}^{-1}$

(ii) $C + O_2 \longrightarrow CO_2$; $\quad \Delta H = -394 \text{ KJ mol}^{-1}$

(iii) $H_2 + \frac{1}{2}O_2 \longrightarrow H_2O$, $\quad \Delta H = -286 \text{ KJ mol}^{-1}$

$$6C + 3H_2 \longrightarrow C_6H_6, \Delta H = ?$$

6 × Eqn (ii)+3×Eqn.(iii) − Eqn (i), gives required equation with $\Delta H = +48 \text{ kJ mol}^{-1}$.

53 (*c*) Statements I and II are the correct while statements III is incorrect. The correct form is as follows

On reversed a reaction, only the sign of ΔH is changed but the magnitude remain same.

54 (*a*) Statement (a) is incorrect.

It's correct form is as follows

The negative sign (−ve) of enthalpy change in the above reaction indicates that this is an exothermic reaction.

55 (*c*) According to Hess's law; the total heat change (ΔH) accompanying a chemical reaction is the same, whether the reaction takes place in one or more steps or follows one or more paths.

Therefore, the correct relation between ΔH and ΔH_1, ΔH_2 will be

$$\Delta H = \Delta H_1 + \Delta H_2$$

56 (*d*) According to the question, the diagrammatic representation of given reaction can be

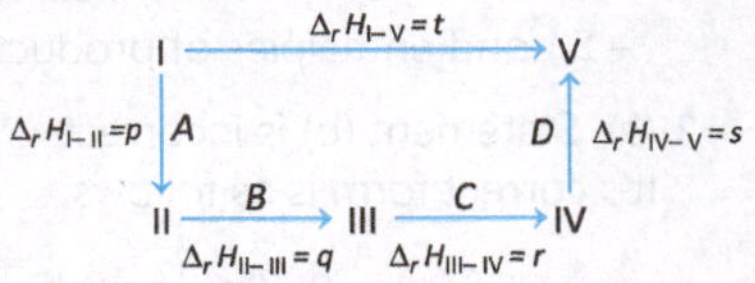

As given, $q = r$ [Hence, (a) is correct]

Using concept of Hess's law,

$$t = p + q + r + s$$

$$\therefore \quad q + r = t - (s + p)$$

[Hence, (b) is correct]

$$2q = t - (s + p) \qquad [\because q = r]$$

[Hence, (c) is correct]

but $q + r = p + s$ is incorrect because exact amount of enthalpy change for each step is not given.

57 (*a*) Using Hess's law,

$$\Delta H_4 = \Delta H_1 + \Delta H_2 + \Delta H_3$$
$$x = 131 + (-282) + (-242)$$
$$x = -393 \text{ kJ}$$

58 (*d*) Given,

∵ We have to find ΔH for the reaction

$$CO + \frac{1}{2}O_2 \longrightarrow CO_2; \Delta H = ?$$

$$\Delta H = \Delta H_2 - \Delta H_1$$

$$\Delta H = -94 - (-26.4) = -67.6 \text{ kcal}$$

59 (*a*) C (graphite) ⟶ C (diamond)

i.e. $\Delta H = [-393.4 - (-395.3)]$ kJ/mol

$= +1.9$ kJ/mol

60 (*b*) Statement (b) is correct, while the other statements are incorrect. Corrected form are as follows

- Combustion reactions are exothermic in nature.
- Our body generates energy from food by the same overall process as combustion.
- The rate of combustion decreases if the supply of oxygen is less.

61 (*c*) $\Delta_r H^\circ =$

Σ bond enthalpies of reactants

$-\Sigma$ bond enthalpies of products.

62 (*b*) Statement (b) is incorrect. It's correct form is as follows

$$\Delta_r C_p^\circ = +\frac{5}{2}R \text{ (for ionisation)}$$

and $\Delta_r C_p^\circ = -\frac{5}{2}R$ (for electron gain)

Rest other statements are correct.

63 (*a*) For the reaction,

$$H_2 + Cl_2 \longrightarrow 2HCl$$

∴ Enthalpy of formation of HCl

$$= \frac{(104 + 58) - (2 \times 103)}{2}$$

$$= -22 \text{ kcal mol}^{-1}$$

64 (*d*) Ethyne molecule breaks as

$$C_2H_2(g) \longrightarrow 2C(s) + H_2(g);$$

$$\Delta H = -225 \text{ kJ/mol} \quad ...(i)$$

$$2C(s) \longrightarrow 2C(g); \Delta H = 1410 \text{ kJ/mol} \quad ...(ii)$$

$$H_2(g) \longrightarrow 2H(g); \Delta H = 330 \text{ kJ/mol} \quad ...(iii)$$

Adding Eq. (i), (ii) and (iii) gives

$$\Rightarrow C_2H_2(g) \longrightarrow 2C(g) + 2H(g); \quad \Delta H = 1515 \text{ kJ}$$

Since,

$$\Delta_r H = \Sigma BE_{(reactants)} - \Sigma BE_{(products)}$$

$$\Rightarrow 1515 \text{ kJ/mol} = 2 \times (C—H)BE + (C{\equiv}C)BE$$

$$\Rightarrow 1515 \text{ kJ/mol} = 2 \times 350 + (C{\equiv}C) BE$$

$$\Rightarrow (C{\equiv}C)BE = 1515 - 700 = 815 \text{ kJ/mol}$$

65 (*b*) Given, I.E. of Xe = 279 kcal/mol

B.E. (F—F) = 38 kcal/mol

Electron affinity of F = 85 kcal/mol

∵ $\Delta_r H$ = Heat supplied − Heat evolved

∴ $292 = (4x + 279) - (38 + 85)$

⇒ $x = 34 \text{ kcal mol}^{-1}$

66 (*b*) ∴ $2H_2(g) \longrightarrow 4H(g); \quad \Delta H = 869.6 \text{ kJ}$

Thus, dissociation energy of H—H bond

$$= \frac{869.6}{2} = +434.8 \text{ kJ}$$

67 (*c*) Let the bond dissociation energy of H — Cl bond be *x*.

For the given reaction,

$$\Delta H_f = \Sigma B.E_{(reactants)} - \Sigma B.E_{(products)}$$

$$-93 = \frac{1}{2}(434) + \frac{1}{2}(242) - x$$

$$-93 = +338 - x$$

$$\Rightarrow x = 431 \text{ kJ/mol}$$

68 (*a*) In the given reactions (i), (ii) and (v) will not have equal ΔH and ΔU as ΔH is zero for them.

69 (*c*)

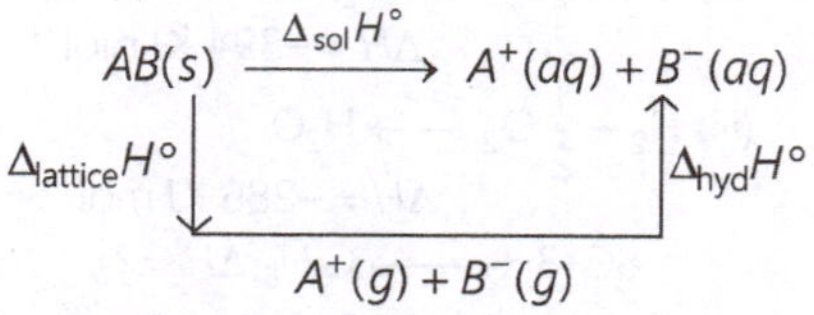

70 (*c*) $\Delta_{sol}H^\circ = \Delta_{lattice}H^\circ + \Delta_{hyd}H^\circ$

∴ $\Delta_{sol}H^\circ = +788 \text{ kJ mol}^{-1} - 784 \text{ kJ mol}^{-1}$

$= +4 \text{ kJ mol}^{-1}$

71 (*d*)

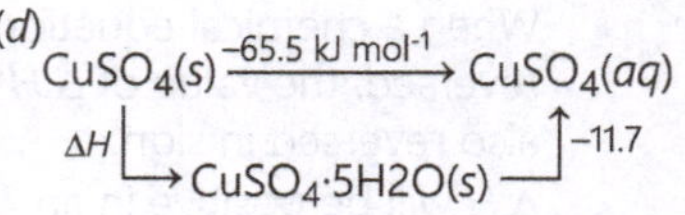

$$-65.5 = \Delta H + (-11.7)$$

$$\Delta H = -53.8 \text{ kJ mol}^{-1}$$

72 (*b*)

73 (*c*) The given reaction is endothermic and spontaneous.

74 (*b*) In exothermic process, heat released increases the disorderness of the surroundings and overall entropy change is positive which makes the reaction spontaneous.

75 (*d*) Decrease of regularity in structure would mean increase in entropy.

76 (*b*) Statement (b) is incorrect. The correct form is as follows

Entropy changes varies inversely with temperature.

77 (*b*) Statement (b) is incorrect. Its correct form is as follows

All naturally occurring processes, whether physical or chemical tend to proceed spontaneously only in one direction.

Rest other statements are correct.

78 (*a*) Statement (a) is incorrect. Its correct form is as follows

The greater the disorder in an isolated system, the higher is the entropy.

Rest other statements are correct.

79 (*b*) Hydrogen (H_2) is only in the gaseous phase here it has maximum entropy.

80 (*b*) Among the given reactions, in the reaction (b) there is decrease in number of moles of the gas and, therefore is accompanied by decrease in entropy, i.e. ΔS will be negative.

81 (*a*) For both reversible and irreversible expansion for an ideal gas, under isothermal conditions, $\Delta U = 0$, but ΔS_{total}, i.e. $\Delta S_{sys} + \Delta S_{surr}$ is not zero for irreversible process.

82 (*a*) Since, entropy is a state function and work done (W) is a path function and, therefore $\Delta S_{A\to C} = \Delta S_{A\to B} + \Delta S_{B\to C}$ is true.

83 (*a*) As we know that,

$$\Delta S_{total} = \Delta S_{sys} + \Delta S_{surr}$$

$$\Delta S_{surr} = -\frac{\Delta_r H^\circ}{T}$$

(at constant pressure)

$$= \frac{-(-1648\times 10^3 \text{ J mol}^{-1})}{298 \text{ K}}$$

$$= 5530 \text{ JK}^{-1} \text{ mol}^{-1}$$

$$\Delta S_{total} = 5530 + (-549.4)$$

$$= 4980.6 \text{ JK}^{-1} \text{ mol}^{-1}$$

Hence, the above reaction is spontaneous.

84 (*b*) Statement II is correct, while the other statements are incorrect. The correct form of I and III is: Flowing of heat from warmer to colder body, expanding of gas and burining of carbon to give carbon dioxide, all are spontaneous processes. While the gas in a container contracting into a corner is a non-spontaneous process.

85 (*a*) Among the given reactions, only in (a) entropy increases because randomness (disorder) increases.

Thus, standard entropy change (ΔS°) is positive. Moreover, it is a combustion reaction and all the combustion reactions are generally exothermic, i.e. $\Delta H^\circ = -$ve.

We know that,

$\Delta G^\circ = \Delta H^\circ - T\Delta S^\circ = -\text{ve} - T(+\text{ve})$

Thus, as the temperature increases, the value of ΔG° become more negative.

86 (*c*) $\because$ $\Delta G^\circ = 0$ at equilibrium,

$$\therefore \quad \Delta S_{vap} = \frac{\Delta H_{vap}}{T}$$

$$= \frac{30\times 10^3 \text{ J mol}^{-1}}{300 \text{ K}}$$

$$= 100 \text{ J mol}^{-1} \text{ K}^{-1}$$

87 (*d*) $\because \Delta S^\circ_{reaction} = \Delta S^\circ_{products} - \Delta S^\circ_{reactants}$

For the reaction,

$$CH_4(g) + H_2O(g) \longrightarrow 3H_2(g) + CO(g)$$

$$\Delta S^\circ_{reaction} = [3\times S^\circ_{H_2} + S^\circ_{CO}] - [S^\circ_{CH_4} + S^\circ_{H_2O}]$$

$$= [3\times 130.6 + 197.6] - [186.2 + 188.7]$$

$$= 589.4 - 374.9$$

$$= 214.5 \text{ JK}^{-1} \text{ mol}^{-1}$$

88 (*c*) Molar entropy change for the melting of ice,

$$\Delta S_{melt} = \frac{\Delta H_{fusion}}{T} = \frac{1.435 \text{ kcal / mol}}{(0+273)\text{K}}$$

$$= 5.26\times 10^{-3} \text{kcal/mol K}$$

$$= 5.260 \text{ cal/mol K}$$

89 (*b*)

ΔH	ΔS	Comment on temperature (T)	ΔG	Comment on the process
<0	>0	at any temp.	<0	spontaneous

90 (*c*) The correct form as (c) is :

For a spontaneous process, $\Delta S > 0$.

91 (*a*) $\Delta G = \Delta H - T\Delta S$

At equilibrium, $\Delta G = 0$, $\Delta H = T\Delta S$

$30000 = T \times 100$; $T = 300$ K or 27°C.

92 (*d*) ΔH is +ve, ΔS is +ve and $\Delta H < T\Delta S$.

Therefore, for ΔG to be negative, $\Delta S > 0$ and $\Delta H < T\Delta S$.

93 (*c*) $\Delta G^\circ_{(reaction)}$

$$= \Sigma G^\circ_f(CO_2) - \Sigma[G^\circ_f(CO) + \frac{1}{2} G^\circ_f(O_2)]$$

$$\Rightarrow -298.4 - [-114.6 + 0]$$

$$[\because G^\circ_f(O_2) = 0]$$

$$\Rightarrow -183.8 \text{ kJ/mol}$$

Also, $\Delta G^\circ = \Delta H^\circ - T\Delta S^\circ$

$$\Rightarrow -183.8 = \Delta H^\circ - [298\times(-0.082)]$$

$$\Rightarrow \quad \Delta H^\circ = -208.24 \text{ kJ/mol}$$

94 (*d*) The equilibrium constant,

$$K = e^{-\frac{\Delta G^\circ}{RT}}$$

95 (*a*) $\Delta_r G^\circ$ is related to the equilibrium constant of the reaction as follows

$$0 = \Delta_r G^\circ + RT \ln K$$

$$\Delta_r G^\circ = -RT \ln K$$

$$\Delta_r G^\circ = -2.303\, RT \log K$$

96 (*c*) $\Delta G = \Delta H - T\Delta S$

The process will be spontaneous, when $\Delta G = -$ ve, i.e. $|T\Delta S| > |\Delta H|$

$$\Rightarrow \quad T > \frac{|\Delta H|}{|\Delta S|} = \frac{200}{40} = 5 \text{ K}$$

97 (*b*) $\Delta G = \Delta H - T\Delta S$

At equilibrium,

$$\Delta G = 0$$

$$\Delta H = T\Delta S$$

$$T = \frac{\Delta H}{\Delta S} = \frac{29.37\times 10^3}{104}$$

$$= \frac{29370}{104} = 282.4 \text{ K}$$

98 (*c*) $\Delta G = \Delta H - T\Delta S$

At equilibrium, $\Delta G = 0$

$$\therefore \quad \Delta H = T\Delta S$$

Given, $\Delta H = -743.1 \text{ J mol}^{-1}$

$$\therefore \quad T = \frac{-743.1}{-17.0} = 43.7 \text{ K}$$

At this temperature, solids I and II are in equilibrium.

99 (*d*) $\because$ $-\Delta G^\circ = 2.303\, RT \log_{10} K_p$

$$\therefore -(-115\times 10^3) = 2.303\times 8.314 \times 298 \log_{10} K_p$$

$$\log_{10} K_p = \frac{115000}{2.303\times 8.314\times 298}$$

$$= 20.15$$

100 (*d*) The plot of the option (d) is representing an exothermic reaction.

$$\ln K_p = -\frac{\Delta H}{RT} + \text{constant}$$

Assertion-Reason

1 (*d*) A is false but R is true.

The correct form of A is:

Volume of water in a pond is a state function because change in volume of its water is independent of the route by which water is filled in the pond, either by rain or by tubewell or by both.

2 (a) Both A and R are true and R is the correct explanation of A.

3 (a) Both A and R are true and R is the correct explanation of A.

4 (d) A is false but R is true. The correct form of A is :
1 mole of acetone requires less heat to vaporise than the 1 mole of water to vaporise.

5 (a) Both A and R are true and R is the correct explanation of A.

6 (c) A is true but R is false. The correct form of R is :
There is a net decrease in potential energy in the direction of change.

7 (b) Both A and R are true but R is not the correct explanation of A.

8 (d) A is false but R is true.
The entropy increases when the temperature of a crystalline solid is raised from 0 K to 115 K.

9 (a) Both A and R are true and R is the correct explanation of A.

Statement Type

1 (b) Statement I is true but Statement II is false. The correct form of Statement II is :
In a closed vessel, $\Delta U = \Delta H$ if pressure and volume inside the calorimeter remains constant.

2 (d) Both statement I and II are true.

3 (c) Statement I is false but Statement II is true. The correct form of Statement I is :
For a chemical reaction at equilibrium, $\Delta G = 0$ but $\Delta G°$ may or may not be equal to zero.

4 (b) Statement I is true but Statement II is false. The correct form of Statement II is :
Entropy of formation of even elementary substances at 298 K and one atmosphere pressure is not zero.

5 (d) Both Statements I and II are true.

6 (b) Among the given statements, Statements I and V are incorrect. While the statements II, III and IV are correct. The correct form of I and V is :
I The greater the disorder in an isolated system, the higher is the entropy.
V In a bomb calorimeter, heat absorbed at constant volume can be measured.

7 (b) Among the given statements, Statements I, III and IV are correct whereas Statement II and V are incorrect. Their correct form is :
II A spontaneous process is a process which takes place by itself.
V Spontaneous reaction occurs at constant temperature and pressure, so that $\Delta H < 0$ and $\Delta S > 0$.

8 (b) Among the given statements, Statement I, II, IV and V are correct whereas, Statement III is incorrect. Its correct form is :
The enthalpy of formation of $H_2O(l)$ is greater than that of $H_2O(g)$.

9 (a) Among the given statements, Statements I, IV and III are incorrect, while the Statements II and V are correct.
The correct form of I and IV are :
I. The standard value of absolute entropy of elementary substances is not zero, it has a definite value.
IV During expansion against vaccum, $p_{ext} = 0$, so work done is zero.
III During adiabatic expansion, the internal energy of the system decreases, which means the enthalpy of the system also changes.

10 (c) Among the given statements, Statements I, II and IV are correct while Statements III and V are incorrect. The correct form of III and V is :
III. Molar property (X_m) is an extensive property.
V. A spontaneous process is an irreversible process.

Matching Type

1 (a) The correct match is
A-1, B-4, C-3, D-2.

2 (b) The correct match is
A-2, B-3, C-1, D-4.

3 (d) The correct match is
A-3, B-4, C-2, D-1.

4 (b) The correct match is
A-4, B-3, C-1, D-2.

5 (c) The correct match is
A-3, B-4, C-2, D-1.

6 (a) The correct match is
A-4, B-2, C-3, D-1.

Numerical Value

1 (1000) $\Delta Q = 3000$ J

$$W = p\Delta V = (2 \times 10^5 \text{ Nm}^{-2})(10 \times 10^{-3} \text{ m}^3) = 2 \times 10^3 \text{ J}$$

$$\Delta U = \Delta Q - w = 3000 - 2000 = 1000\text{J}$$

2 (1070) $\Delta S = \dfrac{\Delta H_{fus}}{T_m}$

$$28.4 \text{ JK}^{-1} \text{ mol}^{-1} = \frac{30.4 \text{ kJ mol}^{-1}}{T_m}$$

$$T_m = 1070.4 \text{ K}$$

3 (400)

$$\Delta H_f^\circ = \Sigma \text{BE}_{\text{Reactants}} - \Sigma \text{BE}_{\text{Products}}$$

$$-200 = (x + 0.5x) - 2x$$

$$-200 = -0.5x$$

$$\Rightarrow \quad x = \frac{-200}{-0.5} = 400$$

4 (4) Intensive properties are independent of the amount of the substance. They don't change with the size of mass of a sample. i.e. Molarity, E°_{cell}, molar mass and molar heat capacity.

5 (4) A, B, C, E are endothermic $C(s) + O_2(g) \longrightarrow CO_2(g)$ is a combustion reaction.

Combustion reactions are generally exothermic.

NCERT Exemplar's

1 (c) Thermodynamics is not concerned with the rate at which a reaction proceeds.

2 (c) Statement (c) is correct, while other statements are incorrect. Corrected form are as follows

Presence of reactive species in a covered beaker is an example of closed system.

3 (d) $pV = nRT$

Thus, p, V, T and n describe the state of the system. So, they are interrelated.

4 (c) The specific heat will remains constant. This is because, specific heat is an intensive property which depends only on the nature of the gas.

5 (c)

6 The correct match is A-2, B-3, C-1.

7 (c) Free expansion, $W = 0$

Adiabatic process, $q = 0$

$\Delta U = q + W = 0$, this means that internal energy remains constant. Therefore, $\Delta T = 0$. In ideal gas there is no intermolecular attraction.

8 (b) The reaction for the combustion of $CH_4(g)$ is given as,

$$CH_4(g) + 2O_2(g) \longrightarrow CO_2(g) + 2H_2O(l)$$

$$\Delta n_g = (n_p - n_R) = 1 - 3 = -2$$

$\because \quad \Delta_f H^\circ = \Delta_f U^\circ + \Delta n_g RT$

As $\quad \Delta n_g = -2$

$\therefore \quad \Delta_f H^\circ < \Delta_f U^\circ$

9 (b) The correct option is

W (= reversible) < W (= irreversible).

This is because area under the curve is always more in irreversible compression.

10 (c) When water freezes in a glass beaker, ΔS (system) decreases because molecules in solid ice are less random than in liquid water. However, when water freezes to ice, heat is released which is absorbed by the surrounding ($\Delta S_{surr} > 0$).

11 (c) Combustion of elements to form a compound can be exothermic or endothermic.

e.g. $C + O_2 \longrightarrow CO_2$ is exothermic.

Whereas, $C + 2S \longrightarrow CS_2$ is endothermic.

Hence, enthalpy of formation may be positive or negative.

12 (c) The algebraic relationships of the given reaction is

equation (1) – equation (2) = equation (3)

$$C(\text{graphite}) + O_2(g) \longrightarrow CO_2(g); \quad \Delta_r H = x \text{ kJ mol}^{-1}$$

$$\underset{(-)}{C}(\text{graphite}) + \underset{(-)}{\frac{1}{2}}O_2(g) \longrightarrow \underset{(-)}{CO}(g); \quad \Delta_r H = y \text{ kJ mol}^{-1}$$

$$CO(g) + \frac{1}{2}O_2(g) \longrightarrow CO_2(g); \quad \Delta_r H = z \text{ kJ mol}^{-1}$$

Hence, $x - y = z$ or $x = y + z$

13 The correct match is A-3, B-1, C-2.

14 (b) ΔG should be (–ve) for a spontaneous reaction.

15 (c) Same bonds are formed in reactions (1) and (2) but no bonds are broken in reaction (1) whereas bonds in the reactant molecules are broken in reaction (2).

As energy is absorbed when bonds are broken, energy released in reaction (1) is greater than that in reaction (2), hence $x > y$.

16 (a) Enthalpy of sublimation

= Enthalpy of fusion + Enthalpy of vaporisation.

17 The correct match is (i)-(b, d), (ii)-(b), (iii)-(c), (iv)-(a).

Past Exams'

1. (d) The correct match is

A-II, B-III, C-IV, D-I.

2 (b) In reversible isothermal process, work done is,

$$W = -2.303 nRT \log_{10}\left(\frac{p_1}{p_2}\right)$$

$$= -2.303 \times 1 \times 2 \times 298 \log_{10}\left(\frac{20}{10}\right)$$

$$= -413.14 \text{ calories}$$

3 (c) The statement given in A, C, D are correct in regard to increase in entropy.

A. When liquid evaporates to vapour, randomness increases, so entropy increases.

C. $\Delta n_g = 2 - 0 = 2$

$\Delta n_g = +\text{ve} \longrightarrow \Delta S = +\text{ve}$

$\Rightarrow$ Entropy increases.

D. $\Delta n_g = 2 - 1 = 1$

$\Delta n_g = +\text{ve} \longrightarrow \Delta S = +\text{ve}$

$\Rightarrow$ Entropy increases.

Statement given in B is incorrect, because, when temperature decreases, entropy decreases.

4 (a) In p-V graph, the area under the curve represents the magnitude of work. The maximum area is covered in graph (a). Hence, it represents maximum work done.

5 (b) For an ideal gas, $C_p - C_V = nR$

(where, n = number of moles of gas, C_p, C_V = specific heat at constant pressure and volume, R = universal gas constant)

As $n = 1$, so $C_p - C_V = R$

6 (c) The change in internal energy depends on the temperature. For isothermal process, $\Delta T = 0$.

So, $\Delta U = 0$.

With an expansion of an ideal gas, more space is available for the gaseous particles.

$\therefore$ Entropy of gas increases so, entropy of system is not zero. i.e. $\Delta S \neq 0$.

7 (a) $\Delta G = \Delta H - T\Delta S$ (Gibbs equation)

For a spontaneous reaction,

$\Delta G < 0$, i.e. $T\Delta S > \Delta H$

$$\Rightarrow \quad T > \frac{\Delta H}{\Delta S} = \frac{30 \times 1000 \text{ J mol}^{-1}}{\Delta S}$$

[Given, $T = 450$ K]

$\Rightarrow \quad \Delta S > \dfrac{30\times 1000 \text{ J mol}^{-1}}{450 \text{ K}}$

$= 66.67 \text{ J mol}^{-1}\text{K}^{-1}$

When $\Delta S > 66.67 \text{ J mol}^{-1}\text{K}^{-1}$, the reaction will be spontaneous.

So, from the options, $\Delta_r S = 70 \text{ J mol}^{-1}\text{K}^{-1}$ indicates spontaneity of the reaction.

8 (*a*) $\underset{[\text{H—H}]}{H_2(g)} + \underset{[\text{Br—Br}]}{Br_2(g)} \longrightarrow \underset{[\text{H—Br}]}{2HBr(g)}$

$\Rightarrow \Delta_r H = (\Sigma \text{BE})_{\text{Reactants}} - (\Sigma \text{BE})_{\text{Products}}$

[$\because$ BE = bond energy]

$\Rightarrow -109 = [(\text{BE})_{H_2} + (\text{BE})_{Br_2}] - (\text{BE})_{HBr} \times 2$

$-109 = (435 + 192) - (\text{BE})_{HBr} \times 2$

$\Rightarrow (\text{BE})_{HBr} = 368 \text{ kJ mol}^{-1}$

9 (*c*) In this reaction, combination of two Cl atoms takes place to give more stable Cl_2 molecule. So, the reaction is exothermic, i.e. $\Delta_r H < 0$.

Here, $\Delta n_g = 1 - 2 = -1$

So, entropy change of the reaction will be, $\Delta_r S < 0$.

10 (*c*) Entropy is negative in case of $2H(g) \longrightarrow H_2(g)$ as the number of moles of gaseous reactants are more than that of gaseous products. i.e. $\Delta n_g < 0$.

11 (*d*) **Key Idea** *For an isothermal irreversible expansion,*

$W_{\text{irrev}} = -p_{\text{ext}}(V_2 - V_1)$

$V_1 = 0.1 \text{ L}; V_2 = 0.25 \text{ L}; p_{\text{ext}} = 2$

We know that,

$W_{\text{irrev}} = -p_{\text{ext}}(V_2 - V_1)$

On substituting the given values in the above equation, we get

$W_{\text{irrev}} = -2 \text{ bar } (0.25 - 0.1) \text{ L}$

$= -2 \times 0.15 \text{ L bar}$

$= -0.3 \text{ L bar}$

$= -0.3 \times 100 \text{ J} = -30 \text{ J}$

[$\because$ 1 L bar = 100 J]

12 (*b*) Given, $p_{\text{ext}} = 10^5 \text{ Nm}^{-2}$, $V_1 = 10^{-3}\text{m}^3$, $V_2 = 10^{-2} \text{ m}^3$

$W = -P_{\text{ext}}(V_2 - V_1)$

We get,

$W = -10^5 \text{ Nm}^{-2}(10^{-2}\text{m}^3 - 10^{-3}\text{m}^3)$

$= -10^5 \text{ Nm}^{-2} \times 10^{-3} (10-1)\text{m}^3$

$= -900 \text{ Nm} = -900 \text{ J}$

(1 J = 1 Nm)

13 (*d*) From first law of thermodynamics, $\Delta U = q + W$

In adiabatic expansion, $q = 0$

$\therefore \quad \Delta U = W$

During expansion of a gas w is negative, i.e $w < 0$ or $\Delta U < 0$.

We know that, $\Delta U = nC_V \Delta T$

$\therefore \quad nC_V\Delta T < 0$ or $\Delta T < 0$

$\therefore \quad T_C - T_A < 0$ or $T_C < T_A$

Thus, option (d) is incorrect while the remaining options are correct.

14 (*a*) Let the bond dissociation energies of X_2, Y_2 and XY are a kJ mol^{-1}, 0.5a kJ mol^{-1} and a kJ mol^{-1}, respectively.

$\therefore \Delta_r H = \Sigma \text{BE}_{\text{Reactants}} - \Delta \text{BE}_{\text{Products}}$

$= \left[\frac{1}{2} \times a + \frac{1}{2} \times 0.5a\right] - [1 \times a]$

$-200 = \frac{a}{2} + \frac{a}{4} - a$

$a = 800 \text{ kJ mol}^{-1}$

$\therefore$ The bond dissociation energy of $X_2 = 800 \text{ kJ mol}^{-1}$

15 (*b*) For a reaction to be spontaneous

$\Delta G < 0.$

i.e. $\quad \Delta H - T\Delta S < 0$

or, $\quad \Delta H < T\Delta S$

or, $T > \dfrac{\Delta H}{\Delta S} = \dfrac{35.5 \text{ kJ mol}^{-1}}{83.6 \text{ JK}^{-1}\text{mol}^{-1}}$

$= \dfrac{35.5 \times 1000 \text{ J mol}^{-1}}{83.6 \text{ J K}^{-1} \text{ mol}^{-1}}$

$= 425 \text{ K}$

$T > 425 \text{ K}$

16 (*b*) The correct thermodynamic conditions for the spontaneous reaction at all temperatures are $\Delta H < 0$ and $\Delta S > 0$.

17 (*c*) Mathematical expression of the thermodynamics equilibrium is $\Delta G = \Delta G° + 2.303RT \log K$

At equilibrium when $\Delta G = 0$

then $\Delta G = \Delta G° + 2.303RT \log K = 0$

$\Delta G° = -2.303RT \log K$

18 (*a*) Given,

$C(s) + O_2(g) \longrightarrow CO_2(g);$

$\Delta_f H = -393.5 \text{ kJ mol}^{-1}$

$\because$ Heat released on formation of 44 g or 1 mole $CO_2 = -395.5$kJ mol

$\because$ Heat released on formation of 35.2 g of CO_2

$= \dfrac{-393.5 \text{ kJ mol}^{-1}}{44\text{g}} \times 35.2 \text{ g}$

$= -315 \text{ kJ mol}^{-1}$

19 (*b*) $\Delta G = \Delta H - T\Delta S$

For adsorption of a gas, ΔS is negative because randomness decreases. Thus, in order to make ΔG negative [for spontaneous reaction], ΔH must be highly negative.

20 (*b*) Given, $\Delta U = 2.1$ kcal,

$\Delta S = 20 \text{ cal K}^{-1}$

$\therefore \quad \Delta H = \Delta U + \Delta n_g RT$

$\Delta n_g = (2-0) = 2$

$\therefore \quad \Delta H = 2.1 + 2 \times 2 \times 10^{-3} \times 300$

$\Delta H = 3.3$ kcal

By using Gibbs equation,

$\Delta G = \Delta H - T\Delta S$

$\Delta G = 3.3 - 300 \times 20 \times 10^{-3}$

$\Delta G = -2.7$ kcal

21 (38) Given,

$\Delta H^{\circ}_{\text{vapour}} = +40.79$ kJ/mol

$T = 100°\text{C} = 373 \text{ K}$

Using enthalpy equation,

$\Delta H^{\circ}_{\text{vapour}} = \Delta U° + \Delta n_g RT$

$\Delta U° = 40.79 - \dfrac{8.3 \times 373}{1000}$

$= 37.67 \text{ kJ/mol} \approx 38 \text{ kJ/mol}$

22 (125) Given, Bond enthalpies of

C—H = 414 kJ; C—C = 347 kJ

H—H = 435 kJ; C=C = 615 kJ

Now, the formation of ethane takes place as follows

$C_2H_4(g) + H_2(g) \rightarrow C_2H_6(g)$

$\Delta H = $ B.E. (C=C) + 4B.E. (C—H) + B.E. (H—H) − B.E. (C—C) − 6B.E. (C—H)

$\Delta H = $ B.E.(C=C) + B.E. (H—H) − B.E. (C—C) − 2B.E. (C—H)

$\Rightarrow \Delta H = 615 + 435 - 347 - 2(414)$

$\Delta H = -125$ kJ

23 (1200) For isothermal expansion at constant pressure, heat is given by

$Q = -p_{ext}(V_2 - V_1)$

$= -80 \times 1000 \times (45 - 30) \times 10^{-3}$

$= -15 \times 80 = -1200$ J

Negative sign indicates heat is lost.

Hence, amount of heat transfer is 1200 J.

24 (150) First of all write the balanced chemical equation, by then by using this equation, calculate the value of Δn_g after that use the equation $\Delta H = \Delta U + \Delta n_g RT$ and substitute the given values.

Then compare the equation obtained with the given equation in question to obtain the value of x.

The complete reaction is as follow,

$C_6H_5COOH(s) + \frac{15}{2}O_2(g) \longrightarrow 7CO_2(g) + 3H_2O(l)$

$\Delta H = \Delta U + \Delta n_g RT$

$= -321.30 - \frac{1}{2}\frac{R}{100} \times 300$

$= (-321.30 - 150R)$ kJ

Matching with equation given in question the value of x is 150.

25 (c) The most appropriate relations are given in B and C only. The correct form of other relations are

(A) $\Delta U = q + W \; (W = -p\Delta V)$

$\Delta U = q - p\Delta V$

(D) $\Delta H = \Delta U + \Delta n_g RT$

26 (b) On dividing equation (A) by 2 and reversing the result and equation we get,

$CO_2(g) \longrightarrow CO(g) + \frac{1}{2}O_2(g)$

$\Delta H_2 = \frac{x}{2}$ kJ/mol ...(iii)

Eq. (i) = Eq. (ii) + Eq. (iii)

$\therefore \; \Delta H = -y + \frac{x}{2} = \frac{x}{2} - y$

$\Rightarrow \Delta H = \frac{x - 2y}{2}$

27 (d) Since in adiabatic system, no heat exchange between system and surrounding takes place. Hence, when methane undergoes combustion, due to exothermic reaction, the temperature rises in container (A).

$CH_4 + 2O_2 \longrightarrow CO_2 + 2H_2O +$ Heat

In diathermic container, heat can exchange between system and surrounding, hence heat releases into the surrounding and temperature of system (B) remains same.

28 (a) Relation given in option (a) is not correct.

According to first law of thermodynamics, the change in heat energy of system is equal to the sum of change in internal energy of system and work done by the system.

i.e. $\Delta H = \Delta U + p\Delta V$

29 (c) Given,

(i) $C_2H_6(g) + \frac{1}{2}O_2(g) \longrightarrow 2CO_2(g) + 3H_2O(l)$,

$\Delta H^\circ_{comb} = -1560$ kJ/mol

(ii) $C(s) + O_2(g) \longrightarrow CO_2(g)$,

$\Delta H^\circ_{comb} = -394.0$ kJ/mol

(iii) $H_2(g) + \frac{1}{2}O_2 \longrightarrow H_2O(g)$,

$\Delta H^\circ_{comb} = -286.0$ kJ/mol

The reaction between carbon and hydrogen is :

$2C(s) + 3H_2(g) \longrightarrow C_2H_6(g)$,

$\Delta H^\circ_{rn} = \Delta H^\circ_{f\,(C_2H_6,\,g)}$

$\Delta H^\circ_r = \Delta H^\circ_c$ (reactant)$-\Delta H^\circ_c$ (Product)

$= 2 \times (-394) + 3(-286) - 1560$

$= -788 - 858 + 1560$

$= -86.0$ kJ/mol

30 (c) $\Delta H_r = 3\Delta H_{c_2} - \Delta H_{c_1}$

$= 3 \times -1300 - (-3268)$

$= -3900 + 3268$

$= -632$ kJ mol^{-1}

31 (b) The correct match is

A-2, B-3, C-4, D-1.

32 (b) All the expression of thermodynamics are correct except $\ln k = \frac{\Delta H^\circ - T\Delta S^\circ}{RT}$

Also,

As we know, $\Delta G = \Delta H^\circ - T\Delta S^\circ$ ...(i)

Also, $\Delta G = -RT \ln k$ ...(ii)

$\therefore$ From (i) and (ii)

$-RT \ln k = \Delta H^\circ - T\Delta S^\circ$

$\because \; \ln k = \frac{\Delta H^\circ - T\Delta S^\circ}{-RT}$

Skill Boosters

1 (d) Energy consumed for walking a distance of 5 km $= 150 \times 5$ kJ

$= 750$ kJ

1 mole of glucose, $C_6H_{12}O_6$ (180 g) gives theroretically energy

$= 3000$ kJ

Actaul energy available

$= \frac{30}{100} \times 3000 = 900$ kJ

Thus, for 900 kJ of energy, glucose required = 180 g

$\therefore$ For 750 kJ of energy, glucose required $= \frac{180}{900} \times 750$ g $= 150$ g

2 (a) $N_2(g) + 3H_2(g) \longrightarrow 2NH_3(g)$;

$\Delta H = -2 \times 46$ kJ mol^{-1}

$\Delta H = \Sigma(\text{BE})_{reactants} - \Sigma(\text{BE})_{products}$

$= (941.8 + 3 \times 436) - 6x$

$= -2 \times 46$

(Here, x = B.E. of N—H bonds)

$x = 390.3$ kJ mol^{-1}

$NH_3 \longrightarrow N + 3(H)$

Heat of atomisation

$= 3 \times 390.3 = 1170.9$ kJ mol^{-1}

3 (b) $\frac{\Delta G_a}{\Delta G_b} = 1$ as Gibbs energy is a state function and initial and final states are same in (i) and (ii).

4 (c) Density $(d) = \frac{\text{Mass}}{\text{Volume}}$

Initial volume of 100 g sample of $H_2O\ (V_1)$

$$= \frac{\text{Mass}}{\text{Density}} = \frac{0.1\ \text{kg}}{1000\ \text{kg m}^{-2}}$$

$$= 1 \times 10^{-4}\ \text{m}^3$$

Since, the efficiency is 60% hence 60g of water is converted to gas and 40 g of water remains same final volume (V_f) = Volume of 60 g gas + Volume of 40 g of water

$$= V_f = \frac{0.06}{0.6} + \frac{0.04}{1000}$$

So, work done $= p_{ext}\ (V_f - V_i)$

$$= -10^5 \left(\frac{0.06}{0.60} + \frac{0.04}{1000} - 1 \times 10^{-4}\right)$$

$$= -10^5\ (0.1 + 4 \times 10^{-5} + 10^{-4})$$

$$|W| = 9994\ \text{J}$$

5 (c) The change take place as follows

(i) 1 mol H_2O (l, 100°C) $\rightarrow$ 1 mol (l, 0°C)

Enthalpy change ΔH_1

1 mol H_2 (l, 0°C) $\rightarrow$ 1 mol H_2O (S, 0°C)

Enthalpy change ΔH_2

Total enthalpy change will be

$$\Delta H = \Delta H_1 + \Delta H_2$$

$$\Delta H_1 = -(18 \times 4.2 \times 100)\ \text{J mol}^{-1}$$

$$= -7560\ \text{J mol}^{-1}$$

$$= -7.56\ \text{kJ mol}^{-1}$$

$$\Delta H_2 = -6.00\ \text{kJ mol}^{-1}$$

Therefore, $\Delta H = -7.56\ \text{kJ mol}^{-1} + (-6.00\ \text{kJ mol}^{-1})$

$$= -13.56\ \text{kJ mol}^{-1}$$

There is negligible change in the volume during the change from liquid to solid state.

Therefore, $p\Delta V = \Delta n_g RT = 0$

$$\Delta H = \Delta U = -13.56\ \text{kJ mol}^{-1}$$

(ii) We can represent the process of evaporation as

$$\underset{(1\ \text{mol})}{H_2O(l)} \xrightarrow{\text{Vapourisation}} \underset{(1\ \text{mol})}{H_2O(g)}$$

No. of moles in 18 g $H_2O(l)$ is

$$= \frac{18\ \text{g}}{18\ \text{g / mol}^{-1}} = 1\ \text{mol}$$

Heat supplied to evaporate 18 g of water at 298 K

$$= n \times \Delta_{vap}H^\circ$$

$$= (1\ \text{mol}) \times (44.01\ \text{kJ mol}^{-1})$$

$$= 44.01\ \text{kJ}$$

6 (c) The reaction is

$$CH_3OH(l) + \frac{3}{2}O_2(g) \longrightarrow CO_2(g) + 2H_2O(l)$$

(i) $\Delta_r G^\circ = \Sigma\Delta_f G^\circ_{(\text{Products})} - \Sigma\Delta_f G^\circ_{(\text{Reactants})}$

$$= [\Delta_f G^\circ_{(CO_2)} + 2\Delta_f G^\circ_{(H_2O)}] - \left[\Delta_f G^\circ(CH_3OH) + \frac{3}{2}\Delta_f G^\circ(O_2)\right]$$

$$= [(-394.4) + 2(-237.1)] - \left[-166.3 + \frac{3}{2}(0)\right]$$

$$\Delta_r G^\circ = -702.3\ \text{kJ mol}^{-1}$$

(ii) $\Delta U^\circ = \Delta H^\circ - \Delta n_g\ RT$

$$= -726\ \text{kJ mol}^{-1} - \left(\frac{-1}{2}\right)\text{mol}\ (8.314 \times 10^{-3}\ \text{k JK}^{-1}\ \text{mol}^{-1})\ (298\ \text{K})$$

$$= -726 + 1.24\ \text{kJ mol}^{-1}$$

$$= -724.76\ \text{kJ mol}^{-1}$$

(iii) $\Delta G^\circ = \Delta H^\circ - T\Delta S^\circ$

or $\Delta S^\circ = \frac{\Delta H^\circ - \Delta G^\circ}{T}$

$$= \frac{-726.0 - (-720.3)\ \text{kJ mol}^{-1}}{298\ \text{K}}$$

$$= \frac{5.7\ \text{kJ mol}^{-1}}{298\ \text{K}}$$

$$= \frac{-5700\ \text{J mol}^{-1}}{298\ \text{K}}$$

$$= -19.1\ \text{JK}^{-1}\ \text{mol}^{-1}$$

7 (b) Given, that Jatin's initial internal energy (U_i) is 500 kJ, he burns 100 kJ of energy during his exercise, and loses 50 kJ of heat to his surroundings.

We can express this as, $U_i = 500$ kJ

Energy expended during exercise $= -100$ kJ

(–ve due to lost of energy by system)

Heat lost to surroundings $= -50$ kJ

The change in internal energy is

$$\Delta U = Q + W$$

$$\Delta U = (-100\ \text{kJ}) + (-50\ \text{kJ})$$

$$\Delta U = -150\ \text{kJ}$$

So, Jatin's final internal energy would be

$$U_f = U_i + \Delta V$$

$$U_f = 500\ \text{kJ} - 150\ \text{kJ}$$

$$U_f = 350\ \text{kJ}$$

8 (c) Let's calculate the heat absorbed by the water using the formula :

$$q_{water} = m \times C \times \Delta T$$

where :

$m = 1000$ g (mass of water)

$C = 4.18$ J/g°C (specific heat capacty of water)

$\Delta T = 45°C - 25°C = 20°C$ (Change in temperature)

$$q_{water} = 1000\ \text{g} \times 4.18\ \text{J/g°C} \times 20°\text{C} = 83600\ \text{J}$$

Next, let's calculate the heat absorbed by the calorimeter

$$q_{calorimeter} = C_{calorimeter} \times \Delta T$$

where,

$C_{calorimeter} = 8.0$ kJ/°C = 8000J/°C (heat capacity of the calorimeter)

$$q_{calorimeter} = 8000\ \text{J/°C} \times 20°\text{C} = 160{,}000\ \text{J}$$

Now, let's find the total heat absorbed

$$q_{total} = q_{water} + q_{calorimeter}$$

$$= 83600 + 160000$$

$$= 243{,}600\ \text{J}$$

Since, we used 1.00 g of the compound, the heat of combustion per gram is

Heat of combustion per gram

$$= \frac{243.6\ \text{kJ}}{1.00\ \text{g}} = 243.6\ \text{kJ/g}$$

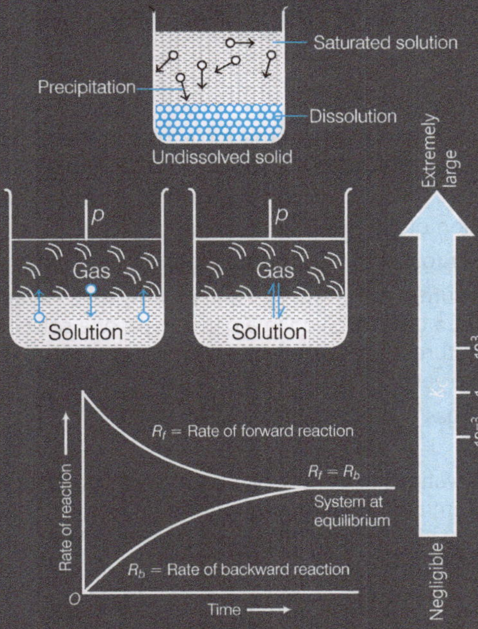

Topicwise No. of Ques asked in 5 Years

Topics	No. of Questions				
	2024	2023	2022	2021	2020
Equilibrium in Physical and Chemical Processes along with Dynamic Equilibrium	–	1	–	–	–
Law of Chemical Equilibrium and Equilibrium Constant	2	1	–	–	–
Homogeneous and Heterogeneous Equilibrium and Application of Equilibrium Constant	1	–	–	–	–
Relationship Between *K*, *Q* and *G* and Factors Affecting Equilibria	–	1	1	–	–
Ionic Equilibrium and Acids, Bases and Salts	–	–	–	–	–
Ionisation of Acids and Bases	–	–	–	–	1
Buffer Solutions	–	–	1	1	–
Solubility Equilibria of Sparingly Soluble salts	–	–	1	–	1

Special Type of Ques asked in 5 Years

Types	Years				
	2024	2023	2022	2021	2020
Statement Based	–	0	–	–	–
A-R	–	–	–	–	–
Matching	–	0	–	–	–

Last 5 Years Weightage (NEET)

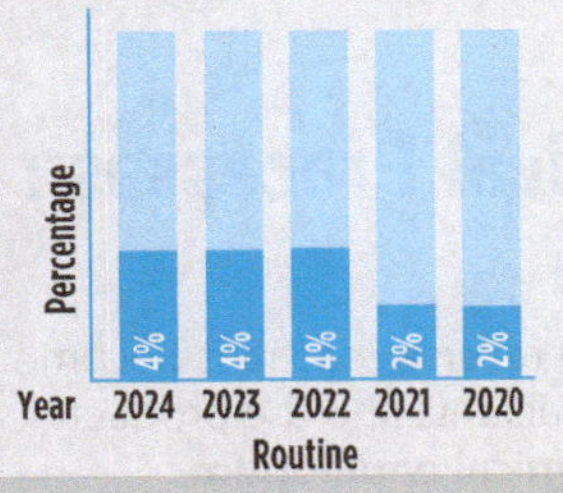

06

Scan for **Chemistry Through Concept Master** *Videos*

Equilibrium

- In a reversible reaction, the point at which there is no further change in concentration of reactants and products is called **equilibrium state.** For example, at equilibrium, the rate of evaporation is equal to the rate of condensation. It may be represented by

$$H_2O(l) \rightleftharpoons H_2O(\text{vap.})$$

- The mixture of reactants and products in the equilibrium state is called an **equilibrium mixture.**
- The concept of equilibrium is applicable for both physical and chemical processes.
- At equilibrium, the forward and reverse process take place at equal rates, hence it is called **dynamic equilibrium.**
- Equilibrium involving ions in aqueous solutions is called as **ionic equilibrium.**

Equilibrium in Physical Processes

A **physical equilibrium** is a state at which two phases of a compound can co-exist and an equilibrium is established between these two states.

The most familiar examples are phase transformation processes

e.g.

$$\text{Solid} \rightleftharpoons \text{Liquid}$$
$$\text{Liquid} \rightleftharpoons \text{Gas}$$
$$\text{Solid} \rightleftharpoons \text{Gas}$$

Solid-Liquid Equilibrium

Ice along with water in a insulated flask at 0°C and atmospheric pressure goes to equilibrium which explains that the mass of ice and water remains constant.

$$\text{Ice} \rightleftharpoons \text{Water}$$

At equilibrium, rate of melting of ice = rate of freezing of water.

Freezing point/melting point The temperature at which the solid-liquid equilibrium is reached for a pure substance under 1 atm is called normal melting/ freezing point of the substance.

Liquid-Vapour Equilibrium

At a particular temperature and normal atmospheric pressure, in a closed container the amount of water, (liquid) and water (vapours) remains constant.

Rate of evaporation of water = rate of condensation of water vapours.

$$H_2O(l) \rightleftharpoons H_2O\text{ (vap.)}$$

At equilibrium, the pressure exerted by the water molecules at a given temperature remains constant and is called the equilibrium vapour pressure of water.

The liquid which has a higher vapour pressure is more volatile and has a lower boiling point.

Boiling point The temperature at which liquid-gas equilibrium is attained for a pure substance under 1 atm is called **normal boiling point** of the substance. It depends on the altitude of the place, at high altitude the boiling point decreases.

Solid-Vapour Equilibrium

Certain solids on heating directly change from solid to vapour state (sublimation), in equilibrium, the concentration of solid becomes equal to gas.

e.g.

$$I_2(s) \rightleftharpoons I_2\text{ (vap.)}$$

$$\text{Camphor}(s) \rightleftharpoons \text{Camphor (vap.)}$$

Equilibrium Involving Dissolution of Solid or Gases in Liquids

Solids in liquids

- When a solution become saturated then, no more solute can be dissolved at a given temperature.
- In a saturated solution, when saturation point is reached, the amount of undissolved solid solute and the concentration of solid solute in the solution remains constant. At this stage a dynamic equilibrium exists between the solute molecules in the solid state and in the solution.

For example, in saturated solution of sugar,

Sugar (solution) $\rightleftharpoons$ Sugar (solid), and the rate of dissolution of sugar = rate of crystallisation of sugar.

Gases in Liquids

- When a soda water bottle is opened, some of the carbon dioxide gas dissolved in it fizzes out rapidly.
- The phenomenon arises due to difference in solubility of carbon dioxide at different pressures.
- There is equilibrium between the molecules in the gaseous state and the molecules dissolved in the liquid under pressure.
- For dissolution of gases in liquids, i.e.

$$CO_2\text{(gas)} \rightleftharpoons CO_2\text{(in solution)}$$

This equilibrium is governed by **Henry's law**, which states that, mass of a gas dissolved in a given mass of a solvent at any temperature is proportional to the pressure of the gas above the solvent.

- Solubility of gas in liquid decreases with increase of temperature.
- All the observations about dissolution of solids or gases in liquids are summarised in following table.

Process	Conclusion
Liquid $\rightleftharpoons$ Vapour $H_2O(l) \rightleftharpoons H_2O(g)$	p_{H_2O} constant at given temperature.
Solid $\rightleftharpoons$ Liquid $H_2O(s) \rightleftharpoons H_2O(l)$	Melting point is fixed at constant pressure.
Solute $(s) \rightleftharpoons$ Solute (solution) Sugar $(s) \rightleftharpoons$ Sugar (solution)	Concentration of solute in solution is constant at a given temperature.
Gas $(g) \rightleftharpoons$ Gas (aq)	[gas (aq)]/[gas (g)] is constant at a given temperature.
$CO_2(g) \rightleftharpoons CO_2(aq)$	$[CO_2(aq)]/[CO_2(g)]$ is constant at a given temperature.

General Characteristics of Equilibria Involving Physical Processes

Some important characteristics of physical equilibrium are as follows

- Equilibrium is possible only in a closed system at a given temperature.
- All the measurable properties of the system remains constant.
- Both the opposing processes occur at the same rate and there is a dynamic but stable condition.
- The physical equilibrium is characterised by constant value of one of its parameter (such as melting point) at a given temperature.
- The magnitude of such quantities at any stage indicates the extent to which the physical process has proceeded before reaching equilibrium.

Equilibrium in Chemical Processes : Dynamic Equilibrium

When the rates of the forward and reverse reactions become equal, the concentrations of the reactants and the products remain constant. This is called **chemical equilibrium**.

- This equilibrium is dynamic in nature as it consists of a forward reaction in which the reactants give products and reverse reaction in which product(s) gives the original reactants.
- The equilibrium can be attained only if the system is a closed one. The variation of concentration of reactants and products in a reversible reaction can be seen as,

$$A + B \rightleftharpoons C + D$$

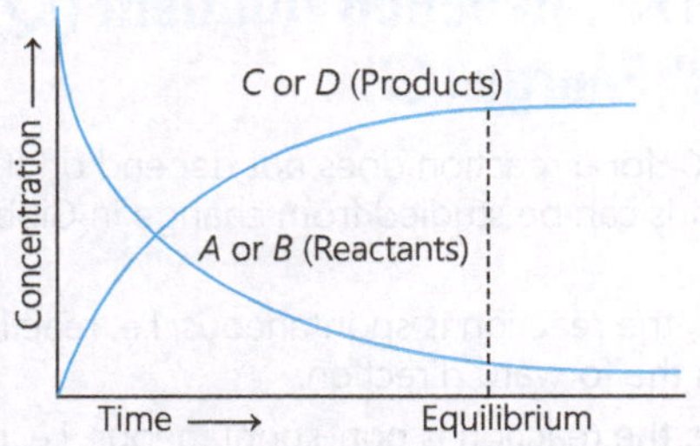

Attainment of chemical equilibrium

Law of Chemical Equilibrium and Equilibrium Constant

Law of chemical equilibrium states that, the value obtained by dividing the product of concentration of the reaction products raised to the respective stoichiometric coefficient in a balanced chemical equation by the product of concentration of reactants raised to their individual stoichiometric coefficients is constant. i.e.

For a reversible reaction,

$$aA + bB \rightleftharpoons cC + dD$$

$$K_C = \frac{[C]^c [D]^d}{[A]^a [B]^b}$$

where, [*A*], [*B*], [*C*] and [*D*] are molar concentration of *a*, *b*, *c* and *d* at equilibrium and K_C is **equilibrium constant**, which is expressed in mol L^{-1}.

Note The above equilibrium equation is also known as law of mass action.

The characteristics of equilibrium constant are as follows

- Expression for equilibrium constant is applicable only when concentrations of the reactants and products have attained constant value at equilibrium state.
- The value of equilibrium constant is independent of initial concentrations of the reactants and products.
- Equilibrium constant is temperature dependent having one unique value for a particular reaction represented by a balanced equation at a given temperature.
- The equilibrium constant for the reverse reaction is equal to the inverse of the equilibrium constant for the forward reaction.
- The equilibrium constant (*K*) for a reaction is related to the equilibrium constant of the corresponding reaction, whose equation is obtained by multiplying or dividing the equation for the original reaction by a small integer.
- Relations between equilibrium constants for a general reaction and its multiples

Chemical equation	Equilibrium constant
$aA + bB \rightleftharpoons cC + dD$	K_C
$cC + dD \rightleftharpoons aA + bB$	$K_C' = \left(\frac{1}{K_C}\right)$
$naA + nbB \rightleftharpoons ncC + ndD$	$K_C'' = (K_C^n)$

Homogeneous Equilibria

For **homogeneous equilibria**, all the reactants and products are in the same phase.

e.g. $\quad N_2(g) + 3H_2(g) \rightleftharpoons 2NH_3(g)$

Equilibrium constant in gaseous system

$$K_p = \frac{[p_{NH_3}]^2}{[p_{N_2}][p_{H_2}]^3}$$

Relation between K_p and K_C is given by

$$K_p = K_C(RT)^{\Delta n}$$

where, Δn = (number of moles of gaseous products) – (number of moles of gaseous reactants).

Heterogeneous Equilibria

Equilibrium in a system which having more than one phase is called **heterogeneous equilibrium**.

It involves pure solids or liquids.

e.g. $\quad CaCO_3(s) \overset{\Delta}{\rightleftharpoons} CaO(s) + CO_2(g)$

$$K_C = \frac{[CaO(s)][CO_2(g)]}{[CaCO_3(s)]}$$

Since, $[CaCO_3(s)]$ and $[CaO(s)]$ are both constant, therefore modified equilibrium constant for the thermal decomposition of calcium carbonate will be

$$\therefore \quad K'_C = [CO_2(g)] \text{ and } K_p = p_{CO_2}$$

Units of Equilibrium Constant

- Concentration of a substance is measured in terms of moles/litre, therefore unit of K_C is $(\text{mol L}^{-1})^{\Delta n}$
- Partial pressure is measured in terms of atmosphere, therefore unit of K_p is $(\text{bar})^{\Delta n}$.

  1 atm = 1.013 bar, 1 bar = 10^5 Pa.

  So, 1 atm = 1.013×10^5 Pa
- If $\Delta n = 0$, both K_C and K_p have no units.
- If $\Delta n > 0$, unit of $K_C = (\text{mol L}^{-1})^{\Delta n}$, unit of $K_p = (\text{bar})^{\Delta n}$
- If $\Delta n < 0$, unit of $K_C = (\text{L mol}^{-1})^{\Delta n_g}$, unit of $K_p = (\text{bar}^{-1})^{\Delta n_g}$

- Equilibrium constants can also be expressed as dimensionless quantities if the standard state of reactants and products are specified.
- Value of equilibrium constant explains the thermodynamic stability of products. Greater the value of K, greater will be the stability of products and instability of reactants.

Applications of Equilibrium Constants

The value of equilibrium constant is helpful in many ways.

Predicting the Extent of a Reaction

- The numerical value of the equilibrium constant for a reaction indicates the extent of the reaction.
- An equilibrium constant does not give any information about the rate at which the equilibrium is reached.
- If $K_C > 10^3$, products predominates over reactants and if K_C is very large,reaction proceeds nearly to completion.
- If $K_C < 10^{-3}$, then reactants predominates over products and reaction proceeds rarely.
- If K_C is in the range 10^{-3} to 10^3, appreciable concentrations of both reactants and products are present.

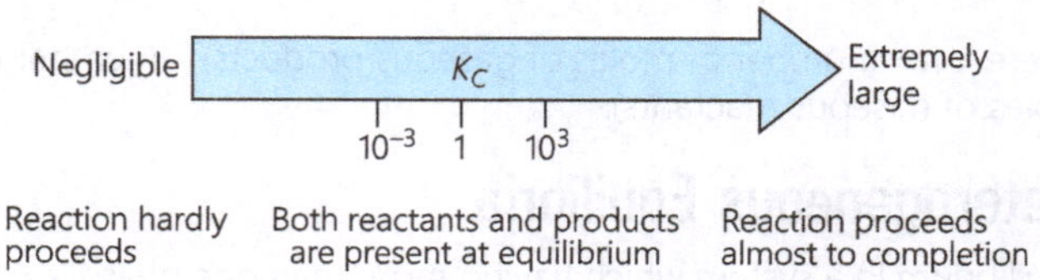

Dependence of extent of reaction on K_C

Predicting the Direction of a Reaction

If the reaction is not at equilibrium, then 'Q' reaction quotient is expressed instead of K_C.

[Q_C with molar concentration and Q_p with partial pressures]

A reaction proceeds as :

$$aA + bB \rightleftharpoons cC + dD$$

$$\text{Thus, } Q_C = \frac{[C]^c\,[D]^d}{[A]^a\,[B]^b}$$

- If $Q = K_C$, reaction at equilibrium.
- If $Q < K_C$, reaction proceeds in forward direction.
- If $Q > K_C$, reaction proceeds in backward direction.

Calculating Equilibrium Concentrations

For the calculation of equilibrium concentration, the following steps shall be followed:

- First of all write the balanced equation for the reaction.
- Check the initial concentration, change in concentrations on going to equilibrium and equilibrium concentration.
- After that, consider the equilibrium concentration as x and put it into the equilibrium equation for getting the value of x.
- Finally check the result by substituting the values into the equilibrium equation.

Relationship between Equilibrium Constant (K), Reaction Quotient (Q) and Gibbs' Energy (G)

The value of K_C for a reaction does not depend on the rate of the reaction. It is can be studied from change in Gibb's energy (ΔG).

- If $\Delta G = -$ve, the reaction is spontaneous, i.e. reaction proceeds in the forward direction.
- If $\Delta G = +$ ve, the reaction is non-spontaneous, i.e. reaction proceeds in the backward direction.
- If $\Delta G = 0$, reaction has achieved equilibrium.
- Gibb's free energy and reaction quotient are related as

$$\Delta G = \Delta G° + RT \ln Q$$

where, $\Delta G°$ = Standard Gibbs energy

At equilibrium, $\Delta G = 0$ and $Q = K$, therefore the equation becomes

$$\Delta G° = -RT \ln K \quad \text{or} \quad \ln K = \frac{-\Delta G°}{RT}$$

Taking antilog on both sides, we get

$$K = e^{-\Delta G°/RT}$$

- The equation, $K = e^{-\Delta G°/RT}$ helps in predicting the spontaneity of the reaction as,
  - If $\Delta G° < 0; e^{-\Delta G°/RT} > 1 \Rightarrow K > 1$

    Therefore, forward reaction is spontaneous i.e. product formed predominantly.
  - If $\Delta G° > 0; e^{-\Delta G°/RT} < 1 \Rightarrow K < 1$

    Therefore, forward reaction is non-spontaneous, i.e. product formed in very less quantity.

Factors Affecting Equilibria

Le-Chatelier's Principle According to this principal, "if any of the factors that determine the equilibrium condition of a system is changed, the system will move in such a direction, so that effect of the change is reduced or nullified or opposed."

Different factors affecting equilibrium are as follows

For Concept Master Video

(i) **Effect of concentration change** Change in the concentration of either reactant(s) or product(s), shift the reaction in such a direction in which the effect of change is minimised or nullified.

For reaction, $PCl_5(g) \rightleftharpoons PCl_3(g) + Cl_2(g); \Delta H = +$ ve

- Addition of PCl_3 or Cl_2 or removal of PCl_5 will shift the equilibrium in backward direction.
- Addition of PCl_5 or removal of PCl_3 and Cl_2 will shift the equilibrium in forward direction.

(ii) **Effect of pressure change** Increase in pressure, shifts the equilibrium in that direction, where the number of moles of the gas or pressure decreases and *vice-versa*.

For reaction,

$$PCl_5(g) \rightleftharpoons PCl_3(g) + Cl_2(g);\ \Delta H = +\text{ ve}$$

- Increase of pressure will favour the reaction in backward direction, with decrease in the number of gaseous molecules.
- Decrease of pressure will favour the reaction in forward direction.

(iii) **Effect of temperature change** High temperature favours endothermic reaction and low temperature favours exothermic reaction.

For reaction,

$$PCl_5(g) \rightleftharpoons PCl_3(g) + Cl_2(g);\ \Delta H = +\text{ ve}$$

The dissociation of PCl_5 is endothermic. Hence, increase of temperature increases the rate of formation of PCl_3 and Cl_2.

(iv) **Effect of inert gas addition** At constant volume, there is no effect of addition of inert gas. While, at constant pressure, when inert gas is added, reaction goes in the direction in which there is an increase in the number of moles of the gases.

For reaction,

$$PCl_5(g) \rightleftharpoons PCl_3(g) + Cl_2(g);\ \Delta H = +\text{ ve}$$

In this reaction, $n_p > n_r$ addition of an inert gas has no effect at constant volume but, at constant pressure, the equilibrium shifts in the forward direction.

(v) **Effect of catalyst** A catalyst increases the rate of forward reaction as well as the backward reaction, so it does not effect the equilibrium and equilibrium constant.

Marks Maximizer

Some important examples of Le-Chatelier's principle.

- **Haber's Process of Synthesis of Ammonia**

$$N_2(g) + 3H_2(g) \rightleftharpoons 2NH_3(g);\ \Delta H = -22.4\text{ kcal}$$

The favourable conditions are

– high concentration of N_2 or / and H_2

– high pressure (as $\Delta n = -2$)

– low temperature (as the reaction is exothermic)

- **Dissociation of HI**

$$2HI(g) \rightleftharpoons H_2(g) + I_2(g);\ \Delta H = +\text{ve}$$

The favourable conditions are

– high concentration of HI

– unaffected by pH

– high temperature (as the reaction is exothermic)

Ionic Equilibrium in Solution

- Equilibria that involve ions only are studied under different class called **ionic equilibrium**.
- Michael Faraday classified the substances into two categories based on their ability to conduct electricity. i.e. **electrolytes** and **non-electrolytes**.
- **Strong electrolytes** on dissolution in water are ionised completely, while the **weak electrolytes** are only partially dissociated.
- In weak electrolytes, an equilibrium is established between ions and unionised molecules, leading to an ionic equilibrium in the aqueous solution. Acids, bases and salts may be classified as weak or strong electrolytes.

Acids, Bases and Salts

- The word "acid" has been derived from a Latin word "acidus" meaning sour. They turn blue litmus paper into red and liberate dihydrogen on reacting with some active metals. e.g. HCl, CH_3COOH etc.
- Bases are known to turn red litmus paper into blue. e.g. NaOH, KOH, $Ba(OH)_2$ etc.
- When acids and bases are mixed in the right proportion they react with each other to give salts. e.g. NaCl, $BaSO_4$ etc.

Different Theories Related to Acids and Bases

There are three main concepts related to acids and bases.

1. Arrhenius Concept of Acids and Bases

- **Acids** Furnish/release H^+ ions in their aqueous solution.
- **Bases** Furnish/release OH^- ions in their aqueous solution.

Examples $\underset{\text{(Acid)}}{HCl} \longrightarrow H^+ + Cl^-$; $\underset{\text{(Base)}}{NaOH} \longrightarrow Na^+ + OH^-$

Limitations of Arrhenius Concept

- It does not explain the acidic character of certain compounds like CO_2, SO_2, $AlCl_3$ etc., and basic character of some compounds like Na_2CO_3, NH_3 etc., which do not give H^+ and OH^- ions respectively.
- It does not explain the behaviour of acids and bases in the absence of water.
- It does not explain the nature of H^+ and OH^- ions in water.

2. The Bronsted-Lowry Acids and Bases

- **Acids** A substance which can give/donate a proton (H^+)
- **Bases** A substance which can accept a proton (H^+)

e.g.

Add proton

$$\underset{\text{Base}}{NH_3(aq)} + \underset{\text{Acid}}{H_2O(l)} \rightleftharpoons \underset{\text{Conjugate acid}}{NH_4^+(aq)} + \underset{\text{Conjugate base}}{OH^-(aq)}$$

Loses proton

- The acid-base pair which differ only by a proton are said to form a conjugate **acid-base pair**.
- If Bronsted acid is a strong acid, then its conjugate base is weak and *vice-versa*.
- Water can donate as well as accept a proton, i.e. water can act both as acid as well as base. Hence, water is **amphoteric** or **amphiprotic** in nature.
- If two acids (with respect to water) are mixed together then the weaker acid will act as a base with respect to the stronger acid. The acid base pair that differs only by one proton **conjugate acid-base pair**.

Conjugate pair

e.g. $$\underset{\text{Acid}_1}{HClO_4} + \underset{\text{Base}_2}{H_2SO_4} \rightleftharpoons \underset{\text{Acid}_2}{H_3SO_4^+} + \underset{\text{Base}_1}{ClO_4^-}$$

Conjugate pair

- All Lewis bases are also Bronsted bases and *vice-versa* because a Lewis base having a tendency to donate a pair of electrons can also accept a proton and can behave as Bronsted base also.

3. Lewis concept

- **Acids** Accept a pair of electrons, i.e. acids are electron deficient compounds.
- **Base** Donate a pair of electrons to form coordinate bonds, i.e. bases are electron rich compounds.

Example $\underset{\text{(Acid)}}{H^+} + \underset{\text{(Base)}}{OH^-} \longrightarrow H_2O$

Types of Lewis Acids Include

- Compounds in which the central atom has incomplete octet, e.g. $GaCl_3$, $MgCl_2$, $BeCl_2$ etc.
- Compounds in which the central atom has available or partially filled *d*-orbital, e.g. PF_3, PF_5, SF_4
- All simple cations like Na^+, Fe^{3+}, Ca^{2+}, H^+, etc.
- Molecules with multiple bonds between dissimilar atoms, e.g. $O=C=O$, $O=S=O$, SO_3 etc.

Types of Lewis Bases Include

- All simple anions, like Cl^-, F^-, OH^-, CN^-, etc.
- Molecules with one or two unshared (lone) pairs, e.g. $H_2\ddot{O}$, $\ddot{N}H_3$, $R\ddot{O}H$, $R_2\ddot{O}$, $R_2\ddot{S}$, pyridine, etc.

Multiple bonded compounds which form co-ordination compounds with transition metals, e.g. CO, NO, etc.

In coordination compounds, the ligands act as **Lewis base**

$$\underset{\substack{\text{Lewis acid}\\\text{(incomplete octet)}}}{BF_3} + \underset{\substack{\text{Lewis base}\\\text{(lone pair)}}}{\ddot{N}H_3} \longrightarrow \underset{\text{Acid base adduct}}{BF_3:NH_3}$$

Ionisation of Acids and Bases

- According to Arrhenius concept, strong acid and bases are that species which able to completely dissociate into their constituent ions is aqueous medium and produce H_3O^+ and OH^- ions respectively in the medium. e.g. $HClO_4$, H_2SO_4 are strong acids and NaOH, KOH are strong bases.
- According to Bronsted-Lowry concept of acids and bases, a strong acid is a good proton donor and a strong base is a good proton acceptor.

$$\underset{\text{acid}}{HA(aq)} + \underset{\text{base}}{H_2O(l)} \rightleftharpoons \underset{\text{Conjugate acid}}{H_3O^+(aq)} + \underset{\text{Conjugate base}}{A^-(aq)}$$

- In above reaction the equilibrium will shift towards the forward direction.
- The conjugate base obtained from a strong acid is weak and that obtained from a weak acid is strong.

e.g. ClO_4^-, HSO_4^- are weak conjugate base.

The Ionisation Constant of Water and its Ionic Product

- **Ionic Product** The product of the concentrations of ions present in a given solution taking the stoichiometry into account is called ionic product.
- The ionisation constant of water and its ionic product is given as

$$K_w = [H_3O^+]\,[OH^-] = [H^+]\,[OH^-] = 1.0 \times 10^{-14}\ M^2 \text{ at } 298\ K$$

where, K_w is the ionic product of water.

- The value of K_w is temperature dependent as it is an equilibrium constant.
- The acidic, neutral and basic aqueous solutions can be distinguished by the relative values of the H_3O^+ and OH^- concentrations.

Acidic	:	$[H_3O^+] > [OH^-]$
Neutral	:	$[H_3O^+] = [OH^-]$
Basic	:	$[H_3O^+] < [OH^-]$

The pH Scale

- In order to represent, the hydronium ion concentration more conveniently in terms of molarity, **Sorensen** introduced scale, called pH scale.

$$pH = -\log [H^+]$$

If $pH < 7$, acidic solution, $pH = 7$ neutral, if $pH > 7$, basic solution.

- pK_w is a very important quantity for aqueous solutions and controls the relative concentrations of hydrogen and hydroxyl ions as their product is a constant. i.e.

$$pK_w = pOH + pH = 14$$

Marks Maximizer

For a binary electrolyte *AB*,

	$AB \rightleftharpoons$	A^+	$+ B^-$
Initial conc.	C	0	0
Conc. at equilibrium	$C(1-\alpha)$	$C\alpha$	$C\alpha$

where, α is degree of dissociation/ionisation.

$$\text{Degree of dissociation }(\alpha) = \frac{\text{Number of moles dissociated}}{\text{Total number of moles taken}}$$

Ionisation Constants of Weak Acids

- For a reaction,

	$HX(aq) + H_2O(l) \rightleftharpoons$	$H_3O^+(aq)$	$+ X^-(aq)$
Initial conc.	C	0	0
Conc. at equilibrium	$C(1-\alpha)$	$C\alpha$	$C\alpha$

The **acid ionisation** or dissociation constant (K_a) is given as,

$$K_a = \frac{[H^+][X^-]}{[HX]} = \frac{C\alpha^2}{1-\alpha}$$

- For a weak electrolyte,

If $\alpha << 1 \Rightarrow (1-\alpha) \approx 1$ and degree of ionisation (α) is given as,

$$\alpha = \sqrt{\frac{K_a}{C}}$$

or $$\propto \frac{1}{\sqrt{C}} \propto \sqrt{V} \qquad \left(\because C \propto \frac{1}{V}\right)$$

- For strong electrolytes, $\alpha = 1$
  - K_a is called the dissociation or ionisation constant of acid *HX*. At a given temperature *T*, K_a is a measure of the strength of the acid *HX*.
  - K_a is a dimensionless quantity. The larger the value of K_a, stronger is the acid.

Marks Maximizer

The degree of dissociation is proportional to the square root of volume for weak electrolytes. This is the statement of **Ostwald's dilution law.**

Ionisation Constant of Weak Base

For a reaction,

	$MOH(aq) \rightleftharpoons$	$M^+(aq)$	$+ OH^-(aq)$
Initial conc.	C	0	0
conc. at equilibrium	$C(1-\alpha)$	$C\alpha$	$C\alpha$

The base ionisation constant is represented by K_b and is given as

$$K_b = \frac{[M^+][OH^-]}{[MOH]} = \frac{C\alpha^2}{1-\alpha}$$

and degree of ionisation is given as, $\alpha = \sqrt{\frac{K_b}{C}}$

Higher the value of K_b, more basic is the base.

Relation between K_a and K_b

- The equilibrium constant for a net reaction obtained after adding two (or more) reactions equal to the product of the equilibrium constants for individual reactions.

$$K_{Net} = K_1 \times K_2 \times \ldots.$$

In case of a conjugate acid-base pair.

$$K_a \times K_b = K_w$$

- **The p*K* value of the conjugate acid and base** are related to each other by the equation :

$$pK_a + pK_b = pK_w = 14 \text{ (at 298 K)}$$

Here, $pK_a = -\log K_a$ and $pK_b = -\log K_b$

Di and Polybasic Acids and Di and Polyacidic Bases

- Acids having more than one ionisable proton per molecule of acids are known as **polybasic** or **polyprotic acids**. For **dibasic acids**, like H_2X have two ionisation constants and for tribasic **acids** like H_3PO_4, have three ionisation constants. Each ionisation has its own ionisation constant.
- It is more difficult to remove a positively charged proton from a negative ion due to electrostatic forces that's why, the higher order ionisation constants (K_{a_2}, K_{a_3}) are smaller than lower order ionisation constant (K_{a_1}).

Factors Affecting Acid Strength

- The extent of dissociation of an acid depends on the strength and polarity of the H — *A* bond.
- When strength of H — *A* bond decreases that is, the energy required to break the bond decreases, *HA* becomes a stronger acid.

- When the H — *A* bond becomes more polar, i.e. the electronegativity difference between the atoms H and *A* increases, cleavage of the bond becomes easier thereby increasing the acidity. e.g.

Size increases →

HF << HCl << HBr << HI

Acidic strength increases →

Electronegativity increases →

$CH_4 << NH_3 < H_2O < HF$

Acidic strength increases →

Common Ion Effect in the Ionisation of Acids and Bases

For Concept Master Video

- A shift in equilibrium on adding a substance that provides more of an ionic species already present in the dissociation equilibrium. This phenomenon is called as **common ion effect**.
- Ionisation of a weak acid (H*A*) decreases in the presence of a strong acid such as HCl because H^+ as common ion combines with A^- to form H*A*.

Hydrolysis of Salts and the pH of their Solutions

- The salts formed by reaction between acids and bases get ionised in water and exist as hydrated ions.
- The reaction of ions with water is known as **hydrolysis** or salt **hydrolysis**.
- The salts formed by reaction between strong acids and strong bases are neutral as the cations of strong bases and anions of strong acids simply get hydrated and do not get hydrolysed.

Depending upon the nature of acid and base from which a salt is obtained, the salts are categorised into three types as tabulated below

Salt of	Example	K_h (hydrolysis constant)	Hydrolysis	Resulting solution	*h* (degree of hydrolysis)	pH of solution
Weak acid and strong base	CH_3COONa	$\frac{K_w}{K_a}$	Anionic	Alkaline, pH > 7	$\sqrt{\frac{K_w}{K_a \cdot C}}$	$\frac{1}{2}pK_w + \frac{1}{2}pK_a + \frac{1}{2}\log C$
Strong acid and weak base	NH_4Cl	$\frac{K_w}{K_b}$	Cationic	Acidic, pH < 7	$\sqrt{\frac{K_w}{K_b \cdot C}}$	$\frac{1}{2}pK_w - \frac{1}{2}pK_b - \frac{1}{2}\log C$
Weak acid and weak base	CH_3COONH_4	$\frac{K_w}{K_a \cdot K_b}$	Anionic and cationic both	Neutral, pH = 7 (If $K_a = K_b$)	$\sqrt{\frac{K_w}{K_a \cdot K_b}}$	$\frac{1}{2}pK_w + \frac{1}{2}pK_a - \frac{1}{2}pK_b$

Buffer Solutions

The solutions which resist change in their pH on dilution or an addition of small amounts of acid or alkali are called **buffer solutions**.

Buffers are classified into two categories

- **Simple buffers** These are the solutions of salts of weak acid and weak base. e.g. CH_3COONH_4.
- **Mixed buffers** These are the mixtures of two solutions.
  The different types of mixed buffer solutions are as follows :
- A buffer solution having pH less than 7 is called as an **acidic buffer**, e.g. $CH_3COOH + CH_3COONa$.
  To prepare a buffer of acidic pH, used weak acid and its salt formed with strong base.
  The pH of an acidic and basic buffer is given by **Henderson-Hasselbalch equation** as

$$pH = pK_a + \log \frac{[\text{Conjugate base}/A^-]}{[\text{Acid}/HA]}$$

or, $$pH = pK_a + \log \frac{[\text{Salt}]}{[\text{Acid}]}$$

- A buffer solution having pH greater than 7 is called as **basic buffer**, e.g. $NH_4OH + NH_4Cl$. The pH of basic buffer is given by

$$pOH = pK_b + \log \frac{[\text{Conjugate acid}/BH^+]}{[\text{Base}/B]}$$

or $$pOH = pK_b + \log \frac{[\text{Salt}]}{[\text{Base}]}$$

In terms of pH, it can be written as

$$pH = pK_a + \log \frac{[\text{Conjugate acid}/BH^+]}{[\text{Base}/B]}$$

Note If molar concentration of base and its conjugate acid is same, then the pH of the buffer solution will be same as the pK_a value for the base.

Marks Maximizer

- Buffer capacity (ϕ)

$$= \frac{\text{Number of moles of acid or base added to 1L of buffer}}{\text{Change in pH}}$$

Buffer capacity is maximum

(i) When [salt] = [acid], i.e. pH = pK_a for acidic buffer

(ii) When [salt] = [base], i.e. pH = 14 – pK_b or $pK_w - pK_b$ for basic buffer

- The ability of buffer solution to resist changes in pH on addition of acid or base is called **buffer action** and range of pH over which the buffer solution remain effective is called **buffer range**.

Buffer	Range in pH
Acidic	$pK_a \pm 1$
Basic	$(pK_w - pK_b) \pm 1$

Solubility Equilibria of Sparingly Soluble Salts

- Lattice enthalpy and solvation enthalpy play a key role in deciding the solubility of salts in a particular solvent.
- As if a salt has to be dissolved in a solvent the strong forces of attraction between its ions (lattice enthalpy) must be overcome by the ion-solvent interactions.

  ∴ Lattice enthalpy < Solvation enthalpy
  - The amount of solvation enthlapy is depend on the nature of the solvent.
  - In case of a non-polar (covalent) solvent, solvation enthalpy is small, i.e., not sufficient to overcome lattice enthalpy of the salt.
  - Salt does not dissolve in non-polar solvent. In this case solvation enthlapy < lattice energy.
- Depending upon the solubility, salts are categorised into three groups.

Category I	Soluble	Solubility > 0.1M
Category II	Slightly soluble	0.01 M < Solubility < 0.1M
Category III	Sparingly soluble	Solubility < 0.01M

Solubility Product Constant

A solid salt of the general formula, $M_x^{p+}X_y^{q-}$ with molar solubility '*S*' in equilibrium with its saturated solution may be represented by the equation.

$$M_xX_y(s) \rightleftharpoons xM^{p+}(aq) + yX^{q-}(aq)$$

$$K_{sp} = [M^{p+}]^x[X^{q-}]^y = (xS)^x(yS)^y = x^x y^y S^{(x+y)}$$

$$S^{(x+y)} = K_{sp}/x^x y^y \Rightarrow S = (K_{sp}/x^x y^y)^{1/x+y}$$

where, K_{sp} is called the **solubility product**.

Common Ion Effect on Solubility of Ionic Salts

- If a common ion is added (increases the concentration) to a solution then solubility of the ions is decreases. This is *vice-versa* of concentration decreases.
- Increases in the concentration of one of the ions, it should combine with the ion of its opposite charge and some of the salt will be precipitated, till once again any salt get added.

$$K_{sp} = Q_{sp}.$$

Applications of K_{sp}

- The value of Q_{sp} (ionic product) and K_{sp} (solubility product) are helpful for **predicting, whether a precipitate is formed or not.**

  In general, – if $Q_{sp} > K_{sp}$, then precipitation takes place.
  – if $Q_{sp} < K_{sp}$, then no precipitation takes place.
  – if $Q_{sp} = K_{sp}$, the reaction is at equilibrium.
- **Predicting solubility of sparingly soluble salt** This can be calculated from its solubility product at a given temperature.

$$AB \rightleftharpoons \underset{S}{A^+} + \underset{S}{B^-}$$

$$K_{sp} = [A^+][B^-] = S^2 \Rightarrow S = \sqrt{K_{sp}}$$

- The solubility of salts of weak acids like phosphates increases with decrease in pH as at lower pH, the anion gets protonated and, hence its concentration decreases.
- **Qualitative analysis** Principle of selective precipitation is used in qualitative analysis of a mixture containing all the common cations.
- **Purification of common salt** HCl gas is circulated through the saturated solution of common salt (NaCl). Thus, the concentration of Cl^- ions increases considerably in the solution due to ionisation of HCl. Hence, the ionic product $[Na^+][Cl^-]$ exceeds for their K_{sp} value and therefore, pure NaCl precipitates out from the solution.

Marks Maximizer

Solubility products of different types of electrolytes.

Type of salt	Example	Solubility (S)	Solubility constant of (K_{sp})
Binary electrolyte 1 : 1 (XY type)	NaCl, AgCl	$\sqrt{K_{sp}}$	S^2
Ternary electrolyte 1 : 2 (XY_2 type)	$Ca(OH)_2$, CaF_2	$\sqrt[3]{K_{sp}/4}$	$4S^3$
Ternary electrolyte 2 : 1 (X_2Y type)	Ag_2CO_3, Ag_2CrO_4	$\sqrt[3]{K_{sp}/4}$	$4S^3$
Quaternary electrolyte 1 : 3 type	$AlCl_3$, $Fe(OH)_3$	$\sqrt[4]{K_{sp}/27}$	$27S^4$
2 : 3 type	Bi_2S_3	$\sqrt[5]{K_{sp}/108}$	$108\,S^5$
3 : 2 type	$Ca_3(PO_4)_2$	$\sqrt[5]{K_{sp}/108}$	$108\,S^5$

Caution Points

- The same equilibrium mixture is achieved with or without the catalyst, but the equilibrium is established more quickly in the presence of a catalyst.
- The solubility in water of a species and extent of ionisation are differ from each other. e.g. NH_3 is very soluble in water (≈ 15 mol L^{-1} at 25°C). However, in 0.1 M solution, NH_3 is only 1.3% ionised and 98.3% non-ionised.
- When the ionic product is less than the solubility product, the solution is unsaturated and the solution contain only ions and no undissociated salt.
- Greater the value of ionisation constant of the acid or base, smaller is the pK_a and stronger is the acid or base.
- A decrease in pH by one unit indicates 10 times increases in hydronium ion concentration.

PYQ Notes

1. Phenolphthalein shows colour change in the pH range of 3.5-/4.6. **JEE 2022**
2. AgCl has most solubility in deionised water. **JEE 2022**
3. Effect of temperature on equilibrium constant is explained with the help of van't Hoff equation. **NEET 2014**

$$\log \frac{K_2}{K_1} = \frac{\Delta H^\circ}{2.303R}\left[\frac{T_2 - T_1}{T_1 T_2}\right]$$

Here, K_1 and K_2 are the equilibrium constants at temperature T_1 and T_2 respectively.

– ΔH° is the enthalpy of reaction.

$R =$ gas constant

– If $T_2 > T_1$ and ΔH° is positive (endothermic reaction), then $K_2 > K_1$.

– If $T_2 < T_1$ and ΔH° is negative (exothermic reaction), then $K_2 < K_1$.

Step by Step

Mastering NCERT

- Concept Builders
- Topical Questions
- Assertion-Reason
- Statement Type
- Matching Type
- Numerical Value
- NCERT Exemplar's
- Past Exams'
- Skill Boosters

Concept Builders

1 The classification of chemical equilibrium is based on the .... (speed/extent) to which the reaction proceeds.

2 The liquid which has higher vapour pressure is less volatile and has lower boiling point. [T/F]

3 Name the equilibrium which is present in 'ice and water, when kept in closed system at 273 K and at atmosphere pressure'?

4 In a saturated solution of sugar, the rate of dissolution of sugar becomes equal to the rate of .... of sugar because of the existence of .... equilibrium.

5 For the equation, $2SO_3(g) \rightleftharpoons 2SO_2(g) + O_2(g)$ the value of K_p is less than K_C. [T/F]

6 For a reaction in which H_2 and I_2 is involved, the equilibrium state of reaction can detected by merely looking at the .... of purple colour.

7 The value of K_C and K_p is same for the reaction, $N_2(g) + 3H_2(g) \rightleftharpoons 2NH_3(g)$. [T/F]

8 The reaction will proceed in the direction of reactants if .... $(Q_C > K_C / Q_C < K_C)$

9 The expression of reaction quotient and equilibrium constant is same for reaction at equilibrium. [T/F]

10 $\Delta G = \Delta G° + RT \ln Q$, where Q is reaction quotient. At equilibrium reaction quotient becomes equal to equilibrium constant K and the value of ΔG ....

11 Direction of a reversible reaction at equilibrium conditions is governed by the principle known as ....

12 The reaction $CaCO_3(s) \rightleftharpoons CaO(s) + CO_2(g)$ has positive value of ΔH. The production of lime can be increased by .... of CO_2. (addition/removal)

13 Addition of inert gas at constant volume and temperature affects the equilibrium as total pressure is increased. [T/F]

14 Catalyst lowers the activation energy of forward reaction but increases the activation energy of backward reaction. [T/F]

15 Adding a catalyst to a reaction at equilibrium changes neither Q nor .... $[K_{eq} / K_C]$.

16 Write the name of one of the species which can act both as a Bronsted acid as well as a Bronsted base.

17 Arrhenius concept of acid and base is applicable to non aqueous solution only. [T/F]

18 Phenolphthalein and bromothymol blue are weak bases and used as indicators in acid-base titrations. [T/F]

19 Given, pK_w $(H_2O) = 6.77$ at 40°C, the nature of the solution having pH = 7 at 40°C.

20 If the concentration of hydrogen ion of soft drink sample is 3.8×10^{-3} M, then its pH is 4.5. [T/F]

21 What is the decreasing order of K_b values of the following bases → Ammonia, Aniline, Pyridine and Urea.

22 The ionisation constant of the 0.08 M acid is 2.5×10^{-5}. Its pH is 2.85 and it's percent dissociation is ....

23 Higher order ionisation constant are smaller in magnitude as compare to lower order ionisation constants of a polyprotic acid. [T/F]

24 A compound of the type ZOH is either a hydroxide or an ....

25 Oxalic acid, sulphonic acid and phosphoric acids are known as .... (polyacidic/polybasic).

26 The interaction of cation/anion of salt with water to form corresponding acid/base is called ....

27 The solution which resist change in pH on dilution or with the addition of small amounts of acid or alkali is called ....

28 The solubility product refers to a saturated solution. [T/F]

29 Write the formula for solubility product constant of the following equation.

$$BaSO_4(s) \xrightleftharpoons[\text{in water}]{\text{Saturated solution}} Ba^{2+}(aq) + SO_4^{2-}(aq)$$

30 The solubility of salts of weak acids like phosphates .... (increases/decreases) at lower pH.

Topical Questions

Equilibrium in Physical and Chemical Process alongwith Dynamic Equilibrium

1 Consider the following statements regarding physical processes. NCERT Pg 169

I. Equilibrium is possible only in a closed system at a given temperature.

II. Both the opposing processes occur at the same rate and there is a dynamic but stable condition.

III. Equilibrium is static in nature.

IV. When equilibrium is attained for a physical process, it is characterised by constant value of one of its parameters at a given temperature.

Which of the following statement is incorrect?

(a) Only II (b) Only I (c) Only IV (d) Only III

2 Which of the following statement is incorrect? NCERT Pg 171

(a) In solid $\rightleftharpoons$ liquid equilibrium, there exists one temperature and pressure at which the two phases can co-exist.

(b) For liquid $\rightleftharpoons$ vapour equilibrium, the vapour pressure is constant at a given temperature.

(c) For dissolution of solids in liquids, the solubility is constant at a given temperature.

(d) For dissolution of gases in liquids, the concentration of a gas in liquid is independent of the pressure of the gas over the liquid.

3 Which one of the following statements is incorrect about chemical equilibrium? NCERT Pg 172

(a) Chemical equilibrium is attained whether we start with reactants or products.

(b) Chemical equilibrium is dynamic in nature.

(c) Chemical equilibrium, $CaCO_3(s) \rightleftharpoons CaO(s) + O_2(g)$ is attained, when $CaCO_3(s)$ is heated in an open vessel.

(d) At equilibrium, the concentration of each of the reactants and products becomes constant.

4 Consider the graph given below and choose the incorrect statement regarding it. NCERT Pg 172

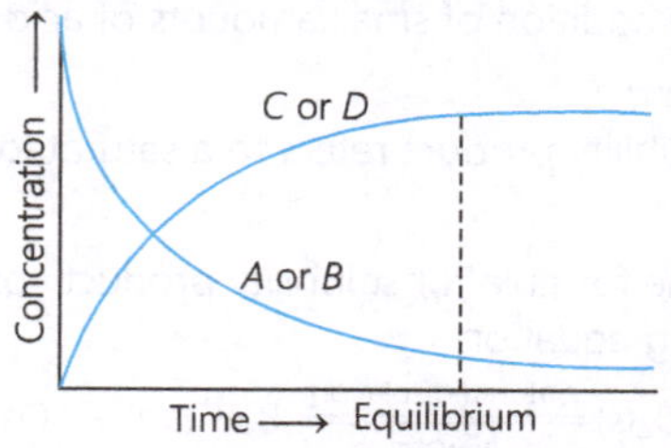

(a) The given graph represents the attainment of equilibrium for a reversible reaction, $A + B \rightleftharpoons C + D$

(b) The rate of forward reaction decreases and that of reverse reaction increases.

(c) The two reactions occur at the same rate.

(d) The reaction can reach the state of equilibrium only if it starts with *A* and *B*.

5 In the chemical reaction,

$$N_2 + 3H_2 \rightleftharpoons 2NH_3$$

at equilibrium point, NCERT Pg 174

(a) equal volumes of N_2 and H_2 are reacting

(b) equal masses of N_2 and H_2 are reacting

(c) the reaction has stopped

(d) the same amount of ammonia is formed, as it is decomposed into N_2 and H_2

6 Consider the following graph and choose the incorrect statements. NCERT Pg 174

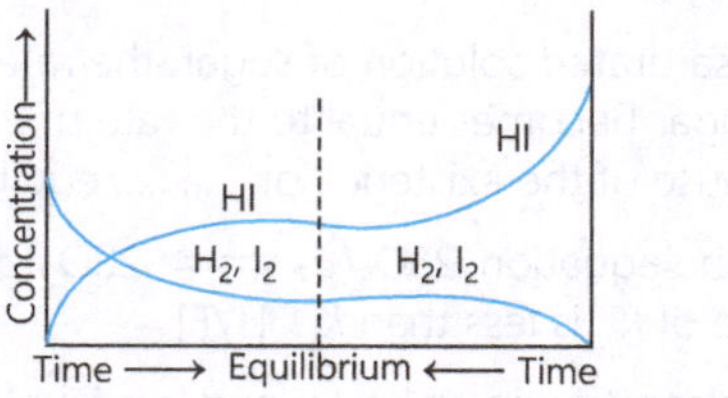

(a) If total number of H and I atoms are same in a given volume, then same equilibrium mixture is obtained.

(b) Chemical equilibrium in the reaction $H_2(g) + I_2(g) \rightleftharpoons 2HI(g)$ can be attained from reactant side only.

(c) The concentration of H_2 and I_2 decreases while that of HI increases with time.

(d) The reaction can proceed in the reverse direction by starting with HI alone.

7 Consider the following graph and mark the correct statement. NCERT Pg 174

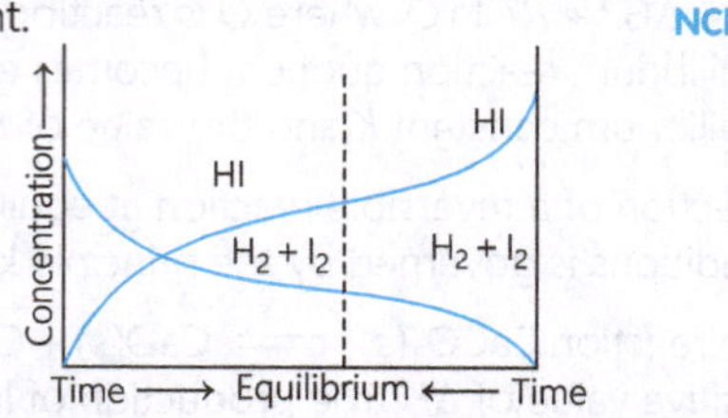

(a) Chemical equilibrium in the reaction, $H_2 + I_2 \rightleftharpoons 2HI$ can be attained from either directions.

(b) Equilibrium can be obtained when H_2 and I_2 are mixed in an open vessel.

(c) The concentrations of H_2 and I_2 keep decreasing while concentration of HI keeps decreasing with time.

(d) We can find out equilibrium concentration of H_2 and I_2 from the given graph.

8 Consider the following statements about the graph given below, NCERT Pg 174

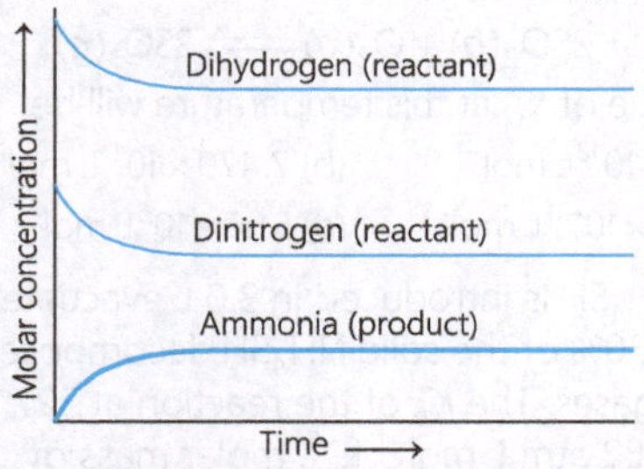

I. After a certain time, the composition of the mixture remains same.

II. The reaction mixture starting with either H_2 or D_2 reach equilibrium with same composition.

III. The constancy in composition indicates that the reaction has reached equilibrium.

Choose the correct answer from the options given below.

(a) Only I (b) Only II
(c) I and III (d) I, II and III

Law of Chemical Equilibrium and Equilibrium Constant

9 In the following equilibrium reaction

$$2A \rightleftharpoons B + C$$

the equilibrium concentration of A, B and C are 1×10^{-3} M, 2×10^{-3} M and 3×10^{-3} M respectively at 300 K. The value of K_C for this equilibrium at the same temperature is

(a) $\frac{1}{6}$ (b) 6 (c) $\frac{1}{36}$ (d) 360

10 Given that, equilibrium constant for the reaction,

$$2SO_2(g) + O_2(g) \rightleftharpoons 2SO_3(g)$$

has a value 278 at a particular temperature.

What is the value of the equilibrium constant for the following reaction at the same temperature?

$$SO_3(g) \rightleftharpoons SO_2(g) + \frac{1}{2}O_2(g)$$ NCERT Pg 176

(a) 1.8×10^{-3} (b) 3.6×10^{-3} (c) 6×10^{-2} (d) 1.3×10^{-5}

11 1.1 mol of A and 2.2 mol of B reach an equilibrium in 1 L container according to the reaction $A + 2B \rightleftharpoons 2C + D$. If at equilibrium 0.1 mol of D is present, the equilibrium constant is NCERT Pg 176

(a) 0.001 (b) 0.002
(c) 0.003 (d) 0.004

12 For the reaction, NCERT Pg 176

$$2SO_2(g) + O_2(g) \longrightarrow 2SO_3(g),$$

$\Delta H = -57.2$ kJ mol^{-1} and $K_C = 1.7 \times 10^{16}$.

Which of the following statement is incorrect?

(a) The equilibrium constant decreases as the temperature increases.

(b) The addition of inert gas at constant volume will not affect the equilibrium constant.

(c) The equilibrium will shift in forward direction as the pressure increases.

(d) The equilibrium constant is large suggestive of reaction going to completion and so no catalyst is required.

13 Two moles of HI were heated in a sealed tube at 440°C till the equilibrium was reached. HI was found to be 22% decomposed. The equilibrium constant for dissociation is NCERT Pg 177

(a) 0.282 (b) 0.0796
(c) 0.0199 (d) 1.99

14 For the reaction,

$$N_2(g) + O_2(g) \rightleftharpoons 2NO(g),$$

the equilibrium constant is K_1. The equilibrium constant is K_2 for the reaction,

$$2NO(g) + O_2(g) \rightleftharpoons 2NO_2(g).$$

What is K for the reaction ?

$$NO_2(g) \rightleftharpoons \frac{1}{2}N_2(g) + O_2(g)$$ NCERT Pg 177

(a) $\frac{1}{(K_1K_2)}$ (b) $\frac{1}{(2K_1K_2)}$ (c) $\frac{1}{(4K_1K_2)}$ (d) $\left[\frac{1}{K_1K_2}\right]^{1/2}$

15 Consider the following reversible chemical reactions,

$$A_2(g) + B_2(g) \overset{K_1}{\rightleftharpoons} 2AB(g) \quad \text{...(i)}$$

$$6AB(g) \overset{K_2}{\rightleftharpoons} 3A_2(g) + 3B_2(g) \quad \text{...(ii)}$$

The relation between K_1 and K_2 is NCERT Pg 177

(a) $K_2 = K_1^3$ (b) $K_1K_2 = 3$
(c) $K_2 = K_1^{-3}$ (d) $K_1K_2 = \frac{1}{3}$

16 For the reaction,

$$I_2(g) \rightleftharpoons 2I(g);\ K_C = 37.6 \times 10^{-6}$$

at 1000 K. If 1.0 mole of I_2 is introduced into a 1.0 L flask at 1000 K, at equilibrium NCERT Pg 177

(a) $[I_2] > [I]$ (b) $[I_2] = [I]$
(c) $[I_2] < [I]$ (d) Unpredictable

17 When 3 moles of ethyl alcohol are mixed with 3 moles of acetic acid, 2 moles of ester are formed at equilibrium. According to the equation, NCERT Pg 177

$$CH_3COOH(l) + C_2H_5OH(l) \rightleftharpoons CH_3COOC_2H_5(l) + H_2O(l)$$

The value of the equilibrium constant for the reaction is

(a) 4 (b) 2/9
(c) 2 (d) 4/9

Homogeneous and Heterogeneous Equilibrium and its Applications

18 In the following reactions/equilibria, the number of reactions in which K_p is less than K_C? **NCERT Pg 178**

I. $N_2O_4(g) \rightleftharpoons 2NO_2(g)$

II. $2HI\ (g) \rightleftharpoons H_2(g) + I_2(g)$

III. $2SO_2(g) + O_2(g) \rightleftharpoons 2SO_3(g)$

IV. $N_2(g) + O_2(g) \rightleftharpoons 2NO\ (g)$

V. $N_2(g) + 3H_2(g) \rightleftharpoons 2NH_3(g)$

(a) 2 (b) 3 (c) 5 (d) 4

19 For reaction in equilibrium,

$$H_2(g) + I_2(g) \rightleftharpoons 2HI(g)$$

Choose the incorrect option. **NCERT Pg 178**

(a) $K_C = \frac{[HI(g)]^2}{[H_2(g)]\ [I_2(g)]}$

(b) $K_p = \frac{[HI(g)]^2\ [RT]^2}{[H_2(g)]RT \cdot [I_2(g)]\ RT}$

(c) $K_p = K_C$

(d) $K_p \neq K_C$, i.e. both equilibrium constants are not equal.

20 For the reaction,

$$SO_2(g) + \frac{1}{2}O_2(g) \rightleftharpoons SO_3(g)$$

if $K_p = K_C(RT)^x$ where the symbols have usual meaning, then the value of x is (assuming ideality). **NCERT Pg 178**

(a) -1 (b) $-\frac{1}{2}$

(c) $\frac{1}{2}$ (d) 1

21 Consider the reaction,

$$N_2(g) + 3H_2(g) \rightleftharpoons 2NH_3(g)$$

The equilibrium constant of the above reaction is K_p. If pure ammonia is left to dissociate, the partial pressure of ammonia at equilibrium is given by (Assume that $p_{NH_3} << p_{total}$ at equilibrium) **NCERT Pg 178**

(a) $\frac{3^{3/2} K_p^{1/2} p^2}{4}$ (b) $\frac{3^{3/2} K_p^{1/2} p^2}{16}$

(c) $\frac{K_p^{1/2} p^2}{16}$ (d) $\frac{K_p^{1/2} p^2}{4}$

22 At a certain temperature and total pressure of 10^5 Pa, iodine vapour contains 40% by volume of I-atoms.

$$I_2(g) \rightleftharpoons 2I(g)$$

The value of K_p for the equilibrium is **NCERT Pg 178**

(a) 2.67×10^4 Pa (b) 7.2×10^5 Pa

(c) 3.67×10^5 Pa (d) 4.66×10^7 Pa

23 At 450 K, $K_p = 2.0 \times 10^{10}\ bar^{-1}$ for the given reaction at equilibrium,

$$2SO_2(g) + O_2(g) \rightleftharpoons 2SO_3(g)$$

The value of K_C at this temperature will be **NCERT Pg 178**

(a) $6.4 \times 10^{12} L\ mol^{-1}$ (b) $7.479 \times 10^{11} L\ mol^{-1}$

(c) $7.00 \times 10^{-11} L\ mol^{-1}$ (d) $5.66 \times 10^6 L\ mol^{-1}$

24 5.1 g NH_4SH is introduced in 3.0 L evacuated flask at 327°C. 30% of the solid NH_4SH decomposed to NH_3 and H_2S as gases. The K_p of the reaction at 327°C is ($R = 0.082$ atm L mol^{-1} K^{-1}, molar mass of $S = 32$ g mol^{-1} molar mass of N = 14 g mol^{-1})

(a) $0.242 \times 10^{-4}\ atm^2$ (b) $0.242\ atm^2$ **NCERT Pg 178**

(c) $4.9 \times 10^{-3}\ atm^2$ (d) $1 \times 10^{-4}\ atm^2$

25 For the following equilibrium,

$$N_2O_4(g) \rightleftharpoons 2NO_2(g)$$

K_p is found to be equal to K_C. This is attained when (where, $R = 0.0821$ atm L $mol^{-1}K^{-1}$

(a) $T = 1$ K (b) $T = 273$ K **NCERT Pg 178**

(c) $T = 12.18$ K (d) $T = 17.15$ K

26 $\frac{K_p}{K_C}$ for the reaction

$$CO(g) + \frac{1}{2}O_2(g) \rightleftharpoons CO_2(g) \text{ will be}$$

NCERT Pg 178

(a) 1 (b) RT (c) $\frac{1}{\sqrt{RT}}$ (d) $(RT)^{\frac{1}{2}}$

27 The equilibrium,

$$N_2(g) + O_2(g) \rightleftharpoons 2NO(g)$$

is established in a reaction vessel of 2.5L capacity. The amount of N_2 and O_2 taken at the start were respectively 2 moles and 4 moles. Half mole of nitrogen has been used at equilibrium. The molar concentration of nitric oxide is **NCERT Pg 179**

(a) 0.2 (b) 0.4 (c) 0.6 (d) 0.1

28 The equilibrium constant for the reaction,

$$H_2(g) + CO_2(g) \rightleftharpoons H_2O(g) + CO(g)$$ **NCERT Pg 179**

is 1.80 at 1000°C. If 1.0 mole of H_2 and 1 mole of CO_2 are placed in 1 L flask, the final equilibrium concentration of CO at 1000°C is

(a) 0.573 M (b) 0.385 M

(c) 5.73 M (d) 0.295 M

29 The partial pressure of carbon monoxide from the following data will be

$$CaCO_3(s) \overset{\Delta}{\rightleftharpoons} CaO(s) + CO_2\uparrow;\ K_{p_1} = 8 \times 10^{-2}$$

$$CO_2(g) + C(s) \rightleftharpoons 2CO(g);\ K_{p_2} = 2$$ **NCERT Pg 180**

(a) 0.2 atm (b) 0.6 atm (c) 0.8 atm (d) 0.4 atm

30 Which of the following statement is incorrect? NCERT Pg 187

(a) In general, the temperature dependence of the equilibrium constant depends on the sign of ΔH for the reaction.
(b) The equilibrium constant for an exothermic reaction (negative, ΔH) increase as the temperature increases.
(c) The equilibrium constant for an endothermic reaction (positive, ΔH) increases as the temperature increases.
(d) Temperature changes affect the equilibrium constant and rates of reactions.

31 The value of K_C for the reaction, $2A \rightleftharpoons B + C$ is 2×10^{-3}. At a given time, the composition of reaction mixture is $[A] = [B] = [C] = 3 \times 10^{-4}$ M. In which direction, the reaction will proceed? NCERT Pg 182

(a) Forward direction
(b) Reverse direction
(c) At equilibrium
(d) Direction of the reaction cannot be predicted.

32 For the reaction,

$H_2(g) + I_2(g) \rightleftharpoons 2HI(g)$; $K_C = 57.0$ at 700 K.

The molar concentration of $[H_2] = 0.10$ M, $[I_2] = 0.20$ M and $[HI] = 0.40$ M.

The reaction quotient, Q_C of the reaction is NCERT Pg 182

(a) 10.0 (b) 7.0 (c) 8.0 (d) 12.0

33 Consider the following figure which shows dependence of extent of reaction on K_C.

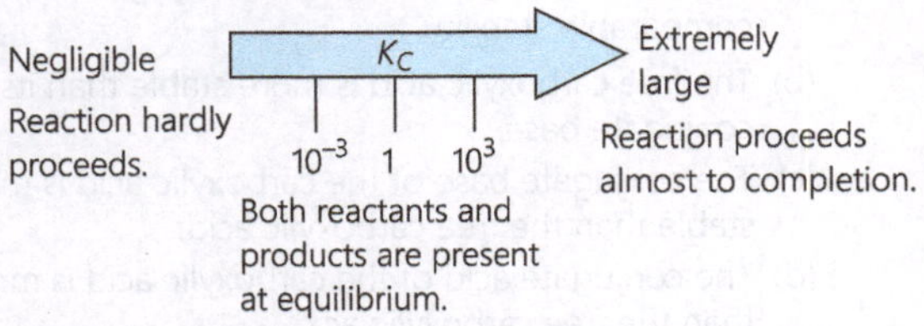

Point out of the incorrect statement for the above graph. NCERT Pg 182

(a) If $K_C > 10^3$, products predominate over reactants, i.e. if K_C is very large, the reaction proceeds nearly to completion.
(b) If $K_C < 10^{-3}$, reactants predominate over products, i.e. if K_C is very small, the reaction proceeds rarely.
(c) If K_C is in the range of 10^{-3} to 10^3, appreciable concentrations of both reactants and products are present
(d) If $K_C > 10^3$, reactants predominate over products, i.e. if K_C is very small, the reaction proceeds nearly to completion.

34 In the following reaction,

$$2NO(g) + Cl_2(g) \rightleftharpoons 2NOCl(g)$$

It is observed that equilibrium is not attained and the rate of forward reaction is greater than rate of backward reaction. Which of the following is true for the reaction? NCERT Pg 182

(a) $K_p = Q_p$ (b) $Q_p > K_p$ (c) $Q_p < K_p$ (d) $Q_p \neq 0$.

Relationship Between *K*, *Q* and *G* and Factors affecting Equilibria

35 The free energy of formation of NO is 78 kJ mol^{-1} at the temperature of an automobile engine (1000 K). What is the equilibrium constant for this reaction at 1000 K?

$$\frac{1}{2}N_2(g) + \frac{1}{2}O_2(g) \longrightarrow NO(g)$$

(Value of antilog is replace by $-4.0237 = 8.439 \times 10^{-5}$)

(a) 8.4×10^{-5} (b) 7.1×10^{-9} NCERT Pg 184
(c) 4.2×10^{-10} (d) 1.7×10^{-19}

36 Using the equation ($K = e^{-\Delta G°/RT}$), the reaction spontaneity can be interpreted in terms of the value of $\Delta G°$ as NCERT Pg 184

(a) if $\Delta G° < 0$, the reaction proceeds in the forward direction to such an extent that the products are present predominantly.
(b) if $\Delta G° > 0$, the reaction proceeds in the backward direction to such a small extent that only a very minute quantity of product is formed.
(c) $\Delta G° < 0$, the reaction yield is very poor.
(d) $\Delta G° > 0$, the reaction is spontaneous at standard conditions.

37 The value of $\Delta G°$ for the phosphorylation of glucose in glycolysis is 13.8 kJ/mol. The value of K_C at 298 K is

(a) 7.72×10^{-4} (b) 5.62×10^{-4} NCERT Pg 184
(c) 4.81×10^{-3} (d) 3.81×10^{-3}

38 Hydrolysis of sucrose gives,

$$\text{Sucrose} + H_2O \rightleftharpoons \text{Glucose} + \text{Fructose}$$

Equilibrium constant (K_C) for the reaction is 2×10^{13} at 300 K. The value of $\Delta G°$ at 300 K is NCERT Pg 184

(a) 3.52×10^5 J mol^{-1} (b) 5.12×10^5 J mol^{-1}
(c) 7.64×10^4 J mol^{-1} (d) -7.64×10^4 J mol^{-1}

39 Which of the following statements is incorrect regarding equilibrium state? NCERT Pg 184

(a) The value of ΔG at equilibrium is zero.
(b) The reaction ceases at equilibrium.
(c) Equilibrium constant is independent of initial concentrations of reactants.
(d) Catalysts have no effect on equilibrium state.

40 Which one of the following informations can be obtained on the basis of Le-Chatelier's principle? NCERT Pg 185

(a) Dissociation constant of a weak acid.
(b) Entropy change in a reaction.
(c) Equilibrium constant of a chemical reaction.
(d) Dissociation constant of a strong acid.

41 For the reaction $PCl_5(g) \rightleftharpoons PCl_3(g) + Cl_2(g)$, the forward reaction at constant temperature is favoured by NCERT Pg 185

(a) introducing an inert gas at constant volume
(b) introducing Cl_2 at constant volume
(c) introducing PCl_5 at constant volume
(d) reducing the pressure of container.

42 A pressure change obtained by changing the volume can affect the yield of products in case of a gaseous reaction, where NCERT Pg 186

(a) the total number of moles of gaseous reactants and total number of moles of gaseous products are different
(b) the total number of moles changes with doubled the volume.
(c) number of moles of reactants > number of moles of products
(d) number of moles of reactants < number of moles of products

43 Which of the following statements for a given reaction is incorrect? NCERT Pg 186

$$\underset{\text{Yellow}}{Fe^{3+}(aq)} + \underset{\text{Colourless}}{SCN^-(aq)} \rightleftharpoons \underset{\text{Deep red}}{[Fe(SCN)]^{2+}(aq)}$$

(a) The equilibrium constant,
$$K_C = \frac{[Fe(SCN)^{2+}(aq)]}{[Fe^{3+}(aq)][SCN^-(aq)]}$$
(b) A reddish colour appears on adding two drops of 0.002 M potassium thiocyanate solution to 1 mL of 0.2 M iron (III) nitrate solution due to the formation of $[Fe(SCN)]^{2+}$. The intensity of the red colour becomes constant on attaining equilibrium.
(c) The equilibrium can be shifted in either forward or reverse directions depending on our choice of adding a reactant or a product.
(d) The equilibrium can be shifted in the same direction by adding reagents that remove Fe^{3+} or SCN^- ions.

44 Ostwald's process for the manufacture of nitric acid involves the reaction,

$$4NH_3(g) + 5O_2(g) \rightleftharpoons 4NO(g) + 6H_2O(l); \Delta H = +Q\,kJ$$

Which of the following factors will not affect the concentration of NH_3 at equilibrium? NCERT Pg 188

(a) Addition of catalyst (b) Decrease of temperature
(c) Increase of pressure (d) Increase of volume

Ionic Equilibrium and Concepts of Acids, Bases and Salts

45 Which of the following statement is incorrect? NCERT Pg 188

(a) Conductance of electricity increases with an increase in concentration of common salt in aqueous glucose solution.
(b) Aqueous solution of acetic acid mainly contains unionised acetic acid molecules and only some CH_3COO^- and H_3O^+ ions.
(c) In weak electrolytes equilibrium is established between ions and unionised molecules.
(d) Aqueous solution of sugar conducts electricity.

46 While, comparing the ionisation of hydrochloric acid with that of acetic acid in water we find that though both of them are polar covalent molecules, former is completely ionised into its constituent ions, while the latter is only partially ionised (< 5%).
The reason is that, NCERT Pg 189

(a) ionisation depends upon the strength of the bond and the extent of solvation of ions produced
(b) ionisation depends upon the strength of the bond only
(c) ionisation depends upon the extent of solvation of ions produced
(d) hydrochloric acid is stronger than acetic acid

47 Carboxylic acids readily dissolve in aqueous sodium bicarbonate, liberating carbon dioxide. Which one of the following statement is correct? NCERT Pg 191

(a) The free carboxylic acid and its conjugate base are of comparable stability.
(b) The free carboxylic acid is more stable than its conjugate base.
(c) The conjugate base of the carboxylic acid is more stable than the free carboxylic acid.
(d) The conjugate acid of the carboxylic acid is more stable than the free carboxylic acid.

48 Which of the following is least likely to behave as Lewis base? NCERT Pg 192

(a) OH^- (b) H_2O (c) NH_3 (d) BF_3

49 Which one of the following is the weakest acid? NCERT Pg 192

(a) HCl (b) HF (c) H_2SO_4 (d) HNO_3

50 Which of the following statement is incorrect regarding the formation of salt NaCl? NCERT Pg 189

(a) It exists in solid state as a cluster of positively charged chloride ions and negatively charged sodium ions.
(b) Sodium and chloride ions are held together due to electrostatic interactions between oppositely charged species.

(c) When sodium chloride is dissolved in water, the electrostatic interactions are reduced by a factor of 80.
(d) Ions of NaCl in water are free to move in the solution.

51 According to Bronsted-Lowry concept of acids and bases a conjugate acid-base pair can exist as

Conjugate pair

$$\underset{\text{Acid}}{HA} + \underset{\text{Base}}{B^-} \rightleftharpoons \underset{\text{Conjugate acid}}{BH} + \underset{\text{Conjugate base}}{A^-}$$

Conjugate pair

Mark the option in which conjugate pair is correctly matched. **NCERT Pg 190,191**

	Species	Conjugate acid	Conjugate base
(a)	HSO_4^-	H_2SO_4	SO_4^{2-}
(b)	H_2CO_3	HCO_3^-	CO_3^{2-}
(c)	HS^-	S^{2-}	H_2S
(d)	HPO_4^{2-}	$H_2PO_4^-$	H_2PO_4

Ionisation of Acids and Bases

52 The correct order of increasing $[H_3O^+]$ in the aqueous solution is
(a) $0.01 M\ H_2S < 0.01\ M\ H_2SO_4 < 0.01\ M\ NaCl < 0.01\ M\ NaNO_2$
(b) $0.01\ M\ NaCl < 0.01\ M\ NaNO_2 < 0.01\ M\ H_2S < 0.01\ M\ H_2SO_4$
(c) $0.01\ M\ NaNO_2 < 0.01\ M\ NaCl < 0.01\ M\ H_2S < 0.01\ M\ H_2SO_4$
(d) $0.01\ M\ H_2S < 0.01\ M\ NaNO_2 < 0.01\ M\ NaCl < 0.01\ M\ H_2SO_4$

53 The concentration of hydrogen ion in a sample of soft drink is 3.8×10^{-3}M. The value of its pH is **NCERT Pg 194**
(a) 4.32 (b) 5.12 (c) 3.31 (d) 2.42

54 2g of NaOH is dissolved in water to make 1L solution. The pH of solution is **NCERT Pg 194**
(a) 10.25 (b) 8.256 (c) 12.70 (d) 10.89

55 The pH of a mixture when a 50 mL solution of pH = 1 is mixed with a 50 mL of pH = 2 is [Given : log 5.5 = 0.74] **NCERT Pg 194**
(a) 0.56 (b) 1.26 (c) 1.76 (d) 2.06

56 Assuming complete ionisation, the pH of 0.1 M HCl is 1. The molarity of H_2SO_4 with the same pH is **NCERT Pg 194**
(a) 0.01 (b) 0.2 (c) 0.05 (d) 2.0

57 The pH 0.005 M codeine ($C_{18}H_{21}NO_3$) solution is 9.95. Its pK_b value is [Given : Antilog $(-4.05 = 8.913 \times 10^{-5})$]]
(a) 8.92 (b) 5.80 (c) 3.76 (d) 4.29 **NCERT Pg 194**

58 If 50 mL of 0.1 HBr is mixed with 50 mL 0.2 M NaOH, find pH of resulting mixture **NCERT Pg 194**
(a) 2.7 (b) 12.7 (c) 10.7 (d) 1.3

59 The dissociation constant of acetic acid at a given temperature is 1.69×10^{-5}. The degree of dissociation of 0.01 M acetic acid in the presence of 0.01 M HCl is equal to **NCERT Pg 195**
(a) 0.41×10^{-2} (b) 0.18×10^{-7}
(c) 0.169×10^{-2} (d) 0.013×10^{-4}

60 A 0.2 molar solution of formic acid is 3.2% ionised. Its ionisation constant is **NCERT Pg 195**
(a) 9.6×10^{-3} (b) 2.1×10^{-4}
(c) 1.25×10^{-6} (d) 4.8×10^{-5}

61 If the ionisation constant of acetic acid is 1.8×10^{-5}, at what concentration will it be dissociated to 2%?
(a) 1 M (b) 0.018 M **NCERT Pg 196**
(c) 0.18 M (d) 0.045 M

62 A 0.01 M ammonia solution is 5% ionised. The concentration of OH^- ion is **NCERT Pg 197**
(a) 0.005 M (b) 0.0001 M (c) 0.0005 M (d) 0.05 M

63 The pK_b for fluoride ion at 25°C is 10.83, the ionisation constant of hydrofluoric acid at this temperature is
(a) 2.72×10^{-5} (b) 3.52×10^{-3} **NCERT Pg 199**
(c) 6.76×10^{-4} (d) 5.38×10^{-2}

64 The equilibrium constants for the reaction,

$Zn(s) + Cu^{2+}(aq) \rightleftharpoons Zn^{2+}(aq) + Cu(s)$ and

$Cu(s) + 2Ag^+(aq) \rightleftharpoons Cu^{2+}(aq) + 2Ag(s)$

are K_1 and K_2 respectively. The equilibrium constant for the combined reaction is **NCERT Pg 199**
(a) $K_1 \times K_2$ (b) $K_1 + K_2$ (c) $K_1 - K_2$ (d) K_1/K_2

65 For the following three reactions (i), (ii) and (iii) equilibrium constants are given
(i) $CO(g) + H_2O(g) \rightleftharpoons CO_2(g) + H_2(g); K_1$
(ii) $CH_4(g) + H_2O(g) \rightleftharpoons CO_2(g) + 3H_2(g); K_2$
(iii) $CH_4(g) + 2H_2O(g) \rightleftharpoons CO_2(g) + 4H_2(g); K_3$
Which of the following relations is correct? **NCERT Pg 199**
(a) $K_3 \cdot K_2^3 = K_1^2$ (b) $K_1\sqrt{K_2} = K_3$
(c) $K_2 \cdot K_3 = K_1$ (d) $K_3 = K_1 \cdot K_2$

66 For a polybasic acid, the dissociation constant have a different values for each step, e.g.

$$H_3A \rightleftharpoons H^+ + H_2A^-; K = K_{a_1}$$
$$H_2A^- \rightleftharpoons H^+ + HA^{2-}; K = K_{a_2}$$
$$HA^{2-} \rightleftharpoons H^+ + A^{3-}; K = K_{a_3}$$

What is the observed trend of pK_a values in successive stages? NCERT Pg 200

(a) $pK_{a_1} > pK_{a_2} > pK_{a_3}$ (b) $pK_{a_1} = pK_{a_2} = pK_{a_3}$
(c) $pK_{a_1} < pK_{a_2} < pK_{a_3}$ (d) $pK_{a_1} = pK_{a_2} + pK_{a_3}$

67 If 0.02 M solution of pyridinium hydrochloride has pH = 3.44, then the ionisation constant of pyridine will be NCERT Pg 202

(a) $10^{-5.45}$ (b) $10^{-8.82}$
(c) $10^{-12.65}$ (d) $10^{-14.14}$

68 A 100 mL, 0.1 M solution of ammonium acetate is diluted by adding 100 mL of water. The pH of the resulting solution will be (pK_a of acetic acid is nearly equal to pK_b of NH_4OH) NCERT Pg 202

(a) 4.9 (b) 5.9
(c) 7.0 (d) 10.0

Buffer Solutions

69 100 mL of a solution contains 0.1 M NH_4OH and 0.1 M NH_4Cl. The pH of the solution will not change on adding. NCERT Pg 203

(a) 20 mL of 0.1 M NH_4OH solution
(b) 20 mL of 0.1 M NH_4Cl solution
(c) 10 mL of 0.1 M NaOH solution
(d) 10 mL of distilled water

70 Which of the following combinations of CH_3COOH + NaOH would result in the formation of acidic buffer? NCERT Pg 203

(a) 1 : 1 mol ratio (b) 2 : 1 mol ratio
(c) 1 : 2 mol ratio (d) 3 : 1 mol ratio

71 pK_a of NH_4^+ is 9.26. Hence, effective pH range for NH_4OH-NH_4Cl buffer is about NCERT Pg 203

(a) 8.26 to 10.26 (b) 4.74 to 5.74
(c) 3.74 to 5.74 (d) 8.26 to 9.26

72 The pH of a buffer solution will be equal to the pK_a of acid, only if NCERT Pg 203

(a) molar concentration of acid is greater than molar concentration of conjugate base
(b) molar concentration of acid is smaller than molar concentration of conjugate base
(c) molar concentration of acid is equal to the molar concentration of conjugate base
(d) molar concentration of acid is almost negligible

73 pH of a buffer prepared by adding 10 mL of 0.10 M acetic acid to 20 mL of 0.1M sodium acetate is equal to (pK_a of CH_3COOH = 4.74) NCERT Pg 203

(a) 4.74 (b) 5.6
(c) 5.04 (d) 6.02

74 The pK_a of HCN is 9.30. The pH of a solution prepared by mixing 2.5 moles of KCN and 2.5 moles of HCN in water and making up the total volume of 500 mL is NCERT Pg 203

(a) 9.30 (b) 7.30 (c) 10.30 (d) 8.30

75 A buffer solution is prepared in which the conc. NH_3 is 0.30 M and the concentration of NH_4^+ is 0.20 M. If the equilibrium constant, K_b for NH_3 equals 1.8×10^{-5}, what is the pH of this solution? NCERT Pg 203

(a) 8.73 (b) 9.08 (c) 9.44 (d) 11.72

76 One litre of a buffer solution containing 0.01 M NH_4Cl and 0.1 M NH_4OH having pK_b of 5 has pH of NCERT Pg 203

(a) 9 (b) 10 (c) 6 (d) 7

77 Which of the following statement is correct? NCERT Pg 203

(a) Acidic buffer consist of a strong acid and its salt with weak base in a fixed proportion.
(b) pH of the buffer solution changes by dilution.
(c) Natural buffer are the solution of salts of weak acid and weak base.
(d) Glycine + glycine hydrochloride is an example of acidic buffer.

78 A mixture of acetic acid and sodium acetate acts as buffer solution around pH *P* and a mixture of ammonium chloride and ammonium hydroxide acts as a buffer around pH *Q*. *P* and *Q* respectively are NCERT Pg 203

(a) 9.25 and 4.75 (b) 4.75 and 9.25
(c) 8.74 and 3.87 (d) 3.87 and 8.74

79 50 mL of 0.1 M NaOH is added to 75 mL of 0.1M NH_4Cl to make a basic buffer. If pK_a of NH_4^+ is 9.26, then the pH of solution is NCERT Pg 203

(a) 4.44 (b) 9.56 (c) 4.74 (d) 5.76

80 In the following solution, how many of them would act as buffer solution?

I. HNO_3 + NaOH
II. NH_4OH(excess) + HCl
III. $CH_3COOH + H_2CO_3$
IV. $\underset{\text{(excess)}}{NaCN}$ + HCN
V. CH_3COOH + NaOH(large excess) NCERT Pg 203

(a) 6 (b) 4 (c) 2 (d) 1

Solubility Equilibria of Sparingly Soluble Salts

81 At 25°C, K_{sp} for $PbBr_2$ is equal to 8×10^{-5}. If the salt is 80% dissociated, what is the solubility of $PbBr_2$ in mol/L? NCERT Pg 205

(a) $\left[\frac{10^{-4}}{1.6 \times 1.6}\right]^{\frac{1}{3}}$ (b) $\left[\frac{10^{-5}}{1.6 \times 1.6}\right]^{\frac{1}{3}}$

(c) $\left[\frac{10^{-4}}{0.8 \times 0.8}\right]^{\frac{1}{3}}$ (d) $\left[\frac{10^{-5}}{1.6 \times 1.6}\right]^{\frac{1}{2}}$

82 Solubility of AgI in presence of 0.2 M NaI solution will be (K_{sp} of AgI $= 8.3 \times 10^{-17}$) NCERT Pg 205

(a) 8.3×10^{-16} M (b) 4.15×10^{-17} M
(c) 4.15×10^{-16} M (d) 8.3×10^{-17} M

83 Calculate the volume of water required to dissolve 0.1g lead (II) chloride to get a saturated solution. (K_{sp} of $PbCl_2 = 3.2 \times 10^{-8}$ and atomic mass of Pb = 207 u) NCERT Pg 205

(a) 100 mL (b) 180 mL
(c) 120 mL (d) 150 mL

84 At 20°C, the Ag^+ ion concentration in a saturated solution of Ag_2CrO_4 is 1.5×10^{-4} mol/L. At 20°C, the solubility product of Ag_2CrO_4 will be NCERT Pg 205

(a) 3.3750×10^{-12}
(b) 1.6875×10^{-10}
(c) 1.6875×10^{-12}
(d) 1.6875×10^{11}

85 Solubility of calcium phosphate (molecular mass, M) in water is W g per 100 mL at 25°C. Its solubility product at 25°C will be approximately. NCERT Pg 205

(a) $10^7\left(\frac{W}{M}\right)^3$ (b) $10^7\left(\frac{W}{M}\right)^5$
(c) $10^5\left(\frac{W}{M}\right)^5$ (d) $10^3\left(\frac{W}{M}\right)^5$

86 If S_1, S_2, S_3 and S_4 are the solubilities of AgCl in water, in 0.01 M $CaCl_2$, in 0.01 M NaCl and in 0.05 M $AgNO_3$ respectively at a certain temperature, the correct order of solubilities is, NCERT Pg 205

(a) $S_1 > S_2 > S_3 > S_4$ (b) $S_1 > S_3 > S_2 > S_4$
(c) $S_1 > S_2 = S_3 > S_4$ (d) $S_1 > S_3 > S_4 > S_2$

87 The solubility product of a salt having general formula MX_2 in water is 4×10^{-12}. The concentration of M^{2+} ions in the aqueous solution of the salt is NCERT Pg 205

(a) 4×10^{-1} M (b) 1.6×10^{-4} M
(c) 1×10^{-4} M (d) 2×10^{-6} M

88 pH of saturated solution of $Ba(OH)_2$ is 12. The value of solubility product of K_{sp} of $Ba(OH)_2$ is NCERT Pg 205

(a) 3.3×10^{-7} (b) 5.0×10^{-7}
(c) 4.0×10^{-4} (d) 5.0×10^{6}

89 Calculate the solubility of A_2X_3 in pure water, assuming that neither kind of ion reacts with water. (Given, the solubility product of A_2X_3, $K_{sp} = 1.1 \times 10^{-23}$) NCERT Pg 205

(a) 2.0×10^{-5} mol L^{-1}
(b) 5.0×10^{-5} mol L^{-1}
(c) 1.0×10^{-5} mol L^{-1}
(d) 4.0×10^{-3} mol L^{-1}

90 What is the pH at which 0.01 M Co^{2+} ions in solution just precipitate as $Co(OH)_2$? K_{sp} of $Co(OH)_2 = 2.5 \times 10^{-16}$ NCERT Pg 205

(a) 6.3 (b) 7.3
(c) 10.8 (d) 7.7

91 The addition of NaCl to AgCl decreases the solubility of AgCl because NCERT Pg 206

(a) solubility product decreases
(b) solubility product remains constant
(c) solution becomes unsaturated
(d) solution becomes supersaturated

92 The solubility product (K_{sp}) of AgCl is 1.8×10^{-10}. Precipitation of AgCl will occur only when equal volumes of solutions of NCERT Pg 206

(a) 10^{-4} M Ag^+ and 10^{-4} M Cl^- are mixed
(b) 10^{-7} M Ag^+ and 10^{-7} M Cl^- are mixed
(c) 10^{-5} M Ag^+ and 10^{-5} M Cl^- are mixed
(d) 10^{-10} M Ag^+ and 10^{-10} M Cl^- are mixed

93 The solubility product (K_{sp}) of the sparingly soluble salt Ag_2CrO_4 is 4×10^{-12}. The molar solubility of the salt is NCERT Pg 206

(a) 1.0×10^{-4} mol L^{-1} (b) 2×10^{-6} mol L^{-1}
(c) 1.0×10^{-5} mol L^{-1} (d) 2×10^{-12} mol L^{-1}

94 The value of molar solubility of $Ni(OH)_2$ in 0.10 M NaOH. If the ionic product of $Ni(OH)_2$ is 2.0×10^{-15}. NCERT Pg 206

(a) 6.0×10^{-12} M (b) 8.0×10^{-13} M
(c) 2.0×10^{-13} M (d) 5.0×10^{-12} M

95 The solubility product (K_{sp}) of solid barium sulphate at 298 K is 1.1×10^{-10}. The molar solubility, (S) of $[Ba^{2+}]$ and $[SO_4^{2-}]$ are NCERT Pg 206

(a) 1.05×10^{-7} mol L^{-1} (b) 1.05×10^{-10} mol L^{-1}
(c) 1.05×10^{-6} mol L^{-1} (d) 1.05×10^{-5} mol L^{-1}

96 Calculate the molar solubility (S) of a salt like zirconium phosphate of molecular formula. $(Zr^{4+})_3(PO_4^{3-})_4$. NCERT Pg 206

(a) $\left(\frac{K_{sp}}{9612}\right)^{1/8}$ (b) $\left(\frac{K_{sp}}{6912}\right)^{1/7}$
(c) $\left(\frac{K_{sp}}{5348}\right)^{1/6}$ (d) $\left(\frac{K_{sp}}{8435}\right)^{1/7}$

97 The values of K_{sp} of two sparingly soluble salts $Ni(OH)_2$ and AgCN are 2.0×10^{-15} and 6×10^{-17} respectively. Which salt is more soluble? NCERT Pg 206

(a) $Ni(OH)_2$ is more soluble than AgCN.
(b) AgCN is more soluble than $Ni(OH)_2$.
(c) Both $Ni(OH)_2$ and AgCN soluble to same extent.
(d) $Ni(OH)_2$ is soluble but AgCN is insoluble.

Assertion-Reason Questions

Directions (Q. Nos. 1-10) *In the following question Assertion (A) followed by Reason (R) is given below. Choose the correct option out of the choices given below.*

(a) Both A and R are true and R is the correct explanation of A.
(b) Both A and R are true but R is not the correct explanation of A.
(c) A is true but R is false.
(d) A is false but R is true.

1 **Assertion** (A) For dissolution of gases in liquids, on increasing the temperature or decreasing the pressure the amount of gas dissolved decreases. NCERT Pg 171

Reason (R) For dissolution of gases in liquids, the concentration of a gas in liquid is inversely proportional to the pressure (concentration) of the gas over the liquid.

2 **Assertion** (A) When Cu(II) and sulphide ions are mixed, they react together extremely quickly to give a solid. NCERT Pg 175

Reason (R) The equilibrium constant of $Cu^{2+}(aq) + S^{2-}(aq) \rightleftharpoons CuS(s)$ is high because the solubility product is low.

3 **Assertion** (A) For any chemical reaction at a particular temperature, the equilibrium constant is fixed and is a characteristic property. NCERT Pg 176

Reason (R) Equilibrium constant is independent of temperature.

4 **Assertion** (A) $N_2O_4(g) \rightleftharpoons 2NO_2(g)$ is the example of homogeneous equilibria. NCERT Pg 178

Reason (R) For this reaction, K_C has unit L/mol and K_p has unit bar.

5 **Assertion** (A) If a volume is kept constant and an inert gas such as argon is added which does not take part in the reaction, the equilibrium remains undisturbed. NCERT Pg 187

Reason (R) The addition of an inert gas at constant volume does not change the partial pressure or the molar concentrations of the substance involved in the reaction.

6 **Assertion** (A) Higher order ionisation constant (K_{a_2}, K_{a_3}) are smaller than the lower order ionisation constant (K_{a_1}) of a polyprotic acid. NCERT Pg 200

Reason (R) It is more difficult to remove a positively charged proton from a negative ion due to Coulombic forces.

7 **Assertion** (A) Common ion effect is defined as a shift in equilibrium on adding a substance that provides more of an ionic species already present in the dissociation equilibrium. NCERT Pg 201

Reason (R) Common ion effect is a phenomenon based on the Le-Chatelier's principle.

8 **Assertion** (A) An aqueous solution of ammonium acetate can act as a buffer. NCERT Pg 202

Reason (R) Acetic acid is a weak acid and NH_4OH is a weak base.

9 **Assertion** (A) A solution containing a mixture of acetic acid and sodium acetate maintains a constant value of pH on addition of small amount of acid or alkali. NCERT Pg 203

Reason (R) A solution containing a mixture of acetic acid and sodium acetate acts as a buffer solution of around pH 4.75.

10 **Assertion** (A) A solution of $FeCl_3$ in water produces brown precipitate on standing. NCERT Pg 205

Reason (R) Hydrolysis of $FeCl_3$ takes place in water.

Statement Type Questions

Direction (Q. Nos. 1-6) *In the following questions, two statements (I & II) are given. In the light of the given statements, choose the correct option given below.*

(a) Both Statement I and Statement II are false.
(b) Statement I is true but Statement II is false.
(c) Statement I is false but Statement II is true.
(d) Both Statement I and Statement II are true.

1 **Statement I** At equilibrium, the reactants and products have reached the equilibrium concentrations. NCERT Pg 172

Statement II At equilibrium, the forward reaction and reverse reaction stop.

2 **Statement I** A large value for the equilibrium constant indicates that products are favoured equilibrium. NCERT Pg 181

Statment II The ratio of products to reactants is less than 1,for the forward reaction.

3 **Statement I** If an inert gas is added to a dissociation equilibrium keeping pressure cosntant, the dissociation increases. NCERT Pg 187

Statement II Inert gas exerts its own pressure in the vessel.

4 **Statement I** For $PCl_5(g) \rightleftharpoons PCl_3(g) + Cl_2(g)$ If more Cl_2 is added, the equilibrium will shift in backward direction hence, equilibrium constant will decrease. NCERT Pg 187

Statement II Addition of inert gas to the equilibrium mixture at constant volume, does not alter the equilibrium.

5 **Statement I** The amphoteric nature of water is explained by using Lewis acid/base concept. NCERT Pg 192

Statement II Water acts as an acid with NH_3 and as a base with H_2S.

6 **Statement I** The pH of water increases with increase in temperature. NCERT Pg 195

Statement II The dissociation of water in H^+ and OH^- is an exothermic reaction.

7 Which of the following statements are correct? NCERT Pg 168, 169, 172

I. The reactions stops to keep the concentrations constant at equilibrium.
II. A reaction at equilibrium means the velocity of both forward and backward reaction are equal.
III. According to law of mass action, the rate of a reaction is directly proportional to molalities of the reactants.
IV. A small value of equilibrium constant shows that the reaction is less in the forward direction and more in the backward direction.
V. At constant temperature, if a small amount of one of the products is removed, the equilibrium constant increases.

Choose the correct answer from the given option.

(a) I, II and III (b) II and IV
(c) I, II and IV (d) III, IV and V

8 Consider the following statements. NCERT Pg 185, 193, 194

I. The pH of a mixture containing 400 mL of 0.1 M H_2SO_4 and 400 mL of 0.1 M NaOH will be approximately 1.3.
II. Ionic product of water is temperature dependent.
III. A monobasic acid with $K_a = 10^{-5}$ has a pH $= 5$. The degree of dissociation of this acid is 50%.
IV. The Le-Chatelier's principle is not applicable to common-ion effect.

Choose the correct answer from the options given below.

(a) I, II and IV (b) II and III
(c) I and II (d) I, II, and III

9 Consider the following statements regarding the equilibrium constants. NCERT Pg 175, 176, 187

I. Expression for the equilibrium constant is not applicable when concentrations of the reactants and products have attained constant value at equilibrium state.
II. The value of equilibrium constant is dependent on initial concentration of the reactants and products.
III. Equilibrium constant is temperature dependent having one unique value for a particular reaction represented by a balanced equation at a given temperature.
IV. The equilibrium constant for the reverse reaction is directly proportional to the equilibrium constant for the forward reaction.
V. The equilibrium constant for a reaction is related to the equilibrium constant of the corresponding reaction, whose equation is obtained by multiplying or dividing the equation for the original reaction by a small integer.

Choose the correct answer from the options given below.

(a) I and II (b) II and III
(c) III and V (d) III and I

10. Select the correct statement from the following. NCERT Pg 204, 205

I. K_{sp} remains constant with changes in temperature.
II. K_{sp} values based on the pH of the solution in which the salt is dissolved.
III. K_{sp} represents the equilibrium constant for the dissociation of ionic solid into its respective ions in a saturated solution.
IV. The molar solubility of a salt directly correlates with its K_{sp} value, higher K_{sp} indicating higher solubility.

Choose the correct answer from the option given below.

(a) I, III and IV (b) II and IV
(c) II and III (d) I and IV

Matching Type Questions

1 Match the Column I with Column II **NCERT Pg 171**

Column I (Process)	Column II (Conclusion)
A. Liquid $\rightleftharpoons$ Vapour	1. Concentration of solute in solution is constant at a given temperature.
B. Solid $\rightleftharpoons$ Liquid	2. [Gas (*aq*)]/ [gas (*g*)] is constant at a given temperature.
C. Solute(*s*) $\rightleftharpoons$ Solute (solution)	3. p_{H_2O} constant at given temperature.
D. Gas (*g*) $\rightleftharpoons$ Gas (*aq*.)	4. Melting point is fixed at constant pressure

Codes

	A	B	C	D		A	B	C	D
(a)	2	3	4	1	(b)	1	2	3	4
(c)	4	3	2	1	(d)	3	4	1	2

2 Match the following graphical variation with their description. **NCERT Pg 172**

Column I	Column II
A. 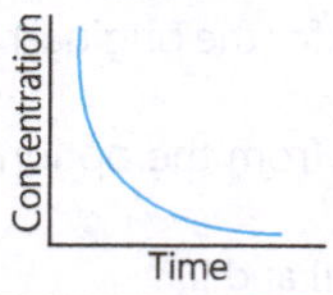	1. Variation in product concentration with time
B. 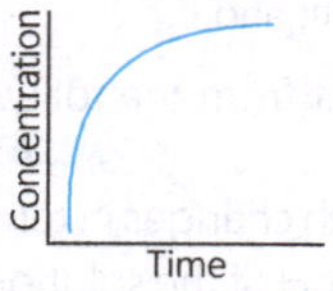	2. Reaction at equilibrium
C. 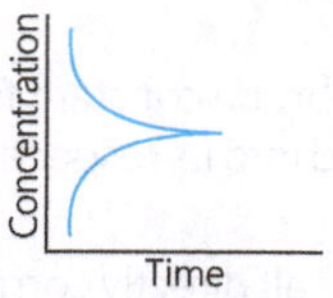	3. Variation in reactant concentration with time
	4. Reaction does not occur

Codes

	A	B	C		A	B	C
(a)	3	1	2	(b)	1	2	3
(c)	2	3	1	(d)	1	2	4

3 Match the Column I with Column II. **NCERT Pg 202**

Column I (Hydrolysis of the salts)	Column II (Example)
A. Weak acid and strong base	1. NH_4Cl
B. Strong acid and weak base	2. CH_3COONH_4
C. Weak acid and weak base	3. CH_3COONa
D. Strong acid and strong base	4. NaCl

Codes

	A	B	C	D		A	B	C	D
(a)	3	4	1	2	(b)	4	2	3	1
(c)	2	3	4	1	(d)	3	1	2	4

4 Match the following species with the corresponding conjugate acid. **NCERT Pg 203**

Species	Conjugate acid
A. NH_3	1. CO_3^{2-}
B. HCO_3^-	2. NH_4^+
C. H_2O	3. H_3O^+
D. HSO_4^-	4. H_2SO_4
	5. H_2CO_3

Codes

	A	B	C	D		A	B	C	D
(a)	4	3	2	1	(b)	2	5	3	4
(c)	1	2	3	4	(d)	5	3	4	2

5 Match the Column-I with Column II. **NCERT Pg 205**

Column-I (Electrolyte)	Column-II (Solubility product)
A. A_2B_3 (2 : 3 type of electrolyte)	1. $4s^3$
B. AB (1 : 1 type binary electrolyte)	2. $27s^4$
C. AB_3 (1 : 3 type quaternary electrolyte)	3. $108s^5$
D. AB_2 (1 : 2 type ternary electrolyte)	4. s^2

Codes

	A	B	C	D		A	B	C	D
(a)	3	2	4	1	(b)	4	2	1	3
(c)	3	4	2	1	(d)	2	3	1	4

Numerical Value Questions

1 A mixture of 1 mole of H_2O and 1 mole of CO is taken in a 10 litre container and heated to 725 K. At equilibrium 40% of water by mass reacts with carbon monoxide according to the equation
$CO(g) + H_2O(g) \rightleftharpoons CO_2(g) + H_2(g)$.
The equilibrium constant $K_C \times 10^2$ for the reaction is .... (Nearest integer) **NCERT Pg 175**

2 4.5 moles each of hydrogen and iodine is heated in a sealed ten litre vessel. At equilibrium, 3 moles of HI were found. The equilibrium constant for
$H_2(g) + I_2(g) \rightleftharpoons 2HI(g)$ is .... **NCERT Pg 175, 176**

3 25.0 mL of 0.050 M $Ba(NO_3)_2$ is mixed with 25.0 mL of 0.020 M NaF. K_{sp} of BaF_2 is 0.5×10^{-6} at 298 K. The ratio of $[Ba^{2+}][F^-]^2$ and K_{sp} is .... (Nearest integer) **NCERT Pg 204**

4 Consider the following equation:
$2SO_2(g) + O_2(g) \rightleftharpoons 2SO_3(g), \Delta H = -190$ kJ
The number of factors which will increase the yield of SO_3 at equilibrium from the following is ....
NCERT Pg 185, 186, 187, 188

A. increasing temperature B. increasing pressure
C. adding more SO_2 D. adding more O_2
E. addition of catalyst

5 20 mL of 0.1 M NaOH is added to 50 mL of 0.1 M acetic acid solution. The pH of the resulting solution is .... $\times 10^{-2}$. (Nearest integer)
Given, pK_a (CH_3COOH) = 4.76 **NCERT Pg 196**
$\log 2 = 0.30$
$\log 3 = 0.48$

NCERT Exemplar's Questions

1 When hydrochloric acid is added to cobalt nitrate solution at room temperature, the following reaction takes place and the reaction mixture becomes blue. On cooling the mixture it becomes pink. On the basis of this information mark the correct answer.

$$\underset{\text{(Pink)}}{[Co(H_2O_6)]^{3+}(aq)} + 4Cl^-(aq) \rightleftharpoons \underset{\text{(Blue)}}{[CoCl_4]^{2-}(aq)} + 6H_2O(l)$$

(a) $\Delta H > 0$ for the reaction.
(b) $\Delta H < 0$ for the reaction.
(c) $\Delta H = 0$ for the reaction.
(d) The sign of ΔH cannot be predicted on the basis of this information.

2 For the reaction, $H_2(g) + I_2(g) \rightleftharpoons 2HI(g)$, the standard free energy is $\Delta G° > 0$. The equilibrium constant (K_C) would be
(a) $K = 0$ (b) $K > 1$ (c) $K = 1$ (d) $K < 1$

3 The ionisation constant of an acid, K_a is the measure of strength of an acid. The K_a values of acetic acid, hypochlorous acid and formic acid are 1.74×10^{-5}, 3.0×10^{-8} and 1.8×10^{-4} respectively. Which of the following order of pH of 0.1 mol dm^{-3} solutions of these acids is correct?
(a) Acetic acid > hypochlorous acid > formic acid
(b) Hypochlorous acid > acetic acid > formic acid
(c) Formic acid > hypochlorous acid > acetic acid
(d) Formic acid > acetic acid > hypochlorous acid

4 Which of the following is not a general characteristic of equilibria involving physical process?
(a) Equilibrium is possible only in a closed system at a given temperature.
(b) All measurable properties of the system remain constant.
(c) All the physical process stop at equilibrium.
(d) The opposing processes occur at the same rate and there is dynamic but stable condition.

5 Which of the following statements is incorrect?
(a) In equilibrium mixture of ice and water kept in perfectly insulated flask, mass of ice and water does not change with time.
(b) The intensity of red colour increases when oxalic acid is added to a solution containing iron (III) nitrate and potassium thiocyanate.
(c) On addition of catalyst, the equilibrium constant value is not affected.
(d) Equilibrium constant for a reaction with negative ΔH value decreases as the temperature increases.

6 PCl_5, PCl_3, and Cl_2 are at equilibrium at 500 K in a closed container and their concentrations are 0.8×10^{-3} mol L^{-1}, 1.2×10^{-3} mol L^{-1} and 1.2×10^{-3} mol L^{-1}, respectively. The value of K_C for the reaction.
$PCl_5(g) \rightleftharpoons PCl_3(g) + Cl_2(g)$ will be
(a) 1.8×10^3 mol L^{-1} (b) 1.8×10^{-3} mol L^{-1}
(c) 1.8×10^{-3} mol^1 L (d) 0.55×10^4 mol L^{-1}

7 We know that, relationship between K_C and K_p is

$$K_p = K_C(RT)^{\Delta n}$$

What would be the value of Δn for the reaction

$$NH_4Cl(s) \rightleftharpoons NH_3(g) + HCl(g)?$$

(a) 1 (b) 0.5 (c) 1.5 (d) 2

8 K_{a_1}, K_{a_2} and K_{a_3} are the respective ionisation constants for the following reactions.

$$H_2S \rightleftharpoons H^+ + HS^-$$
$$HS^- \rightleftharpoons H^+ + S^{2-}$$
$$H_2S \rightleftharpoons 2H^+ + S^{2-}$$

The correct relationship between $K_{a_1}, K_{a_2}, K_{a_3}$ is

(a) $K_{a_3} = K_{a_1} \times K_{a_2}$ (b) $K_{a_3} = K_{a_1} + K_{a_2}$
(c) $K_{a_3} = K_{a_1} - K_{a_2}$ (d) $K_{a_3} = K_{a_1} / K_{a_2}$

9 On increasing the pressure, in which direction will the gas phase reaction proceed to re-establish equilibrium, is predicted by applying the Le-Chatelier's principle. Consider the reaction,

$$N_2(g) + 3H_2(g) \rightleftharpoons 2NH_3(g)$$

Which of the following statement is correct, if the total pressure at which the equilibrium is established is increased without changing the temperature?

(a) K will remain same (b) K will decrease.
(c) K will increase.
(d) K will increase initially and decrease when pressure is very high.

10 In which of the following reactions, the equilibrium remains unaffected on addition of small amount of argon at constant volume?

(a) $H_2(g) + I_2(g) \rightleftharpoons 2HI(g)$
(b) $PCl_5(g) \rightleftharpoons PCl_3(g) + Cl_2(g)$
(c) $N_2(g) + 3H_2(g) \rightleftharpoons NH_3(g)$
(d) The equilibrium will remain unaffected in all the three cases

11 What will be the correct order of vapour pressure of water, acetone and ether at 30°C? Given that among these compounds, water has maximum boiling point and ether has minimum boiling point?

(a) Water < ether < acetone (b) Water < acetone < ether
(c) Ether < acetone < water (d) Acetone < ether < water

12 At 500 K, equilibrium constant, K_C, for the following reaction is 5.

$$\frac{1}{2}H_2(g) + \frac{1}{2}I_2(g) \rightleftharpoons HI(g)$$

What would be the equilibrium constant K_C for the reaction?

$$2HI(g) \rightleftharpoons H_2(g) + I_2(g)$$

(a) 0.04 (b) 0.4 (c) 25 (d) 2.5

13 K_a for CH_3COOH is 1.8×10^{-5} and K_b for NH_4OH is 1.8×10^{-5}. The pH of ammonium acetate will be

(a) 7.005 (b) 4.75
(c) 7.0 (d) between 6 and 7

14 Which of the following options will be correct for the stage of half-completion of the reaction $A \rightleftharpoons B$?

(a) $\Delta G^\ominus = 0$ (b) $\Delta G^\ominus > 0$
(c) $\Delta G^\ominus < 0$ (d) $\Delta G^\ominus = -RT \ln 2$

15 Acidity of BF_3 can be explained on the basis of which of the following concepts?

(a) Arrhenius concept
(b) Bronsted-Lowry concept
(c) Lewis concept
(d) Bronsted-Lowry as well as Lewis concept

16 Which of the following will produce a buffer solution when mixed in equal volumes?

(a) 0.1 mol dm^{-3} NH_4OH and 0.1 mol dm^{-3} HCl
(b) 0.05 mol dm^{-3} NH_4OH and 0.1 mol dm^{-3} HCl
(c) 0.1 mol dm^{-3} NH_4OH and 0.05 mol dm^{-3} HCl
(d) 0.1 mol dm^{-3} CH_4COONa and 0.1 mol dm^{-3} NaOH

17 Match the Column I with Column II.

	Column I		Column II
A.	Equilibrium	1.	$\Delta G > 0, K < 1$
B.	Spontaneous reaction	2.	$\Delta G = 0$
C.	Non-spontaneous reaction	3.	$\Delta G^\ominus = 0$
		4.	$\Delta G < 0, K > 1$

18 In which of the following solvents, silver chloride is most soluble?

(a) 0.1 mol dm^{-3} $AgNO_3$ solution
(b) 0.1 mol dm^{-3} HCl solution
(c) H_2O
(d) Aqueous ammonia

19 Match standard free energy of the reaction with the corresponding equilibrium constant.

A.	$\Delta G^\ominus > 0$	1.	$K > 1$
B.	$\Delta G^\ominus < 0$	2.	$K = 1$
C.	$\Delta G^\ominus = 0$	3.	$K = 0$
		4.	$K < 1$

20 The pH of neutral water at 25°C is 7.0. As the temperature increases, ionisation of water increases, however the concentration of H^+ ions and OH^- ions are equal. What will be the pH of pure water at 60°C?

(a) Equal to 7.0 (b) Greater than 7.0
(c) Less than 7.0 (d) Equal to zero

21 What will be the value of pH of 0.01 mol dm^{-3} CH_3COOH ($K_a = 1.74 \times 10^{-5}$)?

(a) 3.4 (b) 3.6 (c) 3.9 (d) 3.0

Past Exams' Questions

NEET Archive

1 In which of the following equilibria, K_p and K_c are not equal? NCERT Pg 178, NEET 2024

(a) $PCl_5(g) \rightleftharpoons PCl_3(g) + Cl_2(g)$

(b) $H_2(g) + I_2(g) \rightleftharpoons 2HI(g)$

(c) $CO(g) + H_2O(g) \rightleftharpoons CO_2(g) + H_2(g)$

(d) $2BrCl(g) \rightleftharpoons Br_2(g) + Cl_2(g)$

2 For the reaction, $2A \rightleftharpoons B + C, K_C = 4 \times 10^{-3}$. At a given time, the composition of reaction mixture is: $[A] = [B] = [C] = 2 \times 10^{-3}$. NCERT Pg 182, NEET 2024

Then, which of the following is correct?

(a) Reaction is at equilibrium.

(b) Reaction has a tendency to go in forward direction.

(c) Reaction has a tendency to go in backward direction.

(d) Reaction has gone to completion in forward direction.

3 Consider the following reaction in a sealed vessel at equilibrium with concentrations of NCERT Pg 195, NEET 2024

$N_2 = 3.0 \times 10^{-3} M, O_2 = 4.2 \times 10^{-3} M, NO = 2.8 \times 10^{-3} M$

$$2NO(g) \rightleftharpoons N_2(g) + O_2(g)$$

If 0.1 mol L^{-1} of NO (*g*) is taken in a closed vessel, what will be degree of dissociation (α) of NO (*g*) at equilibrium?

(a) 0.00889 (b) 0.0889 (c) 0.8889 (d) 0.717

4 The pH of the solution containing 50 mL each of 0.10 M sodium acetate and 0.01 M acetic acid is [Given : pK_a of $CH_3COOH = 4.57$] NCERT Pg 203, NEET 2022

(a) 3.57 (b) 4.57 (c) 2.57 (d) 5.57

5 The pK_b of dimethyl amine and pK_a of acetic acid are 3.27 and 4.77 respectively at *T*(K). The correct option for the pH of dimethyl ammonium acetate solution is NCERT Pg 204, NEET 2021

(a) 8.50 (b) 5.50 (c) 7.75 (d) 6.25

6 Find out the solubility of $Ni(OH)_2$ in 0.1 M NaOH. Given, that the ionic product of $Ni(OH)_2$ is 2×10^{-15}. NCERT Pg 184, NEET 2020

(a) 2×10^{-8} M (b) 1×10^{-13} M

(c) 1×10^{8} M (d) 2×10^{-13} M

7 Hydrolysis of sucrose is given by the following reaction.

Sucrose + $H_2O \rightleftharpoons$ Glucose + Fructose

If the equilibrium constant (K_C) is 2×10^{13} at 300 K, the value of $\Delta_r G^\ominus$ at the same temperature will be NCERT Pg 184, NEET 2020

(a) $8.314 \text{ J mol}^{-1} \text{K}^{-1} \times 300 \text{ K} \times \ln(2 \times 10^{13})$

(b) $8.314 \text{ J mol}^{-1} \text{K}^{-1} \times 300 \text{ K} \times \ln(3 \times 10^{13})$

(c) $-8.314 \text{ J mol}^{-1} \text{K}^{-1} \times 300 \text{ K} \times \ln(4 \times 10^{13})$

(d) $-8.314 \text{ J mol}^{-1} \text{K}^{-1} \times 300 \text{ K} \times \ln(2 \times 10^{13})$

8 Which will make basic buffer? NCERT Pg 203, NEET 2019

(a) 100 mL of 0.1 M CH_3COOH + 100 mL of 0.1 M NaOH

(b) 100 mL of 0.1 M HCl + 200 mL of 0.1 M NH_4OH

(c) 100 mL of 0.1 M HCl + 100 mL of 0.1 M NaOH

(d) 50 mL of 0.1 M NaOH + 25 mL of 0.1 M CH_3COOH

9 The pH of 0.01 M NaOH (*aq*) solution will be NCERT Pg 194, Odisha, 2019

(a) 7.01 (b) 2 (c) 12 (d) 9

10 Which of the following cannot act both as Bronsted acid and as Bronsted base? NCERT Pg 191, Odisha, 2019

(a) HCO_3^- (b) NH_3 (c) HCl (d) HSO_4^-

11 The solubility of $BaSO_4$ in water is $2.42 \times 10^{-3} \text{g L}^{-1}$ at 298 K. The value of its solubility product (K_{sp}) will be NCERT Pg 204, NEET 2018

(Given : Molar mass of $BaSO_4 = 233 \text{ g mol}^{-1}$)

(a) $1.08 \times 10^{-14} \text{ mol}^2 \text{ L}^{-2}$ (b) $1.08 \times 10^{-12} \text{ mol}^2 \text{ L}^{-2}$

(c) $1.08 \times 10^{-10} \text{ mol}^2 \text{ L}^{-2}$ (d) $1.08 \times 10^{-8} \text{ mol}^2 \text{ L}^{-2}$

12 The equilibrium constants of the following are

$N_2 + 3H_2 \rightleftharpoons 2NH_3; \quad K_1$ ...(i)

$N_2 + O_2 \rightleftharpoons 2NO; \quad K_2$ ...(ii)

$H_2 + \frac{1}{2}O_2 \longrightarrow H_2O; \quad K_3$ ...(iii)

The equilibrium constant (*K*) of the reaction

$$2NH_3 + \frac{5}{2}O_2 \overset{K}{\rightleftharpoons} 2NO + 3H_2O$$, will be NCERT Pg 176, 177, NEET 2017

(a) $K_1K_3^3 / K_2$ (b) $K_2K_3^3 / K_1$

(c) K_2K_3 / K_1 (d) $K_2^3K_3 / K_1$

13 Concentration of the Ag^+ ions in a saturated solution of $Ag_2C_2O_4$ is $2.2 \times 10^{-4} \text{ mol}^{-1}$ solubility product of $Ag_2C_2O_4$ is NCERT Pg 204, NEET 2017

(a) 2.42×10^{-8} (b) 2.66×10^{-12}

(c) 4.5×10^{-11} (d) 5.3×10^{-12}

14 The percentage of pyridine (C_5H_5N) that forms pyridinium ion ($C_5H_5N^+H$) in a 0.10 M aqueous pyridine solution (K_b for $C_5H_5N = 1.7 \times 10^{-9}$) is NCERT Pg 197, NEET 2016

(a) 0.0060% (b) 0.013% (c) 0.77% (d) 1.6%

15 If the value of an equilibrium constant for a particular reaction is 1.6×10^{12}, then at equilibrium the system will contain NCERT Pg 176, CBSE-AIMPT 2015

(a) all reactants

(b) mostly reactants

(c) mostly products

(d) similar amounts of reactants and products

16 The K_{sp} of Ag_2CrO_4, AgCl, AgBr and AgI are respectively, 1.1×10^{-12}, 1.8×10^{-10}, 5.0×10^{-13}, 8.3×10^{-17}. Which one of the following salts will precipitate last if $AgNO_3$ solution is added to the solution containing equal moles of NaCl, NaBr, NaI and Na_2CrO_4? **NCERT Pg 204, CBSE-AIMPT 2015**
(a) AgI (b) AgCl (c) AgBr (d) Ag_2CrO_4

17 For a given exothermic reaction, K_p and K_p' are the equilibrium constants at temperatures T_1 and T_2, respectively. Assuming that heat of reaction is constant in temperature range between T_1 and T_2, it is readily observed that **NCERT Pg 178, CBSE-AIMPT 2014**
(a) $K_p > K_p'$ (b) $K_p < K_p'$ (c) $K_p = K_p'$ (d) $K_p = \frac{1}{K'_p}$

JEE Main Archive

18 For the given hypothetical reactions, the equilibrium constants are as follows: **NCERT Pg 176, JEE Main 2024**

$$X \rightleftharpoons Y;\ K_1 = 1.0$$
$$Y \rightleftharpoons Z;\ K_2 = 2.0$$
$$Z \rightleftharpoons W;\ K_3 = 4.0$$

The equilibrium constant for the reaction $X \rightleftharpoons W$ is
(a) 12.0 (b) 7.0
(c) 6.0 (d) 8.0

19 Given below are two statements: **NCERT Pg 198, JEE Main 2024**
Statement I Aqueous solution of ammonium carbonate is basic.
Statement II Acidic/basic nature of salt solution of a salt of weak acid and weak base depends on K_a and K_b value of acid and the base forming it.
In the light of the above statements, choose the most appropriate answer from the options given below
(a) Statement I is correct but Statement II is incorrect.
(b) Statement I is incorrect but Statement II is correct.
(c) Both Statement I and Statement II are correct.
(d) Both Statement I and Statement II are incorrect.

20 The ratio $\frac{K_P}{K_C}$ for the reaction, **NCERT Pg 178, JEE Main 2024**

$$CO(g) + \frac{1}{2}O_2(g) \rightleftharpoons CO_2(g) \text{ is}$$

(a) 1 (b) $\frac{1}{\sqrt{RT}}$ (c) $(RT)^{1/2}$ (d) RT

21 For a concentrated solution of a weak electrolyte (K_{sp} equilibrium constant) A_2B_3 of concentration 'C', the degree of dissociation 'a' is **NCERT Pg 205, JEE Main 2023**
(a) $\left(\frac{K_{eq}}{108C^4}\right)^{1/5}$ (b) $\left(\frac{K_{sp}}{25C^2}\right)^{1/5}$
(c) $\left(\frac{K_{sp}}{5C^4}\right)^{1/5}$ (d) $\left(\frac{K_{sp}}{6C^5}\right)^{1/5}$

22 Which of the following statement(s) is/are correct?
A. The pH of 1×10^{-8} M HCl solution is 8.
B. The conjugate base of $H_2PO_4^-$ is HPO_4^{2-}.
C. K_w increases with increase in temperature.
D. When a solution of a weak monoprotic acid is titrated against a strong base at half neutralisation point $pH = \frac{1}{2}pK_a$. **NCERT Pg 193, JEE Main 2023**

Choose the correct answer from the options given below.
(a) B, C and D (b) B and C (c) A, B and C (d) A and D

23 K_{a_1}, K_{a_2} and K_{a_3} are the respective ionisation constants for the following reactions A, B, and C.
A. $H_2C_2O_4 \rightleftharpoons H^+ + HC_2O_4^-$
B. $HC_2O_4^- \rightleftharpoons H^+ + C_2O_4^{2-}$
C. $H_2C_2O_4 \rightleftharpoons 2H^+ + C_2O_4^{2-}$
The relationship between K_{a_1}, K_{a_2} and K_{a_3} is given as **NCERT Pg 199, JEE Main 2022**
(a) $K_{a_3} = K_{a_1} + K_{a_2}$ (b) $K_{a_3} = K_{a_1} - K_{a_2}$
(c) $K_{a_3} = K_{a_1} / K_{a_2}$ (d) $K_{a_3} = K_{a_1} \times K_{a_2}$

24 For a reaction at equilibrium, $A(g) \rightleftharpoons B(g) + \frac{1}{2}C(g)$
the relation between dissociation constant (K), degree of dissociation (α) and equilibrium pressure (p) is given by **NCERT Pg 195, JEE Main 2022**
(a) $K = \frac{\alpha^{1/2}p^{3/2}}{\left(1+\frac{3}{2}\alpha\right)^{1/2}(1-\alpha)}$ (b) $K = \frac{\alpha^{3/2}p^{1/2}}{(2+\alpha)^{1/2}(1-\alpha)}$
(c) $K = \frac{(\alpha p)^{3/2}}{\left(1+\frac{3}{2}\alpha\right)^{1/2}(1-\alpha)}$ (d) $K = \frac{(\alpha p)^{3/2}}{(1+\alpha)(1-\alpha)^{1/2}}$

25 4.0 moles of argon and 5.0 moles of PCl_5 are introduced into an evacuated flask of 100 litre capacity at 610 K. The system is allowed to equilibrate. At equilibrium, the total pressure of mixture was found to be 6.0 atm. The K_p for the reaction is [Given, $R = 0.082$ L atm K^{-1} mol^{-1}] **NCERT Pg 178, 179, JEE Main 2022**
(a) 2.25 (b) 6.24 (c) 12.13 (d) 15.24

26 A student needs to prepare a buffer solution of propanoic acid and its sodium salt with pH 4. The ratio of $\frac{[CH_3CH_2COO^-]}{[CH_3CH_2COOH]}$ required to make buffer is [Given, K_a $(CH_3CH_2COOH) = 1.3 \times 10^{-5}$] **NCERT Pg 203, JEE Main 2022**
(a) 0.03 (b) 0.13 (c) 0.23 (d) 0.33

27 The solubility of AgCl will be maximum in which of the following? **NCERT Pg 205, JEE Main 2022**
(a) 0.01 M KCl (b) 0.01 M HCl
(c) 0.01 M $AgNO_3$ (d) Deionised water

28 The K_{sp} for bismuth sulphide (Bi_2S_3) is 1.08×10^{-73}. The solubility of Bi_2S_3 in mol L^{-1} at 298 K is **NCERT Pg 205, JEE Main 2022**

(a) 1.0×10^{-15}
(b) 2.7×10^{-12}
(c) 3.2×10^{-10}
(d) 4.2×10^{-8}

29 The solubility of AgCN in a buffer solution of pH = 3 is x. The value of x is...... .
[Assume : No cyano complex is formed; $K_{sp}(AgCN) = 2.2 \times 10^{-16}$ and $K_a(HCN) = 6.2 \times 10^{-10}$] **NCERT Pg 205, JEE Main 2021**

(a) 0.625×10^{-6} (b) 1.6×10^{-6}
(c) 2.2×10^{-16} (d) 1.9×10^{-5}

Skill Boosters

1 In an experiment, NO_2 gas is prepared and taken into 3 test tubes P, Q and R. NO_2 gas which is brown in colour dimerises into N_2O_4 which is colourless. Test tube P is kept at room temperature, Q is kept in ice and R is kept in hot water. The colour and the reason of its changes are observe respectively.

$$\underset{\text{Brown}}{2NO_2(g)} \rightleftharpoons \underset{\text{Colourless}}{N_2O_4(g)}; \Delta H = -57.2 \text{ kJ mol}^{-1}$$

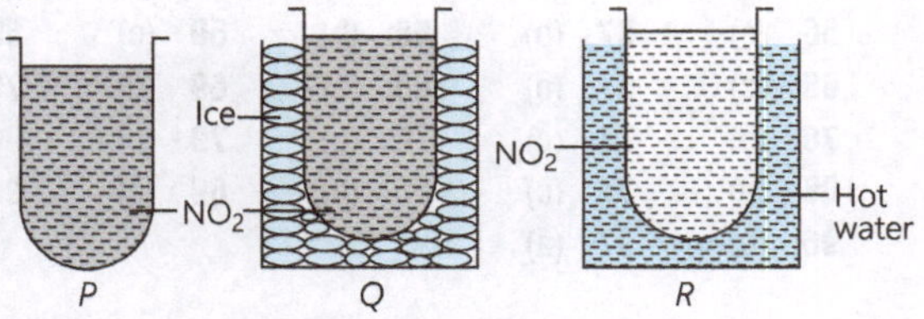

(a) In test tube P, brown colour intensifies since, backward reaction is favoured at low temperature.
(b) In test tube Q, brown colour intensifies since, backward reaction takes place at room temperature.
(c) In test tube R, brown colour intensifies since, high temperature favours the backward reaction.
(d) Brown colour of test tubes P, Q and R remains same since, there is no effect of change in temperature on the reaction.

2. Prerana perform an experiment, she arranged the set up at 27°C as shown below.

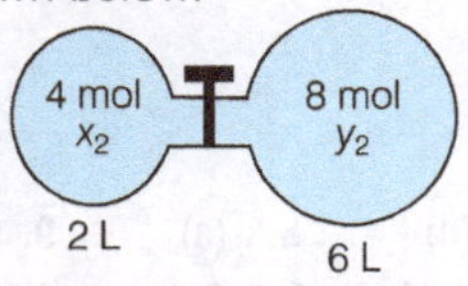

The gas X_2 in the left flask allowed to react with gas Y_2 present in right flask as

$$X_2(g) + Y_2(g) \rightleftharpoons 2XY(g), K_C = 4$$

The equilibrium concentration of [XY] will be

(a) 1.33 (b) 0.66 (c) 0.33 (d) 1.66

3 A compound 'X' is a weak acid and it exhibits colour change at pH close to the equivalence point during neutralisation of NaOH with CH_3COOH. Compound 'X' exists ionized form in basic medium. The compound 'X' is

(a) methyl red (b) erichrome black T
(c) phenolphthalein (d) methyl orange

4 Pooja had taken a vessel for a reaction to form SO_3. Starting with one mole of O_2 and two moles of SO_2, the equilibrium for the formation of SO_3 was established at a certain temperature. If V is the volume of the vessel and $2x$ is the number of moles of SO_3 present, the equilibrium constant will be

(a) $\dfrac{x^2V}{(1-x)^3}$ (b) $\dfrac{4x^2}{(2-x)(1-x)}$
(c) $\dfrac{(1-x)^3}{2V}$ (d) $\dfrac{x^2}{(2-x)(1-x)}$

5 Some students in the class were asked to prepare one litre of buffer solution of pH 8.26 by their chemistry teacher. The amount of ammonium chloride to be dissolved by the student in 0.2 M ammonia solution to make one litre of the buffer is (given $pK_b(NH_3) = 4.74$; Molar mass of $NH_3 = 17$ g mol^{-1}; molar mass of $NH_4Cl = 53.5$ g mol^{-1})

(a) 53.5g (b) 72.3 g
(c) 107.0 g (d) 126.0 g

6 For a hypothetical reaction; $P(g) + Q(g) \rightleftharpoons R(g) + S(g)$, a graph between log K and T^{-1} is a straight line as follows, where $\theta = \tan^{-1} 0.5$ and $OA = 10$. Assuming $\Delta H°$ is independent of temperature, the equilibrium constant at 298 K and 798 K are respectively.

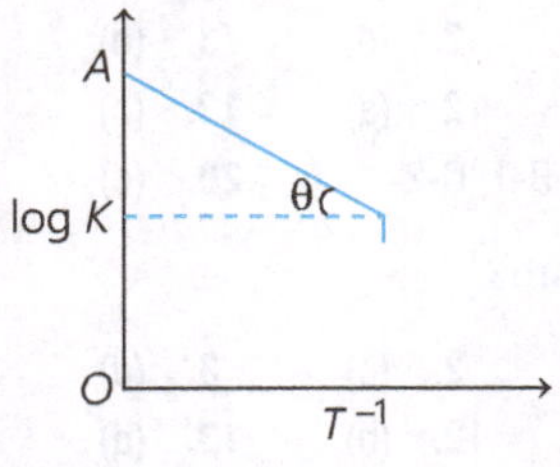

(a) $K_1 = 9.96 \times 10^9$, $K_2 = 2.76 \times 10^{10}$
(b) $K_1 = 3.79 \times 10^8$, $K_2 = 9.98 \times 10^9$
(c) $K_1 = 7.96 \times 10^9$, $K_2 = 7.96 \times 10^9$
(d) $K_1 = 9.96 \times 10^9$, $K_2 = 9.96 \times 10^9$

7 In an experiment with indicator. An acid type indicator, HIn differs in colour from its conjugte base (In^{-1}). The human eye is sensitive to colour differences only when the ratio $[In^-]/[HIn]$ is greater than 10 or smaller than 0.1. The minimum change in the pH of the solution to observe a complete colour change ($K_a = 1.0 \times 10^{-5}$)?

(a) 4, 5 (b) 4, 6 (c) 5, 6 (d) 6, 8

8 Jaya is asked to prepare a 100 mL buffer solution of pH = 5.0 for this purpose, you are supplied with acetic acid ($pK_a = 4.74$), benzoic acid ($pK_a = 4.20$), formic acid ($pK_a = 3.75$) and their sodium salts. She select acid to prepare the most effective buffer is

(a) $pK_a = 3.75$ (b) $pK_a = 4.74$
(c) $pK_a = 4.20$ (d) $pK_a = 4.2$ and $pK_a = 3.75$

Correct Codes

Topical Questions

1 (d)	2 (d)	3 (c)	4 (d)	5 (d)	6 (b)	7 (a)	8 (d)	9 (b)	10 (c)
11 (a)	12 (d)	13 (c)	14 (d)	15 (c)	16 (a)	17 (a)	18 (a)	19 (d)	20 (b)
21 (b)	22 (a)	23 (b)	24 (b)	25 (c)	26 (c)	27 (b)	28 (a)	29 (d)	30 (b)
31 (b)	32 (c)	33 (d)	34 (c)	35 (a)	36 (a)	37 (d)	38 (d)	39 (b)	40 (c)
41 (d)	42 (a)	43 (d)	44 (a)	45 (d)	46 (a)	47 (c)	48 (d)	49 (b)	50 (a)
51 (a)	52 (c)	53 (d)	54 (c)	55 (b)	56 (c)	57 (b)	58 (b)	59 (c)	60 (b)
61 (d)	62 (c)	63 (c)	64 (a)	65 (d)	66 (c)	67 (b)	68 (c)	69 (d)	70 (b)
71 (a)	72 (c)	73 (c)	74 (a)	75 (c)	76 (b)	77 (c)	78 (b)	79 (b)	80 (c)
81 (a)	82 (c)	83 (b)	84 (c)	85 (b)	86 (b)	87 (c)	88 (b)	89 (c)	90 (b)
91 (d)	92 (a)	93 (a)	94 (c)	95 (d)	96 (b)	97 (a)			

Assertion-Reason

1. (c)	2. (b)	3. (c)	4. (c)	5. (a)	6. (c)	7. (a)	8. (b)	9. (a)	10. (a)

Statement Type

1. (b)	2. (b)	3. (d)	4. (c)	5. (c)	6. (a)	7. (c)	8. (d)	9. (c)	10. (a)

Matching Type

1. (d)	2. (a)	3. (d)	4. (b)	5. (c)

Numerical Value

1. (44)	2. (1)	3. (5)	4. (3)	5. (458)

NCERT Exemplar's

1. (a)	2. (d)	3. (d)	4. (c)	5. (b)	6. (b)	7. (d)	8. (a)	9. (a)	10. (d)
11. (b)	12. (a)	13. (c)	14. (a)	15. (c)	16. (c)	17. A-(2, 3), B-4, C-1	18. (d)		
19. A-4, B-1, C-2		20. (c)	21. (a)						

Past Exams'

1. (a)	2. (c)	3. (d)	4. (d)	5. (c)	6. (d)	7. (d)	8. (b)	9. (c)	10. (c)
11. (c)	12. (b)	13. (d)	14. (b)	15. (c)	16. (d)	17. (a)	18. (d)	19. (c)	20. (b)
21. (a)	22. (b)	23. (d)	24. (b)	25. (a)	26. (b)	27. (d)	28. (a)	29. (d)	

Skill Boosters

1. (c)	2. (b)	3. (c)	4. (a)	5. (c)	6. (d)	7. (b)	8. (b)

Step by Step

Decoding the Questions

Concept Builders

1 extent
2 False
3 Physical equilibrium
4 crystallisation, dynamic
5 False [$K_p > K_c$]
6 intensity
7 False
8 $Q_C > K_C$
9 True
10 $\Delta G = 0$
11 Le-Chatelier's principle
12 removal
13 True
14 False
15 K_{eq}
16 HCO_3^-
17 False
18 False
19 Basic
20 False (pH of soft drink is 2.42)
21 Ammonia > Pyridine > Aniline > Urea
22 1.76%
23 True
24 oxoacid
25 polybasic
26 salt hydrolysis
27 buffer solution
28 True
29 $K_{sp} = [Ba^{2+}][SO_4^{2-}]$
30 increases

Topical Solutions

1 (*d*) Statements I, II and IV are correct while statement III is incorrect. The corrected form is as follows :

Equilibrium never be static but it is dynamic in nature as reaction never stops but rate becomes equal after some time.

2 (*d*) Statement (d) is incorrect. Its correct form is as follows

For dissolution of gases in liquids, the concentration of a gas in liquid is proportional to the pressure of the gas over the liquid.

3 (*c*) Statement (c) is incorrect.

It's correct form is as follows

Chemical equilibrium cannot take place in an open vessel if one of the reactants or products is a gas.

Rest other statements are correct.

4 (*d*) Statement (d) is incorrect.

It's correct form is as follows

The reaction can reach the state of equilibrium even if it starts with only *C* and *D*, i.e. there is no *A* and *B* being present initially. This is because, equilibrium can be reached from either direction.

Rest other statements are correct.

5 (*d*)

6 (*b*) Statement (b) is incorrect.

It's correct form is as follows

Chemical equilibrium in the reaction, $H_2(g) + I_2(g) \rightleftharpoons 2HI(g)$ can be attained from either direction.

Rest other statements are correct.

7 (*a*)

8 (*d*) All the given statements are correct.

9 (*b*) For the given reaction,

$$K_C = \frac{[B][C]}{[A]^2}$$

$$K_C = \frac{2 \times 10^{-3} \times 3 \times 10^{-3}}{(10^{-3})^2} = 6$$

10 (*c*) Equilibrium constant for first reaction,

$$K_C = \frac{[SO_3]^2}{[SO_2]^2 [O_2]} \quad \text{...(i)}$$

Equilibrium constant for second reaction is

$$K' = \frac{[SO_2][O_2]^{1/2}}{[SO_3]} \quad \text{...(ii)}$$

On squaring both sides in Eq. (ii), we have

$$(K')^2 = \frac{[SO_2]^2 [O_2]}{[SO_3]^2} = \frac{1}{K_C} = \frac{1}{278}$$

(as $K_C = 278$)

$$\therefore \; K' = \sqrt{\frac{1}{278}} = \sqrt{0.003597}$$

$$= 5.99 \times 10^{-2}$$

or $\approx 6.0 \times 10^{-2}$

11 (*a*)

	A	+	$2B$	$\rightleftharpoons$	$2C$	+	D
At $t = 0$	1.1 mol		2.2 mol		0		0
At eqn.	(1.1 − 0.1) = 1.0 mol		(2.2 − 0.2) = 2.0 mol		0.2		0.1 mol
	left		left		produced (given)		produced (given)

$$K = \frac{(0.2)^2 \times (0.1)}{(1) \times (2)^2} = \frac{0.2 \times 0.2 \times 0.1}{1 \times 2 \times 2}$$

$$= 0.001$$

12 (*d*) Statement (d) is incorrect.

It's correct form is as follows

The reaction takes place in the presence of a catalyst which is $V_2O_5(s)$ in contact process or $NO(g)$ in chamber process. Rest other statements are correct.

13 (*c*)

	$2HI$	$\rightleftharpoons$	H_2	+	I_2
Initial	2 mol		0		0
At equil.	$2 - \frac{22}{100} \times 2$		0.22		0.22

$= 2 - 0.44 = 1.56$

$$\therefore \; K = \frac{[H_2][I_2]}{[HI]^2} = \frac{0.22 \times 0.22}{(1.56)^2} = 0.0199$$

14 (*d*) $N_2(g) + O_2(g) \rightleftharpoons 2NO(g)$, K_1

$2NO(g) + O_2(g) \rightleftharpoons 2NO_2(g)$, K_2

$N_2(g) + 2O_2(g) \rightleftharpoons 2NO_2(g)$,

$K = K_1 \times K_2$

$\therefore$ For $NO_2(g) \rightleftharpoons \frac{1}{2}N_2(g) + O_2(g)$

$$K' = \left[\frac{1}{K_1 K_2}\right]^{1/2}$$

15 (c) (i) $A_2(g) + B_2(g) \rightleftharpoons 2AB(g);$

$$K_1 = \frac{[AB]^2}{[A_2][B_2]}$$

(ii) $6AB(g) \rightleftharpoons 3A_2(g) + 3B_2(g);$

$$K_2 = \frac{[A_2]^3[B_2]^3}{[AB]^6} = \frac{1}{\left(\frac{[AB]^2}{[A_2][B_2]}\right)^3} = \frac{1}{K_1^3},$$

16 (a) As K_C is very low and $K_C = \frac{[I]^2}{[I_2]}$

For the reaction, $I_2(g) \rightleftharpoons 2I(g)$

$\therefore \quad [I_2] > [I]$

17 (a) $CH_3COOH(l) + C_2H_5OH(l) \rightleftharpoons CH_3COOC_2H_5(l) + H_2O(l)$

	$CH_3COOH(l)$	$C_2H_5OH(l)$	$CH_3COOC_2H_5(l)$	$H_2O(l)$
Initial	3 mol	3 mol	0	0
At equil.	1	1	2	2

$$\therefore \quad K = \frac{2 \times 2}{1 \times 1} = 4$$

18 (a) Among the given reactions (III) and (V) have K_p values less than K_C.

From the equation, $K_p = K_C(RT)^{\Delta n}$

III. $2SO_2(g) + O_2(g) \rightleftharpoons 2SO_3(g)$

$$\Delta n = 2 - 3 = -1$$
$$K_p = K_C(RT)^{-1}$$

V. $N_2(g) + 3H_2(g) \rightleftharpoons 2NO_3(g)$

$$\Delta n = 2 - 4 = -2$$
$$K_p = K_C(RT)^{-2}$$

19 (d) For reaction in equilibrium,

$$K_C = \frac{[HI(g)]^2}{[H_2(g)][I_2(g)]}$$

or $K_C = \frac{[p_{HI}]^2}{[p_{H_2}][p_{I_2}]}$

Further, since $p_{HI} = [HI(g)]RT$

$p_{I_2} = [I_2(g)]RT, p_{H_2} = [H_2(g)]RT$

Therefore, $K_p = \frac{[p_{HI}]^2}{[p_{H_2}][p_{I_2}]}$

$$= \frac{[HI(g)]^2[RT]^2}{[H_2(g)]RT \cdot [I_2(g)]RT}$$

$$= \frac{[HI(g)]^2}{[H_2(g)][I_2(g)]} = K_C$$

In this example, $K_p = K_C$, i.e. both equilibrium constants are equal.

20 (b) For the given reaction,

$$\Delta n_g = n_P - n_R$$

$\because \quad K_p = K_C(RT)^{\Delta n_g}$

$\therefore \quad \Delta n_g = -\frac{1}{2}$

Thus, the value of $x = -\frac{1}{2}$

21 (b) $N_2(g) + 3H_2(g) \rightleftharpoons 2NH_3(g)$

At equil. $p_{N_2} = P, p_{H_2} = 3P, p_{NH_3} = 2P$

$\Rightarrow p_{(total)} = p_{N_2} + p_{H_2} + p_{NH_3}$

$\approx p_{N_2} + p_{H_2}$ [$\because P_{(total)} >> p_{NH_3}$]

$= p + 3p = 4p$

Now, $K_p = \frac{p^2_{NH_3}}{p_{N_2} \times p^3_{H_2}} = \frac{p^2_{NH_3}}{p \times (3p)^3}$

$$= \frac{p^2_{NH_3}}{27 \times p^4} = \frac{p^2_{NH_3}}{27 \times \left(\frac{P}{4}\right)^4}$$

[$\because P = 4p$]

$$K_p = \frac{p^2_{NH_3} \times 4^4}{3^2 \times 3 \times P^4}$$

$$\Rightarrow p^2_{NH_3} = \frac{3^2 \times 3 \times P^4 \times K_p}{4^4}$$

$$\Rightarrow p_{NH_3} = \frac{3 \times 3^{1/2} \times P^2 \times K_p^{1/2}}{4^2} = \frac{3^{3/2} \times P^2 \times K_p^{1/2}}{16}$$

22 (a) $\because$ I-atoms in iodine vapours $= 40\%$ by volume

$\therefore$ Iodine vapours of I_2 molecule $= 60\%$ by volume

Now, partial pressure of I-atoms

$$p_1 = \frac{40}{100} \times 10^5 = 0.40 \times 10^5 \text{ Pa}$$

Similarly, partial pressure of iodine molecule (I_2),

$$p_2 = \frac{60}{100} \times 10^5 = 0.60 \times 10^5 \text{ Pa}$$

$$\therefore \quad K_p = \frac{p_I^2}{p_{I_2}} = \frac{(0.40 \times 10^5 \text{ Pa})^2}{(0.60 \times 10^5 \text{ Pa})} = 2.67 \times 10^4 \text{ Pa}$$

23 (b) $2SO_2(g) + O_2(g) \rightleftharpoons 2SO_3(g);$

$$K_p = K_C(RT)^{\Delta n_g}$$

$\because \quad \Delta n_g = 2 - 3 = -1$

$\therefore \quad K_C = \frac{K_p}{(RT)^{\Delta n_g}} = \frac{K_p}{(RT)^{-1}}$

or $\quad K_C = K_p \times RT$

$= 2.0 \times 10^{10} \text{ bar}^{-1} \times 0.0831 \text{L bar K}^{-1}\text{mol}^{-1} \times 450 \text{ K}$

$K_C = 7.479 \times 10^{11} \text{ L mol}^{-1}$

24 (b) Molar mass of $NH_4SH = 18 + 33 = 51 \text{ g mol}^{-1}$

Number of moles of NH_4SH introduced in the

$$\text{vessel} = \frac{\text{Weight}}{\text{Molar mass}} = \frac{5.1}{51} = 0.1 \text{ mol}$$

$NH_4SH(s) \rightleftharpoons NH_3(g) + H_2S(g)$

	$NH_4SH(s)$	$NH_3(g)$	$H_2S(g)$
Number of moles at $t = 0$	0.1	0	0
At $t = t_{eq}$	0.1(1 − 0.3)	30% of 0.1 = 0.03	30% of 0.1 = 0.03
Active mass (mol L^{-1})		$\frac{0.03}{3} = 0.01$	$\frac{0.03}{3} = 0.01$

$$K_C = \frac{[NH_3][H_2S]}{[NH_4HS(s)]} = \frac{0.01 \times 0.01}{1}$$

$$= 10^{-4} \text{ (mol L}^{-1})^2$$

$\Rightarrow K_p = K_C(RT)^{\Delta n_g}$

[where, $\Delta n_g = \Sigma n_{product} - \Sigma n_{reactant}$]
$= 2 - 0 = 2$

$\therefore K_p = K_C(RT)^2$

$= 10^{-4} \times [0.082 \times (273 + 327)]^2 \text{ atm}^2$

$= 0.242 \text{ atm}^2$

25 (c) As we know that, $K_p = K_C(RT)^{\Delta n_g}$

Here, $\quad K_p = K_C, \Delta n_g = 2 - 1 = 1$

$\Rightarrow \quad (RT)^{\Delta n_g} = 1$

$(0.0821 \times T) = 1$

Thus, $\quad T = \frac{1}{0.0821} = 12.18 \text{ K}$

26 (c) As we know,

$$K_p = K_C(RT)^{\Delta n}$$
$$\Delta n = n_p - n_r$$
$$\Delta n = 1 - \left(1 + \frac{1}{2}\right) = -\frac{1}{2}$$

So, $\quad \frac{K_p}{K_C} = (RT)^{-\frac{1}{2}} = \frac{1}{\sqrt{RT}}$

27 (b) $N_2(g) + O_2(g) \rightleftharpoons 2NO(g)$

Initial 2 mol 4 mol 0

At equil. $2-\frac{1}{2}$ $4-\frac{1}{2}$ $2\times\frac{1}{2}=1$ mol

$\therefore$ Molar concentration of NO at equilibrium $=\frac{1}{2.5}=0.4$

[$\because$ Given, $V=2.5$ L]

28 (a)

$H_2(g)+CO_2(g) \rightleftharpoons H_2O(g)+CO(g)$

Initial 1 1 0 0

At equil. $1-x$ $1-x$ x x

$\because$ $K=\frac{x^2}{(1-x)^2}$

$\Rightarrow$ $\sqrt{K}=\frac{x}{1-x}=\sqrt{1.80}=\frac{x}{1-x}$

$\Rightarrow$ $1.34=\frac{x}{1-x}$

This gives $x=0.573$ M

29 (d) From both given reactions

$CaCO_3(s)+C(s) \rightleftharpoons CaO(s)+2CO(g)$

$K'_p=K_{p_1}\times K_{p_2}$

$=8\times10^{-2}\times2=16\times10^{-2}$

$\therefore$ $K'_p=(p_{CO}(g))^2$

$\Rightarrow$ $p_{CO}=\sqrt{K'_p}$

$=\sqrt{16\times10^{-2}}$

$=4\times10^{-1}=0.4$ atm

30 (b) Statements (a), (c) and (d) are correct while statement (b) is incorrect. The corrected form is as :

The equilibrium constant for an exothermic reaction (negative, ΔH) decreases as the temperature increases.

31 (b) The reaction quotient Q_C is given by, $Q_C=[B][C]/[A]^2$

$\because [A]=[B]=[C]=3\times10^{-4}$ M

$\therefore Q_C=\frac{(3\times10^{-4})(3\times10^{-4})}{(3\times10^{-4})^2}=1$

As $Q_C>K_C$, so the reaction will proceed in the reverse direction.

32 (c) Consider the gaseous reaction of H_2 with I_2.

$H_2(g)+I_2(g) \rightleftharpoons 2HI(g); K_C=57.0$ at 700 K

$\Rightarrow Q_C=\frac{[HI]^2}{[H_2][I_2]}=\frac{(0.40)^2}{(0.10)\times(0.20)}=8.0$

33 (d) Statements (a), (b) and (c) are correct while statement (d) is incorrect regarding the given graph.

The corrected form is :

If $K_C>10^3$, products predominate over reactants, i.e. if K_C is very large, the reaction proceeds nearly to completion.

34 (c) For the given reaction,

$$Q_C=\frac{[NOCl]^2}{[NO]^2[Cl_2]}$$

If $Q_p<K_p$, the reaction will proceed in the direction of the products, i.e. forward direction.

35 (a) $K_{eq}=\text{antilog}\left(\frac{-\Delta G°}{2.303RT}\right)$ ...(i)

$\Delta G°=78$ kJ/mol $=78000$ J/mol

$R=8.314$ JK^{-1} mol^{-1}, $T=1000$ K

Putting these value in Eq. (i) we get,

$K_{eq}=\text{antilog}\left[\frac{-78000}{2.303\times8.314\times1000}\right]$

$K_{eq}=\text{antilog}(-4.0737)$

or $K_{eq}=8.4\times10^{-5}$

36 (a)

37 (d) $\because \Delta G°=-RT\ln K_C$

Hence, $\ln K_C=-13.8\times10^3$ J/mol / (8.314 J mol^{-1} K$^{-1}\times$ 298 K)

$\Rightarrow \ln K_C=-5.57 \Rightarrow K_C=3.81\times10^{-3}$

38 (d) Sucrose + $H_2O \rightleftharpoons$ Glucose + Fructose

We know that, $R=8.314$ J mol^{-1}K^{-1}

Given, $T=300$ K; $K_C=2\times10^{13}$

$\because$ $\Delta G°=-RT\ln K_C$

or $-2.303RT\log K_C$

$\therefore \Delta G°=-2.303\times8.314$ Jmol^{-1} K^{-1} $\times300$ K $\times\log(2\times10^{13})$

$\Rightarrow \Delta G°=-7.64\times10^4$ J mol^{-1}

39 (b) Statement (b) is incorrect.

It's correct form is as follows :

The reaction never ceases at equilibrium because equilibrium is dynamic in nature.

Rest other statements are correct.

40 (c)

41 (d) If concentration of PCl_5 is increased, the forward reaction is favoured.

42 (a)

43 (d) Statements (a), (b) and (c) are correct while the statement (d) is incorrect regarding the given reaction.

The corrected form is :

The equilibrium can be shifted in the opposite direction by adding reagents that remove Fe^{3+} and SCN^- ions.

44 (a)

45 (d) A solution of sugar does not conduct electricity because cane sugar is a covalent compound, which is bonded by the sharing of electrons. In the solution, it does not have ions to conduct electrical charges across the solution.

46 (a) **47** (c)

48 (d) Among the given compounds, BF_3 is least likely to behave as Lewis base because it has a capacity of electron accepting instead of donating. As, BF_3 is a Lewis acid.

49 (b) Higher the tendency to give H^+ ion (i.e. to undergo ionisation), stronger will be the acid or *vice-versa*.

HF has poor tendency to give H^+ ion hence, it is the weakest acid among the given.

The order of acidity of given acids is $H_2SO_4>HNO_3>HCl>HF$.

50 (a) Statement (a) is incorrect.

It's correct form is as follows

NaCl exists in solid state as a cluster of negatively charged chloride ions and positively charged sodium ions.

Rest other statements are correct.

51 (a) Bronsted-Lowry acid base conjugate pairs differ by just one proton (acid has the extra proton). Bronsted-Lowry acids are proton acceptors. The conjugate acid of hydrogen sulphate (HSO_4^-) is (H_2SO_4) and conjugate base of hydrogen sulphate is SO_4^{2-}.

52 (c) $NaNO_2$ solution is slightly basic, NaCl solution is neutral, H_2S is weakly acidic, whereas H_2SO_4 is strong acid.

Thus, the correct order of increasing $[H_3O]^+$ in the aqueous solution is

$0.01\,M\,NaNO_2 < 0.01\,M\,NaCl < 0.01\,M\,H_2S < 0.01\,M\,H_2SO_4$.

53 (d) $\because$ $pH = -\log[H^+]$

$\therefore$ $pH = -\log[3.8\times10^{-3}]$

$= -\{\log(3.8) + \log(10^{-3})\}$

$= -\{-2.42\}$

$= 2.42$

Therefore, the pH of the soft drink is 2.42 and it can be inferred that, it is acidic.

54 (c) Weight of NaOH dissolved = 2 g

$\therefore$ Equivalent of NaOH dissolved $= \frac{2}{40}$

$\Rightarrow N_{NaOH} = \frac{2}{40} = 0.05$

$\Rightarrow [OH]^- = 0.05 = 5\times10^{-2}$

$\Rightarrow pOH = -\log[OH^-]$

$= -\log(5\times10^{-2}) = 1.3010$

$\because pH + pOH = 14$

$\therefore pH = 14 - pOH$

$= 14 - 1.3010$

$= 12.70$

55 (b) For pH = 1, $[H^+] = 10^{-1}$ M

For pH = 2, $[H^+] = 10^{-2}$ M

$M_1V_1 + M_2V_2 = M_R(V_1 + V_2)$

$10^{-1}\times 50 + 10^{-2}\times 50 = M_R \times 100$

Thus, $M_R = 5.5\times10^{-2}$ M

$\therefore$ $pH = -\log 5.5\times10^{-2} = 1.26$

56 (c) $[H^+]$ in 0.1 M HCl = 0.1 M

For same pH, $[H^+]$ in H_2SO_4 = 0.1 M

One mole H_2SO_4 gives 2 moles of H^+ ions

$\therefore$ 0.1 M $[H^+]$ will be given by

$= \frac{0.1}{2} = 0.05\,M\,H_2SO_4$

57 (b) $C_{18}H_{21}NO_3 + H_2O \rightleftharpoons \text{Codeine H}^+ + OH^-$

$pH = 9.95$

or $pOH = 14 - 9.95 = 4.05$

$\because$ $pOH = -\log[OH^-]$

$\therefore \log[OH^-] = -4.05$

$[OH^-] = \text{antilog}(-4.05) = 8.913\times10^{-5}$

Now, $K_b = \frac{[\text{Codeine H}^+][OH^-]}{[\text{Codeine}]}$

$= \frac{[OH^-]^2}{[\text{Codeine}]}$

(because $[\text{codeine H}^+] = [OH^-]$)

$\Rightarrow K_b = \frac{(8.913\times10^{-5})^2}{0.005} = 1.588\times10^{-6}$

$\Rightarrow pK_b = -\log[K_b]$

$= -\log[1.588\times10^{-6}]$

$\therefore pK_b = 6 + [-0.2009] = 5.7791 \approx 5.80$

58 (b) $N_{Mix}V_{Mix} = N_1V_1 - N_2V_2$ ... (i)
(Base) (Acid)

Given, $M_1 = 0.2$ M, $N_1 = 0.2$ N

$M_2 = 0.1$ M, $N_2 = 0.1$ N

$V_1 = 50$ mL,

$V_2 = 50$ mL, $V_{mix} = 100$ mL

On substituting the given values in equation (i),

we get $N_{mix}\times 100 = 50\times0.2 - 50\times0.1$

$N_{mix} = \frac{5}{100} = 5\times10^{-2}$

$\therefore$ $[OH^-] = 5\times10^{-2}$

Now, $pOH = -\log[OH^-]$

$= 2 - \log 5 = 1.3$

Also, pH + pOH = 14

$\therefore$ $pH = 14 - 1.3 = 12.7$

59 (c) Given, $K = 1.69\times10^{-5}$

$\because$ $C\alpha << 0.01$

$\therefore$ $K = \frac{C\alpha(C\alpha + 0.01)}{C(1-\alpha)} = 0.01\alpha$

or $\alpha = \frac{1.69\times10^{-5}}{0.01} = 0.169\times10^{-2}$

60 (b) Given, conc. of formic acid solution = 0.2 M

$\alpha = 0.032$

As we know that, $K = C\alpha^2$

$K = 0.2\times(0.032)^2$

$= 2.1\times10^{-4}$

61 (d) $CH_3COOH \rightleftharpoons CH_3COO^- + H^+$

Initial	C	0	0
At equil.	$C(1-\alpha)$	$C\alpha$	$C\alpha$

$\therefore$ $K = \frac{C\alpha\cdot C\alpha}{C(1-\alpha)} = \frac{C\alpha^2}{1-\alpha} = C\alpha^2$

or, $C = \frac{K}{\alpha^2} = \frac{1.8\times10^{-5}}{(0.02)^2} = 0.045$ M

62 (c) $NH_4OH \rightleftharpoons NH_4^+ + OH^-$

Initial conc.	C	0	0
At equil.	$C(1-\alpha)$	$C\alpha$	$C\alpha$

$\therefore [OH^-] = C\alpha = 0.01\times0.05 = 0.0005$ M

63 (c) $F^- + H_2O \rightleftharpoons HF + OH^-$

$K_b = \frac{[HF][OH^-]}{[F^-]}$ ...(i)

$K_w = [H_3O^+][OH^-] = 10^{-14}$ ...(ii)

Dissociation of HF in water is represented by the equation,

$HF + H_2O \rightleftharpoons H_3O^+ + F^-$

$K = \frac{[H_3O^+][F^-]}{[HF]}$ ...(iii)

$K_b\cdot K = [H_3O^+][OH^-] = K_w$

or $\frac{K_w}{K_b} = K$

Taking log on both sides, we get

$\log K = \log K_w - \log K_b$

$-\log K = -\log K_w - (-\log K_b)$

$-\log K = pK_w - pK_a$

$= 14 - 10.83 = 3.14$

or $K = \text{Antilog}(-3.17)$

$= 6.76\times10^{-4}$

64 (a) The equilibrium constant for combined reaction is $K_1\times K_2$. This is because, when two reaction are added, their equilibrium constants are multiplied.

65 (d) Given equations are

$CO(g) + H_2O(g) \rightleftharpoons CO_2(g) + H_2(g)$; K_1 ...(i)

$CH_4(g) + H_2O(g) \rightleftharpoons CO(g) + 3H_2(g)$; K_2 ...(ii)

On adding both equations, we get

$CH_4(g) + 2H_2O(g) \rightleftharpoons CO_2(g) + 4H_2(g)$; K_3

Hence, the correct relation is

$K_3 = K_1\cdot K_2$

66 (c) If the acid is strong then acid conjugate base should be weak.
A^{3-} is a strong base due to its high negative charge and the basic order is

$$A^{3-} > HA^{2-} > H_2A^-.$$

∴ Strength of acids

$$HA^{2-} < H_2A^- < H_3A$$

The value of ionisation constant is

$$K_{a_1} > K_{a_2} > K_{a_3}.$$

Thus, the higher the K_a value, the lower will be the pK_a value. Hence, the correct order is

$$pK_{a_1} < pK_{a_2} < pK_{a_3}.$$

67 (b) Pyridinium hydrochloride is a salt of weak base and strong acid.

So, $pH = \frac{1}{2}[pK_w - pK_b - \log C]$

[Given, pH of pyridinium hydrochloride = 3.44]

$$3.44 = \frac{1}{2}[14 - pK_b - \log(2 \times 10^{-2})]$$

$$pK_b = 8.82 \Rightarrow K_b = 10^{-8.82}$$

68 (c) Ammonium acetate is a salt of weak acid and weak base. When solutions are of weak acid and weak base, pH of solution is calculated from the following relationship.

$$pH = 7 + \left(\frac{1}{2} pK_a - \frac{1}{2} pK_b\right)$$

∵ $pK_a \approx pK_b$ (given)

∴ pH of solution = 7

69 (d) pH of buffer does not change on adding 10 mL of distilled water as there are no ions present in it.

70 (b) When $CH_3COOH + NaOH$ are mixed in the ratio of 2 : 1, they will form acidic buffer. This is because, 1 mole of weak acid will be left unreacted and 1 mole of CH_3COONa will be formed. The reaction is given below.

$$\underset{2\text{ mole}}{CH_3COOH} + \underset{1\text{ mole}}{NaOH} \rightleftharpoons \underset{1\text{ mole}}{CH_3COONa} + H_2O$$

71 (a) As we know,

$$pH = pK_a + \log \frac{\text{salt}}{\text{acid}}$$

And buffer range is $pK_a \pm 1$, so it will work between pH 8.26 to 10.26.

72 (c) Handerson - Hasselbalch equation for acidic buffer solution is given as,

$$pH = pK_a + \log \frac{[\text{Conjugate base}]}{[\text{Acid}]}$$

Therefore, if the molar concentration of acid is equal to the molar concentration of conjugate base, we have

$$pH = pK_a + \log 1$$

or $pH = pK_a$ [∵ log 1 = 0]

Hence, pH of a buffer solution becomes equal to pK_a of acid only if,

[Acid] = [Conjugate base]

73 (c) We can easily calculate the pH by converting the concentration into millimoles.

Millimoles of $CH_3COOH = 0.1 \times 10$
= 1.0 millimole

Millimoles of $CH_3COONa = 0.1 \times 2.0$
= 2.0 millimole

∴Using Henderson-Hassebalch equation,

$$pH = pK_a + \log \frac{[\text{Conjugate base}]}{[\text{acid}]}$$

$$= 4.74 + \log \frac{2}{1}$$

$$= 4.74 + 0.30$$

$$= 5.04$$

74 (a) ∵ $pH = pK_a + \log \frac{[\text{salt}]}{[\text{acid}]}$

As [salt] = [acid]

∴ $pH = pK_a = 9.30$

75 (c) Given, conc. of NH_3 (base) = 0.30 M

Conc. of NH_4^+ (salt) = 0.20 M

$$K_b = 1.8 \times 10^{-5}$$

∵ $pOH = pK_b + \log \frac{[\text{salt}]}{[\text{base}]}$

$$= 4.74 + \log \frac{0.20}{0.30}$$

$$= 4.74 + (0.301 - 0.477)$$

$$= 4.74 - 0.176 = 4.56$$

⇒ $pH = 14 - 4.56 = 9.44$

76 (b) Given,
conc. of $NH_4OH = 0.1$ M
conc. of $NH_4Cl = 0.01$ M

$$pK_b = 5$$

∵ $pOH = pK_b + \log \frac{[\text{salt}]}{[\text{base}]}$

$$= 5 + \log \frac{0.01}{0.1}$$

$$= 5 + \log 10^{-1}$$

$$= 5 - 1 = 4$$

∴ $pH = 14 - 4 = 10$

77 (c) Statement (c) is correct, while the other statements are incorrect.
Corrected form are as follows

(a) Acidic buffer consists of a weak acid and its salt with strong base in a fixed proportion.
e.g. $CH_3COOH + CH_3COONa$

(b) pH of the buffer solution is not affected by dilution because ratio under the logarithmic terms remains unchanged.

(d) Glycine + glycine hydrochloride is an example of basic buffer.

78 (b) A mixture of acetic acid and sodium acetate acts as buffer solution around pH 4.75 and a mixture of ammonium chloride and ammonium hydroxide acts as a buffer around pH 9.25.

79 (b) NH_4Cl reacts with NaOH to form NH_4OH and unreacted NH_4Cl forms a basic buffer.

Millimoles of $NH_4Cl = 75 \times 0.1 = 7.5$

Millimoles of $NaOH = 50 \times 0.1 = 5.0$

	NH_4Cl	+ NaOH ⇌	NH_4OH	+ NaCl
Initial conc.	7.5	5.0	0	0
Change	−5.0	−5.0	+5.0	+5.0
Final conc.	2.5	0	5.0	5.0

Given, $pK_a(NH_4^+) = 9.26$

∴ $pK_b(NH_3) = 14 - 9.26 = 4.74$

⇒

$$pOH = pK_b + \log \frac{[NH_4^+]}{[NH_4OH]}$$

$$= 4.74 + \log \frac{2.5}{5.0}$$

⇒ $pOH = 4.44$

Thus, $pH = 14 - 4.44$

$pH = 9.56$

80 (c) II. $NH_4OH + HCl \longrightarrow NH_4Cl + H_2O$
(Here, NH_4OH is present in an excess amount)

So, the mixture contains weak base and salt of strong acid and weak base ($NH_4OH + NH_4Cl$) which acts as a basic buffer solution.

IV. NaCN is a salt of weak acid and strong base and HCN is a weak acid. Therefore, there can acts as a buffer.

81 (a) For the reaction,

$$PbBr_2 \longrightarrow \underset{S\alpha}{Pb^{2+}} + \underset{2S\alpha}{2Br^{\ominus}} \quad ...(i)$$

Given, $K_{sp} = 8 \times 10^{-5}$

So, $8 \times 10^{-5} = (S\alpha)(2S\alpha)^2$

$8 \times 10^{-5} = 4(S\alpha)^3$

$(S \times 0.8)^3 = 2 \times 10^{-5}$

$$S = \left[\frac{2 \times 10^{-5}}{0.8 \times 0.8 \times 0.8}\right]^{\frac{1}{3}} = \left[\frac{10^{-4}}{1.6 \times 1.6}\right]^{\frac{1}{3}}$$

82 (c) For reaction

$$AgI \rightleftharpoons \underset{S}{Ag^+} + \underset{\substack{(S+0.2)\\ =0.2}}{I^{\ominus}}$$

As, $[Ag^+][I^-] = K_{sp}$

$S \times 0.2 = 8.3 \times 10^{-17}$

$$S = \frac{8.3 \times 10^{-17}}{0.2} = 41.5 \times 10^{-17}$$

$= 4.15 \times 10^{-16}$ M

83 (b) Suppose solubility of $PbCl_2$ in water is S mol L^{-1}.

$$PbCl_2(s) \rightleftharpoons \underset{S}{Pb^{2+}(aq)} + \underset{2S}{2Cl^-(aq)}$$

$K_{sp} = [Pb^{2+}][Cl^-]^2$

$K_{sp} = [S][2S]^2 = 4S^3$

$3.2 \times 10^{-8} = 4S^3$

$$S^3 = \frac{3.2 \times 10^{-8}}{4}$$

$S^3 = 0.8 \times 10^{-8}$

$= 8.0 \times 10^{-9}$

Solubility, $PbCl_2 = S = 2 \times 10^{-3}$ mol L^{-1}

Solubility of $PbCl_2$ in gL^{-1}

$= 278 \times 2 \times 10^{-3} = 0.556$ gL^{-1}

0.556 g of $PbCl_2$ dissolve in 1 L of water

$\therefore$ 0.1 g of $PbCl_2$ will dissolve in $\frac{1 \times 0.1}{0.556}$ L of water $= 0.1798$ L

$= 179.8$ mL ≈ 180 mL

84 (c) $Ag_2CrO_4 \longrightarrow 2Ag^+ + CrO_4^{2-}$

$[CrO_4^{2-}] = \frac{1}{2}[Ag^+]$

$$= \frac{1.5 \times 10^{-4}}{2} = 0.75 \times 10^{-4} \text{ mol/L}$$

$\because K_{sp} = [Ag^+]^2 [CrO_4^{2-}]$

$\therefore K_{sp} = (1.5 \times 10^{-4})^2 (0.75 \times 10^{-4})$

$= 1.6875 \times 10^{-12}$

85 (b) $\because S = \frac{10W}{M}$ mol/L

For $Ca_3(PO_4)_2 \rightleftharpoons \underset{3S}{3Ca^{2+}} + \underset{2S}{2PO_4^{3-}}$

$\Rightarrow K_{sp} = (3S)^3 \times (2S)^2$

$\therefore K_{sp}$ of $Ca_3(PO_4)_2 = 108\,S^5$

$$\Rightarrow 108\left(\frac{10W}{M}\right)^5$$

$$\Rightarrow 10^7\left(\frac{W}{M}\right)^5 \text{ (approximately)}$$

86 (b) $[Ag^+][Cl^-] = K_{sp}$ (constant)

Hence, $S_1 = \sqrt{K_{sp}}$ = maximum;

$$S_2 = \frac{K_{sp}}{0.02} = 50\,K_{sp}$$

$$S_3 = \frac{K_{sp}}{0.01} = 100\,K_{sp};$$

$$S_4 = \frac{K_{sp}}{0.05} = 20\,K_{sp}$$

Thus, the correct order of solubilities is

$S_1 > S_3 > S_2 > S_4$

87 (c) The equation is as

$$MX_2 \longrightarrow \underset{S}{M^{2+}} + \underset{2S}{2X^-}$$

$K_{sp} = (S)(2S)^2 = 4S^3$

$(\because K_{sp} = 4 \times 10^{-12})$

$$\therefore S = \left[\frac{K_{sp}}{4}\right]^{\frac{1}{3}} = \left[\frac{4 \times 10^{-12}}{4}\right]^{\frac{1}{3}} = 10^{-4} \text{ M}$$

88 (b) pOH = 14 − pH = 14 − 12 = 2

We know that, pOH = − log $[OH^-]$

2 = − log $[OH^-]$

$\Rightarrow$ $[OH^-] = 10^{-2}$

$Ba(OH)_2$ dissolve in water as

$$\underset{S \text{ mol } L^{-1}}{Ba(OH)_2} \rightleftharpoons \underset{S}{Ba^{2+}} + \underset{2S}{2OH^-}$$

$[OH^-] = 2S = 10^{-2}$

$K_{sp} = [Ba^{2+}][OH^-]^2$

$$= (10^{-2}) \times \frac{(10^{-2})^2}{2}$$

$= 0.5 \times 10^{-6} = 5 \times 10^{-7}$

89 (c) $A_2X_3 \longrightarrow 2A^{3+} + 3X^{2-}$

$K_{sp} = [A^{3+}]^2[X^{2-}]^3 = 1.1 \times 10^{-23}$

If S = solubility of A_2X_3, then

$[A^{3+}] = 2S;\ [X^{2-}] = 3S$

therefore, $K_{sp} = (2S)^2(3S)^3$

$= (108)\,S^5 = 1.1 \times 10^{-23}$

Thus, $S^5 = 1 \times 10^{-25}$

$S = 1.0 \times 10^{-5}$ mol L^{-1}

90 (b) As, $Co(OH)_2 \rightleftharpoons Co^{2+}(aq) + 2OH^-(aq)$ ...(i)

Given, $K_{sp} = 2.5 \times 10^{-16}$

$= [Co^{2+}][OH^-]^2$ ...(ii)

$[Co^{2+}] = 0.01$ M

Now, put the value of $[Co^{2+}]$ in Eq. (ii) then,

$(0.01)[OH^-]^2 = 2.5 \times 10^{-16}$

$$[OH^-]^2 = \frac{2.5 \times 10^{-16}}{0.01} = 2.5 \times 10^{-14}$$

$[OH^-] = \sqrt{2.5 \times 10^{-14}} = 1.58 \times 10^{-7}$ M

pOH = − log 1.58×10^{-7} = 6.8

As we know, pH + pOH = 14

So, pH = 14 − pOH

= 14 − 6.8 = 7.2

The nearest option given is 7.3.

91 (d) The addition of NaCl to AgCl decrease the solubility of AgCl because solution becomes supersaturated.

92 (a) Precipitation of AgCl will occur only when ionic product is greater than solubility product. This is possible only in case, when 10^{-4} M Ag^+ and 10^{-4} M Cl^- are mixed, i.e. ionic product $= 10^{-4} \times 10^{-4} = 10^{-8}$

93 (a) $Ag_2CrO_4 \rightleftharpoons \underset{2S}{2Ag^+} + \underset{S}{CrO_4^{2-}}$
$\quad\ \ S$

$K_{sp} = (2S)^2 S = 4S^3$

$$\text{or } S = \left(\frac{K_{sp}}{4}\right)^{1/3}$$

$$= \left(\frac{4 \times 10^{-12}}{4}\right)^{1/3} = 1.0 \times 10^{-4} \text{ mol L}^{-1}$$

94 (c) Let the solubility of $Ni(OH)_2$ be equal to S.

Dissolution of S mol/L of $Ni(OH)_2$ provides S mol/L of Ni^{2+} and $2S$ mol/L of OH^-, but the total concentration of $OH^- = (0.10 + 2S)$ mol/L because the solution already contains 0.10 mol/L of $\bar{OH}$ from NaOH.

$$K_{sp} = 2.0 \times 10^{-15} = [Ni^{2+}][OH^-]^2 = (S)(0.10 + 2S)^2$$

As K_{sp} is small, $2S << 0.10$, thus, $(0.10 + 2S) \approx 0.10$

Hence, $2.0 \times 10^{-15} = S(0.10)^2]$

$$S = 2.0 \times 10^{-13}\ M$$

Thus, $[Ni^{2+}] = 2.0 \times 10^{-13}$ M

95 (d) $BaSO_4(s) \xrightleftharpoons[\text{in water}]{\text{Saturated solution}} Ba^{2+}(aq) + SO_4^{2-}(aq)$

If molar solubility is S, then

$1.1 \times 10^{-10} = (S)(S) = S^2$

or, $S = 1.05 \times 10^{-5}$

96 (b) $[Zr^{4+}] = 3S$ and $[PO_4^{3-}] = 4S$

and $K_{sp} = (3S)^3(4S)^4 = 6912\,(S)^7$

or $S = \{K_{sp}/(3^3 \times 4^4)\}^{1/7} = (K_{sp}/6912)^{1/7}$

97 (a) $AgCN \rightleftharpoons Ag^+ + CN^-$

$$K_{sp} = [Ag^+][CN^-] = 6 \times 10^{-17}$$

$$Ni(OH)_2 \rightleftharpoons Ni^{2+} + 2OH^-$$

$$K_{sp} = [Ni^{2+}][OH^-]^2 = 2 \times 10^{-15}$$

Let $[Ag^+] = S_1$, then $[CN^-] = S_1$

Let $[Ni^{2+}] = S_2$, then $[OH^-] = 2S_2$

$S_1^2 = 6 \times 10^{-17}$, $S_1 = 7.7 \times 10^{-9}$

$2S_2^{\ 2} = 2 \times 10^{-15}$, $S_2 = 7.9 \times 10^{-6}$

$\therefore Ni(OH)_2$ is more soluble than AgCN.

Assertion-Reason

1 (c) Dissolution of gases in liquid is that the concentration of a gas in liquid is proportional to the pressure (concentration) of the gas over the liquid.
Thus, A is true but R is false.

2 (b) Both A and R are true but R is not the correct explanation of A.

3 (c) A is true but R is false.
Equilibrium constant of a reaction depends upon temperature.

4 (c) For the homogeneous equilibrium,

$$N_2O_4(g) \rightleftharpoons 2NO_2(g)$$

K_C has unit mol/L and K_p has unit bar.
Thus, A is true but R is false.

5 (a) The reaction quotient changes only if the added gas is reactant or product involved in the reaction.

Both A and R are true and R is the correct explanation of A.

6 (c) Higher order ionisation constants (K_{a_2}, K_{a_3}) are smaller than the lower order ionisation constant (K_{a_1}) of a polyprotic acid.

The reason for this is that, it is more difficult to remove a positively charged proton from a negative ion due to electrostatic forces.
Thus, A is true but R is false.

7 (a) Both A and R are true and R is the correct explanation of A.

8 (b) An aqueous solution of ammonium acetate can act as a natural buffer as it resist changes in pH on dilution or an addition of small amount of acids or alkalies.

Moreover, ammonium acetate is a salt of weak acid (CH_3COOH) and weak base (NH_4OH).

Thus, both A and R are true but R is not the correct explanation of A.

9 (a) Both A and R are true and R is the correct explanation of A.

10 (a) Both A and R are true and R is the correct explanation of the A.

Statement Type

1 (b) Statement I true is but Statement II is false.

The correct form of Statement II is
Chemical equilibrium is dynamic in nature where the concentrations of both reactant and product change constantly with equal speed.

2 (b) Statement I is true Statement II is false.

The correct form of statement II is
The ratio of products to reactants is greater than 1 for the large value of equilibrium in the favour of forward reaction.

3 (d) Both Statement I and II are true.

4 (c) Statement I is false but Statement II is true. The correct explanation is given as :

Addition of Cl_2 will take reaction in backward direction but equilibrium constant will not change as it depends only on temperature.

5 (c) Statement I is false but Statement II is true. The correct explanation is given as:

The amphoteric nature of water can be explained by Bronsted-Lowry concept. Water acts as an acid with NH_3 and as a base with H_2S.

$$\underset{\text{Acid}}{H_2S} + \underset{\text{Base}}{H_2O} \rightleftharpoons H_3O^+ + HS^-$$

$$\underset{\text{Acid}}{H_2O} + \underset{\text{Base}}{NH_3} \rightleftharpoons NH_4^+ + \bar{O}H$$

6 (a) Both Statement I and Statement II are false.

The correct form of statements are

I. Temperature plays a significant role on pH measurements.
As the temperature rises, molecular vibrations increase which results in greater ability of water to form hydrogen ions. As a result, the pH will drop.

II. The dissociation of water molecules into ions is bond breaking and is therefore an endothermic process.

7 (c) Statement I, II and IV are the correct but III and V are incorrect. The correct forms are as follows:

III. According to law of mass action, the rate of a reaction is directly proportional to molarities of the reactants.

V. At constant temperature, if a small amount of one of the products is removed, the equilibrium constant decreases.

8 (*d*) Statements I, II and III are correct while statement IV is incorrect. It's correct form is as follows :
Le-Chatelier's principle is applicable to common ion effect.

9 (*c*) Statements III and V are correct, while the other statements are incorrect.
Corrected form are as follows
I. Expression for the equilibrium constant is applicable when concentrations of the reactants and products have atttained constant value at equilibrium state.
II. The value of equilibrium constant is independent of initial concentrations of the reactants and products.
IV. The equilibrium constant for the reverse reaction is equal to the inverse of the equilibrium constant for the forward reaction.

10 (*a*) Among the given statements I, III and IV are correct whereas II is incorrect.

The correct form is K_{sp} values are not typically influenced by the pH of the solution unless the salt exhibits hydrolysis or react with the solvent.

Matching Type

1 (*d*) The correct match is
A-3, B-4, C-1, D-2.

2 (*a*) The correct match is
A-3, B-1, C-2.

3 (*d*) The correct match is
A-3, B-1, C-2, D-4.

4 (*b*) The correct match is
A-2, B-5, C-3, D-4.

5 (*c*) The correct match is
A-3, B-4, C-2, D-1.

Numerical Value

1 (*44*) $CO(g) + H_2O(g) \rightleftharpoons CO_2(g) + H_2(g)$

At $t=0$	1 mol	1 mol	0	0
At eq.	$1-x$	$1-x$	x	x

Given that 40% by mass, water reacts with CO at equilibrium.

$\Rightarrow \quad x = 0.4$ and $1 - x = 0.6$

So, $K_C = \dfrac{[CO_2]\,[H_2]}{[CO]\,[H_2O]} = \dfrac{0.4 \times 0.4}{0.6 \times 0.6}$

$= 0.44$

or $K_C \times 10^2 = 44$

2 (*1*) $H_2(g) + I_2(g) \rightleftharpoons 2HI(g)$

At $t=0$	4.5	4.5	—
At $t=$ eq.	3	3	3

$K_C = \dfrac{[HI]^2}{[H_2]\,[I_2]} = \dfrac{(3)^2}{3 \times 3} = 1$

3 (*5*) If equal volume are mixed, concentration become half

$Ba(NO_3)_2 \rightleftharpoons Ba^{2+} + 2NO_3^{\ominus}$

Before mixing $= Ba^{2+} = 0.05$ M

After mixing $= \dfrac{0.05}{2} = 0.025$ M ... (i)

$BaF_2 \rightleftharpoons Ba^{2+} + 2F^{\ominus}$

Before mixing, $F^{\ominus} = 0.02$ M

After mixing $= \dfrac{0.02}{2} = 0.01$ M ... (ii)

From Eqs. (i) and (ii),
$Q = [Ba^{2+}]\,[F^-]^2 = [0.025]\,[0.01]^2$
$= [2.5 \times 10^{-6}]$

Since, $[Q > K_{sp}]$
So, precipitation takes place and remaining solution is in equilibrium.

$\therefore \dfrac{[Ba^{2+}]\,[F^-]^2}{K_{sp}} = \dfrac{2.5 \times 10^{-6}}{0.5 \times 10^{-6}} = [5]$

4 (*3*) On increasing pressure, equilibrium will shift in forward direction. Apart from that addition of more SO_2/O_2 will also increase the yield of SO_3 at equilibrium while other factors decrease the yield of SO_3.

5 (*458*) 20 mL of 0.1 M NaOH = 2 m mole of NaOH (base)
50 mL of 0.1 M CH_3COOH = 5 m mole of CH_3COOH (acid)

$CH_3COOH + NaOH \longrightarrow CH_3COONa + H_2O$
(5 m mol, 2 m mol; 3 m mol of (CH_3COOH will left); 2 m mol of salt will formed)

Now, with weak acid and the salt to weak acid, a buffer solution will be formed, pH can be calculated from Henderson equation

$\text{pH} = \text{p}K_a + \log\left[\dfrac{A^{\ominus}\text{ ion}}{HA\text{ acid}}\right]$

$\text{pH} = 4.76 + \log\left[\dfrac{2\text{ mmol}}{3\text{ mmol}}\right]$

$\text{pH} = 4.58$ or (458×10^{-2})

Thus, the value of $x = 458$

NCERT Exemplar's

1 (*a*) On cooling, the equilibrium shifts in backward direction or on heating, the equilibrium shifts in forward direction.

Hence, reaction is endothermic, i.e. $\Delta H > 0$.

2 (*d*) $\Delta G°$ and K_C are related as,
$\Delta G° = -RT \ln K_C$
when $G° > 0$ means $\Delta G°$ is positive.
This can be only, if $\ln K_C$ is negative, i.e. $K_C < 1$.

3 (*d*) As the acidity or K_a value increases, pH decreases, thus the order of pH value of the acids is

hypochlorous acid (3.8×10^{-8}) < acetic acid (1.74×10^{-5}) < formic acid (1.8×10^{-4})

4 (*c*)

5 (*b*) Statement (b) is incorrect.
It's correct form is as follows
In the reaction,

$Fe^{3+} + SCN^- \rightleftharpoons FeSCN^{2+}$ (Red)

When oxalic acid is added, it combines with Fe^{3+} ions, and equilibrium shifts towards backward direction. Therefore, intensity of red colour decreases.

6 (*b*) For the reaction,

$\Rightarrow \quad K_C = \dfrac{[PCl_3]\,[Cl_2]}{[PCl_5]}$

$= \dfrac{(1.2 \times 10^{-3}) \times (1.2 \times 10^{-3})}{(0.8 \times 10^{-3})}$

$= 1.8 \times 10^{-3}$ mol L^{-1}

7 (*d*) For the reaction,

$NH_4Cl(s) \rightleftharpoons NH_3(g) + HCl(g)$;
$\Delta n = 2 - 0 = 2$

8 (*a*) For the reactions,

$$K_{a_1} = \frac{[H^+][HS^-]}{[H_2S]}$$

$$K_{a_2} = \frac{[H^+][S^{2-}]}{[HS^-]}$$

When, the above two given reactions are added, their equilibrium constants are multiplied, thus

$$K_{a_3} = \frac{[H^+]^2 [S^{2-}]}{[H_2S]} = K_{a_1} \times K_{a_2}$$

Hence, $K_{a_3} = K_{a_1} \times K_{a_2}$

9 (*a*) In the reaction,

If the total pressure at which the equilibrium is established is increased without changing the temperature, *K* will remain same. This is because, *K* changes only with change in temperature.

10 (*d*)

11 (*b*) Greater the boiling point, lower is the vapour pressure of the solvent. Hence, the correct order of vapour pressure will be water < acetone < ether.

12 (*a*) For the reaction,

$$\frac{1}{2}H_2(g) + \frac{1}{2}I_2(g) \rightleftharpoons HI(g)$$

$$K_C = \frac{[HI]}{[H_2]^{1/2}[I_2]^{1/2}} = 5$$

Thus, for the reaction,

$$2HI(g) \rightleftharpoons H_2(g) + I_2(g)$$

$$K_C = \frac{[H_2][I_2]}{[HI]^2} = \left(\frac{1}{K_C}\right)^2 = \left(\frac{1}{5}\right)^2 = \frac{1}{25} = 0.04$$

13 (*c*) Given that,

Ammonium acetate is salt of weak and weak base.

For such salts, $pH = 7 + \frac{pK_a - pK_b}{2}$

$$= 7 + \frac{[-\log 1.8 \times 10^{-5}] - [-\log 1.8 \times 10^{-5}]}{2}$$

$$= 7 + \frac{4.74 - 4.74}{2} = 7.0$$

14 (*a*) As we know that, $\Delta G^\ominus = -RT \ln K$

At the stage of half-completion of the reaction,

$$A \rightleftharpoons B, [A] = [B]$$

Therefore, $K = 1$

Thus, $\Delta G^\ominus = 0$

15 (*c*)

16 (*c*) When the concentration of NH_4OH (weak base) is higher than the strong acid (HCl), a mixture of weak base and its conjugate acid is obtained, which acts as basic buffer.

	$NH_4OH +$	$HCl \longrightarrow$	$NH_4Cl + H_2O$
Initially	0.1 M	0.05 M	0
After reaction	0.05 M	0	0.05 M

17 The correct match is

A-(2, 3), B-(4), C-(1).

18 (*d*) Among the given solvents, AgCl is most soluble in aqueous ammonia solution. AgCl react with aqueous ammonia to form a complex, $[Ag(NH_3)_2]^+Cl^-$.

19 The correct match is

A-(4), B-(1), C-(2).

20 (*c*) The pH of neutral water at 25°C is 7.0.

At 25°C, $[H^+] = [OH^-] = 10^{-7}$

and $K_w = [H^+][OH^-] = 10^{-14}$

On heating, K_w increases, i.e.

$[H^+][OH^-] > 10^{-14}$

As $[H^+] = [OH^-]$ or, $[H^+]^2 > 10^{-14}$

$\Rightarrow [H^+] > 10^{-7}$ M

$\therefore$ pH < 7.

With rise in temperature, pH of pure water decreases and it become less than 7 at 60°C.

21 (*a*) Given that, $K_a = 1.74 \times 10^{-5}$

Concentration of $CH_3COOH = 0.01$ mol dm^{-3} $[H^+] = \sqrt{K_a \cdot C}$

$$= \sqrt{1.74 \times 10^{-5} \times 0.01}$$

$$= 4.17 \times 10^{-4}$$

$$pH = -\log [H^+]$$

$$= -\log(4.17 \times 10^{-4}) = 3.4$$

Past Exams'

1 (*a*) In $PCl_5(g) \rightleftharpoons PCl_3(g) + Cl_2(g)$

$$K_p = K_C (RT)^{\Delta n_g}$$

when $\Delta n_g = 0$ then $K_p = K_C$

$\Delta n_g \neq 0$ then $K_p \neq K_C$

In $PCl_5(g)$, $\Delta n_g \neq 0$

$\therefore$ $K_p \neq K_C$

Rest all options has $\Delta n_g = 0$.

So $K_p = K_C$ for them.

2 (*c*) For the given reaction,

$$2A \rightleftharpoons B + C, K_C = 4 \times 10^{-3}$$

At a given time

$[A] = [B] = [C] = 2 \times 10^{-3}$ M

$$Q_C = \frac{[B][C]}{[A]^2} \Rightarrow Q_C = 1$$

As $Q_C > K_C$, reaction has tendency to go in backward direction.

3 (*d*) $2NO(g) \rightleftharpoons N_2(g) + O_2(g)$

$(2.8 \times 10^{-3} M)$ $(3 \times 10^{-3} M)$ $(4.2 \times 10^{-3} M)$

$$K_C = \frac{[N_2][O_2]}{[NO]^2}$$

$$= \frac{3 \times 10^{-3} \times 4.2 \times 10^{-3}}{(2.8 \times 10^{-3})^2} = 1.60 \quad \text{.... (i)}$$

$$2NO(g) \rightleftharpoons N_2(g) + O_2(g)$$

$t = t_{eq}$ $(C - C\alpha)$ $\frac{C\alpha}{2}$ $\frac{C\alpha}{2}$

$$K_C = \frac{(C\alpha)^2}{4C^2(1-\alpha)^2}$$

$$\left(\frac{\alpha}{1-\alpha}\right)^2 = 4 \times 1.6 \text{ [from Eq.(i) } K_C = 1.60]$$

$$\frac{\alpha}{1-\alpha} = 2 \times 1.26 \Rightarrow \alpha = 0.717$$

4 (*d*) pH of acidic buffer solution is given by

$$pH = pK_a + \log\frac{[Salt]}{[Acid]}$$

$$= 4.57 + \log\left(\frac{0.1}{0.01}\right)$$

$$= 4.57 + 1 = 5.57$$

5 (*c*) $pH = 7 + \frac{1}{2}(pK_a - pK_b)$

pK_a of acetic acid = 4.77

pK_b of dimethyl amine = 3.27

$$\text{pH} = 7 + \frac{1}{2}(4.77 - 3.27)$$

$$\text{pH} = 7 + \frac{1}{2} \times 1.50 = 7.75$$

6 (*d*) $NaOH(aq) \longrightarrow \underset{0.1}{Na^+(aq)} + \underset{0.1}{OH^-(aq)}$

$$\underset{S'}{Ni(OH)_2(s)} \rightleftharpoons \underset{S'}{Ni^{2+}(aq)} + \underset{0.1+2S'}{2OH^-(aq)}$$

Ionic product $= (S')(0.1 + 2S')^2$

($\because 2S'$ is very small)

$$2 \times 10^{-15} = S'(0.1)^2$$

$$S' = 2 \times 10^{-13}\ \text{M}$$

7 (*d*) Sucrose + $H_2O \rightleftharpoons$ Glucose + Fructose

For this equilibrium,

$$\Delta_r G^\ominus = -RT \ln K_C$$

$$\Rightarrow \Delta_r G^\ominus = -(8.314\ \text{J mol}^{-1}\text{K}^{-1}) \times (300\ \text{K}) \times \ln(2 \times 10^{13})$$

8 (*b*) 100 mL of 0.1 M HCl + 200 mL of 0.1 M NH_4OH

	HCl	+ NH_4OH	$\longrightarrow NH_4Cl + H_2O$
Initial conc.	100 mL × 0.1 M HCl = 10 mmol	200 mL × 0.1 M = 20 mmol	0 mmol
Final conc.	0	10 mmol	10 mmol

It is basic buffer because final solution contains weak base and its salt with strong acid. Hence, option (b) is correct.

9 (*c*) NaOH is a strong base, thus

$$[OH^-] = 0.01\text{M} = 10^{-2}\ \text{M}$$

$$\text{pOH} = -\log[OH^-] = -\log(10^{-2}) = 2$$

We know that, pH + pOH = 14

$$\therefore \quad \text{pH} = 14 - 2 = 12$$

10 (*c*) HCl can act as Bronsted acid because it can only donate proton.

$$\underset{\text{Acid}}{HCl} + \underset{\text{Base}}{H_2O} \rightleftharpoons H_3O^+ + Cl^-$$

The remaining options contains substances which act both as Bronsted acid and Bronsted base.

11 (*c*) For $BaSO_4$ (binary solute giving two ions)

$$BaSO_4(s) \rightleftharpoons \underset{S}{Ba^{2+}(aq)} + \underset{S}{SO_4^{2-}(aq)}$$

$$\therefore \quad K_{sp} = [Ba^{2+}][SO_4^{2-}]$$

$$= (S)(S) = S^2 \quad \text{...(i)}$$

Given, $S = 2.42 \times 10^{-3}\ \text{gL}^{-1}$

Molar mass of $BaSO_4$ = 233 g mol^{-1}

$\therefore$ Molar solubility of $BaSO_4$ (S)

$$= \frac{2.42 \times 10^{-3}}{233}\ \text{mol L}^{-1}$$

$$= 1.04 \times 10^{-5}\ \text{mol L}^{-1}$$

On substituting the value of S in Eq. (i), we get

$$K_{sp} = (1.04 \times 10^{-5}\ \text{mol L}^{-1})^2$$

$$= 1.08 \times 10^{-10}\ \text{mol}^2\ \text{L}^{-2}$$

12 (*b*) Given,

$$N_2 + 3H_2 \rightleftharpoons 2NH_3,\ K_1 \quad \text{...(i)}$$

$$N_2 + O_2 \rightleftharpoons 2NO,\ K_2 \quad \text{...(ii)}$$

$$H_2 + \frac{1}{2}O_2 \longrightarrow H_2O,\ K_3 \quad \text{...(iii)}$$

To calculate,

$$2NH_3 + \frac{5}{2}O_2 \overset{K}{\rightleftharpoons} 2NO + 3H_2O,$$

$$K = ? \quad \text{...(iv)}$$

On reversing the equation (i) and multiplying the equation (iii) by 3, we get

$$2NH_3 \rightleftharpoons N_2 + 3H_2,\ \frac{1}{K_1} \quad \text{...(v)}$$

$$3H_2 + \frac{3}{2}O_2 \longrightarrow 3H_2O,\ K_3^3 \quad \text{...(vi)}$$

Now, add equation (ii), (v) and (vi), we get the resultant equation (iv).

$$2NH_3 + \frac{5}{2}O_2 \overset{K}{\rightleftharpoons} 2NO + 3H_2O$$

$$\therefore \quad K = \frac{K_2 K_3^3}{K_1}$$

13 (*d*) $Ag_2C_2O_4(s) \rightleftharpoons \underset{2S}{2Ag^+} + \underset{S}{C_2O_4^{2-}}$

$$K_{sp} = [Ag^+]^2[C_2O_4^{2-}] = [2S]^2[S]$$

Given, $2S = 2.2 \times 10^{-4}$

or $\quad S = 1.1 \times 10^{-4}\ \text{M}$

$$\therefore \quad K_{sp} = [2.2 \times 10^{-4}]^2[1.1 \times 10^{-4}]$$

$$= 5.3 \times 10^{-12}$$

14 (*b*) The percentage of pyridine can be equal to the percentage of dissociation of pyridinium ion and pyridine solution as shown below:

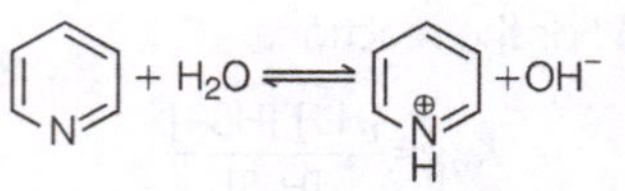

As pyridinium is a weak base, so degree of dissociation is given as

$$\alpha = \sqrt{\frac{K_b}{C}} = \sqrt{\frac{1.7 \times 10^{-9}}{0.10}}$$

$$= \sqrt{1.7 \times 10^{-8}} = 1.3 \times 10^{-4}$$

or, percentage of dissociation

$$= (\alpha \times 100)\%$$

$$= (1.3 \times 10^{-4}) \times 100 = 0.013\%$$

15 (*c*) For a reaction,

$$\underset{\text{Reactant}}{A} \rightleftharpoons \underset{\text{Product}}{B}$$

$$K = \frac{[B]_{eq}}{[A]_{eq}}$$

$$\Rightarrow \quad 1.6 \times 10^{12} = \frac{[B]_{eq}}{[A]_{eq}}$$

$$\therefore \quad [B]_{eq} >> [A]_{eq}$$

This indicates the ratio of product concentration to reactant concentration is very high. So, mostly the product will be present in the equilibrium mixture.

16 (*d*) $Ag_2CrO_4 \rightleftharpoons 2Ag^+ + CrO_4^{2-}$

Solubility product

$$K_{sp} = (2S)^2 \times S = 4S^3 = (1.1 \times 10^{-12})$$

$$S = \sqrt[3]{\frac{K_{sp}}{4}} = 0.65 \times 10^{-4}\ \text{mol L}^{-1}$$

$\because$ Solubility of Ag_2CrO_4 is highest. So, it will precipitate last.

17 (*a*) The equilibrium constant at two different temperatures for a thermodynamic process is given by

$$\log \frac{K_2}{K_1} = \frac{\Delta H^\circ}{2.303R}\left[\frac{1}{T_1} - \frac{1}{T_2}\right]$$

Here, K_1 and K_2 are replaced by K_p and K'_p. Therefore,

$$\log \frac{K'_p}{K_p} = \frac{\Delta H^\circ}{2.303R}\left[\frac{1}{T_1} - \frac{1}{T_2}\right]$$

For exothermic reaction, $T_2 > T_1$ and $\Delta H = -\text{ve}$

$$\therefore \quad K_p > K'_p$$

18 (*d*) $X \rightleftharpoons Y; K_1 = 1.0$

$Y \rightleftharpoons Z; K_2 = 2.0$

$Z \rightleftharpoons W; K_3 = 4.0$

For the equilibrium constant value of

$X \rightleftharpoons W; K = K_1 \cdot K_2 \cdot K_3$

$K = 1 \times 2 \times 4 = 8$

Hence, option (d) is correct.

19 (*c*) Both the Statement I and Statement II are correct.

20 (*b*) Given,

$$CO(g) + \frac{1}{2} O_2(g) \rightleftharpoons CO_2(g)$$

$$\Delta n_g = 1 - \left(1 + \frac{1}{2}\right) = -\frac{1}{2}$$

$$\frac{K_p}{K_c} = (RT)^{\Delta n_g} = (RT)^{-1/2} = \frac{1}{\sqrt{RT}}$$

21 (*a*) We consider following reaction

$$A_2B_3 \rightleftharpoons 2A(g) + 3B(g)$$
$$C(1-\alpha) \quad 2C\alpha \quad 3C\alpha$$

$$K_{eq} = \frac{4C^2\alpha^2 \times 27C^3\alpha^3}{C(1-\alpha)}$$

$$K_{eq} = \frac{108C^5\alpha^5}{C(1-\alpha)}$$

$$\alpha = \left(\frac{K_{eq}}{C^4(108)}\right)^{1/5}$$

(assuming, $1-\alpha \approx 1$)

22 (*b*) Statements (B) and (C) are correct while statements (A) and (D) are incorrect.

(A) pH of 10^{-8} M HCl is in acidic range, i.e. 6.98.

(D) At half neutralisation point, half of the acid is present in the form of salt. $pH = pK_a + \log \frac{1}{1} = pK_a$.

23 (*d*) Ionisation constant can be represented as

$$K_{a_3} = \frac{[H^+]^2[C_2O_4^{2-}]}{[H_2C_2O_4]} \quad ...(i)$$

$$K_{a_1} = \frac{[H^+][HC_2O_4^-]}{[H_2C_2O_4]} \quad ...(ii)$$

$$K_{a_2} = \frac{[H^+][C_2O_4^{2-}]}{[H_2C_2O_4]} \quad ...(iii)$$

Multiply Eq. (ii) and Eq. (iii),

$$K_{a_1} \times K_{a_2} = \frac{[H^+][HC_2O_4^-]}{[H_2C_2O_4]} \times \frac{[H^+][C_2O_4^{2-}]}{[HC_2O_4^-]}$$

$$= \frac{[H^+]^2[C_2O_4^{2-}]}{[H_2C_2O_4]}$$

$$K_{a_1} \times K_{a_2} = K_{a_3}$$

24 (*b*) For the given reaction,

$$A(g) \rightleftharpoons B(g) + \frac{1}{2}C(g)$$

Initial : $p_i \quad 0 \quad 0$

At equili : $p_i(1-\alpha) \quad p_i\alpha \quad p_i \cdot \frac{\alpha}{2}$

Equilibrium pressure $(p) = p_i\left(1 + \frac{\alpha}{2}\right)$

For A, $p_A = \left(\frac{1-\alpha}{1+\alpha/2}\right)p$

For B, $p_B = \left(\frac{\alpha}{1+\alpha/2}\right)p$

For C, $p_C = \left(\frac{\alpha/2}{1+\alpha/2}\right)p$

Now, dissociation constant

$$(K) = \frac{p_C^{1/2} \cdot p_B}{p_A}$$

$$K = \frac{\left(\frac{\alpha/2}{1+\alpha/2}\right)^{1/2} p^{1/2} \cdot \left(\frac{\alpha}{1+\alpha/2}\right)p}{\left(\frac{1-\alpha}{1+\alpha/2}\right)p}$$

$$\therefore K = \frac{\alpha^{3/2}\, p^{1/2}}{(2+\alpha)^{1/2}(1-\alpha)}$$

25 (*a*) $p_{total} = \frac{nRT}{V} = \frac{9 \times 0082.1 \times 610}{100}$

$= 4.5$ atm

$$p_{PCl_5} = \frac{5 \times 4.5}{9} = 2.5$$

$$p_{Ar} = \frac{4 \times 4.5}{9} = 2$$

Now, $PCl_5 \rightleftharpoons PCl_3 + Cl_2$

$2.5 - p \quad p \quad p$

$p_{total} = 2.5 - p + p + p + p_{Ar} = 6$

$p = 1.5$

Now, $K_p = \frac{[PCl_3][Cl_2]}{[PCl_5]}$

$$= \frac{1.5 \times 1.5}{(2.5 - 1.5)} = 2.25$$

26 (*b*) K_a for propanoic acid $= 1.3 \times 10^{-5}$

$pK_a = -\log K_a = -\log(1.3 \times 10^{-5})$

$pK_a = 5 - \log 1.3 = 5 - 0.11 = 4.89$

pH of buffer solution = 4.00

Using Henderson-Hasselbalch equation,

$$pH = pK_a + \log\frac{[CH_3CH_2COO^-]}{[CH_3CH_2COOH]}$$

$$4.00 = 4.89 + \log\frac{[CH_3CH_2COO^-]}{[CH_3CH_2COOH]}$$

$$\log\frac{[CH_3CH_2COO^-]}{[CH_3CH_2COOH]} = -0.89$$

$$\frac{[CH_3CH_2COO^-]}{[CH_3CH_2COOH]} = 10^{-0.89} = 0.13$$

27 (*d*) The solubility of AgCl will be maximum in deionised water as rest all the solution (0.01 M KCl, 0.001 M, HCl and (0.01 N $AgNO_3$) have a common ion with solute being added AgCl.

Thus, AgCl will be most soluble in deionised water.

28 (a) Given, K_{sp} for $Bi_2S_3 = 1.08 \times 10^{-73}$

$$Bi_2S_3(s) \rightleftharpoons 2Bi^{3+}(aq) + 3S^{2-}(aq)$$
$$3S$$

$K_{sp} = [Bi^{3+}]^2\,[S^{2-}]^{3S}$

So, $K_{sp} = [2\,S]^2\,[3\,S]^3$

$K_{sp} = 4S^2 \times 27S^3 = 108\,S^5$

$$\Rightarrow \quad S = \left(\frac{K_{sp}}{108}\right)^{1/5}$$

$$\therefore \quad S = \left(\frac{1.08 \times 10^{-73}}{108}\right)^{1/5}$$

$$= (10^{-75})^{1/5}$$

Hence, solubility, $S = 1.0 \times 10^{-15}$ mol L^{-1}

29 (*d*) pH of AgCN buffer solution = 3

$[H^+] = 10^{-3}$

$AgCN \rightleftharpoons Ag^+ + CN^-$ ...... K_{sp}

$CN^- + H^+ \rightleftharpoons HCN$ ...... $\frac{1}{K_a}$

$AgCN + H^+ \rightleftharpoons HCN + Ag^+$

$$K_{sp} \times \frac{1}{K_a} = \frac{[Ag^+][CN^-][HCN]}{[H^+][CN^-]}$$

$$[S]=\sqrt{\frac{K_{sp}\,[H^+]}{K_a}}$$

$$\Rightarrow \frac{2.2\times 10^{-16}}{6.2\times 10^{-10}}=\frac{S\;\;S}{10^{-3}}$$

$$S^2=\frac{2.2\times 10^{-16}}{6.2\times 10^{-10}}\times 10^{-3}$$

$$S=1.9\times 10^{-5}$$

Skill Boosters

1 (c) It is an exothermic reaction hence at high temperature, backward reaction favoured resulting in formation of NO_2, intensifying brown colour.

2 (b)

$$X_2(g) + Y_2(g) \rightleftharpoons 2XY(g)$$

Moles at equilibrium $\quad 2-x \quad 4-x \quad 2x$

$$K_C=\frac{4x^2}{(2-x)(4-x)}$$

$$\Rightarrow \quad 4=\frac{4x^2}{(2-x)(4-x)}$$

$$x=1.33 \text{ moles}$$

$$[XY]=\frac{x}{2}\Rightarrow\frac{1.33}{2}\Rightarrow 0.66\text{ M}$$

3 (c) Phenolphthalein is weak acid which give colour in basic medium.

4 (a)

$$2SO_2(g)+O_2(g)\rightleftharpoons 2SO_3(g)$$

	$2SO_2(g)$	$O_2(g)$	$2SO_3(g)$
Initial moles	2	1	0
Moles at equilibrium	$(2-2x)$	$(1-x)$	$2x$
Molar conc	$\frac{2(1-x)}{V}$	$\frac{(1-x)}{V}$	$\frac{2x}{V}$

$$K_C=\frac{(2x/V)^2}{\left[\frac{2(1-x)}{V}\right]^2\left[\frac{(1-x)}{V}\right]}=\frac{x^2V}{(1-x)^3}$$

5 (c) $pH + pOH = 14$

$$pOH = 14 - 8.26$$

$$pOH = pK_b + \log\frac{[NH_4^+]}{[NH_3]}$$

$$\Rightarrow \quad 5.74 = 4.74 + \log\frac{[NH_4^+]}{0.2}$$

$$\Rightarrow \quad [NH_4^+]=2\text{ M}$$

Molar mass of $NH_4Cl = 53.5\text{ g mol}^{-1}$

Amount of $NH_4Cl = 2\times 53.5 = 107$ g

6 (d) Using, $\log K = -\frac{\Delta H°}{2.303\,RT}+C$

$$\text{Slope}=\frac{\Delta H°}{2.303\,R}$$

and intercept $= C$

As per question, $C = 10$ and slope $= \tan\theta = 0.5$

So, slope $= 0.5 = \frac{\Delta H°}{2.303\times 8.314}$

$$\Delta H° = 9.574\text{ Jmol}^{-1}$$

$$\log K = 10 - \frac{9.574}{2.303\times 8.314\times 298}$$

$$= 9.9983$$

or $\quad K = \text{Antilog}\,(9.9983)$

$$= 9.96\times 10^9$$

As $\Delta H°$ is independent of temperature, K will also be independent of temperature. Hence, K will be same at 298 K and 798 K.

7 (b) If $K_a = 1\times 10^{-5}$

$\therefore pK_a = 5$

The two conditions when colour indicator will be visible are derived by

$$pH = pK_a + \log\frac{[In^-]}{[HIn]}$$

(i) $pH = 5 + \log 10 = 6$

(ii) $pH = 5 + \log 0.1 = 4$

8 (b) The greater the differene between pH of the solution and pK_a of the acid, the lower is the buffer capacity of the solution.

As given, pH of buffer solution $= 5.0$ of the given acids, acetic acid has its value of $pK_a (4.74)$ nearest to the value of pH of the solution.

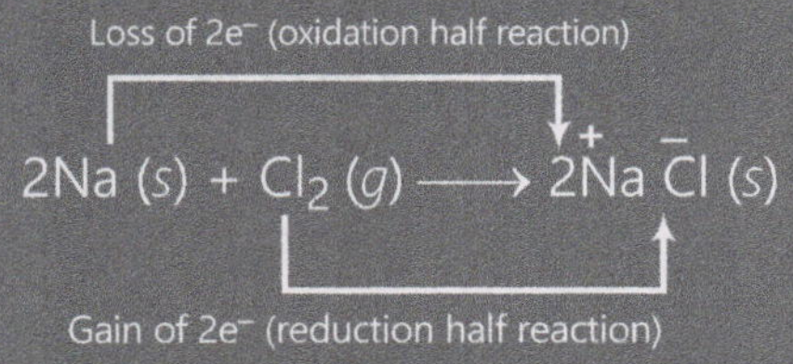

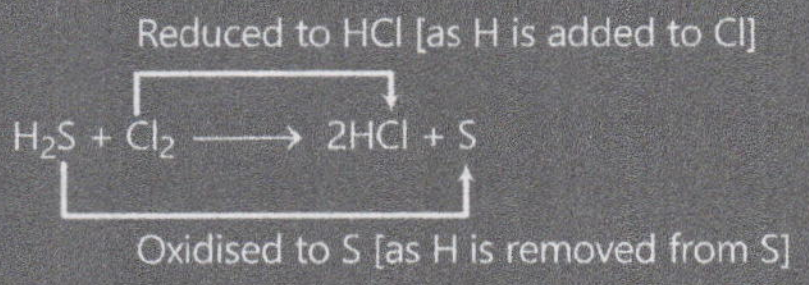

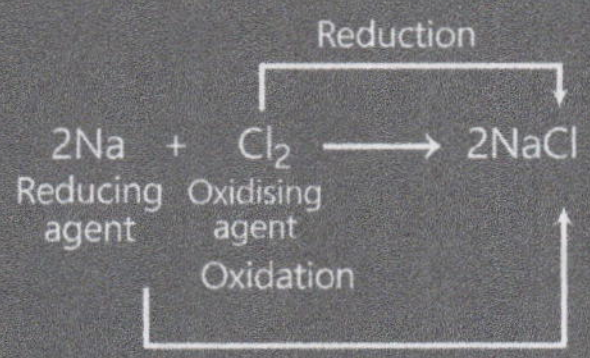

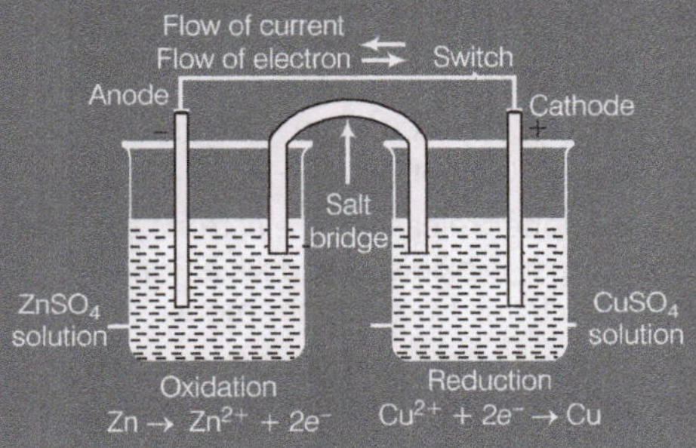

Topicwise No. of Ques asked in 5 Years

Topics	No. of Questions				
	2024	2023	2022	2021	2020
Classical Idea of Redox Reactions-Oxidation and Reduction Reactions	–	–	–	–	–
Redox Reactions in Terms of Electron Transfer Reactions	–	–	–	–	–
Oxidation Number	–	1	–	1	1
Redox Reactions and Electrode Processes	1	–	1	–	1

Special Type of Ques asked in 5 Years

Types	Years				
	2024	2023	2022	2021	2020
A-R	–	–	–	–	–
Statement Based	–	–	–	–	–
Matching	–	–	–	–	–

Last 5 Years Weightage (NEET)

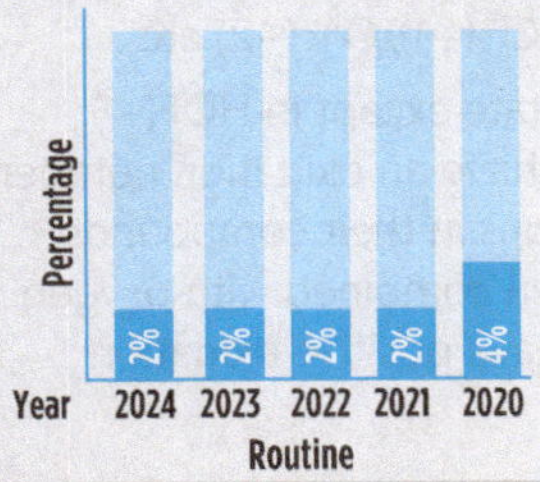

07

Scan for **Chemistry Through Concept Master** Videos

Redox Reactions

Chemistry deals with varieties of matter and change of one kind of matter into the other. Transformation of matter from one kind into another occur through various type of reactions. One of the important category of such reactions is **redox reactions**.

These reactions find extensive importance in pharmaceutical, biological, industrial, metallurgical and agricultural areas.

Previously two major environmental issues like **hydrogen economy** (use of liquid hydrogen as fuel) and growth of **ozone hole** have started noticed out under redox phenomenon.

Classical Idea of Redox Reactions : Oxidation and Reduction Reactions

- **Oxidation** is the removal of hydrogen/electropositive element from a substance or addition of oxygen/electronegative element to a substance.

e.g. $S(s) + O_2(g) \longrightarrow SO_2(g)$ [Addition of oxygen]

$H_2S(g) + O_2(g) \longrightarrow 2S(s) + 2H_2O(l)$ [Removal of hydrogen]

$Fe(s) + S(s) \longrightarrow FeS(s)$ [Addition of an electronegative element]

$2K_4[Fe(CN)_6](aq) + H_2O_2(aq) \longrightarrow 2K_3[Fe(CN)_6](aq) + 2KOH(aq)$

[Removal of electropositive element]

- **Reduction** is the removal of oxygen/electronegative element from a substance or addition of hydrogen/electropositive element to a substance.

e.g. $2HgO(s) \xrightarrow{\Delta} 2Hg(l) + O_2(g)$ [Removal of oxygen]

$2FeCl_3(aq) + H_2(g) \longrightarrow 2FeCl_2(aq) + 2HCl(aq)$

[Removal of electronegative element, chlorine]

$CH_2{=}CH_2(g) + H_2(g) \longrightarrow H_3C{-}CH_3(g)$ [Addition of hydrogen]

$$2HgCl_2(g) + SnCl_2(aq) \longrightarrow Hg_2Cl_2(s) + SnCl_4(aq)$$

[Addition of electropositive element Hg]

- The reactions in which oxidation and reduction occur simultaneously are known as **redox reactions**. NEET 2024

e.g.

Oxidation (Removal of hydrogen)

$$\overset{2-}{H_2S}(g) + \overset{0}{Cl_2}(g) \longrightarrow 2\overset{-1}{HCl}(g) + \overset{0}{S}(s)$$

Reduction (Addition of hydrogen)

Redox Reactions in Terms of Electron Transfer Reactions

- In terms of electron transfer, loss of electrons by any species is called **oxidation** and the half-reaction that involve loss of electrons are called **oxidation reactions**.

e.g. $2Na(s) \longrightarrow 2Na^+(g) + 2e^-$

- Gain of electrons by any species is called **reduction** and the half-reactions that involves gain of electrons are called **reduction reactions**.

e.g. $Cl_2(g) + 2e^- \longrightarrow 2Cl^-(g)$

- Sum of oxidation and reduction half reactions gives overall reaction.

e.g. $2Na(s) + Cl_2(g) \longrightarrow 2Na^+Cl^-(s)$

- A reactant that removes electrons from other reactants in a chemical reaction is called **oxidising agent** or **oxidant.** Oxidising agent cause other substances to be oxidised in a chemical reaction, while they get reduced themselves.
- A **reducing agent** or **reductant** is a substance that reduces another substance by donating electrons to it. Reducing agents cause other substances to be reduced in a chemical reaction, while they get oxidised themselves.

Oxidation (Reducing agent)

$$2Na(s) + Cl_2(g) \longrightarrow 2\overset{+}{Na}\overset{-}{Cl}(s)$$

Reduction (Oxidising agent)

Competitive Electron Transfer Reactions

- The reaction between zinc metal and aqueous solution of copper nitrate as shown below.

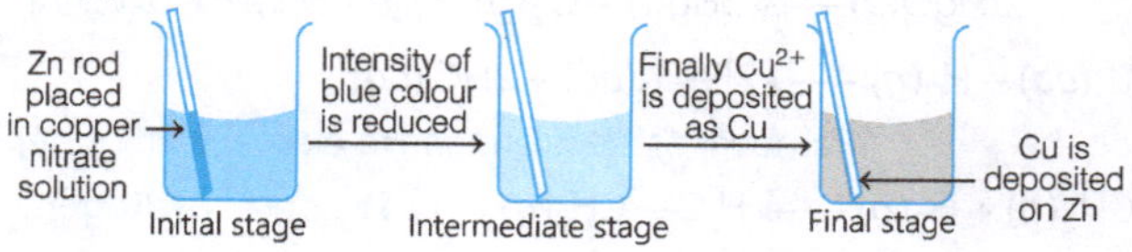

Release of $2e^-$

$$Zn(s) + Cu^{2+}(aq) \longrightarrow Zn^{2+}(aq) + Cu(s)$$

Gain of $2e^-$

- In above reaction zinc is oxidised as it loses electron to form Zn^{2+} ion, whereas copper ion is reduced by gaining electrons from the zinc.
- The reaction between copper metal and aqueous solution of silver nitrate is shown below.

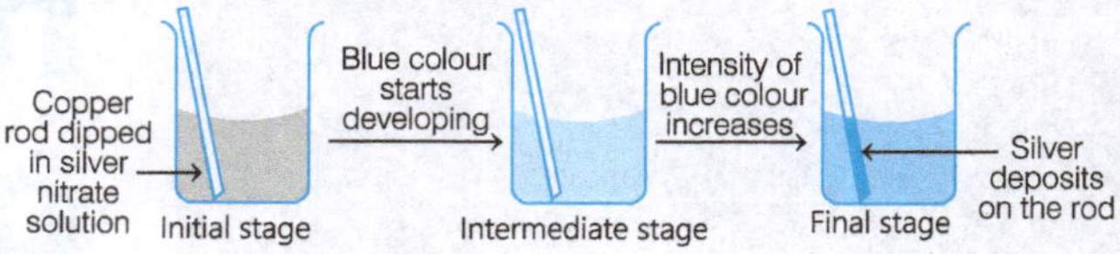

Release of $2e^-$

$$Cu(s) + 2Ag^+(aq) \longrightarrow Cu^{2+}(aq) + 2Ag(s)$$

Gain of $2e^-$

- In above reaction as copper release two electrons to form Cu^{2+} ion therefore copper is oxidised and silver ion is reduced by gaining electrons from copper metal.
- Zinc releases electrons to copper and copper releases electrons to silver and therefore the electron releasing tendency of the metals is in the order

$$Zn > Cu > Ag.$$

- The competition for electrons between various metals helps us to design a class of cells named as galvanic cells in which the chemical reactions become the source of electrical energy.

Oxidation Number

For Concept Master Video

The oxidation number denotes the **oxidation state** of an element in a compound ascertained according to a set of rules formulated on the basis that electron pair in a covalent bond belongs predominantly to more electronegative element. NEET 2018, 19, 20

Some **rules for finding oxidation number** are as follows

- Oxidation number of atom of all the elements in their elementary/free state is 0. e.g. Each atom in H_2, O_2, Cl_2, O_3, P_4, S_8, Na, Mg, Al has the zero oxidation number.
- For ions composed of only one atom, the oxidation number is equal to the charge on the ion.

e.g. $Na^+(+1)$, $Mg^{2+}(+2)$, $Fe^{3+}(+3)$, $Cl^-(-1)$, $O^{2-}(-2)$ etc.

- Fluorine always has –1 oxidation state except in HOF(+1). Other halogens (Cl, Br and I) also have an oxidation number of –1, when they occur as halide ions in their compounds. Chlorine, bromine and iodine when combined with oxygen (like in oxoacids and oxoanions) have positive oxidation numbers.

- Oxidation number of oxygen in most of its compounds is −2. While in peroxides it is −1, in superoxides it is −1/2 and in OF_2 and O_2F_2, it is +2 and + 1, respectively.
- Oxidation number of H is +1 when combined with non-metals and is −1 in metallic hydrides.
- In a compound, the more electronegative atom will have negative oxidation number, whereas the less electronegative atom will have positive oxidation number.
- Algebraic sum of oxidation numbers of all the atoms in a compound must be zero and in an ion, it is equal to charge on the ion.
  e.g. The algebraic sum of the oxidation number of three oxygen atoms and one carbon atom in the carbonate ion, $(CO_3)^{2-}$ is −2.

The idea of oxidation number has been invariably applied to define the following terms

- An increase in the oxidation number of the element in the given substance is called **oxidation** and reagents which can increase the oxidation number is called **oxidising agent** or **oxidants.**
- A decrease in the oxidation number of the element in the given substance is called **reduction** and reagents which lowers the oxidation number of an element is called **reducing agent** or **reductants.**
- **Redox reactions** involve change in oxidation number of the interacting species.

Marks Maximizer

Oxidation number of metals in amalgams (Na—Hg, Zn—Hg) and in metal carbonyls [$Ni(CO)_4$, $Fe(CO)_5$, $Cr(CO)_6$, etc.] is usually zero, since they exist in the elemental state.

Fractional Oxidation State

The average oxidation state of an element is, when two or more of its atoms are present in different oxidation states in a given compound is called **fractional oxidation state.** e.g.

- **Oxidation number of C in C_3O_2** (Carbon suboxide)

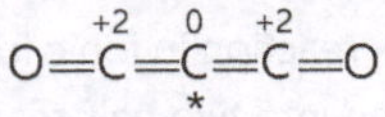

Average oxidation number of C is $= \frac{2+2+0}{3} = \frac{4}{3}$

- **Oxidation number of Br in Br_3O_8** (Tribromo octaoxide)

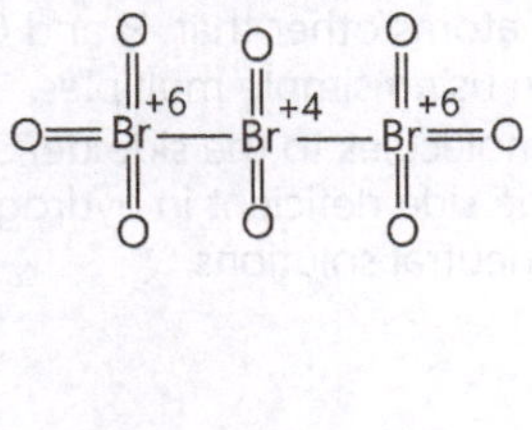

NEET 2019

Average oxidation number of Br in $Br_3O_8 = \frac{6+6+4}{3} = \frac{16}{3}$

- **Oxidation number of S in $S_4O_6^{2-}$** (Tetrathionate ion)

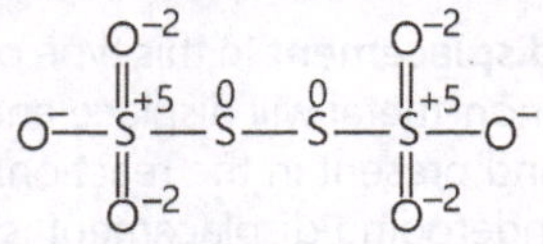

Average oxidation number of S in $S_4O_6^{2-} = \frac{5+0+0+5}{4} = \frac{10}{4}$

- In **stock notation,** the oxidation number/state of a metal in a compound is expressed by putting a Roman numerals, I, II, III etc., within the parenthesis after the symbol of the metal in the molecular formula. e.g. Aurous chloride and auric chloride are written as Au(I)Cl and $Au(III)Cl_3$.

Types of Redox Reactions

Combination Reactions

In these reactions two atoms or molecules combine together to form a third molecule. It may be denoted in the manner,

$$A + B \longrightarrow C$$

e.g. $\overset{0}{C} + \overset{0}{O_2} \xrightarrow{\Delta} \overset{+4-2}{CO_2}$

Either *A* and *B* or both *A* and *B* must be in the elemental form for such a reaction to be a redox reaction.

Decomposition Reactions

In these reactions molecule/compound breaks down to form two or more atoms/molecules. These reactions are the opposite of combination reactions.

In these reactions, it is essential that one of the products of decomposition must be in elemental state.

e.g.
$$AB \longrightarrow A + B$$
$$2\overset{+1-2}{H_2O}(l) \xrightarrow{\Delta} 2\overset{0}{H_2}(g) + \overset{0}{O_2}(g)$$

Note Here, it is not necessary that all decomposition reactions are redox reactions. e.g. Decomposition of calcium carbonate is not a redox reaction.

$$\overset{+2+4-2}{CaCO_3}(s) \xrightarrow{\Delta} \overset{+2-2}{CaO}(s) + \overset{+4-2}{CO_2}(g)$$

Displacement Reactions

In these reactions, an atom (or ion) of a compound is replaced by an atom (or an ion) of another element.

$$A + BC \longrightarrow AC + B$$

Displacement reaction can be categories into two following ways

(i) **Metal displacement reaction** If a metal in a compound can be displaced by another metal in the uncombined state, it is called metal displacement reaction.

e.g. $\overset{+4}{Ti}\overset{-1}{Cl_4}(l) + 2\overset{0}{Mg}(s) \xrightarrow{\Delta} \overset{0}{Ti}(s) + 2\overset{+2}{Mg}\overset{-1}{Cl_2}(s)$

$\overset{+5}{V_2}\overset{-2}{O_5}(s) + 5\overset{0}{Ca}(s) \xrightarrow{\Delta} 2\overset{0}{V}(s) + 5\overset{+2}{Ca}\overset{-2}{O}(s)$

(ii) **Non-metal displacement** In this type of reactions, either a metal or a non-metal will displace another non-metal of a compound present in the reaction. Usually, the non-metal undergoing displacement is hydrogen.

- According to the capability of reducing metal or non-metal, following non-metal displacement reactions cases occurs as follows
  - Good reducing agents like all alkali metals and few alkaline earth metals (Ca, Sr, Ba) displace hydrogen from cold water.

    $2\overset{0}{Na}(s) + 2\overset{+1}{H_2}\overset{-2}{O}(s) \longrightarrow 2\overset{+1}{Na}\overset{-2}{O}\overset{+1}{H}(aq) + \overset{0}{H_2}(g)$

    $\overset{0}{Ca}(s) + 2\overset{+1}{H_2}\overset{-2}{O}(l) \longrightarrow \overset{+2}{Ca}(\overset{-2}{O}\overset{+1}{H})_2(aq) + \overset{0}{H_2}(g)$
  - Less active metals (Mg, Fe) can react with steam to form hydrogen gas.

    $2\overset{0}{Fe}(s) + 3\overset{+1}{H_2}\overset{-2}{O}(l) \xrightarrow{\Delta} \overset{+3}{Fe_2}\overset{-2}{O_3}(s) + 3\overset{0}{H_2}(g)$
  - Metals that cannot displace dihydrogen from cold water but can displace hydrogen from acids.

    $\overset{0}{Zn}(s) + 2\overset{+1}{H}\overset{-1}{Cl}(aq) \longrightarrow \overset{+2}{Zn}\overset{-1}{Cl_2}(aq) + \overset{0}{H_2}(g)$
- Metals like cadmium and tin do not react with cold water or steam are capable of displacing dihydrogen from acids.
- Very less active metals, which may occur in the native state such as silver (Ag) and gold (Au) do not react even with hydrochloric acid.
- In the displacement reactions of chlorine, bromine and iodine, using fluorine is not generally carried out in aqueous solution because fluorine is so reactive that it attacks water and displaces the oxygen of water.

Disproportionation Reactions

- It is a special type of redox reaction in which the same species is simultaneously oxidised as well as reduced.
- In these reactions, one of the reacting substances always contains an element that can exist in atleast three oxidation states.
- The element in the form of reacting substance is in the intermediate oxidation state, and both higher and lower oxidation states of that element are formed in the reaction.

e.g. In the following reaction, the oxygen of peroxide, which is present in –1 state, is converted to zero oxidation state in O_2 and decreases to –2 oxidation state in H_2O.

Reduced

$2\overset{+1}{H_2}\overset{-1}{O_2}(aq) \longrightarrow \overset{+1}{H_2}\overset{-2}{O}(l) + \overset{0}{O_2}(g)$

Oxidised

> **Marks Maximizer**
>
> The reverse of disproportionation reaction is called **comproportionation reaction** in which two reactants each having the same element but in different oxidation state will form a product in which the oxidation state of its both the atoms is similar. e.g. Reaction occurring in lead storage battery.
>
> $\overset{0}{Pb}(s) + \overset{+4}{Pb}O_2(s) + 2H_2SO_4(aq) \longrightarrow 2\overset{+2}{Pb}SO_4(s) + 2H_2O(l)$

Balancing of Redox Reactions

The redox reactions are balanced by two methods. One is **oxidation number method** and second is **half-reaction method** or **ion electron method**.

1. Oxidation Number Method

***Step* I** Write the correct formula for the reactants and the products of the chemical reaction.

***Step* II** Assign oxidation numbers to the atoms in the equation and find out atoms which undergo oxidation and reduction.

***Step* III** Calculate the increase or decrease in the oxidation number per atom and for the entire molecule/ion in which it occurs. If these are not equal then multiply by suitable number so that these become equal.

***Step* IV** Find out the involvement of the ions if the reactions is taking place in water, add H^+ or OH^- ions to the expression on the appropriate side so that the total ionic charges of reactants and products become equal.

If the reaction is carried out in acidic solution, use H^+ ions in the equation; if in basic solution, use $\bar{O}H$ ions.

***Step* V** Make the numbers of hydrogen atoms in the expression on the two sides equal by adding water (H_2O) molecules to the reactants or products.

2. Half-Reaction Method or Ion-Electron Method

In this method, the two half equations are balanced separately and then added together to give balanced equation.

The following steps are involved in this method.

For Concept Master Video

***Step* I** Write down the redox reaction in ionic form.

***Step* II** Split the redox reaction into two half-reactions, one for oxidation and other for reduction.

***Step* III** Balance each half-reaction for the number of atoms of each element. For this purpose,

- Balance the atoms other than H and O in each half-reaction using simple multiples.
- Add water molecules to the side deficient in oxygen and H^+ to the side deficient in hydrogen. This is done in acidic or neutral solutions.

- In alkaline medium, for each H^+ ion, add an equal number of OH^- ions to both sides of the equation, where H^+ and OH^- appear on the same side of the equation, combine to given H_2O.

***Step* IV** Add electrons to the side which is deficient in electrons to equalise the charge on both sides.

***Step* V** Multiply one or both the half-reactions by a suitable number, so that number of electrons become equal in both the equations.

***Step* VI** Add the two balanced half-reactions and cancel the term common to both sides.

Redox Reactions as the Basis for Titrations

Redox titration is a laboratory method of titration for determining the strength of a given analyte (oxidant/reductant) by using a redox sensitive indicator.

The usage of indicators in redox titration is illustrated below

- The reagent which itself is intensely coloured.
  e.g. MnO_4^- can acts as the self indicator.
- If there is no dramatic auto-colour change, there are indicators which are oxidised immediately after the last bit/drop of the reactant is consumed.
  e.g. $Cr_2O_7^{2-}$ oxidises the indicator substance diphenylamine just after the equivalence point to produce an intense blue colour, thus signalling the end point.
- Starch is used as indicator in case of reagents which either oxidise I^- (e.g. Cu^{2+}) or reduce I_2 (e.g. $S_2O_3^{2-}$) as it gives intense blue colour with molecular iodine.

Marks Maximizer

$KMnO_4$ acts as an oxidant in every medium although with different strength follows the order:

Acidic medium > Neutral medium > Alkaline medium

Equivalent mass of oxidising/reducing agent

$$= \frac{\text{Equivalent mass}}{\text{Change in O. S. per mole}}$$

Limitations of Concept of Oxidation Number

The concept of redox processes has been evolving with time. In recent past the oxidation process is visualised as decrease in electron density and reduction process as an increase in electron density around the atom(s) involved in the reaction.

Redox Reactions and Electrode Processes

- It involve the oxidation of one element and reduction of another. Electrode processes include redox reactions where chemical energy turns into electrical energy.
- A **redox couple** is defined as the pair having together the oxidised and reduced forms of a substance taking part in an **oxidation** or **reduction half-reaction**.
  e.g. Two redox couples are represented as Mg/Mg^{2+} and Ag^+/Ag.
- **Salt-bridge** It is a junction that connects the anodic and cathodic compartments (half-cells) in a cell to provides an electric contact between the two solutions without allowing them to mix with each other.

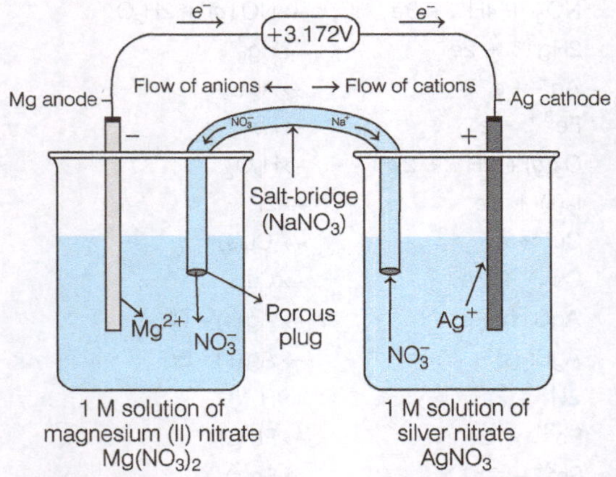

Setup for Daniell cell showing the use of salt-bridge

- The potential difference setup between the metal and its own ions in the solution or potential associated with each electrode is called the **electrode potential**.
- If the concentration of each species taking part in the electrode reaction is unity and further the reaction is carried out at 298 K, then the potential of each electrode is said to be the **standard electrode potential**.

Electrochemical Series

It is a series in which a list of oxidising or reducing agents are arranged in decreasing or increasing order of their strength. It is also called activity or **electromotive series**.

The Standard Electrode Potentials at 298 K.

Ions are present as aqueous species and H_2O as liquid; gases and solids are shown by *g* and *s* respectively.

Reaction (Oxidised form + ne^-	→ Reduced form)	$E°$/V
$F_2(g) + 2e^-$	$\rightarrow 2F^-$	2.87
$Co^{3+} + e^-$	$\rightarrow Co^{2+}$	1.81
$H_2O_2 + 2H^+ + 2e^-$	$\rightarrow 2H_2O$	1.78
$MnO_4^- + 8H^+ + 5e^-$	$\rightarrow Mn^{2+} + 4H_2O$	1.51
$Au^{3+} + 3e^-$	$\rightarrow Au(s)$	1.40
$Cl_2(g) + 2e^-$	$\rightarrow 2Cl^-$	1.36
$Cr_2O_7^{2-} + 14H^+ + 6e^-$	$\rightarrow 2Cr^{3+} + 7H_2O$	1.33
$O_2(g) + 4H^+ + 4e^-$	$\rightarrow 2H_2O$	1.23
$MnO_2(s) + 4H^+ + 2e^-$	$\rightarrow Mn^{2+} + 2H_2O$	1.23
$Br_2 + 2e^-$	$\rightarrow 2Br^-$	1.09
$NO_3^- + 4H^+ + 3e^-$	$\rightarrow NO(g) + 2H_2O$	0.97
$2Hg^{2+} + 2e^-$	$\rightarrow Hg_2^{2+}$	0.92
$Ag^+ + e^-$	$\rightarrow Ag(s)$	0.80
$Fe^{3+} + e^-$	$\rightarrow Fe^{2+}$	0.77
$O_2(g) + 2H^+ + 2e^-$	$\rightarrow H_2O_2$	0.68
$I_2(s) + 2e^-$	$\rightarrow 2I^-$	0.54
$Cu^+ + e^-$	$\rightarrow Cu(s)$	0.52
$Cu^{2+} + 2e^-$	$\rightarrow Cu(s)$	0.34
$AgCl(s) + e^-$	$\rightarrow Ag(s) + Cl^-$	0.22
$AgBr(s) + e^-$	$\rightarrow Ag(s) + Br^-$	0.10
$2H^+ + 2e^-$	$\rightarrow H_2(g)$	0.00
$Pb^{2+} + 2e^-$	$\rightarrow Pb(s)$	–0.13
$Sn^{2+} + 2e^-$	$\rightarrow Sn(s)$	–0.14
$Ni^{2+} + 2e^-$	$\rightarrow Ni(s)$	–0.25
$Fe^{2+} + 2e^-$	$\rightarrow Fe(s)$	–0.44
$Cr^{3+} + 3e^-$	$\rightarrow Cr(s)$	–0.74
$Zn^{2+} + 2e^-$	$\rightarrow Zn(s)$	–0.76
$2H_2O + 2e^-$	$\rightarrow H_2(g) + 2OH^-$	–0.83
$Al^{3+} + 3e^-$	$\rightarrow Al(s)$	–1.66
$Mg^{2+} + 2e^-$	$\rightarrow Mg(s)$	–2.36
$Na^+ + e^-$	$\rightarrow Na(s)$	–2.71
$Ca^{2+} + 2e^-$	$\rightarrow Ca(s)$	–2.87
$K^+ + e^-$	$\rightarrow K(s)$	–2.93
$Li^+ + e^-$	$\rightarrow Li(s)$	–3.05

↑ Increasing strength of oxidising agent

↓ Increasing strength of reducing agent

- A negative $E°$ means that the redox couple is a stronger agent than the H^+/H_2 couple.
- A positive $E°$ means that the redox couple is a weaker reducing agent than the H^+/H_2 couple.

Caution Points

- If an element is in intermediate oxidation state, then that compound can act as both oxidising agent and reducing agent, e.g. H_2O_2.
- Lower the electrode potential, stronger is the reducing agent.
- Higher the electrode potential, stronger is the oxidising agent.
- If a coordinate bond is formed between same atoms or dissimilar atoms but the donor atom is less electronegative than the acceptor atom, assign an oxidation number of +2 to the donor atom and –2 to the acceptor atom.
- If the donor atom is more electronegative than the acceptor atom, neglect the contribution of the co-ordinate bond.

PYQ Notes

1. CrO_5 has butterfly structure having two (—O—O—) bonds.

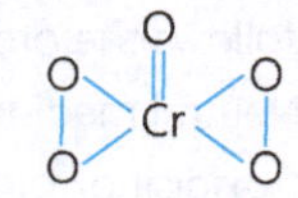

NEET 2014, 2019

2. Cr has +6 oxidation in CrO_6 due to peroxide linkages.

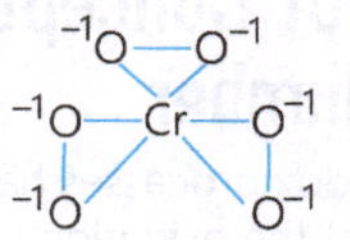

NEET 2019

Step by Step

Mastering NCERT

- Concept Builders
- Topical Questions
- Assertion-Reason
- Statement Type
- Matching Type
- Numerical Value
- NCERT Exemplar's
- Past Exams'
- Skill Boosters

Concept Builders

1 Corrosion is a type of redox reaction. [T/F]

2 Reduction is defined as removal of electropositive element or addition of electronegative element. [T/F]

3 Oxidation is .... of oxygen and .... of hydrogen.

4 Fluorine is a stronger oxidising agent because it is a electropositive element. [T/F]

5 Complete the following reaction,

$$2K_4[Fe(CN)_6](aq) + H_2O_2(aq) \longrightarrow \text{......} + 2KOH(aq)$$

6 The species undergoing reduction in

$H_2S(g) + Cl_2(g) \longrightarrow 2HCl(g) + S(s)$ is ....

7 Write the value of x and y in the following reaction.

Loss of xe^-

$$2Na(s) + S(s) \xrightarrow{\Delta} (Na^+)_2\overset{-2}{S}(s)$$

Gain of ye^-

8 Half-reactions that involve loss of electrons are called oxidation reactions. [T/F]

9 On passing H_2S gas through the solution containing Cu^{2+} ion to produce the .... colour of cupric sulphide.

10 The order of electron releasing tendencies Zn, Cu and Ag is Zn > Cu > Ag. [T/F]

11 Green colour is observed when a strip of metallic copper is placed in zinc sulphate solution. [T/F]

12 The compound NH_4NO_3 exhibit two different oxidation states .... and ....

13 Write the oxidation number of Cl in $HClO_4$ is ....

14 The sum of oxidation number of 3 oxygen atoms and 1 carbon atom in the CO_3^{2-} ion must equal to −3. [T/F]

15 Write the molecular formula of aurous chloride compound using stock notation.

16 The stock notation for $HAuCl_4$ is $HAu(III)Cl_4$. [T/F]

17 ClO_4^- does not disproportionate because chlorine is present in highest oxidation state that is ....

18 The reaction, $P_4 + 3NaOH + 3H_2O \longrightarrow 3NaH_2PO_2 + PH_3$, is an example of disproportionation reaction. [T/F]

19 Copper, gold and silver reacts with water and acid to give salt and hydrogen gas. [T/F]

20 In oxidation number method, use .... or .... to balance ionic charges.

21 Write the value of a, b, c, d and e for the skeletal ionic equation given below.

$$Cr_2O_7^{2-}(aq) + aSO_3^{2-}(aq) + bH^+ \longrightarrow cCr^{3+}(aq) + dSO_4^{2-}(aq) + eH_2O$$

(acidic solution)

22 When Zn is added to $CuSO_4$ solution, metallic copper is formed because of oxidation of Zn. [T/F]

23 Write the name of the method used to find out the strength of one solution against another.

24 Dipping of zinc rod in $CuSO_4$ solution is an exothermic reaction. [T/F]

25 In a Daniell cell oxidation takes place at ....

26 The potential associated with each electrode is known as electrode potential. [T/F]

27 The concentration of each species in electrode reaction is unity and the reaction is carried out at 298 K and 1 atm pressure then the potential of each electrode is called the ....

28 Ammonium nitrate solidified by boiling with .... and later cooling to a jelly like substance.

29 Fluorine is a weaker reducing agent than hydrogen. [T/F]

30 The electrolysis of molten sodium hydride liberates .... at the anode and .... at the cathode.

Topical Questions

Classical Idea of Redox Reactions

1 Which of the following reactions does not represent redox process? NCERT Pg 235

(a) Electrochemical process for extraction of highly reactive metals and non-metals.

(b) Manufacturing of caustic soda.

(c) Corrosion of metals.

(d) Reaction between acids and hydrogen carbonates.

2 In the given reaction,

$$2K_4[Fe(CN)_6](aq) + H_2O_2(aq) \longrightarrow 2K_3[Fe(CN)_6](aq) + 2KOH(aq)$$

Which of the following processes takes place? NCERT Pg 236

(a) Oxidation due to removal of potassium.

(b) Oxidation due to removal of iron.

(c) Reduction due to removal of potassium.

(d) Oxidation due to removal of electronegative element.

3 In the given reaction,

$$2FeCl_3(aq) + H_2(g) \longrightarrow 2FeCl_2(aq) + 2HCl\,(aq)$$

ferric chloride undergoes NCERT Pg 236

(a) reduction process (b) oxidation process

(c) addition process (d) substitution process

4 Consider the following reaction,

$$3Fe_3O_4(s) + 8Al(s) \longrightarrow 9Fe(s) + 4Al_2O_3(s)$$

Identify the species undergoing oxidation and reduction, respectively. NCERT Pg 236

(a) Fe_3O_4 is oxidised and Al in reduced.

(b) Al is oxidised and Fe_3O_4 is reduced.

(c) Both Fe_3O_4 and Al are oxidised.

(d) Both Fe_3O_4 and Al are reduced.

5 Select the incorrect conversion by reduction. NCERT Pg 236

(a) $HgO \longrightarrow Hg$ (b) $FeCl_3 \longrightarrow FeCl_2$

(c) $CH_2CH_2 \longrightarrow CH_3CH_3$ (d) $Hg_2Cl_2 \longrightarrow HgCl_2$

Redox Reactions in Terms of Electron Transfer Reactions

6 In the reaction given below, identify the species undergoing redox reaction. NCERT Pg 237

$$2Na(s) + H_2(g) \longrightarrow 2NaH(s)$$

(a) Na is reduced and hydrogen is oxidised.

(b) Na is oxidised and hydrogen is reduced.

(c) Na undergoes oxidation.

(d) It is not a redox reaction.

7 Identify the correct statement in relation to the following reaction. NCERT Pg 237

$$Zn + 2HCl \longrightarrow ZnCl_2 + H_2$$

(a) Chlorine is acting as an oxidant.

(b) Chlorine is acting as a reductant.

(c) Hydrogen ion is acting as a reductant.

(d) Zinc is acting as a reductant.

8 When a strip of metallic zinc is placed in an aqueous solution of copper nitrate, the ions formed is/are

(a) Zn^{2+} (b) Cu^{2+} (c) NO_2^+ (d) Cu^+ NCERT Pg 238

9 Which of the following change is observed when a clean metallic rod of zinc is placed in a solution of copper nitrate? NCERT Pg 238

(a) Reddish brown copper metal starts depositing on the zinc rod.

(b) Zinc rod gradually starts depositing.

(c) Heat is consumed in the reaction.

(d) Heat is released in the reaction.

10 Identify the redox reaction taking place in the beaker.

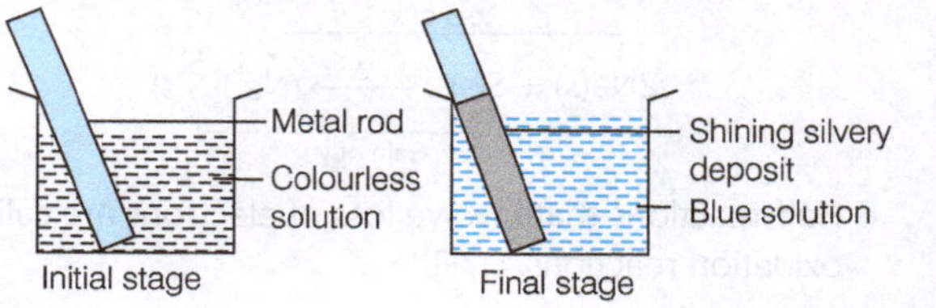

NCERT Pg 238, 239

(a) $Zn(s) + Cu^{2+}(aq) \longrightarrow Zn^{2+}(aq) + Cu(s)$

(b) $Cu(s) + 2Ag^+(aq) \longrightarrow Cu^{2+}(aq) + 2Ag(s)$

(c) $Cu(s) + Zn^{2+}(aq) \longrightarrow Zn(s) + Cu^{2+}(aq)$

(d) $2Ag(s) + Cu^{2+}(aq) \longrightarrow 2Ag^+(aq) + Cu(s)$

11 The correct decreasing order of electron releasing tendency of the given elements is NCERT Pg 239

(a) Ag > Cu > Zn (b) Zn > Cu > Ag

(c) Cu > Ag > Zn (d) Zn > Ag > Cu

Oxidation Number

12 In case of peroxides and superoxides, oxidation number of oxygen respectively are NCERT Pg 240

(a) –1/2 and – 1 (b) –1 and – 1/2

(c) + 1/2 and –1/2 (d) +1 and –1

13 The algebraic sum of the oxidation number of all the atoms in a compound must be NCERT Pg 240

(a) +1 (b) – 1 (c) zero (d) 2

14 The correct sequence of the oxidation state of underlined elements is **NCERT Pg 240**

$$H\underline{Au}Cl_4, K_2\underline{Ta}F_7, Mg_2\underline{P}_2O_7, Na_2\underline{S}_4O_6, \underline{N}_3H$$

(a) +3, +5, +5, +2.5, −1/3
(b) +5, +3, +5, +3, +1/3
(c) +3, +3, +5, +5, −1/3
(d) +5, +5, +3, +2.5, +1/3

15 In which of the following compounds oxygen has highest oxidation state and in which it has lowest oxidation state? **NCERT Pg 240**

$$OF_2, KO_2, O_2F_2, H_2O_2$$

(a) Highest = KO_2, Lowest = H_2O_2
(b) Highest = OF_2, Lowest = K_2O_2
(c) Highest = OF_2, Lowest = KO_2
(d) Highest = H_2O_2, Lowest = KO_2

16 What is the highest oxidation state element in $KMnO_4$ and $K_2Cr_2O_7$? **NCERT Pg 240**

(a) Potassium (b) Manganese
(c) Chromium (d) Oxygen

17 Oxidation states of *X*, *Y*, *Z* are +2, +5 and −2 respectively. The formula of the compound formed by these will be **NCERT Pg 240**

(a) X_2YZ_6 (b) XY_2Z_6
(c) XY_5 (d) X_3YZ_4

18 Which of the following is a decreasing order of oxidation states of the central atoms? **NCERT Pg 240**

(a) $PCl_5, HIO_4, Cr_2O_7^{2-}, CO_2$
(b) $HIO_4, Cr_2O_7^{2-}, PCl_5, CO_2$
(c) $Cr_2O_7^{2-}, CO_2, HIO_4, PCl_5$
(d) $Cr_2O_7^{2-}, HIO_4, CO_2, PCl_5$

19 The species with +6 oxidation is **NCERT Pg 240**

(a) MnO_4^- (b) $[Cr(CN)_6]^{3-}$ (c) $[NiF_6]^{2-}$ (d) CrO_2Cl_2

20 Oxidation number of potassium in K_2O, K_2O_2 and KO_2, respectively is **NCERT Pg 240**

(a) +1, +4 and +2 (b) +1, +2 and +4
(c) +1, +1 and +1 (d) +2, +1 and +1/2

21 The decreasing order of oxidation number of Mn in the given compounds is **NCERT Pg 240**

I. K_2MnO_4 II. Mn_2O_5
III. MnO_4^- IV. $MnCl_2$

(a) IV > II > III > I (b) IV > III > II > I
(c) III > I > II > IV (d) IV > II > I > III

22 Atomic number at an element is 25. The highest O.S exhibited by it in its compound is **NCERT Pg 240**

(a) 3 (b) 5 (c) 6 (d) 7

23 Which of the following reactions doesn't shows any redox process? **NCERT Pg 240**

(a) $VO_2^+ \rightarrow V_2O_3$ (b) $Na \rightarrow Na^+$
(c) $CrO_4^{2-} \rightarrow Cr_2O_7^{2-}$ (d) $Zn^{2+} \rightarrow Zn$

24 Choose the incorrect pair. **NCERT Pg 240**

	Compound	Oxidation state of N atom
(a)	NH_4Cl	−3
(b)	$(N_2H_5)_2SO_4$	+2
(c)	Mg_3N_2	−3
(d)	NH_2OH	−1

25 In which of the following compounds the oxidation number of carbon is maximum? **NCERT Pg 240**

(a) HCHO (b) CH_3OH
(c) $CHCl_3$ (d) $C_{12}H_{22}O_{11}$

26 Which of the following is incorrect? **NCERT Pg 240**

(a) $KMnO_4 \xrightarrow{1e^-} MnO_4^{2-}$
(b) $KMnO_4 \xrightarrow{3e^-} MnO_2$
(c) $KMnO_4 \xrightarrow{6e^-} Mn_2O_3$
(d) $KMnO_4 \xrightarrow{5e^-} Mn^{+2}$

27 The compound that can work both as oxidising and reducing agent is **NCERT Pg 240**

(a) $KMnO_4$ (b) H_2O_2 (c) BaO_2 (d) $K_2Cr_2O_7$

28 The correct explanation about the given reaction, **NCERT Pg 240**

$$Cr_2O_7^{2-} + H_2O \longrightarrow 2CrO_4^{2-} + 2H^+$$ is

(a) chromium is oxidised
(b) chromium is reduced
(c) oxidation number of chromium has neither decreased nor increased
(d) hydrogen is reduced

29 The compound AgF_2 is unstable compound. However, if formed the compound acts as a very strong oxidising agent. Why? **NCERT Pg 240**

(a) The oxidation state of Ag in AgF_2 is + 2 which is unstable.
(b) The oxidation state of Ag in AgF_2 is + 1 which is stable.
(c) The oxidation state of Ag in AgF_2 is + 1 which is unstable.
(d) The oxidation state of Ag in AgF_2 is + 2 which is stable.

30 Which of the following statement is correct regarding the below reaction? **NCERT Pg 241**

$$3N_2H_4 + 2BrO_3^- \longrightarrow 3N_2 + 2Br^- + 6H_2O$$

(a) N_2H_4 is oxidised and BrO_3^- acts as oxidising agent.
(b) BrO_3^- is oxidised and acts as reducing agent.
(c) BrO_3^- oxidised and N_2H_4 acts as a oxidising agent.
(d) N_2H_4 is reduced and act as oxidising agent.

31 The oxide, which is not a reducing agent is NCERT Pg 241

(a) NO_2 (b) SO_2 (c) CO_2 (d) ClO_2

32 Which of the following stock notation is incorrect? NCERT Pg 241

(a) $Na_2Cr_2(VI)O_7$ (b) $Mn_2(VII)O_7$

(c) $V_2(V)O_5$ (d) $Fe_2(III)(SO_4)_3$

33 In the given reaction, NCERT Pg 241

$$FeSO_4 + KClO_3 \longrightarrow KCl + Fe_2(SO_4)_3$$

I. $FeSO_4$ acts as reducing agent.

II. $KClO_3$ is reduced.

III. The change in oxidation number of Fe is 2.

IV. The change in oxidation number of Cl is –6.

Which of the above statements is correct?

(a) I and III (b) II and III (c) I, II and IV (d) I and IV

34 Which of the following statement is incorrect? NCERT Pg 241

(a) The reactants, which undergo oxidation and reduction are called reductant and oxidant respectively.

(b) In redox reaction, the oxidation number of oxidant increases, while that of reductant decreases.

(c) HNO_2 acts as an oxidising as well as reducing agent.

(d) Oxidation is the process, in which electrons are lost.

35 In which of the following reactions the underlined substance is oxidised? NCERT Pg 242

(a) $3\ Ca + \underline{N_2} \longrightarrow Ca_3N_2$

(b) $2\ NaI + \underline{Br_2} \longrightarrow 2NaBr + I_2$

(c) $\underline{ZnO} + H_2 \longrightarrow Zn + H_2O$

(d) $\underline{CO} + Cl_2 \longrightarrow COCl_2$

36 When SO_2 is passed through an acidified solution of $KMnO_4$, manganese sulphate is formed. Change in oxidation state of Mn is NCERT Pg 242

(a) +4 to +2 (b) +6 to +3

(c) +7 to +2 (d) +5 to +2

37 Choose the incorrect statements regarding the given reaction. NCERT Pg 241

$$(CN)_2(g) + 2OH^-(aq) \longrightarrow CN^-(aq) + CNO^{-1}(aq) + H_2O(l)$$

(a) Decomposition of cyanogen in the cyanide ion (CN^-) and cyanate ion (CNO^-) occurs in basic medium.

(b) Cyanogen $(CN)_2$ acts as both oxidising and reducing agent.

(c) Cyanogen $(CN)_2$ acts as oxidising agent only.

(d) It is a decomposition reaction.

38 The reaction, $2H_2O(l) \xrightarrow{\Delta} 2H_2(g) + O_2(g)$ is an example of NCERT Pg 242

(a) addition reaction

(b) decomposition reaction

(c) displacement reaction

(d) combination reaction

39 Which of the following reactions is an example of a redox reaction? NCERT Pg 242

(a) $XeF_4 + O_2F_2 \longrightarrow XeF_6 + O_2$

(b) $XeF_2 + PF_5 \longrightarrow [XeF]^+PF_6^-$

(c) $XeF_6 + H_2O \longrightarrow XeOF_4 + 2HF$

(d) $XeF_6 + 2H_2O \longrightarrow XeO_2F_2 + 4HF$

40 Which of the following will be displaced by all alkali metals from cold water? NCERT Pg 243

(a) Oxygen (b) Hydrogen

(c) Carbon (d) Nitrogen

41 When magnesium and iron react with steam, they produce NCERT Pg 243

(a) H_2 (b) O_2 (c) FeO (d) H_2O_2

42 Which of the following metals do not react with steam? NCERT Pg 243

(a) Cadmium and magnesium

(b) Iron and Tin

(c) Tin and cadmium

(d) Magnesium and tin

43 Which of the following metals do not react with HCl? NCERT Pg 243

(a) Cadmium and tin

(b) Silver and gold

(c) Calcium and magnesium

(d) Iron and silicon

44 Which of the following is disproportionation reaction? NCERT Pg 244

(a) $CH_4 + 2O_2 \longrightarrow CO_2 + 2H_2O$

(b) $CH_4 + 4Cl_2 \longrightarrow CCl_4 + 4HCl$

(c) $2F_2 + 2OH^- \longrightarrow 2F^- + OF_2 + H_2O$

(d) $2NO_2 + 2OH^- \longrightarrow NO_2^- + NO_3^- + H_2O$

45 Breakdown of hydrogen peroxide into water and oxygen is an example of .... NCERT Pg 244

(a) combination (b) decomposition

(c) disproportionation (d) double decomposition

46 Select the compound in which chlorine shows oxidation state of +3? NCERT Pg 244

(a) ClO_4^- (b) ClO_3^- (c) ClO_2^- (d) ClO^-

47 Phosphorus, sulphur and chlorine undergo disproportionation in the NCERT Pg 244

(a) acidic medium (b) alkaline medium

(c) neutral medium (d) presence of platinum

48 Which of the following reactions is responsible for formation of bleaching agent? NCERT Pg 244

(a) $P_4 + 3OH^- + 3H_2O \longrightarrow PH_3 + 3H_2PO_2^-$

(b) $S_8 + 12OH^- \longrightarrow 4S^{2-} + 2S_2O_3^{2-} + 6H_2O$

(c) $Cl_2 + 2OH^- \longrightarrow ClO^- + Cl^- + H_2O$

(d) $H_2SO_4 + P_4 \longrightarrow H_3PO_3 + H_2O$

49 In the reaction,

$3Br_2 + 6CO_3^{2-} + 3H_2O \longrightarrow 5Br^- + BrO_3^- + 6HCO_3^-$ **NCERT Pg 244**

(a) Br is reduced and CO_3^{2-} is oxidised.
(b) Br undergoes disproportionation.
(c) Br is reduced and H_2O is oxidised.
(d) Only H_2O is oxidised to carbonic acid.

50 The reaction of white phosphorus with *aq*. NaOH gives phosphine along with another phosphorus containing compound. This reaction is known as **NCERT Pg 244**

(a) simple redox reaction
(b) disproportionation reaction
(c) decomposition reaction
(d) addition reaction

51 An example of a disproportionation reaction is **NCERT Pg 244**

(a) $2MnO_4^- + 10I^- + 16H^+ \longrightarrow 2Mn^{2+} + 5I_2 + 8H_2O$
(b) $2NaBr + Cl_2 \longrightarrow 2NaCl + Br_2$
(c) $2KMnO_4 \longrightarrow K_2MnO_4 + MnO_2 + O_2$
(d) $2CuBr \longrightarrow CuBr_2 + Cu$

52 Which of the following explanation is incorrect for ClO_4^- species? **NCERT Pg 244**

(a) ClO_4^- shows disproportionation reaction.
(b) ClO_4^- is very stable in water.
(c) The oxidation number of Cl is +7 in ClO_4^-.
(d) ClO_4^- is basic in nature.

53 Which of the following halogens react with alkali like other halogens but does not undergo disproportionation reaction? **NCERT Pg 244**

(a) F_2 (b) Cl_2 (c) Br_2 (d) I_2

54 In the following reaction **NCERT Pg 244**

$$P_4 + 3KOH + 3H_2O \longrightarrow 3KH_2PO_2 + PH_3$$

(a) 'P' is oxidised only.
(b) 'P' is reduced only.
(c) 'P' is oxidised as well as reduced.
(d) 'P' is neither oxidised nor reduced.

55 Consider the following reactions. **NCERT Pg 244**

(i) $H_2O_2 + 2OH^- - 2e^- \longrightarrow O_2 + 2H_2O$
(ii) $H_2O_2 + 2e^- \longrightarrow 2OH^-$
(iii) $H_2O_2 + 2H^+ + 2e^- \longrightarrow 2H_2O_2$
(iv) $H_2O_2 - 2e^- \longrightarrow O_2 + 2H^+$
(v) $2H_2O_2 + 2e^- \longrightarrow H_2O + O_2 + 2H^+$

How many of them are having the reducing nature of H_2O_2?

(a) 2 (b) 3
(c) 4 (d) 5

56 What is the average oxidation number of carbon in carbon suboxide which has the following structure, O=C=C=C=O? **NCERT Pg 245**

(a) $+\frac{4}{3}$ (b) $+\frac{10}{4}$ (c) +2 (d) $+\frac{2}{3}$

57 The oxidation number of sulphur, chromium and nitrogen in H_2SO_5, $Cr_2O_7^{2-}$ and NO_3^- respectively are **NCERT Pg 245**

(a) + 8, + 6 and + 5 (b) +6, −6 and +8
(c) + 6, + 6 and + 5 (d) +8, +6 and +7

58 Compound which has the minimum fractional oxidation number. **NCERT Pg 245**

(a) C_3O_2 (b) C_5O_2
(c) Br_3O_8 (d) $S_4O_6^{2-}$

59 $aK_2Cr_2O_7 + bKCl + cH_2SO_4 \longrightarrow xCrO_2Cl_2 + yKHSO_4 + zH_2O$,

the above equation balances, when **NCERT Pg 246**

(a) $a = 2, b = 4, c = 6$ and $x = 2, y = 6, z = 3$
(b) $a = 4, b = 2, c = 6$ and $x = 6, y = 2, z = 3$
(c) $a = 1, b = 4, c = 6$ and $x = 2, y = 6, z = 3$
(d) $a = 1, b = 6, c = 4$ and $x = 6, y = 2, z = 3$

60 $a Cu + b HNO_3 \longrightarrow c Cu(NO_3)_2 + d NO + e H_2O$

a, b, c, d and *e* respectively are **NCERT Pg 246**

(a) 3, 1, 2, 3, 4 (b) 3, 2, 3, 2, 4
(c) 3, 8, 3, 2, 4 (d) 3, 8, 8, 4, 6

61 For the redox reaction,

$MnO_4^-(aq) + Br^-(aq) + H_2O(l) \longrightarrow MnO_2(s) + BrO_3^-(aq) + 2OH^-(aq)$

The correct coefficients of the reactants for the balance reaction are **NCERT Pg 247**

	MnO_4^-	Br^-	H_2O
(a)	2	1	1
(b)	2	1	2
(c)	1	2	1
(d)	2	3	1

62 BrO_3^- changes into Br_2 in an acidic medium of a unbalanced equation. How many electron should be present in the balanced equation? **NCERT Pg 247**

(a) 10 electron in left (b) 6 electron in left
(c) 3 electron in left (d) 3 electron in left

63 The reaction when HCl is treated with MnO_2 is **NCERT Pg 247, 248**

(a) $MnO_4^- + 5Cl^- + 8H^+ \longrightarrow Mn^{2+} + 5Cl^- + 5H_2O$
(b) $MnO_2 + 2Cl^- + 4H^+ \longrightarrow Mn^{2+} + Cl_2 + 2H_2O$
(c) $2MnO_2 + 4Cl^- + 8H^+ \longrightarrow 2Mn^{4+} + 4Cl^- + 4H_2O$
(d) $MnO_2 + 4HCl \longrightarrow MnCl_4 + Cl_2 + H_2O$

64 During the disproportionation of I_2 to iodide and iodate ions, the ratio of iodate and iodide ions formed in alkaline medium is **NCERT Pg 247**

(a) 1 : 5 (b) 5 : 1 (c) 3 : 1 (d) 1 : 3

65 What is '*A*' in the following reaction ? **NCERT Pg 247**

$$2Fe^{3+}(aq) + Sn^{+2}(aq) \longrightarrow 2Fe^{2+}(aq) + A$$

(a) $Sn^{3+}(aq)$ (b) $Sn^{+1}(aq)$ (c) $Sn^{4+}(aq)$ (d) Sn

66 Choose the correct explanation regarding half-reaction such as $Cr_2O_7^{2-} \longrightarrow Cr^{3+}$ from the following. **NCERT Pg 248**

(a) It is oxidation half-reaction.
(b) Oxidation number is increasing by 3
(c) $Cr_2O_7^{2-}$ is a good reducing agent.
(d) Chromium is being reduced.

67 In the following redox reaction,

$$x\overset{2+}{Fe} + yCr_2O_7^{2-} + zH^+ \longrightarrow x\overset{3+}{Fe} + 2y\overset{3+}{Cr} + z/2H_2O$$

x, *y* and *z* are respectively. **NCERT Pg 248**

(a) 3, 1 and 14 (b) 6, 1 and 7 (c) 6, 1 and 14 (d) 6, 2 and 14

68 In the ionic equation, **NCERT Pg 248**

$BiO_3^- + 6H^+ + xe^- \longrightarrow Bi^{3+} + 3H_2O$, the value of *x* is

(a) 6 (b) 2 (c) 4 (d) 3

69 One mole of acidified $K_2Cr_2O_7$, on reaction with excess KI will liberate *n* moles of I_2, then the value of *n* is **NCERT Pg 249**

(a) 6 (b) 1 (c) 3 (d) 7

70 Which of the following is correct representation of a given molecular equation in ionic form? **NCERT Pg 249**

$$6KI + 2KMnO_4 + 4H_2O \longrightarrow 3I_2 + 2MnO_2 + 8KOH$$

(a) $6I^- + 2MnO_4^- + 4H_2O \longrightarrow 3I_2 + 2MnO_2 + 8OH^-$
(b) $6K^+ + 6I^- + 2K^+ + 2MnO_4^- + 4H_2O \longrightarrow 3I_2 + 2MnO_2$
(c) $6K^+ + 6I^- + 2K^+ + 2MnO_4^- + 4H_2O \longrightarrow 3I_2 + 2MnO_2 + 8K^+ + 8OH^-$
(d) $6I^- + 2K^+ + 4H_2O \longrightarrow 3I_2 + 2MnO_2 + 8K^+$

71 In a solution of $KMnO_4$, MnO_4^- ions produced which act as a **NCERT Pg 249**

(a) induced indicator (b) self indicator
(c) spontaneous indicator (d) oxidising agent

72 The reaction of Cu^{2+}ions with iodide ions gives an intense blue colour when starch is added. By which of the following blue colour disappeared? **NCERT Pg 249**

(a) SO_3^- (b) HSO_4^- (c) $S_2O_3^-$ (d) SO_2

73 Choose the incorrect statement among all, regarding the colour changes shown during redox titration. **NCERT Pg 249**

(a) I^- ions gives blue colour with starch as end point during the formation of iodine by oxidation.
(b) $KMnO_4$ in the form of MnO_4^- ions gives pink colour signs as end point.
(c) The indicator diphenylamine oxidised from $Cr_2O_7^{2-}$ to produce blue colour as end point.
(d) $(S_2O_3^{2-})$ ions gives blue colour as an end point.

Redox Reactions and Electrode Processes

74 In Daniell cell, electrons flow from **NCERT Pg 250**

(a) cathode to anode – through external circuit
(b) anode to cathode – through external circuit
(c) cathode to anode – through internal circuit
(d) anode to cathode – through internal circuit

75 Solution of potassium chloride or ammonium nitrate in salt-bridge usually solidified by boiling with **NCERT Pg 250**

(a) *agar-agar* (b) starch
(c) cellulose (d) glycogen

76 Given below is the set up for Daniell cell, label *p*, *q*, *r* in the given figure. **NCERT Pg 250**

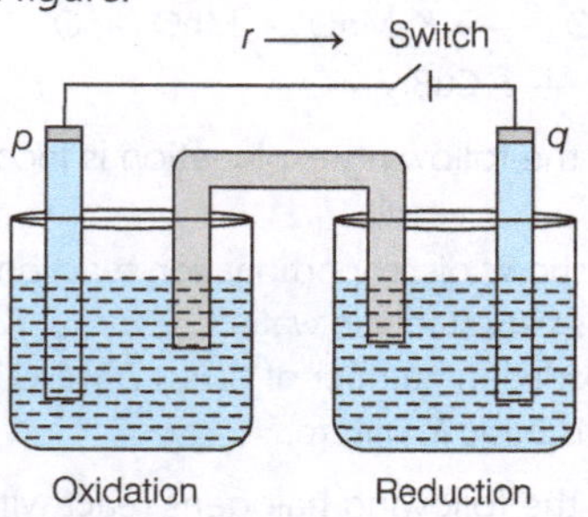

$Zn \longrightarrow Zn^{2+} + 2e^-$ $Cu^{2+} + 2e^- \longrightarrow Cu$

	p	*q*	*r*
(a)	Anode	Cathode	Current flow
(b)	Cathode	Anode	Electron flow
(c)	Anode	Cathode	Electron flow
(d)	Cathode	Anode	Current flow

77 Consider the galvanic cell reaction, **NCERT Pg 250**

$$Zn\,(s) + 2Ag^+(aq) \longrightarrow Zn^{2+}(aq) + 2Ag(s)$$

Which of the following statement is incorrect?

(a) Zinc electrode is positively charged.
(b) The ions carry current in the cell.
(c) At anode, $Zn \longrightarrow Zn^{2+} + 2e^-$
(d) At cathode, $Ag^+(aq) + e^- \longrightarrow Ag(s)$

78 Given, **NCERT Pg 251**

$Co^{3+} + e^- \longrightarrow Co^{2+}; E° = +1.81$ V
$Pb^{4+} + 2e^- \longrightarrow Pb^{2+}; E° = +1.67$ V
$Ce^{4+} + e^- \longrightarrow Ce^{3+}; E° = +1.61$ V
$Bi^{3+} + 3e^- \longrightarrow Bi; E° = +0.20$ V

Oxidising power of the species will increase in the order

(a) $Ce^{+} < Pb^{4+} < Bi^{3+} < Co^{3+}$ (b) $Bi^{3+} < Ce^{4+} < Pb^{4+} < Co^{3+}$

(c) $Co^{3+} < Ce^{4+} < Bi^{3+} < Pb^{4+}$ (d) $Co^{3+} < Pb^{4+} < Ce^{4+} < Bi^{3+}$

79 Given, $E^\circ_{Cl_2/Cl^-} = 1.36$ V, $E^\circ_{Cr^{3+}/Cr} = -0.74$ V

$E^\circ_{Cr_2O_7^{2-}/Cr^{3+}} = 1.33$ V, $E^\circ_{MnO_4^-/Mn^{2+}} = 1.51$ V

Among the following, the strongest reducing agent is **NCERT Pg 251**

(a) Cr (b) Mn^{2+} (c) Cr^{3+} (d) Cl^-

80 A gas *A* at 1 atm is bubbled through a solution containing a mixture of 1M B^- and 1M C^- ions at 25°C. If the reduction potentials of $C > B > A$, then **NCERT Pg 251**

(a) *B* will oxidise *A* but not *C* (b) *B* will oxidise both *A* and *C*

(c) *B* will oxidise *C* but not *A* (d) *B* will reduce both *A* and *C*

81 Consider the following redox couples,

$E^\circ_{Cu^{2+}/Cu} = +0.34$ V, $E^\circ_{Hg^{2+}/Hg} = +0.885$ V, $E^\circ_{Ag^+/Ag} = +0.80$ V

Which of the following statement is correct regarding above values? **NCERT Pg 251**

(a) Mercury can only displace copper from its salt solution.

(b) Mercury can displace silver and copper from their salt solution.

(c) Copper can only displace silver from its salt solution.

(d) Copper can displace mercury and silver from its salt solution.

82 Which of the following is not a correct statement about electrochemical series of reduction potentials? **NCERT Pg 251**

(a) The standard electrode potential of hydrogen is 0.00 volts.

(b) Active non-metals have positive reduction potentials.

(c) Active metals have negative reduction potentials.

(d) Metals which have positive reduction potentials are good reducing agent.

83 The products formed when an aqueous solution of NaBr is electrolysed in a cell having inert electrodes are

(a) Na and Br_2 (b) Na and O_2 **NCERT Pg 250, 251**

(c) H_2, Br_2 and NaOH (d) H_2 and O_2

84 What will be the order of decreasing reducing nature for the given metals? **NCERT Pg 251**

(a) Zn > Na > Fe > Mg > Cu > Ag

(b) Cu > Fe > Mg > Zn > Na > Ag

(c) Ag > Cu > Fe > Zn > Mg > Na

(d) Na > Mg > Zn > Fe > Cu > Ag

85 Predict the products of electrolysis of the following. An aqueous solution of $AgNO_3$ with silver electrodes. **NCERT Pg 251**

(a) Ag from anode dissolves, while Ag^+ ions get reduced and deposited at cathode.

(b) Ag from cathode dissolves, while Ag^+ ions get reduced and deposited at anode.

(c) Ag^+ from anode dissolves while Ag get reduced and deposited at cathode.

(d) Ag^+ from cathode dissolves while Ag^+ ions get oxidised and deposited at anode.

86 Arrange the following metals in the order in which they displace each other from the solution of their salts.

Al, Cu, Fe, Mg and Zn.

Given : $E^\circ_{Al^{3+}/Al} = -1.66$V; $E^\circ_{Cu^{2+}/Cu} = +0.34$ V,

$E^\circ_{Fe^{2+}/Fe} = -0.44$V; $E^\circ_{Mg^{2+}/Mg} = -2.36$V and

$E^\circ_{Zn^{2+}/Zn} = -0.76$V **NCERT Pg 251**

(a) Mg, Zn, Fe, Al, Cu (b) Cu,Zn, Mg, Al, Fe

(c) Mg, Al, Zn, Fe, Cu (d) Al, Mg, Zn, Cu, Fe

87 Given the standard electrode potentials,

$K^+/K = -2.93$ V, $Ag^+/Ag = 0.80$ V, $Hg^{2+}/Hg = 0.79$ V

$Mg^{2+}/Mg = -2.37$ V, $Cr^{3+}/Cr = -0.74$ V

Arrange these metals in their increasing order of reducing power. **NCERT Pg 251**

(a) Ag < Cr < Hg < K < Mg (b) Ag < Cr < Hg < Mg < K

(c) Ag < Hg < Cr < Mg < K (d) K < Mg < Cr < Hg < Ag

88 Consider the following redox couples : **NCERT Pg 251**

I. Zn^{2+}/Zn, $E^\circ = -0.76$ II. Ag^{2+}/Ag, $E^\circ = +0.80$ V

III. Cu^{2+}/Cu, $E^\circ = +0.34$ V IV. Hg^{2+}/Hg ; $E^\circ = +0.885$

Which of the above will act as anode when connected to standard hydrogen electrode which has E° value given as zero?

(a) Only I (b) Only III

(c) I and II (d) II, III and IV

89 A solution contains Fe^{2+}, Fe^{3+} and I^- ions. This solution is treated with iodine at 35°C. E° for Fe^{3+}/Fe^{2+} is 0.77 V and E° for I_2/I^- 0.536 V. The favourable redox reaction is **NCERT Pg 251**

(a) I_2 will be reduced to I^-.

(b) there will be no redox reaction.

(c) I^- will be oxidised to I_2.

(d) Fe^{2+} will be oxidised to Fe^{3+}.

90 How many of the following reactions, have more reduction potential than hydrogen? **NCERT Pg 251**

(i) $E^\circ_{I_2/2I^-}$ (ii) $E^\circ_{Cl_2/2Cl^-}$ (iii) $E^\circ_{Pb^{2+}/Pb(s)}$

(iv) $E^\circ_{Cr_2O_7^{2-}/2Cr^{3+}}$ (v) $E^\circ_{H_2O_2/2H_2O}$

(a) 12 (b) 2 (c) 3 (d) 4

Assertion-Reason Questions

Directions (Q. Nos. 1-10) *In the following question Assertion (A) followed by Reason (R) is given below. Choose the correct option out of the choices given below.*

(a) Both A and R are true and R is the correct explanation of A.
(b) Both A and R are true but R is not the correct explanation of A.
(c) A is true but R is false.
(d) A is false but R is true.

1 **Assertion** (A) The oxidation number of central sulphur in $Na_2S_4O_6$ is 1.5.
Reason (R) Two central S-atoms are not directly linked with O atoms in $Na_2S_4O_6$. NCERT Pg 240

2 **Assertion** (A) Displacement reactions of all halogens using fluorine are not carried out in aqueous solution.
Reason (R) Fluorine attacks water and displaces oxygen of water. NCERT Pg 243

3 **Assertion** (A) Among halogens fluorine is the best oxidant. NCERT Pg 243, 244
Reason (R) Fluorine is the most electronegative atom.

4 **Assertion** (A) The decomposition of hydrogen peroxide to form water and oxygen is an example of disproportionation reaction.
Reason (R) The oxygen of peroxide is in –1 oxidation state and it is converted to zero oxidation state in O_2 and –2 oxidation state in H_2O. NCERT Pg 244

5 **Assertion** (A) Sulphur dioxide and chlorine are both bleaching agents.
Reason (R) Both are reducing agents. NCERT Pg 244

6 **Assertion** (A) In the species, Br_3O_8 each of two extreme bromine exhibits oxidation state of + 6 and the middle bromine of + 4.
Reason (R) The average of three oxidation numbers of bromine of the Br_3O_8 is 16/3. NCERT Pg 245

7 **Assertion** (A) In the reaction between potassium permanganate and potassium iodide, permanganate ions act as oxidising agent.
Reason (R) Oxidation state of manganese changes from +2 to +7 during the reaction. NCERT Pg 248

8 **Assertion** (A) Fe_3O_4 contains iron atoms in two different oxidation numbers.
Reason (R) Fe^{2+} ions decolourise $KMnO_4$ solution. NCERT Pg 249

9 **Assertion** (A) The electrons are transferred from zinc to copper through the wire which connects the two rods in a electrochemical cell.
Reason (R) Electricity flows through the salt-bridge by migration of ions from one beaker to other. NCERT Pg 250

10 **Assertion** (A) A negative value of E° means that the redox couple is a weaker reducing agent than the H^+/H_2 couple.
Reason (R) A positive E° means that the redox couple is stronger reducing agent than the H^+/H_2. NCERT Pg 251

Statement Type Questions

Directions (Q. Nos. 1-6) *In the following questions, two statements (I & II) are given. In the light of the given statements, choose the correct option given below.*

(a) Both Statement I and Statement II are false.
(b) Statement I is true but Statement II is false.
(c) Statement I is false but Statement II is true.
(d) Both Statement I and Statement II are true.

1 **Statement I** The oxidation number of an oxidant decreases in a redox reaction.
Statement II When $K_2Cr_2O_7$ is converted to K_2CrO_4, the charge in the oxidation number of chromium is two. NCERT Pg 241, 239

2 **Statement I** HNO_2 acts both as an oxidising as well as a reducing agent.
Statement II The O.N of N can increase above +3 and can also decrease below +3. NCERT Pg 241

3 **Statement I** All decomposition reactions are redox reactions.
Statement II H_2O, decomposes to give H_2 and O_2. NCERT Pg 242

4 **Statement I** In disproportionation reactions, an element in one oxidation state is only oxidised.
Statement II Decomposition of hydrogen peroxide is an example of disproportionation reaction. NCERT Pg 244

5 **Statement I** The electrochemical cell stops working after sometime.

Statement II The electrode potential of both the electrodes become zero. NCERT Pg 250

6 **Statement I** Silver can be precipitated by adding zinc powder to $AgNO_3$ solution.

Statement II $ZnSO_4$ solution can be stirred with a silver spoon. NCERT Pg 251

7 Which of the following statements are incorrect?

I. Many elements occur on the earth in the form of their oxides because of (~20%) dioxygen in the atmosphere.
II. Addition of electropositive element to a substance is oxidation.
III. Reducing agent is a substance which donates electron.
IV. The competition of electrons between various metals helps us to design a class of cells, named as galvanic cells.
V. The electron releasing tendency of Zn, Cu and Ag is Ag > Cu > Zn.

Choose the correct answer from the options given below. NCERT Pg 235, 236, 237, 239

(a) I, II and III (b) II and V
(c) III, IV and V (d) I and V

8 Select the correct statements from the following.

I. Oxidation state of S in S_8 is –2.
II. All alkali metals compounds have oxidation number +1.
III. Oxidation state of O in O_2F_2 is –2.
IV. The algebraic sum of the oxidation number at all the atoms in a compound must be zero.
V. Stannous chloride can be written as Sn (II)Cl_2.

Choose the correct answer from the options given below. NCERT Pg 240, 241

(a) I and IV (b) II and V
(c) II, IV and V (d) I, II, III and IV

9 Which of the following statements are incorrect?

I. All combustion reactions are combination reactions.
II. All decomposition reactions are redox reactions.
III. For metallurgical processes, metal displacement reactions are beneficial.
IV. Cadmium and tin are capable of displacing hydrogen from acids.
V. Halogens can not show a disproportionation tendency.

Choose the correct answer from the options given below. NCERT Pg 242, 243, 244

(a) I, III and V (b) II and IV
(c) II and V (d) I, II, III and IV

10 Select the correct statements from the following.

I. Fractional oxidation number of Br_3O_8 is $\frac{13}{3}$.
II. MnO_4^- acts as the self-indicator.
III. Adding starch after the liberation of iodine from the reaction of Cu^{2+} ions gives an intense blue colour.
IV. In recent past, the oxidation process is visualised as a decrease in electron density.
V. The standard electrode potential of H^+/H_2 couple is 0.00 V.

Choose the correct answer from the options given below. NCERT Pg 245, 249, 251

(a) I, II, III and IV (b) II, III, IV and V
(c) I, II and IV (d) I, IV and V

Matching Type Questions

1 Match the Column I (Reaction with underlined species) with Column II (Type of change shown by underlined species) and choose the correct option from the codes given below. NCERT Pg 236

Column I (Reactions)	Column II (Type of oxidation process)
A. $\underline{2Mg} + O_2 \longrightarrow 2MgO$	1. Removal of hydrogen.
B. $\underline{Mg} + Cl_2 \longrightarrow MgCl_2$	2. Removal of electropositive element.
C. $\underline{2H_2S} + O_2 \longrightarrow 2S + 2H_2O$	3. Addition of oxygen.
D. $\underline{2KI} + H_2O + O_3 \longrightarrow 2KOH + I_2 + O_2$	4. Addition of electronegative element.

Codes

	A	B	C	D		A	B	C	D
(a)	2	3	4	1	(b)	3	4	1	2
(c)	3	4	2	1	(d)	3	2	1	4

2 Match the Column I with Column II and select the correct option from the codes given below. NCERT Pg 239

Column I (Compounds)		Column II (Oxidation number of nitrogen)
A. N_2O_3	1.	– 3
B. HNO_3	2.	+5
C. NO	3.	+3
D. NH_4OH	4.	+2

Codes

	A	B	C	D		A	B	C	D
(a)	2	3	4	1	(b)	1	2	3	4
(c)	4	1	2	3	(d)	3	2	4	1

3 Match the Column I with Column II and select the correct option from the codes given below. **NCERT Pg 241, 250**

Column I	Column II
A. $KMnO_4$	1. Used in salt-bridge
B. $SnCl_2$	2. Used as an oxidising agent
C. $ZnSO_4$	3. Used as a reducing agent
D. K_2SO_4	4. Used as electrolyte in Daniell cell

Codes

	A	B	C	D		A	B	C	D
(a)	2	3	1	4	(b)	2	3	4	1
(c)	2	4	1	3	(d)	3	4	2	1

4 Match Column I with Column II and select the correct answer from given codes. **NCERT Pg 242, 243, 244**

Column I (Types of redox reactions)	Column II (Redox reactions)
A. Combustion reaction	1. $CH_4(g) + 2O_2 \xrightarrow{\Delta} CO_2(g) + 2H_2O(l)$
B. Disproportionation reaction	2. $2NaH(s) \xrightarrow{\Delta} 2Na(s) + H_2(g)$
C. Decomposition reaction	3. $S_8(s) + 12OH^-(aq) \longrightarrow 4S^{2-}(aq) + 2S_2O_3^{2-}(aq) + 6H_2O(l)$
D. Displacement reaction	4. $Cr_2O_3(s) + 2Al(s) \xrightarrow{\Delta} Al_2O_3(s) + 2Cr(s)$

Codes

	A	B	C	D
(a)	4	2	1	3
(b)	1	2	4	3
(c)	1	3	2	4
(d)	2	1	4	3

5 Match the Column I with column II and select the correct option from the codes given below. **NCERT Pg 245**

Column I (Species)	Column II (Oxidation number of element marked with asterisk)
A. $O{=}C{=}C{=}\overset{*}{C}{=}O$	1. 0
B. 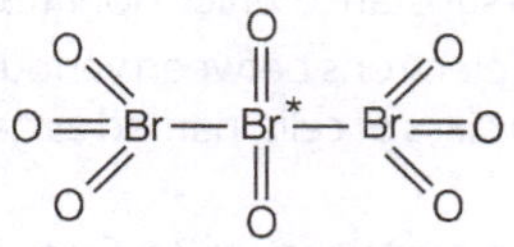	2. +4
C. 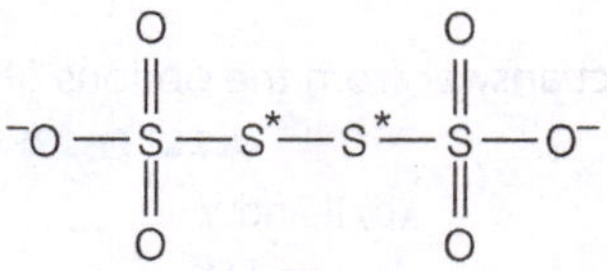	3. +2
	4. +6

Codes

	A	B	C
(a)	2	3	1
(b)	3	2	1
(c)	1	2	4
(d)	3	1	4

Numerical Value Questions

1 The oxidation states of transition metal atoms in $K_2Cr_2O_7$, $KMnO_4$ and K_2FeO_4, respectively, are *a*, *b* and *c*. The sum of *a*, *b* and *c* is .... **NCERT Pg 239**

2 The oxidation states of iron atoms in compounds (*P*), (*Q*) and (*R*), respectively, are *a*, *b* and *c*.

The sum of *a*, *b*, and *c* is

$Na_4[Fe(CN)_5(NOS)]$, $Na_4[FeO_4]$, $[Fe_2(CO)_9]$

[*P*] [*Q*] [*R*] **NCERT Pg 239**

3 The value of *n* in the molecular formula $Be_nAl_2Si_6O_{18}$ is .... **NCERT Pg 240**

4 Among the following the number of elements showing only one non-zero oxidation state is O, Cl, F, N, P, Sn, Tl, Na, Ti, ... **NCERT Pg 240**

5 See the following chemical reaction.

$Cr_2O_7^{2-} + AH^+ + 6Fe^{2+} \longrightarrow BCr^{3+} + 6Fe^{3+} + CH_2O$

The sum of *A*, *B* and *C* is .... **NCERT Pg 247**

6 Consider the following equations:

$2Fe^{2+} + H_2O_2 \longrightarrow aA + bB$ (in basic medium)

$2MnO_4^- + 6H^+ + 5H_2O_2 \longrightarrow a'C + b'D + c'E$ (in acidic medium) **NCERT Pg 247**

The sum of the stoichiometric coefficients *a*, *b*, *a'*, *b'* and *c'* for products *A*, *B*, *C*, *D* and *E* respectively is ....

NCERT Exemplar's Questions

1 Which of the following is not an example of redox reaction?

(a) $CuO + H_2 \longrightarrow Cu + H_2O$
(b) $Fe_2O_3 + 3CO \longrightarrow 2Fe + 3CO_2$
(c) $2K + F_2 \longrightarrow 2KF$
(d) $BaCl_2 + H_2SO_4 \longrightarrow BaSO_4 + 2HCl$

2 The more positive the value of $E°$, the greater is the tendency of the species to get reduced. Using the standard electrode potential of redox couples given below find out which of the following is the strongest oxidising agent.

$E°$ values: $Fe^{3+}/Fe^{2+} = +0.77$; $I_2(s)/I^- = +0.54$;
$Cu^{2+}/Cu = +0.34$; $Ag^+/Ag = +0.80$ V

(a) Fe^{3+} (b) I_2 (c) Cu^{2+} (d) Ag^+

3 $E°$ values of some redox couples are given below. On the basis of these values choose the correct option.

$E°$ values: $Br_2/Br^- = +1.09$; $Ag^+/Ag(s) = +0.80$;
$Cu^{2+}/Cu(s) = +0.34$; $I_2(s)/I^- = +0.54$

(a) Cu will reduce Br^- (b) Cu will reduce Ag
(c) Cu will reduce I^- (d) Cu will reduce Br_2

4 Thiosulphate reacts differently with iodine and bromine in the reactions given below.

$$2S_2O_3^{2-} + I_2 \longrightarrow S_4O_6^{2-} + 2I^-$$
$$S_2O_3^{2-} + 2Br_2 + 5H_2O \longrightarrow 2SO_4^{2-} + 4Br^- + 10H^+$$

Which of the following statements justifies the above dual behaviour of thiosulphate?

(a) Bromine is a stronger oxidant than iodine.
(b) Bromine is a weaker oxidant than iodine.
(c) Thiosulphate undergoes oxidation by bromine and reduction by iodine in these reactions.
(d) Bromine undergoes oxidation and iodine undergoes reduction in these reactions.

5 The oxidation number of an element in a compound is evaluated on the basis of certain rules. Which of the following rules is incorrect in this respect?

(a) The oxidation number of hydrogen is always +1.
(b) The algebraic sum of all the oxidation numbers in a compound is zero.
(c) An element in the free or the uncombined state bears oxidation number zero.
(d) In all its compounds, the oxidation number of fluorine is –1.

6 In which of the following compounds, an element exhibits two different oxidation states?

(a) NH_2OH (b) NH_4NO_3 (c) N_2H_4 (d) N_3H

7 Which of the following arrangements represent increasing oxidation number of the central atom?

(a) $CrO_2^-, ClO_3^-, CrO_4^{2-}, MnO_4^-$
(b) $ClO_3^-, CrO_4^{2-}, MnO_4^-, CrO_2^-$
(c) $CrO_2^-, ClO_3^-, MnO_4^-, CrO_4^{2-}$
(d) $CrO_4^{2-}, MnO_4^-, CrO_2^-, ClO_3^-$

8 The largest oxidation number exhibited by an element depends on its outer electronic configuration. With which of the following outer electronic configurations the element will exhibit largest oxidation number?

(a) $3d^1 4s^2$ (b) $3d^3 4s^2$ (c) $3d^5 4s^1$ (d) $3d^5 4s^2$

9 Identify disproportionation reaction,

(a) $CH_4 + 2O_2 \longrightarrow CO_2 + 2H_2O$
(b) $CH_4 + 4Cl_2 \longrightarrow CCl_4 + 4HCl$
(c) $2F_2 + 2OH^- \longrightarrow 2F^- + OF_2 + H_2O$
(d) $2NO_2 + 2OH^- \longrightarrow NO_2^- + NO_3^- + H_2O$

10 Match Column I with Column II for the oxidation states of the central atoms.

Column I	Column II	
(i) $Cr_2O_7^{2-}$	A.	+3
(ii) MnO_4^-	B.	+4
(iii) VO_3^-	C.	+5
(iv) FeF_6^{3-}	D.	+6
	E.	+7

11 Which of the following elements does not show disproportionation tendency?

(a) Cl (b) Br (c) F (d) I

12 Using the standard electrode potential, find out the pair between which redox reactions is not feasible.

$E^\ominus$ values: $Fe^{3+}/Fe^{2+} = +0.77$; $I_2/I^- = +0.54$
$Cu^{2+}/Cu = +0.34$; $Ag^+/Ag = +0.80$ V

(a) Fe^{3+} and I^- (b) Ag^+ and Cu
(c) Fe^{3+} and Cu (d) Ag and Fe^{3+}

13 Match the items in Column I with relevant items in Column II.

Column I	Column II
(i) Ions having positive charge	A. +7
(ii) The sum of oxidation number of all atoms in a neutral molecule	B. –1
(iii) Oxidation number of hydrogen ion (H^+)	C. +1
(iv) Oxidation number of fluorine in NaF	D. 0
(v) Ions having negative charge	E. Cation
	F. Anion

Past Exams' Questions

NEET Archive

1 Which reaction is not a redox reaction? **NCERT Pg 235, NEET 2024**

(a) $Zn + CuSO_4 \longrightarrow ZnSO_4 + Cu$
(b) $2KClO_3 + I_2 \longrightarrow 2KIO_3 + Cl_2$
(c) $H_2 + Cl_2 \longrightarrow 2HCl$
(d) $BaCl_2 + Na_2SO_4 \longrightarrow BaSO_4 + 2NaCl$

2 On balancing the given redox reaction,

$$aCr_2O_7^{2-} + bSO_3^{2-}(aq) + cH^+(aq) \longrightarrow 2aCr^{3+}(aq) + bSO_4^{2-}(aq) + \frac{c}{2}H_2O(l)$$

the coefficients a, b and c are found to be, respectively

(a) 3, 8, 1 (b) 1, 8, 3 **NCERT Pg 247, NEET 2023**
(c) 8, 1, 3 (d) 1, 3, 8

3 Which of the following reactions is the metal displacement reaction? Choose the right option. **NCERT Pg 242, NEET 2021**

(a) $2Pb(NO_3)_2 \longrightarrow 2PbO + 4NO_2 + O_2\uparrow$
(b) $2KClO_3 \xrightarrow{\Delta} 2KCl + 3O_2$
(c) $Cr_2O_3 + 2Al \xrightarrow{\Delta} Al_2O_3 + 2Cr$
(d) $Fe + 2HCl \longrightarrow FeCl_2 + H_2\uparrow$

4 Identify the reaction from following having top position in EMF series (Standard reduction potential) according to their electrode potential at 298 K. **NCERT Pg 251, NEET 2020**

(a) $Mg^{2+} + 2e^- \longrightarrow Mg(s)$
(b) $Fe^{2+} + 2e^- \longrightarrow Fe(s)$
(c) $Au^{3+} + 3e^- \longrightarrow Au(s)$
(d) $K^+ + 1e^- \longrightarrow K(s)$

5 What is the change in oxidation number of carbon in the following reaction? **NCERT Pg 239, NEET 2020**

$$CH_4(g) + 4Cl_2(g) \longrightarrow CCl_4(l) + 4HCl(g)$$

(a) +4 to +4 (b) 0 to +4
(c) −4 to +4 (d) 0 to −4

6 The correct structure of tribromooctaoxide is **NCERT Pg 245, NEET 2019**

(a) 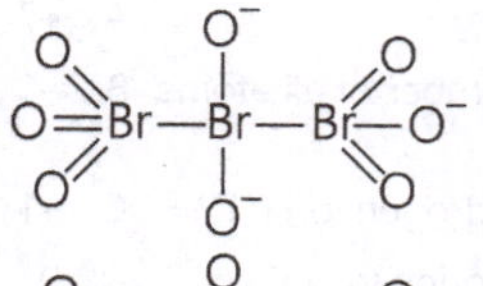
(b) 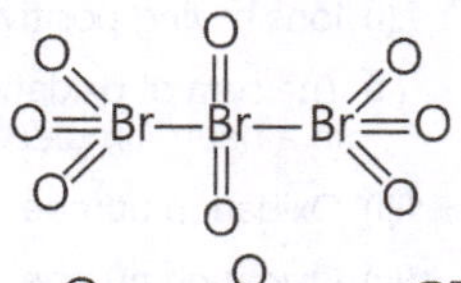
(c) 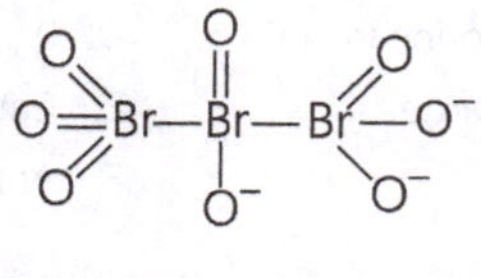
(d) 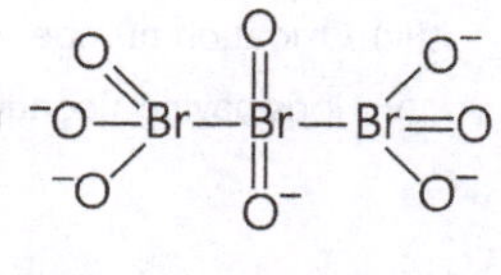

7 Which of the following reactions are disproportionation reaction? **NCERT Pg 244, NEET 2019**

I. $2Cu^+ \longrightarrow Cu^{2+} + Cu^0$
II. $3MnO_4^{2-} + 4H^+ \longrightarrow 2MnO_4^- + MnO_2 + 2H_2O$
III. $2KMnO_4 \xrightarrow{\Delta} K_2MnO_4 + MnO_2 + O_2$
IV. $2MnO_4^- + 3Mn^{2+} + 2H_2O \longrightarrow 5MnO_2 + 4H^{\oplus}$

Select the correct option from the following.

(a) I, II and III (b) I, III and IV
(c) I and IV (d) I and II

8 The standard electrode potential ($E°$) values of (Al^{3+}/Al, Ag^+/Ag, K^+/K and Cr^{3+}/Cr are −1.66 V, 0.80V, −2.93 V and −0.74 V, respectively. The correct decreasing order of reducing power of the metal is **NCERT Pg 251, NEET 2019**

(a) Ag > Cr > Al > K (b) K > Al > Cr > Ag
(c) K > Al > Ag > Cr (d) Al > K > Ag > Cr

9 For the redox reaction,

$$MnO_4^- + C_2O_4^{2-} + H^+ \longrightarrow Mn^{2+} + CO_2 + H_2O$$

the correct coefficients of the reactants for the balanced equation are **NCERT Pg 246, NEET 2018**

	MnO_4^-	$C_2O_4^{2-}$	H^+		MnO_4^-	$C_2O_4^{2-}$	H^+
(a)	2	16	5	(b)	2	5	16
(c)	16	5	2	(d)	5	16	2

JEE Main Archive

10 From the given list, the number of compounds with + 4 oxidation state of sulphur is ..... **NCERT Pg 239, JEE Main 2024**

SO_3, H_2SO_3, $SOCl_2$, SF_4, $BaSO_4$, $H_2S_2O_7$

11 Thiosulphate reacts differently with iodine and bromine in the reactions given below : **NCERT Pg 236, JEE Main 2024**

$$2S_2O_3^{2-} + I_2 \longrightarrow S_4O_6^{2-} + 2I^-$$
$$S_2O_3^{2-} + 5Br_2 + 5H_2O \longrightarrow 2SO_4^{2-} + 4Br^- + 10H^+$$

Which of the following statements justifies the above dual behaviour of thiosulphate?

(a) Thiosulphate undergoes oxidation by bromine and reduction by iodine in these reactions.
(b) Bromine is a weaker oxidant than iodine.
(c) Bromine is a stronger oxidant than iodine.
(d) Bromine undergoes oxidation and iodine undergoes reduction in these reaction.

12 Which of the following reactions are disproportionation reactions? **NCERT Pg 244, JEE Main 2024**

(A) $Cu^+ \longrightarrow Cu^{2+} + Cu$
(B) $3MnO_4^{2-} + 4H^+ \longrightarrow 2MnO_4^- + MnO_2 + 2H_2O$
(C) $2KMnO_4 \longrightarrow K_2MnO_4 + MnO_2 + O_2$
(D) $2MnO_4^- + 3Mn^{2+} + 2H_2O \longrightarrow 5MnO_2 + 4H^+$

Choose the correct answer from the options given below NCERT Pg 244, JEE Main 2024

(a) (A), (D) (b) (A), (B), (C) (c) (B), (C), (D) (d) (A), (B)

13 Match List-I with List-II.

	List-I (Reaction)	List-II (Type of redox reaction)
A.	$N_2(g) + O_2(g) \longrightarrow 2NO(g)$	I. Decomposition
B.	$2Pb(NO_3)_2(s) \longrightarrow 2PbO(s) + 4NO_2(g) + O_2(g)$	II. Displacement
C.	$2Na(s) + 2H_2O(l) \longrightarrow 2NaOH(aq.) + H_2(g)$	III. Disproportionation
D.	$2NO_2(g) + 2\bar{O}H(aq) \longrightarrow NO_2^-(aq) + NO_3^-(aq) + H_2O(l)$	IV. Combination

Choose the correct answer from the options given below. NCERT Pg 242, JEE Main 2024

	A	B	C	D		A	B	C	D
(a)	III	II	I	IV	(b)	IV	I	II	III
(c)	I	II	III	IV	(d)	II	III	IV	I

14 Which of the following options are correct for the reaction?

$$2[Au(CN)_2]^-(aq) + Zn(s) \longrightarrow 2Au(s) + [Zn(CN)_4]^{2-}(aq)$$

A. Redox reaction B. Displacement reaction
C. Decomposition reaction D. Combination reaction

Choose the correct answer from the options given below. NCERT Pg 242, JEE Main 2023

(a) C and D (b) A and B (c) A and D (d) Only A

15 H_2O_2 acts as a reducing agent in NCERT Pg 241, JEE Main 2023

(a) $Na_2S + 4H_2O_2 \longrightarrow Na_2SO_4 + 4H_2O$
(b) $2Fe^{2+} + 2H^+ + H_2O_2 \longrightarrow 2Fe^{3+} + 2H_2O$
(c) $Mn^{2+} + 2H_2O_2 \longrightarrow MnO_2 + 2H_2O$
(d) $2NaOCl + H_2O_2 \longrightarrow 2NaCl + H_2O + O_2$

16 $2IO_3^- + xI^- + 12H^+ \longrightarrow 6I_2 + 6H_2O$

What is the value of x? NCERT Pg 246, JEE Main 2023

(a) 6 (b) 2 (c) 10 (d) 12

17 Which of the given reactions is not an example of disproportionation reaction ? NCERT Pg 244, JEE Main 2022

(a) $2H_2O_2 \longrightarrow 2H_2O + O_2$
(b) $2NO_2 + H_2O \longrightarrow HNO_3 + HNO_2$
(c) $MnO_4^- + 4H^+ + 3e^- \longrightarrow MnO_2 + 2H_2O$
(d) $3MnO_4^{2-} + 4H^+ \longrightarrow 2MnO_4^- + MnO_2 + 2H_2O$

18 Which one of the following is an example of disproportionation reaction? NCERT Pg 244, JEE Main 2022

(a) $3MnO_4^{2-} + 4H^+ \longrightarrow 2MnO_4^- + MnO_2 + 2H_2O$
(b) $MnO_4^- + 4H^+ + 4e^- \longrightarrow MnO_2 + 2H_2O$
(c) $10I^- + 2MnO_4^- + 16H^+ \longrightarrow 2Mn^{2+} + 8H_2O + 5I_2$
(d) $8MnO_4^- + 3S_2O_3^{2-} + H_2O \longrightarrow 8MnO_2 + 6SO_4^{2-} + 2OH^-$

19 Identify the process in which change in the oxidation state is five JEE Main 2021

(a) $Cr_2O_7^{2-} \longrightarrow 2Cr^{3+}$ (b) $MnO_4^- \longrightarrow Mn^{2+}$
(c) $CrO_4^{2-} \longrightarrow Cr^{3+}$ (d) $C_2O_4^{2-} \longrightarrow 2CO_2$

20 Which of the following equation depicts the oxidising nature of H_2O_2? NCERT Pg 241, JEE Main 2021

(a) $KIO_4 + H_2O_2 \longrightarrow KIO_3 + H_2O + O_2$
(b) $I_2 + H_2O_2 + 2OH^- \longrightarrow 2I^- + 2H_2O + O_2$
(c) $2I^- + H_2O_2 + 2H^+ \longrightarrow I_2 + 2H_2O$
(d) $Cl_2 + H_2O_2 \longrightarrow 2HCl + O_2$

21 The species given below that does not show disproportionation reaction is NCERT Pg 244, JEE Main 2021

(a) BrO_4^- (b) BrO^- (c) BrO_2^- (d) BrO_3^-

Skill Boosters

1 MnO_4^- ions are reduced in acidic condition to Mn^{2+} ions whereas they are reduced in neutral condition to MnO_2. The oxidation of 25 mL of a solution X containing Fe^{2+} ions required in acidic condition 20 mL of solution Y containing MnO_4^- ions. What volume of solution Y would be required to oxidise 25 mL of solution X containing Fe^{2+} ions in neutral condition?

(a) 11.4 mL (b) 12.0 mL (c) 33.3 mL (d) 35.0 mL

2 A compound contains atoms of three elements A, B and C. If the oxidation number of A is +2, B is +5 and that of C is −2, the possible formula of the compound is

(a) $A_3(BC_4)_2$ (b) $A_3(B_4C)_2$ (c) ABC_2 (d) $A_3(BC_3)_2$

3 Bleaching powder and bleach solution are produced on a large scale and used in several household products. 25 mL of household bleach solution was mixed with 30 mL of 0.50 M KI and 10 mL of 4N acetic acid. In the titration of the liberated iodine, 48 mL of 0.25 N $Na_2S_2O_3$ was used to reach the end point. The molarity of the household bleach solution is

(a) 0.48 M (b) 0.96 M (c) 0.24 M (d) 0.024 M

4 In metro cities water is a important aspect of living. But dirty water is a problem facing by people in those areas. To overcome this, chlorine is used to purify drinking water. Excess of chlorine is harmful. The excess chlorine is removed by treating with sulphur dioxide. This process is a type of redox reaction that can be expressed as

(a) $Cl_2(aq) + 2SO_2(aq) + 2H_2O(l) \longrightarrow 2Cl^-(aq) + 2SO_4^{2-}(aq) + 4H^+(aq)$

(b) $2Cl_2(aq) + 5SO_2(aq) + 4H^+(aq) \longrightarrow 4Cl^-(aq) + 5SO_2(aq) + 2H_2O(aq)$

(c) $Cl_2(aq) + SO_2(aq) + 2H_2O(l) \longrightarrow 2Cl^-(aq) + SO_4^{2-}(aq) + 4H^+(aq)$

(d) $4Cl_2(aq) + 3SO_2(aq) + 6H_2O(l) \longrightarrow 4Cl^-(aq) + 3SO_4^{2-}(aq) + 12H^+$

5 In redox systems, the titration method can be adopted to determine the strength of a reductant/oxidant using a redox sensitive indicator. An observation is made that, 2.68×10^{-3} moles of a solution containing an ion A^{m+} require 1.61×10^{-3} moles MnO_4^- for the oxidation of A^{m+} to AO_3^- in acidic medium. By using redox reactions find the value of m.

(a) 1 (b) 2 (c) 3 (d) 4

6 Consider the following redox reaction.

$$Cr_2O_7^{2-} + Cl^- \longrightarrow Cr^{3+} + Cl_2$$

In a certain experiment, 0.25 moles of potassium dichromate ($K_2Cr_2O_7$) are reacted with excess hydrochloric acid (HCl). If all the chromium in the dichromate is converted to chromium (III) ions, what volume (in litres) of chlorine gas at STP will be produced?

(a) 22.4 L (b) 15.2 L (c) 10.8 L (d) 16.8 L

7 A compound *XYZ* is having an element *X* of oxidation number X^{n-}. It is oxidised by $Cr_2O_7^{2-}$ in acidic medium. In the experiment, 1.68×10^{-3} mole of $K_2Cr_2O_7$ were used for 3.26×10^{-3} mole of *XYZ*. The new oxidation medium of *X* after oxidation is

(a) $n-3$ (b) 3
(c) $3+n$ (d) $3-n$

Correct Codes

Topical Questions

1. (d) 2. (a) 3. (a) 4. (b) 5. (d) 6. (b) 7. (d) 8. (a) 9. (a) 10. (b)
11. (b) 12. (b) 13. (c) 14. (a) 15. (c) 16. (b) 17. (b) 18. (b) 19. (d) 20. (c)
21. (c) 22. (d) 23. (c) 24. (b) 25. (c) 26. (c) 27. (b) 28. (c) 29. (a) 30. (a)
31. (c) 32. (a) 33. (c) 34. (b) 35. (d) 36. (c) 37. (c) 38. (b) 39. (a) 40. (b)
41. (a) 42. (c) 43. (b) 44. (d) 45. (c) 46. (c) 47. (b) 48. (c) 49. (b) 50. (b)
51. (d) 52. (a) 53. (a) 54. (c) 55. (a) 56. (a) 57. (c) 58. (b) 59. (c) 60. (c)
61. (b) 62. (a) 63. (b) 64. (a) 65. (c) 66. (d) 67. (c) 68. (b) 69. (c) 70. (a)
71. (b) 72. (c) 73. (d) 74. (b) 75. (a) 76. (c) 77. (a) 78. (b) 79. (a) 80. (a)
81. (b) 82. (d) 83. (c) 84. (d) 85. (a) 86. (c) 87. (c) 88. (a) 89. (c) 90. (d)

Assertion-Reason

1. (d) 2. (a) 3. (b) 4. (a) 5. (c) 6. (b) 7. (c) 8. (b) 9. (b) 10. (d)

Statement Type

1. (b) 2. (d) 3. (c) 4. (c) 5. (b) 6. (d) 7. (b) 8. (c) 9. (c) 10. (b)

Matching Type

1. (b) 2. (d) 3. (c) 4. (c) 5. (b)

Numerical Value

1. (19) 2. (6) 3. (3) 4. (2) 5. (23) 6. (19)

NCERT Exemplar's

1. (d) 2. (d) 3. (d) 4. (a) 5. (a) 6. (b) 7. (a) 8. (d) 9. (d)
10. (i)-D, (ii)-E, (iii)-C, (iv)-A 11. (c) 12. (d) 13. (i)-E, (ii)-D, (iii)-C, (iv)-B, (v)-F

Past Exams'

1. (d) 2. (d) 3. (c) 4. (d) 5. (b) 6. (b) 7. (c) 8. (b) 9. (c) 10. (3)
11. (c) 12. (d) 13. (b) 14. (b) 15. (d) 16. (c) 17. (c) 18. (a) 19. (b) 20. (c)
21. (a)

Skill Boosters

1. (c) 2. (a) 3. (c) 4. (c) 5. (b) 6. (d) 7. (d)

Step by Step

Decoding the Questions

Concept Builders

1 True
2 False
3 addition, removal
4 False
5 $2K_3[Fe(CN)_6](aq)$
6 Cl_2
7 $x = 2, y = 2$
8 True
9 black
10 True
11 False
12 −3, 5
13 +7
14 False
15 Au (I) Cl
16 False
17 +7
18 True
19 False
20 H^+/OH^-
21 $a = 3, b = 8, c = 2, d = 3, e = 4$
22 True
23 Titration
24 True
25 anode
26 True
27 standard electrode potential
28 *agar-agar*
29 True
30 H_2, Na

Topical Solutions

1 (*d*)

2 (*a*) In the given reaction, oxidation takes place due to removal of one potassium atom from potassium ferrocyanide to potassium ferricyanide.

3 (*a*) In the given reaction, removal of electronegative element, i.e. chlorine from ferric chloride takes place. Hence, it is an example of reduction process.

4 (*b*) In the given reaction, aluminium is oxidised because oxygen is added to it. Ferrous oxide (Fe_3O_4) is reduced because oxygen has been removed from it. In other words, Al is changing to Al^{3+}, i.e. loss of e^- and Fe^{2+}, Fe^{3+} are converting into Fe, i.e. gain of e^-.

5 (*d*) The incorrect conversion is (d).

$$\overset{+1}{Hg_2Cl_2} \longrightarrow \overset{+2}{HgCl_2}$$

In this process oxidation occurs. The correct form is

$$HgCl_2 \longrightarrow Hg_2Cl_2$$

6 (*b*)

Loss of $2e^-$

$$2Na(s) + H_2(g) \xrightarrow{\Delta} 2Na^+H^-(s)$$

Gain of $2e^-$

Na is oxidised and hydrogen is reduced.

7 (*d*) The oxidation number of Zn increases from 0 to +2 therefore, Zn acts as a reductant.

Oxidation number of H decreases from +1 to 0, so it acts as an oxidant.

8 (*a*) When a strip of metallic zinc is placed in an aqueous solution of $Cu(NO_3)_2$, zinc appears as ions (Zn^{2+}).

$$\overset{0}{Zn}(s) + Cu(NO_3)_2(aq) \longrightarrow \overset{+2}{Zn}(NO_3)_2(aq) + Cu(s)$$

9 (*a*) When rod of metallic zinc is dipped in the solution of copper nitrate, the intensity of blue colour of solution decreases because of the dissolution of zinc rod and finally reddish brown copper metal starts depositing on the zinc rod.

10 (*b*) Copper is more reactive than silver, it displaces Ag^+ ions from its salt solution which get deposited on the copper rod and Cu^{2+} ions form blue colour.

$$Cu(s) + 2Ag^+(aq) \longrightarrow Cu^{2+}(aq) + 2Ag(s)$$

11 (*b*) Zinc releases electrons to copper and copper releases electrons to silver, therefore the electron releasing tendency of the given metals is in the order Zn > Cu > Ag.

12 (*b*) In peroxides (such as H_2O_2, Na_2O_2) each oxygen atom is assigned an oxidation number of −1 and in superoxides (such as KO_2, RbO_2), it is −1/2.

13 (*c*)

14 (*a*) $H\underline{Au}Cl_4 : +1 + x + 4(-1) = 0 \Rightarrow x = +3$

$K_2\underline{Ta}F_7 : 2 + x + (-7) = 0 \Rightarrow x = +5$

$Mg_2\underline{P_2}O_7 : 4 + 2x - 14 = 0 \Rightarrow x = +5$

$Na_2\underline{S_4}O_6 : 2 + 4x - 12 = 0 \Rightarrow x = +2.5$

$\underline{N_3}H : 3x + 1 = 0 \Rightarrow x = \frac{-1}{3}$

15 (*c*) Oxidation state of oxygen in OF_2 is = +2 and in KO_2 is $= \frac{-1}{2}$.

16 (*b*) $KMnO_4 = +1 + x - 8, x = +7$

$K_2Cr_2O_7 = 2 + 2x - 14 = 0, x = +6$

17 (*b*) We know that, the algebraic sum of the oxidation states is always zero in neutral compound.

Oxidation states of $X = +2$

$Y = +5$

$Z = -2$

So, the algebraic sum of total *X*, *Y* and *Z* should be equal to zero which is found in XY_2Z_6.

$$XY_2Z_6 = +2 + (5 \times 2) - (2 \times 6) = +2 + 10 - 12 = 0$$

18 (*b*) $CO_2 \longrightarrow x + 2(-2) = 0 \Rightarrow x = +4$

$Cr_2O_7^{2-} \longrightarrow 2x + 7(-2) = -2 \Rightarrow x = +6$

$HIO_4 \longrightarrow 1 + x + 4(-2) = 0 \Rightarrow x = +7$

$PCl_5 \longrightarrow x + (-5) = 0 \Rightarrow x = +5$

19 (*d*) $CrO_2Cl_2 = x + 2(-2) + 2(-1) = 0$

$= x - 4 - 2 = 0 \Rightarrow x = +6$

20 (*c*) Alkali metal has always (+1) oxidation state. In K_2O, K_2O_2 and KO_2 the oxidation number of potassium is +1, +1 and +1.

21 (*c*) For the given compounds,

I. $K_2\overset{+6}{Mn}O_4$ II. $\overset{+5}{Mn_2}O_5$

III. $\overset{+7}{Mn}O_4^-$ IV. $\overset{+2}{Mn}Cl_2$

The decreasing order is (c).

22 (*d*) Atomic number (25) = Mn

Electronic configuration (Mn) $= [Ar]\, 4s^2 3d^5$

Hence, Mn can attain upto +7 oxidation state.

23 (*c*) CrO_4^{2-} $\quad$ $Cr_2O_7^{2-}$

$x + (-2 \times 4) = -2 \qquad 2x - 14 = (-2)$

$x = +6 \qquad 2x = 12$

$x = +6$

There is no redox reaction occurs.

24 (*b*) Oxidation state of N is $(N_2H_5)_2SO_4$ is –2.

25 (*c*) Oxidation number of C in

$HCHO = 0$

$CH_3OH = -2$

$CHCl_3 = +2$

$C_{12}H_{22}O_{11} = 0$

26 (*c*) $K\overset{+7}{Mn}O_4 \xrightarrow{4e^-} \overset{+3}{Mn_2}O_3$

27 (*b*) H_2O_2 acts as both oxidising and reducing agent.

28 (*c*) Oxidation states of chromium in $Cr_2O_7^{2-}$ and CrO_4^{2-} is +6. Similarly, oxidation states of hydrogen in H_2O and H^+ is +1. Thus, oxidation number of chromium has neither increased nor decreased.

29 (*a*) In AgF_2, Ag is in +2 oxidation state. For Ag, this oxidation state is highly unstable so it readily accepts an electron to attain +1 oxidation state which is more stable.

$$Ag^{2+} + e^- \longrightarrow Ag^+$$

That's why, AgF_2 acts as a strong oxidising agent.

30 (*a*) In the given reaction,

$$3\overset{-2}{N_2}H_4 + 2\overset{+5}{Br}O_3^- \longrightarrow 3\overset{0}{N_2} + 2\overset{-1}{Br^-} + 6H_2O$$

(Oxidation: N, –2 → 0; Reduction: Br, +5 → –1)

Oxidation number at N changes from –2 to 0. It is oxidised and act as a reducing agent.

Oxidation number of Br changes from +5 to –1, it is reduced and acts as an oxidising agent.

31 (*c*) Because in CO_2, carbon is in maximum +4 oxidation state. Hence, it is not a reducing agent.

32 (*a*) The correct form of (a) is $Na_2Cr_2(VI)O_7$.

33 (*c*) Statements I, II and IV are correct, while the statement III is incorrect.

It's correct form is as follows

$$\overset{+2}{Fe}SO_4 + K\overset{+5}{Cl}O_3 \longrightarrow K\overset{-1}{Cl} + \overset{+3}{Fe_2}(SO_4)_3$$

The change in O.S of Fe is $= 3 - 2 = +1$

34 (*b*) Statement (b) is incorrect.

It's correct form is as follows

Oxidation is a process in which electrons are lost whereas reduction is a process in which electrons are accepted/gained.

Rest other statements are correct.

35 (*d*) In (d) reaction CO is oxidised to $COCl_2$.

36 (*c*) The given reaction is represented as

$$K\overset{+7}{Mn}O_4 + H_2SO_4 \longrightarrow \overset{2+}{Mn}SO_4$$

Oxidation number of Mn is changed from +7 to +2.

37 (*c*) $(CN)_2$ (acts) as reducing agent as well as oxidising agent.

38 (*b*)

39 (*a*) The reaction in which oxidation and reduction occur simultaneously are termed as redox reaction.

$$\overset{+4}{Xe}F_4 + \overset{+1}{O_2}F_2 \longrightarrow \overset{+6}{Xe}F_6 + \overset{0}{O_2}$$

Since, Xe undergoes oxidation while O undergoes reduction.

So, it is an example of redox reaction.

40 (*b*) All alkali metals and some alkaline earth metals (like Ca, Sr and Ba) which are very good reductants, will displace hydrogen from cold water.

$$2Na + 2H_2O \longrightarrow 2NaOH + H_2$$

41 (*a*) Less active metals like magnesium and iron reacts with steam to produce dihydrogen gas.

$$Mg(s) + 2H_2O(l) \xrightarrow{\Delta} Mg(OH)_2(s) + H_2(g)$$

$$2Fe(s) + 3H_2O(l) \xrightarrow{\Delta} Fe_2O_3(s) + 3H_2(g)$$

42 (*c*)

43 (*b*) Silver (Ag) and gold (Au) are less reactive metals or noble metals and hence, do not react with HCl.

44 (*d*) Reactions in which the same substance is oxidised as well as reduced are called disproportionation reaction.

$$2\overset{+4}{N}\overset{-2}{O_2} + 2\overset{-2}{O}\overset{+1}{H^-} \longrightarrow \overset{+3}{N}\overset{-2}{O_2^-} + \overset{+5}{N}\overset{-2}{O_3^-} + \overset{+1}{H_2}\overset{-2}{O}$$

(Loss of e^-: N, +4 → +5; Gain of e^-: N, +4 → +3)

Thus, in the reaction of NO_2 and OH^-, N is both oxidised as well as reduced.

45 (*c*)

46 (*c*) $ClO_2^- : x + (-2 \times 2) = -1$

$x - 4 = -1, x = +3.$

47 (*b*) Phosphorus, sulphur and chlorine disproportionate in alkaline medium as shown below :

Oxidation

$$\overset{0}{P_4}(s) + 3OH^-(aq) + 3H_2O(l) \longrightarrow \overset{-3}{P}H_3(g) + 3H_2\overset{+1}{P}O_2^-(aq)$$

Reduction

Reduction

$$\overset{0}{S_8} + 12OH^-(aq) \longrightarrow 4\overset{-2}{S}{}^{2-}(aq) + 2\overset{+2}{S_2}O_3^{2-}(aq) + 6H_2O(l)$$

Oxidation

Oxidation

$$\overset{0}{Cl_2}(g) + 2OH^-(aq) \longrightarrow \overset{+1}{Cl}O^-(aq) + \overset{-1}{Cl}{}^-(aq) + H_2O(l)$$

Reduction

48 (*c*) The reaction (c) describes the formation of household bleaching agents. The hypochlorite ion (ClO^-) formed in the reaction oxidises the colour-bearing stains of the substances to colourless compounds.

49 (*b*) In the given reaction, Br_2 is both reduced and oxidised.

$Br_2(0) \longrightarrow Br^-(-1)$ shows reduction

$Br_2(0) \longrightarrow BrO_3^-(+5)$ shows oxidation

Hence, Br undergoes disproportionation.

50 (*b*)

Oxidation (Loss of e^-)

$$\overset{0}{P_4} + 3NaOH + 3H_2O \longrightarrow \overset{-3}{P}H_3 + 3Na\overset{+1}{H_2}\overset{+1}{P}\overset{-2}{O_2}$$

Reduction (Gain of e^-)

The oxidation number of phosphorus in PH_3 and NaH_2PO_2 is -3 and $+1$, respectively, i.e. here phosphorus is oxidised as well reduced.

Therefore, this reaction is known as disproportionation reaction.

51 (*d*) Among the given reaction, reaction (d) is a disproportionation reaction.

Reduction

$$2\overset{+1}{Cu}Br \longrightarrow \overset{+2}{Cu}Br_2 + \overset{0}{Cu}$$

Oxidation

52 (*a*) ClO_4^- does not show disproportionation reaction because oxoanion of chlorine is present in its highest oxidation state, i.e. +7, so it does not further increase its oxidation number.

53 (*a*) Fluorine does not show a disproportionation reaction.

$$2\overset{0}{F_2} + 2OH^- \longrightarrow 2\overset{-1}{F} + \overset{+2}{O}\overset{-1}{F_2} + H_2O$$

i.e. Here, only reduction is taking place no oxidation.

54 (*c*) Oxidation state of P in $PH_3 = -3$

In KH_2PO_2 O.S. of P = +1

Hence, it gets oxidised as well as reduced.

55 (*a*) Only 2, i.e. (i) and (iv) are correct, these reactions are showing the reducing nature of H_2O_2.

(i) $\underset{\text{reductant}}{(O^{-1})_2} \longrightarrow (O^0)_2 + 2e^-$

(iv) $\underset{\text{reductant}}{(O^{-1})_2} \longrightarrow (O^0)_2 + 2e^-$

56 (*a*) In C_3O_2, two C-atoms linked with oxygen atoms are present in +2 oxidation state and central carbon has zero oxidation state.

So, the average oxidation state of carbon is $= \dfrac{+2+0+2}{3} = +\dfrac{4}{3}$.

57 (*c*) H_2SO_5,

↓

Oxidation no. +6

$2 + x + (-2 \times 3) + (-1 \times 2) = 0,$

$x = +6$

$Cr_2O_7^{2-}$, NO_3^-

↓ +6 ↓ +5

$2x + (-2 \times 7) = -2,$ $x + (-2 \times 3) = -1$

$x = +6$ $x = +5$

Thus, the oxidation number of S, Cr and N in H_2SO_5, $Cr_2O_7^{2-}$ and NO_3^-, respectively are +6, + 6 and +5.

Note In the structure of H_2SO_5, two oxygen atoms form peroxide linkage, so oxidation number of these O-atoms is –1.

58 (*b*) C_5O_2

$$O{=}\overset{+2}{C}{=}\overset{0}{C}{=}\overset{0}{C}{=}\overset{0}{C}{=}\overset{+2}{C}{=}O = \frac{+4}{5}$$

$C_3O_2 = \dfrac{+4}{3}$, $Br_3O_8 = \dfrac{+16}{3}$ and $S_4O_6^{2-} = \dfrac{+5}{2}$

59 (*c*) $\underset{1}{a}\overset{+1}{K_2}\overset{+6}{Cr_2}\overset{-2}{O_7} + \underset{4}{b}\overset{+1}{K}Cl + \underset{6}{c}H_2SO_4$

$\longrightarrow \underset{2}{x}\overset{+6}{Cr}\overset{-2}{O_2}\overset{-1}{Cl_2} + \underset{6}{y}\overset{+1}{K}\overset{+1}{H}S\overset{-2}{O_4} + \underset{3}{z}H_2O$

The balanced equation is,

$$K_2Cr_2O_7 + 4KCl + 6H_2SO_4 \longrightarrow 2CrO_2Cl_2 + 6KHSO_4 + 3H_2O$$

$a = 1, b = 4, c = 6, x = 2, y = 6, z = 3$

60 (*c*)

Increase by 2

$$\overset{0}{Cu} + H\overset{+5}{N}O_3 \longrightarrow \overset{+2}{Cu}(NO_3)_2 + \overset{+2}{N}O + H_2O$$

Decrease by 3

Multiply Cu term with 3 and N term with 2

$$3Cu + 2HNO_3 \longrightarrow 3Cu(NO_3)_2 + 2NO + H_2O$$

Balance H and O

$$3Cu + 8HNO_3 \longrightarrow 3Cu(NO_3)_2 + 2NO + 4H_2O$$

So, *a*, *b*, *c*, *d* and *e* are 3, 8, 3, 2 and 4 respectively.

61 (*b*) The balanced equation is represented as

$$2MnO_4^- + Br^- + 2H_2O \longrightarrow 2MnO_2 + BrO_3^- + 2OH^-$$

62 (*a*) The equation when BrO_3^- changes into Br_2 in an acidic medium is as follows

$$2BrO_3^- + 12H^+ \longrightarrow Br_2 + 6H_2O$$

Add $10e^-$ in LHS to balance the charge on both sides

$$2BrO_3^- + 10e^- + 12H^+ \longrightarrow Br_2 + 6H_2O.$$

∴ 10 electrons should be present on the left side of balanced equation.

63 (*b*) The reaction is

$$MnO_2 + 4HCl \longrightarrow MnCl_2 + Cl_2 + 2H_2O$$

64 (*a*) The balanced equation is

$$6I_2 + 12OH^- \longrightarrow 2IO_3^- + 10I^- + 6H_2O$$

2 : 10

1 : 5

65 (c) Reduction: $2\overset{3+}{Fe} + \overset{2+}{Sn} \longrightarrow 2\overset{2+}{Fe} + \overset{4+}{Sn}$; Oxidation

66 (d) $\overset{6+}{Cr_2O_7^{2-}} \longrightarrow \overset{3+}{Cr}$

Gain of e^- (reduction)

Reduction takes place due to decrease in oxidation number, so chromium is being reduced.

67 (c) The balanced redox reaction by half reaction method.

$$6\overset{2+}{Fe} + Cr_2O_7^{2-} + 14H^+ \longrightarrow 6\overset{3+}{Fe} + 2\overset{3+}{Cr} + 7H_2O$$

$\therefore$ The coefficients x, y and z are 6, 1 and 14 respectively.

68 (b) $BiO_3^- + 6H^+ + xe^- \longrightarrow Bi^{3+} + 3H_2O$

Total charge on LHS = Total charge on RHS

$$-1 + 6 + x(-1) = +3$$
$$-x = +3 - 5$$
$$-x = -2$$
$$\Rightarrow \quad x = 2$$

69 (c) $K_2Cr_2O_7 + KI\text{ (excess)} \longrightarrow Cr^{3+} + H_2O + nI_2$

$$\overset{6+}{Cr} \xrightarrow{+3e^-} \overset{3+}{Cr}$$

Cr^{6+} accepts $3e^-$, so mole of I_2 liberated = 3.

Thus, the value of n is 3.

70 (a) Oxidation half reaction :

$$6I^- \longrightarrow 3I_2 + 6e^-$$

Reduction half reaction :

$$2MnO_4^- + 4H_2O + 6e^- \longrightarrow 2MnO_2 + 8OH^-$$

On adding the above the two half equations.

$$6I^- + 2MnO_4^- + 4H_2O \longrightarrow 3I_2 + 2MnO_2 + 8OH^-$$

71 (b) In a solution of $KMnO_4$, MnO_4^- acts as a self indicator because in redox titrations, these reagents which are itself has intense colour, act as self indicator.

72 (c) The reaction of Cu^{2+} ions with iodide ions gives an intense blue colour when starch is added. When $S_2O_3^-$ is added the blue colour of solution gets disappeared.

73 (d) All the options are correct except (d). The correct form of (d) is as follows

Thiosulphate ($S_2O_3^{2-}$) is not an indicator, thus has no colour change as end point in titrations.

74 (b) In Daniell cell, electrons flow from anode to cathode from external circuit and current flows from cathode to anode.

75 (a) A salt-bridge is a U-tube containing a solution of potassium chloride or ammonium nitrate solidified by boiling with *agar-agar* and later cooling to a jelly like substance.

76 (c)

77 (a) Statements (a) is incorrect. It's correct form is as follows

Zn electrode is negatively charged because of the oxidation of Zn to Zn^{2+} ions, electrons are accumulated on zinc electrode.

78 (b) More positive is the $E°$ value, more is the oxidising power. Hence, the correct order is (b).

79 (a) The substances which have lower reduction potentials are strong reducing agents. Therefore, $Cr(E°_{Cr^{3+}/Cr} = -0.74\text{ V})$ is the strongest reducing agent among all the other given options.

80 (a) Higher the reduction potential, stronger the oxidising agent. Since, reduction potentials decrease in the order $C > B > A$. Hence, B will oxidise A but not C.

81 (b) The reduction potential of mercury is higher than copper and silver. Thus, it can displace both silver and copper from their salt solution.

$$Hg + CuSO_4 \longrightarrow HgSO_4 + Cu$$
$$Hg + AgNO_3 \longrightarrow HgNO_3 + Ag$$

Thus, statement (b) is correct.

82 (d) Metals with negative reduction potentials undergo oxidation and act as good reducing agents.

83 (c) $NaBr \longrightarrow Na^+(aq) + Br^-(aq)$

At cathode

$$2H_2O(l) + 2e^- \longrightarrow H_2(g) + 2OH^-(aq)$$

Since the electrode potential of H_2O (–0.83 V) is higher than that of, Na^+ (–2.71) therefore, H_2O is reduced to H_2 in preference to Na^+ ions.

At anode $2Br^-(aq) \longrightarrow Br_2(g) + 2e^-$

Thus, H_2 is liberated at cathode, Br_2 at the anode and NaOH is left in the solution.

84 (d) Na > Mg > Zn > Fe > Cu > Ag

$E°$(V) –2.71 –2.36 –0.76 +0.44 +0.34 +0.80

85 (a) An aqueous solution of $AgNO_3$ with silver electrode, when undergoes electrolysis, two oxidation and two reduction half-reactions must be considered.

Oxidation (at anode)

(A) $Ag(s) \longrightarrow Ag^+(aq) + e^-$; $E° = -0.80$ V

(B) $2H_2O(l) \longrightarrow O_2(g) + 4H^+(aq) + 4e^-$; $E° = -1.23$ V

Reduction (at cathode)

(C) $Ag^+(aq) + e^- \longrightarrow Ag(s)$; $E° = +0.80$ V

(D) $2H_2O(l) + 2e^- \longrightarrow H_2(g) + 2OH^-(aq)$; $E° = -0.83$ V

86 (c) A metal with more negative value of $E°_{red}$ is a stronger reducing agent than those which have less negative or positive value of $E°_{red}$. Therefore, the order in which they displace each other from the solution of their salts is Mg, Al, Zn, Fe, Cu.

87 (c) More negative $E°$ value means that the redox couple is a stronger reducing agent. The arrangement of metals in their increasing order of reducing power is as follows

$$Ag < Hg < Cr < Mg < K.$$

88 (*a*) When the value of standard reduction potential is negative, the electrode undergoes oxidation and acts as anode. Thus, $Zn^{2+}/Zn; E° = -0.76$ will acts as anode, when connected to standard hydrogen electrode.

Thus, statement I is correct.

89 (*c*) Since, the reduction potential of Fe^{3+}/Fe^{2+} is greater than that of I_2/I^-, Fe^{3+} will reduced and I will be oxidised.

$$2Fe^{3+} + 2I^- \longrightarrow 2Fe^{2+} + I_2$$

90 (*d*) Among the given half-cell reactions, (i), (ii), (iv) and (v) has more reduction potential than hydrogen.

Assertion-Reason

1 (*d*) A is false but R is true.

The correct form of A is :

The oxidation number of central sulphur in $Na_2S_4O_6$ is zero.

2 (*a*) Both A and R are true and R is the correct explanation of A.

3 (*b*) Both A and R are true but R is not the correct explanation of A.

F is best oxidising agent only on the basis of its high hydration energy because its have less electron affinity and bond dissociation enthalpy than chlorine.

4 (*a*) Both A and R are true and R is the correct explanation of A.

5 (*c*) A is true but R is false,

The correct form of R is :

Cl_2 bleaches by oxidation while SO_2 bleaches by reduction.

6 (*b*) Both A and R are true but R is not the correct explanation of A. The correct explanation of A is :

The structure of Br_3O_8 (tribromooctaoxide) is

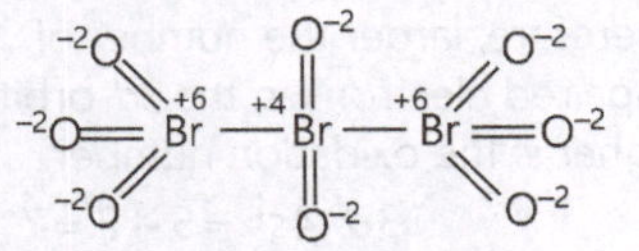

Thus, oxidation state of two corner Br atoms is +6 and of middle one is +4. The difference in oxidation states is due to difference in bonding situations.

7 (*c*) A is true but R is false.

$$10KI + 2K\overset{+7}{Mn}O_4 + 8H_2SO_4 \longrightarrow 2\overset{+2}{Mn}SO_4 + 5I_2 + 6K_2SO_4 + 8H_2O$$

Oxidation state of Mn decreases +7 to +2. So, the decrease in oxidation state introduce the permanganate ions act as oxidising agent.

8 (*b*) Both A and R are true but R is not the correct explanation of A.

The correct explanation of A is :

The decomposition of Fe_3O_4 in $FeO \cdot Fe_2O_3$ having iron in +2 and +3 oxidation states respectively.

Fe^{2+} ion present in FeO being a reducing agent decolourise $KMnO_4$ solution.

9 (*b*) Both A and R are true but R is not the correct explanation of A. The correct explanation of A is :

The electrons are transferred from Zn to Cu^{2+} through the metallic wire which connects the two rods.

While electricity flows through the salt-bridge by migration of ions from one beaker to other.

10 (*d*) A is false and R is true. The correct form of A is :

Ions having negative $E°$ value are stronger reducing agent than H^+/H_2 couple.

Statement Type

1 (*b*) Statement I is true but Statement II is false.

The correct form of Statement II is :

When $K_2Cr_2O_7$ is converted to K_2CrO_4, there is no change in the oxidation number of chromium.

2 (*d*) Both Statements I and II are true.

3 (*c*) Statement I is false but Statement II is true.

The correct form of Statement I is :

Only those decomposition reactions which undergo oxidation reduction are called redox reactions.

4 (*c*) Statement I is false but Statement II is true.

The correct form of Statement I is :

In a disproportionation reaction, an element in one oxidation state is simultaneously oxidised and reduced.

5 (*b*) Statement I is true but Statement II is false.

The correct form of Statement II is :

Electrodes potential of both the electrodes become equal.

6 (*d*) Both Statements I and II are true.

7 (*b*) Among the given statements. Statements II and V are incorrect while the other statements are correct.

Correct form is as :

II. Addition of electropositive element to a substance is reduction.

V. The electron releasing tendency of Zn, Cu and Ag is Zn > Cu > Ag.

8 (*c*) Among the given statements, Statement II, IV and V are correct while I and III are incorrect.

Their correct form is

I. Oxidation state of S in S_8 is 0.

III. Oxidation state of O in O_2F_2 is +1.

9 (*c*) Among the given statements, statements II and V are incorrect while I, III and IV are correct. The correct form of II and V is

II. All decomposition reactions are not redox reaction, e.g. decomposition of $CaCO_3$.

V. Halogens can show a disproportionation.

10 (*b*) Among the given statements. Statements II, III, IV and V are correct while I is incorrect. The correct form of I is

I. Fractional oxidation number of Br_3O_8 is $\frac{16}{3}$.

Matching Type

1 (*b*) The correct match is
A-3, B-4, C-1, D-2.

2 (*d*) The correct match is
A-3, B-2, C-4, D-1.

3 (*c*) The correct match is
A-2, B-4, C-1, D-3.

4 (*c*) The correct match is
A-1, B-3, C-2, D-4.

5 (*b*) The correct match is
A-3, B-2, C-1.

Numerical Value

1 (19)

$$K_2Cr_2O_7 \Rightarrow 2(+1) + 2a + 7 \times (-2) = 0$$
$$a = +6$$
$$KMnO_4 \Rightarrow 1 \times (+1) + b + 4 \times (-2) = 0$$
$$b = +7$$
$$K_2FeO_4 \Rightarrow 2 \times (+1) + c + 4 \times (-2) = 0$$
$$c = +6$$

So, $(a + b + c) = 6 + 7 + 6 = 19$

2 (6) $Na_4[Fe(CN)_5(NOS)] \Rightarrow 4 \times (+1) + a + 5 \times (-1) + (+1) - 2 = 0$

$$a = +2$$
$$Na_4[FeO_4] \Rightarrow 4 \times (+1) + b \times 4 \times (-2) = 0$$
$$b = +4$$
$$[Fe_2(CO)_9] \Rightarrow 2 \times c + 9 \times 0 = 0$$
$$c = 0$$

So, $a + b + c = 2 + 4 + 0 = 6$

3 (3) Since, the net charge on the neutral molecule is 0. Therefore, for the given molecule, $Be_nAl_2Si_6O_{18}$.

$$n(+2) + 2(+3) + 6(+4) + 18(-2) = 0$$
$$2n + 6 + 24 - 36 = 0$$
$$2n - 6 = 0$$
$$n = +3$$

4 (2) Non-zero oxidation states of O are –1, –2; that of Cl are –1, +1, +3, +5 and +7; that of F is –1; that of N and P are –3, –2, +1, +3 and +5; that of Sn are +2 and +4; that of Tl are +1 and +3; that of Na is +1 and that of Ti is +2, +3 and +4. Thus, only F and Na can exist in one non-zero oxidation state.

5 (23) Reduction half reaction can be balanced as

$$Cr_2O_7^{2-} + 14H^+ + 6e^- \longrightarrow 2Cr^{3+} + 7H_2O$$

Oxidation half reaction is

$$Fe^{2+} \longrightarrow Fe^{3+} + e^-$$

On combining both equation and eliminate number of electrons, the overall equation we get

$$Cr_2O_4^{2-} + 14H^+ + 6Fe^{2+} \longrightarrow 2Cr^{3+} + 7H_2O + 6Fe^{3+}$$

Hence, $A = 14, B = 2, C = 7$

$A + B + C = 14 + 2 + 7 = 23$

6 (19) In basic medium, the balanced equation is given by

$$2Fe^{2+} + H_2O_2 \longrightarrow 2Fe^{3+} + 2OH^-$$

In acidic medium, the balanced equation is given by

$$2MnO_4^- + 6H^+ + 5H_2O_2 \longrightarrow 2Mn^{2+} + 8H_2O + 5O_2$$

$\therefore\ a = 2, b = 2, a' = 2, b' = 8, c' = 5$

$\therefore\ a + b + a' + b' + c' = 2 + 2 + 2 + 8 + 5 = 19$

NCERT Exemplar's

1 (*d*) Reaction

$$\overset{+2}{Ba}\overset{-1}{Cl_2} + \overset{+1}{H_2}\overset{+6}{S}\overset{-2}{O_4} \longrightarrow \overset{+2}{Ba}\overset{+6}{S}\overset{-2}{O_4} + 2\overset{+1}{H}\overset{-1}{Cl}$$

Option (d) is not an example of redox reaction.

It is because in this reaction there is no change in oxidation number of the interacting species.

2 (*d*) Since, $E°$ value of the redox couple Ag^+/Ag is the most positive, i.e. + 0.80 V, therefore, Ag^+ is the strongest oxidising agent amongst given species.

3 (*d*) The $E°$ values show that copper will reduce Br_2, if the $E°$ of the following redox reaction is positive.

$$Cu + Br_2 \longrightarrow CuBr_2$$

Now,

$$Cu \longrightarrow Cu^{2+} + 2e^-;\ E° = -0.34\ V$$
$$Br_2 + 2e^- \longrightarrow 2Br^-;\ E = +1.09\ V$$
$$\overline{Cu + Br_2 \longrightarrow CuBr_2;\ E° = +0.75\ V}$$

Since, $E°$ of this reaction is positive, therefore, Cu can reduce Br_2. While other reaction will give negative value of $E°_{cell}$.

4 (*a*) $2\overset{+2}{S_2}\overset{-2}{O_3^{2-}}(aq) + \overset{0}{I_2}(s) \longrightarrow \overset{2.5}{S_4}O_6^{2-}(aq) + 2I^-(aq)$

$$\overset{+2}{S_2}\overset{-2}{O_3^{2-}}(aq) + 2\overset{0}{Br_2}(l) + 5H_2O(l) \longrightarrow 2\overset{+6}{S}\overset{2-}{O_4^{2-}}(aq) + 4Br^-(aq) + 10H^+(aq)$$

Bromine being stronger oxidising agent than iodine, oxidises S (in +2 oxidation state) of $S_2O_3^{2-}$ ion to S (in +6 oxidation state) of SO_4^{2-} ion, whereas I_2 oxidises S from +2 oxidation state of $S_2O_3^{2-}$ to only +2.5 oxidation state of $S_4O_6^{2-}$ ion.

5 (*a*) Oxidation number of hydrogen is always +1 is wrong since, it is +1 in hydrogen halides, –1 in hydrides and zero in H_2 molecule.

6 (*b*) NH_4NO_3 is actually NH_4^+ and NO_3^-. It is an ionic compound. The oxidation number of nitrogen in the two species is different.

Let, oxidation number of N in NH_4^+ is x.

$\Rightarrow x + (4 \times 1) = +1$ or $x + 4 = +1$

or $x = -3$

Let oxidation number of N in NO_3^- is x.

$\Rightarrow\ x + (3 \times -2) = -1$

or $x - 6 = -1$ or $x = +5$

7 (*a*) The oxidation number of Cr, Cl and Mn of each species in the four set of ions, is

$$\overset{+3}{Cr}O_2^-, \overset{+5}{Cl}O_3^-, \overset{+6}{Cr}O_4^{2-}, \overset{+7}{Mn}O_4^-$$

Thus, the correct order is (a).

8 (*d*) Highest oxidation number of any transition element $= (n-1)$ *d*-electrons + *ns*-electrons. Therefore, larger the number of unpaired electrons in the 3*d*-orbitals, higher is the oxidation number.

$$3d^5 4s^2 = 5 + 2 = 7$$

9 (*d*) In reaction (d), N is both oxidised as well as reduced since the O.N. (oxidation number) of N increases from + 4 in NO_2 to +5 in NO_3^- and decreases from +4 in NO_2 to +3 in NO_2^-.

10 The correct matching is (i)-D, (ii)-E, (iii)-C, (iv)-A.

11 (*c*) Cl, Br, I can have –1 to +7 oxidation state. But oxidation state of F is fixed (–1) as it is the most electronegative element and do not loose electron.

Hence, it does not show disproportionation reaction/tendency.

12 (*d*) The order of getting reduced is $Ag^+ > Fe^{3+} > I_2 > Cu^{2+}$

Ag^+ and Fe^{2+} cannot undergo reaction since both have almost the same ability to get reduced and poorability to get oxidised.

Possible reactions are

$$I_2 + Cu \longrightarrow I^- + Cu^{2+}$$
$$Fe^{3+} + I^- \longrightarrow Fe^{2+} + I_2$$
$$Fe^{3+} + Cu \longrightarrow Fe^{2+} + Cu$$
$$Ag^+ + Fe^{2+} \longrightarrow Ag + Fe^{3+}$$
$$Ag^+ + I^- \longrightarrow Ag + I_2$$
$$Ag^+ + Cu \longrightarrow Ag + Cu^{2+}$$

13 The correct matching is

(i) - E, (ii) - D, (iii) - C, (iv) - B, (v) - F

Past Exams'

1 (*d*) $\underset{+2\ -1}{BaCl_2} + \underset{+1\ +6\ -2}{Na_2SO_4} \longrightarrow \underset{+2\ +6\ -2}{BaSO_4} + \underset{+1\ -1}{2NaCl}$

As there is no change in oxidation state of any element, hence it is not a redox reaction.

2 (*d*) The value of *a*, *b* and *c* is 1, 3, 8 the complete balanced equation is as follows

$$Cr_2O_7^{2-} + 3SO_3^{2-}(aq) + 8H^+(aq) \longrightarrow 2Cr^{3+}(aq) + 3SO_4^{2-}(aq) + \frac{8}{2}H_2O\ (l)$$

3 (*c*) Aluminium (Al) can displace chromium (Cr) because Cr is less reactive than Al and placed lower in electrochemical series with respect to Al.

Hence, the correct option for metal displacement reaction is

$$Cr_2O_3 + 2Al \xrightarrow{\Delta} Al_2O_3 + 2Cr$$

4 (*c*) Let us consider the segment of EMF series (standard reduction potential) of the given reduction half-call reactions:

Reduction half reaction	E/V at 298K
(a) $Mg^{2+} + 2e \longrightarrow Mg$	– 2.36
(b) $Fe^{2+} + 2e \longrightarrow Fe$	– 0.44
(c) $Au^{3+} + 3e \longrightarrow Au$	+ 140
(d) $K^+ + e \longrightarrow K$	– 2.93

Hence, option (c) is correct.

5 (*c*) In CH_4, oxidation number of carbon is –4 while in CCl_4, oxidation number of carbon is +4.

Thus, the change in oxidation number of carbon in the given reaction is from – 4 to +4.

6 (*b*) 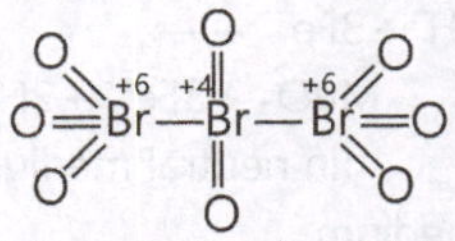

7 (*d*) The reaction in which the same species is simultaneously oxidised and reduced are called disproportionation reactions.

(i) $2Cu^+ \longrightarrow Cu^{2+} + Cu^0$

(ii) $3\overset{+6}{Mn}O_4^{2-} + 4H^+ \longrightarrow 2\overset{+7}{Mn}O_4^- + \overset{+4}{Mn}O_2 + 2H_2O$

8 (*b*) More negative the value of standard reduction potential, higher is the reduction power.

Thus, the correct decreasing order of reducing power of the metal is (b).

9 (*b*) The given redox reaction is

$$MnO_4^- + C_2O_4^{2-} + H^+ \longrightarrow Mn^{2+} + CO_2 + H_2O$$

The reaction can be balanced by half-reaction method to get

$$2MnO_4^- + 5C_2O_4^{2-} + 16H^+ \longrightarrow 2Mn^{2+} + 10CO_2 + 8H_2O$$

∴ The coefficients of the reactants, MnO_4^-, $C_2O_4^{2-}$ ad H^+ are 2, 5 and 16 respectively.

10 (3) Oxidation state of sulphur in given compound is calculated as,

$SO_3 \Rightarrow 0 = x - 6, x = 6$

$H_2SO_3 \Rightarrow 0 = 2 \times 1 + x - (2 \times 3), x = +4$

$SOCl_2 \Rightarrow 0 = x - 2 - (2 \times 1), x = +4$

$SF_4 \Rightarrow 0 = x - 4, x = +4$

$BaSO_4 \Rightarrow 0 = 2 + x - 8, x = +6$

$H_2S_2O_7 \Rightarrow 0 = 2 + 2x - 2 \times 7, x = +6$

Hence, in total 3 compounds sulphur have +4 oxidation state.

11 (*c*) In the reaction of $S_2O_3^{2-}$ with I_2, oxidation state of sulphur change from +2 to +2.5.

In the reaction of $S_2O_3^{2-}$ with Br_2, oxidation state of sulphur changes from +2 to +6.

∴ Both I_2 and Br_2 are oxidant (oxidising agent) and Br_2 is stronger oxidant than I_2.

12 (*d*) **Disproportionation reaction** is a type of reaction in which, the same element is simultaneously oxidised and reduced. In the given options,

$$Cu^+ \longrightarrow Cu^{2+} + Cu$$

$$3\overset{+6}{Mn}O_4^{2-} + 4H^+ \longrightarrow 2\overset{+7}{Mn}O_4^- + \overset{+4}{Mn}O_2 + 2H_2O$$

These two reactions undergoes disproportionation.

13 (*b*) The correct match is

A-IV, B-I, C-II, D-III.

Concept Enhancer All combustion reactions are combination reaction whether there is a use of elemental dioxygen or any other element.

14 (*b*) Consider the following reactions

$$2[\underset{(+1)}{Au}(CN)_2]^-(aq) + \underset{(0)}{Zn}(s) \longrightarrow 2\underset{(0)}{Au}(s) + [\underset{(+2)}{Zn}(CN)_4]^{2-}(aq)$$

Reduction (Au: +1 → 0); Oxidation (Zn: 0 → +2)

Above reaction is redox reaction as well as a metal displacement reaction because Au is displaced by Zn. Hence, option (b) is correct.

15 (*d*) $2NaOCl + H_2O_2 \longrightarrow 2NaCl + H_2O + O_2$

If we calculate the oxidation state of various components in above reaction then H_2O_2 act as reducing agent as it reduces NaOCl and itself gets oxidised.

Reduction (NaOCl → NaCl)

$$\underset{(+1)}{2NaOCl} + \underset{(-1)}{H_2O_2} \longrightarrow \underset{(-1)}{2NaCl} + H_2O_2 + \underset{(0)}{O}$$

Oxidation (H_2O_2 → O)

16 (*c*) Number of iodine on reactant side = Number of iodine on product side

$$2 + x = 6 \times 2$$
$$x = 12 - 2$$
$$x = 10$$

Thus, the equation will be

$$2IO_3^- + 10I^- + 12H^+ \longrightarrow 6I_2 + 6H_2O$$

17 (*c*) $\overset{+7}{Mn}O_4^- + 4H^+ + 3e^- \longrightarrow \overset{+4}{Mn}O_2 + 2H_2O$

So, it is only (*c*) reaction which does not show disproportionation reaction because Mn only gets reduced not oxidised.

18 (*a*)

Reduction (gain of electrons)

$$3\overset{+6}{Mn}O_4^{2-} + 4H^+ \longrightarrow 2\overset{+7}{Mn}O_4^- + \overset{+4}{Mn}O_2 + 2H_2O$$

Oxidation (loss of electrons)

Both oxidation and reduction is shown by same species.

19 (*b*) $MnO_4^- \longrightarrow Mn^{2+}$

$x - 8 + 1 = 0$ $\quad x = +2$

$x = +7$ $\quad (\therefore 5e^-$ change)

Hence, in the process of MnO_4^- to Mn^{2+} the change in oxidation state is five.

20 (*c*) $2I^- + 2H^+ + \overset{1}{H_2}\overset{-1}{O_2} \longrightarrow \overset{0}{I_2} + 2\overset{+1}{H_2}\overset{-2}{O}$

In this reaction, H_2O_2 oxidises I^- to I_2 and itself gets reduced to H_2O, so the reaction depicts oxidising nature of H_2O_2.

While in other reactions H_2O_2 does not oxidise KIO_4, I_2 and Cl_2.

21 (*a*) BrO_4^- will not undergo disproportionation reaction because bromine is in its maximum oxidation state, i.e. + 7.

The maximum and minimum possible oxidation state value for Br are + 7 and + 1 respectively.

So, BrO_4^- cannot oxidise further.

Hence, it cannot show disproportionation reaction.

Skill Boosters

1 (*c*)

$$MnO_4^- + 8H^+ + 5e^- \longrightarrow Mn^{2+} + 4H_2O$$
$$[Fe^{2+} \longrightarrow Fe^{3+} + e^-] \times 5$$

$$MnO_4^- + 5Fe^{2+} + 8H^+ \longrightarrow Mn^{2+} + 5Fe^{3+} + 4H_2O$$

(in acidic medium)

$$MnO_4^- + 4H^+ + 3e^- \longrightarrow MnO_2 + 2H_2O$$
$$[Fe^{2+} \longrightarrow Fe^{3+} + e^-] \times 3$$

$$MnO_4^- + 4H^+ + 3Fe^{2+} \longrightarrow MnO_2 + 3Fe^{3+} + 2H_2O$$

(in neutral medium)

In acidic medium,

$$\frac{M_1V_1}{1} = \frac{M_2V_2}{5} \Rightarrow \frac{M_1 \times 20}{1} = \frac{M_2 \times 25}{5},$$
$$M_1 = \frac{M_2}{4}$$

In neutral medium,

$$\frac{M_1V_1}{1} = \frac{M_2V_2}{3} \Rightarrow \frac{M_2V_1}{4} = \frac{M_2 \times 25}{3}$$
$$= V_1 = 33.3 \text{ mL}$$

2 (*a*) Putting the O.N of all the elements in the molecular formula of all the compounds, we find that in molecular formula $A_3(BC_4)_2$ the sum of O.N. of all the elements comes out of zero.

$$3 \times (+2) + 2 \times (+5 + 4 \times -2) = 0$$

Thus, option (*a*) is correct.

3 (*c*) $N_1V_1[Ca(OCl)_2] = N_2V_2[Na_2S_2O_3]$

$\therefore \quad N_1 \times 25 = 0.25 \times 48$

or $N_1 = \dfrac{0.25 \times 48}{25} = 0.48$ N

Thus, the normality of $Ca(OCl)_2$ solution = 0.48 N

Now, since Eq. (i) is $2e^-$ change

$\therefore$ Eq. wt. at $Ca(OCl)_2 = \dfrac{\text{Mol. wt.}}{2}$

In other words,

$$\text{Molarity} = \frac{\text{Normality}}{2} = \frac{0.48}{2} = 0.24 \text{ M}$$

Thus, the molarity of the household bleach = 0.24 M

4 (*c*) $Cl_2(aq) + SO_2(aq) + 2H_2O(l) \longrightarrow 2Cl^-(aq) + SO_4^-(aq) + 4H^+(aq)$

This represents the balanced redox reaction.

5 (*b*) 1.61×10^{-3} moles of MnO_4^- will oxidise $A^{m+} = \dfrac{5}{5-m} \times 1.61 \times 10^{-3}$ mol ...(iii)

But the no. of moles of A^{m+} actually oxidised $= 2.68 \times 10^{-3}$ moles ...(iv)

Equating the values of Eqs. (iii) and (iv), we have

$$\frac{5}{5-m} \times 1.61 \times 10^{-3} = 2.68 \times 10^{-3}$$
$$5 \times 1.61 = (5 - m) \times 2.68$$
$$2.68m = 5\,(2.68 - 1.61)$$
$$2.68m = 5.35$$
$$m = \frac{5.35}{2.68} \approx 2$$

6 (*d*) $Cr_2O_7^{2-} + 14H^+ + 6Cl^- \longrightarrow 2Cr^{3+} + 3Cl_2 + 7H_2O$

Given, that 0.25 moles of potassium dichromate are reacted, this will produce 0.25 × 3 moles of chlorine gas, which is 0.75 moles of chlorine gas. Now, we can use the ideal gas law to find the volume of Cl_2 at STP.

$$pV = nRT \Rightarrow V = \frac{nRT}{p}$$
$$V = \frac{0.75 \times 0.0821 \times 273.15}{1} = 16.8 \text{ L}$$

So, the volume of chlorine gas produced at STP will be 16.8 litres.

7 (*d*) $Cr_2O_7^{2-} + X^{n-}YZ \longrightarrow Cr^{3+} + X^{n+a}$

Equivalents of $Cr_2O_7^{2-}$ = Equivalents of XYZ.

$$1.68 \times 10^{-3} = 3.26 \times 10^{-3} \times a$$

So, $a = 3$. Hence, O.N $= 3 - n$

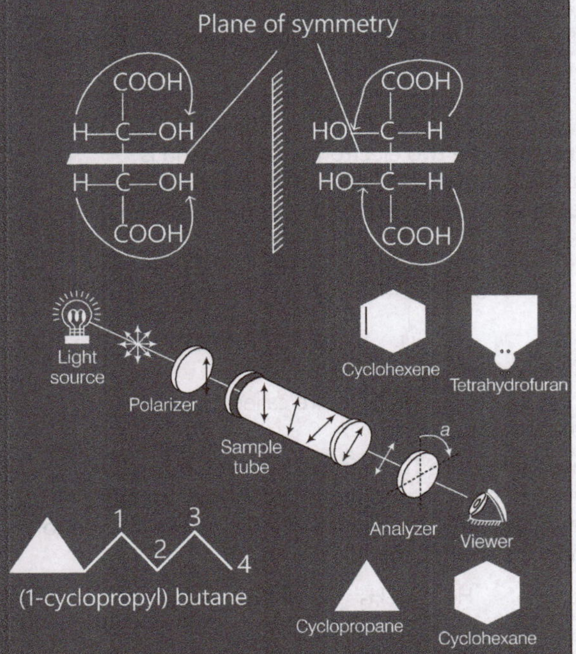

Scan for **Chemistry Through Concept Master** *Videos*

08

Organic Chemistry : Some Basic Principles and Techniques

Topicwise No. of Ques asked in 5 Years (NEET)

Topics	No. of Questions				
	2024	2023	2022	2021	2020
General Introduction Tetravalence of Carbon : Shapes of Organic Compounds	–	–	–	–	1
Structural Representation and Classification of Organic Compounds	–	1	–	–	–
Nomenclature of Organic Compounds	1	–	1	1	–
Isomerism	–	1	–	–	–
Fundamental Concepts in Organic Reaction Mechanism	1	1	–	–	–
Methods of Purification of Organic Compounds	–	–	–	–	1
Qualitative and Quantitative analysis of Organic Compounds	–	1	–	–	–

Special Type of Ques Asked In 5 Years (NEET)

Types	Years				
	2024	2023	2022	2021	2020
A-R	–	–	–	–	–
Statement Based	–	–	–	–	–
Matching	–	–	–	–	–

Last 5 Years Weightage (NEET)

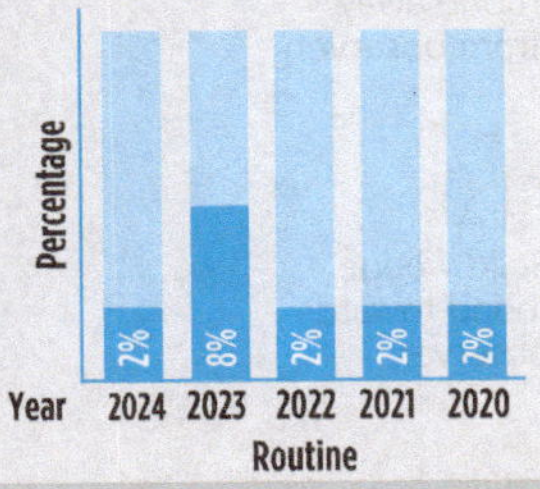

- Carbon has the unique property of '**catenation**' by which it can form large number of covalent compounds.
- **Organic chemistry** deals with the study of such compounds (hydrocarbons) and their derivatives. Some organic compounds may also contain nitrogen, oxygen, sulphur, phosphorus, halogens etc.
- **Berzilius, a Swedish chemist** proposed that a 'vital force' was responsible for the formation of organic compounds.
- **F-Wohler (1828)** synthesised an organic compound, urea from an inorganic compound ammonium cyanate effectively which destroyed the myth of organic compounds being associated with a vital force.

$$\underset{\text{(Ammonium cyanate)}}{NH_4CNO} \xrightarrow{\text{Heat}} \underset{\text{(Urea)}}{NH_2CONH_2}$$

- Synthesis of acetic acid by **Kolbe (1845)** and that of methane by **Berthelot (1856)** showed conclusively that organic compounds could be synthesised from inorganic sources in a laboratory.

Tetravalence of Carbon : Shapes of Organic Compounds

The Shapes of Carbon Compounds

- **Tetravalency of carbon** can be explained in terms of its electronic configuration and the hybridisation of *s* and *p*-orbitals.
- The shape of molecules can be explained in terms of hybridised carbon atoms. Some are given below.

Hybridisation	% *s* character	% *p* character	Shape	Bond strength	Electro-negativity	Example
sp^3	25	75	Tetrahedral	Weak	2.48	Ethane
sp^2	33.3	66.6	Trigonal planar	Stronger	2.75	Ethene
sp	50	50	Linear	Strongest	3.25	Ethyne

Some Characteristic Feature of π-bond

- In π-bond formation, parallel orientation of the two *p*-orbitals on adjacent atoms is necessary for a proper sideways overlap. NEET 2020
- Rotation is restricted around a pi bond due to the presence of both pi and sigma bonds.
- The electron charge cloud of the π-bond is located above and **below the plane of bonding atoms**.
- π-bonds generally provide the most reactive centres in the molecules containing multiple bonds.

Marks Maximizer

As the multiplicity of bond increases, the bond strength increases and the bond length decreases.

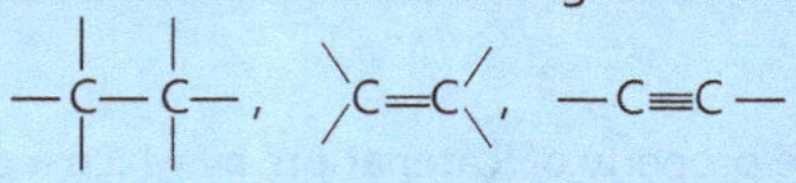

⟶ Increasing bond strength

⟵ Decreasing bond length

Functional group

An atom or a group of atoms joined to the carbon chain which is responsible for the characteristic chemical properties of organic compound is called the functional group. e.g. —OH (hydroxyl group), —CHO (aldehyde group) and —COOH (carboxylic acid) etc.

Homologous Series

A group or a series of organic compounds each containing a characteristic functional group forms a homologous series and the members of the series are called homologues. In this series, the successive members differ from each other in molecular formula by a $—CH_2$ unit. There are a number of homologous series of organic compounds. Some of these are alkanes, alkenes, alkynes, haloalkanes, amines etc.

Structural Representation of Organic Compounds

Complete, Condensed and Bond-line Structural Formulas

Structures are represented in several ways. Some are as follows

- **Lewis structure** Electrons are represented as dots.

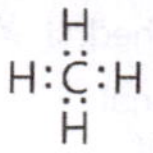

- **Dash structure** The two electron covalent bond is represented by a dash (–). Lone pairs of electrons on hetero atoms may or may not be shown.

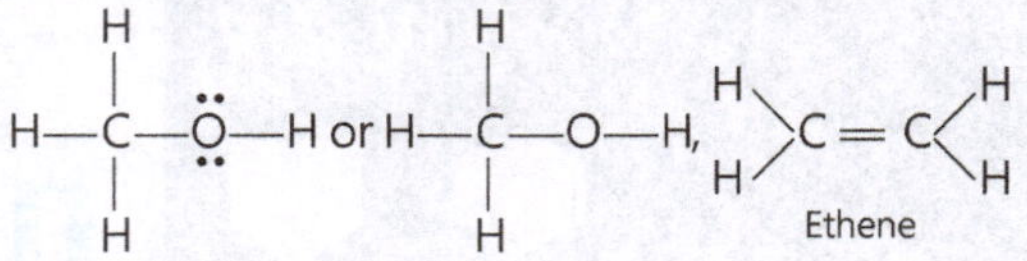

Methanol Ethene

Such structural representations are called complete structural formulas.

- **Condensed structure** The formula is written by omitting some or all of the dashes representing covalent bonds and by representing the number of identical groups attached to an atom by a subscript.

CH_3CH_3 Ethane $H_2C=CH_2$ Ethene $CH{\equiv}CH$ Ethyne CH_3OH Methanol

- **Bond line structure** Carbon and hydrogen are not shown and the lines representing C—C bonds are drawn in a *zig-zag* fashion only heteroatoms are written specifically.

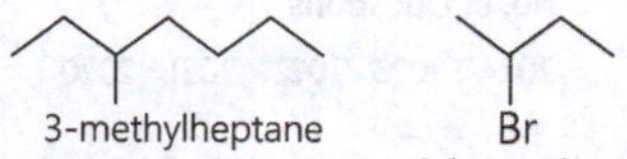

3-methylheptane 2-bromobutane

- In cyclic compounds, the bond-line formulas may be given as follows

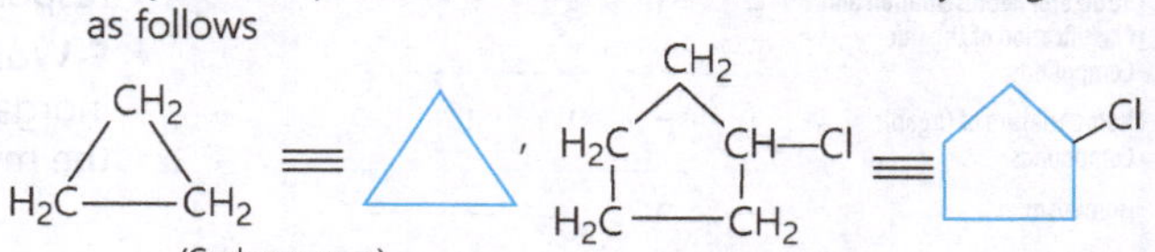

(Cyclopropane) (Chlorocyclopentane)

Three Dimensional Representation of Organic Molecules

- It can be represented on paper (2-dimensional) by using solid wedge (◀) and dashed wedge (⦙⦙⦙⦙) in the formula.
- In these formulas, the solid wedge is used to indicate a bond projecting out of the plane of paper, towards observer and dashed wedge is used to depict the bond projecting away from the observer.
- The bonds lying in the plane of the paper are shown by normal lines (—).

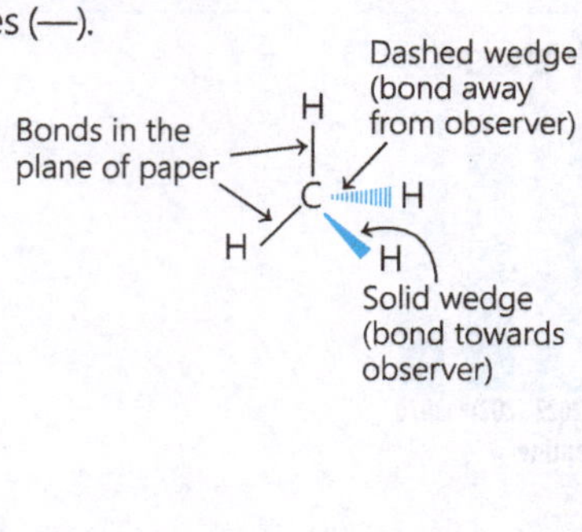

Classification of Organic Compounds

These are broadly classified as follows

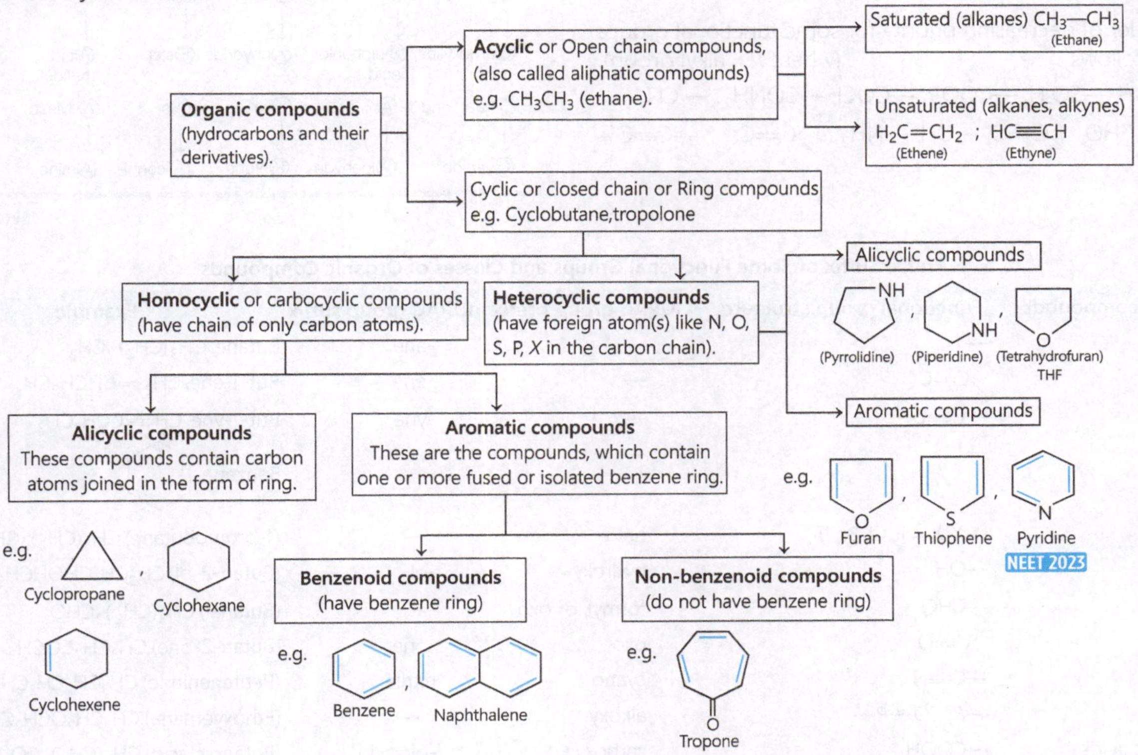

Nomenclature of Organic Compounds

Two system for naming of organic compound are as follows

Trivial or Common system These are generally based on the source or some important property or at the wish of discoverer. These are useful particularly when the alternative systematic names are lengthy and complicated.

e.g. Buckminster fullerene is a common name given to C_{60} cluster.

The IUPAC System of Nomenclature

According to IUPAC, the name of an organic compound consists of following components. NEET 2021, 2022

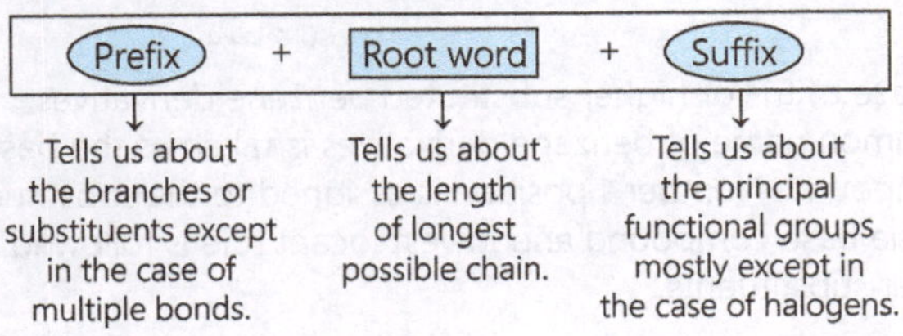

Rules for IUPAC Nomenclature NEET 2024

For branched chain alkanes compounds :

- First of all, the longest carbon chain in the molecule is identified.
- Numbering is started from the terminal carbon from where branching is nearest. While writing the trivial names of substituents in alphabetical order, the prefixes *iso* and *neo* are considered to be the part of the fundamental name of alkyl group. The prefixes *sec* and *tert* are not considered to be the part of fundamental name.
- If the two substituents are found in equivalent positions, the lower number is given to the one coming first in the alphabetical string.
- If there are two chains of equal size, then that chain is to be selected which contains more number of side chains.

For organic compounds having functional group(s) :

- The longest chain of carbon atoms containing the functional group is numbered in such a way that the functional group is attached at the carbon atom possessing lowest possible number in the chain.

- In polyfunctional compounds, one of the functional group is chosen (priority wise) as the principal functional group and the compound is then named on that basis.
- The order of decreasing priority for some functional groups are as follows (where R = alkyl group)

$$-COOH, -SO_3H, -COOR, -COCl, -CONH_2, -CN, -CHO, >C{=}O, -OH, -NH_2, >C{=}C<, -C{\equiv}C-.$$

Mnemonics Trick to remember decreasing priority of functional group.

- (C)ome → (C)arboxylic acid
- (S)oon → (S)ulphonic acid
- (A)jay → (A)nhydride
- (E)at → (E)ster
- (A)n → (A)cid halide
- (A)pple → (A)mide
- (C)haat and → (C)yanide
- (A) → (A)ldehyde
- (K)iur → (K)etone
- (A)s → (A)lcohol
- (A)dvised → (A)mine

Prefix, Suffix of Some Functional Groups and Classes of Organic Compounds

Class of compounds	Functional group structure	IUPAC group prefix	IUPAC group suffix	Example
Alkanes	—	—	-ane	Butane, $CH_3(CH_2)_2CH_3$
Alkenes	$>C{=}C<$	—	-ene	But-1-ene, $CH_2{=}CHCH_2CH_3$
Alkynes	$-C{\equiv}C-$	—	-yne	But-1-yne, $CH{\equiv}CCH_2CH_3$
Arenes	—	—	—	Benzene, 
Halides	$-X$ (X = F, Cl, Br, I)	halo-	—	(1-bromobutane) $CH_3(CH_2)_2CH_2Br$
Alcohols	$-OH$	hydroxy-	-ol	(Butan-2-ol) $CH_3CH_2CHOHCH_3$
Aldehydes	$-CHO$	formyl, or oxo	-al	(Butanal) $CH_3(CH_2)_2CHO$
Ketones	$>C{=}O$	oxo-	-one	(Butan-2-one) $CH_3CH_2COCH_3$
Nitriles	$-C{\equiv}N$	cyano	nitrile	(Pentanenitrile) $CH_3CH_2CH_2CH_2CN$
Ethers	$-R-O-R-$	alkoxy-	—	(Ethoxyethane) $CH_3CH_2OCH_2CH_3$
Carboxylic acids	$-COOH$	carboxy	-oic acid	(Butanoic acid) $CH_3(CH_2)_2CO_2H$
Carboxylate ions	$-COO^-$	—	-oate	(Sodium butanoate) $CH_3(CH_2)_2CO_2^-Na^+$
Esters	$-COOR$	alkoxycarbonyl	-oate	(Methyl propanoate) $CH_3CH_2COOCH_3$
Acyl halides	$-COX$ (X = F, Cl, Br, I)	halocarbonyl	-oyl halide	(Butanoyl chloride) $CH_3(CH_2)_2COCl$
Amines	$-NH_2$ >NH, >N—	amino-	-amine	(Butan-2-amine) $CH_3CHNH_2CH_2CH_3$
Amides	$-CONH_2$, $-CONHR-CONR_2$	-carbamoyl	-amide	(Butanamide) $CH_3(CH_2)_2CONH_2$
Nitro compounds	$-NO_2$	nitro	—	(1-nitrobutane) $CH_3(CH_2)_3NO_2$
Sulphonic acids	$-SO_3H$	sulpho	sulphonic acid	(Methylsulphonic acid) CH_3SO_3H

Nomenclature of Substituted Benzene Compounds

- For substituted benzene compounds, the substituent is placed as prefix to the word benzene.
  However, common names of many substituted benzene compounds are still universally used. e.g. Methylbenzene (toluene)
- In disubstituted benzene ring, the substituents are given the lowest numbers possible while numbering the carbon atoms of the ring.
- In the trivial system of nomenclature, the prefix *ortho* (*o*-) indicates 1, 2-, *meta* (*m*-) indicates 1, 3- and *para* (*p*-) indicates 1, 4-disubstituted benzene ring.

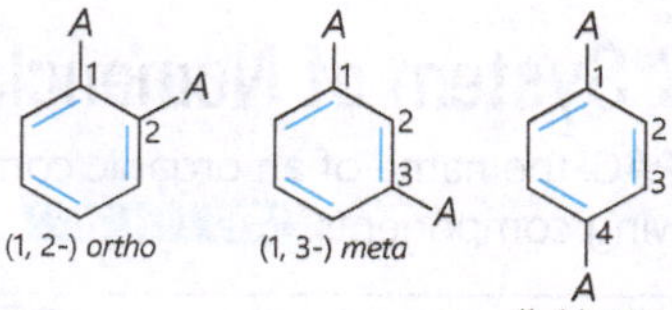

(1, 2-) *ortho* (1, 3-) *meta* (1, 4-)*para*

- In case of tri- or higher substituted benzene derivatives, common name of benzene derivatives is taken as the base compound. Number 1 position is assigned to the substituents of the base compound and lowest locant rule is followed for other substituents.
- Benzene ring is considered as substituent [Phenyl (Ph), $-C_6H_5$] when it is attached to an alkane with a functional group.

Isomerism

The phenomenon of existence of two or more compounds possessing the same molecular formula but different properties is known as isomerism. The following flow chart shows different types of isomerism.

Isomerism

- **Structural isomerism** (have same molecular formula but different structures)
  - **Chain isomerism** (differ in carbon skeleton) e.g. Pentane and 2-methylbutane
  - **Position isomerism** (differ in the position of substituent atom or functional group) e.g. 1-butene and 2-butene
  - **Functional group isomerism** (differ in functional groups attached) e.g. Propanal and propan-2-one
  - **Metamerism** (having different alkyl group on either side of functional group.) e.g. Methoxypropane and ethoxypropane NEET 2023
- **Stereoisomerism** (have same constitution and sequence of covalent bonds but differ in relative position of their atoms or group in space.)
  - **Geometrical isomerism**
  - **Optical isomerism**

For Concept Master Video

Fundamental Concepts in Organic Reaction Mechanism

It is the sequential account of each step, describing details of electron movement, energetics during bond cleavage and bond formations and the rates of transformation of reactants into products. The general reaction is

$$\underset{\text{(Substrate)}}{\text{Organic molecule}} \xrightarrow{\text{Attacking reagent}} \text{Intermediate} \longrightarrow \text{Product(s)} + \text{By product(s)}$$

Note A molecule whose carbon is involved in new bond formation is called **substrate** and other one is called **reagent**.

Fission of a Covalent Bond

The organic reaction begins with the breakage of covalent bond and this breakage or fission are of two types:

1. Homolytic Cleavage or Homolysis

- In this cleavage, one of the electrons of the shared pair in a covalent bond goes with each of the bonded atoms, i.e. symmetrical. It is represented by half headed (fish hook : ⌒) curved arrow.

e.g. $$R-X \xrightarrow[\text{Light}]{\text{Heat or}} \underset{\text{Alkyl free radical}}{R^{\bullet}} + X^{\bullet}$$ NEET 2023

- **Free radical** It is an unchange molecule (highly reactive and short-lived) having an unpaired electron.
- Alkyl free radicals are also classified as *primary*, *secondary* or *tertiary*.

  Like carbocations, the **order of stability of alkyl free radicals** is

$$\underset{\substack{\text{Methyl}\\\text{free radical}}}{\dot{C}H_3} < \underset{\substack{\text{Ethyl}\\\text{free radical}\\(1^\circ)}}{\dot{C}H_2CH_3} < \underset{\substack{\textit{Iso}\text{-propyl}\\\text{free radical}\\(2^\circ)}}{\dot{C}H(CH_3)_2} < \underset{\substack{\textit{Tert-}\text{ butyl}\\\text{free radical}\\(3^\circ)}}{\dot{C}(CH_3)_3}$$

2. Heterolytic Cleavage or Heterolysis

- This cleavage involves breaking of a covalent bond in such a way that shared pair of electrons remains with one of the fragments, i.e. unsymmetrical. The reaction proceed through this cleavage are called ionic or heteropolar or just polar reaction.

$$X-Y \xrightarrow{\text{Heterolysis}} X^{+} + Y^{-}$$ (when X is less electronegative than Y)

$$X-Y \xrightarrow{\text{Heterolysis}} X^{-} + Y^{+}$$ (when Y is less electronegative than X)

For Concept Master Video

Heterolytic cleavage results in formation of two types of species or intermediates. These are as follows

Carbocation	Carbanion
It is an ion containing a **positively charged** carbon atom.	It is an ion containing a **negative charged** carbon atom.
The carbon atom bearing the +ve charge is ***sp***^{2} hybridised.	The carbon atom bearing the –ve charge is ***sp***^{3} hybridised.
The geometry of the carbon atom is **trigonal planar**.	The geometry of the carbon atom is **pyramidal.**
It is **paramagnetic** in nature.	It is **diamagnetic** in nature.
Act as an **electrophile** in chemical reactions.	Act as a **nucleophile** in chemical reactions.
Order of stability (i) $1^\circ < 2^\circ < 3^\circ$ NEET 2023 (ii) $Ph_3C^+ > Ph_2\overset{\oplus}{C}H > (Me)_3\overset{\oplus}{C}H >$ $Ph\overset{\oplus}{C}H_2 > (Me)_2\overset{\oplus}{C}H$ $\overset{\oplus}{C}H_3 > CH\equiv\overset{\oplus}{C} > C_6\overset{\oplus}{H}_5$ NEET 2024 (in gaseous phase)	Order of stability (i) $1^\circ > 2^\circ > 3^\circ$ (ii) $Ph_3C^{\ominus} > Ph_2CH^- > Ph_2\bar{C}H_2$ $> CH_2{=}CH-CH_2^- > HC\equiv C^-$ $> H_2C{=}\bar{C}H > \bar{C}H_3$ $> Me\bar{C}H_2 > (Me)_3C^-$

Nucleophiles and Electrophiles

- **Nucleophiles or Nucleophilic reagents** An electron rich species having a lone pair of electrons is called a nucleophile (Nu**:**), i.e. nucleus loving species.
  e.g. **Negatively charged** species : H^-, Cl^-, Br^-, I^-, carbanions, $\bar{O}H$, $\bar{O}R$, $\bar{S}R$, CN^-.

  Nucleophiles can also be seen in the form of **neutral molecules**.

  e.g. $H_2\ddot{O}$, $\ddot{N}H_3$, $R\ddot{N}H_2$, $R\ddot{O}H$, $R\ddot{S}H$, etc.

- **Electrophiles or Electrophilic reagents** An electrophile is defined as electron deficient species which attacks on electron rich areas, i.e. electron seeking.
- **Positively charged species** H^+, Cl^+, NO_2^+, SO_3^+ and carbocations.
- The electrophiles can also be seen in the form of **neutral molecules**, e.g. carbenes ($:CR_2$), nitrenes ($\ddot{N}R$), BF_3, $AlCl_3$, $FeCl_3$, $RCOCl$, SO_3, CS_2 etc.

Electron Movement in Organic Reactions

It can be shown by curved-arrow notation. It shows how changes in bonding occur due to electronic redistribution during the reaction. Presentation of shifting of electron is given below :

$=Y-$ ↔ $-Y=$ (from π-bond to adjacent bond position)

$=Y-$ ↔ $-\ddot{Y}-$ (from π-bond to adjacent atom)

$-\ddot{Y}-$ ↔ $-Y=$ (from atom to adjacent bond position)

Electron Displacement Effects in Covalent Bonds

These are mainly divided into following categories.

Inductive Effect

It involves partial displacement of σ-electrons towards more electronegative atom or group of σ-bond.

- It is a permanent effect. NEET 2019
- It is distance dependent, the longer the distance, the weaker the effect (becomes vanishingly small after three bonds).

Inductive effect are of two types

- **+*I* effect** The graph which releases or donates electron clouds is known as +*I* group and effect is called +I effect.
- **Decreasing order of +*I* effect**

$NH_2^s > O^\ominus\ -COO^\ominus > -C(CH_3)_3 > -CH(CH_3)_2 >$
$-CH_2-CH_3 > -CH_3 > T > -D > -H$

- **–*I* effect** The atom or graph which withdraws electron clouds is known as –*I* group and effect is called –*I* effect.
- **Decreasing order of –*I* effect**

$-\overset{\oplus}{N}R_3 > -\overset{\oplus}{S}R_2 > -\overset{\oplus}{N}H_3 > -NO_2 > -SO_3R > -CN >$
$SO_2Ar > -COOH > -F > -Cl > -Br > -I > -OBr >$
$-COOR > -OR > -COR > -SH > -SR > -OH >$
$-C\equiv CR > -Ar_2 > C\equiv CR_2$

Resonance Structure

- There are many organic molecules whose behaviour cannot be explained by a single Lewis structure.
- The resonance structures are hypothetical and individually do not represent any real molecule. The actual structure is a **resonance hybrid** of several contributing structure.
- The energy of actual structure (resonance hybrid) is lower than that of canonical structures.
- The difference in energy between the actual structure and the lowest energy resonance structure is called the **resonance stabilisation energy** or **resonance energy**.
- Resonance structure with greater number of covalent bonds are more stable than those with less number.
- Resonance structure with more dispersal of charge is more stable than other.

Resonance Effect or Mesomeric Effect

- It is defined as the polarity produced in the molecule by the interaction of two π-bonds or between a π-bond and lone pair of electrons present on adjacent atom. This effect is transmitted through the chain.
- If the chain or cyclic system consist of alternate single and double bonds then, it is termed as conjugated system.

Resonance effect are of two types

- **+*R* effect** In this effect, the transfer of electrons is always away from an atom of a substituent attached to the conjugated system. Substituents like, halogens, $-OH$, $-OR$, $-OCOR$, $-NH_2$, $-NHR$, $-NR_2$, $-NHCOR$. show this effect.
- **–*R* effect** In this effect, the flow of electrons is towards the atom of a substituent attached to the conjugated system.
  e.g. Substituents like, $-COOH$, CHO, $C=O$, $-CN$, $-NO_2$.

Note The presence of alternate single and double bonds in an open chain or cyclic system is termed as conjugate system.

Electromeric Effect

It is defined as the complete transfer of a shared pair of π-electrons to one of the atoms joined by a **multiple bond** on the demand of an attacking reagent. It is a temporary effect.

Electromeric effect are of two types

- **+*E* effect** In this effect, the π-electrons of the multiple bond are transferred to that atom to which the reagent gets attached.

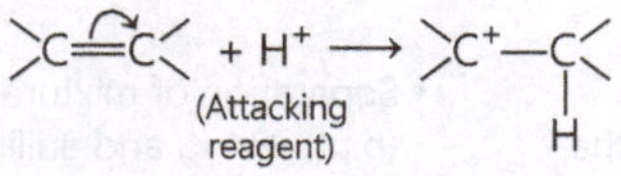

- **–*E* effect** In this effect the π-electrons of the multiple bond are transferred to that atom which is attacked by the chemical reagent.

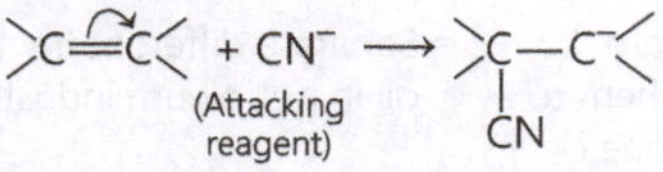

Note When inductive and electromeric effects operate in opposite directions, the electromeric effect predominates.

Hyperconjugation

- It involves delocalisaiton of σ-electrons of C—H bond of an alkyl group directly attached to an atom of unsaturated system or to an atom with an unshared *p*-orbital.
- It is a permanent effect.
- It is also called no bond resonance.
- Greater the number of alkyl groups attached to a positively charged carbon atom, the greater is the hyperconjugation interaction and stabilisation of the cation.

Marks Maximizer

- No. of hyperconjugation structure = No. of alpha hydrogen +1
- Species that behave as an electrophile as well as nucleophiles are known as ambiphiles (ambidents).
e.g.

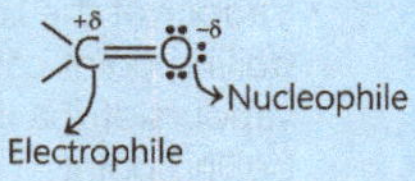

Types of Organic Reactions and Mechanisms

Organic reactions can be classified into the following categories

- Substitution reactions
- Addition reactions
- Elimination reactions
- Rearrangement reactions

Methods of Purification of Organic Compounds

The common techniques used for purification are as follows

Methods	Principle	Process	Applications
Crystallisation	It is based on the difference in the solubilities of the compound and the impurities in the suitable solvent.	• In this method, a hot concentrated solution of the compound is prepared. • This gives the crystals of the pure compound upon filtration and cooling.	Sugar having common salt as impurity can be crystallised through hot ethanol as it is soluble in hot ethanol but common salt does not.
Sublimation	This process is employed to separate sublimable compounds from non-sublimable impurities.	In this process, the impure solid is taken into China dish and on heating, the solid changes to vapour without converting into liquid phase and the vapours upon cooling give back the solid.	Impure samples of naphthalene, anthracene, camphor, benzoic acid, NH_4Cl, dry ice, salicylic acid can be purified by this process.

Methods	Principle	Process	Applications
Distillation	• It is based upon the large difference in the boiling points of two liquids or two components. • It is generally used if an organic liquid contains a non-volatile impurity.	• In this process, vapours of liquids in the mixture formed separately on reaching at their boiling points. • The vapours on cooling condense to give back the original liquid in its pure form.	• Separation of mixture of hexane (b.pt. 342 K) and toluene (b. pt. 384 K). • Separation of mixture of chloroform (b.pt. 334 K) and aniline (b.pt. 457 K).
Fractional distillation	• This method is based upon the separation of two liquids having nearly equal boiling points. • Vapour of the liquid with higher boiling point condense before the vapours of the liquid with lower boiling point.	• The distillation is carried out with the help of specially designed fractionating columns. • Chemical compounds are separated by heating them to a temperature at which one or more fractions of the mixture will vaporise.	• A mixture of acetone and methyl alcohol is separated by this process. • Separate different fractions of crude oil in petroleum industry.
Distillation under reduced pressure	It is used for those liquids which have very high boiling point, and decompose at or below their boiling point.	Under reduced pressure, the liquid will boil at low temperature.	At 12 mm of Hg pressure, glycerol boils at 453 K without decomposition and can be separated from spent-lye in soap industry.
Steam distillation	It is used for steam volatile substances which are immiscible with water.	• Compound is distilled with steam under reduced pressure at a temperature below 373 K. • Pure compound comes out with steam and separates on cooling.	Aniline is separated from aniline water mixture.
Differential extraction	Two immiscible liquids have different solubility in a solvent forms different layer.	The extraction of a organic compound from its aqueous solution can be carried out by shaking it with an organic solvent in which the compound is insoluble.	Benzoic acid is separated from water by using benzene.
Chromatography	It is based upon the principle of distribution of components of a given organic mixture between two phases, i.e. stationary phase and mobile phase.	In this process, the stationary phase can either be solid or liquid supported over a solid. A pure solvent a mixture of solvents or a gas is allowed to move slowly over the stationary phase. The moving phase is called mobile phase.	For separation of sugars and amino acids.
Types of chromatography			
Adsorption chromatography	• Differential adsorption of the various components of a mixture on a suitable adsorbent such as silica gel or alumina.	• Mobile phase is allowed to move over a stationary phase (absorbent) the components of the mixture move by varying distance over the stationary phase.	• Silica gel, cellulose microcrystalline etc.
Column chromatography	• The mixture is passed through adsorbent packed in glass tube.	• It consists of a stationary solid phase that adsorbs and separates the compounds passing through it.	• Mixture of naphthalene and benzophenone.

Thin layer chromatography	• The mixture is passed over adsorbent on a thin glass plate (about 0.2 mm).	• The stationary phase is applied on the surface of thin glass plate then pour the mobile phase into the TLC.	• Amino acids can be detected by spraying the plate with ninhydrin solution. • The relative adsorption of each component of the mixture is expressed in terms of its retardation factor.
Partition chromatography	• It is based on continuous differential partitioning of components of a mixture between stationary and mobile phases.	It mainly includes paper chromatography in which a strip of chromatographic paper is spotted with the solution mixture suspended in a suitable solvent which acts as mobile phase. NEET 2020	• For separation of sugars and amino acids • For separating a coloured ink

Qualitative Analysis of Organic Compounds

It involves the detection and percentage composition of elements present in an organic compound. These are as follows

Element	Method/Detection reagent	Procedure	Chemical reactions
Carbon and hydrogen	• Heat the compound with copper (II) oxide • $C + 2CuO \xrightarrow{\Delta} 2Cu + CO_2$ • $2H + CuO \xrightarrow{\Delta} Cu + H_2O$	• CO_2 reacts with lime water which develops turbidity and confirms carbon. • H_2O reacts with anhyd. $CuSO_4$ and develops blue colour confirms hydrogen.	• $CO_2 + \underset{\text{(Lime water)}}{Ca(OH)_2} \longrightarrow \underset{\text{(Milkiness)}}{CaCO_3} \downarrow + H_2O$ • $5H_2O + \underset{\text{(White)}}{CuSO_4} \xrightarrow{\Delta} \underset{\text{(Blue)}}{CuSO_4 \cdot 5H_2O}$
Nitrogen	• Lassaigne's extract (NaCN) $Na + C + N \xrightarrow{\Delta} NaCN$	• Boil Lassaigne's extract (LE) with $FeSO_4$ and then acidify with conc. H_2SO_4. • Formation of prussian **blue colour** confirms nitrogen.	• $6NaCN + Fe^{2+} \longrightarrow [Fe(CN)_6]^{4-}$ • $3[Fe(CN)_6]^{4-} + 4Fe^{3+} \xrightarrow{xH_2O} \underset{\text{(Prussian blue)}}{Fe_4[Fe(CN)_6]_3 \cdot xH_2O}$
Sulphur	• Lassaigne's extract (Na_2S) • $2Na + S \xrightarrow{\Delta} Na_2S$ (LE)	• Add acetic acid and lead acetate to Lassaigne's extract to get a black precipitate. • Add sodium nitroprusside to Lassaigne's extract to get **violet colour** confirms sulphur.	• $S^{2-} + Pb^{2+} \longrightarrow \underset{\text{(Black)}}{PbS} \downarrow$ • $S^{2-} + \underset{\text{(Nitroprusside ion)}}{[Fe(CN)_5NO]^{2-}} \longrightarrow \underset{\text{(Violet)}}{[Fe(CN)_5NOS]^{4-}}$
Nitrogen and sulphur together	• Lassaigne's extract (NaSCN) • $Na + C + N + S \xrightarrow{\Delta} NaSCN$	• Boil L.E with acetic acid and lead acetate. • Formation of blood red colour and no prussian blue colour.	• $FeCl_3 + NaSCN \longrightarrow \underset{\text{Blood red colour}}{[Fe(SCN)]Cl_2} + NaCl$ NEET 2023
Halogen	• Lassaigne's extract (NaX) • $Na + X \xrightarrow{\Delta} NaX$	• Acidify Lassaigne's extract with HNO_3 and then add $AgNO_3$. A **white ppt**. soluble in NH_4OH shows presence of chlorine. • **Yellow ppt.** sparingly soluble in NH_4OH shows presence of bromine. • A **yellow ppt.** insoluble in NH_4OH shows presence of iodine.	• $X^- + Ag^+ \longrightarrow \underset{\text{(ppt.)}}{AgX}$ • (X represents a halogen Cl, Br or I)
Phosphorus	• Heat the compound with (oxidising agent) sodium peroxide. • $P \xrightarrow[\Delta]{Na_2O_2,\ \text{Boil}} Na_3PO_4$	• Solution is boiled with nitric acid and then treated with ammonium molybdate. • Formation of yellow colouration or ppt. indicate the presence of phosphorus.	• $Na_3PO_4 + 3HNO_3 \longrightarrow H_3PO_4$ • $H_3PO_4 + \underset{\text{Ammonium molybdate}}{12(NH_4)_2MoO_4} + 21HNO_3 \longrightarrow$ $\underset{\text{Ammonium phosphomolybdate (yellow ppt.)}}{(NH_4)_3PO_4 \cdot 12MoO_3} + 21NH_4NO_3 + 12H_2O$

Quantitative Analysis

The percentage composition of elements present in an organic compound is determined by the methods based on the following principles

Element	Procedure with formulas
Carbon and Hydrogen (C and H)	**Liebig's combustion method** • A known mass of an organic compound is burnt in presence of excess of O_2 and CuO. $C_xH_y + \left(x + \frac{y}{4}\right)O_2 \xrightarrow{\Delta} xCO_2 + \frac{y}{2}H_2O$ • CO_2 evolved is absorbed by conc. solution of KOH $\cdot H_2O$ produced is absorbed by anhydrous $CaCl_2$. • Increase in masses of these absorbing compounds gives the masses of CO_2 and H_2O produced. • % of C $= \frac{12}{44} \times \frac{\text{Mass of } CO_2 \text{ formed}}{\text{Mass of compound}} \times 100$, % of H $= \frac{2}{18} \times \frac{\text{Mass of } H_2O \text{ formed}}{\text{Mass of compound}} \times 100$
Nitrogen (N)	**Duma's method** • Nitrogen containing organic compound is heated with CuO in an atmosphere of CO_2. $C_xH_yN_z + \left(2x + \frac{y}{2}\right)CuO \longrightarrow xCO_2 + \frac{y}{2}H_2O + \frac{z}{2}N_2 + \left(2x + \frac{y}{2}\right)Cu$ • N_2 evolved gets collected over conc. KOH solution which absorbs CO_2. • % of N $= \frac{28}{22400} \times \frac{\text{Volume of } N_2 \text{ gas at STP}}{\text{Mass of compound}} \times 100$
	Kjeldahl's method • Organic compound $+ H_2SO_4(\text{conc.}) \longrightarrow (NH_4)_2SO_4 \xrightarrow{2NaOH} Na_2SO_4 + 2NH_3 + 2H_2O$ $2NH_3 + H_2SO_4 \longrightarrow (NH_4)_2SO_4$ • % of N $= \frac{1.4 \times \text{Molarity of acid} \times \text{Vol. of acid used} \times \text{Basicity of acid}}{\text{Mass of compound}}$ • % of N $= \frac{1.4 \times \text{Normality of acid} \times \text{Vol. of acid used}}{\text{Mass of compound}}$ **Limitation** Kjeldahl's method is not applicable to compounds containing nitrogen in nitro and azo groups and nitrogen present in the ring like pyridine.
Halogen (X) [X = Cl, Br, I]	**Carius method** • Halogen in organic compound is precipitated as silver halide by boiling with conc. HNO_3 and then adding $AgNO_3$. • % of Cl $= \frac{35.5 \times \text{Mass of AgCl}}{1435 \times \text{Mass of compound}} \times 100$ • % of Br $= \frac{80 \times \text{Mass of AgBr}}{188 \times \text{Mass of compound}} \times 100$ • % of I $= \frac{127 \times \text{Mass of AgI}}{235 \times \text{Mass of compound}} \times 100$
Sulphur (S)	**Carius method** Sulphur in organic compound is oxidised to H_2SO_4 by boiling with Na_2O_2 or conc. HNO_3 and is precipitated as $BaSO_4$ by adding excess of $BaCl_2$ solution in water. • $S \xrightarrow[\text{(ii) } BaCl_2]{\text{(i) } HNO_3, \Delta} \underset{\text{White ppt.}}{BaSO_4 \downarrow}$ • % of S $= \frac{32}{233} \times \frac{\text{Mass of } BaSO_4 \text{ formed}}{\text{Mass of compound}} \times 100$
Phosphorus (P)	**Ignition method** • $\underset{\text{(Phosphorus)}}{P} \xrightarrow[\Delta]{HNO_3} \underset{\text{(Phosphoric acid)}}{H_3PO_4}$ • $H_3PO_4 + Mg^{2+} + NH_4Cl \xrightarrow{\Delta} \underset{\text{(Magnesium ammonium phosphate (white ppt.)}}{MgNH_4PO_4} + HCl$ • $2MgNH_4PO_4 \xrightarrow{\Delta} \underset{\text{(Magnesium pyrophosphate)}}{Mg_2P_2O_7} + 2NH_3 + H_2O$ • % of P $= \frac{62}{222} \times \frac{\text{Mass of } Mg_2P_2O_7}{\text{Mass of compound}} \times 100$

Note The quantitative analysis of oxygen is given by iodine method.

- Percentage of oxygen = 100 – (Sum of the percentages of all other elements)

Or

- Organic compound $\xrightarrow{\Delta} O_2$ + other gaseous products

$$O_2 + 2C \xrightarrow{1100\,°C} 2CO$$

$$5CO + I_2O_5 \longrightarrow I_2 + 5CO_2$$

$$\% \text{ of O} = \frac{32 \times \text{mass of } CO_2}{88 \times \text{mass of compound taken}} \times 100$$

Or

$$= \frac{5 \times 16}{2 \times 127} \times \frac{\text{mass of } I_2 \text{ formed}}{\text{mass of compound taken}} \times 100$$

- Presently the estimation of elements in an organic compound is carried out by using microquantities of substance and automatic experimental techniques.
- The elements carbon, hydrogen and nitrogen present in a compound are determined by an apparatus known as CHN elemental analyser. The analyser requires only a very small amount of the substance (1-3 mg) and displays the values on a screen within a short time.

Caution Points

- Kjeldahl's method cannot be used to estimate nitrogen of compounds having, nitro group or nitrogen present in ring.
- If resonance, mesomerism, hyperconjugation, inductive effect and electromeric effect is asked in a single problems then their predomination becomes important. So, always remember the following order.

Resonance ≈ Mesomerism > Hyperconjugation > Inductive > Electromeric effect

PYQ Notes

1. Higher the stability of carbocation, lower will be hydride affinity. **JEE 2023**
2. On fusing with Na, $CH_3NH_2 \cdot HCl$ give positive test for both nitrogen and halogen. **JEE 2023**

$$CH_3NH_2 \cdot HCl \xrightarrow[\text{Fusion}]{Na} NaCN + NaCl$$

– NaCN gives positive test for nitrogen.

– NaCl gives positive test for halogen.

3. Crude sodium chloride obtained by crystallisation of brine solution does not contain $MgSO_4$. **NEET 2019**
4. Method of separation of 1:1 mixture of *ortho* and *para*-nitrophenols is steam distillation. **NEET 2017**
5. Nucleophile is not a Lewis acid. **NEET 2015**

Step by Step

Mastering NCERT

- Concept Builders
- Topical Questions
- Assertion-Reason
- Statement Type
- Matching Type
- Numerical Value
- NCERT Exemplar's
- Past Exams'
- Skill Boosters

Concept Builders

1 Write the name of the property of carbon that makes it different from other elements.

2 The hybridisation of ethyne molecule is dsp^2. [T/F]

3 $CH_2{=}C{=}CHCH_3$ has .... σ bonds and .... π bonds.

4 When molecule is represented in *zig-zag* manner and atoms are not shown then the representation is known as .... representation.

5 Write the bond line representation of the given molecule into complete molecule representation.

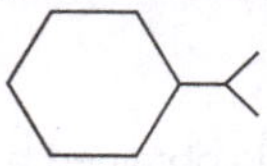

6 In 3D structural representation, dashed and wedge is used to show bond towards the viewer and away from the viewer respectively. [T/F]

7 Cyclic systems having atleast one benzene ring are called .... compounds.

8 Pyridine is an example of heterocyclic aromatic compound. [T/F]

9 A group or series of organic compounds having a characteristic functional group is called ....

10 Thiophene has nitrogen as hetero atom in its ring. [T/F]

11 Write the name of the compound found in red ants.

12 The common name given to the C_{60} cluster is ....

13 The IUPAC name of

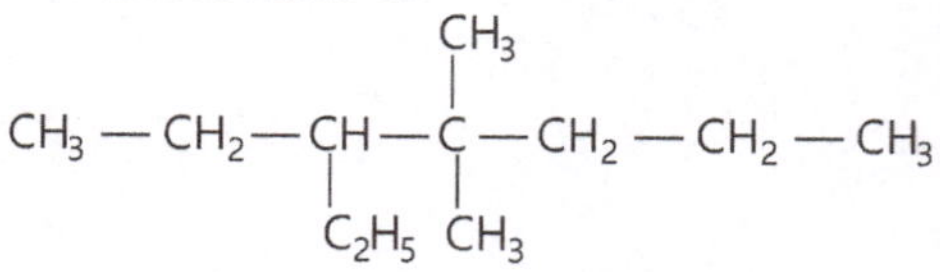

is ....

14 The IUPAC name of $HOCH_2(CH_2)_3CH_2COCH_3$ is 2-oxoheptan-7-ol. [T/F]

15 Write the name of the prefix used for esters.

16 The IUPAC name of

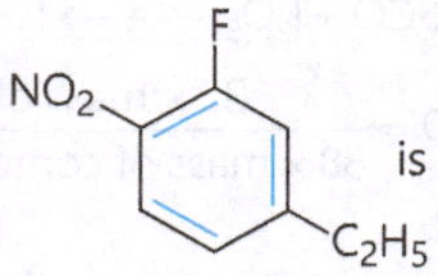

is ....

17 Compound with same molecular formula can show position isomerism. [T/F]

18 Stereo isomerism can be classified as .... and .... isomers.

19 The organic reaction which proceed through heterolytic bond cleavage are .... (homopolar/heteropolar)

20 $AlCl_3$ is an electrophile. [T/F]

21 Pyridine has .... resonance energy than furan but .... resonance energy than benzene.

22 Aniline shows $-R$ effect and nitrobenzene shows $+R$ effect due to the presence of nitrogen containing compounds substitutent group. [T/F]

23 Write the other name of hyperconjugation.

24 Write the name of the apparatus in which vapours of liquid mixture are passed through fractional distillation.

25 Glycerol can be distilled from .... in soap industry.

26 The technique that involves separation of mixture over a column of adsorbent packed is glass tube in partition chromatography. [T/F]

27 A black ppt. is obtained when sodium extract is acidified with acetic acid followed by adding lead acetate to it. This confirms the presence of ....

28 In .... method compound is heated with CuO in the atmosphere of CO_2 and yields nitrogen in addition to CO_2 and H_2O.

29 Give the name of method used for the estimation of halogens.

30 The instrument which is used to determine C, H and N is called ....

Topical Questions

General Introduction and Tetravalence of Carbon

1 Consider the following reaction, NCERT Pg 256

$$\underset{\text{Ammonium cyanate}}{NH_4CNO} \xrightarrow{\text{Heat}} A$$

Here, A refers to

(a) NH_2COCl (b) NH_2COOH

(c) NH_2COCH_3 (d) NH_2CONH_2

2 Which of the following property(s) parameter(s) increases as the s-character of a hybrid orbital decreases?

I. Bond strength II. Bond length NCERT Pg 251

III. Electronegativity IV. Bond angle

Choose the correct answer from the options given below.

(a) I and III (b) II and IV

(c) II, III and IV (d) I and IV

3 The ratio of percentage s -character of C-atom in ethyne and ethene is equal to NCERT Pg 257

(a) 4 : 1 (b) 3 : 1 (c) 3 : 2 (d) 1 : 2

4 The hybridisation and shape of H_2CO is NCERT Pg 257

(a) sp^3, tetrahedral (b) sp^2, bent

(c) sp^2, trigonal planar (d) sp, linear

5 The correct order of electronegativity of carbon in ethane, ethene and ethyne is NCERT Pg 257

(a) ethane < ethene < ethyne

(b) ethyne < ethene < ethane

(c) ethene < ethyne < ethane

(d) ethene < ethane < ethyne

6 The compound which has 10σ and 3π bonds is NCERT Pg 257

(a) $CH \equiv C - CH = CH - CH_3$

(b) $CH_2 = C = CH - CH_3$

(c) $CH_2 = CH - C \equiv C - CH_2 - CH_3$

(d) $CH_2 = \overset{\overset{\large H}{|}}{C} - CH_2 - CH_2 - CH_3$

7 The type of hybridisation of each carbon in $CH_3CH = CHCN$ is NCERT Pg 257

(a) sp^3, sp^3, sp^2, sp^2 (b) sp^3, sp^2, sp, sp^3

(c) sp^3, sp^2, sp^2, sp (d) sp^2, sp^3, sp, sp

Structural Representation and Classification of Organic Compounds

8 Choose the correct bond-line formula for 2-hydroxy-1,2,3-propanetricarboxylic acid. NCERT Pg 258

(a) 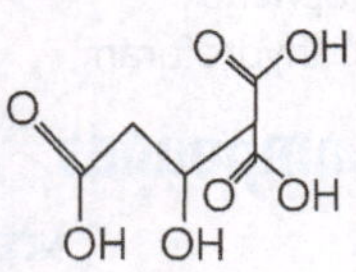

(b) 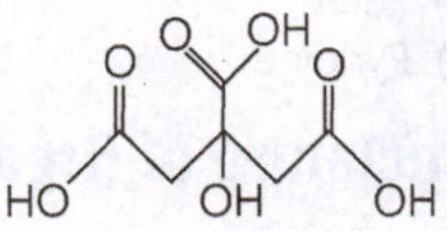

(c) 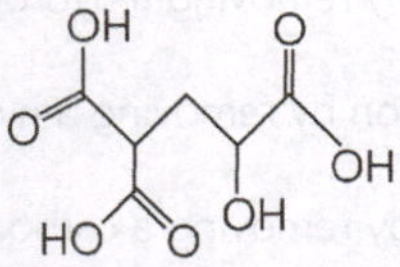

(d) 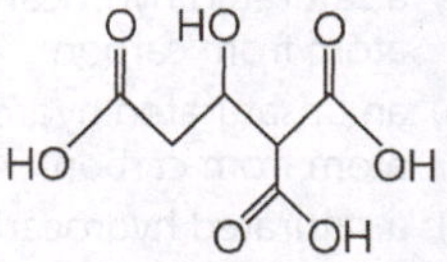

9 In cyclic compounds, the bond-line formula for chlorocyclohexane is represented by which of the following representations? NCERT Pg 259

(a) 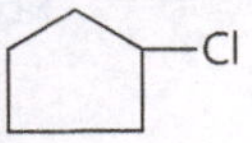

(b) 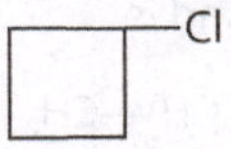

(c) 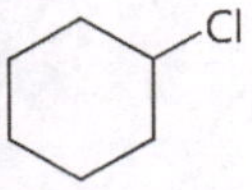

(d) 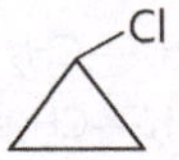

10 The space-filling model emphasises the relative size of each atom based on its NCERT Pg 260

(a) ionic radius (b) van der Waals' radius

(c) atomic radius (d) atomic size

11 Which of the following statements is incorrect? NCERT Pg 261

(a) Aromatic compounds may have hetero atom in the ring.

(b) Tropone is a non-benzenoid compound.

(c) Pyridine is a heterocylic aromatic compound.

(d) Aniline is a non-benzenoid compound.

12 Which of the following is a homocyclic alicyclic compound? NCERT Pg 261

(a) 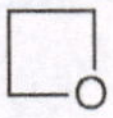

(b) 

(c) 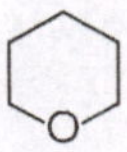

(d) 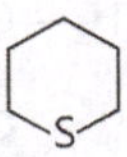

13 Naphthalene is a .... NCERT Pg 261

(a) alicyclic compound
(b) benzenoid aromatic compound
(c) non-benzenoid aromatic compound
(d) acyclic compound

14 Which of the following compound is not heterocyclic aromatic compound? NCERT Pg 262

(a) Furan (b) Thiophene
(c) Pyridine (d) Tetrahydrofuran

Nomenclature of Organic Compounds

15 An alkyl group is derived from NCERT Pg 263

(a) a saturated hydrocarbon by removing a hydrogen atom from carbon
(b) an unsaturated hydrocarbon by removing a hydrogen atom from carbon
(c) a saturated hydrocarbon by removing a carbon atom
(d) an unsaturated hydrocarbon by removing a carbon atom

16 The structure of *iso*-butyl group in an organic compound is NCERT Pg 263

(a) $(CH_3)_2CH—CH_2—$
(b) $CH_3—CH_2—CH_2—CH_3$
(c) $CH_3—CH_2—CH_2—CH_2—$
(d) $CH_3—C(CH_3)_2—$

17 What is the correct IUPAC name of the given compound? NCERT Pg 263

$CH_3—CH(CH_3)—CH_2CH_2CH_2—CH(CH_2CH_3)—CH_2CH_2CH_3$

(a) 6-ethyl-2-methylnonane (b) 2-methyl-6-ethylnonane
(c) 2,6-ethyl-methylnonane (d) 4-ethyl-8-methylnonane

18 The correct way of numbering in the given structure, $CH_3—CH(CH_3)—CH_2—CH_2(CH_3)$ will be NCERT Pg 264

(a) $\overset{1}{C}H_3—\overset{2}{C}H(CH_3)—\overset{3}{C}H_2—\overset{4}{C}H_2—\overset{5}{C}H_3$

(b) $\overset{5}{C}H_3—\overset{4}{C}H(CH_3)—\overset{3}{C}H_2—\overset{2}{C}H_2—\overset{1}{C}H_3$

(c) $\overset{6}{C}H_3—\overset{5}{C}H(\overset{4}{C}H_3)—\overset{3}{C}H_2—\overset{2}{C}H_2—\overset{1}{C}H_3$

(d) $\overset{4}{C}H_3—\overset{3}{C}H(CH_3)—\overset{2}{C}H_2—\overset{1}{C}H_2(CH_3)—$

19 The correct structure for 3-methylpentan-1, 3-diene is NCERT Pg 264

(a) $CH_3CH=C(CH_3)\ CH=CH_2$
(b) $CH_2=CHCH(CH_3)\ CH_2CH_3$
(c) $CH_3CH=C(CH_3)_2$
(d) $CH_2=CH(CH_2)_2CH_3$

20 The correct IUPAC name of the compound,

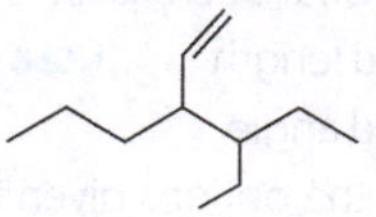

is NCERT Pg 265

(a) 3-(1-ethylpropyl) hex-1-ene
(b) 4-ethyl-3-propylhex-1-ene
(c) 3-ethyl-4-ethenylheptane
(d) 3-ethyl-4-propylhex-5-ene

21 What is the correct IUPAC name of the following? NCERT Pg 265

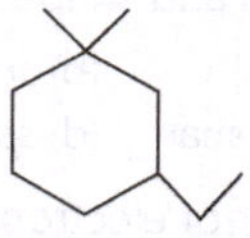

(a) 3-ethyl-1,1-dimethylcyclohexane
(b) 1-ethyl-3,3-dimethylcyclohexane
(c) 1,1-dimethyl-3-ethylcyclohexane
(d) 2-ethyl-4, 4-dimethylcyclohexane

22 The correct decreasing order of priority for the functional groups of organic compounds is NCERT Pg 266

(a) —COOH, —COOR, —CN, $—SO_3H$
(b) —HC=O, $—SO_3H$, COCl, NH_2
(c) —COOR, —COOH, $—SO_3H$, —CN
(d) $—SO_3H$, COCl, —HC=O, $—NH_2$

23 Consider the following statements: NCERT Pg 266

I. The presence of functional group disables systematisation of organic compound into different classes.
II. In polyfunctional compounds, one of the functional group is chosen as the principle functional group.
III. The order of priority for functional group is —COCl > —COOR > $—SO_3H$ > —COOH.
IV. $CH_2(OH)CH_2(OH)$ is named as ethane-1, 2-diol.

Choose the correct statements from the options given below.

(a) I and II (b) II and IV (c) I, II and III (d) I and IV

24 The IUPAC name of the following compound is

$$H_3C—\underset{}{\overset{CH_3}{\overset{|}{C}H}}—\overset{OH}{\overset{|}{C}H}—CH_2—COOH$$

NCERT Pg 266

(a) 4,4 - dimethyl -3-hydroxybutanoic acid
(b) 2-methyl-3-hydroxypentan-5-oic acid
(c) 3- hydroxy -4-methylpentanoic acid
(d) 4-methyl-3-hydroxypentanoic acid

25 The correct IUPAC name of the given structures will be

NCERT Pg 267

$$\text{I. } CH_3—\overset{O}{\overset{||}{C}}—CH_2—CH_2—CH_2—COOH$$

$$\text{II. } CH{\equiv}C—CH{=}CH—CH{=}CH_2$$

Choose the correct option.

	I	II
(a)	Hexane-dione	Hexa-1,3-dien-5-yne
(b)	5-oxohexanoic acid	Hexa-1,3-dien-5-yne
(c)	5-oxohexanoic acid	Hexadiene-5-yne
(d)	3-oxohexanoic acid	Hexadiene-5-yne

26 Which of the following is not in accordance to IUPAC system?

NCERT Pg 267

(a) $Br—CH_2—CH{=}CH_2$
1-bromoprop-2-ene

(b) $$CH_3—CH_2—\overset{CH_3}{\underset{Br}{C}}—CH_2—\underset{CH_3}{CHCH_3}$$
4-bromo- 2, 4-dimethylhexane

(c) 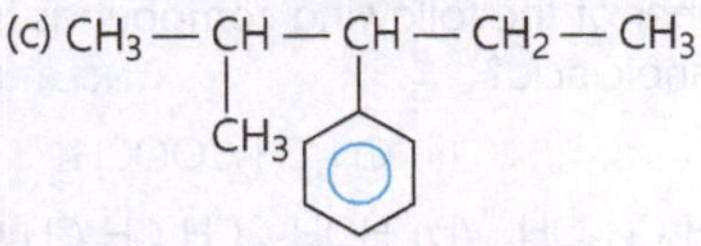
2-methyl-3- phenylpentane

(d) $$CH_3—\underset{O}{\underset{||}{C}}—CH_2—CH_2CH_2COOH$$
5-oxohexanoic acid

27 The IUPAC name of the following compound. $HOCH_2(CH_2)_3CH_2COCH_3$ is

NCERT Pg 267

(a) 7-hydroxyheptan-2-ol (b) 7-hydroxyheptan-2-one
(c) 2-oxoheptan-7-ol (d) Heptan-2-oxo-7-ol

28 The IUPAC name for the following compound is

NCERT Pg 268

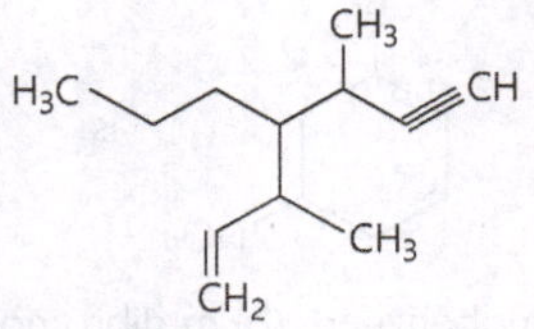

(a) 3-methyl-4-(3-methylprop-1-enyl)-1-heptyne
(b) 3, 5-dimethyl-4-propylhept-6-en-1-yne
(c) 3-methyl-4-(1-methylprop-2-ynyl)-1-heptene
(d) 3, 5-dimethyl-4-propylhept-1-en-6-yne

29 Which of the following names of the given compounds is not correct?

NCERT Pg 269

(a) 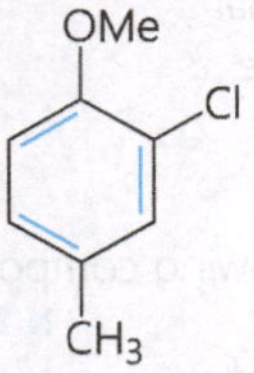 2-chloro-4-methylanisole

(b) 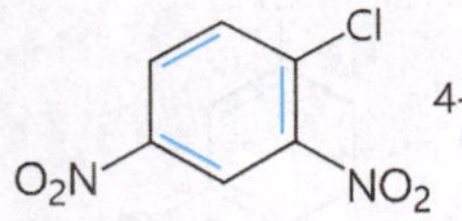 4-chloro-1,3-dinitrobenzene

(c) 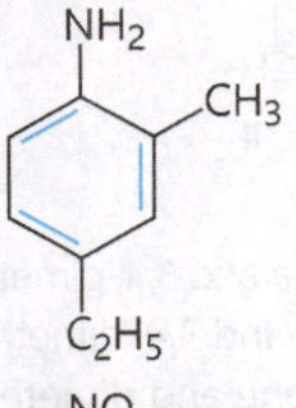 4-ethyl-2-methylaniline

(d) 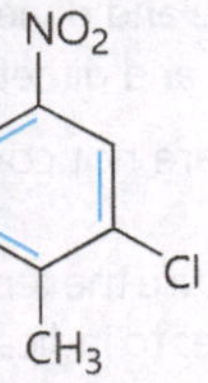 2-chloro-1-methyl-4-nitrobenzene

30 The correct IUPAC name of the given compound is

NCERT Pg 269

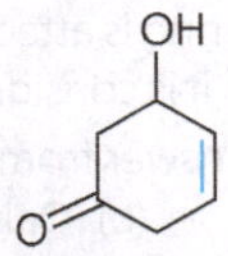

(a) 7-hydroxycyclohex -5-en-1-one
(b) 3-hydroxycyclohex-5-en-1-one
(c) 8-hydroxycyclohex -3-en-1-one
(d) 5-hydroxycyclohex -3-en-1-one

31 The IUPAC name of the following compound NCERT Pg 269

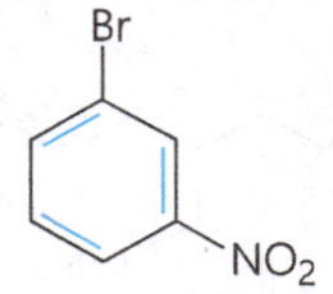

is

(a) 1, 3-dibromobenzene (b) *m*-dibromobenzene
(c) 1, 5-dibromobenzene (d) 1-bromo-3-nitrobenzene

32 Write the IUPAC name of the following. NCERT Pg 269

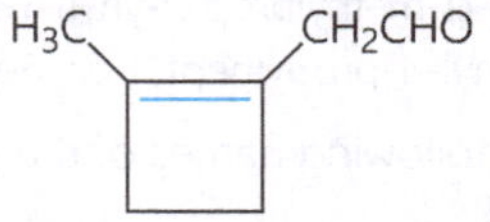

(a) 2-(2-methylcyclobut-1-enyl) ethanal
(b) 2-methyl, 2-ethanalcyclobut-1-ene
(c) Hept-3-en-1-al
(d) 2-methyl, 2-ethylcyclobut-1-enal

33 The correct IUPAC name of the following compounds NCERT Pg 269

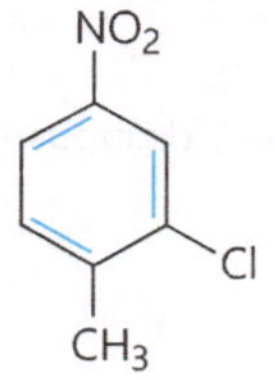

I

and

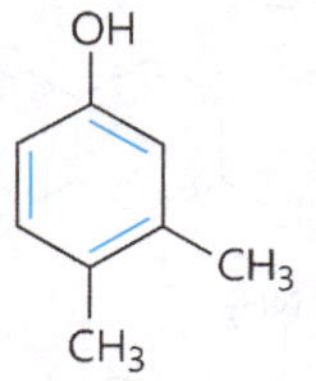

II

respectively are

(a) 2-chloro-1-methyl-4-nitrobenzene and 3,4-dimethylphenol
(b) 4-methyl-5-chloronitrobenzene and 3,4-dimethylphenol
(c) 2-methyl-1-chloro-5-nitrobenzene and dimethylphenol
(d) 3-chloro-4-methyl- nitrobenzene and dimethylphenol

34 Which of the following statements are not correct? NCERT Pg 269

I. In the trivial system of nomenclature the terms *ortho*, *meta* and *para* are used as prefixes to indicate the relative positions 1, 2; 1, 3 and 1, 4 respectively.
II. 1,3-dibromobenzene is named as *o*-dibromobenzene.
III. When a benzene ring is attached to an alkane having a functional group, it is considered as parent.

Choose the correct answer from the options given below.

(a) Only I (b) Only II
(c) Both II and III (d) Both I and III

Isomerism

35 Among the following, which one is an isomer of ethanol? NCERT Pg 270

(a) Methanol (b) Acetone
(c) Diethyl ether (d) Dimethyl ether

36 Which of the following compound is isomeric with 4-*iso*-propylheptane? NCERT Pg 270

(a) 3-ethyl-2,2 dimethylpentane
(b) 5-ethyl-3-methyl-4-*n*-propyloctane
(c) 2,2,4,4-tetramethylhexane
(d) 4-ethyl-3-methyl-4-*n*-propyloctane

37 How many chain isomers are given by the compound, C_5H_{12}? NCERT Pg 270

(a) Three (b) Two
(c) Four (d) Only one

38 The type of isomerism present between $CH_3CH_2CH_2OH$ and $CH_3—\underset{|}{\overset{OH}{CH}}—CH_3$ is NCERT Pg 270

(a) position isomerism
(b) chain isomerism
(c) functional group isomerism
(d) metamerism

39 $C_5H_{10}O$ is a carbonyl compound. The number of carbonyl structural isomers possible for this molecular formula are NCERT Pg 270

(a) 5 (b) 8 (c) 6 (d) 7

40 Study the structures given below carefully and choose the type of isomerism they represent. NCERT Pg 270

$CH_3—C(CH_3)_2—CH_3$ and $CH_3—\overset{CH_3}{\overset{|}{CH}}—CH_2—CH_3$

(a) chain isomerism (b) position isomerism
(c) functional isomerism (d) metamerism

41 How many member of the following compounds is/are isomer(s) of butanoic acid? NCERT Pg 290

(i) CH_3COOCH_3 (ii) $CH_3CH_2COOCH_3$
(iii) $CH_3COCH_2CH_2CH_2OH$ (iv) $HOH_2CCH_2CH_2CH_2OH$
(v) $(OH)_2CHCH_2CH_2CHO$

(a) 1 (b) 2 (c) 3 (d) 4

42 Consider the following isomers of $C_4H_{10}O$. NCERT Pg 271

(i) $CH_3OCH_2CH_2CH_3$ (ii) $CH_3CH_2CH_2CH_2OH$
(iii) $CH_3CH_2OCH_2CH_3$ (iv) $CH_3—\underset{OH}{\underset{|}{CH}}—CH_2CH_3$

The metamers among the given structure is/are

(a) (i) and (ii) (b) (ii) and (iii)
(c) (i) and (iii) (d) (ii) and (iv)

43 Which one of the following exhibits geometrical isomerism? NCERT Pg 271
(a) 1, 2-dibromoprop-1-ene
(b) 2, 3-dimethylbut-2-ene
(c) 2-methylbut-2-ene
(d) 2, 3-dibromobut-1-ene

44 What is the relationship between the structures shown ?

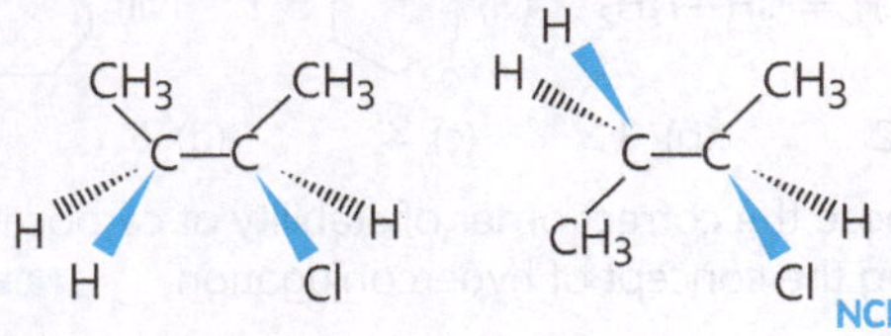

NCERT Pg 271
(a) Structural isomers
(b) Geometrical isomers
(c) Conformational structures
(d) Identical structures

Fundamental Concepts in Organic Reaction Mechanism

45 Relative stabilities of the following carbocations will be in the order NCERT Pg 271

$\overset{\oplus}{C}H_3, CH_3\overset{\oplus}{C}H_2, \overset{\oplus}{C}H_2OCH_3$
(A) (B) (C)

(a) $C > B > A$ (b) $C < B < A$
(c) $B > C > A$ (d) $C > A > B$

46 The correct order of decreasing stability of the following carbocation is NCERT Pg 271

$CH_3-\overset{\oplus}{C}H-CH_3$, (I) $CH_3-\overset{\oplus}{C}H-OCH_3$, (II)
$CH_3-\overset{\oplus}{C}H-CH_2-OCH_3$ (III)

(a) II > I > III (b) II > III > I
(c) III > I > II (d) I > II > III

47 Select the correct statements from the following. NCERT Pg 271, 272
I. In heterolytic cleavage, the bond breaks in such a way that shared pair of electrons remains with one of the fragments.
II. In homolytic cleavage, one of the electrons of the shared pair in a covalent bond goes with each of the bonded atoms.
III. The single electron movement is shown by 'half-headed' (fish hook : ⇀) curved arrow.
IV. Free radicals contain a paired electron.
V. Homolytic fission gives free radical and also called polar reactions.

Choose the correct answer from the options given below.
(a) I, II and III (b) III, IV and V
(c) II, III and IV (d) I, II and V

48 The shape of carbanion NCERT Pg 272
(a) square planar (b) tetrahedral
(c) trigonal planar (d) trigonal pyramidal

49 The stability order of carbanion in the following is NCERT Pg 272

A. $R-C\equiv\overset{\ominus}{C}$; B.  ;

C. $R_2C=\overset{\ominus}{C}H$; D. $R_3C-\overset{\ominus}{C}H_2$

(a) D > B > C > A (b) A > C > B > D
(c) A > B > C > D (d) B > C > D > A

50 The correct order of stability of alkyl radical is NCERT Pg 272
(a) $\dot{C}H(CH_3)_2 < \dot{C}H_3 < \dot{C}H_2CH_3 < \dot{C}(CH_3)_3$
(b) $\dot{C}(CH_3)_3 < \dot{C}H(CH_3)_2 < \dot{C}H_3 < \dot{C}H_2CH_3$
(c) $\dot{C}(CH_3)_3 < \dot{C}H(CH_3)_2 < \dot{C}H_2CH_3 < \dot{C}H_3$
(d) $\dot{C}H_3 < \dot{C}H_2CH_3 < \dot{C}H(CH_3)_2 < \dot{C}(CH_3)_3$

51 Compare stability of free radicals NCERT Pg 272

I. $CH_3-\dot{C}H-CH_3$ II. 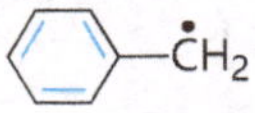

III. $\dot{C}H_2-CH(CH_3)_2$ IV. $\dot{C}H_2-CH_3$

(a) II > I > III > IV (b) II > I > IV > III
(c) I > II > III > IV (d) IV > III > I > II

52 Which of the following is most stable carbocation? NCERT Pg 272

(a) 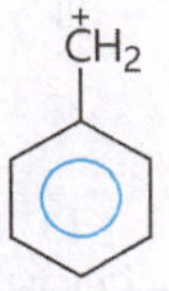 (b) 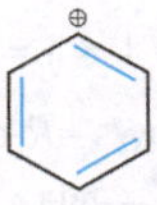 (c) 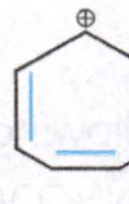 (d) 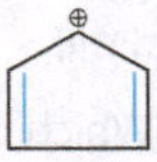

53 Which of the following groups contain only electrophiles? NCERT Pg 273
(a) $BF_3, \overset{+}{C}H_3, NO_2$
(b) $AlCl_3, SO_3, NO_2^+$
(c) $NO_2^+, CH_3^+, R-\ddot{\underset{..}{S}}H$
(d) $C_2H_5^-, \dot{C}_2H_5, C_2H_5^+$

54 Which is not an example of electron withdrawing groups relative to hydrogen are NCERT Pg 274
(a) $-NO_2$ (b) $-COOH$
(c) $-COOR$ (d) $-NH_2$

55 Which of the following pair is not a resonating structure of the each other? **NCERT Pg 275**

I. 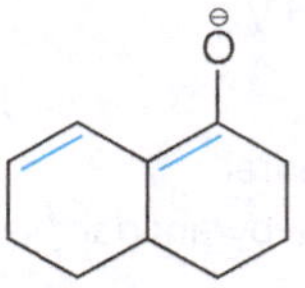 II. 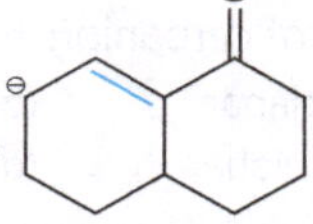

III. 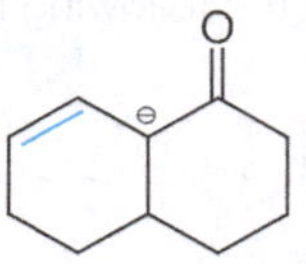 IV. 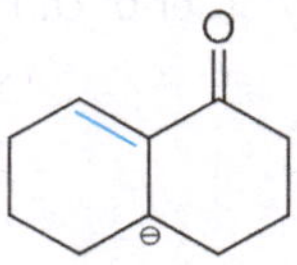

(a) I and II (b) II and III
(c) I and III (d) III and IV

56 Which of the following statement is incorrect? **NCERT Pg 275**

(a) Nitromethane has 2 Lewis structure.
(b) The resonance structure are hypothetical and individually do not represent any real molecule.
(c) Resonance structure contribute to the actual structure in proportion to stability.
(d) Less the number of contributing structures, the more is the resonance energy.

57 The order of relative stability of the contributing structures is **NCERT Pg 275**

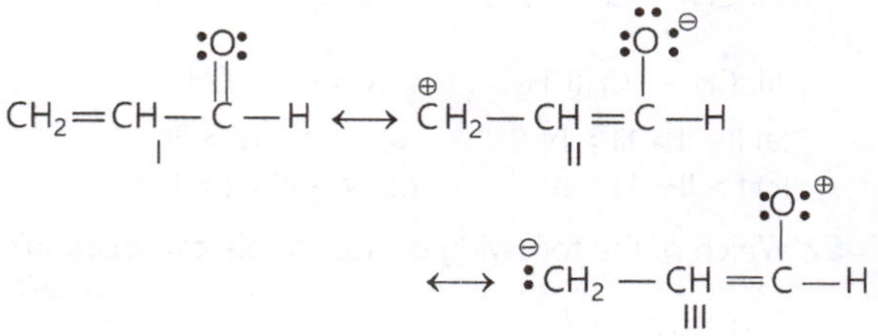

(a) II > I > III (b) I > II > III
(c) III > II > I (d) I = II = III

58 Which of the following shows –*R*-effect? **NCERT Pg 276**

(a) —O*R* (b) —NHCO*R* (c) —NH_2 (d) —COOH

59 Resonance effect of the substituent with benzene ring is not observed in **NCERT Pg 276**

(a) 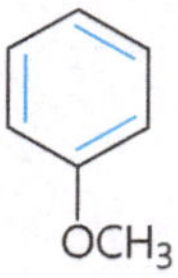 (b) 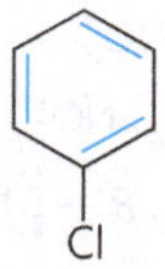

(c) 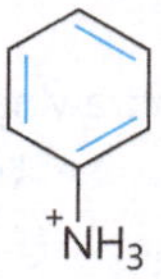 (d) 

60 How many of the following compounds, do not show resonance? **NCERT Pg 276**

(i) $CH_2{=}CH{-}CH_2OH$ (ii) 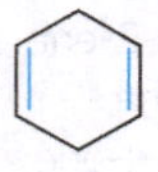 (iii) 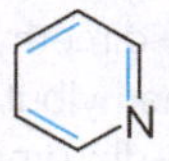 (iv) 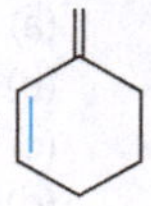

(v) $CH_2{=}CH{-}NH_2$ (vi) 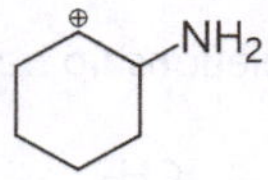 (vii) 

(a) 2 (b) 3 (c) 4 (d) 5

61 Choose the correct order of stability of carbocation using the concept of hyperconjugation. **NCERT Pg 277**

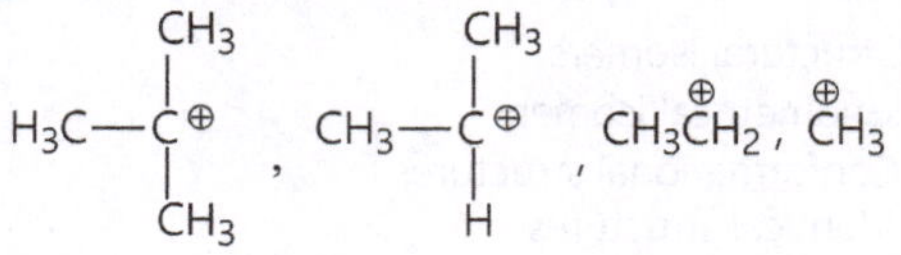

I II III IV

(a) I < II < III < IV (b) IV < III < II < I
(c) III < IV < II < I (d) II < III < I < IV

62 Observe the following species and choose the number of hydrogen atoms involved in hyperconjugation. **NCERT Pg 277**

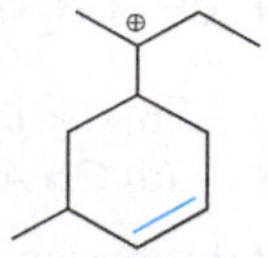

(a) 8 (b) 9 (c) 7 (d) 10

63 Which of the following effect helps in deciding the stability of *iso*-butylene? **NCERT Pg 277**

(a) Inductive effect (b) Mesomeric effect
(c) Hyperconjugative effect (d) Steric effect

Methods of Purification of Organic Compounds

64 Naphthalene can be easily purified by **NCERT Pg 279**

(a) sublimation (b) crystallisation
(c) distillation (d) vaporisation

65 Which of the following process is used to separate volatile liquid from non-volatile impurities? **NCERT Pg 279**

(a) Distillation (b) Sublimation
(c) Differential extraction (d) Crystallisation

66 Which of the following distillation is used if the difference in boiling points of two liquids is not much? **NCERT Pg 279**

(a) Steam distillation
(b) Simple distillation
(c) Fractional distillation
(d) Distillation under reduced pressure

67 The technological applications of fractional distillation is
(a) to separate different fractions of crude oil in petroleum industry **NCERT Pg 279**
(b) to separate different fractions of volatile and non-volatile solvents
(c) to separate mixture of amino acids
(d) to separate glycerol from spent-lye

68 Glycerol can be separated from spent-lye in soap industry by **NCERT Pg 280**
(a) chromatography
(b) sublimation
(c) fractional distillation
(d) distillation under reduced pressure

69 Which of the following processes is suitable for the purification of aniline? **NCERT Pg 281**
(a) Simple distillation
(b) Fractional distillation
(c) Fractional crystallisation
(d) Steam distillation

70 A mixture of *o*-nitrophenol and *p*-nitrophenol can be separated by **NCERT Pg 281**
(a) fractional distillation (b) sublimation
(c) chemical separation (d) steam distillation

71 The technique in which extraction of compound takes place on the basis of more solubility of one compound in another solvent, is **NCERT Pg 281**
(a) differential extraction (b) chromatography
(c) sublimation (d) crystallisation

72 Given below is a diagram of differential extraction. **NCERT Pg 282**

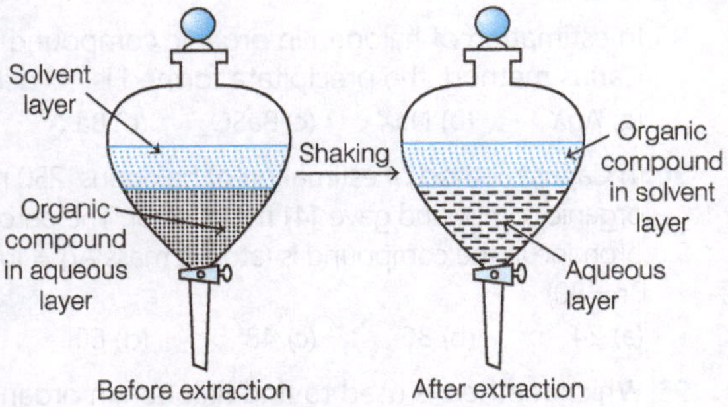

The correct reason of the organic compound present in the aqueous layer moves to the organic solvent is
(a) the organic substance is more soluble in the solvent
(b) the organic substance is insoluble in water hence, organic compound moves up
(c) organic compound being lighter moves in the upper layer
(d) the solute starts diffusing from the supersaturated solution

73 In which technique same solvent is repeatedly used for extraction of the compound? **NCERT Pg 281**
(a) Continuous extraction
(b) Non-continuous extraction
(c) Differential extraction
(d) Non-differential extraction

74 What is the advantage of steam distillation? **NCERT Pg 281**
(a) It reduces decomposition of inorganic compounds.
(b) It increases the decomposition of temperature sensitive compounds.
(c) It increases the decomposition of inorganic compounds.
(d) It reduces decomposition of temperature sensitive organic compounds.

75 Which chromatography is based on the fact that different compounds are adsorbed on an adsorbent to different degrees? **NCERT Pg 282**
(a) Partition chromatography
(b) Adsorption chromatography
(c) Absorption chromatography
(d) Paper chromatography

76 Which of the following adsorbent is used in thin layer chromatography? **NCERT Pg 283**
(a) SiO_2 (b) I_2 (c) C_6H_5COONa (d) SO_2

77 Compound that act as an adsorbent in column chromatography is **NCERT Pg 283**
(a) Na_2O (b) Na_2SO_4 (c) Al_2O_3 (d) NaCl

78 Given below are some column of adsorbent in which the mixture of compounds $A+B+C$ is placed. **NCERT Pg 283**

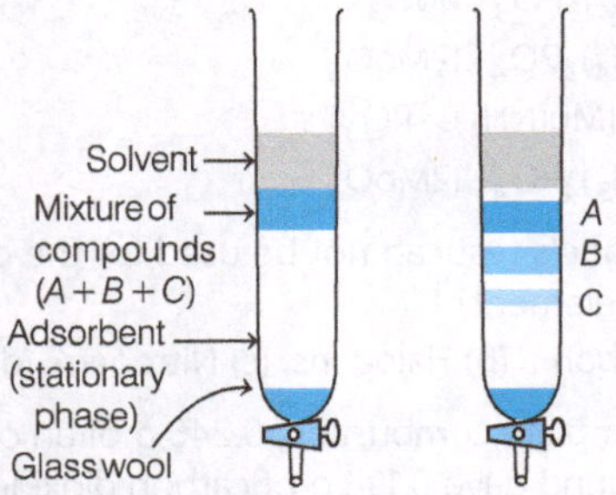

Which of the following statement is correct?
(a) *B* is most strongly adsorbed component.
(b) *A* is the most strongly adsorbed component.
(c) *C* is the most strongly adsorbed component.
(d) *A* is the most weakly adsorbed component.

79 The element filled in the closed jar is .... **NCERT Pg 283**
(a) mixture of gases
(b) mixture of a liquid and a gas
(c) mixture of solids
(d) mixture of liquids

80 In chromatography, which of the following statements is incorrect for R_f? **NCERT Pg 283**

(a) R_f value depends on the type of chromatography.
(b) Higher R_f value means higher adsorption.
(c) R_f value is dependent on the mobile phase.
(d) The value of R_f can not be more than one.

Qualitative and Quantitative; Analysis of Organic Compounds

81 Which of the following should be added in the compound for the detection of carbon and hydrogen? **NCERT Pg 284**

(a) Cu(I) oxide (b) Cu(II) oxide
(c) Zn dust (d) Activated charcoal

82 During the fusion of an organic compound with sodium metal, nitrogen of the organic compound is converted into **NCERT Pg 284**

(a) $NaNO_2$ (b) $NaNH_2$
(c) NaCN (d) NaNC

83 In Lassaigne's test, a blue colour is obtained if the organic compound contains nitrogen. The blue colour is due to the formation of **NCERT Pg 285**

(a) $K_4[Fe(CN)_6]$ (b) $Fe_4[Fe(CN)_6]_3$
(c) $Na_3[Fe(CN)_6]$ (d) $Cu_2[Fe(CN)_6]$

84 In detection of phosphorus in an organic compound, the oxidised phosphorus compound solution is boiled with nitric acid and then treated with ammonium molybdate. Yellow colour is due to the formation of **NCERT Pg 285**

(a) $(NH_4)_3PO_3 \cdot MoO_3$
(b) $(NH_4)_3PO_4 \cdot 12MoO_3$
(c) $Na_4[Mo(NH_4)_3 \cdot PO_3]$
(d) $(NH_3)_4PO_4 \cdot 12MoO_3$

85 Lassaigne's test can not be used for the detection of which element? **NCERT Pg 285**

(a) Carbon (b) Halogens (c) Nitrogen (d) Sulphur

86 On complete combustion, 0.246 g of an organic compound gave 0.198 g of carbon dioxide and 0.1014 g of water. The percentage composition of carbon and hydrogen in the compound respectively are **NCERT Pg 286**

	%C	%H
(a)	21.95	4.58
(b)	21.95	5.58
(c)	11.95	5.58
(d)	11.95	4.58

87 How many grams equal to the 22400 mL N_2 at STP? **NCERT Pg 287**

(a) 26 g (b) 27 g (c) 28 g (d) 29 g

88 An organic compound is estimated through Dumas method and was found to evolved 6 moles of CO_2, 4 moles of H_2O and 1 mole of nitrogen gas. The formula of the compound is **NCERT Pg 287**

(a) C_6H_8N (b) $C_{12}H_8N$ (c) $C_{12}H_8N_2$ (d) $C_6H_8N_2$

89 Quantitative measurement of nitrogen in an organic compound is done by **NCERT Pg 287**

(a) Berthelot method (b) Carius method
(c) Lassaigne method (d) Kjeldahl's method

90 Kjeldahl's method cannot be used to estimate nitrogen for which of the following compounds? **NCERT Pg 288**

(a) $C_6H_5NO_2$ (b) $NH_2—\overset{O}{\overset{\|}{C}}—NH_2$
(c) $CH_3CH_2—C\equiv N$ (d) $C_6H_5NH_2$

91 Which of the following compounds will be suitable for Kjeldahl's method for nitrogen estimation? **NCERT Pg 288**

(a) 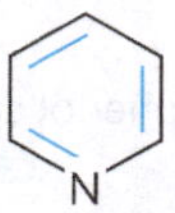

(b) 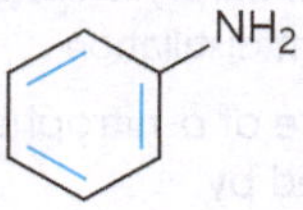

(c) 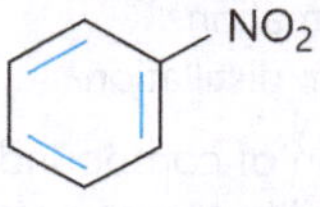

(d) 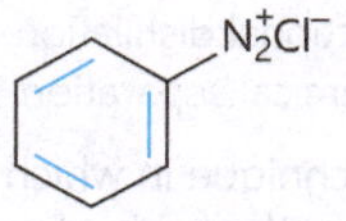

92 0.56 of an organic compound was kjeldahlised. Ammonia evolved was passed in 50 cc of 1 N H_2SO_4. Residual acid needed 60 cc of $\frac{N}{2}$ NaOH. The percentage of 'N' in this compound is **NCERT Pg 288**

(a) 14 (b) 28 (c) 42 (d) 50

93 In estimation of halogen in organic compound by Carius method, the precipitate formed is **NCERT Pg 289**

(a) AgX (b) NaX (c) $BaSO_4$ (d) BaX_2

94 In Carius method of estimation of halogens, 250 mg of an organic compound gave 141 mg of AgBr. The percentage of bromine in the compound is (atomic mass Ag = 108 and Br = 80) **NCERT Pg 289**

(a) 24 (b) 36 (c) 48 (d) 60

95 Which method is used to find halogen in organic compound? **NCERT Pg 289**

(a) Duma's method (b) Leibig's method
(c) Kjeldahl method (d) Carius method

96 What is the name of tube in which a known mass of an organic compound is heated for the quantitative analysis of sulphur? **NCERT Pg 289**

(a) Borosil tube (b) Carius tube
(c) Kjeldahl tube (d) Duma tube

97 In the estimation of sulphur, which reagent is heated alongwith organic compound in a Carius tube? NCERT Pg 289
(a) Sodium peroxide (b) Dil. nitric acid
(c) Silver nitrate (d) Sodium hydroxide

Assertion-Reason Questions

Directions (Q Nos. 1-10) *In the following question Assertion (A) followed by Reason (R) is given below. Choose the correct option out of the choices given below.*

(a) Both A and R are true and R is the correct explanation of A.
(b) Both A and R are true but R is not the correct explanation of A.
(c) A is true but R is false.
(d) A is false but R is true.

1 Assertion (A) In $H_2C=CH_2$ molecule, the rotation about carbon-carbon double bond ($C=C$) is restricted. NCERT Pg 257

Reason (R) Rotation of one CH_2 fragment with respect to other interferes with maximum overlap of *p*-orbitals.

2 Assertion (A) Allyl and benzyl carbonium ions are more stable than propyl carbonium ions. NCERT Pg 271

Reason (R) Electron releasing groups stabilises carbonium ions.

3 Assertion (A) Inductive effect and resonance effect cause permanent polarisation of bond. NCERT Pg 274

Reason (R) These involve electron displacements due to the influence of an atom or a substituted group present in the molecule.

4 Assertion (A) The compound $O_2NCH_2CH_2O^-$ is expected to be less stable than $CH_3CH_2O^-$. NCERT Pg 274

Reason (R) Stability of alkyl carbanion is inversely proportional to the magnitude of negative charge.

5 Assertion (A) Conjugated system show abnormal behaviour, due to alternate single and double bonds in an open chain or cyclic system. NCERT Pg 277

Reason (R) In conjugated system, π-electrons are delocalised and the system develops polarity.

98 In sulphur estimation, 0.157 g of an organic compound gave 0.4813 g of barium sulphate. The percentage of sulphur in the compound is NCERT Pg 289
(a) 42.10% (b) 52.10% (c) 21.05% (d) 40.01%

6 Assertion (A) Simple distillation can help in separating a mixture of propan-1-ol (boiling point 97°C) and propanone (boiling point 56°C). NCERT Pg 279

Reason (R) Liquids with difference of more than 20°C in their boiling points can be separated by simple distillation.

7 Assertion (A) A mixture of *o*-nitrophenol and *p*-nitrophenol can be separated by steam distillation. NCERT Pg 281

Reason (R) *p*-nitrophenol is steam volatile while *o*-nitrophenol is not steam volatile.

8 Assertion (A) Thin layer chromatography is an adsorption chromatography. NCERT Pg 283

Reason (R) A thin layer of silica gel is spread over a glass plate of suitable size in thin layer chromatography which acts as an adsorbent.

9 Assertion (A) $NH_2-\overset{\overset{S}{\|}}{C}-NH_2$ gives red colour in Lassaigne's tets. NCERT Pg 284

Reason (R) Compounds having N along with C give red colour in Lassaigne's test.

10 Assertion (A) Kjeldahl's method is not applicable to compounds containing nitrogen in the form of nitro, azo groups and nitrogen present in the ring (e.g. pyridine). NCERT Pg 286

Reason (R) Nitrogen of nitro and azo group containing compounds does not change to ammonium sulphate by Kjeldahl's method.

Statement Type Questions

Direction (Q. Nos. 1-6) *In the following questions, two statements (I & II) are given. In the light of the given statements, choose the correct option given below.*

(a) Both Statement I and Statement II are false.
(b) Statement I is true but Statement II is false.
(c) Statement I is false but Statement II is true.
(d) Both Statement I and Statement II are true.

1 Statement I Heterolytic cleavage of CH_3Br will give CH_3 and Br. NCERT Pg 271

Statement II A covalent bond may be cleaved either by heterolytic cleavage or by homolytic cleavage.

2 Statement I Polarisation of σ-bond caused by the polarisation of adjacent σ-bond is referred to as electromeric effect. NCERT Pg 274

Statement II $CH_2{=}CH{-}\overset{\overset{\Large O}{\|}}{C}{-}H$ is more stable than $\overset{+}{C}H_2{-}CH{=}\overset{\overset{\Large O^-}{|}}{C}{-}H.$

3 Statement I Stability of isopropyl carbanion increases in the presence of electron withdrawing group but decreases in the presence of electron releasing group.

Statement II Dispersal of the charge leads to the unstability of ion while intensification of negative charge leads to the stability of ion. NCERT Pg 274

4 Statement I The resonance structures have different positions of nuclei. NCERT Pg 275

Statement II Resonance structures have the same number of unpaired electrons.

5 Statement I Retardation factor can be measured in meter/centimeter. NCERT Pg 283

Statement II Retardation factor value of compound remains constant in all solvents.

6 Statement I The formation of NaCN during preparation of sodium extract will give positive Lassaigne's test for nitrogen. NCERT Pg 284

Statement II Phenylhydrazine gives positive Lassaigne's test for nitrogen.

7 Select the incorrect statements form the following. NCERT Pg 257, 276

I. Tertiary butyl carbocation is more stable than a secondary butyl carbocation because of $+R$ effect of $-CH_3$ group.
II. Resonance involves delocalisation at σ-electrons along a conjugated system.
III. Benzene is an alicyclic carbocyclic compound.
IV. The state of hybridisation of C_2 and C_3 carbon in the hydrocarbon $CH_2{=}C{=}CHCH_3$ is *sp* and sp^2.
V. The compound $C_4H_{10}O$ shows metamerism.

Choose the correct answer from the options given below.

(a) I, II and III (b) II, IV and V (c) I, II and IV (d) IV and V

8 Which of the following statements are incorrect? NCERT Pg 265, 269, 271, 272, 280

I. The prefixes *sec*- and *tert*- are considered to be the part of the fundamental name.
II. Benzene ring is attached to an alkane with a functional group, it is considered as phenyl (Ph).
III. Rate of transformation of reactant into products (kinetics) is referred to as reaction mechanism.
IV. Organic reactions, which results in formation of free radicals are called polar reactions.
V. Each successive condensation and vaporisation unit in the fractionating column is called a theoritical plate.

Choose the correct answer from the options given below.

(a) I, II and III (b) I and IV (c) II, III and V (d) III, IV and V

9 Which of the following statements are incorrect? NCERT Pg 270, 271, 277, 279, 288

I. Chain isomers have similar molecular formula but different carbon skeletons.
II. Greater the numbers of alkyl groups attached to a negatively charged carbon atom, greater will be the stabilisation.
III. Geometrical isomerism is a type of stereo isomerism.
IV. Crystallisation is based on the difference in solubilities of the compound and the impurities in a suitable solvent.
V. Pyridine can be used to estimate nitrogen by using Kjeldahl's method.

Choose the correct answer from the options given below.

(a) I and IV (b) II and III
(c) II and V (d) II, III and IV

10 Which of the following statements are correct? NCERT Pg 284, 287, 288, 289

I. Kjeldahl's method is used for the estimation of nitrogen in an organic compound.
II. Carius method is used for the estimation of sulphur in an organic compound.
III. Duma's method is used for the detection of nitrogen containing compound.

IV. In Lassaigne's test, the elements present in an organic compound are converted from ionic to covalent form by fusing with sodium metal.

V. Lassaigne's test is used for the confirmation of nitrogen.

Choose the most appropriate answer from the options given below.

(a) I, II, III and IV (b) II, III, IV and V

(c) II, III and IV (d) I, II, III and V

Matching Type Questions

1 Match the terms of Column I with Column II and choose the correct option from the codes given below.

NCERT Pg 257

Column I (Structure of compound)	Column II (Hybridisation of carbon)
A. CH_3Cl	1. sp^3 and sp^2
B. $(CH_3)_2CO$	2. sp^2
C. CH_3CN	3. sp^3
D. $HCONH_2$	4. sp^3 and sp

Codes

	A	B	C	D
(a)	3	1	4	2
(b)	4	3	2	1
(c)	3	1	2	4
(d)	1	2	3	4

2 Match terms of Column I with Column II and choose the correct option from the codes given below. NCERT Pg 258

Column I (Bond-line formula for the molecule)	Column II (Name of the molecule)
A. 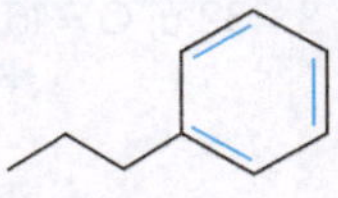	1. 2,5-dimethylheptane
B. 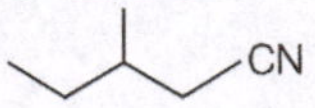	2. 3-methylpentanenitrile
C. 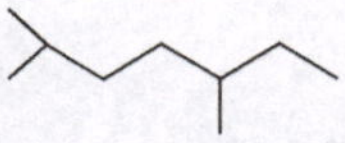	3. 3-bromo-3-chloroheptane
D. 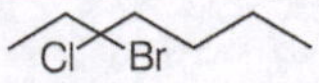	4. Propylbenzene

Codes

	A	B	C	D
(a)	4	2	1	3
(b)	1	2	3	4
(c)	2	3	1	4
(d)	3	1	4	2

3 Match the terms of Column I with Column II and choose the correct option from the codes given below.

NCERT Pg 261, 262

Column I (Definition)	Column II (Type of compounds)
A. Compounds containing only one type of atoms joined in the form of a ring.	1. Homocyclic compounds
B. When atoms other than carbon atoms are present in the ring	2. Non-benzenoid compound
C. Benzene and other related ring compounds	3. Heterocyclic compound
D. Compounds which do not contain benzene ring but aromatic in nature.	4. Benzenoid compound

Codes

	A	B	C	D
(a)	1	3	4	2
(b)	1	2	3	4
(c)	4	3	2	1
(d)	3	1	2	4

4 Match the items of Column I with the Column II and choose the correct option from the codes given below.

NCERT Pg 270, 271

Column I (Structure of compounds)	Column II (Type of isomerism)
A. $CH_3CH_2CH_2CH_2CH_3$ and $CH_3-CH(CH_3)-CH_2CH_3$	1. Chain isomerism
B. $CH_3CH_2CH_2OH$ and $CH_3-CH(OH)-CH_3$	2. Position isomerism
C. $CH_3-C(=O)-CH_3$ and $CH_3-CH_2-C(H)=O$	3. Metamerism
D. $CH_3OC_3H_7$ and $C_2H_5OC_2H_5$	4. Functional group isomerism

Codes

	A	B	C	D
(a)	1	2	3	4
(b)	2	3	1	4
(c)	4	1	2	3
(d)	1	2	4	3

5 Match the items of Column I with the items of Column II appropriately and choose the correct option from the codes given below. **NCERT Pg 286, 287, 288, 289**

	Column I		Column II
A.	Percentage of sulphur	1.	$\frac{1.4 \times M \times 2\,(V - V_1/2)}{m}$
B.	Percentage of phosphorus	2.	$\frac{62 \times m_1 \times 100}{222 \times m}\%$
C.	Percentage of halogen	3.	$\frac{\text{atomic mass of } X \times m_1 \times 100}{\text{molecular mass of Ag}X \times m}$
D.	Percentage of nitrogen	4.	$\frac{32 \times m_1 \times 100}{233 \times m}$

Codes

	A	B	C	D		A	B	C	D
(a)	4	2	3	1	(b)	4	3	1	2
(c)	4	2	1	3	(d)	1	3	2	4

Numerical Value Questions

1 The number of sp^3-hybridised carbons in an acyclic neutral compound with molecular formula C_4H_5N is .... **NCERT Pg 257**

2 Number of carbon atoms present in the parent carbon chain of the given compound is .... **NCERT Pg 264**

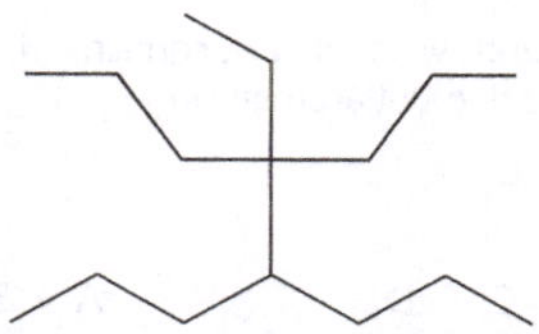

3 Three organic compounds *A*, *B* and *C* were allowed to run in thin layer chromatography using hexane and gave the following result (see figure). The R_f value of the most polar compound is .... × 10^{-2}. **NCERT Pg 283**

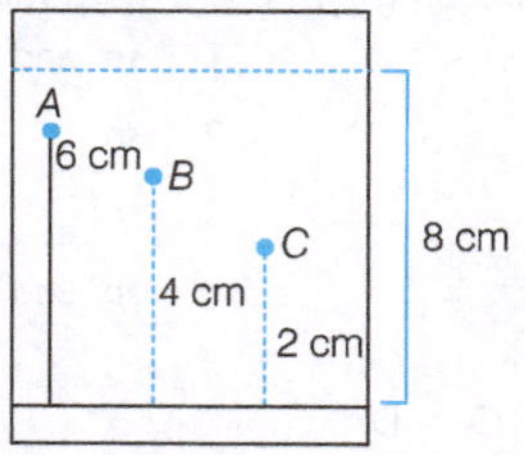

4 0.400 g of an organic compound (*X*) gave 0.376 g of AgBr in Carius method for estimation of bromine. % of bromine in the compound (*X*) is ....
(Given : Molar mass AgBr = 188 g mol^{-1}, Br = 80 g mol^{-1}) **NCERT Pg 289**

5 In sulphur estimation, 0.471 g of an organic compound gave 1.4439 g of barium sulphate. The percentage of sulphur in the compound is .... (Nearest integer)
(Given : Atomic mass Ba = 137 u, S = 32 u, O = 16 u) **NCERT Pg 289**

NCERT Exemplar's Questions

1 Which of the following is the correct IUPAC name?
(a) 3-ethyl-4, 4-dimethylheptane
(b) 4,4-dimethyl-3-ethylheptane
(c) 5-ethyl-4, 4-dimethylheptane
(d) 4,4-*bis*(methyl)-3-ethylheptane

2 The IUPAC name for

$$CH_3-\overset{\overset{\displaystyle O}{\|}}{C}-CH_2-CH_2-\overset{\overset{\displaystyle O}{\|}}{C}-OH \text{ is}$$

(a) 1-hydroxypentane-1,4-dione (b) 1,4-dioxopentanol
(c) 1-carboxybutan-3-one (d) 4-oxopentanoic acid

3 The IUPAC name for

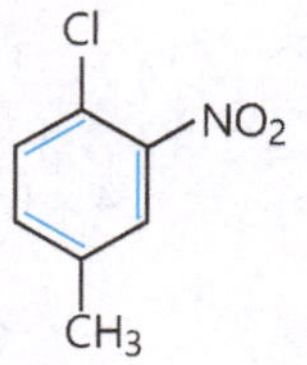

(a) 1-chloro-2-nitro-4-methylbenzene
(b) 1-chloro-4-methyl-2-nitrobenzene
(c) 2-chloro-1-nitro-5-methylbenzene
(d) *m*-nitro-*p*-chlorotoluene

4 Electronegativity of carbon atoms depends upon their state of hybridisation. In which of the following compounds, the carbon marked with asterisk is most electronegative?

(a) $CH_3-CH_2-{}^*CH_2-CH_3$
(b) $CH_3-{}^*CH=CH-CH_3$
(c) $CH_3-CH_2-C\equiv{}^*CH$
(d) $CH_3-CH_2-CH={}^*CH_2$

5 In which of the following, functional group isomerism is not possible?

(a) Alcohols
(b) Aldehydes
(c) Alkyl halides
(d) Cyanides

6 Match the type of mixture of compounds in Column I with the technique of separation/ purification given in Column II.

Column I		Column II	
A.	Two solids which have different solubilities in a solvent and do not undergo reaction when dissolved in it.	1.	Steam distillation
B.	Liquids that decompose at its boiling point.	2.	Fractional distillation
C.	Steam volatile liquid	3.	Simple distillation
D.	Two liquids which have boiling points close to each other.	4.	Distillation under reduced pressure
E.	Two liquids with large difference in boiling points.	5.	Crystallisation

7 In which of the following compounds the carbon marked with asterisk is expected to have greatest positive charge?

(a) ${}^*CH_3-CH_2-Cl$ (b) ${}^*CH_3-CH_2-Mg^+Cl^-$
(c) ${}^*CH_3-CH_2-Br$ (d) ${}^*CH_3-CH_2-CH_3$

8 Ionic species are stabilised by the dispersal of charge. Which of the following carboxylate ion is the most stable?

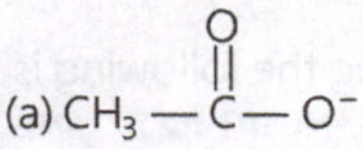

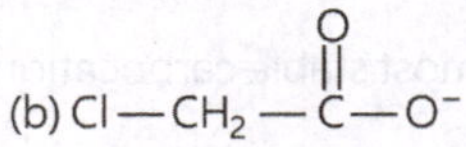

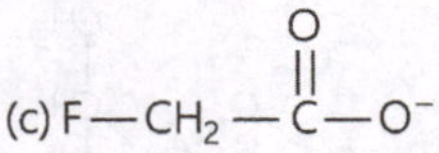

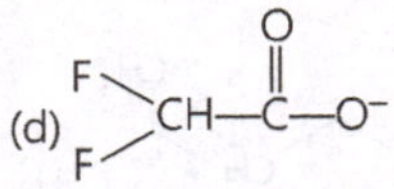

9 Electrophilic addition reactions proceed in two steps. The first step involves the addition of an electrophile. Name the type of intermediate formed in the first step of the following addition reaction.

$$H_3C-HC=CH_2 + H^+ \longrightarrow ?$$

(a) 2° carbanion (b) 1° carbocation
(c) 2° carbocation (d) 1° carbanion

10 The addition of HCl to an alkene proceeds in two steps. The first step is the attack of H^+ ion to $>C=C<$ portion which can be shown as

(a) 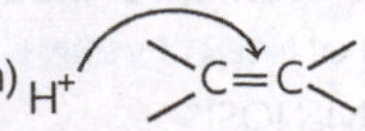
(b) 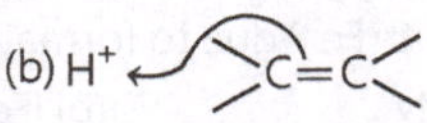
(c) 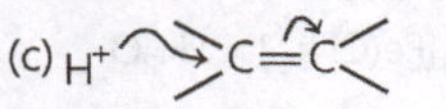
(d) All of these are possible

11 Match the Column I with Column II and choose the correct option from the codes given below.

Column I		Column II	
A.	Duma's method	1.	$AgNO_3$
B.	Kjeldahl's method	2.	Silica gel
C.	Carius method	3.	Nitrogen gas
D.	Chromatography	4.	Free radicals
E.	Homolysis	5.	Ammonium sulphate

Past Exams' Questions

NEET Archive

1 The most stable carbocation among the following is NCERT Pg 271, NEET 2024

(a) 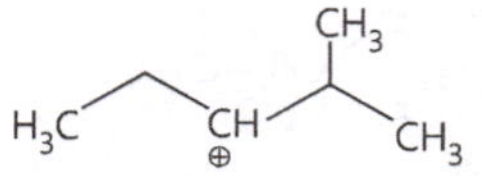 (b) 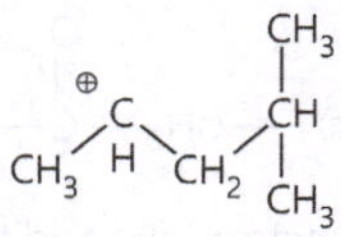

(c) 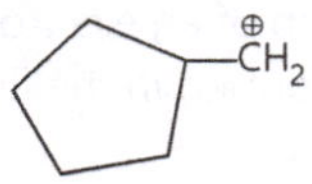 (d) 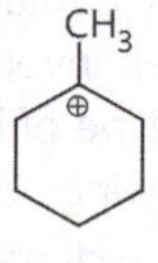

2 A compound with a molecular formula of C_6H_{14} has two tertiary carbons. Its IUPAC name is NCERT Pg 267, NEET 2024

(a) *n*-hexane (b) 2-methylpentane
(c) 2,3-dimethylbutane (d) 2,2-dimethylbutane

3 In Lassaigne's extract of an organic compound, both nitrogen and sulphur are present, which gives blood red colour with Fe^{3+} due to formation of NCERT Pg 284, NEET 2023

(a) NaSCN (b) $[Fe(CN)_5NOS]^{4-}$
(c) $[Fe(SCN)]^{2+}$ (d) $Fe_4[Fe(CN)_6]_3 \cdot xH_2O$

4 The Kjeldahl's method for the estimation of nitrogen can be used to estimate the amount of nitrogen in which one of the following compounds? NCERT Pg 288, NEET 2022

(a) 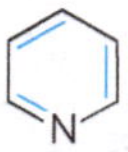 (b) 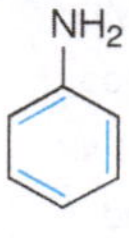

(c) 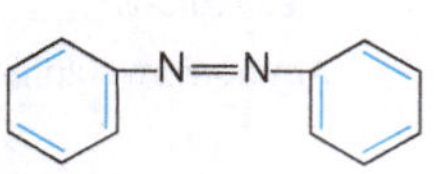 (d) 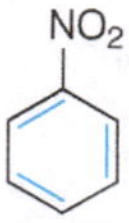

5 The correct structure of 2,6-dimethyl-dec-4-ene is NCERT Pg 267, NEET 2021

(a) 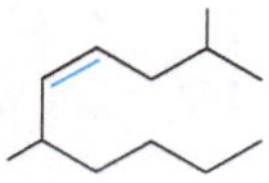 (b) 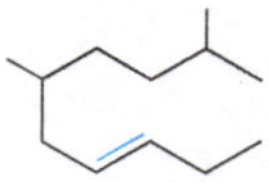

(c) 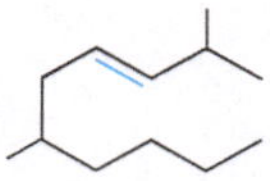 (d) 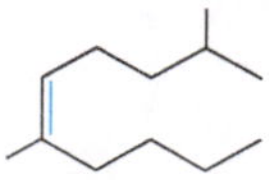

6 The compound which shows metamerism is NCERT Pg 271, NEET 2021

(a) C_5H_{12} (b) C_3H_8O (c) C_3H_6O (d) $C_4H_{10}O$

7 A liquid compound (*x*) can be purified by steam distillation only if it is NCERT Pg 281, NEET 2020

(a) steam volatile, immiscible with water
(b) not steam volatile, miscible with water
(c) steam volatile, miscible with water
(d) not steam volatile, immiscible with water

8 The most stable carbocation, among the following is NCERT Pg 271, NEET 2019

(a) $(CH_3)_3C—\overset{\oplus}{C}H—CH_3$
(b) $CH_3—CH_2—\overset{\oplus}{C}H—CH_2—CH_3$
(c) $CH_3—\overset{\oplus}{C}H—CH_2—CH_2—CH_3$
(d) $CH_3—CH_2—\overset{\oplus}{C}H_2$

9 Which of the following molecules represents the order of hybridisation sp^2, sp^2, sp, sp from left to right atoms? NCERT Pg 257, NEET 2018

(a) $CH_2{=}CH—CH{=}CH_2$
(b) $CH_2{=}CH—C{\equiv}CH$
(c) $CH{\equiv}C—C{\equiv}CH$
(d) $CH_3—CH{=}CH—CH_3$

10 The correct statement regarding electrophile is NCERT Pg 273, NEET 2017

(a) Electrophile is a negatively charge species and can form a bond by accepting a pair of electrons from a nucleophile.
(b) Electrophile is a negatively charged species and can form a bond by accepting a pair of electrons from another electrophile.
(c) Electrophiles are generally neutral species and can form a bond by accepting a pair of electrons from a nucleophile.
(d) Electrophile can be either neutral or positively charged species and can form a bond by accepting a pair of electrons from a nucleophile.

11 In Duma's method for estimation of nitrogen, 0.25g of an organic compound gave 40 mL of nitrogen collected at 300 K temperature and 725 mm of Hg pressure. If the aqueous tension at 300 K is 25 mm of Hg the percentage of nitrogen in the compound is (approximately) NCERT Pg 287, CBSE-AIPMT 2015

(a) 17.36 (b) 18.20
(c) 16.76 (d) 15.76

12 Which of the following statements is not correct for a nucleophile? **NCERT Pg 287, CBSE-AIPMT 2015**

(a) Nucleophile is a Lewis acid.
(b) Ammonia is a nucleophile.
(c) Nucleophiles attack low electrons density sites.
(d) Nucleophiles are not electron seeking.

13 In the Kjeldahl's method for estimation of nitrogen present in a soil sample, ammonia evolved from 0.75 g of sample neutralised 10 mL of 1 M H_2SO_4. The percentage of nitrogen in the soil is **NCERT Pg 288, CBSE-AIPMT 2014**

(a) 37.33 (b) 45.33 (c) 35.33 (d) 43.33

JEE Main Archive

14 Relative stability of the contributing structures is

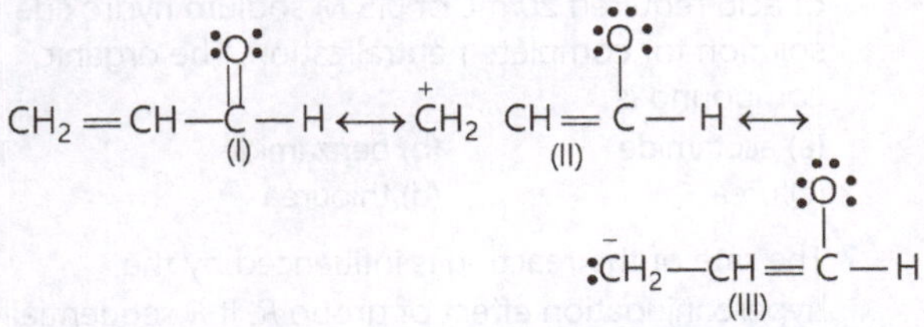

NCERT Pg 266, JEE Main 2024

(a) (II) > (I) > (III) (b) (III) > (II) > (I)
(c) (I) > (II) > (III) (d) (I) > (III) > (II)

15 Which among the following is incorrect statement? **NCERT Pg 277, JEE Main 2024**

(a) Hydrogen ion (H^+) shows negative electromeric effect.
(b) Electromeric effect dominates over inductive effect.
(c) The electromeric effect is, temporary effect.
(d) The organic compound shows electromeric effect in the presence of the reagent only.

16 A species having carbon with sextet of electrons and can act as electrophile is called **NCERT Pg 272, JEE Main 2024**

(a) pentavalent carbon (b) carbon free radical
(c) carbanion (d) carbocation

17 The decreasing order of hydride affinity for following carbocations is **NCERT Pg 272, JEE Main 2023**

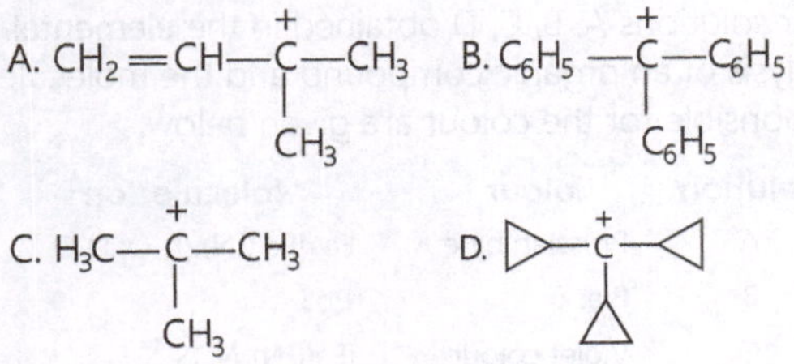

Choose the correct answer from the options given below.

(a) C > A > B > D
(b) C > A > D > B
(c) A > C > D > B
(d) A > C > B > D

18 Thin layer chromatography of a mixture shows the following observation. **NCERT Pg 283, JEE Main 2023**

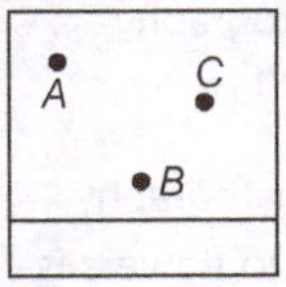

The correct order of elution in the silica gel column chromatography is

(a) *B, C, A* (b) *A, C, B*
(c) *C, A, B* (d) *B, A, C*

19 120 g of an organic compound that contains only carbon and hydrogen gives 330 g of CO_2 and 270 g of water on complete combustion. The percentage of carbon and hydrogen, respectively are **NCERT Pg 286, JEE Main 2022**

(a) 25 and 75 (b) 40 and 60
(c) 60 and 40 (d) 75 and 25

20 In Carius method of estimation of halogen, 0.45 g of an organic compound gave 0.36 g of AgBr. Find out the percentage of bromine in the compound.
(Molar masses of Ag = 188 g mol^{-1}; Br = 80 g mol^{-1}) **NCERT Pg 289, JEE Main 2022**

(a) 34.04% (b) 40.04%
(c) 36.03% (d) 38.04%

21 Which of the following compounds does not exhibit resonance ? **NCERT Pg 275, JEE Main 2021**

(a) $CH_3CH_2OCH{=}CH_2$ (b) 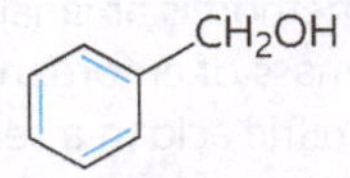

(c) $CH_3CH_2CH_2CONH_2$ (d) $CH_3CH_2CH{=}CHCH_2NH_2$

22 Which one of the following set of elements can be detected using sodium fusion extract? **NCERT Pg 284, JEE Main 2021**

(a) Phosphorus, oxygen, nitrogen, halogens
(b) Nitrogen, phosphorus, carbon, sulphur
(c) Sulphur, nitrogen, phosphorus, halogens
(d) Halogens, nitrogen, oxygen, sulphur

Skill Boosters

1 During the hearing of a court case, the judge suspected that some changes in the documents had been carried out. He asked the forensic department to check the ink used at two different places. According to the situation which technique can give the best results?
(a) Column chromatography
(b) Solvent extraction
(c) Distillation
(d) Thin layer chromatography

2 The fragrance of two flowers is due to the presence of some steam volatile organic compounds called essential oils. These are generally insoluble in water at room temperature but are miscible with water vapour in vapour phase. A suitable method for the extraction of these oils from the flowers is
(a) distillation
(b) crystallisation
(c) distillation under reduced pressure
(d) steam distillation

3 Three students, Manish, Rameh and Rajni experimented with Lassaigne's test extract to determine extra elements. They prepared the extract independently, then added $FeSO_4$ and sulphuric acid, and observe different colours. Manish and Rajni obtained prussian blue colour and Ramesh got red colour.

Choose the correct reason for the red colouration obtained by Ramesh.
(a) Due to the presence of halogen in extract
(b) Lassaigne's extract didn't prepared well
(c) Taking excess sodium to prepare Lassaigne's extract
(d) Due to formation of red ammonium phosphomolybdate

4 Carius method is an analytical method in which the known mass of an organic compound is heated with fuming nitric acid in a sealed carius tube in which carbon gets converted to carbon-dioxide and hydrogen converts into water. The estimation of phosphorus, 0.248 g of an organic compound gave a precipitate of $Mg_2NH_4PO_4$ which on ignition yielded 0.444 g of $Mg_2P_2O_7$. What is the percentage of phosphorus in the compound?
(a) 50% (b) 25%
(c) 45% (d) 60%

5 In a kingdom, a king and his wife lives together. The king had a great knowledge in chemistry and life sciences. You've also a good knowledge in chemistry. Let's try it. What is the IUPAC name of the IInd last letter than comes in alphabetical order in the name of the king's wife?

(a) Butane
(b) 1-methyl bicyclo [1.1.0] butane
(c) 1, 1-dimethylcyclobutane
(d) 2-methylpropane

6 The ammonia evolved from the treatment of 0.30 g of an organic compound for the estimation of nitrogen was passed in 100 mL of 0.1 M sulphuric acid. The excess of acid required 20 mL of 0.5 M sodium hydroxide solution for complete neutralization. The organic compound is
(a) acetamide (b) benzamide
(c) urea (d) thiourea

7 The rate of the reaction is influenced by the hyperconjugation effect of group *R*. If *R* sequentially is

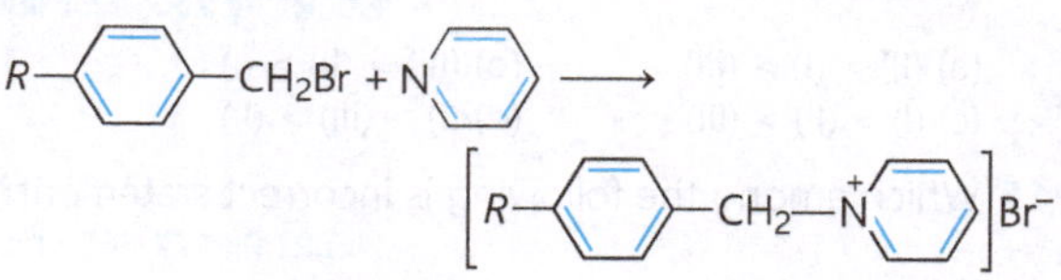

A. CH_3- B. CH_3-CH_2-

C. $CH_3-CH(CH_3)-$ D. $CH_3-C(CH_3)_2-$

The increasing order of the speed of the above reaction is
(a) D < C < B < A (b) A < B < C < D
(c) A < D < C < B (d) C < B < A < D

8 Four solutions A, B, C, D obtained in the elemental analysis of an organic compound and the molecule/ion responsible for the colour are given below.

Solution	Colour	Molecule/Ion
A	Prussian blue	$Fe_4[Fe(CN)_6]_3 \cdot xH_2O$
B	Black	PbS
C	Violet colour	$[Fe(CN)_5NOS]^{4-}$
D	Yellow	$(NH_4)_2MoO_4$

Which of the observations is not correct as per the given data?

(a) Solution A (b) Solution B

(c) Solution C (d) Solution D

9 The phenomena in which two or more compounds having the same molecular formula but different chemical and physical properties.

Mainly two types of isomers acyclic and cyclic are there. By this, a compound with molecular formula, C_3H_6 have how many acyclic and cyclic isomers?

(a) 3 cyclic, 6 acyclic

(b) 4 cyclic, 5 acyclic

(c) 5 cyclic, 4 acyclic

(d) 6 cyclic, 3 acyclic

Correct Codes

Topical Questions

1 (d)	2 (b)	3 (c)	4 (c)	5 (a)	6 (a)	7 (c)	8 (b)	9 (c)	10 (b)
11 (d)	12 (b)	13 (b)	14 (d)	15 (a)	16 (a)	17 (a)	18 (a)	19 (a)	20 (b)
21 (a)	22 (d)	23 (b)	24 (c)	25 (b)	26 (a)	27 (b)	28 (d)	29 (b)	30 (d)
31 (d)	32 (a)	33 (a)	34 (c)	35 (d)	36 (c)	37 (a)	38 (a)	39 (d)	40 (a)
41 (a)	42 (c)	43 (a)	44 (c)	45 (a)	46 (a)	47 (a)	48 (b)	49 (b)	50 (d)
51 (b)	52 (c)	53 (b)	54 (d)	55 (d)	56 (d)	57 (b)	58 (d)	59 (c)	60 (b)
61 (b)	62 (b)	63 (c)	64 (a)	65 (a)	66 (c)	67 (a)	68 (d)	69 (d)	70 (d)
71 (a)	72 (a)	73 (a)	74 (d)	75 (b)	76 (a)	77 (c)	78 (b)	79 (d)	80 (b)
81 (b)	82 (c)	83 (b)	84 (b)	85 (a)	86 (a)	87 (c)	88 (d)	89 (d)	90 (a)
91 (b)	92 (d)	93 (a)	94 (a)	95 (d)	96 (b)	97 (a)	98 (a)		

Assertion-Reason

1. (a)	2. (c)	3. (a)	4. (d)	5. (a)	6. (a)	7. (c)	8. (a)	9. (c)	10. (a)

Statement Type

1. (c)	2. (c)	3. (a)	4. (c)	5. (d)	6. (b)	7. (a)	8. (b)	9. (c)	10. (d)

Matching Type

1. (a)	2. (a)	3. (a)	4. (d)	5. (a)

Numerical Value

1. (1)	2. (8)	3. (25)	4. (40)	5. (42)

NCERT Exemplar's

1. (a)	2. (d)	3. (b)	4. (c)	5. (c)	6. A-5, B-4, C-1, D-2, E-3	7. (a)	8. (d)
9. (c)	10. (b)	11. A-4, B-5, C-1, D-2, E-3					

Past Exams'

1. (d)	2. (c)	3. (c)	4. (b)	5. (a)	6. (d)	7. (a)	8. (c)	9. (b)	10. (d)
11. (c)	12. (a)	13. (a)	14. (c)	15. (a)	16. (d)	17. (a)	18. (b)	19. (d)	20. (a)
21. (d)	22. (c)								

Skill Boosters

1. (d)	2. (d)	3. (c)	4. (a)	5. (b)	6. (c)	7. (d)	8. (d)	9. (b)

Step by Step

Decoding the Questions

Concept Builders

1 Catenation

2 False

3 9, 2

4 bond line

5 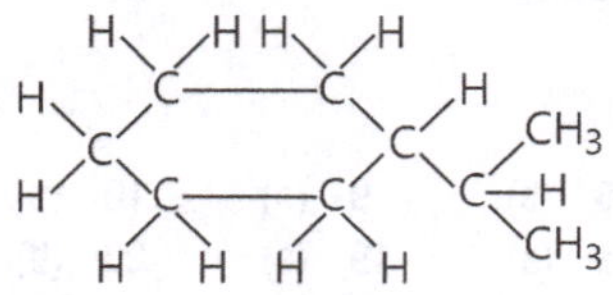

6 False

7 benzenoid

8 True

9 homologous series

10 False

11 Formic acid

12 Buckminster fullerene

13 3-ethyl-4, 4-dimethylheptane

14 False

15 Alkoxycarbonyl

16 5-ethyl-1-fluoro-2-nitrobenzene

17 True

18 geometrical and optical

19 heteropolar

20 True

21 more, less

22 False

23 No bond resonance

24 Fractionating column

25 spent lye

26 True

27 sulphur

28 Duma's

29 Carius method

30 elemental analyser

Topical Solutions

1 (*d*) *A* refers to urea (NH_2CONH_2).

2 (*b*) As the *s*-character of a hybrid orbital decreases,

(i) the bond length increase; triple bond (50% *s*-character) < double bond (33% *s*-character) < single bond (25% *s*-character).

(ii) bond angle increases; the bond angles for *sp*, sp^2 and sp^3 hybrid orbitals are 180°, 120° and 109.5°, respectively.

3 (*c*) The percentage *s*-character of C-atom in ethyne is 50%

The percentage *s*-character of C-atom in ethene is 33%

So, the ratio of percentage *s*-character of C-atom is $= \frac{50}{33} = \frac{3}{2}$

4 (*c*) The carbon in $H_2C{=}O$ is sp^2-hybridised and shape is trigonal planar.

5 (*a*)

Hydrocarbons	Molecular formula	% s-character
Ethane	$CH_3—CH_3$	25%
Ethene	$CH_2 = CH_2$	33%
Ethyne	$CH \equiv CH$	50%

As we know that, electronegativity $\propto$ % *s*-character $\propto$ acidic character. Hence, correct order of electronegativity in the given compounds is

ethane < ethene < ethyne.

6 (*a*) $CH \equiv C—CH{=}CH—CH_3$

7 (*c*) sp^3, sp^2, sp^2, *sp*

8 (*b*)

9 (*c*)

10 (*b*)

11 (*d*) Statement (d) is incorrect while other statements are correct.

The correct form of A is as follows

Aniline is a benzenoid aromatic compound because it contains benzene ring.

12 (*b*) Alicyclic compounds contain carbon atoms joined in the form of a ring.

Homocyclic means it contains only C-atoms in the ring.

Other given compounds contain atoms other than carbon.

13 (*b*) The given compound contains benzene nucleus so, naphthalene is a benzenoid aromatic compound.

14 (*d*) Among the given compounds tetrahydrofuran is not a heterocyclic aromatic compound. It is a heterocyclic alicyclic compound while other are heterocyclic aromatic compound.

15 (*a*)

16 (*a*) '*iso*' means one methyl group is present at side chain.

Hence, the structure of *iso*-butyl group is in option (a).

$(CH_3)_2 > CH—CH_2—$

'yl' suffix is used to represent one —H less than the parent hydrocarbon.

17 (*a*) The correct IUPAC name of the given compound is 6-ethyl-2-methylnonane.

It is shown below :

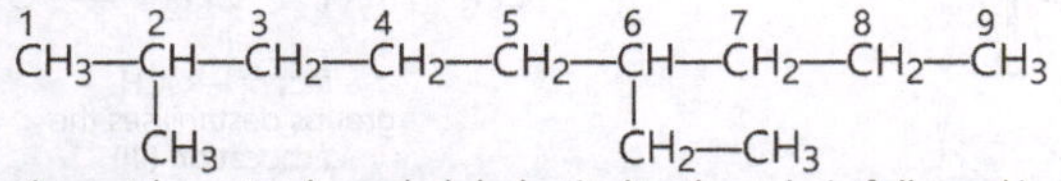

(lowest locant rule and alphabetical order rule is followed.)

18 (*a*) The correct way of numbering the given structure is option (a) to mark the branched C-atom with lowest number.

19 (*a*) The correct structure for 3-methylpentan-1, 3-diene is

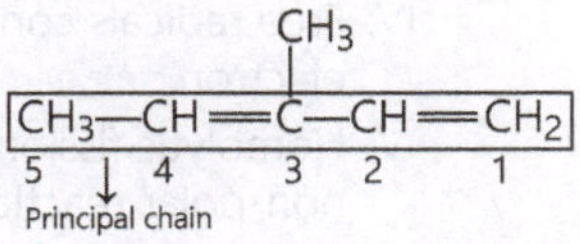

20 (*b*) The correct IUPAC name of the compound is 4-ethyl-3-propylhex-1-ene.

Principal chain should be choosen in such a way that should contain double bond.
It is shown as follows

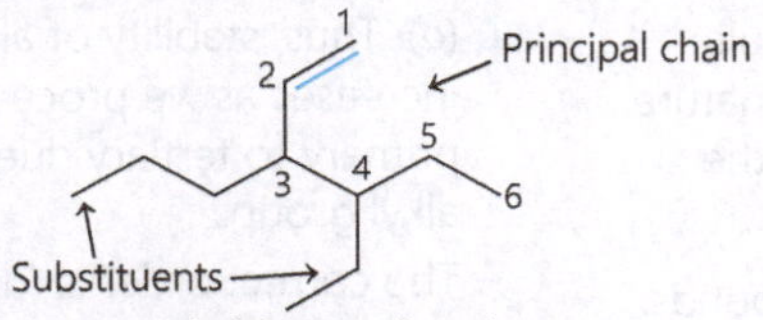

4-ethyl-3-propylhex-1-ene

21 (*a*) A saturated monocyclic compound named by prefixing 'cyclo' to the corresponding straight chain alkane. If side chains are present, then the general rules of naming are applied.
Thus, the correct IUPAC name of the following structure is

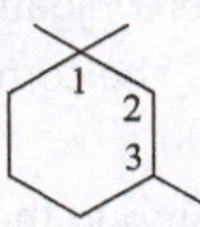

3-ethyl-1,1-dimethylcyclohexane
(Substituent name in alphabetical order)

22 (*d*) The order of decreasing priority for some functional group is
$-COOH, -SO_3H, -COOR, -COCl, -CONH_2, -CN,$
$-HC{=}O, >C{=}O, -OH, -NH_2, >C{=}C<, -C{\equiv}C-$

23 (*b*) Statements II and IV are correct, while the Statements I and III are incorrect.

The correct form of I and III is

I. The presence of functional group enables systematisation of organic compound into different classes.

III. The order of priority of functional groups is
$-COOH > -SO_3H > -COOR > -COCl.$

24 (*c*) The IUPAC name of the given compound is 3-hydroxy-4-methylpentanoic acid.

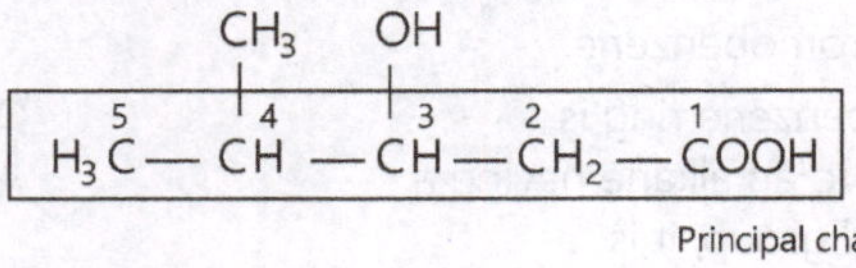

25 (*b*)

26 (*a*) Option (a) is not in accordance with IUPAC system. In IUPAC system of nomenclature, preference is given to multiple bond than halogen substituent, so the correct name is $Br-\overset{3}{C}H_2-\overset{2}{C}H=\overset{1}{C}H_2$.
3-bromoprop-1-ene

27 (*b*) The correct IUPAC name of the given compound $HOCH_2(CH_2)_3CH_2COCH_3$ is 7-hydroxyheptan-2-one. A compound containing both an alcohol and a keto group is named as hydroxy alkanone since the keto group is preferred over hydroxy group.

28 (*d*) The IUPAC name for the given compound is 3, 5-dimethyl-4-propylhept-1-en-6-yne.

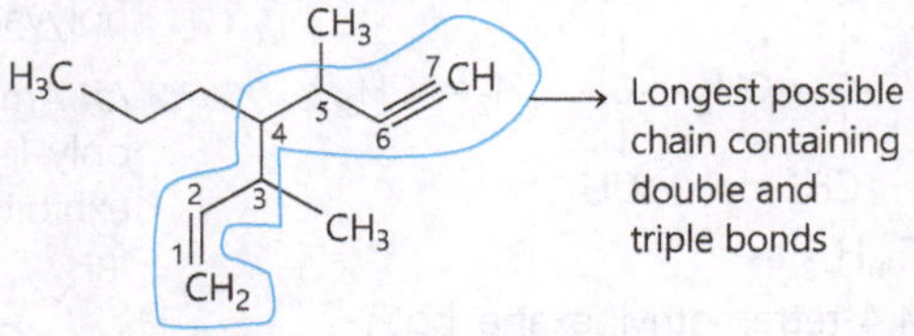

If both double and triple bonds are present in the compound, the endings like-en-yne, a (numeral) dien-(numeral)-yne etc., are used.
Numbers as low as possible are given to double and triple bonds as a set.

29 (*b*) The correct name is 1-chloro-2,4-dinitrobenzene.

30 (*d*) The correct IUPAC name of the given compound is 5-hydroxycyclohex -3-en-1-one.

31 (*d*) The correct IUPAC name of given compound is 1-bromo-3-nitrobenzene.

32 (*a*)

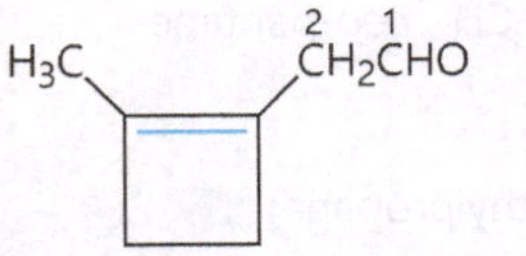

IUPAC name 2-(2-methylcyclobut-1-enyl) ethanal

33 (*a*)

34 (c) Statements II and III are incorrect while I is correct.
The correct form of II and III are as follows
II. 1,3-dibromobenzene is named as *m*-dibromobenzene.
III. When a benzene ring is attached to an alkane having a functional group, it is considered as substituent, instead of a parent.

35 (d) Dimethyl ether is an isomer of ethanol. It is a functional isomer of ethanol.
Both of them have same molecular formula but different functional group.

36 (c) $H_3C—CH_2—CH_2—CH(CH(CH_3)_2)—CH_2—CH_2CH_3$,
i.e. $C_{10}H_{22}$ is 4-*iso*-propylheptane, isomeric with

$H_3C—C(CH_3)_2—CH_2—C(CH_3)_2—CH_2—CH_3$,

i.e. $C_{10}H_{22}$ as 2,2,4,4-tetramethylhexane, both have same molecular formula.

37 (a) Three chain isomers are given by the compound C_5H_{12}. These are as follows
(i) $CH_3CH_2CH_2CH_2CH_3$ (Pentane)
(ii) $CH_3—CH(CH_3)—CH_2—CH_3$
Iso-pentane (2-methylbutane)
(iii) $CH_3—C(CH_3)_2—CH_3$ *neo*-pentane
(2,2-dimethylpropane)

38 (a) The compounds show position isomerism.

39 (d) There are 4 aldehyde forms and 3 ketone forms of $C_5H_{10}O$.

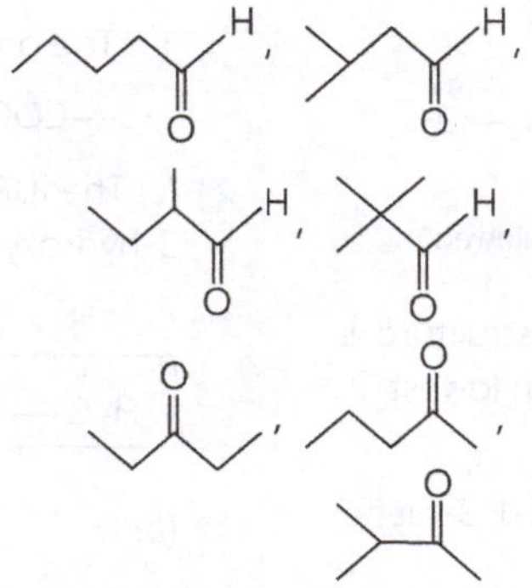

So, total number of structural isomers of C_5H_{10} are 7.

40 (a) The compounds show chain isomerism because they have different carbon chains.

41 (a) Among the given isomers only one (ii) is an isomer of butanoic acid.

42 (c) (i) and (iii) are the metamers of the compound having formula $C_4H_{10}O$ as they differ in the nature of alkyl groups attached to the polyvalent functional group.

43 (a) Among the given compounds, only 1, 2-dibromoprop-1-ene exhibits geometrical isomerism.

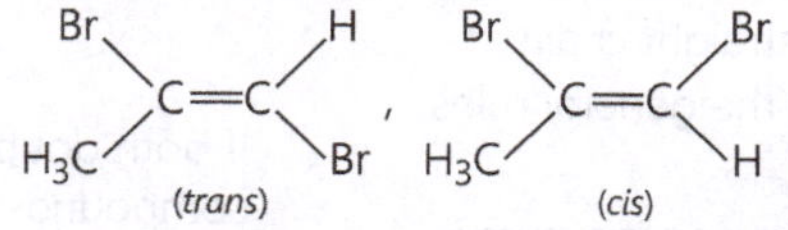

44 (c)

45 (a) The dispersal of the charge stabilises the carbocation. More the number of alkyl groups, the greater is the dispersal of positive charge and therefore, more is the stability of carbocation.
Thus, the correct order is (a).

46 (a) Stability of the given cations can be understood by following structures :

$CH_3 \rightarrow \overset{+}{C}H \leftarrow CH_3$,
I
+I-effect of two methyl groups stabilises the carbocation (I)

$CH_3 \rightarrow \overset{+}{C}H — \ddot{O} — CH_3$,
II
Strong +R-effect of $—OCH_3$ groups stabilises the carbocation (II)

$CH_3 —\overset{+}{C}H — CH_2 \rightarrow OCH_3$
III
−I-effect of $—OCH_3$ groups destabilises the carbocation (III)

Thus, the stability of carbocation decreases in the order (a).

47 (a) Statements I, II and III are correct, while the statement IV and V incorrect. Their correct form is as follows
IV. Free radicals contain unpaired electron.
V. Homolytic fission is also called non-polar reactions.

48 (b)

49 (b) Stability order of carbanion is as
Aliphatic *sp* > Aliphatic sp^2 > Phenyl > Hindered 1° aliphatic sp^3
Thus, the correct order is (b).

50 (d) Thus, stability of alkyl radical increases as we proceed from primary to tertiary due to increase in alkyl group.
The correct order is (d).

51 (b) Among the given free radicals,

$—\dot{C}H_2$ is most stable due to resonance. In the remaining free radicals. Hyperconjugative hydrogen in (I) is 6, in (III) is 1 and (IV) is 3. No. of hyperconjgation ∝ Stability.
Thus, the correct order of stability is (b).

52 (c) Among the given compounds,

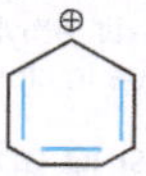

(cycloheptatrienyl cation) is most stable carbocation due to its aromatic nature.

53 (b) $AlCl_3$, SO_3 (Lewis acids), NO_2^+, CH_3^+, $CH_3—\overset{+}{C}=O$ are electron deficient species. Hence, these acts as electrophiles.

54 (d) All the given examples act as electron withdrawing group except NH_2 relative to hydrogen.

—NH_2 group is a donating group due to the lower electronegativity difference between nitrogen and hydrogen.

55 (*d*) Among the given structures, structures III and IV are not resonating structure of each other.

56 (*d*) Statement (d) is incorrect while other statements are correct.

The correct form of (d) is as follows. More the number of contributing structures, the more is the resonance energy.

57 (*b*) The order of relative stability of the contributing structures is I > II > III.

58 (*d*) —COOH is a $-R$-effect showing group, while other options shows $+R$-effect.

59 (*c*) Among the given options, compound (c) does not show resonance effect with benzene ring because N can form maximum of four bonds only.

To do resonance it will have to form a fifth bond which is not possible.

60 (*b*) Among the given species, resonance effect is not shown by (i), (ii) and (vi).

61 (*b*) Greater the number of alkyl groups attached to a positively charged carbon atom, the greater is the hyperconjugation interaction and stabilisation of the cation.

Thus, the correct order of stability of carbocation is (b).

62 (*b*) The given compound is

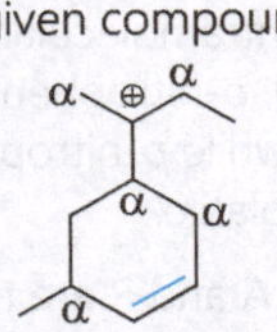

Hence, number of αC—H bond at sp^3-hybridised α—C-atom, which involved in hyperconjugation = 9.

63 (*c*) Hyperconjugative effect helps in deciding the stability of *iso*-butylene. The structures are as follows

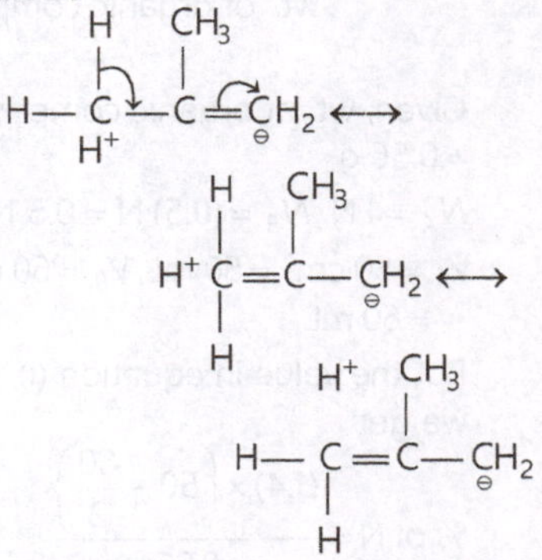

64 (*a*) Substances which sublime on heating are usually purified by sublimation. Hence, naphthalene is purified by sublimation.

65 (*a*) Distillation is based on the difference in the boiling points of liquids. Thus, it is used to separate volatile liquid from non-volatile impurities.

66 (*c*) Fractional distillation is used when the difference in boiling points of two liquids is not much.

67 (*a*) The technological application of fractional distillation is to separate different fractions of crude oil in petroleum industry. Thus, statement (a) is correct.

68 (*d*) Glycerol can be separated from spent-lye in soap industry by distillation under reduced pressure. This method is used because glycerol decomposes at its boiling point.

69 (*d*) The organic compounds, which are volatile in steam are purified by steam distillation. Since, aniline is a steam volatile compound. So, it can be purified by steam distillation method.

70 (*d*) A mixture of *o*-nitrophenol and *p*-nitrophenol can be separated by steam distillation. *o*-nitrophenol is steam volatile due to intramolecular hydrogen bonding.

71 (*a*) Differential extraction is used to extract the compound on the basis of more solubility of one compound in another solvent.

72 (*a*) The organic substance being more soluble in organic solvent is transferred from aqueous layer to the organic layer.

73 (*a*) In continuous extraction same solvent is repeatedly used for extraction of the compound.

74 (*d*)

75 (*b*) Adsorption chromatography.

76 (*a*) Silica gel and alumina is used as an adsorbent in thin layer chromatography.

77 (*c*) Al_2O_3 (aluminium oxide) acts as an adsorbent in column chromatography.

78 (*b*) The most strongly adsorbed component is present near the top while, the weakly adsorbed constituent is formed near the bottom. So, *A* is strongly adsorbed component.

79 (*d*) The element filled in the closed jar is liquid or mixture of liquids.

80 (*b*) Low polarity compounds are weekly adsorbed and has greater R_f value.

81 (*b*) Carbon and hydrogen are detected by heating the compound with Cu(II) oxide.

82 (*c*) When organic compound is fused with sodium metal, nitrogen of the compound is converted into sodium cyanide as

$$Na + C + N \longrightarrow NaCN$$

83 (*b*) The prussian blue colour is obtained due to the formation of complex ferriferrocyanide $[Fe_4[Fe(CN)_6]_3]$.

84 (*b*)Yellow colour is due to the formation of $(NH_4)_3PO_4 \cdot 12MoO_3$. (Ammonium phosphomolybdate).

85 (*a*) Lassaigne's test is not used for the detection of carbon element. It can be used for detection of halogens, nitrogen and sulphur.

86 (*a*) Given mass of CO_2=0.198 g and mass of H_2O=0.1014 g

As we know,

$$\% \text{ of C} = \frac{12}{44} \times \frac{m_{CO_2}}{w} \times 100$$

Percentage of carbon

$$= \frac{12 \times 0.198 \times 100}{44 \times 0.246} \approx 21.95\%$$

Also, $\% \text{ of H} = \frac{2}{18} \times \frac{m_{H_2O}}{w} \times 100$

Percentage of hydrogen

$$= \frac{2 \times 0.1014 \times 100}{18 \times 0.246} \simeq 4.58\%$$

87 (*c*) 22400 mL N_2 denotes 1 mole of N_2 and mass of 1 mole of N_2 i.e. 28 g.

88 (*d*) Let, the molecular formula of the organic compound (1 mol) be $C_xH_yN_z$. In Duma's method,

$$\underset{\text{1 mol}}{C_xH_yN_z} + (2x + y/2)\, CuO \longrightarrow xCO_2 + y/2H_2O + z/2\, N_2 + (2x + y/2)Cu$$

Given, $x = 6$, $\frac{y}{2} = 4$

$\Rightarrow \quad y = 8$ and $\frac{z}{2} = 1$

$\Rightarrow \quad z = 2$

$\therefore$ Molecular formula of the compound is $C_6H_8N_2$.

89 (*d*)

90 (*a*) Kjeldahl's method cannot be used for nitro compounds, diazo compounds and compounds with nitrogen in a ring, because these on reaction with H_2SO_4 do not give ammonium ion.

91 (*b*) Among the given compounds only aniline can be used for estimation of nitrogen by Kjeldahl's method.

92 (*d*) As we know,

Kjeldahl's method formula is

$$\% \text{ of N} = \frac{1.4 \times (N_AV_A - N_BV_B)}{\text{wt. of organic compound}} \quad \text{...(i)}$$

Given, wt. of organic compound = 0.56 g

$N_A = 1\text{ N}$, $N_B = (0.5)\text{ N} = 0.5\text{ N}$

$V_A = 50\text{ cm}^3 = 50\text{ mL}$, $V_B = 60\text{ cm}^3 = 60\text{ mL}$

Put the value in equation (i), we get

$$\% \text{ of N} = \frac{(1.4) \times \left(50 - \frac{60}{2}\right)}{0.56}$$

$$= \frac{140}{56} \times 20 = 50$$

$\therefore$% of N in compound is 50.

93 (*a*) By Carius method, the halogen present in the compound forms the precipitate of corresponding silver halide (Ag*X*).

94 (*a*) $\therefore$According to the formula, % of bromine by Carius method is as follows

$$\% \text{ of Br} = \frac{\text{atomic weight of Br}}{\text{molecular weight of AgBr}} \times \frac{\text{weight of AgBr}}{\text{weight of organic bromide}} \times 100$$

$$\therefore \quad \% \text{ of Br} = \frac{80}{188} \times \frac{141}{250} \times 100$$

$$= \frac{1128000}{47000} = 24\%$$

Thus, the percentage of bromine in the compound is 24.

95 (*d*)

96 (*b*) For the quantitative analysis of sulphur 'Carius tube' is used in which a known mass of an organic compound is heated.

97 (*a*) In the estimation of sulphur, sodium peroxide reagent is heated alongwith organic compound in a Carius tube.

98 (*a*) Percentage of sulphur can be calculated by

Molecular mass of $BaSO_4$

$= 137 + 32 + 64 = 233$ g

233 g $BaSO_4$ contains 32 g sulphur

0.4813 g $BaSO_4$ contains $\frac{32 \times 0.4813}{233}$ g sulphur

Percentage of sulphur

$$= \frac{32 \times 0.4813 \times 100}{233 \times 0.157} = 42.10\%$$

The percentage of sulphur in the compound is 42.10.

Assertion-Reason

1 (*a*) Both A and R are true and R is the correct explanation of A.

2 (*c*) A is true but R is false. The correct form of R is :

The stability of carbonium ions is influenced by both resonance and inductive effects. Allyl and benzyl carbonium ions can be stabilised by resonance but propyl carbonium ion has no resonating structures.

3 (*a*) Both A and R are true and R is the correct explanation of A.

4 (*d*) A is false but R is true.

The correct form of R is :

The compound $O_2N—CH_2—CH_2—O^-$ is expected to be more stable than $CH_3CH_2O^-$ due to $-I$ effect of NO_2.

5 (*a*) Both A and R are true and R is the correct explanation of A.

6 (*a*) Both A and R are true and R is the correct explanation of A.

7 (*c*) A is true but R is false.

The correct form of R is :

Due to intramolecular hydrogen bonding, *o*-nitrophenol is steam volatile while *p*-nitrophenol is not steam volatile.

8 (*a*) Both A and R are true and R is the correct explanation of A.

9 (*c*) A is true but R is false.

The correct form of R is :

Compounds containing N, S and C give red colour in Lassaigne's test.

10 (*a*) Both A and R are true and R is the correct explanation of A.

Statement Type

1 (*c*) Statement I is false but Statement II is true.

The correct form of statement I is

Heterolytic cleavage of CH_3Br will give CH_3^+ and Br^-.

2 (*c*) Statement I is false but Statement II is true. The correct form of statement II is

Polarisation of σ-bond caused by the polarisation of adjacent σ-bond is referred to as inductive effect.

3 (*a*) Statement I is true but Statement II is false.

The correct form of statement II is

Dispersal of the charge leads to the stability of ion while intensification of negative charge leads to the unstability of ion.

4 (*c*) Statement I is false but Statement II is true.

It's correct form is as follows

The resonance structures have same positions of nuclei.

5 (*d*) Both Statement I and Statement II are false.

Their correct form are as follows

I. Retardation factor (R_f) is unitless and dimensionless.

II. Retardation factor (R_f) value will be different for same compounds at different solvent because, it depends on the solubility and polarity with solvent.

6 (*b*) Both Statements I and II are true.

7 (*a*) Among the given statements, IV and V are correct, while I, II and III are incorrect. Their correct form is :

I. Tertiary butyl carbocation is more stable than a secondary butyl carbocation because of hyperconjugation.

II. Resonance involves delocalisation of negative charge along a conjugated system.

III. Benzene is an aromatic carbocyclic compound.

8 (*b*) Among the given statements, statements I and IV are incorrect while II, III and IV are correct. The correct form of I and IV is

I. The prefixes *sec*- and *tert*- are considered to be the part of the fundamental name.

IV. Organic reactions which result in formation of free radicals are called non-polar reactions.

9 (*c*) Statements II and V are incorrect, while other statements are correct.

The correct form of II and V is

II. Greater the number of alkyl groups attached to a positively charged carbon atom, greater will be the stabilisation.

V. Pyridine can't be used to estimate nitrogen by using kjeldahl's method because nitrogen is present in ring.

10 (*d*) Among the given statements I, II, III and V are correct, while IV is incorrect. The correct form of statement IV is :

In Lassaigne's test, the elements present in an organic compound are converted from covalent to ionic form by fusing with sodium metal.

Matching Type

1 (*a*) The correct match is A-3, B-1, C-4, D-2.

2 (*a*) The correct match is A-4, B-2, C-1, D-3.

3 (*a*) The correct match is A-1, B-3, C-4, D-2.

4 (*d*) The correct match is A-1, B-2, C-4, D-3.

5 (*a*) The correct match is A-4, B-2, C-3, D-1.

Numerical Value

1 (*1*) Molecular formula $= C_4H_5N$

Degree of unsaturation

$$= (C+1) - \left(\frac{H+X-N}{2}\right)$$

$$= 4 - \frac{5}{2} + \frac{1}{2} + 1 = 3$$

Compound has one nitrogen, so it must contain CN and it is acyclic.

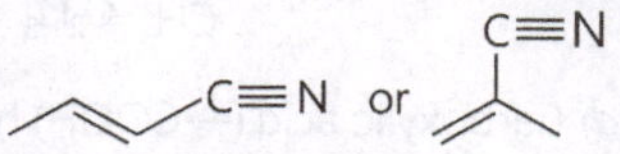

are two possibilities.

Number of sp^3-hybridised carbon = 1

2 (*8*) Parent carbon chain must be the longest chain. So, from the image

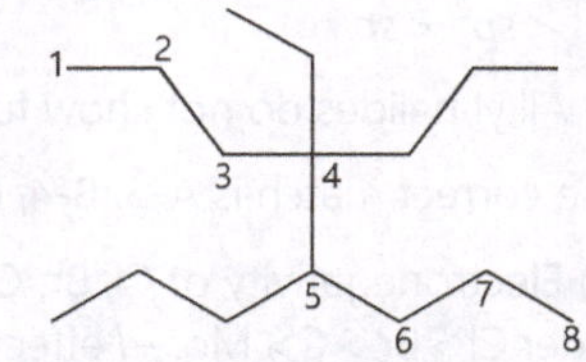

Here, the longest chain has 8 carbon atoms.

3 (*25*) Less R_f value means more polar.

Thus, among *A*, *B* and *C*, *C* will be most polar. Thus,

$$R_f = \frac{\text{Distance travelled by compound}}{\text{Distance travelled by solvent}}$$

$$= \frac{2}{8} = 0.25 = 25 \times 10^{-2}$$

4 (*40*) ∴ Moles of AgBr

$$= \frac{\text{Given mass}}{\text{Molar mass}} = \frac{0.376}{188}$$

$$\text{Moles of bromine} = \frac{0.376}{188} \times 80$$

$$= [0.16 \text{ gram}]$$

∴% of bromine in organic compound (*X*)

$$\Rightarrow \frac{0.16}{0.40} \times 100 \Rightarrow 40\%$$

5 (*42*) To calculate the % of sulphur we use Carius method

$$= \frac{32}{233} \times \frac{\text{Weight of BaSO}_4 \text{ formed}}{\text{Weight of organic compound}} \times 100$$

$$= \frac{32}{233} \times \frac{1.4439}{0.471} \times 100$$

$$= 42.10 \approx 42$$

NCERT Exemplar's

1 (*a*) The correct **IUPAC name** is 3-ethyl-4, 4-dimethylheptane. Its structure is as follows

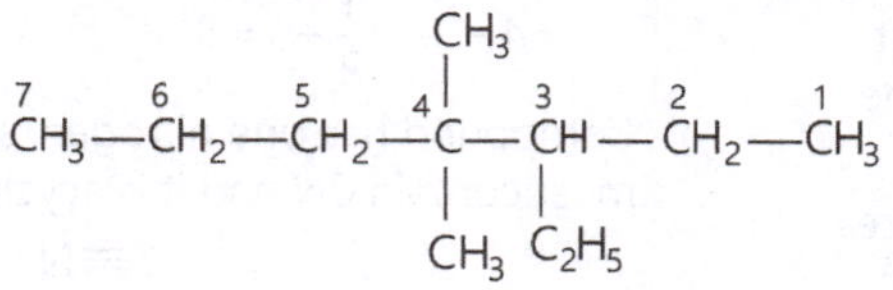

2 (*d*) Carboxylic acid (—COOH) has more priority than ketone $\left(>C=O \right)$. So, the IUPAC name is (d).

3 (*b*)The IUPAC name of given compound is 1-chloro-4-methyl-2-nitrobenzene.

4 (*c*) More the *s*-character, more is the electronegativity $sp^3 < sp^2 < sp$.

5 (*c*) Alkyl halides do not show functional isomerism.

6 The correct match is A-5, B-4, C-1, D-2, E-3.

7 (*a*) Electronegativity of Cl, Br, C and Mg follows the order Cl > Br > C > Mg. −*I* effect of Cl > Br. Hence, $CH_3—CH_2—Cl$ has the greatest positive charge.

8 (*d*)

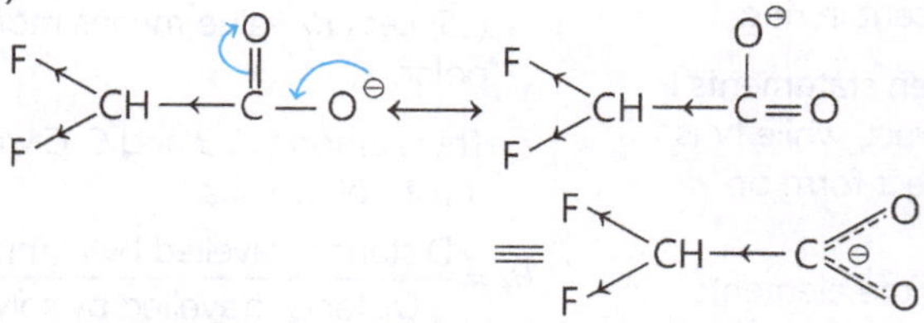

Due to presence of F, the dispersal of negative charge is maximum in (d).

9 (*c*) If unsymmetrical alkene, i.e. $CH_3CH=CH_2$ undergoes electrophilic addition (addition of H^+ ion), then first step could lead to two different carbocation.

$$CH_3—CH=CH_2 + H^+ \longrightarrow CH_3—\overset{\oplus}{C}H—CH_3$$
(2° carbocation)

$$H^+ + CH_3—CH=CH_2 \longrightarrow CH_3—CH_2—\overset{\oplus}{C}H_2$$
(1° carbocation)

As 2° carbocation is more stable than 1° carbocation thus first addition is more feasible.

10 (*b*) π-bonds of the alkene creates an electron cloud and form a bond with the electrophile (H^+) to form a carbocation.

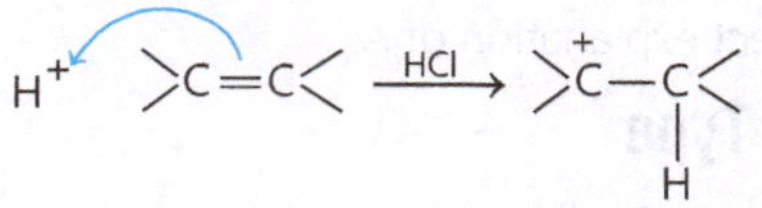

11 The correct match is A-4, B-5, C-1, D-2, E-3.

Past Exams'

1 (*d*) The stability of carbocation is depending on number of α-hydrogen. The more the number of alpha hydrogen atoms, more is the stability of the carbocation.

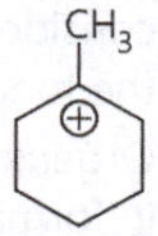 has 7 α-hydrogen, which is highest among all given structures.

2 (*c*) The correct IUPAC name and structure is,

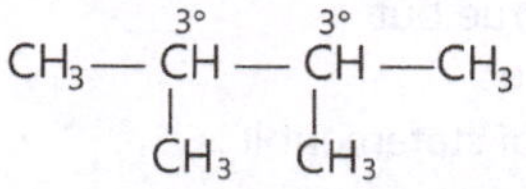

2, 3-dimethylbutane
[2 tertiary (3°) carbon]

3 (*c*) $Fe^{3+} + SCN^- \longrightarrow [Fe(SCN)]^{2+}$
Blood red

4 (*b*) Kjeldahl's method is not applicable to the compounds containing nitrogen as nitro and azo groups and nitrogen present in the ring (e.g. pyridine).

5 (*a*) Structure of 2,6-dimethyl-dec-4-ene is

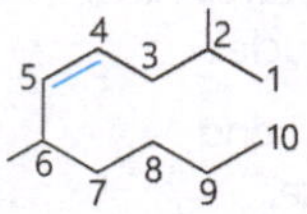

6 (*d*) $C_4H_{10}O$ has ether as functional group for which following two arrangements are possible.

$$CH_3—O—CH_2—CH_2—CH_3$$
Methoxy propane

$$CH_3—CH_2—O—CH_2—CH_3$$
Ethoxy ethane

So, it shows metamerism.

7 (*a*) The purification or separation technique by steam distillation is based on the principle that the liquid should be steam volatile as well as immiscible with water.

8 (*c*) $CH_3\overset{+}{C}HCH_2CH_2CH_3$ is the most stable carbocation among the given species. It is because the number of α-H atom attached to carbocation is maximum in it. Thus, it has the maximum number of hyperconjugating structure. Hence, it is most stable.

9 (*b*) $\overset{sp^2}{C}H_2{=}\overset{sp^2}{C}H{-}\overset{sp}{C}{\equiv}\overset{sp}{C}H$

10 (*d*)

11 (*c*) Experimental values

$p_{N_2} = p_{total} - p_{H_2O}$

$= 725 - 25 = 700$ mm

According to Duma's method for estimation of N, Weight of nitrogen $= \frac{pVM}{RT}$

$= \frac{700 \times 40 \times 28}{760 \times 1000 \times 300 \times 0.0821} \approx 0.0419$ g

$\therefore$ % of nitrogen $= \frac{0.0419}{0.25} \times 100$

$= 16.76\%$

12 (*a*) Nucleophiles are electron rich species. Hence, act as a Lewis base but not Lewis acid.

13 (*a*) In Kjeldahl's method, percentage of N is given by %N

$= \frac{1.4 \times \text{Normality of acid} \times \text{Volume of acid}}{\text{Weight of compound}}$

$1\,M\,H_2SO_4 = 2\,NH_2SO_4$

$\therefore \quad \%N = \frac{1.4 \times 2 \times 10}{0.75} = 37.33\%$

14 (*c*) Generally, neutral structures are more stable than charged ones. Therefore, I is more stable than II and III. While positive charge on less electronegative atom is more stable, i.e. C^+ is more stable than O^+.

Thus, the correct order is I > II > III.

15 (*a*) Among the given statements, incorrect statement is given in option (a). Its correct form is hydrogen ion (H^+) shows positive electromeric effect.

16 (*d*) Carbocations are the species that have sextet of electrons and can act as an electrophile, i.e.

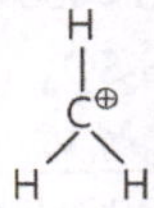

($6e^-$ species)

17 (*a*) The decreasing order of hydride affinity for the given carbocations is C > A > B > D.

The correct hydride affinity order of carbocations will be decided by the stability of carbocation.

Higher the stability of carbocation, lower will be hydride affinity.

18 (*b*) The correct order of elution in the silica gel column chromatography is *A*, *C*, *B*.

According to the observation, *A* is more mobile and interacts with mobile phase more than *C*. Similarly, *C* is more mobile than *B*.

19 (*d*) $C_xH_y + \left[x + \frac{y}{4}\right]O_2 \longrightarrow x\,CO_2 + \frac{y}{2}H_2O$

$\%$ of C $= \frac{\text{Mass of } CO_2 \text{ produced} \times 12}{\text{Mass of organic compound}} \times 100$

$= \frac{330 \times 12}{120 \times 44} \times 100 = 75\%$

$\%$ of H $= \frac{\text{mass of } H_2O \text{ formed} \times 2 \times 100}{\text{mass of organic compound} \times 18}$

$= \frac{270 \times 100 \times 2}{18 \times 120} = 25\%$

20 (*a*) $\therefore$ Moles of AgBr $= \frac{0.36}{188}$

$\therefore$ Mass of bromine

$= \frac{0.36}{188} \times 80 = 0.1532$ g

$\therefore$ % bromine in compound

$= \frac{0.1532}{0.45} \times 100 = 34.04\%$.

21 (*d*) $CH_3CH_2CH{=}CHCH_2NH_2$ will not show resonance as it does not have conjugated system.

22 (*c*) By sodium fusion extract we can detect sulphur, nitrogen, phosphorus and halogens.

Skill Boosters

1 (*d*) Thin layer it can be used to separate the pigments present in the ink.

Hence, the correct option is (d).

2 (*d*) Steam distillation is used to separate substances which are steam volatile and are immiscible with water.

3 (*c*) If the organic compound contains both N and S, then during fusion it may form either sodium thiocyanate (NaSCN) or a mixture of sodium cyanide (NaCN) and sodium sulphide (Na_2S) depending upon the amount of Na used.

If the sodium metal is used less, only NaSCN is produced.

$Fe^{2+} \xrightarrow[\text{Oxidation}]{\text{Aerial}} Fe^{3+}$

$Fe^{3+} + 3NaSCN \longrightarrow \underset{\substack{\text{Ferric thiocyanate} \\ \text{(Red colouration)}}}{Fe(SCN)_3} + 3Na^+$

However, if excess of sodium metal is used.

$\underset{\substack{\text{Soddium} \\ \text{thiocyanate}}}{NaSCN} + 2Na \longrightarrow \underset{\substack{\text{Sodium} \\ \text{cyanide}}}{NaCN} + \underset{\substack{\text{Sodium} \\ \text{sulphide}}}{Na_2S}$

NaCN, thus formed then reacts with $FeSO_4$ more NaCN and Fe^{2+} ions to given ultimately prussian blue colour due to the formation of ferric ferrocyanide or iron (III) hexacyano ferrate (II).

$2NaCN + FeSO_4 \longrightarrow Na_2SO_4 + Fe(CN)_2$

$Fe(CN)_2 + 4NaCN \longrightarrow \underset{\substack{\text{Sodium hexacyano} \\ \text{ferrate (II)}}}{Na_4[Fe(CN)_6]}$

$$3Na_4[Fe(CN)_6] + 4Fe^{3+} \longrightarrow \underset{\text{Iron (III) hexacyano ferrate (II) (Prussian blue)}}{Fe_4[Fe(CN)_6]_3} + 12Na^+$$

From the above discussion, it follows that Manish and Rajni used excess sodium and Ramesh used less sodium.

4 (*a*) Molar mass of $Mg_2P_2O_7$

$= (2 \times 24 + 2 \times 31 + 7 \times 16) = 222$ g

$$n_{Mg_2P_2O_7} = \frac{\text{Mass}_{Mg_2P_2O_7}}{\text{Molar mass}_{Mg_2P_2O_7}}$$

$$= \frac{0.444}{222 \text{ g mol}^{-1}}$$

$$n_P = 2 \times n_{Mg_2P_2O_7} = 2 \times \frac{0.44}{222} \text{ mol}$$

$$\text{Mass}_P = n_P \times \text{Molar mass}_P$$

$$= 2 \times \frac{0.44}{222} \times 31$$

% of P in organic compound

$$= \frac{\text{Mass}_P}{\text{Mass}_{OC}} \times 100$$

$$= \frac{2 \times 0.444 \times 31}{222 \times 0.248} \times 100\%$$

$$= 49.50\% \approx 50$$

5 (*b*) A king's wife is a queen.

The structure of the word queen is

The last letter is U but second last letter is Q in the alphabetical order. The IUPAC name is

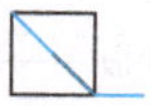

1-methylbicyclo [1.1.0] butane

6 (*c*) Let the vol. of acid left unused $= V$ mL of 0.1 M H_2SO_4

Applying molarity equation

$n_a M_a V_a = n_b M_b V_b$ we have,

$$2 \times 0.1 \times v = 1 \times 0.5 \times 20$$

or $\quad v = 50$ mL

$\therefore$ Vol. of acid used $= 100 - 50$

$= 50$ mL of 0.1 M H_2SO_4

$$\% \text{ N} = \frac{1.4 \times n_a M_a V_a}{\text{Wt. of subtance taken}}$$

$$= \frac{1.4 \times 2 \times 0.1 \times 50}{0.3} = 46.6$$

% N in urea (NH_2CONH_2)

$$= \frac{28}{60} \times 100 = 46.6\%$$

% N in acetamide (CH_3CONH_2)

$$= \frac{14}{59} \times 100 = 23.72\%$$

% N in benzamide $(C_6H_5CONH_2)$

$$= \frac{14}{121} \times 100 = 11.57\%$$

% N in thiourea (NH_2CSNH_2)

$$= \frac{28}{76} \times 100 = 36.84\%$$

Thus, option (c) is correct.

7 (*d*) More the number of H atoms on the α-carbon of the group *R*, more the hyperconjugation structures, weaker is the C—Br bond and hence higher is the rate of the reaction.

Now, since CH_3 has three, ethyl has two isopropyl has one and *tert*-butyl group has no α-hydrogen, therefore, hyperconjugation effect decreases and hence the rate decreases in the same order, i.e. option (b) is correct.

8 (*d*) During the detection of P, the yellow ppt. obtained are due to $(NH_4)_3PO_4 \cdot 12\,MoO_3$ (ammonium phosphomolybdate) and not due to $(NH_4)_2MoO_4$ (ammonium molybdate).

9 (*b*) Double bond equivalents (D.B.E)

$$\text{D.B.E} = \frac{\Sigma n\,(v-2)}{2} + 1$$

where '*n*' is the number of different kinds of atoms present in the molecule and v is the valency of each atom.

$$\text{D.B.E.} = \frac{1}{2}[4(4-2) + 6(1-2)] + 1 = 2$$

Since, D.B.E $= 2$, therefore, C_4H_6 has either two double bonds or one triple bond or one double bond and a ring or two rings.

The following nine isomers are possible :

(i) $CH_2{=}CH{-}CH{=}CH_2$
Buta-1, 3-diene

(ii) $CH_3CH_2{-}C{\equiv}CH$
But-1-yne

(iii) $CH_3{-}C{\equiv}C{-}CH_3$
But-2-yne

(iv) $CH_2{=}C{=}CHCH_3$
Buta-1, 2-diene

(v)

Cyclobutene

(vi)

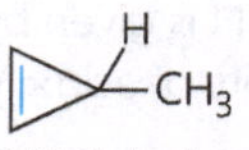

3-Methylcycloprop-1-ene

(vii)

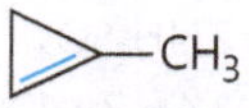

1-Methylcyclopropene

(viii)

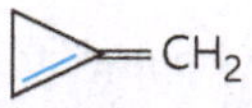

Methylenecyclopropane

(ix)

Bicyclo [1. 1. 0] butane

Scan for **Chemistry Through Concept Master** Videos

09 Hydrocarbons

Topicwise No. of Ques asked in 5 Years

Topics	No. of Questions				
	2024	2023	2022	2021	2020
Classification	–	–	–	–	–
Alkanes	1	–	–	2	1
Alkenes	–	–	1	1	1
Alkynes	1	–	–	–	–
Aromatic Hydrocarbons	–	1	–	1	1
Carcinogenicity	–	–	–	–	–

Special Type of Ques asked in 5 Years

Types	Years				
	2024	2023	2022	2021	2020
A-R	–	–	–	–	–
Statement Based	1	–	–	–	–
Matching Type Case Based	1	–	–	–	–

Last 5 Years Weightage (NEET)

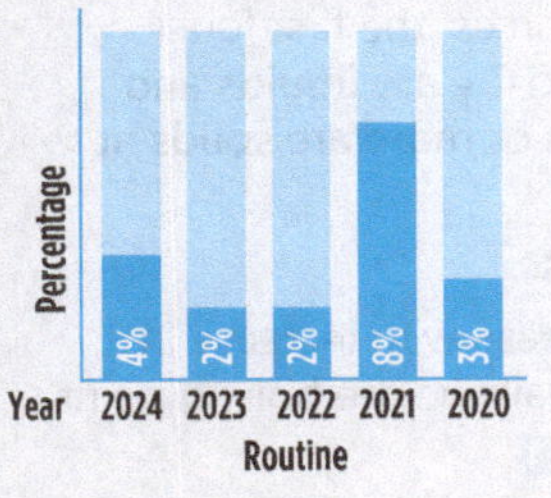

Hydrocarbons means compounds containing only carbon and hydrogen. The main sources of hydrocarbons are coal petroleum and natural gas. They are used for the manufacture of polymers like polyethene, polypropene, polystyrene etc.

Classification

Depending upon the types of carbon-carbon bonds present, hydrocarbons can be classified into three main categories:

(i) Saturated (ii) Unsaturated (iii) Aromatic

- **Saturated hydrocarbons** contain carbon-carbon and carbon-hydrogen single bonds. If different carbon atoms are joined together to form open chain of carbon atoms with single bonds, they are termed as **alkanes**. On the other hand, if carbon atoms forms a closed chain or a ring, they are termed as **cycloalkanes**.
- **Unsaturated hydrocarbons** contain carbon-carbon multiple bonds (double bonds, triple bonds or both).
- **Aromatic hydrocarbons** are a special type of cyclic compounds.

Alkanes

- These are **saturated** open chain hydrocarbons containing C—C single bonds. Chemically, these have very low reactivity and that's why also known as paraffins.
- The general formula is C_nH_{2n+2}. where, $n = 1, 2, 3$ e.g. CH_4 (methane)

  Structure All the C-atoms in alkanes are sp^3-hybridised.
- In alkanes, tetrahedra are joined together in which C—C and C—H bond lengths are 154 pm and 112 pm respectively.

Nomenclature

Steps to be followed while writing IUPAC names are as follows

- First of all, the longest chain of carbon atoms corresponding to the parent alkane is identified.
- The substituents attached to the carbon atoms are numbered such that the branched C atoms get the lowest possible numbers.
- The substituents are written in alphabetical order before the name of parent alkane.

Isomerism

- The phenomenon in which hydrocarbons possess same molecular formula but different structures is known as **isomerism**.
- Alkanes show only chain isomerism which is a type of structural isomerism.

  e.g. Butane has two isomers are given as

  $$C_4H_{10}: \underset{n\text{-butane}}{H_3C—CH_2—CH_2—CH_3}, \quad \underset{iso\text{-butane}}{H_3C—CH(CH_3)—CH_3}$$

- Based upon the number of carbon atoms attached to another carbon atom, the carbon atom is termed as primary (1°), secondary (2°), tertiary (3°) or quaternary (4°).
- Terminal carbon atoms are always primary. Carbon atom attached to two carbon atoms is known as secondary. Tertiary carbon is attached to three carbon atoms and quaternary carbon to four carbon atoms.
- On constructing the structures for higher alkanes, the larger number of isomers are obtained. Although **first three alkanes**-methane, ethane and propane have only one structure, i.e. **do not exhibit isomerism.**
- The groups or substituents are derived from alkanes by removal of one hydrogen atom known as alkyl groups with general formula (C_nH_{2n+1}).

Preparation

- **By hydrogenation of unsaturated hydrocarbons** Dihydrogen gas adds to alkenes and alkynes in the presence of finely divided catalysts (Pt/Pd/Ni) to form alkanes. This process is called **hydrogenation**.

$$\underset{\text{Ethene}}{CH_2{=}CH_2} + H_2 \xrightarrow[\text{(Hydrogenation)}]{\text{Pt/Pd/Ni}} \underset{\text{Ethane}}{CH_3—CH_3}$$

$$\underset{\text{Propene}}{CH_3—CH{=}CH_2} + H_2 \xrightarrow{\text{Pt/Pd/Ni}} \underset{\text{Propane}}{CH_3—CH_2—CH_3}$$

$$\underset{\text{Propyne}}{CH_3—C{\equiv}C—H} + 2H_2 \xrightarrow{\text{Pt/Pd/Ni}} \underset{\text{Propane}}{CH_3—CH_2—CH_3}$$

- **Reduction of alkyl halides** Alkyl halides (except fluorides) on reduction with zinc and dilute hydrochloric acid gives alkanes.

  e.g. $$\underset{\text{Chloromethane}}{CH_3—Cl} + H_2 \xrightarrow{\text{Zn, H}^+} \underset{\text{Methane}}{CH_4} + HCl$$

- **Wurtz reaction** Alkyl halides on treatment with Na metal in dry ethereal solution gives higher alkanes. It is used for the preparation of higher alkanes containing even number of carbon atoms. NEET 2020

$$\underset{\text{Bromomethane}}{CH_3Br} + 2Na + BrCH_3 \xrightarrow{\text{Dry ether}} \underset{\text{Ethane}}{CH_3—CH_3} + 2NaBr$$

- **From carboxylic acids**
  - Sodium salts of carboxylic acids on heating with soda lime gives alkanes containing one carbon atom less than the carboxylic acid. This process of elimination of CO_2 from a carboxylic acid is known as **decarboxylation.**

$$\underset{\text{Sodium ethanoate}}{CH_3COO^-Na^+} + NaOH \xrightarrow[\Delta]{\text{CaO}} CH_4 + Na_2CO_3$$

  - **Kolbe's electrolysis method** This method in used to create a new C—C linkage. In this method, an aqueous solution of sodium or potassium salt of a carboxylic acid on electrolysis gives alkane containing even number of carbon atoms at anode.

$$2CH_3COO^-Na^+ + 2H_2O \xrightarrow{\text{Electrolysis}} CH_3—CH_3 + 2CO_2 + 2NaOH + H_2$$

  - **At anode,**

$$\underset{\text{Acetate ion}}{2CH_3—\overset{O}{\overset{\|}{C}}—\bar{O}} \xrightarrow{-2e^-} \underset{\text{Acetate free radical}}{2CH_3—\overset{O}{\overset{\|}{C}}—\ddot{O}\colon} \longrightarrow \underset{\text{Methyl free radical}}{2\dot{C}H_3} + 2CO_2\uparrow;$$

$$\dot{C}H_3 + \dot{C}H_3 \longrightarrow CH_3—CH_3\uparrow$$

  - **At cathode,**

$$H_2O + e^- \longrightarrow OH^{\ominus} + \dot{H};\ 2\dot{H} \longrightarrow H_2\uparrow$$

Marks Maximizer

- In **Wurtz reaction**, if two different alkyl halides are used, the product is non-separable mixture of unsymmetrical alkanes are produced due to similar boiling points.

$$CH_3X + 2Na + C_2H_5X \xrightarrow[-NaX]{\text{Ether}} CH_3—CH_3 + CH_3—C_2H_5 + C_2H_5—C_2H_5$$

- **Kolbe electrolytic method** is not suitable for the preparation of methane (CH_4). Also, this method is not suitable for alkanes having odd number of carbon atoms as in such cases a mixture of hydrocarbons is formed which is difficult to separate.

Physical Properties

- Alkanes are **non-polar** molecules.
- Due to the weak van der Waals' forces the first four members, C_1 to C_4 are **gases**. C_5 to C_{17} are **liquids** and those containing 18 carbon atoms or more are **solids** at 298 K.
- They are **colourless** and **odourless**.
- The boiling points of alkanes increase with increase in molecular mass and for the same alkane the boiling point decreases with branching. NEET 2024

- Mixture of higher alkanes are non-polar and hence, hydrophobic in nature.

Marks Maximizer

Generally, melting point increases with increase in molecular weights but alkanes with even number of carbon atoms, have higher melting point than the preceding and succeeding odd carbon atom containing members. It is due to their well packed structures.

Chemical Properties

Alkanes are generally inert towards acids, bases, oxidising and reducing agents. However, they undergo following reactions under certain conditions.

Alkanes

- Halogenation
  - $CH_4 + Cl_2 \xrightarrow{h\nu} CH_3Cl \xrightarrow[-HCl]{Cl_2/h\nu}$
  - $CH_2Cl_2 \xrightarrow[-HCl]{Cl_2/h\nu} CHCl_3 \xrightarrow[-HCl]{Cl_2/h\nu} CCl_4$
- Controlled oxidation
  - $2CH_4 + O_2 \xrightarrow{Cu/523K/100\ atm} 2CH_3OH$
  - $CH_4 + O_2 \xrightarrow[\Delta]{Mo_2O_3} HCHO + H_2O$
  - $2CH_3CH_3 + 3O_2 \xrightarrow[\Delta]{(CH_3COO)_2Mn} 2CH_3COOH + 2H_2O$
  - $(CH_3)_3CH + O_2 \xrightarrow[oxidation]{KMnO_4} (CH_3)_3COH$
- Combustion
  - $C_nH_{2n+2} + \left(\frac{(3n+1)}{2}\right) O_2 \text{ (excess)} \xrightarrow[combustion]{Complete} nCO_2 + (n+1)H_2O$
  - $CH_4(g) + O_2(g) \text{ (limited)} \xrightarrow[combustion]{Incomplete} C(s) + 2H_2O(l)$
- Aromatisation
  - $\text{Hexane} \xrightarrow[\substack{Al_2O_3 \text{ or } Cr_2O_3 \\ 773\ K,\ 10\text{-}20\ atm}]{V_2O_5 \text{ or}} \text{Benzene}$
- Isomerisation
  - $CH_3(CH_2)_4CH_3 \xrightarrow[HCl]{Anhyd.\ AlCl_3} CH_3CH(CH_3)(CH_2)_2CH_3 + CH_3CH_2CH(CH_3)CH_2CH_3$
- Reaction with steam
  - $CH_4 + H_2O \xrightarrow[\Delta]{Ni} CO + 3H_2$
- Pyrolysis or Cracking
  - $C_6H_{14} \xrightarrow[6\text{-}7\ atm]{773\ K} C_6H_{12} + H_2$; $C_4H_8 + C_2H_6$; $C_3H_6 + C_2H_4 + CH_4$

Important Points Regarding Above Reactions

- Lower alkanes do not undergo nitration and sulphonation reactions.
- The rate of reaction of alkanes with halogens is $F_2 > Cl_2 > Br_2 > I_2$.
- Rate of replacement of hydrogens of alkanes is 3° > 2° > 1°.
- Fluorination is too violent to be controlled.
- Iodination is very slow and reversible reaction. It can be carried out in the presence of oxidising agents like HIO_3 or HNO_3.

$$CH_4 + I_2 \rightleftharpoons CH_3I + HI, \quad HIO_3 + 5HI \longrightarrow 3I_2 + 3H_2O$$

- Halogenation proceeds *via* free radical chain mechanism. i.e.

Chain initiation step $Cl—Cl \xrightarrow[Homolysis]{h\nu} \dot{Cl} + \dot{Cl}$ (Chlorine free radicals)

Chain propagation step $CH_4 + \dot{Cl} \xrightarrow{h\nu} \dot{C}H_3 + H—Cl$

$\dot{C}H_3 + Cl—Cl \xrightarrow{h\nu} CH_3—Cl + \dot{Cl}$

Chain termination step $\dot{Cl} + \dot{Cl} \longrightarrow Cl_2$

$\dot{C}H_3 + \dot{Cl} \longrightarrow CH_3Cl$

$\dot{C}H_3 + \dot{C}H_3 \longrightarrow CH_3—CH_3$

Conformations

- Spatial arrangements of atoms which can be converted into one another by rotation around a carbon-carbon single bond are called **conformations** or **conformers** or **rotamers**.
- There are infinite number of conformations are possible for alkanes.

Conformations of Ethane

For Concept Master Video

- **Eclipsed conformation** In this rotation about C—C single bond is by an angle such that hydrogen atoms of front carbon atom completely cover or eclipse the hydrogen atoms of rear carbon atom.
- **Staggered conformation** In this rotation about C—C single bond is by an angle so that hydrogen atoms of two carbon atoms are at maximum distance from each other.
- **Skew conformation** Any other intermediate conformation between eclipsed and staggered.

Eclipsed and staggered conformations can be represented by Sawhorse and Newman projections as shown below.

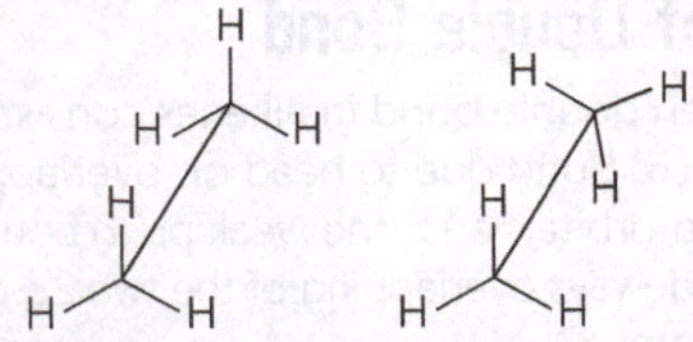

(i) Eclipsed (ii) Staggered

Sawhorse projections of ethane

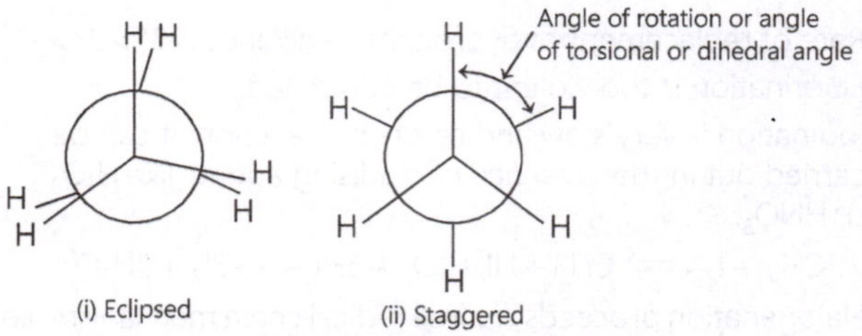

Newman projections of ethane

Relative Stability of Conformations

- In staggered form of ethane, the electron clouds of C—H bonds are as far apart as possible and have minimum repulsive forces and are more stable than other.
- The repulsive interaction between the electron clouds, which affects stability of conformation is called **torsional strain**.
- Magnitude of torsional strain depends upon the angle of rotation about C—C bond. This angle is called **dihedral angle** or **torsional angle.** NEET 2021
- The staggered form has the least torsional strain and the eclipsed form has maximum torsional strain. Thus, eclipsed form is least stable.
- The energy difference between the two extreme forms (eclipsed and staggered) is of the order of 12.5 kJ mol^{-1}.

Marks Maximizer

Conformations of cyclohexane The important conformations for cyclohexane are **chair boat** and **twist boat.** Chair form is the most stable than all other conformation.

Alkenes

- They are unsaturated hydrocarbons containing at least one double bond having general formula C_nH_{2n}.
- They are also known as olefins, since the first member, ethylene or ethene was found to form an oily liquid with chlorine.

Structure of Double Bond

- Carbon-carbon double bond in alkenes consists of one strong sigma (σ) bond due to head on overlapping of sp^2-hybridised orbitals and one weak pi (π) bond obtained by lateral or sideways overlapping of the two 2*p*-orbitals of the two carbon atoms.
- The double bond is shorter in bond length (134 pm) then the C — C single bond (154 pm).
- Due to pi (π) bond, alkenes are easily attacked by reagents or compounds which are in search of electrons. Such reagents are called **electrophilic reagents.**

Nomenclature

- For nomenclature of alkenes in IUPAC system, the longest chain of carbon atoms containing the double bond is selected.
- Numbering is done from the end which is nearer to double bond. The suffix 'ene' replaces 'ane' of alkanes.

Isomerism

Alkenes show both structural isomerism and geometrical isomerism.

- **Structural isomerism** This type of isomerism is shown by those compounds which have more than three carbon atoms. e.g. Ethene and propene can have only one structure but C_4H_8 have different structures and can be written in the following three ways :

I. $\overset{1}{C}H_2{=}\overset{2}{C}H{-}\overset{3}{C}H_2{-}\overset{4}{C}H_3$
But-1-ene

II. $\overset{1}{C}H_3{-}\overset{2}{C}H{=}\overset{3}{C}H{-}\overset{4}{C}H_3$
But-2-ene

III. $\overset{1}{C}H_2{=}\overset{2}{C}(CH_3){-}\overset{3}{C}H_3$
2-methyprop-1-ene

- Structures I and III, & II and III are the examples of **chain isomerism** whereas structures I and II are **position isomers.**
- **Geometrical isomerism** A carbon-carbon double bond is made up of one σ-bond and one π-bond. The presence of π-bond prevents free rotation about the double bond with the result of the type *ABC*=*CAB* can exist in two different geometrical isomeric forms, i.e. *cis*-form and *trans*-form.
- The isomer in which two identical groups lie on the same side of the double bond is called ***cis*-isomer** and the other isomer in which identical groups lie on the opposite sides of the double bond is called ***trans*-isomer**.
- *cis*-form of alkene is found to be more polar than *trans*-form because dipole moment of *trans*-form is almost zero.

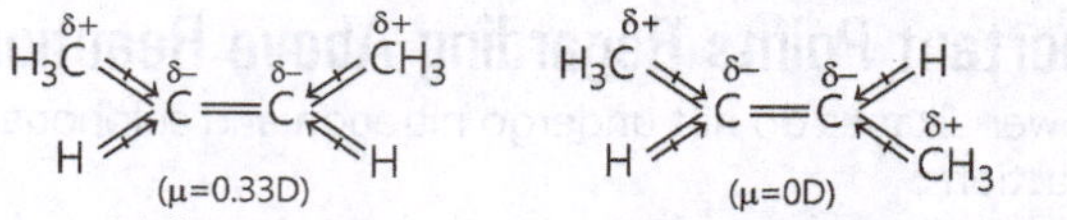

(μ=0.33D) [*cis*-but-2-ene] (μ=0D) [*trans*-but-2-ene]

Preparation

It can be summarised as follows

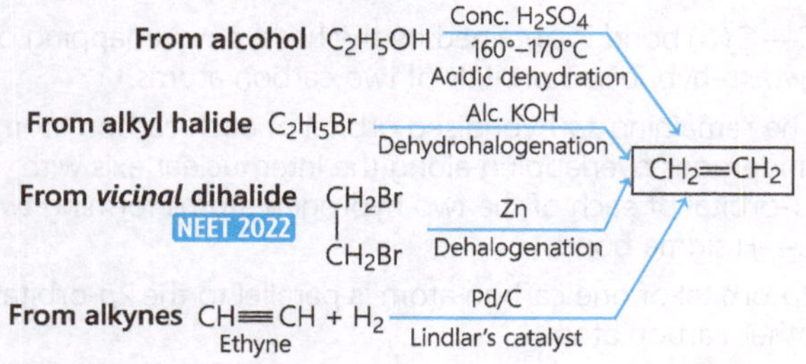

- **Birch reduction**

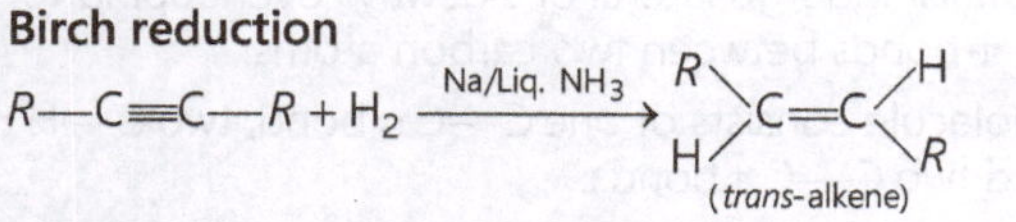

- Alkynes on hydrogenation with Pd/C form *cis*-alkenes, whereas on reduction with Na in liq. NH_3 form *trans*-alkenes.
- Partially deactivated palladised charcoal is known as Lindlar's catalyst.
- Dehydrohalogenation and acidic dehydration of alcohols both are the example of β-elimination. In β-elimination reaction, hydrogen atom is eliminated from the β-carbon atom.
- Nature of halogen atom and alkyl group determine rate of the reaction. It is observed that for halogens, the rate is $I > Br > Cl$, while for alkyl group it is $3° > 2° > 1°$.

Physical Properties

- The first three members are gases, the next fourteen are liquids and higher ones are solids.
- All alkenes are **colourless** and **odourless except ethene** which has faint sweet smell.
- All alkenes are insoluble in water but fairly soluble in non-polar solvents.
- Boiling points of alkenes increase regularly with increase in size and straight chain alkenes have higher boiling points than isomeric branched chain compounds.

Marks Maximizer

Saytzeff rule

- It states that, when in a compound two types of β-hydrogen atoms are present then during elimination two alkenes are formed as a product but the major product is that alkene which has more number of alkyl group attached with carbon-carbon double bond.
- Greater the number of alkyl groups attached to the doubly bonded carbon atoms, more stable is the alkene.

Chemical Properties

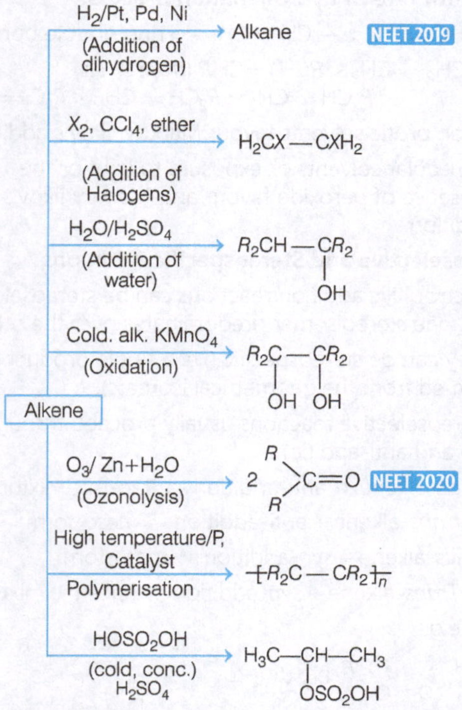

- **Markovnikov's rule** states that, during the addition of hydrogen halides to unsymmetrical alkenes, the negative part of the addendum (adding molecules) gets attached to that carbon atom which possesses lesser number of hydrogen atoms.

For Concept Master Video

$$\underset{\text{Propene}}{H_3CCH{=}CH_2} + HBr \longrightarrow \underset{\text{2-bromopropane}}{H_3C{-}\underset{\displaystyle Br}{\overset{}{CH}}{-}CH_3}$$

NEET 2019

- **Peroxide effect** states that, the presence of peroxide, addition of HBr to unsymmetrical alkenes takes place contrary to Markovnikov's rule. This is also known as **Kharasch effect.**

$$\underset{\text{Propene}}{H_3CCH{=}CH_2} + HBr \xrightarrow{\text{Peroxide}} \underset{\text{1-bromopropane}}{CH_3CH_2CH_2Br}$$

Peroxide effect is observed in case of HBr only, not with HCl and HI.

- The order of reactivity of the hydrogen halides is

$$HI > HBr > HCl.$$

Marks Maximizer

Order for rate of hydrogenation process

- $—HC{=}CH_2 > —CH{=}CH— >$ ring double bond
- $—CH_2{=}CH_2 < RCH{=}CHR$ (*trans* > *cis*) $< R_2CH{=}CH_2 < R_2CH{=}CHR < R_2C{=}CR_2$
- Polar, protic solvents favour Markovnikov's addition :
- Non-polar solvents or exposure to light or the presence of peroxide favour anti-Markovnikov's addition.

Stereoselective and Stereospecific Additions

- Electrophilic addition reactions can be stereoselective (i.e. one stereoisomer predominates over the other).
- They can be stereospecific (i.e. a single product is formed from the geometrical isomers).
- Stereoselective reactions usually proceed through *syn* and anti-addition.
  (i) *cis*-alkene + anti-addition → Racemic mixture
  (ii) *trans*-alkene + anti-addition → *meso*-form
  (iii) *cis*-alkene + *syn*-addition → *meso*-form
  (iv) *Trans*-alkene + *syn*-addition → Racemic mixture

e.g.

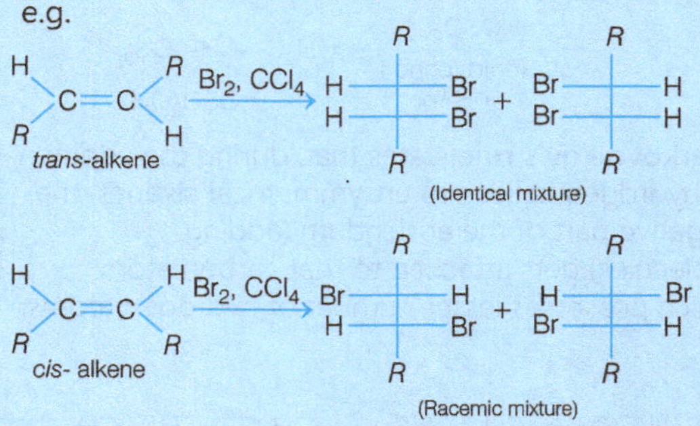

Mnemonics Trick to Remember Stereoselective Addition Reaction

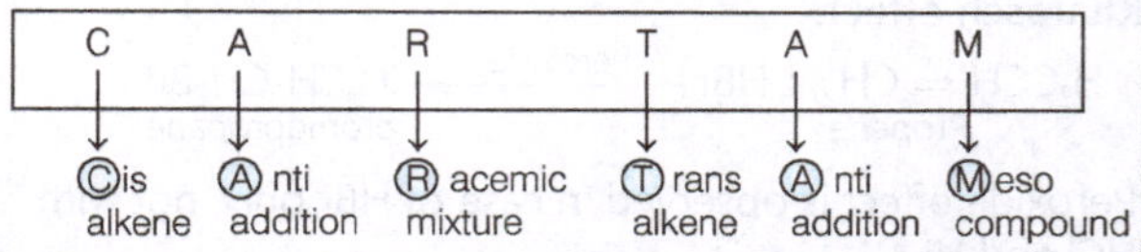

Alkynes

- Alkynes are unsaturated hydrocarbons that contain at least one triple bond between two carbon atoms.
- Their general formula is C_nH_{2n-2}.

Structure of Triple Bond NEET 2024

- Each carbon atom of ethyne has two *sp*-hybridised orbitals.
- C—C (σ) bond is obtained by the head on overlapping of two *sp*-hybridised orbitals of two carbon atoms.
- The remaining *sp*-hybridised orbital of each carbon atom undergoes overlapping along the internuclear axis with 1*s*-orbital of each of the two hydrogen atoms forming two C—H sigma bonds.
- 2*p*-orbital of one carbon atom is parallel to the 2*p*-orbital of other carbon atom.
- These orbitals undergo lateral or sideways overlapping to form two π-bonds between two carbon atoms.
- Ethyne molecule consists of one C—C σ bond, two C—H σ bonds and two C—C π bonds.

Nomenclature and Isomerism

- In IUPAC system, they are named as derivatives of the corresponding alkanes replacing 'ane' by the suffix 'yne'.
- They generally show position isomerism. Here, two compounds differ in their structures due to the position of triple bond. e.g. C_5H_8.

$HC{\equiv}C—CH_2—CH_2—CH_3$, Pent-1-yne

$H_3C—C{\equiv}C—CH_2—CH_3$, Pent-2-yne

$H_3C—CH(CH_3)—C{\equiv}CH$, 3-methyl but-1-yne

- Ethyne does not show any type of isomerism.

Preparation

It can be explained as below.

1. **From calcium carbide** It involves on industrial scale.

$$CaC_2 + 2H_2O \longrightarrow Ca(OH)_2 + C_2H_2$$

2. **From *vicinal* dihalides** *Vicinal* dihalides on treatment with alcoholic KOH undergo dehydrohalogenation.

$$CH_2Br—CH_2Br \xrightarrow{\text{Alc. KOH}} CH{\equiv}CH$$

Physical Properties

- First three members are gases, next eight are liquids and higher ones are solids.
- All alkynes are colourless and odourless except ethyne which has characteristic odour.
- These are weakly polar in nature.

- They are lighter than H_2O and immiscible with water but soluble in organic solvent.
- Their melting and boiling point increases with increase in molar mass.

Chemical Reactions of Alkynes

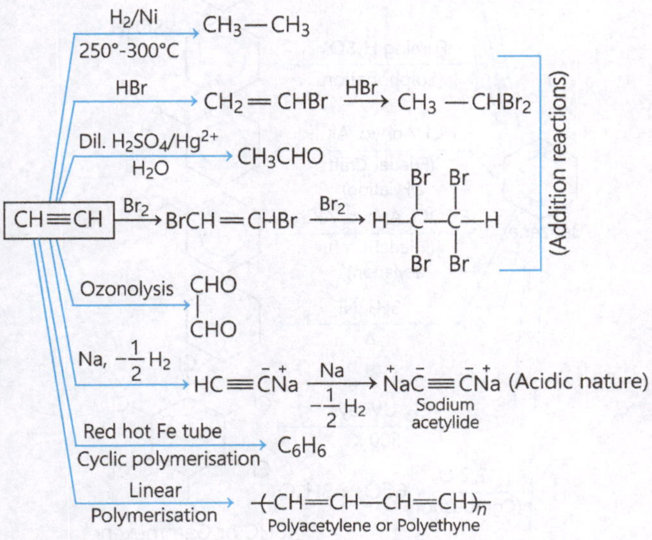

- The acidic character of hydrocarbons decreases in the order : $CH\equiv CH > CH_2=CH_2 > CH_3-CH_3$.
- The group $-C\equiv CH$ (1-alkyne) is acidic in nature due to more *s*-character (50%) of $C\equiv C$ which is *sp*-hybridised. Hence, proton release in $-C\equiv CH$ takes place more readily.
- Acidic trend among different alkynes : $HC\equiv CH > CH_3-C\equiv CH > CH_3-C\equiv C-CH_3$

Aromatic Hydrocarbons

- Aromatic hydrocarbons, also known as **arenes**, were found to contain benzene ring (highly unsaturated).
- Aromatic compounds containing benzene ring are known as **benzenoids** and those not containing a benzene ring are known as **non-benzenoids**.

Nomenclature and Isomerism

- In IUPAC nomenclature, the substituent is placed as prefix to the word benzene.
- When two hydrogen atoms in benzene are replaced by two similar or different monovalent atoms or groups, three different position isomers are possible.
- If one of the hydrogen atom of ring is substituted by an alkyl radical or a group then it is called as **monosubstituted derivative**.

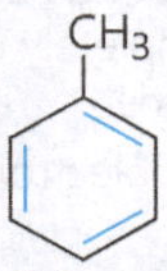

Toluene

- The position of second substituent with respect to first one will form different forms.

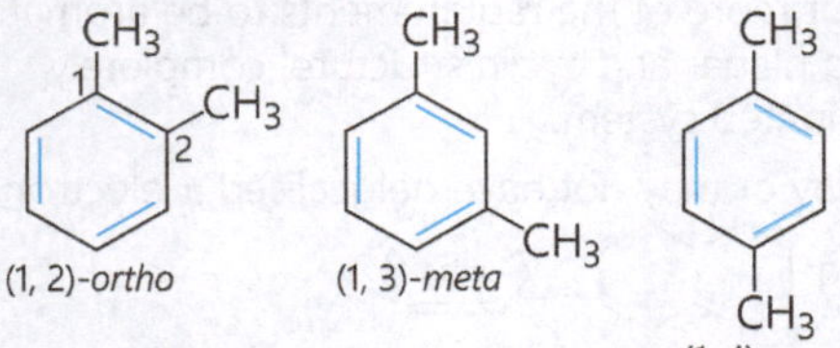

(1, 4)-*para*

- The 1, 2 or 1, 6 is known as the *ortho* (*o*-), the 1, 3 or 1, 5 as *meta* (*m*-) and the 1, 4 as *para* (*p*-) disubstituted compounds.

Structure of Benzene

- In benzene, each carbon is sp^2-hybridised.
- Two of the hybrid orbitals on each carbon are used for the formation of σ-bonds with two adjacent carbon atoms.
- The third sp^2-hybrid orbital overlaps with the *s*-orbital of H-atom to form a σ-bond.
- All lie in the same plane.
- The unhybridised *p* orbital of each C-atom overlaps equally with unhybridised *p*-orbital of both the adjacent C-atoms to which it is bonded.

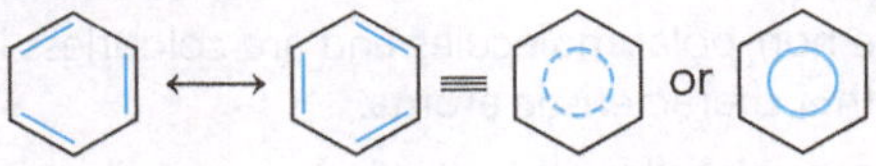

Aromaticity

For Concept Master Video

- For a compound to be aromatic, it must possess the following characteristics :
  - (i) Planarity
  - (ii) Complete delocalisation of the π-electrons in the ring.
  - (iii) Presence of $(4n+2)$ π electrons in the ring, where n is an integer ($n=0, 1, 2, \ldots$) This is referred to as Huckel's rule.

NEET 2023

- Examples of a few aromatic compounds are given below :

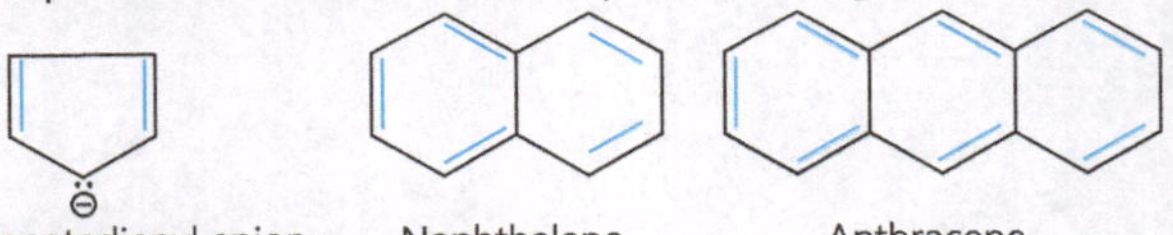

Cyclopentadienyl anion $n=1$ (6π-electrons) | Naphthalene $n=2$ (10π-electrons) | Anthracene $n=3$ (14π-electrons)

Marks Maximizer

- **Anti-aromatic compounds** are molecules that are cyclic, planar and completely conjugated but are consist of $4n\pi$-electrons.
  - → Have delocalised π-electron system and $4n\ \pi$-electrons.
  - → e.g. 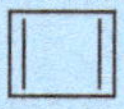 Cyclobutadiene
- **Non-aromatic compounds** are molecules that lack one or more of the requirements to be aromatic, being planar and cyclic structure, completely conjugated system.
  - → May or may not have delocalised π-electron system.
  - → e.g. 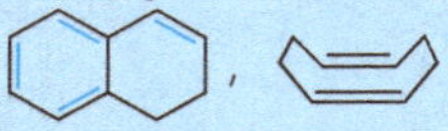

Order of stability : Aromatic > Non-aromatic > Anti-aromatic

Preparation

The summarise form of the preparation is as follows

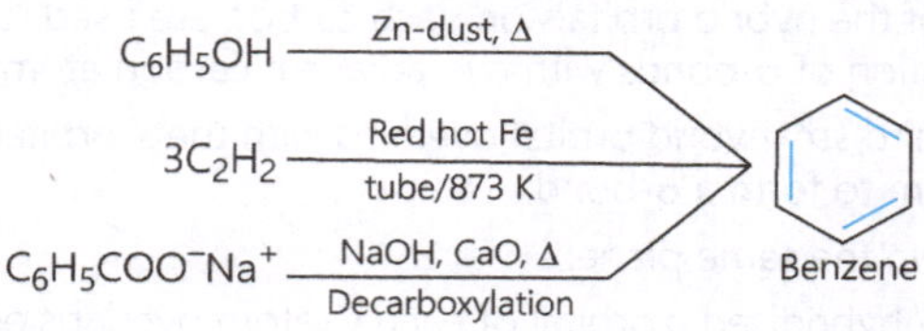

Physical Properties

- These are non-polar molecules and are colourless liquids or solids with a characteristic aroma.
- These are immiscible with water but are readily miscible with organic solvents.
- Boiling point of arenes increases with increase in the molecular size due to increase in van der Waals' forces of attraction.
- Melting point depends on molecular size and symmetry. Among *o*-, *m* and *p*-xylenes, the *p*-isomer has the highest melting point.

Chemical Reactions of Benzene

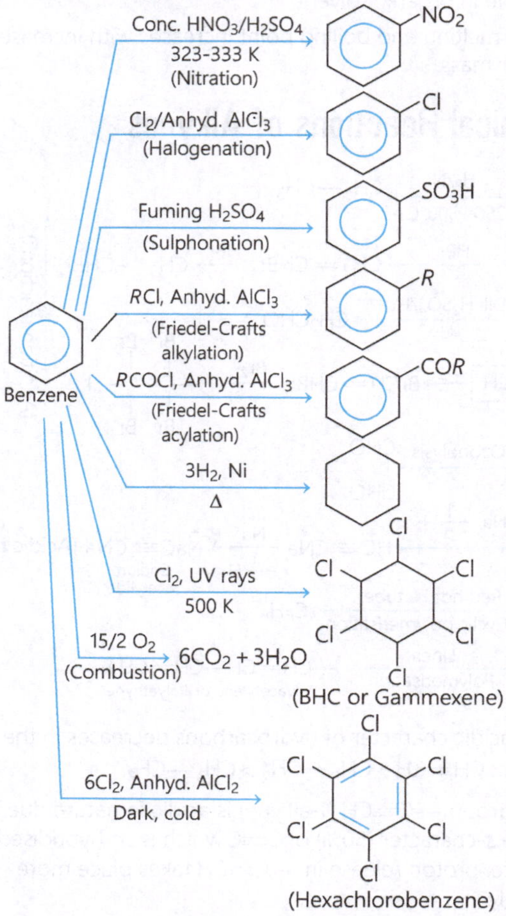

Mechanism of Electrophilic Substitution Reaction

According to experimental evidences, S_E (S = substitution: E = electrophilic) reactions are supposed to proceed *via* the following three steps: **NEET 2020**

(a) Generation of the electrophile.

$$Cl{-}Cl + AlCl_3 \longrightarrow \underset{\text{Chloronium ion}}{Cl^+} + [AlCl_4]^-$$

(b) Formation of carbocation intermediate.

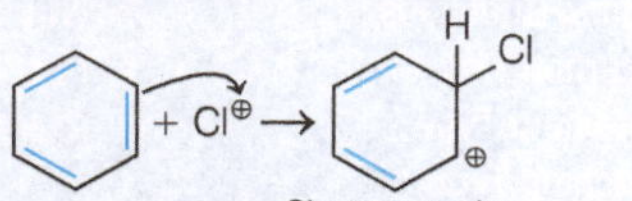

Sigma complex (arenium ion)

(c) Removal of proton from the carbocation intermediate.

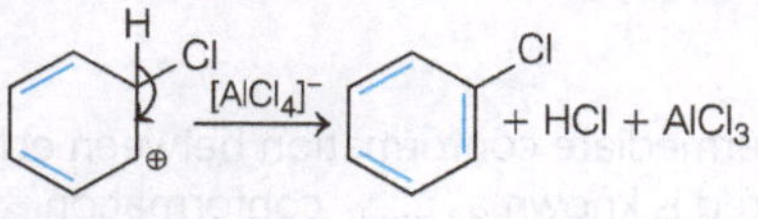

Directive Influence of a Functional Group in Mono-substituted Benzene

ortho and *para*-directing Groups

- Groups with positive mesomeric effect (+*M*) increases electron density at *o*- and *p*-positions due to delocalisation.
- The groups, e.g. — OH, — NH_2, — NH*R*, — $NHCOCH_3$, — OCH_3, — CH_3, — C_2H_5 etc., are called *ortho* and *para*-directing as well as activating groups.
- Phenol is resonance hybrid of following structures.

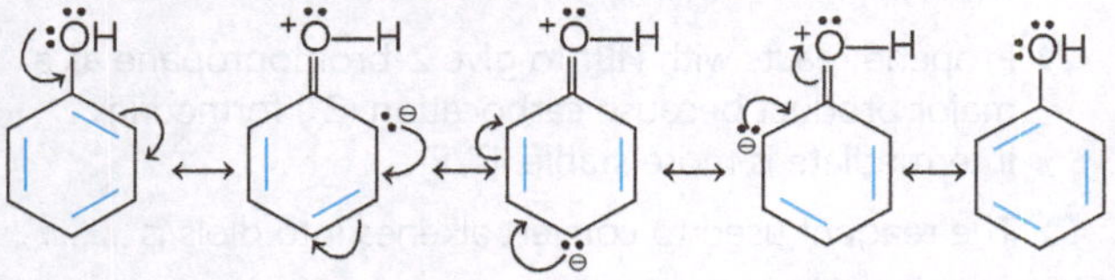

I II III IV V

- They activate benzene ring towards electrophilic substitution.

  Exception In aryl halide halogens are deactivating but they are *ortho* and *para* directing groups.

meta-directing Groups

- Groups with negative mesomeric effect (–*M*) decreases electron density on *o*- and *p*-positions, so electrophile will attack on *m*-position.
- Resonance structures of nitrobenzene are given below.

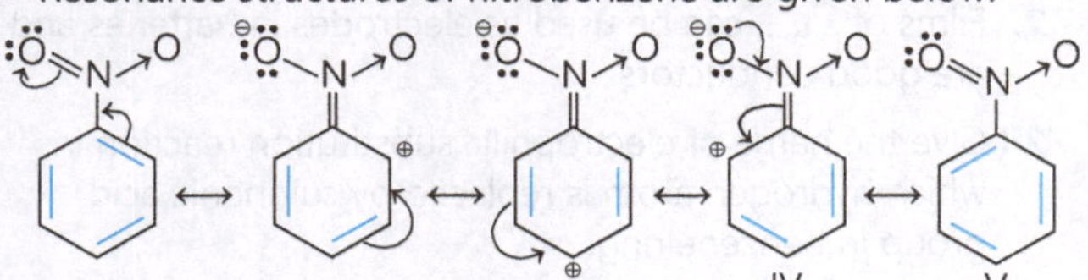

I II III IV V

- The groups, e.g. — NO_2, — CN, — CHO, — CO*R*, — COOH, — COO*R*, — SO_3H etc., are called *meta*-directing as well as deactivating groups.
- They reduce the electron density in the benzene ring due to its strong –*I* -effect.

Carcinogenicity and Toxicity

- Benzene and polynuclear hydrocarbons containing more than two benzene rings fused together are toxic and said to possess cancer producing (carcinogenic) property.
- Such polynuclear hydrocarbons are formed on incomplete combustion of organic materials like tobacco, coal and petroleum.
- They enter into human body and damage DNA.

Caution Points

- Rate of substitution of various hydrogen follows the sequence 3° > 2° > 1° and their relative rates varies with the nature of halogen.
- The structure of cyclohexane in which two or more bulkier groups occupy equatorial position is more stable, then the one in which these occupy axial position.
- If two groups (EWG/EDG) are present, the strongly activating groups generally win over the deactivating or weakly activating group.
- In all the conformations the bond angles and the bond length remains the same.

PYQ Notes

1. Alkyne undergoes hydrogenation reaction to give *cis*-alkene in presence of Lindlar's catalyst. **NEET 2022**
2. Every single bond has one σ-bond and every double bond has one σ, one π-bond and every triple bond has one σ, two π-bonds. **NEET 2015, 2019**
3. The enthalpy of hydrogenation of hydrocarbon is inversely proportional to stability of alkene. **NEET 2015**
4. Ethyne (H—C ≡ C—H) has same hybridisation as its combustion product CO_2. **NEET 2014**

Step by Step

Mastering NCERT

- Concept Builders
- Topical Questions
- Assertion-Reason
- Statement Type
- Matching Type
- Numerical Value
- NCERT Exemplar's
- Past Exams'
- Skill Boosters

Concept Builders

1 Coal gas is obtained by the destructive .... (liquification/distillation) of coal.

2 Hydrocarbons which are inert under normal condition and react with acids, bases and other reagents are known as ....

3 2-Methyl pentane and 3-methyl pentane are stereo isomers of *n*-hexane. [T/F]

4 Write the IUPAC name of the following structure

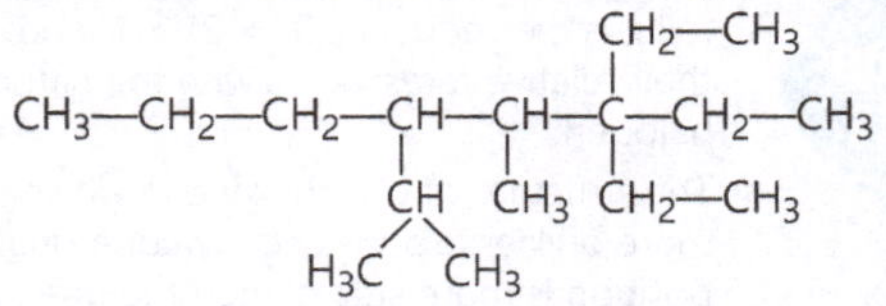

5 Complete the analogy with respect to structural formula and IUPAC names. $(CH_3)_3CCH_2C(CH_3)_3$: 2,2,4,4-tetra methyl pentane :: $(CH_3)_2C(C_2H_5)_2$: ?

6 Find X in the given reaction is,

$$\text{Propyne} + 2H_2 \xrightarrow{\text{Pt/Pd/Ni}} X$$

7 Write the name of the reaction used in the preparation of higher alkanes from alkyl halide.

8 Methane can be prepared using Kolbe's electrolytic reaction. [T/F]

9 Write the name of the following reaction.

$$CH_3COONa + NaOH \xrightarrow[\Delta]{CaO} CH_4 + Na_2CO_3$$

10 Pentane has boiling point more than 2-methyl propane because there is weak intermolecular force between spherical molecules. [T/F]

11 The compound that will react most readily with gaseous bromine has the formula .... (C_3H_6/C_4H_{10}).

12 Write an oxidising agent involved in iodination of alkanes.

13 .... is formed during incomplete combustion of alkanes with insufficient amount of air.

14 The repulsive interaction between adjacent bond in C—C single bond is called torsional strain. [True/False]

15 The intermediate conformation between eclipsed and staggered is known as .... conformation.

16 The energy difference between eclipsed and staggered form is of the order of 12.5 kJ/mol. [T/F]

17 Geometrical isomers have .... (different/same) melting point, boiling point, solubility etc.

18 Write the another name of partially deactivated palladised charcoal.

19 Dehydrohalogenation of alkyl halides to form alkenes in presence of alcoholic potash is an example of ....

20 Write the intermediate formed when alkane reacts with HBr.

21 Propene reacts with HBr to give 2-bromopropane as a major product because carbocation (2°) formed in intermediate is more stable. [T/F]

22 The reagent used to convert alkenes into diols is ....

23 Acetylene is used for arc-welding purpose in the form of oxyacetylene flame. [T/F]

24 Vicinal-dihalides reacts with alc. KOH followed by treatment with sodamide will give alkyne as a final product. [T/F]

25 Write the name of the reagent used to distinguish between alkanes, alkenes and alkynes.

26 Addition of reagent on alkynes are general examples of electrophilic substitution reaction. [T/F]

27 Films of .... can be used as electrodes in batteries and are good conductors.

28 Give the name of electrophilic substitution reaction in which hydrogen atom is replaced by sulphonic acid group in benzene ring.

29 When benzene is treated with excess of chloride in presence of anhyd. $AlCl_3$ in dark, it will yield .... (chlorobenzene/hexachlorobenzene)

30 The arenium ion formed in electrophilic substitution reaction is stabilised by .... (resonance/hyperconjugation).

Topical Questions

Classification

1 Which of the following hydrocarbons is not a saturated hydrocarbon? **NCERT Pg 296**

(a) Butane (b) Cyclohexane
(c) Acetylene (d) Heptane

2 The compounds which have carbon-carbon multiple bonds - double bonds, triple bonds or both are called as **NCERT Pg 296**

(a) saturated hydrocarbons
(b) unsaturated hydrocarbons
(c) aromatic hydrocarbons
(d) assymetric hydrocarbons

Alkanes

3 The given structures, **NCERT Pg 297**

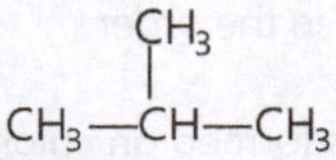 and $CH_3CH_2CH_2CH_3$ are

(a) conformational isomers
(b) chain isomers
(c) position isomers
(d) functional isomers

4 In how many ways you can join five C-atoms and twelve H-atoms of C_5H_{12}? **NCERT Pg 297**

(a) One (b) Two (c) Three (d) Four

5 The IUPAC name of the following compound is

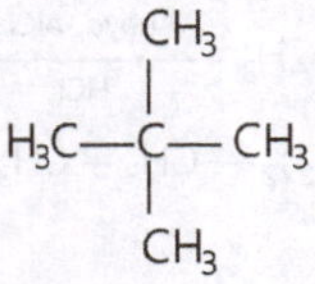

NCERT Pg 297

(a) 1-methyl isobutane
(b) 2, 2-dimethylbutane
(c) 2, 2-dimethylpropane
(d) 2-methyl isobutane

6 The number of possible structural isomers for C_6H_{14} are **NCERT Pg 298**

(a) 4 (b) 9
(c) 22 (d) 5

7 Addition of dihydrogen gas to alkenes and alkynes in the presence of finely divided catalysts like Ni, Pt, Pd is called **NCERT Pg 300**

(a) dehydrogenation (b) catenation
(c) carbonation (d) hydrogenation

8 Which of the following compounds will react with sodium to form 4,5 diethyloctane ? **NCERT Pg 301**

(a) Bromobutane
(b) 1-bromo-3-methyl hexane
(c) 2-bromo hexane
(d) 3-bromo hexane

9 Which of the following alkane will be formed in high yield by Wurtz reaction? **NCERT Pg 301**

(a) 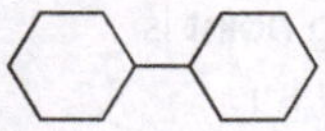 (b) 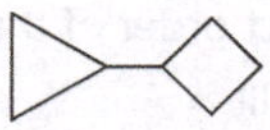

(c) 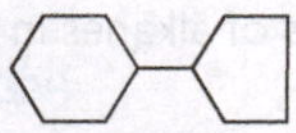 (d) 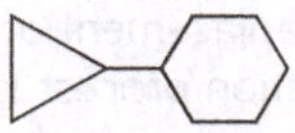

10 Which of the following statements are correct regarding Kolbe's electrolytic process? **NCERT Pg 301**

I. Alkanes containing even number of C-atoms are prepared.
II. Sodium or potassium salts of carboxylic acids are taken as substrate.
III. Methane can be prepared by this method.
IV. H_2 gas is liberated at anode.

Choose the correct answer from the options given below.

(a) I and II (b) II and III
(c) I and III (d) I, III and IV

11 In the given reaction,

(i) Bromomethane $\xrightarrow{\text{Na, ether}} A \xrightarrow[h\nu]{Br_2} B \xrightarrow{\text{Na, ether}} C$

(ii) Acetic acid $\xrightarrow{\text{NaOH}} A \xrightarrow[\text{CaO}]{\text{NaOH}} B \xrightarrow[h\nu]{Br_2} C$

Identify *A*, *B* and *C*

	A	*B*	*C*
(a)	(i) Methane	Methyl bromide	Ethane
	(ii) Sodium acetate	Ethane	Ethyl bromide
(b)	(i) Ethane	Methane	Methyl bromide
	(ii) Sodium actetate	Methane	Propane
(c)	(i) Ethyl bromide	Ethane	Propane
	(ii) Sodium acetate	Methane	Methyl bromide
(d)	(i) Ethane	Ethyl bromide	Butane
	(ii) Sodium acetate	Methane	Methyl bromide

12 Based on branching, isomers of hexane are divided into three distinct classes as shown below: **NCERT Pg 302**

I. 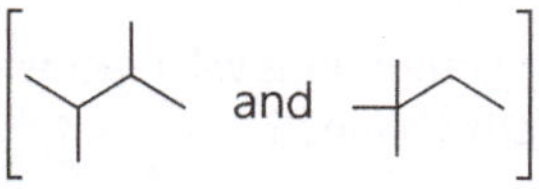

II. 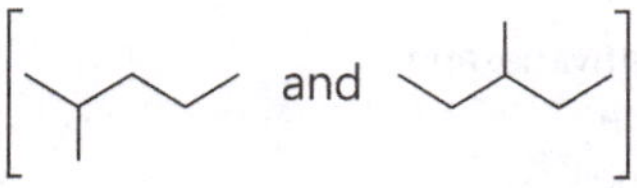

III. 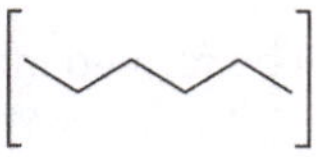

The correct order of their boiling point is

(a) I > II > III (b) III > II > I

(c) II > III > I (d) III > I > II

13 Rate of replacement of hydrogens of alkanes in halogenation process is **NCERT Pg 303**

(a) $1° > 2° > 3°$ (b) $1° > 3° > 2°$

(c) $2° > 1° > 3°$ (d) $3° > 2° > 1°$

14 Iodination of alkanes is always carried out in the presence of some oxidising agents like HIO_3. This is because **NCERT Pg 303**

(a) it is a very fast process

(b) it is a reversible reaction

(c) I—I bond is very weak

(d) it is a irreversible reaction

15 The reactants involved in general combustion equation for any alkane is represented as **NCERT Pg 303**

(a) $C_nH_{2n+2} + \left(\frac{3n+2}{2}\right)O_2$

(b) $C_nH_{2n} + \left(\frac{3n-1}{2}\right)O_2$

(c) $C_nH_{2n} + \left(\frac{3n+2}{2}\right)O_2$

(d) $C_nH_{2n+2} + \left(\frac{3n+1}{2}\right)O_2$

16 Which of the following is the correct order for heat of combustion?

(i) $CH_3—CH_2—CH_2—CH_2—CH_3$

(ii) $CH_3—CH(CH_3)—CH_2—CH_2—CH_3$

(iii) $CH_3—CH_2—CH_2—CH_3$ **NCERT Pg 303**

Choose the correct answer from the options given below.

(a) (i) > (ii) > (iii)

(b) (ii) > (i) > (iii)

(c) (iii) > (i) > (ii)

(d) (ii) > (iii) > (i)

17 Arrange the correct sequence for mechanism of chlorination of methane. **NCERT Pg 303**

I. $CH_4 + Cl^\bullet \xrightarrow{h\nu} \dot{C}H_3 + H—Cl$

II. $Cl—Cl \xrightarrow{h\nu} 2\dot{Cl}$

III. $\dot{C}H_3 + Cl_2 \longrightarrow CH_3—Cl + Cl^\bullet$

IV. $\dot{Cl} + \dot{Cl} \longrightarrow Cl—Cl$

$\dot{C}H_3 + \dot{C}H_3 \longrightarrow CH_3—CH_3$

Choose the correct answer from the options given below.

(a) II, I, III and IV (b) I, II, III and IV

(c) IV, III, II and I (d) II, III, I and IV

18 Which of the following statements is not correct regarding halogenation of alkanes? **NCERT Pg 303**

(a) Br is less reactive than Cl towards a particular alkane.

(b) For a given halogen, the reactivity of hydrocarbon is in the order of $3° > 2° > 1°$.

(c) The reactivity of halogens is in the order $F_2 > Cl_2 > Br_2 > I_2$

(d) Monosubstituted product is formed on chlorination while disulistuted products are formed on iodination.

19 In presence of *X*, ordinary alkanes resist oxidation but alkanes having tertiary H-atom can be easily oxidised to alcohols. Identify '*X*'. **NCERT Pg 304**

(a) Cu/523 K (b) Mo_2O_3

(c) $KMnO_4$ (d) $(CH_3COO)_2Mn$

20 Choose the correct option regarding product (*A* and *B*) of the given reaction. **NCERT Pg 304**

$$\underset{n\text{-hexane}}{CH_3(CH_2)_4CH_3} \xrightarrow[\text{HCl}]{\text{Anhyd. AlCl}_3} A + B$$

(a) $CH_3—CH(CH_3)—(CH_2)_2—CH_3 + CH_3CH_2—CH(CH_3)—CH_2CH_3$

(b) $CH_3CH_2—CH(CH_3)—CH_2CH_3 + CH_3CH_2CH_2CH_3$

(c) $CH_3CH_2CH_2CH_3 + CH_3—CH(CH_3)—CH_3$

(d) $H_3C—CH_2—CH_2—CH_2—CH{=}CH_2 + CH_3—CH_2—CH{=}CH_2$

21 Name the process in which *n*-hexane on heating to 773 K at 10-20 atm pressure in the presence of oxides of vanadium, molybdenum or chromium supported by alumina produces benzene. **NCERT Pg 304**

(a) Pyrolysis (b) Reduction

(c) Aromatisation (d) Oxidation

22 The product(s) obtained in the following reaction is/are

$$C_{12}H_{26} \xrightarrow[973\text{ K}]{Pt/Pd/Ni}$$

NCERT Pg 304

(a) C_7H_{16} (b) C_6H_{10}
(c) C_5H_{12} (d) C_7H_{18}

23 Liquid hydrocarbons can be converted to a mixture of gaseous hydrocarbons by using the process NCERT Pg 304

(a) hydrolysis
(b) oxidation
(c) cracking
(d) distillation under reduced pressure

24 Chlorination of methane does not occur in dark because NCERT Pg 304

(a) substitution reaction can take place only in sunlight and not in dark.
(b) propagation step can not take place in dark. It requires sunlight.
(c) methane can form free radicals in presence of sunlight only.
(d) to get chlorine free radicals form Cl_2 molecules energy is required.

25 Which of the following hydrocarbon will be formed when dodecane is heated to 973 K in presence of palladium? NCERT Pg 304

(a) Propane + Hexane
(b) Heptane + Pentene + Other products
(c) Heptane + Pentane
(d) Hexane + Propene + Other products

26 Complete the following reactions. NCERT Pg 303, 304

(i) $CH_4 + O_2 \xrightarrow[\Delta]{Mo_2O_3} X$

(ii) $CH_3—CH_3 + Cl_2 \xrightarrow{hv} Y$

(iii) $CH_4 + H_2O \xrightarrow[\Delta]{Ni} Z$

(a) $X = HCHO, Y = CH_3CH_2Cl, Z = CO$
(b) $X = HCOOH, Y = CH_3CH_2Cl, Z = H_2$
(c) $X = HCHO, Y = C_2H_6Cl, Z = HCHO$
(d) $X = C_2H_6, Y = CH_4, Z = CO$

27 The possible rotamers of ethane are NCERT Pg 305

(a) 0 (b) 3 (c) 4 (d) ∞

28 The repulsive interaction between the electron clouds, which affects stability of a conformation is termed as NCERT Pg 305

(a) torsional strain
(b) dihedral angle
(c) torsional angle
(d) conformation

29 In the Newman projection for $CH_3—\underset{CH_3}{\overset{CH_3}{\underset{|}{\overset{|}{C}}}}—CH_2CH_3$:

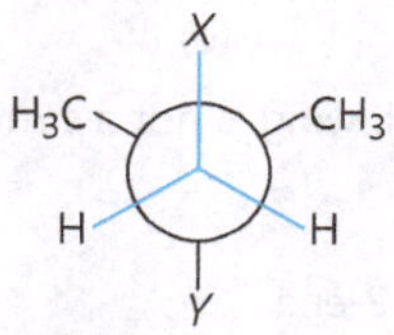

X and Y can respectively be NCERT Pg 305

(a) CH_3 and H (b) CH_3 and CH_3
(c) C_2H_5 and C_2H_5 (d) CH_3 and C_2H_5

30 Which of the following statement(s) is/are correct regarding rotation around internuclear axis of C—C bond?

I. Rotation produces rotamers. NCERT Pg 305
II. Magnitude of torsional strain depends upon the angle of rotation about C—C bond.
III. Repulsive interaction between adjacent bond is termed as torsional strain.
IV. Ethane has only four conformational isomers.

Choose the correct answer from the options given below.

(a) I and II (b) I, II and III
(c) I, III and IV (d) III and IV

31 Which of the following statement is incorrect regarding relative stability of conformations of ethane? NCERT Pg 306

I. There is minimum repulsive force and maximum stability of molecule in the case of staggered form.
II. There is maximum repulsive force and minimum stability of molecule in case of eclipsed form.
III. Due to repulsive force, eclipsed form posseses more energy as compared to staggered form.
IV. Energy of staggered molecule is higher than that of eclipsed form.
V. The staggered form changes into the eclipsed form, the electron clouds of the C—H bonds come closer to each other.

Choose the correct answer from the options given below.

(a) I and V (b) I and II
(c) Only III (d) Only IV

Alkenes

32 The IUPAC name of $CH_2{=}\underset{CH_3}{\underset{|}{C}}—CH_3$ is NCERT Pg 307

(a) 2-methylbutene (b) 1-methylpropene
(c) 2-methylbut-2-ene (d) 2-methylprop-1-ene

33 The number of σ-bonds and π-bonds present in 1,3,5,7 octatetraene **NCERT Pg 307**

	σ-bond	π-bond		σ-bond	π-bond
(a)	17	4	(b)	14	3
(c)	18	4	(d)	15	3

34 Which of the following is not a structural isomer of C_5H_{10}? **NCERT Pg 308**

(a) Pent-1-ene
(b) 2-methylbut-2-ene
(c) 2-methylbut-1-ene
(d) 2,3-dimethylpropene

35 How many species among the following shows geometrical isomerism? **NCERT Pg 308**

(i) But-2-ene (ii) 2-methyl but-2-ene
(iii) 1, 2-dichloroethene (iv) 1-phenyl propene
(v) 3, 4-dimethylhex-3-ene (vi) 2-methyl propene
(a) 2 (b) 3 (c) 4 (d) 5

36 Consider the following reaction,

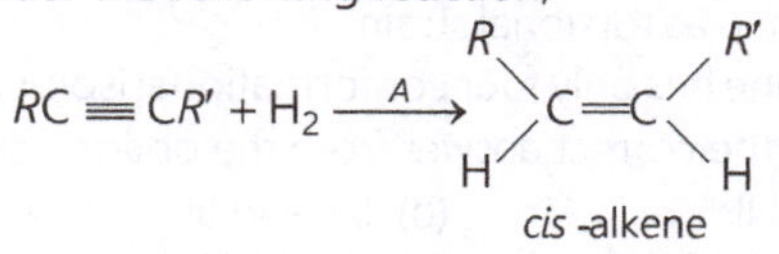

What does A refers to? **NCERT Pg 309**

(a) $Na/liq.\ NH_3$ (b) Pd / C
(c) Alc. KOH (d) Conc. H_2SO_4

37 The *trans*-alkenes are formed by the reduction of alkynes with **NCERT Pg 309**

(a) H_2-Pd/C, $BaSO_4$ (b) $NaBH_4$
(c) Na/liq. NH_3 (d) Sn-HCl

38 Consider the given reactions : **NCERT Pg 309**

(i) $CH_3C{\equiv}C\ C_2H_5 + H_2 \xrightarrow[H_2]{Pd/C} A$

(ii) $CH_3C{\equiv}C\ C_2H_5 + H_2 \xrightarrow[NH_3]{Na/liq.} B$

B and A respectively are
(a) *cis* and *trans*-alkene (b) *trans* and *cis*-alkene
(c) alkane and alkene (d) alkene and alkane

39 Which of the statement is correct regarding the following structures? **NCERT Pg 309**

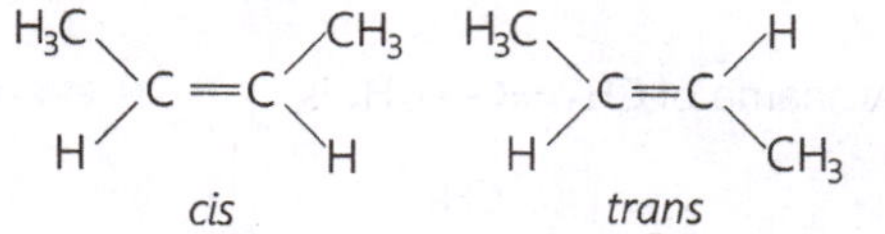

cis *A* *trans* *B*

(a) A and B are stereoisomers of each other.
(b) A and B are not a conformational isomers.
(c) B has more boiling point than A.
(d) A is more stable than B.

40 In the following reaction,

$CH_3{-}CH_2{-}CH_2Br \xrightarrow[\Delta]{Alc.\ KOH} A$, A is **NCERT Pg 310**

(a) $CH_2{=}CH{-}CH_3$ (b) $CH_3CH_2{-}CH_3$
(c) $CH{\equiv}C{-}CH_3$ (d) $H_2C(OH){-}C{\equiv}CH$

41 The product (X) obtained in the following reaction is

$CH_3CHBr{-}CH_2Br + Zn \longrightarrow$ 'X' **NCERT Pg 310**

(a) $CH_3CH_2{-}CH_2Br$ (b) $CH_3CH(Br){-}CH_3$
(c) $CH_3CH{=}CH_2$ (d) $CH_3{-}CH_2{-}CH_3$

42 In the acidic dehydration of alcohols, (ethanol) are heated with conc. H_2SO_4 with the elimination of one water molecule. It gives the product 'A'. What is the another name of the reaction and the product 'A' respectively are ? **NCERT Pg 310**

(a) γ-elimination and ethene (b) γ-elimination and butene
(c) β-elimination and butene (d) β-elimination and ethene

43 The major product formed when 3,3-dimethyl butan-2-ol is heated with concentrated sulphuric acid is **NCERT Pg 310**

(a) 2,3-dimethylbut-1-ene
(b) 2,3-dimethylbut-2-ene
(c) 3,3-dimethylbut-1-ene
(d) *cis* and *trans*-isomers of 2,3-dimethylbut-1-ene

44 Ethene reacts with one mole of bromine in the presence of CCl_4, to give **NCERT Pg 311**

(a) 1,1-dibromoethane (b) 2,2-dibromoethane
(c) 2,2-dibromobutane (d) 1,2-dibromoethane

45 The correct order of reactivity of the hydrogen halides with alkenes is **NCERT Pg 311**

(a) HI > HBr > HCl (b) HCl > HBr > HI
(c) HI > HCl > HBr (d) HBr > HCl > HI

46 What will be the product of the following reaction?

$CH_3{-}CH{=}CH_2 + HBr \xrightarrow{(C_6H_5CO)_2O_2}$ Product **NCERT Pg 312**

(a) $CH_3CH_2CH_2Br$ (b) $CH_3CH(Br)CH_3$
(c) $CH_3CBr_2CH_3$ (d) $CH_3{-}C(H){=}CH_2$

47 Addition of water in presence of conc. H_2SO_4 (few drops) to 2-methyl propene produces alcohols in accordance with **NCERT Pg 312**

(a) Anti-Markovnikov's addition
(b) Markovnikov's rule
(c) Saytzeff's rule
(d) Hofmann rule

48 Which of the following reactions does not show the correct product of the reaction? **NCERT Pg 311, 312**

(a) $CH_3-CH_2-CH=CH_2 \xrightarrow[\text{Peroxide}]{HCl} CH_3-CH_2-CH_2-CH_2-Cl$

(b) $CH_3-CH=CH_2 \xrightarrow{HBr} CH_3-CH(Br)-CH_2Br$

(c) $CH_3-CH=CH_2 \xrightarrow{HCl} CH_3-CH(Cl)-CH_2Cl$

(d) $CH_3-CH_2-CH=CH_2 \xrightarrow[\text{Peroxide}]{HBr} CH_3-CH_2-CH_2-CH_2-Br$

49 But-2-ene on reaction with alkaline $KMnO_4$ at elevated temperature followed by acidification will give **NCERT Pg 313**

(a) $CH_3-CH(OH)-CH(OH)-CH_3$

(b) one molecule of CH_3CHO and one molecule of CH_3COOH

(c) 2 molecules of CH_3COOH

(d) 2 molecules of CH_3CHO

50 Addition of cold conc. H_2SO_4 to alkenes is an example of **NCERT Pg 313**

(a) electrophilic substitution reaction

(b) nucleophilic substitution reaction

(c) electrophilic addition reaction

(d) nucleophilic addition reaction

51 Consider the following reaction,

$$CH_3CH=CH_2 + HOSO_2OH \longrightarrow$$

The product obtained is **NCERT Pg 313**

(a) $CH_3-CH(OSO_2H)-CH_3$ (b) $CH_3-CH_2-CH_2(OSO_2H)$

(c) $CH_3-CH(OSO_3H)-CH_3$ (d) $CH_3-CH_2-CH_2(OSO_3H)$

52 Consider the following reaction. **NCERT Pg 313**

$$CH_3-C(CH_3)_2-CH=CH_2 \xrightarrow{H_2O/H^+} \underset{\text{Major product}}{A} + \underset{\text{Minor product}}{B}$$

The major product A is

(a) $CH_3-C(CH_3)(OH)-CH(CH_3)-CH_3$ (b) $CH_2(OH)-C(CH_3)_2-CH_2-CH_3$

(c) $CH_3-CH(CH_3)-C(CH_3)(OH)-CH_3$ (d) $CH_3-C(CH_3)_2-CH_2-CH_2(OH)$

53 Choose the correct option regarding A and B.

(i) $CH_2=CH_2 + H_2O + [O] \xrightarrow[273\ K]{\text{Dil. } KMnO_4} A$

(ii) $CH_3-CH=CH_2 + H_2O + [O] \xrightarrow[273\ K]{\text{Dil. } KMnO_4} B$

NCERT Pg 313

	A	B
(a)	$CH_2(OH)-CH_3$	$CH_3CH_2CH_2OH$
(b)	CH_3CH_2OH	$CH_3CHOHCH_3$
(c)	$CH_3CH(OH)CH_3$	$CH_3CH(OH)CH_2OH$
(d)	$CH_2(OH)CH_2(OH)$	$CH_3CH(OH)CH_2OH$

54 Consider the reaction given below. **NCERT Pg 313**

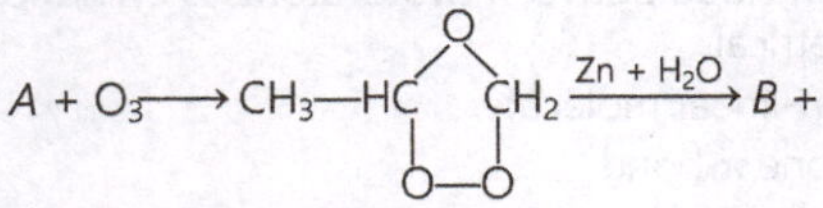

Here, A and B respectively are

(a) propene and methanal

(b) propane and ethanal

(c) propene and ethanol

(d) propene and ethanal

55 Which of the following alkenes on ozonolysis gives a mixture of ketones only? **NCERT Pg 313**

(a) $CH_3-CH=CH-CH_3$ (b)

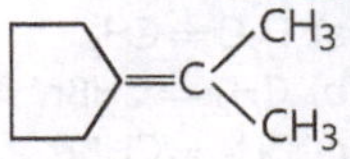

(c) $CH_3-CH(CH_3)-CH=CH_2$ (d) $CH_3-C(H)=C(CH_3)-CH_3$

56 Which compound would give 5-keto-2-methyl hexanal upon ozonolysis? **NCERT Pg 313**

(a)

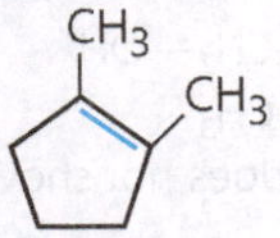

(b)

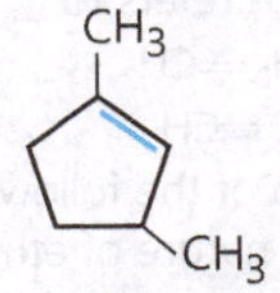

(c)

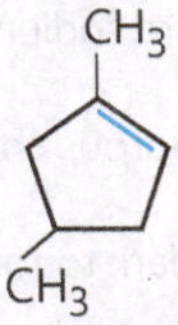

(d)

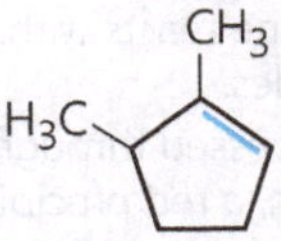

Alkynes

57 The correct IUPAC name of the given structure $H_3C-CH(CH_3)-C\equiv CH$ is **NCERT Pg 314**

(a) 2-methylbut-1-yne (b) 1-methylbut-3-yne

(c) 2-methylbut-3-yne (d) 3-methylbut-1-yne

58 The common name and IUPAC name of $CH_3CH_2—C{\equiv}CH$, are respectively. **NCERT Pg 314**

(a) dimethylacetylene and but-2-yne
(b) ethylacetylene and but-1-yne
(c) acetylene and but-2-yne
(d) methylacetylene and but-2-yne

59 How many isomers are possible for C_6H_{10}? **NCERT Pg 314**

(a) 7 (b) 6
(c) 4 (d) 5

60 Which of the following statement is correct for ethyne molecule? **NCERT Pg 315**

(a) Electron cloud between two C-atoms is cylindrically symmetrical.
(b) It a non-linear molecule.
(c) It has one π-bond.
(d) Ethyne molecule consists of two C—C σ-bonds.

61 What are A and B in following reaction? **NCERT Pg 316**

$$H_2C(Br)—C(Br)(H)—H + KOH \xrightarrow{\text{Alcohol}} A \xrightarrow{NaNH_2} B$$

	A	B
(a)	$H_2C{=}CH_2$	$CH{\equiv}CH$
(b)	$CH_2{=}CHBr$	$CH{\equiv}CH$
(c)	$CH_2{=}CHBr$	$CH_2{=}CH_2$
(d)	$CH_2{=}CH_2$	$CH{\equiv}CBr$

62 Consider the following reaction,

$$\begin{array}{l} CH_2X \\ | \\ CH_2X \end{array} \xrightarrow{\text{Alc. 2KOH}} A$$

Here, A refers to **NCERT Pg 316**

(a) $CH_2{=}CH_2$ (b) $CH_3—CH_2—OH$
(c) $HC{\equiv}CH$ (d) $CH_3—CH_3$

63 Which of the following reactions does not show the acidic nature of ethyne? **NCERT Pg 316**

(a) Acetylene reacts with sodamide to form sodium acetylides.
(b) When passed through ammoniacal cuprous chloride solution, a red precipitate is formed.
(c) Acetylene reacts with chlorine in the dark to form di or tetrachlorides.
(d) Acetylene when passed through ammoniacal silver nitrate gives a white precipitate.

64 Which of the following alkynes is least acidic? **NCERT Pg 316**

(a) $CH_3C{\equiv}CH$
(b) $CH_3C{\equiv}CCH_3$
(c) $CH_3CH_2C{\equiv}CH$
(d) $CH{\equiv}CH$

65 Consider the following reaction,

(i) $CaCO_3 \xrightarrow{\Delta} A + CO_2$
(ii) $A + \text{Carbon} \longrightarrow CaC_2 + CO$

Here, A refers to **NCERT Pg 315, 316**

(a) $Ca(CO)_2$ (b) Ca_2O (c) CaO (d) $Ca(OH)_2$

66 $A \xleftarrow[\text{(ii) } H_2]{\text{(i) Pt/Pd/Ni}} R—C{\equiv}CH \xrightarrow{NaNH_2} B$

Here, A and B refers to **NCERT Pg 317**

(a) $R—CH{=}CH_2$ and $R—C{\equiv}C—NH_2$
(b) $R—CH{=}CH_2$ and $R—C{\equiv}C^-Na^+$
(c) $H—C{\equiv}C—H$ and $R—C{\equiv}C^-Na^+$
(d) $R—C{\equiv}C^-Na^+$ and $R—CH{=}CH_2$

67 $CH_3—C{\equiv}CH + Br—Br \longrightarrow A.$

Here, A refers to **NCERT Pg 317**

(a) $BrCH_2—CH{=}CHBr$
(b) $CH_3—CH{=}CBr_2$
(c) $Br—CH_2—CBr{=}CH_2$
(d) $CH_3—CBr{=}CHBr$

68 When $CH_3—C{\equiv}CH$ reacts with one mole of HBr then product obtained is **NCERT Pg 317**

(a) bromoethene (b) dibromopropane
(c) 2-bromopropene (d) 1-bromopropane

69 Which of the following molecules on passing through red hot iron tube at 873 K undergoes cyclic polymerisation to form benzene? **NCERT Pg 318**

(a) Ethene (b) Methane
(c) Acetylene (d) But-1-ene

Aromatic Hydrocarbons

70 Which of the following statement is correct? **NCERT Pg 318**

(a) Aromatic hydrocarbons are polar molecules.
(b) Aromatic hydrocarbons are coloured liquids.
(c) Aromatic hydrocarbons are immiscible with water.
(d) Aromatic hydrocarbons are immiscible with organic solvents.

71 The common name and IUPAC name of

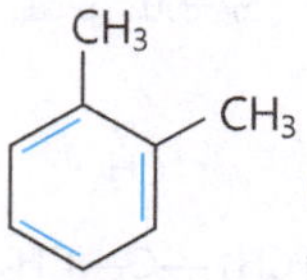

respectively are **NCERT Pg 318**

(a) *o*-xylene and toluene
(b) *o*-xylene and 1,2-dimethylbenzene
(c) *o*-xylene and 1,2-dimethyltoluene
(d) *p*-xylene and 1,2-dimethylbenzene

72 Which reaction confirms the presence of three double bonds in benzene? **NCERT Pg 319**
(a) Oxidation reaction (b) Hydrolysis reaction
(c) Ozonolysis reaction (d) Addition reaction

73 Which one of these is incorrect for benzene? **NCERT Pg 319**
(a) It forms only one type of monosubstituted product.
(b) There are three C—C single bonds and three C—C double bonds.
(c) The heat of hydrogenation of benzene is less than the theoretical value.
(d) The bond angle between the C—C bond is 120°.

74 How many isomers of 1,2-dibromobenzene are possible according to Kekule? **NCERT Pg 319**
(a) 1 (b) 2 (c) 3 (d) 4

75 Which of the following statements are correct regarding structure of benzene? **NCERT Pg 319**
I. All the six carbons in benzene are sp^2-hybridised.
II. sp^2-hybridised orbital of carbon combines with another sp^2-hybridised orbital of carbon to give C—C sigma bonds.
III. C—H σ-bond is obtained by lateral overlapping of sp^2-hybridised orbital of C and 1 *s*-orbital of H-atom.
Choose the correct answer from the options given below.
(a) I, II and III (b) I and II
(c) I and III (d) II and III

76 Which of the following is aromatic? **NCERT Pg 321**
(a)  (b) 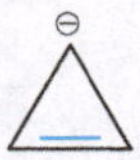 (c) 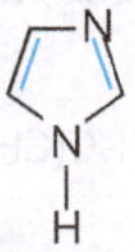 (d) 

77 Which of the following compounds is not aromatic? **NCERT Pg 321**
(a) 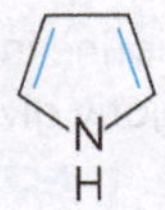 (b)  (c)  (d) 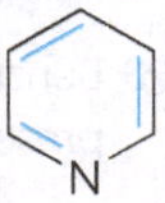

78 Four structures are given in options (a) to (d). Examine them and select the one that is not aromatic. **NCERT Pg 321**
(a)  (b) 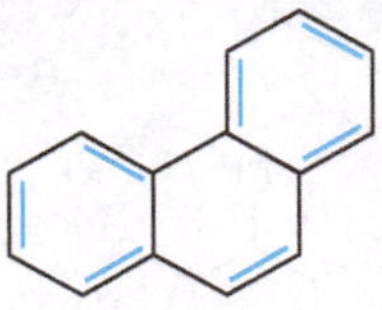
(c)  (d) 

79 Consider the following reaction,

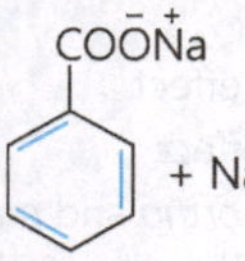 + NaOH $\xrightarrow[\Delta]{CaO}$ A + Na_2CO_3, A is **NCERT Pg 321**

(a) C_6H_6 (b) C_6H_5 — Na
(c) C_6H_5 — ONa (d) C_5H_5 — Na

80 X-ray diffraction study of benzene reveals that **NCERT Pg 321**
I. it is a planar molecule.
II. C—C bond lengths are of the same order which is intermediate between C—C single bond and C—C double bond.
III. benzene is reluctant towards the addition reaction under normal conditions.
IV. it can not explains the unusual behaviour of benzene.
V. Wurtz reaction is used for the preparation of benzene.
Which of the above statements are not true?
(a) II and III (b) Only III
(c) III and IV (d) IV and V

81 For an electrophilic substitution reaction, the presence of a halogen atom in the benzene ring **NCERT Pg 322**
(a) deactivates the ring by inductive effect
(b) deactivates the ring by resonance
(c) decrease the charge density at *ortho*-position relative to *para*-position by resonance
(d) directs the incoming electrophile to *meta*-position by increasing the charge density relative to *ortho* and *para* -position

82 Which one of the following is most reactive towards electrophilic reagent? **NCERT Pg 322**
(a) 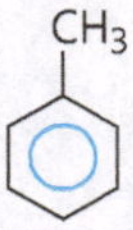 (b) 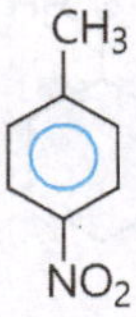 (c) 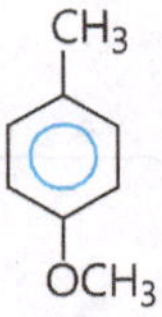 (d) 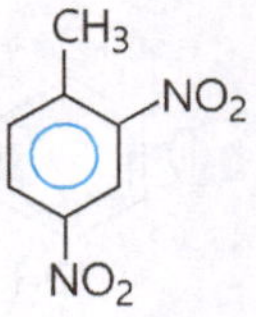

83 Consider the reaction given below. **NCERT Pg 322**

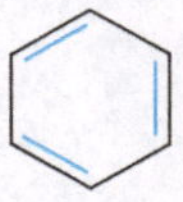 + Conc. HNO_3 + Conc. H_2SO_4 $\xrightarrow{(323–333)\text{ K}}$ A + H_2O,

Here, A refers to
(a) 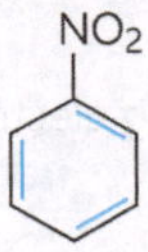 (b) 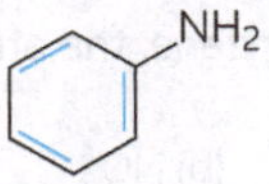 (c) 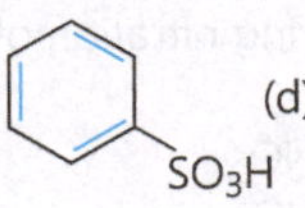 (d) 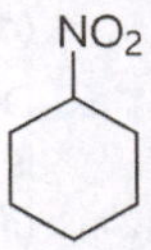

84 In an electrophilic substitution reaction of nitrobenzene, the presence of nitro group **NCERT Pg 322**

(a) activates the ring by resonance effect
(b) activates the ring by inductive effect
(c) decreases the charge density at *ortho* and *para*-position of the ring relative to *meta* -position by mesomeric
(d) increases the charge density at *meta*-position relative to the *ortho* and *para* -positions of the ring by mesomeric

85 Consider the reaction given below. **NCERT Pg 322**

$+ RX \xrightarrow{\text{anhyd. } AlCl_3} A + HCl$, Here, *A* is

(a) methylbenzene (b) toluene
(c) alkylbenzene (d) ethylbenzene

86 In the following reaction,

$$X \xleftarrow{Cl_2} C_6H_6 \xrightarrow[\Delta]{H_2SO_4 \text{ (Fuming sulphuric acid)}} Y,$$

X and *Y* respectively are **NCERT Pg 322**

(a) C_6H_5Cl and $C_6H_5SO_3H$
(b) C_6H_5Cl and C_6H_5OH
(c) $C_6H_4Cl_2$ and $C_6H_5SO_2$
(d) C_6H_5Cl and C_6H_5CHO

87 Identify *X*, *Y* and *Z* in following reactions. **NCERT Pg 322**

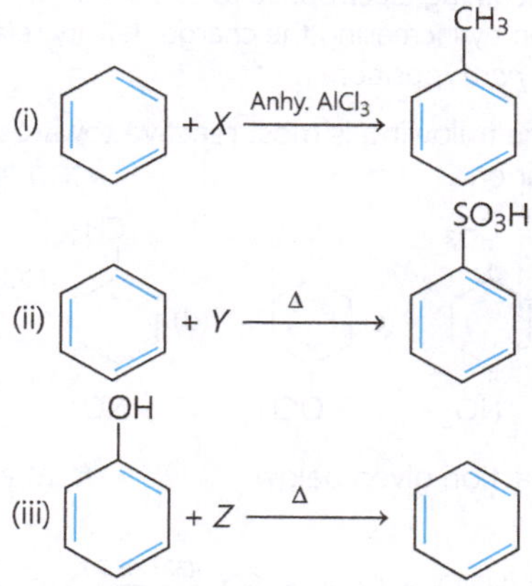

(a) $X = Ni, Y = H_2SO_4, Z = CH_4$
(b) $X = CH_3Cl, Y = H_2SO_4, Z = Zn$
(c) $X = C_2H_5Cl, Y = SO_4, Z = Ni$
(d) $X = H_2SO_4, Y = H_2SO_4, Z = Ni$

88 During nitration of benzene, the attacking electrophile is **NCERT Pg 322**

(a) NO_3^- (b) NO_2^-
(c) NO_2^+ (d) HNO_3

89 Which of the following statement is incorrect regarding nitration of aromatic compounds? **NCERT Pg 322**

I. The rate of nitration of benzene decreases at 323-333 K.
II. The rate of nitration of toluene is greater than that of benzene.
III. The rate of nitration of chlorobenzene is greater than that of benzene.
IV. Nitration is an electrophilic substitution reaction.

Choose the incorrect statement.

(a) I (b) I and III (c) II and IV (d) II and III

90 Consider the following reaction sequence.

$$C_2H_2 \xrightarrow[\text{Fe tube}]{\text{Red hot}} A \xrightarrow[\text{Anhy. } AlCl_3]{CH_3COCl} B \xrightarrow[\text{Conc. HCl}]{\text{Zn-Hg}} C$$

Product *C* is **NCERT Pg 323**

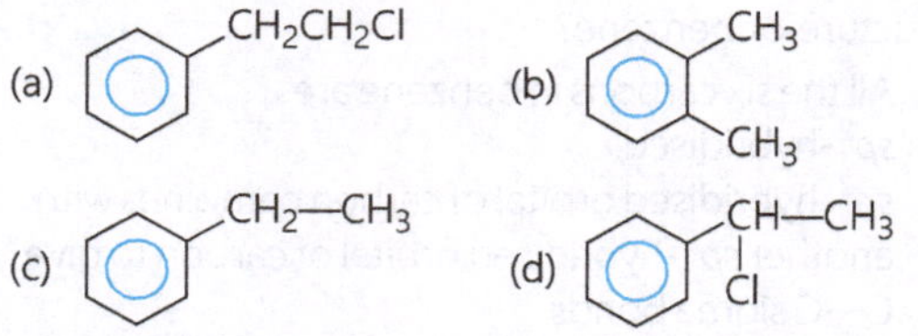

91 Acetophenone ($C_6H_5COCH_3$) is prepared from reaction of benzene (C_6H_6) with *A* in the presence of anhyd. $AlCl_3$. Here, *A* refers to **NCERT Pg 323**

(a) CH_3COCH_3 (b) CH_3CHO
(c) CH_3CH_2CHO (d) CH_3COCl

92 *Neo*-pentyl chloride reacts with benzene in the presence of a Lewis acid ($AlCl_3$) to form **NCERT Pg 323**

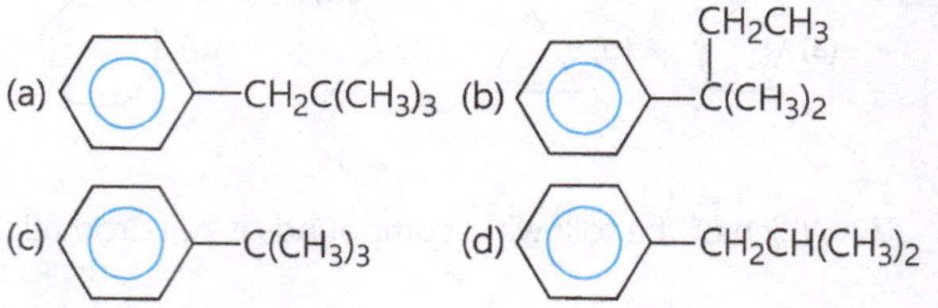

93 Benzene on treatment with excess of chlorine in presence of anhydrous $AlCl_3$ in dark, majorly gives? **NCERT Pg 323**

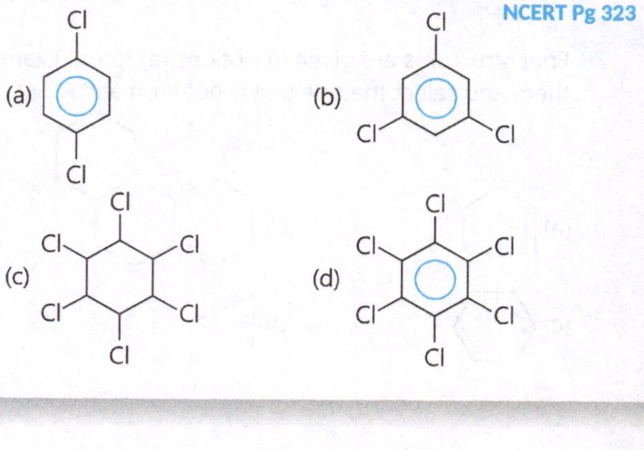

94 The correct order of electrophilic substitution reaction is

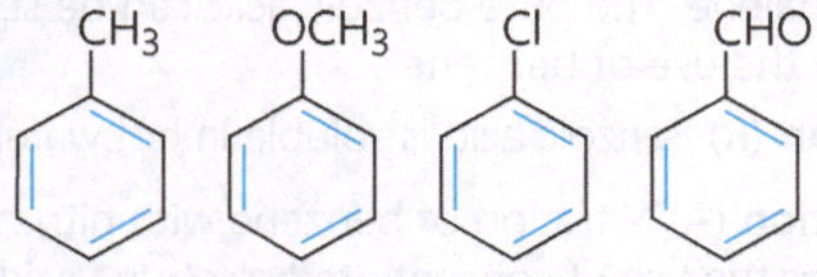

(A) (B) (C) (D)

NCERT Pg 323

(a) $A > B > C > D$ (b) $D > B > A > C$
(c) $B > A > C > D$ (d) $B > A > D > C$

95 Consider the reaction given below. NCERT Pg 324

$$\text{Benzene} + A \xrightarrow{\text{Ni},\ \Delta} \text{Cyclohexane}$$

Here, A is

(a) H_2 (b) $2H_2$ (c) $3H_2$ (d) $4H_2$

96 Polynuclear hydrocarbons are formed by an incomplete process of organic materials. This process is termed as

(a) addition (b) combustion NCERT Pg 324
(c) elimination (d) substitution

97 When benzene is heated in air, it burns with sooty flame producing X and Y, as shown in the given reaction.

$$C_6H_6 + \frac{15}{2}O_2 \longrightarrow X + Y$$

Here, X and Y refer to NCERT Pg 324

(a) C_6H_5—OH, CO
(b) CO_2, H_2O
(c) C_6H_{14}, CO_2
(d) C_6H_5OH, H_2

98 How many species, among the following groups, is/are not an activating group(s)? NCERT Pg 325

(i) —OCH_3 (ii) —NO_2 (iii) —NH_2
(iv) —SO_3H (v) —COOR (vi) —C_2H_5
(vii) —$NHCOCH_3$

(a) 3 (b) 4 (c) 5 (d) 6

99 In nitrobenzene, the X attacks on comparatively electron rich *meta*-position resulting in Y substitution. Here, X and Y refer to NCERT Pg 325

(a) electrophile, *meta* (b) nucleophile, *meta*
(c) deactivating group, *para* (d) activating group, *meta*

Carcinogenicity and Toxicity

100 The correct structure of 1,2,5,6-dibenzanthracene is NCERT Pg 325

(a) 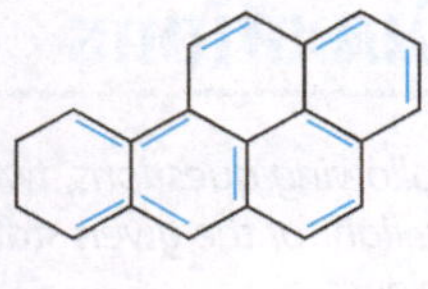 (b) 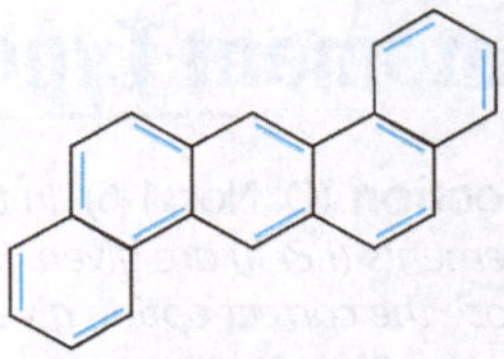

(c) 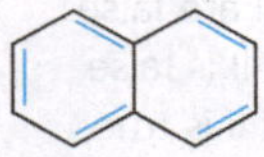 (d) 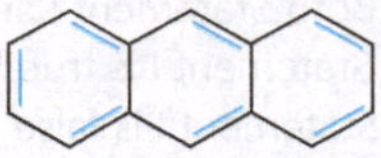

101 Which of the following compound is not a carcinogenic compound? NCERT Pg 325

(a) 1, 2-benzpyrene (b) 3-methyl cholanthrene
(c) 1,2-benzanthracene (d) 3-chloro benzene

Assertion-Reason Questions

Direction (Q.Nos. 1-10) *In the following question Assertion (A) followed by Reason (R) is given below. Choose the correct option out of the choices given below.*

(a) Both A and R are true and R is the correct explanation of A.
(b) Both A and R are true but R is not the correct explanation of A.
(c) A is true but R is false.
(d) A is false but R is true.

1 Assertion (A) Boiling point of alkanes increases with increase in molecular weight. NCERT Pg 302

Reason (R) van der Waal's forces increase with increase in molecular weight.

2 Assertion (A) Among isomeric pentanes, 2, 2-dimethylpentane has highest boiling point. NCERT Pg 302

Reason (R) Branching decreases the boiling point.

3 Assertion (A) 1-butene on reaction with HBr in the presence of a peroxide, produces 1-bromobutane. NCERT Pg 311

Reason (R) It involves the formation of a primary radical.

4 Assertion (A) 1-hexyne is converted to 1-hexene by Lindlar's catalyst. NCERT Pg 317

Reason (R) 1-hexyne is converted to *n*-hexane by the reduction with hydrogen gas in the presence of Pd/Ni.

5 Assertion (A) Toluene on Friedel-Crafts methylation gives *o*-and *p*- xylene. NCERT Pg 318

Reason (R) CH_3 group bonded to benzene ring increases electron density at *o*-and *p*- position.

6 **Assertion** (A) [6] Annulene, [8] Annulene and *cis*-[10] Annulene, are respectively aromatic non-aromatic and aromatic. **NCERT Pg 321**

Reason (R) Planarity is one of the requirements of aromatic systems.

7 **Assertion** (A) The compound cyclooctatetraene has the following structural formula. **NCERT Pg 321**

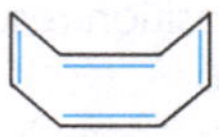

It is cyclic and has conjugated 8π-electron system but it is not an aromatic compound.

Reason (R) $(4n+2)$ π-electron rule does not hold good and ring is not planar.

8 **Assertion** (A) A mixture contains benzoic acid and naphthalene. The pure benzoic acid can be separated out by the use of benzene. **NCERT Pg 322**

Reason (R) Benzoic acid is soluble in hot water.

9 **Assertion** (A) Nitration of benzene with nitric acid requires the use of concentrated sulphuric acid. **NCERT Pg 322**

Reason (R) The mixture of concentrated sulphuric acid and concentrated nitric acid produces the electrophile, NO_2^+.

10 **Assertion** (A) In the electrophilic substitution of aryl halides, the incoming electrophile gets attached to the *meta*-position. **NCERT Pg 323**

Reason (R) Aryl halides are moderately deactivating.

Statement Type Questions

Direction (Q. Nos. 1-6) *In the following questions, two statements (I & II) are given. In the light of the given statements, choose the correct option given below.*

(a) Both Statement I and Statement II are false.
(b) Statement I is true but Statement II is false.
(c) Statement I is false but Statement II is true.
(d) Both Statement I and Statement II are true.

1 **Statement I** Emission of hydrocarbons and carbon monoxide is inherently very low from diesel vehicles. **NCERT Pg 295**

Statement II Diesel driven vehicles are inherently more fuel-efficient compared to petrol driven vehicles.

2 **Statement I** Iodination of methane can be carried out in the presence of HIO_3 or HNO_3^-. **NCERT Pg 296, 303**

Statement II Alkanes are saturated hydrocarbons.

3 **Statement I** Substances that have the same polarity are miscible and can dissolve each other. **NCERT Pg 302**

Statement II Hydrocarbons will dissolve in water.

4 **Statement I** As the branching increases the melting point also increases. **NCERT Pg 302**

Statement II Surface area of the molecule increases the force of attraction increases.

5 **Statement I** The addition of HI to propene in the presence of organic peroxide follow peroxide effect. **NCERT Pg 311**

Statement II Propene reacts with HBr in presence of benzoyl peroxide to give 1-bromopropane as major product.

6 **Statement I** Tropolone is an aromatic compound and has 8π-electrons. **NCERT Pg 321**

Statement II π-electrons of $\rangle C{=}O$ group in tropolone is invovled in aromaticity.

7 Which of the following statements are incorrect? **NCERT Pg 295, 296, 297, 301**

I. The major constituent of the natural gas is methane.
II. Soda lime is a mixture of calcium hydroxide and sodium oxide.
III. *Neo*-pentane contains three different monochloro derivatives product.
IV. Substance that slows down or stops the reaction is known as inhibitor.
V. Alkanes are also referred as saturated hydrocarbons.

Choose the correct answer from the options given below.

(a) I and II (b) II and III
(c) II, III and IV (d) I, III and V

8 Which of the following statements are correct? **NCERT Pg 303, 304, 308**

I. Bromine is less reactive than chlorine towards a particular alkane.
II. Kerosene oil is a mixture of aliphatic hydrocarbons.
III. 2-methyl propene exhibits geometrical isomerism.
IV. Chlorination of methane does not occur in dark.
V. Preparation of oil gas and petrol gas from kerosene and petrol is the example of dehydrogenation reaction.

Choose the correct answer from the options given below.

(a) I, II and III (b) II and IV
(c) I, II and IV (d) III, IV and V

9 Which of the following statements are correct? NCERT Pg 301, 302, 311, 313

I Butane is a liquid hydrocarbon at room temperature.
II 2-methyl propane has the lowest boiling point among the same molecular mass compounds.
III 2-chloro pentane is obtained from the reaction of pent-1-ene with HCl.
IV Presence of unsaturation in organic compounds can be tested with Fittig's reagent.
V Hydrolysis of ozonide of but-1-ene gives propionaldehyde and formaldehyde.

Choose correct answer from the options given below.

(a) I, II and III (b) I and IV
(c) II, III and V (d) IV and V

10 Which of the following statements are correct? NCERT Pg 323, 324, 325

I. The —OH group present in phenol is *ortho* and *para*-directing.
II. Directive influence of a functional group in monosubstituted benzene depends on the nature of the substituent already present in the benzene ring.
III. The —OH group deactivates the benzene ring for the attack by an electrophile.
IV. Groups such as $—NH_2$, —NH*R*, $—NHCOCH_3$, $—OCH_3$, $—CH_3$, $—C_2H_5$ etc., are examples of deactivating groups.
V. Presence of —CHO group in a benzene ring activates the ring towards electrophilic substitution.

Choose the correct answer from the options given below.

(a) I and II (b) II and III
(c) II, IV and V (d) I, III and IV

Matching Type Questions

1 Match the Column I and Column II and choose the correct option from the codes given below. NCERT Pg 302, 303, 304

Column I	Column II
A. $\text{Alkane} + X_2 \xrightarrow{h\nu}$	1. Water + carbon dioxide
B. $\text{Alkane} + O_2 \xrightarrow{\Delta}$	2. Alkanal
C. $\text{Alkane} + O_2 \xrightarrow[\Delta]{Mo_2O_3}$	3. Haloalkane
D. $n\text{-hexane} \xrightarrow[\text{10-20 atm}]{\Delta,\ 773\ K}$	4. Benzene

Codes

	A	B	C	D
(a)	1	2	3	4
(b)	1	2	4	3
(c)	3	1	2	4
(d)	3	1	4	2

2 Match the Column I and Column II and choose the correct option from the codes given below. NCERT Pg 304

Column I	Column II
A. $CH_4 + O_2 \longrightarrow CH_3OH$	1. Cu/523 K/100 atm
B. $CH_4 + O_2 \longrightarrow HCHO$	2. Mo_2O_3, Δ
C. $2CH_3CH_3 + 3O_2 \longrightarrow 2CH_3COOH + 2H_2O$	3. $(CH_3COO)_2Mn$
D. $(CH_3)_3CH \longrightarrow (CH_3)_3COH$	4. $KMnO_4$

Codes

	A	B	C	D
(a)	2	3	4	1
(b)	1	2	3	4
(c)	2	1	3	4
(d)	4	3	2	1

3 Match the Column I and Column II and choose the correct option from the codes given below. NCERT Pg 316, 317

Column I	Column II
A. $RC{\equiv}CR \xrightarrow[CH_3COOH_2O_2,\ NaOH]{BH_3,\ THF}$	1. $CH_3—C{\equiv}C—CH_3$
B. $RC{\equiv}CR \xrightarrow[H_2]{Pd/Ni}$	2. $R—CH_2—\overset{O}{\overset{\|}{C}}—R$
C. $\underset{Br}{\underset{\|}{C}H_2}CH_2Br \xrightarrow[NaNH_2]{Alc.\ KOH}$	3. $R—CH_2—CH_2—R$
D. $CH_3C{\equiv}CH \xrightarrow[(ii)\ CH_3—I]{(i)\ NaNH_2}$	4. $CH{\equiv}CH$

Codes

	A	B	C	D
(a)	2	3	4	1
(b)	2	1	4	3
(c)	3	2	4	1
(d)	2	1	3	4

4 Match the Column I and Column II and choose the correct option from the codes given below. **NCERT Pg 322**

Column I	Column II

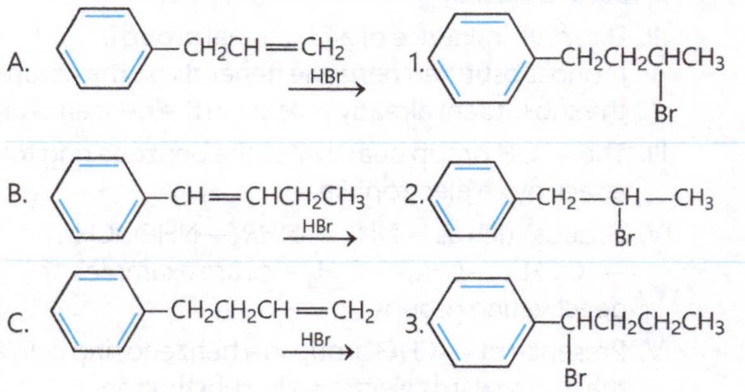

Codes

	A	B	C		A	B	C
(a)	2	3	1	(b)	1	2	3
(c)	1	3	2	(d)	3	2	1

5 Match the Column I and Column II and choose the correct option from the codes given below. **NCERT Pg 322, 323**

Column I	Column II
A. Benzene + Cl_2 $\xrightarrow{AlCl_3}$	1. Benzene sulphonic acid
B. Benzene + CH_3Cl $\xrightarrow{AlCl_3}$	2. Methyl phenyl ketone
C. Benzene + CH_3COCl $\xrightarrow{AlCl_3}$	3. Toluene
D. Benzene $\xrightarrow[\text{Conc./Fuming}]{H_2SO_4}$	4. Chlorobenzene

Codes

	A	B	C	D
(a)	4	3	2	1
(b)	4	3	1	2
(c)	3	4	1	2
(d)	3	4	2	1

Numerical Value Questions

1 The total number of monobromo derivatives formed by the alkanes with molecular formula C_5H_{12} is .... (excluding stereoisomers) **NCERT Pg 297**

2 Number of 3° carbon in the given compound is **NCERT Pg 297**

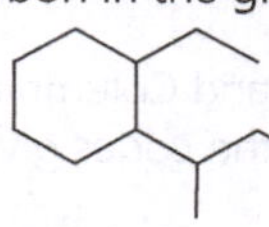

3 The dihedral angle in staggered form of Newman projections of 1,1,1-trichloroethane is .... degree. **NCERT Pg 305**

4 Among the following, the number of aromatic compound(s) is .... **NCERT Pg 321**

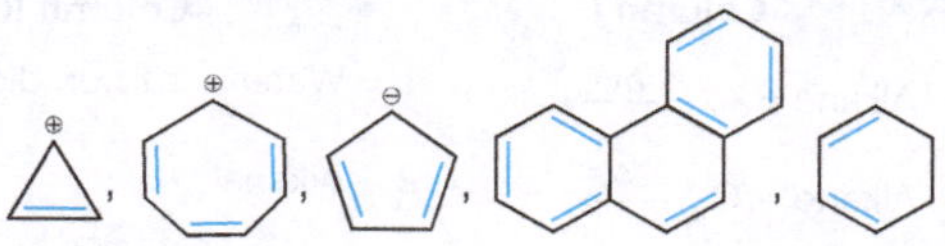

5 In the presence of sunlight, benzene reacts with Cl_2 to give product, *X*. The number of hydrogens in *X* is .... **NCERT Pg 322**

NCERT Exemplar's Questions

1 The addition of HBr to 1-butene gives a mixture of products *A*, *B* and *C*.

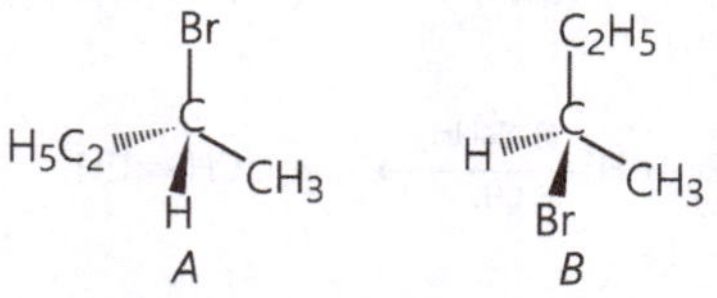

$CH_3—CH_2—CH_2—CH_2—Br$

C

The mixture consists of

(a) *A* and *B* as major and *C* as minor products
(b) *B* as major, *A* and *C* as minor products
(c) *B* as minor, *A* and *C* as major products
(d) *A* and *B* as minor and *C* as major products

2 Arrange the following in decreasing order of their boiling points.

A. *n*-butane *B*. 2-methylbutane
C. *n*-pentane *D*. 2, 2-dimethylpropane

(a) $A > B > C > D$ (b) $B > C > D > A$
(c) $D > C > B > A$ (d) $C > B > D > A$

3 Arrange the halogens F_2, Cl_2, Br_2, I_2 in order of their increasing reactivity with alkanes.

(a) $I_2 < Br_2 < Cl_2 < F_2$ (b) $Br_2 < Cl_2 < F_2 < I_2$
(c) $F_2 < Cl_2 < Br_2 < I_2$ (d) $Br_2 < I_2 < Cl_2 < F_2$

4 The increasing order of reduction of alkyl halides with zinc and dil. HCl is

(a) $R—Cl < R—I < R—Br$
(b) $R—Cl < R—Br < R—I$
(c) $R—I < R—Br < R—Cl$
(d) $R—Br < R—I < R—Cl$

5 Match the reagent from Column I which on reaction with $CH_3—CH{=}CH_2$ gives some product given in Column II as per the codes given below :

Column I	Column II
A. O_3 / Zn + H_2O	1. Acetic acid and CO_2
B. $KMnO_4$ / H^+	2. Propan-1-ol
C. $KMnO_4$ / OH^-	3. Propan-2-ol
D. H_2O / H^+	4. Acetaldehyde and formaldehyde
E. B_2H_6 / NaOH and H_2O_2	5. Propane-1, 2-diol

6 The correct IUPAC name of the following alkane is

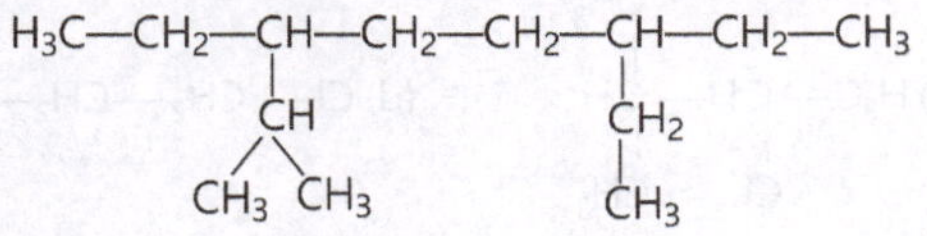

(a) 3,6-diethyl-2-methyloctane
(b) 5-*iso*-propyl -3-ethyloctane
(c) 3-ethyl-5-*iso*-propyloctane
(d) 3-*iso*-propyl-6-ethyloctane

7 Which of the following will not show geometrical isomerism?

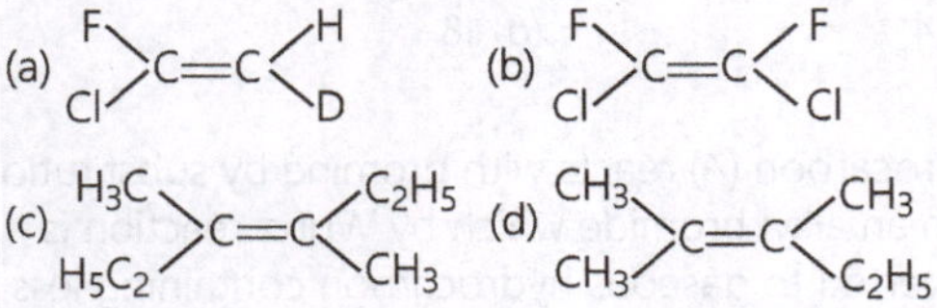

8 Match the reactions given in Column I with the reaction types in Column II.

Column I	Column II
A. $CH_2{=}CH_2 + H_2O \xrightarrow{H^+} CH_3CH_2OH$	1. Hydrogenation
B. $CH_2{=}CH_2 + H_2 \xrightarrow{Pd} CH_3—CH_3$	2. Halogenation
C. $CH_2{=}CH_2 + Cl_2 \longrightarrow Cl—CH_2—CH_2—Cl$	3. Polymerisation
D. $3CH{\equiv}CH \xrightarrow[\text{Heat}]{\text{Cu tube}} C_6H_6$	4. Hydration

9 Arrange the following hydrogen halides in order of their decreasing reactivity with propene.

(a) HCl > HBr > HI
(b) HBr > HI > HCl
(c) HI > HBr > HCl
(d) HCl > HI > HBr

10 Arrange the following carbanions in order of their decreasing stability.

A. $H_3C—C{\equiv}C^-$ B. $H—C{\equiv}C^-$
C. $H_3C—\bar{C}H_2$

(a) $A > B > C$
(b) $B > A > C$
(c) $C > B > A$
(d) $C > A > B$

11 Match the following reactants in Column I with the corresponding reaction products in Column II.

Column I	Column II
A. Benzene + $Cl_2 \xrightarrow{AlCl_3}$	1. Benzoic acid
B. Benzene + $CH_3Cl \xrightarrow{AlCl_3}$	2. Methyl phenyl ketone
C. Benzene + $CH_3COCl \xrightarrow{AlCl_3}$	3. Toluene
D. Toluene $\xrightarrow{KMnO_4/NaOH}$	4. Chlorobenzene
	5. Benzene hexachloride

12 Arrange the following alkyl halides in decreasing order of the rate of β-elimination reaction with alc. KOH.

A. $CH_3—\underset{CH_3}{\overset{H}{\underset{|}{\overset{|}{C}}}}—CH_2Br$ B. $CH_3—CH_2—Br$

C. $CH_3—CH_2—CH_2—Br$

(a) $A > B > C$
(b) $C > B > A$
(c) $B > C > A$
(d) $A > C > B$

13 Which of the following reactions of methane is incomplete combustion?

(a) $2CH_4 + O_2 \xrightarrow{Cu/523\,K/100\,atm} 2CH_3OH$
(b) $CH_4 + O_2 \xrightarrow{Mo_2O_3} HCHO + H_2O$
(c) $CH_4 + O_2 \longrightarrow C(s) + 2H_2O(l)$
(d) $CH_4 + 2O_2 \longrightarrow CO_2(s) + 2H_2O(l)$

Past Exams' Questions

NEET Archive

1 Match List-I with List-II. **NCERT Pg 314, NEET 2024**

List-I (Molecule)		List-II (Number and types of bond/s between two carbon atoms)
A. Ethane	I.	One σ-bond and two π-bonds
B. Ethene	II.	two π-bonds
C. Carbon molecule, C_2	III.	One σ-bond
D. Ethyne	IV.	One σ-bond and one π-bond

Choose the correct answer from the options given below:

(a) A-I, B-IV, C-II, D-III (b) A-IV, B-III, C-II, D-I
(c) A-III, B-IV, C-II, D-I (d) A-III, B-IV, C-I, D-II

2 Given below are two statements: **NCERT Pg 302, NEET 2024**

Statement I The boiling point of three isomeric pentanes follows the order

n-pentane > *iso*-pentane > *neo*-pentane

Statement II When branching increases, the molecule attains a shape of sphere. This results in smaller surface area for contact, due to which the intermolecular forces between the spherical molecules are weak, thereby lowering the boiling point.

In the light of the above statements, choose the most appropriate answer from the options given below:

(a) Both Statement I and Statement II are true.
(b) Both Statement I and Statement II are false.
(c) Statement I is true but Statement II is false.
(d) Statement I is false but Statement II is true.

3 Consider the following compounds/species.

(i) 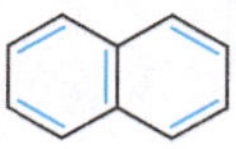 (ii)  (iii)  (iv) 

(v)  (vi) 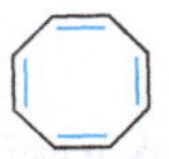 (vii) 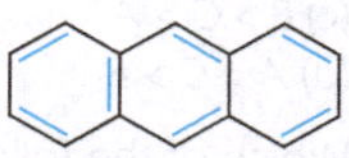

The number of compounds/species which obey Huckel's rule is .... **NCERT Pg 321, NEET 2023**

(a) 6 (b) 2 (c) 5 (d) 4

4 Compound *X* on reaction with O_3 followed by Zn/H_2O gives formaldehyde and 2-methyl propanal as products. The compound *X* is **NCERT Pg 313, NEET 2022**

(a) 2-methylbut-1-ene (b) 2-methylbut-2-ene
(c) pent-2-ene (d) 3-methylbut-1-ene

5 Which of the following is a free radical substitution reaction? **NCERT Pg 312, NEET 2020**

(a) Benzene with $Br_2/AlCl_3$
(b) Acetylene with HBr
(c) Methane with $Br_2/h\nu$
(d) Propene with $HBr/(C_6H_5COO)_2$

6 An alkene '*A*' on reaction with O_3 and $Zn-H_2O$ gives propanone and ethanal in equimolar ratio. Addition of HCl to alkene '*A*' gives '*B*' as the major product. The structure of product '*B*' is **NCERT Pg 313, NEET (National) 2019**

(a) 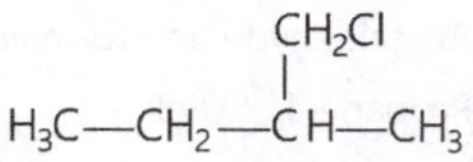 (b) 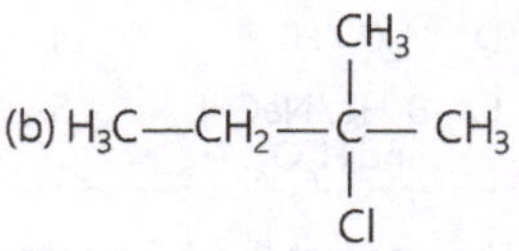

(c) 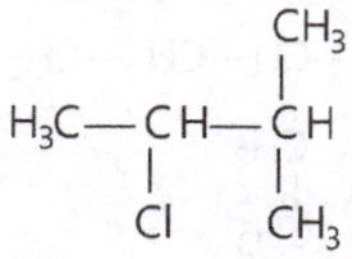 (d) 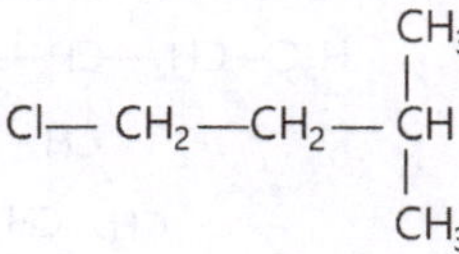

7 In the following reaction,

$$H_3C-C\equiv CH \xrightarrow[873\text{ K}]{\text{Red hot iron tube}} A,$$

the number of sigma(σ) bonds present in the product *A* is **NCERT Pg 318, NEET (Odisha) 2019**

(a) 21 (b) 9
(c) 24 (d) 18

8 Hydrocarbon (*A*) reacts with bromine by substitution to form an alkyl bromide which by Wurtz reaction is converted to gaseous hydrocarbon containing less than four carbon atoms. *A* is **NCERT Pg 301, NEET 2018**

(a) CH_3-CH_3
(b) $CH_2=CH_2$
(c) $CH\equiv CH$
(d) CH_4

9 Predict the correct intermediate and product in the following reaction. **NCERT Pg 317, NEET 2017**

$$H_3C-C\equiv CH \xrightarrow[HgSO_4]{H_2O,\ H_2SO_4} \underset{(A)}{\text{Intermediate}} \longrightarrow \underset{(B)}{\text{Product}}$$

(a) 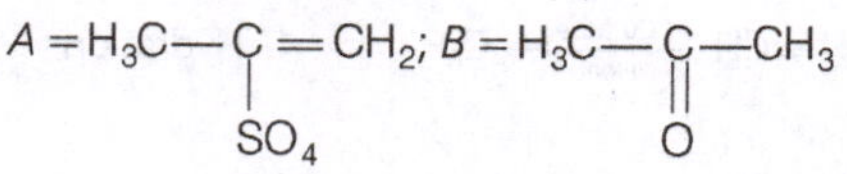

(b) $A = H_3C—\underset{\displaystyle OH}{\underset{|}{C}}=CH_2$; $B = H_3C—\underset{\displaystyle SO_4}{\underset{|}{C}}=CH_2$

(c) $A = H_3C—\underset{\displaystyle O}{\underset{\|}{C}}—CH_3$; $B = H_3C—C\equiv CH$

(d) $A = H_3C—\underset{\displaystyle OH}{\underset{|}{C}}=CH_2$; $B = H_3C—\underset{\displaystyle O}{\underset{\|}{C}}—CH_3$

10 With respect to the conformers of ethane, which of the following statements is true? **NCERT Pg 305, NEET 2017**

(a) Bond angle remains same but bond length changes.
(b) Bond angle changes but bond length remains same.
(c) Both bond angle and bond length change.
(d) Both bond angles and bond length remain same.

11 In the given reaction,

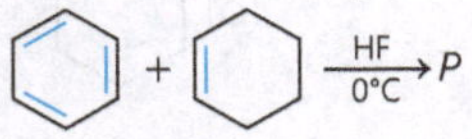

The product *P* is **NCERT Pg 311, NEET 2016**

(a) 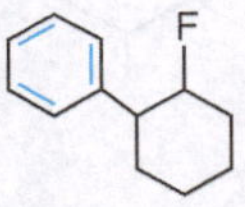 (b) 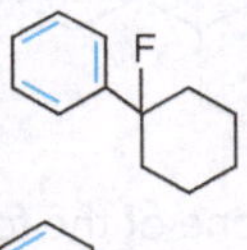

(c) 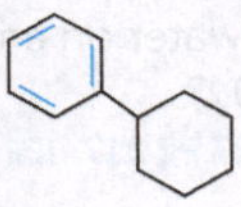 (d) 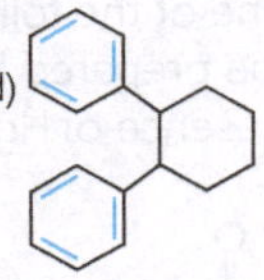

12 In the reaction,

$$H—C\equiv CH \xrightarrow[\text{(ii) } CH_3CH_2Br]{\text{(i) } NaNH_2/\text{Liq.}NH_3} X \xrightarrow[\text{(ii) } CH_3CH_2Br]{\text{(i) } NaNH_2/\text{Liq.}NH_3} Y$$

X and *Y* are **NCERT Pg 316, NEET 2016**

(a) $X = 2$-butyne; $Y = 3$-hexyne
(b) $X = 2$-butyne; $Y = 2$-hexyne
(c) $X = 1$-butyne; $Y = 2$-hexyne
(d) $X = 1$-butyne; $Y = 3$-hexyne

13 In the reaction with HCl, an alkene reacts in accordance with the Markovnikov's rule, to give a product 1-chloro-1-methylcyclohexane. The possible alkane is **NCERT Pg 311, CBSE-AIPMT NEET 2015**

(a) 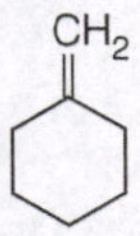 (b) 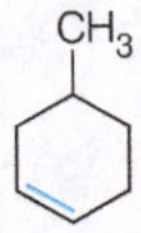

(c) 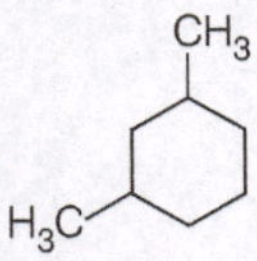 (d) 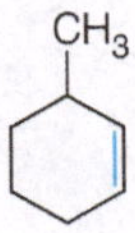

14 Identify *Z* in the sequence of reactions,

$$CH_3CH_2CH=CH_2 \xrightarrow{HBr/H_2O_2} Y \xrightarrow{C_2H_5ONa} Z$$

NCERT Pg 312, CBSE-AIPMT 2014

(a) $CH_3—(CH_2)_3—O—CH_2CH_3$
(b) $(CH_3)_2CH—O—CH_2CH_3$
(c) $CH_3(CH_2)_4—O—CH_3$
(d) $CH_3CH_2—CH(CH_3)—O—CH_2CH_3$

JEE Main Archive

15 The incorrect statement regarding the geometrical isomers of 2-butene is **NCERT Pg 308, JEE Main 2024**

(a) *trans*-2-butene is more stable than *cis*-2-butene.
(b) *cis*-2-butene and *trans*-2 butene are not interconvertible at room temperature.
(c) *cis*-2-butene has less dipole moment than *trans*-2-butene.
(d) *cis*-2-butene and *trans*-2-butene are stereoisomers.

16 Which of the following are aromatic? **NCERT Pg 321, JEE Main 2024**

A. 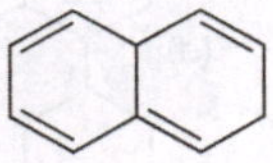 B. 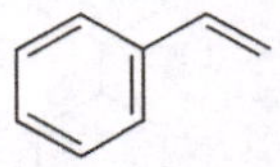

C. 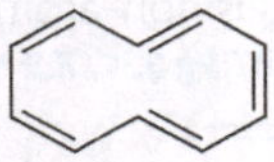 D. 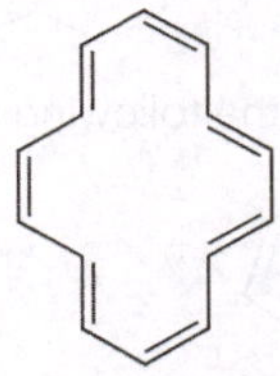

(a) C and D only (b) B and D only
(c) A and C only (d) A and B only

17 Which of the following conformations will be the most stable? **NCERT Pg 305, JEE Main 2023**

(a) 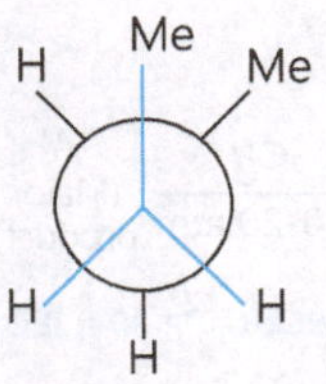

(b) 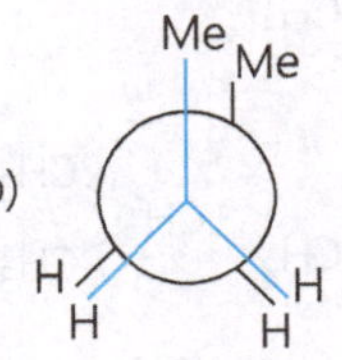

(c) 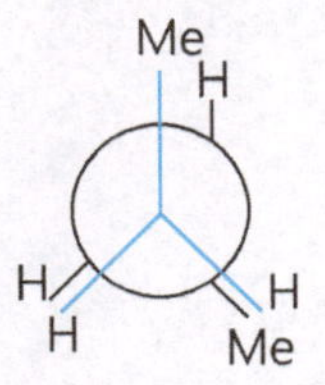

(d) 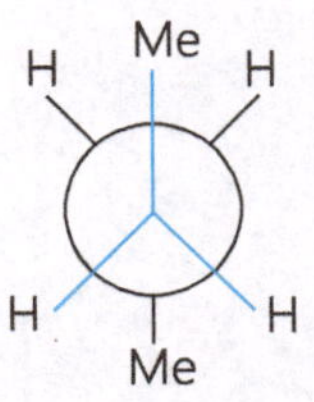

18 In the following given reaction, '*A*' is

NCERT Pg 311, JEE Main 2023

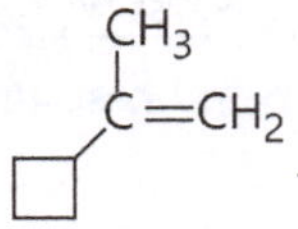 + HBr ⟶ '*A*' (Major product)

(a) 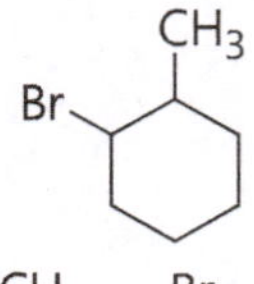
(b) 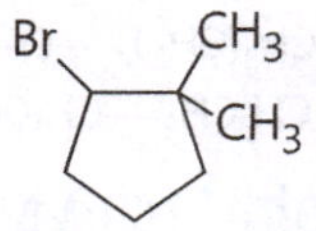
(c) 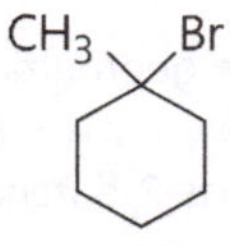
(d) 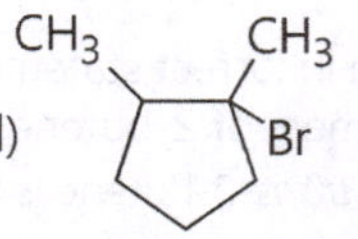

19 '*X*' is : 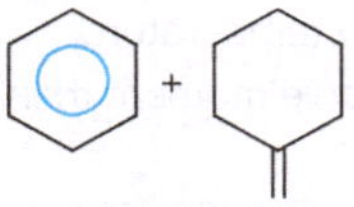 $\xrightarrow[\Delta]{HF}$ *X* Major product

NCERT Pg 311, JEE Main 2023

(a) 
(b) 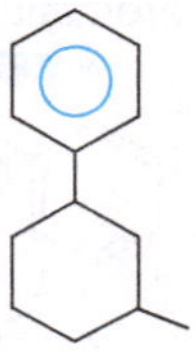
(c) 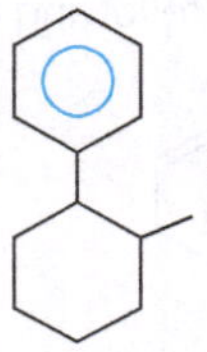
(d) 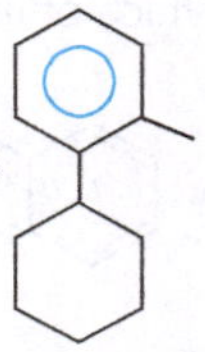

20 Which of the following compounds is non-aromatic?

NCERT Pg 321, JEE Main 2022

(a) 
(b) 
(c) 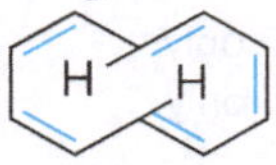
(d) 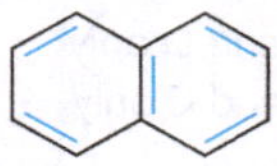

21 Identify *A* in the given chemical reaction.

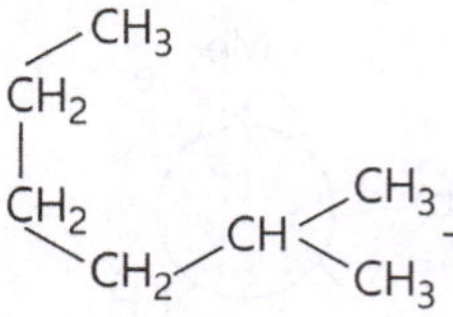 $\xrightarrow[773\text{ K, 10-20 atm}]{Mo_2O_3}$ '*A*' (Major product)

NCERT Pg 304, JEE Main 2021

(a) 
(b) 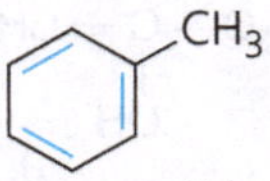
(c) 
(d) 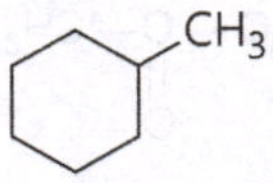

22 The major product of the following reaction is

NCERT Pg 322, JEE Main 2021

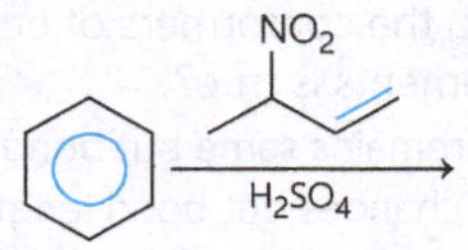

(a) 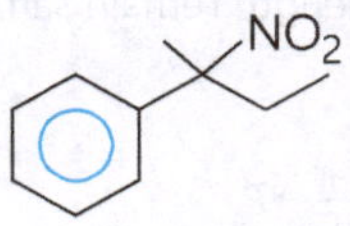
(b) 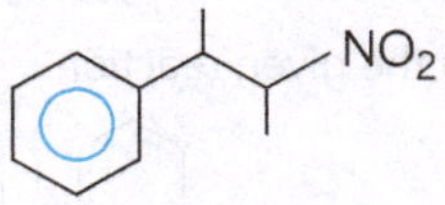
(c) 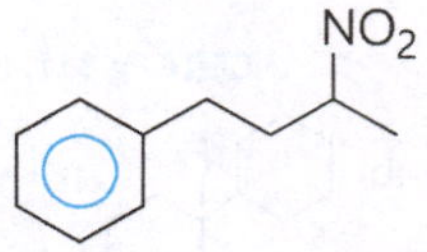
(d) 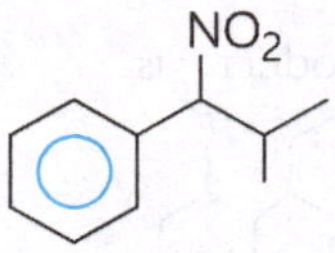

23 Which one of the following carbonyl compounds cannot be prepared by addition of water on an alkyne in the presence of $HgSO_4$ and H_2SO_4?

NCERT Pg 317, JEE Main 2021

(a) $CH_3-\overset{O}{\overset{\|}{C}}-CH_2CH_3$

(b) $CH_3-CH_2-\overset{O}{\overset{\|}{C}}-H$

(c) 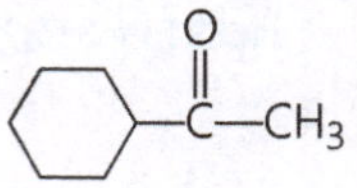

(d) $CH_3-\overset{O}{\overset{\|}{C}}-CH_3$

Skill Boosters

1 Hydrocarbon (C) reacts with bromine by substitution reaction to form an alkyl bromide *D*. *D* undergoes the Wurtz reaction to give a gaseous hydrocarbon containing less than four carbon atoms.

The formula of (C) is

(a) $CH_2{=}CH_2$ (b) $CH{\equiv}CH$
(c) $CH_3{-}CH_3$ (d) CH_4

2 An alkyl halide $C_5H_{11}Br$ (*A*) reacts with ethanolic KOH to give an alkene '*B*', which reacts with Br_2 to give a compound '*C*', which on dehydrobromination gives an alkyne '*D*'. On treatment with Na metal in liq. ammonia, one mole of '*D*' gives one mole of the sodium salt of *D* and half a mole of hydrogen gas. Complete hydrogenation of '*D*' yields a straight chain alkane. *A* and *D* respectively are

(a) alkene and alkyl bromide
(b) alkyl halide and alkyne
(c) alkyne and sodium alkynide
(d) sodium alkynide and alkene

3 A compound *P* decolourises Br_2 water and reacts slowly with conc. H_2SO_4 to give an addition product. *P* reacts with HBr to form *Q*. *Q* reacts with NaOH to form *R*. On oxidation *R* gives hexan-3-one. *P*, *Q* and *R* in the reactions are

- $P \xrightarrow{Br_2\ water}$ Decolourisation
  $\downarrow$ Conc. H_2SO_4
  Addition product
- $P \xrightarrow{HBr} Q \xrightarrow{NaOH} R \xrightarrow{[O]} CH_3CH_2CH_2{-}\underset{\underset{O}{\|}}{C}{-}CH_2CH_3$
  Hexan-3-one

(a) $P = CH_3CH_2CH{=}CHCH_2CH_3$
$Q = CH_3CH_2{-}\underset{\underset{Br}{|}}{CH}{-}CH_2CH_2CH_3$
$R = CH_3CH_2CH_2{-}\underset{\underset{OH}{|}}{CH}{-}CH_2CH_3$

(b) $P = CH_3CH_2{=}CHCH_2CH_2CH_3$
$Q = CH_3CH_2CH_2CH_2CH_2CH_2Br$
$R = CH_3CH_2CH_2OH$

(c) $P = CH_3CH{=}CHCH_3$
$Q = CH_3CH(Br)CH(Br)CH_3$
$R = CH_3CH_2CH_2OH$

(d) $P = CH_3CH_2CH{=}CHCH_3$
$Q = CH_3CH_2CH(Br)CH(Br)CH_2CH_3$
$R = CH_3CH_2CH_2CH_3$

4 An unsatuated hydrocarbon 'H' adds two molecules of H_2 and on reductive ozonolysis gives butane-1, 4-dial, ethanal and propanone. From the structure of 'H', predict its IUPAC name.

(a) 2-methyl-octa-2,6-diene
(b) 3-methyl-octa-3,7-diene
(c) 1-methyl-hept-1,5-diene
(d) Non-3,7-diene

5 An alkene *A* contains three C—C, eight C—H σ-bonds and one C—C π-bond. *A* on ozonolysis gives two moles of an aldehyde of molar mass 44 u. Write IUPAC name of *A*.

(a) Prop-1-ene
(b) But-2-ene
(c) But-1-ene
(d) Pent-1-ene

6 Jay thought to did an experiment in lab as photochemical fluorination of alkane which is explosive in real. While iodination is too slow to occur. He's trying to solve the reason behind it.

(a) Formation of CH_3F is most exothermic.
(b) Formation of H—F is most exothermic while formation of HI is endothermic.
(c) Bond dissociation energy of I_2 is minimum.
(d) F_2 has lower bond dissociation energy than Cl_2 and Br_2.

7 The heat of hydrogenation of 1-hexene is -126 kJ mol^{-1}. When a second double bond is introduced in the molecules the heat of hydrogenation of the resulting compound is -230 kJ mol^{-1}. The resulting compound is

(a) 1,3-hexadiene
(b) 1,4-hexadiene
(c) 1,5-hexadiene
(d) 1,6-hexadiene

8 Raj had done a lab activity for the deduction of structural formula of any substance. For that he took 1 mole of a hydrocarbon '*A*', which on treatment with 1 mole of Br_2 gives a dibromo compound, $C_5H_{10}Br_2$.

Compound '*A*' react with cold, dil. $KMnO_4$ solution to form $C_5H_{12}O_2$. On ozonolysis, '*A*' gives equivalent quantities of propanone and ethanal. He finally deduced the structure of '*A*' which is

(a) 1-methyl ethanol
(b) 1-methyl butene
(c) 2-methyl but-2-ene
(d) 2-methyl prop-2-ene

Correct Codes

Topical Questions

1 (c)	2 (b)	3 (b)	4 (c)	5 (c)	6 (d)	7 (d)	8 (d)	9 (a)	10 (a)
11 (d)	12 (b)	13 (d)	14 (b)	15 (d)	16 (b)	17 (a)	18 (d)	19 (c)	20 (a)
21 (c)	22 (a)	23 (c)	24 (d)	25 (b)	26 (a)	27 (d)	28 (a)	29 (b)	30 (b)
31 (d)	32 (d)	33 (a)	34 (d)	35 (c)	36 (b)	37 (c)	38 (b)	39 (a)	40 (a)
41 (c)	42 (d)	43 (b)	44 (d)	45 (a)	46 (a)	47 (b)	48 (a)	49 (c)	50 (c)
51 (c)	52 (c)	53 (d)	54 (d)	55 (b)	56 (b)	57 (d)	58 (b)	59 (a)	60 (a)
61 (b)	62 (c)	63 (c)	64 (b)	65 (c)	66 (b)	67 (d)	68 (c)	69 (c)	70 (c)
71 (b)	72 (c)	73 (b)	74 (b)	75 (b)	76 (c)	77 (b)	78 (d)	79 (a)	80 (d)
81 (a)	82 (c)	83 (a)	84 (c)	85 (c)	86 (a)	87 (b)	88 (c)	89 (b)	90 (c)
91 (d)	92 (b)	93 (d)	94 (c)	95 (c)	96 (b)	97 (b)	98 (a)	99 (a)	100 (b)
101 (d)									

Assertion-Reason

1 (a)	2 (d)	3 (c)	4 (b)	5 (a)	6 (d)	7 (a)	8 (c)	9 (a)	10 (d)

Statement Type

1 (a)	2 (a)	3 (b)	4 (b)	5 (c)	6 (b)	7 (b)	8 (c)	9 (c)	10 (a)

Matching Type

1 (c)	2 (b)	3 (a)	4 (a)	5 (a)

Numerical Value

1 (8)	2 (3)	3 (60)	4 (4)	5 (6)

NCERT Exemplar's

1 (a) 2 (d) 3 (a) 4 (b) 5 A-(4), B-(1), C-(5), D-(3), E-(2) 6 (a) 7 (d)

8 A-(4), B-(1), C-(2), D-(3) 9 (c) 10 (b) 11 A-(4), B-(3), C-(2), D-(1) 12 (d) 13 (c)

Past Exams'

1 (c)	2 (a)	3 (d)	4 (d)	5 (c)	6 (b)	7 (a)	8 (d)	9 (d)	10 (d)
11 (c)	12 (d)	13 (a)	14 (a)	15 (c)	16 (b)	17 (d)	18 (d)	19 (a)	20 (c)
21 (b)	22 (b)	23 (b)							

Skill Boosters

1 (d)	2 (b)	3 (a)	4 (a)	5 (b)	6 (b)	7 (a)	8 (c)

Step by Step

Decoding the Questions

Concept Builders

1 distillation
2 paraffins/Alkanes
3 False
4 3, 3 diethyl-5-*iso*-propyl-4-methyl octane
5 3,3-dimethyl pentane
6 Propane
7 Wurtz reaction
8 False
9 Decarboxylation
10 True
11 C_3H_6
12 HIO_3 or HNO_3
13 Carbon black
14 True
15 skew
16 True
17 different
18 Lindlar's catalyst
19 β-elimination reaction
20 Carbocation
21 True
22 cold dil. $KMnO_4$
23 True
24 True
25 Bromine water test method
26 False
27 polyacetylene
28 Sulphonation
29 hexachloro benzene
30 resonance

Topical Solutions

1 (*c*) Acetylene (CH≡CH) is an unsaturated hydrocarbon.

2 (*b*) Unsaturated hydrocarbons have multiple bonds.

3 (*b*) In the given compounds, the molecular formulas are same but the chain of C-atoms is different, these are chain isomers.

4 (*c*) Five C atoms and twelve H atoms of C_5H_{12} can be joined in following three ways :

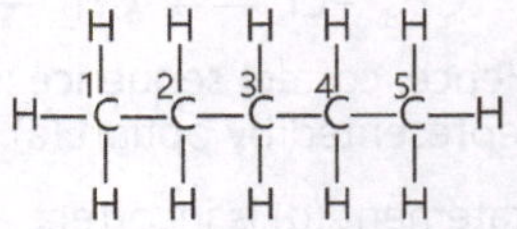

Pentane (*n*-pentane)

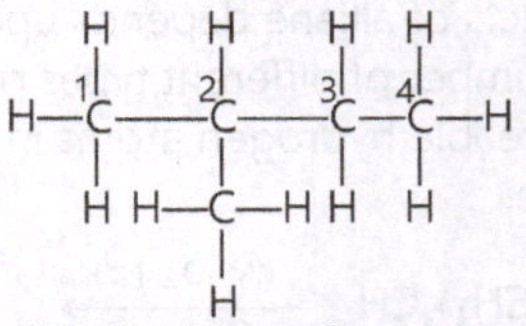

2-methyl butane (*iso*-pentane)

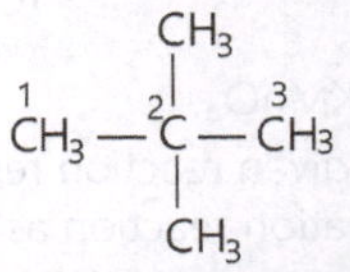

2, 2-dimethyl propane (*neo*-pentane)

5 (*c*) The IUPAC name of the given compound is 2, 2-dimethylpropane.

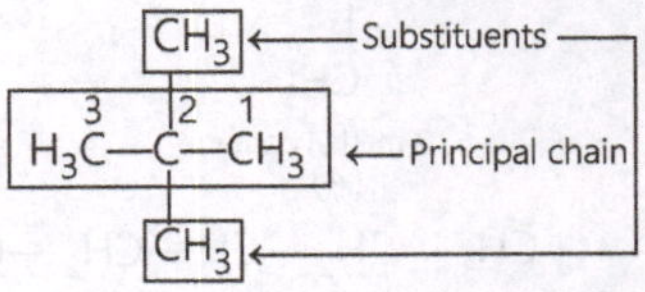

6 (*d*) Possible structural isomers for C_6H_{14} are five.

These are as shown below.

(i) $CH_3—CH_2—CH_2—CH_2—CH_2—CH_3$

Hexane

(ii)
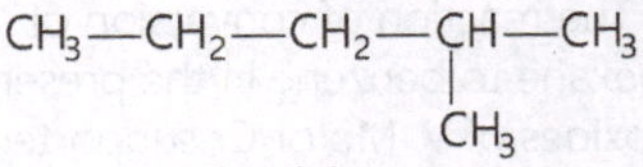

2-methylpentane

(iii)
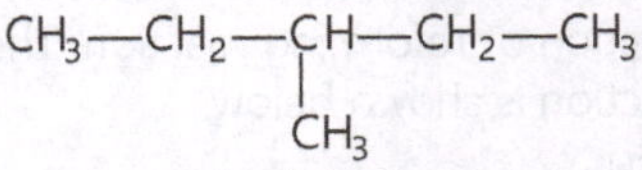

3-methylpentane

(iv)
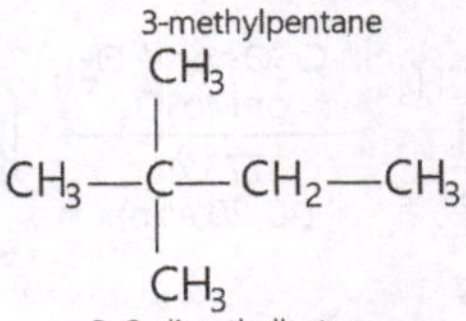

2, 2-dimethylbutane

(v)
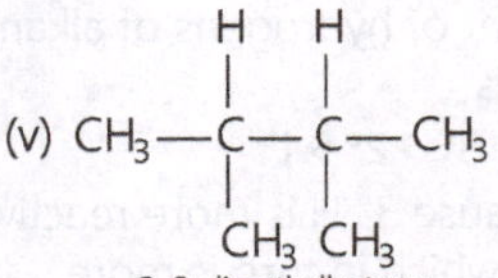

2, 3-dimethylbutane

7 (*d*) Hydrogenation.

8 (*d*) The reaction is Wurtz reaction and proceeds as follows

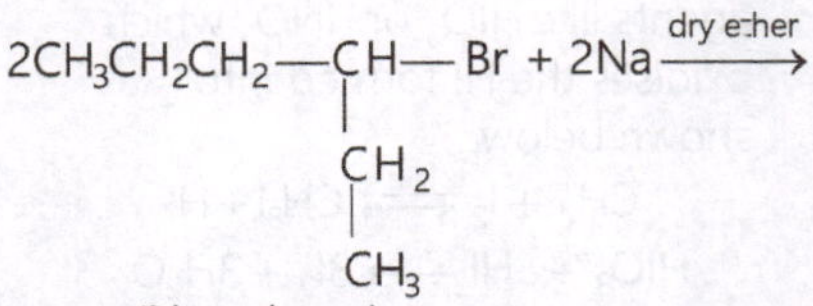

(3-bromohexane)

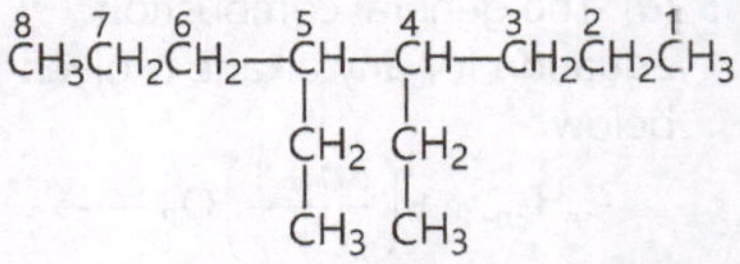

(4,5-diethyloctane)

9 (*a*) Among the given alkanes, only 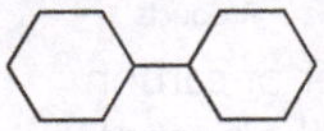 alkane contain even number of carbon atoms. Hence, it will be formed in high yield by Wurtz reaction.

10 (*a*) Statements I and II are correct, while the statements III and IV are incorrect.
Corrected form are as follows
III. Methane cannot be prepared by Kolbe's electrolytic process.
IV. CO_2 gas is liberated at anode.

11 (*d*)

12 (*b*) The correct order of boiling points is given below :

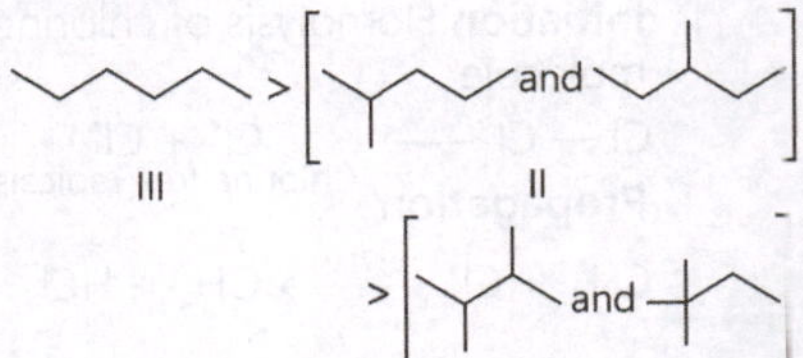

As the branching branching increases, surface area decreases and hence, boiling point decreases.

13 (*d*) In halogenation process, rate of replacement of hydrogens of alkanes is as follows

$$3° > 2° > 1°$$

This is because 3° H is more reactive than 2° H, which in turn is more reactive than 1° H.

14 (*b*) Iodination is very slow and a reversible reaction. It can be carried out in the presence of oxidising agents like HIO_3 or HNO_3 which oxidises the HI formed into I_2 as shown below.

$$CH_4 + I_2 \rightleftharpoons CH_3I + HI$$

$$HIO_3 + 5HI \longrightarrow 3I_2 + 3H_2O$$

15 (*d*) The general combustion equation for any alkane is given below :

$$\underbrace{C_nH_{2n+2} + \left(\frac{3n+1}{2}\right)O_2}_{\text{Reactants}} \longrightarrow \underbrace{nCO_2 + (n+1)\,H_2O}_{\text{Products}}$$

16 (*b*) More the number of carbon atoms, more will be the heat of combustion. For compounds, of same number of carbon atoms heat of combustion decreases with increase in branching.

- Pentane-5 carbon atoms.
- 2-methyl pentane-6 carbon atoms and 1 branching.
- Butane- 4 carbon atoms.

Hence, the correct order of combustion is (ii) > (i) > (iii).

17 (*a*) Halogenation (chlorination here) of alkane proceeds through free radical mechanism as follows

II. **Initiation** Homolysis of chlorine molecule

$$Cl - Cl \longrightarrow \underset{\text{Chlorine free radicals}}{Cl^\bullet + Cl^\bullet}$$

I. **Propagation**

$$CH_4 + Cl^\bullet \xrightarrow{h\nu} \dot{C}H_3 + HCl$$

III. $\dot{C}H_3 + Cl - Cl \longrightarrow CH_3Cl + \dot{C}l$

$$CH_3Cl + Cl^\bullet \longrightarrow \dot{C}H_2Cl + HCl$$

$$\dot{C}H_2Cl + Cl - Cl \longrightarrow CH_2Cl_2 + \dot{C}l$$

IV. **Termination**

$$Cl^\bullet + Cl^\bullet \longrightarrow Cl - Cl$$

$$H_3\dot{C} + \dot{C}H_3 \longrightarrow CH_3 - CH_3$$

$$\dot{C}H_3 + \dot{C}l \longrightarrow CH_3 - Cl$$

Hence, correct sequence is represented by option (a).

18 (*d*) Statement (d) is incorrect because number of monohalogen products of alkane depends upon the number of different types of replaceable hydrogen atoms in the alkane.

19 (*c*) $\underset{\text{2-methylpropane}}{(CH_3)_3CH} \xrightarrow[\text{Oxidation}]{KMnO_4\ (X)} \underset{\text{2-methylpropan-2-ol}}{(CH_3)_3COH}$

So, *X* is $KMnO_4$.

20 (*a*) The given reaction represents isomerisation reaction as shown below.

$$\underset{n\text{-hexane}}{CH_3(CH_2)_4CH_3} \xrightarrow[\text{HCl}]{\text{Anhyd. } AlCl_3}$$

$$\underset{\text{2-methyl pentane } (A)}{CH_3-\underset{\displaystyle CH_3}{\underset{|}{CH}}-(CH_2)_2-CH_3} + \underset{\text{3-methyl pentane } (B)}{CH_3-CH_2-\underset{\displaystyle CH_3}{\underset{|}{CH}}-CH_2-CH_3}$$

Here, *A* and *B* are chain isomers of each other.

21 (*c*) The reaction of conversion of *n*-hexane to benzene in the presence of oxides of V, Mo or Cr supported by alumina is called aromatisation reaction or reforming reaction. The reaction is shown below.

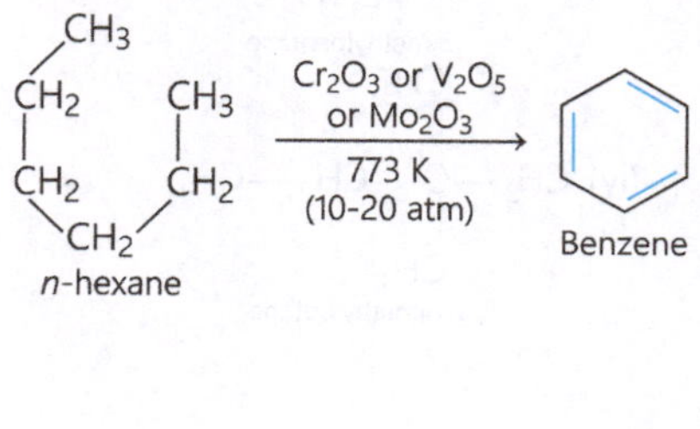

22 (*a*) Dodecane ($C_{12}H_{26}$) on heating to 973K in the presence of Pt, Pd, Ni gives a mixture of heptane, pentene and other products. Reaction involved is as follows

$$C_{12}H_{26} \xrightarrow[973\text{ K}]{Pt/Pd/Ni} C_7H_{16} + C_5H_{10} + \text{Other products}$$

The principle involved in this reaction is pyrolysis.

23 (*c*) Cracking is the process of breaking a heavier hydrocarbon into two or more smaller hydrocarbons.

e.g. Liquid H.C → Gaseous H.C.

24 (*d*) Chlorination of methane is a free radical substitution reaction.

Chlorine is not able to convert into free radicals in the dark, so the reaction does not happen.

Hence, presence of sunlight is must for the reaction to occur.

25 (*b*) The given reaction is pyrolysis

$$\underset{\text{Dodecane}}{C_{12}H_{26}} \xrightarrow{Pt,\ 973K} \underset{\text{Heptane}}{C_7H_{16}} + \underset{\text{Pentene}}{C_5H_{10}} + \text{Other products}$$

26 (*a*) The given reaction represented as

(i) $CH_4 + O_2 \xrightarrow[\Delta]{Mo_2O_3} \underset{\text{(Methanal)}}{\underset{X}{HCHO}} + H_2O$

(ii) $CH_3-CH_3 + Cl_2 \xrightarrow{h\nu} \underset{\text{(Chloroethane)}}{\underset{Y}{CH_3-CH_2Cl}} + HCl$

(iii) $CH_4 + H_2O \xrightarrow[\Delta]{Ni} \underset{\text{(Carbon monoxide)}}{\underset{Z}{CO}} + H_2$

27 (*d*) Infinite number (∞) of conformations/rotamers of ethane are possible due to rotation around C—C single bond by every small change in angle between two C—H bonds.

28 (*a*)

29 (*b*) The structure of 2, 2-dimethylbutane is

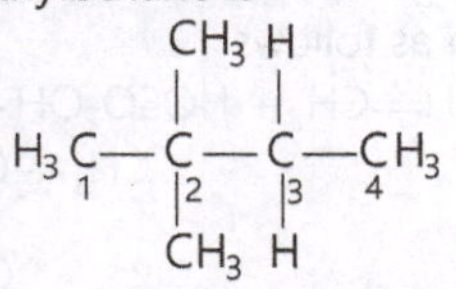

Newman projection for this structure with respect to C_1 - C_2 bond axis is

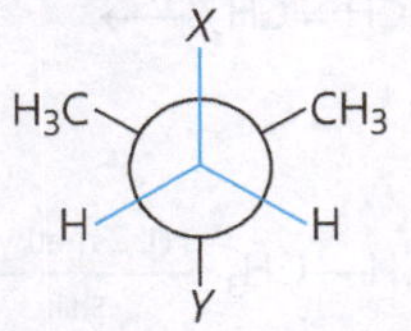

; $X = H$, $Y = C_2H_5$

Similarly, with respect to C_2 and C_3 bond axis is

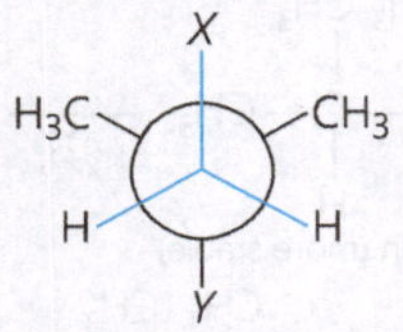

; $X = CH_3$, $Y = CH_3$

Hence, only option (b) is correct in which *X* and *Y* are H_3C and CH_3 respectively.

30 (*b*) Statements I, II and III are correct, while the statement IV is incorrect.

It's correct form is as follows

Alkanes can have infinite number of conformations by rotation around C— C single bonds.

Ethane has infinite number of conformers.

31 (*d*) Statements I, II, III and V are correct while statement IV is incorrect. The corrected form is

The eclipsed conformation is the least stable with the maximum energy whereas the staggered conformation is relatively more stable with less energy.

32 (*d*) 2-methylprop-1-ene

33 (*a*)

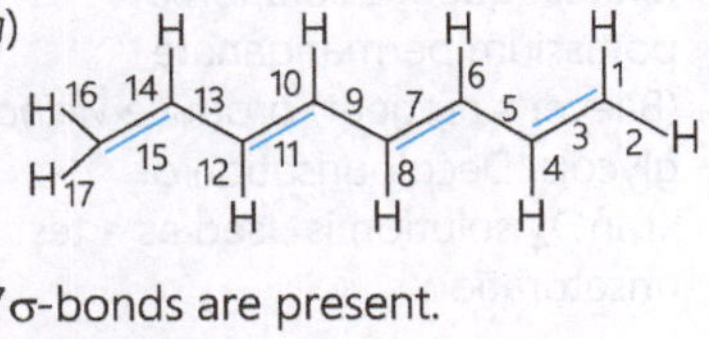

17σ-bonds are present.

The π-bonds can be represented as shown below.

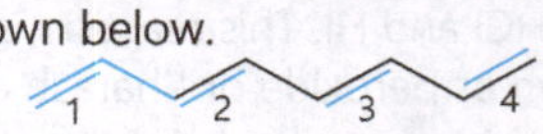

Hence, 4π-bonds are present.

34 (*d*) Possible structural isomers of C_5H_{10} are

(i) $CH_2=CH-CH_2-CH_2-CH_3$
Pent-1-ene

(ii) $CH_3-CH=CH-CH_2-CH_3$
Pent-2-ene

(iii) $CH_3-C(CH_3)=CH-CH_3$
2-methylbut-2-ene

(iv) $CH_3-CH(CH_3)-CH=CH_2$
3-methylbut-1-ene

(v) $CH_2=C(CH_3)-CH_2-CH_3$
2-methylbut-1-ene

Hence, 2, 3-dimethylpropene is not a structural isomer of C_5H_{10}.

35 (*c*) Among all species only, 4 compounds. [(i), (iii), (iv) and (v)] show geometrical isomerism, while (ii) and (vi) do not.

36 (*b*) The complete reaction is shown below.

$$\underset{\text{Alkyne}}{RC\equiv CR'} + H_2 \xrightarrow{\text{Pd/C }(A)}$$

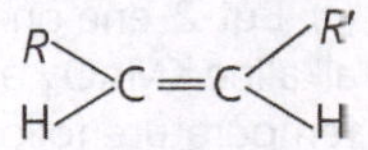

cis-alkene

Reduction of alkyne using Pd/C gives *cis*-alkene as major product whereas, reduction by using Na in liquid, ammonia gives *trans*-alkene as major product.

37 (*c*) Sodium metal in liquid ammonia reduces alkynes with *anti* stereo-chemistry to give *trans*-alkenes. The reduction is selectively *anti* since the vinyl radical formed during reduction is more stable in *trans* configuration.

$$\underset{\text{Alkyne}}{RC\equiv CR'} + H_2 \xrightarrow[\text{Liq. NH}_3]{\text{Na}}$$

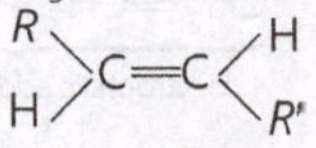

trans-alkene

38 (*b*) The complete reactions are shown below.

(i) $CH_3\ C\equiv C\ C_2H_5 + H_2 \xrightarrow{\text{Pd/C}}$

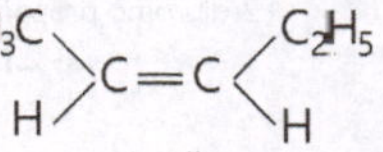

cis-alkene
(*A*)

(ii) $CH_3C\equiv C\ C_2H_5 + H_2 \xrightarrow{\text{Na/Liq. NH}_3}$

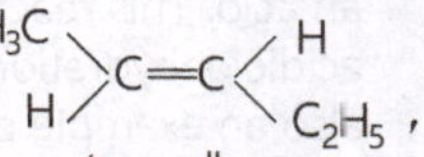

trans-alkene
(*B*)

Hydrogenation of alkynes in the presence of Pd/C forms *cis*-alkene as the major product, whereas hydrogenation in the presence of Na in liquid NH_3 forms *trans*-alkene as the major product.

39 (*a*) Statement (a) is correct, while the statements (c), (b) and (d) are incorrect. It's correct form is as follows :

Arrangement of atoms or groups in space in the two structures is different.

Therefore, they are stereoisomers and conformational isomers.

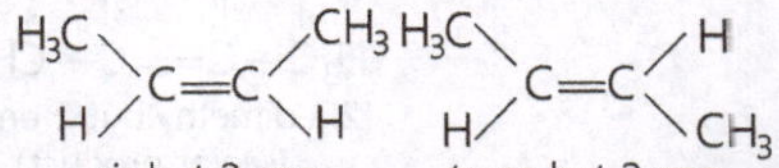

cis-but-2-ene (b.p. 277 K) *trans*-but-2-ene (b.p. 274 K)

Boiling point of *cis*-form is higher than that of *trans*-form.

trans-form is more stable than *cis* due to less crowding.

40 (*a*) The complete reaction is shown below.

$$\underset{\text{1-bromopropane}}{CH_3-CH_2-CH_2Br} \xrightarrow[\text{(Dehydrohalogenation)}]{\text{Alc. KOH}, \Delta} \underset{\substack{\text{Prop-1-ene} \\ (A)}}{CH_3CH=CH_2} + KBr + H_2O$$

Hence, *A* is $CH_2=CH-CH_3$.

41 (*c*) Dihalides in which two halogen atoms are attached to two adjacent carbon atoms are known as *vicinal* dihalides. On reaction with Zn, these form alkene by losing a molecule of ZnX_2 as shown below :

$$\underset{\text{1,2-dibromo propane}}{CH_3CHBr{-}CH_2Br} + Zn \longrightarrow \underset{\text{Propene}}{CH_3CH{=}CH_2} + ZnBr_2$$

42 (*d*) In the given reaction, water molecule is eliminated from the alcohol molecule in the presence of an acid. This reaction is known as acidic dehydration of alcohols. It is also an example of β-elimination reaction since —OH group takes out one hydrogen atom from β-carbon atom as shown below.

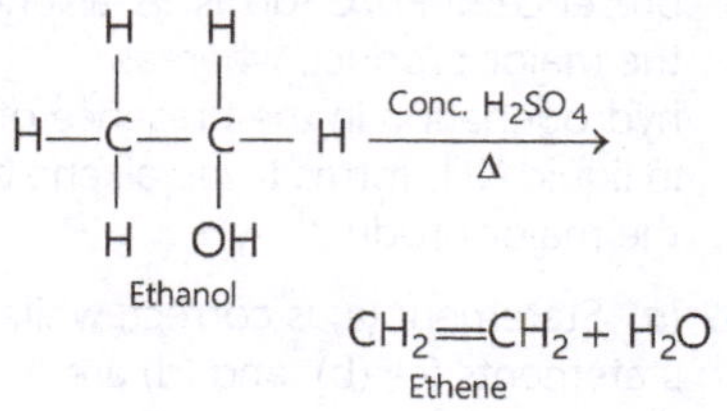

43 (*b*)

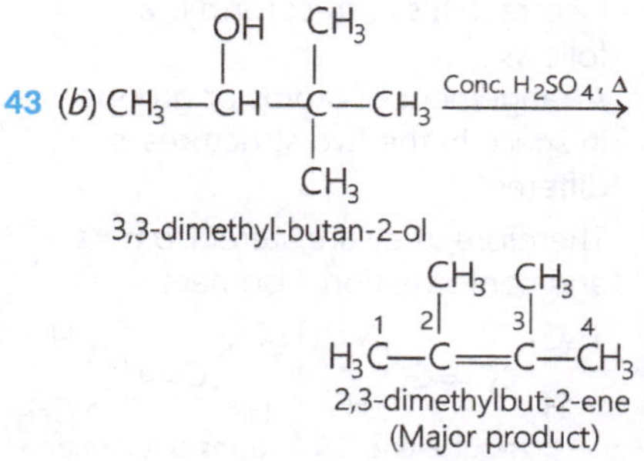

44 (*d*) The complete reaction is shown below.

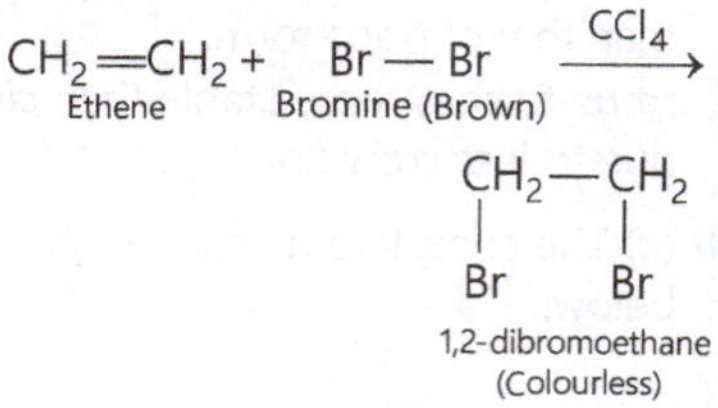

45 (*a*) As the size of halogen atom increases, H—*X* bond length increases, thus reactivity increases. Hence, the order of reactivity of hydrogen halides towards alkenes is HI > HBr > HCl.

46 (*a*) In the presence of peroxide, addition of HBr to unsymmetrical alkenes like propene takes place contrary to the Markovnikov's rule. This happens only with HBr but not with HCl and HI. This reaction is known as peroxide or Kharash effect or anti-Markovnikov's rule.

The reaction is shown below.

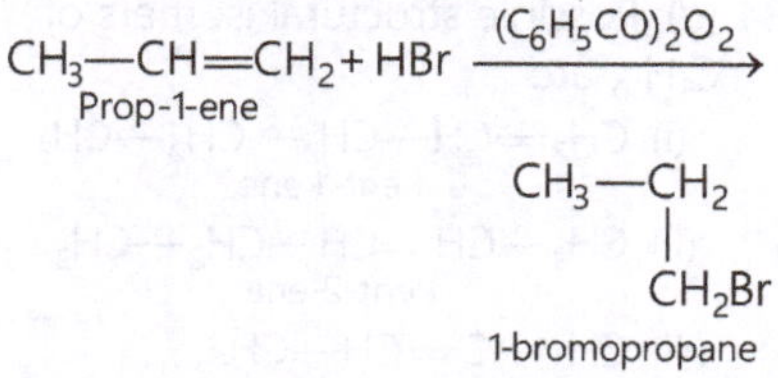

47 (*b*) In the presence of few drops of conc. H_2SO_4, alkenes react with water to form alcohols, in accordance with Markovnikov's rule. The reaction is given below.

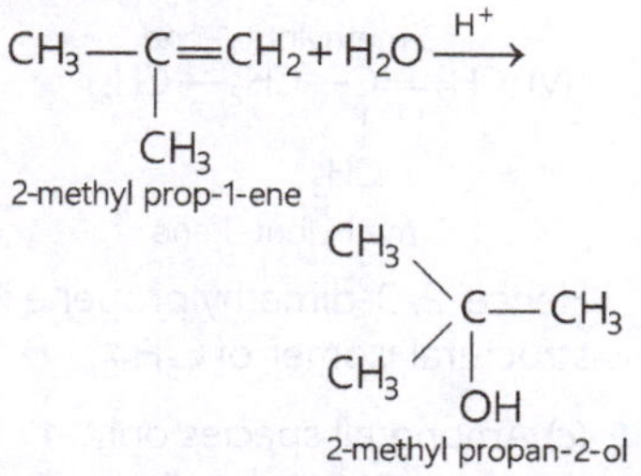

48 (*a*) Addition of HBr gives anti-Markownikoff's product in presence of peroxide only presence of peroxide does not make any difference while reacting with HCl. So, (a) is the correct option.

49 (*c*) But-2-ene on reaction with alkaline $KMnO_4$ at elevated temperature followed by acidification will give acetic acid (CH_3COOH). Hot alkaline solution of potassium permanganate followed by acidification oxidatively cleaved alkenes. The reaction proceed as follows

$$\underset{\text{But-2-ene}}{CH_3{-}CH{=}CH{-}CH_3} \xrightarrow[H_3O^+]{\text{Alk. }KMnO_4\text{, Heat}} \underset{\text{Acetic acid}}{2CH_3COOH}$$

50 (*c*) Cold conc. H_2SO_4 adds to alkenes electrophilic addition reaction in accordance with Markovnikov's rule to form alkyl hydrogen sulphate.

$$\underbrace{CH_2{=}CH_2 + HO{-}SO_3H \longrightarrow}_{\text{Electrophilic addition reaction}} \underset{\text{Ethyl hydrogen sulphate}}{CH_3{-}CH_2{-}OSO_2OH}$$

51 (*c*) The product obtained is propyl hydrogen sulphate. The reaction is given as follows

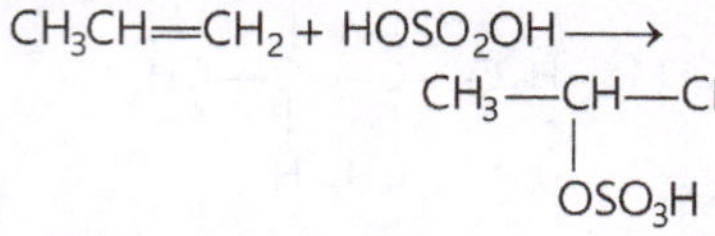

52 (*c*)

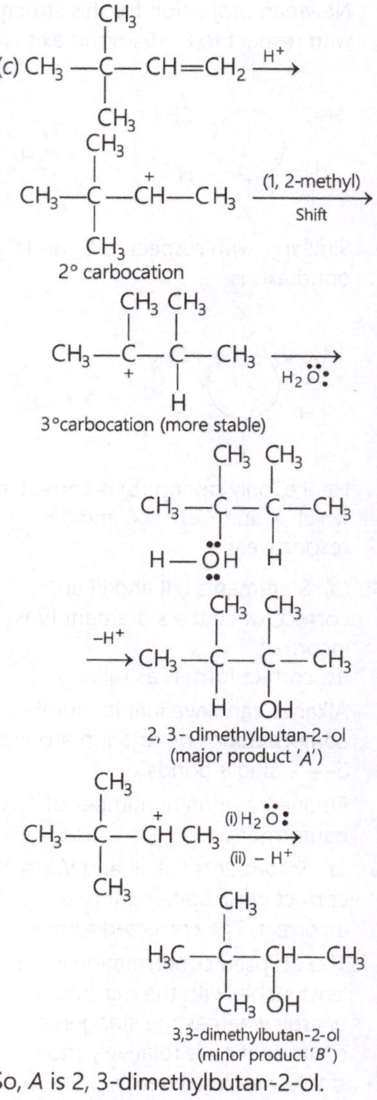

So, *A* is 2, 3-dimethylbutan-2-ol.

53 (*d*) Alkenes on reaction with cold, dilute, aqueous solution of potassium permanganate (Baeyer's reagent) produce *vicinal* glycols. Decolourisation of $KMnO_4$ solution is used as a test for unsaturation.

$$CH_2{=}CH_2 + H_2O + [O] \xrightarrow[273\ K]{\text{Dil. } KMnO_4} \underset{\substack{\text{Ethane-1,2-diol}\\ \text{(Glycol) } (A)}}{\underset{OH\quad OH}{\underset{|\qquad |}{CH_2{-}CH_2}}}$$

$$CH_3{-}CH{=}CH_2 + H_2O + [O] \xrightarrow[273\ K]{\text{Dil. } KMnO_4} \underset{\text{Propane-1,2-diol } (B)}{CH_3CH(OH)CH_2OH}$$

So, *A* is ethane-1, 2-diol and *B* is propane-1, 2-diol.

54 (*d*) Ozonolysis takes place in alkenes. So, *A* will be a double bond containing compound. The complete reaction is shown below.

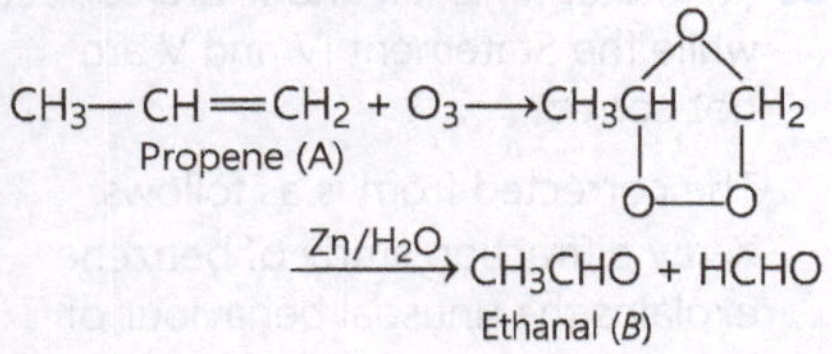

So, *A* is propene and *B* is ethanal.

55 (*b*) Alkenes which have two substituents on each C-atom of the double bond, give mixture of ketones on ozonolysis.

Thus, option (b) gives mixture of ketones as shown below :

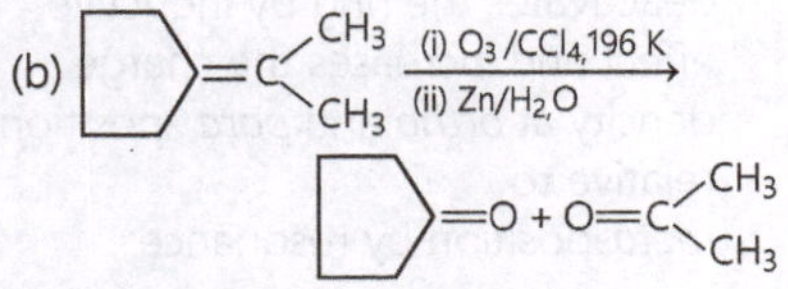

On the other hand, alkenes (a), (c) and (d) give a mixture of two aldehydes.

56 (*b*) The compound (b) on ozonolysis gives 5-keto-2-methyl hexanal as shown below.

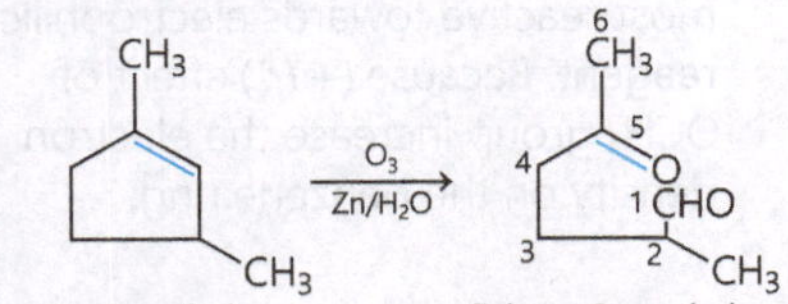

1,3-dimethyl cyclopent-1-ene   5-keto-2-methyl hexanal

57 (*d*) $\overset{4}{H_3C}{-}\underset{\underset{CH_3}{|}}{\overset{3}{C}H}{-}\overset{2}{C}{\equiv}\overset{1}{C}H$.

The IUPAC name of the given compound is 3-methyl but-1-yne.

58 (*b*) The given compound is $CH_3{-}CH_2{-}C{\equiv}CH$.

The common name is ethylacetylene and IUPAC name is but-1-yne.

59 (*a*) Possible isomers of C_6H_{10} are 7. These are as shown below.

1. $HC{\equiv}C{-}CH_2{-}CH_2{-}CH_2{-}CH_3$
Hex-1-yne

2. $CH_3{-}C{\equiv}C{-}CH_2{-}CH_2{-}CH_3$
Hex-2-yne

3. $CH_3{-}CH_2{-}C{\equiv}C{-}CH_2{-}CH_3$
Hex-3-yne

4. $HC{\equiv}C{-}\underset{\underset{CH_3}{|}}{CH}{-}CH_2{-}CH_3$
3-methylpent-1-yne

5. $HC{\equiv}C{-}CH_2{-}\underset{\underset{CH_3}{|}}{CH}{-}CH_3$
4-methylpent-1-yne

6. $CH_3{-}C{\equiv}C{-}\underset{\underset{CH_3}{|}}{CH}{-}CH_3$
4-methylpent-2-yne

7. $HC{\equiv}C{-}\underset{\underset{CH_3}{|}}{\overset{\overset{CH_3}{|}}{C}}{-}CH_3$
3,3-dimethylbut-1-yne

60 (*a*) Statement (a) is correct, while the other statements are incorrect. Corrected form are as follows

(b) Ethyne is a linear molecule.

(c) Ethyne has two π-bonds.

(d) Ethyne molecule consists of one C—C σ bond.

61 (*b*) *Vicinal* dihalides on treatment with alcoholic potassium hydroxide undergo dehydrohalogenation. One molecule of hydrogen halide is eliminated to form alkenyl halide which on treatment with sodamide gives alkyne.

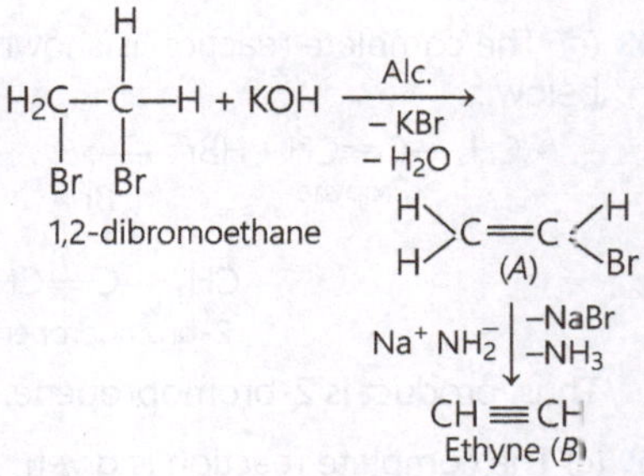

Hence, *A* is $CH_2{=}CHBr$ and *B* is $CH{\equiv}CH$.

62 (*c*) The complete reaction is shown below.

$$\underset{CH_2X}{\overset{CH_2X}{|}} \xrightarrow{\text{Alc. } 2KOH} \underset{\substack{\text{Ethyne}\\ (A)}}{CH{\equiv}CH} + 2KX + 2H_2O$$

63 (*c*) Reaction of acetylene with chlorine in dark is an addition reaction, so it does not show the acidic nature of ethyne.

64 (*b*) But-2-yne has no hydrogen attached to *sp* hybridised carbon. So, all other compounds are more acidic than it.

65 (*c*) The complete reaction is shown below.

$$CaCO_3 \xrightarrow{\Delta} \underset{(A)}{CaO} + CO_2$$

$$CaO \xrightarrow{\text{Carbon}} CaC_2 + CO$$

Hence, *A* is CaO.

66 (*b*) $\underset{\text{Terminal alkyne}}{R{-}C{\equiv}CH} \xrightarrow[H_2]{Pt/Pd/Ni} \underset{(A)}{R{-}CH{=}CH_2}$

$R{-}C{\equiv}CH \xrightarrow{NaNH_2} \underset{(B)}{R{-}C{\equiv}C^- Na^+}$

Thus, *A* is $R{-}CH{=}CH_2$ and *B* is $R{-}C{\equiv}C^-Na^+$.

67 (*d*) The complete reaction is shown below.

$$\underset{\text{Propyne}}{CH_3{-}C{\equiv}CH} + Br{-}Br \longrightarrow \underset{\substack{A\\ \text{1, 2-dibromopropene}}}{CH_3CBr{=}CHBr}$$

Thus, *A* is $CH_3CBr{=}CHBr$.

68 (*c*) The complete reaction is shown below :

$$CH_3—C \equiv CH + HBr \longrightarrow \underset{\text{2-bromopropene}}{CH_3—\overset{\overset{Br}{|}}{C}=CH_2}$$

Propyne

Thus, product is 2-bromopropene.

69 (*c*) The complete reaction is given below .

$$\underset{\text{Acetylene or ethyne}}{3H—C \equiv C—H} \xrightarrow[\text{873 K, }\Delta\text{ Cyclic polymerisation}]{\text{Red hot iron tube}}$$

Benzene

70 (*c*) Statement (c) is correct, while other statements are incorrect.

Corrected form are as follows

(a) Aromatic hydrocarbons are non-polar molecules.

(b) Aromatic hydrocarbons are usually colourless liquids or solids with a characteristic aroma.

(d) Aromatic hydrocarbons are readily miscible with organic solvents.

71 (*b*) The given compound is shown below

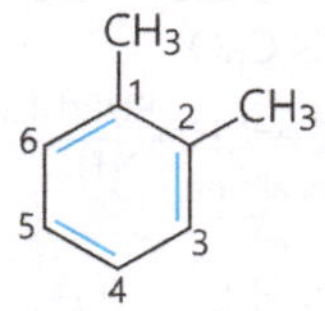

The common name of the compound is *o*-xylene and IUPAC name of the compound is 1,2-dimethylbenzene.

72 (*c*) Benzene forms a triozonide which indicates the presence of three double bonds and reaction involves triozonolysis.

73 (*b*) Statement (b) is incorrect for benzene.

It's correct form is as follows

There are six C—C single bonds and three C—C double bonds in benzene.

Rest other statements are correct.

74 (*b*) The Kekule structure indicates the possibility of two isomeric forms of 1,2-dibromobenzenes. In one of the isomers, the bromine atoms are attached to the doubly bonded carbon atoms, whereas in the other, they are attached to the singly bonded carbons as shown below.

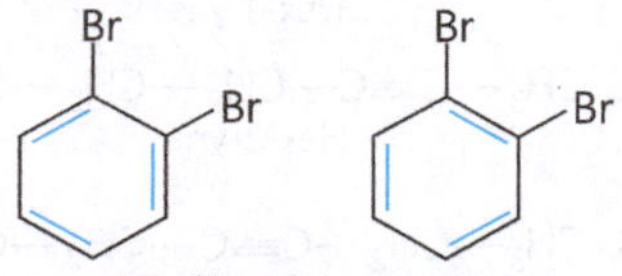

1, 2-dibromobenzene

75 (*b*) Statements I and II are correct, while the Statement III is incorrect.

It's correct form is as follows

C—H σ-bond is obtained by head on overlapping of sp^2-hybridised orbital of C and 1*s*-orbital of H-atom.

76 (*c*)

- 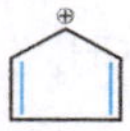 — Anti-aromatic
-  — Anti-aromatic
- 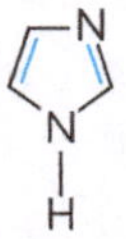 — Aromatic
-  — Non-Aromatic

77 (*b*) Aromaticity of a compound can be decided by Huckel's rule $(4n + 2)$ π electrons

So,  is anti-aromatic does not follow Huckel's rule as it has conjugated 4π-electron $(4n\pi, n = 1)$ system.

78 (*d*) The compound  is not aromatic as there is no delocalisation of pi (π) electrons in the ring.

79 (*a*) The complete reaction is given as follows

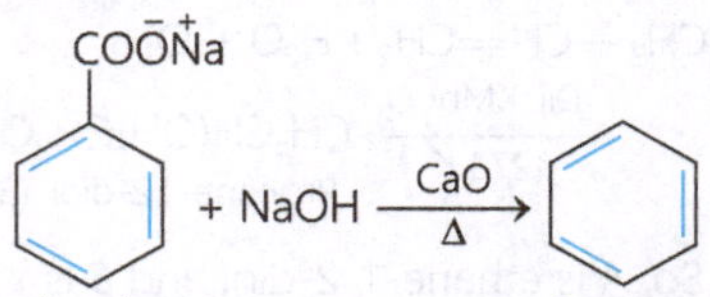

Sodium benzoate Benzene (*A*) + Na_2CO_3

The above reaction is known as decarboxylation of aromatic acids.

80 (*d*) Statements I, II and III are correct while the Statement IV and V are not correct.

The corrected from is as follows:

X-ray diffraction study of benzene explains the unusual behaviour of benzene.

Wurtz reaction is used for the preparation of higher alkanes containing even number of carbon atoms.

81 (*a*) For an electrophilic substitution reaction, the presence of halogen atom in the benzene ring deactivates the ring by inductive effect and increases the charge density at *ortho* and *para* -position relative to *meta*-position by resonance.

82 (*c*) Among the given compounds,

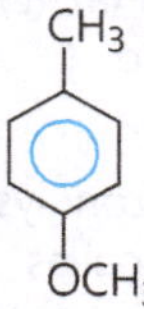

compound is most reactive towards electrophilic reagent. Because (+ *M*) effect of OCH_3 group increase the electron density on the benzene ring.

83 (*a*) The complete reaction is given below.

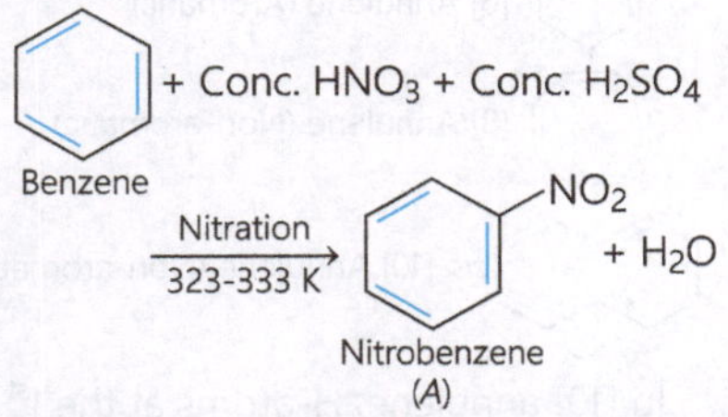

Thus, nitrobenzene is formed and the correct option is (a).

84 (*c*) Nitro group by virtue of –*M*-effect withdraws electron from the benzene ring and decreases the charge density on *ortho* and *para*-position as shown below.

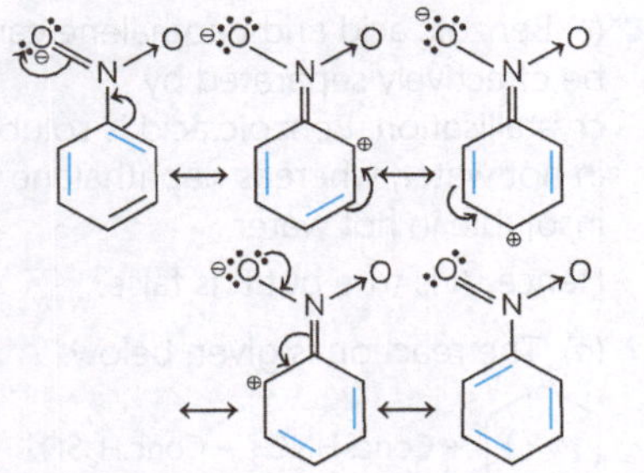

Thus, electron density decreases at *o*/*p*-positions in case of $—NO_2$ and, hence the electrophile attacks at comparatively electron rich *meta*-position.

85 (*c*) When benzene is treated with an alkyl halide in the presence of anhydrous aluminium chloride, alkylbenzene is formed. This reaction is called Friedel-Craft's alkylation reaction as shown below.

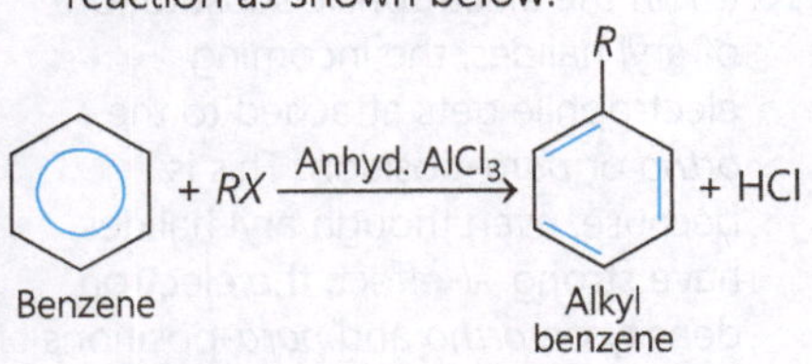

86 (*a*) The complete reaction is shown below.

$$\underset{(Y)}{C_6H_5SO_3H} \xleftarrow[\Delta]{H_2SO_4\,(\text{Fuming})} C_6H_6 \xrightarrow{Cl_2} \underset{(X)}{C_6H_5Cl}$$

Hence, *X* is C_6H_5Cl and *Y* is $C_6H_5SO_3H$.

87 (*b*) The given reaction is represented as

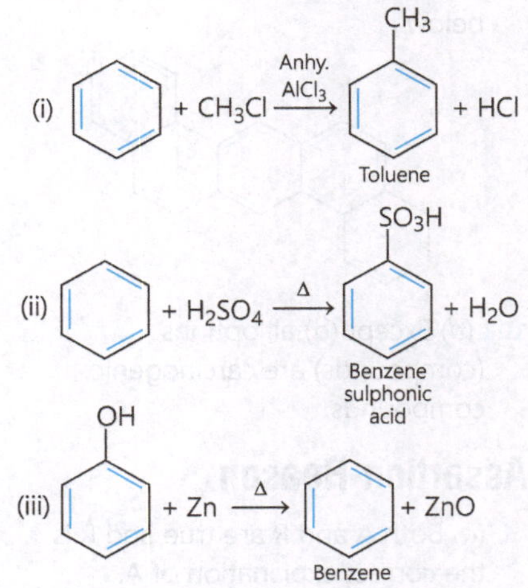

88 (*c*) During nitration of benzene, the attacking electrophile is NO_2^+. It is formed by the reaction between HNO_3 and H_2SO_4 as shown below :

$$HNO_3 + H_2SO_4 \rightleftharpoons H—\overset{+}{O}(H)—NO_2 + HSO_4^-$$

$$H—\overset{+}{O}(H)—NO_2 \rightleftharpoons H_2O + \underset{\text{Nitronium ion}}{NO_2^+}$$

89 (*b*) Statements I and III are incorrect.

It's correct form is as follows

I. The rate of nitration of benzene increases at high. temperature, i.e. 323-333 K.

III. The rate of nitration of chlorobenzene is lower than that of benzene.

Rest other statements are correct.

90 (*c*) The mechanism of the given reaction is follow as

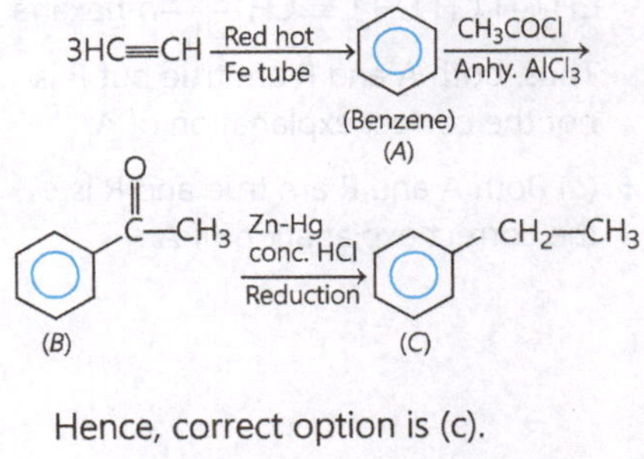

Hence, correct option is (c).

91 (*d*) This reaction is called Friedel-Craft's acylation reaction as shown below.

$$\underset{(A)}{C_6H_6 + CH_3COCl} \xrightarrow{\text{Anhyd. } AlCl_3} \underset{\text{Acetophenone}}{C_6H_5COCH_3} + HCl$$

92 (*b*) The complete reaction is shown below.

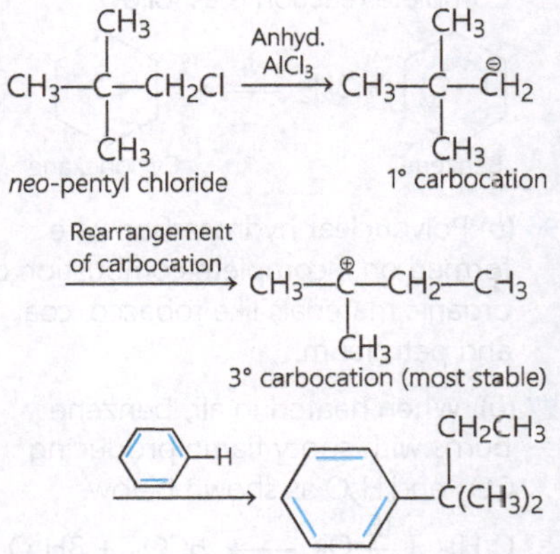

93 (*d*) The reaction is given as

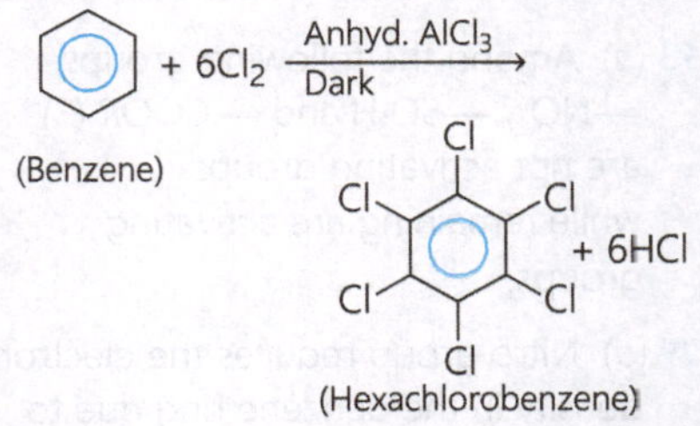

94 (*c*) Electron donating group when bonded with benzene ring will activate the ring and show better electrophilic substitution reaction, whereas electron withdrawing groups deactivate the ring and decreases the nature of electrophilic substitution.

1. Here, alkyl group (i.e. $—CH_3$) show (+*I*) effect and it is an activating group that increases the reactivity of benzene.
2. Chlorine, i.e. Cl show –*I* and +*R* effect due to presence of lone pair of electrons, while —CHO group is of –*R* nature. Thus, C_6H_5Cl show more electrophilic substitution than C_6H_5—CHO.

Groups that show (+*I*) and (+*R*) effect have more electrophilic substitution tendency than those that show either or (−*I*) and (−*R*) effect.

Hence, correct order is $B > A > C > D$ and option (c) is correct.

95 (*c*) *A* is three moles of H_2.

Complete reaction is as follows

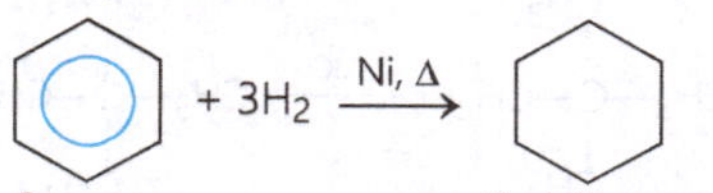

Benzene Cyclohexane

96 (*b*) Polynuclear hydrocarbons are formed on incomplete combustion of organic materials like tobacco, coal and petroleum.

97 (*b*) When heated in air, benzene burns with sooty flame producing CO_2 and H_2O as shown below.

$$C_6H_6 + \frac{15}{2}O_2 \longrightarrow 6CO_2 + 3H_2O$$

Hence, *X* and *Y* refer to CO_2 and H_2O.

98 (*a*) Among the following groups, $—NO_2$, $—SO_3H$ and —COO*R* (3) are not activating groups while remaining are activating groups.

99 (*a*) Nitro group reduces the electron density in the benzene ring due to its strong −*M*-effect. Nitrobenzene is a resonance hybrid of the following structures:

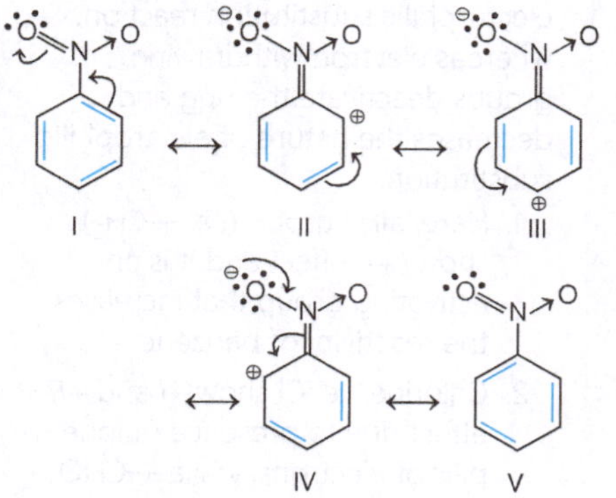

100 (*b*) The correct structure of 1, 2, 5, 6-dibenzanthracene is shown below.

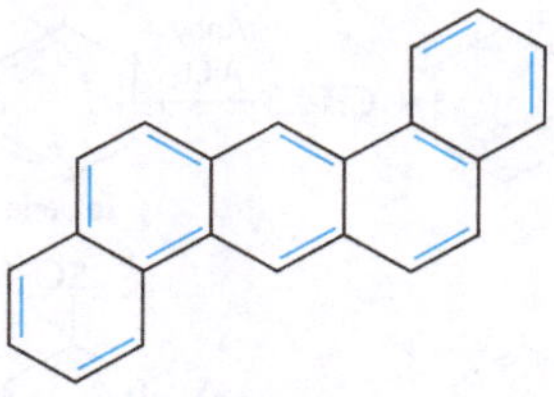

101 (*d*) Except (d) all options (compounds) are carcinogenic compounds.

Assertion-Reason

1 (*a*) Both A and R are true and R is the correct explanation of A.

2 (*d*) Correct form is as follows

Among isomeric pentanes, 2, 2 - dimethylpentane has the lowest boiling point.

3 (*c*) The complete reaction is given below.

$$\underset{\text{But-1-ene}}{CH_2{=}CHCH_2CH_3} + HBr \xrightarrow[\text{Anti-Markovnikov's rule or Kharasch effect}]{H_2O_2} CH_3CH_2CH_2CH_2Br$$

$$\downarrow \dot{B}r$$

$$\underset{\text{Br}}{CH_2}—\dot{C}H—CH_2—CH_3 \xrightarrow{HBr} CH_3CH_2CH_2CH_2Br$$

(Secondary radical) (more stable)

Thus, A is true but R is false.

4 (*b*) The reactions for the given statements are shown below.

$$\underset{\text{Hex-1-yne}}{CH_3CH_2CH_2CH_2C{\equiv}CH} \xrightarrow[\text{catalyst }(H_2)]{\text{Lindlar's}} \underset{\text{(Hex-1-ene)}}{CH_3CH_2CH_2CH_2CH{=}CH_2}$$

$$CH_3CH_2CH_2CH_2C{\equiv}CH \xrightarrow[2H_2]{Pd / Ni} n\text{-hexane}$$

Thus, both A and R are true but R is not the correct explanation of A.

5 (*a*) Both A and R are true and R is the correct explanation of A.

6 (*d*)

[6] Annulene (Aromatic)

[8] Annulene (Non-aromatic)

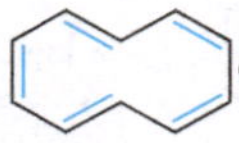

cis-[10] Annulene (Non-aromatic)

In [10] annulene, H-atoms at the 1st and 6th position interfere will each other and force the molecule out of planarity. Planarity is one of the requirement of aromatic system. Hence, A is false and R is true.

7 (*a*) Both A and R are true and R is the correct explanation of A.

8 (*c*) Benzoic acid and napthalene can be effectively separated by crystallisation. Benzoic acid is soluble in hot water, whereas naphthalene is insoluble in hot water.

Hence, A is true but R is false.

9 (*a*) The reaction is given below.

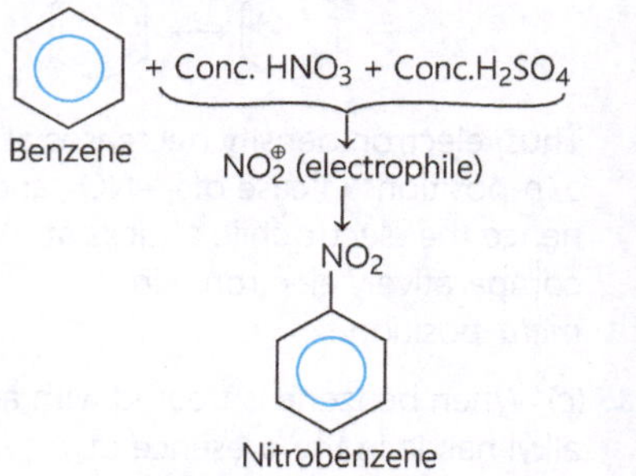

Thus, both A and R are true and R is the correct explanation of A.

10 (*d*) In the electrophilic substitution of aryl halides, the incoming electrophile gets attached to the *ortho* or *para*-position. This is because, even though aryl halides have strong −*I*-effect, the electron density on *ortho* and *para*-positions is greater than that at *meta*-position due to resonance.

Thus, R is true but A is false.

Statement Type

1 (*a*) Both Statement I and Statement II are false.

2 (*a*) Both Statement I and Statement II are false.

3 (*b*) Statement I is true but Statement II is false.

The correct form of it is as follows :

Hydrocarbons are non-polar molecules and water is polar, hence these cannot dissolve with each other as "like dissolves like".

4 (*b*) Statement I is true but Statement II is false.

The correct form of it is as follows

Due to branching, surface area of molecules decreases which makes it more compact and it will be hard to break so melting point increases.

5 (*c*) Statement I is false but Statement II is true.

The correct form of Statement I is

Peroxide effect is not observed in addition of HI because H—I bond is weaker than H—Br bond.

6 (*b*) The structure of tropolone is given as

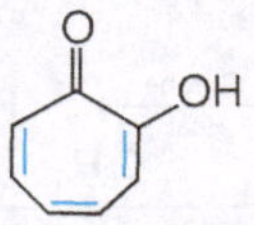

Statement I is true but Statement II is false. Tropolone is an aromatic compound and has 8π electrons (6πe^- are endocyclic and 2πe^- are exocyclic) and π-electrons of

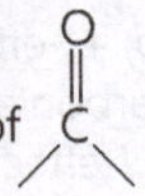

group in tropolone is not involved in aromaticity.

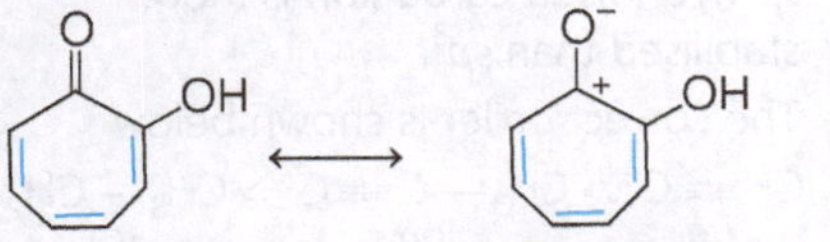

Aromatic compound (6πe^-)

7 (*b*) II and III are the incorrect statements, while I, IV and V are correct statements. The correct form of Statement II and III is as follows.

II. Soda lime is a mixture of NaOH and CaO.

III. *Neo*-pentane contains only one monochloro product.

8 (*c*) Statements I, II and IV are correct but Statement III and V are incorrect. The correct form is as follows

III. 2-methylpropene has identical hydrogen atom so, does not exhibit geometrical isomerism.

V. Preparation of oil gas and petrol gas from kerosene and petrol is the example of pyrolysis.

9 (*c*) The correct statements are II, III and V, while I and IV are incorrect. The correct form of it as follows :

I. Pentane is a liquid hydrocarbon at room temperature.

IV. Presence of unsaturation in organic compounds can be tested with Baeyer's reagent.

10 (*a*) Among the given Statements I and II are correct while Statements III, IV and V are incorrect.

The corrected form is as

- The —OH group activates the benzene ring for the attack by an electrophile and the groups such as —NH_2, —NH*R*, —$NHCOCH_3$, —OCH_3, —CH_3, —C_2H_5 etc., are examples of activating groups.
- Presence of —CHO group in a benzene ring deactivates the ring towards electrophilic substitution.

Matching Type

1 (*c*) The correct match is A-3, B-1, C-2, D-4.

2 (*b*) The correct match is A-1, B-2, C-3, D-4.

3 (*a*) The correct match is A-2, B-3, C-4, D-1.

4 (*a*) The correct match is A-2, B-3, C-1.

5 (*a*) The correct match is A-4, B-3, C-2, D-1.

Numerical Value

1 (*8*)

= 3 monosubstituted products

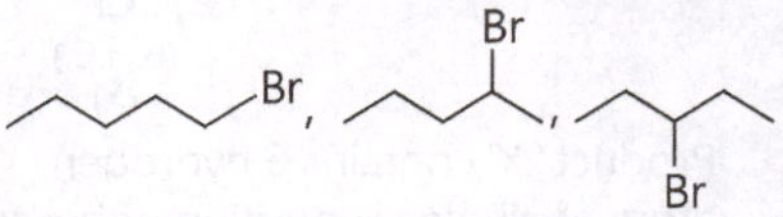

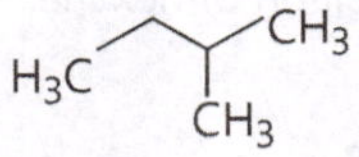

= 4 monosubstituted product

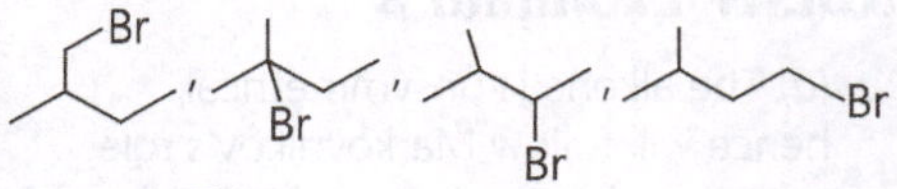

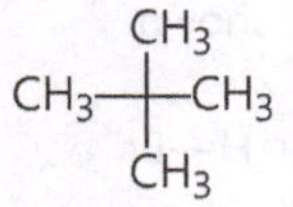

= 1 monosubstituted product

Total derivatives = 3 + 4 + 1 = 8

2 (*3*) There are 3 tertiary carbon atom present in the given compound.

3 (*60*) Staggered form is produced when the rearrangement of atoms or group takes place by an angle of 60°.
1, 1, 1-trichloroethane (CCl_3—CH_3) in eclipsed form on rotation by 60° gives staggered form.

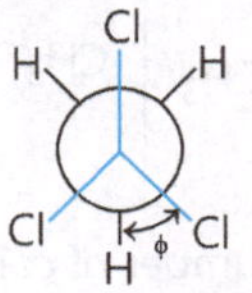

Dihedral angle (ϕ) = 60°

4 (*4*) The number of aromatic compounds are 4.

→ (2πe^-s, planar, conjugated) Aromatic

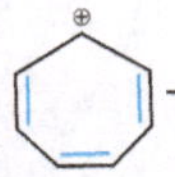

→ (6πe^-s, planar, conjugated) Aromatic

→ (6πe^-s, conjugated, planar) Aromatic

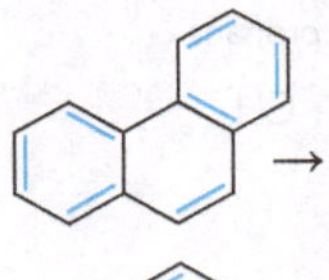

→ (14πe^-s, planar, conjugated) Aromatic

→ (4πe^-s, non-planar) Non-aromatic

5 (*b*)

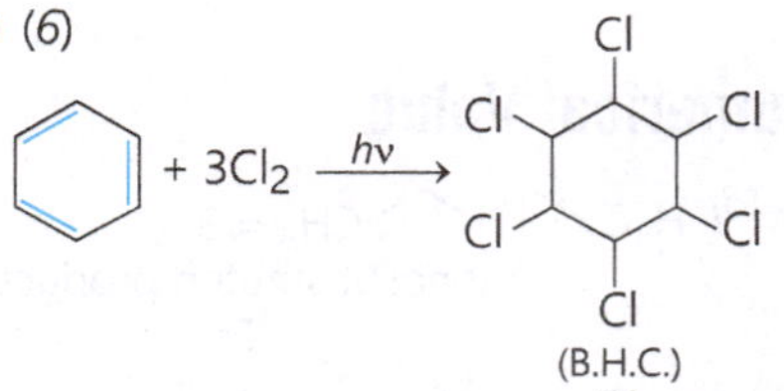

Product '*X*' contains 6 hydrogen atom at all the six position of hexane ring.

NCERT Exemplar's

1 (*a*) The alkene is unsymmetrical, hence will follow Markovnikov's rule to give major product as shown below .

$$CH_3—CH_2—CH{=}CH_2 + H—Br$$
But-1-ene

$$\longrightarrow CH_3—CH_2—CHBr—CH_3$$
(Major product) (*A*)

$$+ CH_3—CH_2—CH_2—CH_2Br$$
(Minor product) (*C*)

Since, *A* contains a chiral carbon, it exists in two enantiomeric forms (*A* and *B*) which are mirror images of each other.

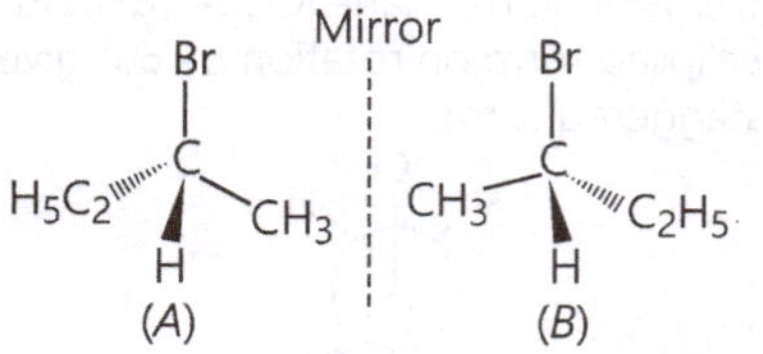

2 (*d*) As the number of carbon atom increases, boiling point increases. Boiling point decreases with branching.

$$H_3C—C(CH_3)_2—CH_3,$$
b.pt. = 282.5 K
(*D*)

$$H_3C—CH_2—CH_2—CH_2—CH_3,$$
b.pt. = 309.1 K
n-pentane
(*C*)
2, 2-dimethyl propane

$$H_3C—H_2C—HC(CH_3)—CH_3,$$
b.pt. = 301 K
2-methyl butane (*B*)

$$H_3C—H_2C—CH_2—CH_3$$
b.pt. = 273 K
(*A*)
n-butane

Thus, the order of boiling point is

$$C > B > D > A$$

3 (*a*) Rate of reaction of halogens with alkanes is,

$$F_2 > Cl_2 > Br_2 > I_2$$

Alkanes react with F_2 vigorously. It is because of the high electronegativity of fluorine. With I_2, the reaction is too slow and it requires a catalyst. Reactivity decreases with decrease in electronegativity which decreases down the group.

4 (*b*) The reactivity of halogens toward alkane is $F_2 > Cl_2 > Br_2 > I_2$. Hence, reduction of alkyl halide with Zn and dil. HCl follows reverse order, i.e. $R—I > R—Br > R—Cl$. Further, the reactivity of this reduction increases as the strength of $C-X$ bond decreases.

5 The correct match is A-(4), B-(1), C-(5), D-(3), E-(2).

	Reagent	Reaction with propene
A.	$O_3/Zn + H_2O$	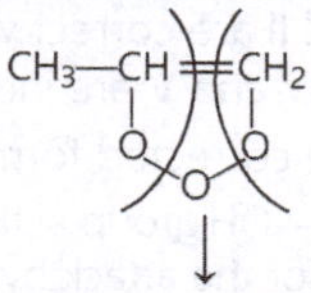 HCHO Formaldehyde + CH_3CHO Acetaldehyde
B.	$KMnO_4/H^+$	$CH_3CH{=}CH_2 \xrightarrow[H^+]{KMnO_4} CH_3COOH + CO_2$ (Acetic acid)
C.	$KMnO_4/OH^-$	$CH_3—CH{=}CH_2 \xrightarrow[OH^-]{KMnO_4} CH_3CH(OH)—CH_2(OH)$ Propan-1, 2-diol
D.	H_2O/H^+	$CH_3CH{=}CH_2 \xrightarrow[\text{(Markovnikov addition)}]{H_2O/H^+} CH_3—CH(OH)—CH_3$ Propan–2–ol
E.	$B_2H_6^+/NaOH^+$ and H_2O_2	$CH_3CH{=}CH_2 \xrightarrow[\text{(ii) NaOH/}H_2O_2 \text{ (Hydroboration-oxidation)}]{\text{(i) }B_2H_6} CH_3CH_2CH_2OH$ Propan-1-ol

6 (*a*) The correct IUPAC name is

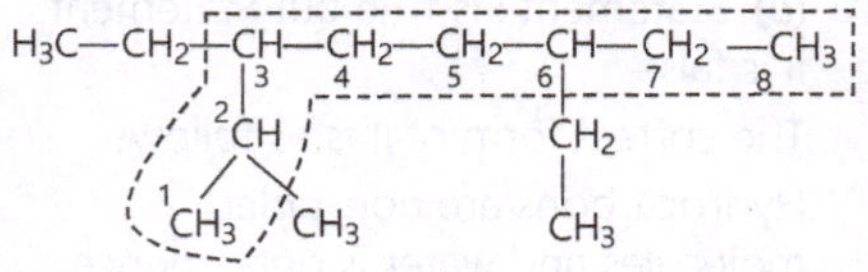

3, 6-diethyl-2-methyl octane.

7 (*d*) Carbon attached with double bond has two same groups (CH_3). Thus, the rotation around carbon will not produce a new compound. Hence, geometrical isomerism is not possible.

8 The correct match is A- (4), B-(1), C-(2), D-(3).

	Reactions	Types of reaction
A.	$CH_2{=}CH_2 + H_2O \xrightarrow{H^+} CH_3CH_2OH$	Hydration (Addition of water)
B.	$CH_2{=}CH_2 + H_2 \xrightarrow{Pd} CH_3—CH_3$	Hydrogenation (Addition of hydrogen)
C.	$CH_2{=}CH_2 + Cl_2 \longrightarrow Cl—CH_2—CH_2—Cl$	Halogenation (Addition of halogen)
D.	$3CH{\equiv}CH \xrightarrow[\text{Heat}]{\text{Cu tube}} C_6H_6$	Polymerisation

9 (*c*) Bond energy of HI is 296.8 kJ/mol, HBr is 367 kJ/mol and HCl is 430.5 kJ/mol. Hence, HI > HBr > HCl is the order of reactivity with propene.

10 (*b*) +*I*-effect decreases the stability of carbon anion. Since, (CH_3) group has + *I*-effect, therefore it intensifies the negative charge and hence destabilises (*A*) relative to (*B*). *sp*-hybridised carbanion is more stabilised than sp^3.

The correct order is shown below :

$$\underset{(B)}{CH \equiv C^-} > \underset{(A)}{CH_3—C \equiv C^-} > \underset{(C)}{CH_3—CH_2^{\ominus}}$$

Hence, the order *B* > *A* > *C* is correct.

11 The correct match is
A-(4), B-(3), C-(2), D-(1).

Reactants	Products
A. Benzene $+ Cl_2 \xrightarrow{AlCl_3}$	Friedel-Craft's reaction 
B. Benzene $+ CH_3Cl \xrightarrow{AlCl_3}$	Friedel-Craft's alkylation reaction 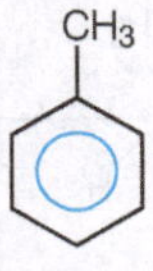 Toluene
C. Benzene $+ CH_3COCl \xrightarrow{AlCl_3}$	Methyl phenyl ketone (Friedel-Craft's acetylation reaction) 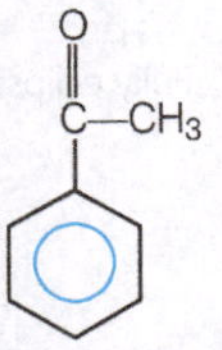
D. Toluene $\xrightarrow{KMnO_4/NaOH}$	Oxidation reaction 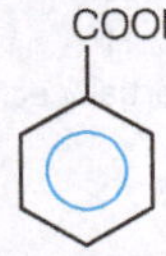 Benzoic acid

12 (*d*) Alkyl halides on heating with alcoholic potash eliminates one molecule of halogen acid to form alkene. Hydrogen is eliminated from β-carbon atom.

Nature of alkyl group determines rate of reaction.

i.e. 3°> 2°> 1°

or $CH_3—\underset{CH_3}{\underset{|}{CH}}—CH_2Br$, (*A*) 3°β-carbon

$CH_3—CH_2—CH_2—Br$, (*C*) 2° β-carbon

$CH_3—CH_2—Br$ (*B*) 1°β-carbon

Thus, decreasing order of rate of reaction is $A > C > B$.

13 (*c*) During incomplete combustion of alkanes with insufficient amount of air or dioxygen, carbon black is formed which is used in the manufacture of ink, printer ink, black pigments and as filters.

Thus, $CH_4(g) + O_2(g) \xrightarrow[\text{combustion}]{\text{Incomplete}} C(s) + 2H_2O(l)$

Past Exams'

1 (*c*) The correct match is
A-III, B-IV, C-II, D-I.

Molecule	Structure	(Type of bonds between two carbon atoms)
A. Ethane	$H_3C—CH_3$ (H—C—C—H with three H on each C)	1σ
B. Ethene	$H_2C=CH_2$	1 σ, 1 π
C. C_2	C=C	2π (as per MOT)
D. Ethyne	H—C≡C—H	1 σ, 2π

2 (*a*) Both Statement I and Statement II are true.

3 (*d*) Among the given options, species that follows Huckel's rule are given as

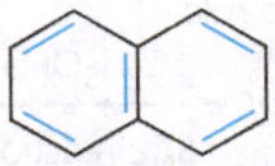
Naphthalene
[No. of π e^-=10]

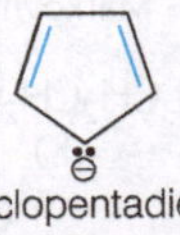
Cyclopentadienyl
[No. of π e^-=6]

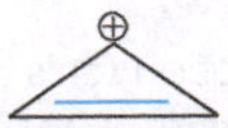
Cyclopropenyl cation
[No. of π e^-=2]

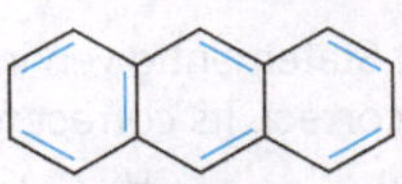
Anthracene
[No. of π e^- =14]

Whereas all other are not-aromatic and does not follows Huckel rule, as (iii), (iv) and (vi) have 4, 4 and 8π-electrons respectively.

4 (*d*) The compound '*X*' that reacts with O_3 followed by reaction with Zn/H_2O gives formaldehyde and 2-methyl propanal as products is 3-methyl but-1-ene. The ozonolysis reaction that involves in this is as follows

$$CH_3—\underset{CH_3}{\underset{|}{CH}}—CH=CH_2 \xrightarrow[\text{(ii) Zn+H}_2\text{O}]{\text{(i) O}_3} (CH_3)_2CH—CH=O + H—CHO$$

2-methyl propanal; Formaldehyde

5 (*c*) $CH_4 \xrightarrow[h\nu]{Br_2} CH_3Br + HBr$

It is a free radical substitution reaction, which have free radical intermediates like $Br^\bullet$, $CH_3^\bullet$ etc.

6 (*b*) The given reaction is represented as

$$\text{Alkene } (A) \xrightarrow[Zn/H_2O]{O_3} (H_3C)_2C=O + O=CH—CH_3$$

Propanone; Ethanal

Alkene (*A*) $\xrightarrow{\text{HCl, Addition reaction}}$ *B* (Major product)

The products of first reaction, i.e. ozonolysis can give an idea about the probable alkene as >C=O group of these arose from the π-bonds of alkene. Thus, most probable alkene will be

$(H_3C)_2C=O \; O=C(H)CH_3 \longrightarrow (H_3C)_2C=C(H)CH_3$ (Alkene)

The reaction taking place will be

$$(H_3C)_2C=CHCH_3 \xrightarrow[Zn/H_2O]{O_3} (H_3C)_2C=O + O=CHCH_3$$

2-methyl but-2-ene (*A*); Propanone; Ethanal

$$(H_3C)_2C=CHCH_3 \xrightarrow{\text{HCl, Addition reaction}} (H_3C)_2\underset{Cl}{\underset{|}{C}}—CH_2—CH_3 + (H_3C)_2CH—\overset{Cl}{\overset{|}{CH}}—CH_3$$

2-chloro-2-methylbutane (*B*) (major product)

2-chloro-3-methylbutane (minor product)

7 (*a*) Alkynes form aromatic compounds when their vapours are passed over red hot copper or iron tubes

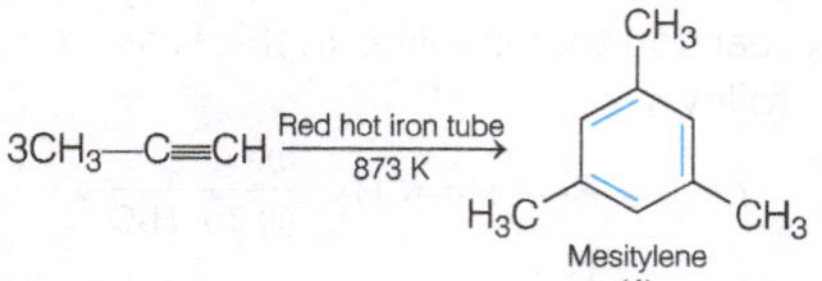

The number of sigma (σ) bonds present in the product (*A*) is 21.

8 (*d*)The given reaction takes place as follows

$$\underset{(A)}{CH_4} \xrightarrow[\text{Step 1}]{Br_2\,/h\nu} CH_3Br \xrightarrow[\text{(Step 2)}]{\text{Na/Dry ether} \atop \text{Wurtz reaction}} CH_3-CH_3$$

9 (*d*) $CH_3-C\equiv CH$

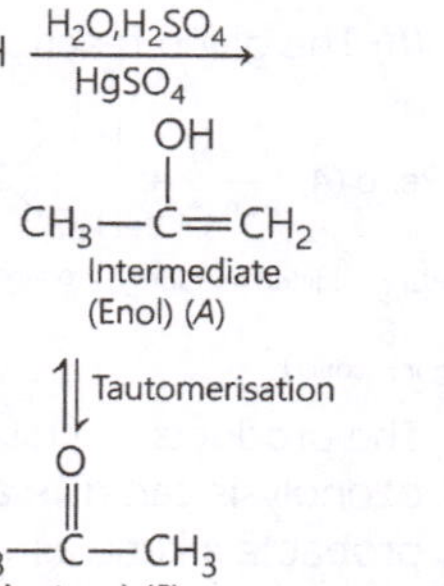

10 (*d*) Isomers which are possible by rotation about single bonds without cleavage of any bond are called conformers.

In ethane, an infinite number of conformations are possible.

So, both bond angle and length remain same.

11 (*c*) First π-electrons of cyclohexene attack at H^+ ion of HF and form carbocation. This carbocation further reacts with benzene and forms addition product.

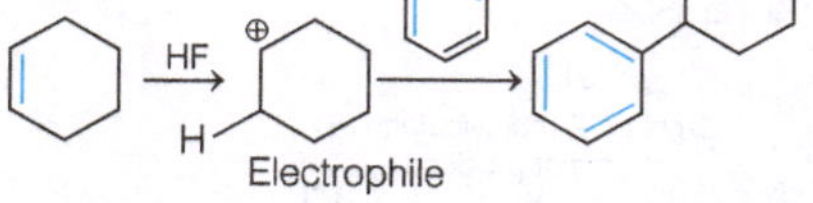

Thus, the correct option is (*c*).

12 (*d*)

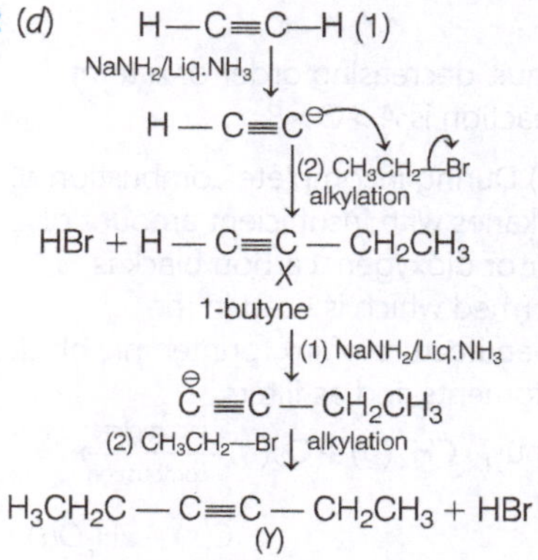

13 (*a*) For structure *A*,

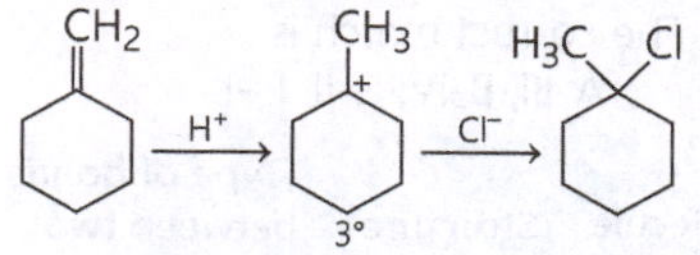

For structure *B*, rearrangement of carbocation occur because 3° carbocation is more stable than 2° carbocation.

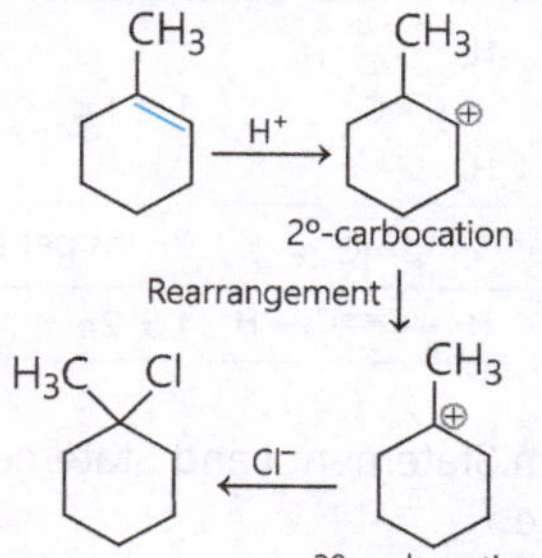

14 (*a*) $CH_3CH_2CH{=}CH_2 \xrightarrow[\text{Anti - Markovnikov's rule}]{HBr\,/H_2O_2} \underset{(Y)}{CH_3CH_2CH_2CH_2Br} \xrightarrow[S_N2\ \text{reaction}]{C_2H_5ONa} \underset{(Z)}{CH_3CH_2CH_2CH_2OC_2H_5}$

15 (*c*) Statement given in option (*c*) is incorrect. Its correct form is,

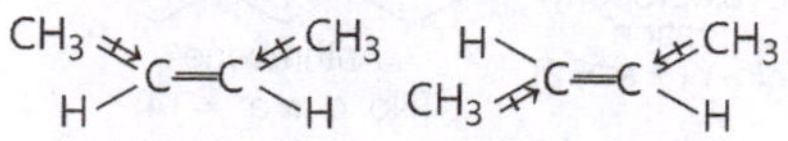

cis but-2-ene has higher dipole moment than *trans* but-2-ene.

16 (*b*) Any compound can be aromatic if it follows the given conditions

- The compound should be cyclic and planar.
- The compound should follow Huckle rule, i.e. have $4n + 2\pi$ electrons.

Structure in B and D are aromatic compound.

Whereas structure in A and C are non-aromatic compound.

17 (*d*) *n*-butane forms more than one type C_2-C_3 rotational conformers.

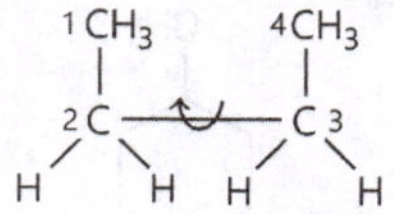

(*n*-butane)

(b)

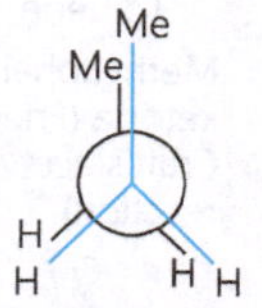

Fully eclipsed form

Fully eclipsed form has maximum steric repulsion between alkyl group (CH_3). So, it is least stable.

(c)

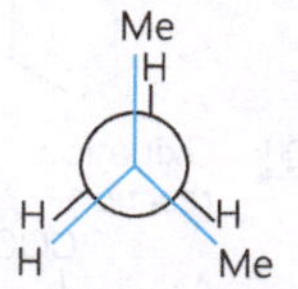

Partially eclipsed form

Partially eclipsed form has lesser steric repulsion than the eclipsed form. So, it is more stable than the eclipsed form.

(a)

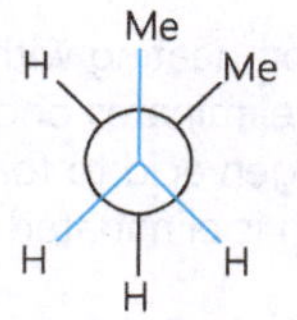

Gauche form

Gauche form is more stable than the eclipsed form.

(d)

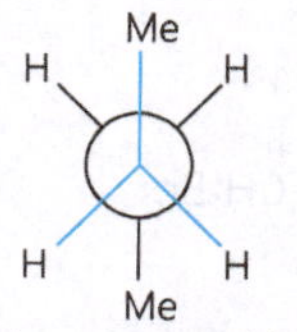

Anti or staggered form

Anti or staggered form is most stable due to lowest steric and torsional strains.

18 (*d*)

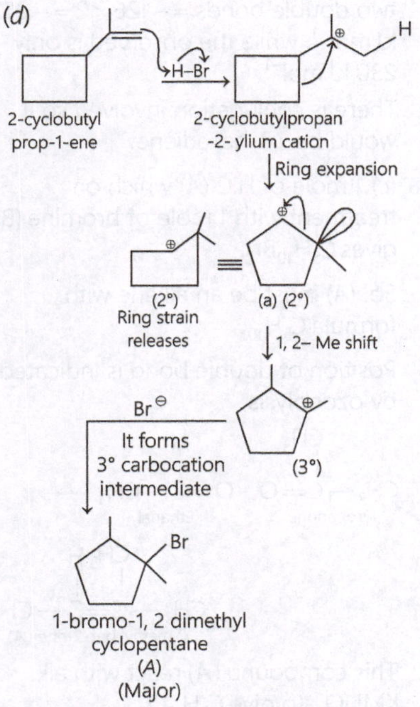

19 (*a*) The correct option is (a).
Mechanism involve in the reaction of cycloalkene with acid hydrogen fluoride so that a proton is abstracted from hydrogen fluoride to form cation of cyclohexene is as follows

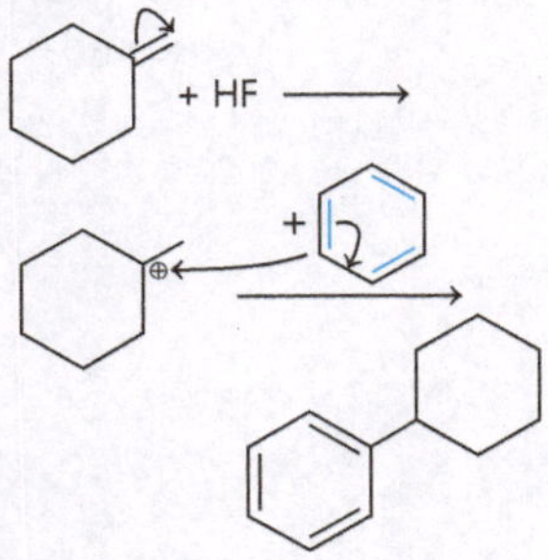

The benzene attacks on the cyclohexyl cation to form the product with two rings joined to each other.
The positive charge is stabilised by the delocalisation in benzene ring.
The abstraction of hydrogen from benzene ring gives final product as shown above.

20 (*c*) Among the given options only (c) is non-aromatic while other are aromatic.

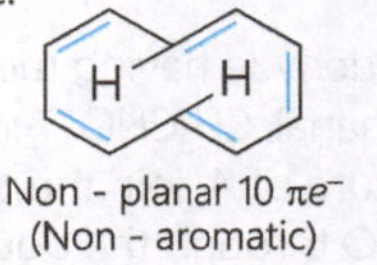

21 (*b*)

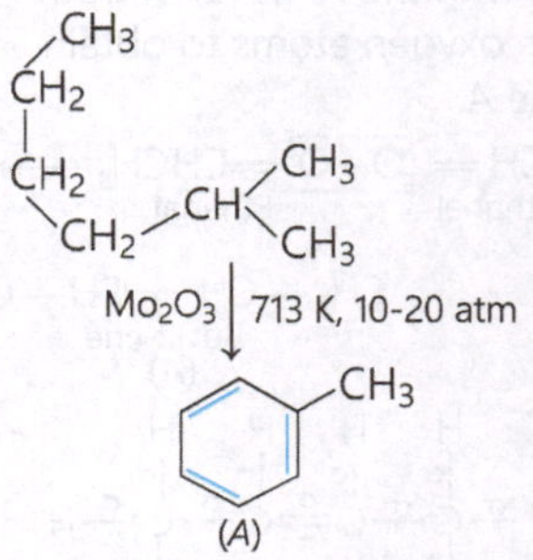

22 (*b*) The reaction take place as follows

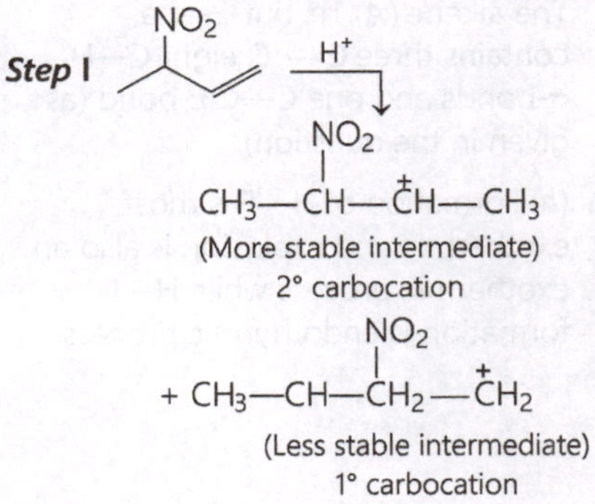

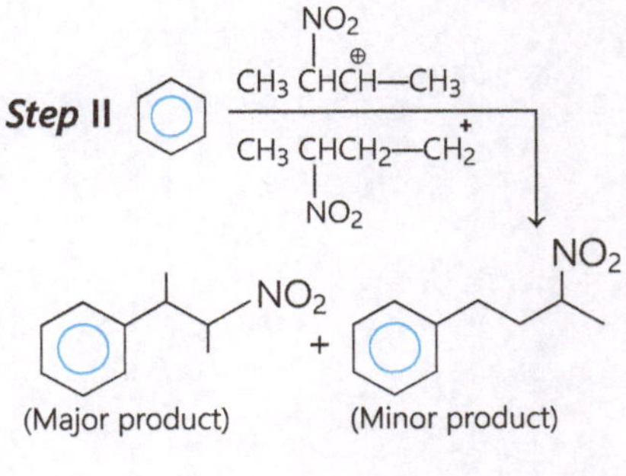

23 (*b*)

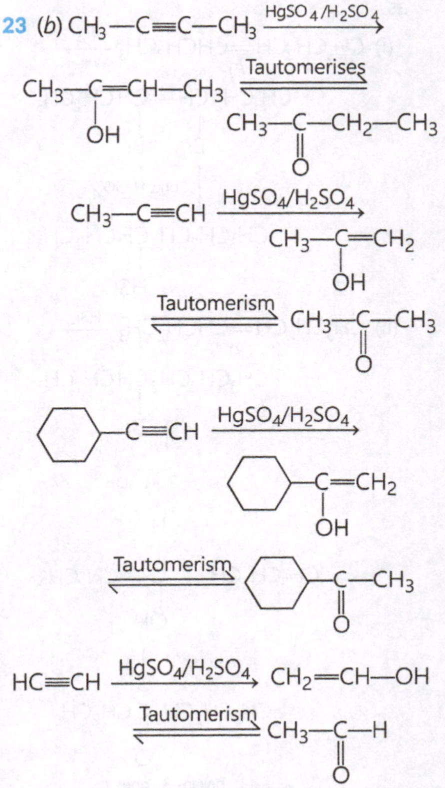

Hence, CH_3CH_2CHO cannot be prepared.

Skill Boosters

1 (*d*) Hydrocarbon (c) is CH_4

$$CH_4 + Br_2 \longrightarrow CH_3Br + HBr$$

CH_3Br by Wurtz reaction is converted to a gaseous hydrocarbon containing less than 4 carbon atoms.

$$2CH_3Br + 2Na \rightarrow CH_3—CH_3 + 2NaBr$$

2 (*b*) The reactions outline is given as

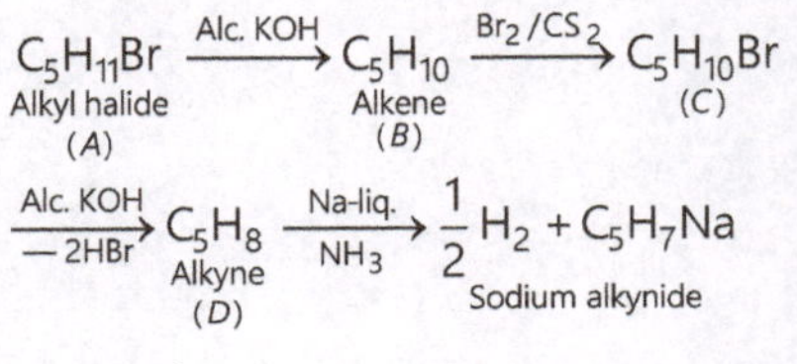

3 (*a*) The given reaction is represented as

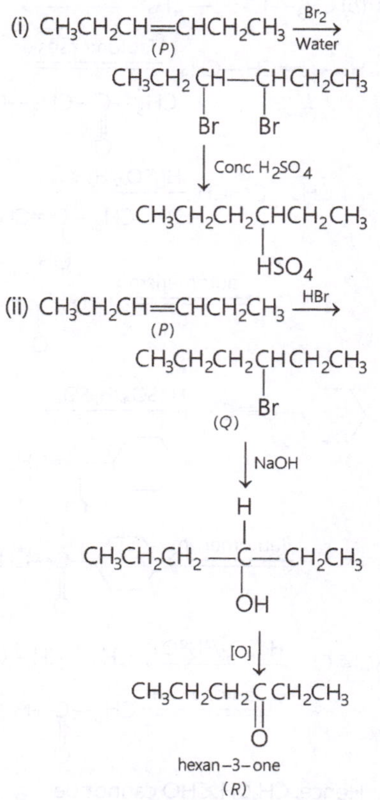

4 (*a*) Two molecules of hydrogen add on 'H', this shows that 'H' is either an alkadiene or an alkyne.

On ozonolysis, compound 'H' gives

$CH_3CHO + OCH—(CH_2)_2—CHO + OC(CH_3)CH_3 \longrightarrow CH_3—CH{=}CH—CH_2—CH_2—CH{=}C(CH_3)—CH_3$

Hence, IUPAC name of the compound 'H' is 2-methyl-octa-2, 6-diene.

5 (*b*) The aldehyde having molar mass 44 v is ethanal, CH_3CHO. To obtain the structure of *A*, join the two ends of CH_3CHO through the double bond with the removal of both of the oxygen atoms to obtain alkene *A*.

$\underset{\text{Ethanal}}{CH_3CH{=}}\boxed{O+O}\underset{\text{Ethanal}}{{=}CHCH_3} \longrightarrow \underset{\underset{(A)}{\text{But-2-ene}}}{CH_3—CH{=}CH—CH_3}$

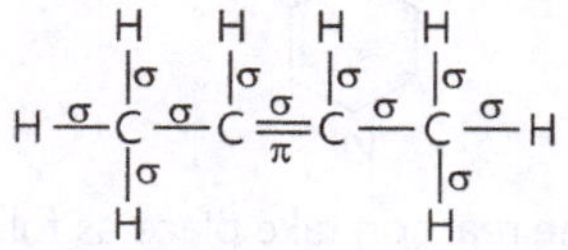

The alkene (*A*), i.e. but-2-ene contains three C— C, eight C—H, σ-bonds and one C—C π-bond (as given in the question).

6 (*b*) Formation of H—F is most exothermic and explosion is also an exothermic process while H—I formation is endothermic process.

7 (*a*) Since, the Δ*H* value expected for two double bonds = – 126 × 2 = – 252 kJ mol^{-1}, while the observed is only 230 kJ mol^{-1}.

There is conjugation involved so it would be 1,3-hexadiene.

8 (*c*) 1 mole of H.C (*A*) which on treatment with 1 mole of bromine (Br_2) gives $C_5H_{10}Br_2$.

So, (*A*) must be an alkene with formula C_5H_{10}.

Position of double bond is indicated by ozonolysis

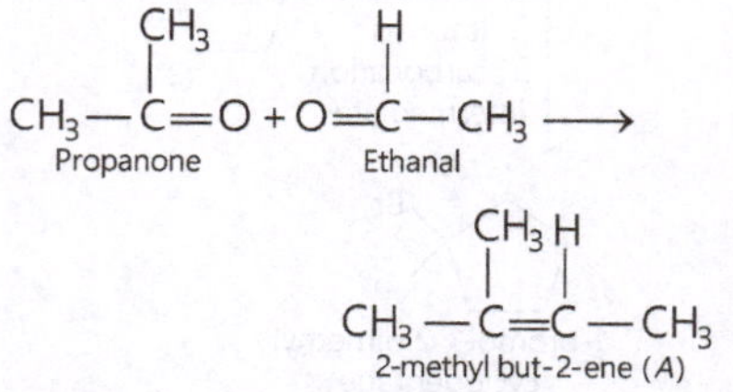

This compound (*A*) react with alk. $KMnO_4$ to give $C_5H_{12}O_2$.

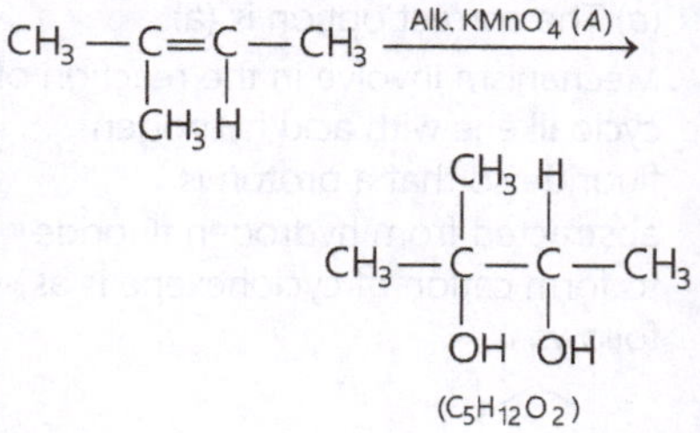

Chapter at a Glance

Completely Coloured Glorified Infographics to map all the Key points of the chapters for quick review.

Some Basic Concepts of Chemistry (Chapter at a Glance)

Physical Properties of Matter

- **Mass and Weight**
  - Mass of a substance is the amount of matter present in it.
  - Weight of a substance is the force exerted by gravity.
- **Volume**
  - Amount of space occupied by a substance.
  - Denoted by cm^3 or dm^3.
  - Litre is used extensively where, $1L = 1000\ cm^3 = 1\ dm^3$
- **Density**
  - $\text{Density} = \frac{\text{Mass}}{\text{Volume}}$

SI Units

Length	l	metre	m
Mass	m	kilogram	kg
Time	t	second	s
Electric current	I	ampere	A
Thermodynamic Temperature	T	Kelvin	K
Amount of substance	N	mole	mol
Luminous intensity	I_V	candela	cd

Prefixes

10^{-1}	deci	d	10^{1}	deca	da
10^{-2}	centi	c	10^{2}	hecto	h
10^{-3}	milli	m	10^{3}	kilo	k
10^{-6}	micro	µ	10^{6}	mega	M
10^{-9}	nano	n	10^{9}	giga	G
10^{-12}	pico	p	10^{12}	tera	T

Significant Figures

- All non-zero digits are significant.
- Zeroes preceding to first non-zero digit are non-significant.
- Zeroes between two non-zeroes are significant.
- Zeroes on the right side of decimal are significant.

Scientific Notation

- Representation of large numbers in form of $N \times 10^n$, where, n can be negative or positive.
- If decimal moves towards right, n is positive. If decimal is moved towards left, n is negative.
- In multiplication, n is added.
- In division, n is subtracted.

Classification of Matter

- **Mixtures**
  - **Homogenous mixtures** are mixtures in which components completely mix with each other.
    e.g. Air, tea, sugar solution etc.
  - **Heterogeneous mixtures** are mixtures in which composition is not uniform throughout and do not mix with each other.
    e.g. Salt and sugar, stone and pulses etc.
- **Pure Substances**
  - **Elements** are species containing only one type of particles.
    These may exist as atoms or molecules.
    e.g. Na, K, H_2, O_2 etc.
  - **Compounds** are species which are obtained from combination of 2 or more atoms.
    e.g. H_2O, NH_3, CO_2 etc.

Empirical Formula

It shows simplest whole number ratio of different atoms present in a compound.
It is obtained by following steps.

- Divide mass of all elements by atomic weight.
- Divide all the obtained values with lowest obtained value.
- Make the obtained number, a whole number if not.
- Write the obtained number below the symbol of the element in subscript.

Molecular Formula

It is the formula showing exact number of atoms present in a molecule.
Molecular formula = $n \times$ empirical formula

$$n = \frac{\text{Molecular formula mass}}{\text{Empirical formula mass}}$$

Mole Concept

Mole Base quantity for amount of substance.

(i) 1 mole of particles 6.023×10^{23} particles or 1 mol = 22.4 L (for gases)

(ii) **Number of moles** $= \frac{\text{Mass}}{\text{Atomic or molar mass}}$

(iii) **Number of molecules** $= N_A \times$ Number of moles

(iv) **Number of atoms** = Number of molecules × Atomicity

States of Matter

- **Solids**
  - Particles are held very close.
  - Have definite volume and shape.
  - Not much freedom of movement of particles.

- **Liquids**
  - Particles are close
  - Have freedom to move
  - Have definite volume
  - Takes shape of container

- **Gases**
  - Particles are distanced
  - Have freedom to move
  - No definite volume or shape
  - Completely fill the space they are in.

- **Plasma**
  - No distinct shape e.g. Lightening.
  - States of matter are inter convertible.

$$\text{Solid} \underset{\text{Cool}}{\overset{\text{Heat}}{\rightleftharpoons}} \text{Liquid} \underset{\text{Cool}}{\overset{\text{Heat}}{\rightleftharpoons}} \text{Gas}$$

Masses

- **Atomic Mass**
  - Represents the mass of an atom.
  - Denoted by amu (Atomic mass unit)
  - $1\ \text{amu} = \frac{1}{12}(\text{Mass of an atom of C-12}) = 1.660 \times 10^{-24}$ g
- **Average atomic mass**
  - Defined for elements existing in more than one isotopes.
  - Each isotope has different mass.
  - Average atomic mass is calculated by taking into account the masses and the % abundance of these isotopes.
    $\frac{\Sigma x_i A_i}{\Sigma x_i}$ (x_i = % abundance, A_i = mass)
- **Molecular Mass**
  - Defined for a molecule.
  - Is equal to sum of atomic masses of all the elements present.
- **Formula Mass**
  - Defined for molecules like, NaCl which does not exist as a single entity.
  - It is taken in terms of amu or u (Unified mass).

Dalton's Atomic Theory

- **Postulates**
  - Matter consists of indivisible atoms.
  - All the atoms of a given element have identical properties including identical mass. Atoms of different elements differ in mass.
  - Compounds are formed when atoms of different elements combine in a fixed ratio.
  - Chemical reactions involves rearrangement of atoms. These are neither created nor destroyed in a chemical reaction.
- **Limitations**
  - Could not explain law of gaseous volumes.
  - Could not explain why atoms combines.

Laws of Chemical Combination

- **Law of Conservation of Mass**
  - Given by Antoine Lavoisier, 1789
  - Matter can neither be created nor be destroyed.
  - There is no net change in mass during a chemical change or physical change.
- **Law of Definite Proportions**
  - Given by Joseph Proust.
  - A compound always contains exactly the same proportions of elements by weight e.g.
    H_2O (from tap)–H–22.22%, O –77.78%.
    H_2O (from lab)–H – 22.22%, O –77.78%
- **Law of Multiple Proportions**
  - Given by Dalton, 1803
  - If two elements can combine to form more than one compound, the masses of one element that combine with a fixed mass of the other element, are in the ratio of small whole numbers.
- **Gay Lussac's Law of Gaseous Volumes**
  - Given by Gay lussac, 1808.
  - When gases combine or produced in a chemical reaction, they do so in a simple ratio by volume provided all gases are at same temperature and pressure.
- **Avogadro's Law**
  - Given by Avogadro's, 1811
  - Equal volumes of gases at same temperature and pressure should contain equal number of molecules.
- **Law of Reciprocal Proportions**
  - When two elements combine separately with a fixed mass of third element, then the ratio between their masses will be either same or simple multiple.

Stoichiometric Calculations

- **Various steps involved in calculations are**
  - Write balanced chemical equation.
  - Write the relative number of moles or relative masses of reactants and products involved below their formulae.
  - In case of gases write 22.4 L at STP in place of 1 mole.
  - Apply unitary method to make required calculations.

Limiting Reagent

- The reactant which gets consumed completely and limits the amount of product formed is called limiting reagent.
- Amount of H_2O is determined by amount of O_2 present.

$$\underset{\substack{(6g)\\(\text{Excess})}}{2H_2} + \underset{\substack{(32g)\\(\text{Limiting})}}{O_2} \longrightarrow \underset{(36g)}{2H_2O}$$

Reactions in Solutions

Reactions occurring in aqueous medium.

- **Mass Percent**
  It is the mass of substance per 100 g of solution.
  $\text{Mass (\%)} = \frac{w_{solute}}{W_{solution}} \times 100$
- **Mole Fraction**
  It is the ratio of moles of a substance to the total number of moles present in the solution.
  Mole fraction of $X_A = \frac{\text{Moles of } A}{\text{Total moles}}$
  Mole fraction of $B\ (X_B) = 1 - X_A$
  Mole fraction can not exceed 1.
- **Molarity** (M)It is moles present per litre of solution. $M = \frac{w \times 1000}{M \times V(\text{mL})}$
- **Molality** (m)
  It is moles present per kg of solvent. It does not vary with temperature.
  $m = \frac{w \times 1000}{M \times W(g)}$
- **Percentage Composition**
  - Shows mass of a constituent in 100 parts of a compound.
  $\text{Mass \%} = \frac{\text{Mass of element in a compound}}{\text{Molar mass of compound}} \times 100$
- **Normality**
  - It is defined as the number of gram-equivalents of solute per litre of solution. $N = \frac{\text{Gram equivalents of solute}}{\text{Volume of solution (in L)}}$

Structure of Atom (Chapter at a Glance)

Subatomic Particles

Particle	Charge	Mass (kg)	Location	Discovery
Electron (e)	-1.6×10^{-19}	9.1×10^{-31}	Outside nucleus	J.J Thomson
Proton (p)	$+1.6\times10^{-19}$	1.67×10^{-27}	Nucleus	E. Rutherford
Neutron (n)	0	1.67×10^{-27}	Nucleus	J. Chadwick

Rutherford's Atomic Model

- Given in 1911
- Based on α-particle scattering experiment
- Positive charge and most of the mass of atoms was densely concentrated in extremely small region (i.e.) **nucleus**.
- Nucleus is surrounded by electrons that move around the nucleus with high speed in circular path called **orbits**.
- Resembles solar system.

Drawback

Failed to explain.
- Stability of atom
- Electronic structure of atom.

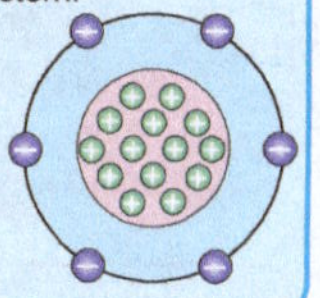

Bohr's Atomic Model

- Electrons revolve around nucleus in orbits. Energy of electron do not change with time.
- Angular momentum is quantised.
  $mvr = \frac{nh}{2\pi}$ $(n = 1, 2, 3)$
  Here, n is principle quantum number,
- Each orbit has a definite amount of energy and definite set of electrons.

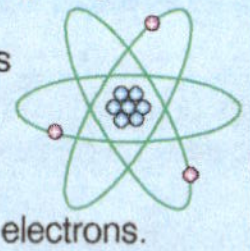

- **Drawbacks** Failed to explain finer details of H atom.
- Could not explain the ability of atoms to form molecules by chemical bonds

Line spectrum of Hydrogen

- Given by H_2 molecules when dissociated into excited H-atoms. Consists of several series of lines. Series of lines are expressed by

$$\bar{v} = \frac{R_H}{hc}\left(\frac{1}{n_1^2} - \frac{1}{n_2^2}\right) \text{cm}^{-1}$$

- Rydberg constant, $R_H = 109677\ \text{cm}^{-1}$
- For absorption spectrum $n_2 > n_1$
- For emission spectrum $n_1 > n_2$

Series of Lines	n_1	n_2	Spectral Region
Lyman series	1	2, 3... ∞	UV light < 4000 Å
Balmer series	2	3, 4... ∞	Visible 4000 – 7000 Å
Paschen series	3	4, 5... ∞	Near IR >7000 Å
Bracket series	4	5, 6... ∞	IR > 7000 Å
Pfund series	5	6, 7... ∞	Far IR > 7000 Å

For absorption spectra, number of lines $= \frac{n(n-1)}{2}$

For emission, number of lines $= \frac{(n_2 - n_1)(n_2 - n_1 + 1)}{2}$

Property	Formulae	Numerical value
• Bohr radius	$r_n = \frac{n^2h^2}{4\pi^2Kme^2Z}$	$r = 0.529\left(\frac{n^2}{Z}\right)$ Å
• Total energy $E = KE + PE$	$E = \frac{-2\pi^2mK^2Z^2e^4}{n^2h^2}$	$E = -13.6\left(\frac{Z^2}{n^2}\right)$ eV atom^{-1} $= -21.8\times10^{-19}\left(\frac{Z^2}{n^2}\right)$ J atom^{-1}
• Velocity of electron (v_n)	$v_n = \frac{2\pi KZe^2}{nh}$	$v_n = 2.188\times10^{-5}\left(\frac{Z}{n}\right)$ ms^{-1}

Developments Leading to Bohr's Model

- **Dual nature of EM radiation**
  Possess both wave like and particle like character.
- **Wave nature** Given by James Maxwell Electrically charged particle under acceleration produces electromagnetic waves. $c = v\lambda$ and $v = 1/\lambda$.
- **Particle nature**
- **Black body radiation** Radiation emitted by a black body.
- **Planck's theory**
  - Energy emitted or absorbed in discrete packets called **quanta**.
  - Quanta of light is called **photon**.
  - Energy is proportional to frequency of radiation.
  - Energy is quantised and cannot be fractional. $E = nhv$
- **Photoelectric effect**
  - Phenomenon of ejection of electrons when light of certain frequency strikes on metal surface.

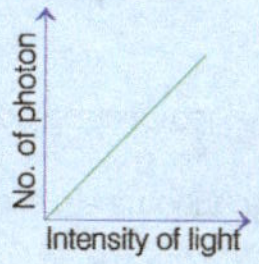

  - Below a threshold frequency (υ_0), effect is not observed.
  - Kinetic Energy of photoelectron (K.E) $= h\upsilon - h\upsilon_0$

Quantum Mechanical Model

- Takes into account dual behaviour of matter.
- Schrodinger equation for any system (atom) whose energy does not change is as $\hat{H}\psi = E\psi$.
- **Schrodinger equation**
  - Energy of electrons is quantized. Follows Heisenberg principle and only talks about probability. Defines ψ as wave function for any electron in an atomic orbital as $\frac{\partial^2\Psi}{dx^2} + \frac{\partial^2\Psi}{dy^2} + \frac{\partial^2\Psi}{dz^2} + \frac{8\pi^2m}{h^2}(E - V)\Psi = 0$
- **Dual behaviour of matter**
  - Given by de- Broglie in 1924.
  - Proposed that electrons should also have momentum as well as wavelength. $\lambda = \frac{h}{mv} = \frac{h}{p}$

Shapes of Atomic Orbitals

- **s-orbital**
  - Boundary surface diagram is centered on nucleus.
  - The sphere has a region having probability of finding an e^- about 90%.
  - With n, size increases. $4s > 3s > 2s > 1s$

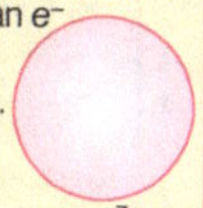

- **p-orbital**
  Are like the shape of dumbell. Has lobes on either side of plane passing through nucleus.

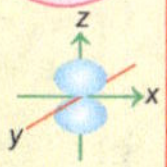

- **d-orbital**
  Are 5 in numbers.
  Given as $d_{xy}, d_{yz}, d_{zx}, d_{x^2-y^2}, d_{z^2}$
  - Represented by the plane in which the orbital lies.
  - Has shape of a double dumbell.

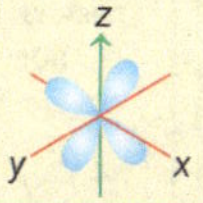

Quantum Numbers

- **Principle Quantum Number (n)** tells size and energy of an orbital.
  $n = 1\ 2\ 3\ 4 \ldots$
  Shell = $K\ L\ M\ N \ldots$
- **Azimuthal Quantum Number (l)**
  - Tells number of subshells and shapes of orbitals.
  $l = 0 \ldots n-1$
  For s-orbital, $l = 0$
  For p-orbitals $l = 1$
  For d-orbitals $l = 2$
- **Magnetic Orbital Quantum Number (m):**
  - Tells number of orbitals in any subshell.
  - For any l, $(2l + 1)$ values of m_l are possible.
- **Electron Spin State (m_s)**
  - Two states are possible.
  + 1/2 for spin up (↑)
  – 1/2 for spin down (↓)

Nodes

- Regions where probability of finding an electron is zero.
- Total nodes in an orbital $= n - 1$
- **Radial Nodes**
  Regions of zero probability across an axis. Is calculated by $(n - l - 1)$
- **Angular Nodes**
  Regions of zero probability across a plane is given by value of 'l'.

Energy of Orbitals

- The orbitals having same energy are called **degenerate orbitals**.
- Existing state of any electron is ground state
- Any other state is excited state.
- For a shell number n, $s < p < d < f$ (Order of energy)
- Effective nuclear charge (Z_{eff}): $Z_{eff} = Z - \sigma$ (σ-shielding)
- Electrons in the outer shells experience less nuclear charge due to shielding by electrons in inner shells. $Z_{eff} \propto \frac{1}{l}$ value, hence $s < p$ (Energy)

Filling of Orbitals

Orbitals are arranged on basis of $(n + l)$ rule $1s < 2s < 2p < 3s < 3p < 4s < 3d < 4p$

- **Aufbau principle**
  Atoms are filled in order of increasing energies.
- **Pauli's Principle**
  - No two electrons in an atom can have same set of quantum numbers.
  - Only two electrons can occupy the same orbitals. Maximum electrons in a shell $= 2n^2$.

Hund's Rule

Pairing of electrons (e^-) in a subshell (s,p,d,f) does not take place until each orbital get one e^- in that subshell or singly occupied.

e.g. [↿⇂] [1 | 1] ; [↿⇂] — Correct; [↿⇂ | |] — Incorrect

Symmetric Distribution
- Symmetry leads to stability
- Electrons in the same subshell do not shield one another effectively. Experience equal nuclear charge.

Exchange Energy
- Electrons having same spin tend to exchange positions. Energy released due to this exchange provide stability. More exchanges possible when the subshell is fully or half-filled and so on giving a total of 10 exchanges.

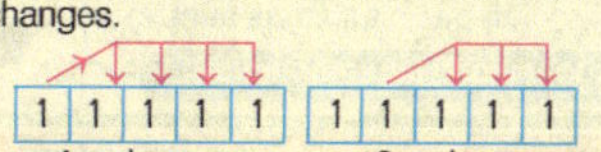

Heisenberg's Uncertainty Principle

- It is impossible to determine exact position and momentum simultaneously.
  $\Delta x . \Delta p_x \geq \frac{h}{4\pi} \equiv \Delta v . \Delta x \geq \frac{h}{4\pi m}$
- Rules out existence of definite trajectories of electrons.

Classification of Elements & Periodicity in Properties (Chapter at a Glance)

Genesis of Periodic Classification

- **Dobereiner's Triads**

Element	At. wt.	Element	At. wt.
Li	7	Ca	40
Na	23	Sr	88
K	39	Ba	137

- Put elements in several groups of triads.
- Atomic weight and properties of middle element was an average of the other two elements.
- Worked only for a few elements.

- **Newland's Octaves**
- Based on law of octaves.
- Arranged elements in increasing order of atomic weights.
- Made observation that every 8th element had properties similar to first element.
- Worked only for element upto calcium.

Mendeleev's Periodic Table

- **Periodic Law**
- Properties, both physical and chemical are a periodic function of their atomic weights.
- Arranged elements in horizontal rows and vertical columns in order of increasing atomic weights.
- Elements with similar properties occupied the same group.
- Emphasis was put on similarities in properties rather than atomic weights.

- **Limitations**
- I with lower atomic weight placed ahead of Te with higher atomic weight.
- Irregularities in properties of lanthanides and actinides.

In Groups

s-block no. of valence electrons in *ns*-orbital.
p-block 10 + number of valence electrons in *np*-orbital.
d-block number of valence electrons in $(n-1)d$ and *ns*-orbitals.

Group 1 - Alkali metals → ns^1
Group 2 - Alkaline earth metals → ns^2
Group 11- Coinage metals → $ns^1\ (n-1)d^{10}$
Group 12- Zinc family → $ns^2\ (n-1)d^{10}$
Group 13 - Boron Family → $ns^2 np^1$
Group 14 - Carbon Family → $ns^2 np^2$
Group 15 -Pnictogens → $ns^2 np^3$
Group 16 - Chalcogens → $ns^2 np^4$
Group 17 - Halogens → $ns^2 np^5$
Group 18 - Noble gases → $ns^2 np^6$

Modern Periodic Law

- **Development Leading to Modern Periodic Law**
- Irregularities in X-ray spectra of elements observed by Henry moseley in 1913.
- For ν frequency, $\sqrt{\nu}$ vs atomic number gave a straight line
- **Periodic Law** Physical and chemical properties of the elements are periodic function of their atomic number.
- Nomenclature of element with atomic number > 100.

Atomic No.	Name
101	Unnilunium (Unu)
102	Unnilbium (Unb)
103	Unniltrium (Unt)
104	Unniquadium (Unq)
105	Unnilpentium (Unp)
106	Unnilhexium(Unh)
107	Unnilseptium (Uns)
108	Unniloctium (Uno)
109	Unnilennium (Une)
110	Ununnillium (Uun)
111	Ununnium (Uuu)
112	Ununbium (Uub)
113	Ununtrium (Uut)
114	Ununquadium (Unq)

Electronic Configuration

In Periods

- **Periodic Number** Highest principle quantum number (*n*) of the elements of the periodic table.
- Number of elements in each period is twice of the atomic orbitals available in the energy level that are being filled.
- 1 (n = 1) 2-elements $1s^{(1\text{-}2)}$
- 2 (n = 2) 8-elements $2s^{(1\text{-}2)}, 2p^{(0\text{-}6)}$
- 3 (n = 3) 8-elements $3s^{(1\text{-}2)}, 3p^{(0\text{-}6)}$
- 4 (n = 4)18-elements $4s^{(1\text{-}2)}, 3d^{(0\text{-}10)}$
- 5 (n = 5)18-elements $5s^{(1\text{-}2)}, 4p^{(0\text{-}6)}, 4d^{(0\text{-}10)}, 5p^{(0\text{-}6)}$
- 6 (n = 6) 32-elements $6s^{(1\text{-}2)}, 5d^{(0\text{-}10)}, 6p^{(0\text{-}6)}$
- 7 (n = 7) 32-elements $7s^{(1\text{-}2)}, 6d^{(0\text{-}10)}, 7p^{(0\text{-}6)}$

Lanthanoids 14 elements of period 6. General configuration $4f^{1\text{-}14}, 5d^{0\text{-}1}, 6s^2$
Actinoids 14 elements of period 7 General configuration $5f^{1\text{-}14}, 6d^{0\text{-}1}, 7s^2$
(Placed in the bottom of the periodic table separately)

Periodic Trends in Physical Properties

- **Atomic Radius**
- It may be covalent, metallic or van der Waals' radii.
- It decreases along a period from left to right but increases on moving down the group.
- Atomic size $\propto \dfrac{1}{Z_{eff}}$

$Z_{eff} = Z - \sigma$

- $Z_{eff} \propto \dfrac{+\text{ve charge}}{-\text{ve charge}}$
- σ is defined as shielding of nuclear charge.

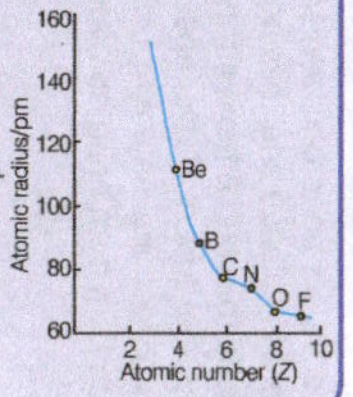

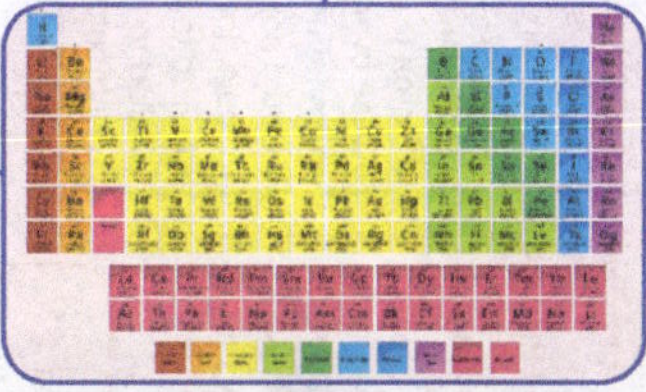

Ionic Radius
- It also follows the same trends as atomic radius.
- A cation is smaller than its parent atom but an anion is larger than its parent atom.

Ionisation Enthalpy
- It is the energy required to remove an electron from isolated gaseous atom.
- It decreases in a group and increases along a period from left to right.

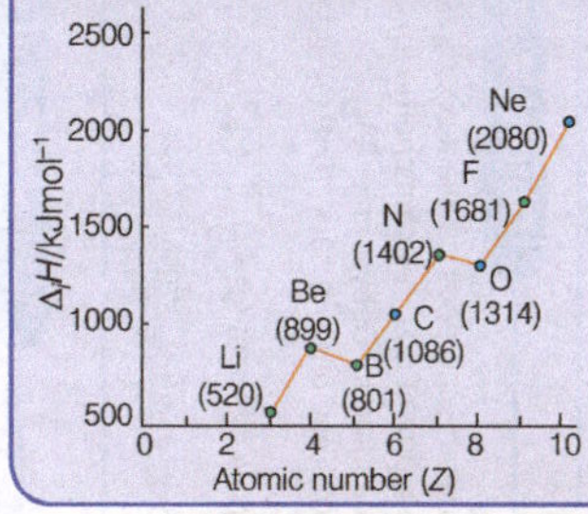

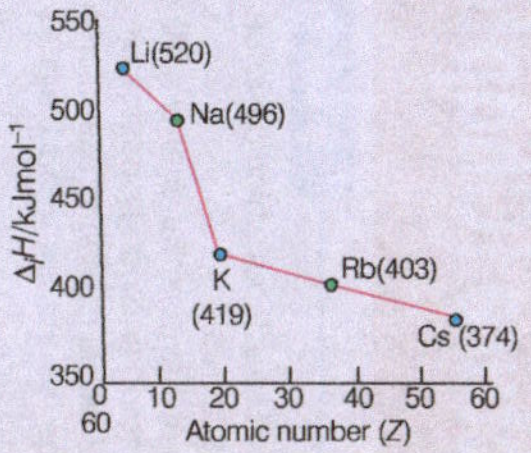

Electron Gain Enthalpy

- It is the energy change occuring during the conversion of an atom into anion. It also follows the same trends as IE.

Element	$\Delta_{eg}H$	Element	$\Delta_{eg}H$
H	–73	F	– 328
Li	–60	Cl	– 349
Na	–53	Br	– 325
O	–141	He	+ 48
S	–200	Ne	+116

Electronegativity

It is the electron attracting power of an element in a compound. It also follows the same trend as IE.

A — B → $A^+ + B^-$ (E.N. of B > E.N. of A)
A — B → $A^- + B^+$ (E.N. of A > E.N. of B)

Atom	EN Value	Atom	EN Value
Li	1.0	F	4.0
Na	0.9	Cl	3.0
N	3.0	Br	2.8

$$EN \propto \frac{1}{\text{Atomic size}}$$

$$E.N \propto Z_{eff} \propto \frac{\text{Positive charge}}{\text{Negative charge}}$$

Periodic Trends in Chemical Properties

Periodicity of Valence State
Valency is the number of electrons in the outermost orbital.

Group	Formula of Hydride	Formula of Oxide
1	LiH, NaH, KH	Li_2O, K_2O
2	CaH_2	MgO,CaO
13	B_2H_6, AlH_3	B_2O_3, Al_2O_3
14	CH_4, SiH_4	CO_2, SiO_2
15	NH_3, PH_3, AsH_3	As_2O_3, N_2O_3, N_2O_5
16	H_2O, H_2S, H_2Se	SO_3, SeO_3
17	HF, HCl	Cl_2O_7

Diagonal Relationship
Found in elements of second period.
Ist element of II period has more similarities in properties of elements of III period.

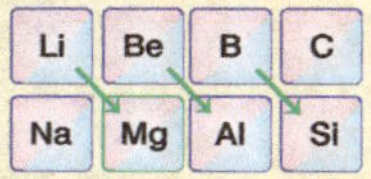

Trends in Reactivity

- **Metallic and Non-Metallic Character**
Metallic character increases on moving down a group and decreases along a period. Reverse is true for non-metallic character.
- **Oxidising and Reducing Property**
In *s*-block, the reducing property increases but oxidising decreases down the group. In case of *p*-block, the order is reverse.

$$\text{Reducing power} \propto \frac{1}{\text{Ionisation enthalpy}}$$

Oxidising power ∝ Electron gain enthalpy

- **Nature of Oxides**
Acidic nature of oxides increases along a period from left to right but decreases on moving down the group. Opposite is true for basic nature. e.g. Na_2O is basic, Cl_2O_7 is amphoteric.

Chemical Bonding & Molecular Structure (Chapter at a Glance)

Kossel-Lewis Approach

- **Atoms** can combine either by transfer of valence electrons from one atom to another or by sharing of valence electrons in order to have a complete octet in their valence shell. This is known as **octet rule**.
- Valence shell electrons are outer shell electrons that take part in reactions.
- **Limitations of Octet Rule**

Not applicable on atoms/molecules which
- have less than four outer electrons. e.g BF_3
- have an extra energy level to accept electrons e.g. PF_5
- have odd number of electrons e.g NO, ClO_2
- could not explain shape, relative stability of molecules.

Covalent Bond

- Electrostatic force of attraction between the nucleus of one atom and electron cloud of another atom having shared equal number of electrons.
- **Polar covalent bond** shared electron are directed more towards the atom having greater electronegativity. e.g NH_3, H_2O etc.
- **Non-polar covalent bond** shared electrons are equally attracted by the two atoms as they have same electronegativity e.g. H_2, Cl_2 etc.

Electrovalent or Ionic Bond

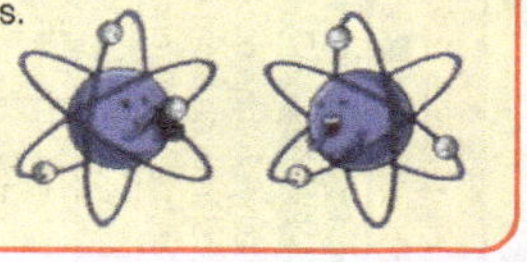

- The electrostatic force of attractions between an anion and a cation formed by complete transfer of electrons.
- Difference in electronegativities of two atoms must be about two or more. e.g. NaCl, $MgCl_2$ etc.
- Electropositive atom forms a cation while electronegative forms an anion.

Fajans' Rule

- Magnitude of covalent character in an ionic bond depends upon the extent of polarisation caused by cation.

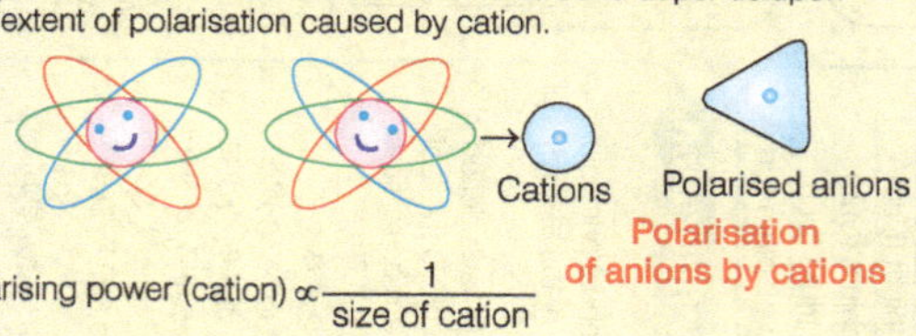

- Polarising power (cation) $\propto \dfrac{1}{\text{size of cation}}$
- Polarisability (anion) $\propto$ size of anion.

Coordinate Bond

- Formed between atoms having excess and deficiency of electrons.
- One atom completely transfers its electrons into an empty orbital of another atom. e.g. NH_4^+, CO.

Bond Parameters

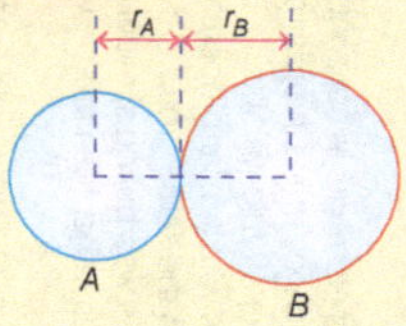

- **Bond Length** The equilibrium distance between the nuclei of two bonded atoms in a molecule.
- **Bond Angle** Angle between the orbitals containing bonding electron pairs around the central atom.
- **Bond Enthalpy** Energy required to break one mole of bond in gaseous state.
- **Bond Order** Number of bonds between two atoms in a molecule e.g $H—C{\equiv}C—H$, B.O = 3
  $H—S—H$, B.O = 1

Resonance

A number of structures which describe a molecule accurately.
All structures have similar energy and similar bonding and non-bonding pairs.
A hybrid of all the resonating structures is known as **resonance hybrid**. e.g.

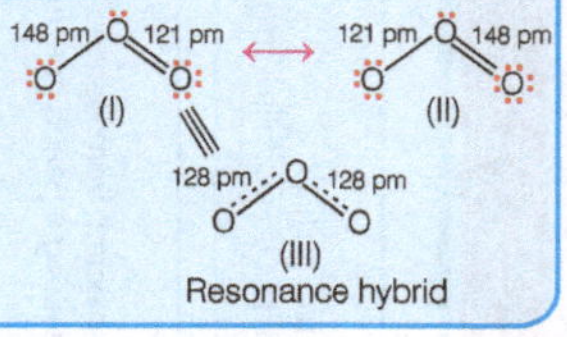

Dipole Moment

- Molecules having polar covalent bonds possess dipole moment.
- Dipole moment (μ) = electric charge (q) $\times$ separation (d)
- It is measured in 'Debye' unit. (D).
- $1D = 10^{-18}$ esu cm $= 3.33 \times 10^{-30}$ C-meter

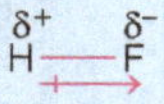

- Net dipole moment $(\mu) = \sqrt{\mu_1^2 + \mu_2^2 + 2\mu_1\mu_2 \cos\theta}$

% ionic character $= \dfrac{\mu_{obs}}{\mu_{ionic}} \times 100$

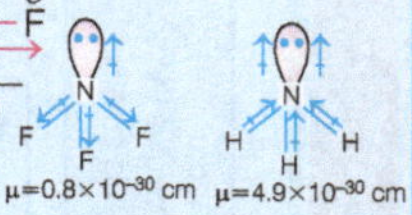

Valence Bond Theory

- Formation of a covalent bond between two atoms occurs by pairing of electrons present in valence shell having opposite spins.
- Directional orbitals (p, d and f) have stronger overlaps while non-directional(s) have weaker overlaps.
- Bond strength $\propto$ directional nature $\propto$ 1/size of orbital
- Sigma (σ) bonds form from head on overlap while π-bond form from side wise overlap.
- **Limitations**
- Could not explain paramagnetism of O_2.
- Could not explain formation of odd e^- bond.
- Failled to explain bonding in electron deficient molecules like B_2H_6.
- Failed to explain formation of coordinate bond in which both electrons are contributed by one of the bonded atoms.

Conditions for Hybridisation

- The orbitals present in the valence shell of the atom are hybridised.
- Orbitals undergoing hybridisation should have nearly same energies.
- Promotion of electron is not essential before hybridisation occurs.
- It is not necessary that only half-filled orbitals participate in hybridisation. In some cases, even filled orbitals of valence shell take part in hybridisation.

Hybridisation

Mixing of different shapes and approximate equal energy atomic orbitals, and redistribution of energy to form new orbitals, of same shape & same energy known as hybrid orbitals.

Hybridisation $H = \frac{1}{2}[V + M - C + A]$

where, V = Valence electrons
M = Monovalent atoms
C or A = Number of Cations or Anions

e.g. NH_4^+, Hybridisation $= \frac{1}{2}[5 + 4 - 1] = \frac{8}{2} = 4 = sp^3$

$H = 2 \rightarrow sp$
$H = 3 \rightarrow sp^2$
$H = 4 \rightarrow sp^3$
$H = 5 \rightarrow sp^3d$
$H = 6 \rightarrow sp^3d^2$

Types of Hybridisation	No. of Hybrid Orbitals	Shape of Molecule	Bond Angle
sp	2	Linear	180°
sp^2	3	Trigonal planar	120°
sp^3	4	Tetrahedral	109.5°
dsp^2	4	Square planar	90°
dsp^3 or sp^3d	5	Trigonal bipyramidal	120° and 90°
d^2sp^3 or sp^3d^2	6	Octahedral	90°

VSEPR Theory

- The shape of the molecules is determined by repulsions between all of the electron pairs present (lone pairs as well as bonded pairs)
- The order of strength of these repulsion is as
  $lp - lp > lp - bp > bp - bp$
- Magnitude of repulsion is dependent on E.N difference between central atom and side atoms.
- Multiple bonds cause more repulsion than single bond.
- **Geometries on VSEPR Theory**

Type of molecule	No. of Bonding pair	No. of Lone pair	Structure and Geometry	Shape	Example
AB_2E	2	1	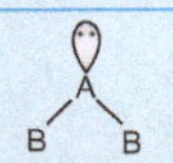 Trigonal planar	Bent	SO_2, O_3
AB_3E	3	1	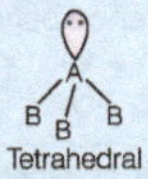 Tetrahedral	Trigonal pyrami -dal	NH_3, PCl_3
AB_2E_2	2	2	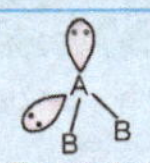 Tetrahedral	Bent	H_2O,
AB_4E	4	1	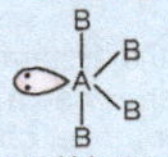 Trigonal bipyramidal	See -saw	SF_4
AB_3E_2	3	2	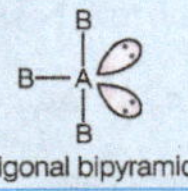 Trigonal bipyramidal	T-shape	ClF_3
AB_5E	5	1	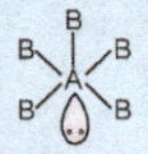 Octahedral	Square pyram -idal	BrF_5
AB_4E_2	4	2	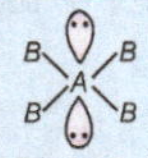 Octahedral	Square planar	XeF_4

Bent's Rule

It explains the relationship between the orbital hybridisation of central atom and electronegativities of substituents in a molecule

- % s-character ∝ bond strength, % s-character ∝ bond angle
- % s-character ∝ 1/bond length $\cos\theta = \frac{s}{s-1}$ or $\frac{p-1}{p}$
- In sp-hybridisation, $s = 0.5$ or 50%, $p = 50\%$
- In sp^2 hybridisation, $s = 33.33\%$, $p = 66.66\%$

Drago's Rule

- Element of 3rd period or below do not allow hybridisation in molecule when they form compound with less electronegative elements. e.g PH_3, SiH_4, AsH_3 do not undergo hybridisation.
- Bond angle observed in drago molecules is nearly equal to 90°.

Types of Overlapping

- **Sigma (σ) bond**
  - A bond formed between two atoms by the overlap of single occupied orbitals along their axes (end to end overlap) is called sigma (σ) bond.
  - Free rotation about σ bonds are possible.

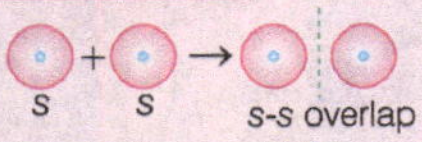

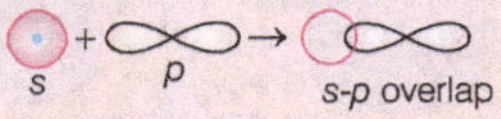

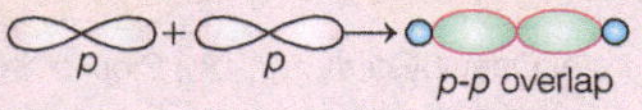

- **π-bond**
  - π bonds are those which are formed by the side wise or lateral overlapping of p and d-orbitals.
  - Free rotations are not possible.
  - π bonds are weaker than σ bonds but multiple bonds are stronger than single bonds.
  Triple bond > Double bond > Single bond.

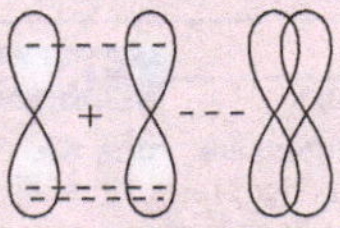

LCAO

- Molecular orbitals are formed by the linear combination of atomic orbitals. The number of molecular orbitals formed is equal to the number of atomic orbitals combined.
- When two atomic orbitals combine they form one bonding molecular orbitals of lower energy and one anti-bonding molecular orbital of higher energy. The molecular orbitals are filled in accordance with Aufbau principle obeying Pauli's exclusion principle and Hund's rule.
- **Condition For LCAO** The combining atoms orbitals must have the same or nearly the same energy.
  The combining atomic orbitals must have the same symmetry about the molecular axis. e.g having the same z-axis as molecular axis.
  The combining atomic orbitals must overlap to the maximum extent.

Molecular Orbital Theory

Element	With 2s-2p Mixing			Without 2s-2p Mixing		
	B_2	C_2	N_2	O_2	F_2	Ne_2
Bond order	1	2	3	2	1	0
Magnetic Properties	Paramagnetic	Diamagnetic	Diamagnetic	Paramagnetic	Diamagnetic	–
Valence electron Configur-ation	$(\sigma 2s)^2(\sigma^*2s)^2(\pi 2p)^2$	$(\sigma 2s)^2(\sigma^*2s)^2(\pi 2p)^4$	$(\sigma 2s)^2(\sigma^*2s)^2(\pi 2p)^4(\sigma 2p)^2$	$(\sigma 2s)^2(\sigma^*2s)^2(\sigma 2p)^2(\pi 2p)^4(\pi^*2p)^2$	$(\sigma 2s)^2(\sigma^*2s)^2(\sigma 2p)^2(\pi 2p)^4(\pi^*2p)^4$	$(\sigma 2s)^2(\sigma^*2s)^2(\sigma 2p)^2(\pi 2p)^4(\pi^*2p)^4(\sigma^*2p)^2$
Interpretation	A	B	C	D	E	F

A Molecule exists stable with single bond. Two electron in π-bonding molecular orbital are unpaired, hence it is paramagnetic

B Molecule exists stable with a double bond. It has 0 unpaired electrons hence, diamagnetic.

C Molecule exists, stable having a triple bond. It has 0 unpaired electrons hence, diamagnetic in nature.

D Molecule exists, stable with a double bond. It is paramagnetic in nature as it has two unpaired electrons in its π-electron antibonding molecular orbital.

E Molecule exists, stable with a single bond. It is diamagnetic in nature as no unpaired electrons are present.

F Molecule unstable and does not exist. As it's non-existent, it's magnetic character can't be determined.

Application

- Bond order $= 1/2\,(N_b - N_a)$
  N_b = number of bonding electrons.
  N_a = number of antibonding electrons.

Nature of bond

Integral bond order values of 1, 2, 3 correspond to single, double and triple bonds.

Bond length

Bond order can be taken as an approximate of bond length.
Bond order ∝ 1/bond length.

Hydrogen Bond

Binds H-atom of one molecule with electronegative atoms (mainly F, O, N) of another molecule.

- **Intramolecular H-bonding**
  Formed between H-atom and an electronegative atom within the same molecule.
- **Intermolecular H-bonding**
  Formed between two different molecules of same or different compounds.

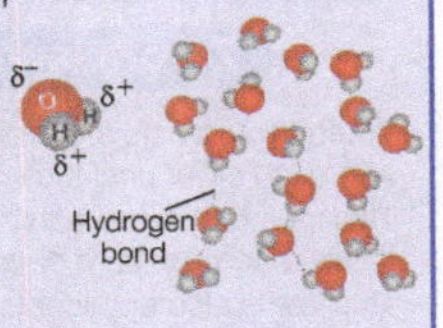

Thermodynamics (Chapter at a Glance)

Thermodynamic Terms

- **System**
  Specified part of the universe which is under investigation.
- **Surroundings**
  Remaining part of the universe which can interact with the system.
- **Boundary** The wall that separates the system from the surroundings.

Types of System

- **Open system** Can exchange both matter and energy.
- **Closed system** Can exchange energy but not matter.
- **Isolated system** Neither matter nor energy can be exchanged.

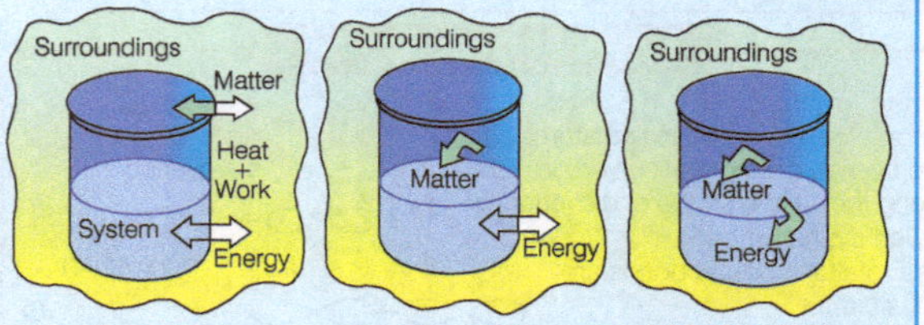

(a) Open System (b) Closed System (c) Isolated System

Thermodynamic Properties

- **Intensive properties** Do not depend upon the quantity or size of matter present in the system. e.g., pressure, temperature, density, surface tension, viscosity, specific heat, melting and boiling points, etc.
- **Extensive properties** Depend upon the quantity or size of matter present in the system, e.g. mass, volume, internal energy, entropy, enthalpy, etc.
- Extensive properties are additive but intensive properties are not.

Thermodynamic Processes

Isobaric process
Thermodynamic process in which the pressure remains constant is known as isobaric process.

$dp=0$

Isochoric process
Thermodynamic process in which the volume remains constant is called isochoric process.

$dV=0$

Thermodynamic process in which there is no heat transfer involved is called **adiabatic process.**

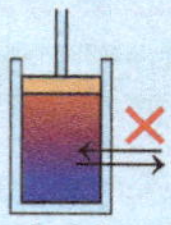

$dq=0$

The process in which the temperature remains constant is known as **isothermal process.**

$dT=0$

- **Reversible process** Direction may be reversed at any stage
- **Irreversible process** Proceeds only in one direction and can not be reversed
- **Cycle process** A system that undergoes a number of states and finally returning to its intial state

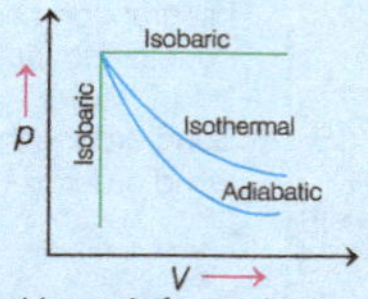

pV graph for various thermodynamic processes

Zeroth law of Thermodynamics

- When two objects are brought in thermal contact, they exchange heat with each other until they reach a state of thermal equilibrium.
- This idea of thermal equilibrium is called **zeroth law of thermodynamics** or law of temperature or law of thermal equilibrium.
- This law is also applicable for more than two objects. If each of the two objects is in thermal equilibrium with a third object then they are also in thermal equilibrium with each other.

State & Path Functions

State function Properties which depend only on the initial and final states of a system. e.g. Pressure (p), Volume (V), Temperature (T), Entropy (S), enthalpy (H)
Path function Properties which depend upon the path followed.
e.g Work and Heat

- **Work** (W)
  It is the mode of transfer of energy.
  $W = p_{ext}(V_f - V_i)$ **(for irreversible process.)**
  $W = -2.303\, nRT \log \frac{V_f}{V_i}$ **(for reversible process).**
  In vacuum, $p_{ext} = 0$, so $W = 0$
  Work done by the system = – ve
  Work done on the system = + ve

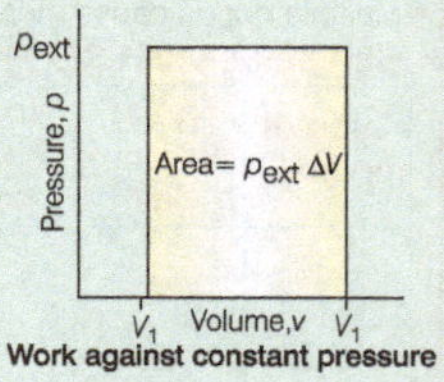

Work against constant pressure

- **Heat** (q)
  Mode of energy exchanged between the system and the surroundings as a result of temperature difference between them.
  - Heat given out by the system is – ve.
  - Heat absorbed by the system is + ve.

First Law of Thermodynamics

- Energy can neither be created nor be destroyed although it can be changed from one form to another.
  Expression : $\Delta U = q + w$ where, $\Delta U = (U_2 - U_1)$
- **Internal energy change** (ΔU)
  - Heat absorbed or evolved by the system at constant volume.
  - It is the sum of all types of energies as a system.
  - It changes with heat or work or matter changes in system.
  - For all isothermal processes, $\Delta U = 0$.
- **Enthalpy Change** (ΔH) It is the total heat content of a system at constant pressure.

$$\Delta H = \Delta U + \Delta n_g RT \; [\Delta n_g = n_p - n_R]$$

where, $\Delta H = \Delta U + p\Delta V$
n_p = number of moles of product and
n_R = number of moles of reactants.

- **Case I** When $\Delta n_g = 0$, then $\Delta H = \Delta U$
- **Case II** When $\Delta n_g < 0$, then $\Delta H < \Delta U$
- **Case III** When $\Delta n_g > 0$, then $\Delta H > \Delta U$
- For reactions involving only solids or liquids, $\Delta V = 0$, $\Delta H = \Delta U$

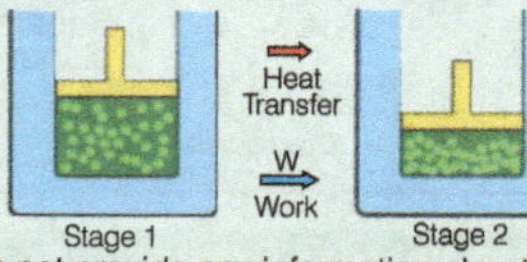

- **Limitation** It does not provide any information about the feasibility of a reaction on process.

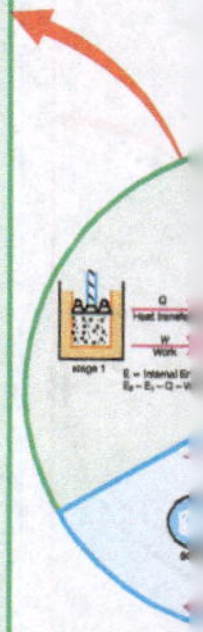

Reaction Enthalpy

Standard enthalpy of reaction ($\Delta_r H^\circ$) Enthalpy change of a reaction when all the participating substances are in their standard states.
Standard Enthalpy of Formation ($\Delta_f H^\circ$) Enthalpy change accompanying the formation of one mole of a substance from its constituents in their standard states.
Enthalpy change during phase transformation Enthalpy change accompanying the conversion of 1 mole of a substance from one state to another.

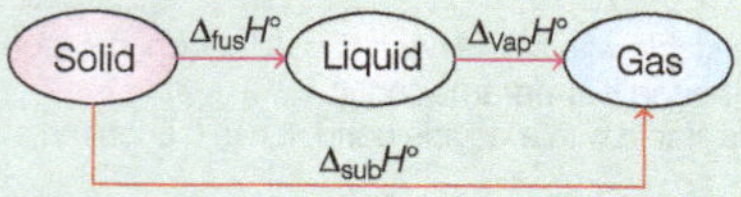

Enthalpy of fusion $(\Delta_{fus}H^\circ) = T_m \Delta S^\circ$
Enthalpy of vaporisation $(\Delta_{vap}H^\circ) = T_b \Delta S^\circ$
Enthalpy of sublimation $(\Delta_{sub}H^\circ) = T_{sub} \Delta S^\circ$

- **Resonance energy**
  - Defined for systems having extra stability.
  - Resonance energy = Experimental heat of formation – Calculated heat of formation.

Enthalpy of Different Reactions

Enthalpy of combustion ($\Delta_c H$) Change in enthalpy when one mole of a substance is completely burnt in oxygen.

$$C(s) + O_2(g) \longrightarrow CO_2(g)\ (\Delta_c H).$$

Enthalpy of atomization ($\Delta_a H$) Change in enthalpy on breaking one mole of bonds completely to obtain atoms in gas phase.

$$CH_4(g) \longrightarrow C(g) + 4H(g)\ (\Delta_a H)$$

Bond enthalpy Standard enthalpy of reaction is related to bond enthalpies of reactant and product in gas phase.

$$\Delta_r H^\circ = \Sigma B.E_{reactants} - \Sigma B.E_{products}$$

Enthalpy of neutralisation Enthalpy change occurred. when one equivalent of an acid is neutralised by one equivalent of a base.

Enthalpy of solution Enthalpy change when one mole of a substance dissolves in a fixed amount of solvent.

$$\Delta_{sol} H^\circ = \Delta_{lattice} H^\circ + \Delta_{hyd} H^\circ$$

Spontaneity & Entropy

- Defined as the property of a system which measures the degree of randomness in a system.
- $\Delta S = S_{Final} - S_{Initial}$, unit = J/K mol
- Order of entropy of states gas > liquid > solid.

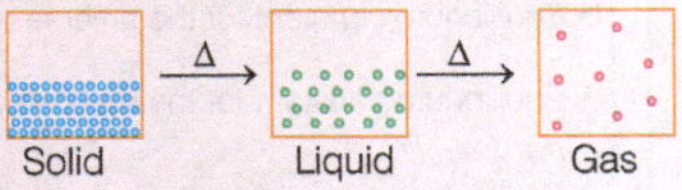

$$\Delta S = \frac{q_{rev}}{T} = \frac{\Delta H}{T}$$

- Entropy change for an ideal gas.

$$\Delta S = nC_V \ln\frac{T_2}{T_1} + nR\ln\frac{V_2}{V_1} = C_p \ln\frac{T_2}{T_1} + nR\ln\frac{p_1}{p_2}$$

- Vaporisation and fusion results in increase in entropy.
- In crystallisation, entropy decreases.
- At equilibrium, $\Delta S = 0$
- For spontaneous change, $\Delta S > 0$.
- For non-spontaneous reactions, $\Delta S < 0$.

Gibbs Energy and Spontaneity

– Gibbs free energy (G) is the net energy available to do useful work.

- $\Delta_r G = \Sigma\Delta_f G^\circ$product $- \Sigma\Delta_f G^\circ$ reactants.
- Gibbs-Helmholtz equation:

$$\Delta G = \Delta H - T\Delta S$$
$$\Delta G^\circ = \Delta H^\circ - T\Delta S^\circ \text{ (standard)}$$
$$\Delta G^\circ = -nFE^\circ, E^\circ = E^\circ_{cell}$$

- If $\Delta G > 0$, process is non-spontaneous
- If $\Delta G < 0$, process is spontaneous.
- If $\Delta G = 0$, process is in equilibrium.

Second Law of Thermodynamic

- All spontaneous processes are accompanied by an increase in total entropy of the universe. $\Delta S_{uni} = \Delta S_{sys} + \Delta S_{surr}$
- No system is 100% efficient.
- It is impossible for a cyclic process to transfer heat from a body at lower temperature to one at higher without conversion of some work to heat.

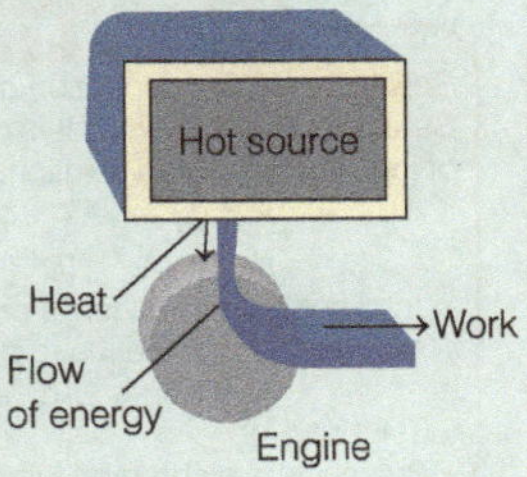

Third Law of Thermodynamics

- The entropy of a perfectly crystalline substance approaches zero as the absolute zero temperature is approached.

$$\text{At } T \to 0\text{K}, S=0$$

Relationship Between ΔG & Spontaneity of a Process

ΔS	ΔH	ΔG	Spontaneous/Non-spontaneous process
+	–	–ve at all temperatures	Spontaneous at all temperature
–	–	–ve at low temperature but +ve at high temperature	Spontaneous at low temperature but non-spontaneous at high temperature
–	+	+ve at low temperature and –ve at high temperature	Spontaneous at high temperature
–	+	+ve at all temperature	Non-spontaneous at all temperature

Gibbs Energy & Equilibrium

ΔG°	log K	K	Comment
$\Delta G^\circ = 0$	$\log K = 0$	1	The equilibrium mixture contains comparable amounts of reactants and products (for 1 M concentration and 1 atm partial pressures).
$\Delta G^\circ < 0$	$\log K > 0$	$K > 1$	The equilibrium mixture contains mainly products, exothermic reactions.
$\Delta G^\circ > 0$	$\log K < 0$	$K < 1$	The equilibrium mixture contains mainly reactants, endothermic reactions.

Heat Capacity

– The quantity of heat required to raise the temperature of system by one degree is called heat capacity of that system.

– This is denoted by C and it is a path function.

Heat capacity $C = \frac{dq}{dT}$, $q = C \times m \times \Delta T$

– If C is the heat capacity of mol of the system, then its molar heat capacity C_m is given by $C_m = C/n$.

– The speacfic heat capacity of water is 1 cal g^{-1} K^{-1}.

- **Heat capacity at constant pressure (C_p)**

$$C_p = \left(\frac{dQ}{dT}\right)_p \text{ when } \Delta p = 0;\ C_p = \left(\frac{dH}{dt}\right)_p$$

- **Heat capacity at constant volume (C_V)** $C_V = \left(\frac{dq}{dT}\right)_V, \Delta V = 0,\ C_V = \left(\frac{dU}{dT}\right)_V$
- **Relation between C_p and C_V** : $C_p - C_V = R$
- C_p/C_V ratio, $\frac{C_p}{C_V} = \gamma$
- The value of γ gives information about the atomicity of gases.
- C_p is always greater than C_V.

Hess's Law

- Total heat change (ΔH) accompanying a chemical reaction is the same whether the reaction takes place in one or more steps.

$$\Delta H = \Delta H_1 + \Delta H_2 + \Delta H_3$$

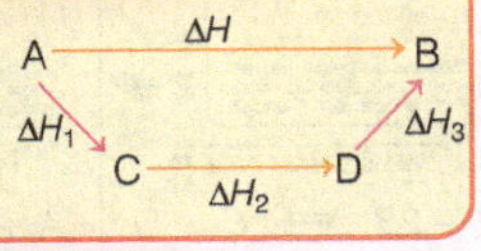

Born-Haber cycle

- Lattice enthalpy change of one mole of an ionic compound dissociating into its ions in gaseous state.
- It is calculated using Born-Haber cycle. e.g. for NaCl

$$\Delta_f H^\circ(\text{NaCl}) = \Delta_{sub} H^\circ(\text{Na}) + \frac{1}{2}\Delta_{sub} H^\circ(\text{Cl}_2) + \Delta_{ion} H^\circ(\text{Na}) = \Delta_{eg} H^\circ(\text{Cl}) + \Delta_{lattice} H^\circ(\text{NaCl})$$

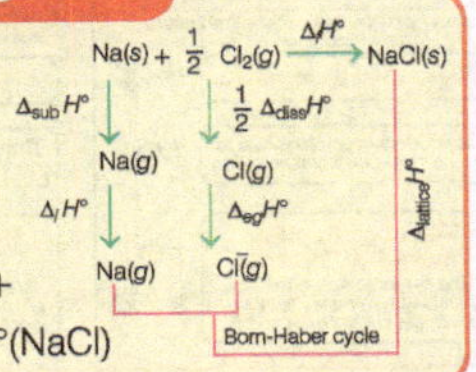

Equilibrium (Chapter at a Glance)

Physical Equilibrium

- Generally observed in phase transformation processes.
- Solid-liquid equilibrium
  Ice (s) $\rightleftharpoons$ Water (l) (in an insulated flask)
  $r_{\text{melting of ice}} = r_{\text{freezing of water}}$
  At fixed temperature and pressure, the change is at equilibrium.
- Liquid-Gas Equilibrium:
  Water (l) $\rightleftharpoons$ Vapour (g)
  $r_{\text{boiling of water}} = r_{\text{condensation}}$
- Solid-Gas Equilibrium:
  I_2 (solid) $\rightleftharpoons$ I_2 (vapour)
  $r_{\text{sublimation}} = r_{\text{condensation}}$

Relation between *K*, *Q* and *G*

$\Delta G = \Delta G^\circ + RT \ln Q$.

- At equilibrium, when $\Delta G = 0$ and $Q = K_C$
  $\Delta G^\circ = -RT \ln K_C$
  $\ln K_C = -\Delta G^\circ/RT$
  If $\Delta G^\circ < 0$, $K_C > 1$. The reaction is spontaneous and forward.
- If $\Delta G^\circ > 0$, $-\Delta G^\circ/RT =$ negative, hence $K_C < 1$. $K_C = e^{-\Delta G^\circ/RT}$ The reaction is non-spontaneous and forward only to a small extent.
- At $K_C = 1$, the reaction is at equilibrium.

Le-Chatelier's Principle

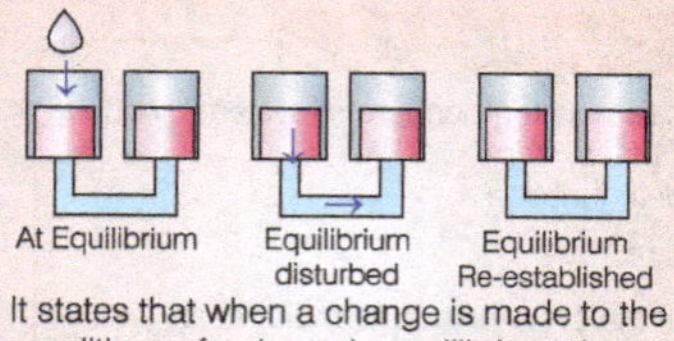

It states that when a change is made to the conditions of a dynamic equilibrium, the system moves to counteract the change, causing changes in quantities of reactants and products.

This is applicable to all physical and chemical equilibrium.

Chemical Equilibrium

- Analogous to physical equilibrium.
- Involves chemical changes.
- When rates of forward and backward reactions become equal, concentration of reactants and products remain constant.

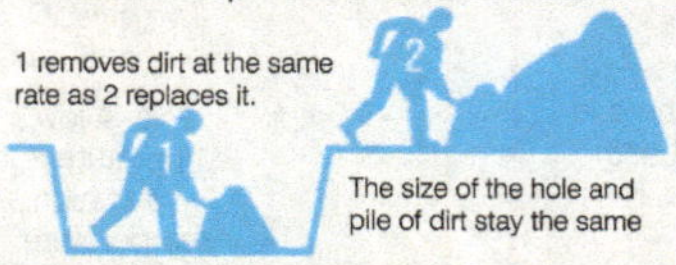

- **Homogeneous Equilibrium** All the reactants and products are in the same phase.
  $H_2(g) + 3H_2(g) \rightleftharpoons 2NH_3(g)$
- **Heterogeneous Equilibrium** Reactants and products are in two or more different phases.
  $C(s) + H_2O(g) \rightleftharpoons CO(g) + H_2(g)$

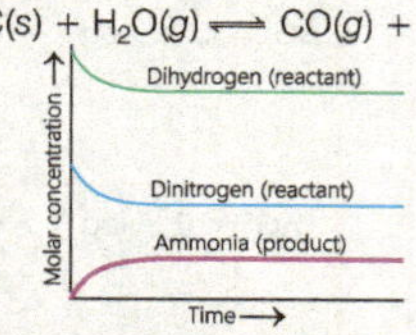

- For heterogeneous equilibrium processes , concentration of solid species and pure solvents are not considered, as they do not change in considerable amount.

Equilibrium Constant

- **For reactions in solutions**, For the reaction,
  $aA(aq) + bB(aq) \rightleftharpoons xX(aq) + yY(aq);\ K_c = \dfrac{[X]^x[Y]^y}{[A]^a[B]^b}$
  K_c = equilibrium constant in terms of molar concentration and this equilibrium equation is also known as law of mass action.
- **For reactions involving gases**
  For the reaction, $aA(g) + bB(g) \rightleftharpoons yY(g);\ K_p = \dfrac{[p_Y]^y}{[p_A]^a[p_B]^b}$
  K_p = equilibrium constant in terms of partial pressure.
- **Units of Equilibrium constant**
  – If $\Delta n_g = 0$, both K_c and K_p have no units
  – If $\Delta n_g > 0$, unit of $K_c = (\text{LmolL}^{-1})^{\Delta n_g}$, unit of $K_p = (\text{atm})^{\Delta n_g}$
  – If $\Delta n_g < 0$, unit of $K_c = (\text{L mol}^{-1})^{\Delta n_g}$, unit of $K_p = (\text{atm}^{-1})^{\Delta n_g}$
- Relation between K_p and K_C
  $K_p = K_C(RT)^{\Delta n}$; If $\Delta n = 0, K_p = K_C$; If $\Delta n = +$ ve, $K_p > K_C$
  If $\Delta n = -$ ve, $K_p < K_C$
- Equilibrium constant for the reverse reaction $K'_C = \dfrac{1}{K_C}$
- Equilibrium constant for the reaction which is divisible by $n, K'_C = n\sqrt{K_C}$
- Equilibrium constant for the reaction which is multiplied by n, $K'_C = (K_C)^n$
- Equilibrium constant for the reaction taking place in n steps $K'_C = K_1 \times K_2 \times K_3 \ldots K_n$

Applications of Equilibrium Constants

- **Predicting the extent of reaction:**
  $K_C > 10^3$ [Forward reaction is favoured.]
  $K_C < 10^{-3}$ [Reverse reaction is favoured.]
  $10^{-3} < K_C < 10^3$ [Both reactants and products are present in equilibrium]
- **Predicting the direction of reaction:**
  For this, reaction quotient Q is defined.
  Q is same as K however in Q, concentrations are not necessarily equilibrium concentration.

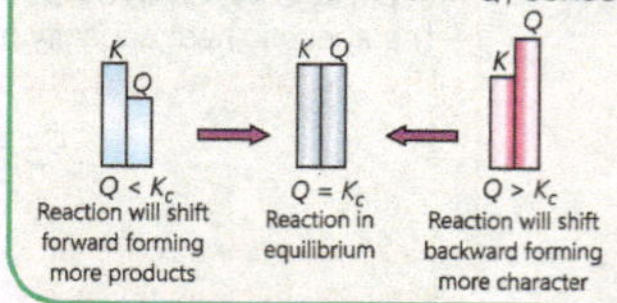

- *Step 1* Write the balanced equation for the reaction.
- *Step 2* Make a table that lists for each substance involved in reaction.
  Initial concentration, change in concentration, equilibrium concentration.
- *Step 3* Substitute the equilibrium concentrations into the equilibrium equation for the reaction and solve.
- *Step 4* Calculate equilibrium concentrations from the calculated value of concentration of substance.
- *Step 5* Check results by substituting them into the equilibrium equation.

Chemical Equilibrium

Factors Affecting Equilibrium

Concentration

Reactant concentration increased
↓
The equilibrium position shifts to reduce the reactant concentration
↓
Reaction forming Products favoured
In the example below the new equilibrium mixture will contain a higher concentration C and D.

Reduces Reactant concentration
$A + 2B \rightleftharpoons C + D$
Reduces Product concentration

Increasing concentration of one side favours the other

Product concentration increased
↓
The equilibrium position shifts to reduce the product concentration
↓
Reaction forming Reactants favoured
In the example above the new equilibrium mixture contain a higher concentration A and B.

Temperature

Temperature increased ↑°C
↓
The equilibrium position shifts to reduce the temperature. ↓°C
↓
The endothermic reaction will be favoured ENDO
In the example below the new equilibrium mixture will contain more A and B and less C and D.

Exothermic *(increases temperature)*
$A + 2B \rightleftharpoons C + D$
(decreases temperature) Endothermic

If the forward reaction is exothermic the backward reaction will be endothermic , and vice. versa

Temperature decreased ↓°C
↓
The equilibrium position shifts to increase the temperature. ↑°C
↓
The exothermic reaction will be favoured EXO
In the example above the new equilibrium mixture less contain more C and B and less A and B.

Pressure

Pressure increased ↑Pa
↓
The equilibrium position shifts to reduce the pressure. ↓Pa
↓
Side of reaction with fewer gas molecules favoured
In the example below the new equilibrium mixture will contain more C and D, and lesser A and B.

Decreases Pressure *(fewer gas molecules on right)*
$A + 2B \rightleftharpoons C + D$
(more gas molecules on left) Increases Pressure

If the number of gas molecules is the same on either side then changing pressure will have no effect.

Pressure decreased ↓Pa
↓
The equilibrium position shifts to increase the pressure. ↑Pa
↓
Side of reaction with more gas molecules favoured
In the example above the new equilibrium mixture will contain more A and B, and less C and D.

Solubility and Solubility Product

Solubility (S) Concentration of a substance in a saturated solution
Solubility Product (K_{sp}) It is defined as the product of concentration of ions in a saturated solution.

$A_xB_y(s) \rightarrow xA^{y+} + yB^{x-}$
$K_{sp} = [A^{y+}]^x.[B^{x-}]^y$

- Total solubility of an ion is product of solubility of salt and the stoichiometry of the ion. e.g
  $Ag_2CO_3 \rightarrow 2Ag^+ + CO_3^{2-}$
  Solubility S $\quad 2S \quad S$
- Presence of a common ion decreases the solubility.

Prediction of Precipitate Formation

- For a solution, at any time, the ionic product (K_{IP}) can be calculated.
- If $K_{IP} > K_{sp}$, the precipitation will take place.
- If $K_{IP} < K_{sp}$, no precipitation will occur.
- If $K_{IP} = K_{sp}$, the reaction is at equilibrium.

Ionic Equilibrium

- Substance that conduct electricity in their aqueous solutions or in molten state are called electrolytes..
- Strong electrolytes are completely ionised in aqueous solutions. e.g. H_2SO_4.
- Weak electrolytes are only partially ionised in aqueous solutions. e.g $Ba(OH)_2$.

Arrhenius Concept of Acids and Bases

- Acids are substances that dissociates in water to give $\rightarrow H^+$ ions.
- Bases are substances that dissociates in water to give $\rightarrow OH^-$ ions.
- H^+ being reactive binds with H_2O to form hydronium ions.

$HX(aq) \longrightarrow H^+(aq) + X^-(aq)$

$H^+ + H_2O \longrightarrow H_3O^+(aq)$

$MOH(aq) \longrightarrow M^+ + OH^-(aq)$

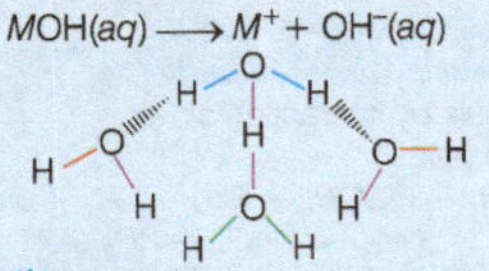

Limitations

- Free H^+ and OH^- do not exist in water.
- Concept is limited to aqueous solutions only.
- Can not explain acidic character of $AlCl_3$, BF_3.

Bronsted-Lowry Acids and Bases

- Acid is a substance that is capable of donating a H^+ ion.

$$HCl\,(aq.) + H_2O\,(l) \rightleftharpoons H_3O^+(aq.) + Cl^-(aq.)$$

(HCl: Acid; H_2O: Adds proton; Cl^-: Conjugate base; HCl Loses proton)

- Base is a substance that is capable of accepting a H^+ ion.

$$NH_3\,(aq.) + H_2O\,(l) \rightleftharpoons NH_4^+\,(aq) + OH^-\,(aq)$$

(NH_3: Base, Adds proton; NH_4^+: Conjugate acid; H_2O Loses proton)

Lewis Acids and Bases

- Acids are defined as species which accepts electron pair.
- Bases are defined as species which donates electron pair.

$$\underset{\text{Lewis base}}{NH_3} + \underset{\text{Lewis acid}}{BF_3} \longrightarrow BF_3 : NH_3$$

Limitations

- Can not explain the strength of acids and bases.
- Does not explain the behaviour of protonic acids such as HNO_3, HCl, H_2SO_4 etc.
- Catalytic activity of acids can't be explained.

Ionisation of Acids and Bases

$$HA \rightleftharpoons H^+ + A^-, K_a = \frac{[H^+][A^-]}{[HA]}$$

Degree of Ionisation, $\alpha = \sqrt{\frac{K_a}{C}}$ where C = concentration

For base, $BOH \rightleftharpoons B^+ + OH^-$, $K_b = \frac{[B^+][OH^-]}{[BOH]}$

- Degree of dissociation, $\alpha = \sqrt{\frac{K_a}{C}}$
- K_a, K_b are acid and base dissociation constants respectively.
- Greater K_a and K_b, stronger is the acid or base.
- $K_w = K_a \cdot K_b$, $pK_a + pK_b = pK_w = 14$
- K_w is the constant of ionic product of water. $K_w = [H^+][OH^-] = 10^{-14}$ or $[H^+] = [OH^-] = 10^{-7}$ M

Factors Affecting Acid Strength

- **Polarity** Strength of HA acid depends on the strength and polarity of H—A bond.
- As size increases, polarity increases and strength increases.

Size increases

$HF << HCl << HBr << HI$

Acid strength increases

- As electronegativity increases, acid strength increases. Electronegativity increases

$CH_4 << NH_3 << H_2O < HF$

Acid strength increases

- **Common Ion Effect** Presence of a common ion suppresses the dissociation of weak electrolytes due to common ion effect. e.g. $CH_3COOH + CH_3COONa$

$CH_3COOH \rightleftharpoons CH_3COO^{\ominus} + H^{\oplus}$

$CH_3COONa \rightleftharpoons CH_3COO^{\ominus} + Na^{\oplus}$

($CH_3COO^{\ominus}$: Common ion)

Salt Hydrolysis

- Salt + Water $\rightleftharpoons$ Acid + Base

Hydrolysis constant: $K_h = \frac{[Acid]\,[Base]}{[Salt]}$

- Degree of hydrolysis (h) is the fraction of total salt that has undergone hydrolysis.

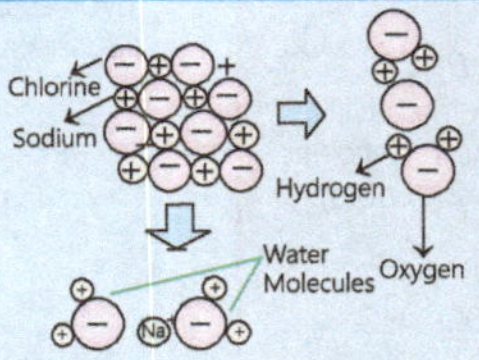

Various Formulae for Salt Hydrolysis

Salt	Nature	Degree of Hydrolysis	pH	K_h
NaCl (strong acid + strong base)	Neutral	No hydrolysis	——	——
CH_3COONa (weak acid + strong base)	Basic	$h = \sqrt{\frac{K_w}{CK_a}}$	$pH = \frac{1}{2}[pK_w + pK_a + \log C]$	$\frac{K_w}{K_a}$
NH_4Cl (strong acid + weak base)	Acidic	$h = \sqrt{\frac{K_w}{CK_b}}$	$pH = \frac{1}{2}[pK_w - pK_b - \log C]$	$\frac{K_w}{K_b}$
CH_3COONH_4 (weak acid + weak base)	*	$h = \sqrt{\frac{K_w}{K_a \times K_b}}$	$pH = \frac{1}{2}[pK_w + pK_a - pK_b]$	$\frac{K_w}{K_a \times K_b}$

* can be neutral, acidic or basic.

pH and pOH Values

- For a weak monobasic acid:

$pH = -\log[H_3O^+], = -\log\sqrt{K_a \cdot C}$

$pH = \frac{1}{2}(pK_a - \log C)$

- For a monoacidic base:

$pOH = -\log[OH^-] = -\log\sqrt{K_b \cdot C}$

$pH = 14 - pOH = 14 - \frac{1}{2}[pK_b - \log C]$

- For mixture of acids and bases

$[H^+] = \sqrt{C_1K_{a_1} + C_2K_{a_2}}$

- where, C_1 = Concentration of acid 1, C_2 = Concentration of acid 2. K_{a_1} and K_{a_2} are dissociation constants of acid 1 and 2 respectively.

$[OH^-] = \sqrt{C_1K_{b_1} + C_2K_{b_2}}$

Buffer Solutions

- Solutions which resist change in pH on dilution or with addition of small amounts of acids or base.
- **Simple buffers** These are the solutions of salts of weak acid and weak base. e.g. CH_3COONH_4 (ammonium acetate).
- **Mixed buffers** These are mixtures of two solutions.
  - **Acidic buffers** These are the solutions of mixtures of weak acid and salt of this weak acid with strong base. e.g $CH_3COOH + CH_3COONa$
  - **Basic buffers** These are the solutions of mixtures of weak base and salt of this weak base with strong acid. e.g. $NH_4OH + NH_4Cl$.

$$pH = pK_a + \log\frac{[Salt]}{[Acid]} = pK_b + \log\frac{[Conjugate\ base]}{[Acid]}\ ;\ pOH = pK_b + \log\frac{[Salt]}{[Base]} = pK_b + \log\frac{[Conjugate\ base]}{[Acid]}$$

Application of Buffer Solutions

- Normal blood have a pH of 7.4 due to buffer nature. This pH is maintained by
  (a) buffer of carbonic acid ($H_2CO_3 + NaHCO_3$)
  (b) buffer of phosphoric acid ($N_2PO_4^-$, HPO_4^{2-})
- Acetate buffer ($CH_3COOH + CH_3COONa$) is used for precipitation of lead chromate quantitatively.
- Buffers are used as preservatives of foods and fruits.
- Buffers are used in paper manufacture, drugs, dyes, inks, electroplating etc.

onic
librium

Some Basic Principles & Techniques (Chapter at a Glance)

Nomenclature

- Complete IUPAC name of an organic compound consists of five parts. Secondary prefix + Primary prefix + Word root + Primary suffix + Secondary suffix
- For naming of benzene compounds, substituents is placed as prefix to word benzene.
- In case of disubstituted benzene, 1, 2; 1, 3 and 1, 4 are used to indicate the position.
- Decreasing priority order for selection of a principal functional group is COOH > — COOR > — COCl > — $CONH_2$ — CN > — CHO > — C== O > — OH > — NH_2 > Alkene > Alkyne

Rules for IUPAC Naming

Rule 1 Select the longest possible carbon chain.

Rule 2 Numbering of parent chain is done from that side where functional group, multiple bond and substituents get the lowest number.

Rule 3 Lowest sum rule—If first substituents sets same number from all side then chain selected should have lowest sum of all substituents numbering.

Rule 4 Alphabet Rule—Naming should be done in alphabetical order if the numbering of all substituents is same.

Rule 5 If the molecule have more than one functional group, the functional group with highest priority assigned the lowest number.

Attacking Reagents

Electrophiles These are positively charged or neutral molecules having electron deficient atom, seeking a site of high electron density.

Positively Charged H_3O^+, X^+ (where *X* = Cl, Br, I) $\overset{+}{N}O_2$, $\overset{+}{N}O$, NH_4^+, SO_3H^+, $C_6H_5N_2^+$, R^+, RCO^+

Neutral BF_3, $AlCl_3$, $FeCl_3$, $BeCl_2$ $ZnCl_2$, SO_3, CO_2, CS_2, CX_4, *R*COCl, :CCl_2

Nucleophiles They are negatively charged or neutral molecules having electron-rich atom with unshared electron pair, seeking electron deficient site to attack. They are also called **Lewis bases** (Electron-pair donors).

Negatively Charged H^-, OH^- X^-, CN^-, N_3^-, RO^-, R^-, RS^-, SH^-, HSO_3^-, NO_2^-, NH_2^-, $RCOO^-$, $HC \equiv C^-$

Neutral NH_3, $H_2\ddot{O}$, $R\ddot{O}H$, $R\ddot{O}R$, $R\ddot{S}H$, *R*MgX, $Ph_3\ddot{P}$, *R*Li, $LiAlH_4$ etc.

Reaction Intermediates

Free radical	Carbocation	Carbanion	Carbene
Electrically neutral, highly unstable, e^- deficient	- + ve charge on C, - Electrophilic, Lewis acid	- –ve charge on C, - Nucleophilic, Lewis base	- Neutral, divalent with 2-unshared electrons -Both nucleophilic and electrophilic
sp^2, planar	sp^2, planar	sp^3 (Non-conjugated), pyramidal sp^3 (Conjugated), planar	(i) sp^2 (singlet): 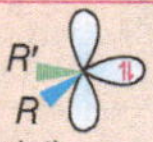 (ii) *sp* (triplet) : $R—\ddot{C}—R$
Paramagnetic	Diamagnetic	Diamagnetic	(i) Diamagnetic (ii) Paramagnetic
Order $Ph_3C > Ph_2CH > PhCH_2 < CH_2 = CH - CH_2 > 3° > 2° > 1° > CH_3 > CH_2 = CH_2$ e.g.-Wurtz reaction – Anti-Markovnikov's addition – Kolbe's electrolysis	**Order** 3°>2°>1° e.g. Pinacol-pinacolone rearrangement – Electrophilic addition reaction of alkenes, alkynes and alkadienes.	**Order** 1°>2°>3° e.g. Aldol condensation – Cannizzaro's reaction – Perkin reaction – Knoevenagel reaction	e.g. Carbylamine reaction – Reimer-Tiemann reaction – Wittig reaction – Wolff rearrangement

Inductive Effect

Inductive Effect Displacement of σ electrons along a saturated C-chain towards electronegative atom.

– *I* effect Order of decreasing strength of –*I* effect due to EWG is0 — NO_2 > — CN > — COOH > — F > — Cl > — Br.

+*I* effect Order of decreasing strength of +*I* effect due to EDG is $(CH_3)_3C—$ > $(CH_3)_2CH—$ > $CH_3CH_2—$ > CH_3 > H—

Electromeric Effect

A temporary effect that involves transfer of -electrons of a multiple bond towards one of the bonded atoms in the presence of an attacking reagent.

+*E* effect $CH_3—CH=CH_2 + H^{\oplus} \longrightarrow CH_3—\overset{\oplus}{C}H—CH_3$

–*E* effect 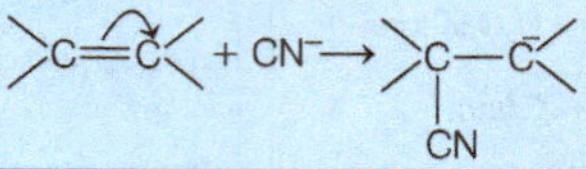

Resonance or Mesomeric Effect

Defined as polarity developed in a molecule by interaction of two π-bonds or between a π bond and a lone pair.

+ *R* or + *M* effect groups — OH, — O*R*, — OCO*R*, — SH, — S*R*, — NH_2, — NH*R*, — NR_2 etc.

– *R* or –*M* effect groups — COOH, — CO, — CHO, — COO*R*, — CN, — NO_2 etc.

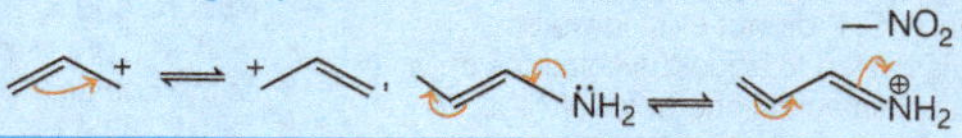

Hyperconjugation

Involves delocalisation of σ electrons of C—H bond of an alkyl group attached to an atom or system with unshared *p*-electrons.

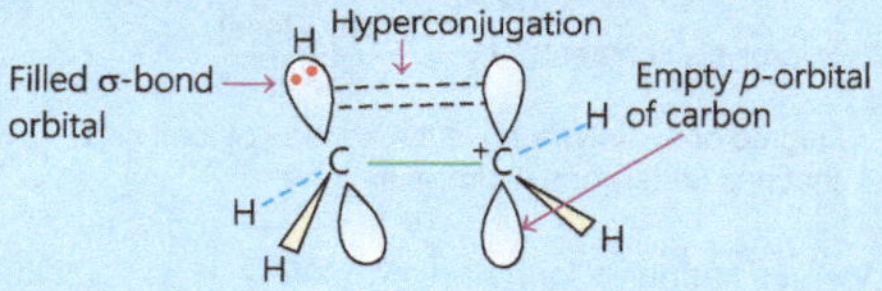

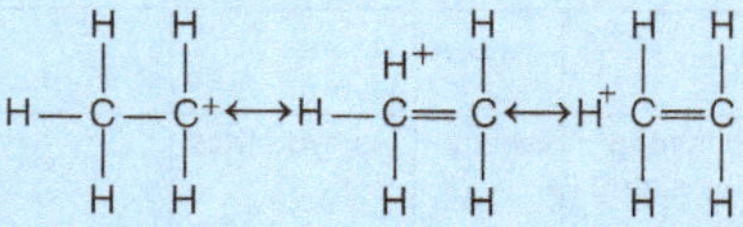

Quantitative Analysis

- **Carbon and Hydrogen** Liebig's method

$$\%C = \frac{12 \times M_2 \times 100}{44 \times M}, \%H = \frac{2 \times M_1 \times 100}{18 \times M}$$

M-Mass of org. compound; M_1-Mass of CO_2 produced; M_2-Mass of H_2 produced

- **Nitrogen** Dumas methods, Kjeldahl's method

$$\%N = \frac{28 \times V \times 100}{22400 \times M}, \%N = \frac{1.4 \times N \times V}{M}$$

M-Mass or org. compound; *N*-Normality of acid; *V*-Volume of acid

- **Halogen** Carius method,

$$\% \text{ halogen} = \frac{\text{atomic mass of halogen} \times M_1 \times 100}{\text{molar mass of Ag}X \times M}$$

M-Mass of org. compound taken; M_1-Mass of Ag*X* formed

- **Sulphur** Carius method,

$$\%S = \frac{32 \times M_1 \times 100}{233 \times M}$$

M-Mass of org. compound; M_1-Mass of $BaSO_4$ formed

- **Phosphorus** Ignition method,

$$\%P = \frac{62 \times M_1 \times 100}{222 \times M}$$

M-Mass of org. compound taken; M_1-Mass of $BaSO_4$ formed

- **Oxygen** Iodine method,

$$\%O = \frac{5 \times 16}{2 \times 127} \times \frac{\text{Mass of } I_2 \text{ formed}}{\text{Mass of org. compound taken}} \times 100$$

Structural Isomerism

- **Chain Isomerism** Having different carbon skeletons. e.g.

Pentane, 2-methyl butane, 2-2 dimethyl propane

- **Position Isomerism** Having different positions of functional group on the carbon chain. e.g

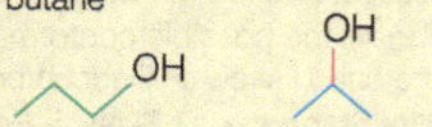

Propan -1-ol, Propan -2-ol

- **Functional Isomerism** Having different functional groups but same formula e.g.

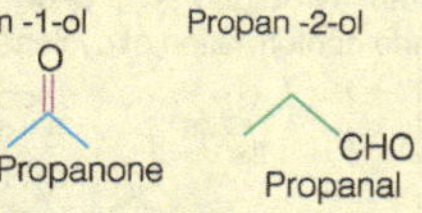

Propanone, Propanal

- **Metamerism** Having different alkyl group on either side of the functional group. e.g.

Methoxy propane, Ethoxyethane

- **Ring Chain Isomerism** Same molecular formula but have open form (chain) isomer as well as in ring isomer. e.g C_4H_8

But-1-ene, Cyclobutane

- **Tautomerism** Arises due to migration of H-atom from one atom to the other within the same molecule. e.g

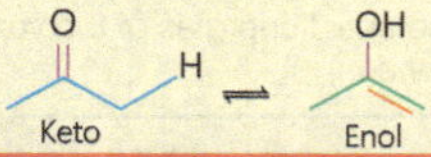

Keto, Enol

Stereo Isomerism

Compounds have that same chemical formula and sequence of covalent bonds but differ in spatial arrangement are called **stereoisomers**.

- **Geometrical Isomerism**
  - Are of types of *cis* and *trans*.
  - *Cis* isomers have same groups on same side of double bond
  - *Trans* isomers have same groups on anti to each other.
  - For compounds not having same groups, the priority of each groups are considered according to CIP rule.
  - E/Z notation is followed in case of different substituents.

e.g.

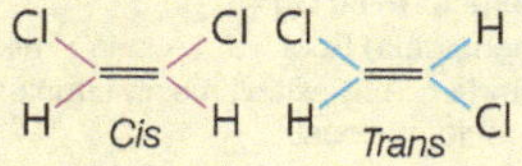

Cis, *Trans*

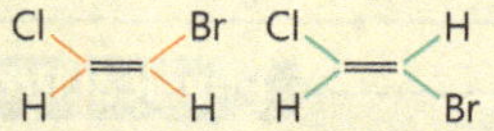

(*Z*) - zusammen, (*E*)-entgegen

- **Optical Isomers**
  - **Enantiomers** Non-superimposable mirror image of a compound are called enantiomers. e.g

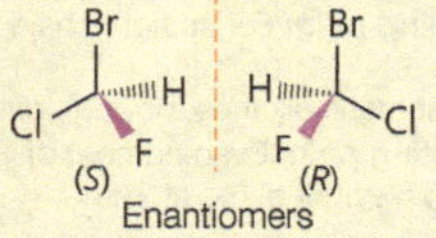

(*S*), (*R*)

Enantiomers

Diastereomers In compounds having at least two chiral carbon atoms. Isomers having different configuration about one carbon atom. e.g

Meso Compounds These are compounds which having at least two centres which are having same substituents but different configuration around carbon centre.

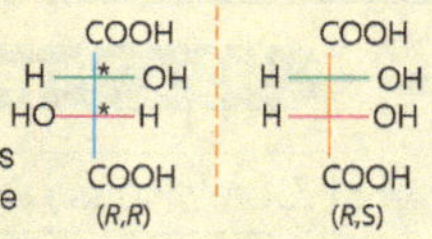

(*R,R*), (*R,S*)

Diastereomers

Purification Methods of Organic Compounds

- **Crystallisation** Differential solubilities of a given organic compounds and its impurities in the same solvent.
- **Sublimation** To separate sublimable compound from non-sublimable impurities.

Distillation Methods

- **Fractional Distillation** It is used when difference in boiling points is not much.
  - Vapours of liquid with higher boiling points condense before the vapours of the liquid with lower boiling point.
- **Distillation Under Reduced Pressure**
  - It is used to purify liquids
  - Having very high boiling points.
  - Which decompose at or below their boiling point.
- **Steam Distillation**
  - This method is used to separate substances which are steam volatile, immiscible with water, possess a vapour pressure of 10-15 mm Hg at 373 K and contain non-volatile impurities.

Chromatography

- **Adsorption Chromatography**
  Differential adsorption of the various components of a mixture on a suitable adsorbent such as silica gel or alumina.
- **Column Chromatography**
  The mixture is passed through adsorbent packed in glass tube.
  e.g. Mixture of naphthalene and benzophenone
- **Thin Layer Chromatography**
  The mixture is passed over adsorbent on a thin glass plate.
  e.g. Detection of amino acids using ninhydrin solution.
- **Partition Chromatography**
  Differential partitioning of components of a mixture between stationary and mobile phase.
- **Paper Chromatography** A special quality paper known as chromatography paper is used. It contains water trapped in it, which acts as the stationary phase.
  e.g. Separation of sugars from amino acids.
- **Retardation Factor (R_f)** Express degree of adsorption of each component.

$$R_f = \frac{\text{Distance moved by component of mixture from base line}}{\text{Distance moved by mobile phase}}$$

Types of Organic Reaction

Substitution Reactions

(Replacement of an atom by different atoms.)

Reaction is done by—

- Free radical (e.g., Wurtz reaction)
- Ionic
  - Electrophilic (by electrophiles), S_E
  - Nucleophilic (by nucleophiles), S_N

S_N1	S_N2
Unimolecular	Bimolecular
First order	Second order
Two steps reaction	One step reaction
(i) $R:X \xrightleftharpoons{\text{Slow}} R^+ + X^-$ (ii) $R^+ + Nu^- \xrightarrow{\text{Fast } R:Nu}$	$R:X + Nu \longrightarrow R:Nu + :X^-$ **(Through transition state)**
Low and milds concentration of nucleophile.	High and strong concentration of nucleophile.
Solvent of high polarity.	Solvents of low polarity.
Catalysed by Lewis and Bronsted acids.	Catalyst not involved.
e.g., Hydrolysis of *tert*-butyl halide.	e.g. Hydrolysis of methyl halide.

Addition Reactions

(Compounds containing $=$ or $\equiv$ bonds.)

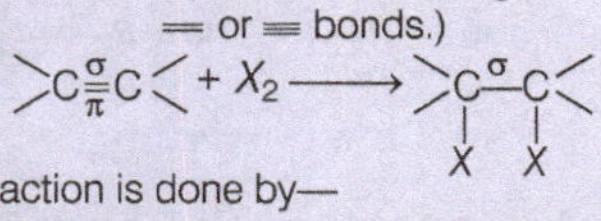

Reaction is done by—

- Free radical—(e.g. Peroxide effect)
- Ionic
  - Nucleophilic (A_N)
  - Electrophilic (A_E)
  (e.g., Markovnikov's rule)

Elimination Reactions

(Reverse of addition reaction.)

- **α-elimination** Two atoms or groups are lost from the same carbon atom to form carbene.

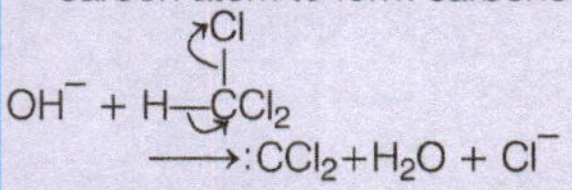

- **β-elimination** Two atoms or groups are lost from adjacent carbon atoms to form an unsaturated compound.

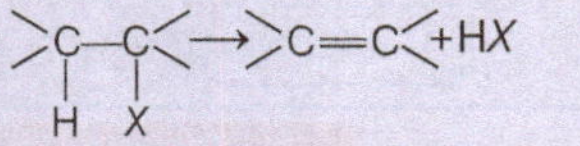

Rearrangement Reactions

(Migration of an atom/group within the molecule).

$$NH_4CNO \xrightarrow{\Delta} NH_2CONH_2$$

Hydrocarbon (Chapter at a Glance)

Alkanes

- **Structure** They have tetrahedral geometry with sp^3 hybridisation and 109°28′ bond angle.
  Contains only single bond between carbon atom.
- **General formula** C_nH_{2n+2}
- **Nomenclature** Root word + ane = alkane name
- **Isomerism** They exhibit mainly structural isomerism, i.e. chain and conformational.

Physical Properties

- First four alkanes are gases, next thirteen are colourless liquids and rest higher ones are waxy solids.
- **Boiling point** For straight chain alkanes, boiling point ∝ molecular size.
  In isomeric alkanes, boiling point ∝ 1/branching.
- **Melting point** Even number of C-atoms ⟶ Higher melting point.
  Odd number of C- atoms ⟶ Lower melting point.

Preparation

Alkane

- **Corey House Synthesis**
  $R—Li + CuI + R'X \xrightarrow{\text{Ether}} R—R'$
- **From unsaturated hydrocarbon**
  $CH_2{=}CH_2 + H_2 \xrightarrow{\text{Pt/Pd/Ni}} CH_3—CH_3$
- **Wurtz Reaction**
  $R—X + 2Na + R—X \xrightarrow[\text{ether}]{\text{dry}} R—R + 2NaX$
- **Decarboxylation**
  $R\,COONa + NaOH \xrightarrow{\text{CaO, 630K}} R—H + Na_2CO_3$
- **Kolbe Electrolysis**
  $R\,COONa + 2H_2O \xrightarrow{\text{Electrolysis}} R—R + 2CO_2 + 2NaOH + H_2$

Chemical Properties

Alkane

- **Halogenation** $CH_4 \xrightarrow[h\nu]{Cl_2} CH_3Cl$
- **Combustion** $C_nH_{2n+2} + \left(\frac{3n+1}{2}\right)O_2 \longrightarrow nCO_2 + (n+1)H_2O$
- **Nitration** $C_2H_6 + HONO_2 \longrightarrow C_2H_5NO_2 + CH_3NO_2 + H_2O$
- **Oxidation** $(CH_3)_3CH + [O] \xrightarrow{\text{Alc.KMnO}_4} (CH_3)_3COH$

Physical properties

- The first three members are gases, the next fourteen are liquid and the higher ones are solids.
- All alkenes are colourless and odourless except ethene & they are insoluble in water.
- Their boiling point and melting point increases with increase in molar mass. Boiling point of *cis* form is higher but melting point is higher for *trans* forms.

Conformations

- **Staggered** The most stable form in which groups are as far apart as possible.
- **Eclipsed** The least stable form in which groups are as close as possible.
- **Skew or Gauche** All the possible conformation between the above conformation are called skew or Gauche conformations.
- **Order of Stability** Staggered > Skew > Eclipsed > Fully eclipsed
- Stability of the conformation of cyclohexane.

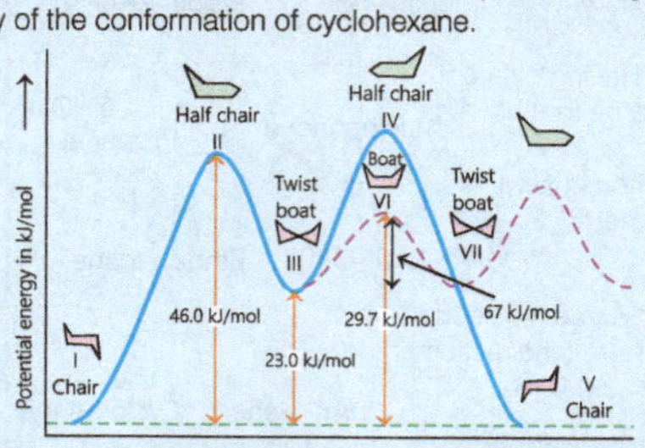

- Relative potential energies of the various conformations of cyclohexane.

Alkane / Alkene

Alkenes

- **Structure** Double bonded C are sp^2 hybridised with trigonal planar shape and 120° angle.
- **General formula** C_nH_{2n}
- Nomenclature Root word + ene = Alkene name
- Exhibit positional chain isomerism
- Exhibit geometrical isomersim

Preparation of Alkenes

Alkene

- **By Dehydrohalogenation**
  $CH_3CH_2Br \xrightarrow[\Delta]{\text{Alc.KOH}} CH_2{=}CH_2 + KBr + H_2O$
- **Birch Reduction**
  $R—C{\equiv}C—R \xrightarrow{\text{Na/Liq.NH}_3}$ (R)(H)C=C(H)(R)
- **Hydroboration**
  $3H—C{\equiv}C—H \xrightarrow{\text{BH}_3\text{in THF}} CH_2{=}CH_2 + CH_2{=}CH—CH{=}CH_2$
- **Hydrogenation**
  $R—C{\equiv}C—R + H_2 \xrightarrow[\text{or Ni—B}]{\text{Lindlar's catalyst}}$ R—C—H ‖ R—C—H

Chemical Properties

Alkenes

- **Hydrogenation** ⟶ Alkanes
  With H_2—Ni/250°C
- **Catalytic oxidation** ⟶ Cyclic ether
  With Ag/ 250-400°C
- **Ozonolysis** ⟶ Carbonyl compounds
  O_3 / with Zn/H_2O
- **Hydroboration** ⟶ Alkanes or alcohols
  BH_3 in THF/H_2O_2

Alkynes

- **Structure** Triple bonded C are *sp* hybridised with linear shape and 180° bond angle. Have atleast one C≡C bond
- **General Formula** C_nH_{2n-2}
- **Nomenclature** Root word + yne
- **Isomerism** Exhibit chain and position isomerism

Preparation

CH≡CH is obtained from:

- $(CH_3COOK)_2$ — Kolbe's electrolysis
- $CaC_2 + 2H_2O$
- $(CH_2Br)_2$ — (i) Alc. KOH (ii) $NaNH_2$, Δ
- $2CHI_3 + 6Ag$ — Alc. KOH
- $2C + H_2$ — Berthelot reaction

Acidic Strength

Acetylene and terminal alkynes are acidic in nature.
Acidic nature is due to *sp*-hybridisation present.
Internal alkynes are non acidic in nature as they lack replaceable H.
The order of pK_a of alkynes, alkene and alkane is in the order alkyne > alkene > alkane

nes

natic

Aromatic Hydrocarbon

Physical Properties

- Aromatic hydrocarbons are non-polar molecules.
- These are colourless liquid or solids with a characteristic aroma.
- These are immiscible with water but miscible with organic solvents and burn with sooty flame.
- **Boiling point** of arenes increases with increase in the molecular size due to increase in van der Waal's forces of attraction.
- **Melting point** depends on molecular size and symmetry. Among *o*-,*m*- and *p* xylenes, the *p* isomer has the highest melting point.

Chemical Properties

- Aromatic hydrocarbons are less reactive than alkenes and alkynes because their π-electrons are involved in delocalisation and not available for addition reactions.
- Under special conditions, they can also undergo addition and oxidation reactions.

Aromaticity

- An aromatic molecule
  —Planar, cyclic and completely conjugated.
  —Contains $(4n+2)\pi$ electrons. (where *n* is an integer)
  —If, on ring closure, the π electron energy of an open chain polyene decreases.

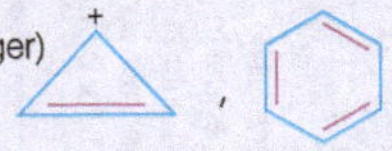

(Aromatic)

- An anti-aromatic molecule
  —Planar, cyclic acid and completely conjugated.
  —Contains $4n\pi$ electrons, (where *n* is an integer)
  —If, on ring closure, the π electron energy increases.

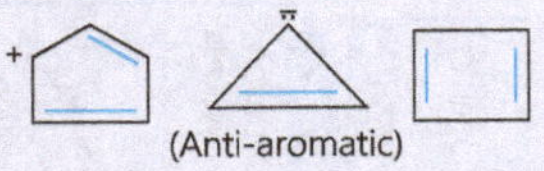

(Anti-aromatic)

- A non-aromatic molecule
  —Non-planar, non-cyclic and not completely conjugated.
  —If, on ring closure, the π electron energy remains the same e.g. Alkanes and alkenes.

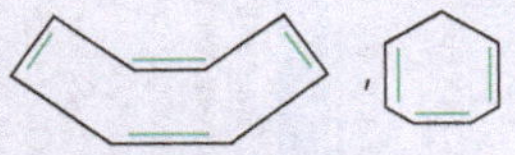

(Non-aromatic)

Chemical Properties

Alkynes:

- Ozonolysis
  - $O_3/Zn, CH_3COOH$
  - $O_3/Zn/H_2O_2$
  - $O_3/LiAlH_4$

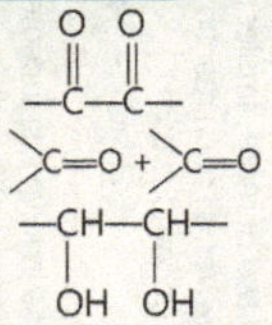

- $KMnO_4$ → Carboxylic acid
  $R—C≡C—R \xrightarrow[\Delta]{KMnO_4}$

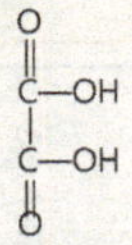

- Carbonyl compounds
  $R—C≡C—H \xrightarrow[HgSO_4]{H_2O, H_2SO_4}$

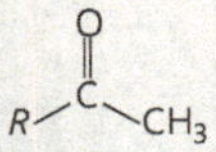

Preparations

Benzene is obtained from:

- Phenol — Dehydroxylation, Zn/dust, Δ
- Acetylene — Polymerisation, Red hot Cu/Fe
- Benzene diazonium chloride — Reduction, H_3PO_2/H_2O
- Halobenzenes — Hydrogenation
- Phenyl magnesium chloride — Hydrolysis
- Sodium salt of carboxylic acids — Decarboxylation, NaOH/CaO

Chemical Properties

Benzene:

- Halogenation → Halobenzene (Cl_2/Fe or $FeCl_3$ or $AlCl_3$, Br_2/Fe or $FeCl_3$ or $AlCl_3$)
- Dark nitration → Nitrobenzene (HNO_3/H_2SO_4)
- Sulphonation → Sulphonic acid (H_2SO_4)
- Friedel-Crafts' alkylation → Alkyl benzene (*RX*/Lewis acid)
- Friedel-Crafts' acylation → Acyl benzene (*R*COCl/Lewis acid)
- Friedel-Crafts' carbonylation → Benzoyl chloride ($COCl_2$/Lewis acid)
- Gattermann synthesis → Benzaldehyde (HCN + HCl + $AlCl_3$)

Directive Influence of Functional group

Towards electrophilic substitution
(i) $—NH_2$, —NH*R*, $—NHCOCH_3$, —OH, $—CH_3$, $—C_2H_5$ etc, are *o/p* directing activating groups.
(ii) Halogens are *o/p* directing but deactivating.
(iii) $—NO_2$, —CN, —CHO, $—CO_2$, —COOH, $—SO_3H$ etc. are *meta* directing and deactivating groups.

Redox Reactions (Chapter at a Glance)

Oxidation

- **Addition of oxygen or other electronegative element**
  $2Mg + O_2 \rightarrow 2MgO$
  $SnCl_2 + Cl_2 \rightarrow SnCl_4$
- **Removal of H or other electropositive element**
  $H_2S + Cl_2 \rightarrow 2HCl + S$
  $2KI + Cl_2 \rightarrow 2KCl$
- **Loss of electron**
  $K \rightarrow K^+ + e^-$
- **Oxidising agent or oxidant**
  It is the species, which reduces, i.e. undergoes reduction.

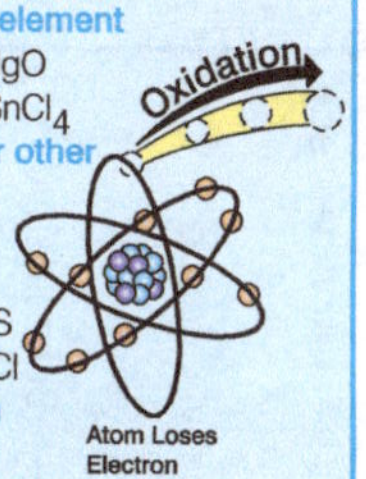

Reduction

- **Addition of Hydrogen or other electropositive element**
  $Cl_2 + H_2 \rightarrow 2HCl$
  $HgCl_2 + Hg \rightarrow Hg_2Cl_2$
- **Removal of oxygen or other electronegative element**
  $CuO + C \rightarrow Cu + CO$
  $2FeCl_3 + H_2 + \rightarrow 2FeCl_2 + 2HCl$
- **Gain of electron**
  $Br_2 + 2e^- \rightarrow 2Br^-$
- **Reducing agent or Reductant**
  Substance which supplies hydrogen or removes oxygen.
  It is itself oxidised after the reduction.

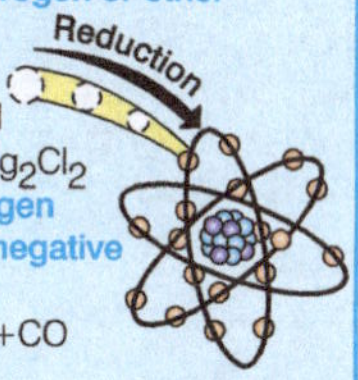

Application of Oxidation Number

- **Acidic Character** Greater the oxidation number of the element forming oxyacids, greater the acid strength except for oxyacids of phosphorus.
  Order : $H_2S_2O_3 < H_2SO_3 < H_2SO_4$
  $HCl < HClO < HClO_2 < HClO_3 < HClO_4$
- **Basic Strength** Greater the oxidation number of the element in conjugate bases, smaller the basic strength.
  – Basic strength of conjugate bases of oxyacids of Cl will be in the order
  $ClO_4 < ClO_3^- < ClO_2^- < ClO^-$.
- **Prediction of Oxidising and Reducing Agent**
  – Oxidising agent in the substance whose oxidation number decreases in the chemical reaction.
  – Reducing agent is the substance whose oxidation number increases in the chemical reaction.

Oxidation Number Method

Steps involved in it are
(i) Write ionic equation.
(ii) Assign oxidation number and balance all other atoms except H and O.
(iii) Predict change in oxidation number.
(iv) Balance charge.
(v) Balance H and O.
e.g. $Zn + HNO_3 \rightarrow Zn(NO_3)_2 + NH_4NO_2 + H_2O$

- **Skeleton equation with oxidation number**
  $\overset{0}{Zn} + \overset{+1+5-2}{HNO_3} \rightarrow \overset{+2+5-2}{Zn(NO_3)_2} + \overset{-3+1+5-2}{NH_4NO_3} + \overset{+1-2}{H_2O}$
- **Change in oxidation number**
  $\overset{0}{Zn} \longrightarrow \overset{+2}{Zn}(NO_3)_2,\ H\overset{+5}{N}O_3 \longrightarrow \overset{-3}{N}H_4NO_3$

– Increase in oxidation number of Zn = 2
Decrease in oxidation number of N = 8,
then $4Zn + NHO_3 \rightarrow 4Zn(NO_3)_2 + NH_4NO_3$
– Addition of HNO_3 on LHS, addition of H_2O on RHS to balance the equation:
$4Zn + 10HNO_3 \rightarrow 4Zn(NO_3)_2 + NH_4NO_3 + 3H_2O$

Oxidation Number

– It is the charge that an atom appear to have in a compound when all other atoms are removed.
– It is zero for free elements.
e.g., P_4, O_2, S_8 etc.
It is – 2 for O, + 1 for H and – 1 for F (generally).
– It is equal to group number for elements of group 1 and 2.
Algebraic sum of oxidation numbers = 0 (for compound) = charge (for ion)

Ion Electron Method

Steps involved in it are
(i) Write ionic equation.
(ii) Split it into two halves.
(iii) Balance all other atoms except H and O.
(iv) Balance charge.
(v) Add half equation.
(vi) Verify balanced equation.
(vii) Convert ionic equation into molecular form.
e.g. $MnO_2 + HCl \longrightarrow MnCl_2 + H_2O + Cl_2$

- **Ionic form**
  $MnO_2 + H^+ + Cl^- \longrightarrow Mn^{2+} + H_2O + Cl_2$
- **Half reactions**
  $Cl \longrightarrow Cl_2,\ MnO_2 + H^+ \longrightarrow Mn^{2+} + H_2O$
  Balance half reaction
  $2Cl^- \rightarrow Cl_2,\ MnO_2 + 4H^+ \rightarrow Mn^{2+} + 2H_2O$
- **Addition of e^-s and balanced reaction**
  $2Cl^- \longrightarrow Cl_2 + 2e^-$
  $MnO_2 + 4H^+ + 2e^- \longrightarrow Mn^{2+} + 2H_2O$
- **Addition of both half-reactions**
  $2Cl^- + MnO_2 + 4H^+ \longrightarrow Cl_2 + Mn^{2+} + 2H_2O$
  $MnO_2 + 4Cl^- + 4H^+ \longrightarrow Cl_2 + Mn^{2+} + 2Cl^- + 2H_2O$
- **Molecular form**
  $MnO_2 + 4HCl \longrightarrow MnCl_2 + Cl_2 + 2H_2O$

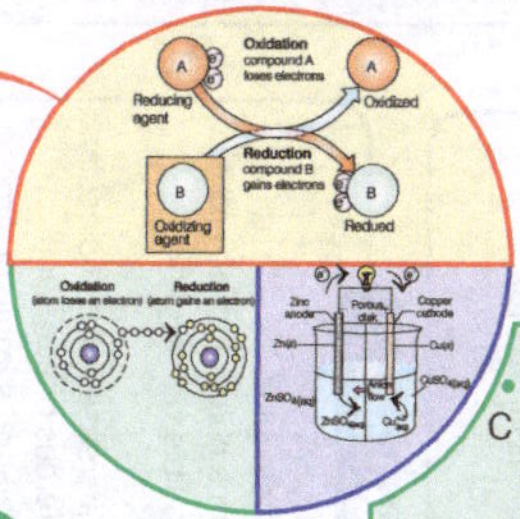

Electrode Process

- **Electrode** It is a metal rod dipped in its salt solution.
- **Anode** The electrode at which oxidation occurs.
- **Cathode** The electrode at which reduction occurs.
- **Redox Couple** It is the combination of oxidised and reduced forms e.g., Zn^{2+}/Zn
- **Electrode Potential** It is the potential associated with an electrode.
- **Standard Electrode Potential** It is the electrode potential measured in standard conditions.
- **Electrolytic Cell** It converts electrical energy into chemical energy.
- **Electrochemical Cell** It converts chemical energy into electrical energy e.g. Daniell cell, lead storage battery etc.
- **Salt Bridge** It completes the circuit and maintain electrical neutrality.
- **Electrochemical Series** A series of decreasing $E°$, e.g., $F^- > Au > Br^- > Cu > Ag > H_2 > Pb > Sn > Fe > Cr > Zn > Al > Mg > Na > Ca > K > Li$.
- **Applications**
  1. Element with more negative $E°$ is good reductant.
  2. Element with less $E°$ can displace the metal with high $E°$ from their salt solution.
  3. $E°_{cell} = E°_{cathode} - E°_{anode}$
  For feasible reaction, $E°_{cell} = +ve$.

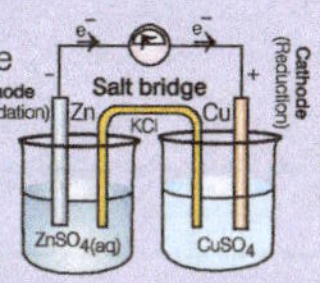

Types of Redox Reactions

- **Combination Reactions**
  These involve combination of two or more atoms to give a single product.
  $2Mg + O_2 \longrightarrow 2MgO$
- **Decomposition Reactions**
  These involve splitting of a compound into two or more simpler products. However, all such reactions are not the decomposition.
  $2H_2O_2 \xrightarrow{\Delta} 2H_2 + O_2$
- **Displacement Reactions**
  These involve displacement of one atom (or ion) by other.
  (i) **Metal displacement reaction**
  Here, one metal displaces the other metal.
  $CuSO_4 + Zn \longrightarrow Cu(s) + ZnSO_4$
  (ii) **Non-metal displacement reaction**
  Here, non-metal is displaced by metal or non-metal.
  $Mg + 2H_2O \longrightarrow Mg(OH)_2 + H_2$
- **Disproportionation Reactions**
  In this reaction, the same element is oxidised as well as reduced.
  $3MnO_4^{2-} + 2H_2O \longrightarrow MnO_2 + 2MnO_4^- + 4OH^-$
- **Comproportionation Reaction**
  This reaction is the reverse of disproportionation reaction. e.g Br^- and BrO_3^- in acidic medium undergoes oxidation and reduction respectively to given Br_2.
  $5Br^- + BrO_3^- + 6H^+ \longrightarrow 3Br_2 + 3H_2O$ (Reduction: $BrO_3^- \rightarrow Br_2$; Oxidation: $Br^- \rightarrow Br_2$)

Redox Reactions in Titrations

The titration involving redox reactions are called redox titration, e.g. titration of MnO_4^- with Fe^{2+} or $C_2O_4^{2-}$, iodometric titrations etc.

Stock Notation

- Oxidation states are written in Roman numeral after the symbol of metal in molecular formula.
- Cation + (Oxidation number in Roman Numeral) + anion. e.g. Au(I) Cl.

Naming the Acid and its Ions

Oxoanions	Formula	Acids	Formula
Bromate (I)	BrO^-	Bromic (I)	HBrO
Bromate (III)	BrO_2^-	Bromic (III)	$HBrO_2$
Bromate (V)	BrO_3^-	Bromic (V)	$HBrO_3$
Bromate (VII)	BrO_4^-	Bromic (VII)	$HBrO_4$
Chromate (VI)	CrO_4^{2-}	Chromic (VI)	H_2CrO_4

Assigning Oxidation Number

Rules	Oxidation Number	Example
Elements	Zero (0)	N_2, Cl_2, O_2, P_4, S_8
Monoatomic ions	Same as charge	$Na^+(+1)$, $Mg^{2+}(+2)$
Hydrogen		
With non-metals	+ 1	H_2O, H_2S, HCl
with metals	+ 1	LiH, CaH_2, KH
Oxygen	– 2 (mostly)	H_2O, CaO, NaOH
In peroxides	– 1	H_2O_2, BaO_2
In superoxides	–1/2	KO_2, CsO_2
In fluorides	+ 1, + 2	O_2F_2, OF_2(respectively)
Alkali metals	+ 1	Li, Na, K, etc.
Alkaline earth metals	+ 2	Be, Mg, Ca, etc.
Fluorine (most electronegative)	– 1 (always)	HF, OF_2, LiF
Sulphides	– 2	H_2S, ZnS

Paradox of Fractional O.N.

- In C_3O_2, oxidation number of two C atoms is + 2 and one C atom is 0.
  O═C═C═C═O
- In $S_4O_6^{2-}$, oxidation number of two S atoms is five and other two S is zero.

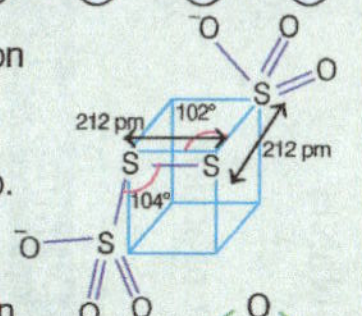

- In Fe_3O_4, oxidation number of two Fe atoms is +3 and one Fe is +2.

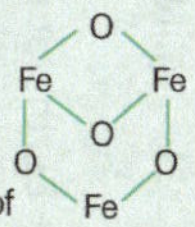

- In Br_3O_8, oxidation number of two Br atoms have +6 while other one has +4. Average oxidation number of Br in $Br_3O_8 = \frac{16}{3}$

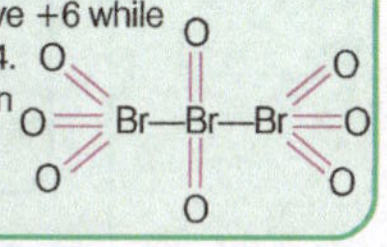